ZHUANGZI

TRANSLATIONS FROM THE ASIAN CLASSICS

ZHUANGZI

A New Translation of the Sayings of Master Zhuang as Interpreted by Guo Xiang

TRANSLATED AND
WITH AN INTRODUCTION
BY RICHARD JOHN LYNN

Columbia University Press
New York

Columbia University Press wishes to express its appreciation for assistance given by the Pushkin Fund and by the Wm. Theodore de Bary Fund in the publication of this book.

Columbia University Press
Publishers Since 1893
New York Chichester, West Sussex
cup.columbia.edu

Library of Congress Cataloging-in-Publication Data
Names: Guo, Xiang, 265–312 author. | Lynn, Richard John, translator.
Title: Zhuangzi : a New Translation of the Sayings of Master Zhuang as Interpreted by Guo Xiang / Translated by Richard John Lynn.
Other titles: Zhuangzi zhu. English | New Translation of the Sayings of Master Zhuang as Interpreted by Guo Xiang | Translations from the Asian classics.
Description: New York : Columbia University Press, 2022. | Series: Translations from the Asian classics | Includes bibliographical references and index.
Identifiers: LCCN 2021041833 (print) | LCCN 2021041834 (ebook) | ISBN 9780231123860 (hardback) | ISBN 9780231123877 (trade paperback) | ISBN 9780231556453 (ebook)
Subjects: LCSH: Zhuangzi. Nanhua jing.
Classification: LCC BL1900.C576 G83513 2022 (print) | LCC BL1900.C576 (ebook) | DDC 299.5/1482—dc23/eng/20211029
LC record available at https://lccn.loc.gov/2021041833
LC ebook record available at https://lccn.loc.gov/2021041834

Cover image: Ho Huai-shuo (He Huaishuo) 何懷碩 (1941–)
吾安得夫忘言之人而與之言哉
"Where, oh, where can I find someone who will forget words so I may have a word with him?" (*Zhuangzi*, Chapter 26)
己亥孟冬何懷碩書於澀盦 "First month of winter in the year *jihai* [November 2019], composed by He Huaishuo at [his studio] the Cloister of Astringency"
Seals: (upper right) *Zengjing sanqian shijie* 曾經三千世界 ; (lower left above) He 何; (lower left below) Huaishuo 懷碩
Zengjing sanqian shijie 曾經三千世界"Experienced the entire trichiliocosm"

This book is for Sonja,
with love ~

CONTENTS

ACKNOWLEDGMENTS

I owe many debts of gratitude to colleagues who helped this book come into existence. Work began more than two decades ago in 1998, immediately following my completion of *The Classic of the Way and Virtue: A New Translation of the* Daode jing *of Laozi as Interpreted by Wang Bi*, when the contract for this book, also with Columbia University Press, was signed. Progress since then was intermittent, with long periods of interruption due to other obligations, both professional and personal. First came the move from the University of Alberta to the University of Toronto in 1998, where from 1999 to 2005, I served as East Asian Studies Graduate Studies Coordinator and Professor of Chinese Thought and Literature. My retirement in June 2005 occasioned a move to Gabriola Island, British Columbia. During 2006–2007, I also served as Visiting Professor at the Department of Asian Studies, University of British Columbia, in nearby Vancouver. During this time, earlier professorial visiting appointments were also held for shorter periods at the City University of Hong Kong and at Peking University (Beijing Daxue). Nevertheless, from the start, Jennifer Crewe, first as editor and later as the director of Columbia University Press, supported and encouraged the project through the years with more forbearance than I deserved. More recently, Christine Dunbar, its final editor, guided the project through to its end with a judicious hand and gracious advice. At various stages of completion, the manuscript was sent out to anonymous readers. I am grateful to their many expert and thoughtful suggestions.

My participation in two international conferences provided opportunities to interact with fellow scholars of the *Zhuangzi* and Wei-Jin *xuanxue* (arcane learning) thought, providing much new information and insight: International Conference on "Wang Bi and Guo Xiang: Commentaries and Philosophy Construction," at the Chinese University of Hong Kong Research Centre for Chinese Philosophy and Culture (2005); and "Global Reception of the Classic *Zhuangzi*: Han to Tang," at the Center for Chinese Studies, University of California at Berkeley (2019). At these and other occasions, conversations with friends and colleagues about the *Zhuangzi* and Guo Xiang contributed in countless ways, and I wish to thank in particular Zhang Longxi, Liu Xiaogan, Tim Barrett, Wang Baoxuan, Karl-Heinz Pohl, Brook Ziporyn, Michael Nylan, Esther Klein, Mark Csikszentmihalyi, Charles Muller, David Chai, Wendy Swartz, Robert Jackson, Martin Kern, David Knechtges, Qian Nanxiu, Victor Mair, Peipei Qiu, Peter Zhang, Stuart Sargent, Tom Tillemans, and Tobias Zürn.

The library of the University of Toronto has provided essential services throughout the course of this project. In particular, I wish to thank Lucy Gan, Information Services Librarian, and Stephen Qiao, Chinese Studies Librarian, for their help in making Internet resources readily available to me over the years. I am also grateful to Itō Moriyuki and Itō Takako for their help in Japan by arranging a lecture for me at Hirosaki University in Aomori on Guo Xiang and the *Zhuangzi* in 1999 and obtaining print research materials and securing Internet connections for me during later visits to Gakushūin University in Tokyo. I also owe special thanks to Hugh Moss for allowing calligraphy in his collection by Ho Huai-shuo to grace the cover of this book and for providing the photographic reproduction.

Donald Holzman, Tang Yijie, and Vincent Shen provided well-needed advice and criticism toward the beginning of this project, for which I shall always be grateful. Although my treatment of the life and times of Guo Xiang in the "Introduction" is based on a wide variety of premodern and modern sources, I am particularly indebted to Wang Xiaoyi, *Guo Xiang pingzhuan fu Xiang Xiu pingzhuan* (Critical biography of Guo Xiang, with critical biography of Xiang Xiu appended) for both general observations and specific details.

Finally, to my wife, Sonja Arntzen, I owe the most. Her patience and understanding, encouragement and unwavering support, constructive criticism, and heartfelt reassurance when the going got tough all mean more to me than I can ever express.

TRANSLATOR'S NOTE

The arrangement and formatting of this translation follow my earlier translations of Wang Bi's commentaries to the *Zhouyi* and the *Laozi*: *The Classic of Changes: A New Translation of the* I Ching *as Interpreted by Wang Bi* (New York: Columbia University Press, 1994) and *The Classic of the Way and Virtue: A New Translation of the* Daode jing *of Laozi as Interpreted by Wang Bi* (New York: Columbia University Press, 1999). As such, this work forms another companion volume and completes my translation of all the *Sanxuan* (Three Arcane Classics), a term used both throughout the tradition and still common today, whose *locus classicus* is probably the *Yanshi jiaxun* (Family instructions for the Yan clan) of Yan Zhitui (531–591).[1] Several works were instrumental in the preparation of this translation: *Sōji* (*Zhuangzi*), by Akatsuka Kiyoshi (1913–1983); *Guo Xiang Zhuangzi zhu jiaoji* (Guo Xiang's commentary to the *Zhuangzi*, with collation notes), by Wang Shumin (1914–2008); *Sōji no shisō to sono kaishaku: Kaku Shō Sei Gen'ei* (The thought of the *Zhuangzi* and its interpretation: Guo Xiang and Chen Xuanying), by Seki Masao; *Guo Xiang yu Wei-Jin xuanxue* (Guo Xiang and arcane learning in the Wei-Jin period), by Tang Yijie (1927–2014); and *Xuanxue tonglun* 玄學通論 (General survey of arcane learning), by Wang Baoxuan. Translated excerpts of Guo Xiang's commentary by Akatsuka and Seki often proved extremely helpful, the extensive commentary of Wang Shumin and his collation notes also greatly helped with interpreting the text of the *Zhuangzi*, and works by Tang Yijie and Wang Baoxuan have elucidated much concerning the basic assumptions, goals, rhetoric and modes of argument, and conclusions of *xuanxue* thinkers, thus providing meaningful parameters for Guo Xiang's own thought.

I have, of course, looked carefully at earlier translations of the *Zhuangzi*, particularly those by Burton Watson, *Chuang-tzu: The Complete Works*, and Victor Mair, *Wandering on the Way: Early Taoist Tales and Parables of Chuang Tzu*. It seems to me that both versions are heavily indebted to the Japanese translations of Fukunaga Mitsuji (1918–2001), *Sōji* (*Zhuangzi*) (Watson), and Akatsuka (Mair). Since Fukunaga and Akatsuka largely follow the interpretive reading of the text by Lin Xiyi (ca. 1210–ca. 1273), *Zhuangzi Juanzhai kouyi jiaozhu* (Juanzhai's vernacular explications of the *Zhuangzi*), which is heavily influenced by neo-Confucian and Buddhist thought (especially Chan/Zen thought), their reading, as well as those by Watson and Mair, are radically different from that of Guo Xiang in many places, and thus equally different from my translation of the text, based as it is on Guo's commentary rather than on Lin Xiyi's. Nevertheless, referring to Watson's and Mair's versions greatly facilitated my treatment of many passages, especially those that tend more to narrative content than philosophical import.

As for the commentary itself, I am much indebted to Brook Ziporyn, who in his *The Penumbra Unbound: The Neo-Taoist Philosophy of Guo Xiang* uses a skillful inductive method based on a host of translated and interpreted passages to define both the general thrust of Guo's thought and the specific parameters of his modes of argument. Directed to such ends instead of focusing directly on the relationship between the commentary and the text of the *Zhuangzi*, Ziporyn's translations are inevitably often different from mine; but having got there first, his pioneering work has proved extremely helpful. I also must acknowledge my acquaintance with other prior translations of passages of Guo's commentary by Birthe Arendrup, Fung Yu-lan (Feng Youlan, 1895–1990), and Frederick W. Mote (in Hsiao Kung-ch'üan [Xiao Gongquan], *A History of Chinese Political Thought*). The translations of the *Zhuangzi* by James Legge and Herbert Giles also were occasionally consulted. Fung Yu-lan's *Chuang Tzu: A New Selected Translation with an Exposition of the Philosophy of Kuo Hsiang*, despite the promise of its title, proved disappointing: Only translations of the first seven "Inner" chapters of the text of the *Zhuangzi* are presented, and only those passages of Guo's commentary with which Fung agreed are included, and they are so abbreviated and paraphrased that their usefulness is rather limited.

I found the best modern annotated Chinese translation of the *Zhuangzi* to be *Zhuangzi* (1996), by Zhang Gengguang, and accordingly I often consulted it. However, the greatest assistance in translating Guo's commentary came from the subcommentary of Cheng Xuanying (ca. 600–ca. 660), contained in its entirety in *Zhuangzi jishi* (Collected explanations of Master Zhuang), compiled by Guo Qingfan (1844–1896), the base text for my translation of both the text of the *Zhuangzi* and Guo's commentary. Cheng's seventh-century prose expands on Guo's terse and too often opaque discourse of the late third–early fourth century, which is so ambiguous in places that its meaning is far from clear. In such cases, I largely allowed Cheng to be my guide. My translation of institutional terms and official titles essentially follows Charles O. Hucker, *A Dictionary of Official Titles in Imperial China*, supplemented for the Wei-Jin era by reference to Michael Loewe, *The Men Who Governed Han China: Companion to a Biographical Dictionary of the Qin, Former Han and Xin Periods*, since the rendering of such terms in Loewe's work seem more accurate for the times in which Guo Xiang lived.

The translation technique here is the same as in *Classic of Changes* and *Laozi*: the text of the *Zhuangzi* and Guo's commentary are fully integrated, so the interpretation of the one is dependent on interpretation of the other. Adjusting what the text means in translation with the meaning of the commentary (and vice versa) demanded that I continuously had to ensure that the two complemented each other and were not at odds. Such a technique, of course, precludes independent presentation of either the *Zhuangzi* text or Guo's commentary; that is, translation of the commentary cannot simply be attached to some other translation of the *Zhuangzi* by Watson or Mair, for example—it just would not fit.

Guo's commentary is a long and difficult text. Even with all the exegetical help, from both traditional and modern scholarship, I am sure that errors in translation and interpretation have crept in despite my every effort—sometimes involving hours and even whole days of painful puzzling over single terms or phrases. Nevertheless, the many years of scholarly labor involved have afforded me far more joy than pain—it has been an incredibly enriching and fulfilling experience, for which I am most grateful.

Note

1. Yan Zhitui, *Yanshi jiaxun*, A: 35a: "The *Zhuang*, *Lao*, and *Zhouyi* are called as a group the *Sanxuan*."

INTRODUCTION

A "New" Translation

The word "new" here carries several meanings: (1) This translation of the *Zhuangzi*, "Sayings of Master Zhuang," is "new" in that it differs significantly from previous translations; (2) this difference is due to a "new" translation technique based on one particular traditional Chinese commentary, that of Guo Xiang (265–312). The reading of the *Zhuangzi* presented here is thus how Guo interpreted the text. To my knowledge, no previous translation of the *Zhuangzi*, into English or any other language, either in the modern East or West, has been based entirely on Guo's commentary. (3) The translation technique used here is also "new," in that the text of the *Zhuangzi* and its commentary are fully integrated; that is, the meaning of the one is determined by that of the other. Such a translation technique precludes independent presentation of either the *Zhuangzi* text or the commentary. Therefore, translation of the commentary cannot simply be attached to some other translation of the *Zhuangzi* (such as by Burton Watson or Victor Mair,[1] the two most popular English versions) because neither interprets its text consistently in terms of Guo's commentary, which makes many renditions of passages incompatible with it. Whereas some of Watson's and Mair's passages—mostly those involving straightforward narratives or parables—seem similar not only to each other but to those translated here, others with more philosophical content differ considerably because they are either based on different commentaries or are interpretations arrived at independently. Such independent interpretations are more apparent in A. C. Graham's translations of passages[2] and thus are usually quite different from Guo Xiang's readings presented here. (4) "New" does not necessarily mean "better" (that is, supposedly closer to the "original" meaning of the *Zhuangzi*). But what that original meaning might be has been a contentious issue throughout the centuries up to now, complicated, of course, by what role Guo Xiang played in the recension of its text.

In light of Guo's editing of the much larger but long-lost fifty-two-chapter version of the *Zhuangzi* that apparently existed in his own time into his thirty-three-chapter version, we might ask, as does the prominent scholar of early Chinese thought and literature Professor Martin Kern, whether Guo's editing and reading of the text transform it from a late Warring States work from the third century BCE into one shaped by the intellectual context of the Western Jin era of the early fourth century CE. And, if it does, does this mean that the text and its interpretation by Guo presented here remove the text that much farther from its original meaning?[3] Two opposing answers are possible: If one sides with hostile critics of Guo, both traditional and modern, who judge that he plagiarized the commentary from Xiang Xiu (ca. 223–ca. 275) and even twisted that into a new vehicle just to suit his own philosophy, then the *Zhuangzi* that I present has little in common with the original meaning. But if one believes that despite his radical editing and innovative commentary, Guo still preserved the drift of its basic integrity, then the text and commentary of this translation should embody both.

Although commentaries to the *Zhuangzi* appeared both before and after Guo Xiang, Guo's is the earliest to be preserved in its entirety. Moreover, his is almost entirely an interpretive commentary, with little concern about the identification of persons, places, and things. This deficiency was filled admirably by Cheng Xuanying (ca. 600–ca. 660), a scholarly Daoist priest from the early Tang dynasty, whose subcommentary I often quote in notes both for their factual information and for the light they cast on the more cryptic of Guo's interpretive passages. Cheng's prose consists of a far more standard vocabulary and syntax than does Guo's; thus, because it is easier to read, it often clarifies what is opaque in Guo's text.

Although Guo's commentary was never completely supplanted by later commentaries, its importance was considerably diminished by the *Zhuangzi Juanzhai kouyi* (Juanzhai's vernacular explications of the *Zhuangzi*) by Lin Xiyi (ca. 1210–ca. 1273), which incorporated Song-dynasty concepts and terminology from both Chan Buddhism and Neo-Confucianism, the dominant discourses of the time. Lin's reading of the *Zhuangzi* is very different from Guo's, and thus would result in an equally different translation.[4] Such differences are already reflected in the translations by Burton Watson and Victor Mair, whose works are significantly shaped by two Japanese translators and annotators of the *Zhuangzi*, Fukunaga Mitsuji (1918–2001)[5] for Watson and Akatsuka Kiyoshi

(1913–1983) for Mair.[6] Both Fukunaga and Akatsuka were themselves greatly influenced by Lin's commentary to the *Zhuangzi*, and their respective translations into Japanese generally follow his readings closely. Since translations into modern Chinese also tend to follow Lin Xiyi's commentary, the modern reception of the *Zhuangzi* during the most recent two or three generations undoubtedly knows it more through Lin's reading than Guo's.

Nevertheless, Guo Xiang is immensely important in his own right, both for his commentary to the *Zhuangzi* and his contributions to the Chinese tradition of philosophy. The development of Chinese thought through the centuries was carried far more by commentaries to the foundational texts of Confucianism, Daoism, and Buddhism than by stand-alone philosophical treatises. Guo's commentary surely must be counted among the most important in this regard, for it significantly advanced the tenets of arcane learning [*xuanxue*], the dominant discourse of the third to the sixth century CE, which not only linked essential features of Daoist metaphysics with Confucian morality and political philosophy to create a new worldview of its own, but also served as the basis for how concepts of Buddhism were received and developed in China. Later, such concepts and terminology made their way, either directly or via Buddhism, into the formulation of Neo-Confucianism during the Song era (the tenth to the thirteenth century). Therefore, ample reasons exist for focusing so much attention on Guo Xiang here.

After much consideration, I have settled on "arcane" to translate the *xuan* of *xuanxue*, which perhaps differs from the majority of current Western scholars of early medieval Chinese thought, who prefer "mystery" for *xuan* and "mystery learning" for *xuanxue*. *Xuan* has a wide range of meanings: "black," "dark," "dark color," "obscure," "hidden," "deep," "profound," "occult," "mysterious," "abstruse," "north/northerly," "deep understanding," "quiet/still," "marvelous," "sublime," "subtle," and "the color of the heavens and (figuratively) of Heaven." Moreover, the old term "Neo-Taoism"/"Neo-Daoism" for *xuanxue* is particularly misleading, since it suggests that *xuanxue* is primarily a renewal of the pre-Han thought of the *Laozi* and *Zhuangzi* and fails to account for the amalgamation of that tradition of thought with many tenets of Confucianism. "Mystery," to my way of thinking, is also a misleading tag for *xuan* since, for students of comparative thought, it might well suggest aspects of the secret cults and mystery religions of the Greco-Roman world. "Arcane" seems more neutral in this respect, but this may be more based on personal preference than on firm heuristic principle. In any case, *xuan* translates as "arcane" throughout this introduction, the appendixes, and the translation of the texts of the *Zhuangzi* and Guo's commentary.

Adherents of the *xuanxue* tradition such as Guo Xiang are usually referred to in contemporary and later Chinese sources as belonging to the Daojia, a term that seems to have been invented by Sima Tan (ca. 165–110 BCE) as one of the traditions of thought included in what he termed the "Essentials of the six *jia*" (*Liujia zhi yaozhi*), discussed in the *Shiji* (Records of the historian),[7] which was completed by his son, Sima Qian (ca. 145–ca. 86 BCE), after his father's death. Kidder Smith translates Daojia as "men of Dao" in his analysis of Sima Tan's use of the term,[8] and Mark Csikszentmihalyi and Michael Nylan use the romanized term "Dao jia" throughout as they argue in their more recent and detailed analysis of the same material that *jia* in the *Shiji* refers to "the methods of individual persuaders, rather than established 'schools' or 'lineages.'[9] However, in one note, they do refer to Dao jia as "philosophical Taoism" in distinction to "religious Taoism."[10] Such a distinction has a long history and was first articulated in detail by Holmes Welch's *Taoism: Parting of the Way* (first published in 1957).[11] Nathan Siven revisited the issue in 1978 and did some much needed fine-tuning, but he still maintained the general distinction between *tao chia* [*Daojia*], the "Taoist school" (philosophical Daoism), and *tao chiao* [*Daojiao*], the "Taoist Sect" (religious Daoism). However, he also warned that the relationship between the two was often ambiguous, and much interaction occurred through the premodern era.[12]

In any event, I have found no evidence in the particular case of Guo Xiang that he was ever a "religious Daoist" involved in such activities as alchemy, hygiene, magic, religious ritual, or any quest for "transcendence" or "immortality" [*xian*], all of which are associated with religious Daoism. Therefore, since the terms "Daoism" and "Daoist" in the scholarly literature of recent years have largely been identified with religious Daoism, when the sources refer to Guo Xiang and other arcane learning [*xuanxue*] figures as "Daojia," or belonging to the "Daojia," to avoid confusion with religious Daoism, its adherents might best be translated as "Dao Scholastics" and their tradition of thought as "School of the Dao."

Sections of This Introduction

The sections of this introduction attempt to account for the sociopolitical context in which the basic assumptions and objectives of Guo's thought were founded, the conditions under which his commentary took shape, and his rise to political power and the effect it had on the commentary. All these topics are covered in "The Life and Times of Guo Xiang," "Guo Xiang's Commentary to the *Zhuangzi*," "Patronage of Sima Yue," and "Guo Xiang's Rise to Power." A major controversy that has lasted from Guo's own day until now concerns the authorship of the commentary. The following sections provide both an account of the controversy and an attempt to settle the debate: "Guo Xiang as Alleged Plagiarist, His Accusers," "Plagiarism Challenged: Doubtful Sources," "The Charge of Plagarization and Its Refutation," "The Modern

Rehabilitation of Guo Xiang: Textual Comparisons," and "Comparison of Interpretive Content: Innovations in Guo's Commentary." Several sections then follow, which attempt to identify and explore the essential features of Guo's thought and to situate it both in the context of thinkers of his own time and to analyze it in terms of modern philosophical categories: "Created or Self-generated, Immanence or Transcendence, Immanent Transcendence," "The Universal and Particular Dao," "Transcendent Naturalism Versus Immanent Naturalism," "Pei Wei, Material Existence, and "Immanent Monism," "Immanent Transcendence in the Writings of Ruan Ji," "Xiang Xiu and Xi Kang on Perspicacity (Zhi)," "Immanent Transcendence and Guo Xiang's Immanent Monism," and, finally, "Xiang Xiu and Guo Xiang: Major Differences and Similarities." The next section, "Guo Xiang and the Zhuangzi," examines the relationship between the *Zhuangzi* and Guo's commentary: Did Guo get its real meaning? Did he distort it completely? Or does the truth lie somewhere in between? Then, "Guo Xiang and Buddhism" describes Guo's general connections with Buddhism and directs the reader to detailed scholarship on the subject. The introduction closes with a section called "Master Zhuang and the Text Attributed to Him," which examines the history and recension of the text and provides a brief account of its essential features.

The Life and Times of Guo Xiang

Guo Xiang[13] (personal name Zixuan) was born between 262 and 269 and died in 311 or 312, with modern scholarship largely agreeing on 265–312 for his lifespan. As for his native place, whereas one source locates it in Yingchuan commandery (present-day central Henan)[14] and another in Henei, "Inside the Yellow River," commandery[15] (present-day northern Henan), most simply say that it was Henan. The connection with Yingchuan perhaps can be inferred from Guo's known close association with fellow arcane learning [*xuanxue*] master Yu Ai (262–311), who hailed from there. His family background, completely obscure, is never addressed in any sources, which suggests that no family members had ever been officials and Guo was originally without elite rank or title. However, his family, probably rural landlords or owners of some kind of commercial enterprise, must have had the resources to provide Guo with an elite education, resources that continued to support him through his maturity and allowed him for years to spurn offers of lower provincial and prefectural offices as he led a cultured and learned lifestyle at home.

As someone who by birth seems to have lacked close elite connections, in an era dominated by great clans and the aristocracy, Guo's chances to achieve high office were slim. However, two avenues did exist: (1) building a reputation as a learned and eloquent proponent of arcane learning [*xuanxue*], the dominant intellectual discourse of the day; and (2) being recruited to and rising within the staff of one of the Jin princes, either in the fief administration or in posts associated with the prince if he held positions in the central government. The former could attract a recommendation to office by a well-placed person, who in Guo's case was Wang Yan (256–311), then a doyen of arcane learning and a man who wielded enormous influence when it came to appraisal of personal character [*pinping*]. When Wang made Guo's acquaintance in the 290s, he was the defender-in-chief [*taiwei*], the highest military officer in the land, and personally well connected at court. The empress, Jia Nanfeng (257–300), who ruled between 291 and 300 in the name of her husband, the mentally defective Emperor Hui (Sima Zhong (259–307)), had had one of Wang's daughters married to Crown Prince Yu, Sima Yu (278–300), and another to her nephew, Jia Mi (d. 300). Wang's influence resulted in Guo receiving offers of several provincial and prefectural offices, which he refused because he was still biding his time. A few years later, with his reputation further enhanced, Guo found a patron in the prince of Donghai, Sima Yue (d. 311), who fostered his career from 302 on.

What little is known about Guo's early life indicates that he was extremely intelligent, devoted to foundational Daoist texts, and a keen scholar of arcane learning [*xuanxue*]:

> Xiang, whose personal name was Zixuan, was a native of Henan. From an early age he had a capacity for analytical thinking [*caili*], which he used to pursue the Dao. Devoted to learning, he assiduously applied himself to the *Laozi* and the *Zhuangzi*. His contemporaries all regarded him as second only to Wang Bi.[16]

Since Wang Bi (226–249), along with He Yan (190–249), was one of the most significant figures in the earlier *xuanxue* tradition,[17] this was indeed high praise. Guo also became known as a voluble virtuoso of "pure discourse" [*qingyan*]. Both qualities came to the attention of Wang Yan:

> From an early age, Guo Xiang, personal name Zixuan, had a capacity for analytical thinking. Dedicated to the *Laozi* and the *Zhuangzi*, he excelled at pure discourse. Defender-in-chief [*taiwei*] Wang often said of him, "When listening to Xiang talk, he seems like a great waterfall pouring out inexhaustibly." Although recruited for provincial and prefectural offices, he would not serve but went on living a free life at home so he could enjoy writing and discussion.[18]

In connection with this passage, Yu Jiaxi (1884–1955) points out that the *Beitang shuchao* (Excerpts from books in the Northern Hall), compiled by Yu Shinan

(558–638), cites a passage in the *Yulin* (Grove of anecdotes) of Pei Qi (second half of the fourth century):

> Grand Guardian Wang asked Sun Xinggong [Sun Chuo (310/314–371)], "What kind of a man is Guo Xiang?" Sun replied, "His use of words is refined and elegant, overflowing with energy, forming coherent discourse as fast as they are uttered, like a waterfall gushing water, they pour out inexhaustibly."[19]

This passage actually appears twice in the *Beitang shuchao*,[20] but it is either corrupt or a later invention, for the exchange between Wang Yan and Sun Chuo, who was born either about the year Wang died or two to four years later, could not have occurred. However, it is likely that a tradition of describing Guo's rhetorical power, in more or less the same words, existed at least until Sun Chuo's time, the generation following Guo's death.

In any case, Guo seems to have been well acquainted with Wang Yan. For example, probably in 297, he was invited to a large Wang family gathering:

> Three days after the marriage of Cavalier Attendant Pei [Pei Xia] to a daughter of defender-in-chief Wang, a grand party was held for his sons-in-law, to which eminent literati of the day and junior members of the Wang and Pei clans were also invited. Guo Zixuan, who attended, challenged Pei to a debate. Despite Zixuan's rich endowment of talent, during several exchanges at the start he was not quite at the top of his form, thus, although the propositions he set forth were extremely rich and pithy, Pei easily handled what he first proposed and argued with such subtlety that it made all those present sigh with pleasure.[21]

Guo's presence at such a gathering suggests that by the mid-290s, he enjoyed a considerable reputation among arcane learning circles. That he could challenge Pei Xia, a prominent expert of "pure discourse" or "pure conversation" [*qingtan*] and scion of the well-established Pei clan, which included masters in *qingtan* such as his father, Pei Chuo, and uncle, Pei Kai (237–291), indicate both daring and confidence. Guo had obviously climbed into their ranks:

> Kai's younger brother Chuo, personal name Jishu, was a man of great breadth of mind and expansive personality, whose highest offices were "attendant gentleman of the yellow gate" [*huangmen shilang*] and commandant [*xiaowei*] of troops in Changshui [southwest of Luoyang]. Zhuo's son Xia excelled at discussing arcane principles [*xuanli*], which he enunciated in a clear and fluent voice, sharp and cool as the notes of a balloon lute. When he once debated such things with Guo Xiang from Henan, the whole assembly present could only sigh in submission. Another time when seated as a guest of Pacifier of the

East General Zhou Fu [d. 311] and playing *weiqi* [capture chess, Japanese *go*] with someone, Commander Fu toasted him to have a drink, but because he did not respond immediately, the commander, in a drunken rage, pulled him over so he fell down. However, Xia slowly got up, merely resumed his seat, not changing his expression, and continued playing just as before. His nature was as void and placid as that.[22]

The offers of provincial and prefectural posts that now came Guo's way were surely due to Wang Yan's influence. It is significant that Guo spurned them all. The cynic might conclude that he extended his period of self-cultivation not in the search for wisdom, but to further enhance his reputation and gain entry to the upper echelons of government. Such a view shapes the few surviving sources that address his life, particularly passages in Liu Yiqing (403–444), the nominal author of *Shishuo xinyu* (A new account of tales of the world), and Fang Xuanling (579–648), the principal editor of *Jinshu* (History of the Jin), a biography of Guo Xiang. Although both works accuse Guo of being "mean and insincere" [*xingbo*] and are often cited to prove that his commentary to the *Zhuangzi* is only a small part his and most of it actually the work of Xiang Xiu (ca. 223–ca. 275), enough evidence exists to refute both assertions. However, before exploring this issue, we should first consider his climb to high office.

It was not until 302, when Sima Yue became minister of works [*sikong*], that Guo began his official career; it is recorded in the *Wenshi zhuan* (Biographies of literary men), edited by Zhang Yin (late fourth century) and Zhang Zhi (act. ca. 401), that "Guo was then summoned to office as a section administrator in the ministry of works [*sikong yuan*]. . . ."[23] A section administrator [*yuan*] was at rank seven [*qipin*], already two ranks up from nine, the lowest rank. The years between 300 and 304 were a favorable time for someone from the fringes of privilege to enter officialdom, even at a rank usually reserved for young men from elite families, since (1) Chaotic internal war conditions due to the "Rebellions of the Eight Princes" [*bawang zhi luan*][24] resulted in a relaxation of conventions and rules governing recruitment to the bureaucracy. (2) Two men sympathetic to Guo then held powerful positions in government. The wealthy aesthete, once a general and now minister of education [*situ*] Wang Rong (234–305), was an older, distant cousin of Wang Yan. The other, of course, was Guo's patron, Sima Yue. Wang Rong, remembered as one of the "Seven Sages of the Bamboo Grove" and affiliated with *xuanxue* from his early years, was surely aware of Guo's own promotion of *xuanxue* and his commentary to the *Zhuangzi*. However, since Wang Rong is not known to have directly sponsored men such as Guo to office, it is more likely that it was Sima Yue, the sponsor of many such men, who first brought him into government. For the next eight years, Guo's fate is inextricably linked to Sima Yue's growing consolidation of power. The last decade of his life is so intertwined with that of Sima Yue that

Guo's personal rise to power and the effect this had both on his *Zhuangzi* commentary and its subsequent reception cannot be fully appreciated unless we examine Sima Yue's own story.

Some two years later, in 304, we find Sima Yue, still minister of works in Luoyang, executing the orders of the regent and crown prince Sima Ying, prince of Chengdu, who at the time was leading military operations in the field from his headquarters in Yecheng (modern Handan, Hebei). It was then that Sima Yue had Guo promoted to "gentleman in attendance of the yellow gate" [*huangmen shilang*][25]—that is, supervising secretary of the chancellery, at rank five [*wupin*]. As one of several officials who handled memorials to the emperor, this placed him close to the pinnacle of power. In 306, when Sima Yue finally put an end to the rebellions of the eight princes and became senior tutor [*taifu*], he made Guo his recorder [*taifu bu*], which enhanced his position even further.

Guo Xiang's Commentary to the *Zhuangzi*

It was also about this time that Guo completed his commentary to the *Zhuangzi*, evidence for which appears in the account of Xiang Xiu's work on the *Zhuangzi* that was included in Xiang's biography in the *Jinshu*:

> Although readers throughout the ages applied themselves to the several tens of inner and outer chapters of Zhuang Zhou's work, no one ever succeeded in expounding its overall intent. But then Xiang Xiu explained its hidden aspects, which so clarified its profound meaning that it excited a vogue for arcane learning. Its readers had then acquired such an extraordinarily clear and heartfelt understanding of it that for a time no one thought it deficient in any respect. However, during the reign of Emperor Hui [r. 290–306], Guo Xiang went on to bring out such an expansion of Xiang's work that people henceforth scorned all footprints left behind by the Confucians and Mohists, and School of the Dao [*Daojia*] sayings flourished instead.[26]

It is actually possible to narrow down the time for the completion of the commentary to approximately 302–306. Although the reign of Emperor Hui began in 290, evidence from Guo's own writings suggests that his commentary could not have been completed during the early part of that reign: in his commentary to 33.23, the last passage in the *Zhuangzi*, Guo acknowledges:

> Earlier, when I had not yet myself examined the *Zhuangzi*, I occasionally heard people engaged in discussion and arguing about the meaning of such things as "a stick a foot long" and "linked rings," which they all said were from the *Zhuangzi*. I consequently thought that Master Zhuang belonged to the tradition

> of the rhetoricians. However, once I noted that the current chapter, which compares and critiques various philosophical masters, in this passage states that the way of the rhetoricians is so confused and contradictory that what they say misses the mark completely, I realized how possible it was that heeding such rumors harmed the truth.

Although Guo does not say when he began his study of the *Zhuangzi*, he likely was well into his exploration of philosophical thought before he had even begun to read the works of Master Zhuang. Note also that these remarks were composed only after he had first read much, if not all, of the text available to him. Assuming that Guo did not begin his commentary until he had read through the material at least once, work on the commentary itself, either concurrent with or subsequent to his massive editing of the *Zhuangzi* material, is unlikely to have been a project of his youth. By 290, Guo was twenty-five but still living at home and studying. By then, he had a reputation as a fast thinker and talker, but no evidence has come to light that he was also a fast writer. Whereas it is quite possible that he began the commentary by 290, it likely took at least a decade to complete, given the enormous task of editing the material from fifty-two chapters to thirty-three and composing a commentary that almost rivals the length of the *Zhuangzi* itself as he edited it.[27]

Other evidence also suggests that the commentary was a product of his later years, for running through the entire commentary is an undercurrent of statecraft pragmatism that was likely to have grown along with his involvement with the politics and military strife that marked the years 300 to 306. By the time he composed the commentary, he seemed to have moved away from disengaged philosophical speculation to embrace politics, eager to join in the search for practical solutions. He thus not only found Master Zhuang wanting but also realized that he could remedy the work that Zhuang left by creating a commentary that converted its perceived impracticalities into a treatise of effective statecraft, for as Guo states in his preface to the *Zhuangzi*:

> We can say of Master Zhuang that he did indeed understand the underlying basis of things [*ben*]. As such, he never kept wild talk about it to himself. His words are those of one who responds to things in a unique way but fails to identify with them. Since he so responded but failed to identify with them, his words may be apt but have no practical use, and since what he says fails to address practical matters, though lofty it has no application. A gap certainly exists between one such as he who quietly refrains from action and one who does start to act but only because it is inevitable—for him it may be said his awareness is unselfconscious. When mind functions in terms of unselfconscious action, one responds as he is immediately affected, his response varying according to the moment involved. Such a one speaks only with utmost caution. As such, he forms one body with transformation and, flowing through a

> myriad ages, arcanely merges with things. How could such a one just playfully talk about otherworldly things only in terms of his own individual experience![28]

According to Guo, Master Zhuang is deficient in three respects: (1) Although he responds spontaneously and uniquely to things (without prejudice and free of influence), he fails "arcanely to merge" or "become one" with them. As such, his words never quite attain sagely wisdom, the articulation of which is the most practical advice possible. (2) Guo sees Master Zhuang as essentially disengaged from worldly affairs, one who "quietly refrains from action," whereas the truly enlightened sage does act, but only "because it is inevitable" or when "there is no alternative" [*budeyi*]. (3) Whereas Master Zhuang engages in "wild talk" couched in terms of his own personal experience, the truly enlightened sage, identifying perfectly with things in all space and time, "speaks only with the utmost caution."

Beginning in 306, Guo held high office, close to the center of power. By this time, he had likely concluded his work on the *Zhuangzi* and put it aside, finished or not. The state of the commentary itself supports this view, for the last of the three sections, the "Miscellaneous Chapters" [*zapian*], especially chapters 28–33, show markedly less attention than all the earlier parts of the work: only three passages in chapter 28, "Refusing Rulership" [*Rangwang*], receive comments, as do only another three in chapter 29, "Robber Zhi" [*Dao Zhi*]. Chapter 30, "Discourse on Swords" [*Shuojian*], lacks commentary entirely. Chapter 31, "The Old Fisherman" [*Yufu*], has only a single comment attached to its last passage, which in a few brief sentences attempts to sum up the meaning of the entire chapter. For chapter 32, "Lie Yukou," most passages have comments, but compared with earlier chapters, they seem rather sketchy. Although most of the passages in chapter 33, "All Under Heaven" [*Tianxia*], receive comments, most of them tend to be brief, while the comment attached to 33.23, one of the longest in the entire commentary, does not address this, the last passage in the work, but instead provides Guo's opinion of Master Zhuang in general. Overall, the comments for chapters 28–33, compared to those for most earlier parts of the work, show signs of haste. Therefore, Guo's commentary received the last of his attention either just before or after he was appointed recorder for the senior tutor in 306. It was then that Guo tried to finish what he could of the commentary, which he then soon abandoned, for his attention was focused elsewhere and he was just too busy.

Patronage of Sima Yue

In 307, Emperor Hui was poisoned, likely on the orders of Sima Yue and possibly with the connivance of the crown prince, Sima Chi (284–313), who then became Emperor Huai.[29] Sima Yue, determined on acquiring power himself, immediately tried to dominate him, but the new emperor proved to be no pushover, for he enjoyed long and close connections with the Luoyang imperial guard and, as a son of the previous emperor, elicited strong support from many in the capital who championed succession legitimacy. He was also an experienced military leader and an energetic and engaging political figure, who enjoyed a considerable personal following, both before and after his ascension. Moreover, he gained followers from among opponents of the machinations to grasp power by the empress dowager, Yang Xianrong (d. 322), and her clique. Sima Yue was even found among these opponents of Yang, for it is thought that he considered the emperor easier to deal with than the empress dowager.[30]

While it may have been due to the emperor's strong support at the time that Sima Yue decided to leave Luoyang, shelving his plans to take immediate control, he had another more pressing concern. In March and April of 307, Wang Mi (d. 311) led a rebellion in Sima Yue's Donghai domain, which succeeded in taking Qingzhou and Xuzhou and killing their governors. Xuzhou, at the heart of the domain, was the primary source from which Sima Yue drew his standing army and on which he depended for political power. But when he asked permission to return to Donghai, the emperor, aware of its importance to him, refused. Sima Yue instead established his headquarters at Xuchang, about 100 miles southeast of Luoyang, taking his princely court with him, including the office staff of the senior tutor [*taifu fu*], which now included Guo Xiang.[31] His choice of Xuchang seemed sound at the time, for it lay within striking distance of the rebellion to the east, and from Xuchang, he could oversee his troops deployed on all sides of Luoyang, which were commanded by his three younger brothers. These forces controlled all the approaches to Luoyang, including the most important, the one from the southeast, the only route by which the capital could then be supplied since all the western sources for supplying the capital were cut off by the Xiongnu, led by Liu Yao (d. 329), and all sources to the north were in the hands of the Jie people, led by Shi Le (274–333).

However, despite extensive military campaigning over the next two and a half years, much of it led in person by Sima Yue, all efforts proved futile, since he was gradually deprived of territory and driven westward toward Xuchang during 307–308 by the combined forces of Liu Yao and Shi Le, who now controlled most of the land north of the Yellow River. In the spring of 309, Sima Yue, still garrisoned in Xuchang, dispatched three thousand heavily armed soldiers into Luoyang, and at the court, had them kill most of the emperor's supporters. He then returned to Luoyang and made himself chancellor [*chengxiang*], assuming control of all civil and military affairs for the central government. Guo Xiang, now well established as one of Sima Yue's intimate advisors, returned with him to Luoyang, where his duties as recorder extended to the office of the chancellor. From then on, Sima Yue seems to have held two offices concurrently: he kept his position of grand tutor while assuming the new position of chancellor. He also apparently kept the staff of his office of grand tutor intact, now seconding its members to his new office, which resulted in Guo becoming recorder for the chancellor [*chengxiang zhubu*].[32]

Guo Xiang's Rise to Power

Guo Xiang's own rise to power is remarkable, for a recorder [*zhubu*] was subordinate to three higher positions in a princely court [*gongfu*]: chief clerk [*zhangshi*], major [*sima*], and palace guard administrator [*congshi zhonglang*]. Moreover, Guo was just one of five recorders who held that post during 306–310/311; the others were Pian Dun (d. 329), Liu Yan (dates unknown), Xun Kai (d. 324), and Pei Xia, the *xuanxue* rhetorician who had bested Guo at the wedding party of 297. Men who filled the senior positions then included Chancellor Pan Tao (d. 311), who had been on Sima Yue's princely staff since before 300; major and gentleman of the palace Liu Qia (dates unknown), Sima Yue's superintendent of the capital [*zhongwei*]; and Major Yu Ai (262–311), Guo's friend and fellow *xuanxue* thinker.[33] Since these seven men were all scions of elite families and highly experienced senior military leaders or administrators, Guo was very much the odd man out. Nevertheless, Sima Yue, who spent most of the first decade of the fourth century out in the field, delegated most of the administration of his court and government during this time to Guo Xiang before, during, and after his usurpation of the complete power of the Jin state:

> When Prince Yue of Donghai appointed Guo recorder for the senior tutor [*taifu zhubu*], as his most trusted deputy, he began to wield such power that its touch smoked or singed [*xunzhuo*] those inside and outside the court. However, because general opinion later turned against him, he was removed from office.[34]

The metaphor "smoke and singe" indicates the effect of great power: like fire, it smokes those at a distance, "outside the court," and singes those nearby, "inside the court." This account in the *Jinshu* is corroborated by a fragment from another work of the same title, the *Jinshu* (History of the Jin) of Zang Rongxu (415–488): "When Guo Xiang, personal name Zixuan, was appointed recorder for the senior tutor [Sima Yue] he so enjoyed his confidence that he was able to use his office to control the military of the entire government [*zhuanling jun yifu*].[35] Wang Xiaoyi interprets in detail what *zhuanling jun yifu* means:

> During the Western Jin, the imperial palace guard consisted of the Left and Right Guards and the Resolute Cavalry of the Van, Rear, Left, and Right, seven garrisons in all, known as the "Seven Armies of the Imperial Guard."[36] The most

important units in the entire imperial palace guard were the two Guards of the Left and Right, whose commanders-in-chief were the Left General and Right General of the Guards. The entire "Seven Armies of the Imperial Guard" were under the authority of a commander-in-chief, the Capital Commandant (also called "General of the Palace Guard" or "Watch Officer of the Northern Army"). According to the *Jin jiang xiang dachen biao* (Chronological table of Jin dynasty generals, ministers, and high officials) of Wan Sitong (1638–1702), while Sima Yue was dictator from the Guangxi era to the fourth year of the Yongjia era [306–310], the position of commander-in-chief of the imperial palace guard went unfilled, either as Capital Commandant, General of the Palace Guard, or Watch Officer of the Northern Army,[37] and one of the Senior tutor's [Sima Yue] individual assistants instead served as such an Imperial Palace Guard Supervisor. The trusted aid who then filled this crucial position was none another than Guo Xiang. . . . The expression *zhuanling jun yifu* means that circumstances were such that no formally appointed senior official was in charge of the imperial palace guard, and Guo Xiang as Sima Yue's deputy had total authority over all military garrisons associated with it. The normal role of a recorder was management of the routine work of the department involved and supervision of its subordinate officials. However, during exceptional conditions stemming from the chaos of war, especially if the department head had also actually taken control of the imperial government, the role of such a subordinate official becomes rather flexible, and, as the department head's deputy, could become commander-in-chief of the army and even administer the puppet court. . . . Therefore, it is evident that it was entirely possible for Guo Xiang, holding the position of recorder for the senior tutor, to carry out the duties of "capital commandant" as his deputy. It was exactly because Guo Xiang had this extraordinary position that the "Guo Xiang biography" in the *Jinshu* states that "he began to wield such power that its touch smoked or singed those inside and outside the court." This happened while Guo Xiang was associated with Sima Yue's faction when it had reached its peak of political power, but, just as in the dramatic climax of a play, he was inextricably dragged along in its swift downfall that soon occurred afterwards.[38]

Guo Xiang as Alleged Plagiarist and His Accusers

The *Jinshu* biography then goes on to close its account of Guo's life and shifts the focus to his *Zhuangzi* commentary:

Toward the end of the Yongjia era [307–313] Guo fell ill and died, leaving a work, *Beilun* (Tombstone Discourses) in twelve chapters.[39] Up to then, dozens

> had written commentaries on the *Zhuangzi*, but all had failed to master its overall intent. But Xiang Xiu [ca. 221–ca. 300], taking an approach different from these old commentaries, explained its meaning in a marvellously new and wonderfully engaging way, which resulted in a great development of arcane learning. When Xiang Xiu died, only the two chapters "Autumn Floods" and "Perfect Joy" remained undone. Since his sons were then too young to do anything about it, his interpretation remained incomplete and piecemeal. However, quite a few copies of this separate version of Xiu's work began to circulate. Guo Xiang was a man whose conduct was reprehensible, so when he saw that Xiang Xiu's interpretation had not achieved proper circulation, he plagiarized the commentary and passed it off as his own work. He composed his own commentary to only two chapters, "Autumn Floods" and "Perfect Joy," and modified just one chapter, "Horses' Hooves." For all other chapters, he probably just edited the wording. Later on, Xiang Xiu's own interpretation also appeared as a separate work, so two versions of the *Zhuangzi* now exist, Xiang's and Guo's, but interpretation of it is one and the same.[40]

This passage is copied almost verbatim from an account in the *Shishuo xinyu*, differing only in one sentence: "As for Guo Xiang, he was a man whose conduct was contemptible, though he possessed great talent, so when he saw that Xiang Xiu's interpretation had not achieved proper circulation . . ."[41] However, that people thought Guo's conduct contemptible was not just because of this supposed act of plagiarism; the act itself was considered characteristic of a far greater fault. Such a negative view of Guo seems to have derived from both his perceived desertion of the lofty principles of Lao-Zhuang philosophy by striving for high office and, even more serious, the way that he acted once he held a position of power. Such was the view, for example, of his erstwhile friend, Yu Ai:

> Then, joining the office of senior tutor for military affairs [*taifu junshi*] of Prince Yue of Donghai [Sima Yue], Yu was transferred to the post of military consultant libationer [*junzi jijiu*]. At that time, the court of Prince Yue was filled with many men of exceptional talent. Although Yu Ai was one of them, he always kept his hands inside his sleeves [observed but took no active part]. Guo Xiang from Henan, then an aide [*zhangshi*] to the regional governor of Yuzhou [a province comprising Henan and northern Hubei], was considered by his contemporaries a second Wang Bi [226–249]. Ai, who knew him well, often said, "Why should Guo Zixuan be thought a lesser man than I, Yu Zisong!" But later, when Guo had become recorder for the senior tutor and used his official appointment to usurp autocratic power, it prompted Ai to say to him, "Henceforth you may be a man of great ability for our present age, but the high opinion I formerly had of you now is all gone!"[42]

At the end of the *Jinshu*, fascicle 50, which contain the biographies of Yu Ai, Guo Xiang, Yu Chun (Yu Ai's uncle), and the upright official Qin Xiu (later third to the early fourth century), the chief editor, Fang Xuanying (578–648), as court historian [shichen] proclaimed:

> For centuries, Master Yu [Ai] has carried a reputation for pure virtue and been praised by the whole world. The area between the Ru and the Ying rivers [Henan] produced many men of extraordinary ability, so how could such a man have been found elsewhere? Mofu [Yu Chun, the uncle of Yu Ai] had always detested the obsequious and wicked, but he only divulged this when he had indulged in food and drink. Therefore, as when shooting at rats one fears to break vessels, how can we make rash accusations? But just as someone who steals another's property is justly called a thief, Zixuan [Guo Xiang] borrowed another's reputation and claimed credit due to him, so why should we not take him for a thief!

In the "Appraisal" [*zan*] of these figures, which immediately follows, Fang delivers the final blow: "Whereas [Guo] Xiang claimed credit due to another, Qin Xiu was a man who hated wickedness."[43] Guo's biography is sandwiched between those of Yu Ai and Yu Chun, a high official (governor of Henan) whose reputation for lofty integrity also stands in great contrast to the one that Fang thrust upon Guo, which was designed to denigrate him as much as possible. Never questioned, the *Shishuo xinyu* passage and Guo's *Jinshu* biography were often repeated in sources for the rest of the tradition and into modern times, albeit at times reworded slightly differently or abbreviated.[44]

The view that Guo had usurped and abused his authority tarnished his reputation for centuries; for example, Yan Zhitui (531–591), staunch Confucian that he was, included Guo in a general diatribe against figures prominent in *xuanxue* thought, which Yan considered inimical to good government and society:

> The writings of Masters Lao and Zhuang teach perfection of authenticity, nourishment of original nature, and aversion to entanglement by things. As such, the one hid from fame as a court archivist and finally went off to tread desert sands, while the other concealed himself as clerk of the lacquer garden and in the end rejected the prime ministership of Chu. This is exactly how the truly unfettered should behave.
>
> However, the likes of He Yan (190–249) and Wang Bi [226–249] transmitted what they taught as "arcane tradition" [*xuanzong*], which, among themselves, they flaunted and promoted, sticking together like shadows of one another or so much grass bending to the wind. Believing that the transformative power

of the Divine Farmer [Shennong] and the Yellow Thearch inhered in them all, they discarded the tradition of the Duke of Zhou and Confucius as unworthy of attention. Nevertheless, Pingshu [He Yan] was executed because he was associated with Cao Shuang [d. 249] and, when he got caught in the net of the law, died for the sake of power. Fusi [Wang Bi] provoked resentment because he too often ridiculed others, and the trap he fell into was his excessive desire to win. Shan Juyuan [Shan Tao (205–283)] incurred ridicule for amassing wealth, for he had violated the maxim, "much hoarding is sure to result in heavy loss."[45] Xiahou Xuan (209–254) was killed because of his talent and popularity, which means he did not follow the examples of Zhili [Shu] and "the unspoiled simple" and "useless wood" [*yongzhong*].[46] When the wife of Xun Fengqian [Xun Can (ca. 209–ca. 237)] passed away, he was so wounded in spirit that he himself died, which is not at all the character of one who drums on an earthenware vessel![47] When Wang Yifu [Wang Yan (256–311)] mourned his son, he was so grief-stricken that he could not bear it, which was completely unlike Dongmen [Wu] with his consummate insight.[48] When Xi Shuye [Xi Kang] disdained conventional behavior, how was he the kind of person who "merges with the brilliant and becomes one with the very dust"![49] When Guo Zixuan went after autocratic power that made people alarmingly upset, how was that the way to "place himself in the rear" and "put aside his person"![50] Ruan Sizong [Ruan Ji (210–263)] immersed himself in wine and lived a disordered life, which was contrary to the advice: when the road is feared, people should take warning.[51] Xie Youyu [Xie Kun (282–324)] was cashiered from office because he took bribes, which ran counter to what was meant when he [Master Zhuang] threw back his extra fish.[52]

These men were all leading figures to whom adherents of arcane doctrine gravitated. As for other such lesser figures, who, shackled by the dust and filth of the world and thoroughly confounded by fame and profit, how can I possibly address all of them! Such people do nothing but take up pure conversation [*qingtan*] and elegant views [*yalun*] to analyze the utmost subtleties of arcane doctrine. Host and guest may go back and forth with all this, but it only delights the mind and pleases the ear and has nothing to do with the essentials for saving the world and establishing good moral habits.[53]

Yan Zhitui seems to have been so determined to denigrate *xuanxue* that he refused to entertain the possibility that it might contribute to effective statecraft and a good society, which, after all, was the apparent intent of Guo's commentary to the *Zhuangzi*.

Other detractors embellished the plagiarism accusation with unsubstantiated elaborations of their own. For example, Chen Jiru (1558–1639), the prominent painter, calligrapher, essayist, and arbiter of taste and culture, not only condemned Guo for stealing the commentary from Xiang Xiu, but also denounced the very idea that commentaries helped one to understand the *Zhuangzi*:

> Forty-nine different commentaries to *Zhuangzi* exist in a total of five hundred sixteen fascicles. Although the "wings" to *Laozi* and *Zhuangzi* as a pair have received much praise recently,[54] my friend Zou Mengyang [1575–1643] told me that all such commentaries should be discarded, except for the one by Guo Zixuan, for it alone is all we need. Yu Shanfu [Yu Ai (262–311), who was fond of reading the *Laozi* and *Zhuangzi*, said, "This is exactly the way I think!" And Xi Shuye [Xi Kang[55] (223–262)] asked "Why must this book [*Zhuangzi*] have any commentary added to it?" This means that only if one tries to understand it without such explanation will an intrinsically marvelous understanding of it emerge, for just as a good military strategy teacher might get half his troops killed, so a commentary on a work might lose half its substance. It was the way that Guo blatantly took it on himself to violate its actual gist that allowed him his supposedly marvelous explication of the *Zhuangzi*. As for the study of Master Zhuang, later generations condemned Guo for gross error, judging him as bad as the wife of Xu Zao, who when she wrote to her younger sister, said that she regarded them [the *Laozi* and *Zhuangzi*] as just so much trivial nonsense.[56] Nevertheless, Dao scholastics [Daojia] went on promoting Guo by attaching his commentary to the work of that supremely perfected one—how ridiculous! . . .
>
> It is to be regretted that *Zhuangzi* commentators were not only the likes of Guo Zixuan! When he was made recorder to the senior tutor by the Prince of Donghai [Sima] Yue, [Guo] Zixuan usurped such power that it smoked and singed. After popular general opinion turned against him, he was removed from office. How could anyone such as [Guo] Zixuan ever have composed an explication of the *Zhuangzi*! He just stole the commentary from Xiang Ziqi [Xiang Xiu]. Since Guo was incapable of conveying the meaning of the *Zhuangzi*, was Xiang equally incapable as well? Earlier commentators of the *Zhuangzi* rarely plumbed its overall meaning, but Ziqi's explication of its hidden meaning went so far beyond these older commentaries that it stirred up extraordinary interest. When Xiang died, only the two chapters "Autumn Floods" and "Perfect Joy" remained undone. Although Zixuan composed his own commentaries to these two chapters, for all the rest he merely edited the wording. Even though Guo could not long conceal the lie that it all was his own work, why was the commentary never attributed to Xiang? As Guo Xiang stole it from Xiang Xiu, Xiang Xiu stole it from Master Zhuang. As Master Zhuang stole it from Old Longears [Master Lao], Old Longears stole it from the *Changes*. And the *Changes* stole it from Heaven and Earth. As the *Yinfu jing* (Scripture of the Hidden Accordance) has it, Heaven and Earth steal from

> man,[57] so why go on to blame [Guo] Zixuan? This is why today it is still called the "Guo commentary."[58]

Another late Ming scholar, the Confucian moral philosopher Liu Zongzhou (1578–1645), after repeating the damning remarks, goes on to characterize Guo as beset first by arrogance and then by shame:

> He [Guo] plagiarized it as his own commentary and bragged about it to all the world. Then, Xiu's disciples, who managed to obtain drafts of his work, placed it in circulation so people could examine and compare the two, and, since the part that Guo had done consisted only of the "Autumn Floods" and "Perfect Joy" chapters, he was so shamed that he wished to die.[59]

Reading through these passages, the rationale underlying such denigration unfolds: Guo could not have composed most of the commentary to the *Zhuangzi* because he was such a devious, mean, and worldly ambitious man that he must have plagiarized it. Not only did he become a high official, he also usurped autocratic power, in great contrast to Xiang, who, although he accepted office, did so only out of fear for his own safety, and, once in office, took no part in its affairs:

> Once Xi Kang [223–262] had been executed, Xiang Xiu, responding to a recommendation for office from the local commandery accounts clerk, went to Luoyang, where [posthumously entitled] Emperor Wen [Sima Zhao (211–265)] said to him, "I have heard that your will was fixed on Jishan [present-day Zhili], so what are you doing here?" Xiang Xu replied, "It is my opinion that Father Chao and Xu You may have been stubbornly upright but never quite understood what Yao had in mind, so why should they be greatly admired!"[60] At that, the emperor was most pleased, and from then on Xiu served as an official. . . . Later, although he was appointed a gentleman cavalier attendant and senior recorder [*sanji shilang*], transferred to the post of gentleman attendant at the palace gate [*huangmen shilang*], and then to cavalier attendant-in-ordinary and senior recorder [*sanji changshi*], at court he had no official duties and did nothing more than just take his place there.[61]

Plagiarism Challenged: Doubtful Sources

However, the accusation that Guo plagiarized Xiang's earlier work appears only in the *Shishuo xinyu*, and, since it obviously copies its account from that work, the *Jinshu* version does not provide independent corroboration. In fact, no such evidence exists for the claim in any other source. Of all the official dynastic histories, the compilation of the *Jinshu* (648) is furthest chronologically from the time it addresses, 229 years (the Jin ended in 420), and more than three centuries from Guo's own time during the Western Jin (265–316). Moreover, it has often been criticized for its failure to corroborate evidence, stick to verifiable facts, and maintain standards of the historiographical tradition. As early as the generation following its completion, the historiographer Liu Zhiji (661–721) criticized it roundly:

> When the *History of the Jin* [*Jinshu*] was edited during our great Tang dynasty, those who drafted it were all literary men who ignored the *Records of the Historian* [*Shiji*, by Sima Qian] and the work of the Ban family in the distant past[62] and instead made the Xu and Yu families in recent times their patriarchs.[63] As such, embellishing what they did with frivolous and flimsy diction, their rendering of the text is no different from applying makeup to a fit man in his prime or clothing a person of lofty integrity in fine silks.[64]
>
> . . . . .
>
> As for the recently appeared history of the Jin produced under imperial auspices, its sources consist mostly of shorter, undemanding and easy to read minor works such as the *Yulin* [Grove of anecdotes by Pei Qi (2nd half 4th cent.)], *Shishuo* [*xinyu*], *Soushen ji* [Record of searching the spirit realm, by Gan Bao (d. 336)], and *Youming lu* [Accounts of the hidden and visible worlds, by Liu Yiqing]. But from works such as the [*Jin*] *ji* (*Annals of the Jin*) by the two masters, Cao [Jia (fl. 250–296)] and Gan [Bao (d. 336)] and the two [*Jin*] *yangqiu* (*Annals of the Jin*) by Sun [Sheng (302–373)] and Tan [Daoluan (5th cent.)], it took nothing.[65] As a result, a great many fine things that it should have been included were left out.[66]

This negative view of the *Jinshu* persisted, for example, in the *Jiu Tangshu* (Old history of the Tang), completed in 945, where Fang Xuanling (579–648), editor-in-chief of the *Jinshu*, and his subordinates were again attacked:

> Historians involved [in the *Jinshu*] were mostly literary men who liked to include unusual, even bizarre, anecdotal odds and ends in order to broaden the appeal of the narrative. Moreover, while they vied to make their discussions and judgements ever more elaborate and dazzling, they failed to seek solid fact. For all these reasons this work has been criticized harshly.[67]

While reiterating much of what Liu Zhiji said centuries before, the editor-in-chief Ji Yun (1724–1805) of the *Qinding siku quanshu zongmu* (Comprehensive catalog of the complete four treasures library, authorized by His Majesty), judged the *Jinshu* even more harshly:

> As for the sources it [the *Jinshu*] chose to use, it disregarded authentic records and instead cited minor anecdotal works. . . . In general, what it chose to include strongly promoted the romantic and unconventional, which it used to liven up the narrative. Passages taken from the *Shishuo xinyu* by Liu Yiqing and the commentary of Liu Xiaobiao [462–521], which one after the other reinforce one another, are included almost entirely without change. Such manner of composition is nothing but the style of commonplace storytellers, so how can anyone look at it and call it a real history! . . . It is simply because the works of the eighteen historians [who compiled histories of the Jin] had all been lost that anyone wishing to investigate the history of the Jin had no other way to get at it than with this, is the only reason it has been preserved down through the ages and not dispatched to oblivion.[68]

Although fragments of some of these eighteen lost Jin histories do exist, only one brief passage from the *Jinshu* of Zang Rongxu (415–488) survives, the one cited here.[69]

It should be noted that a key historiographical concern of the compilers and writers of the *Jinshu* was to explain the downfall of the Western Jin regime. Timothy M. Davis has succinctly summarized how this concern shaped the content and thrust of its biographies:

> The medieval historians [Fang Xuanling et al.] who sought to explain the instability of the Western Jin regime faced a number of challenges. Most pressing was the need to supply reasons for the imperial administration's inability to preserve territorial sovereignty. It was assumed that the psychologically stunning loss of the traditional Chinese heartland to non-Chinese peoples could only have been brought about by the immoral and seditious behavior of key individuals holding positions of authority and influence. Readers of the *Jin shu* should bear this in mind when evaluating the accuracy of the many dramatic accounts of wrongdoing contained therein. The biographical section of the *Jin shu* was one venue for fleshing out (in selective detail) the actions, words, and motives of a whole cast of personalities who were perceived as contributing to the dynasty's demise. Faced with such moral obligations, the medieval historiographer often subordinated "historical truth" to "ethical truth" when handling the more unsavory details of an individual's life.[70]

Since Guo Xiang was a major player in the political and military life of the Western Jin regime during the decade leading up to its demise, he was inevitably targeted as a villain. Not only was he perceived as a usurper of power, he did so as deputy of the greatest usurper of all, Sima Yue, whose intrigues, murders, and subordination of Emperor Huai, as well as his failure to repel foreign threat in the field, all led to the Jin's loss of north China. Guo himself is said to have died of natural causes about 312, the year that Luoyang was attacked and occupied by the Xiongnu. Five years later, the final collapse of the Western Jin occurred with the fall of Chang'an in 316.

Other Works by Guo Xiang

Besides his commentary on the *Zhuangzi*, Guo is known to have composed the following works: *Laozi zhu* (Commentary to the *Laozi* [Sayings of Master Lao]), *Zhuangzi yin* (Pronunciation [of names and terms] in the *Zhuangzi*), *Lunyu tilue* (Essentials of the Lunyu [Analects]), Lunyu yin (What is hidden in the *Lunyu* [Analects]), *Guo Xiang ji* (Collected works of Guo Xiang), which probably contained the following three titles: *Zhiming youji lun* (Resultant fate depends on the individual self, a discourse), *Beilun* (Tombstone discourses), and *Lun Xi Shao* (A discussion of Xi Shao [253–304]). For details, see appendix B.

The Charge of Plagiarism and Its Refutation

Here again is the exact charge:

> When Xiang Xiu died, only the two chapters "Autumn Floods" and "Perfect Joy" remained undone. Since his sons were then too young to do anything about it, his interpretation remained incomplete and piecemeal. However, quite a few copies of this separate version of Xiu's work began to circulate. Guo Xiang was a man whose conduct was reprehensible, so when he saw that Xiang Xiu's interpretation had not achieved proper circulation, he plagiarized the commentary and passed it off as his own work. He composed his own commentary to only two chapters, "Autumn Floods" and "Perfect Joy," and modified just one chapter, "Horses' Hooves." For all other chapters, he probably just edited the wording.[71]

As we have seen, many throughout the ages accepted the truth of the accusation, but some did not. For example, the bibliophile and great book collector Qian Zeng (1629–1701),[72] in his *Dushu minqiu ji* (Record of my earnest search through reading books) quotes the previous passage and then observes:

> When I look into Master Lu's [Lu Deming (556–627)] *Jingdian* [*shiwen*][*Textual explications for*] *classics and scriptures*, I see that the Xiu commentary that it cites is not the least like Guo's, so I suspect that Xiang's existed as a different

> version then still in circulation. Since it was such a long time ago and so subject to discrepancies of rumor and hearsay, I fear that what the *Jinshu* has to say need not be trusted.[73]

However, the editors of the *Qinding siku quanshu zongmu tiyao* (completed 1781–1783) rejected Qian Zeng's judgment and declared that the *Jinshu* accusation against Guo Xiang was reliable, despite the strong doubt they cast on the general reliability of the *Jinshu* elsewhere. After repeating the accusation in Guo's *Jinshu* biography and noting that it is almost identical to what the *Shishuo xinyu* has to say, the *Qinding siku quanshu zongmu tiyao* continues:

> Qian Zeng in his *Dushu minqiu ji* takes exception and says that "since it was such a long time ago and so subject to discrepancies of rumor and hearsay that what the *Jinshu* has to say need not be trusted." [*Siku* editor's note:] According to Chen Zhensun [ca. 1183–1262], Xiang Xiu's commentary was already lost by the Song dynasty, "though it is seen sporadically in Master Lu's *Textual explications* [for classics and scriptures].[74] [Here follows more than a dozen comparisons of identical or almost identical excerpts from the two commentaries.]. . . . Therefore they [the two commentaries] are both virtually the same and differ only in small ways. The assertion that Guo plagiarized what Xiang had written and merely edited the wording is thus certainly not unfounded." . . . So how could Qian Zeng have made such a doubtful judgement of it?[75]

The compilers of the *Qinding siku quanshu zongmu tiyao* thus reinforced the centuries-long bias against Guo Xiang as author of the commentary, but if they had considered other early passages in other works that address Guo and his commentary, they might have been more inclined to agree with Chen Zeng. Such reconsideration should actually begin with the *Jinshu* biography of Xiang Xiu, for in it Guo's commentary, clearly identified as his, is given high praise:

> Although throughout ages there had been readers among the learned and talented intelligentsia of the inner and outer several tens of chapters of the work that Zhuang Zhou had composed, no one had ever succeeded in expounding its overall intent. However, Xiang Xiu then composed an "Explanation of its hidden meaning" [*Yinjie*] for it,[76] which cast such light on its profound meaning that it stirred up a vogue for arcane learning. Although readers then got such a extraordinarily clear and heart-felt understanding of it that for a time none thought it deficient in any way, during the reign of Emperor Hui [r. 290–307], once Guo Xiang again transmitted it in an expanded version, this brought scorn on all footprints that Confucians and Mohists left behind and instead made School of the Dao [Daojia] teachings flourish.[77]

These two contradictory claims, either that Guo plagiarized Xiang's commentary and merely edited the wording or he enlarged and developed it to the extent that his new version greatly enhanced School of Dao teachings, formed the basis of a controversy that lasted throughout the rest of the traditional era and endures to this day. Such modern and contemporary Chinese scholars fall into three groups: (1) those who ignore all evidence to the contrary and simply claim that Guo plagiarized Xiang's commentary—these include Qian Mu (1895–1990) and Hou Wailu (1903–1987); (2) those who take into account a wider range of evidence and conclude that the commentary should be ascribed jointly to Xiang and Guo—these include Feng Youlan (Fung Yu-lan, (1895–1990), Feng Qi (1915–1995), Ren Jiyu (1916–2009), and Tang Yongtong (1893–1964); and (3) those who conclude that because Xiang's commentary was lost before the Tang but Guo's survived fully into the Song and the age of print, the two must have been very different overall, and Guo's was surely superior, the commentary should be ascribed to Guo alone—these include Tang Yijie (1927–2014), Xiao Jiefu (1924–2008), Pang Pu (1928–2015), and Wei Zhengtong (1927–2018).[78] However, to fully understand the issues involved and the conclusions drawn, the controversy should be traced to earlier times.

It should first be noted that the *Wenshi zhuan* (Biographies of literary men) of Zhang Yin (from the late fourth century) pays tribute to Guo's commentary entirely, without mention of Xiang Xiu: "The commentary composed by Guo Xiang to the *Zhuangzi* consists of the most sublime meaning expressed in the clearest diction [*qingci qiuzhi*]."[79] Therefore, even at this early date, the charge that Guo simply incorporated Xiang's earlier commentary into his own with little or no change seems utterly unfounded. However, it was also argued that the preference for Guo's commentary may have also been because Guo's edition of the *Zhuangzi*, to which it is attached, was considered the better version. As Lu Deming, in his preface to the *Jingdian shiwen* (Textual explications for classics and scriptures) (ca. 583), states:

> The *Zhuangzi* in fifty-two chapters listed in the dynastic bibliography in the *History of the Former Han* [206 BCE–24 CE], the *Hanshu yiwen zhi*,[80] is the work to which Sima Biao [240–306] and Mengshi [Master Meng, name and dates unknown] later wrote commentaries. It contains much strange and incredible material, sometimes resembling the *Shanhai jing* [Classic of Mountains and Waters (compiled probably in the third century BCE) and sometimes works concerned with dream divination. As such, these commentators selected and rejected parts based on their opinion of them. Although the inner chapters are the same for all versions, as for the rest of the work, some have the outer chapters but lack the miscellaneous chapters, so it is only Zixuan's [Guo Xiang's] commentary edition that entirely captures Master Zhuang's real meaning, which is why it is universally admired.

> When Xu Xianmin [Xu Mian (344–397)] and Li Hongfan [Li Gui (early fourth century)] prepared their pronunciation editions, they both used Guo Xiang's version, and I too now use it as the base text here.[81]

Lu Deming then goes on to compare editions of the *Zhuangzi* that were known to him and notes that Xiang Xiu's commentary version consists of twenty fascicles and twenty-six chapters, adding his own comment that a variant version also exists in twenty-seven fascicles and twenty-eight chapters and they both lack the miscellaneous chapters. Therefore, Guo's edition, with thirty-three fascicles and thirty-three chapters, is at least five chapters longer than either of the known Xiang versions, and Guo's division of his into seven "Inner Chapters," fifteen "Outer Chapters," and eleven "Miscellaneous Chapters" likely resulted in a book that was better organized, easier to use, and more appealing. Lu Deming began a trend that soon made Guo's edition the definitive version of the *Zhuangzi* for all time, a trend much enhanced when Cheng Xuanying (ca. 600–ca. 660) added his generally admired subcommentary to Guo's during the Tang dynasty.

Once determined as the definitive version of the *Zhuangzi*, Guo's attached commentary acquired an authority of its own that dominated the interpretation of the *Zhuangzi* for much of the later tradition.[82] For example, in his preface to Gui Youguang's (1507–1571) *Nanhua zhenjing pingzhu* (Commentary to the true classic of Nanhua), Feng Mengzhen (1546–1605), the prominent scholar and noted diarist, whose highest office was chancellor of the National University in Nanjing, unequivocally places Guo's commentary at the center of *Zhuangzi* exegesis, leaving in abeyance the question of how much of it was Guo's and how much Xiang's. Note that Feng also moves the commentary at the end of his essay away from a statecraft focus to one of his own personal cultivation and self-fulfillment:

> None of the dozens of *Zhuangzi* commentators since Guo Zixuan have matched his subtlety and profundity, which at their best he used to explain the meaning of the *Zhuangzi* in ways others failed to reach. Now then, if the text of the *Zhuangzi* is the sun, then Zixuan's commentary is the moon, and all other commentators are just stars in the sky, which at most are but lit torches or glowing fireflies. As long as Zixuan's commentary was there before them, they did not let their own lights go out, for, just like ladies other than the beauties Mao Qiang and Xi Shi at court, their faces whitened and brows darkened, who time and again never gave up competing against them for imperial favor.
>
> In recent times Jiao Ruohou [Jiao Hong (1540–1620)] brought out a joint edition entitled *Lao Zhuang yi* (Wings to the *Laozi* and the *Zhuangzi*), which though it contains the entire Guo commentary, includes comments by others only as marginalia. These others, like the Woman Zhao and Doll of Wu,[83] are

assigned to low rank. As for the rest, he did away with them all and made Master Guo his sole patriarch. All it took was one look back to him, and in all the Nine Palaces [bedchambers of the emperor's nine wives and concubines], no beauty existed for him.

Now here the main text is set out first with Guo's commentary copied one character space beneath it. Both texts are printed in large characters exactly the same size in order to promote it [Guo's commentary]. Someone long ago once said, "It is not that Guo Xiang comments on Master Zhuang, but that Master Zhuang comments on Guo Xiang." What a perceptive thing to say! This is why we should promote the commentary, and promote it as equal to the *Zhuangzi* itself.

Some say that his commentary came from Xiang Xiu and that Master Guo stole it, merely adding his own commentary to two chapters, "Autumn Floods" and "Perfect Joy," and then called it all his own work. However, although one might never quite know whether or not this is true, people now only know the commentary as Guo Xiang's and not as Xiang Xiu's—good fortune for the one and misfortune for the other.

About the time I was capped [twenty *sui*, nineteen years], the time was so troubled that I stayed behind our shut gate and read the *Zhuangzi* with Guo's commentary.[84] I so immersed myself in it for almost two months that I neglected all social intercourse. After that, though I must have seemed foolish and wild, I was no longer contrary with family members or even with the world at large. No matter what happened, I became entirely compliant, and I have been at peace right up to now. Although it was later when I was reading Buddhist scriptures that all doubts and misgivings melted away, might it not have been the *Zhuangzi* and Guo's commentary that served as vanguards for the Buddha's teachings?[85]

The Modern Rehabilitation of Guo Xiang: Textual Comparisons

Suspicion that Guo was being treated unfairly and that the commentary should principally be attributed to him began to emerge more frequently during the late Qing and early Republic eras. For example, when the eminent scholar Wang Xianqian (1842–1918),[86] published his *Zhuangzi jijie* (Master Zhuang, collected explications) in 1909, he compared similar comments by Guo and Xiang to a particular passage, to which he himself added the note, "Although people in the past say that Guo plagiarized Xiang's commentary, this is probably wrong."[87]

Qian Zeng's defense of Guo Xiang and its rejection by the editors of *Siku quanshu zongmu tiyao* attracted the attention of Takeuchi Yoshio (1866–1966), a scholar of Chinese philosophy who in work published in 1926 examines evidence for both the charge and the exoneration in considerable detail. Concentrating on passages quoted in Zhang Zhan's (fl. 350–400) commentary to *Liezi* and Lu Deming's *Jingdian shiwen*, he concludes that whereas Guo borrowed much from Xiang Xiu, he also added much of his own work to it.[88] Takeuchi's findings a few years later in 1933 prompted Wu Chengshi (1885–1939), in his *Jingdian shiwen xulu shuzheng* (Prefatory treatise to textual explications for classics and scriptures, critical annotations), to undertake his own survey of the evidence, from which he came to much the same conclusion. He added that although Guo certainly borrowed from Xiang, both commentaries were shaped by general trends in contemporary thought, and since such borrowing was then pervasively practiced, the accusation of "plagiarism" was inappropriate:

> Note: In the *Shishuo* [*xinyu*] where Chancellor Wang maintains that "music has nothing to do with either joy or sorrow," [Liu Jun, better known as Liu Xiaobao (462–521)] notes that just as this concept began with Xi Kang, "nurturing life" [*yangsheng*] began with Ruan Ji and "words fully express idea" [*yan jin yi*] began with Ouyang Jianshi [268–300].[89] Thus it turns out that when a distinctive new idea occurred but words for it were still lacking, those involved relied for its articulation on something already written. This was how the arcane learning movement grew ever stronger. As for the Guo-Xiang case, it was entirely fitting that the one resembled the other, and such a one should not be accused of plagiarism. A further note: When people long ago elucidated classic works, besides explicit explanations, they composed pronunciation guides to works [*yinshu*]. Therefore, when the [*zongmu*] *tiyao* ([*Comprehensive*] *critical catalogue* [*of the complete four treasures library*]) uses as evidence the fact that the [*Jingdian*] *shiwen* (*Textual explications* [for classics and scriptures of Lu Deming]) cited Xiang's *Pronunciation* [of names and terms in the *Zhuangzi*][90] to prove that Xiang had also composed a commentary to the "Autumn Floods" chapter is in error as well.[91] The *Shishuo* also states, "The *Xiaoyao* (Spontaneous Freedom) chapter of the *Zhuangzi* has in the past always been so troublesome that, though various eminent worthies intensively scrutinized and appreciated it, none could extract anyway to understand it other than the way Guo and Xiang did. However Zhi Daolin [Zhidun (314–366)] proposed a superb new way to understand it beyond these two masters and established a new interpretation that went farther than all other famous worthies, a way of approaching it that despite all their ponderings they failed to reach."[92] Therefore, that the Liu [Jun] commentary here cites Guo's and Xiang's explanation of *Xiaoyao* (Spontaneous Freedom) without distinguishing between them can serve as evidence that it was Xiang who first postulated meaning and then Guo who followed up on it. It is generally certain that since in substance their respective writings were not entirely the same, the way they were worded, of course, must have

> been rather different too. This was the usual way such things were done, so one should not find it particularly surprising.[93]

Although Wu intended to absolve Guo from the charge of plagiarism, he failed to make specific comparisons between Guo's and Xiang's commentaries, so his conclusions seem weak. However, several years earlier, in 1927, the classical scholar and bibliophile Liu Pansui (1896–1966) wrote *Shen Guo pian* (On exonerating Guo),[94] which, after quoting the *Shishuo xinyu*, accuses its author, Prince Kang of Linchuan (Liu Yiqing), of egregiously fabricating a trumped-up charge. Liu then declares that both the conception and plan of the commentary were purely Guo's own, and he achieved its final form independently. Wu proposed that this terrible injustice can be put right by looking at three pieces of evidence:

1. The versions of the *Zhuangzi* that Guo and Xiang used were very different. According to the *Suishu jingji zhi* (History of the Sui, "Treatise on classics and scriptures," completed 641–656), Xiang's version comprised twenty fascicles and was already lost by then. Guo's version comprised thirty fascicles and a table of contents in one fascicle. Lu Deming's *Jingdian shiwen shuzheng* (Prefatory treatise to textual explications for classics and scriptures) has it that whereas Xiang's commentary comprises twenty-six fascicles in twenty-six chapters, Guo's version comprises thirty-three fascicles in thirty-three chapters. Moreover, whereas Xiang's version of a *Zhuangzi yin* (Pronunciation guide to Zhuangzi) consisted of one fascicle, Guo's version consisted of three fascicles. All three titles thus indicated very different texts. Since the size of the works differed, their contents must have differed accordingly. Lu Deming also stated that whereas Xiang's version lacked all the miscellaneous chapters [*zapian*], Guo's included eleven chapters, leaving twenty-two chapters for the rest, the inner [*neipian*] and outer chapters [*waipian*]. The Xiang version thus contained four chapters of text not included in Guo's, and the additional eleven chapters in Guo's had attached to them much commentary material that were not present in Xiang's.[95] Such discrepancies clearly indicate that much of the commentary attributed to Guo could not have been written by Xiang Xiu, and the accusation that Guo "composed his own commentary to only two chapters. . . . and modified just one chapter. . . . for all other chapters, he probably just edited the wording" is manifestly groundless.
2. The content of the phrase and passage interpretive comments [*zhangju shiyi*] that comprise the two commentaries mostly differ. Liu Pansui presents comparisons of a dozen or so selected passages from both and concludes that overall, only one to two out of ten seem closely similar or identical. He then notes that excerpts of Guo's and Xiang's commentaries quoted in Zhang Zhan's (fl. 350–400) commentary to the *Liezi* (Master Lie), though often different, are

occasionally similar or even identical, but then he goes on to suggest that this is because they both belong to the same Wei-Jin mainstream of thought, not because Guo plagiarized Xiang. One scholar borrowing from another was commonly done in the early tradition of letters, and others did it both more closely and more extensively than Guo. For example, Fu Qian borrowed much of his commentary to the *Zuozhuan* from Zheng Xuan (127–200), and Yan Zhou [Yan Shigu (581–645)] based his commentary on the *Hanshu* (History of the Former Han) on his uncle Yan Youqin's *Hanshu jueyi* (Resolving doubtful passages in *History of the Former Han*). Liu concludes: "If such matches were their doing, even though they did it by the handfuls, what harm did it do? And how much the less should Zixuan be blamed, for whatever he gleaned from Ziqi was never as great as that which Fu and Yan got that way. So why should such evidence be used to bring a case against Zixuan that he connived to plagiarize!"

3. No one before Liu Yiqing had ever accused Guo of plagiarism. Liu quotes the positive appraisal of Guo by Zhang Yin (late fourth cent) in the *Wenshi zhuan* (Traditions of literary men),[96] and then cites Lu Deming, who explained that his reason for using Guo's version of the *Zhuangzi* in his *Jingdian shiwen* was that Xu Mian (344–397) and Li Gui (early fourth century)] had both prepared their own pronunciation editions based on it:

> Zhang Yin, Xu Mian, and Li Gui, who lived at the beginning of the Eastern Jin [(317–420), were all eminent learned Confucians earlier than Liu Yiqing [403–444] and all had exactly the same good opinion of Guo. When Master Lu compiled his textual explications for *Zhuangzi with Guo's commentary*, although he cited Master Xiang's works on pronunciation and commentary, he never mentioned anything about Guo Xiang's having plagiarized them. That being so, we can know that Guo's commentary was the unique product of his genius and that the Prince Kang's [Liu Yiqing's] accusation was utterly unfounded. Investigating the many such mistakes that occur in the *Shishuo*, Liu Xiaobiao in his commentary sifted out quite a few such errors for censure. However, he did not include this passage about Guo, and that must be acknowledged here. Nevertheless, taking these three points into consideration, it is still perfectly obvious that Guo Xiang did not plagiarize Xiang's interpretation—obvious as if posted at the city gate tower. However, in preparing the *Jinshu* biography of Guo during the Tang, the slander against him in the *Shishuo* was included in its entirety, with no attention as to whether it was true or not. As such, Zixuan was condemned to suffer this injustice, denied vindication for the next thousand years![97]

As zealous as Liu Pansui was in Guo's defense, his brief comparison of passages was still too brief to exonerate Guo completely. However, a much larger investigation was published a few years later in 1940 by the eminent philologist Yang Mingzhao (1909–2003). Yang first notes that among all the fragments of Xiang's commentary, thirty-seven have no counterpart in Guo's, so these play no part in the study. Yang then goes on to list forty-seven passages that are almost exactly the same, only differing slightly in the wording: "In some cases explanatory comments [*jiegu*] match, while in others arguments [*chilun*] are similar. Of similar mind they seem to reason in the same way."[98] Next comes a list of fifteen passages that seem only somewhat similar: "Although explanations differ in these, they seem to follow almost the same gist, as if they were archers shooting at the same target who hit it not far apart."[99] His third comparison lists twenty-seven passages that differ completely. Liu concludes:

> Of these eighty-nine passages, forty-seven are similar in both commentaries, fifteen are close, and twenty-seven are completely different. Overall, more than half are the same or similar. Although this still fails to explore all aspects of comparison and settle things once and for all, it does give a partial view of it that allows summing up: As sure as a river divides off one hill from another or when spring turns seared stubble green, suspicion cast on Zixuan [Guo Xiang] led to a false accusation against which he never had redress.[100]

However, Yang then reiterates Liu Pansui's observation that Liu Xiaobao, despite his many corrections to the *Shishuo xinyu*, failed to address the passage that accuses Guo of plagiarism. That, coupled with how Guo and Xiang get lumped together, where Zhidun's exegesis is judged better than "theirs,"[101] and how eight out of ten comparable passages in Guo's commentary and those of Xiang quoted in Zhang Zhan's (fl. 350–400) commentary to the *Liezi* are virtually the same, lead him to conclude that later scholars should not be blamed for judging the two commentaries more similar than different, or even finding the compilers of the *Jinshu* at fault for following the *Shishuo xinyu* without correction or dissent. Moreover, it seems that Liu Xiaobao, who lived so close in time to Guo, had nothing to go by to determine whether the accusation was true—implying that this might be why he said nothing about it. Yang's final words suggest that Guo probably took over Xiang's commentary and expanded on it, adding new elements of his own, but even this, he says, is not entirely certain.[102]

The next major contribution, and the most important for comparison of the two commentary texts, was published in 1947 by Wang Shumin (1914–2008) in his "*Zhuangzi* Xiang Guo yitong kao" (Investigation of differences and similarities in Xiang's and Guo's commentaries on *Zhuangzi*).[103] Wang not only includes more fragments of Xiang's commentary in his survey, thus providing a larger range of comparative material, but he also provides more detailed comparative analysis. I have prepared a slightly edited and condensed version of Wang's study as appendix C of this book.

Wang's investigation consists of four sections: I. included in Xiang's commentary but not in Guo's (forty-eight places); II. Xiang's and Guo's comments differ completely (thirty places); III. similar comments by Xiang and Guo (thirty-two places); and IV. comments by Xiang and Guo with almost identical wording (twenty-eight places). The original Chinese texts involved by Guo and Xiang are all provided, translated into English, and, where possible, keyed to the numbering system for the translated passages of the *Zhuangzi* and Guo's commentary.

Wang Shumin determines that not one of the forty-eight fragments of Xiang's commentary listed in section I appears anywhere in Guo's commentary, and this, coupled with the thirty places listed in section II where the two commentaries differ completely, amply refute the accusation that Guo plagiarized Xiang's commentary out of whole cloth: that Guo composed his own commentary to only two chapters, "Autumn Floods" and "Perfect Joy," and modified just one chapter, "Horses' Hooves," is manifestly false. As for similar and almost identical places listed in sections III and IV, whereas Guo's comments do seem based on Xiang's, Guo often altered Xiang's exact words to formulate something of his own and did not, as the *Shishuo* and *Jinshu* assert, merely edit the wording and do nothing more. It is also likely that Guo's borrowed material was not always directly from Xiang's commentary, whatever the wording, but rather was assimilated from the general discourse of contemporary *xuanxue* thought, which they both contributed to and drew upon.

Although we can never know all the written sources from which Guo and Xiang might have borrowed, such evidence still exists in a few cases. For example, eight citations to Xiang's commentary in the *Jingdian shiwen* are also attributed to Cui Zhuan (late third–early fourth centuries), whose own twenty-seven-fascicle version of the *Zhuangzi* with his commentary has long been lost.[104] It is also recorded by Liu Xiaobao (462–521) that Xiang largely based his commentary on Cui's: "Although Xiu wandered among numerous worthies seeking support, throughout life he found them all drab and dreary, only loved the *Zhuangzi*, and, largely in accord with what Cui Zhuan had done, composed a commentary to it to guard against forgetting what it meant."[105] We also know that Guo borrowed from Sima Biao's (240–306) fifty-two-chapter *Zhuangzi* commentary. Although this work has long been lost, many fragments of the commentary survive in other works. One such fragment is particularly telling:

> (Guo, 4.0) It is impossible for one who associates with others to live apart from men. However, vicissitudes that beset the human world are such that different measures are appropriate in each and every age. It is only if one remains unselfconscious and so holds not to his own purposes and opinions who can follow wherever vicissitudes lead and yet not be burdened with their entanglements.

> (Sima Biao) This addresses the appropriate way to live in the human world. It is a principle for life during an age of chaos that anyone associating with others will find it impossible to live apart from men. However, the vicissitudes that beset mankind are such that appropriate measures of what to do differ from age to age. It is only if one remains unselfconscious and so holds not to his own purposes and opinions who can change in ways that are exactly right. What may entangle such a one then![106]

Whereas adherents of the plagiarism theory view this instance of Guo's borrowing from Sima Biao as just that much more evidence that he must be guilty,[107] this seems too simplistic. My view is that he synthesized what was available and pertinent from all such sources to enhance his own personal readings of the *Zhuangzi*, and this was how his commentary was composed.

Concerning textual discrepancies that indicate Guo's and Xiang's commentaries must have been significantly different, Tang Yijie (1927–2014) has the last word:

> If the two commentaries were really so similar that Guo Xiang merely "edited the wording," their two editions of the *Zhuangzi* could not possibly have both survived for the more than 300 years from the Jin to the Tang [when Xiang's was lost]. Only if the two commentaries were significantly different could they both have survived separately for so long—only that makes sense.[108]

Such synthetization and adaptation are, of course, not unique to Guo Xiang and Xiang Xiu, for the era in which they lived, or for the Chinese tradition as a whole. Such habits can also be found in the West, as practiced, for example, by one of its most eminent essayists, Michel de Montaigne (1533–1592):

> I leaf through books, I do not study them. What I retain of them is something I no longer recognize as anyone else's. It is only the material from which my judgment has profited, and the thoughts and ideas with which it has become imbued; the author, the place, the words, and other circumstances, I immediately forget.[109]

Created or Self-Generated, Immanence or Transcendence, Immanent Transcendence

Fukunaga Mitsuji seems to have been the first to draw attention to the identification and analysis of the fundamental philosophical propositions, the basic assumptions and presuppositions, that underpin Guo's interpretive comments and how they differ from Xiang's. Fukunaga's reasons for exonerating Guo from the accusation of plagiarism, succinctly set out in a 1964 article, develop an argument that he introduced in a study published in 1954, in which he cites Guo's postscript [*houyu*] to the handwritten text of the *Zhuangzi* preserved in the Kōzanji Temple (Kyoto) (see appendix A.3). The postscript contains a detailed description of how Guo edited the text, which indicates both his vision of the text and his plan for the commentary's overall design, and, because the terminology and reasoning in interpretive passages throughout the commentary is consistent with that vision and design, Fukunaga concludes that Guo should be credited with its overall authorship, regardless of how much he may have borrowed from Xiang.[110] Fukunaga then points out that the commentary also became a vehicle for Guo's own philosophical views:

> Moreover, his *Zhuangzi* commentary is not simply an annotation of the *Zhuangzi*, for he also uses it as a medium through which he conveys his own speculative thought. As such, his *Zhuangzi* commentary becomes an important source by which we may explore the way he thought. Therefore, along with its being a commentary to the *Zhuangzi*, thanks to its systematic treatment and unified interpretation, it also became a work that expressed his own ideas.[111]

In his 1964 study, Fukunaga quotes a passage in Zhang Zhan's (fl. 350–400) commentary to the *Liezi* that, while praising Guo, also suggests that a major difference exists between his and Xiang's interpretations of the *Zhuangzi*:

> Where a form exists a shadow inevitably appears, and where a sound happens an echo inevitably occurs. These both come into existence spontaneously, and both appear and disappear together. How could they possibly exist separately or sequentially depend on each other? And how detailed and comprehensive is Guo Xiang's analysis of this issue in his *Zhuangzi* commentary! Nevertheless, the conventional view is that when a form moves, a shadow follows, and when a sound is made, an echo consequently responds. But here the sage finds a model, since, as an analogy, he understands it to mean that when one is agitated, he loses his foundation, but, if tranquil, he reverts to his roots. So never again misinterpret what shadow and echo actually mean![112]

While specifically referencing both the famous conversation between Shadow and Penumbra (2.33–2.34.4) and the relationship between the mind of the sage and his teachings (11.32.1), the passage also alludes to Guo's basic insistence on the spontaneous self-generation [*zisheng*] of all things (e.g., 2.4.1, 2.5, 2.8.9, and 2.8.21) and his exclusion of deliberate action (along with causal effects) from the rule of the enlightened sovereign (e.g., 1.13.3, 7.13.1–7.13.5, 12.1.3–12.2.1, 13.3.8). That Zhang Zhan cites Guo's commentary but not Xiang's implies that Zhang ascribed such views exclusively to Guo.

However, compare another passage from Xiang's commentary that Zhang quotes (see appendix C, "Texts not included in the Guo Xiang 33 chapter edition," first entry) with Guo's commentary to 2.5–2.6. Although Guo obviously borrowed Xiang's words almost verbatim, a subtle but significant difference emerges: Xiang has it that the generator of things [*shengwuzhe*], the source or initiator of material existence, exists, but is itself "without material substance" [*wuwu*]. That is, *shengwuzhe* designates an ultimate and all-pervasive principle that is both transcendent to and also immanent in the physical world. Using modern terminology, Xiang may be said to have adopted an "immanent transcendence" position. Instead, Guo insists that no external generator exists because for him, no existence is possible apart from material reality; as such, designations such as Heaven [*Tian*], Dao, Creator [*zaowuzhe*], or Great Ultimate [*taiji*] refer not to any universal principle transcendent to physical reality but to one immanent in everything. Guo's position is thus one of "immanent monism" [neizai yiyuanlun].[113] It follows that since the Dao is inherent in all things, it is identical with both their self-generation [*zisheng*] and self-transformation [*zihua*].

The discrepancy between Guo's strict immanence and Xiang's immanent transcendence can be discussed in several ways. Let us first situate it in the modern debate in both China and the West over the roles of transcendence, immanence, and immanent transcendence in the Chinese tradition.[114] "Immanent transcendence" translates as "*neizai chaoyue*," a term that emerged from the New Confucianism [*xinruxue*] movement during the 1950s in Taiwan, Hong Kong, and the West. The movement was led by the philosophers and historians of Chinese thought Tang Junyi (1909–1978),[115] Mou Zongsan (1909–1995),[116] Xu Fuguan (1904–1982), and Carsun Chang (Zhang Junmai) (1886–1969), and later was popularized further by the eminent scholar of Chinese intellectual history Yu Yingshi (b. 1930)[117] and the historian and philosopher Tu Wei-ming (Du Weiming), a close student of Mou Zongsan.[118] Dissatisfied with the rigid dichotomy between transcendence and immanence, characteristic of Western philosophy and religion, which they considered inappropriate for the Chinese tradition, such scholars instead proposed "immanent transcendence" as an alternative to concepts of strict or absolute "external transcendence" [*waizai chaoyue*]—that is, a universal principle or being, "God," or absolute "other" that governs the phenomenal universe and exists strictly apart from it. Although "immanent transcendence" [*neizai chaowu*] is a modern term, its advocates in both China and the West regard it as a concept that can be traced through the tradition to the earliest stages of Chinese philosophical and religious thought.[119]

The Universal and Particular Dao

A different, though still sympathetic, view of transcendence in early Chinese thought, particularly in Huang-Lao metaphysics and its concept of the natural order of the Dao, appeared in several scholarly articles during the 1980s written by Randall Peerenboom, whose research culminated in 1993 in a major monograph, *Law and Morality in Ancient China: The Silk Manuscripts of Huang-Lao*. Huang-Lao thought was a syncretic school that arose during the Han dynasty, which drew on the philosophy of the *Laozi* and the *Zhuangzi* and combined with it legends and sayings associated with Huangdi (the Yellow Thearch), together with views of legalist thinkers. Peerenboom claims that the Dao in Huang-Lao thought is "descriptively immanent" and "prescriptively transcendent":

> Normatively, the natural order is transcendent in two senses. First, it is transcendent in that it is privileged as the fundamental realm of value. That is, the natural realm is transcendent in its normative priority. Its value is independent of human value judgments. Humans do not determine the value of the natural order. Rather, it is simply taken to be good, indeed, to be the good. It is the right Way.[120]

Peerenboom also claims that the natural order is also "transcendent" in either a "correspondence" or an "interpretive" sense:

> Both correspondence and interpretive naturalism are naturalisms in that they conceive of humans as part of the natural order, privilege the natural order and insist that the human order be compatible with the natural order. . . . the former conceives of the natural order as predetermined whereas the latter does not. . . . correspondence naturalists contend that there is a single, preconfigured, normatively correct Way, dao, cosmic natural order. Just as nature is rule governed, . . so is human society governed, structured by constant, impersonal laws. . . . interpretive naturalisms reject that there is a single correct order . . . [but instead] contend that that there are, at least in theory, many possible natural orders.[121]

Peerenboom next defines Huang-Lao naturalism as a "correspondence naturalism," in which "there is a correct Way (*zheng dao*)." I can easily agree with this, but then he goes on to claim that "this differentiates the dao of Huang-Lao from the multiple daos of Zhuang Zi [*Zhuangzi*]," maintaining that in the *Zhuangzi*, each person has his own way, his own dao, and that there are as many rights and wrongs as there are daos—whereas in Huang-Lao thought, "there is just one."[122] This seems to misconstrue the role of immanence as it appears in the text of the *Zhuangzi* and Guo's commentary, for both demonstrate the complete fallacy and futility of trying to formulate "right" and "wrong," condemned as conscious and artificial constructs inimical to the true, correct, and uniquely single Dao, and one single natural order, the Dao itself, is always "right" or "suitable," but that "suitability," inconceivable and inexpressible, is attained only through unself-conscious thought and in spontaneous action—the only ways that humans have full access to and can perfectly correspond with the immanent presence of the Dao in them.[123] What happens is not that each person has a different dao particular to him, but that once natural endowment is received from the Dao, the Dao as a process delineates what is "suitable" for each. Such a natural "right" has nothing to do with the supposed "right" artificially formulated by the Confucians and Mohists (see 2.9.10, 2.9.11, 2.10.3, 11.7.3, 11.7.4, 11.8.1, 14.39.9, 14.39.10, 24.43.7, 29.31), who, like Huang-Lao thinkers, claimed their notions of "right" enjoyed the authority of Heaven [*tian*]. What is "right" or "wrong" for each individual is thus not determined by standards external to him, but rather by manifestation of the Dao immanent in one's natural endowment.

Herein lies a paradox: *xuanxue* theory, whether associated with the immanent transcendence of Wang Bi and He Yan or the immanent monism of Pei Wei and Guo Xiang, conceives of the Dao as both overarching and universal on the one hand, and as particularly manifest in each individual thing through its natural endowment on the other. In each person, it thus delineates original generation and subsequent transformation of all physical and nonphysical traits, all of which are realized spontaneously/naturally [*ziran*]. In other words, there is one single natural order that, in its individual manifestations, differentiates one particular individual from another. Moreover, this universal-particular paradox carries over to the issue of values—that is, what is "good" for both individual and society. Again, we must be careful not to confuse external, artificial standards of "good" with the inherent and natural "good" that exists for each individual thanks to his particular natural endowment. Brook Ziporyn rightly draws attention to the difference:

> While the *Daodejing* seems to take for granted the universal validity of the standard values of the culture—life, longevity, social harmony—while offering contrarian and counterintuitive strategies for attaining them, the *Zhuangzi* for the first time raises questions about these values themselves, focusing on their dependence on particular points of view, and affirming the value-to-themselves of all possible value perspectives. Zhuangzi's idea that a thing's value derives not from its accordance with a single pre-existing universal norm of what is desirable, but rather from its inalienable relation to the standard of rightness implicit in the being of its own quiddity, would become the central pillar of all Guo Xiang's thinking.[124]

However, Ziporyn fails to take into account the paradoxical universal *and* particular nature of the *xuanxue* Dao, in which the universal norms of an overarching Dao are reconciled with the particular corresponding rightness inherent in the individual. Guo Xiang reconciles the two by first rejecting the artificial norms of society and then extolling the innate tendency in individual personal nature to the good:

> "Government" means establishing invariable rules, which are used to rectify the common folk, and "punishment" means promoting criminal law, which is used to determine innocence and guilt. When rules are invariable, people can feign compliance, and when criminal law is promoted, people can evade it. But being able to evade it, they violate innate character in order to avoid trouble. Capable of pretense, one casts off one's original nature in order to comply with the rules. One's outer self may be rectified by complying with the rules, but no submission occurs in the innermost heart. If one harbors the intention to avoid trouble, he will have no sense of shame when it comes to others. As far as moral transformation is concerned, is this not a flimsy way to go about it! Therefore, the text [*Analects* (*Lunyu*) "Conduct Government" part 2 ("*Weizheng dier*")] says, "the common folk will evade both without shame." "Virtue" allows them to embody their original natures, and "propriety" allows them to realize the potential of their innate characters. Innate character has its own sense of shame, and original nature has its own source of being. When one fulfills his original nature, its source provides perfection, and when one embodies his innate character, he has a sense of shame. With this sense of shame, one regulates himself without threat of punishment, and with one's source providing perfection, one rectifies himself without need for rules. This is how "one leads them with virtue and regulates them with propriety, and they have a sense of shame and become rectified."[125]

That is, if each person is allowed to fulfill his innate nature, endowed to him by the Dao, as each individual "rightness" is achieved and maintained, the rightness of the whole society inevitably takes place. And when the whole of society is "right," the entire world, both nature and human, conforms in perfect unity with the universal norms of the Dao.

Transcendent Naturalism Versus Immanent Naturalism

Peerenboom's contrasting definitions for "correspondence naturalism" or "Huang-Lao naturalism" and "interpretive naturalism" given in the following pages seem overly complex, opaque in places, and rather extraneous to understanding transcendence and immanence in the thought of Guo Xiang. Essential differences come to light more when he compares his basis of distinction with that proposed by David Hall and Roger Aimes:

> As a rule of thumb, what I would call a *foundational, correspondence theory*, Hall and Aimes would call a *logical order*; what I would call a *pragmatic, interpretive* or *coherence theory*, Hall and Aimes would call an *aesthetic order*.[126]

Whereas a full account of what Hall and Aimes mean by "logical" and "aesthetic" theories is beyond the scope of this introduction, the essential difference between them is succinctly summarized by Carine Defoort:

> The "logical" order could be characterized as appealing to "transcendent" essences or principles—Platonic Forms, the Unmoved Mover, atoms in classical materialism, the modern rational or volitional ego, human nature, and so forth—for analyzing or explaining something, while the "aesthetic" order is radically immanent in the sense that it completely lacks recourse to such "transcendence."[127]

As such, this brings us back to our principal concern here: issues of transcendence and immanence, immanent transcendence, and immanent monism.

At first, the term and concept of "immanent transcendence" was either ignored or rejected in the West, where, for example, David L. Hall, Roger T. Aimes, and François Jullien, like Immanuel Kant (1724–1804), Georg Wilhelm Friedrich Hegel (1770–1831), and Maximilian Karl Emil Weber (1864–1920) before them, continued to insist that the concept of a universal principle that exists apart from yet universally governs material existence was entirely absent from the Chinese philosophical tradition. In their influential *Thinking Through Confucius* (1987), Hall and Aimes specifically argue against the immanent transcendence of Mou Zongsan and Tu Wei-ming:

> There is considerable confusion among commentators concerning the applicability of "transcendence" to the classical Chinese tradition. For example, although the unity of *t'ien* [*tian*] and man is a central feature of Tu Wei-ming's interpretation of early Confucianism, he insists on numerous occasions that *t'ien* has a transcendent dimension. Mou Tsung-san [Mou Zongsan], using Kant to illuminate the distinctive characteristics of Chinese philosophy, observes: "The way of *t'ien* as . . . high above denotes transcendence. When the way of *t'ien* is invested in the human person and resides internally in him as human nature, it is then immanent. On this basis, we can use an expression that Kant liked to use, and say that in one sense the way of *t'ien* is transcendent, and in another it is immanent (immanent and transcendent are opposites)."[128]

Moreover, Hall and Aimes define "transcendence" strictly in terms distinguishing it from the "radical immanence" that they claim characterizes the Chinese philosophical tradition as a whole :

> Perhaps the most far-reaching of the uncommon assumptions underlying a coherent explication of the thinking of Confucius is that which precludes the existence of any transcendent being or principle. This is the presumption of radical immanence . . . Strict transcendence may be understood as follows: a principle, A, is transcendent with respect to that, B, which it serves as principle if the meaning or import of B cannot be fully analyzed and explained without recourse to A, but the reverse is not true. . . . as we discuss Confucius' thinking in subsequent chapters that attempts to articulate his doctrines by recourse to transcendent beings or principles have caused significant interpretive distortions. Employing the contrast between "transcendent" and "immanent" modes of thought will assist us materially in demonstrating the inappropriateness of these sorts of transcendent interpretations.[129]

Hall and Aimes also insist on maintaining a clear distinction between philosophical and religious thought: whereas they acknowledge the role of a transcendent creative and nourishing source in Chinese religious traditions, they claim that whenever such transcendence appears in philosophical texts, it is but a transitory aberration. Using the *Huainanzi* (Master of Huainan) as an example, they claim that this recourse to transcendence here is characteristic of a shift from what they call an "aesthetic" to a "rational" or "logical" sense of order that occurred due to the influence of Han-state Confucianism, which tended to formulate its tenets in terms of dualistic distinctions, such as two-world cosmogony (other world–this world), yin-yang dualism, Heaven-earth or Heaven-human reciprocity, all of which are rational/logical (and thus literal) constructs. "Aesthetic," on the other hand, supposedly characterizes mainstream Chinese philosophical thought in general, in which terms such as "creator" [*zaowuzhe*] are not used literally but figuratively and should be understood as such:

> On the Taoist side, we can witness a similar shift if we track the movement from the immanental cosmos of the *Lao Tzu* [*Laozi*] and *Chuang Tzu* [*Zhuangzi*] "Inner Chapters" in the direction of the two-world orientation of religious Taoism. An interesting illustration of this shifting orientation can be found in the *Huai Nan Tzu's* reiteration and reinterpretation of the *Chuang Tzu*. While the intention of the *Chuang Tzu* passage is to challenge the principle of an absolute beginning, the *Huai Nan Tzu*, Ch. 2,[130] assumes precisely the opposite position and uses it to describe a series of increasingly abstruse stages in a cosmogonic

evolution of existence. Significantly, it was during this late Ch'in [Qin] and early Han period that various cosmogonic theories appear and are developed in the early Chinese corpus, for cosmogonic theories are primary signals of the conception of logical order.[131]

Moreover, Hall and Aimes assert not only that since such a creative transcendent principle is entirely absent from Chinese philosophical thought, whether Daoist or Confucian, its essential character as a whole can only be characterized as immanently monistic:

> *T'ien* [Tian] is not a preexisting creative principle which gives birth to and nurtures a world independent of itself. *T'ien* is rather a general designation for the phenomenal world as it emerges of its own accord. *T'ien* is wholly immanent, having no existence independent of the calculus of phenomena that constitute it. There is as much validity in asserting that phenomena "create" *t'ien* as in saying that *t'ien* creates phenomena; the relationship between *t'ien* and phenomena, therefore, is one of interdependence. The meaning and value of *t'ien* is a function of the meaning and value of its many phenomena, and the order of *t'ien* is expressed in the harmony that obtains among its correlative parts.[132]

Five years later, Jullien, apparently influenced by Hall and Aimes, delineated the role of Heaven [*tian*] in much the same way—as a presence entirely immanent in things and transcendent only in a figurative sense:[133]

> Il n'"agit" pas, ne fait rien de lui-même (à partir de lui-même), et son efficacité est à la mesure de cette non-ingérence: car, de sa corrélation avec le réel embrassé dans sa totalité résulte un pouvoir d'influence qui peut être à la fois invisible, infini et parfaitement spontané. Par rapport à l'action ou à la causalité, qui sont transitives, il n'y a d'efficacité qu'intransitive, et le "Ciel"—qui s'érige en Transcendance par rapport à l'horizon humain—n'est lui-même que la totalisation—ou l'absolutisation—d'une telle immanence.[134]

> It [*tian*, Heaven] does not "act," does nothing on its own (separate from itself), and its effectiveness is commensurate with this noninterference: because, from its correlation with the reality that it embraces in its totality a power of influence results, which can at the same time be invisible, infinite, and perfectly spontaneous. In contrast to action or causation, which are transitive, it only possesses an intransitive efficiency, and the "Heaven"—which rises up in Transcendence in relation to the human horizon—is itself only the totalization—or absolutization—of such immanence.

Aimes continued to assert a similar view in the years since these remarks were made. These he eventually refined and expanded in *Confucian Role Ethics: A Vocabulary* (2011), where he began using the term "strict transcendence" to qualify why "transcendence," in the Western conventional sense, has no place in Chinese philosophical thought. Coupled with "strict transcendence," Aimes would also banish "strict dualism" from Chinese philosophical thought:

> Such an exclusive mind/body and theory/praxis dualism has never been a distraction in a Chinese correlative yinyang cosmology in which mind/body (*shenxin*) and theory/praxis (*zhixing*) have been taken to be collaborative, coterminous, and mutually entailing aspects of experience. Indeed, the continuity and wholeness of experience is defined in terms of "forming and functioning" (*tiyong*), and "flux and persistence" (*biantong*)—cosmological assumptions that preclude any strictly dualistic categories.[135]
>
> . . . as we have explained the asymmetry in strict transcendence between God and world, God has a free hand in determining and sustaining the world while conversely the world does not have any effect on the perfection that is God. Hence God and world stand in a dualistic relationship. God stands independent of the world, and negates it in the sense that the world has no independent existence outside of God's perfection. An alternative to such strict transcendence is the correlative relationship between *tian* and the human experience captured in the familiar expression used to characterize classical Chinese cosmology, *tianren heyi*, "the continuity between the natural and cultural context and the human experience."[136]

However, implicit in these remarks is the recognition that some kinds of "nonstrict transcendence" and "nonstrict dualism" exist in Chinese philosophical thought: The transcendent both exists apart from and is immanent in the material cosmos—as two distinguishable counterparts that interact in interdependent relationship. Such "nonstrict" concepts of transcendence and dualism can also define the key elements of "immanent transcendence," where the interaction between the transcendent *Tian* or Dao with the material extant is conceived in much the same way. However, like Jullien, Aimes never swerves from treating Chinese philosophical thought as the dichotomous opposite of that of the West; thus, a few years later, he again insisted on characterizing Western philosophical thought exclusively in terms of a "strict transcendence" supposedly not found in the Chinese tradition:

> Strict philosophical or theological transcendence is to assert that an independent and superordinate principle A originates, determines, and sustains B, where the reverse is not the case. Such transcendence renders B absolutely

> dependent upon A, and thus, nothing in itself. The formalist notion of eidos that is foundational in Plato as antecedent "ideals" that together constitute the single Good or the notion of an independent, absolute, eternal, self-sufficient, and hence unchanging creator God that emerges in mainstream Christian theology would be two philosophical and theological examples of such strict transcendence.[137]

Evidence is presented next that such "strict transcendence" does occur in the Chinese philosophical tradition, albeit only in a limited sense, but first we should consider a related issue that is germane to understanding the course of Wei-Jin *xuanxue* thought, to which Aimes shifts his attention—to the relationship between *you* (being, phenomenal existence) and *wu* (non/not being, nothingness):

> Because the determinate and indeterminate—*youwu*—are always mutually entailing *yinyang* correlative categories required to describe the unfolding process of experience, there is no such thing as "being" as something that is independently permanent and unchanging and no such thing as "not being" as a gaping void or an absolute nothingness. *You* describes a persistent yet always changing determinate pattern or rhythm within the flux and flow of experience.[138]

Whereas such a claim accurately describes imminent monism in Chinese thought, with which Guo Xiang and Pei Wei were affiliated, it fails to account for the presence of immanent transcendence found throughout the tradition from the early Confucian and Daoist classics to the Neo-Confucians of the Song to Qing eras. It also fails to explain why such an "immanental cosmos," which is supposedly the fundamental characteristic of Chinese philosophical thought, necessarily precludes transcendence entirely. For example, Hall, Aimes, and Jullien ignore evidence in both the *Laozi* and its early commentary tradition that the Dao, as the prime mover, is thought to have existed *prior* to Heaven, Earth, and all things—the "immanental cosmos" of which they speak. In such texts, the Dao, declared to have existed prior to things, is ipso facto "strictly transcendent"—at least chronologically. Consider the following from the *Laozi* and the commentary of Wang Bi:

> Nameless, it [the Dao] is the Origin of the myriad things; named, it is the mother of the myriad things. [Wang Bi:] Anything that exists originates in nothingness [wu], thus, before it has forms and still nameless, it serves as the origin of the myriad things, and, once it has forms and is named, it grows them, rears them, ensures them their proper shapes, and matures them as their

> mother. In other words, the Dao, by being itself formless and nameless, originates and brings the myriad things to completion.[139]

He Yan, Wang Bi's contemporary, similarly equated nothingness with the Dao and asserted that it was the creative principle or force responsible for the origin of everything:

> In his *Daolun* (On the Dao), He Yan states: "For the extant to exist, its generation depends on nothingness [*wu*]. When something happens, its realization is contingent on nothingness. Say what it is, but there are no words for it. Name it, but there are no names for it. Look for it, but it has no form. Listen for it, but it makes no sound. Nevertheless, since the Dao is present in everything, it thus can manifest sounds and echoes, produce the [twenty-four] seasonal pneuma and all things [*qiwu*], encompass their physical forms and animating spirits [*xingshen*], and display their images and shadows. As black results from its black profundity [*xuan*], so does white results from its white simplicity [*su*];[140] as square results from its squaring, so does round result from its rounding. Although the round and the square thus get their forms, it has no form itself; although the white and the black thus get their names, it has no name itself."[141]

However, whether or not such a transcendent Dao is immanent in things, the very idea of a Dao that exists apart from the material cosmos offends some modern students of the Daoist tradition. For example, the practicing Daoist priest and eminent scholar Kristofer Schipper has declared that Wang Bi was not a Daoist at all, but actually a Confucian whose commentary to the *Laozi* should be condemned for "rationalizing explanations" that "completely miss the point," as well as for conceiving of the Dao as "a kind of god."[142] Schipper is in good company, for back in the Wei-Jin era, Pei Wei and Guo Xiang likewise denied the existence of Wang Bi's "strict" transcendent Dao.

Pei Wei, Material Existence, and Immanent Monism

The trend to conceive of the Dao as transcendent persisted well into the time of Guo Xiang and two significant contemporaries, Wang Yan, a strong proponent of a nonmaterial Dao equated with nothingness, and the immanent monist Pei Wei (267–300), who utterly rejected transcendence in any form and would banish all notions of "nothingness" from the well-managed state, all of which he sets out in an essay largely compatible with the gist of Guo's commentary, his "*Chongyou lun*" (On venerating material existence). An account in the *Jinshu* (History of the Jin) succinctly sums up the situation:

> During the Zhengshi [240–249] era of the Wei, people such as He Yan and Wang Bi followed the teachings of Masters Lao and Zhuang and honored them as patriarchs. They founded a doctrine that taught that "Heaven, earth, and the myriad things all have their roots in nothingness. As for this nothingness, from the start of things to the completion of affairs, no undertaking takes place in which it is not integrally present. The yin and yang rely on it to create things; the myriad things rely on it to attain mature physical existence; worthies rely on it to complete their virtue; and the antisocial rely on it to avoid harm. Therefore, it is because nothingness functions in this way that, though invaluable, it is never honored." Wang Yan thought very highly of this teaching, but Pei Wei thought it all wrong and even wrote a treatise ridiculing it, but Wang Yan, unruffled, persisted in upholding it.[143]

Pei Wei's immanent monism is so similar to Guo Xiang's that it is likely that the one influenced the other—though it is unclear who was first to oppose the earlier immanent transcendent thought represented by Wang Bi and He Yan.

Although few of Pei Wei's writings survive, "On venerating materiality" was fortunately copied into his *Jinshu* biography. Because the arguments Pei uses to castigate "nothingness" illustrate what was politically and socially at stake during these the last years of the Western Jin state, why this philosophical standoff between adherents and opponents of "nothingness" [*wu*] actually occurred, and what the terms and concepts involved actually meant, thereby casting much light on Guo's own use of them, it is here translated and analyzed in its entirety, including the *Jinshu* introduction:[144]

> [Pei] Wei found current trends to dissipation and licentiousness profoundly disastrous. Whereas people no longer respected Confucian learning, He Yan and Ruan Ji continued to enjoy the highest of reputations during that age, though what they had to say was just showy, devoid of substance and failed to follow the rules of propriety. They held sinecures and enjoyed imperial favor, but while in office failed to attend to duties. As for men such as Wang Yan, the more their reputations swelled, the higher their positions, and the greater their power, the less they allowed themselves to be constrained by government duties. As such, mimicking one another, moral standards kept on deteriorating. Thereupon Pei Wei composed this "On venerating materiality" to free people from such foolish falsehood.
>
> The tap root of everything in all its diversity is the prime ultimate Dao. It is the way by which things are differentiated into different categories, within which are different levels of rank. Forms of physical existence clearly differ one from another, for this is the way physical bodies exist. Although the way things change and interact is intricate and complex, these are imprinted by principles inherent in their root origin. Since things in their categories exist at different

> ranks, natural endowment is proportioned accordingly. If endowment leaves something inadequate, it thus must rely on external resources. As such, once alive, things may be investigated through what we know as "principles" [*li*]. The embodiment of principles is identified by the term "material existence" [*you*]. What "material existence" provides may be identified by the term "resources" [*zi*]. When "resources" and "material existence" match, this is identified by the term "suitability" [*yi*]. When one chooses what is suitable for himself, this is identified by the term "natural inclination" [*qing*]. Once one is bestowed with intelligence, going out or staying still may be different ways of life, and remaining silent or speaking out may mean different paths,[145] but the natural inclination to maintain oneself in what is innately suitable, thereby treasuring life, is one and the same.

Here, Confucian social and political hierarchy is justified in School of Dao [Daojia] terms: the ideal society results by everyone filling the position in life that suits his natural endowment or allotted capacity. Moreover, sagehood is achieved because of natural endowment, not because of effort or learning. However, if people try to exceed the limits of natural endowment or allotted capacity, individual life is ruined and social and political chaos ensues. Guo Xiang agrees; see, for example, 1.0–1.7.1, 2.8.15, 3.1.1–3.1.2, 3.8, 4.24.2, 4.45.5, 5.8.3–5.8.5, 5.2.8.8, 5.28.8, 10.5.12–10.5.13, 11.3.1–11.3.3.

> Because principles governing everything act concurrently and do so without damage or obstruction, physical existence, whether noble or base, takes its shape from them. Because success or failure are determined by the particular physical existence one receives, good fortune and bad may be predicted accordingly. Therefore, the worthy or noble man, realizing that desire cannot entirely be eliminated, at times forms friendships with others, and, observing what happens in such interactions, carefully consider what they should do. Acting in accord with the Dao of Heaven and sharing in the goods of earth, they bend themselves to duty with all their strength, and only turn to the joys of pleasure after labors are done. They perform official duties in compliance with benevolence, live simple lives with courtesy, obey with loyalty and sincerity, and act with reverence and deference. Their goal is not to acquire everything they desire and work not to have more than they need. As such, this is how they alleviate the troubles of the world. Therefore, to establish widely the highest standard of moral virtue, to pacify and govern the myriad folk, and to display a model to teach the people, all this is found here—it is the way the sage conducts government.

Although these observations of Pei Wei are echoed in Guo's commentary (e.g., at 11.7.7 and 13.6), Guo also emphasizes that the ideal fit of a person to his position in life depends on his spontaneous recognition of and adherence to individual natural allotment or capacity, a practice that once prevailed in sagely antiquity and now must be recovered in the present. Pei Wei addresses such concerns in the next section of his essay:

> But when it comes to malicious confrontation and arrogant, willful behavior, these are the sprouts of dangerous harm. As such, the more they spread, the quicker disaster arrives; the more people are inclined to dissipation, the more resentment and complain grow. The more people do as they please without constraint, the more prone they are to attack one another. The more advantage is monopolized, the more thievery spreads. One may say that by so trying to enhance life, life is actually lost. The common run of people, shocked at these bloody quarrels, seek reasons why such hard strife occurs. They examine how excessive emphasis on material existence is harmful and thus see the good in simplification and reduction, but they then fall in with expositions of theories that revere nothingness, whose aim is to denigrate material existence. Once they denigrate material existence, they are sure to distance themselves from how they appear to others; once they distance themselves from how they appear to others, they are sure to discard the rule of law; once they discard the rule of law, they are sure to disregard precautions; once they disregard precautions, they are sure to forget all about propriety. Once people no longer maintain propriety and the rule of law, no way remains to conduct government. The masses follow the example of superiors just as water fills the shape of a vessel. Therefore, since it is the nature of the mass of common folk to trust what they are accustomed to, being so accustomed, they are reconciled to their occupations, and, reconciled to their occupations, they say this is the right and natural thing to do. Therefore, the ruler must take care with their moral guidance. He tends to all duties, such as promulgating government decrees and dealing with the penal code, sees that the common folk are separated into households and that each fill one of the four vocations [scholar, farmer, artisan, merchant]. He should ensure that those who receive his orders need not act with undue severity, and he should leave them so secure in their posts that, utterly unmindful that one is different from another, no one wishes to transfer. How much the more true this is for those who fill the exalted positions of the three dukes, for, thanks to the venerable inclinations they harbor at heart, they too should serve as moral guides. Since these are the steps to either benighted or enlightened rule,[146] one cannot fail to treat them with the utmost caution.

Pei Wei would have the ideal ruler rely more on established and conventional rules and regulations, with far less stress on spontaneity and natural inclination, than does Guo Xiang, who insists throughout the commentary on the role of unself-conscious rule for the true sovereign: he should rule by not ruling, and thus shape his people by exemplifying such unself-consciousness.

> Although desire for repletion can be reduced, merely having something should not be rejected entirely; although excessive consumption can be decreased, this should not mean that to have nothing at all need be venerated. For the most part, those who have a talent for disputation, on the one hand, go to extreme lengths to expose abuses inherent in advocating material existence and, on the other, can only praise how admirable the notion of absolute nothingness [*kongwu*] is. But whereas material things have verifiable characteristics, absolute nothingness is impossible to examine. Since disputatiously clever discourse may delight, and words that seem true may lead one astray, everyone may become so bedazzled by them that they get thoroughly taken in by the conventional arguments involved. Even though someone might think differently, such dissent will be to no avail. Held in thrall to what they are accustomed, they say that the theory of pure nothingness [*xuwu*] cannot really be eclipsed. Whenever someone chants it, others chime in, so many set off in that direction never to turn from it. Consequently, they neglect to heed worldly duties, denigrate the need to achieve anything, esteem aimless behavior that drifts this way and that, and disparage pragmatic men of worth. What people will risk their lives for is fame and fortune, which is why writers exaggerate the truth in what they say, but the inarticulate so admire their opinions that everyone in general is infected by them. This is how they establish their arguments, based on pure nothingness, which they say deals with "arcane marvels" [*xuanmiao*]. In office, they pay no heed to responsibilities, which they say is to keep "elegant distance." They maintain themselves in such a way that they lose all sense of honesty and honor, which they say is to be "broad minded." Therefore, such abrasive practices wear away ever harder. As for the unrestrained who follow this trend, some act contrary to the rules of propriety and ceremony governing auspicious and inauspicious events, disregard how their looks and demeanor appear, irreverently ignore the proper order of the old and young, and utterly confuse the social status of the noble and lowly. The worst of them go around naked, talking and laughing heedless of what is appropriate. Thinking that unscrupulous behavior is something grand, the conduct of the intelligentsia keeps on degenerating.

To frame his arguments, Pei Wei manipulates the range of meanings for *you*, which include "actuality," "being," "existent," "material/physical existence," "possess," "possession(s)," "something," and "somethingness," and *wu*, which include "be/do without," "emptiness," "empty," "free from," "lose," "nonexistent," "nonexistence," "nothing," "nothingness," and "without." Although these ranges of meaning for *you* and *wu* also appear in Guo's writings, he never uses them in such a rhetorical strategy. By "manipulate," I mean that Pei has one meaning slide into another so that one set of associations merges with another. However, such pseudologic may have been the order of the day, for Pei may have employed it in this particular essay to parody those he rails against, who move from the denigration of excessive *possessions* to extoling *none at all*, from *nothing at all* to an appeal to an ontological pure or absolute *nothingness*, which they then use to justify *freedom from* conventions in order to pursue an indulgent lifestyle *empty* of all moral and ethical concerns. Nevertheless, Pei's assertions still have affinities with Guo's thought, for the self-conscious self-indulgence, which Pei condemned, was also anathema to Guo Xiang, whose commentary is replete with injunctions to follow unself-conscious spontaneity in all things while never violating one's natural limits:

> The text that Master Lao composed in five thousand characters explicitly exposes all foul and confusing harmful practices, while expounding what tranquillity in singular totality means and how it relieves perplexity, allows for self-equanimity and for accord with the essential directives of *Sun* [Diminution, Hexagram 41], *Qian* [Modesty, Hexagram 15], *Gen* [Restraint, Hexagram 52], and *Jie* [Control, Hexagram 60], of the *Changes*. Moreover, this maintenance of original nature [*shouben*] through tranquillity of singular totality has nothing to do with any "pure nothingness." What such hexagrams as *Sun* and *Gen* actually indicate is one particular Dao for the sovereign; it is not that they serve as a medium for some original nothingness inherent in the *Changes*. When we examine Master Lao's book, although it is profoundly knowledgeable from start to finish, it nevertheless asserts that "existence arises from nothingness,"[147] which puts vacuity [*xu*] in charge of things, and, with bias, sets up a proposition favored by one particular school of thought. How could anything be possibly right about that! Once one comes to life, its full span is achieved by safeguarding it. To take steps to achieve its full span, one should make compliant response to things his chief concern. But if one's taste for the fondly familiar causes neglect of duties, overwhelming disaster will arise. If by paying such heed to details one becomes unmindful of fundamentals, the truth of natural principles will vanish. Depending on how one's actions engage others, results may lead either to survival or to destruction. . . . [148] This is why Master Lao exposed the snares of decadence and unrestraint and composed a text that venerated nothingness, whose aims were to end the utter mistake of living to excess, which he so condemned, to encourage perfect equanimity, which he considered the greatest good, to restrain indulgence in pleasure from going too far, and to re-establish purity and rectitude in one's heart and mind. Although it suited him to employ "nothingness" [*wu*] as a term here, his aims remained entirely with material existence [*you*], which is why, he said, "they [such terms] serve as mere decoration."[149] As such, what is recorded is but discourse with a particular biased perspective.

Extant fragments of Guo's *Laozi zhu* (Commentary to the *Laozi*) are presented, translated, and analyzed in appendix C.1. For similar comments concerning the nonexistence of the Dao as creator or generator, see C.1. *Laozi* 4; for praise of frugality and modesty, see C.1, *Laozi* 10 and 24:

> If it were declared that the ultimate principle of things really depended on nothingness as its progenitor, such biased perspective would harm the truth. The worthy of former times had such thoroughgoing understanding that, no way confined, they profoundly discussed everything. However, only Ban Gu wrote to refute this assertion, but he failed to analyse what it really meant. Although Sun Qing [Xun Kuang (ca. 314–217 BCE), Xunzi] and Yang Xiong [53 BCE–18 CE)] basically denigrated it, they still approved of some aspects. However, use of the term "pure nothingness" spread day by day, and this so stimulated interest among many thinkers that they all set forth theories about it, which, from explaining creative transformative power above covered the myriad things below. Not a one failed to venerate nothingness, with every view of it exactly the same. By nature inflexible, many proclaimed that every advocacy of the principles of material existence as debased in meaning and thus merely superficial and crude. As a consequence, those learned in the Confucian classics, whose avocation had been the debate over human relations, shifted their affiliation to them. This so struck me with fear that I had to express my heartfelt thoughts, which while many gathered to attack, some dismissed them as just some personal grumblings of no lasting significance. Someone good enough to visit me was so upset by what he saw happening that he asked me to compose an essay that enumerated how all evidence proved that "pure nothingness" was untenable, because as long as all aspects of it were not analytically corrected, what partisans of "nothingness" meant by it would be impossible to refute. I then withdrew to think it over: Although the noble man should heed his true inclinations, he should not seek prominence, so when he states his opinions, he should do no more than communicate what he means. However, we are now so distant from the time of sagely wisdom that one's differences from and similarities to it are inescapably mixed together. Nevertheless, even something somewhat compatible should serve to venerate and supplement those canonical works of ancient times, support the clarity of their great enterprise, and be of benefit to the present. As such, though my only worry is that my words will fail, how can I remain silent! Though I fail to lift even one corner of the problem, let me at least briefly express my views on it!

Pei Wei seems much more in the Confucian camp than Guo Xiang, and far more concerned with the formulated wisdom of that tradition, which Guo denigrates as mere "footprints" that only serve to mislead and confuse. For example, see 1.13.7, 6.48, 7.2.1, 8.4.2–8.4.4, 8.6.2:

As for absolute nothingness, since it cannot possibly generate anything, the start of generation must come from the self-generation of things themselves. Once self-generated things surely embody material existence, but if no material existence is there, no source of generation is there either. Since the individual capacity produced by generation consists of material existence, "pure nothingness" just means the "absence" of material existence, as mentioned above. As for "material existence," if "material existence" were not opposed to "nothingness," it would not be "material existence." And as for "nothingness," if "nothingness were not opposed to "material existence," it would not be "nothingness."[150] Therefore, the material extant, which develops when it is nourished, cannot be kept intact by that which has no means to do so. The masses, which exist as long as order is maintained, cannot be kept in compliance by something that has no means to act. The mind is not phenomenal matter yet managing matters must proceed from the mind. However, although managing matters is done by something other than the phenomenal, one cannot say that the mind consists of "nothingness." An artisan is not an implement, yet the making of a tool surely must be done by the artisan. However, though the making of an implement is done by something other than an implement, one cannot say that the artisan does not exist. In like manner, one might wish to catch a deep-water fish, but it cannot be caught by an indolent person, or to shoot down a bird atop a high wall cannot be done by someone who keeps his hands clasped quietly together. Carefully examine how one must apply himself to the operation of bow and bait: these cannot be mastered by "not knowing." Looking at it from this perspective, everything that sustains the material existent must materially exists itself—so how could "pure nothingness" be of any benefit to all the living things that already exist!

Pei's view that "nothingness" cannot be the source of materiality and that things exist only because they self-generate is similarly found in Guo's commentary, where it is most forcefully asserted at 2.5: "Nothingness is just that—nothing—so it cannot generate phenomenal reality [the extant or "somethingness"]. Before anything phenomenally extant is generated, it cannot generate anything else." See also 2.34.4, 11.12.2, 12.18.2–12.18.3, 22.34.3–22.34.4, 23.30.9–23.30.12, 23.38.6.

Immanent Transcendence in the Writings of Ruan Ji

This last section of Pei's essay and comparable passages from Guo's *Zhuangzi* commentary illustrate how both differ from the earlier tradition of *xuanxue* thought, represented first by Wang Bi and He Yan, and later by Xiang Xiu and his contemporaries such as Ruan Ji and Xi Kang. Turning first to Ruan Ji, we find that for him, things do not generate themselves; rather, they are subject to external generation, as this passage from his "Da Zhuang lun" (On understanding Master Zhuang) clearly states:

> As Heaven and Earth are generated by the Natural [*ziran*], so the myriad things are generated by Heaven and Earth. As for the Natural, since nothing exists outside it, "Heaven and Earth" is the name for it. As for Heaven and Earth, since everything extant [*you*] exists within them, the myriad things are generated by them. If the former is deemed to be that outside which nothing exists, who may take issue with that? If the latter is deemed to be that inside which everything exists, who may say otherwise?[151]

However, Donald Holzman interpreted Ruan's position entirely differently—as allied with the immanent monism of Guo Xiang. In doing so, he translated *ziran* as "spontaneity" and asserted that the text should mean "Heaven and Earth are born of themselves.' "[152] Although such a reading of the text is possible, other passages in Ruan's writings unambiguously place him in the immanent transcendence camp. Moreover, since the term *zisheng* ("self-generation" or "self-generate") never appears in Ruan's works, it is more likely that *ziran* as it appears in the previous passage is not equivalent to *zisheng*, and thus is not a process but rather indicates an entity, the prime mover that generates all things. Ruan seems here to have had in mind a section in the *Laozi* that refers to the "Natural" in the same way:

> Man takes his models from Earth; Earth takes its models from Heaven; Heaven takes its models from the Dao; and the Dao takes its models from the Natural [*ziran*].

Ruan seems also to have been influenced by Wang Bi, whose commentary further clarifies that *ziran* is the prime entity upon which all else sequentially depends:

> "The Natural" is a term for that for which no equivalents exist, and expression for that which has infinite reach and scope . . . The Dao complies with the Natural, which results in Heaven having something to rely on [the Dao]; Heaven takes its models from the Dao, which results in Earth having something to emulate [Heaven], which results in Man finding images there [on Earth].[153]

Similarly, Ruan combines references to the *Laozi*, sections 25 and 37, near the beginning of his "Tong Lao lun" (On understanding Master Lao):

> "The Dao takes its models from the Natural" as it effects transformation. If any prince or lord could hold on to it, the myriad folk would undergo moral

> transformation spontaneously."[154] The *Changes* calls this the "Great Ultimate" [*taiji*];[155] the *Spring and Autumn Annals* calls it the "Origin" [*yuan*];[156] and the *Laozi* calls it the "Dao."[157]

For Ruan, "the Natural," "the Great Ultimate," "the Origin," and "Dao" are all provisional names for the prime entity, the name for one of which, "Origin," he expands to "Amorphous Origin" [*hunyuan*] in the fortieth of his "Poems Singing My Feelings" [*Yonghuai shi*]: "Amorphous Origin generated the Two Exemplars (Heaven and Earth)."[158] Also apparent is his writings is Ruan's belief in a causal sequence: the Natural causes the generation of Heaven and Earth, which in turn causes the generation of the myriad things. As for the Dao, its place in Ruan's system is ambiguous: it is either a term interchangeable with the Natural as the prime entity or the name for its immanent process.

Xiang Xiu and Xi Kang on *Perspicacity* (*Zhi*)

Besides the remnants of Xiang's *Zhuangzi zhu* (Commentary to the *Zhuangzi*) various other writings reveal important aspects of his thought. Among the existing fragments of his *Zhouyi Xiangshi yi* (Master Xiang's explications of the *Changes of the Zhou*), only one passage seems philosophically significant—a comment addressed to Hexagram 42 *Yi* (Increase), *Commentary on the Judgements*, "*Yi* [Increase] is such that it means diminution for those above and Increase for those below, so the delight of the common folk is without bounds." Xiang comments: "According to the Dao of the enlightened sovereign, he should aspire to treat those below with kindness. Therefore, his catering to the interests of those below means his diminution, and his giving to those below means their increase."[159] "Should aspire to" [*zhi zai*], also may be translated "should be determined to," "should intend to," "should set his will on," all of which involve conscious intentionality and thus inimical to Guo's basic tenet that the enlightened sovereign or sage ruler should be free of conscious mind and never act with deliberate intent.[160] It is impossible to know if this fragment, utterly devoid of *xuanxue* thought and entirely Confucian in direction, is representative of Xiang's overall approach in his *Changes* commentary, but his view of enlightened rulership here seems typical of an earlier stage of statecraft thinking that harks to the original Confucian classics and their Han dynasty exegetes, and also probably reflects an early stage in Xiang's own thought.

Xiang also addresses the role of perspicacity in his "Nan Yangsheng lun" (Refutation of "On nurturing life"), by Xi Kang:

> A man receives his form from the Former-and-Transformer [*zaohua*] and thus exists among the myriad things. However, he differs from plants and trees, for

> plants and trees can neither avoid wind or rain nor avoid hatchet or axe, and also differs from birds and beasts, which can neither elude traps or nets nor escape from cold or heat. He possesses both mobility to interact with things and the perspicacity to shift himself elsewhere. As such, he has both the advantage of mind and the faculty of perspicacity. But if one shuts these down and silences them, he would be the same as things that lack all perspicacity. So what can be more valuable than perspicacity![161]

Although nothing is said here about unself-conscious mind, which is so important to Guo Xiang, both in his *Zhuangzi* commentary[162] and his *Lunyu tilue* (Essentials of the Lunyu [Analects]),[163] Xiang does say much the same thing in his own *Zhuangzi* commentary,[164] which we know was completed before 262, the year of Xi Kang's death, and that Xi had commented specifically on it:

> At first, when Xiang Xiu wanted to do his commentary, Xi Kang said, "Why must this book have a commentary added to it? That would do nothing but hinder others from using it to play their own music." But once Xiang had finished, he showed it to Xi, saying, "As an exception, this might even be up to it, might it not?" He then went on to discuss "Nurturing Life" with Xi in words that confounded both questions and answers, for he wanted Xi to give it his most lofty consideration. When Xi Kang tended his forge, Xiang Xiu assisted him, and they interacted so cheerfully it was as if no one else was there with them.[165]

Xiang's refutation of Xi's "On nurturing life" was thus written later than his *Zhuangzi* commentary. Although Xiang's commentary to the *Changes*, in which he clearly commends conscious thought and purposeful initiative, might represent an earlier stage in Xiang's thought, much the same view is promoted here. However, this seems at odds with his *Zhuangzi* commentary, where instead he exalts unself-conscious action and freedom from conscious mind. Xiang Xiu and Xi Kang were close friends, so I suspect that their exchange of essays, including also Xi's "*Da nan yangsheng lun*" (Rejoinder to the refutation of "On nurturing life"),[166] constitutes a debate between polemicists who were more interested in "pure conversation" [*qingtan*] competition than in stating opinions of conviction. They also often seem to be talking past one another in order to score points instead of answering or refuting specifics made by the other.

Xi actually says little concerning mind and perspicacity in his two essays, but what he does say seems largely compatible with Xiang's pronouncements in his *Zhuangzi* commentary. Xi first criticizes the common man who

> lets delight and anger violate his correct pneuma [*zhengqi*], lets selfconscious ratiocination [*silü*] ruin his essential spirit, and lets grief and happiness upset

> his stable essence [*pingcui*]. Now, although his is just a tiny body, its attackers do not take a single path to assault it, so his easily exhausted person has to suffer enemies both inside and out.[167]

One who excels at nurturing life, by contrast, has the mind of a sage:

> Because external things entangle the mind, they do not exist for him. Instead, because divine pneuma [*shenqi*] in its purity lodges there, it alone leaves impressions. Unconcerned, it is free from suffering and misery; utterly still, it is free from selfconscious ratiocination [*silü*]. Moreover, he guards it with unity and nurtures it with harmony. Harmony with principle thus daily accrues, which is the same as Vast Compliance.[168]

Moreover, Xi does not denigrate all perspicacity, but only self-conscious, deliberate ratiocination, referred to in his "Rejoinder" as "foresight" [*qianshi*]:

> The reason why we value perspicacity and esteem action is because they can enhance life and improve one's person. However, as soon as desire acts, regret and remorse arise. As perspicacity functions, foresight develops, and once foresight develops, intention begins, which allows external things entrance. When regret and remorse arise, worries mount and one's person is placed in jeopardy. As for the two [perspicacity and action], if one fails to store them within but allows them to engage without, all they will manage to do is visit disaster on one's person while doing nothing to improve life.[169]

"Foresight" involves deliberation, planning, judgment, weighing options, and other kinds of ratiocination—all of which are anathema to spontaneous and unself-conscious thought and action, which both Xiang Xiu and Guo Xiang championed in their *Zhuangzi* commentaries.

Immanent Transcendence and Guo Xiang's Immanent Monism

Whereas Xi Kang never uses the term "self-generate" [*zisheng*], his occasional references to generation suggest instead that it is subject to dependency. For example, in his "Sheng wu aile lun" (On neither grief nor joy exists in music), he states: "It is on the merger of virtues by Heaven and Earth that the myriad things rely for generation."[170] He also refers to dependence in "*Ming dan lun*" (On Elucidating Courage): "It is the molding and smelting of the primordial undifferentiated pneuma [*yuanqi*] on which all living things depend for their endowments."[171] We saw previously that the same kind of causal sequence appears in Ruan Ji's writings. Xi's "*Taishi jian*" (Admonitions of the Grand

Tutor) also contains a passage that alludes to immanent transcendence: "From the vast and majestic grand basis [*taisu*], came luminosity of yang and coalescence of yin, which the Two Exemplars [Heaven and Earth] molded and transformed to give humankind its start."[172]

The sequence of such causality and dependence leads back, either implicitly or explicitly, to a prime creative entity that is both temporarily and ontologically transcendent to phenomenal reality. However, such transcendence for Ruan Ji, Xi Xang, and Xiang Xiu seems equally immanent in things, and so their position seems entirely compatible with the "transcendent immanence" view of modern and contemporary scholars of Chinese thought. By contrast, every time Guo Xiang refers to a supposed creator/transformer, whether it is "Dao," "Heaven," "Nothing(ness)," "Creator," "Nature," or "Former-and-Transformer," he either refutes its independent existence[173] or interprets or uses the term figuratively, as a metaphor for innate spontaneity.[174] Such contrast is particularly apparent in Xiang Xiu's and Guo Xiang's use of the term "Former-and-Transformer" [*zaohua*]. With Xiang, it is both an entity and a process, apparently synonymous with "Creator" or "Dao," and thus transcendent as well as immanent, but with Guo, it is exclusively a process, equivalent to "spontaneity" [*ziran*],[175] and thus solely immanent in material existence.

Xiang Xiu and Guo Xiang: Major Differences and Similarities

While it is undeniable that Guo incorporated parts of Xiang's commentary, how much Guo may have borrowed is unknown because most of Xiang's commentary is lost. Comparison of extant Xiang passages corresponding to Guo's (see appendix C) discloses much similarity, but also reveals many differences, both obvious and subtle:

1. It is likely that Guo at times altered the text of the *Zhuangzi* as he edited it so that it better supported his own interpretations. One telling example is 2.33, which begins the famous conversation between Shadow and Penumbra. Xiang's comments that survive are found in C.I.2.33, 27.14.1, and C.II.2.33. In the first two, Xiang's comments, less precise than Guo's, add nothing to philosophical interpretation, but in the latter, Xiang indicates that his text of the *Zhuangzi* has Penumbra exclaim, "How you [Shadow] lack control [*wuchi*]!" Guo's edited text instead reads, "How you lack independent control [*wu techi*]!" Unfortunately, nothing else remains of Xiang's commentary here, so we do not know if he shared Guo's extreme view that all things were absolutely free of dependency, like Shadow, and thus not only self-generate, but also self-transform throughout their existence.

2. However, shortly later at 2.5–2.6, another opportunity for such comparison occurs since a fragment of Xiang's commentary to the same passage survives:

> My generation is not caused by me; such generation just generates itself. As for that which generates generation, how can it be a thing! Therefore, it is not material. My transformation is not caused by me. Such transformation just transforms itself. As for that which transforms transformation, how can it be a thing! Therefore, it has no materiality [*wuwu*]. If that which generates things were also subject to generation and that which transforms things were also subject to transformation, how could it differ from material things? It is thus clear that only something subject to neither generation nor transformation may serve as the root source of generation and transformation.[176]

Although both Xiang and Guo similarly assert that generation and transformation are immanent in things, Guo also insists that neither external agency nor dependency is involved. I suspect that his lengthy comment here was to refute Xiang's assertion that a "root cause of generation and transformation" did exist, which though immaterial itself was still immanent in things, a position that is anathema to Guo. Xiang instead accepts that such a role commonly exists, such as in C.I.2.7.12. Moreover, even when a comment is attributed to both, it does not necessarily mean the same thing, such as at 6.18.1 (see note 61 and C.IV.6.18.1), where both Xiang and Guo say, "Arcane Obscurity [the Dao] is a name for that which is nothingness [*wu*] and yet not nothingness." I interpret this to mean that whereas Xiang viewed the Dao as a nonmaterial entity, "nothingness," and thus "immanently transcendent," Guo believed that the Dao had no existence apart from its immanent presence in things; as such, as "nothing," it confirms Guo's immanent monism.

3. A major similarity is Xiang's and Guo's promotion of spontaneous, unself-conscious thought and action. Many examples are found in both commentaries; see C.I.19.5.2, C.II.3.4.5, C.II.6.5.3, C.III.3.1.4, C.III.3.4.5, C.III.4.17.1, C.III.4.24.4, C.III.7.15.2, C.III.7.24.2, C.III.7.24.4, C.IV.3.4.4, among many others.
4. Fundamental in Guo's commentary is his concept of "footprints" [*ji*]—that is, the recollections in legends and accounts of sagely thought, action, behavior, and pronouncement that, since these always fall short of the realities involved, falsely establish standards for people to follow, which then corrupt natural inclinations to the good and damage original personal nature. Reference to such "footprints" occurs 11 times in the text of the *Zhuangzi* itself, and 151 times in Guo's commentary. Although the *Zhuangzi* itself provided a precedent for Guo to follow (see especially 14.42.1), Xiang Xiu also used

"footprints" in the same sense as did Guo, though only one such instance is found among the fragments of Xiang's commentary (see C.III.7.21.1), so perhaps the difference here is essentially one of degree and not in kind.

5. The "transcendent immanence" (Xiang) versus "immanent monism" (Guo) divide covered in point 2 extends to their different uses of epithets for the Dao: whereas Xiang tends to regard the Dao, whatever it is called, literally as the ultimate generator and transformer, Guo instead always uses such epithets figuratively, so "Creator" [*zaowuzhe*], "Former-and-Transformer" [*zaohua*], "Great Ultimate" [*taiji*], "Heaven" [*tian*], or "Nature" [*ziran*] alike signify the Dao directly as the immanent process of generation and transformation.
6. Appendix C.II lists thirty known instances where the same passage in the *Zhuangzi* is addressed completely differently in Guo's and Xiang's commentaries. Overall, Xiang seems more interested in the semantics of words and expressions; Guo seems more interested in larger philosophical issues of meaning.

Guo Xiang and the *Zhuangzi*

The relationship between the text of the *Zhuangzi* and Guo's commentary has been the focus of controversy throughout the centuries, with some praising the commentary for its accurate interpretation, as did Lu Deming when he wrote that Guo's commentary "entirely captures Master Zhuang's real meaning, which is why it is universally admired." Others took the opposite view—namely, that Guo, in promoting his own ideas, completely distorted the original meaning of the *Zhuangzi*. For example, the prominent literatus and Neo-Confucian philosopher Yao Nai (1731–1815) reckoned that Guo, in trying to elucidate the *Zhuangzi*, "got four parts of ten wrong."[177] And the erudite scholar and exegete Fang Qian (1805–1868) thought that Guo got it completely wrong:

> The world praises Guo Xiang for his fine understanding of the *Zhuangzi*, but what did Guo Xiang ever know about the *Zhuangzi*! . . . What did Guo Xiang ever know about what Master Zhuang meant as the essence of things!. . . . Were not people like Guo Xiang criminals in their treatment of Master Zhuang! . . . As for Guo Xiang's commentary to the *Zhuangzi*, it is not worth discussing.[178]

The most radical of Guo's critics hold that, like all commentaries, his text distorts the meaning of the *Zhuangzi*, and they insist that the text must be experienced exclusively on its own. A particularly telling example of this view appears in a witty exchange between two Chan masters during the Southern Song dynasty:

Wuzhuo said, "I once took a look at Guo Xiang's commentary to the *Zhuangzi*, about which erudites say should actually be Master Zhuang's commentary to Guo Xiang." Although this old monk found what she said quite strange, I did not ask about it but instead cited the story of Yantou and the old woman. Wuzhuo then composed this *gāthā*:

Let your boat drift alone, leaflike
 on the vast and vague,
For to ply oars and make them dance
 creates a different music of its own,
And once cloudy peaks and water moon's reflection
 are all cast aside,
Win a long time for yourself in Zhuang Zhou's
 butterfly dream![179]

Wuzhuo ("Free of Attachments") is the nun and Chan Master Wuzhuo Miaozong (1095–1170), and Yantou is the Chan Master Yantou Quanhuo (828–887). The text is from the "recorded conversations" [*yulu*] of Wuzhuo's teacher, Chan Master Dahui Zonggao (1089–1163), who refers to himself here as "this old monk." The story of Yantou and the old woman is an obvious parable:

When Yantou took up duties at Shatai he served as ferryman at the side of Lake Ezhu, where on both sides of the lake a wooden board was hung so that when people wanted to cross the lake they struck the board. The Master would then ask, "Who is it?" And the reply was "I want to go to that side." The Master then made oars dance and went to meet them. One day, holding a child in her arms, an old woman arrived and said, "To ply oars and make them dance, I don't care about that. Just tell me where I got this child that I hold in my arms." But the Master immediately started to row anyway. The old woman then said, "I gave birth to seven children. With the first six I never encountered one who understood my music [*zhiyin*]. Just this last one does, but now I find I can do without it." She immediately threw it into the water.[180]

That the text of the *Zhuangzi* can serve as a practical guide to interpreting Guo's commentary is actually quite perceptive—I have certainly found it so (more about this in the "Translator's Note," earlier in this book). Dahui did not ask Wuzhuo what she meant; rather, he cited the parable, which in this context implies the question: Like the old woman who tried various ways to enlightenment and finally found the right one, which once found became superfluous, did you, Wuzhuo, try various commentaries on the *Zhuangzi*, and when you finally found the right (or at least the best) one (namely, Guo Xiang's), did you realize that you no longer needed it? Wuzhuo's response in her *gāthā* suggests something quite different: "Your boat" means "your reading of the *Zhuangzi*," which should be unself-conscious and directionless; one should just wander aimlessly about in it. To "ply oars and make them dance," since it "makes a music of its own," differs from the "music" of the *Zhuangzi* itself, and thus is useless as a way to understand it.

An erudite herself, Wuzhuo surely knew Xi Kang's initial reaction to Xiang Xiu's announcement that he intended to compose a commentary on the *Zhuangzi*, which Xi cast in terms of music: "Why must this book have a commentary added to it? That would do nothing but hinder others from using it to play their own music."[181] Rowing is not drifting but self-conscious and directed momentum, equivalent metaphorically to directed reading and manipulated understanding. The third and fourth lines suggest that if one is not distracted by the attractive tropes, parables, and imagery—all the beauty that permeates the text of the *Zhuangzi*—a truly realized, even "enlightened," experience of interacting with the *Zhuangzi* will occur, one that goes on to enhance all of life itself.[182] However, since a translator must make conscious choices and direct his version in certain directions, he cannot drift aimlessly but must pick up oars and row in one direction instead of another. The oars that I choose to use for this work are borrowed principally from Guo Xiang, who unquestionably shaped an understanding of the text that differs both from that of other commentaries, before and after him, and surely to some extent also from the so-called original meaning of the *Zhuangzi* itself—whatever that might have been.

Guo Xiang and Buddhism

Guo's impact on the introduction and early development of Buddhism in China was complex and profound, the principal conduit of which were Eastern Jin scholarly monks, who, though influenced by the *Laozi*, *Zhuangzi*, and *xuanxue*, in general drew especially on the *Zhuangzi* and Guo's commentary for terms and concepts, resulting in a significant convergence of *xuanxue* and Buddhist thought during this, the first great era of translation of Buddhist literature from Sanskrit and Prakrit.[183] Such eminent monks included Zu Daoqian (286–374), Zhu Fayi (307–380), Dao'an (312–385), Zhidun (Zhi Daolin) (314–366), who also composed a commentary to the first chapter of the *Zhuangzi*, *Xiaoyao you* (Spontaneous Free Play),[184] Huiyuan (334–416), Huiyan (363–443), and Sengzhao (384–414).

Since enough material is involved here to fill another book, and thus far beyond the scope of this introduction, the reader is directed to the following relevant sources. For a general comparison of Guo's thought and Buddhism, see Erik Zücher, "Buddhism at Jiankang and in the South-East"[185]; for a discussion of "nothingness" [*wu*] in Guo Xiang and Buddhism, Guo and Zhidun, Guo and Mādhyamika Buddhism, and Guo and other Eastern Jin monks, see Isabelle Robinet, "Kouo Siang ou le monde comme absolu (Guo Xiang or the world as absolute)"; for comparisons of Guo's thought and Huayan, Tiantai, and Chan Buddhism, see Brook Ziporyn, *The Penumbra Unbound: The Neo-Taoist Philosophy of Guo Xiang* and "Guo Xiang: The Self-So and "The Repudiation-cum-Reaffirmation of Deliberate Action and Knowledge";[186] for a detailed discussion of the influence of Guo's terminology on Chinese Buddhist thought and translation, see Hans-Rudolf Kantor, "The Daoist-Buddhist Discourse(s) on Things, Names, and Knowing in China's Wei Jin Period";[187] for Guo and monks of the Eastern Jin, concepts, terms, and translation, see Livia Kohn, "The Buddhist Connection," chapter 13 in *Zhuangzi: Text and Context*; and for a detailed discussion of Guo Xiang and Zhidun, see Ellen Y. Zhang, "Zhi Dun on Freedom: Synthesizing Daoism and Buddhism."[188]

Although modern Chinese studies of Guo's relation to Buddhism are legion, only two of the most significant are listed here. Although highly speculative, Wang Xiaoyi has devoted a large part of *Guo Xiang pingzhuan fu Xiang Xiu pingzhuan* (Critical biography of Guo Xiang with critical biography of Xiang Xiu appended) to the possibility of Buddhist influence on Guo Xiang (pp. 175–199). On the other hand, Guo's influence on Buddhism via Eastern Jin monks is treated in detail in Tang Yijie, *Guo Xiang yu Wei-Jin xuanxue* (Guo Xiang and arcane learning in the Wei-Jin Period) (pp. 81–97).

Master Zhuang and the Text Attributed to Him

Although the *Zhuangzi* has been popularly regarded in both traditional and modern times as the work of a single author, Master Zhuang, Zhuang Zhou (fourth century BCE), the overwhelming modern scholarly consensus is that it was compiled probably over at least two centuries. However, concerning the text, which (except for fragments) exists only in the thirty-three-chapter recension of Guo Xiang that is divided into three sections, *Neipian* (Inner Chapters), *Waipian* (Outer Chapters), and *Zapian* (Miscellaneous Chapters), agreement has never been reached either on how its chronological layers should be stratified or who contributed to its compilation, either individually or as members of schools of thought. Different ways of approaching the text, based on textual analysis, have been proposed, resulting in the reassignment of some passages in the Inner Chapters to the Outer and Miscellaneous Chapters, the movement of passages in them to the Inner Chapters, and the classification of all chapters in terms of both chronological layers and "school of thought" affiliations. Earlier modern scholars tended to accept that the Inner Chapters were largely authored by Master Zhuang in the fourth century BCE, and the other two sections were product by later "schools" of Master Zhuang's followers; but eventually, more sophisticated approaches appeared that resulted in more detailed conclusions, first significantly by Guan Feng (1919–2005) in 1961.[189] Guan's work was developed further by A. C. Graham in "How Much of Chuang Tzu Did Chuang Tzu Write?" (1980) and *The Seven Inner Chapters and Other Writings from the Book Chuang Tzu* (1981). Working independently of Graham, Liu Xiaogan covered similar ground but came to somewhat different conclusions in his Peking University doctoral dissertation (1985), directed by Professor Zhang Dainian (1909–2004), published *as Zhuangzi zhexue ji qi yanbian* (Philosophy of the *Zhuangzi* and its evolution). The first three chapters of Liu's work were translated as *Classifying the Zhuangzi Chapters with an Afterword* (1994), in which Liu contrasts his dating and classification scheme with Graham's.

Graham proposes seven strata and kinds of authorship in the Zhuangzi as follows:

(1) The Inner Chapters (1–7) represent the actual writings of Master Zhuang, including some passages in the Miscellaneous Chapters in Guo Xiang's recension that rightly belong in the Inner Chapters.
(2) Chapters 8–10 and the first part of 11 are authored by an individual "Primitivist" influenced by the *Laozi*.
(3) Parts of chapter 11, chapters 12–16, and chapter 33 are composed by an early Han school of eclectic Daoists or"Syncretists" (early third century BCE).
(4) Chapters 17–22 expound on and further develop material in the Inner Chapters, and as such, are from the later "School of Master Zhuang" (third to second century BCE, perhaps into the early Han period).
(5) Chapters 23–27 and 32 consist of heterogeneous fragments, including some early material that rightfully belong to the Inner Chapters (fourth-second centuries BCE).
(6) Graham attributes chapters 28–31 to the "Yangists," narratives that are supportive of Yang Zhu's (370–319 BCE) ethical egoism and can be dated to the same time as the "Primitivists" (205 BCE).
(7) The Syncretists" is a collection of passages, probably all from the early Han period, that synthesize Confucian, Legalist, and Daoist thought found in chapters 12, 13, and 14.

Liu proposes four divisions for the Zhuangzi:

(1) Inner Chapters (1–7) (mid–Warring States period, fourth century BCE), records of Master Zhuang's own teachings;
(2) Group I Outer Chapters (17–22), Miscellaneous Chapters (23–27 and 32), are composed and compiled by "Transmitters and Expositors of Master

Zhuang"(late Warring States period before 235 BCE), who explained and developed thought from the Inner Chapters, as well as initiating thoughts of their own that are different from that of the Inner Chapters, and essentially tried to transcend the conflicts between Confucians and Mohists;

(3) Group II Outer Chapters (11B, 12–16, and 33) (late Warring States period before 235 BCE) represent the "Huang-Lao School" and assimilate and accommodate several Confucian and Legalist points of view, emphasizing the arts of the ruler and expounding the principle that he should be inactive while his ministers are active;

(4) Group III Outer Chapters (8–11A), Miscellaneous Chapters (28–31) (late Warring States period before 235 BCE) represent "The Anarchists," who reject "reality" as illusory, seek the freedom of human nature, and promote the idea that in a society of highest virtue, neither distinction of ruler and subjects nor class consciousness exists.

Liu also insists that all of the *Zhuangzi* was completed by 241 BCE, and none of it dates from as late as the early Han.

In the meantime, Harold Roth in "Who Compiled the *Chuang Tzu*?" (1991) largely follows Graham's scheme, but he also argues, agreeing with Guan Feng, that the compilation of the *Zhuangzi*, which contains material composed and transmitted for about two centuries (fourth to second century BCE) should be attributed to Liu An (179–122 BCE), the king of Huainan, and the Huainan scholars, and the actual date of compilation can be narrowed down to about 130 BCE

It is beyond the scope of this introduction to analyze and evaluate the methodologies used and the conclusions arrived at by these scholars. However, for a comprehensive critique of Graham's, Liu's, and Roth's work, among others, as well as new perspectives and conclusions, the reader is directed to Brian H. Hoffert, "Chuang Tzu: The Evolution of a Taoist Classic" (PhD dissertation, Harvard University, 2001). After sifting through all the evidence and arguments presented, Hoffert concludes that the fifty-two-chapter *Zhuangzi* listed in the *Hanshu* (History of the Former Han) *Yiwen zhi* (Treatise on Arts and Letters) was indeed likely compiled by "Syncretists" at the court of the prince of Huainan.[190] However, despite all this effort, much of the evidence remains ambiguous as to which parts were originally composed when, and by whom. Fortunately for the purposes of this study and translation, Guo Xiang, like so many before and after him, regarded Master Zhuang as the single author of the work that bears his name.

The most significant early attribution of such a body of writings to Master Zhuang appears in the biography prepared for him in the *Shiji* (*Records of the Historian*) completed in 104 BCE by Sima Qian.[191] Although the fifty-two-chapter version of the text apparently did not yet exist in Sima's own day, it did come down to the time of Guo Xiang, who, when he revised and edited everything down to thirty-three chapters, also attributed it all to "Master Zhuang."[192] Let us now consider what Sima Qian made of it.

Sima Qian referred to only four sections or chapter titles: *Yufu*, "The Old Fisherman" (Guo's chapter 31), *Dao Zhi*, "Robber Zhi" (chapter 29), *Quque*, "Ransack Chests" (chapter 10), and *Weilei xu Kangsang zi*, "Master Kangsang of Weilei Mountain" (apparently similar to "Gengsang Chu," chapter 23),[193] all of which belong to Guo's edited *Waipian*, "Outer Chapters" and *Zapian*, "Miscellaneous Chapters." None of these four belong to the first set of layers, considered the most representative of the core ideas of the *Zhuangzi* in the *Neipian* "Inner Chapters." Although surprising, this strongly suggests that the "Inner Chapters" compiled by Guo Xiang did not yet exist in a coherent form during Sima Qian's lifetime.

However, it is also obvious that Sima Qian was very familiar with a body of writings associated with Master Zhuang, for not only does his "Biography of Master Zhuang" consist of much detailed factual information, but elsewhere, in other parts of the *Records of the Historian*, he quotes or paraphrases passages that appear later in the Guo Xiang version of the *Zhuangzi*.[194]

Sima Qian recognized that Master Zhuang "excelled at style and diction" and at "clarifying the principles underlying things through analogy," and, although "his words unrestrained flowed as a great ocean just to please himself" and "such writings as 'Master Kangsang of Weilei Mountain' were all fictional fabrications," he effectively used his skills to "excoriate the Confucians and Mohists," while "clarifying the teachings of Master Lao." Sima goes on to say that although Master Zhuang's scope of interest was vast, his teachings ultimately had their origin in the naturalistic thought of Master Lao, and so he contributed nothing fundamentally new. Moreover, Sima thought that Master Zhuang's thought was narrower than that of Master Lao and it lacked practical applications. Such a view had an enormous influence on the later tradition, including Guo Xiang, whose commentary on the *Zhuangzi* is significantly shaped to supplement and correct what he, like Sima Qian, regarded as Master Zhuang's shortcomings.

Key to understanding this last point is the correct reading of Sima Qian's judgment of Master Zhuang that appears at the end of the "Grouped biographies of Master Lao and Han Fei":

> Master Lao emphasized the absolute emptiness of the Dao and that it is by resonating with the Natural in non-purposeful action that one keeps in step with all possible change and transformation. Thus the work he wrote is judged so marvelously subtle that it is hard to understand. Although Master Zhuang separated Dao from Virtue [*san daode*], and freely indulged in high-flown talk, he still fixed his essential thought on the Natural.

"*San daode*" is a troublesome phrase. Although in one modern Chinese translation of the *Shiji*, Xu Jialu and his associates glossed it as "Master Zhuang wandered far off from the Dao-and-Virtue" (i.e., digressed drastically from such a focus),[195] most recent Chinese scholarship on this passage tends to gloss it in various other ways. A few examples follow:

> Master Lao concentrated on the basic meaning of the Dao and Virtue, but as for Master Zhuang, he destroyed the concept of Dao and Virtue that had been handed down [from Master Lao] [or, "fragmented the unified concept of Dao-and-Virtue handed down from Master Lao"].[196]

Although *san* as *pohuai* (meaning "break apart/destroy the unity of") differs from my reading, it similarly criticizes Master Zhuang for harming the tradition of thought associated with Master Lao.

Another reading tries to temper the negative connotations of *san* and *fang* and turn them into positive features of discourse:

> To address how Master Zhuang theorized about things as opposed to how Master Lao did, we should say he went on to develop Master Lao's thought more fully. . . . It was with "recklessness" and "lack of restraint" that Zhuang Zhou derived his thought from Master Lao and expanded on it. In terms of the form his discourse took, adopting an expressive literary style, he used a great many images of natural creatures, all brimming over with life and energy, to expound his Daoist philosophical thought.[197]

Liu Kunsheng reads *san daode* and *fanglun* as parallel verb-object phrases, splitting the verbal compound *sanfang* into "reckless and unrestrained," and apparently reading this term as it appears in Ge Hong's (283–343) *Baopu zi* (The Master who embraces simplicity):

> A gentleman might show abundant respect in his outer appearance, expression reverent and his words circumspect, yet the way he thinks is negligent and careless, his inner self reckless and unrestrained [*zhonghuai sanfang*]; as such, if he were appointed to office he would not manage it properly. . . . [198]

As such, this reading seems to imply that Sima Qian thought that Master Zhuang's work, although rightly inspiring for the free-thinking individual in his personal life, was utterly at odds with standards of thought and behavior for the responsible serving official—and thus, by extension, for the good society as a whole.

However, in another modern annotated Chinese translation of the *Shiji* prepared by Yang Yanqi, the expression *san daode* is glossed differently yet again:

san as both *kuosan*, "diffuse, promulgate," and *tuiyan*, "derive," "evolve," and "develop." Yang settles on *tuiyan* in his modern Chinese translation of the passage, the pertinent part of which may be translated as "Master Zhuang derived the theory of Dao and Virtue [from Master Lao] and developed it further."[199]

Glosses such as "develop," "expand on," and "extend" tend to be favored by modern commentators, a trend that is reflected in Western scholarship, such as that of Esther Klein, who renders the passage as "Zhuangzi extended and developed *dao* and *de*, and discussed them at length; essentially [his thought] also goes back to *ziran* (the self-so/natural)."[200] It is likely that this general modern tendency to read *san* as *tuiyan* can be traced back to the *Shiji zhu buzheng* (Supplements and corrections to annotations of the *Records of the Historian*) of Fang Bao (1668–1749), where Fang uses the *tuiyan2* cognate of *tuiyan1*, to gloss *san*: "*San* means *tuiyan*. [Master Zhuang] derived the concept of Dao and Virtue from Master Lao and developed it further, about which he discoursed in a grand and free manner."[201]

Nevertheless, I still prefer to understand *san daode* as "separated Dao from Virtue," and I suggest that the key to understanding the sentence "*Zhuangzi san daode fanglun yao yi gui ziran*" is the function word *yi*, which here seems to indicate an adverse relationship between the two clauses, "but still" or "nevertheless" (i.e., "although/despite A, B happens/is so"). Thus, the first clause ascribes negative qualities to Master Zhuang, but nevertheless, the second clause concludes on a positive note: "Although Master Zhuang separated Dao from Virtue [*san daode*], and freely indulged in high-flown talk, in essentials he still kept returning to the Natural."

Sima Qian, as is well known, largely identified with the Huang-Lao tradition of thought, which emphasized, among other things, the unity of the inner man (cultivation of sagehood) and external action (nonpurposeful action, *wuwei*) resulting in harmonious and perfect government, in other words, the *neisheng waiwang* "inner sageliness and outer kingliness" ideal. This tradition, of course, has its origin in the *Laozi* (Sayings of Master Lao), with regard to which Sima seems to have understood *dao* and *de* as complementary, two sides of the same coin, a fusion of inner and outer, essence [*ben*], and its practical ramifications [*mo*]. Therefore, as Sima Qian found that Master Zhuang failed to maintain the unity of Dao and Virtue, so did Guo Xiang later, as he states in his preface to his edition of the *Zhuangzi*:

> We can say of Master Zhuang that he did indeed understand the underlying basis of things [ben]. As such, he never kept wild talk about it to himself. His words are those of one who responds to things in a unique way but fails to identify with them. Since he so responded but failed to identify with them, his words may be apt but have no practical use, and since what he says fails to address practical matters, though lofty it has no application.[202]

Tang Yijie has insightfully commented on this passage:

> According to Guo Xiang, although Zhuang Zhou understood the essence of things [*genben*], he still tried to recognize such essence in terms of independent concrete entities [*shiti*], and in so doing he split essence and ramification into two. This was why Zhuang Zhou's view of things "may be apt [*dang*] but has no practical use [*yong*] and "though lofty it has no application [*xing*].[203]

Thus, Sima Qian, Guo Xiang, and now the modern historian and critic of Chinese philosophy Tang Yijie all come to the same conclusion: although the *Zhuangzi* contains much wisdom for the cultivation of the enlightened individual self, it still fails to serve as a means to create the ideal society through sagely rulership (i.e., it may lead to sageliness but not kingliness). Therefore, Guo Xiang composed his commentary as a corrective and supplement to the *Zhuangzi*—he did not merely explain what he thought Master Zhuang is supposed to have "said." Guo rendered for the *Zhuangzi* what Wang Bi provided for the *Daode jing*: he composed a commentary that turned the *Zhuangzi* into a treatise on statecraft, to serve as "advice for the prince." However, such an interpretation does not preclude the reader from delving into it for wisdom to enhance personal thought and behavior, for it was commonplace throughout the ages to read Confucian and Daoist works of philosophy, including the *Zhuangzi*, on more than one level. As the traditional Chinese view had it that the state was the family writ large, so the sage ruler of "all under Heaven" was regarded as a model for the aspiring individual sage in his private life. The *Zhuangzi* thus can be read this way, just like many other early texts.

Notes

1. Burton Watson, trans., *Chuang-tzu: The Complete Works* (1968); Victor Mair, trans., *Wandering on the Way: Early Taoist Tales and Parables of Chuang Tzu* (1998).
2. A. C. Graham, trans., Chuang-tzu: *The Seven Inner Chapters and Other Writings from the Book* Chuang-tzu (1981).
3. Remarks following the presentation of "Whose *Zhuangzi*? Master Zhuang's, Guo Xiang's, or Cheng Xuanying's? Who Says What in the Commentary Tradition," by Richard John Lynn at Ca' Foscari University of Venice, May 27, 2019.
4. Such a translation is currently in progress by Peipei Qiu, Louise Boyd Dale and Alfred Lichtenstein Chair Professor of Chinese and Japanese, Vassar College.
5. Fukunaga Mitsuji, trans., *Sōji* (*Zhuangzi*) (1966–1967); Watson, *Chuang-tzu*, 26.
6. Akatsuka Kiyoshi, trans., *Sōji* (*Zhuangzi*) (1974); Mair, *Wandering on the Way*, liii–liv.
7. Sima Qian, *Shiji*, 130: 3288.
8. Kidder Smith, "Sima Tan and the Invention of Daoism, 'Legalism,' et cetera," 129–156.
9. Mark Csikszentmihalyi and Michael Nylan, "Constructing Lineages and Inventing Traditions Through Exemplary Figures in Early China," 67.

10. Csikszentmihalyi and Nylan, "Constructing Lineages and Inventing Traditions," 60, note 3.
11. See especially Holmes Welch, *Taoism: The Parting of the Way*, 89–105.
12. Nathan Siven, "On the Word 'Taoist' as a Source of Perplexity. With Special Reference to the Relations of Science and Religion in Traditional China," 303–30. It is interesting to note that recent scholars of religious Daoism tend to blur this distinction, while those of philosophical Daoism tend to insist on strictly maintaining it.
13. The following biographical material is largely based on Wang Xiaoyi, *Guo Xiang pingzhuan fu Xiang Xiu pingzhuan* (Critical biography of Guo Xiang with critical biography of Xiang Xiu appended), especially 372–397.
14. Huang Kan (488–545), *Lunyu jijie yishu* (Collected explications and expository commentaries to the *Analects*), *Preface*, 5b.
15. Lu Deming (556–627), *Jingdian shiwen* (Textual explications for classics and scriptures), 1: 40a.
16. Zhang Yin (late fourth century) supplemented by Zhang Zhi (act. ca. 479–502), *Wenshi zhuan* (Biographies of literati), quoted in Liu Yiqing, *Shishuo xinyu* (A new account of tales of the world); see *Shishuo xinyu jiaojian* (A new account of tales of the world, collation and commentary), original commentary by Liu Jun (462–521), collation and new commentary by Yu Jiaxi (1884–1955), ed. Zhou Zumo, Yu Shuyi, Zhou Shiqi, et al., part 4: *Wenxue* (Letters and learning), no. 17, 206; cf. Richard B. Mather, trans., *Shih-shuo Hsin-yü: A New Account of Tales of the World, by Liu I-ch'ing*, 105–106.
17. See Richard John Lynn, *The Classic of Changes: A New Translation of the* I Ching *as Interpreted by Wang Bi*, 10–15, and *The Classic of the Way and Virtue: A New Translation of the* Tao-te ching *of Laozi as Interpreted by Wang Bi*, 5–20.
18. Fang Xuanling et al., ed., *Jinshu* (History of the Jin), 50: 1396–397.
19. *Shishuo xinyu*, part 8: *Shangyu* (Appreciation and praise), 32, B: 438; cf. Mather, *Shih-shuo Hsin-yü*, 219.
20. Yu Shinan, *Beitang shuchao* (Excerpts from books in the Northern Hall), 98: 3a and 100: 5b.
21. Liu Yiqing, *Shishuo xinyu*, part 4: *Wenxue* (Letters and learning), no. 19, 209; cf. Mather, *Shih-shuo Hsin-yü*, 107.
22. Xuanling et al., *Jinshu*, 35: 1052.
23. Quoted in *Shishuo xinyu*; see Liu Yiqing, *Shishuo xinyu jiaojian*, part 4, 206.
24. Albert E. Dien and Keith Nathaniel Knapp, ed., *The Cambridge History of China. Vol. 2: The Six Dynasties, 220–589*, 93: "The Disturbances of the Eight Princes resumed later at a higher level of intensity; from 301 to 307 there was a cascade of assassinations, power grabs, and counterattacks. The scenario was always the same: as soon as one prince succeeded in taking power, the others formed a coalition against him and did all they could to bring him down. As soon as that goal was attained, the coalition broke apart."
25. Xuanling et al., *Jinshu*, 50: 1397.
26. Xuanling et al., *Jinshu*, 49: 1374.
27. See appendix A.3 of this book.
28. See appendix A.2.
29. Both of these assertions are based on contemporary hearsay; see Xuanling et al., *Jinshu*, 4: 108 and 59: 1623.
30. Chen Suzhen, "*Sima Yue yu Yongjia zhi luan* (Sima Yue and the turmoil of the Yongjia era [307–313])," 119; Zhao Yixin, "*Jin Huaidi, Sima Yue yu Xi Jin zhongshu zhengquan de bengkui*" (Jin emperor Huai, Sima Yue, and the collapse of Western Jin central state power), 75–76.

31. Xuanling et al., *Jinshu*, 5: 116, 59: 1623–1624.
32. Wang, *Guo Xiang pingzhuan*, 386.
33. Yu Ai's "Rhapsody on the Way to Think" [*Yifu*] is replete with *xuanxue* terms and concepts; see Xuanling et al., *Jinshu*, 50: 1395; Wendy Swartz, *Reading Philosophy, Writing Poetry: Intertextual Modes of Making Meaning in Early Medieval China*, 264, note 7.
34. Xuanling et al., *Jinshu*, 50: 1397.
35. Citing Yu Shinan (558–638), ed., *Beitang shuchao* (Books copied in the Northern Hall), 69: 2b, cited in Tang Qiu 湯球 (1804–1881) ed., *Jiujia jiu jinshu jiben* (Collected fragments of old histories of the Jin era by nine authors), 9: 80.
36. For more on the Jin imperial guard, see Edward L. Dreyer, "Military Aspects of the War of the Eight Princes 300–307," in *Military Culture in Imperial China*, ed. Nicola Di Cosmo, 119–20.
37. During 304–306, Zhang Fang was general of the palace guard. In 306, Sima Yong had him executed, and the position of commander-in-chief of the imperial palace guard went vacant until 301, when it was filled by Hua Heng (267–335). See Wan Sitong, *Jin jiang xiang dachen biao* (Chronological table of Jin dynasty generals, ministers, and high officials), 3: 3336–37.
38. Wang, *Guo Xiang pingzhuan*, 39–40.
39. See appendix C.5.
40. Xuanling et al., *Jinshu*, 50: 1396–97.
41. Liu Yiqing, *Shishuo xinyu jiaojian*, part 4, 206; cf. Mather, *Shih-shuo Hsin-yü*, 105–6.
42. Xuanling et al., *Jinshu*, 50: 1396. The *Shishuo xinyu* passage on which this part of Guo's *Jinshu* biography is taken also contains the sentence "Guo Zixuan, who had the talent of genius, excelled at discussing Lao-Zhuang learning." See part 8: *Shangyu* (Appreciation and praise), no. 26, 435; cf. Mather, *Shih-shuo Hsin-yü*, 234. Yu Ai's evaluation of Guo is often repeated, for example, in Xuanling et al., *Jinshu*, 50: 1396; *Beitang shuchao* (Excerpts from books in the Northern Hall), ed. Yu Shinan (558–638), 69: 2b; Zheng Qiao (1104–1162), *Tongzhi* (Comprehensive history of institutions), 123: 94b; Gao Sisun (ca. 1160–ca. 1220), *Zilue* (Summary of the philosophers), 2: 9b; and, under the entry "usurp authority" [*zhuanshi*], *Yuding peiwen yunfu* (Pendant literary culture treasury of rhymes, authorized by His Majesty [Kangxi]), 67.2: 6a.
43. Xuanling et al., *Jinshu*, 50: 1406–7. For Qin Xiu, see 50: 1404–6.
44. Bai Juyi and Kong Chuan, ed., *Bai Kong liutie* (Six noteboards of Bai and Kong), 86: 15b–16a; *Cefu Yuangui* (Prime perspicacious tortoise guide to the storehouse of letters), (compiled 1005–1013), ed. Wang Qinruo et al., 605: 16a–16b; Gao Sisun (ca. 1160–ca. 1220), *Zilue* (Summary of the philosophers), 2: 6b; Wang Yinglin (1223–1296), *Kunxue jiwen* (Record of information about learning painfully acquired),10: 29a; Ma Duanlin (1254–1323), *Wenxian tongkao* (Comprehensive examination of documentary sources), 211: 25b; Hu Yinglin (1551–1602), *Sibu zheng'e* (Correct guide to forgeries in the four branches of literature) (1586), in *Xiaoshi shanfang bicong* (Collectanea of jottings from the Little House mountain lodge), 30: 1b; Chen Yumo (1548–1618), *Pianzhi* (Extraneous records), 5: 14b–15a; Jiao Hong (1540–1620), *Bisheng* (Brush vehicle of Master Jiao), 2: 30; Xie Zhaozhe (1567–1624), *Wenhai pisha* (Sand sifted for gold in the sea of letters), 2: 11b; Wang Chang (1725–1806), *Chunrong tang ji* (Literary collection from Spring Warmth Hall), 43: 12a–12b; Yuan Shouding (1705–1782), *Zhanbi congtan* (Collected discussions for casual reading), 5: 14a, Lu Yitian (*jinshi* 1836), *Lenglu zashi* (Sundry notices from Cold Hermitage), 4: 31b.
45. *Laozi*, section 44; Lynn, *The Classic of the Way and Virtue*, 138.

46. For Zhili Shu, see 4.44.1 and 18.9–18.10; for *yongzhong*, "the unspoiled simple," see 1.16; for the meaning "bulges so much in whorls and blisters" (wood useless to the carpenter), see 23.1.2.
47. See 18.6.
48. *Liezi* (Sayings of Master Lie); Yang Bojun, ed., *Liezi jishi* (Collected explications of the *Liezi*), 6: 214: "There was a certain Dongwu Wu who, when his son died, showed no grief, so his wife asked, 'No one in the world loved a son more than you did, yet now that he has died, why are you not sad?' Dongmen Wu replied, 'When I yet had no son, I was not sad, so now that my son has died it is just the same as when I did not have a son, so why should I grieve about it?'"
49. *Laozi*, section 4; Lynn, *The Classic of the Way and Virtue*, 57.
50. *Laozi*, section 7: "As such, the sage places himself in the rear yet finds himself in front. He puts aside his person, yet his person is preserved." See also Lynn, *The Classic of the Way and Virtue*, 63.
51. See 19.19.5.
52. He Ning, comp., *Huainan zi jishi* (Collected Explanations of the *Huainanzi* [Master of Huainan]), 2: 818: "As Master Hui, followed by one hundred carriages, was passing through [the marsh of] Mengzhu, when Master Zhuang saw him, he threw back his extra fish." A comment, probably by Xu Shen (ca. 55–ca. 149), explains: "Master Zhuang, given name Zhou, a recluse who would not serve in office, threw back his extra fish because he saw how insatiable Hui Shi was." Another comment, probably by Gao You (fl. ca. 160–220) and preserved in the *Taiping yulan*, *juan* 935, 8: 503, says that Master Zhuang threw back the fish because "he was so revolted by Hui Shi." Master Zhuang, having caught too many fish, was reminded when seeing the insatiable Hui Shi that he should not take any more than he actually needed. Cf. John S. Major, Sarah A. Queen, Andrew Seth Meyer, Harold D. Roth, Michael Puett, and Judson Murray, trans. and ed., The *Huainanzi: Liu An, King of Huainan: A Guide to the Theory and Practice of Government in Early Han China*, 424 and notes 92 and 93.
53. Yan Zhitui, *Yanshi jiaxun* (Family instructions for the Yan clan), part 8, *Mianxue* (Encouragement to learning), 3: 19a–20a.
54. Jiao Hong (1540–1620), ed., *Laozi yi* (Wings to *Laozi*) and *Zhuangzi yi* (Wings to *Zhuangzi*), prefaces dated 1587 and 1588, respectively. Jiao consulted forty-nine earlier commentaries when compiling the *Zhuangzi yi*.
55. Despite good historical phonological evidence that the surname should be pronounced "Xi," the convention in modern China and elsewhere is to pronounce it "Ji." Note that all instances of the surname in this book gives it as "Xi." See David R. Knechtges and Taiping Chang, ed., *Ancient and Early Medieval Chinese Literature: A Reference Guide*, 2: 1407.
56. Chen Jiang (*jinshi* 1544), *Jinlei zi* (Master of the golden wine jar), B *pian* (chapter), 5: 24b–25a.
57. Cf. *Huangdi yinfu jing* (Scripture of the Yellow Thearch's hidden accordance), 6a.
58. Chen Jiru (1558–1639). *Xu kuangfu zhi yan* (Supplement to the words of a crazy fellow), 4: 22b–23a.
59. Liu Zongzhou, *Renpu leiji* (Classified records of human behavior), A: 74b.
60. Father Chao and Xu You were hermits in remote antiquity, who refused to serve Yao and chose instead to live as recluses on Mount Ji.
61. Xuanling et al., *Jinshu*, 49: 1374–75.
62. The *Hanshu* (History of the Former Han) was jointly authored by Ban Biao (3–54), his son Ban Gu (32–92), and Gu's younger sister, Ban Zhao (ca. 49–ca. 120).

63. Liu Zhiji seems to be associating Xu Chi (471–551) and his son Xu Ling (507–549) and Yu Jianwu (487–551) and his son Yu Xin (513–581) essentially with elaborate, palace-style poetry.
64. Liu Zhiji, *Shitong* (Comprehensive account of historiography), 4: 2b.
65. These five works, long lost, exist now only in fragments, none of which refer to Guo Xiang.
66. Liu Zhiji, *Shitong*, 16: 5a.
67. This quote comes from the biography of Fang Xuanling in *Jiu Tangshu* (Old history of the Tang), 66: 2463.
68. Ji Yun et al., ed., *Qinding siku quanshu zongmu tiyao* (Comprehensive catalog of the complete four treasures library, authorized by his majesty), 45: 37b–38b.
69. Yun, *Beitang shuchao*, 98: 3a and 100: 5b.
70. Timothy M. Davis, *Entombed Epigraphy and Commemorative Culture in Early Medieval China*, 257.
71. *Jinshu*, 50: 1397.
72. See Arthur W. Hummel, ed., *Eminent Chinese of the Ch'ing Period*, 1: 157–58.
73. Qian Zeng, *Dushu minqiu ji* (Record of my earnest search through reading books), 3: 8b.
74. Chen Zhensun, *Zhizhai shulu tijie* (Annotated library catalog from the Studio of Straightforward Sincerity), 9: 287.
75. Ji Yun et al., *Qinding siku quanshu zongmu tiyao*, 146: 221–24a.
76. Xiang Xiu's commentary edition is almost always referred to in Tang-era sources and earlier as *Zhuangzi Xiang Xiu zhu* (Zhuangzi with the commentary of Xiang Xiu); his commentary is called "Explanation of its hidden meaning" only in his biography in the *Jinshu*. However, Jiao Hong in his *Bisheng* (Brush vehicle) calls it *Zhuang yi* (Meaning of *Zhuangzi*); see 2: 29.
77. Xuanling et al., *Jinshu*, 49: 1374.
78. For a detailed discussion of these sources, see Kang Zhongqian, *Cong Zhuangzi dao Guo Xiang: Zhuangzi yu Zhuangzi zhu bijiao yanjiu* (From the *Zhuangzi* to Guo Xiang: Comparative study of the *Zhuangzi* and *Commentary to Zhuangzi*), 32–33.
79. Quoted in Liu Yiqing, *Shishuo xinyu* (A new account of tales of the world); see *Shishuo xinyu jiaojian* part 4, 206; cf. Mather, *Shih-shuo Hsin-yü*, 107.
80. Ban Gu, *Hanshu* (History of the Former Han), 30: 1730.
81. Lu Deming, *Jingdian shiwen*, 1: 39b–40a.
82. After the thirteenth century, Lin Xiyi (ca. 1210–ca. 1273). *Zhuangzi Juanzhai kouyi jiaozhu* (Juanzhai's vernacular explanations of the meaning of the *Zhuangzi*) also became popular and influential, though more in Japan than China. It significantly shaped the two most influential annotated translations of the *Zhuangzi* by modern Japanese scholars, Fukunaga Mitsuji (1918–2001), *Sōji* (*Zhuangzi*), 6 vols. (1966–1967; reprint. 1992); and Akatsuka Kiyoshi (1913–1983), *Sōji* (*Zhuangzi*), 2 vols. (1974). These in turn shaped the translations into English by Burton Watson (Fukunaga) and Victor Mair (Akatsuka).
83. Of these two women performers, one could only sing, the other only dance: this served as a metaphor for commentators who could explain the text only in a limited way.
84. Feng Mengzhen was a native of Xiushui in Zhejiang, just north of Hangzhou Bay. The trouble he refers to was probably the Japanese pirate raids that were still common about 1565.
85. Gui Youguang, *Nanhua zhenjing pingzhu* (Commentary and marginal comments to the *True Classic of the* [*Authentic Man*] *of Nanhua*), *Jiuxu* (Old prefaces), Feng Mengzhen,

Preface, 1a–1b; Feng Mengzhen, "*Zhuangzi Guozhu xu* (Preface to *Zhuangzi* with Guo's commentary)," (*Kuaixue tang ji* (Literary collection from Sudden Snow Hall), 1: 9a–10a.

86. For Wang Xianqian's "Preface to *Zhuangzi jishi*" (Collected commentaries to the *Zhuangzi*), edited by Guo Qingfan, see appendix A.1.
87. Wang Xianqian, *Zhuangzi jijie*, 2: 73.
88. Takeuchi Yoshio, *Rōshi genshi: fu Shoshi kōryaku* (*Laozi*, origins, with *Brief examination of the philosophers* appended), 147–156. Takeuchi presents much the same material and arguments four years later in *Rōshi to Sōshi* (Master Lao and Master Zhuang).
89. Liu Yiqing, *Shishuo xinyu jiaojian*, part 4, 220; cf. Mather, *Shih-shuo Hsin-yü*, 108–9.
90. Although Xiang Xiu's *Zhuangzi yin* (Guide to names and terms in the *Zhuangzi*) is listed as extant during the Liang dynasty (502–557) in *Suishu jingji zhi* (History of the Sui, treatise on classics and scriptures), *Suishu*, 34: 1001, it does not seem to have survived beyond the Tang.
91. *Siku quanshu zongmu tiyao*, 146: 23b. The editors imply here that Guo did not even compose the commentary to "Autumn Floods," but rather that Xiang did.
92. Liu Yiqing, *Shishuo xinyu jiaojian*, part 4, no. 32, 211; cf. Mather, *Shih-shuo Hsin-yü*, 115.
93. Wu Chengshi, *Jingdian shiwen xulu shuzheng*, 143.
94. Liu's *Shen Guo pian* first appeared in *Wenzi tongmeng* (Written alliance) 10 (1927) and later was included in his "*Shishuo xinyu jiaojian*," published in 1939.
95. A similar comparison of Guo's and Xiang's versions of the *Zhuangzi* appears in Livia Kohn, *Early Chinese Mysticism: Philosophy and Soteriology in the Taoist Tradition*, 107–8.
96. Welch, *Taoism: The Parting of the Way*, 89–105.
97. Liu, "*Shishuo xinyu jiaojian*," 71–74.
98. Yang Mingzhao, "*Guo Xiang Zhuangzi zhu shifou qie zi Xiang Xiu jiantao*" (Critical discussion of whether or not Guo Xiang stole his commentary of the *Zhuangzi* from Xiang Xiu), 80.
99. Yang, "*Guo Xiang Zhuangzi zhu shifou qie zi Xiang Xiu jiantao*," 83.
100. Yang, "*Guo Xiang Zhuangzi zhu shifou qie zi Xiang Xiu jiantao*," 88.
101. Kang, *Cong Zhuangzi dao Guo Xiang*, 32–33.
102. Yang, "*Guo Xiang Zhuangzi zhu shifou qie zi Xiang Xiu jiantao*," 88.
103. The first draft of Wang's investigation was completed in 1942, revised in 1946, and published in *Zhongyang tushuguan guankan* (National Central Library bulletin) 1: 4 (1947), 1–8. It was reprinted without change in 2007 in Wang's *Zhuangxue guankui* (Studies of the *Zhuangzi*, limited views), 113–30.
104. See appendix C.I.8.2.3, C.I.33.8.2, C.1.6.24.6, C.II.6.8.6, C.II.23.8.4, C.III. 4.17.1, C.IV.23.5.1, and C.IV.23.17.1–23.17.2.
105. Liu Yiqing, *Shishuo xinyu jiaojian*, part 4, no. 17, 206; cf. Mather, *Shih-shuo Hsin-yü*, 106.
106. Guo Qingfan, *Zhuangzi jishi*, 1: 131.
107. Luo Yanmin, "Sima Biao *Zhuangzi zhu kaolun*" (Critical examination of Sima Biao's commentary on the *Zhuangzi*), 35.
108. Tang Yijie, *Guo Xiang*, 14–15.
109. Michel de Montaigne, *Complete Essays of Montaigne*, trans. Donald Frame, 494.
110. Fukunaga Mitsuji, "*Kaku Shō no Sōji kaishaku*" (Guo Xiang's interpretation of the *Zhuangzi*), *Tetsugaku kenkyū* 37: 2–37: 3 (1954), 46–62; 167–77; for analysis of the postscript, see p. 51 and note 6 on that page.
111. Fukunaga, "*Kaku Shō no Sōji kaishaku*," 51.
112. Yang Bojun, ed., *Liezi jishi*, 1: 18. Fukunaga, "*Kaku Shō no Sōjichū to Shō Shū no Sōjichū*," 190–91.

113. For example, Yang Rubin so designates this aspect of Guo Xiang's thought in *Wuxing yuanlun: Xian Qin sixiang de taichu cunyou lun* (Essential theory of the five phases: Ontology of the absolute beginning in pre-Qin thought), 98.
114. A good survey of this issue, especially for the Confucian and Neo-Confucian traditions, is provided by essays in Nathan Brown and William Franke, eds., *Transcendence, Immanence, and Intercultural Philosophy.* Unfortunately nothing of significance is addressed concerning arcane thought [*xuanxu*].
115. Tang devoted an entire book to the subject: *Ru Dao Shi yu neizai chaoyue wenti* (Issues concerning Ruism, Daoism, and Buddhism and imminent transcendence) (1991).
116. For an analysis of Mou Zongsan's view of immanent transcendence in Chinese thought, see Ady Van den Stock, " 'Immanent Transcendence': toward a genealogical analysis of a key concept in the philosophy of Mou Zongsan (1909–1995)," *Asian Philosophy* 31, no. 2 (2021): 195–209.
117. Karl-Heinz Pohl, " 'Immanent Transcendence' in the Chinese Tradition: Remarks on a Chinese (and Sinological) Controversy," 107.
118. In particular, see Wei-ming Tu, *Centrality and Commonality: An Essay on Confucian Religiousness*, first published in 1976 and updated in 1989.
119. Pohl, " 'Immanent Transcendence' in the Chinese Tradition," 112–19.
120. Randall Peerenboom, *Law and Morality in Ancient China: The Silk Manuscripts of Huang-Lao*, 31.
121. Peerenboom, *Law and Morality in Ancient China*, 32.
122. Peerenboom, *Law and Morality in Ancient China*, 32. Peerenboom's complex and pithy book is not an easy read, but an articulate and insightful guide to it is found in Carine Defoort's review article, "The 'Transcendence' of *Tian*."
123. For example, see 2.1.2, 2.8.24–2.8.25, 2.9.6, 2.9.11, 2.31.5, 2.32.3–2.32.5, 5.6.2, 6.7.5.
124. Brook A. Ziporyn, "Guo Xiang: The Self-So and the Repudiation-cum-Reaffirmation of Deliberate Action and Knowledge," 398.
125. See appendix B.3.2.
126. Peerenboom, *Law and Morality in Ancient China*, 33.
127. Defoort, "The 'Transcendence' of Tian," 365, note 2.
128. David L. Hall and Roger T. Aimes, *Thinking Through Confucius*, 204–5.
129. Hall and Aimes, *Thinking Through Confucius*, 13.
130. Cf. 2.13.
131. Hall and Aimes, *Thinking Through Confucius*, 353, note 4.
132. Hall and Aimes, *Thinking Through Confucius*, 207.
133. A comparative analysis of immanent transcendence in Confucian thought, which also contains an insightful critique of Jullien's position on immanence and transcendence, appears in Fabian Heubel, "Immanente Transzendenz im Spannungsfeld von europäischer Sinologie, kritischer Theorie und zeitgenössischem Konfuzianismus" (Immanent transcendence as a field of controversy in European sinology, critical theory, and contemporary Confucianism), *Polylog: Zeitschrift für interkulturelles Philosophieren* 26 (2011): *Selbstkultivierung und Politik im zeitgenössischen Konfuzianismus* (Self-cultivation and politics in contemporary Confucianism), 125–65.
134. François Jullien, *La propension des choses: Pour une histoire de l'efficacité en Chine* (The propensity of things: For a history of efficiency in China), 265.
135. Roger T. Aimes, *Confucian Role Ethics: A Vocabulary*, 33–34.
136. Aimes, *Confucian Role Ethics*, 302, note 6.
137. Roger T. Aimes, "Getting Past Transcendence: Determinacy, Indeterminacy, and Emergence in Chinese Natural Cosmology," 3.

138. Aimes, "Getting Past Transcendence," 24.
139. *Laozi*, section 1; Lynn, Richard John, trans., *The Classic of the Way and Virtue*, 51.
140. Traditional Chinese thought has it that black is the presence of all colors and white is the absence of all colors.
141. Yang Bojun, ed., *Liezi jishi*, 1: 10–11. Cf. Alan K. L. Chan, "Sage Nature and the Logic of Namelessness," 25.
142. Kristofer Schipper, *The Taoist Body*, 192–93.
143. Xuanling et al., *Jinshu*, 43.1236.
144. Unless otherwise indicated, all quotations in this section are from Xuanling et al., *Jinshu*, 35.1044–1047.
145. Cf. *Yijing* (Classic of Changes), "Commentary on the Appended Phrases" [*Xici zhuan*], Part One: "In the Dao of the noble man/There's a time for going forth/And a time for staying still,/A time to remain silent/And a time to speak out./But for two people to share mind and heart,/Such sharpness severs metal,/And the words of those sharing mind and heart,/Such fragrance is like orchids." Lynn, *The Classic of Changes*, 58.
146. Cf. *Yijing* (Classic of Changes), "Commentary on the Appended Phrases" [*Xici zhuan*], Part One: "The Master said, 'As for how disorder arises, well, what one says is considered the steps to it. If the sovereign is not circumspect, he will lose his ministers; if a minister is not circumspect, he will lose his life; and if the crux of a matter is not kept circumspect, harm will result. This is why the sovereign takes circumspection as a caution and is not forthcoming.'" Lynn, *The Classic of Changes*, 59.
147. Cf. *Laozi*, section 40: "The myriad things under Heaven achieve life in existence. Existence arises from nothingness." Lynn, *The Classic of the Way and Virtue*, 130.
148. A passage of sixteen characters that appears here is judged corrupt by Feng Youlan, who suggests that their transcription from an early time was in disorder; he also suggests that, reworded, they should be transferred to the end section of Pei's essay. Feng Youlan, "*Pei Wei Chongyou lun jiaoshi* (Collation and annotation of Pei Wei's 'Discourse on venerating material existence)'," *Zhongguo zhexueshi xinbian* (History of Chinese philosophy, new edition), 2: 498.
149. Cf. *Laozi*, section 19: "Excise sagehood and purge yourself of intelligence, and the people would benefit a hundredfold. Excise benevolence and purge righteousness, and the people would again be obedient and kind to each other. Excise cleverness and purge sharpness, and thieves and robbers would not exist. As for these three pairs of terms, Since they serve as mere decoration, / Give people the chance to identify with something else: / Exemplify simplicity, embrace the uncarved block. / Curtail self-interest and have few desires." Lynn, *The Classic of the Way and Virtue*, 82.
150. Beginning with "As for," this is the translation of the sixteen inserted characters, following the previously cited suggestion of Feng Youlan.
151. Ruan Ji, *Ruan Ji ji jiaozhu* (Collected works of Ruan Ji, collated and annotated), 1: 138. Unless otherwise indicated, subsequent citations in this section are to this work.
152. Cf. Donald Holzman, *Poetry and Politics: The Life and Works of Juan Chi (A.D. 210–263)*, 100.
153. *Laozi*, section 25; Lynn, *The Classic of the Way and Virtue*, 96–97.
154. *Laozi*, section 37; Lynn, *The Classic of the Way and Virtue*, 118.
155. *Yijing* (Classic of Changes), "Commentary on the Appended Phrases" [*Xici zhuan*], Part One: "Therefore, in change there is the great ultimate. This is what generates the two modes [the yin and yang]." Wang Bi: "Being [*you*] necessarily has its origin in nonbeing [*wu*]. Thus, the great ultimate generates the two modes. Great ultimate is the term for that for which no term is possible. As we cannot lay hold of it and name it, we think of

it in terms of the ultimate point to which we can extend being and regard this as equivalent to the great ultimate." Lynn, *The Classic of Changes*, 65.

156. *Chunqiu Gongyangzhuan zhushu* (Commentaries and subcommentaries to the Spring and Autumn Annals with the commentary of Gongyang), 1: 2196a.
157. Ruan Ji, *Ruan Ji ji jiaozhu*, 1: 159.
158. Ruan Ji, *Ruan Ji ji jiaozhu*, 2: 356.
159. Xiang Xiu, *Zhouyi Xiangshi yi* (Master Xiang's explications of the *Changes of the Zhou*), 3b. See also Lynn, *The Classic of Changes*, 396.
160. For example, cf. 7.13.1, 12.1.3, 13.1.2, 13.12.1–13.12.2, 17.9.5, 26.9, 28.2–28.8.5, and 32.22.1.
161. This text is recorded in Xi Kang, *Xi Kang ji jiaozhu*, 4: 162.
162. For example, cf. 2.11.13–2.11.14, 3.6.3, 4.8.1–4.8.2, 4.24.7, 7.26.4, 11.28.2, 12.5.2, 12.8.3–12.8.5, 12.20.7.
163. See appendix C.3.7 and C.3.9.
164. See appendix D.3.4.5, D.6.5.3, D.7.21.1, D.14.24.4, D. 19.4.1, D. 19.5.1, D.19.5.2.
165. Xuanling et al., *Jinshu*, 49: 1374.
166. For Xiang's and Xi's essays, I have consulted Donald Holzman, *La vie et la pensée de Hi K'ang*: 92–96, 83–91, and 97–121, and Robert G. Henricks, *Philosophy and Argumentation in Third-Century China: The Essays of Hsi K'ang*: 21–30, 31–70.
167. Xi Kang, *Xi Kang ji jiaozhu*, 3: 151–52.
168. Xi Kang, *Xi Kang ji jiaozhu*, 3: 156. This passage ends in a phrase identical to *Zhuangzi* 12.18.10.
169. Xi Kang, *Xi Kang ji jiaozhu*, 4: 168.
170. Xi Kang, *Xi Kang ji jiaozhu* (Collected works of Xi Kang, collated and annotated), 5: 197.
171. Xi, *Xi Kang ji jiaozhu*, 6: 249.
172. Xi, *Xi Kang ji jiaozhu*, 10: 309.
173. See especially 2.34.4.
174. See especially 2.5, 3.12.7, 6.20.4, 6.24.4, and 7.7.2.
175. Cf. 3.12.7 and 6.12.7; note also that in the text of the *Zhuangzi* at 6.23.2, where *zaohua* is obviously addressed as a creative entity, Guo is silent.
176. See the passages immediately following C.I.33.8.2.
177. Yao Nai, *Zhuangzi yizhang xu* (Preface to the *Zhuangzi*, meaning by sections), *Xibao xuan wenji* (Collected prose from the Cherished Embrace Studio), 3: 5b.
178. Fang Qian, afterword to *Nanhua jingjie* (Explication of the Classic of Nanhua), quoted in Fang Yong, *Zhuangzi xueshi* (History of the study of the *Zhuangzi*), 3: 186.
179. Dahui Zonggao (1089–1163), *Dahui Pujue changshi yulu* (Recorded conversations of Chan Master Dahui Pujue), 22: 903c.
180. *Wudeng huiyuan* (Combined sources for the five lamps), 7: 143c.
181. Cf. 2.11.13–2.11.14, 3.6.3, 4.8.1–4.8.2, 4.24.7, 7.26.4, 11.28.2, 12.5.2, 12.8.3–12.8.5, 12.20.7.
182. My interpretation of the exchange between Wuzhuo and Dahui and the translation of Wuzhuo's *gāthā* both differ significantly from those in provided in Wilt Idema and Beata Grant, *The Red Brush: Writing Women of Imperial China*, 326–27.
183. For a succinct summary of the similarities and differences between Guo's thought and those of Buddhists, see Brook Ziporyn, "Guo Xiang: The Self-So and the Repudiation and Reaffirmation of Deliberate Action and Knowledge," 409, n. 14 and 420.
184. See Erik Zücher, *The Buddhist Conquest of China: The Spread and Adaptation of Buddhism in Early Medieval China*, 129.
185. Zücher, *The Buddhist Conquest of China*, 81–179, especially 87, 90–92, 102, 123–124, 129–130.

186. Isabelle Robinet, "Kouo Siang ou le monde comme absolu (Guo Xiang or the world as absolute)," in *Dao Companion to Daoist Philosophy*, ed. Xiaogan Liu 73–107; Brooke Ziporyn, "Guo Xiang: The Self-So and the Repudiation-cum-Reaffirmation of Deliberate Action and Knowledge," in *Dao Companion to Daoist Philosophy*, ed. Xiaogan Liu, 397–423, especially 409, note 14.
187. Hans-Rudolf Kantor, "The Daoist-Buddhist Discourse(s) on Things, Names, and Knowing in China's Wei Jin Period," in *Dao Companion to Chinese Buddhist Philosophy*, ed. Youru Wang, and Sandra A. Wawrytko, 103–34.
188. David Chai, ed., *Dao Companion to Xuanxue (Neo-Daoism)*, 501–23.
189. Guan Feng, *Zhuangzi neipian yijie he pipan* (1961); "*Zhuangzi wai zapian chutan*" (Preliminary discussion of the outer and miscellaneous chapters of the *Zhuangzi*) (1961); *Zhuangzi zhexue taolun ji* 莊子哲學討論集 (Collected essays on the philosophy of the Zhuangzi) (Beijing: Zhonghua shuju, 1961), 62–98.
190. Brian H. Hoffert, "*Chuang Tzu*: The Evolution of a Taoist Classic," 346–347.
191. See appendix D.
192. Much work has been done to recover the larger, pre–Guo Xiang version of the *Zhuangzi*; for the most up-to-date findings (2016), see Stephan Peter Bumbacher, "Reconstructing the *Zhuang zi*: Preliminary Considerations," 611–74.
193. The *Shiji suoyin* (Explicating obscurities in the *Records of the Historian*) of Sima Zhen (early eighth century) interprets *Weilei xu* and *Kangsang zi* as two separate chapters of the *Zhuangzi*, the former identified with the sayings of a disciple of Master Lao, known only as someone who supposedly lived on Weilei Mountain; and the latter identified with Master Gengsang. However, the *Shiji zhengyi* (Correct meaning of the *Records of the Historian*) of Zhang Shoujie, with a preface dated 737, parses and interprets the text as I have rendered it previously, as "Master Kangsang of Weilei Mountain," which is exactly how Gengsang Chu is identified (though with variant characters) at the very beginning of the *Gengsang Chu* chapter in Guo Xiang's recension. See *Shiji*, 63: 2144.
194. Wang Shumin, in *Zhuangzi guankui* (*Zhuangzi*, a limited view), 89–95, tracks parallel passages shared by the *Zhuangzi* and the *Huainanzi*, the Han Feizi, *Shiji*, and other early texts. Esther Klein has also tracked parallel passages shared by the *Zhuangzi* and the *Shiji* in "Were There 'Inner Chapters' in the Warring States? A New Examination of Evidence About the *Zhuangzi*," 327–31.
195. Xu Jialu and An Pinqiu, eds., *Ershisi shi quanyi: Shiji* (Complete translation of the twenty-four histories: *Records of the Historian*), 2: 892.
196. Wang Yunsheng, "*Zhuangzi waipian cunzai de wenti* (External chapters of the *Zhuangzi*, existing problems)," 12.
197. Liu Kunsheng, "*Shilun daojia zhexue yu ziran de guanxi jiqi biaoda fangfa* (On the relationship between the philosophy of the Daoists and the Natural, including their manner of philosophical expression: General discussion of the 'Three Arcane Works,' part 1), 57.
198. Ge Hong, *Baopu zi waipian xiaojian* (Master who embraces simplicity, outer chapters, collation and annotation), edited by Yang Mingzhao, 22: 550.
199. Yang Yanqi, *Shiji quanyi* (*Records of the Historian*, a complete translation), 63: 2565–66.
200. Klein, "Were There 'Inner Chapters' in the Warring States?" 327.
201. Fang Bao, *Shiji zhu buzheng* (Supplements and corrections to annotations of the *Records of the Historian*), 38b.
202. See appendix A.2.
203. Tang Yijie, *Guo Xiang yu Wei Jin xuanxue* (Guo Xiang and arcane learning of the Wei and Jin eras), 39.

ZHUANGZI

PART I

THE SAYINGS OF MASTER ZHUANG, THE INNER CHAPTERS

CHAPTER 1

XIAOYAO YOU [SPONTANEOUS FREE PLAY]

1.0 Although the small and the great differ, as long as they let themselves go in the realm of self-fulfillment [*zide*], creatures shall abide by their natures [*xing*], their behavior shall correspond to their abilities [*neng*], and each shall fulfill its allotted capacity [*fen*], for spontaneous free play [*xiaoyao you*] is the same for all; how could success or failure have any place here?

1.1.1 In the North Sea there is a fish, whose name is the Kun. The Kun's size is so great that no one knows how many tricents big it is. It changes into a bird, whose name is the Peng.

Whether the Kun and the Peng really exist I really don't know. The main idea [*dayi*] in the *Zhuangzi* is that one should let himself go in spontaneous free play [*xiaoyao you*] and achieve self-fulfillment [*zide*] through the practice of unself-conscious action [*wuwei*]. Therefore, the text focuses on the most extreme examples of small and great in order to illuminate what is appropriate to one's natural capacity [*xingfen*] . Scholars who look at things with equanimity and insight should concentrate on the deep and universal significance of what is said [*huigui*] and disregard the particular words that convey it. One should not have to come up with something to say for every little detail, for as long as such omissions do no harm to the main idea [*hongzhi*], they are always acceptable.

1.1.2 The Peng's back is so big that no one knows how many tricents wide it is. When it is roused and takes flight, its wings are like clouds hanging down from the sky. This is such a bird that, spiraled by the sea,[1] it goes to move its abode to the South Sea. The South Sea is the Pool of Heaven.

As only the vast sea has the means to convey the Kun's body, so only ninety thousand tricents of wind have the means to support the Peng's wings. How can such matters be dismissed as mere overfondness for the fantastic! It is simply because huge creatures must themselves live in huge places and huge places must themselves produce these huge creatures. Since their principles of behavior [*li*] are inherently natural [*ziran*], they worry not about making mistakes; even more to the point, how could deliberate thought [*cuoxin*] have any place here?

1.2.1 The *Comic Stories of Qi* [*Qixie*],[2] a book that records anomalies, has this to say: When the Peng travels to the South Sea, it whips the water three thousand tricents high as it flaps up a whirlwind and rises to a height of ninety thousand tricents.

As its wings are huge, it finds it difficult to rise. Therefore, only after flapping up a whirlwind is it able to ascend on it, and only ninety thousand tricents are enough for it to get itself under control. Since it has such wings, how could it ever manage suddenly to burst upward? Or get down in just a few yards? When it does all this, it is because it can't do otherwise and not that it takes delight in doing so.

1.2.2 One going takes the breath of six months.

One going for this great bird takes half a year. When it reaches the Pool of Heaven, it takes a breather. One flight for a little bird takes half a morning, and, when it dashes against an elm or a sandalwood, it stops. If we compare the capabilities [*neng*] of these two, there certainly is a difference, but in suiting their natures [*xing*], they are one and the same.

1.2.3 That is, it takes the "wild horses," the dust, and the breath that all living creatures have been using for each other to breathe.[3]

All these are what the Peng depends on in order to fly. "Wild horses" are moving vapors.[4]

1.2.4 The deep azure of the sky, is this its true color? Or is this the result of its extending so far that its limits can never be reached? When the Peng looks down and sees what is below in just the same way, it then ceases climbing.

Now, when we look at the deep azure of the sky, we never really know whether this is the true color of the sky or if this is because it extends so far that its distance from us is infinite. When the Peng looks down on the ground from above and sees it just as we humans see the sky from here, it then stops and takes aim at the South. In other words, the Peng, without knowing how far its journey might be, just sets forth when enough room to maneuver allows it to get itself under control.

1.3.1 Moreover, if an accumulation of water is not ample enough, it won't have the strength to support a big boat. Upset a cup of water onto a dip in the hall floor, and a mustard seed can serve as a boat on it, but if you place a cup

there, it will get stuck, for the water will prove too shallow and the boat too big.

All this clarifies how the Peng flies high because of the huge size of its wings. Now, what the small in mass have to rely on need not be great, and what the great in mass have to use need not be small. Therefore, as principles [*li*] define the absolute capacity [*zhifen*] of things, so things have fixed limits [*dingji*], but each thing's capacity is sufficient for it to behave as it should; thus the way things operate is the same for all. However, when a thing fails to keep control over forgetting life and instead belabors life beyond limits appropriate to it, then its behavior won't suit its potential and its actions won't accord with its innate tendencies [*qing*].[5] When this happens, even wings so big they hang down from the sky will fail to avoid exhaustion, and flyers that suddenly burst upward will fail to avoid coming to grief.

1.3.2 So if the accumulation of wind is not ample enough, it won't have the capacity to support the Peng's great wings. This is why it takes ninety thousand tricents to provide such wind beneath, for only then will nothing block its progress when it strikes at the wind and bears the blue sky on its back. Only then does it take aim at the South.

The reason that "only then does it take aim at the South" is not because it is fond of great heights and longs for distant places but because, as long as the wind had not accumulated amply enough beneath, the way forward had remained blocked. This is the way the great Peng achieves spontaneous freedom [*xiaoyao*].

1.4.1 A cicada and a turtledove laughed at it, saying: "We just suddenly burst upward and fly, dashing toward an elm or a sandalwood, and, sometimes before we make it, we're dragged down to the ground and finish up there! Why do you have to go up ninety thousand tricents and then head South?"

If one is sufficient unto one's own nature, then the great Peng will have no reason to think itself more noble than the little bird, and the little bird won't covet the Pool of Heaven, for each will have more than enough to fulfill its desires. Thus it is that although the small and great differ, spontaneous freedom is the same for all.

1.4.2 When one goes off to the near countryside, if three meals are provided for the round trip, his belly will still stay full; when one makes a journey of one hundred tricents, he has to pound enough grain the night before; and when one makes a journey of one thousand tricents, he has to gather enough grain to last three months.

The farther one has to go, the more grain has to be gathered. Thus it is that the larger the wings, the greater the thickness of accumulated air has to be.

1.4.3 But when it comes to these two creatures, what do they even understand?

The "two creatures" refers to the Peng and the cicada. By contrasting the great to the small, the text demonstrates how they have their own different, equal predilections. As for why their predilections differ, when does it ever happen that they differ because they self-consciously understand that they should differ? These are always naturally so [*ziran*] without their understanding why they are so. To be naturally so indicates unintentionality [*buwei*], with the main idea [*dayi*] underlying spontaneous freedom [*xiaoyao*].

1.5.1 One of little intelligence may not attain great intelligence, and one of short years of life may not attain long years of life.

Each thing has its own nature [*xing*], and each by nature has its own limits [*ji*]; thus everyone has his own amount of intelligence and years of life, so how could more ever be attained by raising up on tiptoes [*qi*] to hope for something better [*shang*]![6] From this point on to the passage about Master Lie [Liezi], the text repeatedly cites anecdotes about different lengths of life and amounts of intelligence, and in these, trusting to one's own way of doing things [*fang*], a protagonist of one point of view never has the wherewithal to overturn the other. After that, we meet the man who governs free of dependence [*wudai*], disregards others and forgets himself, and merges all such differences. Such a one achieves the same success, though he goes at it in different ways and keeps himself free from all thought of merit and fame. For this reason, one who regards the small and the great as the same is free of any thought of small and great. But if one is occupied with considerations of small and great, although it might be the great Peng compared to the tiny quail or the government official compared to the one who rides the wind [Liezi], they all suffer the same entanglement with things. One who regards life and death as equal is free of any thought of life and death. But if one is occupied with considerations of life and death, although it might be the Great Cedrela [Dachun] compared to the cicada, or Pengzu compared to the morning mushroom, they all equally find their lives cut short. Thus it is that one who plays where great and small don't exist becomes inexhaustible, and one who merges with the state where life and death don't exist becomes limitless. If one enjoys spontaneous freedom, yet is tied to some way of practicing it, even had he let himself go so that full play comes about, he would have limitations, for he still could not do without reliance on something.

1.5.2 How do we know this is so? The morning mushroom knows not evening and dawn; the cicada knows not spring and autumn, for they are so short-lived. South of Chu there is the Arcane Numinous [Mingling], which knows five hundred years as its spring and five hundred years as its autumn, and in remote antiquity there was the Great Cedrela [Dachun], which knew eight thousand years as its spring and eight thousand years as its autumn—such was its great age, yet up to now it is Pengzu who is particularly famous for longevity,[7] but if people in general were to equal him in this, would they still not find it reason for regret!

Length of life and amount of awareness are such that some fall far short of others in just this way. Compared to things that people in general might regret, this is certainly something to regret. However, that people in general have never regretted this occurs because each by nature has limits, and if people understand that limits as such don't permit them anything the least extra, why should anyone in the whole world have anything to regret! People never desire to be small because they are great but surely envy greatness because they are small. This is why the text refers to how the difference between small and great is a matter of fixed allotment [*dingfen*] and not something that desire or envy can do anything about. It is this realization that allows one to sever entanglement with desire and envy. Regret is born of entanglement, so when entanglement is severed, regret disappears. For regret to disappear and life yet remain uneasy [*buan*] is something that never happens!

1.6.1 All this was already covered in King Tang's questions to Ji.

Tang's questions to Ji also say that each thing has its own limitations, and that if these are complied with, everything will go smoothly for it. Therefore, Master Zhuang takes the arguments of the questions to be correct.

1.6.2 North of the barren wastelands is a dark sea, the Pool of Heaven, in which exists a fish whose breadth is several thousand tricents wide, and no one has ever figured out how long it is. Its name is Kun. A bird is also there, whose name is Peng. Its back is like Mount Tai, and its wings are like clouds hanging down from the sky. It beats up a whirlwind upon which it mounts to a height of ninety thousand tricents, where it breaks free of the clouds and bears the blue sky on its back. Only then does it take aim at the South and starts off to the Southern Sea. The marsh quail laughed at it, saying: "Where is that one going? I get up with a jump, never get farther than a few yards, and then come down. To flutter through a stretch of wild grasses—this is really is the best kind of flying. So where is that one going?" Such is the distinction between small and great.

Each fulfills its nature [*dexing*] to the utmost and spontaneously realizes the full extent of its limits [*ji*]. Earlier, the text said that since the two creatures have different wing powers, the destinations they can reach differ accordingly. The one soars off to the Pool of Heaven; the other fulfills its ambition by just going as far as an elm or a sandalwood. It is simply that each finds what matches its embodiment [*chengti*] to be enough, yet is utterly unaware why it is so. But now the text discusses how the difference between the small and the great is determined by the natural basic allotment [*ziran zhi su*] involved. Since this is not attainable by hope or envy, each is content with its inherent nature [*tianxing*] and feels no regret how it might differ. This is why the same material is mentioned a second time here.

1.7.1 Thus it is that whether it is one whose knowledge is up to the responsibilities of one office, one whose conduct can unite the people in one district, or one whose virtue meets the needs of rulership so that he can mobilize an entire state, all these regard themselves is just the same way.

That is, they are like birds that find self-fulfillment [*zide*] in one way of doing things [*fang*].

1.7.2 Nevertheless, Song Rongzi still laughed at this.

He still could not regard all things as equal; this was why he had occasion to laugh.[8]

1.7.3 Though the whole world praised him, he was not any the more encouraged; though the whole world condemned him, he was not any the more discouraged.

He was one who really understood what self-fulfillment means.

1.7.4 He fixed what belongs to the inner and the outer

"The inner" [*nei*] pertains to the self [*wo*], and "the outer" [*wai*] pertains to the other [*wu*].

1.7.5 and differentiated the boundary between honor and disgrace

He honored himself but held others in disgrace.

1.7.6 but stopped at that.

He still could not continue beyond this.

1.7.7 Although he was never anxious and calculating in regard to the world,

Since he was sufficient unto himself, he kept himself separate from the world.

1.7.8 there was still something about which he was not sound.

He could only affirm himself [*zishi*] but failed to realize that nothing exists that is not affirmable [*wusuo buke*].

1.7.9 When Master Lie rode the wind and traveled about, cool and collected, he excelled at it,

"Cool and collected" [*lengran*] means in a light and marvelous manner.

1.7.10 but after fifteen days of this he had to return.

Since he was still subject to dependency [*youdai*] on something, although he did ride the wind and travel about, he could not thus get around everywhere all at once.

1.7.11 He never fussed and worried about attaining such a state of blessing and happiness.

He rode the wind naturally; it was not that he fussed and worried about trying to do it.

1.7.12 Although this meant that he was spared the need to walk anywhere, there was still something on which he had to depend.

If it were not for the wind, he could not manage to travel, which meant that he had to be subject to dependency [*youdai*]. Only one who can ride on absolutely anything is free from dependency [*wudai*].

1.7.13 But if one conveys himself on the rectitude [*zheng*] of Heaven and Earth, rides the interactions among the six pneumas, and so roam about endlessly, on what would such a one then ever need to depend?

"Heaven and Earth" is the general term for the myriad things. Heaven and Earth take the myriad things as physical embodiment [*ti*], and the myriad things must behave naturally [*ziran*] in order to achieve rectitude [*zheng*]. "Naturally" refers to what occurs spontaneously [*ziran*] and without intent [*buwei*]. This is the reason why the Peng can go high and the quail low, the cedrela tree can be long-lived, and the morning mushroom short-lived. In all such cases, it is a matter of what a thing is naturally capable of and not something done by self-conscious effort. Not use self-conscious effort, and yet spontaneously be capable of something, is how rectitude works. Thus it is by "conveying himself on the rectitude of Heaven and Earth" that one complies with the nature [*xing*] of the myriad things; it is by "riding the interactions among the six climatic phenomena" [*liuqi*][9] that one wanders down the road of change and transformation [*bianhua*]. If one were to set out in this way, what venture would ever come to an end? If one were to convey himself on whatever vehicle he met, would he ever have to depend on anything else? This is nothing other than the spontaneous freedom [*xiaoyao*] of the man of perfect virtue [*zhide*], who arcanely unites the other with the self [*xuantong biwo*]. But subject to dependency [*youdai*] on something, even Master Lie, with his easy and marvelous manner, could not travel without the wind. Thus he had to have access to something on which to depend before he could enjoy spontaneous freedom. And how much more this is true for the great Peng! Only one who arcanely merges [*ming*] with things and abides with [*xun*] great transformation [*dabian*] can be free from dependency and thus always keep in step [*changtong*] with things. How could this ever be just the result of self-made success [*zitong*] and nothing more! Furthermore, if one complies with that on which one depends and never lets such dependency slip, what is depended on won't be lost, and, as such, he will become one with the great thoroughfare [*datong*] [the Dao]. Therefore, although I find being subject to dependency and being free from dependency impossible to equate, when an individual is content with his own nature [*xing*], lets his celestial mechanism [*tianji*][10] operate spontaneously, and remains unself-conscious of endowment received, I find it impossible to discern any difference between them. Not only is there insufficient means to distinguish freedom from dependency and subjection to dependency, it is even harder with dependency to determine how much or little of it is involved.

1.7.14 Therefore, I say that the Perfected one [*zhiren*] has no self [*wuji*];

Since he has no self, he complies with things and so attains perfection.

1.7.15 the Divine man [*shenren*] shuns achievement;

No ordinary person ever entrusts his life to nature but instead is sure to rely gladly on stone probes.[11] Thus it is that when principle [*li*] is perfectly realized [*zhi*], all footprints [*ji*] left in association with it vanish. Now, such a one complies and does not try to help, becoming one with a perfectly realized principle, and this is how he shuns achievement.

1.7.16 and the sage [*shengren*] has no name [*wuming*].

"Sage" is nothing more than the name for someone who has fulfilled his nature, a term insufficient to indicate how he attained this.

1.8 When Yao tried to yield the whole world to Xu You,[12] he said, "When the sun or the moon has come out but torches remain unextinguished, will it not be difficult for them to furnish light? When seasonal rains have fallen but one still irrigates fields, will it not be a waste of labor to try to provide moisture? Now, since you, Master, have appeared, the whole world has been well ordered, but I still hold sinecure over it. Since I look upon myself as inadequate, I request, Master, that I be allowed to return the whole world to you."

1.9.1 Xu You replied, "You have been governing the whole world, and it already is in good order.

One who can bring about good order for the whole world does not try to govern the whole world. Thus it was that Yao governed it by not trying to govern it; he did not govern it by trying to govern it. Now, Xu You squarely realizes that since it already is in good order, no reason exists to take Yao's place, for the good order is actually all due to Yao. This is the reason for the words, "you have been governing the whole world." We should forget these words, for then we can search out the circumstances that gave rise to them. However, some say in consequence of these words that the one who governs by trying to govern is Yao, and the one who does not try to govern, yet provides Yao with the way to govern, is Xu You. This is to misconstrue what is meant by a wide mark. When good order stems from not trying to govern, one accomplishes it through unself-conscious action [*wuwei*]. For this, it would have been enough to cite Yao as an example, so why does Xu You need to be brought into it at all? If it had been declared that one should be called a master of unself-conscious action only after he has folded his hands and keeps silent deep in mountains and woods, such a statement would have provided a reason to have the sayings of Master Zhuang and Master Lao rejected by those who hold power. Those who hold power regard themselves as necessarily involved in the realm of self-conscious action [*youwei*] from which there is no turning back. This is the reason [why Xu You was brought into it].

1.9.2 However, were I still to take your place, would I do it for the sake of name? "Name" [*ming*] is the guest of reality [*shi*]. Would I do it for the sake of guesthood?[13]

One who acts to suit himself [*ziren*] is in dualistic opposition with things [*duiwu*], but one who acts in accordance with things is free from such dualistic opposition. Thus it was that Yao was not in dualistic opposition with the whole world, but Xu You was but a match for Ji or Xie.[14] What can we say is the reason for this? It is because once one arcanely merges with things, it is no longer possible to exist apart from all things. As such, one arcanely responds to them [*xuanying*] unself-consciously [*wuxin*] and then but follows the course of that response. If one floats about in an untethered boat, whether one goes east or west won't depend on the person himself. Thus it is that one who never acts except in harmony with the common folk never sets out to do something that is not an act of a true sovereign over the whole world. If one rules as sovereign in this way, just as Heaven remains high of its own accord, such a one shall realize the virtue [*de*] of a true sovereign. However, if someone all on his own proudly sets himself up on top of a high mountain, if it were not a matter of having been moved to protect just himself, it would have been because of predilection to protect just his own individual family—but how could one be as exclusive as that! But this is the very reason why a fellow from a common background could still became an outer minister [*waichen*] for Yao. As such an outer minister, if he were to take the place of an inner ruler [*neizhu*], he might have the title of ruler but would lack the realization [*shi*] to serve as a true sovereign.

1.9.3 The tailorbird builds its nest in the deep forest but uses no more than one twig; the mole shrew[15] drinks from the river but drinks no more than to fill its belly.

The nature [*xing*] of each thing has its own limits [*ji*]. Once contentment reaches these limits, anything more is material [*cai*] that belongs to the whole world.

1.9.4 Return and desist, My Lord, for the whole world is of no use to me whatsoever!

They equally regard it as of no use, yet Yao himself has it. How clear it is that those who are perfectly unbiased [*huaihuo*] are boundless [*wufang*]! Therefore, they happily reject the whole world without the least aversion.

1.9.5 Although the cook might neglect the cookery, the impersonator of the dead or the master of prayer should not go beyond the wine vessels and the meat carving blocks to take his place.

As for the cook, the impersonator of the dead, and the master of prayer, each should be satisfied with the scope of his duties, just as a bird, a beast, and each of the myriad things is content with its own natural endowment. Emperor Yao and Xu You both react to their lot in life with tranquility, so theirs is the most perfect realization [*zhishi*] to be had in the whole world. Since each achieves such realization, why should they ever get involved in anything else? Each achieves self-fulfillment—that is all there is to it! Therefore, although the position of Yao and Xu differ, they are one as far as spontaneous freedom [*xiaoyao*] is concerned.

1.10 Jianwu[16] asked Lian Shu, "I heard things from Jieyu[17] that were quite grand but utterly erroneous—but he just went on and on without ever turning back. I was shocked at his words, for they stretched out like the endless reaches of the Milky Way: wholly poles apart from us and nothing in them to do with the doings of benevolence [renqing]."

1.11 Lian Shu said, "What did his words convey?"

1.12.1 Jianwu replied, "On far distant Guye Mountain[18] there lives a Divine man [*shenren*] whose skin is like ice and snow and who is as delicate and graceful as a maiden.

All of this should be understood metaphorically. "Divine man" [*shenren*] is what nowadays is meant by "sage" [*shengren*]. Although a sage might be found at the imperial court, his mind [*xin*] is no different than what it would be out in the midst of forests and mountains. How could the common run of people ever recognize this! All they see is that he has a yellow carriage canopy over his head and has a jade seal hung at his belt, and then say that these are sufficient to strap and bind his mind. They see him making tours of inspection of mountains and rivers and that he identifies with the affairs of the common folk, and then say that these are sufficient to wear out his spirit [*shen*]. How could they ever comprehend that such a one has reached the point of perfection where he is inexhaustible! That the text now talks about a man of kingly virtue and has him dwell on this mountain demonstrates that the common run of people have no means to recognize him. Therefore, it relegates him to beyond the bounds of the world and promotes him to supersensory powers. "Maiden" refers to how such a one does not allow the outer [*wai*] to harm the inner [*nei*].

1.12.2 He does not eat the five grains but only imbibes the wind and drinks the dew.

That everyone eats the five grains, but such a one alone is a Divine man, demonstrates that a Divine man does not result from the five grains but from a special natural [*ziran*] endowment of marvelous vital force [*miaoqi*].

1.12.3 Riding on clouds and driving flying dragons, he wanders forth beyond the four seas. His spirit [*shen*] is so concentrated that he causes things to stay free of disease and annual crops ripen." I think this is crazy and don't believe it.

Although one who embodies the divine [*shen*], dwells in the numinous [*ju ling*], plumbs principle to the utmost [*qiong li*], and reaches absolute marvelousness [*ji miao*] might calmly keep quiet within the halls of his palace, he still arcanely identifies [*xuantong*] with all within the Four Seas outside. Thus it is that he rides on the two modes [*liangyi*, the yin and yang] and drives the six climatic phenomena [*liuqi*], identifies with the mass of benevolence, and urges on the myriad things. If never a thing exists but that such a one complies with it, the floating clouds shall be his carriage; if never anything with bodily form [*xing*] exists but that such a one gives it a ride, flying dragons shall be his steeds. He casts aside self [*yishen*] and achieves self-fulfillment [*zide*]. Although he is utterly unmindful and needs nothing on which to depend, abiding in forgetfulness [*zuowang*] or acting in forgetfulness [*xing wang*], he accomplishes things having forgotten about them. He thus moves as if he were a dragged piece of dried-up wood and remains still as if a heaped pile of dead ashes. This is what is meant where the text says "his spirit [is] concentrated." It is because his spirit is concentrated that the nonconcentrated achieve self-fulfillment. The common run of people all look at what they see the same way and judge it accordingly, so how could he [Jianwu] have ever believed this!

1.13.1 Lian Shu said, "Be that as it may, it is impossible to provide the blind with the means to enjoy the sight of decorative patterns or to provide the deaf with the means to hear the notes of bells and drums. And is it that deafness and blindness exist but for the physical body alone? The understanding also suffers such afflictions.

He [Jianwu] does not understand that the absolute marvel of perfect expression [*zhiyan*] has been reached here, and so thinks it crazy and does not believe it. Such is the deafness and blindness of the understanding.[19]

1.13.2 How correct [*shi*] his words are; they are like a maiden.

This means that what Jieyu gives an account of here will naturally be sought after by people. However, one whose understanding is deaf and blind will say that it is nonsense.[20]

1.13.3 Such a man with such virtue will merge the myriad things together and make them a single entity, so when the common run of people entreat him about disorder, who is he to belabor himself about it and take the whole world as his duty!

The mind of the sage perfectly comprehends the ultimate union [*zhihui*] of the two modes [yin and yang] and completely grasps the marvelous aptitude [*miaoshu*] with which the myriad things are governed. Therefore, he is able to embody transformation and join in perfect harmony with change [*ti hua he bian*]. No venture is impossible for him, and he merges the myriad things together as one, denying nothing. Let the world seek me to deal with disorder, but as I am utterly unself-conscious [*wuxin*] and not self-consciously mindful, how could I ever fail to respond to the world! This being so, this is one who embodies the arcane [*ti xuan*] and reaches absolute marvelousness [*ji miao*]. The way he perfectly understands the nature [*xing*] of the myriad things and becomes a mold or cast of the transformations [hua] that occurs all over the world—which is how he gets named a "Yao" or a "Shun"[21]—is always because he acts without intent [*buwei wei zhi*]. So who is he to belabor himself about such things, wearing out his spirit and subjecting his thoughts to toil, taking duties as duties, and only then having success!

1.13.4 As for such a man as this, absolutely nothing harms him.

He is at ease with harm, thus harm can't harm him, and, since harm can't harm him, things don't harm him either.

1.13.5 Let a flood be so great as to reach the sky, and he shall not drown. Let a great drought be so hot that rocks of ore melt and mountains of earth scorch, and he shall not burn.

No venture he makes disturbs his ease, thus wherever he finds himself is always suitable for him. Life and death have no effect on him, so it matters even less when he is threatened by drowning or burning! Therefore, the reason why the Perfected one does not react as an infant to misfortune or trouble is not that he avoids them, but that he infers what principles are at work, forges straight ahead, and so naturally finds himself in step with good fortune.

1.13.6 Such are his dregs and chaff that one could even mold or cast a Yao or a Shun out of them! So who is he to be willing to take mere things as his duty!"

"Yao" and "Shun" are just names associated with human affairs [*shishi*]. Since that which produces a name is never equivalent to the name, how could "Yao" and "Shun" ever directly convey who the real Yao and Shun were? For surely the authenticity [*shi*] of the Divine man [*shenren*] inhered in them, so that which people nowadays refer to as "Yao" and "Shun" are merely names for the dregs and chaff they left behind.

1.13.7 A man of the state of Song who sold ceremonial caps took them to Yue, but the people of Yue cut their hair short and tattooed their bodies, so had no use for them. When Yao got the people of the whole world in good order and brought stability to all government within the Four Seas, he set forth to Guye Mountain to see the Four Masters, and once back at the north side of the Fen River [Fenshui][22] he became so utterly detached that the whole world ceased to exist for him.

That Yao had no use for the whole world is just like the people of Yue having no use for ceremonial caps. However, one who casts aside the whole world is inherently someone whom the whole world takes as their exemplary ruler [*zong*]. Although the whole world made Yao its exemplary ruler, Yao never possessed the whole world. Thus it was that it ceased to exist for him, and it became his wont to let his mind wander off to the realm of absolute mystery [*jueming*]. Although he occupied a seat at the pinnacle of the myriad things, from first to last, he never ceased exercising spontaneous freedom [*xiaoyao*]. The "Four Masters" is nothing but a metaphorical expression [*jiyan*] used to illustrate the fact that Yao was not the selfsame thing as "Yao." The actual Yao is a mystery [*ming*], and it is merely the footprints [*ji*] he left behind that constitute "Yao." If one moved from looking at these footprints to observing the mystery that he was, it should be no surprise that the inner and the outer turn out to be different realms. Since the common run of people merely saw the "Yao" that was "Yao," how could they have ever recognized the mystery that he was! This is why they had him seek the Four Masters beyond the seas, while investing "Yao" in what they saw of him. This is why they said that he suffered the same vicissitudes of life as ordinary people and completely missed how he exercised spontaneous freedom. This is because they failed to understand that the way to comply with the most far-reaching is to revert to what is close at hand, and the way to join with the most lofty is to return to what is lowly. If one rigidly holds that only the lofty is perfect and won't come level with the realm of vulgar attachments, such a gentleman of mountains and valleys will never be free from dependency [*dai*], so how could he possess the wherewithal to talk about such things as "reaching the ultimate" [*zhiji*] and "wandering in the limitless" [*you wuqiong*]!

1.14 Huizi [Master Hui][23] said to Master Zhuang: "King Wei[24] presented me with seeds of a giant calabash, and, when I planted them, they produced gourds that weighed five piculs. I tried to use them to hold liquid, but they were not sturdy enough to hold themselves up. I split them to make ladles, but they were too shallow to contain anything. They certainly were great big empty things, but since I thought they were useless, I smashed them up."

1.15.1 Master Zhuang said: "You certainly are inept when it comes to putting great things to use. There was a man of Song who excelled at making salve to prevent hands from chapping and splitting, and, generation after generation, his family made bleaching silk its occupation.

Because this salve could render hands resistant to chapping and splitting, one could keep on bleaching silk in the bleaching solution.

1.15.2 Then a stranger heard about it and offered to buy the recipe for one hundred ounces of gold. The clan assembled to discuss the offer, and concluded: 'We have been engaged in bleaching silk for generation after generation and have never made more than a few catties of gold out of it, but now in one morning we can sell the technique for one hundred catties of gold,[25] so let us give it to him.' When the stranger obtained it, he told the king of Wu about it. Then, when Wu had trouble with Yue, the king of Wu appointed him commander in chief. That winter Wu had a water battle with the people of Yue and won a great victory over them. An area of land was divided off, and he was enfoeffed with it. The power to prevent hands from chapping and splitting always remained the same, but the one used it to get a fief, and the other never managed to get out of the silk bleaching business, so the ways it was put to use were quite different. Now, you had some five piculs calabashes, so why did you not think to make them into giant basins so you could float around on rivers and lakes? Instead, you were upset that ladles made from them were too shallow to contain anything! So, after all, you have a mugwort plant for a mind, don't you!"

Mugwort is not a plant that grows straight and attains length [*zhida*].[26] This section tells us that each thing has its own kind of suitability [*yi*]. If one can take advantage of the suitability involved, what venture would ever fail to result in spontaneous freedom [*xiaoyao*]?

1.16 Huizi [Master Hui] said to Master Zhuang: "I have a great tree, which people call the *shu* [*ailanthus*, tree of Heaven]. Its great trunk bulges so much in whorls and blisters that one can't take a carpenter's marking line to it, and its smaller branches are so rolled up and curled they defy compass and square. Even though it stands right by the roadside, carpenters pay no

attention to it. Now, your words are great too but equally useless, which is why everybody alike rejects them."

1.17 Master Zhuang replied: "Is it just you who has never seen the wildcat or weasel? They crouch down in ambush and lie in wait for an overconfident victim. They leap and jump around east and west, shunning neither high nor low, yet they get caught in snares or die in nets. Now then, there is the yak, big as clouds hanging down from the sky; it can certainly be big, but it can't catch mice. Now here you have a great tree and regard its uselessness as a calamity. Why don't you plant it in the Land of Nothingness or the Wilds of Broad Nothing and make of its side a place to idle about in unselfconscious action [*wuwei*] or make of its cover a bed to lie down in where you can enjoy spontaneous freedom? It finds not a premature death in axes and hatchets—nothing will harm it. Since it does not possess anything of use, what grief will it ever befall it?

Whether a thing is big or small, if one violates its limits [*ji*], the principles [*li*] of benefit and harm [*lihai*] shall equally apply, but, when one finds ways of use appropriate to them, all things shall provide spontaneous freedom [*xiaoyao*].

Notes

1. "Spiraled by the sea" translates *haiyun*, an interpretation suggested indirectly by Guo Xiang's commentary and by Sima Biao's [240–306] and Xiang Xiu's [ca. 221–ca. 300] glosses on *haiyun* quoted in Lu Deming's commentary, and by Cheng Xuanying's subcommentary: [Sima] "The *yun* [in *haiyun*] means *zhuan* [to spiral]"; [Xiang] "If it were not for the sea, it [the Peng] would not *xing* [move], which is why the text says "*haiyun* [spiraled by the sea]"; [Cheng] "*Yun* means *zhuan* [to spiral]. *Shi* [this is such] is an expression of rebuke; that is, this Peng bird, whose bodily form is so heavy and large that if it were not for spiraling around out in the middle of the sea would have no means to get itself up to great heights. This means that it can't help but behave like this—not that it takes delight in it." However, Guo Qingfan rejects all this and says, referring to the *Yupian* [Tablets of Jade, a sixth-century dictionary], "*Yun* means *xing* [move]. The entry on the *huntianyi* [armillary sphere] reads: 'Heaven revolves [*yun*] like the hub of a wheel,' which means that the movement of Heaven never ceases. So the word *yun* here must be glossed as *xing* [move]. Master Zhuang talks about how the Peng, moving without taking a breather [*xi*, rest] over the sea, goes to move its abode to the Pool of Heaven, where it only then rests." See Guo Qingfan, ed., *Zhuangzi jishi* (Collected Explanations of the *Zhuangzi*), 1: 4.
2. It is uncertain whether *Qixie* is the title of a book or whether Qi Xie is a person's name. The subcommentary of Cheng Xuanying [fl. 631–655], which expands on Lu Deming's [556–627] commentary, states: "This person's surname was Qi and name was Xie [Qi the Joker], but it is also said that this refers to the title of a book, for this humorous work did exist in the state of Qi. . . . The book that Qi Xie wrote is mostly about fantastic phenomena, but the *Zhuangzi* cites it here as evidence." See Guo, *Zhuangzi jishi*, 1: 5.
3. "Breath" and "breather" translate *xi* [to breathe, breath, to rest, a rest], and the passage can be reconciled with Guo's commentary only if we read the occurrences of *xi* as puns:

the Peng takes a *xi*, a breather [rests], only after it has used, along with the airborne dust and vapors, the *xi*, breath [air], that all living creatures have been using to breathe for six months.

4. "Moving vapors" translates *youqi*, which might refer to mirages created by rising hot air, for this seems to be the meaning in early Chinese translations of Buddhist texts. See Zhu Qingzhi, "*Yema yizheng* (Evidence for interpretation of the expression "wild horses"), *Guhanyu yanjiu* 7 (1990), 17–18.
5. Cf. Guo commentary, 33.6.1.
6. Cf. Guo commentary, 17.2.4.
7. Pengzu supposedly lived seven hundred or eight hundred years.
8. Although Song Rongzi (ca. 370–ca. 292 BCE) is known in other early texts as Song Rong, Song Xing, or Song Keng, Cheng Xuanying construes the name to mean "Master Rong of Song," a native of the state of Song whose surname is Rong, about whom he says: "Although Master Rong could forget about being, he still could not discard nothingness, which is why he laughed." Guo, *Zhuangzi jishi*, 1: 17.
9. Yin [darkness], yang [daylight], *feng* [wind], *yu* [rain], *hui* [cloudy], and *ming* [clear] are the six climatic phenomena.
10. Fabrizio Pregadio, *The Encyclopedia of Taoism*, 2: 536: "The term *ji* designates the mechanism of the crossbow, hence the spring of something. In Daoism, since the *Zhuangzi* and the *Huainan zi*, it has the sense of 'spring of the world,' or its activating force. The term is cognate to *tianji* (Celestial Mechanism, mentioned in the *Zhuangzi*), *shenji* ("divine" or "spiritual mechanism"), and *ji*, a word that denotes a subtle, incipient movement whose inward spring isn't yet visible outside. Ji is the dynamic aspect of the Dao, the motive force of the world that never ceases to function. . . ."
11. "Stone probes" translates *zhenshi*, the ancient precursor of acupuncture needles, a means to recover health and extend life artificially. Unlike ordinary people, the Divine man eschews all artificial means to assist the course of nature and instead, perfectly in step with it, attempts no efficacy of his own.
12. Cheng Xuanying: "Xu You was a hermit whose surname was Xu and given name You. His courtesy name Zhongwu, he was a native of Yangcheng in Yingchuan [Henan], where he secluded himself on Jishan [present-day Zhili] and found a teacher in Nieque. He relied on the mountain for food and the river for drink. Once Yao learned of his worthiness [*xian*], he tried to yield the emperorship to him, but when Xu You heard of it, he went to the river to wash out his ears. Chaofu went to water a calf there but led it away to avoid him, saying, 'You are ruining my water!' After Xu You died, Yao bestowed a noble tomb on him and gave him the posthumous title of Duke of Qi, for he had been Yao's teacher." Guo, *Zhuangzi jishi*, 1: 23.
13. It is uncertain whether this sentence should read *wu jiang wei bin hu* [would I do it for the sake of guesthood?], which is how the received text has it, or *wu jiang wei shi hu* [would I do it for the sake of reality], which is how the influential late Qing scholar Yu Yue [1821–1907] reads it, since this reading parallels *wu jiang wei ming hu* [would I do it for the sake of name?]. By contrast, Chen Xuanying defends the received text: "However, it is because of the reality that a name occurs: a name arises in response to a reality. As a reality, what is inside is the host, but as a name, what is outside is the guest. If one were to discard the host and accept the guest, it would mean losing what is inside for the sake of pursuing what is outside. Since this isn't what a hermit would ever value, he [Xu You] thus says, 'would I do it for the sake of guesthood?' " Guo, *Zhuangzi jishi*, 1: 25–26.
14. "Ji" and "Xie" refer to Hou Ji, the first ancestor of the Zhou people, and Xie, the first ancestor of the Yin-Shang people, respectively. Tradition has it that they both were

ministers of Yao. Although they were the best of virtuous advisors to Yao, neither had the capacity to rule in his place.

15. Most commentators identify *yanshu* as the common mole or mole shrew, but Cheng Xuanying offers a different identification: "The *yanshu* is about the size of an ox and is of a reddish-black color, with the hooves of a river deer, each hoof ending in three nails. Its ears resemble those of an elephant; the tip of its tail is white; and it likes to enter the river to drink water." Guo, *Zhuangzi jishi*, 1: 25. This seems an approximate description of the Asian tapir (*Tapirus indicus*).
16. Jianwu is the God of the Sacred Mountain of the East, Taishan (Mount Tai).
17. This same name appears below in 4.43, where Cheng Xuanying identifies it as the courtesy name of Lu Tong, a recluse to whom an entry is devoted in Huangfu Mi's (215–282) *Gaoshi zhuan* (Biographies of lofty scholars [scholars who spurn official appointment]), A: 9a–9b. Jieyu also appears as a critic of Confucius in the *Lunyu* (Analects), 18: 2529.
18. Guye Mountain is located somewhere beyond the edge of the world, out in the boundless reaches of the great North Sea. It is one of the realms of the transcendents [*xian*].
19. Cf. 23.8.1.
20. Cheng Xuanying: "The word 'correct' [*shi*] is a term of rebuke. A 'maiden' is a young girl who still lives in her parents' home and here stands for what Ji Yu has said, for his words are like a slender and attractive girl, delicate and soft, whom the *junzi* [noble man] should seek. However, one whose understanding is deaf and blind says that this is nonsense. Guo, *Zhuangzi jishi*, 1: 31.
21. "Becomes a mold or cast" translates *taochu*, which seems to refer to the ability of the sage to reshape himself in automatic response to the transformations that take place in the world so that the actions he takes are always in perfect accord with them. Such moldings and castings surely refer to the outer manifestations of the sage and are metaphors for his actions—the responses to transformation that take "concrete form." These concrete forms are what the world knows of the sage—it can know what he does, but not what he is [a Divine man, his true reality]. As occurs a few lines later in the text of the *Zhuangzi*, the world "molds or casts" a "Yao" or a "Shun" out of the dregs and chaff [actions as outer manifestation of a true sage], for these are what a "Yao" or a "Shun" manifest and leave behind.
22. The Fenshui in Shanxi is a tributary of the Yellow River; tradition has it that Yao's capital was located somewhere north of the Fen.
23. Cheng Xuanying identifies Master Hui [Huizi] as Hui Shi [fourth century BCE], native of Song and prime minister to the state of Liang. Guo, *Zhuangzi jishi*, 1: 36.
24. Cheng Xuanying identifies King Wei as King Hui of Liang. Guo, *Zhuangzi jishi*, 1: 36.
25. According to Cheng Xuanying and other commentators, the gold here is measured in jin [the catty, a pound, 0.5 kg.]. Guo, *Zhuangzi jishi*, 1: 38.
26. Cheng Xuanying: "It [the mugwort] rolls up in curls and does not grow straight." Guo, *Zhuangzi jishi*, 1: 39.

CHAPTER 2

QI WU LUN [ON REGARDING ALL THINGS EQUAL]

2.0 To affirm that one is a "this one" [*shi*] and deny that one is a "that one [*bi*],"[1] to praise oneself and to vilify the other, no one ever fails to behave like this. However, although affirming and denying inherently differ, other [*bi*] and self [*wo*] are really equal.

2.1.1 Ziqi of Southwall [Nanguo Ziqi] sat slumped on his writing table. Looking up, he slowly exhaled, so utterly blank that he seemed to have lost his other half.[2]

He looked upon Heaven and man as one, regarded other and self as equivalent. Therefore, nothing external provides him with pleasure. As such, utterly blank, he dissolves himself [*jieti*], and it is as if he has lost his partner.[3]

2.1.2 Yan Cheng, Ziyou,[4] **who was standing in attendance before him, said, "How can this be? Can the body really be made like dead wood and the mind like lifeless ashes?**

"Lifeless ashes" and "dead wood" capture his solitude and dispassion [*wuqing*]. As for one who complies with the natural and forgets right and wrong, his embodiment allows for nothing but natural authenticity [*tianzhen*], so what else could possibly be in it! Therefore, when he stops, it is as if he stands like a dead tree, and when he moves his limbs, it is as if he brandishes dried-up branches; when he sits, it is as if he has become lifeless ashes; when he walks, it is as if he has become meandering dust. Although his appearance in activity and repose is something that I can't reduce to a single description, his unself-consciousness [*wuxin*] and self-fulfillment [*zide*] are impossible to render in any other way.

2.1.3 He who slumps on his writing table now is not the same as those who hitherto have slumped on writing tables."

Ziyou has seen those who slump on writing tables but never such a one as Ziqi.[5]

2.2.1 Ziyou said, "Yan, is not it good that you ask about this! Just now I lost myself—do you understand what this means?

"I lost myself" means that I forgot myself. Since I forgot myself, what of the whole world is worth remembering! Therefore, only after forgetting everything external and internal does one transcendently [*chaoran*] obtain everything in both.

2.2.2 You may have heard the pipes of Man but never heard the pipes of Earth, or you may have heard the pipes of Earth but never heard the pipes of Heaven."

"Pipes" [*lai*] are the same as panpipes [*xiao*]. Since the pipes of the panpipes are irregular in size, it is capable of notes of different pitch. Therefore, long or short, high or low, it produces an infinitely different number of sounds. Although its sounds may infinitely vary, the rule that it follows is one and the same for all. Therefore, whether excellent or poor, players are allowed no margin of error. How much the more this is true for the elements of nature: as their different tones are equally correct, all must derive spontaneously from it [a single rule], thus it is that the pipes of Heaven and Earth manifest themselves.

2.3 Ziyou said, "May I be so bold as to ask how this happens?"

2.4.1 Ziqi said, "When the Great Clod [Dakuai] sighs, it is called 'wind.'

The "Great Clod" is immaterial [*wuwu*], and as for its sigh, how could that ever involve material substance [*youwu*]! The air clod-like [*kuairan*, intrinsically] just gushes out by itself. The way things come into existence is such that everything generates itself in this clodlike way, thus it is that this clodlike embodiment is so vast that it takes "Great Clod" as its name.[6]

2.4.2 It only acts without intent [*wuzuo*], yet when it does act, a myriad hollows angrily howl.

Here the text says that the wind only acts without intent, though when it does act, a myriad hollows are angrily moved to make sounds.[7]

2.4.3 Is it only you who hasn't heard how long drawn out it is?

This is the sound of the long wind.

2.4.4 As great waves spread through mountain forests,

This is the fanning action of the great wind.

2.4.5 the holes in giant trees a hundred spans in girth become like nostrils, like mouths, like ear canals, like beam brackets, like circular animal pens, like mortars, like water holes, like drainage pits.

This gives an abbreviated description of what all the hollows resemble.

2.4.6 These roar like rushing water, whiz like flying arrows, curse, pant, shout, cry, some deep as a valley, some painfully sad.

This gives an abbreviated account of the differences among all the sounds the hollows make.

2.4.7 As ones in front sing *gheeyoo*, ones behind sing *nheeyuu*. Light breezes result in minor harmony, whirlwinds in great harmony [*dahe*].

Although notes that sounds make can exist in infinite combinations, whether lead and response harmonies be minor or major, none ever fails to match its natural endowment, and each always fulfills its capacity.

2.4.8 When such a fierce wind passes by, all the hollows become empty.

Ji [pass by] means stop. When a fierce wind acts up, all the hollows are filled, but when it stops, all the hollows become empty. Although to be full or empty constitutes a difference, as for the potentiality of each [*gede*], it is always the same.[8]

2.4.9 Is it just you who hasn't seen how it makes things sway and shake, rustle and swish?"

Tiaotiao [sway and shake] and *diaodiao* [rustle and swish] describe how things look in agitation. That is, not only are the sounds of things different, the kind of agitation their bodily forms [*xing*] undergo also differ. Although their movements differ, they achieve an overall uniformity [*deqi*]. So how could "sway and shake" ever be singled out as "correct" [*shi*] and "rustle and swish" as "incorrect" [*fei*]!

2.5 Ziyou said, "Then the pipes of Earth are just all the hollows, and the pipes of Man, are just bamboo panpipes, but may I be so bold as to ask what the pipes of Heaven are?" Ziqi said, "They blow through the myriad things differently since they allow them all to act on their own.[9]

This explains the pipes of Heaven. How could the pipes of Heaven ever be something yet again separate and different? Things such as "all the hollows" and "bamboo panpipes" are categories of phenomenal existence, which all together constitute a single "Heaven" [Tian]. Nothingness [*wu*] is just that—nothingness—so it can't generate phenomenal reality [the extant or "somethingness"] [*you*]. Just as generation of the extant is not caused, something extant cannot cause anything else to generate. Since this is so, what is it then that generates this generation? Actually, clodlike [*kuairan*, "intrinsically"] things generate themselves.[10] Things just self-generate and do not cause themselves to generate. Since I cannot generate something else, something else cannot generate me either; as such, I am spontaneously what I am [*ziran*]. When something is so by itself [*ziji er ran*], we call it "natural" [*tianran*]. The natural is not made or caused [*wei*], and that is why it is referred to by the term "Heaven" [*tian*], an expression used to clarify the spontaneity [*ziran*] involved. How could "Heaven" here mean the sky with its deep azure color! Yet some say that the pipes of Heaven control things and make them obey Heaven. Heaven can't even cause itself to exist, so how much the less can it cause anything else to exist! Therefore, "Heaven" is the general term for the myriad things, and, since not any one thing corresponds to "Heaven," what master is there to control things? Thus it is that everything generates itself—there is no other source from which things come—such is the Dao of Heaven.[11]

2.6 Since it is universal that things initiate themselves, to rouse them, whatever need do that!

Everything can do this entirely by itself, so what master is there to rouse them and make them so! This again clarifies what the pipes of Heaven are.

2.7.1 Great intelligence is broad and deep,
Petty intelligence involves nit-picking.

This addresses the difference in intelligence.

2.7.2 Great words burn brightly,
Petty words just run on and on.

This addresses the difference in the use of words.

2.7.3 Asleep, the spirit remains engaged,
Awake, the person is all too susceptible.

This addresses the difference between being asleep and awake.[12]

2.7.4 Whenever one interacts with others, it becomes a pitfall
In which one struggles daily in heartfelt strife,
Whether accommodating, crafty, or secretive.

This addresses the different ways people interact.

2.7.5 Little fears produce continuous anxiety,
Great fears leave one thoroughly depressed.

This addresses the different kinds of fear.

2.7.6 When starting like an arrow released by a crossbow trigger, it means they would assert mastery over "right" and "wrong." When holding back as if bound by sworn treaty, it means they would preserve a victory already won.

This addresses the difference between action and inaction.

2.7.7 Their ruination is like the withering of autumn and winter, that is, they steadily deteriorate day by day.

Their ruination becomes more pronounced day by day—such is how some fare.

2.7.8 They are so obsessed with what they are doing it's impossible to have them recover.

They are obsessed with their pursuits—such is how some behave.

2.7.9 They are so satiated that it is as if they are sealed up in it—which is a way to describe their aging occlusion.

They are so satiated with desire that the older they are, the more occluded they become.[13]

2.7.10 When a mind is so close to death, there is no way to have it recover the yang [life] force.

Trying to turn calamity to advantage and thinking light of disaster, yin [death] ties off attempts to fulfill ambition—such is how some behave.

2.7.11 One is either joyful, angry, prone to grief, delighted, worried, regretful, hesitant, obstinate, personable, self-indulgent, high-spirited, or posturing.

This accounts for differences in innate personality [*xingqing*].

2.7.12 Music comes from emptiness; steamy air forms mushrooms.

This accounts for the differences arising from the mutability of worldly affairs [*shibian*]. From this point above, the text addresses the boundlessness [*wufang*] of the pipes of Heaven; from this point below, the text clarifies the spontaneity [*ziran*] of this boundlessness. Each and every thing is spontaneous, but we don't know why they are as they are. Therefore, however more bodily forms [*xing*] differ, the way they are what they are [*ran*] is ever more the same.[14]

2.7.13 Day and night replace each other before us, yet no one knows how such generation occurs.

"Day and night replace each other," that is, the old is replaced by the new. Heaven and Earth and the myriad things undergo transformation and are renewed each day, accord with the proper time and all together go forth, but what thing could ever make them generate! Things just happen this way spontaneously.

2.7.14 Have done with it! Have done with it! Since mornings and evenings achieve this, are they not themselves the source of their generation?

This means that they are self-generating [*zisheng*].[15]

2.8.1 If it were not for that [*bi*], there would be no I; if there were no I, there would be nothing for it to endow, so it is, indeed, close by.

"That" [*bi*] refers to Nature [*ziran*]. Since Nature begets me, I spontaneously generate. Therefore, this Nature is my own Nature, so how could it be thought something distant![16]

2.8.2 We know not how it serves as the cause.

All things as such are spontaneously so [*zier*]; they don't serve as causes for one another. Therefore, left alone, their principles [*li*] spontaneously fulfill themselves [*zizhi*].

2.8.3 A true lord [*zhenzai*] might seemingly exist, except we can't find any evidence for it.

Taking the myriad tendencies of the myriad things into consideration, their inclinations and disinclinations are all different, and there might seemingly exist a true lord to cause them all to behave in such ways, but when we look for evidence of this true lord, from beginning to end we never can find any. Thus it is clear that everything behaves spontaneously and nothing causes things to behave as they do.

2.8.4 That it can move is self-evident, 2.8.5 but we see not anything physical to it,

Well, now concerning that which moves, it is evident that it can move by itself.

2.8.6 For it has properties [*qing*] but lacks bodily form [*xing*].

Properties coincide with the thing itself, thus the bodily form for these properties does not appear as something separate.

2.8.7 The body has its hundred joints, nine apertures, six viscera, and all continue to survive together in it.

Complying with what is natural to them, none fails to survive.

2.8.8 So with which should I form a particularly intimate relationship?

One simply preserves himself.

2.8.9 Are you equally fond of them all, or are there among them those to which you are partial?

Even to be fond of them all still means that partiality exists, and, as long as partiality exists, it will be impossible for one to survive. Therefore, one avoids any fondness and so preserves himself, and, not doing nothing about them, just goes on living spontaneously.

2.8.10 If so, are you going to treat all of them as your male and female servants?

If one is partial to them all, your ambitions for them will exceed their capabilities; those more important and less important will usurp each other's responsibilities; and none will actually turn out to be your servants. If the talents among your different servants are such that they are not content with their respective responsibilities, you are handling things badly. Know therefore that rulers and subjects, superiors and inferiors, hands and feet, and the outer and the inner are all results of the spontaneous workings of natural principles [*tianli ziran*]—how could an authentic person ever be consciously involve with that![17]

2.8.11 Do these servants lack the wherewithal to manage one another other?

As long as each servant acts according to his or her allotted capacity, they never fail to manage each other. Managing one another other means, for example, that each hand, foot, ear, eye, each of the four limbs and each of the hundred joints in addition to each having its own jurisdiction also exercises mutual sovereign control over the others.

2.8.12 Or do they take turns in being ruler and subject?

Those who the times regard as worthies become rulers; those whose talents don't answer the need of the age become subjects. As Heaven is naturally high and Earth is naturally low, so the head is naturally located above and the feet are naturally located below, so how could they take turns replacing each other! Though they make no effort to fulfill duties, each is sure to fulfill duties spontaneously.

2.8.13 Or does a true ruler exist there among them?

As long as they are left to function spontaneously, it won't be inauthentic.

2.8.14 It would not matter whether we ascertain or fail to ascertain the facts [*qing*] here, for neither would increase or diminish the truth involved.

Whosoever fulfills his true nature [*zhenxing*] and functions in terms of spontaneous action [*ziwei*], though he reverts to the most menial of positions, will be indifferent to all considerations of denigration and praise and remain content with his own lot. Therefore, whether such a one understands this or not, either way he will remain completely at ease. However, if one were instead to take up the road of hoped for favor and usurps a superior position with inferior talent, such a fellow would lose his authenticity [*zhen*], and, when a man forgets his original nature [*ben*], there in an environment of denigration and praise, he will immediately start making mistakes.

2.8.15 Once one has received his physical body [*chengxing*], he lives out his life to the end by never forgetting what he is.

This means that each person's nature has an allotted capacity; therefore, the intelligent live out life to the end by holding on to their intelligence, and the stupid arrive at death by cherishing their stupidity. How could anyone ever change his nature in mid-course![18]

2.8.16 Whether people interact with others in terms of confrontation or compliance, their progress toward the end is as if they were in a race to get there, and not a one of them is able to stop—is this not sad!

All kinds of people exists in infinite profusion, but whether they interact with others in terms of confrontation or acquiescence, each trusts to his own prejudices, indulges himself in what he is doing, and none are capable of self-reflection. As something which should be sad for everybody, it is indeed pitiable. However, that no one ever thinks of this as something sad is because of temperament [*xingran*]. Since each person has his own temperament, who is left with the wherewithal to be sad about it!

2.8.17 They belabor themselves their whole lives but we never see their success,

Human inclinations [*qing*] being infinite, those who know sufficiency [*zhizu*] are rare. This is why when they get this, they don't stop but once again pursue that. All wear themselves out their whole lives, never tiring of their ambitions, and only cease when they are dead. Therefore, there never comes a time when their "success" is seen.

2.8.18 And, worn out with unrelenting effort for the sake of what they are fond of, they know not where they will finish up—is this not pitiful!

People in general all belabor their bodies for the sake of what they think they want, even to the point of wearing themselves out completely, and they don't know how they will eventually end up as the result of thinking they want "this."

2.8.19 People say that they won't die of it, but what's the good of that!

This means that they really might as well be dead.[19]

2.8.20 As their bodily forms [*xing*] change, at the same time so do their minds [*xin*].

Their minds and bodies rush along together, and, though in great distress, they never turn back. Compared with what ordinary people feel sad about, this is truly a great reason for sadness, but ordinary people never regard this as something sad, for what they feel sad about is not worth the sadness.

2.8.21 Human life, is it inherently as dull-witted as this? Or is it I alone who am dull-witted, while others are not?

Regarding all these matters just mentioned, none involved know why they are as they are; thus we call them "dull-witted." Now, what everyone yet fails to understand is that one does not know how he knows anything yet just spontaneously knows it—just as all living things don't know how they live yet just naturally live. Although the myriad things are all different, in respect to life not depending on knowing how to do it, they are all exactly the same. Therefore, not a creature in the world is not dull-witted.[20]

2.8.22 If one follows his formed mind [*chengxin*] and makes it his teacher, will anyone ever be without a teacher?

A mind that is sufficient to control the activities of a single person is called the "formed mind." As people make the formed mind their own teachers, everyone has a teacher for himself. Since each person has his own teacher, he trusts in it and so considers himself correct.

2.8.23 "What need to know alternatives since the mind should make its own choices?" There are such people, and the stupid are to be found among them.

To exchange the unformed for the formed is not how knowing works, for the mind gets from itself. Therefore, the stupid also make their formed minds their teachers, never willing to use what they refer to as "shortcomings" [of others] and discard what they refer to as [their own] "strengths."

2.8.24 However, for right and wrong to exist without first being formed in the mind is to leave today for Yue and yet arrive there yesterday,

If one were to go to Yue today, how could one arrive yesterday?[21] If not first formed in the mind, where could right and wrong come from? It is obvious that right and wrong as such are things that all kinds of people can't do without. Therefore, the Perfected one [*zhiren*] follows along the course of both.

2.8.25 that is, this is to regard that which has no existence as something which does. When the non-existent is believed to exist, even if it were the Divine Yu, he could not know what to do about it, so how could I ever hope to do so!

The principles of things [*li*] are such that "it is" [right] and "it is not" [wrong] don't exist, but the deluded think that they do, which is to regard that which has no existence as something which does. The minds of the deluded are already formed, and even the sage is unable to make them understand. Therefore, he lets people go their own unhindered way [*ziruo*] and refrains from forcing them to understand.[22]

2.9.1 Speech is not the blowing of air; speech consists of something said,

Each instance consists of something said, thus it differs from the blowing of air.[23]

2.9.2 but what speech discourses about is characteristically indeterminate.

I think that something is so, but he thinks it is not so, and what he takes as right I again consider wrong. Thus speech is indeterminate, and this indeterminacy is the result of his and my different predilections [*qingpian*].

2.9.3 So, does it, after all, consist of discourse,

We might assume that it consists of discourse, but we can't go so far as to assume that it possesses determinacy.

2.9.4 or does it never consist of discourse?

We might assume that it does not consist of discourse, but we still have to take into consideration that for each person it does consist of discourse as an accomplished fact.[24]

2.9.5 We might assume that it is different from the sounds made by hatchlings, but is there really a difference, or is there no difference?

Speech and the sounds made by hatchlings ultimately come to one and the same thing. Whether a difference exists between them or not can never be truly determined. The predilections [*qing*] of everyone in the world are not necessarily the same, yet their speech can't differ.[25] Therefore, rights and wrongs are always so profuse and confusing that no one knows how they should be determined.

2.9.6 Where does the Dao hide so that truth and falsehood thus arise? Where does [perfect] speech hide so that right and wrong occur?

Where is the Dao not present! Where does [perfect] speech hide so that truth and falsehood occur and terms for right and wrong arise in profusion?[26]

2.9.7 Where does the Dao go that it does not exist?

It exists always and everywhere.

2.9.8 Where does [perfect] speech exist yet prove incapable?

It is capable always and everywhere.

2.9.9 The Dao hides within the lesser completions.[27] [Perfect] speech hides within flowery rhetoric.

It is the lesser completions and flowery rhetoric that would hide themselves in the Dao, but the Dao can't really hide them. Thus it is that "truth" and "falsehood," "right" and "wrong" are advanced by flowery rhetoric [*ronghua*] but halted by substantial and fitting expression [*shidang*] to appear in the lesser completions but vanish in great completeness [*daquan*].[28]

2.9.10 Therefore, the rights and wrong of the Confucians and the Mohists are such that each regards the wrong of the other as right and the right of the other as wrong.

The Confucians and the Mohists mutually switched right for wrong, yet the whole world became either Confucians or Mohists. Thus it was that a hundred schools of thought arose together, and, as each had a proprietary stake in its own views, it never reached beyond its own limits.

2.9.11 If one wishes to affirm what they deny and to deny what they affirm, nothing is better than to let them cast light in this way.

To have right and wrong is something which the Confucians and Mohists affirm; not to have right and wrong is something which the Confucians and Mohists deny. Now, if one wishes to affirm what the Confucians and Mohists deny and deny what the Confucians and Mohists affirm, this actually means that one wishes to clarify that right and wrong don't exist, and if one wishes to clarify that right and wrong don't exist, nothing is better than to let the Confucians and the Mohists keep casting such clarifying light back and forth between them. If you let them cast clarifying light one on the other, what is affirmed won't be right, and what is denied won't be wrong. Since wrong turns out not to be wrong, this means that "wrong" does not exist, and, since wrong does not turn out to be right, this means that "right" does not exist either.

2.10.1 There is no one who is not an "other" [*bi*]; there is no one who is not a "this one" [*shi*]. If it is from the point of view of the other, then one does not see it; if it is from what oneself knows, then one knows it.

Everyone affirms himself as a "this one," thus there is no one who is not a "this one"; everyone thinks of everyone else as an "other," thus there is no one who is not an "other." Since there is no one who is not an "other," this then means that among everyone in the world there is no one who is a "this one"; but, since there is no one who is not a "this one," this then means that among everyone in the world there is no one who is an "other." Freedom from the "other" and "this one" is how one achieves arcane unity [*xuantong*].

2.10.2 Thus I declare that the "other" depends for its existence on "this one" and "this one" also depends for its existence on the "other."

The prejudice of people is such that no one sees things from the point of view of others but only knows things in terms of what oneself knows. Since one only knows in terms of what oneself knows, he regards himself as "this one." Since he regards himself as "this one," he has to think the other is not. "Thus I declare that the "other" depends on "this one" for its existence and 'this one' depends on the 'other' for its existence."[29]

2.10.3 Such is the doctrine of immediate mutual generation of the "other" and "this one" [*bishi fangsheng zhi shuo*]. Nevertheless, as soon as "it's life," immediately "it's death," or as soon as "it's death," immediately "it's

life," or as soon as "it's possible," immediately "it's impossible," or as soon as "it's impossible," immediately "it's possible." "What is" for its existence depends on "what is not," and "what is not" for its existence depends on "what is."

The changes that occur between life and death are like the movements among the four seasons—between Spring and Autumn or Winter and Summer. Therefore, although life and death are different conditions, as states with which each person should engage with equanimity, they are one and the same. Now, as soon as the living themselves say that life is life, the dead immediately would themselves say that life is death—so there is no such thing as life. Or as soon as the living themselves say that death is death, the dead would immediately themselves say that death is life—so there is no such thing as death either. Since there are no life, no death, nothing to approve, nothing to disapprove [*wuke wubuke*], the distinctions made by the Confucians and the Mohists are such that I can't agree with them. However, as for each person having to tally arcanely [*ming*] with his allotted capacity [*fen*], this is something with which I can't differ.

2.10.4 Therefore, the sage follows not such a path but instead illuminates things with the light of Heaven and indeed depends on this."

To stay perfectly unbiased [*huaihuo*] means following the "what is" and "what is not" of the whole world so that one stays free of any "what is" and "what is not" of one's own. Therefore, once one avoids the path of "what is" and "what is not," he finds that "what is" and "what is not" are rendered harmless and no longer impediments, and this is why such a one can simply comprehend the inherent naturalness [*tianran*] of things without forcing anything.[30]

2.10.5 "Both this one is an "other";

I [*wo*] too am regarded by an "other" [*bi*] as an "other" [*bi*].

2.10.6 and an "other" is "this one."

An "other" [*bi*] too is regarded by the person himself [*zi*] as a "this one" [*shi*].

2.10.7 There are both an "I am" [*shi*] and an "I am not" [*fei*] for the "other" [*bi*] as well as an "I am" [*shi*] and an "I am not" [*fei*] for "this one" [ci].[31]

"This one [*ci*] regards himself as a "this one" [*shi*] and regards the other [*bi*] as not a "this one." But the other [*bi*] also regards himself as a "this one" [*shi*] and regards this one [*ci*] as not a "this one." So this one [*ci*] and the other [*bi*] both have a "this one" [*shi*] and a "not a this one" [*fei*] in what they embody [*ti*].

2.10.8 So, after all, do "other" [*bi*] and "this one" [*shi*] really exist, or, after all, do "other" and "this one" not really exist?

Now, one might wish to refer to the "other" as the "other," but that "other" will again regard himself as "this one." One might wish to refer to "this one" [oneself] as "this one," but "this one" [oneself] will again be regarded as the "other." Therefore, whether "other" and "this one" exist or not really can never be determined.

2.10.9 Where "other" and "this one" don't find respective mates is called the pivot of the Dao [*daoshu*].

"Mates" mean pairs. "Other" and "this one" are paired counterparts, yet the sage moves along the course of both. Therefore, as one with no mind he arcanely merges [*ming*] with things and never forms dualistic opposition with anything in the world. "Pivot" means the essential. Here one occupies the place of pivotal primacy [*shuyao*] and merges with the arcane ultimate [*xuanji*]. As such, his resonance [*ying*] with things is boundless [*wufang*].

2.10.10 As one's pivot reaches the center of the circle [*huanzhong*], his resonance [*ying*] becomes correspondingly inexhaustible.

"It is" and "it is not" go around and around, chasing each other inexhaustibly, which is why the text refers to them as forming a circle. The center of a circle is empty. Now, if one lets "is" and "is not" form a circle while reaching the center of that circle, such a one will free himself from "it is" and "it is not." Free from "it is" and "it is not," one can thus respond effectively [*ying*] to what "is" and what "is not." Since what "is" and what "is not" are inexhaustible, one's resonance [*ying*] also becomes inexhaustible.

2.10.11 Both "it is" exists in an inexhaustible quantity and "it is not" exists in an inexhaustible quantity.

Of everyone in the world, none fail to regard himself as "is so," and none fail to regard each other as "is not so." Therefore, the two courses [*lianghang*], one of which is "it is" and one of which is "it is not," are endless. It is only by engaging with emptiness and reaching the center, utterly free from personal concerns, that one can ride on them and so roam freely about.[32]

2.10.12 Therefore, I say that nothing is better than to let them cast light on each other. To use my finger as basis to determine that another's finger is not a finger is inferior to using what is not my finger as basis to determine that my finger is not a finger; to use a given horse as basis to determine that another horse is not a horse is inferior to using what is not a given horse as basis to determine that a given horse is not a horse.[33] Heaven and Earth are one finger; the myriad things are one horse.

To affirm oneself as a "this one" and to deny that he is a "that one" [*bi*] is the common lot of mankind when it comes to the "other" and the "self." Therefore, if I use my finger as basis to determine what another's finger is, that other's finger in comparison to my finger in this particular context will turn out not to be a finger. This is to use one's own finger as basis to determine that a finger is not a finger, but, again, if one conversely were to use his finger as basis to determine what my finger is, my finger in comparison to his finger would turn out not to be a finger either. This is to use what is not my finger as basis to determine that a finger is not a finger. To clarify that there is neither "this is" nor "this is not," nothing is better than to let these two go back and forth in the attempt to define each other. If they go back and forth in attempting to define one another, the relation of "that one" to "this one" will be such that not only will each be the same when it comes to affirming for himself that "this is so," each equally will also deny that "this is so" for the other. Since each equally denies that "this is so" for the other, this means that there is no such thing as "this is so" anywhere in the world. And, since they also are the same when it comes to affirming that for each himself "this is so," this means that there is no such thing as "this is not so" in the whole world. How can one clarify [*ming*] the truth of this? If "this is so" really is "this is so," in the whole world there can't exist anyone who would deny that it is so, and if "this is not so" really is "this is not so," in the whole world there can't exist anyone who would affirm that it is so. Now, "is so" and "is not so" have no master but instead continually arise in great confusion. It is clear that though such petty-minded people rely only on their own prejudiced views, yet there is but only the same ultimate congruence [*yizhi*], because, wherever one looks, it always turns out this way.[34] This is why the Perfected one knows that Heaven and Earth might as well be "one finger" and that the myriad things might as well be "one horse." Therefore, the Perfected one with great oceanic serenity [*haoran daning*] allows each of the myriad things in Heaven and Earth to act according to its allotted capacity and equally achieve self-fulfillment, since he himself stays free of "this is so" and "this is not so."

2.11.1 Suitability [*ke*] derives from what suits,

That which is suitable for oneself—one calls this "suitable."

2.11.2 and unsuitability [*buke*] derives from what does not suit.

That which is unsuitable for oneself—one calls this "unsuitable."[35]

2.11.3 Although things become what they are through the operation of the Dao,

None fail to become what they are.

that they become "so" [*ran*] is because of what people say of them.

None escape becoming "so."

2.11.4 What makes them "so"? Their being "so" is based on being deemed "so." What makes them "not so"? Their being "not so" is based on being deemed "not so."

Since the mind [*xin*] and the external world [*jing*] are both unreal [*kong*] and things [*wu*] and the self [*wo*] are both illusions [*huan*], on what could a law [*fa*] governing "so" be based on that one should obey it and establish that something is "so"? And on what could "not so" be based that one should establish that something is "not so"?

2.11.5 People obstinately regard some things as "so"; people obstinately regard some things as "suitable." But no thing fails to be "so"; no thing fails to be "suitable."[36]

Each regards as "so" that which he deems "so"; each regards as "suitable" that which he deems "suitable."[37]

2.11.6 Because of what the deeming "it is" signifies, let us cite as evidence a crossbeam and a pillar, a leper and a Xi Shi,[38] for these may be deemed oversized, deviant, deceptive, or strange, but pervading all things the Dao treats them as one and the same.[39]

A crossbeam is horizontal, and a pillar is vertical;[40] a leper is repulsive and Xi Shi is pleasing. This regarding things as equal of which we speak, how can it mean they must have the same size and shape—as if they should have the same measurements of compass and square! This is why the text cites the horizontal, the vertical, the pleasing, the repulsive, the oversized, the deviant, the deceptive, and the strange, for each person regards as "so" that which is deemed by him to be "so" and "suitable" that which is deemed by him to be "suitable." By contrast, although the principles governing physical appearance and behavior vary infinitely, individual nature has the same potential for fulfillment, which is why the text says "pervading all things the Dao treats them as one and the same"[41]

2.11.7 Disintegration [*fen*] means integration [*cheng*];

Something might disintegrate [*san*] from one point of view, but might be whole [*cheng*] from another point of view.[42]

2.11.8 Integration means destruction.

What I say is whole someone else might instead say is destroyed.[43]

2.11.9 Nothing exists exclusively whole or exclusively destroyed since these states continually interchange while consisting of one and the same thing.

"Whole" and "destroyed" are generated from one's own point of view while disregarding other points of view, and this is why "nothing exists exclusively whole or exclusively destroyed"; in the same way "it is" and "it is not" don't exist either.

2.11.10 Only one of perfect comprehension understands how such interchange comprises one and the same thing, so he does not use things because he thinks they are "right" [*shi*] for it but instead dwells in the ordinary.[44] The ordinary [*yong*] is what is inherently useful [*ziyong*];[45] the inherently useful is what is interchangeably expedient [*tong*]; and what is interchangeably expedient has the potential for fulfillment [*de*].

One of perfect comprehension does not get stuck in one point of view, thus in immediately forgetting himself he can identify [*ji*] perfectly with what in itself is useful [*ziyong*]. What in itself is useful always goes smoothly and provides its own self-fulfillment [*zide*].

2.11.11 When fulfillment happens, it does so about like this.

Ji [about] signifies complete realization [*jin*]. The ultimate principle of things [*zhili*] is completely realized when self-fulfillment [*zide*] occurs.

2.11.12 This is just to follow "it is" and do nothing more.

One of perfect comprehension follows [*yin*] but does not initiate [*zuo*].[46]

2.11.13 To do nothing more while remaining unaware of doing so may be called the Dao. To belabor the divine intelligence [*shenming*] to make things one while remaining ignorant that they are already one and the same may be called "three in the morning."

When one of perfect comprehension follows "it is," how could such a one ever follow it out of an awareness that it was for the sake of doing some good! He does nothing more than spontaneously follow [*ziyin*] without knowing the reason why he follows. This is why it [such procedure] "may be called the Dao."

2.11.14 What does "three in the morning" mean? When the monkey keeper was distributing nuts, he said, "Three in the morning and four in the evening," and all the monkeys were angry. He then said, "If that's how you feel, I'll make it four in the morning and three in the evening," and all the monkeys were pleased. No discrepancy in name or reality [*mingshi*] ever occurred, yet pleasure and anger occurred as if there had been—and this also is to follow "it is."[47]

The manner in which one of perfect comprehension engages with the unity of all things is such that how could it be a question of ever belaboring the spirit about it! If one has to belabor the divine intelligence in order to deem things one, such a one is not worth relying on, for he is not any different from someone who fails to regard things as one. He also suffers from the same confusion as that of the monkeys, for he follows that which gives him pleasure and deem this "it is [so]."

2.11.15 In such a way the sage brings about harmony by taking "it is" and "it is not" and lets them rest on the potter's wheel of Heaven.[48]

Such a one never employs them ["it is" and "it is not"] unilaterally. Therefore, he consigns them to innate equilibrium [*zijun*], where they come to a stop.

2.11.16 This is called the two courses [*lianghang*] approach.

That is, one employs the "it is" and "it is not" of everyone in the world.

2.12.1 What the people of antiquity knew reached the ultimate. What was this ultimate that they reached? It was that things never yet existed for them: this is the ultimate reached, the utmost perfection achieved, to which nothing can be added.

This is to forget Heaven and Earth and abandon the myriad things. Externally they made no inquiry into the physical universe, and internally they remained unselfconscious of their individual selves. Therefore, they could remain utterly free from all attachments, set forth together with things, always absolutely in perfect resonance [*ying*] with them.

2.12.2 Next came those for whom things existed,[49] **but that boundaries were never involved.**

Although they never managed to forget everything, they were still able to forget the distinction between this and that.

2.12.3 Next came those who had it that boundaries did exist between things but that no "it is" and "it is not" ever applied to them.

Although they never managed to forget the distinction between this and that, they were still able to forget the "it is" and the "it is not" as they might apply to this and that.

2.12.4 The manifestation of "this is" and "this is not" is the reason why the Dao was diminished.

Only when free of "this is" and "this is not" does the Dao remain whole.

2.12.5 As the Dao is diminished in this way, so is emotional attachment [*ai*] produced.

When the Dao diminishes, predilections [*qing*] become subject to prejudice and emotional attachments [*ai*] are fully realized [*cheng*], with the result that people can no longer forget emotional attachments, free themselves from selfish considerations, and arcanely unite the other with the self [*xuan tong biwo*].

2.12.6 But do such diminution and completion really exist, or do such diminution and completion not really exist?

Whether they exist or not, this is impossible to know—this is as far as we go here.[50]

2.12.7 Allow that diminution and completion exist—thus we have Master Zhao playing the zither. Allow that diminution and completion don't exist—thus we have Mr. Zhao not playing the zither.

So much music exists that it can never all be played. Therefore, in playing woodwinds and strings, no matter how many and varied the players, much music will always be left out. The purpose of playing woodwinds and strings is to perform music. When some music is performed, other music is left out, but when no music at all is performed, [the whole body of all potential] music is left whole. Therefore, if we want diminution to occur because completion takes place, we should have Zhao Wen[51] play the zither. But if we want no diminution to occur since completion does not take place, we should have Zhao Wen not play the zither.

2.12.8 Zhao Wen playing the zither, Music Master Kuang [Shi Kuang] propping himself up on his baton, and Master Hui[52] slumped on his writing table—what these three masters knew just about covers it.

Ji [about it] signifies complete usage [*jin*]. These three masters all wished to dispute what they themselves were unclear about in order to clarify it. Therefore, their knowledge was all used up, their powers of ratiocination exhausted, their bodies worn out, and their spirits fatigued—so while one might have propped himself up on his baton to take a nap, another might slump on his writing desk so he could close his eyes.

2.12.9 Because for all three it was achieved during the prime of life, this carried them to the end of their years.

It was because they relied on the achievements of their prime that they were able to last long, for otherwise they would have come to early grief.

2.12.10 It was only what they were fond of that distinguished themselves from others.

That is, these three masters were only fond of what they understood, and it was this that they used to distinguish themselves from everybody else.

2.12.11 Since they were fond of it, they wished to clarify it.

They generally clarified it for everyone for they wished to make them have the same preferences as themselves.

2.12.12 They tried to clarify it without others gaining clarity, so they finished up by becoming as obscure as the "Treatise on Hardness and Whiteness."[53]

This was not any more effective than trying to play reed music for cows. Others gained no clarity in the end, so their own techniques of the Dao [*daoshu*] finished up by becoming utterly obscure.

2.12.13 And even his son also tried to finish Wen's tradition [*lun*],[54] but he spent his entire life at it without completion.

It was Zhao Wen's son who also tried to finish his tradition [*xu*], but he too died without completing it.

2.12.14 As such, can they be said to have reached completion? If so, even I may reach completion.

Although these three masters tried to bring clarity to others, in the end no one else achieved clarity. Therefore, they finished their lives without reaching completion. Nevertheless, if these three masters can be said to have reached completion, then even though I have not reached completion, I may still be said to have reached completion.

2.12.15 As such, can they not be said to have reached completion? If so, no one else nor I may ever reach completion either.

Each person might himself achieve clarity but will still fail to bring clarity to others. If others don't achieve clarity, we then can say that they fail to reach completion—which means that none of the myriad things in mutual relation to anything else can ever reach completion. This is why the sage does not cast light on this in order to clarify that, does not abandon himself to chase after something else. Left to one's own resources, each person should just comply with his innate potential, so that perfect completion occurs with nothing left out. Now, these three masters wish to take what they are fond of and clarify it to others—is this not indeed foolish![55]

2.12.16 Therefore, the brightness [understanding] created by slipperiness and uncertainty is what the sage charts. As for deeming things "right," he does not do this but instead entrusts himself to the ordinary. This may be said to be the way to make things clear.

The sage is someone who has freed himself from self [*wuwo*]. Therefore, when it comes to the clarity created by slipperiness and uncertainty [*huayi*], he charts and makes it his realm,[56] and when it comes to the lenient, the amazingly facile, the weird, and the pernicious, he regards them as interchangeable and thus makes them all one. He allows every single individual to find contentment in what makes him content and ensures that no one ever has to deny what he himself deems "right." Thus, no individual will ever be made use of by anyone else, and the usefulness of all the myriad folk becomes useful. When all people themselves become useful, who ever will be "right" or who ever "wrong"! Therefore, even if an utterly unconventional situation or crookedly bizarre set of circumstances arise, such a one will be able to follow their every twist and turn, temporarily lodging in what in itself is useful. As a result, although the useful prove to be infinitely varied, each instance in turn will clarify itself.[57]

2.13.1 Now that I have had this to say about it, I am not so sure if what I assert is of the same category as "is so" or whether it is not of the same category as "is so." Since "it is of the same category" and "it is not of the same category" create a category to which they mutually belong, my assertion and its opposite are mutually indistinguishable.

Now, by saying that "is so" and "is not so" don't exist, I am not sure if my assertion is of the same category as when one says that they do exist. One might want to say that they are of the same category, but since I regard that their non-existence as "so," while one in opposition regards their non-existence as "not so," this means that they are not of the same category. However, although these instances of "is so" and "is not so" differ, my assertion surely still fails to escape the parameters of "is so" and "is not so" as such, which means that my assertion is of the same category as its opposite. Therefore, since "it is of the same category" and "it is not of the same category" create a category to which they mutually belong, my assertion and its opposite have nothing to distinguish between them. However, to consider them in universal terms free from categories [*dabulei*], nothing is better than to be unselfconscious [*wuxin*]. Once one has eliminated "is so" and "is not so," one goes on to eliminate their elimination, and one keeps on eliminating this and eliminating that until the point is reached where there is nothing left to eliminate, for only then when nothing is left to eliminate and nothing remains which has not been eliminated will "is so" and "is not so" get themselves gone.

2.13.2 Nevertheless, let me try to put this into words.

There are no words to express the ultimate principle of things [*zhili*], for by using words one thereby groups things into categories [*yulei*]. As such, I but try to use words as expedient means to speak of it [*jiyan*].[58]

2.13.3 Is it that "things had a beginning"?

If there was a beginning, then there will be an end.[59]

2.13.4 Or is it that "things never had [*weishi*] a beginning"?

This means that since there is neither beginning nor end, life and death should be regarded as one and the same.[60]

2.13.5 Is it that "it was never so that things never had a beginning"?

As far as regard them as one and the same, it would be better to let them innately be equal [*ziqi*] without imputing unity to them, for this goes further to allow one to forget they are one and the same.[61]

2.13.6 Is it that "things really exist"?

If there is existence, then the admirable and the detestable, the "is so" and the "is not so" become concrete realities [*ju*].[62]

2.13.7 Is it that "things don't really exist"?

Allow that non-existence exists and one will still fail to realize that such non-existence does not exist either. As long as this is the case, the "it is" and the "it is not," likes and dislikes will never cease to be concerns.[63]

2.13.8 Is it that "it has never been so that things don't really exist"?

One might realize that non-existence does not exist but still fail to free himself from the realization that this is so.[64]

Is it that "it has never been so that it has never been so that things don't really exist"?[65]

2.13.9 At the same moment, things exist yet don't exist, so I am not quite sure that of such existence and non-existence, what really exists and what really does not.

This is to forget all one's understanding, and, in such a state, suddenly for the first time everything vanishes. It is with this utter vanishing that the myriad things of Heaven and Earth, other and self, "is so" and "is not so" in an instant are truly extinguished [*quesi*].[66]

2.13.10 And now that I've had something to say,

He has just declared that "is so" and "is not so" don't exist, but then immediately says they do exist.

2.13.11 I am not quite sure that as the result of my having said this whether I mean they exist or whether I mean they don't exist.

Again he is not so sure whether he is saying they exist or not, and, in such a state, with them utterly gone, he does not let their least trace enter his breast.

2.13.12 In the whole world nothing is any larger than the tip of an autumn hair, yet Mount Tai[67] is small, and no one is more long-lived than a dead infant, yet Pengzu died young. Heaven and Earth share the same life with me, and the myriad things are one with me.

If one contrasts things on the basis of physical form [*xing*], then Mount Tai is certainly larger than an autumn hair, but if a thing arcanely fulfills its limits according to its natural capacity [*xingfen*], then something with a large bodily form will never have too much of it, and something with a small bodily form will never find it insufficient. If each thing is sufficient in terms of its own nature, then an autumn hair won't find even its small size small, and a Mount Tai won't find even its large size large. If it is sufficiently large according to its own nature [*xing*], no amount of sufficiency of anything in the whole world will ever surpass that of an autumn hair, but if something is not as large as the sufficiency of its nature prescribes, even Mount Tai can still be called small. Thus it is that the text says, "In the whole world nothing is any larger than the tip of an autumn hair, yet Mount Tai is small." Since Mount Tai is considered small, nothing in the whole world can be large, and, since an autumn hair is considered large, nothing in the whole world can be small. It is because nothing is small and nothing large, and no one is long-lived and no one dies young that neither does the cicada covet the Great Cedrela but instead happily achieves self-fulfillment, nor does the quail find going to the Pool of Heaven more noble but instead has enough to fulfill its own desires. Therefore, if I find my natural capacity [*tianran*] sufficient and am content with my natural endowment [*xingming*], even Heaven and Earth will lack the means to be thought long-lived and so will share the same life with me, and even the myriad things will lack the means to be thought different and so will share the same potential for fulfillment [*tongde*] with me. How then could I ever fail either to share the same life as Heaven and Earth or to have one and the same potential for fulfillment as the myriad things!

2.13.13 Since they already are one with me, how do I manage to say anything about it?

Though the myriad things have a myriad different bodily forms, they are all the same when it comes to self-fulfillment [*zide*], so their potential is one and the same. Now, since I already am one with them, there can be nothing to say about the principle [*li*] involved.

2.13.14 But since I have already referred to this as "one," how do I manage not to say anything about it?

Now, names and terms are produced out of lack of understanding. Since people sometimes can't understand this oneness spontaneously, they have to use "this" to pursue "that" [make distinctions]. Therefore, they have to refer to this state as "one" to rectify what it is. Once such people have referred to it as "one," it means that they have something to say about it.

2.13.15 One and the saying of it make two; two and one make three. To go on from this point in such a manner, even a clever calculator could do it—let alone an ordinary one!

Here a word is used to say one, but one itself is not a word, thus one and the word for it make two. Since one is already one, to say it in addition makes two. And now, since there is both one and now two, can we not refer to them as three! Since to use one word to say one, as such, makes three, how much more is involved to keep track of the ramifications involved! Since each and every thing has a different name, even the most excellent mathematician will never be able to account for them all. Therefore, referring to it as "one" is no different from making a "that" [*bi*] out of it, but forgetting "one" is to have nothing to say about it while spontaneously realizing oneness.

2.13.16 Therefore, by going on from having no words to having words brings us to three, so how much the more will result by going on from having words to having words!

Oneness does not involve words at all, but as soon as words are used for it, we arrive at three, so how much the more will result by trying to track down the end sum of it all—could this ever be reached![68]

2.13.17 Don't go on to having them—comply with what things are and go no further.

For each thing, stop at what it is capable of, for this is considered its maximum limit.[69]

2.14.1 The Dao never had boundaries.

Arcanely [*mingran*] it is present without exception everywhere.

2.14.2 Words have never had constancy.

It is because they are said by first one and then another that "it is" and "it is not" are never fixed.

2.14.3 It is because of "it is" that boundaries exist.

It is because the Dao has no boundaries that each of the myriad things can fully realize the limits its own potential.

Let me talk about such boundaries. There is left and there is right.

Each presents different distinctions [*yibian*].[70]

2.14.4 There is normal behavior; there is inclination.

All things are subject to principle [*li*]; every matter is subject to inclination [*yi*].[71]

2.14.5 There are divisions; there are distinctions.

Things divide up according to kind and distinctions are made according to category.

2.14.6 There is competition; there is contention.

To chase after one another is what is called "competition"; to dispute with one another is what is called "contention."

2.14.7 These are called the "eight virtues."

If one identifies general distinctions, there are these "eight virtues" [*bade*].[72]

2.14.8 As for that which is outside the six directions, the sage lets that exist without discussing it.

That which is outside the six directions [*liuhe*][73] refers to what lies beyond the natural capacity [*xingfen*] of the myriad things. Although inherent principles [*li*] exist there beyond the nature of things, since these are not found within the natural capacity of things, they never, as such, have any effect on the sage, which is why he never discusses them. If he did, this would be to cite the myriad things and make one study what they are incapable of. This is why he does not discuss what is outside them, for the eight boundaries coincide with the limits of self-fulfillment [*zide*].

2.14.9 As for that which is within the six directions, the sage discusses this without considering it in detail.

He is content to explain the nature [*xing*] of things.

2.14.10 As for the records of the former kings related to governing the world during the Spring and Autumn era,[74] the sage considers them in detail but without making distinctions.

He follows the evidence of the past but concentrates only on utmost examples of the most appropriate behavior and does not use what is regarded there as "right" [*shi*] to judge everyone else "wrong" [*fei*].

2.14.11 Therefore, in such "division" there is a failure to divide; in such "distinction" there is a failure to distinguish.

All things spontaneously divide up themselves, and all matters spontaneously differentiate themselves. However, one who wants to divide up things and differentiate matters on the basis of his own individual views won't recognize this process of self-differentiation.

2.14.12 You may ask, "What does this mean?"

This is a rhetorical question posed to elicit meaning

2.14.13 The sage holds things in his bosom.

Since the sage regards not making distinctions as that which he should hold in his bosom, he actually holds nothing in his bosom.

2.14.14 Everyone else distinguishes things in order to impose their views on each other. Therefore, I say that in such "distinction" there is a failure to recognize.

It is because they don't recognize that things spontaneously distinguish themselves that they make distinctions made on the basis of their own understanding and use these to impose their views.[75]

2.14.15 The great Dao does not correspond [*cheng*] to anything.

Entrust it to find a name for itself, but no corresponding name exists.[76]

2.14.16 Great distinction does not use words.

This is because things have already differentiated themselves.

2.14.17 Great benevolence is not benevolent.

People take care of themselves without any compassion shown them.

2.14.18 Great uprightness is not humble.

One perfectly content [*zhizu*] realizes that comings and goings depend not on the person he himself is [*wo*].[77] Therefore, there is nothing for him to invest either humility or arrogance in.

2.14.19 Great courage is not recalcitrant.

Because no venture is ever made without compliance [*shun*], every venture undertaken is free of danger.[78]

2.14.20 When the Dao would be made clear, it won't be the Dao.

When "this" is used to clarify "that," both this and that get lost.

2.14.21 When words would make distinctions, they will fall short.

As such, they can't reach the level of the self-differentiation of things themselves.

2.14.22 When benevolence [*ren*] would be constant, it won't be universal [*zhou*].

Others lack a sense of constant compassion [*ai*], so constant compassion surely can never be universal [*zhou*].[79]

2.14.23 When uprightness would display its cleanliness, it won't inspire trust.

One who makes it perfectly obvious that he is morally clean merely covets a good reputation, so his is not genuine uprightness.

2.14.24 When bravery would spend itself in recalcitrance, it won't succeed.

Bravery characterized by contrariness is something for which everyone in the whole world shares a common hatred, for it leaves no place where anyone would dare move his foot.

2.14.25 These five are round but the tendency is to try to make them square.

These five [the Dao, words, benevolence, uprightness, bravery] all harm one's fundamental nature [*dang*] when they are put to selfconscious purpose [*youwei*], for then one can't stop at the limits of one's fundamental nature [*benxing*] but endlessly seek outside it to become something else. To seek that which can't be sought outside is analogous to being a round which emulates the square or a fish which yearns to be a bird. Although the one might hope to become a phoenix and the other try to be as perfectly round as the sun or moon, the closer they approximate these other things the further they distance themselves from their own reality [*shi*], and the more emulation is achieved the more their own nature [*xing*] is lost. Thus it is that by regarding all things as equal that one eliminates all ties with deviant tendencies [*pianshang*].

2.14.26 Therefore, to know that one must stop at what one does not know is to have reached perfection.

That which one does not know always pertains to what is outside one's natural capacity [*xingfen*]. Therefore, it is by stopping within the limits of what one knows that knowledge is perfectly realized [*zhi*].[80]

2.14.27 Who understands the distinction not spoken, the Dao not rendered in words? If anyone can so understand, such understanding is called the Storehouse of Heaven.

With vast and unimpeded scope, such a one lets everything take its own course.

2.14.28 Pour into it, but it never fills; pour from it, but it never empties.

The mind [*xin*] of the Perfected one [*zhiren*] is like a mirror: it reflects but does not retain. Therefore, it is so vast that no change in increase or decrease affects it.

2.14.29 Yet one knows not whence this understanding comes.

The coming of the ultimate principle of things [*zhili*] is spontaneous [*ziran*] and leaves no impressions [*ji*].[81]

2.14.30 This is called preserving the gleam.

Such a one lets it brighten itself, thus its gleam never grows dull.[82]

2.15.1 Thus it was long ago that Yao posed the question to Shun: "I wish to attack and subdue Zong, Kuai, and Xu'ao, but, [here on the throne] facing south, I feel uneasy. Why is this?"

Faced with the Dao as it bears on calm acceptance [*anren*] not yet having spread far and thus uneasy at holding court, Yao decided to entrust clarification of the principle [*li*] of regarding all things equal and as one [*qiyi*] to the great sage. Therefore, he posed this question, which expresses his own puzzlement, in order to elicit an answer.

2.15.2 Shun replied: "These three lords still live among the bitter fleabane and artemisia,

Where someone finds contentment no foulness exists, so to live among the bitter fleabane and artemisia is indeed a marvelous place for the three lords.

2.15.3 So what reason should you have to feel uneasy? In the past ten suns appeared together, and the myriad things were all illumined,

Multiple luminaries ascended the sky, and the six directions [*liuhe*, all phenomenal reality] were all illumined, so no place that fleabane and artemisia grew was not covered with light.

2.15.4 but how much the more powerful is your virtue [*de*] than those suns!"

Although the sun and the moon are impartial [*wusi*] when it comes to illumining things, there are still things that they don't reach, but when it comes to virtue [*de*], there is nothing that it fails to effect. However, now you want to abrogate their wish to live among fleabane and artemisia and so would attack them, subduing them to your rule, but how could this ever help to spread the perfect Dao! As for being uneasy, you need do nothing more than let your innate understanding awake [*shenjie*]. If people are allowed to express their natures [*xing*] fully, each finding contentment in what makes them content, and, regardless of distance and degree of seclusion, and you let them go their own unhindered way [*ziruo*] so that all fulfill their limits, then none of them will ever fail to do what is appropriate and your own self will never fail to be at ease.[83]

2.16 Front Teeth Missing [Nieque] asked Wang Ni: "Do you know what all people alike agree on as "right" [*shi*, "it is"]?"

2.17 Wang Ni replied: "How should I know that?"

What they agree on is not necessarily "right" [*shi*], and not just what they disagree about is "wrong" [*fei*], thus others and a person oneself can never correct each other. Therefore, there is no way to put such knowledge to use.

2.18 "Do you know that you don't know?"

2.19 But he replied: "How should I know that?"

If he himself knew that he did not know it, this would mean that he had knowledge of it, and, having knowledge of it, he could not allow what is inherently fitting [*zidang*] for all other persons of talent to assert itself.

2.20 "If this is so, then does no one know?"

2.21 But he replied: "How should I know that?

Since he stays free of all such knowledge, he is so free and vast that he can make allowance for all.

2.22.1 Nevertheless, let me try to put this into words.

Since he does not know, he dares not make definite assertions but merely tries to put it into words.

2.22.2 How can I know that what I mean by "I know it" is not really that I don't to know it?

It is the common experience of water creatures to be fish swimming in water, and, as such, this is always said to be what they know. However, looking at it from a bird's point of view, what has just been defined as to know now becomes not to know. What the dung beetle knows pertains to rolling pellets, but those who laugh at the dung beetle themselves regard storax as something of great value.[84] Therefore, knowledge which agrees that something is so can never be considered actual proof of anything.

2.22.3 How can I know that what I mean by "I don't know it" is not really that I do know it?

What is meant by "not to know" is simply a matter of "it is" not being shared in common and is derived from the way one particular person knows things.

2.23.1 Now I am going to try to ask you some questions.

Since I myself don't know what the truth is here, I'll try to ask you about it.

2.23.2 If a human being beds down in a damp place, his back will ache so that he will finish up half dead, but is this so for the loach? If a human lives up in a tree, he'll be so beset with worry and fear that he'll shudder and tremble, but is this so for the ape? Of these three, which knows the right place to live?

Cursory citation of these three is used to exemplify the fact that suitability for the myriad things differs one from the other.

2.23.3 Human beings eat the meat of animals that feed on grass and grain; reindeer and deer eat grass; centipedes find snakes delicious;[85] owls and crows relish mice. Of these four, which knows the right taste?

Cursory citation of these four is used to exemplify the fact that no arbiter of taste presides over likes and dislikes.

2.23.4 The female ape is regarded by the dog's head monkey as a proper mate; reindeer roam with deer; the loach swims together with fish. Mao Qiang and Imperial Concubine Li [Liji] were thought beautiful by everyone, but if fish saw them, they would dive deep, if birds saw them, they would fly high, and if reindeer or deer saw them, they would dash off. Of these four, which knows the right standard for beauty for the whole world?

Cursory citation of these four is used to exemplify the fact that what the whole world prefers is not the same, and, when it is not the same it is refuted. Therefore, nothing is necessarily so just because knowledge about it agrees that it so.

2.23.5 From the way I see it, the doctrines of benevolence [*ren*] and righteousness [*yi*] and the paths of "it is" [*shi*] and "it is not" [*fei*] are too confused and crooked—how should I know how to make distinctions among them?

What is of advantage to that one is perhaps harmful to this one, yet the others and selves in the whole world are infinite in number. Therefore, since after all no constancy exists for "it is" and "it is not," the only thing to do is make no such distinctions and let instances of "it is" just happen as such, for only then will all such distinctions vanish, allowing one always to succeed.

2.24 Front Teeth Missing asked: "Since you don't know the difference between advantage and harm, does this mean that the Perfected one [*zhiren*] definitely does not know the difference between them?"

Front Teeth Missing still can't appreciate the marvelousness [*miao*] of Wang Ni's not knowing the difference. Therefore, he continues to suspect that the Perfected one ought to know it, which means that his mind is still beset with a lack of understanding.

2.25.1 Wang Ni replied: "The Perfected one is divine [*shen*].

Since he is utterly unselfconscious [*wuxin*], he never fails to be compliant [*shun*].[86]

2.25.2 The Great Marshland might blaze, yet he can't be burned; the Yellow and Han Rivers might freeze, yet he can't be chilled; thunderclaps might split mountains or typhoons thrash the sea, but he can't be alarmed.[87]

For one with divinity [*shen*] intact and bodily form [*xing*] whole, his individual embodiment [*ti*] arcanely merged [*ming*] with all other things, though he undergo the most extreme change, he never fails to be his real self [*wo*]. Therefore, as if they all vanish troubles never pain his breast.

2.25.3 Such a one as this drives the clouds as carriage,

Since he entrusts himself to the people when he acts, it is not he personally who acts.[88]

2.25.4 rides astride the sun and the moon,

He experiences day and night but is free from life and death.[89]

2.25.5 and so travels beyond the bounds of the four seas.

It is only by nullifying his own knowledge and thus allowing the whole world to act spontaneously [*ziwei*] that he can drive the myriad things fast without ever becoming exhausted.[90]

2.25.6 Since life and death are no change for him,

Since he keeps recreating his embodiment [*ti*] in response to change [*bian*], it is as if life and death are one and the same for him.

2.25.7 how much less likely are considerations of advantage or harm to have an effect!"

Compared to life and death, advantage and harm are even less adequate to trouble one's thoughts.

2.26.1 Master Quque [Master Startled Magpie] asked Master Tall Parasol Tree [Changwu zi] "I have heard it from you, Master, that the sage does not make selfconscious work of the affairs of the world.[91]

He does nothing more than let affairs of the world [*wu*] happen as is their wont and with appropriate principles [*li*] spontaneously responds [*ziying*] to them—never does he make a selfconscious effort to work at them.

2.26.2 Neither does he pursue advantage nor avoid harm.

He just lets things take their own course and keeps going straight ahead, with nothing to avoid or pursue.

2.26.3 Neither does he take delight in being sought after,

Since he takes no delight in being sought after, he simply never gets angry.

2.26.4 nor does he follow the Dao by clinging to it.

It is only such as he who travels it perfectly.[92]

2.26.5 He never says what is said, and what he has to say is never said,

What people in general say to be so is never what I say, for it is nothing more than the pronouncements of individual peculiar notions. Therefore, I stay free of what they have to say and instead have this which is never said to say.

2.26.6 and, as such, wanders off beyond the dust and dirt.

Whenever something fails to realize its true nature [*zhenxing*], it becomes dust and dirt.

2.26.7 You, Master, thought these rash and simplistic words, but I think they are how to practice the marvelous Dao. What do you think, my master, of that?"[93]

2.27.1 Master Tall Parasol Tree replied: "Since it would have been perplexing to hear them even if they came from the Yellow Thearch, how could I, Qiu, ever understand them![94] **You really plan too far in advance! You see a chicken egg and demand of it the hour that ends the night, or see a crossbow pellet and demand of it a dove to roast.**

As things are provided with particular natural endowments [*ziran*], so their principles [*li*] establish their ultimate limits [*chiji*]. If one proceeds straightforwardly in compliance with [*xun*] both, a spontaneous union with them arcanely results—but this can't be expressed in words. Therefore, anything said about it will be vague and simplistic, and those who hear it will be perplexed at what is said. Even if the Yellow Thearch were to come again, he could not free the myriad folk from selfconscious involvement with things [*wuhuai*], and in the end they would remain perplexed at what he said. Therefore, the sage places his fundamental nature [*dang*] beyond the dust and dirt and arcanely merges with what lies outside the reach of sight and hearing. He goes with the natural inclination of things and never plans in advance [*niji*],[95] lets them be as they are and never explains. But now Quque has just heard these rash and simplistic words and immediately regards them as how to practice the marvelous Dao, which is no different from seeing a chicken egg and demand that it have the power to announce the dawn or see a crossbow pellet and demand that it results in a dove to roast. Those unable to find contentment in the moment and reside in compliance but instead keep trying to meddle with and change things, who worry about death in the midst of life, and who cling to their "this is" to distinguish the "it is not," all are disciples of planning in advance.

2.28.1 I am going to try to discuss it for you in illogical terms,

To talk about it [the Dao] is to be rash and simplistic. Therefore, he tries to talk about it illogically [*wang*].

2.28.2 so you listen to it as such. How about that?[96]

If you were to hear these illogical statements as rational [*zheng*], it would again tend to make you plan too far in advance. Therefore, why don't you also listen to them as irrational?

2.28.3 He sidles up to the sun and the moon
and carries the universe under his arm.

To regard life and death as day and night is expressed in the metaphor [*yu*] "to sidle up to the sun and the moon," and to regard the myriad things as one body is expressed by the analogy [*bi*] "to carry the universe under his arm."

2.28.4 To form a perfect union with them,
accept their lack of definition and disorderliness,
and regard inferiors as superiors.

It is because some things are scorned that notions of superiority and inferiority arise, but these are so indefinite [*huahun*] and disorderly that no one can rectify them, for what each individual takes to be so depends on a particular viewpoint. Therefore, to merge perfectly with the Dao as it bears on spontaneous union [*zihe*] nothing is better than to accept things as they are without a word and to entrust them to their own spontaneity. The quality *hun* [indistinct, unsettled] is used to describe the appearance of water when no definition exists between one wave and another.[97]

2.28.5 While everyone else belabors himself,

They race around like horses or flee like frightened flocks of wild geese in the realm of "it is" and "it is not."

2.28.6 The sage stupidly goes his own way.

Witless as a plant in first growth, he just keeps on going his own way.

2.28.7 He identifies with a myriad ages yet,
Integrally one with them, is pure.

Chun [pure] means unadulterated, unmixed. Taking up the myriad ages, he identifies with all the transformations that took place in them, so everyone calls him eclectic [*za*]. Thus it is that they so belabor themselves that they wear out their bodies and are reduced to grief, yet they continue on rejecting that and turning to this. Only the sage stays free of such commitments and, as such, stupidly goes his own way remaining one with the transformation of things. Since he remains one with the transformation of things, he always travels in the realm of independent spontaneity [*du*]. Therefore, though he identifies eclectically with countless differences throughout infinite time, he maintains his integrity [*cheng*] by acting on them in accordance with the Dao, and, since he maintains his integrity [*cheng*], he remains integrally one with both past and present. If what people call him [eclectic] turns out to be so [*ran*], then the myriad things are so in exactly one and the same way. When one is so just as absolutely everything else is so, and when one is integrally one with every moment of time, such a one may be called "pure."

2.28.8 The myriad things are all so,

Nothing fails to be so.

2.28.9 Thus, he takes up instances of "this is" and lets them accumulate.

Yun [accumulate] means *ji* [gather together]. As he gathers together all instances of "this is" [*shi*] from throughout myriad ages, he finds there is only one "this is" for the myriad ages as a whole. As he gathers together all instances of it is "so" [*ran*] as it is applied to the myriad things, he finds that the myriad things are all "so." Therefore, he knows nothing of wherein lies the order of precedence of life over death or what it might be like for another to experience victory and oneself defeat.

2.29.1 How do I know that to love life is not a delusion?

Life and death are one and the same, so to love life alone tends to place one in opposition to the process of transformation [*bianhua*]. Therefore, I am not sure but that this is not a delusion.

2.29.2 How do I know that to hate death is not to suffer youthful loss and thus know not where to return?"

To lose one's native place when young is called *ruosang* [youthful loss]. One who suffers youthful loss tends to become so content with where he consequently finds himself that he knows not to return to his native place. So how do I know that life is not such youthful loss! And how do I know that death would not be such a return that we instead hate!

2.29.3 Concubine Li was the daughter of the Ai district border defense commandant. When the state of Jin first captured her, she cried so much that tears soaked the whole front of her garment, and it was only after she had arrived at the palace, shared his master bed with the ruler, and eaten his fine meats that she regretted she had ever cried.

Throughout a lifetime, one's emotions [*qing*] change as much as this. Since on any given day one never knows how he might feel on any other day, how much the less can one know what the change between life and death might bring!

2.29.4 How do I know that the dead don't regret that they had ever first begged for life!

Qi[98] means *qiu* [beg, seek].

2.30.1 Someone who dreams he is drinking wine when dawn comes might start weeping, and someone who dreams that he is weeping when dawn comes might go out hunting.

This is about how experiences change from when one is awake to when one is sleeping. As experiences change, so one's emotions also change, thus what one desires in life and what one desires in death can't possibly be the same. As one takes pleasure in life when alive, so might one take pleasure in death when dead. Although life and death differ, since one equally gets what one desires in each, what bonds [*xi*] need there be![99]

2.30.2 Just when he is dreaming, he is unaware that he is dreaming.

Looking at it from this point of view, when one is dead, one also might not be aware that he is dead but still feel that everything is going just right for him.

2.30.3 So while in one dream he might go on to divine another dream he has in it.

Since the dreamer has another dream and divines that dream while still in the first dream, this is no different from being awake.

2.30.4 It is only after he wakes up that he realizes that he has been dreaming.

If one finds suitable whatever he encounters, nothing will ever fail to yield contentment, so why worry about death just because one is in the midst of life!

2.30.5 Moreover, only after one has experienced a great awakening will he realize that this is all a great dream.

One who experiences a great awakening is a sage. Once one has had a great awakening, he realizes that it is always the unawakened who carry around cares and worries in their bosoms.

2.30.6 Yet the stupid think that they are awake, something they know with absolute clarity [*qieqie*], so their "Ah, Master" and "Ah, herdsman" are obstinately superficial.

The stupid exists in a great dream but think themselves awake. Therefore, with perfect clarity they regard those whom they esteem as if they were monarchs and those they despise as if they were cow or horse herders. Since they happily trust their own individual prejudices, they can be called obstinately superficial.

2.30.7 I, Qiu, and you are both dreaming.

He is still unable to forget words and let his innate spirit awake [*shenjie*], so it is not as if he has had a great awakening.[100]

2.30.8 And when I say that you are dreaming, this too is a dream.

This means while in a dream to divine another dream. He himself thinks that he is dreaming, which is the same as remaining unawakened, but how much worse off with all their supposed perfect clarity are those who think they are awake!

2.30.9 So, this is the way I talk about it, the name for which is "talk that is bizarre as can be" [*diaogui*].

This is extraordinary talk, so it is something only for an extraordinary person to understand. Therefore, people call it the most bizarre talk possible and fail to recognize its power to free one from bonds [*xuanjie*].

2.30.10 If after a myriad generations, a great sage is encountered only once but knows how to interpret what I say, this would be to encounter him as if between dawn and dusk.

This is a way of saying that those who can cicada-like slough off all bonds and thus arcanely unite [*xuantong*] life and death are extremely rare.[101]

2.31.1 Suppose you and I have an argument, and you beat me and I don't beat you—does this result in you being right and I wrong? Or, I beat you and you don't beat me—does this result in my being right and you wrong?

Ruo [common meanings "if" and "as if [like]] and *er* [common subordinate conjunction] here both mean "you" [*ru*].[102]

2.31.2 Is one of us right and one wrong? Are both of us right? Are both of us wrong? If you and I can't come to a mutual understanding, others will certainly suffer from the obscurity of what we say, so whom shall we appoint to decide who is correct?

This is to judge without first having the necessary knowledge and to dispute without first having the necessary experience; that is, to argue about something without sufficient means to justify one's own self-confidence [*zixin*] and yet do so in opposition to others. People argue opposing views all day long in such obscurity that finally no one is able to judge what is correct. Therefore, one should do nothing but trust people to find their own self-resolution [*zizheng*].

2.31.3 Should we appoint someone who agrees with you to decide? But since such a one would agree with you, how could he decide it? Should we appoint someone who agrees with me? But since such a one would agree with me, how could he decide it?

When people agree, they think what they agree on is right, but this is not quite worth trusting.

2.31.4 Should we appoint someone who disagrees with both you and me to decide? But since such a one would disagree with both you and me, how could he decide it?

When people disagree, they think each other wrong, but this too falls short as a means to rely on.

2.31.5 Should we appoint someone who agrees with both you and me to decide it? But since such a one would agree with both you and me, how could he decide it?

If right really were to turn out to be right, then in the whole world no one could ever again succeed at deeming it wrong. If wrong really were to turn out to be wrong, then there would be no reason for anyone ever again to deem it right. However, here is someone who deems right that which he agrees with and deems wrong that which he disagrees with, but because he provides both disagreement and agreement, he can be no proper judge of what is right or wrong. Thus it is that the phenomenon of right and wrong is born in the love of disputation and vanishes on the potter's wheel of Heaven [*tianjun*], where one entrusts it to the simultaneous pursuit of two courses [*lianghang*] and then lets it come to rest in self-resolution [*zizheng*].

2.31.6 If all this is so, since neither I nor you nor anyone else can come to a mutual understanding, should we depend on yet someone else?

Since each will regard himself as correct, to depend on yet someone else would still fall short as a means to decide what is right. Therefore, since no one in the whole world can ever have a mutual sense of what is correct, one should just let people find their own self-resolution [*zizheng*] and so reach perfection.

2.32.1 What does it mean to be in accord with Heaven's distinctions?

Heaven's distinctions [*tianni*] are the natural divisions [*ziran zhi fen*] between things.

2.32.2 I say that what is deemed right is not right, and what is deemed so is not so. If right really turned out to be right, there would be no dispute between right and not right. If so really turned out to be so, there would be no dispute between so and not so.

As for "right" and "wrong," "so" and "not so," let other and self change positions, for then there would be no dispute. Once free of disputation, one finds oneself in accord with Heaven's distinctions, and, content with nothing other than these natural divisions, one need not depend on anyone else to decide what is right.[103]

2.32.3 The mutual dependence of changing pronouncements is such that they seem not to depend on each other.

The dispute over right and wrong is what causes changing pronouncements, but the mutual dependence of changing pronouncements is such that it is never provides sufficient means to use one to correct the other. Therefore, they seem not to depend on each other.[104]

2.32.4 Be in accord with Heaven's distinctions and comply with their continuous transformations [*manyan*], for this is the way that one may exhaust the limits of one's years.[105]

If one is in accord with the natural division of things [*ziran zhi fen*], trusts to their infinite potential for transformation, and proceeds through life in this way, the realm of right and wrong will vanish by itself, and one may thus as a matter of course exhaust one's natural limits of life.

2.32.5 Forgetting years, forgetting judgment, one takes action [*zhen*] in the limitless [*wujing*]. Therefore, one who lodges [*yu*] there has no limits.

One forgets years and thus arcanely unites [*xuantong*] life and death; one forgets judgment [*yi*] and thus perfectly merges together [*miguan*] right and wrong. When right and wrong, life and death all merge together and become one, this constitutes the ultimate principle of things [*zhili*]. Ultimate principle flourishes without limit [*wuji*], thus one who lodges [*ji*] there can't possibly be subject to limits.

2.33 Penumbra asked Shadow: "A short time ago you were moving, but now you are stopped. A short time ago you were sitting, but now you are standing up. How you lack independent control!"

A penumbra is the faint aura of darkness on the outside of a shadow.[106]

2.34.1 Shadow replied, "Is it that I have something on which to depend [*you-dai*] that I behave as I do?

That is, since its celestial mechanism [*tianji*] operates spontaneously, Shadow's sitting or standing up does not depend on anything else. As it is free of any dependence and thus the result of independent realization [*dude*], who could possibly know the reason for it and so assign responsibility for how it happens?

2.34.2 And does that on which I depend have something else on which to depend that it behaves as it does?

If one were to try to assign responsibility for what it depends on and seek the reason why it is as it is, there would be no end to such seeking and assigning responsibility, so ultimately one would finish up at the point where no dependency [*dai*] exists, which makes the principle [*li*] of independent transformation [*duhua*] readily apparent.

2.34.3 Is my dependency that of the snake scales on the snake or the cicada wings on the cicada?

If its dependency were like that of the snake's skin on the snake or the cicada wings on the cicada, this would be the reason why it had no particular functionality of its own, which it should have had no difficulty in understanding. But its failure to understand here is exactly because it does not depend on anything like that but instead undergoes independent transformation on its own.[107]

2.34.4 How should I know why I behave so? How should I know why I don't behave so?"

Some people in the world say that the penumbra depends on the shadow, the shadow on the bodily form [*xing*], and the bodily form on the Creator [*zaowuzhe*]. But may I ask whether this Creator is something existent [*you*] or is it nothingness [*wu*]? If it is nothingness, how can it create anything? If it is something existent, it will fall short of being a thing that could manifest all bodily forms. Therefore, we must clarify that all bodily forms first have to derive from things themselves before we can begin to speak with such people about any Creator. This is why when involvement with the realm of extant things occurs, although we get a penumbra again and again, this never happens but that it is occasions of self-transformation operating within arcane obscurity [*xuanming*]. Therefore, the Creator is no master, for all things create themselves, and, since all things create themselves, they don't depend on anything else for this to happen—such is the true way of Heaven and Earth. It follows that the self and the other might be related casually, and bodily forms and shadows might come into existence together, but although such arcane coincidences occur again and again, no dependency is ever involved.

Be clear about what this principle is, for it allows each of the myriad things to revert to its own embodiment [*ti*] to find its progenitor and thus need not depend on anything external; as such, external things have no need to refuse, and the inner self has no need to feel proud. This is always why things exist as if they were induced to do so and yet remain unaware how it is that existence happens. Since all equally share this trait, each thing thrives and yet remains unaware how it is that it thrives. Now, to say that the penumbra is in a causal relationship with the shadow is like saying that they both exist but no dependency is involved between them. Thus it is that although the myriad things all collectively develop fully thanks to Nature, each one appears independently, one after the other. Therefore, the penumbra is not something made by the shadow, the shadow is not ordered about by the bodily form, and the bodily form does not owe it transformation to nothingness. Thus it is that whether transformation takes place or not or whether behavior is so or not depends on a thing's innate tendencies [*youji*]. Without exception this always happens spontaneously, so, as such, how may it be understood? Therefore, leave things alone and don't attempt to assist them, for then essentials and details, the inner and the outer, shall all be unselfconsciously realized and tally perfectly together [*minran*] with no impressions left [*wuji*] in the process. However, if one were to invest this immediate cause with responsibility for making things happen, while forgetting that they actually happen spontaneously, this would be to take a progenitor [*zong*] from something external and abandon the master that exists within, which results in the creation of something to cherish and exalt. Although one might wish to promote and make this something universally applicable, what is so exalted actually already exists in one's own breast, so how could anything foreign to you manage to have it!

2.35.1 Once Zhuang Zhou dreamt that he was a butterfly, a butterfly happy as can be, and was himself fully aware how well this suited his disposition!

Happy and content with himself, he flutters about with pleasure.

2.35.2 But he was not aware that he was Zhuang Zhou.

His dreaming that he was a butterfly and thus unaware that he was Zhuang Zhou is no different than if he were dead. However, no matter which state he was in it never failed to suit his aspirations. Therefore, as one when alive is attached to life, so when dead one has to love death. Looking at it from this point of view, we realize that to be distressed about death while one is alive is to be in error.

2.35.3 When he awoke suddenly, he was astonished to be Zhuang Zhou,

It is only because this is addressed from Zhuang Zhou's point of view that it is said that "he awoke." He was not yet certain that it had not been a dream.

2.35.4 but he did not know whether he was Zhuang Zhou who had dreamt that he was a butterfly or a butterfly which was dreaming that he was Zhuang Zhou.

His not being selfconscious of being a butterfly now is no different from his not being selfconscious of being Zhuang Zhou while he was dreaming. However, since each state suited his aspirations at the time, there is no way to be sure that he was not a butterfly now dreaming that he was Zhuang Zhou. It commonly happens in the world that someone takes a nap and dreams the experiences of a lifetime, so there is no way to be sure that one's present lifetime is not just something dreamed during a nap.

2.35.5 Between Zhuang Zhou and the butterfly there had to be a boundary.

The separation between being awake and dreaming is no different from the distinction between life and death. The reason why he is selfconscious that one state suits his aspirations is because it is set off from the other—and not because of a lack of differentiation between them.[108]

2.35.6 And this is known as the transformation of things [*wuhua*].

Since time does not stop even for an instant, we can't preserve the present no matter how much we might wish to do so, which is why the dream last night was transformed into the present. As for the change between life and death, how could it be any different! Yet people worry so much about the gap between them! Just now one is in this state and thus unselfconscious of that state—which is what dreaming of being a butterfly signifies. And taking an example from human experience, throughout life one never knows now what might happen later—which is what the story of Concubine Li signifies. However, the stupid think with absolute clarity that they know that life is delightful and death is painful—this because they have never heard about the transformation of things.

Notes

1. *Zi shi er fei bi* [to affirm that one is a "this one" and deny that one is a "that one"] could equally be rendered as "to regard oneself as right and the other as wrong," but, given the contrast argued next in both the *Zhuangzi* and in Guo's commentary between "this one" [*shi*] and "that one" [*bi*], the first is more likely.
2. Cf. 24.39.
3. "Other half" translates *ou*, and "partner" translates *peipi*. Comments by Cheng Xuanying and Yu Yue cast an interesting light on the passages involved: Cheng Xuanying: "Utterly blank" [*tayan*] signifies an appearance of complete impassiveness [*jieshi mao*]. "Other half" [*ou*] means "one of a matched pair [*pi*]; that is, as the body [*shen*] and the

spirit [*shen*] form a matched pair so that the other [*wu*] and oneself [*wo*] also form two halves of a pair [*ou*]. Ziqi leaned on his writing table and sat in complete oblivion, spirit perfectly concentrated in trance. Looking up at the sky, he sighed, marvelously enlightened [*miaowu*] and spontaneous [*ziran*]. Separated from his bodily form and freed from intellectual knowledge, mind utterly blank and person fallen inert, body and mind both discarded, the other and the self both forgotten, thus 'he seemed to have lost his other half.'" Yu: " 'Lost his other half' means the same thing as the 'I have lost myself' [*wu sang wo*], which occurs later in the text. Guo's commentary says it is 'as if he had lost his partner,' but this does not quite accord with what 'lost myself' means. Sima [Biao] says that 'other half" [*ou*] means the body [*shen*], which is to understand it correctly. However, to say that the body and the spirit form two halves of a pair [*ou*] is wrong. *Ou* should be read as *yu* [dwelling], and *yu* means *ji* [temporary lodging]. The spirit temporarily lodges in the body, and this is why we may say that the body is its dwelling." Whereas Yu Yue, following Sima Biao, understands Ziqi to have "simply" emancipated himself from bodily existence, Cheng Xuanying seems to have a more sophisticated understanding of the passage: Ziqi has transcended the dualism of body and mind, physical existence and spirit, as well as the dualism of self and other, individual existence and all external things, which is what Guo Xiang also seems to be getting at, given his gloss of *ou* [other half] as *peipi* [partner], both of which are rooted in the idea of duality. *Zhuangzi jishi*, 1: 43–44.

4. Lu Deming: "According to Li, he was a disciple of Ziqi. His surname was Yan, and had the given name Yan, posthumous title Cheng, and personal name Ziyou." *Zhuangzi jishi*, 1: 44. Lu quotes from the commentary of someone surnamed "Li" hundreds of times, but it is impossible to determine whether this "Li" refers to Li Yi or Li Gui. However, since Li Yi's work was much longer than Li Gui's, it is more likely that such quotations are from Li Yi's work; thus, "according to Li" henceforth will be taken to refer to Li Yi.
5. Cheng Xuanying expands on Guo's comment: "Ziyou had previously seen people sitting in forgetfulness, but these had never perfectly attained a state of arcane marvelousness [*xuanmiao*]. Now he encountered a leaning on a writing table that was really different from these previous instances, and he so marveled at Ziqi's solitude and dispassion that he had to express his astonishment." *Zhuangzi jishi*, 1: 44.
6. Cheng Xuanying: "The 'Great Clod' is both a name for the Creator [*zaowuzhe*] as well as a term for Nature [*ziran*], the natural/spontaneous principle [*li*] by which the myriad things come into existence, but we know not why this happens as it does. . . ." *Zhuangzi jizhi*, 1: 46.
7. Cheng Xuanying: "To 'act' here means 'rise.' The text states that a great wind does not rise save when it is inherently right [*dang*] for it to do so, but if it does so act, then a myriad hollows all bellow out in angry howl." *Zhuangzi jishi*, 1: 46. Both Guo and Cheng suggest that though the great wind blows aimlessly, with no intent to make hollows howl, they nevertheless do howl. Such opposition to interpret the relationship between wind and howl in terms of cause and effect is comparable to the later account of the relations among object, light, shadow, and penumbra; cf. 2.34.
8. Cheng Xuanying: "How much the more so when it comes to the burgeoning and withering effected by the four seasons, the begetting and ruination done by Heaven and Earth—since they have no selfconscious interest in nurturing things, why should they ever deliberately think about killing them!" *Zhuangzi jishi*, 1: 49.
9. "Allow them to act on their own" reads the text as *shi qi ziji*, which accords with the commentaries of Guo Xiang and Cheng Xuanying, and not as *shi qi ziyi*, "allow them to stop by themselves," which is how Guo Qingfan and a long tradition of other commentators

read it. *Zhuangzi jishi*, 1: 50. Wang Shumin also judges *shi qi ziji* (allow them to act on their own) to be correct; see *Zhuangzi jiaoquan* (Collation and interpretation of the *Zhuangzi*), 48 and note 1.

10. Cf. 12.18.2, Guo commentary, 23.30.11–12; and 23.38.6, Guo commentary.
11. Guo Xiang rejects any role for "nothingness" [*wu*] in his metaphysics—no existence is possible other than physical, phenomenal existence—so his reading of the *Zhuangzi* in this respect fundamentally differs, except for Cheng Xuanying's commentary, from much of the rest of the commentary tradition, as well as translations into modern languages, East and West, which tend to grant "nothingness" transcendent existence as the primordial creative power from which all phenomenal existence flows.
12. Cheng Xuanying: "With the common run of people, one's intelligence [*xinling*] rushes about impetuously utterly trapped in immediate circumstances, unable to stop even for a moment. Therefore, even when asleep and dreaming, the spirit of one's evanescent soul [*hunshen*] remains engaged with others in ridiculous ways, and, when awake, one's person [*xingzhi*] is wide open to indiscriminate influence [*quran*]." *Zhuangzi jishi*, 1: 52.
13. "Occlusion" and "occluded" translate as *xu*, the basic meaning of which is "field ditch." An aging field ditch is liable to get silted up and blocked, just as the aging unwise are ever more sealed up in their own obsession with meddling in worldly affairs. Cheng Xuanying elaborates: "Satiated [*yan*] means "drowned in." Like backed up water, they are so sunk in desire that their muddle-headedness becomes solidly fixed, as if they were sealed and tied up in it. And how could this just refer to the willfulness of those in their prime, for such occlusion increases with age!" *Zhuangzi jishi*, 1: 54.
14. Cheng Xuanying: "The interior of woodwind instruments consists of emptiness, thus it [emptiness] emerges as elegant music; in humid summer the air is steamy, thus it forms into morning mushrooms. This is very similar to way of Heaven and Earth and the myriad things: it has about it the unreality of illusion [*xujia buzhen*], as if from nothingness [*wu*] phenomenal reality [*you*] were produced—as, for example, how mushrooms and music come into existence. As such ephemerality and illusion are involved, why should one ever engage in joy or anger!" *Zhuangzi jishi*, 1: 55.
15. Cheng Xuanying: "One might try to reason out the day and the night, but it will always prove impossible to understand, and, since this causes nothing but worry, it would be best to refrain from doing it. If one further attempts to find out about the morning and evening or investigates the darkness and light, no one will ever fathom what causes them to happen either—it is impossible to discover any clue to this. If one wishes to understand the myriad laws governing the world, know that they are illusionary and unreal; if one wishes to find out about life and death, know that all physical embodiment is subject to extinction [*ji*]. Thus it is that the *Classic of Master Lao* says, 'Try to meet it, but you won't see its head. Try to follow it, but you won't see its tail [so hold on to the Dao of old to preside over what exists now].' The truth of it [*liyou*] is just like this." *Zhuangzi jishi*, 1: 55. That is, the source of the perpetual replacement and renewal of morning and night—and extending to the mutability of Heaven and Earth and myriad things—is the Dao of spontaneity and self-generation. Cheng quotes from the *Laozi*, section 14; see Richard John Lynn, *The Classic of the Way and Virtue*, 73.
16. Cf. 24.66.4.
17. Cheng Xuanying: " 'Male and female servants' signify menial occupations filled by men and women. Moreover, a person's body also contains within it distinctions such as exist between ruler and subject; for example, when one looks at a scene, the eye becomes ruler and the ear becomes subject, or, when one walks, the foot becomes ruler and the hand becomes subject. These result from natural principles [*tianli*]—how could they

ever be the inventions of any man! The reason why these become ruler and subject is exactly because no relationship based on concepts of 'close' and 'distant' is involved. As Guo's commentary states [two lines later], 'Those who the times regard as worthies become rulers; those whose talents don't answer the need of the age become subjects.' Whether ruling a country or ruling one's own body, inner or outer, there is no difference." *Zhuangzi jishi*, 1: 58.

18. "Arrive at death" [*zhisi*] implies an untimely death. Cheng Xuanying: "The bodily form and personal nature with which one is endowed has in each case limited capacity. One can't change one's stupidity into wisdom, and how could one ever change one's ugliness into beauty! Therefore, once one's body and personal nature form, one never loses them in mid-course. If one can just keep within their capacity, he will live out the natural span of his years." *Zhuangzi jishi*, 1: 59–60.
19. A more literal translation of Guo's comment would be, "it is really the same as death," the "it" being the hectic, grasping, and ultimately miserable lifestyle of most people. Cheng Xuanying: "They are so trapped in self-indulgence as this that their distress never ends; this does harm to their life's works and does no good to their spirits. One may say that though this be the days of life for them, it is like the years of death." *Zhuangzi jishi*, 1: 60.
20. Cheng Xuanying is dissatisfied with Guo's comment here: "*Mang* [dull-witted] means *anmei* [ignorant, stupid], which speaks to how people in life are all dull-witted as this. Since the whole world is deluded and confused, how could a single person exist who isn't dim-witted! However, Master Zhuang was an authentic person [*zhenren*] who embodied the Dao, and his wisdom and its application were thoroughly perspicacious and all-inclusive. It was because he condescended to become one with the vulgar world that he asks, 'is it I alone who am dull-witted?' Guo's commentary here is rather forced and peculiar, so I don't follow it." *Zhuangzi jishi*, 1: 61.
21. Cf. 33.20.
22. Cheng Xuanying: "Persisting in such error over time, the deluded mind becomes so entrenched that even the Great Yu, Divine man [*shenren*] that he was, could not make such people understand. Although Master Zhuang had a profound sense of compassionate salvation [*ciqiu*], how could he be an exception and do anything about it? Therefore, he just trusted people to follow their own natural inclinations and did not force them to understand." *Zhuangzi jishi*, 1: 62.
23. Cheng Xuanying: "If we compare the saying of something with the blowing of the wind, both involve the shaping of sounds, but speech must consist of meaningful discourse [*quanbian*], and this is why the text states that it "contains words." *Zhuangzi jishi*, 1: 63. Luo Miandao (fl. ca. 1270), in his commentary to the *Zhuangzi*, reminds us of the context involved: "This again follows from the statement above, 'they blow through the myriad things differently.' The speech of humans isn't like how the pipes of Heaven blows equally the same for the myriad things, for they are unselfconscious [*wuxin*]. . . ." See *Nanhua zhenjing xunben* (Tracing the original meaning of the true classic of the [Authentic Man of] Nanhua), 2: 162b.
24. Cheng Xuanying: "Since the right or wrong of speech can't be determined, what does speech ever really convey! Therefore, we can't go so far as to judge that speech consists of discourse. However, given the opposition of particular perspectives, each person holds to his own version of right and wrong, so we have to take into consideration what each of them says. Therefore, we can't assume that speech does not consist of discourse." *Zhuangzi jishi*, 1: 63.
25. That is, although their opinions differ, they all make the same kind of squabbling sound. The resemblance of human speech to the chirping of hatchlings is more than

the sounds they make; hatchlings chirp in order to get fed—"feed me, feed me"—and human speech seems ultimately to serve the same kind of purpose—"I'm right; you're wrong, serve my interests, serve my interests."

26. Cheng Xuanying: "Since consummate teaching [*zhijiao*] and perfect speech [*zhiyan*] have nothing to do with "wrong" and "right," where could they hide? And could 'right' and 'wrong' as such then exist?" *Zhuangzi jishi*, 1: 64.
27. Cheng Xuanying: "The elements of the 'lesser completions' [*xiaocheng*] are humanity [*ren*], righteousness [*yi*], and the five virtues [*wude*] [the five agents [*wuxing*]: water, fire, wood, metal, and earth]. Complete achievement within this lesser dao [*xiaodao*] is called a 'lesser completion.' When the world enters into decadent times, one may only practice humanity and righteousness, for it is no longer possible to act in terms of the great Dao. This is why the text says 'The Dao hides in the lesser completions.' But the Dao can't really hide. Therefore, as Lord Lao says, 'It is when the great Dao is forsaken that humanity and righteousness appear.'" *Zhuangzi jishi*, 1: 64. Cheng quotes from the *Laozi*, section 18; see Lynn, *The Classic of the Way and Virtue*, 80.
28. Cheng Xuanying: " 'Flowery rhetoric' means puerile disputation, elaborate, decorative speech. It is because it gets bogged down in flowery disputation that perfect speech [*zhiyan*] gets hidden. This is why Lord Lao says, "Sincere words are not beautiful. beautiful words are not sincere." *Zhuangzi jishi*, 64–65. Cheng quotes from the *Laozi*, section 81; see Lynn, *The Classic of the Way and Virtue*, 190.
29. Cheng Xuanying: "To have the 'other' [*bi*] stand in opposition to 'this' [*ci*] and have "what is so' [*shi*] depend on 'what isn't so' [*fei*] are essential strategies of writers. The statement here that 'the "other" depends on "this one" for its existence' involves a pithy use of language and a subtle form of reasoning, for citing the 'other' indicates contention for supremacy. The statement's intention is to demonstrate that by citing the 'other' one can clarify what 'this' is and by citing what this is one can clarify what it isn't is. However, 'other' and 'this' and what 'is so' and what 'isn't so' depend on each other for existence. Nevertheless, once we try to analyze the true state of things, all are determined substantially void and unreal." *Zhuangzi jishi*, 1: 67.
30. Cheng Xuanying: "'Light of Heaven' [*tian*] means naturalness [*ziran*]. The sage's penetrating understanding is such that he does not depend on 'what is' to determine 'what isn't' but simply trusts to the empty mind [*xuning*] and illuminates things with the wisdom [*zhi*] of naturalness. It is just because of this kind of 'what is' and 'what isn't' that he finds himself free from both 'what is' and 'what isn't' and so never has to seize on the existence of the one to prove the lack of existence of the other." *Zhuangzi jishi*, 1: 67.
31. A. C. Graham distinguishes between *shi* and *ci*—here both rendered as "this one"—as follows: *shi* is "the said thing" (what is meant by a name), and *ci* is "this (the thing here)," as an independent pronoun. See *Later Mohist Logic, Ethics and Science*, 120–22. The argument presented in the *Zhuangzi* seems to make the same distinction: *shi*, whether it means "this one" or "this is such/so, "right" and is something purported, assumed, or invested with subjective value, stands in opposition to the equally subjective *bi*, "that one," "that is so," as well as to *fei*, "that isn't so," "wrong"; on the other hand, *ci* signifies an actual physical presence/existence, is the "near demonstrative" and stands in opposition to *bi*, the "far demonstrative," which equally signifies an actual physical presence/existence.
32. "Ride on them," from the context, seems to mean to ride on the infinite courses of "what is" and "what isn't," on "right" and "wrong," as if they were highways or waterways leading everywhere; cf. 23.32. However, Cheng Xuanying explains "them" differently: "One can thus comprehensively go with the ways of all people and ride on them [or, more likely, their inclinations] to roam freely about." *Zhuangzi jishi*, 1: 69.

33. Although both methods are fallacious, it is more effective to use "the other" to negate "this one" than to use "this one" to negate "the other"—this is in order to demonstrate the futility of subjective judgment as a whole. Lin Xiyi adds a useful perspective in *Zhuangzi Juanzhai kouyi*, 25, and both Cheng and Lin take "horse"[*ma*] to mean "gambling chip," *xichou* [Cheng] and *bosai zhi chou* [Lin]: "horse" [*ma*] as "counter" [*ma*]. However, none of the commentaries by Guo, Cheng, or Lin relate this passage to the *Baima lun* (Treatise on the White Horse), in which occurs the famous axiom "a 'white horse' isn't the same as a 'horse,' " or the *Zhiwu lun* (Treatise on Designating Things [in terms of attributes]) [section 3] of the *Gongsun Longzi* (The sayings of Master Gongsun Long [d. 251 BCE]), the best known of the School of Names [Mingjia] texts, which many modern glosses tend to do, but instead insist that "horses" are chips or counters and not horses as such, and "fingers" [*zhi*] are literally fingers, not "attributes" or "meanings" [*zhi*].
34. Cf. *Yijing* (Classic of Changes), "Commentary on the Appended Phrases" [*Xici zhuan*], Part Two: "What does the world have to think and deliberate about? As all in the world ultimately comes to the same end, though the roads to it are different, so there is an ultimate congruence in thought, though there might be hundreds of ways to deliberate about it." About which Wang Bi comments: "Although deliberations may take hundreds of different forms, what they ultimately reach admits no division. If indeed one knows what the essential is—that it isn't to be found in wide searching but something strung together by the One—then without any deliberating, he will get it completely." Richard John Lynn, *The Classic of Changes*, 81.
35. Cheng Xuanying: "No right or wrong exists in the principles of things [*li*], yet that which accords with one's intentions is called 'suitable,' and that which thwarts one's inclinations is called 'unsuitable.' Since such opposition and accord are themselves unreal [*kong*], we know that 'suitability' and 'unsuitability' are both arbitrary notions." *Zhuangzi jishi*, 1: 70.
36. Cheng Xuanying: "All kinds of people exist in infinite profusion, but each takes a personal and private view of that which he sees, so everyone regards as 'so' that which he deems 'so' and regards as 'suitable' that which he deems 'suitable.' " *Zhuangzi jishi*, 1: 71.
37. Cheng Xuanying: "People's inclinations [*qing*] are stubbornly immovable, so when they run up against the external world, they all become befuddled and obstinately say that something is 'so' or that something is 'suitable.' How could they ever understand that by deeming something 'suitable' it becomes unsuitable [for someone else], that by deeming something 'so' it becomes 'not so' [for someone else]!" *Zhuangzi jishi*, 1: 71. Cf. 33.12.3.
38. This refers to a famous beauty from Yue, who became the concubine of King Fuchai of Wu (r. 495–473 BCE), who so bewitched him that it caused his downfall and the demise of Wu. Cf. 14.21.
39. "Pervading all things the Dao treats them as one and the same" is translated as "the Dao gives them a common identity and makes them one" in Lynn, *The Classic of Changes*, 374, note 13.
40. Despite disagreement in later commentaries over how to read *ting* [crossbeam] and *ying* [pillar]—as "small" and "great," or "stalk" and "pillar," etc., Guo's and Cheng's "crossbeam" and "pillar" seem more likely, for surely the contrasted secondary, derived meanings for *heng* [horizontal] "cruel," "harsh," and "tyrannical," and for *zong* [vertical], "be soft on," "indulge," and "pamper" make good sense here. *Zhuangzi jishi*, 1: 71.
41. Cheng Xuanying: "Now *zong* [indulgent] now *heng* [harsh], now beautiful now repulsive—it is in terms of these that infinite variations occur in how people appear. Now

leniency, now hypocrisy, now exoticism, now the inauspicious omen—the way of the world is such that these are used to distort the facts. Therefore, it is by applying 'it is so,' 'it isn't so,' 'suitable,' or 'unsuitable' that one erroneously persists in such dividedness. Now, if we look at things from the perspective of the Dao, they are inherently free of all such dualistic distinctions [*benlai wuer*]. Therefore, although the appearance of beauty and ugliness varies infinitely, the innate tendency to self-fulfillment [*zide zhi qing*] is always one and the same. Thus it is that the text says 'pervading all things the Dao treats them as one and the same.'" *Zhuangzi jishi*, 1: 71.

42. Guo Xiang and Cheng Xuanying explain how *fen* as "disintegration" relates to *fen* as "natural allotment" in their comments on 23.29.
43. Cheng Xuanying provides two examples: wool is pulled apart [destroyed] to make whole carpets; trees are cut down [destroyed] to make whole houses. *Zhuangzi jishi*, 1: 72.
44. Cheng Xuanying: "*Yu* [dwell] means *ji* [temporarily lodge]. The *yong* [ordinary] means the *yong* [inherently useful]. Only one who travels the true path of the Dao with perfect concentration of spirit and arcane discernment [*ningshen xuanjian*] can thus free himself from the dual one-sidedness of this versus that [*bi'erpian*] and see how they interchange to comprise one and the same thing. To fulfill this truth, he does not permanently house success in things but uses them in such a way that their use is immediately forgotten, for he but temporarily depends on the usefulness inherent in all the natural utility [*quncai*] of things." *Zhuangzi jishi*, 1: 72.
45. Cf. 24.66.7.
46. Cheng Xuanying elaborates: "A gentleman who masters the Dao does so without intent [*wuzuo*] and utterly unselfconsciously [*wuxin*]. Therefore, he can follow "it is" and "it isn't" and yet be free from "it is" and "it isn't" and thus can agree with the other and the self and yet be free from the other and the self. Since I do nothing but follow and agree, how could such a one as I ever try to abuse the natural tendencies of others [*qing*]!" *Zhuangzi jishi*, 1: 73.
47. The same anecdote occurs, with variations, in the *Liezi*, where it is used to exemplify how the sage ruler uses his wisdom to control the stupid multitudes. See *Liezi* (Sayings of Master Lie); Yang Bojun, ed., *Liezi jishi* (Collected explications of the *Liezi*), 2: 86.
48. The "potter's wheel of Heaven" [*tianjun*] is glossed by Cheng Xuanying as *ziran pingjun zhi li* "the equitable principles of Nature," *Zhuangzi jishi*, 1: 74. While all the rest whirls around, the exact center of the potter's wheel is stationary, so anything placed there is at rest. Cf. 23.25.
49. The text of 2.12 up to this point is identical to the text of 23.31.1–4.
50. Cheng Xuanying: "It isn't the Dao that has increase or decrease; it is things that diminish and reach completion. Therefore, once completion in the emotional attachment to things occurs we say that the Dao is damaged, but the Dao really has no diminution. This is why the text proposes a hypothetical argument in order to clarify the truth involved. Since whether they exist or not can't be determined, any principle [*li*] governing such diminution and completion should not be recorded as fact." *Zhuangzi jishi*, 1: 76.
51. According to Cheng Xuanying, Zhao Wen was a virtuoso zither player of antiquity. *Zhuangzi jishi*, 1: 76.
52. Cheng Xuanying identifies Shi Kuang (courtesy name Ziye) as the music master of Duke Ping of the state of Jin (fifth century BCE) and confirms that Master Hui is Hui Shi. *Zhuangzi jishi*, 1: 76.
53. The *Jianbai lun* (Treatise on hardness and whiteness) (section 5) in the *Gongsun Longzi* (The sayings of Master Gongsun Long), 9a–11b, consists of an elaborate and obscure

argument whose aim was to prove that it is impossible to grasp the three essential properties of a white rock at the same time—its hardness, whiteness, and the fact that it is a rock.

54. Both Guo Xiang and Cheng Xuanying gloss *lun* [silk thread, cord, tassel] as *xu* [thread] in its extended sense of "tradition." *Zhuangzi jishi*, 1: 77.
55. Cf. 24.66.15.
56. "Charts" translates *tu*, which some commentators and translators interpret in the negative sense of "plan against" or "take steps against," for they regard slipperiness and uncertainly as chaos, which the sage should eschew, and the "brightness" they cast as "flashy show," "glibness." However Guo Xiang has got it right: the sage thrives on slipperiness and uncertainty, for these continually save him from taking fixed positions, and the "light" thus cast is the light of true wisdom. *Zhuangzi jishi*, 1: 78–79.
57. Cheng Xuanying: "The sage ensures that his virtue stays in step with Heaven and Earth, keeps his brightness even with that of the sun and moon. Therefore, he hides outward signs of his activity thus merging imperceptibly into the ordinary. He conceals his brightness when interacting with others, so never bedazzles anyone whatsoever, nor baffles or misleads the mass of common folk. Moreover, since he is never so arrogant as to try to lead others, each person can stay within the bounds of his own natural allotment, and since he unconsciously lets himself be led by the myriads of people, 'doing right' for him is to trust to the collective skills of everyone else. Since he employs his mind in this way, it may be said of it that it consists of sagely intelligence and true knowledge." *Zhuangzi jishi*, 1: 78.
58. Cheng Xuanying: "Although fundamentally there are no words to express ultimate principle [*zhili*], the only way to explain the principles of things [*li*] is to use words. Therefore, we try to use words as an expedient means of expression to provide a semblance of what it might be like." *Zhuangzi jishi*, 1: 79.
59. Cheng Xuanying: "This poses a rhetorical question designed to make one understand that the perfect Dao has neither beginning nor end, which purges one of the notion that it has a beginning and an end." *Zhuangzi jishi*, 1: 80. Guo and Cheng
60. Cheng Xuanying: "Here 'not yet' [*weishi*] means the same as 'never' [*weizeng*]. This again is a rhetorical question: 'Has it [the Dao] never had a beginning and end or not?' This purges one of the notion that it has no beginning or end." *Zhuangzi jishi*, 1: 80.
61. Cheng Xuanying: "This poses another rhetorical question: 'Is it that things both have and never have a beginning?' This purges one of the notion that they are both beginningless and endless." *Zhuangzi jishi*, 1: 80.
62. Cheng Xuanying: "The myriad things of phenomenal existence in all their formidable array are all without exception illusory and insubstantial. Therefore, when the text targets this 'existence,' it clearly does so to indicate that such embodiment of existence is unreal. This sentence purges one of the notion of 'existence.'" *Zhuangzi jishi*, 1: 80.
63. Cheng Xuanying: "This poses the rhetorical question, 'does this "non-existence" exist or not,' to clarify that not only does 'existence' not exist but that 'non-existence' does not exist either. This sentence purges one of the notion of 'non-existence.'" *Zhuangzi jishi*, 1: 80.
64. Cheng Xuanying: "This poses the rhetorical question, 'is it so or never so that non-existence exists or not?' This sentence purges one of the notion of 'isn't so.'" *Zhuangzi jishi*, 1: 80.
65. Cheng Xuanying: "This poses the rhetorical question, 'is it the case that never has non-existence never existed or not?' This sentence purges one of the notion of negating the negation of non-existence. As such, the argument proceeds from shallow to deep,

from the elementary to the profound, beginning with the existence of existence and finishing with the negation of non-existence. Hence we realize that we must dispense with the hundred negations [*baifei*] and transcend the four propositions (tetralemna) [*siju*]. The earlier passage addresses beginning and end, which clarifies the role of time [*shi*], and this passage addresses existence and non-existence, and thus explicates the role of phenomenal constructs [*fa*]. Since all things are but products of time and construct, one should always react to them with emptiness and quietude [*xujing*]." *Zhuangzi jishi*, 1: 80. "Hundred negations" [*baifei*], "fourfold propositions" [*siju*], "time" or "situation" [*shi*], and "phenomenal constructs" [*fa*] are all terms borrowed from Buddhist thought. *Siju* is actually a contraction of *siju fenbie* [the fourfold propositional distinctions], the "tetralemma," often referred to simply as "the fourfold negation"—that is, A, not-A, both A and not-A, neither A nor not-A ; or as here, "things exist," "things don't exist," "things both exist and don't exist," "things neither exist nor don't exist."

66. "Extinguished" reads *si* [this] as *si* [extinguish]; Cheng Xuanying: "The previous passage starts from phenomenal appearance [*ji*], characterized by existence and non-existence, and proceeds to fundamental original nature [*ben*], where the negation of existence and non-existence is itself negated. Now this passage starts from substance [*ti*], which isn't characterized by the negation of existence and nothingness, then goes on to function [*yong*] as it exists or does not exist. Moreover, as for saying 'at the same moment [*e*]', this clarifies that as soon as substance occurs function also appears, for they occur together simultaneously with no gap between them. The arcane Dao is dark and fathomless, and its true teaching is subtle and marvelous. Therefore, when function suddenly appears, it both isn't subject to existence and non-existence yet still is subject to existence and non-existence, and, as soon as substance occurs along with function, it too is both subject to existence and non-existence and not subject to existence and non-existence. Therefore, since such existence and non-existence are not fixed states, substance and functionality have no permanence, so who can determine if they don't exist, and who can determine if they do exist? As such, this passage also avails itself of how function is both extant and non-extant to clarify substance as something both not extant and not non-extant." *Zhuangzi jishi*, 1: 80–81.

67. This passage of the *Zhuangzi*, as well as the attached commentaries by Guo Xiang and Cheng Xuanying, all read *dashan* [Great Mountain], though apparently the text of the *Zhuangzi* that Cheng knew must have had Taishan, written with the character *tai*, meaning "too much" or "great"—that is, the Eastern Marchmount in Shandong, because he includes a remark on *tai* [too much, great] that it means *da* [great, large]; see *Zhuangzi jishi*, 1: 81. However, elsewhere in Cheng's commentary [*Zhuangzi jishi*, 3: 564 and 4: 1103], reference is made to this same passage, and in both these places, the text reads "Taishan, Mount Tai," which is written in the more usual way, with *tai* meaning "peaceful, grand." We should also remember that Mount Tai is first mentioned in the *Zhuangzi* in comparison to the great Peng bird (*Zhuangzi jishi*, 1: 14)—obviously with the sense that Mount Tai is the largest thing imaginable. Therefore, it is likely that *dashan* here should be understood as Dashan, the "Great Mountain"; that is, as the alternative name for Taishan, Mount Tai, and so I shall render it accordingly.

68. Cheng Xuanying: *Zi* [from; myself] means *cong* [from], and *shi* [go; suit] means *wang* [go on]. There are no words for the ultimate principle of things [*zhili*]. Once words are used names [*ming*] arise. Therefore, it is just by going on from not having words to having words that such words result that bring us to three, so how much the more of them will result when going on from having words to having words, with all their ramifications and re-ramifications—could the end of these ever be reached! This clarifies that

for all the myriad phenomenal constructs [*wanfa*] originally there are no names, so it is from not having them that having them is produced, and we eventually end up at such an extreme as this [having names for them all]." *Zhuangzi jishi*, 1: 82–83.

69. Cheng Xuanying: "All phenomenal constructs [*zhufa*] are unreal, so why should names ever be an exception! From this we know that not to have them isn't really not to have them, and to have them isn't really to have them, so, whether we have or don't have names and numbers, the fundamental nature or aptness of things [*dangti*] itself always remains silent. Since one already should not go on to have them by starting from not having them, why should one ever go on further to have them by starting from having them! Therefore, one should pay no heed to such comings and goings and instead do nothing but just comply with the nature of things [xing]." *Zhuangzi jishi*, 1: 83.
70. Cf. 17.6.2–17.6.3, Guo commentary.
71. Cheng Xuanying: "*Lun* [normative behavior] should be read as *li* [principle]. *Yi* [righteousness; meaning] should be read as *yi* [inclination]. All things are in conflict, for there is a principle for this inherent in them. All matters are in disorder, for each person tends to pursue individual advantage." *Zhuangzi jishi*, 1: 84. However, it is common in modern Chinese glosses and *baihua* [vernacular translations], Japanese translations, and translations into Western languages to ignore Guo and Cheng's readings and instead follow the text as it is recorded in the fragments of Cui Zhuan's [third to fourth century] commentary edition of the *Zhuangzi* quoted in Lu Deming's reading notes and promoted by Yu Yue: *youlun youyi* [there are discussions; there are debates]." See *Zhuangzi jishi*, 1: 84.
72. Cheng Xuanying: " 'Virtue' [*de*] is a name for efficacy or potentiality [*gongyong*]. The potentialities of all living things are endless in their transformations, so they can only be set out here in general terms, namely, these 'eight virtues.' This is a way to explicate what the 'boundaries' referred to above mean." *Zhuangzi jishi*, 1: 85.
73. The six correspondences are the four directions (north, east, south, and west), plus Heaven (up) and Earth (down): the bounds of phenomenal reality.
74. That is, the early eighth to late sixth centuries BCE.
75. "Impose views" translates *shi* [demonstrate, instruct, show], which Cheng Xuanying glosses as *shijian yu wu* [impose one's views on things]. *Zhuangzi jishi*, 1: 86.
76. Cheng Xuanying: "The Great Dao still and vast, its marvels transcending bodily form [*xing*] and name [*ming*], is both invisible and soundless. Therefore, no correspondence [*cheng*] can be found for it. As for what to call those who embody the Dao, one should keep silent about them in exactly the same way." *Zhuangzi jishi*, 1: 86.
77. Cf. *Liezi* (The sayings of Master Lie), *Liezi jishi*, 4: 115: "One who cultivates himself, whether in favorable or unfavorable circumstances, realizes that his past and future depend not on the person he himself is [*wo*]"
78. Cheng Xuanying: "*Zhi* [recalcitrant] means *ni* [disobedient]. Within, one cultivates mercy and kindness, while, without, one engages with others with open expansiveness. Therefore, such a one can yield to the wishes of the common world, compassionately succor all living things, stay empty [*xu*] and so remain perfectly in step with the subtleties of all situations [*douji*], and to the end never become contrary [*wuni*]." *Zhuangzi jishi*, 1: 87.
79. The text that Guo Xiang knew apparently read as *zhou* [universal], which is also how the text reads in the so-called *Jiangnan guzang ben* [the old edition preserved in Jiangnan] cited by Yang Shen [1488–1559] in his *Zhuangzi quewu* [Omissions and errors in the text of the *Zhuangzi*]; see *Zhuangzi jishi*, 1: 89. All other versions read as *cheng* [success, successful], which is the reading apparently available to Cheng Xuanying because

the gloss in his commentary, *chenggong* [success], surely refers to the standard *cheng* reading: *Zhuangzi jishi*, 1: 87. Therefore, the text for Cheng would have read something like: "As for humanity, one might apply it constantly, but it won't be successful."

80. Cf. 23.25.2.
81. Cheng Xuanying: "It [the mind of the great sage (the perfect one)] is analogous to a mirror suspended in a high hall, which only shines when things come into it. It isn't known whence comes intelligence that can so shine forth, all we can say of it is that once it shines forth, it forgets what it shone forth and, having forgotten, is able to shine forth again." *Zhuangzi jishi*, 1: 88–89.
82. Cheng Xuanying: "*Bao* [preserve] is *bi* [cover, shelter]. Having attained forgetfulness it shines forth, and, once it shines forth, it forgets, thus by being able to keep its gleam hidden, it becomes ever more bright. This passage pulls together what is meant by "Storehouse of Heaven" mentioned above." *Zhuangzi jishi*, 1: 89.
83. Although Guo confirms the potential of a ruler's virtue as a charismatic power to reach everywhere, more pervasive even than the Sun and the Moon, he does not emphasize the dangers involved in its misuse, which reference to the ten suns surely suggests. Cheng Xuanyin, however, does draw our attention here: "The myriad folk are illumined by the sun in such a way they none can escape their shadows, but if ten suns are added together extra to this, all of which succeed at seeking out and illumining them, then the spirits [*shen*] of the myriad folk would surely be ruined. The illuminating power of the sun is unselfconscious [*wuxin*], but when virtue seeks to make distinctions on the basis of 'it is' and 'it isn't,' and only then selfconsciously [*youxin*] lets loose its power, this is even more powerful than the illuminating power of the sun, for what room does it allow for anyone to turn hand or foot?" *Zhuangzi jishi*, 1: 90.
84. That is, human beings roll beads of aromatic gum resin from the *liquidambar orientale* tree [storax] and collect them for the manufacture of incense. What is of value to the dung beetle is of no value to humans, and vice versa.
85. The text reads *jiju gan dai* [centipedes find snakes delicious], but an old South China folk expression, *jiju qian dai* ["the centipede uses its pincers on the snake"—the propensity for one creature to conquer another], suggests that *gan* might also be read as *qian* [pincers] here. In either case, centipedes eat snakes, or, more accurately, they grip snakes with their pincers and suck out the blood.
86. Cheng Xuanying: " 'Perfect' [*zhi*] refers to his embodiment [*ti*] of the ultimate degree of marvelousness [*miaoji*]; 'divine' [*shen*] refers to the unfathomable way he functions [*yong*]. The sage keeps himself empty [*xu*], responds to things boundlessly [*wufang*], knows without knowing, and distinguishes without distinctions. How could the name 'perfect one' ever convey that the processes of his thought [*xinlü*] have such scope of infinite degree?" *Zhuangzi jishi*, 1: 96.
87. Cf. sections 16 and 52 of the *Laozi*; Lynn, *The Classic of the Way and Virtue*, 75–76 and 151–52.
88. Guo Xiang glosses "drives the clouds as carriage" as "entrusts himself to the people" [*jiwu*], which can also be rendered as "uses the people as vehicle." That is, in governing them, the ruler should identify with the common folk, merge with them, and think as they do.
89. Cheng Xuanying: "Though darkness and light succeed one another and can be divided into day and night, when one resides in compliance [*shun*] and contentment [*an*], there is nothing that can differentiate death from life. In this way such a one stays in control of all things and uses them to transport his innate selfconsciousness [*hanling*]. This is why in the text the terms 'drives' and 'rides astride' occur." *Zhuangzi jishi*, 1: 97.

90. Cheng Xuanying: "Action and quiescence form an undifferentiated unity [*xiangji*] in arcane response [*mingying*] to the circumstances of the moment, so while such a one sits upright in the very center of the universe, his mind travels beyond the boundaries of the four seas." *Zhuangzi jishi*, 1: 97.
91. Although most modern commentaries and translations interpret "Master" to mean Confucius, traditional commentaries are divided between this view and interpreting the word to refer to Master Changwu himself. However, this involves assigning the courtesy name Qiu, which occurs later in the same passage as the courtesy name of Confucius, also to Changwu, for which there seems no external verification. A survey of such contrasting views is provided in *Zhuangzi jishi*, 1: 98. In any event, Cheng Xuanying sides with the latter view and clearly states: "Quque was the disciple of Changwu, and this is why he addressed his teacher as 'Master.' . . . It is because he wished to ask for more instruction from his teacher that he restated what he had heard from him previously." *Zhuangzi jishi*, 1: 98.
92. Cheng Xuanying: "Concentrated in tranquil profundity, his sagely intelligence reflects things free of predilection [*qing*], toward which it neither advances nor with does it engage, neither giving rise to nor extinguishing them, so such a one certainly does not travel on the perfect path [*zhidao*] of emptiness [*xu*] and interchangeable expedience [*tong*] with a mind [*xin*] that clings to the objects of phenomenal reality [*panyuan zhi xin*]." *Zhuangzi jishi*, 1: 98. Note that *panyuan zhi xin* is another instance of Cheng's using Buddhist terms to describe the Daoist sage.
93. Cheng Xuanying elaborates: "Quque regards them as expressing the practice of the marvelous Dao, but Tall Parasol Tree takes them to be rash and simplistic chatter, thus Quque still does not know the truth of it and so asks what Tall Parasol Tree thinks about it." *Zhuangzi jishi*, 1: 99.
94. The commentaries by Guo and Cheng here clearly indicate that the Yellow Thearch would have been perplexed at hearing such words—often the way the passage is read—but that even he could not have avoided making a description of the Dao perplexing when attempting to render it in words for others.
95. Because the basic meaning of *ni* is "move in the opposite direction" or "disobey," *niji* probably also connotes the sense of planning perversely—futile planning.
96. "How about that" translates *xi*, which seems to echo the *wuzi yiwei xiruo* [What do you think, my master, of that?] uttered shortly before by Quque. It is obvious from their commentaries that both Guo Xiang and Cheng Xuanying read the text this way, but others place the *xi* instead at the beginning of the next sentence, which results in the reading "How does he [the sage]. . . .?"
97. Guo's gloss on *hun* refers to the expression *huahun* in the text of the *Zhuangzi*, which he also uses earlier in this same passage of commentary. "No definition exists between one wave and another" translates *wuboji*, literally "no edge to the waves" or "no boundary between waves," which suggests continuous agitation and recombination—nothing ever being settled.
98. *Qi*, written with the grass significant, is an aromatic herb, *ligusticum acutilobum* (Chinese angelica root), but it is used here as *qi*, without the grass significant, meaning the verb "beg," "pray."
99. Cheng Xuanying: "The change that takes place between life and death is just like the difference between being awake and being asleep. Since experiences while awake and experiences while dreaming differ, so the emotions one has while dead and while alive will also differ. Nevertheless, since the world commonly has it that unfortunate things happen while awake and fortunate things happen while dreaming, what is to prevent

death from being the happy state and life from being the unhappy state! From this we should realize that during wakefulness or during sleep neither state has the power to bond one to it." *Zhuangzi jishi*, 1: 105.

100. Cheng Xuanying: "Qiu is the courtesy name of Changwu (Tall Parasol Tree). Here is someone who has penetrated with all perspicuity to the source of truth yet still declares that he is dreaming, so how much the less likely is it that those disciples of stupidity, with all their supposed perfect clarity, will ever experience awakening!" *Zhuangzi jishi*, 1: 106.
101. That is, although such enlightened persons might only be encountered once in a myriad generation, given how rare and wonderful they are, even that lengthy wait should be judged brief. For "slough off," see 15.4, Guo Xiang commentary.
102. All but the last "you," which translates *er*, are translations of *ruo*.
103. Cheng Xuanying: "*Bian* [dispute] here means *bie* [make distinctions]. "Right" and "wrong," "so" and "not so" are all products of false discrimination [*wangqing*]; examine them in terms of principle [*li*], and one finds that they are completely unreal [*xuhuan*]: what is deemed 'right' isn't right, and what is deemed 'so' isn't so. How does one know that this is actually the case? If 'right' really were right, right would be different from wrong, and, if 'so' really were so, 'so' would be different from 'not so.' But here we have this one call something 'right' while someone else call it 'wrong,' and what someone else deems 'so,' this one regards as 'not so.' Therefore, one should realize that when it comes to 'right,' 'wrong,' 'so,' and 'not so,' the truth of it is found in non-discrimination [*bushu*]. But when other and self change places, this makes nonsense of such distinctions, and disputation will thus vanish." *Zhuangzi jishi*, 1: 109.
104. Cheng Xuanying: "Right and wrong, other and self depend on each other for existence, but if you examine them in terms of principle [*li*], this dependence actually turns out to be unreal. Therefore, changing pronouncements have these dependent names, but, since the names fail to signify anything real, the dependency is illusory [*xu*], and since such dependency isn't really dependency, we know that they really don't depend on each other." *Zhuangzi jishi*, 1: 109.
105. Cf. 27.4.1.
106. Cheng Xuanying: "Master Zhuang uses fables and parables [*yuyan*] to express [*chang*] the arcane principles of things [*xuanli*], which is why he relies here on Shadow and Penumbra to clarify the meaning of independent transformation [*duhua*]." *Zhuangzi jishi*, 1: 110.
107. Cheng Xuanying: "When former commentators come upon Master Guo's commentary here, they all take 'snake scales' to mean the teeth-like scales on the snake's belly and the 'cicada wings' as the wings of the cicada and explain that as the snake depends on these scales to move and the cicada depends on these wings to fly, so the shadow depends on the bodily form for its existence. But this is all wrong! If it were just a matter of depending on wings to fly, or feet to move, kinds of creatures that fly and beasts that move are infinite in number, so why does the text go to the trouble of citing the snake and cicada in particular to form the analogy? Now, let me explain that the 'snake scales' refer to the sloughed off skin of the snake, and the 'cicada wings' refer to the shell of the cicada: the snake sheds its old skin and the cicada produces a new shell, but no one knows the reason for it or can explain how it happens, for these are produced by independent transformation, which means they are free from all dependency. Therefore, these two creatures, the snake and the cicada, since they shed skin and shell in this way deserved to be called exceptional animals, which is why they are cited here and why it is said in an outer chapter, 'I am as a cicada shell, a snake slough' [27.14]. Thus we know that

the relation of 'shadow' to 'bodily form' here means exactly the same thing as that of sloughed off snake skin to snake and discarded shell to cicada." *Zhuangzi jishi*, 1: 111. Cf. 24.65.1, Guo commentary.

108. That is, each state—awake or dreaming—provides its own self-consciousness, and it is these various states of self-consciousness that differentiate one state from the other.

CHAPTER 3

YANGSHENG ZHU [THE MASTERY OF NURTURING LIFE]

3.0 When life is preserved through nurturing, life so nurtured fulfills its limits as ordained by principle [*li*]. But if it turns out that nurturing attempts to exceed these limits, injury to life will occur through such nurturing, which is not the mastery of nurturing life.

3.1.1 For our lives there is a limit,

Each allotted capacity [*fen*] has its own limits [*ji*].

3.1.2 but for knowledge [*zhi*][1] there are no limits.

Whether one lifts heavy weights or carries light things around, if one's spirit pneuma [*shenqi*], remains completely at ease [*ziruo*], one will stay within the bounds of one's strength. By contrast, he who esteems fame and loves to win, although he continuously saps all his strength, never will he satisfy his desires. This is what it means to say that there are no limits to knowledge. Thus it is that as a term, "knowledge" is born in inappropriateness and dies with the arcane fulfillment of limits [*mingji*]. The arcane fulfillment of limits means that one acts within the ultimate reach of one's allotted capacity without trying to increase it by the smallest amount. Therefore, although one might bear a myriad catties on his back, if this is appropriate for his capabilities, in an instant, he won't know of the heavy weight on his back. And although one might be responsible for the myriad affairs of state, as he perfectly identifies [*minran*] with them he will remain unaware that they depend on him. This is what "mastery of nurturing life" means.

3.1.3 To pursue the limitless
With the limited,
This is but danger.

To seek knowledge that has no limits with a nature [*xing*] that has limits—how could anyone ever manage not to bring trouble on himself doing this!

3.1.4 To be in such a state and yet keep on trying to know,
This is nothing but danger!

Already in trouble because of knowledge, yet one knows not to stop but brings ever more knowledge to bear in order to rescue himself from his predicament. This is how one injures life through attempting to nurture it, for this truly means great danger.

3.1.5 In doing "good" don't come within reach of fame.
In doing "evil" don't come within reach of punishment.

Forget about "good" and "evil" and stay the middle course [*juzhong*]. Allow everything spontaneous action [*ziwei*] and, keeping it all to yourself, become one with what is perfectly appropriate. Therefore, punishment and fame will stay far from you, while you fully realize principle [*quanli*] in your own person.

3.1.6 Follow the governor tract,[2] making it your main path.

Follow the middle path and make it your norm [*chang*].

3.1.7 You can thereby protect your person,
keep life whole, care for your parents,

One cares for parents in order to please them.

3.1.8 and live out your natural span of years.

If one can attain the middle way and arcanely travel [*mingdu*] on it, nothing will prove impossible. The nurturing of life means not to try to exceed one's allotted capacity [*fen*], for it is nothing more nor less than to realize fully principle [*quanli*] and live out one's natural span of years.

3.2.1 Cook Ding[3] was cutting up an ox for Lord Wenhui [King Hui of Liang][4] in such a way that with:

Each stroke of the hand,
Each thrust of the shoulder,
Each stamp of the foot,
Each jab of the knee,

3.2.2 Matched a sharp sound of rending, as he played his knife, swishing in and out, always in perfect tune, right in step for the Mulberry Grove Dance and in perfect rhythm with the Jingshou Melody.

That is, he exercises his skill with the greatest of ease and never fails to make absolutely the right cut. Since he has perfectly grasped the principle involved, not only is he in perfect harmony with the principle of the ox, he also keeps in perfect rhythm with it.

3.3 Lord Wenhui said, "Wow! Terrific! How could skill ever go so far as this?"

3.4.1 Cook Ding put his knife down and replied, "What I am good at is the Dao, for I have advanced beyond skill.

He simply lodged the principles of the Dao in his skill, so what he was good at was not the skill itself.

3.4.2 When I first began to cut up oxen, what I saw was nothing but the whole ox as such,

He could not yet see the interstices in its natural configuration.

3.4.3 but, after three years, I no longer saw the whole ox as such.

He only saw the interstices in its natural configuration.

3.4.4 And now, I encounter it with my spirit [*shen*] and don't see it with my eyes.

He arcanely fuses with its principle/natural configuration.

3.4.5 When sense and knowledge stop, the divine is ready to act.

As the senses which govern scrutiny quit working, he loosens his mind and accords with principle/natural configuration.

3.4.6 In accord with the natural principle [configuration] [*tianli*],

He does not cut arbitrarily.

3.4.7 I strike at the gaps.

These are the places of juncture, which he follows to strike at the ox and so cause it to come apart.

3.4.8 Following the large openings,

These are the empty places where the joints come apart, which he accordingly follows to cause it to sever.

3.4.9 I abide where inherent certainty leads me.

The knife is not applied rashly.

3.4.10 It never happens that my plying encounters the joints,

Such is the marvelousness of his technique that he always plies the knife edge in emptiness and never lets it come up against the slightest obstacle.

3.4.11 So how much the less likely am I to encounter a big bone!

Gu [big bone] here means to encounter a big bone, which would defeat the knife edge.

3.4.12 A good cook has to change his knife once a year, this because he cuts through [the meat].

He fails to hit the interstices in the natural configuration.

3.4.13 The ordinary cook has to change his knife once a month, this because he hacks.

He hits bones and so breaks the knife.

3.4.14 Now, my knife has lasted nineteen years, and the oxen I have cut up number in the thousands, yet the edge of my knife is as if it had just left the whetstone.

Xing is a whetstone.

3.4.15 The joints have spaces in them, but the knife edge has no thickness. To insert what has no thickness into what has a space means that it will be so spacious that there will be more than enough room to ply the knife. This is why even after nineteen years my knife edge is as if it had just left the whetstone. However, whenever I come to a grouping, I note that it presents difficulties,

Where things intersect and come together is a "grouping."

3.4.16 fearfully take warning, my look stopped,

He no longer applies his eyes to anything else.

3.4.17 my action slowed,

He slows down his hand.

3.4.18 I just have to move my knife the slightest amount, and, with a sharp rending sound, it's already come apart,

Since he gets it just right, he has to use very little effort.

3.4.19 as if it had been dirt clumped into earth.

The natural configuration comes apart yet there's no trace of the knife, as if it had been clumped earth.

3.4.20 Raising my knife and standing there, as a result I look all around and linger awhile filled with satisfaction because of what I have done.

This indicates one self-fulfilled with all his sense of preeminence and feeling of pleasure.

3.4.21 I set my knife right and put it away."

He wipes his knife clean and places it in its sheath.

3.5 Lord Wenhui then said, "Excellent! I have heard Cook Ding's words and learned how to nurture life from them."

Since one can do such nurturing with the knife, he realized that life too can so be nurtured.

3.6.1 When Gongwen Xuan saw the Commander of the Right [Youshi], he was startled to say: "What kind of man are you? How is it that you have one foot [*jie*]?

Jie is a term for having one foot cut off.

3.6.2 Was it Heaven's doing or was it man's?"

If it is something that knowing can do nothing about, it would be Heaven's doing, but if it is the result of going contrary to what one knows, it would be man's doing.

3.6.3 He replied, "It was Heaven's doing, not man's. It was the way that Heaven begot me that caused me to be one-footed [*du*].

To have one foot cut off is called *du*. With all the intelligence he had, he still was incapable of preserving both feet, which means that it was something that his intelligence could not help. If, based on the intelligence he possessed, the Commander of the Right felt he had to seek to keep both his feet, his mind [*xinshen*] would have come to grief within and his body would have lost parts without—how could this ever have stopped with the loss of just one foot![5]

3.6.4 The bodily form of a man includes having two feet [*youyu*].

To have two feet to walk on together is called *youyu*. One never doubts that the bodily form that includes having two feet is not the result of fate [*ming*].

3.6.5 This is how I know that it is Heaven's doing and not man's doing."

To have two feet is a matter of fate [*ming*]. Therefore, he knows that to be one-footed also is not a matter of his own doing. This is why one who understands the conditions of life [*sheng zhi qing*] does not labor at what for life nothing can be done, and one who understands the conditions of fate [*ming zhi qing*] does not labor at what for fate nothing can be helped. He fully realizes his natural endowment [*ziran*] and does nothing more.

3.7.1 The wild pheasant takes a peck every ten steps, a drink every hundred steps, and it does not beg [*qi*] to be raised in a cage [*fan*].

Qi [beg] means seek, and *fan* [cage] is something in which to confine a pheasant. Starting and stopping anywhere in Heaven and Earth, enjoying spontaneous freedom [*xiaoyao*] in the open fields of self-fulfillment [*zide*], all this certainly indicates a marvelous situation for nurturing life, so why should it seek further to enter a cage and so submit to being raised!

3.7.2 Although its spirit [shen] prospers [*wang*], it does not think this good [*shan*].

One who starts in fitness [*shi*] and never fails to remain fit forgets all about fitness. The mind [*xinshen*] of the pheasant prospers [*changwang*] and its will [*zhiqi*] is fully satisfied [*yingyu*]. As soon as it lets itself go free in the wide open spaces, it suddenly no longer is aware that such goodness [*shan*] is good.[6]

3.8 When Lao Dan died, Qin Yi mourned him and giving three cries went out.

As others mourned, so he mourned; as others cried out, so he cried out.

3.9 A disciple said, "Were you not the master's friend?"

The disciple was surprised that Qin Yi did not lean against the doorway and just observe Lao Dan's transformation instead of going so far as to cry out three times.

3.10 He replied, "That is so [*ran*]."

Ran is the same as saying *shi* [it is so]. Qin Yi replies to the disciple, saying "Yes, I am a fellow other-worldly [*fangwai*] friend."

3.11 That being so, is it possible for you to mourn him like this?

That is to say, "Here you are an other-worldly person performing worldly ritual [*li*], crying out and mourning like this—is this possible in terms of principle [*li*]?" Such a person still fails to understand what "merging with the brilliant" [*he guang*] means[7] and so even goes so far as to ask this kind of question.

3.12.1 He replied, "That is so [*ran*]."

This Perfected one [*zhiren*] has no emotions [*qing*] and does nothing more than cry out along with everyone else. Therefore, it is possible to behave like this.

3.12.2 At first, I thought that these were his people, but now I see that they are not. Before, when I had gone in to mourn for him, the old were there weeping over him as if they were weeping for their children, and youngsters were there weeping over him as if they weeping for their mothers. The reason why they had made an assembly of it should have been to speak without being begged [*qi*] to speak and weep without being begged to weep.[8]

He dislikes the way they carry out acts of goodness in anticipating things [*xian wu*]. It is because they don't set forth on the path of principle [*li*] that they arrive at this state of extreme devotion.

3.12.3 Such people try to escape from nature and multiply the scope of their innate tendencies/emotions [*qing*], which is to forget what they have been endowed with.

The inherent nature [*tianxing*] with which one is endowed has in each instance a fundamental allotted capacity [*benfen*] from which one can't escape and to which one can't add.

3.12.4 In ancient times this was called the "punishment of escaping from nature."

To be so greatly and profoundly moved by things that one does not stop at what is right is what is meant by "escaping from nature." If one is going to run amuck in the realm of grief and joy, though he does not yet have painful death inflicted on him, his innate personality [*xingqing*] will already be sorely troubled, so how could this not be a punishment!

3.12.5 He came when it was just right, for the Master was timely.

In step with the moment he underwent self-generation [*zisheng*].

3.12.6 He departed when it was just right, for the Master was compliant.

In step with principle [*li*] he died when it was right.

3.12.7 Content with his time, he abided in compliance, so neither grief nor joy could intrude on him.

Grief and joy are born in loss and gain. Now, a master who arcanely identifies with things [*xuantong*] and stays in step with transformation [*hebian*] will never experience a time when he is not content, never have an occasion for compliance that he does not meet. Once he arcanely becomes one with the Creator [*zaowuzhe*], no path does he take but that it is his own path, so what gain, what loss does he ever have? What death or what life? Therefore, acting in accord with his received endowment, grief and joy find no place to intrude.

3.12.8 In ancient times this was called "ties untied by the Thearch."[9]

If we regard something with ties as "tied," then that which has no ties is "ties untied." With one's ties untied, the innate true state [*qing*] of one's naturally endowed life [*xingming*] are realized. This is the prime directive [*yao*] for nurturing life.[10]

3.13.1 That fingers are used completely in providing firewood is how fire is transmitted,

Qiong [used completely] means *jin* [exhausted]; *wei xin* [provide firewood] is like saying *qian xin* [add firewood]. One adds firewood with the fingers, and the fingers exhaust [*jin*] the principle [*li*] of adding firewood. Therefore, fire is transmitted and so does not go out. Therefore, the mind [*xin*] manages to get just the right amount of nurturing so life continues and is not terminated. How clear it is that nurturing life is the means by which the living have life.[11]

3.13.2 but people don't understand what such exhaustion [*jin*] means.

A moment never comes again, and "now" does not stop for an instant. Therefore, the life of a man consists of nothing more than getting a bit of it with each breath. The breath taken before is not the breath taken now. Therefore, it is by obtaining nurture that life continues. The fire before is not the fire later. Therefore, one provides firewood so that the fire is transmitted. That fire is transmitted and life continues is due to the fact that nurturing fulfills their limits—but how could the common run of mankind ever understand how such exhaustion occurs yet one keeps putting forth new life![12]

Notes

1. "Knowledge" here seems to mean objective knowledge or self-conscious awareness, which is useful for nurturing life up to the capacity of natural endowment but dangerous when used to push beyond that capacity
2. "Governor tract" translates *du* (governor, supervisor), reading it as short for *dumai*, one of the *qijing bamai* (eight extraordinary tracts [channels, meridians]), which runs through the back of the human body from just below the navel, along the spine, through the neck and terminating in the brain. See *Huangdi suwen: gukong lun* (Basic questions of the Yellow Thearch: Discussion of bone orifices) (first century CE), cited in *Zhuangzi jishi*, 1: 117, and the remarks also quoted there by Wang Fuzhi (1619–1692): "The central tract along the back of the body is called the *du* (governor), and this governor dwells there in quietude, dependent on neither right nor left. Though it has the status of a tract [*mai*], it has no physical substance, so one who follows the governor has to do so with the most subtle and marvelous of pneumas [*qi*], which allows one to act while abiding in perfect emptiness. Since such a one halts when he should not act and acts only in terms of spontaneous compliance, he suitably manages to stay right in the center of it."
3. Although it has been the convention to read Ding as a name and Pao as a title, *paoding* probably originally meant "a cook," for *ding* is a male domestic servant: "male domestic servant in/in charge of the kitchen."
4. Sima Biao first makes this identification, and later commentators take it as a given, although no hard evidence exists to support the claim. *Zhuangzi jishi*, 1: 118.
5. Cheng Xuanying elaborates: "Whether a person's intelligence [*zhi*] is bright or stupid, his body incomplete or whole, both are due to the natural endowment of Heaven and

have nothing to do with the doings of men. If one violates the ruler's laws, so that he incurs such mutilation as this, it too is the result of the stupidity begot in him by Heaven. When one's plans for one's own preservation prove insufficient, he simply knows that mutilation suffered is due to others and does not realize that it is due to Heaven having darkened his intelligence. This is to know that whether one has both feet [*youyu*] or is one-footed [*du*] it can't but be the result of fate." *Zhuangzi jishi*, 1: 125.

6. Both Guo Xiang and Cheng Xuanying gloss *wang* as *changwang*, literally "long" and "king," which makes no sense. Lin Xiyi's commentary glosses *wang* also as *changwang*, but he uses the characters *changwang*, which forms a compound meaning "prosper" or "thrive," and this suggests that he read Guo's and Cheng's uses of the term *changwang* in the same way. That *changwang* is a compound stative verb is supported by the fact that it is parallel to the *yingyu* [fully satisfied] in the next phrase—in both Guo's and Cheng's commentary. Therefore, it seems obvious that Guo read *wang* [king] as *wang* [prosper] in the text of the *Zhuangzi*. *Zhuangzi jishi*, 1: 126; Lin Xiyi, *Zhuangzi Juanzhai kouyi*, 53.
7. Cf. *Laozi*, section 4: "The vessel of the Dao. . . . merges with the brilliant, and becomes one with the very dust." Wang Bi's comment: ". . . it merges with the brilliant but does not soil its power to embody." *Laozi*, section 56: "Merge with the brilliant." Wang Bi's comment: "If one has no particular eminence of his own, people will have no predilection to contend." See Richard John Lynn, *The Classic of the Way and Virtue*, 57–58 and 157–58. Guo Xiang's allusion to the *Laozi* implies that otherworldly sages should blend in with others, whether it means glorification or abasement, and that is why Qin Yi goes along with the conventions of mourning.
8. Cheng Xuanying: "When Qin Yi first went in to mourn, he referred to those who were weeping as other-worldly disciples, but when he saw that their grief and pain were excessive, he realized that they were not actually disciples of Lao Jun [Master Lao]." "*Qi* [beg] means 'request,' and *bi* [they] means 'everyone there.' The Sage's [*shengren*] heart was empty and freely receptive [*xuhuai*] and so responded to things with perfect resonance [*wugan siying*]. He pitied the masses of millions and had sympathy for all the living, and so did not have to wait upon earnest requests before he made speeches on their behalf. Therefore, his death was such that everyone who gathered there cried out and wept with such grief and pain that it was as if they were his mother or his child. But this is to be stuck among the obstacles of common emotion and to look on life and death as fools do; they were so moved by his sagely mercy that they mourned with such an extreme of grief as this. As he plumbed the situation from this point of view, he realized that these people were not the disciples of Lord Lao." *Zhuangzi jishi*, 1: 128.
9. *Di* [Thearch] is glossed by Cheng Xuanying as *tian* [Heaven, nature]. *Zhuangzi jishi*, 1: 129. Cf. 21.29.6.
10. The Dao, of course, is the "prime directive."
11. Cheng Xuanying: "*Qiong* [used completely] means *jin* [exhausted]; *xin* [firewood] means *chaiqiao* [firewood]. *Wei* [provide] means *qian* [add]. This is to say that when someone makes a fire burn, he uses his hands to add to it. The way one is able to exhaust the principle [*li*] of making fire burn works this way: although firewood added earlier is fully consumed, firewood added later is used to make it continue. It is because of this continuity of firewood added earlier and firewood added later that the fire does not go out. In just the same way, one who is good at nurturing life stays in step with change and goes along with the transformation of things. Since such a one is always shifting from one state to another in step with things, neither the 'old I' nor the 'new I' ever gets involved in emotional attachments—while never failing to be 'I.' This is how one continues on and never ceases to be." *Zhuangzi jishi*, 1: 130.

12. Cheng Xuanying: "These deluded and forgetful disciples are firmly enslaved to their emotions [*qing*], so how could they ever understand that constant renewal never ceases as one's mental state keeps shifting from one state to another. The 'I' of yesterday is all used up by today, and the 'I' of today will put forth new life after that." *Zhuangzi jishi*, 1: 130.

CHAPTER 4

RENJIAN SHI [THE WAYS OF THE WORLD]

4.0 It is impossible for one who associates with others to live apart from men. However, vicissitudes that beset the human world are such that different measures are appropriate in each and every age. It is only if one remains unselfconscious [*wuxin*] and so holds not to his own purposes and opinions [*ziyong*] who can follow wherever vicissitudes lead and yet not be burdened with their entanglements.

4.1 Yan Hui went to see Zhongni [Confucius] and asked permission to travel.

4.2 Confucius asked, "Where are you going?"

4.3 Yan Hui replied, "I am going to go to Wei."

4.4 "What are you going to do there?"

4.5.1 "I have heard that the ruler of Wei, young and dynamic, acts out of personal motives [*du*],

He does not share in the common aspirations of his people.

4.5.2 uses his state carelessly,

Whenever a ruler of men acts, others are sure to bear the brunt of it. For his moment of anger, prostrate corpses gush blood; for his moment of pleasure, official carriages and caps block roads. Therefore, the way a ruler of men uses his state must not be done carelessly.

4.5.3 and does not see his own faults.

This is because none dare remonstrate.

4.5.4 With such careless use, his people die.

He uses them so carelessly that he takes them to the land of death.

4.5.5 As for his dead, he reckons his state were a marsh and they like the worthless grasses in it.

He mobilizes his entire state's population and conveys it to the land of death, so the dead, impossible to count, he regards as just so much worthless grasses.

4.5.6 How his people now are without recourse!"

They have no refuge.

I have once heard you say, Master, "If a state is well-governed, leave it; if a state is ill-governed, go to it, for at a physician's gate one should have many patients." 4.5.7 I wish to use what I have heard, pondering the rules inherent in it, so that, perhaps, I might find a cure for such a state![1]

4.6 Zhongni said, "Pah! You probably won't do anything but get yourself executed going there.

His grasp of the Dao is insufficient to relieve the disaster that such a one as that has caused there.

4.7.1 The Dao wants no mixing.

It should be the pure [*zheng*] to win over such a man.

4.7.2 If mixed, it becomes manifold; if manifold it becomes troublesome; if troublesome, it becomes worrisome; if worrisome, it offers no relief.

But if one fails to win over such a man, the numerous remedies tried and all the care taken will just serve to provoke suspicion, and it will thus prove impossible to bring about even one cure.

4.7.3 The Perfected one [*zhiren*] of antiquity first stores it in himself and only then would try to have others store it in themselves.

Only after one has fully realized it himself can he use it to deal with others.

4.7.4 If what one amasses in oneself is not quite firm, what use is there in his trying to deal with the actions of a tyrant!

Such a one fails to engage with others with an empty mind [*xuxin*] but instead enlists selfconscious thought [*si*] and so takes risks to overcome obstacles. Therefore, we know that what he has stored in himself is not yet firm. But if one expels what he selfconsciously knows and as such nourishes his authenticity [*zhen*], invests [*ji*] all his talents with his own marvelous aptness [*miaodang*], and allows merit and reputation to revert to others while keeping worries of calamity far from his own person, only then can one extend himself to dealing with the actions of a tyrant.

4.8.1 Moreover, do you know also how virtue [*de*] is dissipated and how intelligence [*zhi*] is made to appear? Virtue is dissipated by reputation, and intelligence appears from competition.

It is because one takes pride in reputation [*ming*] that virtue is dissipated; it is because one competes at doing good [*shan*] that intelligence perversely appears. But even if it brought back King Jie and Robber Zhi, what people would still cherish is nothing other than reputation and goodness.[2]

4.8.2 Reputation as such is something to harm one another; intelligence as such is a tool used to compete. These two are tools of misfortune and not the means to fulfill one's actions.

Reputation and intelligence are commonly used in the world, but when "reputation" arises, it means mutual strife, and when "intelligence" is put to use, competition flourishes. Therefore, only after one discards reputation and intelligence can one's actions be fulfilled.[3]

4.9.1 Even if your virtue were firm and sincerity certain, he would never appreciate your spirit [*qi*]; even if you had a fine reputation for avoiding contention, he would never appreciate your frame of mind [*xin*]. 4.9.2 And yet there you would be, insisting on preaching in the presence of this tyrant about the carpenter's marking line laid down by benevolence [*ren*] and righteousness [*yi*]—which would be taken as using his ugliness to enhance your own beauty.

Well, if one were to throw down the Shines at Night for people, very few would not put their hands on their swords—because they would never appreciate what it is.[4] Now, Yan Hui's virtue and sincerity as well as his reputation for avoiding contention all fail to be appreciated by him [the ruler of Wei], yet were Yan Hui to insist on applying the guidelines laid down by benevolence and righteousness to him, the ruler of Wei would say that Yan Hui wished to besmirch him so as to promote himself. It is for such a reason that the Perfected one [*zhiren*] does not try to rely on his own personal ambitions to put the world in order but instead responds to others with an empty mind [*xuxin*]. Only after his sincerity becomes well known throughout the world and his fame for refraining from contention spreads to all, then all will follow with minds won over, and none between Heaven and Earth will disobey. Thus it is that the whole world will harmoniously chime in with it when one's note of virtue rings out, and all within the six directions [*liuhe*] [all phenomenal existence] will resonate with it when one's noble behavior manifests itself. And only then can one put things in order from beginning to end, involve oneself in turning chaos into order, and yet manage not to rub the reverse scales of the dragon the wrong way.[5]

4.9.3 He will call you a bringer of disaster, and as a bringer of disaster you are sure to have him bring disaster back on you.

Since he will just not bear you with trust, he will say that you are competing with him for reputation and so will harm you back.

4.9.4 You are almost sure to have him inflict disaster on you, will you not! But even if he turns out to delight in the worthy and to hate the wicked, why would he ever seek to use someone different by employing you?

If he could delight in the worthy and hate deceivers, listen to the claims of righteousness and submit to them, then he would be an enlightened sovereign. But if he were an enlightened sovereign, it would not be as if he had no worthy courtiers, so if you go to him, you would not prove to be any more remarkable.

If he were not so, going to him would surely result in your suffering harm. Therefore, if you set out selfconsciously [*youxin*], no matter where you would go it would prove unsuccessful, but if you respond [*ying*] to things unselfconsciously [*wuxin*], the other's resonance [*ying*] would bring you there spontaneously, so no matter where you would go it would a success.

4.9.5 Just don't you make any pronouncements, for this aristocrat will be sure to bully you as a way to win any argument.

You should only keep quiet and not speak, for if you were to speak, this aristocrat would take advantage of you with his ruler's powers and by bullying his way to win the dispute, ward off your remonstrations while covering up his errors.

4.9.6 Your eyes he will dazzle;

His words will be so compelling and quick-witted that they will make your eyes dizzy.

4.9.7 Your expression he will make on a par with his;

You will be unable to keep on making it different from his.

4.9.8 Your mouth he will control;

You will be too busy to save yourself.

Your deportment he will shape;

4.9.9 Your mind he will form.

Now you will put aside your very self so that you conform to him.

4.9.10 This is to fight fire with fire or water with water; we call this "adding more to what is already there."

Though you fall short of rescuing the situation, you are more than capable of making him fully realize his might.

4.9.11 Endless is your submission to precedent.

You resort to the usual and hold firm to precedents, never willing to change.[6]

4.9.12 Since he won't believe your profound words, it is certain you will die in the presence of this tyrant.

If you remonstrate without obtaining his confidence, whatever words you speak will mean harm.

4.10.1 Moreover, long ago Jie had Guan Lingfeng put to death, and Zhou had Prince Bigan put to death.[7] They both were people who had cultivated their persons and out of their lowly status bent down to comfort their [Jie's and Zhou's] common folk and out of their lowly status defied their rulers.

The grief suffered by Longfeng and Bi Gan, who were of lowly status yet filled lofty positions, happened because they did things that were not theirs to do.[8]

4.10.2 Therefore, their rulers used how they had cultivated themselves as the means to destroy them, for they were rulers who loved reputation.

They did not wish to allow their ministers to have fame superior to them as rulers.

4.10.3 Long ago when Yao attacked Congzhi and Xu'ao, and Yu attacked Youhu, these states became desolate and ghost-ridden and the rulers themselves were executed, for they had employed military force without cease, and there had been no end to their greed for profit. All of them were so greedy for reputation and profit—is it you alone who has not heard of them?

These tyrants not only sought to indulge their desires, they also were greedy for reputation, but what they sought has simply nothing to do with the Dao.

4.10.4 One who lives for reputation and profit would be too much for the sages to get the better of—so how much the less could you deal with such a one!

A ruler who so loves reputation and has such insatiable desires—even if Yao and Yu were to return, they could not get the better of such a one with moral transformation and so would have to attack them with massed troops. And yet you now actually wish to set forth empty handed and try to transform such a one with the Dao!

4.11 However, you surely have a plan, so try to put it in words for me."

4.12 Yan Hui replied: "If I efface myself with an upright and proper demeanor and maintain a unitary focus with utmost diligence, will this do?"

His words would be modest and unequivocal.

4.13.1 Zhongni said: "Pah! How could that do!

That is, it would never do.

4.13.2 Pumped up with yang, he manifests it to the utmost.

That is, the Wei ruler's extremely virile [*yang*] nature expands and fills his inner self and powerfully manifests itself in his outer expression, so he behaves with the utmost of tough defiance.

4.13.3 His facial expression is unsettled,

He shows pleasure and anger without constancy.

4.13.4 which is why people never oppose him.

None dare oppose him.

4.13.5 Therefore, he suppresses attempts by others to move his feelings so he can seek to think and feel whatever he wants to.

He is stubborn to an extreme, so when others try to use things they think joyful to move his feelings, he feels humiliated and so suppresses them so he can let himself go and follow his own dissolute mind.[9]

4.13.6 Since that which is called 'virtue absorbed day after day' would not work with him, how much the less likely would an appeal to great virtue![10]

However few or many his words, Yan Hui had not the competence to overcome him.[11]

4.13.7 He will be stubborn and so prove untransformable.

He will preserve his own opinions [*benyi*].

4.13.8 To suit his wishes outwardly and refrain from criticizing him inwardly—how would that ever do!"

"To suit his wishes outwardly and refrain from criticizing him inwardly" refers to how he [Yan Hui] would approach him [the ruler of Wei] by effacing himself with an upright and proper demeanor while maintaining a unitary focus with utmost diligence [as Yan Hui suggests above].[12]

4.14.1 "If so then I would be straight inwardly but bend outwardly, and what I accomplish will conform to ancient precedent.

Yan Hui suggests these three additional approaches.

4.14.2 By being straight inwardly I shall become a disciple of Heaven. As a disciple of Heaven I know that a Son of Heaven and I are both equally regarded by Heaven as its children, so why should I alone entreat this man to approve or disapprove my words?

People are neither lofty nor lowly, for they achieve life in one and the same way. Therefore, approval or disapproval should be entrusted to none other than the impartial judgment of all and not once ever sought from anyone in particular.

4.14.3 Someone like this people call an infant—this is what is meant when one becomes "a disciple of Heaven."

In accord with natural principle [*tianli*], he would let his own natural endowment [*xingming*] drive him on just as it does in the straightforward and spontaneous behavior of the infant.

4.14.4 By bending outwardly I shall be a disciple of men. Respectfully kneeling and bowing with hands curled constitute the ritual behavior [*li*] of a minister at court. Everyone behaves this way, so why should I alone dare not do it! When one who does what others do, others will find no fault in him; 4.14.5 this is what is meant when one becomes "a disciple of men."

He would be someone who, outwardly yielding and tactful, would do what he was supposed to do in conformity with the ways of the world.

4.14.6 To have one's accomplishments conform to ancient precedent is to become "a disciple of antiquity."

That is, make present accomplishment conform to ancient precedent.

4.14.7 Although the words involved seem but teachings, their actual effect will be to rebuke.

Although these may consist of conventional teachings, they actually have as their main purpose remonstration by analogy and rebuke.

4.14.8 They belong to antiquity; they don't belong to me.

4.14.9 As such, although direct I won't be blamed.

Because I use antiquity as the vehicle [*ji*] for such directness, none of it can be used to blame me.

This is what is meant when one becomes "a disciple of antiquity." If my approach is like this, will it do?"

4.15.1 Zhongni [Confucius] said: "Pah! How could that do! With too many rules your method [*fa*] is thus not coherent [*die*].

There is one and only one way to accord with principle [*li*], yet Yan Hui here sets out three approaches for rectification, so he would fail to merge arcanely [*ming*] with the task at hand.[13]

4.15.2 But crude [*gu*] as it is, it should still spare you blame.

Although it would never amount to anything great, he still would not get blamed or rebuked.

4.15.3 Even so, it would just go no further than that; how could it ever go so far as to effect any transformation!

Whereas he would have been spared blame, transformation would not have happened.[14]

4.15.4 This is because you still use your selfconscious mind [*xin*] as your teacher."

If Yan Hui were to go to him [the ruler of Wei] relying on these three approaches, it means that he has not unselfconsciously [*wuxin*] given himself over to the world.

4.16 Yan Hui then said: "Since I have nothing further to go on, may I dare ask what the proper method would be?"

4.17.1 Zhongni [Confucius] replied: "Fast! That's what I have to tell you! But to apply yourself to it selfconsciously [*youxin*], you think this an easy thing to do?

To apply oneself to it with selfconscious mind would certainly never make it easy.

4.17.2 Those who think this should be easy, bright Heaven won't accommodate [*yi*] them."

To think that acting with selfconscious purpose [*youwei*] makes it easy is never suitable [*yi*].[15]

4.18 Yan Hui said: "My family is poor, so since I have neither drunk wine nor eaten rich foods for several months, can such behavior be considered fasting?"

4.19 Confucius replied: "This is the fast associated with the offering of sacrifice; it is not the fast of the mind [*xinzhai*]."

4.20 Yan Hui then said: "May I presume to ask what the fast of the mind is?"

4.21.1 Zhongni [Confucius] replied: "You make your will [*zhi*] one.

This is to rid oneself of extraneous ways of thinking [*yiduan*][16] and give oneself over to spontaneity [*rendu*].

4.21.2 Don't listen with your ears but listen with your mind [*xin*]; don't listen with your mind but listen with your pneuma [*qi*]. Listening stops with the ears, and the mind stops with correspondences [*fu*]. But when it comes to the pneuma, being empty [*xu*] it is at the service of things [*daiwu*].

Discard the ears and eyes and rid yourself of conceptual thought [*xinyin*] so that you tally with the spontaneous receptivity [*zide*][17] of your pneuma nature [*qixing*]—this is what it means to be at the service of things with emptiness.[18]

4.21.3 The Dao will only gather together in emptiness [*xu*], and emptiness is the fast of the mind."

Once one empties one's mind, the perfect Dao will gather in one's bosom.

4.22.1 Yan Hui then said: "As long as I have never been able to do this, I was in fact just Yan Hui,

He had not yet begun to use fast of the mind; therefore, his self [*shen*] still existed for him.[19]

4.22.2 but once I am able to do this, never has Yan Hui existed.

Once he can use of fast of the mind, his self ceases to exist.

Can this be what you mean by 'emptiness' "?

4.23.1 The Master replied: "That sums it up perfectly!" 4.23.2 Here is what I have to tell you. If you can enter and move about freely inside such a cage, don't use the reputation [*ming*] you might have there to gain influence.

In this situation in which he should let the selfconscious mind go [*fangxin*] and become spontaneously receptive [*zide*], he should conform to [*dang*] who he really is [*shi*] and not go beyond that.[20]

4.23.3 If you get through to him, sing out, but if you don't get through to him, desist.

Speaking analogously in terms of music, in which responses [*ying*] should be done unselfconsciously [*wuxin*], the text thus says "sing out." One who responds [*ying*] unselfconsciously [*wuxin*] does nothing but yield utterly to the other and never forces his response.[21]

4.23.4 Don't make doors; don't try remedies [*du*].

To let people go their unhindered way [*ziruo*] is what "don't make doors" means; to trust in the world to find its own spontaneous tranquility [*zian*] is what "don't try remedies" means.[22]

4.23.5 Make unity your dwelling place and dwell in the inevitable.

"The inevitable" [*budeyi*] is the necessity [*biran*] of principle [*li*]. One should locate himself in the dwelling place of perfect unity [*zhiyi*] and match up with the tally of necessity.

4.23.6 If you do that, it should just about do.

The principle is completely realized in this.[23]

4.24.1 To stop making footprints is easy, but to refrain from walking on the ground is impossible.

To refrain from walking is easy, but if you want to walk without leaving footprints, it will prove impossible. To act unselfconsciously [*wuwei*] is easy, but if you want to act with selfconscious purpose and yet harm not your nature, it will prove impossible to do.

4.24.2 When one is commanded by men, it is easy to play them false, but when commanded by Heaven, it is impossible to play it false.

What people obtain by sight and sound is so crude that it is easy to deceive them, but when it comes to reports to nature, these are in such minute detail that it is impossible to play it false. Thus for those who violate the truth [*zhen*] a little their deficiencies are marked slight, and for those who violate the truth a great deal, their deficiencies are marked great. One's report of success and failure never fails to agree with one's allotted capacity [*fen*]. Even so, if one might wish to disobey Heaven and play it false, but would that not be simply impossible!

4.24.3 You've heard of flying with wings but never heard of flying without wings; you've heard of knowing with knowledge but never heard of knowing without knowledge.

Words must have their effective content [*ju*], for only then can they be up to the task. Now, Yan Hui lacks a dwelling place of perfect emptiness [*zhixu*], which means that he is without a source upon which to draw to effect the transformation of others.

4.24.4 Look there behind that closed door into the empty chamber where radiance lives.

Where nothing seems to exist when peered into is an empty chamber. It is only in an empty chamber that pure radiance [*bai*] lives.[24]

4.24.5 Good fortune is still, utterly still,

Where good fortune gathers has to be utterly empty, utterly still.

4.24.6 But as for not being still, this we call "galloping around while sitting."

As for you who fails to stop at your fundamental nature [*dang*] and stay with its limits [*ji*], this means that you gallop wildly around without cease on days when you should be sitting still. Thus it is that the enemy without has not yet arrived, but within you are already suffering distress—so how can you ever transform anyone else!

4.24.7 If you let your eyes and ears reach into yourself while operating beyond the reach of intelligence, then since even the demonic and divine [*guishen*] will come to you for shelter, how much the more shall men!

One whose reception [*de*] occurs spontaneously [*ziran*] with eyes and ears shut operates beyond the use of intelligence [*xinzhi*]. Therefore, trusting to his nature [*renxing*], he connects directly with things, so in no venture does he fail to merge arcanely with it [*ming*]. Since such a one will even avoid punishment from the abstruse workings of the Dao [*youmei*], how much the less likely will he have trouble in the human world!

4.27.8 This is the transformation of the myriad things, out of which Yu and Shun made bonds, and which Fu Xi and Ji Qu used to practice their entire

lives—so how much easier it should it be to deal with someone who has broken free of it![25]

That is, people are neither lofty nor lowly, for without exception they all learn about things through their intelligence [*xinzhi*] and senses. Therefore, those whom the world calls "wise" [*zhi*], did they ever become wise because they wanted to become wise? And those called " keen-eyed" [*jian*], did they ever become keen-eyed because they made themselves keen-eyed? If wisdom or being keen-eyed could just be had by the wanting of it, could anyone who wanted to become a worthy [*xian*] become one just by the wanting of it, or could anyone who wanted to become a sage [*sheng*] become one just by the wanting of it? Certainly not! But the people of the world, not knowing that knowing occurs by just spontaneously knowing, want to use knowledge deliberately to know things; not seeing that seeing occurs by just spontaneously seeing, want to use seeing deliberately to see things; not knowing that growth occurs by just spontaneously growing, also try deliberately to make things grow. Therefore, they see with their eyes and try to have the eye power of a Li Zhu;[26] they listen with their ears and try to put Master Kuang's[27] sharp hearing to shame. This is why their minds [*xinshen*] gallop around within and their eyes and ears are exhausted without, get involved in wrong situations and fail to merge arcanely [*ming*] with others. Never has anyone ever existed who though failing to merge arcanely in this way still manages to stay in step with changes in the human world and resonate with the rhythm of the ages!

4.25.1 When Zigao, the Duke of She, was about to go on a mission to Qi, he inquired of Zhongni: "The mission on which the king dispatches me, Zhuliang, I take very seriously.

He considers his mission serious, for he wants to have what he seeks.

4.25.2 From the way Qi entertains emissaries, I shall probably be treated with great respect but not given priority.

He is afraid that Qi will simply treat him with an empty show of politeness and prove unwilling to respond quickly to what he requests.

4.25.3 Since even a common man can't be moved, how much less likely can one move a feudal lord! So I am greatly alarmed over it. 4.25.4 You once said to me: 'About all things, whether great or small, rarely does one not say that happiness depends on the outcome.

Although things are really neither great nor small, rarely does one not say that happiness is had through their outcome. This is what Zhongni [Confucius] once told Zhuliang [Zigao].

4.25.5 If a successful outcome is not had, one will surely suffer disaster inflicted by the way of men.

One who regards an outcome as something to be happy about will be angry when failure occurs—about which the King of Chu could not help himself.

4.25.6 Even if a successful outcome is had, one's yin and yang surely will suffer disaster.

Although disaster inflicted by the way of men may be avoided, joy and fear will still continue to battle within one's breast, and by then it is already certain they will solidify as ice and charcoal in the five viscera.

4.25.7 Whether successful outcome or failure results, one who stays free of disaster afterwards can only be a possessor of virtue [*de*].'

If successful outcome or failure depend for their determination on some other person yet both lack the power to trouble one's mind [*xin*], such a one can only be a possessor of virtue.

4.25.8 What I eat is not fine food since I insist on simple fare, so there is no one at the stove who longs to be cool.

To be at the stove and yet not long to be cool clearly implies that what is cooked is frugal fare.

4.25.9 But this morning I received orders from court and by evening am drinking ice water—how hot my insides are!

What he eats is frugal fare, yet his insides become so hot he drinks ice water, which means that he truly is worried about the difficulty of his task and that it is not caused by rich food.

4.25.10 I have not yet reached the point where I am actually engaged in the matter but already my yin and yang suffer disaster! And if I fail to secure a successful outcome, I shall surely suffer disaster inflicted by the way of men, which means I might have to suffer both!

Before a successful outcome is had, he just fears that he might not accomplish it, but if after all he really fails to accomplish it, his fear will have both solidified in his insides and the net of punishment will ensnare him from without.

4.25.11 As a minister of the court I am not up to bearing this responsibility, so, Master, I hope you have something to advise me!"

4.26.1 Zhongni [Confucius] then said: "For the whole world there are two great precepts: the command of fate [*ming*] and the command of righteousness [*yi*]. 4.26.2 A son's love for parents is a command from fate and is inseparable from the mind [*xin*].

Tied tight by nature [*ziran*], it can't be undone.

4.26.3 A minister's service to his ruler is a command of righteousness. No matter where one goes, there the ruler reigns, and there is no escaping him anywhere between Heaven and Earth.

Anywhere a thousand people gather, if they don't make one man the ruler, they either fall into chaos or scatter. Therefore, though many worthies exist it is impossible to have many rulers, and though no worthy exists it is impossible to be without a ruler. So these belong respectively to the natural Dao and the human way [*tianren zhi dao*] and operate with inevitable appropriateness [*bizhi zhi yi*].

4.26.4 This is what is meant by 'great precepts.'

If one could escape from one's ruler and if one could untie himself from love for parents, what is commanded by righteousness and fate would not be up to serving as precepts.

4.26.5 As such, in serving one's parents, one finds contentment [*an*] wherever they select to live, for this is the perfection of filial piety; 4.26.6 in serving one's ruler, one finds contentment in whatever he selects for him to do, for this is the perfect fulfillment of loyalty; 4.26.7 and in serving one's own mind [*xin*], one stays free from the fluctuations of sorrow or joy regardless of whatever happens before one, realizes that whatever happens can't be helped and yet remains content with it as it accords with fate [*ming*], for this is the perfection of virtue [*de*].

If one realizes what can't be helped is due to fate and yet remains content with it, then, free from sorrow and free from joy, how could such a one ever fluctuate between them! Therefore, arcanely [*mingran*] take whatever one encounters as fated yet never engage in it with one's mind [*xin*]—one is thus so perfectly identified with it [*minran*] that he becomes one with what is perfectly appropriate [*zhidang*] and stays free from joy or sorrow while this happens. Therefore, although one might serve some ordinary fellow, he shall always act with perfect appropriateness whatever he sets out to do—so how much more likely will he succeed when it comes to ruler or parents!

4.26.8 As someone's minister or son there inherently [*gu*] will be things for which no alternative exists, so one should act on things as they really are and forget all about his own person [*shen*].

Things have their inevitability [*bizhi*], and principle [*li*] inherently always fulfills itself [*tong*]. Therefore, if one does his duty by them, his service will have successful conclusions. It never happens that one reaches successful conclusions and yet fails to preserve himself, so why should he ever again belabor his mind about his own person!

4.26.9 Then why bother to love life and hate death? This is how you should act!

No principle [*li*] ever fails to fulfill itself; therefore, one should just give oneself over to what one encounters and move straight ahead. However, if one's trust in the Dao is not sincere and such fondness and hate still occupy his bosom, he will prove incapable of moving forward together in step with what is perfectly appropriate [*zhidang*] and so will both plot how to live and worry about death—I have never seen such a one capable of success.

4.27.1 Let me, Qiu [Confucius], report what I have heard. Ordinarily when people live in close proximity, they must lightly yield to one another in good faith.

Close neighbors get to meet; therefore, relying on good faith, they should personally yield to one another.

4.27.2 But when they live far apart, they must express such fidelity in words.

At a distance, words have to be used to transmit intentions.

4.27.3 And words must have someone to transmit them. To transmit words when both sides are pleased or when both sides are angry is the hardest thing to do in the whole world.

If words expressing pleasure or anger exceed the real substance [*shi*] of the situation, he who transmits them ought to ensure that the two sides don't violate the mean [*shizhong*]. This is why it is never easy.

4.27.4 When both sides are pleased, much language overflowing with praise is sure to be used, and when both sides are angry, much language overflowing with loathing is sure to be used.

"Overflowing" [*yi*] means "exaggerated" [*guo*].[28] Both pleased and angry language often exceeds what is appropriate [*dang*].

4.27.5 Whenever language is made so to overflow, it will appear irresponsible.

It will be suspected that it is not really the other party's words but seem instead an irresponsible fabrication of the transmitter.

4.27.6 If thought irresponsible, its credibility will be treated with silence.

It will be suspected in silence [*moran*].[29]

4.27.7 And if treated with silence, the transmitter will be faced with disaster.

Because exaggerated words are transmitted, it will seem as if it were irresponsible fabrication. Once the recipient has this suspicion, the transmitter will be unjustly accused of treating serious subjects of concern too lightly.

4.27.8 The old adage says: 'If you transmit the sensible truth and don't transmit overflowing words, this will just about keep you whole.'

Although one might hear exaggerated words said on the spur of the moment, they should not be transmitted. One must weigh such words in terms of the sensible truth [*changqing*] and sum up the gist of their sincere implications [*chengzhi*] , for this will keep one close to keeping oneself whole.

4.28.1 Moreover, those who compete in some skill begin in openness [*yang*]

Originally they share their delight in play.

4.28.2 but often finish in stealth [*yin*].

But when the desire to win reaches an extreme, each hides his enthusiasm to harm another.[30]

4.28.3 And when this goes too far, they resort to much clever trickery.

They no longer comply with principle [*li*].

4.28.4 Drinking according to the rules of ritual behavior [*li*] begins in well-governed fashion,

Superiors and inferiors maintaining distinctions, the exchange of invitations to drink follows proper order.

4.28.5 but often finishes in disorder.

Overindulgence in drink results in drunkenness.

4.28.6 And when this goes on too far, much improper amusement occurs.

Debauchery so runs rampant that no extreme is beyond reach.

4.28.7 All subjects of concern happen in just the same way. They begin in honesty [*liang*] but often end despicably. When they start up, they are simple, but by the time they finish they surely achieve gigantic proportions.

As the vexatious is born from the simple, so subjects of concern arise from tiny origins—these are inevitable tendencies.

4.29.1 Words are wind-driven waves, and to engage with them is to lose what is real.

Words are wind-driven waves; therefore, if one engages with them, what is real will be lost.[31]

4.29.2 As it is easy to be moved by wind-driven waves, so it is easy to fall into danger by the loss of real substance [*shi*].

Therefore, one should avoid wind-driven waves and not engage with them, for then what is real won't be lost. When one gets at the real substance of matters, danger can be rendered harmless and agitation can be stilled.

4.29.3 Therefore, the onset of anger has no other origin than clever words and deviant language.

The onset of anger has no other origin than clever words that exaggerate real substance. Deviant language violates what is appropriate [*dang*].

4.29.4 When wild beasts die, they don't choose the sounds they make and their breath is filled with pent-up fury. In consequence, they indiscriminately turn vicious at heart.

The analogy involves how wild beasts when run to earth make sounds of desperation, their resources finished. Agreeable sounds are utterly beyond them, and their breath becomes chaotic. In anguish and overcome with rage, they respond to all with ferocity.

4.29.5 If one goes too far in forcing one's argument, the other will surely respond with an unseemly state of mind—and even unaware that he does so.

If one accommodates people with generosity, they surely will come around, but if one is too unsparing about every little thing, this will provoke an ugly temper in people without them even being aware of it. Therefore, the great one [*daren*] generously permits them conditions under which they can achieve self-fulfillment [*zide*]. Since such a one neither strains their capacities nor drains them of good cheer, he can establish good relations with everyone within the four seas.

4.29.6 If even he is unaware that he does so, who can know how it will end!

If such a one is not himself aware, how could he ever understand how misfortune and good fortune extend equally to all![32]

4.29.7 The old adage says: "Don't alter the command,

That is, transmit the real substance [*shi*] about which he [the emissary's ruler] is concerned.

4.29.8 and don't force an outcome,

Allow it to fulfill itself [*zicheng*].

4.29.9 for to exceed the measure of things results in overflow [*yi*]."

Such overflow means one does not place one's trust in the real substance [*shi*] of the matter.

4.29.10 Altering the command and forcing an outcome places the subject of concern in jeopardy.

This means danger for the matter involved.

4.29.11 A praiseworthy outcome takes time,

A praiseworthy outcome trusts to the transformative effect of time [*shihua*]—it is analogous to planting something that can't be made to mature in a single morning.

4.29.12 but by the time a hateful outcome occurs, it is already too late to change it.

As it would be what he [the emissary's ruler] found hateful,[33] if the emissary forced such an outcome, regret for failure would quickly arrive.

4.29.13 So how can one not take care! 4.29.14 Moreover, in driving the people as your carriage let your mind wander freely among them.

When using the people as a vehicle, make them your mind.[34]

4.29.15 It is by trusting to the inevitable [*budeyi*] that one cultivates the mean [*zhong*] so that perfection [*zhi*] is had.[35]

It is by trusting to the inevitability of principle [*li*] that a perfect tally with the mean [*zhongyong*] is effected, which is the perfect way to interact with others.[36]

4.29.16 Why should you do anything about the response?

He should just give himself over to the way Qi's response actually turns out—why should he scheme to manipulate how this happens for Qi?

4.29.17 The best thing to do would be to go about fulfilling your fate [*ming*], but this surely is difficult!

If one simply went about fulfilling one's fate, this would be most easy, but because pleasure and anger affect the mind, it is actually difficult.

4.30 Yan He was going to become tutor to the son and heir of Duke Ling of Wey,[37] so posed a question to Qu Boyu: "There is a man here whose virtue [*de*] by nature [*tian*] makes him a killer.[38] If I just let him act unruly [*wufang*], he will endanger our state, but if I provide him with rules, I shall endanger my own person.

A petty man's [*xiaoren*] nature [*xing*] is such that if you try to impose rules on him, he will hate you, but if you indulge his lawlessness, such a ruler will reduce the country to chaos.

4.30.4 He knows just enough to be aware of the faults of others but remains unaware of how he is at fault.

He does not realize that the faults of his people are all due to him. Therefore, he blames his people for crimes but does nothing to reform himself.

4.30.5 Since he is someone like this, what can I do about it?
4.31.1 Qu Boyu replied, "What a good question! Protect yourself from him, treat him with care, for this will keep your own self true [*zheng*]![39]

In his repeated interaction with him, this is always the way to keep his own self true.

4.31.2 For demeanor [*xing*], nothing is better than intimacy [*jiu*]; for state of mind, nothing is better than to be composed [*he*].

His demeanor should not be contrary; he should be composed but maintain a difference.

4.31.3 Nevertheless, disaster lurks in these two approaches. 4.31.4 You should be intimate [*jiu*] but not wish to fit in [*ru*].

Intimacy means maintaining a yielding demeanor, but fitting in means conforming to the point of complete agreement.

4.31.5 You should be agreeable [*he*] but not wish to stand out [*chu*].

To be agreeable means working reform through the power of righteousness [*yi*], but to stand out means engaging in self-display.

4.31.6 If you are intimate and just fit in, you will be both overturned and destroyed, both utterly ruined and trampled flat.

If he conforms to the point of complete agreement, he will be ruined and no longer be in a position to provide reform, and thus will be destroyed together with him [the heir to the throne, Kuaikui]. Therefore, he should emulate Heaven and Earth, not deviating from them in the least.

4.31.7 If you maintain an agreeable state of mind and yet stand out, you will both be held in poor repute and made infamous, bring both ruinous and evil consequences on yourself.

If he makes self-display of being agreeable, he will both develop a disgraceful reputation and become infamous for wanting to reform him [the heir to the throne]. He [the heir] will hate this attempt to prevail over him, and this will rashly provoke evil consequences. Therefore, he should behave stupidly as if he were utterly in the dark, arcanely merging with both the brilliant and the dust,[40] for only then could he manage to avoid appearing either intimate or aloof, or appearing either beneficial or harmful.

4.31.8 When he behaves as a child, you too be a child with him. When he behaves as if he were out in the open country, you too be out there with him in the open country.[41] **When he behaves as if he had no banks, you too with him have no banks.**[42] **To get through to him, penetrate in such a way that it does not hurt.**

Don't in the least hold up a pointed jade tablet to ruffle his dragon's scales.[43]

4.32.1 Don't you know about the praying mantis? It raised its arms in anger to block the turn of a wheel in a carriage rut, but failed to realize that it was

not up to such a task—because of the splendid opinion it had of its own resourcefulness.

As for the praying mantis raising its arms in anger, it is not that it is not splendid, but it is just not equal to the task of blocking a carriage rut. Now here, realizing that nothing may be done about it, if he [Yan He] obstinately insists in fulfilling his obligations, this would be just like a praying mantis raising its arms in anger.

4.32.2 Protect yourself from him and treat him with care! As for the resources pent up in you, by bragging about how splendid they are you will offend him, which will be just about be the end of you!

To offend this man by bragging about your store of resourcefulness and how splendid you are is to pursue the path of danger.

4.33.1 Don't you know about the tiger keeper?[44] He dares not provide it with live animals because of the rage it will feel when killing it.

He fears that because it has a mind bent on killing, this will provoke its rage.

4.33.2 And he dares not provide it with a whole animal because of the rage it will feel when tearing it apart.

As soon as he allows the tiger to tear it apart with its own teeth, the effort involved would provoke its rage.

4.33.3 He keeps track of the times it is hungry or full, and so gets at what makes its mind angry.

Knowing what makes it angry, he complies with it.

4.33.4 Although the tiger is a different kind of creature from man, the reason it still fawns on its keeper is because he complies with it. Therefore, the reason it would kill a keeper is because he thwarts it.

If one complies with principle [*li*], this provokes love in different kinds, but if one thwarts natural law [*jie*], this results even in close friends taking up arms against each other.

4.34.1 A horse lover uses a basket to hold its dung and a large clam shell to hold its urine.

Dung and urine are the lowliest of things, yet he uses valuable containers to hold them—such is the extreme to which love for horses goes.

4.34.2 But if by chance mosquitoes or flies swarm onto it

They irritatingly swarm onto it.

4.34.3 and one happens to slap at them at an inopportune moment,

Although he tries to save it from suffering, he slapped the horse in such a way that he caught it unaware.

4.34.4 it will break out of its bit and injure his head and crush his chest.

It is because he slapped it when it was unprepared that it became as alarmed as this.

4.34.5 For intention, there was success, but for love, there was failure. So how can one not take care!"

His intention aimed at the elimination of the horse's suffering, so he rashly slapped it, but this succeeded at his getting injured and crushed—the result of his having failed to maintain the means to deliver his love. Therefore, when one takes a place in the world and interacts with others, one can't fail to take care when either thwarting or complying with them.

4.35 Carpenter Shi [Jiang Shi] was on his way to Qi, and when he reached Crooked Shaft [Quyuan] he saw the great gnarled oak with its shrine to the tree spirit. Big enough to shelter several thousand oxen, its girth measured some thirty yards, so tall it overlooked the hills and was limbless up to a height of some twenty yards. It had enough wood in it to make close to ten or more boats. Although people gaping at it were as many as people at market, the master carpenter paid it no heed and just walked past without stopping.

4.36 After his apprentices had satisfied their desire to look at it, they hastened to catch up to Carpenter Shi and said: "Since we took up axes to follow you, master, we have never seen such fine wood as this, but you sir don't wish to look and just walk past it without stopping—why is that?"

4.37 "Stop! Don't speak any more about it! It is an unfit tree. If you use it to make boats, they will sink; if you use it to make coffins, they will quickly rot; if you use it to make vessels, they will be quickly ruined; if you use it to make doors, and they will ooze sap; if you use it to make posts, they will be riddled with bugs. It a worthless tree, for it is utterly useless, and that is why it has been able to live so long as this."

It can't be counted among the useful, so this is why it is called an unfit tree.[45]

4.38.1 After Carpenter Shi returned home, the great gnarled oak appeared to him in a dream as the shrine spirit, saying, "With what would you compare me? Would you compare me to the grainy trees?

All useful trees are grainy trees.

4.38.2 When it comes to the hawthorn, the pear, the orange, the pomelo, species that bear fruit large or small, 4.38.3 when the fruit is ripe, they are stripped, and when stripped they are injured, with large branches broken and small branches ripped off. They are such that their lives are made miserable because of their capabilities. Therefore, they don't live out their natural life spans but die young in mid-course, for they attract abuse and attack from the crass and the vulgar—this is the same for all things.

All things suffer because of their innate usefulness [*ziyong*].

4.38.4 So I have long been trying to become useless, and, though close to death,

There had often been those who had designs on it, and it was only Carpenter Shi who understood it.

4.38.5 I now have succeeded in doing so, and this has been of great use to me.

Its increasing uselessness actually proved of great use in saving its life.[46]

4.38.6 But if I too had been useful, how could I have ever managed to grow so large as this?

If it had been useful, surely it would have been cut down long ago.

4.38.7 Moreover, you and I are both things, so how, indeed, can you judge another thing? Since you are an unfit man close to death, it is even more doubtful you can know anything about an unfit tree!"

This is how it pokes fun at Carpenter Shi.

4.39 When Carpenter Shi awoke, he divined what the dream meant, but his apprentices said, "If it prefers to choose uselessness, how can it serve as the shrine spirit?"

They still suspect that it seeks to glorify itself by serving as the shrine spirit and does not simply prefer to choose uselessness.

4.40.1 He replied, "Not so loud! You had better not say such a thing! It is just that it is lodging in it.

It was the shrine spirit that came of its own accord to lodge in it; it was not that this tree sought to serve as the shrine spirit.

4.40.2 Because this failure to understand occurred, it resulted in dishonor.

That is, this tree was dishonored by the shrine spirit failing to understand it—how did this ever glorify it![47]

4.40.3 And even if it had not been serving as the shrine spirit, would it ever have come close to being cut down?

Since the tree regarded uselessness as useful, even if it had not served as the shrine spirit, it would in the end not have been threatened that it would be cut down.

4.40.4 Even so, the way it protects itself is different from the common run of things.

It uses defenselessness as defense, whereas the common run of things uses defensibleness as defense.[48]

4.40.5 If you try to understand it in terms of beneficence [*yi*], would this indeed not be far off the mark!"

To benefit people so they have more than enough to live on and to prevent the common folk from doing wrong, such is the beneficence [*yi*] of the shrine spirit. But tranquil and without intent [*buwei*], it keeps all aspects of its natural endowment [*quncai*] for its own use. Such uses may all be accounted for, but it does not concern itself with them. This is how the useless manage to live out their lives to the full. Your praising it as the shrine spirit shows you lack the means to approach what it really is!

4.41.1 When Senior of the South Ziqi [Nanbo Ziqi][49] was wandering on a hill in Shang,[50] he saw there a great tree that was different from others. A thousand chariots with teams of four horses could have found shade in the shadow it cast.

The shade that its branches cast could provide enough cover to shelter a thousand chariots.

4.41.2 Ziqi said, "What tree is this? I would guess that it must consist of unusual timber!" But when, looking up, he observed that its small limbs were so curled up that they could not be made into posts or beams, and when, looking down, he observed that its great roots were so disintegrated in their cores that the wood could not be made into inner or outer coffins. When he tasted its leaves, it so burned his mouth that it caused real harm. When he smelled it, it made him so violently ill as if from too much drink that even after three days he did not get over it.

The shadow cast by its branches could provide shade for a thousand carriages.

4.42 Ziqi said, "This is, after all, a tree that is good for nothing [*bucai*], which is how it succeeded in reaching such a great size as this. Ah! This is the good of nothingness that the Divine man [*shenren*] makes good use of."

It is because the ruler to his officials is good for nothing [*bucai*] that they manage his affairs—so that the perspicacious observe for him, the acute listen for him, the knowledgeable plan for him, and the brave defend for him. How does this happen? He does nothing other than practice arcane quietude [*xuanmo*], yet all the natural utility [*quncai*] they have fails not to realize what is appropriate [*dang*] to it—this is how good for nothingness actually takes perfect advantage of natural utility [*cai*]. Therefore, everyone in the world happily support such a one yet never tire of it, and he takes full advantage of the myriad things yet causes no harm.

4.43.1 Jingshi in Song is good for catalpas, cypresses, and the mulberries, but any larger than the span of two hands are cut down for monkey perches. Those three or four spans in circumference are cut down for ridgepoles in houses of those of high rank. Those seven or eight spans in circumference are cut down for the sides of coffins used by families of nobles and wealthy merchants. Thus it is that these trees never live out their natural span of years but fall to axes and hatchets, cut down while still young in the mid-course of life. Such is the peril inherent in natural utility [*cai*].

Those things which possesses natural utility can never avoid cause for regret.

4.43.2 Thus it is that in the Expiation Sacrifice [Jie] oxen with white foreheads, pigs with turned up snouts, as well as humans suffering from piles may not be used as sacrificial items consigned to the God of the Yellow River.[51]

When shamans and invocators offer the Expiation Sacrifice, they reject these three, for they must fastidiously select just perfectly reddish-brown items [unmarked oxen, in the one case], for only then do they dare use them.

4.43.3 It is because shamans and invocators know that this is so for all these things

As far as these things are concerned, shamans and invocators also understand that the good for nothing should remain whole.

4.43.4 that they regard them as inauspicious—though they are actually regarded by the Divine man [*shenren*] as greatly auspicious.

Those things that manage to live out their entire lives are called auspicious by the whole world. Shamans and invocators may regard the good for nothing as inauspicious and so not use them, but those things themselves manage to live out their entire lives because they are good for nothing, so they are actually greatly auspicious. The Divine man by staying fee of selfconscious mind complies with things. Therefore, the Divine man never opposes that which the whole world calls "greatly auspicious."

4.44.1 Disjointed Shu [Zhili Shu][52] was such a man that his chin was hidden in his navel, and his shoulders were higher than the top of his head. His hair knot pointed straight up to Heaven, his five arterial points were on top, and his two hips became his flanks.[53] By doing sewing and laundry he managed to feed himself, and the rice he gleaned out by agitating a winnowing basket was sufficient to feed ten people.[54] When the ruler called up soldiers, Disjointed Shu would push up his sleeves and bare his arms, freely mixing among them.

Because he could rely on his uselessness, he had no need to hide himself.

4.44.2 When the ruler had some large conscript labor project to undertake, because of Disjointed Shu's chronic disability he was exempt from service.

This was because he did not have to perform conscript labor.

4.44.3 When the ruler gave grain to the ill and infirm, he received three big bushels and ten bundles of firewood.

Although he supplied no conscript labor, he did get handouts.

4.44.4 The physical form that Disjointed Shu had was still good enough for him to take care of himself and for him to live out his life to the end. So could anyone be better off than someone with such virtue [*de*] as Disjointed Shu!

The Divine man [*shenren*] does not make use of others, which allows all others to realize their innate usefulness [*ziyong*]. He lets achievements and honors revert to the natural usefulness of all [*quncai*] and arcanely merges with others—thus leaving no footprints of his own. Therefore, he avoids harm from the human world and dwells among results that are constantly pleasing to him. Such is the virtue possessed by Disjointed Shu.

4.45.1 When Confucius had gone to Chu, Jieyu, a madman of Chu,[55] wandered by his gate saying:[56]

> **Phoenix, oh, phoenix, oh,[57] why try to do something about**
> **the decline of virtue [*de*]?**

He should comply with the times and just keep on going forward, in perfect step with how things are inclined [*yi*] to come together and go smoothly [*huitong*].[58] As for whether the world prospers or declines, he should ignore this as unworthy to teach about. Therefore, the text says "why try to do something?"

4.45.2 You can't wait for the future nor chase after the past.

Your own inclination to act should be in perfect step with the inclination [*yi*] of things at the very moment they happen.

4.45.3 When the Dao prevails in the whole world,
the sage is successful in it.
When the Dao is absent in the whole world,
the sage preserves his life in it.

Entrust yourself to spontaneity [*zier*], and principle [*li*] will spontaneously generate success [*cheng*]. But since this generating of success is not your own doing, what have you to do with bringing order to chaos or change to regulations! When order prevails, spontaneously seek success, for then you will abandon success yet not fail. When chaos prevails, spontaneously seek life, for then you will forget life yet not die.

4.45.4 But in this present age, you may only escape execution in it.

Don't look forward to the future nor look back on the past but identify completely with the present, arcanely [*mingran*] becoming one with the current age, for only then can your marvelous aptness [*miaodang*] remain intact and you escape the penal code.

4.45.5 Good fortune is lighter than a feather, yet none know to carry it.

As the feet are able to walk, let them go; as the hands are able to grasp, let them hold. Listen to what the ears hear; look at what the eyes see. Let knowing stop at what can't be known; let abilities stop at what can't be done. Make use of what is innately useful [*ziyong*]; do things that are innately doable [*ziwei*]. Do as you please within the limits of your nature but go not the least bit outside your allotted capacity. All this results in the perfect ease inherent in unselfconscious action. It never happens that one's naturally endowed life has not been kept whole when one practices unselfconscious action. Never have we heard of such a principle that when naturally endowed life is kept whole it yet fails to yield good fortune. Therefore, good fortune is nothing other than the tendency to what we call wholeness. Since it does not make use of anything else, how could it ever have even the weight of a goose feather! One who follows his nature and never tries to do anything that lies outside his allotted capacity finds that whatever he does is the easiest thing in the whole world. One who lifts whatever is innately within his capacity to lift and carries whatever is innately within his capacity to carry finds it the lightest thing in the whole world. However, when one's knowledge violates its limits, it harms one's nature; when one's mind craves evil, it destroys one's authenticity. When this happens, one abandons that which for unselfconscious action is most easy and tries instead to do that which for selfconscious action is most difficult; one ignores that which for one's innate capacity to lift is the lightest and instead selects that which is the heaviest. This has been a constant source of disaster for the entire world.

4.45.6 Misfortune is heavier than the Earth, yet none know to avoid it.

If the lifting lies within the limits of one's nature, even if it were a burden of 30,000 catties, it would not seem heavy, but if it were a weight present in something outside the limits of one's nature, though it be less than a few ounces, one would find he is not up to the task. Staying within one's nature results in good fortune, thus good fortune is the lightest thing possible; going outside one's nature results in misfortune, thus misfortune is the heaviest thing possible. Misfortune is the heaviest thing possible, yet none know to avoid it. This is the great mistake that besets the world.

4.45.7 Be done with it, be done with it,
trying to rule people with virtue!
How dangerous, how dangerous,
drawing a line on the ground and have them follow it!

If you draw a line on the ground and try to get people to comply with it, your footprints no longer can be concealed. To take something of your own and try to rule others with it now means that you will fail to merge arcanely with others. Therefore, the great one does not light up himself in order to shine on others but allows others light up themselves. He does not use the virtue in himself to rule others but allows others exercise their own virtue. He can thus comprehensively interrelate with the myriad folk and so arcanely fuse other and self, perfectly identify with them, becoming one with the whole world, so that inner and outer share the same good fortune.

4.45.8 Obscure your brilliance,
Obscure your brilliance,
And don't harm your own progress.

"Obscure your brilliance" [*miyang*] means the same as "disown your brilliance" [*wangyang*]. Disown your brilliance and give yourself over to independent spontaneity [*rendu*], for if you spread not beyond your own boundaries, my progress can take its complete course. If everyone in the whole world were allowed to complete what their "I" can be, then no one who calls himself "I" would fail to achieve completeness.[59]

4.45.9 Your own progress is gapped and circuitous,
But harm not your own self-sufficiency [*zizu*].

That such a one accomplishes his progress circuitously is due to his self-sufficiency [*zizu*].[60]

4.46 Mountain trees cause themselves to be robbed, and the grease-fed flame consumes itself. The cinnamon can be used for food so people peel it; the lacquer tree can be used, so it is pared away. Everyone knows about the use of usefulness, but no one knows about the use of uselessness.

If something is useful, it will be of merit to others, but if it is useless, it will be allowed to live out life spontaneously to the full. When it comes to cutting off one's flesh and skin for the sake of all the world,[61] everyone in the world knows about this, but when it comes to preventing the common folk from losing the means to keep themselves whole and safe, while self and other both achieve what is fitting [*shi*] for them, all are perplexed, unaware that this marvel [*miao*] resides in their very own persons [*shen*].

Notes

1. Cheng Xuanying: "Master Yan now would go to transform Wei, this by transmitting what he had heard in the past, pondering the exemplary sayings he had been taught, to assist him [the ruler of Wei] to get close to the Dao of goodness." *Zhuangzi jishi*, 1: 133.
2. King Jie was the last, tyrannical king of the Xia dynasty, vicious and steeped in self-indulgence and pleasure. Robber Zhi is treated in detail in *Zhuangzi*, chapter 29.
3. Cf. 26.28.
4. This alludes to Zou Yang's [d. 120 BCE] letter to Han dynasty prince Xiao of Liang (enfoeffed 168–144 BCE), who had thrown Zou into prison because he believed the slander of sedition again him. Zou declared that he was a bright gem, unrecognized as such and wrongly suspected: "I have heard that if one were to take the Moon Bright Pearl or the Shines at Night Jade Disk and throw either of them down in the dark for people on the road, without exception they will put their hands on their swords and look askance at each other. Why so? Because without reason it had arrived there in front of them." Sima Qian, *Shiji*, 83: 2476. The expression *mingzhu antou* (bright pearl thrown down in the dark) became a metaphor for talent unrecognized or suspected of sedition, unused and abused.
5. Cheng Xuanying: "Even though his virtue might have been pure and firm, his trustworthiness accepted and secure, his reputation splendid for the avoidance of contention with others, since the ruler of Wei's basic nature [*suxing*] was obstinate and stupid, cruel, and violent with little discernment, as he could never could have appreciated Yan Hui's temperament [*yiqi*], how could he ever understand how his mind [*xin*] was set on providing corrective help!" *Zhuangzi jishi*, 1: 136. Both Guo and Chen clearly take the ruler of Wei as the one who never could have appreciated the kind of person Yan Hui really was. However, most modern interpreters take Yan Hui as the subject—he is the one who fails to appreciate the temperament of others, including the ruler of Wei—which follows the tradition of exegesis begun by Lin Xiyi in the Song. See *Zhuangzi Juanzhai kouyi*, 58.
6. Guo's reading of the text observes Yan Hui as a prisoner of tradition, whose inflexibility would lead inevitably to his downfall; this stands in contrast to other readings, which have the ruler of Wei so dominating Yan Hui from the beginning that he would not stand a chance, an interpretation that seems to have begun with Lin Xiyi; see *Zhuangzi Juanzhai kouyi*, 59.
7. Cf. 20.23.3.
8. Cheng Xuanying: "As a way to refer to them posthumously, Jie means to exploit the common folk and indulge in mass killings, and Zhou means to pervert righteousness [*yi*] into cruelty and goodness [*shan*] into brutality. Guan was the man's surname, and his courtesy name was Longfeng, the worthy minister of King Jie of Xia, who thanks to his utmost sincerity was decapitated. Bi Gan was the younger half-brother by a concubine of the father of King Zhou of Yin [Shang], who because of his loyal remonstration had his heart cut out.... These two men were both good ministers of antiquity,

who cultivated their persons and acted boldly with loyalty and integrity. Out of their subservient positions they grieved at the conditions of their ruler's common folk. Whereas these ministers had virtue [*youde*], their rulers lacked the Dao [*wudao*]. They opposed the wickedness of their rulers, so both suffered ignominious execution. To use the past to bear witness to the present, these episodes amply serve as perspicacious mirrors, that is, we know from them that were Yan Hui to try to transform the state of Wei, in principle [*li*] he could never do it." *Zhuangzi jishi*, 1: 139.

9. This reading of the text is also supported by Cheng Xuanying, *Zhuangzi jishi*, 1: 142; Luo Miandao, *Nanhua zhenjing xunben*, 5: 180a; and Lin Xiyi, *Zhuangzi Juanzhai kouyi*, 60.
10. "Great virtue" [*dade*] here has a cosmic significance that links the sage ruler with the very power of the Dao itself; cf. *Yijing* (Classic of Changes), "Commentary on the Appended Phrases" [*Xici zhuan*], Part Two: "The great virtue of Heaven and Earth is called 'generation.' " Richard John Lynn, *The Classic of Changes*, 76.
11. Guo's comment suggests that whether Yan Hui gradually cultivated the Wei ruler or made an immediate appeal to a supposed sagely intelligence potentially lying in him, neither approach would work. Cheng Xuanying takes a different approach: "The Wei ruler's lack of the Dao was long standing, and since it was impossible for him to absorb virtue day after day even over this long time, how much the less could one hope that a large scale appeal to sagely intelligence [*shengming*] would ever succeed!" *Zhuangzi jishi*, 1: 142.
12. Cheng Xuanying reads the text as does Guo Xiang: he refers to Yan Hui's proposed approach to the ruler of Wei, not to the state of mind and behavior of the ruler of Wei. The latter interpretation, favored by later traditional and modern commentators and translators, requires that we read "refrain from criticizing" [*bushi*] as an antonym expression, in which *bu* is redundant and should be ignored and *shi* means "secretly criticize/criticize behind one's back." This argument, including its origins in commentaries by Lin Yunming (*jinshi* of 1658), *Zhuangzi yin* (Causes and reasons underlying the *Zhuangzi*) (1663), Yao Nai (1732–1815), *Zhuangzi zhangyi* (Meaning of the *Zhuangzi*, arranged by section), and Ma Xulun (1884–1970), *Zhuangzi yizheng* (The *Zhuangzi*, with verifications of meaning), is laid out in detail in Akatsuka Kiyoshi, *Sōji*, 166; however, I find the argument tortuous and unconvincing and believe that the earlier commentary tradition is correct.
13. Cheng Xuanying elaborates: "*Die* (document, report) here means *tiaoli* (be coherent), that is, to accord [*dang*]. If the method [*fa*] accords with principle [*li*], it should not wait upon complications. However, Yan Hui establishes three approaches how he would do rectification, all of which fail to accord with principle and have nothing to do with equanimity. Therefore, how could it ever do!" *Zhuangzi jishi*, 1: 145.
14. Cheng Xuanying expands on Guo's comments but seems unsure how to read this last passage, for he suggests two interpretations: "As for Yan Hui's transformation of Wei, he should not go beyond this method, for only then could he maintain his own moral integrity [*dushan*]. But since it falls short of extending relief to others, how could it go so far as to effect any transformation? Another way of interpreting the text is: If he stops and does not go, this would be the correct course as far as principle [*li*] is concerned, but if he goes to Wei, he would be sure to incur blame." *Zhuangzi jishi*, 1: 145.
15. It is uncertain how Guo Xiang reads this passage—is it about how one should not approach "fasting" with self-conscious purpose, how one should not try to act with regard to anything with self-conscious purpose, or it is specifically about how Yan Hui should not try to transform the ruler of Wei with self-conscious purpose? Cheng Xuanying reads it only in reference to "fasting": "To think it is easy to practice the Dao

with a mind characterized by selfconscious purpose never appears suitable anywhere under bright Heaven. That is to say, it is unsuitable to practice fast of the mind [*xinzhai*] with selfconscious purpose." *Zhuangzi jishi*, 1: 146.

16. I hesitate to translate *yiduan* conventionally as "heterodoxy" or "heresy" because the context seems to call for a more literal rendering.
17. The more usual meaning of "self-fulfillment" for *zide* does not fit here. Cf. 27.11, Guo commentary.
18. Cheng Xuanying: "To correspond or tally with [*fu*] means to match [*he*]. When the mind [*xin*] begins its calculations it has to match up with one's external conditions [*jing*]. One should let all its commands freeze to a halt and become still, no longer allowing it to find correspondences in external conditions. This is how to interpret 'wait for things to come with emptiness.'" *Zhuangzi jishi*, 1: 147.
19. Cheng Xuanying: "He has not yet received instruction in fast of the mind and still harbors a mind filled with boundaries and impediments. Since he is unable to let his physical embodiment [*ti*] crumble away and in so doing forget his self [*shen*], it may still be said that Yan Hui has a real existence." *Zhuangzi jishi*, 1: 148.
20. Guo's comment and his reading of the text become clearer when we note what Cheng Xuanying says about the proper approach that Yan Hui should take: "hiding his efforts and working imperceptibly, he should not try to use reputation and knowledge to gain influence over others." *Zhuangzi jishi*, 1: 149.
21. Cheng Xuanying: "If what he has said puts him on intimate terms with the ruler of Wei, then he can sing out words of rescue, but if his remonstrance does not get through to him, then it would be best if he were to shut his mouth and forget how to talk. Any forced display of loyalty would be sure to inflict disaster on him." *Zhuangzi jishi*, 1: 149.
22. Cheng Xuanying: "*Du* [poison] here means remedy. One should be like water or a mirror in that one's responses should take place with an empty and freely receptive mind [*xuhuai*] with no preparation." *Zhuangzi jishi*, 1: 149. Earlier modern scholars such as Xi Tong (1917) and Zhang Binglin (1918) amend the text to read *wudou* [no opening, no outlet] instead of *wudu* [don't try remedies]; see Wang Shumin, *Zhuangzi jiaoquan* (Collation and interpretation of the *Zhuangzi*), 133, note 16.
23. Cheng Xuanying: "'Just about do' [*ji*] means completely realize [*jin*], that is, the principle [*li*] of how one should respond to others is completely realized in this." *Zhuangzi jishi*, 1: 150.
24. "Radiance" [*bai*] is commonly equated with the Dao in many commentaries, including the one by Cheng Xuanying. Note, however, that Cheng glosses *que* [closed door] as "emptiness" [*kong*], as many other commentaries do. *Zhuangzi jishi*, 1: 151. The "empty chamber," of course, refers to the mind of the sage.
25. "How much easier should it be to deal with someone who has broken with it" translates *kuang sanyanzhe*, which follows the commentary of Cheng Xuanying, whose gloss reads: "So how much easier, as far as it concerns some mean and despicable person of the world who has thrown off the harness [*shusan*], to follow in the tracks laid down by this Dao when one wants to transform him." *Zhuangzi jishi*, 1: 152. This seems a likely way to deal with *sanyanzhe*, literally as "one who has come loose from it," the "it" being the Dao. However, "one who has come loose/loosened himself from them" also makes sense, if we take "them" to refer to the bonds of the Dao recognized and implemented by Yu and Shun. In either case, it is likely that the ruler of Wei, the despicable fellow who has become a renegade from the Dao, is meant here.
26. Li Zhu (Li Lou), a mythic figure from the era of the Yellow Thearch, supposedly could see the tip of an autumn hair at more than 100 paces.

27. Master Kuang was the court music master for the state of Jin during the Spring and Autumn era; he was renowned for his ability to distinguish minute differences in intonation.
28. "Overflow" [*yi*] is written both with and without the water significant, and in either case it means the same thing: exaggeration at the expense of the real substance of matters.
29. Cheng Xuanying: "*Mo* [usually "none," "no one," "nothing"] here signifies the way people look when they express suspicion or doubt. Since it seems that the transmitter has irresponsibly fabricated it, this creates a state of mind in which trust is withheld, thus it is suspected in silence [*moran*]." *Zhuangzi jishi*, 1: 158. That is, its veracity is so completely in doubt that no question or argument need be addressed to it.
30. From his commentary, it is clear that Guo Xiang understands *yin* to mean "stealth," which suggests that he reads *yang* in the previous line as "openness." However, "openness" is easily associated with notions of good cheer and happiness, also alluded to by Guo in his commentary on that line. By contrast, Cheng Xuanying simply glosses *yang* as "happiness" and *yin* as "anger." *Zhuangzi jishi*, 1: 158.
31. Cheng Xuanying: "Water is stirred up into waves due to wind, which serves as metaphor for the mind [*xin*] moved to pleasure or anger due to words. Therefore, one who engages in pleasure or anger because of such wind driven waves of words will find that real principles [*shili*] are lost to him." *Zhuangzi jishi*, 1: 160.
32. Guo's comment should be read in conjunction with his comment on the previous sentence: The ruler [great one] who treats his subjects with generosity and allows them the opportunity for self-fulfillment generates and extends good fortune to all, but the ruler who treats them meanly and prevents their self-fulfillment creates misfortune, which affects everyone. For Guo, the analogy is clear: as the pressing of an argument too far generates ill will in one's opposite, so overly strict rule generates recalcitrance within the ruled.
33. Not only do Guo Xiang and Cheng Xuanying read the text as *wu* (hateful), and not *e* (bad), but Lu Deming's *yinyi* (pronunciation and meaning) commentary also indicates that it should be read as *wu*. *Zhuangzi jishi*, 1: 162.
34. Cf. 27.5.2, Guo commentary.
35. Cf. *Lunyu* (Analects), 6: 2479c: "As virtue the mean [*zhongyong*] is indeed perfect!"
36. Cheng Xuanying: "When one entrusts himself to the inevitable unfolding of events while cultivating a mind infused with central harmony [*zhonghe*], this results in the perfect realization of authentic principle [*zhenli*], which allows one to respond to things with absolute marvelousness [*zhimiao*]." To gloss "the mean" as "central harmony" in Cheng's Daoist tradition of thought is to equate it with *yuanqi*, cosmological "primordial undifferentiated pneuma," as well as the physiological "original breath." *Zhuangzi jishi*, 1: 161. However, He Yan (190–249), in his commentary to the *Lunyu* passage just cited, says of the mean that, practiced by the former kings, it epitomizes "central harmony as virtue that may always be practiced," which suggests more of a Confucian interpretation.
37. Cheng Xuanying: "Surname Yan and given name He, he was a worthy of the state of Lu. Kuaikui was the son and heir [of Duke Ling of Wey by a concubine]. Traveling from Lu to Wey, Yan He was going as tutor to the heir apparent there." *Zhuangzi jishi*, 1: 164. Cf. 28.11, 29.14.
38. Cheng Xuanying: "Surname Qu and given name Yuan, his courtesy name was Boyu. He was a worthy grandee of Wey. Kuaikui was naturally endowed with a virtue of viciousness [*xiongde*], so he took heartfelt delight in slaughtering people. Since he was a native

of Wey, Yan He said, 'there is a man here.' Because Yan was going to become tutor to the heir to the throne, he went to a wise and learned man for advice." *Zhuangzi jishi*, 1: 164.

39. Cheng Xuanying glosses "keep your own self true" as "keep yourself treading the correct path [*zhengdao*]." *Zhuangzi jishi*, 1: 165.
40. That is, glorification and abasement, a paraphrase of the *Laozi* or *Daodejing*, section 4; Richard John Lynn, *The Classic of the Way and Virtue*, 57.
41. "Open country" translates *wu tingxi*, "fields with neither large nor small boundary paths," which serves as a metaphor for reckless behavior that respects no distinction between one's own person and property and those of others.
42. "Have no banks" translates *wuya*, which serves as a metaphor for boundless appetite—just as a river without banks would overflow without limit.
43. Such jade tablets have sharp points and edges: Yan He is thus advised not to rub Kuaikui the wrong way with the conventional morality befitting his office.
44. The same passage, with variants, occurs in the *Liezi* (Sayings of Master Lie); *Liezi jishi*, 2: 58–59.
45. "Unfit tree" translates *sanmu*; Cheng Xuanying glosses *sanmu* as a loose-grained tree with soft, fragile wood. *Zhuangzi jishi*, 1: 171.
46. Cheng Xuanying indicates that it is on Carpenter Shi's authority that, with his having declared that the tree is useless, it is will be judged useless from then on; thus, its life is no longer threatened. See *Zhuangzi jishi*, 1: 173. Luo Miandao, *Nanhua zhenjing xunben*, 5: 186b–87a, makes the same point.
47. Cheng Xuanying: "The tree thinks: 'Since this spirit fails to understand that I regard uselessness as useful and that I place value on living out my life to the full, against my wishes it came to take refuge in me, which has profoundly dishonored me. On the contrary, I have been shamed—how does this ever glorify me!' " *Zhuangzi jishi*, 1: 175.
48. Cheng Xuanying: "As an unfit tree, it uses its uselessness to defend its life, whereas grainy trees are cut down young because of their usefulness, so this is how it is different from them." *Zhuangzi jishi*, 1: 175.
49. Cheng Xuanying notes that Nanbo Ziqi (Senior of the South Ziqi) is the same person as Nanguo Ziqi (Southwall Ziqi). *Zhuangzi jishi*, 1: 176.
50. This refers to Shangqiu (present-day Suiyang in Shangqiu county, Henan).
51. The God of the Yellow River is Hebo.
52. "Disjointed" translates Zhili," and even Shu the surname, if it is that, seems here to mean "slack," "floppy," or "baggy, a variant of which is Zhili Shu, "Disjointed Decrepit," cf. 18.9–18.10, and "Slippery Operator," 24.16.2.
53. Cheng Xuanying: "His hair knot seemed to rise vertically. The "five arterial points [*wuguan*] indicate the vital acupuncture points for the five viscera. The five vital acupuncture points are all located on his back. Hair knots for the ancients were always located close to the back of the top of the head, but here Disjointed Shu was so crippled, a hunchback with head forced downwards, that all this forced the vital acupuncture points for the viscera as well as his hair knot all to turn upwards. His two legs and hips were so jammed together that they were forced up into his flanks." *Zhuangzi jishi*, 1: 180.
54. An alternative tradition of commentary interprets "agitate a winnowing basket" [*guce*] instead to mean the casting of milfoil stalks to divine fortunes, another way that Disjointed Shu might have earned more than enough for his own immediate needs. Cheng Xuanying gives priority to the first interpretation but also presents the second as a possibility. The first seems more likely, for as Cheng remarks, "After Disjointed Shu swept the marketplace, he gleaned out rice by using a winnowing basket to separate it from the dust and dirt." *Zhuangzi jishi*, 1: 180.

55. Cheng Xuanying identifies Jieyu as the courtesy name of Lu Tong, a worthy of Chu. *Zhuangzi jishi*, 1: 183. See above, 1.10.
56. What follows is an abbreviated paraphrase of a passage in the *Lunyu* (Analects) 18: 2529a: "Phoenix, oh, Phoenix, oh, How virtue has declined! As for the past, redemption is impossible, though the future might yet be pursued. But give it up, give it up. Only danger awaits those who engage in government."
57. Conventionally translated as "phoenix," the *feng* in China is a fabulous bird that makes its appearance as a harbinger of good times and hides when times are bad. Calling Confucius a *feng* here can only be sarcasm.
58. "How things come together and go smoothly" translates *huitong*, an allusion to the *Yijing* (Classic of Changes), Appended Phrases" [*Xici zhuan*], Part One: "The sages had the means to perceive the activities taking place in the world, and, observing how things come together and go smoothly [*huitong*], they thus enacted statutes and rituals accordingly." Lynn, *The Classic of Changes*, 68.
59. Cheng Xuanying: " 'Obscure' [*mi*] means lose, and 'brilliant' [*yang*] means bright [*ming*] and dynamic [*dong*]. Lu Tong [Jieyu] admonishes Father Ni [Confucius]: 'Hide your outward signs [*ji*] and conceal your brilliance, the better to set free the unselfconscious action [*wuwei*] that one alone should give oneself over to [*duren*]. Once you forget all about the bright wisdom with which to respond to things, you will go no further than your allotted capacity [*fen*] and so won't harm my progress to live out life to the full.' " *Zhuangzi jishi*, 1: 185.
60. "Gapped" [*xi*] means emptiness [*kong*], and "circuitous" [*qu*] means compliant [*congshun*]. If one empties his mind [*xin*] and complies with the natures [*xing*] of others, then whosoever calls himself an "I" will be self-sufficient [*zizu*]. *Zhuangzi jishi*, 1: 185. It is likely that the *Zhuangzi* is punning on *xing*, "progress," which can literally mean "walk," and *zizu*, "self-sufficiency," which can literally mean "one's own feet." It is also likely that both Guo and Cheng were aware of such double entendres, for their comments could equally mean "that he finishes his route circuitously is due to his own feet" (Guo) and "whosoever calls himself "I" will use his own feet" (Cheng). That is, one can live out one's life to the full only if one's self-sufficiency is allowed free play: one must use his own feet to walk his own path. However, Cheng's glossing of *xi*, (gap, crack, space) as *kong* (empty) seems far-fetched. It is more likely that it means "intermittently," which extends in meaning to "erratically" and "leisurely." Since Guo reduced *xiqu* (gapped and circuitous) simply to *qu* (circuitous), he might have thought that *xi* was superfluous and *qu* covered all aspects of the free individual's circuitous path through life, as crooked, intermittent, erratic, and leisurely as it might be.
61. That is, self-sacrifice for what is perceived as the common good.

CHAPTER 5

DECHONG FU [TALLY OF VIRTUE REPLETE]

5.0 The inner [*nei*] replete with virtue [*de*] and the outer [*wai*] resonating [*ying*] with things, inner and outer arcanely merge [*xuanhe*]. As proof that this is as certain as the auspicious signs of fate,[1] such a one casts aside his physical body [*yi qi xinghai*].

5.1.1 In Lu there was Wang Tai [Wang the Nag], who had had his foot cut off.[2] His followers were like those of Zhongni [Confucius].

The number of his disciples was equal to those of Confucius.

5.1.2 Chang Ji said to Zhongni, "Wang Tai is someone who has had a foot cut off, yet his followers and yours, Master, divide Lu in half. Standing, he does not teach, sitting, he does not discuss, yet they go to him empty [*xu*] and return from him full [*shi*].

Each achieves self-fulfillment [*zide*] and so finds sufficiency.

5.1.3 He surely has a teaching that does not use words, but how can his mind [*xin*] be completely whole [*cheng*] though he lacks physical form? So what kind of man is this?"

Chang Ji marvels at how with such a ruined body, Wang Tai's mind [*xin*] could be so satisfied. With such completeness of mind he casts aside his physical form [*shenxing*], forgets his five viscera, and, when suddenly striking out all on his own, none in the whole world can leave him.

5.2 Zhongni said, "This master is a sage [*shengren*]. It is just that I have lagged behind and so have not yet gone to him. As I was going to take him as my teacher, how much more should those lesser than I! And why

let it stop with Lu? I am going to lead the whole world to become his followers!"

With spirit [*shen*] whole and mind [*xin*] complete, his body [*ti*] arcanely merges with all others. One who merges arcanely with all others is someone the whole world can't keep at a distance—so how could it stop just at one state!

5.3 Chang Ji then said, "Though he has had a foot cut off, he still bests you, sir, so how much farther from the ordinary [*yong*] must he be! Someone like this then, how does he ever use his mind?"

5.4.1 Zhongni replied, "Life and death are indeed great,

Although people change daily, the change between life and death is the greatest of all changes.

5.4.2 but he is not changed with them.

Since he stays in perfect step with change, life and death produce no change in him.[3]

5.4.3 Even if Heaven were to overturn and Earth sink, he still would not be made to perish with them.

This is because he complies [*shun*] with them.[4]

5.4.4 Since he clearly knows what it is to be free from falsehood,

He understands the inherent aptness [*gudang*] of his natural endowment [*xingming*].

5.4.5 he is not altered by things.[5]

He gives himself over to [*ren*] the spontaneous altering of things [*ziqian*].[6]

5.4.6 He ascribes the transformation of things to fate,

He regards transformation [*hua*] as fate [*ming*] so does not oppose it.

5.4.7 And so preserves the progenitor [*zong*][7] in him."

He does not go counter to the limits [*ji*] of what is perfectly appropriate [*zhidang*] for him.

5.5 Chang Ji then asked, "What do you mean?"

5.6.1 Zhongni replied, "If you look at them in terms of difference, although things might be as close as liver and gall bladder, people regard them as far apart as Chu and Yue.

As contentment and suffering differ in nature [*xing*], so tendencies [*qing*] to esteem or detest operate in opposition.

5.6.2 But if you look at them in terms of sameness, the myriad things are all one.

Although people differ in what they esteem [*mei*], they are all the same in having something to esteem. Since each esteems what he regards as estimable, the myriad things as one share the same esteem. Since each affirms [*shi*] what he regards as affirmable, the whole world as one share the same affirmation. Since people regard things as different from the point of view of what they consider different, nothing in the world fails to be different. However, when one takes an oceanic view of things, such a one regards the whole world as one's office and the myriad things as one's duty and thus knows that differences don't amount to real differences. Therefore, whereas people regard things to be the same from the point of view of what they consider to be the same, so nothing in the world fails to be the same, such a one instead knows that sameness does not really amount to anything real either. Therefore, since such a one regards them as non-existent [*wu*] on the basis of what he considers non-existent, the affirmable [*shi*], the deniable [*fei*], the estimable *mei*], and the detested [*wu*] never really exist for him. To regard oneself as right and the other wrong, to esteem oneself and despise the other, from those of middling intelligence on down to insects, all without exception behave like this. But this is to understand just themselves and fail to understand others. However, those who arcanely interchange [*xuantong*] and merge imperceptibly with things [*minhe*] understand the whole world from the point of view of the whole world. Since none in the whole world says, "I am wrong," it is clear that none in the world are ever wrong, and, since none says "the other is right," it is clear that none in the world are ever right. It is by freeing oneself from right and wrong and blending them together so they become one that one may ride change [*bian*] and trust to transformation [*hua*] and so encounter anything without fear.

5.6.3 And if you regard them this way, you will become unselfconscious of what the ears and eyes might find suitable,

Suitability [*yi*] arises from the unsuitable, but if one is free of both esteem [*mei*] and detestation [*wu*], nothing fails to be suitable. It is because one has become free from the unsuitable that suitability is forgotten.

5.6.4 and so your mind will be set free to play about in the harmony [*he*] of virtue [*de*]

It is by forgetting all about suitability [*yi*] that one can trust to absolutely everything. It never happens that one trusts to everything and yet not succeeds, and it is unheard of that one succeeds in everything and yet fails to achieve harmony [*he*]. Therefore, when one lets one's mind loose in the realm of the Dao and its virtue, he so expands that everything without exception is appropriate and so empties himself that absolutely everything is fitting.

5.6.5 As for things, he heeds how they are all one and the same and so heeds not their loss, thus he looks on the loss of a foot as if it were the discarding of a piece of dirt."

It is because he embodies a marvelous mind of infinite potential that he can identify with absolutely everything. Since he identifies with absolutely everything, though life and death effect change and transformation, no matter which way they go, there his I will be. Therefore, life makes his I timely, and death makes his I compliant. Timeliness allows him to preserve the aggregate of his I, and death allows him to accept the dispersal of his I. Although aggregation and dispersal are different, since his I makes an I of both of them, life accordingly constitutes his I, but it never means gain to him, and death too may constitute his I, but it never means loss to him. Change occurs with life and death, yet he regards them as one, and, aware they are one, he sloughs them off and has no ties to either. Arcanely merging [*xuantong*] self and other, he regards life and death the same as being awake or asleep, physical existence as a journey, the discarding of life as the taking off of a shoe, and having a foot cut off as the discarding of a piece of dirt. I have never seen any of these sufficient to entangle his mind.

5.7.1 Chang Ji then said, "He uses his knowledge for his own sake

He suspects that Wang Tai still can't forget knowledge and, as such, spontaneously exist.

5.7.2 and uses his mind to obtain his mind.

He suspects that he is still unable to set aside his mind and thereby achieve self-fulfillment.

5.7.3 If he has realized his constant mind, why ever should they gather to him!"

One who has realized his constant mind [*changxin*] interacts in an ordinary way, but Chang Ji suspects that he is unable to interact in an ordinary way when encountering others, which is why he always causes others to gravitate to him.

5.8.1 Zhongni replied, "One would not mirror himself in moving water but instead mirrors himself in still water.

The perfect ability of still water to mirror is not due to its seeking to become a mirror by making itself still. Thus it is that Wang Tai's gathering of large numbers to him is due to them gravitating to him of their own accord, so how could it ever be said that he ever attracted them to make them his disciples!

5.8.2 Only the still can make everyone stop and be still.

If it were to try to do this while moving, it would be unable to provide a place for everyone to stop.[8]

5.8.3 Among those that receive life from Earth, only the pine and cypress remain perfectly green from summer to winter.

The pine and the cypress are especially endowed with concentrated pneuma [*qi*] from Nature [*ziran*] and thus are able to become just the most outstanding of all trees. However, it is not that they are able to achieve this state by trying to do so.

5.8.4 Among those who receive life from Heaven, it is only a Shun who is correct.

That is, those who receive correct pneuma [*zhengqi*] from nature are so extremely rare. Looking down, there are only the pine and cypress, and looking up, there are only the sages. This is why all those that are not correct come to them to seek correctness. If all things kept their greenness intact, none would esteem the pine and cypress, and if all people rectified themselves, none would admire the great sages and so gravitate to them.

5.8.5 It is because such a one is favored with the ability to keep his own life correct that he may correct the lives of all.

It is just that such a one is favored with the spontaneous ability to keep himself correct and not that he deliberately practices correctness in order to be correct.

5.8.6 Proof of one's preserving his initial state [*shi*] is had in the concrete manifestation of fearlessness. Say a warrior fiercely dashes into the ranks of a nine-fold army. Though he may be set on gaining a reputation by doing so, he can still do this as a spontaneous pursuit [*ziyao*]—so even he behaves in the same way.

Even though such a one can't discard reputation, yet he never fails to trust to [*ren*] everything.[9]

5.8.7 But how much the more true should this be for one who governs the whole world and holds the myriad things in his treasury,

He arcanely [*mingran*] embodies [*ti*] absolutely everything.

5.8.8 who but lodges temporarily in the six parts of his body,

They constitute what might be called a traveler's inn.[10]

5.8.9 seems to use ears and eyes,

Others use ears and eyes, and so he too uses ears and eyes—but not because he needs ears and eyes.

5.8.10 and whose mind never dies because he renders all that he knows into unified knowledge [*yizhi*].

Since his knowledge [*zhi*] stays perfectly in step with change and transformation [*bianhua*], whichever way they go it never fails to merge arcanely [*minghui*]with them. This is what is meant by "unity of knowledge." Since the mind [*xin*] complies perfectly [*shun*] with life and death, it will at no time cease to live. This is what it meant by "the mind never dies."[11]

5.8.11 As if he were about to choose a day to ascend on high—this is why these others become his followers.

One simply makes choices in order not to miss opportunities, but this man has nothing to do with choices but instead gives himself over to the course of nature [*tianxing*] and the dynamics of the moment [*shidong*]. Therefore, people who would make use of him accordingly gather to him.[12]

5.8.12 But why would he ever be willing to regard others as his concern!"

Such is his utter detachment [*tianmo*] that he is complete unto himself [*quan*].

5.9.1 Shentu Jia was someone who had had a foot cut off, yet he together with Zichan of Zheng Sun Qiao had Bohun Wuren [Elder Muddled None His Other] as teacher.[13] Zichan said to Shentu Jia, "If I withdraw first, you remain, but if you withdraw first, I remain."

He is ashamed to walk with someone who has lost a foot.

5.9.2 The next day they were again seated together in the same hall and on the same mat. Zichan said to Shentu Jia, "If I withdraw first, you remain, but if you withdraw first, I remain. Now I am going to withdraw, so will you remain or not?

He asks him this direct question because he wants to make sure that he does not accompany him.

5.9.3 Moreover, when you come into the presence of a head of government, you don't dodge out of the way. So do you regard yourself as the equal of a head of government?"

He always uses being head of the government to make much of himself, and this is why he comes right out and says "Do you regard yourself as the equal of a head of government." As such, we can say that this amply illustrates how immodest he is.

5.10.1 Shentu Jia replied, "Within our master's gate, is there really a place here for such a head of government?"

This is a place for the discussion of virtue and not evaluating positions.

5.10.2 Is it because you are so pleased with being head of government that you thrust people behind you?

Shentu Jia laughs at how boastful and pleased Zichan is about his position and how he wants to place himself before others.

5.10.3 I've heard it said that if a mirror is kept bright, dust does not settle on it, but if dust does settle on it, it is not bright. So it is that if one keeps company for a long time with worthy men, he will be without fault. Now, the great one you have chosen to learn from is our master, yet you still bring out words such as these—indeed, is this not a fault!"

He serves such a brilliant teacher but has not yet rid himself of such a vulgar mind as this, which truly is a fault.

5.11.1 Zichan replied, "Here you are such as this,

That is, with such a crippled body as this.

5.11.2 and yet you would even rival Yao in goodness. Evaluate your virtue! Are you not up to self-reflection?"

That is, he so lacks self-understanding that he not only is inclined to despise those in authority but even to regard himself as an equal to the virtuous: "Evaluate your virtue! You still are not up to correcting the fault that caused crippling of your body."

5.12.1 Shentu Jia then replied, "Legion are those who excuse their transgressions because they think they don't deserve to perish,

Legion are those who make much of themselves and talk about how they committed transgressions because they think they don't deserve to perish.

5.12.2 but rare are those who don't excuse their transgressions because they think they don't deserve to live.

Few are those who are aware of their transgressions yet keep quiet about them because they think they deserve to die.

5.12.3 As for those who understand that nothing can be done about it and so are content to comply with fate, only those possessed of virtue can do this. Suppose you happen to wander within the bow range of Yi, right there in the center where you should be hit—and if you are not hit, it will be due to fate [*ming*].

Yi was an excellent archer in antiquity. The reach of an arrow shot from a bow is its bow range. When it comes to benefit or harm, everyone in the world is a Yi. If you don't discard the self [*shen*], forget awareness [*zhi*], and merge perfectly with the rise and fall of things, you end up wandering within the bow range of Yi. Even if you went out like a Zhang Yi or stayed in like a Shan Bao,[14] you won't be spared the place where you might be hit—but whether you are hit or not, all simply depends on fate. Though everyone no matter how insignificant has such things befall them, no one realizes that this is due to the spontaneity [*zier*] of fate. Therefore, when one is spared the harm of getting hit by an arrow, he thinks it is because of his skill—happily he makes much of himself. But when he is not so spared, he is chagrined at himself for his blunder, his will [*zhi*] wounded and spirit [*shen*] humiliated. All this indicates someone who yet fails to comprehend the tendencies [*qing*] of fate [*ming*]. One's life is not generated by oneself, thus within an entire lifetime, even within one hundred years, whether one is content where one is or gets up to get going, whether one does or desists, whether active or passive, or whether inclined toward or prone to reject, one's fundamental nature [*qingxing*] and mental powers [*zhineng*], whatever one has, whatever one has not, whatever one does, whatever one encounters, none of any of this is up to the person himself but instead is due to nothing other than the spontaneity [*zier*] of principle [*li*]. Nevertheless, people allow their lives to teem with happiness and unhappiness—which is a failure resulting from opposition to spontaneity [*ziran*].

5.12.4 Legion are those who, because their feet are whole, laugh at me for failing to keep my feet whole.

Because no one understands fate, they all have this tendency to laugh at him.

5.12.5 It upsets me so much I get angry.

The fact that he gets angry when he sees others failing to understand fate means that he too fails to understand fate.

5.12.6 But if I go to our Master's place, I calm down and recover myself,

Since he sees how this Perfected one [*zhiren*] understands fate and discards physical form it so dissipates the anger that came upon him earlier that he recovers his normal state [*chang*].

5.12.7 Perhaps this happens because our Master washes me with his goodness?

Perhaps this is because the Master washes him with the Dao of goodness? Is this why he can recover himself [*zifan*]? This is to forget about physical form and discards all worldly ties.

5.12.8 I have associated with our Master for nineteen years, and he has never once noticed that I have lost a foot.

This is because he has forgotten all about physical form.

5.12.9 Now, you and I should associate in terms of what is interior to the physical body [*xinghai*], yet you pursue what I am in terms of what is exterior to the physical body—is this too not a fault!"

The physical body belongs to the outer, and its virtue belongs to the inner. Now you and I should only associate in terms of virtue; ours should not be an association based on physical forms, yet you pursue what I am in terms of my outer goodness—it this not a fault!

5.13 Startled and embarrassed, Zichan changed his attitude and altered his expression, saying, "Perhaps you might not say anything more about it."

Once he understood, he became disgusted at how much he had said.

5.14.1 In Lu, Shushan the No-Toes, who had had his foot cut off, often kept trying to see Zhongni.

Zhong (often) means *pin* (frequently).

5.14.2 Zhongni said to him, "Since you did not take care, you committed a crime in the past and so came to such grief as this. Although you have come to me now, what can be done about it!"

5.15.1 No-Toes replied, "It is just that I did not understand what I really should be concerned about and so regarded my body lightly, which is why I lost my foot.

Since one's life self-generates [*zisheng*] according to principle [*li*], one simply should not selfconsciously interfere with it in any way but just let it self-generate. This is to regard one's person [*shen*] highly and to understand what one should really be concerned about. But if one forgets about its self-generation and instead tries to treat it dutifully and with care, this is to regard one's person lightly and fail to understand what one really should be concerned about. As a result, the five viscera war with each other inside, and one's hands and feet suffer harm outside.

5.15.2 The reason I have come to you now is because I still have something to preserve that I revere more than a foot.

To have had a foot cut off did not prove sufficient to damage his virtue [*de*], which clearly indicates that the physical body [*xinghai*] is but a traveler's inn.

5.15.3 Therefore, I am concerned to keep it intact.

To rid oneself of dutifulness and care and instead trust to life's self-generation—this is what is meant by concern to keep it intact.

5.15.4 There is nothing that Heaven fails to cover, nothing that Earth fails to carry,

Heaven does not cover with selfconscious purpose [*wei*], thus it can always cover; the Earth does not carry with selfconscious purpose, thus it can always carry. If Heaven and Earth were allowed to cover and carry with selfconscious purpose, there would be times when they would desist from doing so. If boats were able to submerge themselves and only selfconsciously floated for our sake, there would be times when they would sink. Thus it is that when people apply themselves to it selfconsciously, they never manage to reach the end of their natural span of life.

5.15.5 Since I took you, master, for the Heaven and Earth, how could I have expected that you were such a man as this!"

He reproaches him for his lack of solicitude, that is, for failing to measure up to Heaven and Earth.

5.16 Confucius replied, "I have indeed been rude! Why don't you enter? And please let me discourse on what I know."[15]

5.17.1 When No-Toes had withdrawn,

When No-Toes heard what Confucius had to say, he withdrew, which kept his unselfconscious action [*wuwei*] intact.

5.17.2 Confucius said, "Be diligent, disciples! No-Toes has had a foot cut off, but still he is concerned about learning how to make amends for the evil he had formerly practiced—so how much the more should those whose virtue is still intact do so!"

One whose virtue is really intact lives the better to forget life.

5.18.1 No-Toes then spoke to Lao Dan [Old Long Ears, Laozi], "Kong Qiu [Confucius] compared to a Perfected one [*zhiren*], still fails to measure up, does he not? So why does he come so often to study with you?

No-Toes is puzzled why Confucius now keeps coming to study with Lao Dan.

5.18.2 He just wants to be famous for being unconventional and bizarre [*chugui*],[16] but does he not realize that the Perfected one [*zhiren*] regards such fame as hand fetters and foot shackles?"

As someone unselfconscious, he too emulates just as people in general emulate. However, emulators in antiquity emulated for themselves, whereas emulators nowadays emulate for others—and such degeneration even goes so far as to behave with the behavior of others. To make others one's teachers in order to achieve one's own self-fulfillment, this is what one who holds fast to his original and constant nature [*changran*] does, whereas to discard self, imitate others and so chase after external things, this is what one who pursues fame for not conforming to constant nature [*feichang*] does. Fame gained for not conforming to constant nature actually starts in one's constant nature [*chang*]. Therefore, emulation is not practiced in order to become bizarre, yet being bizarre necessarily starts in emulation—just as civility [*li*] is not practiced in order to become floridly decorous, yet the rise of florid decorum necessarily starts in civility. Such is the inevitability of the principles involved, about which the Perfected one can do nothing—and this is why he regards such fame as fetters for his hands and shackles for his feet.

5.19 Old Long Ears replied, "Why not just get him to regard life and death as a single thread and suitability [*ke*] and unsuitability [*buke*] as strung on a single cord—and so release him from his hand fetters and foot shackles? Surely this is possible!"

He wants Confucius to merge arcanely [*ming*] with people via unswerving principle in the hope that he will leave no footprints for them to follow.

5.20 No-Toes then said, "Since Heaven is punishing him, how could he ever be released!"

Now, it is not that Zhongni failed to merge arcanely, for, in accordance with natural principle, when he acted it was as a shadow that tagged along, and when he spoke it was as an echo that followed. It was by so complying with others that his fame and achievement [*ji*] became established as they did. However, his complying with others was not done in order to achieve fame, and, since it was not done in order to achieve fame, it reached perfection—and in the end this did not spare him from fame. As such, who would have ever been able to release him! Therefore, his fame consisted of shadows and echoes, and these shadows and echoes became the hand fetters and foot shackles for his demeanor [*xing*] and voice [*sheng*]. If one understands this principle, fame and achievement can be discarded. Once achievement is discarded, esteem for others can be terminated. Once esteem for others is terminated, one's naturally endowed life [*xingming*] can remain intact [*quan*].

5.21.1 Duke Ai of Lu asked advice of Zhongni [Confucius], "In Wei there is an ugly man, whose name is Doleful Camelback [Ai Taituo].[17]

E [ugly] [should not be read as *wu* (hate) but as the stative verb] meaning *chou* [ugly].

5.21.2 Men who kept company with him become so fond of him that they can't leave him, and when women of marriageable age see him, more than ten so far have begged their parents, saying, 'I would rather become the Master's concubine than the wife of anyone else.' No one has ever heard him take the lead, and all he does is chime in with others. He has neither position of ruler that he might use to save peoples' lives

This makes it clear that it is not because of his power and influence that people flock to him.

5.21.3 nor accumulated official salary that he might use to fill their bellies.

This make it clear that it is not because they seek something to eat that they flock to him.

5.21.4 Moreover, though he could terrify the whole world with his ugliness,

This makes it clear that it is not because of his handsome appearance that they flock to him.

5.21.5 though he but chimes in and does not take the lead,

It is not that they come to him because he summons them.

5.21.6 and though he knows nothing beyond his immediate surroundings,

He does not think of things beyond his allotted lot in life [*fen*].

5.21.7 yet male and female gather before him.

One whose innate talents [*cai*] are all intact [*quan*] never causes anything harm. Therefore, when he comes among beasts, he never disturbs their flocks, and when he comes among birds, he never disturbs their ranks—but instead becomes a wilderness refuge for the myriad creatures.

5.21.8 This means that he surely consists of something different from other men.

5.21.9 When I summoned him to an audience, as expected he turned out to be someone who could terrify the whole world with his ugliness. But when he had stayed with me for less than a month, I became interested in his innate nature [*weiren*].

Before a month had elapsed, he already had begun to realize that Ai Taituo possessed real profundity.

5.21.10 And before a year had passed, I trusted him. Since my state was without a chief minister, I decided to turn the state over to him.

He would entrust him with the governance of his state.

5.21.11 But he accepted only after expressing indifference,

Favor and humiliation failed to disturb his spirit [*shen*].

5.21.12 and, as if it were unsuitable for him, first declined.

He too declined just as people in general would have declined.[18]

5.21.13 I was embarrassed, but in the end turned the state over to him anyway. Not very long afterward he up and left me. I was as sad about this as if I had suffered a real loss and as if I no longer had someone with whom to enjoy my state. What kind of a man is this?"

5.22.1 Zhongni [Confucius] replied, "Once when on a mission to Chu I happen to see piglets suckling at their dead mother.

They were feeding on its milk.

5.22.2 After a short time, as if in the wink of an eye, they all abandoned her and ran away, simply because she no longer appeared as one of them, that is, no longer belonged to their own kind.

Alive, the mother belonged to their same kind because of the talents and virtues [*caide*] she possessed, but once she died, these talents and virtues vanished. Therefore, the living ones ran away because she no longer belonged to their own kind. Thus it is that one possessed of a rich store of virtue is comparable to a newborn child—no matter where he goes he remains a newborn child. As such, no one in the world ever harms him, for it is as one whom they all identify as of their own kind that such a one clearly reveals himself. If one's innate character [*qing*] is of the same kind as that of another, even if he fails to share the same physical appearance [*xing*], that other will have no harmful designs on him, but if one's innate character fails to be of the same kind, though the physical appearance be the same as that of mother and offspring, this will prove inadequate to control the direction the will [*zhi*] takes.[19]

5.22.3 What they loved in their mother was not her bodily form [*xing*], what they loved was that which used her bodily form.

That which uses the bodily form are the talents and virtue [*caide*].[20]

5.22.4 When a man dies in battle, war plumes are not furnished at his burial,

War plumes are furnished as decorations for martial prowess [*wu*]. One who dies in battle no longer has martial prowess, so why should war plumes be furnished?

5.22.5 and there is no longer any reason for one who has had feet cut off to love shoes.

The sole reason why one loves shoes is for the sake of his feet.

5.22.6 since for both no basis [*ben*] any longer exists.

War plumes and shoes have as their bases military prowess and feet.

5.22.7 Palace women who serve the Son of Heaven neither cut their nails nor pierce their ears,

They keep their physical appearance [*xing*] intact [*quan*].

5.22.8 and men who have just taken wives are kept on only in extraneous capacity and may not continue in proper duties.

This is out of fear that their physical appearance would be harmed.[21]

5.22.9 Since perfection of physical appearance is as important as this,

The selection of lower ranked concubines and happy newly married men for palace service is based on the criterion that their physical appearance [*xing*] be pleasing. Therefore, keeping one's physical appearance perfect [*quan*] serves as a metaphor to humble the attitude [*qing*] of the most exalted [the ruler] and have him return to the conduct [*cao*] of an innocent virgin.

5.22.10 how much more important should it be for the man of complete virtue!

By keeping his virtue complete the people love him [the ruler]—how fitting!

5.22.11 Now, before Doleful Camelback spoke he was already trusted, before he achieved merit was so beloved that he caused someone to turn his state over to him, fearing only that he would not accept it. This surely is an example of how innate talent [*cai*] is kept perfectly intact [*quan*] yet virtue [*de*] does not manifest itself in physical appearance [*xing*]."

5.23 Duke Ai then said, "What do you mean by 'innate talent is kept perfectly intact'?"

5.24.1 Zhongni [Confucius] said, "Life or death, survival or destruction, obscurity or eminence, poverty or wealth, worthiness or unworthiness, slander or praise, hunger or thirst, heat or cold, such changes as these are all the workings of fate [*ming*].

The principles involved operate with inherent aptness [*gudang*], from which there is no escape. If one lives, it is not life that happens by mistake, and what occurs in life does not happen at random. Although Heaven and Earth are great and the myriad things many, all that one might encounter appropriately happens according to these principles. Therefore, although it be all the gods and divinities of Heaven and Earth or all the sages and worthies involved in the governance of the world, even if they exert all their strength and intelligence, they would still find it impossible to violate these principles. Whatever one does not encounter can't ever have been encountered, and whatever one does encounter can't fail to have been encountered. Whatever does not happen can't ever have happened, and whatever does happen can't fail to have happened. Therefore, one submits to it and spontaneously tallies with it [*zidang*].

5.24.2 Such things supersede one another day and night, as time moves on,

Driven by fate, change in things ceases neither day nor night. Reject it and it won't go away; detain it and it won't stay. This is why one whose innate talent [*cai*] is perfect [*quan*] goes along with whatever he encounters and just trusts [*ren*] to it.

5.24.3 but knowledge [*zhi*] can't perceive how change begins [*shi*].

The initial state [*shi*] of change is imperceptible to knowledge, which is why change can't be stayed by one's predilection [*qing*] to do so. We know from this that fate [*ming*] works inevitably and things inevitably change, so when change has already reached an end point, how could one ever expect to perceive its initial state, or when it is already in a new state, how could one ever long for what used to be! Even if one had perfect knowledge, he still could not perceive such a thing, and, as for the passing away of what used to be, how could one ever do anything about that!

5.24.4 Therefore, they should not disturb one's harmony [*he*],

If one understands the inherently appropriate [*gudang*] for one's naturally endowed life [*xingming*], though it be life or death, obscurity or eminence, a thousand changes or ten thousand transformations, placidly such a one will feel completely at ease [*ziruo*] and harmony with principle [*heli*] will pervade his person [*shen*].

5.24.5 and they must not enter the numinous storehouse [*lingfu*].

The "treasure house of the spirit" is the dwelling place for one's essence and spirit [*jingshen*]. When this reaches perfect capacity, it does not allow such concerns to reach the spirit [*shen*], and they just seem to pass by outside one's skin.

5.24.6 If one ensures that his spirit remains harmonious and content, things will go smoothly [*tong*] and happiness will be unimpaired,

If one ensures that his harmonious nature [*hexing*] is not disturbed and treasure house is filled with ease and contentment, though involved in the utmost change, such a one won't impair his happiness.

5.24.7 and if one does this day and night without interruption,

One should identify perfectly [*minran*] with things and just let them happen.

5.24.8 he will provide a springtime for all things.

It shall be on him that all living things rely.[22]

5.24.9 Such a one gives succor as he lets the seasons grow in his heart and mind [*xin*].

In compliance with the four seasons, he and their transformations [*hua*] are one.

5.24.10 This is what I mean by 'innate talent is kept perfectly intact' "

5.25 "What do you mean by 'virtue [*de*] does not manifest itself in physical appearance [*xing*]?' "

5.26.1 He replied, "When it is level, water is in an absolutely state of stillness; as such, it can serve as a standard [*fa*].

Because it utterly free of bias [*qing*] and absolutely level, everyone in the world finds what is true [*zheng*] in it.

5.26.2 Inside it preserves such a state so outside shows no agitation.

Inwardly preserving its brightness and outwardly free from discrepancy [*qingwei*], it is an arcane mirror [*xuanjian*] that clearly shines forth [*dongzhao*] impartial [*wuqing*] toward everything. Therefore it can keep its level intact [*quan*] and so operate as a standard [*fa*].

5.26.3 Virtue is the cultivation [*xiu*] of success [*cheng*] and harmony [*he*].

The capacity [*de*] to succeed at things and to stay in harmony with people is called "virtue."

5.26.4 Such a one whose virtue is not manifest in physical appearance, is one people can't do without."

Never to fail at anything and never failing to stay in harmony with people signifies someone whose virtue is not manifest in physical appearance. "Therefore everyone in the world happily promote him without ever tiring of it."[23]

5.27 On another day, Duke Ai related this to Master Min [Minzi],[24] "When I first faced south and ruled the whole world, I took personal charge of rules and regulations for the common folk and out of worry for their untimely deaths. I thought this was the most expeditious [*tong*] policy. Now that I have heard what the Perfected one [*zhiren*] had to say, I feared that I had failed to grasp the truth [*shi*] about it and was treating my own person carelessly and endangering my state. My relationship to Kong Qiu [Confucius] as such was not that of ruler and subject but simply one of friendship based on virtue."

Here is someone who heard about virtue complete, and even though it was still Duke Ai, he wanted to detach himself from his physical existence [*xinghai*] and forget about eminence and humility.

5.28.1 After some shapeless fellow with curled under toes and who was without lips explained things to Duke Ling of Wey, Duke Ling became so pleased with him that when he looked at men with normal bodies, their necks seemed too long and thin for him. And after some fellow with a goiter as large as a big bellied jug explained things to Duke Huan of Qi, Duke Huan became so pleased with him that when he looked at men with normal bodies, their necks seemed too long and thin for him too.

Once partiality [*pianqing*] operates in a certain direction, the ugly [*chou*] is transformed into the pleasing and the pleasing transformed into the ugly.

5.28.2 Therefore, as their virtue was deemed strong, their physical appearance was deemed forgettable.

When the strength of one's virtue lies in complying with others, others forget how ugly he looks; when the strength of one's virtue lies in opposing others, others forget about how fine he looks.

5.28.3 When people don't forget what is forgettable and instead forget what is unforgettable, this is called the truly forgettable.

While alive, people cherish it [physical appearance] but when dead, they discard it. It follows from this that what common people of the world find unforgettable in one is virtue and what principle [*li*] does not preserve in one is physical appearance. Therefore, when it is just one's physical appearance that is forgotten, this does not signify the truly forgettable, but when it is one's virtue that is forgotten while his physical appearance is not forgotten, this does signify the truly forgettable.[25]

5.28.4 Therefore, since the sage has his place to wander about in,

The sage wanders about in the realm of self-fulfillment [*zide*], and wherever he lets himself go, he never fails to achieve perfect realization [*zhi*], since his talents and virtues [*caide*] always remain intact [*quan*].

5.28.5 for him knowledge [*zhi*] would mean calamity [*nie*], regulations [*yue*] would mean glue [*jiao*], virtue would mean bonds [*jie*], and skill would mean a commodity [*shang*].

That these four spontaneously [*ziran*] give rise to one another, is because their principles [*li*] already provide for it.

5.28.6 Since the sage makes no plans, what use has he for knowledge? He does not chop things up, so what use has he for glue? He never loses, so what use has he for virtue? He does not sell, so what use has he for commodities?

His nature [*ziran*] is already complete, therefore the sage finds such things no use to him.

5.28.7 These four are the gruel of Heaven. The gruel of Heaven is nourishment that Heaven provides.

This means the endowment that Nature [*ziran*] provides.

5.28.8 Since he receives nourishment from Heaven, what further use has he for human action?

Thanks to his natural endowment, the principles of his existence are already fully sufficient. Therefore, although he might deeply ponder so as to avoid trouble or take cognizance of warning so as to seek refuge from disaster, he never makes a false step, for in all cases, he merges with Heaven and Earth and with the innate tendencies of perfect principle. When this involves things that he himself must ponder, it is not that he ponders them with a personal self, and when this involves things that he himself must not ponder, it is not that he refrains from pondering them with a personal self either. Sometimes he ponders and so avoids something, sometimes he ponders and does not avoid something, sometimes he does not ponder and yet avoids something, and sometimes he does not ponder and yet does not avoid something. In all these cases it is not his personal self that is responsible for anything, so what more should he do! He just lets things spontaneously fulfill themselves.

5.28.9 He may have the physical appearance of a man,

Looking at him, he seems to have the appearance of a man.

5.28.10 but he has no human predilections [*qing*].

He is withered as the branches of a dead tree.

5.28.11 Since he has the physical appearance of a man, he keeps company with other men.

That things both gather together and separate by kind is due to the natural Dao.

5.28.12 Since he has no human predilections [*qing*], right [*shi*] and wrong [*fei*] have no effect on him.

Since he is impartial [*wuqing*], he just goes along with things.

5.28.13 He is so trivial, so insignificant that he belongs with everyone else.

In appearance he is just like everyone else.

5.28.14 He is so great, so significant that he alone perfectly realizes [*cheng*] his natural endowment [*tian*].

It is because he is utterly impartial [*wuqing*] that he can give himself flood like [*haoran*] over to absolutely everything. To give oneself over to absolutely everything is impossible if one is partial [*youqing*]. This is why it is the impartial alone who perfectly fulfills his natural endowment.

5.29 Huizi [Master Hui] said to Master Zhuang, "Can a man really be completely dispassionate [*wuqing*]?"

5.30 Master Zhuang replied, "That's right."

5.31 Master Hui then asked, "To be a man and yet be dispassionate—how can such a one be called a man?" Master Zhuang replied, "The Dao gave him a face, Heaven gave him a physical form, so how can he not be called a man?"

One's life is not lived out of a predilection [*qing*] to live, so how could one's expertise [*zhi*] in life ever be because of predilection? Therefore, one might have the predilection [*youqing*] to become a Li Zhu or a Master Kuang but would be incapable of it, yet Li Zhu and Master Kuang themselves had keen eyesight and sharp hearing without the predilection [*wuqing*] to have them. One might have the predilection to become a sage or worthy but would be incapable of it, yet sages and worthies become sages and worthies without the predilection to become so. And why must it just involve the enormous discrepancy that sets one off from the sages and worthies or the impossible envy one might feel towards a Li Zhu or a Master Kuang? Though it be as lowly as becoming an imbecile or a deaf or blind person or even a cock that crows or a dog that barks, no matter how much one might have the predilection to become one of these, it would always prove impossible. No matter whether it be near or far, and even if only the slightest difference as say between Yan Hui and Confucius, no one could ever manage it. These examples involve relationships with the myriad things, but let us now draw examples from within one's own body. The ear and the eye can't exchange duties and still function properly; the hands and the feet can't exchange responsibilities and still operate properly. Therefore, when a child is first born, it does not use its eyes to try to nurse, does not use its ears to determine which way to look, does not use its feet to grasp things, or does not use its hands to try to walk. How is it possible that each part of the human body does not have its own definite function or that one's physical form is not foreordained, and instead assert that these are arbitrarily controlled by one's own predilections?

5.32 Master Hui then said, "Since you have already said that it is a man, how can he manage to be free from predilections?"

He still fails to understand that physical form is not the result of predilection.

5.33.1 Master Zhuang replied, "The tendency to approve [*shi*] and disapprove [*fei*] is what I mean by predilection [*qing*].

Since it is the propensity to approve or disapprove that constitutes predilection, one who stays free of approval and disapproval, like and dislike, though he has a physical appearance, he is nothing other than what he himself is, so what room could predilection find in him?

5.33.2 When I say that one should be without predilections [*wuqing*], I mean that one should not allow likes and dislikes to harm his inner self

To accept [*ren*] what is appropriate for one [*dang*] and just keep moving forward has nothing to do with predilection.

5.33.3 but that instead he should rely on [*yin*] spontaneity [*ziran*] and not try to augment life."

Such a one stays with what is appropriate [*dang*] for him.

5.34 Master Hui then said, "If one does not augment life, how can he maintain his person?"

He still fails to understand that life is self-generated [*zisheng*] and that principle [*li*] is self-sufficient [*zizu*].

5.34.1 Master Zhuang replied, "The Dao gave him a face, Heaven gave him a physical form,

One's life principle [*shengli*] is such that one's self-sufficiency [*zizu*] exists within one's own physical form, so one has only to trust to it for his person to be preserved.

5.34.2 and he is free from any tendency within to harm his person with like and dislike.

The reason why predilection to like and dislike is not the means to augment life but can only harm one's person is because one's life is fated.[26]

5.34.3 Now here you are so estranged from your spirit [*shen*] and so belabor your vital essence [*jing*] that you have to lean against trees and moan, slump on your desk, and doze.

When one fails to keep his spirit [*shen*] within one's natural capacity, this is estrangement [*wai*]. When one fails to keep his vital essence [*jing*] from extending beyond the limits of one's self-generation [*zisheng*], this is to belabor it. Therefore, when walking, one will have to lean on trees and moan, and when sitting, one will have to slump on one's writing desk and nap. That is, having predilections results in self-inflicted distress [*zikun*].

5.34.4 Heaven gave you physical existence [*xing*], yet you use it to jabber on about hardness and whiteness."[27]

This addresses the fact that in whatever you do, you are estranged from your spirit [*shen*] and belabor your vital essence [*jing*]. Leaning on trees or slumped on your writing desk, now moaning, now napping, this is what the world means by predilection [*qing*]. Yet the text says "Heaven gave," which makes it clear that "predilection" is not generated by predilection, so how much less likely by anything else! Therefore, although the myriad things have myriad different physical existences, the text says that when it comes to choosing or rejecting anything, this always happens when no predilection is involved—why should it depend further on predilection whether one does one thing instead of another!

Notes

1. "Auspicious sign of fate" translates *fuming*, which usually refers to the manifestation of a good omen that signifies a perfect match between a sovereign destined to rule and his fated appearance in the world—based on the belief that Heaven sends down positive omens to rulers as evidence that they are true sovereigns, fit to rule.
2. Lu Deming reads Wang's name as *tai* [worn out or inferior horse] and not *dai* [indolent, unconventional]. *Zhuangzi jishi*, 1: 187. His foot was amputated as punishment.
3. This and similar paradoxical statements that immediately follow, all of which follow the pattern "being perfectly in step with change, he isn't changed," resolve this paradox by understanding the distinction between the Divine man [*shenren*], who arcanely merges with things and so spontaneously changes with them, and the ordinary man,

who self-consciously maintains his distinction from things and so, against his will, is changed by them.

4. Cheng Xuanying: "Since he arcanely merges [*ming*] with safety or danger, his self [*wo*] never perishes." *Zhuangzi jishi*, 1: 190.
5. Cf. 13.31.6.
6. Cheng Xuanying: "His numinous mind [*lingxin*] tranquilly comprehending [*anshen*], he marvelously embodies [*miaoti*] his true origin [*zhenyuan*]. It is because he resonates with [*xiangying*] the Dao that he isn't altered by things." *Zhuangzi jishi*, 1: 190.
7. Cf. *Laozi* or *Daodejing*, section 4; Richard John Lynn, *The Classic of the Way and Virtue*, 57: "The vessel of the Dao is empty, so use it but don't try to refill it. It is such an abyss, oh, that it appears to be the progenitor [*zong*] of the myriad things."
8. Cheng Xuanying: "*Wei* (only) means *du* (uniquely); 'only the still' refers to water in its original tranquil state; 'can make stop' refers to how it can detain people to mirror themselves; 'everyone stop and be still' refers to those who come to mirror themselves. Wang Tai has forgotten all personal involvement with things [*wanghuai*] and is empty and tranquil [*xuji*], so he can provide a place for all the disciples to stop. It is because of this latent power [*gongneng*] that everyone is made to gather to him." *Zhuangzi jishi*, 1: 194.
9. The issue isn't about discarding the need for reputation, but rather about keeping faith with one's original nature. The warrior described behaves as he does, including his pursuit of reputation, entirely spontaneously. He may acquire fame in the process, but this is a by-product of keeping faith with himself. So it is with Wang Tai, who keeps faith with his own nature and in the process happens to acquire disciples. Cheng Xuanying elaborates: "Say there is someone endowed with a martial pneuma [*qi*], who preserves his mind [*xin*] in its initial state of goodness [*shanshi*] and whose sincerity [*xin*] creates an integrity [*jie*] that carries him through to the end. Inwardly he harbors a fearless will, while outwardly he manifests an appearance of fierce bravery. As such, he dashes straight into the ranks of a nine-fold army. Although by doing this he may be set on gaining name and rank, it nevertheless is his ability to submit to his mind as he pursues praise that allows him to forget all about life and death. So how much the more true is this for Wang Tai!" *Zhuangzi jishi*, 1: 195.
10. The six parts of the body are the four limbs, the trunk, and the head.
11. Cheng Xuanying: " 'Unified knowledge' refers to the manner of his knowing, and 'all that he knows' refers to its scope [*jing*]. Because knowledge of what he can know reflects the scope of what is known in such a way that knowledge and scope so arcanely merge that not the least discrepancy exists between them, knowing and not knowing interpenetrate [*tong*] and become one. Even though he continues to exhibit outward manifestations of principles [*jili*] inherent in the transformation of things [*wuhua*], his mind never dies. So how could there ever be room in it for such notions as wholeness or one-footedness!" *Zhuangzi jishi*, 1: 196.
12. Cheng Xuanying: "How could such a one as Wang Tai still simply choose a good day to ascend to the Arcane Dao [*xuandao*]—it isn't at all what he would do! He just abides in emptiness [*xu*] and placidity [*dan*], forgets all personal involvement with things [*wanghuai*] and merges with it [the Arcane Dao]. This perfect one [*zhiren*], utterly unselfconscious [*wuxin*], is as still water in which a reflection lingers, yet people of the world in their delusion become his followers because of it." *Zhuangzi jishi*, 1: 196.
13. Cheng Xuanying: "Surnamed Shentu and given name Jia, he was a worthy of the state of Zheng who had had his foot cut off. Surnamed Sun, given name Qiao, and personal name Zichan, he was also a worthy of Zheng. Bohun Wuren was the worthy title of their

teacher. *Bo* means elder, and *hun* means muddled. As he grew older and virtue accumulated, he kept his light hidden so seemed dim. Because he was absolutely unmindful of the distinction between self and other, he was called 'Elder Muddled None His Other.'" *Zhuangzi jishi*, 1: 197. However, he appears again in 32.1, but with the *wu* written with a character usually pronounced *mao*, meaning dim or dim-sighted, confused, or stupid; thus there, it can be rendered as "Elder Muddled Dim to Others."

14. Zhang Yi and Shan Bao are discussed in chapter 19 of this book, *Dasheng* (Understand Life), in 19.18. Zhang Yi took care to ingratiate himself with the rich and powerful, taking care of the "outer," and yet he died early of illness; Shan Bao chose to become a hermit in the wilds, taking care of the "inner," and yet he died before his time because he was eaten by a hungry tiger.
15. Cheng Xuanying: "What Zhongni had to propound involved nothing more than the mere footprints of sagehood. No-Toes asking to study with him was because he was concerned about how to keep his life intact, but all he got was a shallow response to a profound question—it just amounted to worthless superficiality." *Zhuangzi jishi*, 1: 203.
16. Cf. 33.19.11.
17. Cheng Xuanying and Lu Deming, citing earlier opinion, read the name as Aitai Tuo [Ugly Tuo]; but note that shortly afterward, Cheng also refers to him neither as Aitai nor Tuo, but as Taituo. *Zhuangzi jishi*, 1: 207–208. Therefore, it is also possible to read the name as Ai Taituo: Ai as the surname, its literal meaning "doleful," and Taituo as the given name, "camelback."
18. Cheng Xuanying: "*Fanruo* (as if it were unsuitable) signifies an attitude that it was unsuitable and not his place. Although he was disturbed by neither favor nor humiliation, he still modestly declined. Therefore, as if it were unsuitable, becoming one with the very dust, he declined as anyone in general might have declined." *Zhuangzi jishi*, 1: 209. To "become one with the very dust" is a tenet of the *Laozi*, section 4; Lynn, *The Classic of the Way and Virtue*, 57.
19. Cheng Xuanying adds: "This is a metaphor for Duke Ai, who since he basically lacks all talent and virtue, isn't at all Camelback's own kind, so Camelback gave up on him and left. Since Camelback's talents and virtues are perfectly intact [*quan*], he is comparable to a newborn child. That others love him dearly is, of course, entirely appropriate." *Zhuangzi jishi*, 1: 210.
20. Cheng Xuanying equates talents and virtue with "essence and spirit" [*jingshen*]. *Zhuangzi jishi*, 1: 210.
21. Cheng Xuanying: "At the monarch's palace, as for palace women who are selected, if they had ears pierced or nails cut, he feared their physical appearance would be harmed, and, as for commoner men [servants] who have just taken wives, these are kept on only for ancillary duties, for since their duties [inside the palace] would make them busily dash around, he was concerned that their faces would grow pale. The text thus again cites examples to serve as metaphors for keeping innate talent intact." *Zhuangzi jishi*, 1: 211.
22. Cheng Xuanying: "Shining his kindness on all that lives, his mercy watering all flora and fauna, he treats everything with benevolence, so everything burgeons with the youthful vigor of spring." *Zhuangzi jishi*, 1: 214.
23. Cf. 21.31.3. Guo Xiang quotes from the *Laozi* or *Daodejing*, section 66; Lynn, *The Classic of the Way and Virtue*, 173.
24. Cheng Xuanying: "Surnamed Min, with given name Sun and personal name Ziqian, he was a disciple of Xuan Ni [Confucius]. As for the four categories of moral expertise, he most possessed the virtue of filiality. He was a native of the state of Lu." *Zhuangzi jishi*, 1: 216.

25. Cheng Xuanying: "*Cheng* [truly] is the same as *shi* [really]. 'What is forgettable' refers to physical appearance [*xing*], and 'what is unforgettable' refers to virtue [*de*]. To forget physical appearance is easy but to forget virtue is hard. This is why it is said that physical appearance is forgettable but virtue is unforgettable. So when one has his virtue forgotten while his physical appearance isn't forgotten, such a one has become truly forgettable. This is what 'virtue [*de*] does not manifest itself in physical appearance [*xing*]' means." *Zhuangzi jishi*, 1: 218. Guo's and Cheng's argument can be reworded as follows: The virtue of the true sage isn't manifest; people should be unaware that it even exists. The grotesques who so impressed Duke Ling and Duke Huan could not have been true sages because they did not hide their virtue, but merely succeeded in having the two dukes forget that their ugliness was ugliness and become fond of them personally because of their supposed virtue. However, the true sage, by contrast, does not manifest his virtue in recognizable form no matter what he looks like—he is truly forgettable.
26. "Is fated" translates *youfen*: one can harm himself only if he tries to shape his person or life in ways foreign to his fated nature.
27. Guo Xiang remains silent here, but Cheng Xuanying elaborates: "Yet you turn your naturally endowed intelligence to distinguish names and analyze principles, stubbornly upholding your own virtue to bedazzle everyone. How is this any different from Master Gongsun Long composing his 'White Horse Discourse' in which he said that a 'white horse' isn't the same as a 'horse' and which he stubbornly insisted on, using it to aggrandize himself. One gave credence to his words but not to the substance of what he said, so he was able to defeat everyone in argument but unable to defeat the way everyone thought. Now, here you are outside your allotted capacity [*fen*] bragging away, so you are just the same as he." *Zhuangzi jishi*, 1: 223.

CHAPTER 6

DA ZONGSHI [THE GREAT EXEMPLARY TEACHER]

6.0 No matter how large Heaven and Earth are or how plentiful are the myriad things, what they all take as model [*zong*] and follow as teacher is done unselfconsciously [*wuxin*].

6.1.1 To know how Heaven acts and how man acts is to reach perfection [*zhi*].

One who knows how Heaven and man act always acts spontaneously [*ziran*]. Therefore, inwardly he lets himself go [*fangshen*] and outwardly he arcanely merges [*ming*] with others, and, once arcanely united [*xuantong*] with everyone, he gives himself over [*ren*] to them and so never fails to reach perfection.

6.1.2 To know how Heaven acts is to live in step with Heaven.

"Heaven" [*tian*] is a way of referring to the natural [*ziran*]. One who tries selfconsciously to act fails to act, for he should do nothing but act spontaneously [*ziwei*]. One who makes selfconscious attempts to know can't know, for he should do nothing but know spontaneously [*zizhi*]. To do nothing but know spontaneously means not to know. By not knowing, knowledge emerges from not knowing. To do nothing but act spontaneously means not to act. Since it is by not acting that action emerges from not acting, not to act is used as one's guiding principle [*zhu*]. Since knowledge emerges from not knowing, not to know is taken as one's model [*zong*]. This is why the authentic man [*zhenren*] knows by discarding knowledge, acts by not acting, lives only spontaneously [*ziran*], and achieves by situating himself in forgetfulness [*zuowang*]. Thus it is that for such a one the term "knowledge" is expelled and the word "action" is eliminated.

6.1.3 When it comes to knowing how man should act, he takes what his knowing knows and uses it to know what he does not know and so lives out

the full span of his years without dying young in mid-course; such is his fullness of knowledge.

For the life of a human being, though his stature be only seven *chi* in height [about 5 feet, 3 inches], the five agents [*wuchang*, metal, wood, water, fire, earth] must all be present in him. Therefore, though he has but this insignificantly small body, it still takes all the resources of Heaven and Earth to provide it. Thus it is for the myriad things of Heaven and Earth: whatever exists can't even for one day do without any of them [the five agents], for were even one agent [*wu*] not present, a living thing would lack the wherewithal to stay alive, and when something does not perfectly realize even one single principle [*li*], it loses the means to fulfill its natural span of years. However, the constituents of the body are either the means of knowing [*zhi*] or not, and the principles [*li*] that inhere in it are either result in action or not. Therefore, what is known to knowing is little though the constituents of the body are legion, and what actions that may result from its acting are few though the principles involved are great in number. No ruler has ever been able to enlist them as useful tools [*qi*] and in that way seek universal sufficiency [*bei*]. What people know is not necessarily the same, but how they act dares not differ, for if they acted differently, it would be a false result—and never has it happened that one may indulge in false results and yet not lose his authenticity [*zhen*]. Some people love knowledge so much that they never tire of straining every part of their bodies to get it, though what they love is nothing more than one branch, had at the expense of the entire root becoming corrupt, which is to use what one knows to harm what one does not know. As for the fullness of knowledge, one should realize that there is an allotted capacity [*fen*] that limits how one should act, and one should allow this to determine what one does and not try to force it. One should also realize that what one can know has limits [*ji*] and when knowledge is put to use, one should not drift beyond those limits. In this way, what one knows does not let a boundless appetite for knowledge bring about its own grief. Therefore, knowing and not knowing then imperceptibly coincide, resulting in perfect wholeness. This is how one uses what one knows to nourish what one does not know.[1]

6.2.1 However, there is still a problem:

Although fullness of knowledge is achieved, this is not as good as discarding knowledge entirely and trusting instead to the problem free workings of Heaven.[2]

6.2.2 When knowledge makes correspondences [*dang*], it does so only thanks to its dependency [*dai*] on something.

Knowledge can never reach the point where it finds nothing to approve, nothing to disapprove [*wuke wubuke*], thus it must always be dependent. But if one lives by trusting to Heaven, it will make correspondences with whatever is encountered.

6.2.3 Such dependency can only be indeterminate.

As soon as dependency exists, indeterminacy [*wuding*] occurs.[3]

6.2.4 And how do I know that when I call Heaven's doing, it is not actually my doing, and what I call my doing, it is not actually Heaven's doing?

That one's life has limits is "Heaven's doing," and when my mind [*xin*] wants to augment it, it is "my doing." However, though this is how I refer to them, nothing ever happens except for "Heaven's doing." "Heaven" is the natural [*ziran*]. Since everything that happens to me happens naturally, whether order or chaos, success or failure, whatever encountered or not encountered, nothing is ever "my doing," for everything that happens only occurs naturally.

6.3.1 Moreover, only with the advent of an authentic man [*zhenren*] will authentic knowledge [*zhenzhi*] prevail.

Only with the advent of an authentic man[4] will what everyone knows achieve such truth, thus rendering the world incapable of disorder.

6.3.2 What is an "authentic man"? 6.3.3 The authentic man of antiquity did not oppose minorities,

Since such a one never opposed any minority, those who placed their hopes in him were legion.

6.3.4 did not use his success to become leader,

Such a one did not depend on his success to take the lead over others.

6.3.5 and did not scheme to recruit the learned [*shi*] to serve his interests.

Giving his mind [*xin*] free play, he went straight ahead, and all the learned gathered to him spontaneously—it was not that he schemed to bring them hither.

6.3.6 Such a one as this neither had to feel regret about mistakes nor feel any sense of self accomplishment about being right [*dang*].

It was simply that since he spontaneously was always perfectly right, he never made mistakes, and he did not belabor his mind [*xin*] about success or failure.[5]

6.3.7 Such a one as this climbed high yet trembled not with fear, entered water yet did not drown, and entered fire yet did not burn. This is what he whose knowledge ascended to the Dao was like.[6]

This describes how one whose knowledge [*zhi*] ascended to the Dao could go so far as this. It was his inherent realization of principle [*li*] that kept himself whole and safe and not his fear of death. Therefore, when the authentic man traveled by land, it was not to avoid drowning; when he kept away from fire, it was not to escape getting burned; and when he kept free from error, it was not to make things right [*cuodang*]. Therefore, though he did not think of getting burned as getting burned, yet he never went through fire; though he did not think of drowning as drowning, yet he never treaded water; and though he did not think of dying as dying, yet he never lost his life. Therefore, as for life, why did he ever have to try to live in order to keep on living! And as for success, why did he ever have to try to be successful in order to achieve success! Therefore, just to let things happen and yet have everything turn out perfectly—such was the authentic man. Why would such a one ever need weigh his thoughts when encountering any situation!

6.4.1 The authentic man of antiquity while sleeping did not dream

He kept himself free of anticipation [*yixiang*].

6.4.2 and while awake was free of worry.[7]

He was equal to the moment of whatever he encountered.

6.4.3 His food was not consciously delicious to him.

According to principle [*li*], it was just that he had to eat.

6.4.4 His breathing was deeper than deep. The authentic man's breathing was done with the heels.

It came from where the very root of his being [*genben*] was located.

6.4.5 The common run of men breathe with their throats, and those who waver and quaver hold their words in the throat as if choking.[8]

Their pneuma [*qi*] does not flow smoothly.

6.4.6 And as for those sunk in sensual desire, their celestial mechanism [*tianji*] is meager.

Only when one has make the root of existence deep and lets quietude extend to its utmost limits [*shengen ningji*] will he recover unity with all things [*fanyi*] and be free from desire [*wuyu*].

6.5.1 The authentic man of antiquity knew neither to love life nor hate death.

Such a one had formed one body [*ti*] with transformation [*ti*].

6.5.2 He felt no elation at being born and when dying he resisted not.

Calm and self-possessed, he just gave himself over [*ren*] to it.

6.5.3 Carefree he went as carefree he came—that was all there was to it.

Since he entrusted [*ji*] himself to the ultimate principle of things [*zhili*], his going and coming was no problem to him.

6.5.4 He neither forgot how he began nor sought how he should end.

Such a one forgot all about the change and transformation [*bianhua*] of both his beginning and his end—how could he, contrary to expectations, just forget about his birth and still keep on trying to understand the meaning of his death![9]

6.5.5. Receiving, he took delight in it.

He questioned not what he was offered, so whatever he encountered always suited [*shi*] him.

6.5.6 Forgetting, he returned to it.

Since returning to it was done unselfconsciously [*buyou yu shi*], it was perfectly done [*zhi*].[10]

6.5.7 This means not using the mind to abandon the Dao and not using man to assist Heaven—which is what it means to be an authentic man.

One is born quiet [*jing*], for this is one's original nature [*xing*] as endowed by Heaven. Stimulated by things, one becomes agitated [*dong*], which is due to the desire [*yu*] in one's nature. Things that stimulate one are infinite in number, so if one pursues one's desires without restraint, one's sense of natural principle [*tianli*] will be ruined. The authentic man understands that to use the mind is to abandon the Dao and that to assist Heaven is to harm life. Therefore he does not do it.

6.6.1 Such a one as this—his mind is determined [*zhi*].

Wherever he finds himself, contentment [*an*] is his goal [*zhi*].[11]

6.6.2 His expression is calm [*ji*].

Although he acts, he never does harm to his quietude [*jing*].

6.6.3 His forehead looks like the great uncarved block [*kui*].

Kui [cheekbones] here indicates the way the great uncarved block [*dapu*] looks.[12]

6.6.4 Chilly like autumn,

He kills not because of power [*wei*].

6.6.5 Warm like spring,

He nourishes life not because of benevolence [*ren*].

6.6.6 His pleasure and anger stay in step [*tong*] with all four seasons.

One who embodies the Dao and stays in step [*he*] with change [*bian*] synchronizes his warmth and severity with the hot and cold seasons—but never does so selfconsciously [*youxin*]. Nevertheless, since he has warm or severe expressions and has occasions when he either nourishes or takes life, he is metaphorically associated with the terms "pleasure" and "anger."

6.6.7 He allows people to live as it suits them [*youyi*], yet no one is ever aware of his infinite capacity to do so.

Since such a one treats people unselfconsciously [*wuxin*], he never robs them of living as it suits their natures [*wuyi*], and since all can live as it suits their natures, no one knows his limits [*ji*].[13,14]

6.7.1 Thus it is that the sage uses military force in such a way that he may destroy states but does not lose the hearts of their inhabitants. He may bestow benefit and favor on ten thousand ages, but does not do so because he loves the people.

He only destroys them because he follows the heartfelt desire of their people that they be destroyed—this is why he does not lose their hearts.[15] Though the bright sun ascends the sky and shines equally in all directions, it does not shine on people because it loves them. Thus it is that the sage takes his place in the world to cast his warmth on it as if he were the natural gentleness of spring sunshine. Therefore, those who enjoy his favor thank him not, and, when he casts his chill on the world as if he were the natural fall of autumn frost, those who wither and fall resent not what he does.

6.7.2 Therefore, one who takes delight in expediting [*tong*] the lives of the people is not a sage.

The sage does not feel delight—it is just that he does not impede anyone, so the people fulfill themselves [*zitong*].

6.7.3 One who feels partiality [*youqin*] is not benevolent [*ren*].

As perfect benevolence [*zhiren*] is free from partiality [*wuqin*], one trusts to principle and lets others spontaneously exist.

6.7.4 One who times himself according to Heaven's moments [*tianshi*] is not a worthy [*xian*].

Timing oneself according to Heaven is inferior to the worthy who forgets all about timing and achieves spontaneous union [*zihe*] with it.[16]

6.7.5 One for whom advantage and harm are not one and the same [*tong*] is not a noble man [*junzi*].

One who can't unify the paths of right and wrong [*shifei*] and instead pursues advantage and avoids harm, damages his virtue [*de*] and depletes his fundamental nature [*dang*].

6.7.6 One who pursues reputation at the loss of self [*ji*] is not a proper person of learning [*shi*].

One who excels at becoming a person of learning achieves self-fulfillment [*zide*] by discarding reputation, and, as a result, his reputation corresponds to who he really is and blessings follow from the nature of his person.

6.7.7 If one lets himself perish and is not authentic [*zhen*], he won't make use of others.

One who discards his own personal nature and in violation of it attaches himself to others is often used by them. How could such a one make use of others!

6.7.8 People such as Hu Buxie, Wu Guang, Bo Yi, Shu Qi, Master Ji, Xuyu, Ji Tuo, and Shentu Di forced themselves to do what served others, suited themselves to what suited others and so did not suit what suited themselves.

They all discarded themselves in devotion to others and harmed themselves by submitting to them.[17]

6.8.1 The authentic man [*zhenren*] of antiquity was such that:

> **His outward signs manifested righteousness [*yi*]**
> **and he formed no cliques.**

He merged his inclinations [*yi*] with those of others but shunned cliques.[18]

6.8.2 He seemed to have less than enough
> **yet did not take.**

His perfect emptiness [*chongxu*] left no room for anything else, thus he seemed to have not enough. He lowered himself so much that none failed to rise, thus, though he seemed to have not enough, he did not take from them.[19]

6.8.3 How carefree and easy he was in his independence,
> **yet he did not cling to it.**

He always roamed freely in independence yet did not cling to it.[20]

6.8.4 How vast his emptiness,
yet he did not show it off.

Only when one is utterly void and free of selfconscious involvement with things [*wuhuai*], shall he realize perfect fullness [*shi*].

6.8.5 How carefree he was as he seemed to be happy!

The Perfected one [*zhiren*] did not experience happiness, but because he was so free from care [*changran*] and in such harmony with things [*heshi*] that he did seem happy.

6.8.6 How absolute [*cui*] he was in circumstances inevitable!

His activity and behavior were always governed by the absolutely inevitable [*biran zhi ji*].[21]

6.8.7 How he brought things together [*chu*] in enhancing [*jin*]
his expression!

He did not harm himself for the sake of others.[22]

6.8.8 How carefree and spontaneous [*yu*] he was in staying
within his own virtue [*de*]!

He had no biases.

6.8.9 How in danger [*li*] he was in being just like the rest of the world!

The Perfected one [*zhiren*] was not in danger [*li*], but because he was just like the rest of the world, he seemed in danger.[23]

6.8.10 How great he was in being unrestrainable!

Noble and bold in action, he achieved self-fulfillment [*zide*].

6.8.11 How much continuity he had while seeming
to like his gate shut.

He was so long-lasting and far-reaching that no one could discern the gate that led to him.

6.8.12 How dispassionate [*men*] he was in neglecting to speak.

Unselfconscious and unaware, his celestial mechanism [*tianji*] bestirred itself; therefore, he was "dispassionate."

6.8.13 He regarded punishment as embodied.

Punishment for him was embodied in governance; it was not something he engaged in personally.

6.8.14 He regarded rites [*li*] as the wings.[24]

Ritual behavior for him was nothing other than what people of the world do spontaneously [*zixing*] and not for him to institute it.

6.8.15 He regarded knowledge as a function of the moment.

Knowledge for him was prompted by the moment; it was not for him to initiate it.

6.8.16 He regarded virtue as a matter of compliance.

Virtue for him proceeded from complying with others; it was not for him to invoke it.

6.8.17 Because he regarded punishments as the body, he was lenient when it came to killing.

Because he let governance itself do the killing, killing was done, but it was done leniently.

6.8.18 Because he regarded rites as the wings, they were commonly practiced in the world.

They complied with the common practices of the world, therefore none failed to practice them.

6.8.19 Because he regarded knowledge as a function of the moment, he applied himself only when it became inevitable.

That the high and the low exchange places is an irreversible course; that the small and the great replace each other among the masses is an inevitable trend. Being utterly void and impartial [*wuqing*], such a one became a storehouse of collective wisdom [*qunzhi*]; being a confluence that receives the flow of all streams, he occupied the very apex of the teachers of men. How did he do this? He gave himself over to the wisdom of the world in his time, complied with the inevitability of circumstances, and accommodated himself to the whole world—nothing other than that!

6.8.20 That he regarded virtue as a matter of compliance meant that he joined with those who achieved satisfaction and in doing so fulfilled [*zhi*] his own limits [*qiu*].

Qiu [hill, an earthen ridge between fields][25] is the reason original nature [*ben*] is what it is. In terms of individual nature [*xing*], it is the basis [*ben*] of individual nature. Each person is satisfied [*zu*] when he is satisfied in terms of his original nature [*ben*]. When such a one lets everyone comply spontaneously with the virtue [*de*] they have, he participates in their satisfaction and so fulfills [*zhi*] his own original nature. When original nature is fulfilled [*zhi*], its principle [*li*] is thus completely realized [*jin*].

6.8.21 Yet people actually thought that he diligently worked at what he did.

All that he did were accomplishments from the point of view of others, but since what he accomplished had nothing to do with himself, although he found himself at the pinnacle of countless matters of administration, he was always so relaxed and comfortable with himself [*zishi*] that, unselfconscious, he was unaware that matters passed through him, dispassionate, he was oblivious to the words in his mouth. However, since people were so greatly deluded, they actually said that the Perfected one [*zhiren*] diligently worked at what he did.

6.8.22 Therefore, what he liked was whole and complete [*yi*], and what he disliked was whole and complete.

Always unselfconscious [*wuxin*], he complied [*shun*] with others; therefore, his liking and disliking, what he found good and what he loathed, were no different from those of others.

6.8.23 His unity [*yi*] was whole and complete [*yi*], and his disunity [*buyi*] was also whole and complete.

His unity was his identification with Heaven, and his disunity was his identification with man. The authentic man regarded Heaven and man as one, other and self as equal, and for him such unity was no different from disunity.[26]

6.8.24 His unity came from his perfect identification with Heaven.

To regard everything without exception as a unity pertains to Heaven.

6.8.25 His disunity came from his perfect identification with man.

To regard the other as other and the self as self pertains to man.

6.8.26 For him Heaven and man were not in contention; this is why he was called an authentic man.

The authentic man regarded both Heaven and man as the same and countless different tendencies [*wanzhi*] as all equal. For him these countless different tendencies did not negate one another and Heaven and man were not in contention; therefore, utterly void, he regarded absolutely everything as one and arcanely united the other with the self [*xuantong biwo*].

6.9.1 That one lives or dies is a matter of fate [*ming*]. That this is as inevitable as day and night is due to Heaven.

That this is as inevitable as day and night is due to the Dao of Heaven. Therefore, we know that whether one lives or dies is set by the limits [*ji*] of fate [*ming*] and does not happen at random [*wang*]. Since their succession is just like that of day and night, what bonds [*xi*] need there be [to life]!

6.9.2 That this is something that people can't cope with is always due to their emotional bias [*qing*].

When the authentic man found himself in daytime, he coped with the day, and when he found himself at night, he coped with the night—how could this have been anything beyond his control! But when people are confronted with what lies beyond their control and find themselves reacting emotionally [*youyu zai huai*] to it, this always happens because of emotional bias—and has nothing to do with the principle involved [*li*].

6.9.3 They regard Heaven in particular as their father and even personally love it, so how much the more should they love that which towers majestically [*zhuo*]![27]

That which *zhuo* [towers majestically] refers to independent transformation [*duhua*]. For effectiveness [*gong*] arising from following [*yin*] nothing is better than the perfection [*zhi*] of independent transformation. Therefore, what man should follow is Heaven, for what Heaven gives rise to is independent transformation. Everyone regards Heaven as father. Therefore, when day and night change places or the seasons shift from cold to hot, none dare despise what happens but follows Heaven and is content with it—so how much the more should one follow independent transformation, which towers majestically! Even if it leads to the land of arcane obscurity [*xuanming*] [death], how could one fail to give oneself over [*ren*] to it! And once one gives oneself over to it, when the change and transformation [*bianhua*] from life to death occur, it is just a matter of obeying fate.

6.9.4 People regard the ruler they have as superior to themselves and even personally die for him, so how much the more should they be willing to do this for the authenticity [*zhen*] he embodies.

Authenticity means not pretending to be something else and thus is what is natural [*ziran*]. One can't possibly spurn what is natural, so how could one just do such a thing simply because his ruler commanded it!

6.10.1 When springs dry up and fish find themselves stranded together on land, they spew moisture on each other and wet each other with foam from their mouths, but it would be better if they could just forget about one another in rivers and lakes.[28]

How could not having enough so that they have to care for each other ever compare to having more than enough so that they can forget each other!

6.10.2 Compared with praising Yao and condemning Jie, it would be better to forget both and follow the transformations of the Dao.

Condemning and praising arise from insufficiency. Therefore, one who has wholly enough, forgets good and bad, discards life and death, and becomes one with change and transformation [*bianhua*]. With perfect magnanimity such a one is perfectly comfortable with absolutely everything, so beyond this why should he heed whether a Yao or a Jie might be in power?

6.10.3 The Great Clod[29] **burdens me with physical form [*xing*], tires me with life, gives me ease with old age, and allows me rest with death.**

Physical form, life, old age, and death—all these are what I am. Therefore, my body is something for me to carry; my life provides the way for me to labor; my old age allows me leisure; and death brings me to an end. Although these four involve change, I never stop being who I am, so why should I have any regrets!

6.11.1 One might hide a boat in a ravine or a mountain in a marsh, and say they are safe.

This is a folk saying that means that one can't escape the changes and transformations of life and death. Therefore, it first cites the most extreme examples of what one might escape with, after which one is supposed to understand that one should conform to [*fu*] inevitable change [*bian*], and by giving oneself over to transformation [*hua*] stay free of attachment.

6.11.2 Nevertheless, in the middle of the night someone strong might shoulder them and run off with them. The stupid don't understand how this happens.

As for the strength of that which is without strength, none is greater than change and transformation [*bianhua*]. Therefore, such strength takes up everything in Heaven and Earth in pursuing the new and carries mountains with it in discarding the old. Never resting for a moment, suddenly new things thus happen, and so it is that the myriad things of Heaven and Earth never cease their transformation. Everyone in the world is continually something new, yet they think of themselves as something old. A boat moves every day, but looking at it, it seems to be just as it was before; a mountain changes every day, but looking at it, it seems to be just as it had been. Now, here is someone who all he can do is fold his arms and suffer their loss, for both are taken from him in the dark. Thus it is that the I who existed before is no longer the I who exists now. Since every such I continually escapes from the present, how can one ever preserve what he used to be! Yet no one in the world understands this but unreasonably says that one can remain attached to what one happens to be in the present and stay the way he is. Is this not stupid!

6.11.3 If one hides something small in something large, though it fits there, it can still slip away.

If one does not understand that he should form one body with transformation [*hua*] and instead thinks that hiding will allow him to escape transformation, though it involves the most secluded and secure places, into which he always manages to fit, this is still no way to prevent change [*bian*] from happening to him every day. Thus it is that hiding to keep oneself intact can't prevent oneself from slipping away. However, when one does not try to hide but instead gives himself over to transformation [*renhua*], change [*bian*] can't change him.

6.11.4 But to hide the world in the world so nothing can slip away is the great truth [*daqing*] of things as they constantly endure [*hengwu*].

With nothing hidden and giving oneself over to everything, such a one neither fails to merge arcanely with things nor becomes one with transformation. Therefore, nothing is outer or inner to him. Free from life and death, he embodies Heaven and Earth and joins in perfect harmony with change and transformation. If one tries to find anything that might slip away from such a one, he can't find it. Such is the great truth [*daqing*] of constant existence [*changcun*]—and not just some small point of the truth [*yiqu*] for the small-minded.[30]

6.11.5 When one happens to take on a human physical form [*xing*], he thus is excessively delighted with it. However, outcomes as good as a human physical form, which are the results of myriads of transformations, are without limit.

A human physical form is nothing more than a single outcome from among myriads of possible transformations, so it is not worth being particularly delighted about. From among this limitlessness [*wuji*], all outcomes are just as good as a human physical form, so why should the human form in particular be cause for delight and anything else not be cause for joy!

6.11.6 And this is cause for joy beyond calculation!

One originally was not a human being and then was transformed into a human being, and, with transformation into a human being, one incurs the loss of the former state of being. It is losing the former state of being that causes one delight—one finds the outcome joyful. Since change and transformation are inexhaustible, is there any outcome that could not occur! And since any outcome would be joyful, how could the joy involved ever come to an end!

6.11.7 Therefore, the sage wanders where things can't slip away and everything is preserved.

The sage wanders along the path of change and transformation and so allows himself go in a current new each day. As the myriad things undergo myriads of transformations, so he undergoes myriads of transformations along with them. Since such transformations are limitless, he too is limitless in step with them—so what could such a one have slip away on him! In life lost so in death preserved—so whenever would such a one not be preserved!

6.11.8 Though such a one but makes the best of early death and makes the best of old age, makes the best of his beginning and makes the best of his ending, people should still emulate him.

This means that one should maintain innate equilibrium [*zijun*] throughout the span of one hundred years, neither making the best of early death nor being negative about old age, for one who does so is neither capable of embodying change and transformation nor regarding life and death as equal. However, for his calmness and simplicity he still is a worthy teacher of men.

6.11.9 So how much the more should they when it is one who bonds with the myriad things and unites with that on which transformation depends.

This is to merge arcanely [*xuantong*] with the myriad things and form one body with transformation. It is for this reason that such a one is venerated as model [*zong*] by the whole world—is this not indeed fitting [*yi*]!

6.12.1 Although the Dao has an innate character and is faithful, it acts unselfconsciously and has no discernible form.

It has predilection [*qing*] free from predilection [*qing*], thus it acts unselfconsciously [*wuwei*]; it has faithfulness free from constancy, and it is without discernible form.[31]

6.12.2 It can be conveyed but not possessed.

People throughout ancient and modern times convey it and so give it temporary lodging, but none are able to acquire it and so possess it.

6.12.3 One can attain it, but it is invisible.

All can internalize [*zirong*] it, but none sees its form.

6.12.4 Self-rooted and taking hold all by itself, it has inherently existed [*gucun*] from time immemorial before there were Heaven and Earth.

This makes it clear that its non-existence [*wu*] does not depend on existence [*you*] for its non-existence [*wu*].

6.12.5 It endows demons [*gui*] and thearchs [*di*] with divinity and begot Heaven and Earth.

Since it is non-existent, how could it cause divinity and birth? It does not endow demons or thearchs with divinity [*shen*], yet demons and thearchs are themselves divine, which means they are divine without being caused to be divine. It did not beget Heaven and Earth, yet Heaven and Earth were born, which means they were born without being caused to be born. Therefore, whereas the result of attempts to make them divine would fail to make them divine, they become divine without being caused to be divine. How could the power it has ever prove enough and how could the effort it makes ever prove reliable enough to accomplish all this!

6.12.6 Beyond the supreme ultimate [*taiji*] is not too high for it; below the absolute reach of the six directions [*liuji*] is not too deep for it.[32] Born before Heaven and Earth, this is not too long a time for it; older than remote antiquity, this is not too old for it.

That is, there is no place where the Dao does not exist. Therefore, any height is not too high for it; any depth is not too deep for it; any duration of time is not too long for it; any age is not too old for it. There is no place where it does not exist, yet wherever it is it is nothing. Moreover, measure every up and down of it, yet one can't say what its height and depth are; visit it everywhere inside and outside, yet one can't put name to what its inside and outside are; as it shifts with each and every transformation, one can't say how long it has endured; as it never had a beginning or ending, one can't say how old it is.

6.12.7 Sire Boar Hide got it and thus supported [*qie*]
Heaven and Earth in his hands.[33]

6.12.8 Fu Xi got it and thus made combinations [*xi*]
from the mother of pneuma [*qimu*].[34]

6.12.9 The Pathfinder Dipper thus got it and
thus forever never erred.[35]

6.12.10 The sun and moon got it and
thus forever never rested.[36]

6.12.11 Kanpi got it and thus entered Kunlun.[37]

6.12.12 Feng Yi got it and thus courses through
the Great River.[38]

6.12.13 Jianwu got it and thus dwelt
on the Great Mountain.[39]

6.12.14 The Yellow Thearch got it and
thus ascended to the cloudy Heavens.[40]

6.12.15 Zhuanxu got it and thus dwelt in the
Black Palace [Xuangong].[41]

6.12.16 Yuqiang got it and thus took a position
at the Extreme North [Beiji].[42]

6.12.17 The Queen Mother of the West [Xi Wang Mu]
got it and thus sits atop Shaguang,
and no one knows her beginning,
no one knows her end.[43]
6.12.18 Pengzu got it and lived from the time of Yu
to the time of the Five Tyrants [Wuba].[44]
6.12.19 Fu Yue got it and thus became minister to Wu Ding,
who then all of a sudden came to possess
the whole world.
Fu Yue then rode the Guardians of the
East [Dongwei] by straddling Ji And Wei [Sagittarius and Scorpio],
and thus joined the ranks of the stars.[45]

The Dao itself has no capability [*neng*]. To say here that they achieved [*de*] it from the Dao is just a way of elucidating that they achieved it spontaneously [*zide*]. They just achieved it spontaneously, and that is all there was to it. The Dao can't make one achieve anything, and what I myself am not up to achieving I can't make myself achieve either. That being so, whatever can be achieved [*de*], externally does not depend on the Dao and internally does not depend on the self [*ji*]. Vacuously one but achieves it spontaneously [*zide*] and in so doing undergoes independent transformation [*duhua*]. As difficult as it is to have existence [*sheng*], nevertheless through independent transformation such existence is spontaneously realized [*zide*]. Once one has achieved existence, why should one any longer worry that it is impossible for such existence to be had through selfconscious effort [*wei*]! Therefore, making selfconscious effort to exist, as one might expect, is an ineffective way to keep one's existence whole and safe because existence is not the result of self effort [*jiwei*], and if one works selfconsciously at it, this will harm one's authentic existence [*zhensheng*].

6.13 Nanbo Zikui[46] asked Woman Loner [Nü Yu], "You are quite advanced in years, yet your complexion seems that of an infant—why is that?"

6.14 She replied, "I have heeded the Dao."

"To have heeded the Dao" means that she gave herself over [*ren*] to self-generation [*zisheng*], and this is why her complexion remains perfect [*quan*].

6.15.1 Nanbo Zikui then asked, "Is the Dao something that can be learned?"

6.16.1 She replied, "Ha! How can it! You are not the man to do it. Whereas Buliang Yi has the talent [*cai*] of a sage but not the Dao of a sage, I have the Dao of a sage but not the talent of a sage.[47] I wanted accordingly to teach it to her, but how could I have hoped that she might really turn out to be anything close to a sage! Nevertheless, since it is easy to teach one who has the talent of a sage about the Dao of a sage, I still persisted in telling her about it, and after three days she was able to put the whole world outside herself.

"To put outside" [*wai*] means "to cast aside" [*yi*].[48]

6.16.2 Once she had put the whole world outside herself, I had her keep at it, and after seven days she was able to put things outside herself.

"Things" means the things one needs from morning to night, with which one is intimately involved and so are hard to forget.

6.16.3 Once she had put things outside herself, I again had her keep at it, and after nine days she was able to put existence [*sheng*] outside her."

That is, she cast everything aside.

6.16.4 Once she has put existence outside her, she could discern with the light of the rising sun.

Once she had cast aside existence, she did not hate death, and since she did not hate death, she was content [*an*] with whatever she encountered. Suddenly free of all obstruction [*wuzhi*], she acted only when she distinguished the incipience of the moment [*ji*]. This is what "discern with the light of the rising sun" [*chaoche*] means.[49]

6.16.5 Once she discerned with the light of the rising sun, she became aware of her perfect independence [*jiandu*].

Content with whatever she encountered, she forgot all relationships in both past and present—as such, she became aware of her perfect independence.

6.16.6 Once she became aware of her perfect independence, she could free herself from past and present.

She ventured forth with her perfect independence intact.

6.16.7 Once free of past and present, she was able to reach the state where one neither lives nor dies.

It is because one is attached to life that one experiences death. Because one hates death, one is conscious of life. Therefore, only after one is free of such attachment and hatred can one be free of life and death.

6.16.8 One who kills[50] life does not die, but one who is conscious of life as life does not live. This is the way one should treat things: never fail to send them off;

Let things send themselves off [*zijiang*], so nothing fails to be sent off.

6.16.9 never fail to welcome them;

Let things welcome themselves, so none fails to be welcomed.[51]

6.16.10 never fail to destroy them;

Let things destroy themselves, so none fails to be destroyed.

6.16.11 never fail to fulfill them.

Let things fulfill themselves [*zicheng*], so none fail to be fulfilled.

6.16.12 The name for this is 'serene in disturbance' [*yingning*]

For one who merges arcanely [*ming*] with things, though when they entangle [*ying*] he surely gets entangled, such a one never fails to be serene.[52]

6.16.13 One serene in disturbance achieves fulfillment [*cheng*] only after such disturbance."

If things entangle but one does not get entangled, he will fail. This is why when entanglement happens, one should let it happen, for then such a one will never fail to achieve complete fulfillment [*qucheng*].[53]

6.17 Nanbo Zikui then said, "Where did you ever hear that?"

6.18.1 She replied, "I heard it from the son 'Ink as Aid' [Fumo].[54] The son 'Ink as Aid' heard it from the grandson 'Repetitive Reciter' [Luosong].[55] The grandson of 'Repetitive Reciter' heard it from 'Seeing Distinct' [Zhanming].[56] 'Seeing Distinct' heard it from 'Whispered Approval' [Niexu].[57] 'Whispered Approval' heard it from 'Must Practice' [Xuyi].[58] 'Must Practice' heard it from 'Singing' [Ou].[59] 'Singing' heard it from 'Arcane Obscurity' [Xuanming].

Arcane Obscurity is a name for that which is nothingness [*wu*] and yet not nothingness.[60]

6.18.2 'Arcane Obscurity' heard it from 'Triple Voidance' [Canliao].

If one attempts to reach nothingness [*wu*] by stepping up to it on terminology [*ming*], he is sure to grasp only what nothingness means from the expression of such terminology. Therefore, although such a one has still failed to attain to the furthest reaches of arcane obscurity, he still has entrusted himself fully to triple intangible—also referred to as the "mystery upon mystery" [*xuan zhi you xuan*].[61]

6.18.3 'Triple Voidance' heard it from 'Distrust Origin' [Yishi]."

The principles [*li*] of Nature are such that sometimes one becomes successful [*cheng*] at them only through accumulated practice [*jixi*], just as one reaches the distance by climbing the near or gets at the fine by grinding the coarse. Thus it is that only after seven layers does one reach the term "nothingness" [*wu*] and only after nine layers does one distrust the assertion that nothingness is the origin [*shi*] of them [the principles of Nature].[62]

6.19 Master Si, Master Yu, Master Li, and Master Lai were all four talking together, when someone said, "Who can regard 'things don't exist' " as the head, life as the backbone, and death as the buttocks? Who understands that life and death, existence and extinction all come to the same thing? I would be his friend."[63] The four looked at each other and smiled. Since no one felt otherwise, they all became friends.

6.20.1 After a while, Master Yu took ill, so Master Si went to inquire how he was.

6.20.2 Master Yu said, "How great the Creator [*zaowuzhe*] is, for it has made me all bent over like this! My back is hunched up so that it sticks out and the acupuncture points for my five viscera are all on top, and my chin is hidden in my navel, so my shoulders are higher than the top of my head, which makes my neck just a bulge pointing up at the sky. It must be that the combination of my yin and yang pneumas [*qi*] is in disharmony [*zhen*]."

Zhen [disrupted flow, disharmony] means "confused" [*lingluan*].

6.20.3 His mind [*xin*] at ease and disengaged [*wushi*],

He did not think it was something to be anxious about.

6.20.4 He dragged himself over to see his reflection in a well, where he said, "What a pity! The Creator [*zaowuzhe*] went on to make me as bent over as this!"

One who gives himself over to natural change is free from self-pity but sighs in pity for things in general.

6.21 Master Si asked, "Do you resent it?"

6.22.1 "Not at all, why should I resent it? If my left arm gradually [*qin*] evolves into a rooster, I shall thus demand of it the hour that ends the night. If my right arm gradually evolves into a crossbow pellet, I shall thus demand of it a dove to roast.[64] If my buttocks gradually evolve into wheels, I shall use my spirit [*shen*] as a horse and thus mount them for a ride—why then should I ever need a carriage again!

Qin [soak] means "gradually" [*jian*]. Since such a one embodies transformation and merges with change, wherever they lead him, he is sure to comply, and wherever such compliance leads, it will suit [*ke*].

6.22.2 Moreover, 'gain' as such happens when the time is right for it,

When just the time for it happens—this the world calls "gain."

6.22.3 and 'loss' as such occurs in compliance [*shun*] with it.

Time never stops even for an instant, so one must comply with its going and just let it go—this the world calls "loss."

6.22.4 Content with my time, I abide in compliance, so neither grief nor joy can intrude on me.[65] This the ancients called 'ties untied.' However, if one can't untie them himself, things will bind him.

Once one fails to untie them himself, everything at once will bind him. Therefore, if one can do the untying, nothing will remain untied, but if he does not do the untying, nothing will ever be untied.

6.22.5 Moreover, people can't get the better of Heaven—this has always been so. Therefore, why should I still feel resentment about it?"

As Heaven can't be without the alteration of day and night, why should I, not free from the alteration of life and death, resent it?

6.23.1 Sometime later, Master Lai took ill, panting rapidly and on the point of death. His wife and children crowded around him and cried out in grief. Master Li, who had gone there to inquire how he was, said, "Hey! Get you gone! Don't upset his transformation [*hua*] with your grieving!"

As life and death are just like wakefulness and sleep, so according to principle [*li*] he should sleep and thus not want people to upset him. That he was about to undergo transformation and die was indeed fitting—there should be no grief over it.

6.23.2 Leaning on the doorway, he addressed Master Lai thus: "How great the Former-and-Transformer [*zaohua*] is! What is he going to make out of you

next? And what path is he going to have you follow? Will he make you into a rat's liver, or will he make you into a bug's arm?"

6.24.1 Master Lai replied, "Parents have such control over a child that whether east or west, north or south, he can only obey when they order him to go there; that being so, can yin and yang have less control over a man than his parents!

Although since ancient times there might have been those who managed to defy the orders of parents, there has never been anyone who has managed to defy change between yin and yang or oppose the rhythm of day and night.

6.24.2 He has brought me unto death, and if I don't obey, that would be brash and unreasonable of me—how could I ever blame him for this!

Life and death, just like day and night, can't be reckoned distant. When the time comes to die, there is no way to resist it. However, if one is perversely minded to disobey, just being this brashly recalcitrant alone will hasten one's death. Such hastened death is all due to the individual's brashness and not something to blame on death. "It" [*bi*] just refers to death. Because the person is still alive, death is thus referred to as "it."[66]

6.24.3 The Great Clod burdens me with physical form [*xing*], tires me with life, gives me ease with old age, and allows me rest with death. Therefore, if I regard my life to be good, for the same reason I should likewise regard my death to be good.

The principle [*li*] is the same for both.

6.24.4 Suppose a great smelter was casting metal, if the metal should jump up and declare 'You must make me into a Moye!'[67] The great smelter would surely think it inauspicious metal. Now suppose for once someone were to take on a physical form—if he were to declare 'Nothing but a man, nothing but a man!' The Former-and-Transformer [*zaohua*] would surely think him an inauspicious man.

"Nothing but a man, nothing but a man!" means that he only wants to be a man—just like the metal jumping up [just wanting to be a Moye]. Everyone knows that metal is inauspiciousness and that it must not be allowed self-transformation [*zihua*].[68] The Dao of change and transformation [*bianhua*] is such that there is no form that one might not happen on. Now, if for once one takes on the physical form of a man, how could that have ever been done deliberately! Life does not happen deliberately but just happens when it is the time is right for self-generation [*zisheng*]. To strive to have life—is that not absurd!

6.24.5 Now I regard Heaven and Earth as a great furnace and the Former-and-Transformer [*zaohua*] as a great smelter, so where could I be sent that would not suit me?

Everyone knows that it is because of its inherent attachments [*xi*] that metal is inauspicious. Therefore, Master Lai clarifies that as he is no different from metal, he had to free himself from bias [*qing*] due to attachments, and thus free nothing would fail to suit him.[69]

6.24.6 So I just peacefully go to sleep,
and wake up pleasantly surprised."

He is completely at ease [*ziruo*] whether awake or sleeping and binds not his mind with thoughts of life and death.[70]

6.25.1 Master Sang Hu,[71] Mengzi Fan, and Master Qinzhang, the three being friends, were talking and someone said, "Who can interact [*xiangyu*] without selfconsciously interacting, care for one another [*xiangwei*] without selfconsciously caring for one another?"

One who embodies Heaven and Earth and arcanely merges [*ming*] with change and transformation [*bianhua*] does so just as hands and feet, with their different functions, and the five viscera, with their different offices, never selfconsciously interact [*xiangyu*], yet all the joints in the body work together harmoniously. This is what "interact without selfconsciously interacting" means. They never help one another yet inner and outer both find succor. This is what "help without helping" means. If one selfconsciously employs one's will to help out one's hands or feet, or works one's thighs or arms to meddle with the five viscera, the more intense such meddling is, the more inner and outer will come to grief. This is why one who regards the entire world as the same single entity [*yiti*] performs no act of sympathy [*aiwei*] for anyone in it.

6.25.2 "Who can climb up to Heaven and wander freely in the mists, circling around at ease in the infinite,

There is nothing that such a one does not give himself over to [*ren*].[72]

6.25.3 and so forget life and nowhere ever reach an end?"

If one forgets life, there is absolutely nothing that such a one fails to forget. Therefore, keeping in step with change [*bian*] and giving oneself over to transformation [*hua*], he is entirely free of any limits [*jing*].

6.25.4 The three looked at each other and laughed, for there was nothing to the contrary in their hearts and minds [*xin*]. Consequently they became friends.

If this is the way that it was, how could they have become friends? It was that, relying on their perfect sagacity and vision, they were free of any close feelings of sympathy [*aiwei*].

6.26.1 In no time at all Master Sang Hu died. Before the burial Confucius heard of it and so sent Zigong to assist with things, where he found the one there weaving a screen[73] while the other played a zither—together they sang this song:

Ah, Sang Hu!
Ah, Sang Hu!
You have already returned to your authentic state
But we still exist as men.

People weep, so they weep too, for this is an outward sign [*ji*] manifested within the common world of men, but they regard life and death as equal [*ji*] and have forgotten joy and sorrow, so in the presence of a corpse they can sing, which is the epitome of other-worldliness [*fangwai*].

6.26.2 Zigong hurried forward and said, "May I presume to ask, does singing in the presence of a corpse indicate propriety [*li*]?"

6.27 The two looked at each other and laughed, then one of them said, "What does this fellow know about the meaning of propriety!"

One who understands the real meaning of propriety must attend to worldly conventions [*jingnei*] only from the perspective of wandering beyond worldly conventions [*youwai*] and by preserving the child by holding fast to the mother.[74] Such a one is equal to his natural inclinations [*chenqing*] and simply goes out and does it. But as for those who take pride in reputation and let themselves be led by form and appearance, for them filial piety [*xiao*] proceeds not out of commitment to sincerity, and paternal compassion [*ci*] proceeds not from honesty, so fathers and sons and older and younger brothers keep their true feelings hidden and bully and deceive one another—what does this have to do with the meaning of propriety in the large sense of the word!

6.28 Zigong returned and told Confucius about this, saying "What kind of people can they be? There is nothing to their moral conduct, and they don't care about their physical appearance. They even sing in the presence of a corpse, with no change in their facial expressions, so there is just no name for them. What kind of people can they be?"

6.29.1 Confucius answered, "They are wanderers beyond the scope of worldly conventions, while I am someone who wanders within the scope of worldly conventions.

When principle realizes absolute perfection, what is beyond worldly conventions and what is within worldly conventions arcanely merge the one into the other. One who wanders with absolute freedom beyond worldly conventions never fails to merge arcanely with what is within worldly conventions, and one who can arcanely merge with what is within worldly conventions never fails to wander beyond worldly conventions. Thus it is that the sage constantly wanders outside worldly conventions so that he may arcanely merge with what is within worldly conventions, unselfconsciously complying with what is there. Therefore, although all day long such a one might employ his physical form in this way or that, his spirit pneuma undergoes no change, and although he might handle a myriad tasks he remains utterly calm and completely at ease. To see his physical form yet fail to reach his spirit is the constant shortcoming of all in the world. Therefore, when they see him just going along with everyone else, they fail to realize that he has cast things aside and detached himself from the human world. When they see him embody transformation and respond to matters, they fail to realize that he abides in forgetfulness and achieves things spontaneously. And why should they merely say that this is not the way a sage is! They surely must also say that this is not the way perfectly realized principle is realized either. Therefore, Master Zhuang's intent here is to cite models that everyone can commonly agree to emulate in order to illustrate his explanation so that the whole world can understand. If he had simply declared that Confucius was like this [i.e., an otherworldly sage], this might be rejected on the evidence of how Confucius had actually appeared. Therefore, Master Zhuang transcended the outward signs that Confucius left behind in the conventional realm and instead used these masters as vehicles to express what "other-worldliness" means. But one should forget the vehicles involved so the better to get at the main message of the narrative, for then the Dao as it bears on wandering beyond the scope of worldly conventions, while arcanely merging with it, becomes abundantly clear. Herein surely lies the reason why the book of Master Zhuang, though involved with the common and vulgar, is praised as the best expository work of its age.

6.29.2 Without and within don't mix, yet I sent you there to take part in the mourning—I must have been simple-minded!

Mourning is a familiar practice within the realm of worldly conventions, so trying to extend it to those beyond the realm of worldly conventions would indeed be simple-minded.

6.29.3 As men who will join with the Creator [*zaowuzhe*] they now wander about in the primal and unitary pneuma of Heaven and Earth.

They have both arcanely merged [*ming*] them,[75] so no dualistic distinctions [*wuer*] exist between them.

6.29.4 They regard life as an appended tumor or as an attached pimple,

It is like a pimple which attaches itself or a tumor which appends itself—it is a temporary coalescence [*ju*] of pneuma [*qi*] and nothing to be happy about.

6.29.5 And death as a ruptured swelling or a burst boil.

Like a swelling which self-ruptures or a carbuncle which bursts all on its own—it is a self-dispersal of pneuma and nothing to regret.

6.29.6 Since this is the way they are, why should they care anything about in which the better or the worse is located, life or death?

Life and death supersede one another without ever any end to it. If one just goes along together with them, anything can happen, so why should one care about which is better and which worse?

6.29.7 They may avail themselves of different things but lodge themselves in the same all-inclusive body.

Jia [borrow, avail of] means *yin* [avail of, rely on]. Now, change and transformation [*bianhua*] associated with the coalescence and dispersal attendant on life and death, being boundless [*wufang*], always keeps resulting in different things, so nothing different fails to avail itself of something. Therefore, although that which things avail themselves of differ, all together they form one body.[76]

6.29.8 They forget their liver and gall and cast aside their ears and eyes,

Giving themselves over to principle, they arcanely set forth [*mingwang*].

6.29.9 and go to and fro from beginnings to ends, unaware of when these begin or end [*duanni*].

Since they had forgotten their own five viscera, whatever else could possibly warrant their selfconscious attention [*shi*]? Because they never had been selfconsciously aware of anything, this gave them complete freedom [*fangren*] on the path of change and transformation [*bianhua*], allowing them to merge arcanely [*xuantong*] with them as they undulate back and forth, unaware of when they begin or end.[77]

6.29.10 Far and wide they leisurely wander beyond the dust and dirt, spontaneous and free [*xiaoyao*] as they engage in unselfconscious action [*wuwei*].

What is referred to here as "engage in unselfconscious action" does not mean that they do nothing more than just clap their hands together and keep silent, and "beyond the dust and dirt" does not mean that they hide themselves away in mountain forests.

6.29.11 Furthermore, how could they be so muddleheaded as to get involved with such commonplace propriety as this and in so doing make a spectacle of themselves for the eyes and ears of the mass of ordinary people!"

That which becomes a spectacle for the mass of ordinary people is never anything other than dust and dirt of the common world, which has nothing to do with the arcane merging with things that takes place beyond the realm of worldly conventions.

6.30 Zigong then asked, "If this is the case, what is the method [*fang*], Master, that you are an adherent of?"

Zigong had never had original nature [*xing*] and the Dao of Heaven explained to him, so he just sees that he [*Confucius*] is an adherent but does not see how he goes about adhering. The way he goes about adhering it is to remain free of adherence—but how could the vulgar world ever appreciate this!

6.31.1 Confucius replied, "I am just someone punished by Heaven,

The fact that he regards the realm of worldly conventions as shackles makes it clear that what he esteems lies beyond worldly conventions. As one who wanders freely beyond worldly conventions he still adheres to what lies within them, and as one who abandons humankind he still conforms to vulgar custom. This is the reason why one who possesses the world has no use for it, why it is only after one has cast people aside that one can participate in human society, why it is only after one abides in forgetfulness that one can respond properly to the demand of duties. The more one casts things aside, the more one is successful at them. But as he resides within these limits [*ji*],[78] even though he might wish to escape them, the principle [*li*] involved will always spontaneously apply, for it is something that neither Heaven nor man can have waived.[79]

6.31.2 but even so I shall share this with you."

"Although I am shackled by worldly concerns, I am simply going to share this with you." This clearly indicates that he always located himself beyond the realm of worldly conventions.[80]

6.32 Zigong replied, "May I be so bold as to ask what method [*fang*] may do this?"

He asks what it means to be able to wander at ease beyond the realm of worldly conventions and yet shares in worldly conventions.

6.33.1 Confucius said, "As fish do best for themselves in water, so men do best for themselves in the Dao.[81] Those that do best for themselves in water make their way through ponds and so find sufficient sustenance; those who do best for themselves in the Dao remain disengaged [*wushi*] and so find tranquility [*ding*] of life.

Although "to do best" here differs, it is through disengagement [*wushi*] that success is had [*deshi*] and it is through other-worldliness [*fangwai*] that one takes part in worldly conventions, for only then does one have sufficient sustenance, and with it tranquility [*ding*] of life—this without exception is the same for all. It is because none are themselves aware of it that all are capable of unselfconscious action [*wuwei*].

6.33.2 Thus it is said that as fish forget one another in rivers and lakes, so men forget one another in the techniques of the Dao [*daoshu*]."

That each is self-sufficient [*zizu*] and so forgets one another is so for all in the world without exception. It is because the Perfected one [*zhiren*] is always self-sufficient that he always so forgets.

6.34 Zigong then asked, "May I be so bold as to ask about the eccentric individual [*jiren*]?"

His question is concerned with what is referred to as someone who has nothing to do with common custom since he lives beyond worldly conventions, so in what does his way consist?

6.35.1 Confucius replied, "The eccentric individual is at odds with people but one with Heaven.

One who merges arcanely [*ming*] with worldly conventions wanders at ease beyond worldly conventions. It is only because he can wander freely beyond worldly conventions that he merges arcanely with worldly conventions, and, as such, he lets everyone behave naturally [*ziran*] so that the inherent nature [*tianxing*] of each is fulfilled and the Dao of true rulership [*diwang dao*] is perfectly realized [*cheng*]. This is what it means to be "at odds with people but one with Heaven."

6.35.2 Thus it is said that the petty man [*xiaoren*] of Heaven is a noble man [*junzi*] among men and that the noble man among men is a petty man of Heaven."

Speaking in terms of the natural [*ziran*], no man is petty or noble, but in terms of the principles of human behavior [*renli*], only one who is one with Heaven may be called a "noble man."

6.36 Yan Hui asked Confucius, "As for Mengsun Cai,[82] when his mother died, he wailed but shed no tears, felt no heartfelt grief, and mourned her with no appearance of sadness. Though deficient in these three ways, he had the very best reputation in all of Lu for the way he mourned. Did he really gain this reputation without actually doing anything to warrant it? I certainly find this strange!"

Whereas those in the state of Lu observed his attention to ritual, Yan Hui examined his state of mind.

6.37.1 Confucius replied, "Master Mengsun did everything and had actually progressed beyond selfconscious awareness of it!

He completely realized [*jin*] the principles of dealing with life and death and brought into resonance [*ying*] what was suitable [*yi*] for both beyond worldly conventions and within them. When he acted, he moved in step with Heaven [*tianxing*] and was not married to selfconscious understanding [*zhi*].

6.37.2 Even if he tried to choose between them, he could not,

Had he the choice between life or death, he would not find any difference between them since they are like spring or autumn, winter or summer in the progress of the four seasons.[83]

6.37.3 for a choice had already been made. Master Mengsun was unconcerned why he lived or why he would die.

As the choice had already been made, of which he was incapable, nothing failed to make him content [*an*], and since nothing failed to make him content, he did not burden his self-transformation [*zihua*] with concerns of life and death.[84]

6.37.4 He was unconcerned about reaching either what was before him or the hereafter.

Whatever he encountered left him content.

6.37.5 He complied with transformation [*hua*] and became the thing he should.

He did not go against transformation.

6.37.6 As such, he just awaited the unknown transformation that was in store for him—that's all there was to it!

Through all the twists and turns of life and death he remained one with transformation. Since he had forgotten about what he knew about the present, why should he have any worries beforehand while waiting for the yet unknown!

6.37.7 Moreover, since just for the time being transformation had occurred, how can he know about the state he was in before that transformation had happened? And now for the time being before transformation occurs how can he know about the state he will be in after that transformation happens?

Having undergone the transformation that brought him life, how could he know about the state he was in before he was born? And before undergoing the transformation that would bring him death, how could he know about the state he would be in after death? Therefore, as there was nothing he tried to avoid, he went forward in step with transformation.

6.37.8 You and I simply have never awoken from this dream of ours,

Life and death are just like being awake and being in dream. Now while in dream one thinks he is awake, so there is nothing then to verify that this being awake is not actually dreaming. If there is no way to verify that being awake is not a dream, then there is also no way to verify that being alive is not actually being dead. Since it is impossible to know where one is, whether in life or in death, or whether awake or dreaming, whatever one encounters, one should never fail to be open to spontaneous receptivity [*zide*]—so why should one worry about what will happen in the other state while still here in this state!

6.37.9 Moreover, although he suffered shock to the body, no harm came to his mind.

Change and transformation are nothing more than a shock to the physical body, so he did not let thoughts of life and death harm or bind his mind.

6.37.10 Although he had a temporary lodging, he was dispassionate [*wuqing*] toward death.

He thought the change that the physical body undergoes does nothing more than provide a new temporary lodging—as if it were something changed each day. His innate character [*qing*] was such that he did not regard this as death.

6.37.11 Mengsun alone was awake, so when people wailed, he too wailed—it was because of this that he behaved so.

As he was always awake, he never took exception to whatever there was to do, which is why when people wailed he also wailed. It was in just this way that he accommodated himself to others.

6.37.12 Moreover, his 'I' was there in both states alike.

In the change and transformation that life and death undergo, his "I" was always there as an "I," and since he was always there as an "I," how could his "I" ever be lost? And since his "I" was never lost, why should his "I" ever feel grief? Thus it was that since he never took exception to anything, when people wailed, he wailed, and since he never grieved, he could wail yet be not sad.

6.37.13 But why should he care about what I mean by "his 'I' was there?

Since there was no state in which he was not an "I," he could arcanely unite [*xuantong*] inner and outer, perfectly merge [*miguan*] past and present, and stay in step with transformation [*hua*] as he became something new each day—so why should he have ever cared where his "I" was located![85]

6.37.14 And then one might dream that he is a bird that darts through the sky, or dream that he is a fish swimming freely in the depths.

That is, in everything one might do, self-fulfillment [*zide*] is achieved.

6.37.15 But who knows when one talks about such things whether one is awake or dreaming.

Since when one is dreaming one thinks he is awake, how can one know that he is not now actually dreaming? And so in the same way, how can one know that he is not now actually awake? When being awake is transformed into dreaming, whatever happens always turns out all right, so when change takes place from life to death, it is not worth feeling grief over.

6.37.16 Realizing suitability is not as good as a good laugh, and giving a good laugh is not as good as just going along with things.

Once what one realizes [*zao*] always proves suitable [*shi*], one can forget all about suitability—but this still is not as good as a good laugh. *Pai* [follow in order] should be read as *paiyi* [go along with]. When propriety [*li*] demands wailing, one must wail, and when one gives a good laugh, one must be happy, but when sadness and happiness are harbored in one's bosom, such a one can't just go along with what is suitable. Now here is Mengsun who suits every occasion, thus he wails while not being sad, for he always stays perfectly in step with transformation.

6.37.17 Content with just going along with things and so proceeding in step with transformation, one thus joins in oneness with intangible nature [*liaotian*]."

Content with going along with things [*tuiyi*] and so proceeding in step with transformation, one thus assimilates himself into what is without physical form or substance [*jiliao*][86] and becomes one with nature [*tian*]. From here back to the appearance above of Master Si, the text consistently addresses the same issue. It is just because those involved handled mourning in different ways that they changed between singing and wailing.

6.38 When Master Yier went to see Xu You, Xu You said, "What did Yao give you for assistance [*zi*]?"

Zi means to give help.

6.39 Master Yier replied, "Yao said to me, 'You must personally practice benevolence [*ren*] and righteousness [*yi*] and clearly differentiate right from wrong."

6.40 Xu You then said, "So what are you doing coming to see me? Since Yao has already tattooed you with benevolence and righteousness and cut off your nose with right and wrong, how are you going to roam about on the road that allows you utter freedom to wander freely as you might!"

This means that he is going to ruin himself with punishments and moral teachings and thus never again be capable of roaming in the realm of self-fulfillment [*zide*] on the road that frees one from all attachments [*xi*].

6.41 Master Yier said, "Nevertheless, I would still like to wander along the edges of this realm."

He dares not try again to take up the way through its center and wants nothing more than to try to wander along the margins of this realm.

6.42 Xu You replied, "That's ridiculous! The blind have no means to relate to the allure in a face with beautiful features, and the sightless have no means to relate to the way colorful embroidery looks."

6.43.1 Master Yier then said, "But there was Wuzhuang who lost her sense of beauty, Juliang who lost his sense of strength, and the Yellow Thearch who forgot all about his wisdom—all this due to nothing other than their undergoing smelting and forging.

That is, everything in the world does not necessarily have to fulfill itself [*zicheng*], for it is also a natural principle that some must undergo smelting and forging before they realize their capacity [*qi*]. Therefore, it was only after these three had heard the Dao that they forgot all about what they were striving to achieve [*wu*]. All this is a metaphor for discarding bondage [*lei*] to what one would do.

6.43.2 So how do you know that the Creator [*zaowuzhe*] won't remove my tattoo and mend my nose, thus allowing me to ride upon my realizable potential [*cheng*] and follow you, sir?"

To follow one's original nature [*xing*] and just straightaway set about doing things is to be natural [*ziran*]. But when one has been doing things so that it harms one's original nature, even with one's original nature thus harmed, if one can reform, this too is to be natural. "How do you know that my natural endowment [*ziran*] is such that my tattoo can't be removed and my nose not repaired, so I can ride on the Dao as it bears on realizable potential and follow you master? Instead, you want to reject me and tell me nothing—I fear that you are not an epitome [*zhi*] of the Creator.

6.44.1 Xu You replied, "Ah! That remains to be seen, but I shall tell you about the general gist of it anyway. Oh, this teacher of mine. Oh, this teacher of mine.[87] When it crushes the myriad things it does so not from a sense of moral justice [*yi*]; when it extends favor and grace to a myriad ages it does so not out of a sense of benevolence [*ren*].

In both cases it just acts spontaneously [*zier*], and since there is no emotional attachment [*ai*] in all this, what role is there for benevolence or moral justice?

6.44.2 Though older than remote antiquity, it is not old.

It is renewed each day.

6.44.3 It covers and carries Heaven and Earth and carves the forms of everything yet is not skilled [*qiao*].[88]

It is spontaneous [*ziran*], so no skill is involved.

6.44.4 It is only in this that I wander."

He wanders in unintentionality [*buwei*] so finds a teacher where no teacher exists.

6.45 Yan Hui said, "I am gaining."

He regards his loss as gain.[89]

6.46 Confucius then said, "What do you mean?"
6.47 Hui replied, "I have forgotten all about benevolence [*ren*] and righteousness [*yi*]."
6.48 Confucius then responded, "That's good, but you still haven't gone far enough."

Benevolence [*ren*] is the outward sign/footprints [*ji*] of universal love [*jian'ai*], and righteousness [*yi*] is the outward manifestation [*gong*] of people being fulfilled [*cheng*]. Love does not depend on benevolence, for benevolence just consists of the footprints [*ji*] that are made by it [love]. Fulfillment does not depend on righteousness, for righteousness is but the outward manifestation in which it [fulfillment] appears. If one is focused on benevolence and righteousness, he won't be up to realizing that love and benefit [*li*] come unselfconsciously [*wuxin*]. Therefore, to forget all about them is a good thing, but Yan Hui has still only forgotten about their outward manifestations, and thus he still fell short of arcane understanding [*xuanda*].

6.49 Another day Yan Hui again went to see him, and he said, "I am gaining."
6.50 Confucius asked, ""What do you mean?"
6.51 Hui replied, "I have forgotten all about ritual [*li*] and music [*yue*]."
6.52 Confucius then said, "That's good, but you still haven't gone far enough."

Ritual is the means [*yong*] to shape physical comportment, and music is a devise to bring joy to life. To forget all about these devices is not as good as forgetting about the underlying reasons why these devices exist.

6.53 On yet another day Yan Hui again went to see him, and he said, "I am gaining."
6.54 Confucius asked him, "What do you mean?"
6.55 Hui replied, "I sit in forgetfulness."
6.56 Startled, Confucius said, "What do you mean by 'sit in forgetfulness'?"
6.57 Yan Hui replied, "I discard my limbs and trunk and banish intelligence [*congming*]. Separate from my physical body and with awareness cast out, I become one with the great thoroughfare [*datong*]. This is what I mean by 'sit in forgetfulness.' "

In sitting in forgetfulness what is not forgotten! He forgot both the footprints he had made and what had made them [*suoyi ji*]. Once inwardly [*nei*] he lost selfconsciousness of his entire body and outwardly [*wai*] no longer had any awareness of Heaven and Earth, he became so utterly expansive that he formed one body with change and transformation [*yu bianhua wei ti*] and integrated [*tong*] perfectly with everything.

6.58.1 Confucius said, "Since you have become one with everything, you must be free of preference,

Since he has become one with absolutely everything, nothing ever fails to be suitable [*shi*], and since nothing ever fails to be suitable, how could he have had any preferences or dislikes!

6.58.2 and since you are perfectly in step with transformation, you have no constant state [*chang*].

Since he was perfectly in step with transformation, it was with transformation that he conformed [*shi*], thus he had no constant state.

6.58.3 So you certainly are a worthy! I request that I be allowed to become your follower."

6.59.1 Master Yu and Master Sang[90] were friends. Once when it had been raining incessantly for ten days, Master Yu said, "Master Sang is probably ill with hunger" and, wrapping up some cooked rice, took it for him to eat.

These two took care of one another without selfconsciously taking care of one another [*xiangwei*]. That the one now wrapped up cooked rice to take care of the other was a matter of giving himself over [*ren*] to the natural principle [*tianli*] involved and just acting spontaneously [*zier*]; it was not a matter of going to him only after he had selfconsciously thought to take care of him.

6.59.2 When he arrived at Master Sang's gate, it seemed he was either wailing or singing as he played a zither:

> **Was it Father?**
> **Was it Mother?**
> **Was it Heaven?**
> **Was it Man?**

As if he could not bear the sound of it and was rushing through the words.

6.60 When Master Yu entered, he asked, "This song you are singing, why do it like this?"

He suspected there was some emotional bias [*qing*] to it, so he sought out what distant principle [*li*] might have prompted it.

6.61 Master Sang replied, "I was thinking about what had made me finish up as bad as this but could not figure it out. How could my mother and father have wished me this poor? Heaven impartially covers all, and Earth impartially carries all, so how could Heaven or Earth have wished me this poor? I was trying to figure out what had made me so but could not do so. However, since I did finish up as bad as this it must be fate [*ming*].

He means that everything follows the way of nature [*ziran*] and so it was done unselfconsciously [*wuwei*].

Notes

1. Cheng Xuanying: "'How man should act' refers to how each of the four limbs and all the other parts of the body has its own function. 'What is known to knowing' refers, for example, to the eye gaining knowledge of the phenomenal appearance of things [*se*],

which means that it is the phenomenal appearance of things that is known to it. 'What isn't known to knowing' refers to how the eye can know the phenomenal appearance of things but can't know sound, which means that it is sound that isn't known to it. Consequently, the eyes see on behalf of the hands and feet, and the feet provide movement on behalf of the ears and nose. Even though these interact [*xiangwei*] unselfconsciously [*wuxin*], they each facilitate the success of the other. Therefore, the eyes, ears, nose, and tongue as well as the four limbs and all the other parts of the body may take turns enlisting each other's services, but each remains in control of itself. Whether intelligent or stupid, the mind too has its limits, so one should employ it only within the limits allotted to it and never try to force it to know more." *Zhuangzi jishi*, 1: 225.

2. Cheng Xuanying interprets Guo's comment to mean that one should "give oneself over to spontaneity" [*rendu*]. *Zhuangzi jishi*, 1: 226.
3. Cheng Xuanying: "Knowledge must adjust itself to external conditions [*jing*], for without external conditions correspondences don't occur. But since the continued existence or disappearance of external conditions is indeterminate, knowledge also has to depend on seizing something inconstant. Only when external conditions and knowledge are both forgotten and subject and object [*nengsuo*] are both banished, can one reach the point where there is nothing to approve, nothing to disapprove, and only after that will he become problem free." *Zhuangzi jishi*, 1: 226.
4. Cheng Xuanying glosses true man [*zhenren*] as sage [*shengren*]. *Zhuangzi jishi*, 1: 226.
5. At first glance, the statement in the *Zhuangzi* seems to mean: "Such a one when making mistakes felt no regret, and when right felt no sense of self-accomplishment," but Guo Xiang, alert to the overall assertion in the *Zhuangzi* that the sage, always perfectly in step with the moment and perfectly attuned to the situation, never makes mistakes, insists on reading it differently. Cheng Xuanying also rejects the ostensible meaning and attempts to explain it in yet another way: "Though Heaven's moment [*tianshi*] might have already past, his mind [*xin*] never felt regret, and when fate [*fenming*] by chance made him equal to the moment [*dang*], he never regarded it as self-accomplishment worthy of praise." *Zhuangzi jishi*, 1: 226. Other traditional commentators, as well as modern translators, usually ignore this problem and interpret the statement in its ostensible sense.
6. Cf. 1.13.5.
7. Cf. 15.4.17.
8. The reading here follows Cheng Xuanying; see *Zhuangzi jishi*, 1: 228.
9. Cheng Xuanying: "*Shi* [beginning] means birth, and *zhong* [end] means death. Since he had discarded all concern for both birth and death, he was never encumbered by either. So how could he exclusively forget about his birth and on the contrary seek to find out about his death? His beginning and his end meant exactly the same thing to him, so whatever happened to him he found fitting [*shi*]." *Zhuangzi jishi*, 1: 230.
10. Cheng Xuanying: "He returned to not having yet been born." *Zhuangzi jishi*, 1: 230.
11. Cheng Xuanying: "If one has such a mind as stated above, one that does not abandon the Dao, this state of mind [*xinhuai*] has such power of will [*zhili*] that is can reach perfection [*zhi*]. As it is said in the classic of Master Lao, 'one who acts with power has his goal fulfilled.'" *Zhuangzi jishi*, 1: 231. See also *Laozi*, section 33; Richard John Lynn, *The Classic of the Way and Virtue*, 111. Modern commentators and translators usually follow the tradition of commentary that begins with Lu Deming, who reads *zhi*, "determined," as a scribal error for *wang*, "forget."
12. Although Guo and Cheng both gloss *kui* here as the look of the great uncarved block, later in chapter 13, *Tiandao* [The Dao of Heaven], where Master Lao castigates

Shi Chengqi for his arrogant look, including his forehead with its *kuiran [kui*-like] appearance, Guo glosses *kuiran* as "high and handsome," and Cheng glosses it as "high and magnificent." *Zhuangzi jishi*, 2: 458. For these two commentators, at least, *kui* can have both positive and negative connotations: the sage's forehead is broad and plain—perhaps because it has no wrinkles of worry—but the forehead of this failure at sagehood might be magnificent, but it only expresses arrogance.

13. Cf. 24.66.8.
14. Cheng Xuanying uses Buddhist terms to describe the Daoist sage: "The true man resonates with the world in such a way that his response stays in step with it. When he interacts with people, he is sure to accommodate himself to what suits them. However, with his empty mind [*xuxin*] and compassionate love [*ciai*], he always excels at saving people. Because his capacity is as large as the Great Void [Taixu], no one knows his limits." *Zhuangzi jishi*, 1: 232.
15. Cheng Xuanying: "When Yao attacked the Congzhi, Yu attacked the Youfu, Cheng Tang destroyed Xia, and King Wu of Zhou attacked Yin, all of them acted in step with the moment of Heaven above and conformed to the way human affairs were situated below. Accordingly, they rose up in arms, consoled their people and condemned the crimes of their rulers. Therefore, even though they destroyed the states involved, they did not lose the good will and support of their people." *Zhuangzi jishi*, 1: 232.
16. Cheng Xuanying: "To divine the waxing and waning of the arcane images [sun, moon, and stars] to time the comings and goings of Heaven's moments is but trivial knowledge—how could these signify a great worthy!" *Zhuangzi jishi*, 1: 233. Cf. *Yijing* (Classic of Changes), *Wenyan* (Commentary on the words of the text) to Qian (Pure Yang, hexagram 1): "The great one is someone whose virtue is consonant with Heaven and Earth, his brightness with the sun and moon, his consistency with the four seasons, and his prognostications of the auspicious and inauspicious with the workings of gods and spirits. When he precedes Heaven, Heaven isn't contrary to him, and when he follows Heaven, he obeys the timing of its moments." Richard John Lynn, *The Classic of Changes*, 138.
17. Cheng Xuanying: "Surnamed Hu with courtesy name Buxie, he was a worthy of antiquity; it is also said that he was a worthy at the time of Yao, who would not accept Yao's abdication and so threw himself into the Yellow River and drowned. Wu Guang, who lived at the time of the Yellow Thearch, was seven *chi* in height [about 5 feet, 3 inches]; it is also said that he lived during the Xia dynasty, ingested potions to nourish his nature, and liked to play the zither. When Tang tried to abdicate in his favor, he would not accept it and so weighed himself down with stone and drowned himself in the Lu River. Bo Yi and Shu Qi were the two sons of Lord Guzhu of Liao West, a descendent of Shennong (The Divine Farmer) of the surname Jiang. When their father died, the two brothers mutually gave way, neither willing to succeed to the title. When they heard that the Earl of the West [later King Wen of Zhou] had the Dao, they went there to see if this were true. It so happened that it was then that King Wen died and King Wu was going to attack King Zhou [of the Shang]. Bo Yi and Shu Qi held back his horses and tried to dissuade him from doing so, but King Wu would not agree. They thereupon became hermits on Shouyang Mountain in Hedong, where, unwilling to eat the grain of Zhou, they ended up hungry and so died. Master Ji was the worthy minister of King Zhou of the Yin [Shang], who admonished Zhou to change his ways, but Zhou would not listen, so he met with a slave's death. Xuyu was the given name of Master Ji. However, this name is also explained as that of the son of Grand Master Wu She [died 522 BCE] of the state of Chu, whose given name was Yun and whose courtesy name was

Xuyu. He was the minister of King Fuchai of Wu [ruled 495–473 BCE], who would not heed his loyal admonitions, so he had his eyes gouged out and died, his corpse sunk in the Yellow River. Ji Tuo was surnamed Ji, and his given name was Tuo. He was a hermit at the time of King Tang, who when he had heard that Tang had tried to abdicate in favor of Wu Guang, afraid that he would be next, took his disciples and they all threw themselves into the Kuan River and drowned. When Shentu Di heard of this, he threw himself into the Yellow River for the same reason. All of these masters violated their natures and acted falsely. Obstinately determined to establish reputations for themselves, they raised themselves to such an extraordinary pitch that they finished up like this. Starving themselves, drowning themselves, they brought about their early deaths, yet their good names and fine reputations are handed down in history books. Since this was all due to their having been prompted by others, how could they ever make use of them! They may have brought delight to the eyes and ears of others, but how could they have ever suited their own temperaments [*qingxiang*]?" *Zhuangzi jishi*, 1: 233–34.

18. Cheng Xuanying: "*Zhuang* [outward signs] means *ji* [outward signs]; *yi* [righteousness] means *yi* [inclination, what is suitable]. The outward signs that he left behind fit in perfectly with the whole world, since he accommodated himself to the inclinations [*yi*] of others. Moreover, emptying himself [*xuji*] and evenly balanced, he never forms biased associations." *Zhuangzi jishi*, 1: 235.
19. "Left no room for anything else" translates *wuyu* (free of excess, literally "free of having more than enough"); cf. the *Laozi*, section 77: "The Dao of Heaven is it not like when a bow is pulled? As the high end gets pulled down, the low end gets pulled up: so those who have more than enough are diminished, and those who have less than enough get augmented." Lynn, *The Classic of the Way and Virtue*, 185.
20. Cheng Xuanying: "*Gu* [goblet; writing tablet] should be read as *du* [independence] and *jian* [firm; to persist] as *gu* [obstinate]. Carefree and spontaneous, self-fulfilled [*zide*] without restraint [*rongyu*], such a one roamed freely about in the field of independent transformation [*duhua*] yet did not cling to it." *Zhuangzi jishi*, 1: 235. "How carefree and easy" translates *yuhu*, the *yu* of which, as the common function word "with, and," and so on, makes no sense, so Cheng seems to think that *yu* is an abbreviation for *rongyu* [without restraint], which does seem likely. For other explanations, see *Zhuangzi jishi*, 1: 235–36.
21. Guo Xiang does not explain *cui*, here translated as "absolute," but from the rest of his comment, he seems to equate *cui* with *ji* [extremity] in the phrase *biran zhi ji* [the absolutely inevitable]. *Cui*, literally "the lofty reaches of a mountain," does equate with "extremity" or the "absolute" limits of something, which is what Guo seems to mean here: the way that the authentic man responds to the absolute demands of the inevitable. By contrast, Cheng Xuanying glosses *cui* as *dong* [dynamic], probably following Xiang Xiu, which would result in "How dynamic he was when. . . ." *Zhuangzi jishi*, 1: 236.
22. Cheng Xuanying: "*Chu* [bring things together] means *ju* (gather); *jin* [enhance, literally "advance"] means *yi* [augment]. Since his mind [*xin*] is like still water, he can thus gather in it all living things [*qunsheng*] [i.e., reflect all things perfectly, as in a mirror]. Therefore, he responded to things impartially [*wuqing*], was kind without any expenditure of self, did what suited himself, did what augmented himself, and so his expression never deteriorated." *Zhuangzi jishi*, 1: 236.
23. Cf. The *Classic of Changes*, hexagram 1 (Qian, Perfect Yang), Third Yang: "The noble man makes earnest efforts throughout the day, and with evening he still takes care; though [seemingly] in danger [*li*], he will suffer no blame." Lynn, *The Classic of Changes*, 134.

Cheng Xuanying seems to have had this passage in mind when he comments: "*Li* [most common meaning "harsh"] means *wei* [in danger]. The authentic man [*zhenren*] is one with safety or danger, merges with disaster or good fortune, and 'merges with the brilliant and becomes on with the very dust,' so as such seems in danger, just like when Confucius got into difficulties with the people of Kuang or when King Wen was imprisoned in Youli. Although they were in danger, they did not neglect to address their situations with unselfconscious action [*wuwei*]." *Zhuangzi jishi*, 1: 237. The embedded quotation is from *Laozi*, 4; Lynn, *The Classic of the Way and Virtue*, 57.

24. "Wings" indicates supplementary institutions—secondary to punishments—specifically rites and music, which mold civil behavior.
25. Guo Xiang seems to have read *qiu* [hill] in the derived meaning of an earthen ridge between fields. Since such ridges define the boundaries of a field, *qiu* as such defines the bounds or limits of one's original nature [*ben*].
26. Cheng Xuanying: "His unity involved sagely wisdom [*shengzhi*]; his disunity involved all common human tendencies [*fanqing*]. Consequently, because the common and the sagely differed not with him, disunity was always a unity." *Zhuangzi jishi*, 1: 240.
27. Guo Xiang seems to have read into the passage an allusion to the *Analects*: "I [Yan Yuan] want to desist but can't, and when I have utterly exhausted my capacity, it still seems that there is something there, towering up majestically [*zhuoer*], and though I want to go toward it, there is no path to follow." Translation by E. Bruce Brooks and A. Taeko Brooks, *The Original Analects: Sayings of Confucius and His Successors*, 53; *Lunyu* (Analects), 9: 2490c. That is, the Dao of Heaven is everywhere present, majestically obvious, but there is no way to grasp it intellectually, and the abstraction "Heaven" accordingly can't command the same love as the reality of the Dao with which people are immediately familiar with on a daily basis.
28. Cf. 14.31.11 and 24.59.3.
29. Cheng Xuanying glosses "Great Clod" as Nature [*ziran*]. *Zhuangzi jishi*, 1: 243.
30. Cf. the *Xunzi:* "It is the common flaw of men to be blinded by some small point of the truth [*yiqu*] and to shut their minds to the Great Ordering Principle [*dali*]." John Knoblock, trans., *Xunzi: A Translation and Study of the Complete Works*, 3: 100.
31. Cheng Xuanying: "Its predilection is that of a bright mirror that reflects perfectly; its faithfulness is that of an echo that responds on impulse. Utterly serene and still, it acts unselfconsciously. Look for it and it isn't seen since it is without discernible form." *Zhuangzi jishi*, 1: 247.
32. From the context, *taiji* apparently designates the highest height and *liuji* designates the lowest depth, both spatial distinctions. *Liuji* corresponds to the *liuhe*, the "six correspondences," east, west, north, south, up, and down, the six directions that define the bounds of the Earth, all of physical reality. The Dao thus exists even below Earth itself. Similarly, if the Dao is out there beyond the *taiji*, it means that it exists above Heaven, beyond the sky. This sense of *taiji* must be distinguished from *taiji* as the unseparated state of Heaven and Earth and the initiator of yin and yang and all that is numinous or divine, the locus classicus of which is the *Classic of Changes*, "Commentary on the appended phrases" [*Xici zhuan*], Part One: "how much the less can we understand what the numinous [*shen*] is. It is for this reason that, in order to clarify the polarity of yin and yang, we take the great ultimate [*taiji*], the initiator of it, and, in addressing change and transformation, we find that an equivalent for them is best found in the term *numinous* [*shen*]." Lynn, *The Classic of Changes*, 55.
33. Although Guo Xiang does not comment on any of the mythical heroes mentioned here, Cheng Xuanying addresses all of them, beginning with Boar Hide [Xiwei]: "Boar Hide

is the name of a ruler in remote antiquity. Because he got the Dao replete with numinous conductivity [*lingtong*], he was able to control everything in all its diversity and manage [*tiqie*] the two great exemplars [*eryi*] [Heaven and Earth]. It [*qie*, support in his hands] may also be written with the character *qi* (tally, fit together). Qi means *he* (combine); that is to say, he was able to merge and combine the myriad things and adjust and accommodate the Two Exemplars the one with the other." *Zhuangzi jishi*, 1: 248; however, see also 25.44.

34. Cheng Xuanying: "Fu Xi was one of the three monarchs of remote antiquity. He was able to domesticate the ox and harness the horse to conveyances, and because he domesticated [*yangfu*] animals suitable for sacrifice [*xisheng*], he was called Fu Xi (Domesticator of Sacrificial Animals). *Xi* (make combinations) means *he* (combine). *Qimu* (mother of pneuma) is the mother of the primordial undifferentiated pneuma [*yuanqi*], which resonates with the Dao. It was because he was able to obtain the perfect Dao [*zhidao*], it enabled him to draw the eight trigrams, develop them into the six lines, regulate yin and yang, and regulate the primordial undifferentiated pneuma." *Zhuangzi jishi*, 1: 248. Accounts of deities and mythical heroes provided for this passage by Cheng may be supplemented by Anne Birrell, *Chinese Mythology: An Introduction*, where legends are comprehensively sorted and reconciled (where possible) with good sense and erudition.
35. Cheng Xuanying: "The Pathfinder Dipper [Weidou] is the same thing as the North Pole Star, which is the overall leader of all the stars, and this is why it is called the Pathfinder Dipper. . . . Since it was able to get the perfect Dao [*zhidao*], it has safeguarded Heaven and Earth throughout all time, its heart [*xin*] never off center." *Zhuangzi jishi*, 1: 249.
36. Cheng Xuanying: "The lights of sun and moon follow the standard of the single Dao [a pun that also means "single unvarying path"], which is why they have been able to shine light down forever, never resting even once." *Zhuangzi jishi*, 1: 249.
37. Cheng Xuanying: "Kunlun is the name of mountains located to the north of the North Sea. Kanpi is the name of a god [*shen*] who dwells in the Kunlun mountains. *Xi* here means 'enter.' Kanpi has a human face and the body of an animal, who was able to enter the Kunlun mountains and become a god." *Zhuangzi jishi*, 1: 249.
38. Cheng Xuanying: "Surname Feng and personal name Yi, he was from the embankment at Tong town, Huayin county, Hongnong prefecture [Henan]. He weighed himself down with eight stones [threw himself into the river] and became a water immortal. The 'Great River' is the Yellow River. The Celestial Thearch [Tiandi] made Feng Yi the Earl of the Yellow River, [Hebo], where he subsequently roves in the Great River at Meng Crossing [Mengjin]." *Zhuangzi jishi*, 1: 249.
39. Cheng Xuanying: "Jianwu is the name of a god [*shen*]. When he got the Dao, he came to dwell on the Sacred Mountain of the East [Dongyue] as the God of Taishan." *Zhuangzi jishi*, 1: 249.
40. Cheng Xuanying: "The Yellow Thearch is Xuanyuan. He gathered copper from Head Mountain [Shoushan, Henan] and cast a tripod at the foot of Mount Jing [Jingshan, Henan]. When the tripod was finished, a dragon descended to the tripod to greet him. The emperor then took both his ministers and women from the inner palace, seventy-two in all, and in broad daylight rode up on clouds in a carriage pulled by dragons and ascended to Heaven—having been deified he thus departed." *Zhuangzi jishi*, 1: 250.
41. Cheng Xuanying: "Zhuanxu was a grandson of the Yellow Thearch, that is, he was the Emperor Gaoyang, also called the Black Emperor [Xuandi]. He was capped at eleven, when fourteen he assisted Emperor Shaohao, and at nineteen became emperor.

He gathered copper at Mount Yu [Yushan, which straddles the Shandong-Jiangsu border] and made it into tripods. Able to summon gods from all parts of the world, he had numinous powers [*lingyi*]. He physically died when ninety-six, but as he had got the Dao, he became Emperor of the North. *Xuan* [arcane, dark, black] is the color of the north; therefore, he dwells in the Black Palace [Xuangong]." *Zhuangzi jishi*, 1: 250.

42. Cheng Xuanying: "Yuqiang is the name of the God of Waters; he is also called Yujing. He has a human face and the body of a bird and travels about riding on a dragon. He is the joint progeny of Zhuanxu and Xuanyuan. Although he recovered the Dao, he did not become emperor but instead became the God of Waters. Since water is associated with the north, the title of his position is 'Extreme North.'" *Zhuangzi jishi*, 1: 250.
43. Cheng Xuanying: "Shaguang is the name of a mountain at the Extreme West [Xiji]. The Queen Mother is the vital essence [*jing*] of Grand Darkness [Taiyin]. She has the tail of a leopard, the teeth of a tiger, and is in the habit of laughing. At the time of Shun, she dispatched envoys and presented a jade bracelet; at the time of Emperor Wu of the Han she presented fresh peaches. Her face is like that of a fifteen- or sixteen-year old girl, and she looks very upright and proper. She sits atop the mountain at Shaguang in the west and is no longer subject to life and death; therefore, no one knows her beginning or ending." *Zhuangzi jishi*, 1: 250.
44. Cheng Xuanying: "Pengzu was the great-great-grandson of Zhuanxu. He was enfoeffed at Peng City, and since his practice of the Dao was worthy of veneration [*zu*], he was called Pengzu. Good at nourishing his original nature [*yangxing*], he was one who had got the Dao. The Five Tyrants [Wuba] were Kunwu, who was tyrant during the Xia, Dapeng and Shiwei, who were tyrants during the Yin, and Huan of Qi [Qi Huan] and Wen of Jin [Jin Wen], who were tyrants during the Zhou—together they are considered the Five Tyrants. Since this is so, as Pengzu had got the Dao, he thereby attained long life—from back to the time of Yu to down to the time of the Yin and Zhou dynasties, all together 800 years." *Zhuangzi jishi*, 1: 250–51. Shiwei is likely an alternative name for Xiwei (Boar Hide).
45. Cheng Xuanying: "Wu Ding is the name of a Yin [Shang] king, whose title was Gaozong (Eminent Ancestor). Gaozong dreamt that he would find Fu Yue, so he sent emissaries throughout the whole world to search for him, and they finally found him living in a house with walls of rammed earth at Fuyan in Hebei county, Shanzhou [Henan]. Once he became minister to Wu Ding, great peace and calm suddenly reigned everywhere. Fu Yue is a star spirit [*xingjing*], and his star is located above Ji and Wei [Sagittarius and Scorpio]. However, as members of the twenty-eight lunar mansions, Ji and Wei safeguard the east, and this is why the text says that Fu Yue 'rode the Guardians of the East by straddling Ji and Wei,' for it joined their ranks and marched together with Jiao and Kang [Spica and Virgo] and the other stars [in the eastern quadrant]. This is why the text says 'joined the ranks of the stars.'" *Zhuangzi jishi*, 1: 251.
46. It is likely that Nanbo Ziqi, Nanguo Ziqi, and Nanbo Zikui are all variants of the same name—or they may be scribal errors. See remarks from Cheng Xuanying and Lu Deming as quoted in *Zhuangzi jishi*, 1: 252.
47. Cheng Xuanying: "Buliang is the surname of a woman, Yi her given name. Empty mind [*xuxin*] and utter calm [*ningdan*] characterize the Dao, and the exercise of wisdom [*zhiyong*] and the resources of intelligence [*mingmin*] characterize talent. This speaks on the one hand to how Liang has the talent to deal with external things but not the Dao of internal calm, and on the other to how Woman Loner has the Dao that allows for placidity but not the talent to exploit the resources of intelligence. So each is hindered by being one-sided and thus not quite perfect in all respects. However, if you compare talent to the Dao, talent is inferior and Dao superior. *Zhuangzi jishi*, 1: 253.

48. Cheng Xuanying elaborates, interpreting the passage in terms of Buddhist thought: "Put things outside oneself means to forget about them [*yiwang*]. Just being a teacher isn't easy, and to transmit the Dao is the hardest of all. Since she [Woman Loner] was going to teach her [Buliang Yi], she had her perfectly concentrate her spirit and eliminate all thought [*ningshen jinglü*]. Keeping on with such cultivation for all of three days, once her [Buliang Yi's] mind had become empty and tranquil [*xuji*], all possible realms of existence [*wanjing*] were void to her, and so all things below Heaven and on Earth became non-existent [*feiyou, abhāva*]." *Zhuangzi jishi*, 1: 253. The *jing* (realms) in *wanjing* can also be read as the short form of *jingjie* (realms of perceptual objects), the Chinese translation of the Sanskrit *viṣaya*.
49. Cheng Xuanying equates "discern with the light of the rising sun" [*chaoche*] with the Buddhist term *huizhao* [light of wisdom]. *Zhuangzi jishi*, 1: 254.
50. Cheng Xuanying glosses "kill" as "extinguish" or "do away with" [*mie*], and Lu Deming glosses it as "destroy" or "lose" [*wang*]. *Zhuangzi jishi*, 1: 255. "Lose awareness of" seems an appropriate interpretation.
51. Cheng Xuanying: "*Jiang* [take, take along, lead] here means *song* (send off). The Dao treats things in such a way that it succors [*zhengji*] them boundlessly [*wufang*], so even though it neither makes them live nor causes them to perish, they still keep on living and keep on perishing. As such, it welcomes an inexhaustible number to life and sends off an immeasurable number to death." *Zhuangzi jishi*, 1: 255.
52. Note that Guo Xiang equates disturbance with entanglement—to be disturbed by things [*ying*] is to be entangled with them [*ying*].
53. Cheng Xuanying: "Only after one is able to 'merge with the brilliant and become one with the very dust' so he can act yet always remain calm, can such a one go along with the disturbance of things and become adept at providing for the fulfillment of life." *Zhuangzi jishi*, 1: 255. Cf. *Laozi*, section 4: "It [the vessel of the Dao] blunts the sharp, cuts away the tangled, merges with the brilliant, and becomes one with the very dust." Lynn, *The Classic of the Way and Virtue*, 57.
54. Cheng Xuanying: "Ink here signifies brush and ink, that is, writing. Principles [*li*] can generate teaching, which is why the text says that writing is an aid. Just as by means of the trap that the fish is caught, so it is by means of teaching that principles are made clear. The reason why they are 'heard' from brush and ink is because before they are clarified they have to be explained by writing." *Zhuangzi jishi*, 1: 256.
55. Cheng Xuanying: "Copying texts is what is meant by 'Ink-as-Aid,' whereas reciting from memory is what is meant by 'Repetitive-Recitation.' At first, since explanation is generated by texts, one takes up the reading of texts and masters them. Next, one gradually understands the principles involved, which is why one should recite them repeatedly. Moreover, since teaching is generated by principles, this is why it is called 'son,' and since recitation arises from teaching, it is referred to as 'grandson.'" *Zhuangzi jishi*, 1: 256.
56. Cheng Xuanying: "*Zhan* [look at] means *shi* [see, sight], which also implies the sense of 'attain to, reach' [*zhi*]. Having become highly proficient at reading and reciting and after a long accumulation of accomplishment, one's sight gradually attains to the principles of things and one's intelligence [*lingfu*] becomes perfectly clear [*fenming*]." *Zhuangzi jishi*, 1: 256.
57. Cheng Xuanying: "*Nie* has the sense here of 'ascend' [*deng*] as well as 'whisper words close to the ear.' Once one achieves some measure of profundity in reciting and begins to comprehend principles through teaching, joy and happiness grow in heart and mind [*xin*]. Privately approving that he has got it, he secretly whispers this close to the ear. Though such a one has heeded the Dao, he dare not yet practice it openly, and this too

signifies his gradual ascent to wonderful arcane truth [*xuanqing*]." *Zhuangzi jishi*, 1: 256–57.

58. Cheng Xuanying: "*Xu* [require] means *xu* [must], and *yi* [implement] means *yong* [practice]. Even though one privately enjoys self-approval and gradually is increasing his clarity of wisdom, he still must depend on teaching and comply with it, practice diligently and must not become lax. If he becomes lazy and does not practice, he will lack the means to gain the Dao." *Zhuangzi jishi*, 1: 257.
59. Cheng Xuanying: "'Singing' [Ou] means *ouge* songs of praise. Once one understands principles thanks to teaching and practices according to his understanding of them, he thereupon allows his magnificent wisdom [*shenghui*] to manifest itself, which causes songs of praise to fill the highways and byways." *Zhuangzi jishi*, 1: 257.
60. Cheng Xuanying: "'Arcane' [*xuan*] is a term for utter profundity [*shenyuan*], and 'obscurity' [*ming*] is an expression for abstruse quietude [*youji*]. Once virtuous practice prospers within and glorious reputation is manifest without, such a one thus gradually ascends to the ultimate of emptiness [*xuji*], even going so far as to reach arcane obscurity." *Zhuangzi jishi*, 1: 257. However, "Arcane Obscurity" is also an epithet of the Dao. Guo's commentary here is also attributed jointly to Xiang Xiu in Lu Deming's *Jingdian shiwen* (see appendix C.IV.6.18.1). Therefore, for Guo, the Dao as "nothingness yet not nothingness" should mean that it is "nothingness" apart from things, but extant when immanent in them, but for Xiang, as "nothingness" it exists both immaterially apart from things and immanently extant in them.
61. *Laozi*, section 1: "Nameless, it [the Dao] is the origin of the myriad things; named, it is the mother of the myriad things. . . . These two emerge together, but have different names. Together, we refer to them as mystery: the mystery upon mystery and gateway of all subtleties." Lynn, *The Classic of the Way and Virtue*, 51–52. Commenting on the same passage in the *Zhuangzi*, Cheng Xuanying says, "*Can* [accompany, join] is the same as *san* [three, triple], and *liao* [intangible, profound, void/voidance] means *jue* [cut off, reject]: the first is to reject existence [*jue you*]; the second is reject nothingness [*jue wu*]; and the third is [to reject] both the negation of existence and the negation of nothingness [*feiyou feiwu*]. This is why they are referred to as the 'three rejections' [*sanjue*]. The realm of arcane obscurity is such that although one still fails to attain to the furthest reaches of its marvels [*miao*], if he still manages to get as far as the three rejections, he will here have just arrived at the twofold arcane [*chongxuan*]." *Zhuangzi jishi*, 1: 257.
62. Cheng Xuanying: "*Shi* [begin, initial state] here means *ben* [root]. The Dao transcends such four-fold propositions [*siju*] as this and has nothing to do with such hundred negations [*baifei*] as that. With verbal articulation [*mingyan*], the way to the Dao is severed, and with the operation of intelligence [*xinzhi*], one's security [*chu*] is destroyed. Even though one gets as far as the three rejections [*sanjue*], he has yet to grasp completely [*qiong*] all its [the Dao's] subtleties [*miao*]. However, beyond the three rejections lies the fundamental essence [*genben*] of the Dao, the realm of the twofold arcane [*chongxuan*], and the gate of all subtleties [*zhongmiao*], which are impossible to grasp by thought and articulate in words. It [the Dao] takes root without taking root, for its root has nothing to take root in, so one has to distrust the use of the name "root," for surely there is no referent [*di*, literally "target"] that "root" can refer to. This is why this one is called 'Distrust Origin.'" *Zhuangzi jishi*, 1: 257–58.
63. Cheng Xuanying: "A person emerges from utter nothingness [*xuwu*], so nothingness is what is first there, which is why nothingness is regarded as the head. From nothingness existence is born, so existence is what is there next, which is why existence is regarded

as the backbone. Having lived, one dies, so death occupies the last position, which is why death is regarded as the buttocks. Therefore, although the head and the buttocks are separated from one another, to be sure they still belong to the same single body. Likewise, although life and death may be different, they both have their source in the same single entity [*yiti*]. One who can arrive at this insight will have every situation he encounters go well [*shi*] for him. How could such a one allow existence and extinction or likes and dislikes ever to interfere with this! Whoever can understand this, he I would make my friend." *Zhuangzi jishi*, 1: 258. The wording of the text in the *Zhuangzi* here is almost identical to a passage in 23.31.

64. Cf. 2.27.2.
65. Cheng Xuanying: "'Gain' means life, and 'loss' means death. Suddenly gain happens, and life occurs when the time is right for it. All of a sudden loss occurs, and death happens in accordance with principle [*li*]. Therefore, content with one's time, one does not take pleasure in life, and abiding in compliance, one does not resent death. Once one is free from such pleasure and resentment, what grief or joy would ever intrude on him!" *Zhuangzi jishi*, 1: 261.
66. Cheng Xuanying: " 'It' [*bi*] refers to the Former-and-Transformer [*zaohua*]. Here he is in the midst of being former-and-transformed, which orders him to approach death. If he had resented death and disobeyed, the blame would have been his, so how could he ever have blamed it for it! Guo's commentary states that 'it' refers to death." *Zhuangzi jishi*, 1: 263.
67. Moye is the name of a famous ancient sword.
68. Metal is the material for weapons and other instruments of killing, and thus it is inauspicious.
69. "Attachments" [*xi*] seems to refer to the objects of "innate tendencies" [*qing*]. As a man is "attached" to, is fond of, or prefers human form, so metal is "attached" to its shape as a weapon—as mentioned previously, the shape of a Moye.
70. "Peacefully" translates *chengran*, which Lu Deming thinks might be a mistaken translation for *eran* [suddenly]. However, since Guo Xiang describes Master Lai as "completely at ease" [*ziruo*] and Cheng Xuanying as "relaxed" [*xianfang*], "peacefully" is preferred. *Zhuangzi jishi*, 1: 264.
71. Cf. 6.59 and 20.18
72. Cheng Xuanying: "To 'climb up to Heaven' expresses how, pure and lofty, he lightly lifts himself above the world; to 'wander freely in the clouds and mist' expresses how he encounters no obstacles there. As such, he limitlessly keeps in step with change and transformation [*bianhua*], lets the Former-and-Transformer [*zaohua*] take the lead, and so circles around at ease." *Zhuangzi jishi*, 1: 265.
73. This follows the commentary of Cheng Xuanying; see *Zhuangzi jishi*, 1: 266.
74. That is, to attend to details from the perspective of the Dao; cf. Wang Bi's commentary to the *Laozi*, section 38; Lynn, *The Classic of the Way and Virtue*, 123.
75. That is, Heaven, the realm beyond worldly conventions, and Earth, the realm within worldly conventions.
76. Cheng Xuanying: "Water, fire, metal, wood—different things avail themselves of these in turn, and as each and every thing finds a place to lodge itself, all together they form one body. From this we know that one's physical body [*xinghai*] is illusory [*xuwei*]." *Zhuangzi jishi*, 1: 270.
77. Cheng Xuanying: "*Duan* [beginning] means *xu* [beginning], and *ni* [boundary, limit] means *pan* [boundary, end, limit]; *fanfu* [go to and fro] is the same as *wanglai* [come and go]; "beginning and end" is the same as "life and death." Since they have forgotten

the stuff of their physical forms [*xingzhi*], obliterating their bodies and discarding intelligence, they can send life off and welcome death, and just go along in step with transformation [*hua*]. Since transformation also is without limits, no one knows where this begins or ends." *Zhuangzi jishi*, 1: 270.

78. That is, limits imposed by worldly conventions.
79. Cheng Xuanying: "The outward signs [*ji*] of the sage are propriety and rites [*liyi*], and it is these that shackle his physical body and personal nature [*xingxing*]. Since Confucius is an adherent of the realm of worldly conventions, it is a natural principle that he should be punished." *Zhuangzi jishi*, 1: 271.
80. The "this" Confucius is going to share with Zigong is an account of how he manages to be in but not of the world. Cheng Xuanying clarifies: "Confucius was a sage who dealt with matters by merging with the brilliant, sharing the same world with all its disorder and trouble, and esteeming the propriety of common custom. Although he left such outward signs [*ji*] in the realm of worldly conventions, he said "I shall share this with you." As such, he was one who let his mind wander beyond the realm of worldly conventions, leisurely and carefree, untrammeled and free." *Zhuangzi jishi*, 1: 272. Cf. *Laozi*, section 56, where the text advises: "Merge with the brilliant," and Wang Bi's commentary states: "If one has no particular eminence of his own, people will have no predilection to contend." Lynn, *The Classic of the Way and Virtue*, 157.
81. Cheng Xuanying: "*Zao* (do best) means *yi* (attain). As for what fish might attain, to suit [*shi*] their natures [*xing*] nothing is better than deep water. As for what men might realize [zhi], to achieve satisfaction, nothing is better than the techniques of the Dao [*daoshu*]." *Zhuangzi jishi*, 1: 272.
82. According to Cheng Xuanyin, Mengsun Cai was a worthy of the state of Lu. *Zhuangzi jishi*, 1: 274.
83. Cheng Xuanying: "A person comes with life and goes with death, analogous to the sequence of the four seasons. Therefore, had Mengsun Cai been given the choice between them [life or death], he would not distinguish one from the other." *Zhuangzi jishi*, 1: 275.
84. Cheng Xuanying: "Even if he again had a choice to make, in the end, since he did not recognize any difference between life and death, he could find contentment in change and transformation [*bianhua*] and was unconcerned about things that made people happy or sad." *Zhuangzi jishi*, 1: 275. The choice that "had already been made" must refer to Mengsun's mother's death—there was nothing that Mengsun could do about it; it was not up to him. Therefore, his own death and any other death were no concern of his.
85. Cheng Xuanying: "*Yong* [ordinary people] means the common people whose knowledge and insight are both shallow and narrow, so how could they understand what I mean by 'there is no place where I am not to be found'! Even if one undergoes a thousand changes or ten thousand transformation, one's 'I' is yet present in them all, so whether one is a new 'I' or an old 'I,' why should one feel any like or dislike about either!" *Zhuangzi jishi*, 1: 277.
86. Cf. *Laozi*, section 25: "There is something, amorphous and complete, that was born before Heaven and Earth. Obscure, oh, and immaterial, oh, it stands alone, unchanged." Wang Bi's commentary here states: "*Jiliao* [ordinarily, "silent and empty/vague"] means 'without physical form or substance.'" Lynn, *The Classic of the Way and Virtue*, 95.
87. Cheng Xuanying explicitly identifies "my teacher" with the "perfect Dao" [*zhidao*]. *Zhuangzi jishi*, 1: 282.
88. Cf. 13.2.4.

89. Cheng Xuanying: "Master Yan received his teaching from Confucius and was committed wholeheartedly to asking about the Dao. Here he feels he has made progress, so he wants to present an explanation to his teacher. Loss means to become increasingly empty [*kong*], so he regards his loss as gain." *Zhuangzi jishi*, 1: 283. Cf. *Laozi*, section 48: "The pursuit of learning means having more each day, but the pursuit of the Dao means having less each day." Lynn, *The Classic of the Way and Virtue*, 143.
90. Cf. 6.25 and 20.18.

CHAPTER 7

YING DIWANG [FIT TO BE SOVEREIGNS]

7.0 One who is unselfconscious [*wuxin*] and thus given over to [*ren*] self-transformation [*zihua*] should be fit to be a ruler.

7.1 Nieque [Front Teeth Missing] in questioning Wang Ni asked four questions, but Wang knew not how to answer any of the four. This made Nieque hop around in great glee and go to tell Master Puyi [Puyi zi, Cattail Clothes][1] about it.

7.2.1 Master Puyi said to him, "Did you just realize this now? The Sire of Yu [Shun] was inferior to the Sire of Tai [Fu Xi].

All comparisons of the Sire of Yu with the Sire of Tai involve nothing more than footprints [*ji*] left behind in the realm of human affairs and have nothing to do with the actual makers of the footprints [*suoyi ji*]. Those who supposedly made the footprints actually left no footprints [*wuji*], so who in the world gave them such names! And since such names were never actually given, how is any inferior or superior involved? However, to leave no footprints means to ride on collective change [*qunbian*] while treading a path through countless ages. But some ages are safe while others dangerous, so just by following footprints you shall never catch up.

7.2.2 As for the Sire of Yu, he still harbored a sense of benevolence, by which he won over people to him. He certainly won people over but never escaped from the sense of what it was not to be a man.

One who thinks that what one would like is to be to be a man [*shi ren*] and what one would not like is not to be a man [*fei ren*] is circumscribed by the bounds of "is" and "is not." One who can break free from the bounds of "is not a man" can only do so by entering the realm where "is not a man" does not exist. Thus it is that neither achievement nor failure or neither the suitable nor the unsuitable exist for such a one, so how could it have simply been that he [Shun] won over people thanks to the sense of benevolence he harbored?

7.2.3 As for the Sire of Tai, he lay down utterly at peace and woke up utterly contented. At one time he thought he was a horse; at another time he thought he was a cow.

As such, how much the less could he have ever had the notion that he was a man [*shiren*] or not a man [*feiren*]. This is why it can be said of him that he escaped from the bounds of "is not a man."

7.2.4 His understanding was genuine and trustworthy;

He gave himself over to [*ren*] spontaneous understanding; as a result it was genuine and trustworthy [*qingxin*].

7.2.5 his virtue [*de*] thoroughly authentic [*zhen*],

He followed his authentic knowledge [*zhenzhi*], which freed his attitude [*qing*] from falsehood and artificiality, so a result was that it was real and trustworthy [*shixin*].

7.2.6 and he never had anything to do with "is not a man."

It is because he never had anything to do with the bounds of "is" and "is not" that he severed all ties with the world of the Sire of Yu.

7.3 Jianwu went to see crazy Jieyu, who said to him, "What did Sire Midday Start [Rizhong Shi][2] tell you?"

7.4 Jianwu replied, "He told me that the ruler over men issues something of his own for rules and standards to serve as models of conduct and morality such that no one dare ignore them and fail to be transformed by them."

7.5.1 Crazy Jieyu then said, "This is to pervert virtue.

If one tries to control people through his own efforts, people will lose their authenticity [*zhen*].

7.5.2 This way of his to govern the world is like trying to dig a canal across the ocean or get a mosquito to carry a mountain on its back.

For one who identifies [*ji*] perfectly with the myriad things, no task fails to fulfill itself [*zicheng*], but if he tries to control the world with his own person, no success will be his, and he will fail to be up to the task.

7.5.3 The way the sage governs, does it come from beyond him?

He just fully realizes the potential of his natural capacity [*xingfen*], and that's all there is to it.[3]

7.5.4 Only when he is true to himself does he act

In every instance he is true to the allotted capacity [*fen*] of his natural endowment [*xingming*].

7.5.5 and just does exactly what he can really do and nothing more!

He does not try to do what he can't do.

7.5.6 But the bird flies high lest it come to harm by harpoon arrows, and the field mouse burrows deep beneath the sacred hill[4] lest it come to grief by being smoked out or dug up.

Just as birds and beasts all have the wherewithal to take care of themselves [*zicun*], so rulers should allow people to act as they would [*ren zhi*] and not force them to do things, for in this way they fulfill themselves [*zicheng*].

7.5.7 How is it that you don't know about these two creatures!

That is, how can you not know how both these two creatures preserve themselves without depending on being taught to do so?

7.6 Skyroot [Tiangen] went wandering to the south of Mount Yin, and when he reached the Liao River, he met by chance Nameless Man [Wuming Ren], to whom he said, "May I ask how to govern all under Heaven?"

7.7.1 Nameless Man replied, "Be gone, you vulgar little man! What a disagreeable question!

To ask how to govern all under Heaven is not to start from the great beginning [*dachu*] and stop in arcane obscurity [*xuanming*].

7.7.2 I am just about to become someone at one with the Creator [*zaowuzhe*],

That is, he gives himself over [*ren*] to acting spontaneously [*ziwei*].

7.7.3 and when I am sated with that I shall ride on the bird that takes me to the amorphous and infinitesimally fragmentary [*mangmiao*] beyond the absolute reach of the six directions [*liuji*] to roam where nothing exists at all, there to dwell within the precincts of infinity [*kuanglang*].

"Amorphous and infinitesimally fragmentary [*mangmiao*] refers to the "odds and ends of existence" [*qunsui*]. It is by riding on the odds and ends of existence [*qunsui*] and galloping along on the myriad things that one sources himself in the "always in step" [*changtong*], where neither restraint nor obstruction exist.[5]

7.7.4 So despite that, why do you insist on disturbing my mind with your rules and standards for governing the world!

That is, if all are allowed self-fulfillment [*zide*], they will govern themselves [*zizhi*] without being governed.

7.8 But when he still asked about it again,

7.9.1 Nameless Man said, "Let your mind wander in the dispassionate [*dan*]

If one follows his own nature [*renxing*] and keeps it free of all embellishment, it will indeed be "dispassionate."[6]

7.9.2 and let your pneuma [*qi*] merge with perfect quietude [*mo*],

In silence [*moran*] invest your original nature [*xing*] with quietude [*jing*] and stop there.

7.9.3 comply with the spontaneity [*ziran*] of things and don't allow anything personal to intrude, and with this the whole world will come to order.

When one follows his own nature [*renxing*] and lets self-generation [*zisheng*] occur, this is public and for everyone [*gong*]; when the mind wishes to augment life, this is private and selfish [*si*].[7] If people yield to private and selfish tendencies, they shall lack the means to live life to the fullest [*shengsheng*], for it is this that allows compliance with the public good [*gong*] to reach all.

7.10 Yang Ziju[8] went to visit Lao Dan and said to him, "Supposing there is someone quick witted and strong as a beam, with penetrating insight into things, and who untiringly studies the Dao, could such a man compare with the enlightened sovereigns?"

7.11.1 Lao Dan replied, "Compared with the sages, such a man is but a common clerk, face distorted with effort and tied to skill, body belabored and mind in a state of alarm.

That is, since he can't even preserve his own person with such effort, of course he fails to compare with the sage sovereigns.

7.11.2 It is the markings on the tiger or leopard that bring hunters after them [*lai tian*], and it is the nimbleness of monkeys and the tendency of dogs to catch foxes that gets them leashed [*lai jie*],[9] so how can anyone alike compare with the enlightened sovereign?"

All these so encumbered, either because of their markings or because of their skills, don't cross into nothingness [*xu*] to operate there in the boundless [*wufang*].[10]

7.12 Shocked, Yang Ziju said, "May I presume to ask what the government of the enlightened sovereign does consist of?"

7.13.1 Lao Dan replied, "The government of the enlightened sovereign is such that his achievement [*gong*] covers the entire world yet it seems not of his own doing.

When the world lacks an enlightened sovereign, no one can attain self-fulfillment [*zide*]. Making it possible for them to attain self-fulfillment really marks the enlightened sovereign's achievement, for such achievement lies in unselfconscious action [*wuwei*], which returns responsibility [*ren*] for all in the world to themselves. It is because all in the world thus attains self-empowerment [*ziren*], it seems this does not depend on the enlightened sovereign.

7.13.2 He bestows his transformative power [*hua*] on the myriad things yet the people don't selfconsciously rely on it.

The enlightened sovereign allows for everyone to satisfy his own nature, thus everyone says "I am free" [*wo zier*], yet no one realize that this depends on the enlightened sovereign.

7.13.3 Though never commended for it, it is he who is responsible for the people making themselves happy.

Although his achievement covers the entire world, he is never commended for being responsible for it, which is why each person thinks it is he who is responsible for making himself happy.

7.13.4 He stands in the unfathomable [*buze*]

He locates himself on the path of change and transformation [*bianhua*], constantly renewed and boundless [*wufang*].

7.13.5 and wanders in the nonexistent [*wuyou*].”

Since he forms one body with the myriad things [*yu wanwu wei ti*], where he wanders is void [*xu*]. But if he could not arcanely merge with things [*mingwu*], he would be too busy being at odds with them to have any time to wander the void [*youxu*]!

7.14.1 In Zheng there was a shaman with divine powers [*shenwu*] named Ji Xian,[11] who knew if one would live or die, survive or perish, whether enjoy good fortune or suffer misfortune, live long or die young, predicting the year, month, and day of the month as if godlike. When the people of Zheng saw her, they avoided her and ran away.

They did not like to hear the day of their own deaths.

7.14.2 But when Master Lie saw her, he was utterly fascinated by her. On returning, he reported to Master Hu,[12] “I used to think, Master, that your way was the ultimate, but now there is someone that even surpasses it.”

That is, the attainment [*zhi*] of Ji Xian’s surpasses that of his master.

7.15.1 Master Hu replied, “What I have conveyed to you so far is entirely the outer form of it but not yet all its inner substance, so are you sure that you really have mastered the Dao as such? You might have all the hens but no rooster, so then what fertile eggs are you going to get from them?

That is, Master Lie has not yet fully internalized the Dao [*huai Dao*].

7.15.2 Yet you take such a way and flaunt it at the world, determined to be trusted, which allowed this person to examine you physiognomically.

As he had not fully internalized the Dao, he still remained selfconscious [*youxin*], and selfconsciously flaunted one aspect of it, determined that he would be trusted by the world, which is why he could be judged physiognomically.

7.15.3 Try to bring her here and show her to me.”

7.16 The next day Master Lie did bring her to see Master Hu, and when they came out she said to Master Lie, “Alas, your master is dying! There is no indication of life, and he shall not last more than ten days! I saw something strange in him: I saw wet ashes in him.”

7.17.1 Master Lie then went back in and, tears soaking his lapels, reported this to Master Hu, but Master Hu said, “What I have showed her was myself as outer signs of the Earth [*diwen*], like a bud neither stirring nor governed [*zheng*].

Like a bud motionless and not governing itself [*zizheng*],[13] he is a match for an old tree not in flower or for the wet ashes equal to a forlorn earth-bound soul [*po*],[14] for such is the state of a Perfected one [*zhiren*] free of thoughts and feelings [*wugan*]. A Perfected one acts as does Heaven, is quiescent as is Earth, moves as does water, and is still as is the silence of the abyss. Whether the abyss is still or the water flows, whether Heaven acts or Earth rests are all identical in that they are free from intent [*buwei*] and function spontaneously [*zier*]. Now Ji Xian saw him there like a corpse abiding in forgetfulness [*zuowang*] and so said that he was about to die, but if she had seen how his spirit [*shen*] moved in compliance with Heaven [*tiansui*], she would have said that he had life to live. One who truly can respond to things without using selfconscious mind [*xin*] and whose comprehension spontaneously tallies arcanely [*xuanfu*] with them, one who takes the measure of the world in step with increases and decreases arising from change and transformation [*bianhua*], only such a one is up to mastery over them and can infinitely [*wuji*] comply with the demands of the moment [*shunshi*]. Therefore, he is just not to be examined physiognomically. And this is the basic gist of "Fit to be Sovereigns."

7.17.2 So she probably saw me in a state of sealed up vitality [*dudeji*]. Try to bring her here again."

Vitality [*deji*] unexpressed is said to be "sealed up" [*du*]

7.18 The next day he again brought her to see Master Hu, and this time when they went out she said to Master Lie, "How fortunate that your master met me, for this was his cure, and now he has all life in him! When I saw him before he was he in a state of sealed up transformative vigor [*duquan*]."

"Transformative vigor" [*quan*] here is the same as "activating force" [*ji*]. Now she realizes that what she saw the day before was him in a state of sealed up transformative vigor, which is why she said that he was about to die.

7.19.1 Master Lie then went back in and reported this to Master Hu, but Master Hu said, "What I have showed her was myself as Heaven and Earth [*tianrang*],

Right at the center of Heaven and Earth, his effectiveness [*gong*] at protecting and nourishing became apparent. Like his outer signs of Earth [*diwen*], is not this state still an outer aspect? But this is how he looks when he reacts and responds [*ganying*].

7.19.2 into which neither reputation nor benefit [*mingshi*] enter,[15]

When he protects and nourishes by giving himself over to [*ren*] spontaneity [*ziran*], it is his celestial mechanism [*tianji*] that arcanely responds [*xuanying*] to things.

7.19.3 and so, as activating force [*ji*] started up from my heels,[16]

But it always starts at the very highest level.

7.19.4 She probably saw that the good in me was this activating force.

When activating force started up it did him good, and so she saw it.[17]

7.19.5 Try to bring her here again."

7.20 The next day he again brought her to see Master Hu and again when they went out she said to Master Lie, "Your master is so irregular [*buqi*] that I have nothing with which to examine him physiognomically. Try to get him to stabilize [*qi*][18] **and I shall again examine him physiognomically."**

7.21.1 Master Lie then went back in and reported this to Master Hu, but Master Hu said, "What I then showed her was that my great empty vessel [*taichong*] had no room for victory.

He dwells in the infinite capacity [*ji*] of the great empty vessel [*taichong*], where oceanically [*haoran*] he moors his mind and arcanely unites [*xuantong*] with the infinite methods [*wanfang*], so there is no room in him for either victory or defeat.

7.21.2 so she probably saw me with activating force [*ji*] in balanced pneuma [*hengqi*].

No venture of his is done without equanimity [*ping*], for he merges with all in one integral whole [*hunran yizhi*]. No one who peers at the sky through a tube ever sees its limits, which is why he seems irregular [*buqi*] to her.

7.21.3 A whale swirled whirlpool gathered to form my abyss, then still waters gathered to form my abyss, and then flowing water gathered to form my abyss. Though the abyss exists in nine kinds, here I distinguished only three of them,

The abyss signifies quiet passivity [*jingmo*]. Water always behaves unselfconsciously [*wuxin*], so accommodates itself to whatever is outside it. Therefore, whether it flows or is still, whether swirled by whale or made to leap by dragon, abyss-like it always is just as before [*ziruo*], never losing its quiet passivity [*jingmo*]. When a Perfected one [*zhiren*] is called upon [*yong*] he acts; when he is set aside [*she*] he desists.[19] Although such acting and desisting differ, they are identical in their quiet passivity. Therefore, he cited in brief these three different kinds to illustrate what he meant. Although the flow of water exists in nine different transformations, still and disturbed all mixed up together, one who dwells in infinite capacity [*ji*] will always placidly achieve self-fulfillment [*zide*] and moor himself in unselfconscious effort [*wangwei*].

so try to bring her here again."

7.22 The next day he again brought her to see Master Hu, but before coming to a standstill she just lost self-possession and fled. Master Hu said, "Run after her!"

7.23 But though Master Lie chased after her, he failed to catch her, and on his return reported to Master Hu, "She's vanished! I've lost her! I just couldn't catch up with her!"

7.24.1 Master Hu said, "What I already showed her never revealed my Progenitor [*zong*].

Although his change and transformation [*bianhua*] occurred without constancy, he always remained deeply rooted in the utmost arcane [*mingji*].[20]

7.24.2 I was so empty [*xu*], with her, wriggling as compliant as a snake is to the ground Unselfconsciously [*wuxin*] he kept transforming in step with the other [Ji Xian].

7.24.3 that she did not know what kind of a person I was.

He was so unstable that there was nothing by which he could be bound.

7.24.4 As such I became utterly flexible, as such I drifted identical to the current, and that was why she ran away."

He freely submits to change and transformation, drifts in step with the affairs of the world, so nothing he ventures to do fails to comply. Though a Perfected one remains integrally one, he resonates with worldly vicissitudes and so acts in step with them. Therefore, the physiognomist had nothing to set the eyes to and, losing self-possession, just ran away. This illustrates how someone fit to be a sovereign stays free of set methods.

7.25.1 After this, Master Lie thought that he had never learned anything and so went home, which he did not leave for three years, tending the fire and cooking for his wife, feeding the pigs as if he were feeding people.

He forgot about all distinctions between noble and base.

7.25.2 In regard to affairs, he had no preferences,

He just took things as he encountered them.

7.25.3 From the carved and polished he returned to pristine simplicity [*pu*],

He rejected gorgeous elaboration and adopted unadorned simplicity.

7.24.4 Clod-like [*kuairan*] to stand alone in his physical form [*xing*],

All external embellishment had been eliminated.

7.24.5 though engaged in turmoil he kept himself gathered together,

Although he acted, his authenticity [*zhen*] remained intact [*busan*].

7.24.6 And in unity with all things [*yi*] he lived out his life as such to the end.

He allowed all others to live out their natural lives to the end [*zizhong*].

7.26.1 Don't play a role befitting reputation [*mingshi*].

If people are left alone, each one will spontaneously live up to his reputation.[21]

7.26.2 Don't be the repository of deliberation.

Allow each person to deliberate for himself.

7.26.3 Don't be responsible for affairs.

Allow people to be responsible for their own affairs.

7.26.4 Don't be a master of intelligence [*zhi*].

If one is unselfconscious [*wuxin*] oneself, each person shall then spontaneously master his own intelligence.

7.26.5 Since their embodiments are completely realized [*tijin*], they are free from exhaustion [*wuqiong*],

It is because he allows all under Heaven to act spontaneously [*ziwei*] that he may gallop along on the myriad folk and never be exhausted [*wuqiong*].[22]

7.26.6 While you wander among them seamlessly,

It is because he trusts the people to do for themselves [*renwu*] that he leaves no footprints [*wuji*].

7.26.7 Fully realize what you have received from Heaven,

As it is sufficient, stop within it.

7.26.8 But don't look on it as something obtained.

If he looks on it as something obtained, he won't know when to stop.

7.26.9 Just be empty [*xu*], that is all.

If he is not empty, he will fail to allow everyone to fulfill oneself [*shi*].

7.26.10 The Perfected one uses his mind just as a mirror works,

It mirrors things impartially [*wuqing*].

7.26.11 neither sending anything off nor welcoming anything hither, it responds but never retains [*zang*].[23]

When something comes, it responds; when something goes, it stops.

7.26.12 Therefore he is up to dealing with things and is never injured by them.

When something comes, he mirrors it, but the mirroring is not done with selfconscious mind [*xin*]. Therefore, though the world be wide, he never is tired by distress of spirit [*shen*].

7.27 The Emperor of the Southern Sea was Shu (Quick); the Emperor of the North Sea was Hu (Sudden); and the Emperor of the Center was Hundun (Primal Chaos). Shu and Hu met from time to time in Hundun's territory, where he treated them very well. Shu and Hu deliberated how they could repay Hundun's kindness, "All men have seven apertures so they can see, hear, eat, and breathe, but he alone has none, so let us try to bore them in him." Each day they bored one aperture, and on the seventh day Hundun died.

Selfconscious effort [*wei*] destroyed him.[24]

Notes

1. Cheng Xuanying: "Master Cattail Clothes was a worthy of the time of Yao, who at the age of eight was regarded by Shun as his teacher, and when Shun tried to yield rule to him, he refused. This is the same person as Master Commoner Clothed [Piyi *zi*]." *Zhuangzi jishi*, 1: 287.
2. Rizhong Shi [Midday Start] seems a fanciful name of the sort that Master Zhuang seems to have been fond of inventing. Cheng Xuanying interprets it so, as does Li Yi before him. However, Yu Yue, among others, thinks that only Zongshi [Mid-Start] is a name and that *ri* (day, sun) isn't part of the name but rather is equivalent to *rizhe* [previously]. See *Zhuangzi jishi*, 1: 290.
3. Cheng Xuanying elaborates: "He governs according to his allotted capacity [*fen*] and certainly does not try to govern people from beyond it; one who tries to govern from beyond it may be said to not govern them at all." *Zhuangzi jishi*, 1: 291.
4. "Sacred hill" refers to the raised plot of ground on which the altar to the god of the soil is situated.
5. Cf. 13.3.13.

6. Cheng Xuanying: "If one could let the spirit of his mind [*xinsi*] wander in the realm of the utterly dispassionate [*tiandan*] and merge body and pneuma [*xingqi*] with the state of absolute quietude [*jimo*], then both body and pneuma shall achieve emptiness and quietude [*xujing*], and, as such, the whole world will then undergo self-transformation without any need for governance." *Zhuangzi jishi*, 1: 294. It is likely that both Guo and Cheng read the *Zhuangzi* here in the light of the *Laozi*, section 63, and Wang Bi's commentary on it: "Act by not acting; do by not doing; find flavor in that which has no flavor." [Wang:] "To handle matters without selfconscious effort [*wuwei*], practice the teaching that isn't expressed in words, and have a taste for the utterly dispassionate [*tiandan*] is the ultimate of government." Richard John Lynn, *The Classic of the Way and Virtue*, 168.
7. Cf. Guo Xiang: "That one's life has limits is Heaven's doing, and when my mind [*xin*] wants to augment it, it is my doing." *Zhuangzi jishi*, 1: 226.
8. Cheng Xuanying identifies Yang Ziju as the ethical egoist philosopher Yang Zhu (370–319 BCE, but according to Li Yi, "*Ju* is a given name, and *zi* is a general title for men," a reading resulting in "Yang, Master Ju." *Zhuangzi jishi*, 1: 295.
9. Cheng Xuanying elaborates: "Since monkeys tend to jump about and are so nimble, they are always restrained by tethers; because dogs are wont to chase after foxes, they are always tied by the neck." *Zhuangzi jishi*, 1: 296.
10. "The boundless" [*wufang*] can also be rendered as "without method," which is especially apt in this context.
11. The same passage occurs, with variations, in the *Liezi* (Sayings of Master Lie); *Liezi jishi*, 2: 70–73.
12. Cheng Xuanying: "Master Hu was a man of Zheng who had attained the Dao. Sobriquet Huzi (Master Hu) and given name Lin, he was the teacher of Master Lie." *Zhuangzi jishi*, 1: 298.
13. That is, he is like a dormant tree bud in the dead of winter, seemingly dead but full of life's potential. However, "governed" [*zheng*] is written as *zhi* (cease, pause) in some editions of the *Zhuangzi*, a reading supported by the text of Guo's commentary, which is attributed to Xiang Xiu in Zhang Zhan's (fourth century CE) commentary on the *Liezi* (Sayings of Master Lie), which is exactly the same as Guo's except that "keeping itself still" [*zizhi*] appears instead of "governing itself" [*zizheng*]. See Wang Shumin, *Guo Xiang Zhuangzi zhu jiaoji* (Collation notes for the Guo Xiang commentary to the *Zhuangzi*), 2: 15, and a full treatment of the textual variants *zheng* and *zhi*, which appears in Wang's *Zhuangzi jiaoquan*, 292, note 14. These readings would result in "like a bud neither stirring nor paused [*zhi*]" (*Zhuangzi*) and "like a bud motionless yet not keeping itself still [*zizhi*]" (Guo's commentary). Nevertheless, *zizheng* (govern oneself; self-rectification, self-rectify) often appears in other places in Guo's commentary; it is a term likely borrowed from the *Laozi*, section 37: "Achieving tranquility by keeping them [the myriad folk] free from desire, all under Heaven would govern themselves [*zizheng*]." Lynn, *The Classic of the Way and Virtue*, 118.
14. The earthbound soul is attached to the physical body, which becomes wet ashes after death.
15. Given the context, it is most likely that "neither reputation nor benefit" [*mingshi*] alludes to a passage in the *Mengzi* (Mencius); see Zhao Qi and Sun Shi, *Mengzi zhushu* (*Mencius*, with commentary and subcommentary), 12A: 2757b: "He who gives first priority to reputation and benefit works for the sake of others, but he who gives secondary priority to reputation and benefit works for himself."
16. Cf. 6.4.4.

17. Cheng Xuanying: "When he showed his power to do good [*shanji*] in resonance with these two modes [*yin* and *yang*, Heaven and Earth], Ji Xian saw the appearance of this in him and so said that this was good. To have all life in him is what is meant by 'saw the good in me.'" *Zhuangzi jishi*, 1: 302.
18. Cheng Xuanying explains "stabilize" [*qi*] as "stabilize the true state of his mind [*xinji*]." *Zhuangzi jishi*, 1: 302.
19. Cf. *Lunyu* (Analects), 7: 2482a: "The Master [Confucius] said to Yan Yuan, 'When called upon, act; when set aside, seclude yourself.'"
20. Cheng Xuanying: "Rooted in the arcane wellspring [*xuanyuan*], his marvelousness [*miao*] is so obscure and faint that it transcends the *siju* [tetralemma], is free from the hundred negations [*baifei*], and can't be comprehended in thought, so how could it ever be captured in form or name! Since it lies beyond the reach of words or images, no way exists to understand the path of the Progenitor [*zongtu*]. And because she could not fathom where he was coming from, she gave up and went away." *Zhuangzi jishi*, 1: 304. Elsewhere, *mingji* seems to mean "arcane limits," but here the expression "deeply rooted in the arcane ultimate" [*shen'gen mingji*] should be understood as being parallel to a similar expression used several times by Guo Xiang, "deeply rooted in the tranquil ultimate" [*shen'gen ningji*]. See Jiang Longxiang, "*Xiang Xiu benti sixiang shangque* (Deliberating Xiang Xiu's ontology)," 48–49. Wang Shumin actually prefers to read *shen'gen mingji* as *shen'gen ningji* because the fragment of Xiang Xiu's commentary on this passage reads *shen'gen ningji*, which Wang indicates was partially appropriated by Guo. However, Wang also points out that Cheng Xuanying obviously based his remarks on the reading of *shen'gen mingji*. See Wang Shumin, *Zhuangzi jiaoquan*, 258, note 6 and *Zhuangzi zhu jiaoji*, 2: 16a–16b.
21. Cheng Xuanying shifts his emphasis from the enlightened ruler as the arbiter of reputation among his subjects to his own transcendence of personal reputation: "*Shi* (corpse; ceremonial stand-in for the deceased; master, arbiter) is equivalent to *zhu* (master). If the self [*shen*] has been forgotten and abandoned, where would reputation reside? Thus it is that such a one no longer would be master of reputation." *Zhuangzi jishi*, 1: 307.
22. Cheng Xuanying again shifts the emphasis back to the enlightened ruler: "It is because he forms one body with the true wellspring [*zhenyuan*] that he can arcanely unite [*minghui*] with the objects of cognition [*zhijing*], which is why the text states, 'he never becomes exhausted.'" *Zhuangzi jishi*, 1: 308.
23. Cf. 22.60. Cheng Xuanying glosses *zang* as "conceal." *Zhuangzi jishi*, 1: 309.
24. Cheng Xuanying elaborates: "The Southern Sea is a place of brightness and clarity, thus Shu acts in terms of existence [*you*]. The North is the realm of darkness, thus Hu acts in terms of nonexistence [*wu*]. The Center is neither North nor South, thus Hundun acts in terms of neither existence nor nonexistence. When existence and nonexistence, these two states of mind [*xin*], met in the territory of neither existence nor nonexistence, it merged the two partial states of mind in the embrace of one single intermediate [*zhong*] disposition [*zhi*]. This is why the text states 'treated them very well.' But the two, Shu and Hu, still inflexibly stuck at what they were and, unable to unite, thought up a plan based on what they had learned. Since they took a rash dislike to Hundun's unselfconsciousness [*wuxin*], they said that to bore holes in him would be beneficial. They used their four limbs to overstay their welcome there and bored seven apertures in him, allowing him to be infected with the impure world. They perverted his absolute purity and would have had him conform to making choices based on existence and nonexistence. As such he did not live out his natural span of years but died young in midcourse. So rouse yourselves, students, and make every effort! This is why Guo's commentary states that 'selfconscious effort destroyed him.'" Cheng's exhortation is, of course, sarcastic. *Zhuangzi jishi*, 1: 310.

PART 2

THE SAYINGS OF MASTER ZHUANG, THE OUTER CHAPTERS

CHAPTER 8

PIANMU [WEBBED TOES]

8.1.1 Webbed toes and extra fingers do indeed come from one's inborn nature [*xing*] but are extra to the virtues [*de*].[1] Attached lumps and appended warts do come from one's physical body but are extra to the inborn nature.

As the long are never provided with too much and the short never with not enough, so webbed toes and extra fingers or lumps and warts also all come from the inborn nature of one's physical body [*xingxing*] and are not artificial [*jiawu*].[2] However, whether webbed toes or not, the inborn nature [*xing*] provides just enough in both cases, and it is only because webbed toes and extra fingers are thought excessive, compared to everyone in general, that it is said that they are "extra." The deluded sometimes even say that since they don't originate in the inborn nature, they should be cut away, which would have it that things exist in which the Dao is not present and which virtue [*de*] does not support. If so, then people might exist who as resources [*cai*] may be dispensed with, and things might exist whose use [*yong*] may be done without. But how could this ever be the intent [*yi*] of perfect order [*zhizhi*]![3] A person might have some small or large trait, and might have some potential [*neng*] in scant or ample amount. Here what are considered too large are webbed toes and extra fingers, and what are considered too ample are lumps and warts. As for an allotted capacity [*fen*] for webbed toes and extra fingers or lumps and warts, anyone at all might have it, so whenever these are not allowed [*ren*], it rejects the inborn nature [*xing*] that exists in everyone.

8.1.2 When one has extra measures [*fang*] of benevolence [*ren*] or righteousness [*yi*] and as such would apply them, though to be sure they still rank

among his five viscera, they don't represent the correctness [*zheng*] of the Dao and its Virtue.

To merge arcanely [*ming*] with others, nothing should ever be extra, so one who has extra measures of benevolence or righteousness, though these should still rank among his five viscera, they are "correct" only for him as an individual and can never be used to engage with others, which should be without set measures [*wufang*], whereby each person's natural endowment [*xingming*] achieves its own correctness. This is why the text says "they don't embody the correctness [*zheng*] of the Dao and its Virtue." As for how much is right for the measure [*fang*], this varies infinitely throughout the world, with each person's a fixed amount [*dingfen*] with only a hair's breadth of difference between too little and too much, so no "extra digit" [*qi*] may ever be added. If each person is allowed to abide by the measure that is right for him, be it little or much, each and every person will realize it spontaneously [*zide*]. However, when the deluded hear that those with much are incapable of correcting those with little, they want to dispense with those endowed with much and tolerate those with little, which would lose them the entire world—is that not absurd![4]

8.1.3 Therefore, a web between the toes connects a useless piece of flesh, and an extra digit on the hand erects a useless finger.

It is simply due to one's natural endowment [*xingming*] that these inevitably occur, and not because they serve a useful purpose.

8.1.4 To add extra measures, "webs" and "extra digits" as it were, to the innate properties [*qing*] of the five viscera will invest the practice of benevolence [*ren*] and righteousness [*yi*] with wickedness and perversity

The properties of the five viscera come in just certain innate amounts, but those who have less unreasonably persist in augmenting them to the point where they become wicked and perverse, thus violating the ultimate fitness of their innate embodiment.[5]

8.1.5 and to invest the functions [*yong*] of hearing and vision with increased measures [*fang*].

As for the functions of hearing and vision, each person has a fundamental allotted capacity [*benfen*] such that however much a measure, it is never excessive, however scant a measure, it is never inadequate. However, the surge of desire never fails to make people denigrate the less and esteem the more, so when they see something they so envy [in others], they work themselves up to augment it [in themselves], and by trying to aggrandize their fundamental functions [*benyong*], they distress the original nature [*xing*] they have by nature [*ziran*]. But if they would forget about what they esteem and instead safeguard their own fundamental allotted capacity [*sufen*], then, free of anything extraneous to their original natures, all their various measures would remain whole and safe [*quan*].

8.2.1 Therefore, an added "web" to vision, does this not throw the five colors into confusion, cause licentious enjoyment of designs [*wen*]and emblems [*zhang*], as well as green and yellow axe-shape and *yi*-shape embroidery that bedazzle the eye? All this has happened just because of Li Zhu![6] As for an addition to hearing, does this not throw the five tones into confusion, cause licentious enjoyment of the six yang pitches [*liulü*] and, played on metal, stone, strings, and bamboo, the sounds of "yellow bell" [*huangzhong* (great yang pitch)] and "great yin pitch" [*dalü*]? All this happens just because of Music Master Kuang [Shi Kuang]![7]

Those with ears and eyes never inflict distress on themselves [*zikun*] by envying the deaf and blind; their distress stems from admiring Li Zhu and envying Master Kuang. Therefore, though Li and Kuang are keen of eye and acute of ear, they are actually the root causes of confusion for ear and eye.

8.2.2 Those who add an "extra digit" to benevolence [*ren*] pull up their virtues and boost their original natures[8] in order to garner reputation, but does this not cause the world, spurred on by panpipe and drum, to pursue unattainable models? All this happens just because of Zeng and Shi!

It just so happened that Zeng Shen and Shi Qiu, in their original natures, were strong in benevolence, but those not strong in it unreasonably persist in envying them, but the benevolence produced by such envy is truly false. The world never envies King Jie and Robber Zhi [Dao Zhi] but instead surely envies Zeng Shen and Shi Qiu, so it is Zeng and Shi, having thus stirred up the world with panpipe and drum, who cause people to abandon their original natures—which makes them worse than Jie and Zhi!

8.2.3 Those who add a "web" to their powers of disputation improvise on language by tying it up in stacks of tiles, as their minds wander amidst "hard," "white," "identical," and "difference," but does this not just wear them out in useless words that provide but fleeting reputation? All this happens just because of Yang and Mo!

Those who wantonly use their extraordinary powers of disputation, even to the point where words cause danger, heed not the maw of the *Taowu* but must compete in disputation with the likes of Yang and Mo. Therefore, Yang and Mo are the root cause of confusion in all discourse![9]

8.2.4 Therefore, since all these represent the way of extra webs and excess digits, they don't represent what is perfectly correct [*zhizheng*] for all under Heaven.

All these masters complied with their inherent natures [*tianxing*], which just happened to include extra "webs" and "digits," and these were correct only for each as an individual. As such, if these individual instances of correctness were used to correct a myriad others, the myriad others would, of course, not be correct. Therefore, one who is perfectly correct does not use his own correctness to correct everyone else but does nothing more than allow each other person to achieve his own correctness.

8.3.1 Those for whom correctness is perfectly fulfilled [*zhengzheng*] lose not the true state [*qing*] of their natural endowment [*xingming*]. It is when each person is allowed to trust to his own nature [*renxing*] that correctness is perfectly fulfilled. When one reads the text from this point on, what "perfect correctness" [*zhizheng*] means becomes readily apparent.

8.3.2 As such, joining [*he*] does not involve a "web,"

If the correctness of joining were judged from the viewpoint of the branched out, such a one would say that the joining is a "web."

8.3.3 branching out does not involve an "extra digit,"

If the correctness of branching out were judged from the viewpoint of the joined, such a one would say that the branching out is an "extra digit."[10]

8.3.4 being long does not involve excess,

If the correctness of being long were judged from the perspective of being short, such a one would say that the long is too long.

8.3.5 and being short does not involve inadequacy.

If the correctness of being short were judged from the perspective of being long, such a one would say that the short is not long enough.[11]

8.3.6 Thus it is that although the wild duck's neck is short, to extend it would result in its grief, and, although the crane's legs are long, to shorten them would result in its grief.

Each has its own correctness, thus it won't do to correct the one in terms of the other, thereby diminishing one and increasing the other.

8.3.7 Therefore, if what is long by nature should not be cut short and what is short by nature should not be extended, there will be no reason to banish grief.

If one realizes that his natural capacity [*xingfen*] should neither be cut short nor extended but trusted to as such, there will be no need to banish grief, for grief will stay away by itself.

8.3.8 Alas! Don't benevolence and righteousness belong to one's innate character [*qing*]!

Benevolence and righteousness naturally belong to one's fundamental nature [*qingxing*], so one should do nothing more than trust to them as such.

8.3.9 Those who would make people benevolent, how much grief they suffer!

Those who fear that benevolence and righteousness don't belong to one's innate character and so grieve over it really can be said to suffer much grief.

8.4.1 Moreover, one who has a web between the toes weeps when it is severed, and one who has an extra finger on the hand cries out when it is bitten off. As for these two, whether an excess in number or a deficiency, in distress they are one and the same.

It is because it is said that the one has not enough [toes] that, weeping, he severs it [the web], and because the other is considered to have too many [fingers] that, crying out, he bites one off. Despite the fact that all living things differ in countless ways, this certainly demonstrates a lack of understanding wherein grief lies. If only each would be content with his inherent nature [*tianxing*], neither severing webs nor biting off digits, complete fulfillment [*qucheng*] would be achieved with no injury suffered—so what grief would ever result then!

8.4.2 Nowadays the benevolent look with unclear eyes at the world's troubles.

It is indeed when the footprints of universal love [*jian'ai*] enjoys esteem that the eyes of the world become unclear, and it is because such footprints should be esteemed that the unclear cause disaster, which they then grieve over. But this is to trap people in trouble and afterwards try to deliver them from it. Nevertheless, nowadays everyone just says that this is "benevolence."

8.4.3 People who are not benevolent have broken with their innate characters [*qing*] in their greed for eminence and wealth.

That eminence and wealth can inspire such greed is all because of those who suffer unclear vision. If there were no such footprints to esteem, people would be content with their allotted capacities [*fen*], whose limits they would measure and to which they would commit themselves—would there ever again be anyone who abandons self and imitates others as he greedily thieves things beyond his appropriate expectations?

8.4.4 Therefore, alas, do not benevolence and righteousness belong to one's innate character [*qing*]!

8.4.5 But ever since the Three Dynasties, how much noisy contention has occurred throughout the world over them!

Benevolence and righteousness naturally belong to one's innate character [*qing*], but beginning with the Three Dynasties, people have perversely joined in such noisy contention over them, abandoning what is in their innate characters to chase after the footprints [*ji*] of them elsewhere, behaving as if they would never catch up, and this too, has it not, resulted in much grief!

8.5.1 Moreover, depending on curve and straight line or compass and square to achieve correctness is to pare away original nature [*xing*]. To depend on ropes and cords or glues and lacquers to achieve firmness is to corrode virtue [*de*]. To use rites and music to make people bow and scrape, to use benevolence and righteousness to make people nurturing and empathetic, in order to comfort the hearts of all in the world, is to violate original and constant nature [*changran*]. Everything in the world has an original and constant nature—thus the curved is so without using a curve, the straight is so without using a straight line, the round is so without using a compass, the square is so without using a square, the attached is so without using glues and lacquers, and the bound is so without using ropes and cords. Therefore, everyone in the world, unaware, all may live but know not how they happen

to live, and, sharing this same trait, all may be fulfilled [*de*] but know not how this happens.

People have an original and constant nature [*changran*], and if they give themselves over to it without assistance, perfectly identified [*minran*] with it, they will achieve self-fulfillment [*zide*] free of self-awareness.

8.5.2 Therefore, throughout past and present, such non-duality [*buer*] should never fail.

It is by merging [tong] with others that such non-duality [*wuer*] allows for constant wholeness [*changquan*] with them.

8.5.3 So why do benevolence and righteousness, continuous as glue and lacquer or rope and cord, still wander on, mingled with the Dao and its Virtue!

If one trusts to the Dao and so achieves self-fulfillment [*de*], he shall embrace simplicity [*baopu*] and venture forth independently [*duwang*], so as for continued dependence on these other things, none of that happens here.

8.5.4 This causes all in the world to be confused.

All that this continuity of benevolence and righteousness does is just confuse people and cause them to lose their authenticity [*zhen*].

8.6.1 Little confusion changes one's direction, but great confusion changes one's original nature [*xing*].

To change direction from east to west does not go so far as to harm one's body [*ti*], but to parade benevolence and flaunt righteousness causes one to lose his original and constant nature [*changran*], thereby conveying him to the land of death; this is great confusion indeed!

8.6.2 How do we know this is so? Ever since the Sire of Yu [Yu shi][12] summoned up benevolence and righteousness to confuse and obstruct the world, the whole world never fails to rush and obey the dictates of benevolence and righteousness.

Engaging with others so no harm is done them has nothing to do with benevolence, yet the footprints of "benevolence" are left in the process. That which always has principles of behavior appropriately applied has nothing to do with righteousness, yet as an outcome, "righteousness" appears in the process. Therefore, to behave appropriately so that no harm is done has nothing to do with any summons to benevolence and righteousness. Nevertheless, people of the whole world rush around, abandoning their real selves [*wo*] and conforming to those of others, which causes them to lose their original and constant natures [*changran*]. Therefore, confusion of mind does not come from bad people but always rests with those who seem to be good. Thus "benevolence" and "righteousness" are tools that confuse and obstruct the world.

8.6.3 Thus is it not for the sake of "benevolence" and "righteousness" that people's original nature [*xing*] has been changed!

Although the Sire of Yu had it not in his innate character [*qing*] to change them,[13] yet the original nature found in everyone in the world was certainly changed because of him.

8.6.4 Therefore, I shall try to discuss why this is so. Ever since the Three Dynasties, not one in the whole world, indeed, has neglected to change his original nature for the sake of something else.

Before the Three Dynasties, there were, in fact, footprints [*ji*] of unselfconscious action [*wuwei*], and such footprints of unselfconscious action, after all, were esteemed by practitioners of selfconscious action [*youwei*], but with such esteem that they violated their natural basic allotments [*ziran zhi su*]. Even sages [*shengren*] were thus inevitably affected by this, sometimes even exchanging their original natures [*xing*], characterized by "sleeves hanging down over clasped hands," for flesh-wounding engagement with affairs,[14] and how much the more affected were those who worried all the time!

8.6.5 If ordinary people, they sacrificed themselves [*xun*] for advantage; if the learned [*shi*], they sacrificed themselves for reputation; if officers of state, they sacrificed themselves for family; if sages, they sacrificed themselves for all under Heaven.

One who "lives as a quail and eats as a fledgling, a bird in flight leaving no tracks"[15] never sacrifices himself, no matter for what prize it might be! Therefore, one who is always in arcane fusion [*ming*] with the world conforms to it just as it changes, but the footprints [*ji*] so made appear as those of someone who sacrifices himself to save the world. What such a one encounters sometimes might involve flesh-wounding and shinbone-baring exigency, so such footprints would then be those of one wounded to his very nature. However, even if this involves rushing off to the eight ends of the earth, his spirit pneuma [*shenqi*] undergoes no change; though his hands and feet are covered with wounds, the situation he finds himself in troubles him not. So what after all had been the sacrifice! No sacrifice had actually occurred, so don't regard the supposed sacrifice as real sacrifice, though such footprints are identical to what the world thinks indicate sacrifice.[16]

8.6.6 Therefore, although the occupations of these several varied and the regard in which they are held was bruited about differently, the way they all harmed their original natures by sacrificing themselves for something was one and the same. A domestic slave and a houseboy were the two of them together tending sheep, and both lost the sheep. When the domestic slave was asked how it happened, it turned out he was busy holding bamboo slips to read a book. When the houseboy was asked how it happened, it turned out he was playing a game of chance for fun. Although the way they were occupied differed, their loss of the sheep was equally the same. Bo Yi died for the sake of reputation below Mount Shouyang; Robber Zhi

died for gain atop Dongling. Although what these two died for differ, the way they destroyed their lives and harmed their original natures was equally the same, so why must it be approval for Bo Yi and disapproval for Robber Zhi!

What all in the world cherish is life, but here these sacrifice themselves for wanting too much of something, so since both destroyed their lives, whether their sacrifices merit approval or disapproval is not worth further discussion.

8.6.7 Everyone in the world sacrifices himself for something, but if what one sacrifices oneself for is benevolence and righteousness, one who does so is commonly called a "noble man," but if what one sacrifices oneself for is money and goods, one who does so is called a "petty man." Since those who sacrifice themselves include one and all, both the noble man and the petty man are found among them. When it comes to destroying one's life and harming one's original nature, Robber Zhi too is just another Bo Yi, so how can we single out the "noble men" and the petty men among them?

Everyone in the world regards avoidance of such destruction as good, but here these are all the same when it comes to destroying their own lives, so although what they sacrifice themselves for differs, it is not worth taking account of this aspect any further. But how does such destruction of life happen? How does such harm of original nature occur? Both come from esteem for the footprints left by unselfconscious action. Once one realizes that these footprints are but formed as the result of unselfconscious action, one ceases such esteem, avoids trying to exceed himself, and again arcanely fulfills [*ming*] the limits of the true self [*wo*]. Yao and Jie aimed equally at achieving self-fulfillment [*zide*], so what is there to distinguish between the noble man and the petty man!

8.7.1 Moreover, one who subordinates his original nature to benevolence and righteousness, though he becomes as expert at them as Zeng and Shi, is not someone I would say succeeds.

To attach this to that is to "subordinate." To subordinate one's original nature to benevolence is to sacrifice oneself for benevolence, which is the reason such a one does not succeed.

8.7.2 One who subordinates his original nature to the five flavors, though he becomes as expert at them as Yu Er,[17] is not someone I would say succeeds.

To be expert in flavors by original nature, now that is success!

8.7.3 One who subordinates his original nature to the five tones, though he becomes as expert at them as Music Master Kuang, is not someone I would say is acute of ear. One who subordinates his original nature to the five colors, though he becomes as expert at them as Li Zhu, is not someone I would say is keen of sight.

If one depends for these not on one's own self but on others, though one becomes as expert as those others, his own self would be lost. This is why each should trust to the use of his own ears and eyes and not subordinate himself to the likes of Li Zhu and Shi Kuang, for it is this way that keen hearing and acute sight might be had.

8.7.4 What I mean when I call someone "successful" does not refer to "benevolence" and "righteousness" but to the successful realization of the virtues one has, exactly this and nothing more.

If one is good at self-fulfillment, he shall forget all about benevolence and yet be benevolent.

8.7.5 What I mean when I call someone "successful" does not refer to "benevolence" and "righteousness" but to one who trusts in the innate character [*qing*] of his natural endowment [*xingming*], exactly this and nothing more.

If it were said that someone was successful at benevolence and righteousness, it would mean one who harms his own self in order to sacrifice himself for them, which as far as one's natural endowment is concerned is to turn around and be unbenevolent to oneself. Since such a one is unbenevolent to his own person, how else would he treat others! Therefore, it is the one who trusts in his natural endowment who can extend himself to others. Such extension to others frees one from bondage to self so that others and self share equally in self-fulfillment, which can really be said to constitute success!

8.7.6 What I mean when I call someone "acute of hearing" does not refer to one who would hear with the hearing of another but with his own hearing, exactly this and nothing more. What I mean when I call someone "keen of eyesight" does not refer to one who would see with the sight of another but with his own sight, exactly this and nothing more.

When people reject Li Zhu and abandon Shi Kuang and trust to their own powers of hearing and sight, acuteness of hearing and the keenness of sight of everyone everywhere [*wanfang*] shall be kept whole and safe [*quan*].[18]

8.7.7 One who does not see with his own sight but would see with the sight of another fails to fulfill himself but tries instead to achieve another's fulfillment; such a one tries to achieve what another achieves and thus fails to achieve what he himself should achieve. In trying to suit himself to what would suit another he fails to suit himself to what would suit himself.

This is to abandon one's own self and imitate someone else. Although the imitation might exactly match the other person, one's own self is completely lost in the process.[19]

8.7.8 One who tries to suit himself with what suits another and thus fails to suit himself with what suits himself, whether he be a Robber Zhi or a Bo Yi,[20] is equally wicked and perverse.

To become obstructed and perverse through loss of original nature, though the route to the loss might differ, the loss is one and the same for all.

8.7.9 I am shamed before the Dao and its Virtue, thus, above, dare not engage in the practice of "benevolence and "righteousness" or, below, dare not engage in acts of wickedness and perversity.

He is shamed by the unintentionality of the Dao and its virtue and feels apologetic before how arcanely they continually leave no footprints [*wuji*]. Therefore, one should reject selfconscious moral conduct [*caoxing*], forget reputation and gain, and, light and easy as dust drifting about, abandon self and forget other—be just like this, that's all there is to it!

Notes

1. Cheng Xuanying glosses "virtues" as the "five virtues" [*wude*]: benevolence [*ren*], righteousness [*yi*], propriety [*li*], wisdom [*zhi*], and trustworthiness [*xin*], which "are stored in the five viscera [*wuzang*]" (heart, liver, spleen, lungs, and kidneys). "Extra to the virtues" means extra measures of inherent natural virtues, which some might have, just as people might have extra digits and other appendages.
2. "Not artificial" alludes to the *Liezi* (Sayings of Master Lie); *Liezi jishi*, 5: 179–80, where an account appears of Master Craftsman Yan's fabrication of a lifelike automaton singer that so fooled King Mu of Zhou that he was convinced that it was human until it was shown to be "artificial" [*jiawu*] when Yan took it apart in the king's presence.
3. That is, the consignment of man and nature to the perfect order of the Dao; cf. 10.6.
4. "The deluded" refers to deluded rulers, whose mistaken attitudes and policies alienate "the entire world." Cheng Xuanying: "'Measures' [*fang*] are 'techniques of the Dao' [*daoshu*]. This passage speaks to the virtues [*de*] of Zeng and Shi, whose original natures [*xing*] were endowed with extra benevolence [*ren*] and righteousness [*yi*], which, ranked as such among their viscera, they tried to apply to others. But as these represented just what they as individuals knew, they never could achieve grand arcane fusion with all others. One who can naturally fuse arcanely with others, positions himself not with 'benevolence' and 'righteousness,' yet the amounts of benevolence and righteousness with which response is made are never excessive or inadequate, so, infinitely capable of change and transformation, such a one inexhaustibly engages with others free from the least prejudice or predilection. This is what the text means by 'the correctness of the Dao and its Virtue.'" *Zhuangzi jishi*, 2: 313. Zeng Shen, a favorite disciple of Confucius, and Shi Qiu (Scribe Qiu), of the court of Duke Ling of Wey, were both praised as paragons of virtue by Confucius.
5. This alludes to ancient Chinese correlative cosmology thought that links correspondences among the five agents/phases [*wuxing*]: wood [*mu*], fire [*huo*], earth [*tu*], metal [*jin*], and water [*shui*]; the five viscera [*wuzang*]: heart [*xin*], liver [*gan*], spleen [*pi*], lung [*fei*], and kidney [*shen*]; the five humors [*wuye*]: sweat [*han*], nasal mucus [*ti*], tears [*lei*], saliva [*yan*], and spittle [*tuo*]; the five emotions [*wuqing*]: joy [*xi*], anger [nu], sorrow [*ai*], pensiveness [*si*], and fear [*kong*] (variants include worry [*you*], pleasure [*le*], fondness [*hao*], hate [*wu*], and love [*ai*]); the five sense organs [*wuguan*]: eyes [*mu*], nose [*bi*], tongue [*she*], mouth [*kou*], and ears [*er*]; and the five constant virtues [*wude*]: benevolence [*ren*], righteousness [*yi*], propriety [*li*], wisdom [*zhi*], and trust [*xin*]. Since imbalance or corruption in any one of the viscera, for example, will result in corruption in the others, any attempt to augment the viscera (or immediately below the

sense organs) with their correspondences to humors, emotions, and constant virtues will result in unnatural and harmful behavior.

6. Cheng Xuanying: "Axe-shape is called '*fu*[3]-embroidery'; two *yi*-characters back-to-back-shape is called 'fu[2]-embroidery.' The 'five colors' are blue, yellow, red, white, and black. Whereas designs consist of blue and red, emblems consist of red and white. . . . Li Zhu, also known as Li Lou, was a person at the time of the Yellow Thearch of such keen eyesight that he could discern the tip of an autumn hair at the distance of 100 *li*." *Zhuangzi jishi*, 2: 314.
7. Master Kuang had a perfect ear for all technical aspects of music; see 2.12.
8. "Pull up their virtues and boost their original natures" translates *zhuo de qian xing*, which reads as "boost" [*qian*] for the standard version "obstruct" or "stop up" [*sai*], which follows Wang Niansun (1744–1832), who cites the wording of similar passages in the *Huainan zi* (Master of Huainan), where *qian* appears instead of *sai*. Wang Shumin agrees; see *Zhuangzi jiaoquan*, 311, note 8. However, Cheng Xuanying preserves the *sai* reading: "They promote false virtues and stop up their original natures." *Zhuangzi jishi*, 2: 315.
9. The *Taowu* is the title of the historical annals of the ancient state of Chu, which was named for a vicious and untamable mythical animal, a text that records the deeds of evildoers and warns against them. See Zhao Qi and Sun Shi, *Mengzi zhushu* 8A: 2727c–2728a: "When the tradition of the *Odes* died out, only then were the *Chunqiu* (Spring and Autumn Annals) composed. The *Sheng* of Jin, the *Taowu* of Chu, and the *Chunqiu* of Lu are all the same kind [of annals]."
10. Cheng Xuanying: "One who regards joining from the perspective of branching out would say that the joining is a 'web,' but the joining is actually not a 'web'; one who regards branching out from the perspective of joining would say that the branching out is an 'extra digit,' but the branching out is actually not an 'extra digit.' " *Zhuangzi jishi*, 2: 317.
11. Cheng Xuanying: "The 'long' refers to Zeng, Shi, Kuang, Yang, and Mo, all whose inherent natures [*tianxing*] were so endowed with either latent benevolence [*ren*] and righteousness [*yi*], or keen eyesight, or superiority in disputation that when compared with the rabble of ordinary people, they are said to be 'long,' but since they acted perfectly in step with their natures, no excess ever occurred. As for the 'short,' people in general don't measure up to the likes of Zeng and Shi, so they are said to be 'short,' but even so if their celestial mechanisms [*tianji*] are allowed to operate spontaneously [*zizhang*], no inadequacy will occur." *Zhuangzi jishi*, 2: 318.
12. Yu was the name of the fiefdom that the ancient sage-king Shun received from Yao.
13. This phrase can also be translated as "although the Sire of Yu had no predilection [*qing*] to change them."
14. Cheng Xuanying: "Yu of Xia exchanged his effortless action way of ruling for painfully laborious engagement with affairs so that 'wind combed his hair and rain washed his face' and 'his hands and feet were covered with calluses.' Since the ruler above was like this, the common folk below could not help but be the same." *Zhuangzi jiaoquan*, 2: 324.
15. This is the true sage; cf. 12.13.5–12.13.6.
16. Cheng Xuanying: "*Xun* [sacrifice oneself for] is to 'follow' or 'go after' [*cong*], 'seek' or 'strive for' [*ying*], 'seek'[*qiu*], or 'pursue' [*zhu*], used here to address what it is that a person may go after. The petty man is greedy for advantage; the man of principle values reputation, the officer of state sacrifices himself for his particular family; the monarch strives for all within the four seas. Though what they sacrifice themselves for differs, in trying to change their inborn natures [*yixing*] they are all the same. However, since the

sage remains always in arcane fusion with the world, his footsteps there may indicate self-sacrifice, but its flesh-wounding and shinbone-baring exigencies never entangle his spirit." *Zhuangzi jishi*, 2: 325. Cf. 17.16, note 27.

17. Yu Er was a connoisseur of flavors active at the court of Duke Yuan of Qi (d. 643 BCE), though some sources have him living at the time of the Yellow Thearch; see *Zhuangzi jishi*, 2: 328.
18. Cheng Xuanying: "It is admiration for Li Zhu and envy for Shi Kuang that leads to trying to see with the sight of the one and hear with the hearing of the other, so the mind [*xinshen*] races about and hearing and sight wear out and fail. This is really stupid, so how can one ever say that such people are "acute of hearing" and "keen of eyesight"! However, if people listen to just what their ears hear and look at just what their eyes see, while preserving their allotted capacities [*fen*] and trusting to their authenticity [*zhen*], they won't be agitated by exterior influences; it is then that acute hearing and keen sight will be available to all." *Zhuangzi jishi*, 2: 329.
19. Cheng Xuanying: "One who fails to see what his vision sees but would instead see with eyes that strive for the keenness of Li Zhu, or one who fails to know what his intelligence knows but instead subordinates his intelligence out of envy for the righteousness of Shi Yu [Shi Qiu], such people thus falsify their own innate characters and try to achieve what others achieve. It certainly can't be said that they follow their original natures and achieve what they themselves should achieve. But once they do so, they make themselves into counterfeit copies of how others seem to appear. By so imitating others they might please people, but making such counterfeit copies wears out their minds and hearts, thus they fail to suit themselves to what would suit themselves." *Zhuangzi jishi*, 2: 329. The fact that Cheng links "knowing" and "intelligence" with "righteousness" suggests that he regards all of them here as aspects of moral wisdom.
20. Cf. 6.7.8, 8.6.6.–8.6.7, 17.1.2, 17.2.6, 28.55–28.56, 29.17.

CHAPTER 9

MATI [HORSES' HOOVES]

9.1.1 As for the horse, its hooves allow it to tread the frost and snow, and its hair allows it to withstand the wind and cold. It bites off grass and drinks water, lifts its feet, and prances about. This is the true nature of the horse.

Whether nag or great steed, each horse does what is suitable for itself and is thus content.

9.1.2 Were it provided with great ceremonial terraces and grand halls for sleeping, it would have no use for them.

The true nature of the horse is such that though it does not reject saddle or hate to be ridden, it is free of envious desire for glory and splendor.

9.1.3 Then came Bole, who said "I am good at looking after horses." So they were singed, clipped, pared, branded, yoked with bridles and hobbles, and lined up in stables and on wooden flooring, with the result that two or three of ten horses died.

To maintain them with such deliberation is no maintenance at all! They are so maintained as to do them good, but such maintenance does no good.

9.1.4 They were starved, made to go thirsty, forced to gallop, to halt and move in unison, for those in front the scourge of bit and head ornament, for those behind the threat of leather whip and bamboo crop, with the result that more than half of horses died.

He who is good at riding horses does so by letting them completely realize [*jin*] their capability, and such complete realization of potential consists in letting them act to suit themselves. However, if when horses would walk they are forced to gallop fast, this tries to exceed the use for which they are capable, which is why it happens that, unable to bear it, many of them die. But, if horses, whether nag or great steed, were allowed to employ their strengths accordingly and suit their allotted capacities for speed, although their hoof prints might stretch out to beyond the eight ends of the earth, the original nature of each and every horse would surely be kept whole and safe. Nevertheless, the deluded, when they hear about horses being allowed to suit their own natures, take this to mean that they should be freed and no longer ridden. When they hear talk of unselfconscious action, they are wont to say that this means it is better to lie down and rest than to get up and act. And how they do go on and on without ever turning back! But this is surely to miss completely what Master Zhuang means by far!

9.1.5 The potter says, "I am so good at working clay that my round pieces fit the compass and my square pieces match the square." The carpenter says, "I am so good at working wood that my curved pieces fit the curve and my straight pieces match the straight line." But how could the nature of clay and wood be such that the one needs to fit the compass and square and the other the curve and straight line? Nevertheless, age after age praises them, saying, "As Bole was good at maintaining horses, the potter and carpenter are good at working clay and wood." This too is the error committed by those who govern the world.

The world commonly thinks that to allow people to follow their natural course and refrain from adding to their effectiveness is not a good way to govern. Bend the curved to make it straight or train the nag to make of it a great steed. One can try to use compass and square to force the nature of these to be what it is not, only stopping when they cause death, but to say that this is good government, is that not surely in error!

9.2.1 In my opinion, those who are really good at governing the world don't do it this way.

To govern by not selfconsciously governing, this then is to be good at governing.

9.2.2 It is in the constant nature [*changxing*] of the common folk that they weave to make clothes and plow to provide food—these are known as their "common virtues" [*tongde*].

Although the virtues of the common folk differ in detail, they are the same in general. Therefore, what must not be denied to them by nature include the need to be clothed and fed, so occupations they must not be prevented from perusing include plowing and weaving. As this is the same for all in the world, as such it is fundamental [*ben*]. To abide by the Dao in this way achieves the perfection [*zhi*] of unselfconscious action [*wuwei*].

9.2.3 When they are allowed to remain one and the same in these and thus stay free from partiality, this is called the "natural state of freedom" [*tianfang*].

It is by leaving them alone that they spontaneously remain one and the same—simple as that. Since this is characterized by impartiality, it is called the "natural state of freedom."

9.2.4 So it was in an age of perfect virtue [*zhide*] that they acted with complete satisfaction and looked with complete absorption.

Since they were self-sufficient [*zizu*] within, they presented no appearance of craving for anything without.

9.2.5 At such a time as that, mountains had no paths or trails through them and waters had no boats on or bridges over them.

Since no one tried to gain anything beyond his appropriate expectations, everyone was content to stay in their own homes.

9.2.6 The myriad folk lived together with all living creatures as neighbors in such a land.

In primal and unselfconscious chaos [*hunmang*] when everyone had the same chance for fulfillment [*tongde*], since everyone was at one with the world, all were indifferent to gain from it, so how could states have existed apart or families differed?

9.2.7 Birds and beasts formed multitudes, and plants and trees grew to maturity.

Since people did not go beyond the satisfaction of their original natures, they stayed free of inordinate desires, thus everything was whole and safe [*quan*].

9.2.8 As such, one could tie and tether birds and beasts and wander about with them, could climb up to the nests of crows and magpies and peer into them.

Since no harm was done to creatures, they were tame.

9.3.1 In such a world of perfect virtue [*zhide*], people lived together with the birds and beasts, joined in kinship with the myriad creatures, so how would there be any awareness of the "noble man" or the "petty man" then? Identical in their freedom from selfconscious awareness of them, they were not estranged from their virtue.

When people have such selfconscious awareness, they estrange themselves from the Dao by trying to be "good."[1]

9.3.2 When people were identical in their freedom from desire, this state is called the "simple uncarved block" [*supu*].

When people have desires, they estrange themselves from their original natures by trying to embellish themselves.

9.3.3 In this state of the "simple uncarved block," the original nature of the common folk was fulfilled.

They were untroubled by awareness and desire.

9.3.4 But when the "sage" arrived,

"The sage" means nothing but footprints left indicating that the common folk had fulfilled their original nature; it does not indicate the maker of the footprints. When the text states, "but when the 'sage' arrived," it means "but when his footprints appeared."

9.3.5 benevolence was practiced with such toil and effort, righteousness with such self-importance and confidence that the world began to have doubts. Such histrionic music was made, such picky and obscure rites were performed that all the world began to fragment.

Once the footprints of "the sage" were manifest, benevolence and righteousness became inauthentic and rites and music so estranged people from their original nature that all they could manage was but to feign outer appearance. Once "sages" appear, such fraud happens, but though this is so, what can be done about it?

9.3.6 Therefore, as long as the plain uncarved block remained unspoiled, who would have made it into a sacrificial vessel? As long as the white jade remained intact, who would have made it into a ceremonial tablet? As long as the Dao and its Virtue were not abandoned, what need was there to resort to benevolence and righteousness? As long as people were not estranged from their innate personalities [*xingqing*], what need was there to resort to rites and music? As long as the five colors did not confuse, who would have formulated patterns for color? As long as the five tones did not confuse, who would have established the six yang pitches [*liulü*] for resonance?

All these refer to transforming pristine simplicity [*pu*] into showy embellishment [*hua*], to discarding roots and venerating branch tips, which for inherent nature [*tiansu*] does but maim and cripple. Although the world esteems such things, there is nothing of value in them.

9.3.7 As to spoil the uncarved block by making it into a vessel was the fault of the carpenter, so to ruin the Dao and its Virtue by devising "benevolence" and "righteousness" was the crime of "the sage."

As the artisan resorts to the control of compass and square, so "the sage" resorts to footprints that he esteems.

9.4.1 Now as for horses, when they live out on the open plain, they graze on grass and drink water. When happy they rub their necks on each other; when angry they turn back to back and kick at each other. What horses know is just this and nothing more.

If one drives them in accord with that authentic knowledge [*zhenzhi*] of theirs and rides them in harmony with what is natural to them, one can have them last to the end of a myriad tricents route without violating the original nature that all horses have.

9.4.2 But when they are hampered with shaft yokes or beset with harnesses, forced to stay in unison by means of engraved metal moon head insignias, all that horses then know what to do, looking askance with fear and anger, is try to twist out of yokes and break out of harnesses, or, careening about madly, try to spit out bits and throw off halters. As a result, what horses know then creates such inauthentic attitude [*tai*] that they try to usurp control.

The original nature of horses differs from one to another, so if one tries to make use of them all in the same way, it will result in their assuming inauthentic attitudes [*tai*], which exhausts their strength.[2]

9.5.1 At the time of Sire Hexu [Hexu shi],[3] the common folk stayed at home, unselfconscious of what they were doing; moved, unselfconscious of where they were going; happy their mouths were full of food, they wandered about drumming on their full bellies. What the common folk then were capable of was just this.

These suited the true capabilities of the common folk.

9.5.2 But when "the sage" arrived, he had people bow and scrape to rites and music in order to rectify the demeanor [*xing*] of all in the world and had them stretch up on tiptoe for "benevolence" and "righteousness" beyond reach in order to make the hearts and minds of all in the world kind. Only then did the common folk instead began to leap and prance after coveted knowledge, which had them so competing at reaching positions of advantage that they could not bring themselves to stop. This too was the crime of "the sage."

These faults all occurred because footprints should be esteemed.

Notes

1. Cheng Xuanying: "One who sacrifices himself for something, being wicked and perverse, is a 'petty man'; one who treads the correct path, being square and upright, is a 'noble man.' But once when people lived in tree nests and dwelt in caves, not separate from birds and beasts, 'mouths full of food and drumming on filled bellies,' creatures all mixed together with no way to tell one from another, how could they recognize who was a 'noble man' or distinguish who was a 'petty man'?" *Zhuangzi jishi*, 2: 337.
2. Cheng Xuanying: " 'Inauthentic attitude' signifies 'treachery and falsehood.' The true knowledge of horses is suited to the open plain, so if they are forced to gallop faster than their allotted capacity to do so, this produces false and treacherous attitude in them, and the blame for such treachery and falsehood must be assigned to Bole." *Zhuangzi jishi*, 2: 340.
3. Cheng Xuanying: "Hexu was a monarch of remote antiquity, about whom it is also said that his virtue, ardent as flame, compelled folk from afar to gravitate to him in submission, which was why he was called Hexu [literally "Ardent Attractor of Followers"]. No doubt he was the same person as Yandi (Flame Thearch)." *Zhuangzi jishi*, 2: 341. The current scholarly consensus is that Yandi, so far as the written record is concerned, can be identified with Shennong, the "Divine Farmer," one of the Three Sage-Kings of remote antiquity.

CHAPTER 10

QUQUE [RANSACK CHESTS]

10.1 To guard against petty thieves who ransack chests, delve into bags, or open strongboxes, one who is sure to bind them tightly with ropes and cords or belt them securely with buckles and hasps will be called by ordinary people of the world "knowledgeable" [*zhi*]. But if a great robber comes along, he will place the chest on his back, pick up the strongbox, or place the bag on a carrying pole and make off with them, concerned only that ropes and cords, buckles and hasps might not be secure. As such, the one who previously had been called "knowledgeable," is not he now just someone who collected things for a great thief?

This exemplifies how "knowledge" is insufficiently reliable.

10.2.1 Therefore, let me try to discuss what this means. Those whom ordinary people of the world call "knowledgeable," do they not collect things for the great thief? Those whom they call "sage," do they not stand on guard for the great thief? How do we know that this is so? Long ago in the state of Qi, neighboring villages had sight of each other and could hear each other's chickens and dogs. Where nets were spread on water and where plows and hoes pierced soil, the area covered more than two thousand square tricents. Everywhere within its four borders, wherever they founded ancestral shrines and altars to the gods of soil and grain, and wherever they established places for governing village, hamlet, or rural district, when did they ever fail to emulate "the sages"! Yet in the space of a day, Lord Cheng of Tian killed the ruler of Qi and stole his state.[1]

To emulate "the sages" amounts to nothing more than emulating the footprints they left behind. Now footprints are things of the past and are done with, not devices used to respond to the vicissitudes of the moment, so why should people adhere to them with such esteem? Devotion to footprints already made as means to control the infinitely changeable [*wufang*] is such that, when the infinitely changeable arrives, to follow these footprints are sure to get one bogged down. Therefore, safeguarding one's state turns out to be safeguarding the state for someone else.

10.2.2 But what he stole, how could it have been only his state? He stole it along with methods derived from wisdom of "the sages."

If he had not stolen the methods of "the sages," he would not have had the means to usurp his state.[2]

10.2.3 Therefore, although Lord Cheng of Tian was labeled a robber and a thief, he nevertheless occupied a position as secure as Yao or Shun. Smaller states dared not censure him and greater states dared not punish him, and for twelve generations his people possessed the state of Qi. And he did not just steal the state of Qi, for along with it, did he not also steal methods derived from wisdom of "the sages" to safeguard the robber and thief that he personally was?

That is, the methods of "the sages" can only be of use to such a man and can't serve as devices that are always perfectly appropriate [*quandang*].

10.3.1 Let me try to discuss what this means. Those whom ordinary people of the world call "perfectly knowledgeable" [*zhizhi*], do they not collect things for the great thief? Those whom they call "perfect sages," do they not stand on guard for the great thief? How do we know that this is so? Long ago Longfeng was beheaded, Bi Gan had his heart cut out, Chang Hong was disemboweled, and Zixu's corpse was left to rot.[3] So despite these four being such worthies, they themselves could not avoid being slaughtered.

That is, ruthless and arbitrary rulers too can rely on the monarch's power to slaughter such worthies so that no one dares mount opposition, all thanks to the methods of "the sages." If methods of "the sages" had not existed, how could Jie and Zhou ever have been able to safeguard their own positions as they committed such cruel murder, while making all in the world look the other way?

10.3.2 So it was that one of Robber Zhi's gang asked him, "Do even robbers have a sagely way?" To which he replied, "No matter where one goes, there is always a sagely way! His reckoning of what valuables might be kept in a building indicates sageness; that he breaks in first indicates courage; that he leaves last indicates righteousness; knowing whether or not it can be done indicates wisdom; dividing the spoils equally indicates benevolence. To be deficient in these five and yet become a great robber, no such thing ever happens in the world.

Though these five are supposed to provide the means to suppress the robber, on the contrary they are actually the robber's assets.

10.3.3 Looking at it from this point of view, just as the good man can't establish himself without having attained the way of "the sages," so too Robber Zhi can't ply his trade without having attained the way of "the sages." In all the world, good men are few and bad men many, thus it rarely happens that "the sages" benefit the world, though they often harm it.

How true these words are! However, as true as they may be, it yet won't do to get rid of "the sages." Since it is not yet possible to rid the world of selfconscious knowledge, the way of "the sages" must be used to keep it under control. If the world is not rid of all other forms of selfconscious knowledge but only rid of the wisdom of "the sages," more harm would be done to the world than when there was sageness involved. That being so, though harm caused by "the sages" is great, this is still better than the disorder that would result if "the sages" were done away with. Though better than getting rid of "the sages," this still is not as good as freeing the world completely of harm by ridding it of all selfconscious knowledge. Is not it too bad! In all the world, no one fails to strive for gain yet no one can get rid of all selfconscious knowledge! How confused they are, how lost to the truth!

10.3.4 Thus it is said, "when lips are gone, teeth grow cold";[4] "when wine of Lu was diluted, Handan was besieged";[5] and "when the sages appeared, great robbers arose."

Doing away with lips is not done to make the teeth cold, but teeth do become cold; when the wine of Lu was diluted, it was not done to cause the siege of Handan, but Handan was besieged; when the sages appeared, it did not happen to make great robbers arise, but great robbers did arise, for such is spontaneous mutual generation, the inevitable propensity of things. Although the sages did not establish themselves so they could be esteemed by people, yet they could not prevent people from esteeming them. Therefore, regardless of whether they were eminent or humble, or whether what they did really happened or not, if one [a ruler] emulates the example of the sages, all in the world will suppress complaint and obey without understanding—it is just this that supplied the means whereby Robber Zhi became a great robber.

10.3.5 Attack and abuse "the sages" and let robbers and thieves do whatever they want, then the world would start to come to order.

Since it is "the sages" that the world esteems, if we end our esteem for them and instead abide by the simple uncarved block [*supu*] in our own selves, abolish their prohibitions, and replace them with diminished desires, such attacking and abusing "the sages" will allow the simple uncarved block in us to be kept whole and safe.

10.3.6 As valleys empty when rivers run dry, as chasms are filled when hills are leveled, so once sages die, great robbers would no longer arise,

Rivers dry up not to make valleys empty, but valleys do become empty; hills are leveled not to make chasms filled, but chasms are filled; sages are rejected not to bring an end to robbers, but robbers are brought to an end. Thus it is that bringing an end to robbers depends on the elimination of desire and not on the promulgation of sagely wisdom.

10.3.7 and the whole world would be at peace yet without reason for being so.

It is not merely that robbers would cease, the reason why people so compete to esteem the footprints [of the sages] would all be gone too.[6]

10.4.1 As long as sages don't die, great robbers won't cease, and the more importance is placed on "the sages" in governing the world, the more advantages accrue to Robber Zhi.

Increasing the importance of "the sages" in governing the world only results in people of the ilk of King Jie and Robber Zhi usurping their methods as devices for their own use. So if what they usurp as devices is increased in importance, how can the advantages derived possibly be less?

10.4.2 If bushels and pecks are used for measuring, the robber will even include bushels and pecks in what he steals; if steelyard scales are used for weighing, he will even include steelyard scales in what he steals; if official tallies and seals are used to engender trust, he will even include tallies and seals in what he steals; if benevolence and righteousness are used to rectify behavior, he will even include benevolence and righteousness in what he steals.

Although these are the means whereby petty thieves are brought to grief, they are also what great robbers use as devices for their own advantage.

10.4.3 How do we know this is so?

> **Steal a belt hook and you're put to death,**
> **But steal a state and you're a feudal lord.**
> **And within your gates of a feudal lord**
> **There keep benevolence and righteousness safe.**

As such, is this not stealing sagely wisdom for its benevolence and righteousness?[7] Therefore, one who makes every effort to become a great robber or would usurp the position of a feudal lord will steal benevolence and righteousness, along with the advantage of using bushels and pecks, steelyard scales, and tallies and seals. No matter what reward of official carriages and caps is offered, nothing can deter him; no matter what intimidation of executioner's axe is made, nothing can stop him.

Official carriages and caps and the execution's axe represent substantial rewards and punishments, made substantial in order to thwart robbers, but as great robbers will just keep on doing their utmost until they manage to steal them, these then instead become devices for robbers themselves to use. What they have to use is then so substantial that it provides the means for them to become great robbers. Those who are "great robbers" are sure to use benevolence and righteousness to make people behave, use steelyard scales to enforce fairness, use tallies and seals to guarantee trust, use official carriages and caps to deter, and use executioner's axes to intimidate. They first have to steal these public instruments [*gongqi*], for only then can they manage to usurp the position of a feudal lord. This is why, whether benevolence and righteousness or reward and punishment, such measures are only effective in eliminating the theft of belt hooks.

10.4.4 Providing Robber Zhi with such substantial advantages that he cannot be stopped is a crime for which no one but "the sages" are responsible.

The reason why Robber Zhi can't be stopped is because the advantages stolen by him are so substantial, and the reason why these advantages are so substantial is because "the sages" don't belittle them. Therefore, putting an end to robbers depends on devaluing the worth of things and not on stressing the importance of "the sages."

10.5.1 Thus it is said, "As fish may not quit the safety of the depths, sharp instruments of the state may not be disclosed to the people."

If fish quit the safety of the depths, they will be caught by men; if the sharp instruments of the state are readily apparent, they will be appropriated by robbers. This is why they may not be disclosed to the people.[8]

10.5.2 "The sage" is a term for the sharp instruments for the world,

A real sage truly can reject sageness and abandon wisdom, and instead allow people to fulfill their own arcane limits to perfection. Once the limits of everyone are arcanely fulfilled, footprints thus made indicate only that the people have been benefited [*li*]. "Instruments" [*qi*] are nothing other than footprints left in the process; if these are held for use, they become "instruments."[9]

10.5.3 and not something that may be disclosed to the world.

By disclosing these sharp instruments to the world, robbers and thieves are provided with assets.

10.5.4 Therefore, reject sageness and abandon wisdom, for then great robbers will cease.

If they are divested of such assets as these, without any ban enacted against them, they will stop of their own accord.

10.5.5 Discard jades and destroy pearls, for then petty thieves won't arise.

If what they value is devalued, without threat of punishment they will cease of their own accord.

10.5.6 Burn tallies and smash seals, for then the common folk will be simple and unwitting.

If what people rely on to be false and treacherous is removed, they no longer will have the means to practice their cheating and knavery.

10.5.7 Bust the bushels and break the scales, for then the common folk will no longer argue.

These may be fair for the little but are used unfairly by the great.

10.5.8 Utterly destroy the methods of the sages all over the world, for then it becomes possible to discuss things with the common folk.

Once they are freed of external corrective measures, their own internal uncarved block will be whole and safe, so no talk of loss of self [*zishi*] will occur.

10.5.9 Discard the six yang pitches [*liulü*] and let tones be confused, burn up woodwinds and strings, stop up blind Kuang's ears, for only then will people all over the world come into possession of their own innate sense of hearing. Get rid of formulated patterns, banish all discrimination among the five colors, paste up the eyes of Li Zhu, for only then will people all over the world come into possession of their own sense of sight.

As long as there are Li Zhu and Master Kuang for sounds and colors, they will enjoy the esteem of those who have ears and eyes. Although people are endowed with individual innate allotments, what they value leads them astray, resulting in loss of their natural endowments. So if what they value is done away with and people abandon what others have and trust only what they have themselves, with the hearing and sight of everyone kept whole and safe, people will come into possession of their own authenticity.

10.5.10 Destroy the curve and straight line and abandon compass and square, twist off the fingers of Artisan Chui [Gong Chui], for only then will people all over the world come into skills of their own. For thus it is said, "Great skill seems unskilled."[10]

As mean and lowly as they are, spiders and dung beetles spin perfect webs and roll perfect pellets without seeking the skill of a master craftsman, so it is that each of all the myriad creatures has its own specific capability. Although capabilities differ, as for what they practice, creatures dare not do anything else, and that is why though they seem skillful they are really unskilled. Therefore, one good at employing the masses, allows those who can shape squares make things square, those who can shape rounds make things round, so that each person commits himself to his own capability and everyone is content with his own original nature; he does not demand of the common folk the skill of an Artisan Chui. Therefore, whereas the mass crafts, involving as they do non-interchangeable capabilities, all might still seem unskilled, yet when all in the world fulfills personal potential a great overall skill would be achieved. Since people would now employ just what they themselves are capable of, compass and square may be abandoned and the fingers of the marvelous craftsman may be twisted off.

10.5.11 Cut away the behavior of Zeng and Shi, plug the mouths of Yang and Mo, and discard "benevolence" and "righteousness," for only then will the virtues of all in the world arcanely unite [*xuantong*].[11]

Once rid of their leadership, which misleads the masses, everyone in the world will recover his own way and thus unite with arcane virtue [*xuande*].

10.5.12 Once people come into possession of their own keen eyesight, the world will no longer melt into blur; once people come into possession of their own acute hearing, the world will no longer be troubled; once people come into possession of their own wisdom, the world no longer will be confused; once people come into possession of their own virtue, the world no longer will go astray. Zeng, Shi, Yang, Mo, Master Kuang, Artisan Chui, and Li Zhu all might have established their virtues for external show, thereby bedazzling the world into chaos,

All these were endowed with so much versatility that they made everyone in the world dance after them in emulation, but in emulating them, people lost what they themselves were. It was this loss of self due to them that made them masters of chaos, and the great disaster that has so afflicted the world is caused by just this loss of self.

10.5.13 but to emulate them is absolutely no use!

Methods that may be used are as follows: when vision tries not to exceed what one can see, the vision of all never fails to be keen; when hearing tries not to exceed what can be heard, the hearing of all never fails to be acute; when whatever is done tries not to exceed what one is capable of, the crafts of all never fail to be skillful; when knowing tries not to exceed what one can know, the original nature of everyone never fails to be in accord; when virtue is not forced to exceed its potential, the virtues of everyone never fail to be apt. So what use is there to set up models beyond one's natural capacity to reach and make the world so chase after them that it can't find its way back!

10.6.1 Do even you not know about the age of perfect virtue? Long ago, just at the time of the clansmen Rongcheng, Dating, Bohuang, Zhongyang, Lilu, Lixu, Xuanyuan, Hexu, Zunlu, Zhurong, Fu Xi, and Shennong,[12] the common folk knotted cords and used them as reminders.

Just these sufficed to record essential events.

10.6.2 They found their food so delicious, their clothes so beautiful,

Since they found delicious what they had always eaten and found beautiful what they had always worn, as for any inclination to wasteful extravagance, they would never be content with that.

10.6.3 their customs so delightful, and their dwellings so satisfying that, though neighboring states might provide distant views of each other and the sounds of each other's chickens and dogs might even be heard, the common folk would reach old age without ever going back and forth between such places.[13]

This represents absolute freedom from covetousness.

10.6.4 At a time such as this, there was nothing but perfect order. But then it came to pass that the common folk were made to crane their necks and rise up on tiptoe, when someone said "There is a worthy in some place or other," so they hoisted what provisions they could carry and went off in pursuit of

him, deserting their parents within and abandoning service to their lord without, their footprints extending to the very borders of the feudal states, their cart ruts ranging across more than a thousand tricents.

The footprints left by perfect order caused evil as bad as this.

10.6.5 Thus it was that rulers [*shang*] who loved knowledge were responsible for such crime.

"Rulers" [*shang*] refers to monarchs who loved knowledge. If one comes to know something and then falls in love with that something, this leads to such crime as this.[14]

10.7.1 As long as rulers love knowledge yet are without the Dao, the whole world will be beset by great chaos. How do we know that this is so? The more people know about devices such as bows, crossbows, bird nets, and harpoon arrows, the more birds will find ways to confound them in the sky; the more people know about hooks, bait, fish nets, and fish traps, the more fish will find ways to confound them in the water. The more people know about cage traps, net traps, and rabbit snares, the more beasts will confound them in the marshes.

The more meticulous ways are devised to go after them, the more clever they will become at escaping them. Since one can't use knowledge to scheme against birds and beasts, how much the less will this work for men! Therefore, the only thing to do for one who would govern the world is to avoid relying on knowledge, for nothing good comes from reliance on it.

10.7.2 The more different forms occur in plots of trickery, in the muddling of "hard" and "white," and in the fraud of uniting "same" and "difference,"[15] the more ordinary people will be confused by disputation.

Because rulers indulge in many of these, those below find it impossible to remain content with the few they have, but since they have few by nature, when they try to have many, it only makes them confused.

10.7.3 Therefore, blame for why the world, made dim-witted and dull, suffers great confusion must be assigned to the love of knowledge. As a result, all people in the world know only to strive after what they don't know, but no one knows to strive after what he already knows;

To fail to strive after what one already knows and instead strive after what one does not know means that one has discarded his own self to imitate others, and tries to exceed the limits of his own endowed allotment.

10.7.4 all know to condemn what they regard as not good, but no one knows to condemn what they already regard as good.

Regarding as good what is generally regarded as good is the origin of the competition to esteem it.[16]

10.7.5 And this was how the great confusion occurred, why the brightness of sun and moon above was made deviant, the essence was melted out of hills and streams below, and the four seasons were made to lag in between.

Not even a single insect that squirmed along, not even a single creature that fluttered around managed to avoid having its original nature violated. How great the confusion was that fondness for knowledge inflicted on the world!

Though good fortune or misfortune, remorse and regret all stem from human behavior, the trouble that knowledge is capable of stirring up is really enough to shake Heaven and Earth, effecting the behavior of every living thing, so how can anyone not forget about all he would know!

10.7.6 Ever since the Three Dynasties, it has only been thus, the pristinely simple common folk are abandoned but cunning sharpers are favored; peaceful unselfconscious action is abolished and intent fostered by continuous harangue [*tuntun*] is preferred. It is just this continuous harangue that has so confused the world!

"Continuous harangue" [*tuntun*] means to instruct others by going on about oneself.

Notes

1. "Lord Cheng" is the posthumous title of Chen Heng (Lord Cheng of Tian [Tian Chengzi] or Tian Heng), whose forebears were enfoeffed in Tian, a district in the state of Qi, who killed the ruler, Duke Jian, in 481 BCE. Members of the Chen clan, who also took Tian as their surname, had been gaining power in Qi long before Chen Heng, then a grand master at the Qi court, killed Duke Jian, who was plotting to expel them. Thereafter, the Chen/Tian clan became de facto rulers of Qi.
2. Cheng Xuanying: "What Tian Heng stole, how could it merely have been the state of Qi? He first stole the wisdom of the sages, which he used to obtain the support of the feudal lords. Thus we know that the footprints left behind of benevolence and righteousness perfectly form the basis of robbery." *Zhuangzi jishi*, 2: 345.
3. For Guan Longfeng and Bi Gan, see chapter 4, note 8. Concerning Chang Hong (d. 492 BCE), Cheng Xuanying quotes from Liu Xiang's *Shuoyuan* (Garden of Persuasions): "Shu Xiang [died ca. 528 BCE] of Jin had Chang Hong killed: Since he had seen Chang Hong several times at the Zhou court, Shu Xiang pretended to have lost a letter there in which Chang Hong is supposed to have told him, 'You should raise troops in Jin to attack Zhou, so we can get rid of Sire Liu and replace him with Sire Dan.' The Liu crown prince reported this to the Zhou king, adding, 'This was said by Chang Hong.' So the king had Chang executed." *Zhuangzi jishi*, 2: 347. Zixu is the personal name of Wu Yun (d. 484 BCE); cf. 6.7,8, 29.18.
4. Duke Xi of Lu, Fifth Year (654 BCE): "When Duke Xian of Jin again asked for grant of passage through Yu so he could attack Guo, Gong Ziqi argued against it, saying 'Guo is a buffer that protects Yu, so if Guo perishes, Yu is sure to fall with it. Jin is such that we should neither encourage its greed nor take its pillaging lightly. Once is already taking too much of a chance, so how could we now risk it yet again! Heed how the proverb goes, "Just as wheel struts and wheel [*fuju*] depend on each other, once lips are gone teeth are cold." This sums up the relationship between Yu and Guo exactly!' " Du Yu and Kong Yingda, *Chunqiu Zuozhuan zhengyi* (Correct meaning of the *Spring and Autumn Annals* with *Zuo's Commentary*), 12:1795b. For *fu* as "wheel struts," see Joseph Needham

and Wang Ling, *Science and Civilization in China*, vol. 4: *Physics and Physical Technology*; Part II: *Mechanical Engineering*, 79, where *fu* is explained as "quasi-diametral struts" [*jiafu*].

5. Lu Deming: "When King Xuan of Chu invited the feudal lords to court, Duke Gong of Lu was the last to arrive; moreover the wine he brought was weak. King Xuan was angry and tried to shame him, but Duke Gong did not accept the rebuke, saying, 'As direct descendent of the Duke of Zhou and thus superior to all the feudal lords, when I commit acts of etiquette and have music performed, it is as a Son of Heaven, thus bringing merit to the house of Zhou. My gift of wine to you is already a breach of etiquette, and you now rebuke me that it is weak—is that not going too far!' Thereupon without apology he returned home. Fueled by anger, King Xuan dispatched troops and, allied with Qi, attacked Lu. King Hui of Liang had been wanting to strike a blow at Zhao but had feared that Chu would come to its rescue. Now because Chu was occupied with Lu, Liang could lay siege to Handan [in Zhao]. This speaks to how events have their origin in one another, which, of course, is a matter of stimulus and response [*ganying*]. . . . [However,] Xu Shen in his commentary to the *Huainan zi* (Master of Huainan) says: 'When Chu held a meeting of the feudal lords, Lu and Zhao both presented wine to the king of Chu. The Lu wine was weak, the Zhao wine strong. The principal wine steward of Chu asked the Zhao to give him some wine, but the Zhao refused. Angered, the steward, switching the strong wine of Zhao for the weak wine of Lu, submitted it to the king. Because the king of Chu thought the Zhao wine was deliberately diluted, he besieged Handan.' " *Zhuangzi jishi*, 2: 349.
6. Although other commentators, traditional and modern, as well as modern translators tend to read the passage something like "the whole world would be at peace without troubles [*wugu*]," neither Guo Xiang nor Cheng Xuanying does so. Tang Yijie notes how Guo often links *wugu* "without reason"/"without cause" with another favorite term, "spontaneously so" [*zier*]; see *Guo Xiang yu Wei-Jin xuanxue* (Guo Xiang and the Learning of the Arcane in the Wei-Jin Period), 157, 233–34, 237, 282, 284, 317. So for Guo, once the sages were rejected, the world would achieve peace *spontaneously*. Cheng has yet another interpretation: "Reason" [*gu*] here means "matter" [*shi*]. Once the sages were rejected and wisdom abandoned, the whole world would be at peace so that people would sing and beat on earthenware pots, thus nothing would be done with selfconscious artificiality [*youwei*]." *Zhuangzi jishi*, 2: 350.
7. Cheng Xuanying: "If benevolence and righteousness were not preserved, such a one would have no way to become a mass leader of men. Hence the text says, how can this not be a matter of stealing the footprints of the sages and using them to steal a state?" *Zhuangzi jishi*, 2: 351.
8. Cheng Xuanying: "The 'sharp instruments of the state' [*liqi*] are the footprints left by the sages." *Zhuangzi jishi*, 2: 353. Here, "sharp" [*li*], as in English, has overtones of "deceit" or "fraud." Moreover, the saying quoted, although phrased only slightly differently in *Laozi*, section 36, is interpreted by Wang Bi entirely differently from the way that Guo and Cheng read it here. Cf. Richard John Lynn, *The Classic of the Way and Virtue*, 116–17.
9. Guo distinguishes between the real sage and the footprints left by him, which become "the sage" and mislead people into perverting their original natures in trying to live up to the wisdom associated with "the sage." Guo also takes advantage of the range of meanings of *li*: "sharp," when applied to the harmful and fraudulent instruments associated with "the sage," but "benefit" when describing what happens when people are allowed to fulfill their own natures. Cf. *Laozi*, chapter 36: "The sharp instruments of the

state may not be disclosed to the people." Wang Bi: "Sharp instruments are devices used to profit the state. Act only in accordance with the nature of the people and don't rely on punishment to keep them in order. It is by ensuring that these devices can't be seen, thus allowing everyone to obtain his proper place, that they are the 'sharp instruments' of the state. Disclosing them to the people means relying on punishment." Lynn, *The Classic of the Way and Virtue*, 116.

10. "*Laozi*, section 45; Lynn, *The Classic of the Way and Virtue*, 139, where "unskilled" [*zhuo*] is translated as "clumsy."
11. *Laozi*, section 56; Lynn, *The Classic of the Way and Virtue*, 158, where *xuantong* is rendered as "one with mystery."
12. Cheng Xuanying: "The above mentioned twelve clansmen were all monarchs of remote antiquity. Since at that time written records were not yet kept, we don't know their chronological sequence." *Zhuangzi jishi*, 2: 358.
13. *Laozi*, section 80; Lynn, *The Classic of the Way and Virtue*, 189.
14. Cheng Xuanying: "It was because of esteem for the footprints of perfect order and love for wisdom relating to the governance of men that such crime occurred as this." *Zhuangzi jishi*, 2: 359.
15. For "hard" and "white," see chapter 2, note 53; uniting "same" and "difference" is one of the paradoxical ploys used by Hui Shi to confound his interlocutors.
16. Cheng Xuanying: "Those from whom esteem is withheld are Jie and Shi, and the reason why esteem is accorded elsewhere is that it is directed at footprints of the sages. The conduct of Robber Zhi was 'not good,' thus he came to grief at Dongling; Tian Heng followed the footprints of the sages, thus he was able to steal the state of Qi. Therefore, although the way they were occupied differed, the loss of the sheep by the domestic slave and the houseboy too was equally the same. One might think that the conduct of Bo Yi and Robber Zhi differed, but the harm they did to their original natures was exactly the same. It is the disciples of ignorance and the commonplace who started the notions of goodness and evil, but what is good or bad has really never been settled." *Zhuangzi jishi*, 2: 362.

CHAPTER 11

ZAIYOU [LET THINGS FREELY BE]

11.1.1 I have heard about letting the world be [*you*] but have never heard about putting the world in order [*zhi*].

Letting it be [*you*] allows it to exist freely on its own [*zizai*], which results in order, but if one tries to put it in order, disorder [*luan*] results. Human life is inherently simple and straightforward [*zhi*], so if nothing tries to lead it astray, one won't attempt to exceed one's natural endowment [*xingming*], and natural desires and aversions won't be distorted. If those in authority don't practice unselfconscious action [*wuwei*], actions taken by them will result in everyone conforming to them. This is why having been seduced into liking and desiring things people are wont to exceed the limits of their natural endowment. Therefore, what is valued in the sage king is not his ability to put things in order but the fact that by practicing unselfconscious action, he allows people to behave spontaneously [*ziwei*].

11.1.2 One leaves it alone out of fear that the people of the world would exceed the limits of their own natural endowments, and lets it be out of fear that the people of the world would stray from the merits of their own innate virtues. But if people of the world exceed not their natural endowments and stray not from the merits of their innate virtues, then, as such, the world achieves order.

With unselfconscious rule [*wuzhi*], people neither exceed nor stray.

11.1.3 Long ago, the way Yao ruled the world made everyone so happy that it delighted their original natures, which disturbed their equanimity; the way

Jie ruled the world made everyone so miserable that it embittered their original natures, which made them unhappy.

Even though Yao let the world freely be, the footprints he left behind came to mean "order." Although the order of the former and the disorder of the latter certainly differed, it is just that the two were the same, in that they both inflicted loss of happiness on later ages and in the way they both denied self-realization to people, who either competed to esteem the one or were filled with fear and revulsion for the other. Therefore, instead of praising Yao and condemning Jie, it would be better just to forget about both of them.

11.1.4 To deny people equanimity and happiness is to violate Virtue. To violate Virtue and yet manage to last long, this has never happened in the world.

It is only when people with equanimity and happiness achieve self-fulfillment that one [a ruler] can last long.

11.2.1 Are people too happy? This weakens the yang element. Are people too angry? This weakens the yin element. When both yin and yang are weakened, farm work goes out of kilter and the harmony of cold and hot seasons fails, so people surely bring about their own physical harm! When the happiness or anger of people become so immoderate that their daily lives are disrupted, their selfconscious thoughts so alienate them from self-fulfillment that normal behavior is no longer manifest.

This passage refers to both Yao and Jie, kinds of rulers who caused people such greatly excessive amounts of happiness and anger that disasters of this order occurred. Between Heaven and Earth, mankind, due to the happiness and anger associated with numinous awareness [*lingzhi*], is the most capable of throwing all living creatures into chaos and destabilizing yin and yang. Therefore, when it comes to success or failure, if happiness or anger excessively mounts up in the hearts of the common folk, the harmony of cold and hot seasons will break down, the sequence of the four seasons will go awry, time itself becomes completely muddled, and every human effort will miserably fail.

11.2.2 It was then that all in the world started to become indignant at imagined injustices and arrogant about how special they were, which led to the behavior of both Robber Zhi and of Zeng and Shi. As a result, even if the good were rewarded with what the whole world contained, it would not be enough,

If people are good only because they covet reward, no amount of rewards could ever supply enough.

11.2.3 and even if the bad were punished with every punishment in the world, it would not be enough.

If people desist only because they fear punishment, no amount of punishments could ever meet the need.

11.2.4 Therefore, as great as the whole world is, it can adequately provide neither such rewards nor such punishments. Ever since the Three Dynasties, people have been in such tumult over rewards and punishments that these finally became their entire concern, so what chance have they ever had to be content with the true state [*qing*] of their own natural endowments [*xingming*]!

When rewards and punishments are forgotten so that goodness is achieved spontaneously, natural endowment should provide all that is needed. Rewards and punishments were used by the sage kings to recompense achievement and penalize error; they were not used to express encouragement and instill fear. Therefore, once such principles [*li*] were perfectly realized [*zhi*], they were cast aside, for only then could things return to perfect unity [*zhiyi*]. However, ever since the Three Kingdoms, people have tried to follow the footprints left by those attending to these matters, which resulted in such tumultuous pursuit of the footprints that in the end, dependence on them became their entire concern. As for the true states [*qing*] of their own natural endowments [*xingming*], what chance had they to be content with them!

11.3.1 Moreover, do people admire keen eyesight? This is to be besotted with colors. Do they admire acute hearing? This is to be besotted with sounds. Do they admire the benevolent? This is to be muddled by "virtue." Do they admire the righteous? This is to be perverted by what is "right." Do they admire ritual behavior? This is to lend assistance [*xiang*] to dishonesty. Do they admire music? This is to lend assistance to licentiousness. Do they admire sageness? This is to lend assistance to craftiness. Do they admire wisdom? This is to lend assistance to error.

Being so besotted never occurs when one is perfectly in accord with the principles involved, but once besotted with any of these, disasters such as licentiousness and perversity occur. Here "lend assistance" [*xiang*] means "help" [*zhu*].

11.3.2 As long as everyone in the world remains content with the true state of his own natural endowment, to keep these eight may be all right or to discard them may be all right.

Such keeping or discarding does not depend on anything, for all anyone has to do is trust to his allotted capacity, and his own natural endowment will provide contentment.[1]

11.3.3 But as long as everyone in the world fails to be content with the true state of his own natural endowment, these eight will twist people up tight and make them hard-pressed, thus throwing the whole world into confusion.

If it is insisted that people avail themselves of these eight, they will be denied the freedom to trust to their own natural endowments, since they are twisted up tight and so hard-pressed.

11.3.4 But then everyone in the world even began to venerate and treasure them. Their misunderstanding is, indeed, as extreme as that!

That they could not discard them was already a mistake, but then they went on even to venerate them as objects of esteem, so was that not the worst kind of misunderstanding?

11.3.5 And when have people just left them once they are finished? Instead they fast when discussing them, kneel reverently when presenting them, and drum and sing when celebrating them in dance. What can we possibly do about that!

It is not as if they just depend on them for temporary shelter and leave when finished with them, instead they treasure them as much as this!

11.4.1 Therefore, when no alternative exists for the noble man but to take charge of the world, nothing is better than unselfconscious action [*wuwei*], for it is only with unselfconscious action that in its true state, everyone's natural endowment finds ease.

Unselfconscious action does not mean to fold one's hands and just keep silent. As long as everyone is allowed to do what is innately doable, each natural endowment shall be at ease. One for whom no alternative exists shuns coercion based on the threat of punishment and instead maintains the Dao, internalizes pristine simplicity, and surrenders to the absolutely inevitable. If so, the whole world will submit themselves to him spontaneously [*zibin*].[2]

11.4.2 Therefore:

> **One who values his life more than the chance to gain the**
> **world may be entrusted with the world.**
> **One who cherishes his life more than the chance to gain**
> **the world may have the world rendered to his care.**[3]

As for one who makes light of his own life as he risks it for the sake of gain, who discards his own true self in sacrificing it for something else, since even his own person fails to find ease, how could he possibly bring ease to the world!

11.4.3 Therefore, if the noble man can avoid distinguishing among his five viscera and avoid trying to elevate [*zhuo*] his hearing and eyesight,

Such distinguishing and boosting result in harm.[4]

11.4.4 he shall be still as a ceremonial stand-in for the deceased [*shi*] yet with the look of a dragon, utterly silent yet sounding like thunder,[5]

Whether he goes forth or stays still, whether remains silent or speaks out,[6] he always stays free of selfconscious mind, consigning himself to spontaneity.

11.4.5 his spirit moving in step with Heaven,

As his spirit moves in step with things, he acts in compliance with Heaven.

11.4.6 and utterly at ease, he acts free of selfconscious purpose, at which the myriad things become freely drifting dust.

They seem just like drifting dust freely moving about on its own.

11.4.7 So more than that, why should I bother myself about governing the world!"

He just trusts to his natural endowment and does nothing else.

11.5 Cui Qu questioned Lao Dan, "If one does not govern the world, how does one make men's minds good?"

11.6.1 Lao Dan replied, "One must be careful not to muddle their minds."

To muddle them damages their spontaneous goodness.

11.6.2 A man's mind is such that if held back he feels down; if advanced he feels up.

"If held back he feels down; if advanced he feels up" addresses how easily one is swayed.

11.6.3 But whether up or down, it results in care and vexation.

It is only if there is nothing either to hold one back or to advance him that one can find perfect contentment.

11.6.4 It is gentleness and pliancy that softens the hard and forceful.

That is, if one can be gentle and pliant, the hard and forceful will become soft.[7]

11.6.5 But if one carves and polishes them with sharp instruments, their heat becomes as hot as blazing fire, its chill enough to freeze ice.

The heat of blazing fire, the chill of frozen ice, are both generated by the accumulation of delight and anger. But if one neither carves nor polishes, the pristine simplicity of everyone would remain perfectly intact, and what chill of ice or heat of coal could ever happen then!

11.6.6 Happening as fast as the nod of the head, it keeps reoccurring and spreads to beyond the bounds of the four seas.

Such is how the mood of the common folk moves.

11.6.7 Let it be still, and it will be as serene as a deep pool, but stir it and it will reach the distant sky.

If allowed to be serene, it can resemble a deep pool, but if stirred, it leaps up to the distant sky.

11.6.8 Thus agitated it will erupt in arrogance, defying all restraint. Such is the mind of man!

The mind of man is so capable of change that there is nothing it would not do, but if left alone to go its own way, it remains serene and, as such, fulfills itself [*zitong*]. However, if restrained by the bonds of government, it becomes so diverted as to erupt in arrogance, and this eruption of arrogance will have such force that no amount of restraint can control it.

11.7.1 Long ago, the Yellow Thearch began to use benevolence and righteousness to meddle with the minds of men.

The Yellow Thearch did not selfconsciously practice benevolence and righteousness; it was just that in merging arcanely with others, the footprints of benevolence and righteousness spontaneously appeared. Once these footprints spontaneously appeared, the minds of people in later ages were inevitably sacrificed in devotion to them. So, after all, it was the footprints that the Yellow Thearch left behind that muddle people.

11.7.2 After that, Yao and Shun worked off all flesh from the inside of their thighs and all hair from their shins in nourishing the physical needs of all in the world, but they also filled their five viscera with worry and grief by practicing benevolence and righteousness and belabored their essential vigor with the laws they established. However, there were still those who would not submit; Yao had to banish Huan Dou to Mount Chong, expel Sanmiao to Sanwei, and exile Gonggong to Youdu, which means, after all, that they failed to make the whole world submit. As such, this continued down to the three kings, by which time the whole world was in a real panic.[8]

The names for the monarchs "Yao" and "Shun" never indicate more than the footprints they left behind. Though they themselves filled these footprints, the footprints should not be mistaken for those who made them. Therefore, the panic was caused by the world itself, and the more the world panicked the more crude the footprints became. Now, the reason footprints appear crude or fine is only because the path on which they are made is either safe or dangerous.[9] How instead could it be because the traveler on it kept changing his feet! This is why though the sage has always been one and the same, differences came to exist between "Yao," "Shun," "Tang," and "Wu," differences which, when understood, turn out to be just a matter of names supplied in different ages, all of which fail to designate the true authenticity of the sage. Therefore, how could the names "Yao" or "Shun" ever simply have meant one particular Yao or one particular Shun? This is why, though their appearance might be marked by distress and grief and the footprints they left might seem like benevolence and righteousness, they who made the footprints, as always, remained perfectly intact.[10]

11.7.3 Low down were Jie and Robber Zhi,
High up were Zeng and Shi,
Then finally Confucians and Mohists arose.

11.7.4 Consequently,

The happy and the angry suspected each other,
The stupid and the wise bullied each other,
The good and the bad condemned each other,
The charlatans and the trustworthy sneered at each other,
And so the whole world declined.

No one could find stability in self-fulfillment.

11.7.5 As great virtue lost its harmony, so natural endowment fragmented.[11]

Though differing only in minor ways, people failed to limit themselves to their own allotted capacities.

11.7.6 As the whole world came to covet knowledge, so the common folk exhausted themselves in seeking it.

Though knowledge is infinite it was still coveted, so nothing could satisfy those who sought it.

11.7.7 Consequently,

> **Axes and saws were used to cut and trim them,**
> **The carpenter's ink line was used to partition [sha] them,**[12]
> **Hammer and chisel were used to sever them apart.**

Their natural endowments were carved and polished so much that it reached such an extreme as this.

11.7.8 So everyone in the whole world trampled on each other in great confusion, the blame for which lies with such meddling with men's minds. As a result, worthies went to live in seclusion below cliffs of great mountains, while rulers who mastered a myriad chariots suffered grief and fear up in their ancestral halls.

If people are allowed to trust to their natural endowments and so dwell in what is appropriate for them, then, complying with their innate tendencies, the worthy and the stupid, the eminent or humble will all take their rightful places. Whether monarch or minister, the high or the low, "none shall fail to fulfill themselves to the utmost,"[13] and all the world shall be free from peril. But it is these footprints that meddle with the minds of all in the world, causing them to rush about so much that they can't stop. Thereupon, of those with middling knowledge or less, none failed to gild over their original natures in order to hoodwink the masses, so that "those that hate the honest and detest the just"[14] led each other on in enormous numbers. Consequently, while those committed to authenticity lost all they could rely on, those who venerated falsehood stole all authority for it. It was because of this that rulers suffered grief and fear above, while the common folk became hard-pressed below.

11.8.1 Nowadays those condemned to death lie pillowed on one another, those forced into cangues jostle one another, and those punished for crimes never lose sight of one another. Nonetheless the Confucians and Mohists, stretching up on tiptoes and rolling up their sleeves, got busy amidst all these shackles and fetters. Alas! It was as bad as that! They behaved so very shamefully yet with no sense of shame!

It was because the footprints were preserved by dogmatic Confucians that such a terrible disaster occurred. They never thought to discard the footprints and recover unity with all things but instead just kept on rolling up their sleeves in the effort to use the footprints to control how footprints should be made [how government should be conducted]. So it may be said of them that "they behaved so very shamefully yet had no sense of shame."

11.8.2 I am not so sure that sagely wisdom is not the yoke for cangues and benevolence and righteousness are not the mortise and tenon for shackles.

Cangues are locked with yokes, and fetters and shackles work thanks to mortise and tenon. Sagely wisdom with its benevolence and righteousness have left footprints far removed from blame, and being thus far removed from blame the common folk venerated them, but it was from such veneration that falsehood was born. And since this birth of falsehood, have devices to prevent evil ever been found wanting? Therefore, if what people thus venerate is discarded, falsehood would not occur, and when falsehood does not occur, cangues and shackles would disappear—then what use would there exist for yoke or mortise and tenon?

11.8.3 And how do I know that Zeng and Shi are not whistling signal arrows for Jie and Robber Zhi!

Whistling signal arrows are arrows that make a fierce sound. Here, the text addresses how Zeng and Shi were exploited by Jie and Robber Zhi.

11.8.4 Therefore I say, abandon sageness and discard wisdom, for then the whole world will find great and perfect order.

Get rid of what does the muddling.

11.9 The Yellow Thearch had been the Son of Heaven for nineteen years, and his decrees prevailed throughout the world. He then heard that Master Guangcheng was on Mount Kongtong, so he went to see him and addressed him thus: "I have heard that you, sir, have realized the perfect Dao [*zhidao*], so I dare to ask what the vital essence [*jing*] of the perfect Dao is, for I wish to take the vital essence of Heaven and Earth and use it to assist the growing of the five grains and so nourish the common folk. I also wish to control the yin and yang and so comply with the needs of all living things [*qunsheng*]. How can this be done?"

11.10.1 Master Guangcheng replied: "Though what you wish to ask me about pertains to the intrinsic nature [*zhi*] of things,

His asking what the vital essence of the Dao is can but pertain to the intrinsic nature of things.

11.10.2 what you wish to control means only the ruin [*can*] of things.

He would not allow them their spontaneity [*zier*] but wishes to control them, which would thus mean their ruin.

11.10.3 Your own governing of the world would have it rain before the vapor of clouds gathers; leaves would fall before they turn yellow; and the light of sun and moon would become increasingly dim.

11.10.4 Your sycophant's mind is so very narrow that how after all could you ever be up to talk of the perfect Dao!"

11.11 The Yellow Thearch thereupon withdrew, abandoned his rule of the whole world, built a place to live alone in, spread a mat of white rushes, dwelt there in seclusion for three months, and then again ventured forth to seek instruction.

11.12.1 Master Guangcheng was reclining with his head toward the south as the Yellow Thearch, adopting a humble manner, advanced on his knees, twice kowtowed prostrating himself and then presumed to ask, "I have heard, my master, that you have realized the perfect Dao, so I dare to ask how I should cultivate myself that I may have a long life." At that Master Guangcheng suddenly rose up and said, "How excellent is your question!

If everyone cultivated themselves and did not try to put the world in order, the world would itself find order. This is why he thought it excellent.

11.12.2 Come here, and let me tell you about the perfect Dao.

> **Elusive and profound, the vital essence of the perfect Dao,**
> **Imperceptible and unfathomable, its infinite capacity,**

It is elusive and unfathomable because it consists entirely of absolutely nothing. Master Lao and Master Zhuang repeatedly declare that it consists of nothingness, and why is that? They understand that things are generated without anything doing it, for things just generate themselves. Since things just generate themselves and are not made to generate, why should further selfconscious effort be expended on them [*youwei*] once they are generated?

11.12.3 So try not to see it, try not to hear it,
But wrap your spirit with quietude,
For then your bodily form shall rectify itself.

Become unselfconscious of eyesight and you shall see with your own eyesight; become unselfconscious of hearing and you shall hear with your own hearing. Then your spirit shall be freed from disturbance, and your physical form shall commit no wrong.

11.12.4 You must be still, you must be pure,
Labor not your bodily form,
Trouble not your vital essence,
For then you may live long.

Because you allow yourself to act spontaneously, carefree and tranquil, you won't die young.

11.12.5 If your eyes have nothing to see, if your ears have nothing to hear, if your mind has nothing to know,
Your spirit shall guard your bodily form,
And your bodily form shall live long.

It is because this all complies with your original nature that you shall live long.

11.12.6 Carefully abide by what is inside you,

Keep your authenticity whole and safe.

11.12.7 And close yourself to what is outside,

Abide by your allotted capacity.

11.12.8 For much knowledge would be your downfall.

Because knowledge knows no limit, it shall lead to your downfall.

11.12.9 I shall lead you out to great luminescence above, reaching there the source of perfect yang, and through the gate of the abstruse and the remote, reaching there the source of perfect yin.

It is by plumbing the ultimate source of yin and yang to the utmost that leads to great luminescence above and allows one to enter the gate of the abstruse and the remote.[15]

11.12.10 Heaven and Earth have their supervisors, and yin and yang have their storehouse.

All one has to do is comply with them.[16]

11.12.11 Carefully guard your bodily form, and things shall prosper on their own. By complying with the unity of all things I dwell in harmony with them. Thus I have cultivated myself for twelve hundred years, and my bodily form has never aged."

It is by fulfilling one's natural endowment to the utmost that one attains the ultimate of longevity, and, since such a one does not die young, he can extend the chance to do the same to others.

11.13 The Yellow Thearch twice kowtowed prostrating himself, and then said "You, Master Guangcheng, may be said to be Heaven itself!"

By "Heaven" he means the personification of unselfconscious action [*wuwei*].

11.14.1 Master Guangcheng said, "Come here, and let me tell you. Things are infinite, yet everyone supposes them finite; things are unfathomable, yet everyone supposes they have limits.[17]

They merely are aware of their individual transformations.

11.14.2 Those who attained my Dao, above became 'Heavenly monarchs' and below became 'Earthly kings.'

Rulers are judged "Heavenly Monarch" or "Earthly King" only because the former lived during superior ages and the latter lived during inferior ages, but they were all one and the same when it came to their attainment of the Dao with its seamless adaptation to circumstances so one resonates perfectly with things.[18]

11.14.3 Those who fail to attain my Dao may shine with glory above but become one with the Earth below.

One who fails to attain the infinite Dao places all his trust in what constitutes his own individual transformation and, as such, can't regard the exalted and the lowly as equally the same. Therefore, when he looks up at the one or down at the other, he thinks of them differently.[19]

11.14.4 **Now,**

> **As everything that flourishes in life**
> **Is born from the Earth**
> **And returns to the Earth,**
> **So I shall leave you.**

The Earth has no mind, so since I am born from that which has no mind, I should again guard such state of no mind and carry on alone.

11.14.5 **I shall enter the gate of the inexhaustible**
And thereby wander through infinity,
Such a one merges perfectly with transformation.

11.14.6 **To shine just like the sun and moon,**
Endure as long as Heaven and Earth.
He lets everything just take care of itself.

11.14.7 **If anything comes toward me,**
I stupidly merge with it!
If anything goes away from me,
I stupidly take no notice!
Whether things approach or depart, he pays them no heed.

11.14.8 **Though all other men may die,**
I alone continue to survive!"
Since he regards life and death as essentially one and the same, no matter what venture embarked on, he never fails to survive.

11.15 **While traveling east and passing through the branches of the Fuyao tree, Cloud General encountered Hong Meng [Grand Obscurity], who just then was amusing himself by slapping his thighs and hopping about like a sparrow. Astonished, he came to a halt and standing stock-still asked, "Venerable sir, who are you? And why are you doing this?"**[20]

11.16 **Grand Obscurity without ceasing how he slapped his thighs and hopped about like a sparrow replied to Cloud General, "I'm just having fun."**

11.17 **Cloud General then said, "I would like to ask you something."**

11.18 **Grand Obscurity looked up at Cloud General and said, "Uh-oh!"**

11.19 **Cloud General then said, "The pneuma of Heaven is in disharmony, the pneuma of Earth is clotted; the six climatic phenomena [*liuqi*] are out of sync; and the four seasons out of whack. Now I want to bring the essences of the six climatic phenomena into harmony in order to nurture all living things. How should that be done?"**

11.20 **Grand Obscurity, still slapping his thighs and hopping about like a sparrow, shook his head and said, "I know nothing about that! I know nothing about that!"**

11.21 So it was that Cloud General did not get an answer to his question. After another three years, once more he traveled east, and when passing through the open country of Song, just happened to meet Grand Obscurity again. Greatly delighted, Cloud General quickly stepped forward to him and said, "Have you, oh Heaven, forgotten me? Have you, oh Heaven, forgotten me?" Then he twice kowtowed and prostrated himself, wishing to hear Grand Obscurity's instruction.

11.22.1 At this Grand Obscurity said,

"Wandering aimlessly,
Unselfconscious of what I seek,

Nevertheless, he spontaneously obtains what is sought.

11.22.2 Wild and free,
Unselfconscious of where I am going,

Nevertheless, he spontaneously succeeds in reaching his destination.

11.22.3 My wanderings, so extensive,
Afford me vision free from error.

One whose inner being is content finds his vision spontaneously true wherever he casts his gaze.[21]

11.22.4 So what more should I know!"

This is all there is to it.

11.23.1 Cloud General then said, "I also consider myself wild and free, but the common folk follow me wherever I go, so I can't help it that they now emulate me.

In governing the people, though he deliberately makes no footprints yet footprints are left. His wild and free behavior is not done to summon the common folk yet the common folk gravitate toward him. Therefore, he is emulated by the common folk and there is nothing he can do about it.

11.23.2 Please favor me with a word of advice."

11.24.1 Grand Obscurity replied,

"If the warp of Heaven is disordered
And the innate character of things violated,
Arcane Heaven is denied its potential.

If one complies with the innate character of things and thus avoids selfconscious control, their innate character won't be violated, and, its warp not disordered, the arcane and silent fully realizes its potential and Nature is thus fulfilled.

11.24.2 Beasts that live together will scatter,
And birds will all sing at night.

They are denied the conditions to be calm.

11.24.3 Disaster will extend to plants and trees,
And calamity will befall insects.

Since these are all sedentary, they will suffer harm.

11.24.4 Ah! Such is the calamity caused by the control of people!"

It is because of footprints left by selfconscious control that disorder is born.

11.25 Cloud General then asked, "Since this is so, what should I do?"

11.26.1 Grand Obscurity replied, "Ah! How poisonous you are!

This refers to the severity of the disaster that would be caused by his trying to control people.

11.26.2 How you bob up and down! Just go home!"

"Bob up and down" [*xianxian*] describes someone sitting down and standing up. Since Grand Obscurity is displeased with Cloud General's failure to be flexible and keep in step with things, he orders him to go home.[22]

11.27 Cloud General then said, "It has been so difficult for me to meet you, oh Heaven, so please favor me with a word of advice."

11.28.1 Grand Obscurity replied, "Ah! Let your mind be nourished:

Since it is by using the mind that harm is done, the way to "nourish the mind" can only be not to use it!

11.28.2 Dwell only in unselfconscious action,
And let the myriad things transform themselves.

11.28.3 Shed your bodily form,
Spit out your intelligence,
Let moral principles and others be forgotten.

If one does not allow moral principles and others a place in one's mind and, free of selfconscious intention [*an*], submits to Nature, he shall act unselfconsciously and self-transformation shall occur.

11.28.4 Join the great harmony in amorphous unity,

Let there be no border between you and things.

11.28.5 Release your mind, free your spirit,
Senseless, be free of selfconscious life [*wuhun*].

Abide in forgetfulness [*zuowang*] and give yourself over to independent spontaneity [*rendu*].

11.28.6 Flourish as do the myriad things,
Each reverting to its roots.[23]
Each returns to its roots yet is completely unaware.

Revert without awareness, only this is authentic reversion.

11.28.7 Be primordially amorphous,
And thus throughout life never part from your roots.

Primordially amorphous and free of selfconscious mind, thus trusting to spontaneous reversion, only then can one throughout life never part from his roots.

11.28.8 But once you're aware of them,
You've already parted from your roots.

To try to revert while being aware of it, this is to be at odds with reversion.

11.28.9 Ask not the name for this,
Investigate not its true state,
And things shall certainly live successfully on their own."

If you investigate and ask, things will lose the power to live successfully on their own.[24]

11.29.1 Cloud General then said,

"You, oh Heaven, have conferred this virtue on me,
Shown me the way of arcane quietude.
Humbling myself I have searched for this,
And now I have obtained it."

If one so becomes aware but still lacks quietude, he inevitably shall violate who he really is [*zishi*].

11.29.2 Then he bowed twice prostrating himself, got up to take his leave, and went away.

11.30.1 An average person always likes it when others agree with him, and dislikes it when others disagree. That someone wishes others to agree and does not wish others to disagree is because he has his mind set on standing out from the masses.

At heart he wishes to stand out from the crowd and become a person of eminence above the masses.

11.30.2 But when has anyone who has his mind set on standing out from the masses ever really managed to stand out from them!

It is actually because all ordinary people have their minds set on standing out from the masses that keeps them among the ranks of the ordinary. Therefore, if I too wish to stand out from the masses, I am no different from them, so I really have no chance of really standing out. Now, let all ordinary people set their minds on standing out from one another, but I shall differ from them by refusing to do so; then, completely different from the masses, I shall become their master.

11.30.3 It is by complying with the masses that one is safe, for what one otherwise might know never matches the great quantity of their collective ingenuity.

What I as a single person might know falls far short of the collective ingenuity of the masses. Therefore, compliance with the masses results in safety. But if I don't comply with the masses, all the massed multitudes shall be my enemy.[25]

11.30.4 Nevertheless, when someone wants to govern a state, it will be one who covets such profits as the three kings had and disregards the disasters they caused.

One who wants to govern a state does so not in order that the masses themselves govern it but so he himself governs it. This approach to governing only covets such profits as the three kings had but ignores the disasters they caused. That being so, how did the three kings have such profits? It was surely not because they themselves created them, but only because the world was allowed to create them itself.

11.30.5 If such a one risks his state in the attempt to better his fortunes, what are the chances that he might avoid losing his state? There is not one chance in ten thousand that he will keep his state, and, in losing his state, though only he alone may fail, more than ten thousand shall lose their lives!

Both parties, the individual ruler and his entire populace, prosper only by relying on one another. But if a ruler, a single person, tries to exercise autocratic control over the entire populace, the entire populace will be held down. So how then could he alone make things go smoothly! Therefore, not only would he a single person fail, of everyone everywhere more than enough would perish.

11.30.6 What a pity that those who possess land don't understand this!

11.31.1 One who possesses land possesses the greatest of all things, but one who possesses the greatest of all things may not do so as a thing.

One who can't control things but is controlled by things is just such a thing himself, so how could he ever let things be things! Since he can't let things be things, he is unfit to possess the great thing.[26]

11.31.2 But if one though a thing is yet not a thing, he thus can let things be things.

One who uses things is not used by things; not used by things makes him not a thing. And since not a thing, he may allow each one self-fulfillment.[27]

11.31.3 Since one who understands how to let things be things is not a mere thing himself, how can he as such be limited just to governing all the common folk of the world! He will move in and out of the six directions [*liuhe*, all phenomenal existence] and wander throughout all the nine regions of the world.

Because he lets the whole world act spontaneously, he may gallop along on the myriad things and never be exhausted.[28]

11.31.4 He goes forth alone and returns alone, so this may be called "unique existence."

Though everyone else is separate from one another, he alone wanders together with everyone, which is why "he goes forth alone and returns alone." Since he alone has such independence, this may be called "unique existence."[29]

11.31.5 Someone who "alone has it" is said to have attained "perfect esteem."

Though one who arcanely unites with the masses seeks not esteem from them, the masses can't help but accord him esteem. However, if one trusts to his own prejudices and is selfconscious that he alone is different, though he be perfectly one with them, he will after all be just another person among the common herd, not someone with "unique existence." If one is incapable of "unique existence" and yet greedily tries to usurp the canopied carriage and headdress of a monarch, scheming his way to them beyond his allotted capacity, how could the masses ever naturally gravitate to such as him! Therefore, such a one does not attain "perfect esteem."

11.32.1 The teachings of the great one occur just as solid objects relate to shadows or sounds relate to echoes.

The minds of the common folk are the solid objects and sounds; the teachings of the great one are the shadows and echoes. How does the mind of the great one relate to those of all under Heaven? It is like the shadows or echoes that occur along with solid objects or sounds.[30]

11.32.2 When questioned, he responds to it, fulfilling completely what people aspire to

He has people with their aspirations the chance fulfill themselves completely.[31]

11.32.3 and so becomes companion of all under Heaven.

Since the one who asks is the master, the one who responds is the companion.

11.32.4 Passive, he exists where he echoes not,

Passive, he waits on things.[32]

11.32.5 active, he moves in the infinitely changeable.

He keeps transforming himself in response to things

11.32.6 He leads you by the hand so you can recover your spontaneous behavior [*naonao*].

"Random, chaotic" [*naonao*] here means spontaneous behavior [*zidong*]. He leads the myriad folk by the hand so they recover their naturally endowed capacity for spontaneous behavior, that is, the perfect realization of unselfconscious action.

11.32.7 He wanders with the infinite [*wuduan*],

United with transformation, he is with the infinite.

11.32.8 enters and leaves as if no boundaries existed [*wupang*],

Free of boundaries, he arcanely unites.[33]

11.32.9 and, with the sun, never has a beginning,

Since such a one is renewed together with the sun, never has he a beginning.[34]

11.32.10 His facial features and bodily form merge with the great thoroughfare [*datong*],

His appearance differs not from Heaven and Earth.

11.32.11 And in the great unity has no self.

If he had a self, he would be unable to achieve great unity.

11.32.12 Since he has no self, how could phenomenal existence exist for him?

The most difficult thing in the world to relinquish is the self, but once the self ceases to exist, all extant things will lack the means to exist any longer.

11.32.13 If you look at those for whom phenomenal things exist, they were the monarchs of yore.

They succeeded in gaining fine reputations.[35]

11.32.14 If you look at those for whom they did not exist, they were the friends of Heaven and Earth.

If you look at those for whom they did not exist, they allowed things to exist independently [*zisheng*].

11.33.1 That which, though considered lowly yet must be used, are the myriad things; that which, though humbled yet must be complied with, are the common folk.

If one [the ruler] uses them in compliance with their original natures, order will result; if he bullies them to go against their original natures, disorder will arise. The reason why the common folk and the myriad things are demeaned and humbled is because one fails to use them in compliance with their natures [*yinren*]. But when one uses the demeaned with compliance, he esteems them, and when he complies with the humble, he venerates them. These are certain correlations.

11.33.2 That which is concealed yet must be allowed to function [*wei*] is the capacity to do things [*shi*].

Because the capacity to do things is hidden in a person, the text says it is "concealed." Since all persons have an innate capacity to do things [*ziwei*], this must be allowed to function, and to do so one must only use them in compliance with their natures [*yinren*].

11.32.3 That which, though crude yet must be set forth in words, are laws [*fa*].

Laws are footprints left by marvelous works [*miaoshi*], and as crude as these footprints may be, why should such marvelous works not be set forth in words![36]

11.33.4 That which, though distant yet by which one must abide, is righteousness.

One should abide by it only if it is appropriate, which is why it is kept at a distance.[37]

11.33.5 That which, though close yet must be expanded [*guang*], is benevolence.[38]

When close it is severely partial, which is why only when expanded does it become real benevolence.

11.33.6 That which, though it consists of rules yet must amass, is ritual behavior.

The rules of ritual behavior harm unity with all things, which is why only when everyone embodies them do they amass and become universal.

11.33.7 That which, though apt yet must be aimed high, is virtue.

If one does something vile, though done aptly, this is not real virtue.

11.33.8 That which, though unifying yet must be simple and easy, is the Dao.

If one finds something hard to do, though merged in unity with it, this has nothing to do with the Dao—even less if not merged in unity!

11.33.9 That which, though divine yet must act, is Heaven.

If one has an intention yet acts not, though it be divine, this has nothing to do with Heaven—even less if not divine!

11.33.10 Therefore, the sage observes Heaven but does not try to assist it.

He does nothing other than comply with its spontaneous action.

11.33.11 Perfect in virtue, he is not flawed;

He merges splendidly with Nature.[39]

11.33.12 emerging from the Dao, he is without selfconscious intention;

Free of selfconscious intention, he achieves unity, thus things are simple and easy for him.

11.33.13 he tallies with benevolence but relies not on it;

If he selfconsciously relied on it, it would not expand [impartially].

11.33.14 he rests lightly on righteousness, so is not impeded by it;

He complies with the original nature of people and keeps righteousness at a distance, so it fails to impede him.

11.33.15 he responds with ritual behavior, but is free of prohibitions;

He responds spontaneously with ritual behavior, which does not originate in prohibitions and taboos.

11.33.16 he engages with matters, and shirks them not;

He engages with matters in accord with the principles involved and trusts himself as to whether he can do them or not, so since he acts only when he should act, the chance to shirk anything never arises.

11.33.17 he regulates with laws but causes no disorder;

It is because he manages these crudities with marvelous skill that no disorder occurs.

11.33.18 he relies on the common folk and is not careless with them;

It is because he does nothing other than rely on the way they spontaneously behave that they are never employed carelessly.

11.33.19 he complies with everything so no loss occurs.

It is because he employs them in compliance with what they are, they are not made to lose their original natures.[40]

11.33.20 Although no thing can adequately be made to function yet function it must.

As for functioning, does anything really function because it can be made to do so! It is instead because they inherently embody certain functions that things can't help but function.

11.33.21 One who fails to understand Heaven is not pure in virtue.

It is failure to understand the Natural that leads to selfconscious action, and with selfconscious action one's virtue is no longer pure.

11.33.22 One who can't stay in step with the Dao lacks a place from which to start.

If one can't empty oneself in engaging with others, he will always be out of step with things as they happen.[41]

11.33.23 How pitiable is he who fails to understand Heaven!

11.34.1 What does "Dao" mean? There is the Dao of Heaven and the dao (way) of man. To act unselfconsciously and be thus venerated, such is the Dao of Heaven.

This refers to a ruler who places his trust in the spontaneous behavior of the myriad folk.

11.34.2 To act selfconsciously and become thus enmeshed, such is the way of man.

One who acts selfconsciously and so becomes enmeshed in it will fail to fulfill his own potential.

11.34.3 For the ruler, it is the Dao of Heaven.

One who trusts the people to do for themselves as does Heaven will spontaneously take his place above them.

11.34.4 For the minister, it is the way of man.

Each should fulfill his responsibilities.

11.34.5 The Dao of Heaven and the way of man are far apart.

The ruler on his throne comporting himself with unselfconscious action delegates to his numerous officials, and though his numerous officials have their responsibilities, the sovereign does not interfere with them. If both ruler and ministers achieve success free of selfconscious effort, the way of the ruler will be one of ease and that of ministers one of toil. Such toil and ease are so different that they may not be spoken of together on the same day!

11.34.6 One must distinguish between them clearly!

If one does not distinguish clearly between them, the positions of ruler and minister will be thrown into disorder!

Notes

1. Cheng Xuanying: "Acute hearing, keen eyesight, benevolence, righteousness, ritual behavior, music, sageness, and wisdom constitute 'these eight.' The text discusses how since the natural allotments of people vary, their innate personalities differ accordingly. For Li Zhu, Master Kuang, Zeng Shen, and Shi Qiu, such dimensions were available in

their fundamental allotted capacities, thus for them they may be kept. However, they are not available in the natural capacities of people in general, who so admire them that they pervert their own authenticity, thus for them they may be discarded." *Zhuangzi jishi*, 2: 368.

2. Cf. *Laozi*, section 32: "Although the uncarved block is small, none under Heaven can make it his servitor [*chen*], but, if any lord or prince could hold on to it, the myriad folk would submit spontaneously [*zibin*]." Richard John Lynn, *The Classic of the Way and Virtue*, 108.
3. Cf. 28.1 and *Laozi*, section 13: "Therefore, since such a one values his own person as much as anything under Heaven, he may be entrusted with All Under Heaven. Since such a one cherishes his own person as much as anything under Heaven, he may have All Under Heaven rendered to his care." Lynn, *The Classic of the Way and Virtue*, 71–72. Both the *Laozi* and the *Zhuangzi* passages are beset with ambiguous textual variants; see Wang Shumin, *Zhuangzi jiaoquan*, 2: 377–78, note 9.
4. Cheng Xuanying: "The five viscera are the domains wherein selfconsciousness resides; hearing and seeing are the functions of ears and eyes. If one distinguishes [*fenbian*] among the kinds of perception and knowledge provided by the five viscera or shows off how he boosts [*zhuo*] his powers of hearing and eyesight, his selfconsciousness will run amuck within and his ears and eyes will exhaust themselves without." *Zhuangzi jishi*, 2: 370. Cf. 8.2
5. Cf. 14.33.
6. Cf. *Classic of Changes*, "Commentary on the appended phrases" [*Xici zhuan*], Part One: "In the Dao of the noble man / There's a time for going forth / And a time for staying still, / A time to remain silent / And a time to speak out." Richard John Lynn, *The Classic of Changes*, 58.
7. Cf. *Laozi*, section 36: "Softness and pliancy conquer hardness and forcefulness." Lynn, *The Classic of the Way and Virtue*, 116.
8. Cheng Xuanying: "Long ago Sire Dihong [the Yellow Thearch] had a good-for-nothing son, known to the world as Primal Chaos [Hundun], that is, Huan Dou, who when he formed a clique with Gonggong, was banished to the border at the far south. Sire Jinyun [summer (war) minister of the Yellow Thearch] had a good-for-nothing son, known to the world as Taotie, and this was Sanmiao. He was enfoeffed by Yao with the domain of Sanmiao. . . . Sanwei is the name of a mountain on the border to the far west. Sire Shaohao [son of the Yellow Thearch] had a good-for-nothing son, known to the world as Qiongqi, and this was Gonggong. He was minister of waters for Yao. Youdu is in the far north." *Zhuangzi jishi*, 2: 374. The "three kings" are the kings of the Xia, Shang, and Zhou.
9. Cf. 7.2.
10. The distinction between the plural "sages" and a single "true sage" is addressed by Wang Baoxuan: "The [Guo Xiang] commentary clearly indicates there is only one [true] sage, namely the intrinsic 'authentic substance [*shi*] of the Divine man [*shenren*]' or the 'authentic substance of the sage [*shengren*],' so 'Yao,' 'Shun,' 'Tang,' 'Wu,' and so forth are nothing but the extrinsic manifestations of the 'authentic substance of the sage.'" Wang Baoxuan, *Xuanxue tonglun* (General survey of arcane learning), 551.
11. "Great virtue" is the power of the Dao itself; cf. 4.13. When the harmony of the Dao is so disrupted, as Cheng Xuanying observes, "the natural span of lives is cut short." *Zhuangzi jishi*, 2: 375.
12. Cheng Xuanying glosses "partition" [*sha*] in terms of "elaborate and spare" [*longsha*]: "As the carpenter's ink line is used to confirm that wood is straight and true, so ritual and ceremony are used to let one know whether performance should be elaborate

or spare." This alludes to the *Liji* (Record of Ritual), *Xiangyin jiuyi* (Ceremonial wine drinking in the districts): "As for the mass of guests, they ascend and accept drink, kneel and perform libation, stand and drink, then descend without saluting the host in return. Elaborate or spare, such distinctions are thus made for participants in the ceremony." That is, for those of high rank, ritual is more elaborate; for those of low rank, ritual is spare. See Zheng Xuan (127–200) and Kong Yingda, *Liji zhengyi* (Correct meaning of the *Record of Ritual*), 61: 1683c–1684a, and *Zhuangzi jishi*, 2: 376. As such, "partition" distinguishes one rank of person from another.

13. This line is a quote from the ode *Siwen*, "How fine and good you are," *Zhousong* (Hymns of Zhou), *Shijing* (Classic of Odes); see Zheng Xuan and Kong Yingda, *Maoshi zhengyi* (Correct meaning of the *Mao edition of the Odes*), 19. 2:590a.
14. The locus classicus of this phrase is *Zuo's Commentary* to the *Spring and Autumn Annals*, eighteenth year of Duke Shao; see Du Yu and Kong Yingda, *Chunqiu Zuozhuan zhengyi*, 52: 2118a.
15. Cf. *Laozi*, section 21: "Abstruse, oh, indistinct, oh, but within it the essence of things is there." Lynn, *The Classic of the Way and Virtue*, 87. Cheng Xuanying: "When the perfect one [the true sage ruler] acts in resonance with things, he shines like the sun and moon, thus the name for this is 'great luminescence.' " *Zhuangzi jishi*, 2: 383.
16. Cheng Xuanying: "The celestial supervisors are the sun, moon, and stars, which shine down on the whole world below, and because they manage the myriad things, they are called 'supervisors.' The terrestrial supervisors are metal, wood, water, fire, and earth, which have the power to manage animals and plants and as they convey everything, they also are called 'supervisors.' Yin and yang, the two pneuma, have control over each of the four seasons, spring, summer, autumn, winter, and, as such, act like storehouses for them. If all these receive your compliance, nothing shall fail to go well, for how would you then go against creative transformation or alter the offices of these supervisors? All you have to do is practice effortless action, carefully guard your bodily form, and all the myriad things shall flourish spontaneously. So why belabor yourself with intentionality and 'give yourself nothing but distress'?" *Zhuangzi jishi*, 2: 383. Cheng's quote at the end is from the ode *Xiaoming* (Little brightness), *Xiaoya* (Lesser elegentiae), *Shijing* (Classic of Odes); see Zheng Xuan and Kong Yingda, *Maoshi zhengyi* (Correct meaning of the *Mao edition of the Odes*), 13.1: 464c.
17. Cheng Xuanying: "Change and transformation, birth and death go on without end according to the natural principles of things, yet the common mass of people, stupid and deluded, say they have a beginning and an end." *Zhuangzi jishi*, 2: 384.
18. Cf. 16.4. Cheng Xuanying: "As for those who attained the Dao of Nature, in superior times, encountering an age of pristine simplicity, Fu Xi and Shennong appeared, and, in inferior times, encountering an age of degenerate superficiality, Tang and Wu were there to respond to it. Whether the footprints are made by a Heavenly monarch or an Earthly king depends on whether the conditions are either safe or dangerous; nevertheless the Dao [path] they travel on are always one and the same." *Zhuangzi jishi*, 2: 384.
19. This passage addresses the state of mind of rulers who fail to attain the Dao, whose "individual transformation" happens to result in their becoming rulers, whose attitude toward things is restricted to self-centered concerns for personal security and exalted power and glory. Cheng Xuanying elaborates: "Those who disregard the Dao of effortless action, mired in minds filled with desire, while alive may appear glorious and magnificent but when dead just get transformed into soil. They are so obstinately obsessed with life and death that they can't regard the exalted and the lowly as equally the same." *Zhuangzi jishi*, 2: 384.

20. Cheng Xuanying: "This is an allegory. Pneuma is the basis of all living things; clouds are the source of nourishing rain; the tree represents the yang force of spring [caring, nurturing government]; the east represents where benevolence and kindness are practiced. These four are cited to indicate a monarch who rules his people first of all with kindness and charity." *Zhuangzi jishi*, 2: 385.
21. Cheng Xuanying: "As Grand Obscurity lets his mind wander through areas great and wide, his sight plays on enormous numbers of things, so the perception that his powers of sight provide is such that his field of vision is free from error. 'Weary' [*yangzhang*] here means 'extensive' [*zhongduo*]." *Zhuangzi jishi*, 2: 388.
22. Cheng Xuanying: "*Xianxian* describes an appearance of lightly rising. Because he is displeased that Cloud General has caused disaster by [inadvertently] controlling people, he tells him to rise up lightly, then strongly urges him to stop making footprints and return to his original nature [*guiben*]." *Zhuangzi jishi*, 2: 390. Whereas Guo glosses *xianxian* as "bob up and down," perhaps Cheng's gloss is more accurate because Cloud General, as a cloud, can "rise up lightly" and thus avoid leaving any footprints.
23. Cf. *Laozi*, section 16: "All things flourish, but each returns to its roots." Lynn, *The Classic of the Way and Virtue*, 76. See also Wang Shumin, *Zhuangzi jiaoquan*, 402, note 14.
24. Cheng Xuanying: "Since the Dao defies description and its principles transcend human consideration, if one employs names to ask about the Dao or employs human consideration to investigate its principles, will that not be far off the mark! But if one can banish human consideration, forget all about names, and just allow things their independent transformation, they shall fulfill their life principle by themselves." *Zhuangzi jishi*, 2: 392.
25. Cheng Xuanying: "To use the collective ingenuity of the masses means to comply with what the masses see and hear, for then there will be no angry altercation with them. One called 'perspicacious' has the masses see for him; one called 'wise' has the masses plan policy for him." *Zhuangzi jishi*, 2: 393. Cheng's last sentence closely paraphrases a brief passage about the enlightened sovereign in Tao Hongjing's (456–536) commentary on the *Guigu zi* (Master of the valley of demons); see Xu Fuhong, *Guigu zi jiao jizhu* (Collected commentaries to the collated *Guigu zi*), chapter 12: *Fuyan* (Tally words), 178.
26. Cheng Xuanying: "One who willfully covets a state such as those the three kings possessed is incapable of allowing things to act spontaneously, so instead he is used by things. Since he himself is just another thing, how could he let things be things! He is utterly incapable of it!" *Zhuangzi jishi*, 2: 394.
27. The text here exploits the range of meanings for *wu*, especially the ambiguity between "other persons" or "the people" versus "things," which could encompass creatures, plants, or climate as well as humans. It is thus possible also to render Guo's remarks as "One who can't control others but is controlled by others is just such an 'other' himself, so how could he ever let others be others! Since he can't let others be others, he is unfit to possess the great other." "The great other," of course, thus means "the people" and all their works.
28. Cf. 20.4.5 and 22.35.8.
29. Paradoxically, only one who can merge perfectly with everyone else can attain perfect independence from them, and such perfect independence makes him unique.
30. Cheng Xuanying: "The 'great one' is the sage, who free of selfconscious mind resonates with things. Because he resonates free of selfconscious mind, the minds of the common folk are as if solid objects and sounds, and the teachings of the great one become shadows and echoes that arise in response to them." *Zhuangzi jishi*, 2: 395. However, this surely relates to the passage about the shadow and the penumbra; see 2.33–2.34.

31. Cheng Xuanying: "The mind of the sage not only moves in response to people it also perfectly tallies with how they think at the moment, so the aspirations of the people achieve perfect fulfillment." *Zhuangzi jishi*, 2: 396.
32. Cheng Xuanying: "When not moved to respond, his mind is like a dead tree. Utterly still, it makes neither shadows nor echoes." *Zhuangzi jishi*, 2: 396.
33. Cheng Xuanying: "He enters and leaves the world of dust, arcanely united with nature as he lives and dies, aware of no boundaries at all." *Zhuangzi jishi*, 2: 397.
34. Cheng Xuanying: "Since such a one is renewed together with the sun, he has neither beginning nor end. *Zhuangzi jishi*, 2: 397.
35. Cheng Xuanying: "They practiced benevolence and righteousness, maintained ritual relationships between ruler and minister, and never abandoned selfconscious action." *Zhuangzi jishi*, 2: 397.
36. Cheng Xuanying: "A 'law' means something taught, used to give a distant view of principle, but though principles may be marvelous, laws are crude. However, analogous to fish traps and rabbit snares, one should thus comply with them as set forth in words." *Zhuangzi jishi*, 2: 398.
37. Cheng Xuanying: "Although righteousness is remote from the Dao, if in accord with principle one should use it to make judgments." *Zhuangzi jishi*, 2: 399.
38. Cf. 14.30.
39. Cheng Xuanying: "Capable of arcanely merging selfconsciousness with external conditions, since perfect virtue is thus achieved he is freed spontaneously from flaw or error." *Zhuangzi jishi*, 2: 399.
40. Cheng Xuanying: "Since he abides by the natural inclinations of the common folk and complies with the original natures of the myriad things, although he might apply laws and teachings, this does not make people or things forsake their fundamental natures." *Zhuangzi jishi*, 2: 401.
41. Cheng Xuanying: "If one lets his empty and arcane Dao-nature [*daoxing*] be blocked, whatever situation such a one encounters will leave him facing a wall, for he has no starting point from which to act." *Zhuangzi jishi*, 2: 401. Cf. 14.41.

CHAPTER 12

TIANDI [HEAVEN AND EARTH]

12.1.1 Great as Heaven and Earth are, their transformative power is impartial.

Such impartiality depends on unselfconscious action that allows for self-transformation.

12.1.2 Numerous as the myriad things are, their regulation is one and the same for all.

In the same one way, self-fulfillment regulates them.

12.1.3 Countless as the mass of common folk are, it is the true sovereign who is their master.

Since all in the world selfconsciously think differently about things, someone free of selfconscious mind becomes their master.

12.1.4 The true sovereign has his source in Virtue and thus fulfills the course of Heaven.

Since he makes Virtue the source [*yuan*], no thing fails to realize its potential. It is in realizing potential that self-fulfillment is achieved; as such, fulfillment never fails, which is how the course of Heaven is fulfilled.[1]

12.1.5 Thus it is said, those in remote antiquity who ruled the world as true sovereigns did so with unselfconscious action, that is with the Virtue of Heaven and nothing more.

They trusted to the course of natural spontaneity.

12.2.1 It is by using words from the point of view of the Dao that the sovereign of the world is really true.

One who rules with unselfconscious action becomes a true sovereign spontaneously, and thus never does anything contrary.

12.2.2 It is by making distinctions from the point of view of the Dao that the relative status of sovereign and minister is clarified.

When each matches his status, the one situated above comports himself with unselfconscious action, and the one situated below comports himself with selfconscious action.

12.2.3 It is by judging abilities from the point of view of the Dao that officials all over the world are well ordered.

When each official is matched with his capabilities, all are well ordered.

12.2.4 It is by looking at everything in general from the point of view of the Dao that all the myriad things respond perfectly.

When one [the ruler] responds to things with unselfconscious action, everything in the world responds to them with its own capacity for unselfconscious action.[2]

12.2.5 Therefore, that which allows Heaven and Earth to interflow is Virtue.

It is when all the myriad things without exception achieve fulfillment that Heaven and Earth interflow.

12.2.6 That which acts through the myriad things is the Dao.

It is when the course of the Dao is not constrained that the myriad things spontaneously fulfill their power to act.

12.2.7 The way the ruler should govern the people is to allow them their proper activities.

He lets everyone accomplish their proper activities spontaneously.[3]

12.2.8 When one's capabilities include some skill, this is true craft.

"Craft" for the myriad folk is unessential.[4]

12.2.9 Craft involves activity; activity involves righteousness; righteousness involves Virtue; Virtue involves the Dao; the Dao involves Heaven.

Roots and branch tips [essentials and details/ramifications] are related the way hand and arm are attached to one another. Therefore, just as when a body exists in harmonious unity, so its hundreds of joints all work smoothly together so when one [the ruler] complies with the Dao of Heaven, both roots and branch tips thrive.

12.2.10 Thus it is said of those in antiquity who nurtured the world:

> **They were so free from desire**
> **That all in the world were content,**
> **So practiced unselfconscious action**
> **That the myriad things transformed as they should,**
> **Projected such serene equanimity**
> **That all the common folk calmly settled down.**

12.2.11 As it is recorded,

> **"Merge with all as one,**
> **And everything shall be fulfilled.**
> **Stay free of mental attainment,**
> **And the demonic and divine shall submit."**

When he [the ruler] merges as one with all and practices unselfconscious action, every principle shall be fulfilled.

12.3.1 The Master said,[5] "The way the Dao covers and carries the myriad things, how great it is, like an immense ocean! The noble man must not fail to cleanse his mind in it.

If one remains selfconscious [*youxin*], it entangles his natural endowment, which is why he must cleanse it away.

12.3.2 To act with unselfconscious action indicates 'Heaven.'

Only when one acts without intent so such action spontaneously occurs does it accord with the Dao of Heaven.

12.3.3 To speak without intent indicates 'Virtue.'

Only when one speaks without intent so such words spontaneously occurs do they accord with true Virtue.

12.3.4 To love the people and benefit them indicates 'benevolence.'

This is to love and benefit them in accord with tendencies innate to their natural endowments.

12.3.5 To treat the dissimilar as similar indicates 'greatness.'

Only when he [the noble man] allows all the myriad folk in their myriad forms to abide by their allotted capacities, never forcing anyone to be the same as anyone else, shall such a one be "great."[6]

12.3.6 To act without contrariety, this indicates 'generosity.'

If one [the ruler] arcanely unites himself with others, the myriad folk shall all have their own means of support [*zirong*], thus he does more than enough for them.

12.3.7 To possess the myriad different things indicates 'wealth.'

If one [the ruler] unites himself with absolutely everything, he alone can possess such a myriad of things.

12.3.8 Therefore, to hold fast to Virtue indicates the 'master guide.'

Virtue is the master guide for everyone.

12.3.9 To fulfill Virtue indicates 'establishment.'

Fulfillment contrary to virtue must not be called 'establishment.'[7]

12.3.10 To comply with the Dao indicates 'universal sufficiency.'

The Dao is not partial to people or things.[8]

12.3.11 Not to be deterred indicates 'complete perfection.'

Self-realization takes place entirely within.[9]

12.3.12 When the noble man exhibits these ten characteristics, he embodies the greatest capacity for attention to things,

He is so huge-minded that nothing is beyond his capacity.

12.3.13 and he forms a great surge that carries the myriad folk along.

The surging momentum of his virtuous beneficence is due to his allowing the myriad folk to go their own way.

12.3.14 Such a man as this leaves gold hidden in the mountains and pearls hidden in the depths,

He does not value things difficult to obtain.

12.3.15 finds no profit in goods,

Since he can forget self, how much the more has he forgotten all about goods!

12.3.16 draws not near to eminence and wealth,

Whatever happens to come to him on its own stays but temporarily with him since his mind always keeps it far away.

12.3.17 delights not in long life, grieves not in early death,

This is what is referred to as "ties untied."[10]

12.3.18 feels no splendor in affluence, is shamed not by poverty,

Since at heart he has forgotten all about long life and early death, would he have any place for poverty and affluence there!

12.3.19 grabs not the profits of the entire world as his own private share,

He entrusts them all to the myriad folk.

12.3.20 and does not use kingship of the world as an opportunity to glorify himself.

He has no selfconscious awareness that glory is attached to his person.

12.3.21 Flaunting glory, he would be conspicuous,

He shuns glory and just remains obscure.

12.3.22 But since he stores himself as one with the myriads of everything else, life and death seem the same to him."

Sloughed off, they no longer exist for him.

12.4.1 The Master said, "The Dao, how deep its tranquility, how sharp its clarity! If they fail to achieve this, metal or stone chimes have no way to make sounds.

Sounds starts from silence.

12.4.2 Therefore, if metal or stone chimes are to make sounds, it does not happen unless they are struck.

This is used as a metaphor for one who embodies the Dao, who responds to things only in reaction to them.

12.4.3 But for the myriad things, who could ever define rules for this.

No set methods exist for reaction and response.

12.4.4 A man of true kingly virtue maintains his natural simplicity as he undertakes things and thus would be ashamed to be thoroughly conversant with affairs.

He does nothing but trust to his natural simplicity [*su*] as he undertakes things so delights not in being thoroughly conversant with affairs.

12.4.5 He takes his stand in the root source [*benyuan*] thus his intelligence accesses the divine.

So rooted, his intelligence is never contrary to it.

12.4.6 Therefore, his virtue extends everywhere.

As the result of his natural simplicity and access to the divine it extends everywhere.

12.4.7 His mind emerges only because the people stir it to action.

It only emerges after the people stir it to action; he never takes the initiative in advance of them.

12.4.8 Thus it is, if it were not for the Dao his body would have no life, and if it were not for virtue he would manifest no brightness. He safeguards his body and lives life to the full, establishes virtuous works and brightly manifests the Dao—does this not indicate true kingly virtue! How his effect vastly spreads! He emerges all of a sudden, acts all in a flash, and the myriad folk just follow him! Such a one is called a man of kingly virtue.

"All of a sudden" and "all in a flash" both describe how he responds free of selfconscious mind, and, because his actions arise unselfconsciously, the myriad folk follow him and his effect spreads everywhere. It is thus that he can safeguard his body and live life to the full, realizing the virtue of a true king by establishing virtuous works and brightly manifesting the Dao.

12.4.9 He sees into the utterly dark and listens to the absolutely soundless.
12.4.13 Where it is utterly dark he alone sees the brightness; where there is no sound he alone hears the harmony.

If he looked and listened without giving himself over to passive quietude [*ji*], it [the Dao] would only consist of dark obscurity and no harmony.

12.4.10 And so, there in depths below depth he finds he can let things be,

Once he has plumbed the source to its beginning he can let things be things.[11]

12.4.11 there in the divine beyond divinity he can realize its vital essence.

Once he reaches the ultimate of compliance its marvelous power can completely be his.

12.4.12 Therefore, he interacts with the myriad folk in such a way that he meets all their wants out of perfect emptiness [*zhiwu*].

With his self truly extinguished [*quesi*], he thus always yields to others, so the wants of others are spontaneously met.

12.4.13 With timeliness and indulgence he regards their fulfillment as essential, whether great or small, whether superior or inferior, no matter how far away they are.

Always indulgent, he yields to them and lets them fulfill their limits, nothing more.[12]

12.5.1 When the Yellow Thearch wandered north of the Red River, he climbed Mount Kunlun for a view to the south, but when returned home he discovered he had lost his black pearl.

This is a metaphor for the source from which one understands how to attain authenticity.

12.5.2 He dispatched Intelligence to look for it, but he failed.

This means that the use of intelligence is insufficient to attain authenticity.

12.5.3 He dispatched Li Zhu to look for it, but he failed; he dispatched Chigou [Argumentation] to look for it, but he failed.

From the acute in sight and hearing to argumentation, they miss authenticity by an ever wider mark.

12.5.4 Then he dispatched Wangxiang [Mindless], and he found it. The Yellow Thearch then exclaimed, "How strange! It was Mindless who found it!

Understanding how to attain authenticity has nothing to do with using one's mind. Only a "Mindless" is authentic.[13]

12.6 Yao's teacher was called Xu You;[14] Xu You's teacher was called Nieque [Front Teeth Missing]; Nieque's teacher was called Wangni [Princeling]; Wangni's teacher was called Piyi [Clothed].

12.7.1 Yao asked Xu You, "Can Nieque be a companion to Heaven?"

He means, should he become Son of Heaven.

12.7.2 I would rely on Wangni to invite him to take my place.

Since Wangni was his teacher, the Yellow Thearch wanted to dispatch him to invite Nieqie.

12.8.1 Xu You replied, "What a risk! It would put the world in danger [ji]!

Ji [steep] means "danger" [*wei*].

12.8.2 Nieque is a kind of man who by inborn nature is so quick-witted in intelligence that he surpasses other men,

Because he surpasses others in intelligence, this causes others to make an extra digit of him, which repeatedly does harm to the common folk.[15]

12.8.3 and besides that he tries to use what he is as a man to recover Heaven.

He tries to use his intelligence to seek to recover his natural endowment.[16]

12.8.4 He is careful about preventing error but fails to understand the source from which error arises.

Error arises from intelligence, but he still tries to employ intelligence to prevent it, so the error just becomes ever more severe. Thus it is said, freedom from error depends on banishing intelligence and not on trying more strongly to prevent it.

12.8.5 Let him be a companion to Heaven? He would just bring about the loss of Heaven by reliance on such a human quality.

If given the whole world, he would just cause people of later ages to rely on intelligence and thus lose their authenticity.

12.8.6 He would take his own person as the basis and regard other persons as different [*yixing*].

When they [the sage kings] took the myriad folk as the basis, all change could take place in unity and all different persons [*yixing*] could merge as one, but this left an impression that then caused later generations [of rulers] to try to govern the people on the basis of their own views of it [such an impression], which caused the myriad folk to be at odds.[17]

12.8.7 He would venerate intelligence, creating a trend which would spread like fire.

When such a "worthy" takes his place to lead in front, intelligence will be venerated by those who follow behind, who will so contend with one another in pursuit of it that the trend would spread like fire.

12.8.8 He would get involved with administrative servitude.

He would be the inspiration for the administrative servitude of [rulers of] later ages.

12.8.9 He would be fettered by things.

He would cause [rulers of] later ages to be utterly preoccupied with government administration.

12.8.10 He would scrutinize the four directions and ensure that all people comply with him.

He would cause [rulers of] later ages to try to influence how people behave through their personal direction, to make them comply with their efforts from above.

12.8.11 He would respond as it suits the masses.

He would ensure that [rulers of] later ages can't forget goodness and so would respond expediently with benefit and benevolence.

12.8.12 He would just follow along as things change,

He would then cause [rulers of] later ages to try to keep up with things and thus fail to achieve self-fulfillment within.

12.8.13 and thus never would have consistency.

This means always doing what seems expedient for the moment, but, as such, though today might enjoy the virtue he bestows, tomorrow might suffer the harm he causes. Therefore, the text states "he never would have consistency."

12.8.14 So how could he ever be a worthy companion to Heaven! Nevertheless, there are multitudes of people and their chiefs.

A person of his caliber has the ability to fulfill the duties of a chief.

12.8.15 So he could be a 'father of the multitudes' but not the 'father of the father of the multitudes.'

It was by the "father of the father of the multitudes" that footprints were left.[18]

12.8.16 His rule would be the harbinger of chaos,

He would not only be the ruling master but also the harbinger of chaos.[19]

12.8.17 leading to disasters for those who face north

Jie and Zhou could not have killed their worthy ministers had they not relied on footprints left by sagely wisdom, which they used to inflict disaster on them.

12.8.18 and to robbery for those who face south."

Tian Heng could not have killed his ruler had he not relied on benevolence and righteousness, which he used to rob him.[20]

12.9 Yao was on a tour of inspection in Hua,[21] where a boundary sentry said to him, "Ah, a sage! May I pray that you be blessed, oh sage.

12.10 May the sage have long life!" Yao said, "I decline." "May the sage be wealthy." Yao said, "I decline." "May the sage have many sons." Yao said, "I decline."

12.11 The border marker then said, "Long life, wealth, and many sons are what all men desire, so why do you alone not desire them?"

12.12 Yao replied, "Many sons means more worry; wealth means more trouble; long life means more chance for insult. These three are no way to cultivate virtue, so I decline them."

12.13.1 The border marker then said, "At first, I took you for a sage, but now it seems you are just a noble man. In begetting the myriad folk, Heaven is sure to assign everyone something he can do, so if you had many sons and were to assign them something to do, what would there be to worry about!

When each person is allowed the place right for him, his ambition will be focused there.

12.13.2 If you were wealthy and allowed others to share, what trouble would there be!

If he were to give it away to all in the world, he would have no trouble.[22]

12.13.3 The sage lives like a quail,

Free of selfconscious thought, he is always content.[23]

12.13.4 feeds like a hatchling,

Face upwards to others, he is satisfied.[24]

12.13.5 and travels as a bird does to leave no tracks.

Since he acts in compliance with his original nature, he leaves no lasting footprints [*changji*].[25]

12.13.6 When the world has the Dao,
he prospers along with everyone else.

Utterly without restraint he behaves freely and thus treads the great method [of the Dao]. [*dafang*].[26]

12.13.7 When the world is without the Dao,
he cultivates his virtue and reverts to leisure.

Even though it be the doings of Tang and Wu, if one complies with Heaven and accords with the wishes of mankind,[27] no act is done without leisure. Therefore, one who acts without selfconscious purpose yet who accomplishes everything is never without leisure.

12.13.8 After a thousand years, tired of the world,
he leaves it and ascends to the immortals,

That the Perfected one extends longevity to the utmost is because he gives himself over to all change, whether it means affluence or poverty, so his life progresses spontaneously, and his death occurs as a transformation of things. Therefore, this is what the text means when it says that he grows tired of the world and ascends to the immortals.

12.13.9 Riding on those white clouds
to reach the realm of the thearchs.

When pneuma disperses, there is no place it does not reach.

12.13.10 The three causes for worry never touch him,
and misfortune never befalls him,
so what chance for insult ever comes his way!"

12.14 As the border marker was leaving, Yao followed him and said, "May I ask about it?"

12.15 But the border marker just said, "Withdraw and be done with it!"

12.16 When Yao governed the world, he enfoeffed Bocheng Zigao one of his feudal lords, but after Yao yielded rule to Shun and Shun yielded to Yu, Bocheng Zigao resigned and became a farmer. When Yu went to see him, he found him tilling out in the country. Humbling himself, Yu hastened to him, stood there and asked him, "In the past, when Yao governed the world, you, sir, were enfoeffed as a feudal lord, but after Yao yielded rule to Shun and Shun yielded to me, you, sir, resigned and became a farmer. May I dare to ask the reason why?"

12.17 Zigao replied, "In the past when Yao governed the world, he made no rewards yet the people were still diligent; he carried out no punishments yet the people were awestruck. Now you make rewards and carry out punishments, but the people are still not benevolent. From now on virtue will decline and punishment increase, and the disorder of later ages will have its origin right here. Why don't you just go away and stop interrupting my work!" He then busily went back to tilling and no longer paid him any attention.

By the time of Yu, the Three Sage Kings [Yao, Shun, and Yu] successively achieved rule and fully manifested virtue, but as for how their excellence of achievement gradually failed, historical accounts record nothing of this, and Zhongni [Confucius] could not distinguish among them. Therefore, although they possessed the world, they did not concern themselves with it, that is, they possessed it but regarded it as naught. Those who hitherto investigated those times found that Yu was the best, and reckoned that these men were three sages, but actually they were all just one "Yao." As long as there were no sages, the minds of all in the world gravitated back to their pristine state, and, utterly impartial, someone [among them] took his rightful place [as ruler], who gave the world to the common folk. Since receiving or giving it away had nothing to do with him personally, when he lost it, he did not try to get it back, and when he received it, he did not decline to have it. Unselfconsciously he let it go, childishly unaware he let it come, which is why in receiving the world he did no harm to honest members of the elite and no surprise that he was named to the rank of the Three Sage Kings. Master Zhuang accordingly brought to light the harm that "Yao" as such did, for the harm began with a "Yao" and reached a perfect evil with a "Yu." When the distant footprints they had made were entrusted to Zigao, he refused to follow them and would not rule, for by repudiating sagehood, he intended to recover unity with all things, and by discarding wisdom, he intended to achieve the utmost serenity—but we have never heard if he actually did so. As for what Master Zhuang said, it can't be probed as if it follows only one path. Sometimes he has it that the footprints left by the Yellow Thearch made Yao and Shun work off all hair from their shins,[28] so how could it be said that he just esteemed Yao and denigrated Yu! Therefore, we should disregard the content of his metaphors and instead concentrate on the significance of "repudiate sagehood and discard wisdom."[29]

12.18.1 In the great beginning [*taichu*] nothing existed,
and since nothing existed there is no name for it.

Because nothing existed there was nothing to name.[30]

12.18.2 From it the One arose,[31]
so the One existed but not yet forms.

The One at the beginning of being represents a state of absolute marvelousness, and because it was a state of absolute marvelousness, forms that follow the principles of things did not then yet exist. As to what the One arose from, it arose from perfect unity and not from any "nothingness." But then why does Master Zhuang repeatedly equate "nothingness" with the beginning? The "beginning" represents the time when the One had not yet come into existence but just then acquired existence. As difficult as it was for it to acquire existence, it neither relied on any "nothingness" prior to it nor depended on any knowledge that came later with it—it just spontaneously acquired existence all by itself. Why keep on looking for its origin in something that supposedly existed prior to it in order to deny its own self-generation![32]

12.18.3 That from which things acquired existence is called Virtue.

"Nothingness" could not have begotten things, yet the text uses the expression "that from which things acquired existence." It does so only in order to clarify that the existence of things was spontaneously acquired, that is, they were empowered to acquire it themselves, and this can be called Virtue.

12.18.4 Before things had forms they had their allotments, and even so, no separations yet existed among them,

These are called their natural endowments.

As they fluxed and flowed, things came into existence, and, as things were formed, the principles involved were created.

These are called their forms.

Bodily form protects the spirit, each of which has certain limits [*yize*].

These are called their original natures.

Virtue, form, original nature, and natural endowment are names assigned to different aspects, but all belong to one natural whole.

12.18.5 Cultivation of original nature recovers virtue, and perfect virtue allows one to merge with the Beginning.

If one is constant in practicing unselfconscious action, one spontaneously realizes this state.

12.18.6 So merged, one becomes empty, and being empty, one's capacity becomes vast,

If one does not merge with the Beginning but along the way engages in selfconscious action, the mind will certainly become preoccupied with things, and being so occupied, the virtue cultivated is small.

12.18.7 and he joins the chirping of the birds.

If one is not selfconscious of what he is saying but just speaks spontaneously, he shall join the chirping of the birds.

12.18.8 Joining the chirping of the birds, he merges with Heaven and Earth.

Heaven and Earth also are free of selfconscious mind and thus behave spontaneously.

12.18.9 Such merger renders one befuddled and unselfconscious

As though one were utterly stupid, utterly a dolt.

Abiding in forgetfulness, one just merges spontaneously; one does not merge by selfconsciously striving for it.

12.18.10 This is called Arcane Virtue,

Which is the same as Vast Compliance.

When one's virtue attains the arcane, his capacity for compliance, indeed, becomes vast.

12.19.1 The Master [Confucius] asked Lao Dan, "Someone who governs as if he were following a model makes the impermissible permissible and the not so to be so,

If one follows a model and forces people to do what should not be done and to accept what is not so to be so, this warps their innate natures.

12.19.2 as such, a disputer of whom it is claimed that he 'distinguishes hardness and whiteness as clearly as if they were suspended in the sky.'[33]

This claims that such distinctions are as easy to see as if they were displayed on high.

12.19.3 Can someone such as this be called a sage?"

12.20.1 Lao Dan replied, "Such a man is but a common clerk, face distorted with effort and tied to skill, body belabored and mind in a state of alarm, as if he were a dog brought out to hunt foxes or a monkey whose nimbleness gets it leashed.

This means that these all lose their original and constant natures. The text reads "get worried" [*chengsi*], which is an error and should be "brought out to hunt" [*lai tian*]; it reads "brought out from mountain forests" [*zi shanlin lai*], which is an error and should be "gets him leashed" [*lai jie*].[34]

12.20.2 Qiu [Confucius], what I am going to tell you is something you are neither capable of hearing nor of saying yourself. Those who have heads and feet but lack minds and ears exist in masses,

"Heads and feet" means the same as "beginnings and ends." That they "lack minds and ears" addresses their own self-transformation [*zihua*].[35]

12.20.3 but it is impossible that those with bodily form can exist in the same way as that which is free of form or shape.

Because those who have bodily form easily change, they can't have the same kind of existence as that which is free of form or shape. Therefore, one who excels at governing does not restrict himself to precedent but instead only complies with transformation as it newly occurs each day.

12.20.4 Whether they are active or at rest, whether they live or die, whether they prosper or fail, all this too is beyond their control.

That is, whether people need act or can enjoy repose, whether live or die, whether they prosper or fail, all these never happen with constancy but just occur spontaneously without their doing anything about it. Therefore, just let it happen and allow them to achieve self-realization in the process.

12.20.5 But sovereignty lies with the people.

It does not lie with the ruler for his personal use.

12.20.6 To forget things, to forget Heaven, the name for this is Forget Self.

When Heaven and things are both forgotten, not only does one forget self, what else is there left?

12.20.7 Someone who has forgotten self may be said to have merged with Heaven.

What people can't forget is the self, so when one as an exception does forget it, what further awareness is there! Only a state so free of awareness and intelligence as this allows one to achieve arcane fusion with the Natural.

12.21 Jianglü Mian went to see Ji Che and said, "The Lord of Lu[36] said to me, 'May I ask for your teachings?' I tried to decline but failed to get excused, so I had to tell him something after all. But I know not whether it was right or not, so may I try to tell you about it? This is how I addressed the Lord of Lu: 'You must practice respect and thrift, select the fair and faithful as your subordinates and eschew favoritism, for then who among your people would dare be troublesome?' "

12.22.1 Ji Che, bent over with laughter, replied, " In speaking thus about the virtue of true sovereigns you are like a praying mantis excitedly waving its arms to try to block a cart track—not at all up to the task!

If one needs to practice respect and thrift, this means he will practice them while still selfconscious of them; if one needs to appoint the fair and the faithful, this means he will make appointments while still selfconscious of these qualities. Therefore, although he might avoid favoritism, he won't be up to the task of dealing with falsehood and treachery

12.22.2 If he were to do as you say, it would place him in a high and dangerous position—what an observation tower he would make!

All these actions would place him in a high and conspicuous position, where he could be seen from afar like an observation tower.

12.22.3 People would gravitate in his direction,

He would cause people to exceed the allotment of their fundamental natures, and, making much of their false "digits," they would flock to him.

12.22.4 and those prompted to start out would form a multitude."

They would raise their feet high and rush toward him because they had become discontent with the steps their own fundamental natures were taking.

12.23 Shocked by surprise, Jianglü Mian then said, "To me, what you say seems really opaque. Nevertheless, I hope that you, sir, will tell me how it would affect people for the better."

12.24.1 Ji Che replied, "When a great sage governs the world, he lets the minds of the common folk waver and drift this way and that, allowing them thus to form their own teachings as customs change. As this eradicates any inclination to thievery, everyone advances to fulfill his own unique ambition. Though in this way they behave spontaneously according to their original natures, the common folk are unaware of why this is so.

Each person's ambition has its own particular inclination, so it won't do that anyone imitates someone else. Therefore, if people are allowed to waver spontaneously, though they waver they are not made to do so, and if they are allowed to drift spontaneously, though they drift they are not moved to do so. As a result, any inclination to thievery spontaneously vanishes, unique ambition advances to its own fulfillment, teachings form as customs change, and all this happens unselfconsciously and without following any footprints. People thus act according to their original natures, unaware why this is so, and, as such, they all say "I am spontaneously what I am!"

12.24.2 This being so, why honor Yao and Shun as elder brothers for the way they taught the common folk and with the greatest of esteem [*mingxing*] play younger brothers to them!

Mingxing [obscure and chaotic] here means "the greatest of esteem" [*shengui*]. Refuse to feel grateful to Yao and Shun and promote them as elder brothers.

12.24.3 One should just share in the same Virtue, for then the mind shall find repose [*ju*]."

"Find repose" [*ju*] means not to pursue anything outside. If the mind does not find repose, Virtue can't be shared.

12.25 When Zigong had travelled south to Chu and was returning through Jin, he passed the south bank of the River Han, where he saw an old fellow who, for his raised rows of vegetable beds, had dug a trench though them down to the water in a well. He appeared from it carrying a big jug to water the vegetables, exerting an enormous amount of effort to scarcely any effect. Zigong addressed him, "A machine exists for such a purpose, which in one day can irrigate a hundred gardens. Since it takes little effort yet has great effect, would you, sir, not like to have one?"

12.26 The gardener raised his head, looked at him and asked, "How does it work?" Zigong replied, "A timber is shaped into a pole heavy at back and light in front, which picks up water just as you pull it up, but as fast as if it were overflowing on its own. It is called a well sweep." The gardener first got angry and then laughed, "I heard from my teacher that someone who has a machine will surely have machine things to do, and someone who has machine things to do is sure to have a machine-like mind. When one harbors a machine-like mind in one's breast, his pure simplicity [*chunbai*] becomes impaired, and when one's pure simplicity is impaired, his spiritual life [*shensheng*] becomes unstable. One whose spiritual life is unstable won't be supported by the Dao. It's not that I don't know about it, I just would be ashamed to use it."

One who uses something only at the time it should be used does preserve perfection of simplicity. This fellow in his desire to cultivate perfection of simplicity would embrace the One by abiding by ancient precedent, which misses the point entirely.

12.27 Utterly ashamed, Zigong looked down and did not reply.

12.28 After a short time the gardener asked, "What do you do?"

12.29 Zigong replied, "I am a disciple of Kong Qiu [Confucius]."

12.30.1 The gardener said, "Then you must be one of those who broaden their learning so to appear like the sages, fawn and flatter so to rise above the masses, strumming and singing sad solos so to peddle their reputations to the world! Would that you soon forget your spirit, discard your body, and perhaps then you might get close to it!

Without such forgetting and discarding, no close way to the Dao exists for him.

12.30.2 Since you can't govern your own person, it goes without saying that you could never govern the world! Get you gone! Don't waste my time!"

12.31 Zigong then went pale with shame, and, utterly at a loss [*bu zide*], travelled some thirty tricents before recovering.

12.32 One of his disciples asked him, "What was that fellow back there doing? Why did you lose composure and go pale when you saw him, and not recover after such a long time?"

12.33.1 Zigong replied, "I used to think that there was only one such man in the world

He means Kong Qiu [Confucius].

12.33.2 and had not known there was also this man. I heard it from the Master [Confucius] that in handling affairs, one tries for what should be done and in undertakings, one tries for success, thus with little effort one's merit should be great—such is the Dao of the sage.

The Dao of the sage means using the minds of all the common folk.

12.33.3 Now it seems this is not so. One who abides by the Dao keeps his virtue perfectly intact, and one whose virtue is perfectly intact keeps his physical body whole and safe. One whose physical body is whole and safe keeps his spirit in perfect condition; keeping one's spirit in perfect condition is the Dao of the sage. One thus casts his lot with the common folk and moves along with them, unaware where he is going, so lost is he in the obscure vastness of perfect purity! This man then would put out of mind any thought of advantageous craftiness.

This is the Dao of the sage but not that fellow's way. When Zigong heard what he had to say about reliance and cultivation, he agreed with it but still failed to realize that pure simplicity is actually had by merging perfectly with the world.

12.33.4 For someone like him, if something does not suit his goal, he won't pursue it; if it does not suit what he thinks, he won't do it. Be he praised by all the world in words that are apt, he loftily heeds it not; be he censured by all the world in words that miss the mark, he disregards it with indifference. Since the censure and praise of the whole world neither benefit nor harm him, he should be called a person of perfect virtue! Whereas I should be called a common fellow, just a wind-driven wave."

As a disciple of Song Rongzi, this fellow still lacks the means to achieve perfect virtue. The way Zigong was led astray by him was just like the way Master Lie became utterly fascinated with Ji Xian.[37]

12.34.1 When he returned to Lu, he reported all this to Confucius, who said, "That fellow is someone who tries to rely on and cultivate the techniques of Sire Primal Chaos [Hundun shi].

Because he turns his back on the present and faces the past, he is ashamed to do things like the rest of the contemporary world. As such, we know he is not a true Hundun.

12.34.2 He knows about the one thing but not about the second.

He only knows about cultivating the pristine simplicity of watering by hauled jug and nothing about the ease of using things when and how they should be used.

12.34.3 He may control his inner self but fails to control what is outside.

A true Primal Chaos tries to control neither, so how could such a one have anything to do with distinguishing inside from outside and controlling one at the expense of the other!

12.34.4 Someone who attains natural simplicity though brightness and clarity, recovers pristine simplicity through unselfconscious action, and safeguards his spirit though embodiment of original nature, and who thanks to all that can wander freely throughout the common world—why should someone like this surprise you?

This is a true Primal Chaos. Therefore, though he merges with the waves of the world, he never violates who he really is [*zishi*], and, though he wanders freely throughout the common world, he is so completely one with it that he leaves no footprints in it. Why should such a one cause you to feel surprise?

12.34.5 Moreover, as for the techniques of Sire Primal Chaos, how could you or I be up to knowing anything about them!"

Addressing that, he becomes that, and addressing this, he becomes this; such is the way a Primal Chaos arcanely unites with things. So who could ever know how it is done? All that one can know about it is nothing, but the footprints are left behind.

12.35 When Simple Dim-wit [Chun Mang] was on his way to the Great Drain, by the shore of the Eastern Sea he happened to meet Whirlwind [Yuanfeng], who asked, "Where are you going?"

12.36 Simple Dim-wit replied, "I am going to the Great Drain."

12.37 Whirlwind asked, "What are you going to do there?"

12.38 He replied, "The Great Drain is something into which water pours but is never filled, out of which water is taken but never runs dry, so I am going there to play in it."

12.39 Whirlwind then said, "But have you no concern, sir, about level-eyed mankind? I wish to hear about the government of the sage."

12.40.1 Simple Dim-wit replied, "What about government of the sage? He has officials appointed so that no one suitable is neglected and makes selections of them so no one of ability is left out. He thoroughly examines circumstances and then lets happen what should be done.

He uses everyone in compliance with his nature.

12.40.2 His words and deeds allow people to act on their own, thus the whole world is transformed.

He allows the people to act on their own, thus he himself does not transform them.

12.40.3 He but lifts his hand to point, turns his head to look, and common folk from the four quarters without exception all come to him. This is called the government of the sage."

This means with the wave of his hand or the turn of his head, each and every one of the common folk perfectly fulfills his original nature, for he allows them to act on their own.

12.41 "I wish to hear about the man of virtue."

12.42.1 "What about the man of virtue? In repose he is free of selfconscious thought; in activity he is free of selfconscious deliberation.

In everything he is simply spontaneous.

12.42.2 He harbors no sense of right or wrong, thinks not in terms of good or evil.

Since no sense of right or wrong exists in his heart and mind, he entrusts the world to them [the people].

12.42.3 But to share benefits with all in the world makes him happy, and to provide for all makes him content,

No selfishness exists in him.

12.42.4 though he remains as concerned as a child who has lost his mother or anxious as a traveler who has lost his way.[38] **12.42.5 His wealth and goods are more than enough, yet he knows not whence they arise; he gets all the food and drink he needs, yet he knows not whence they come. All this describes the appearance [*rong*] of the man of virtue."**

Because "virtue" is nothing but the footprints left by the Divine man [*shenren*], the text says "appearance."

12.43 "I wish to hear about the divine man."

He wants to hear about the maker of the footprints.

12.44.1 Simple Dim-wit replied,

As his most exalted divinity mounts on radiance,
Along with his body he ceases to exist.

Once mounted on radiance he has no radiance of his own.[39]

12.44.2 As such he is called "Light of the Vast World."

Free of self and given over to the people, his heart and mind are completely void, but this does not mean that he is stupid and ignorant.

12.44.3 Natural endowment completely fulfilled,
innate character perfectly realized,
Joy pervades Heaven and Earth
and the myriad cares vanish.

With character perfectly realized and natural endowment completely fulfilled, Heaven and Earth are suffused with joy. Since nothing happens to impede such joy, this means he is utterly disengaged.[40]

12.44.4 When the myriad folk recover their innate characters,
This is called "Inchoate Arcane Fusion [*hunming*]."

With him comes recovery of innate character, and inchoate arcane fusion occurs without his leaving any footprints.

12.45 While Men Wugui and Chizhang Manji were observing the army of King Wu, Chizhang Manji said, "He does not measure up to the man of the Yu clan,[41] which is why he has encountered such a disaster as this."

12.46 Men Wugui then said, "Was the world in peaceful good order and only then did the man of the Yu clan take over governing it, or did he take over only after it was in disorder?"

This addresses how both the two sages took over governing because the world was in disorder, the former through abdication by his predecessor and the latter through force of arms, the difference due only to different circumstances and not that the one was better than the other.

12.47.1 Chizhang Manji replied, "If all in the world desired that peaceful good order prevail, why would anyone go on to think that the Sire of Yu should be called on to manage it?

If peaceful good order had prevailed, the desires of each and every person would have been satisfied, so why should anyone go on to think that the virtue of the Sire of Yu was such that he should be promoted as ruler! We have to admit that what Wugui said is correct.[42]

12.47.2 But the way the Sire of Yu treated scabies was to let someone first go bald and then provide him with a wig, let him first get sick, and then seek a remedy.

Because all in the world were suffering the disaster of disorder, they sought medicine from the Sire of Yu.

12.47.3 He was a 'filial son' who picks medicinal herbs to cure a kind father, his face haggard with grief. A true sage would be ashamed to do such a thing.

One who brings enlightened rule to the world does not do so for the sake of a lofty reputation.

12.48.1 In an age of perfect virtue the worthy are not esteemed,

The worthy just live up to the position they fill, so no inclination exists to esteem them.

12.48.2 and the capable are not assigned duties.

The capable just act spontaneously, so no need exists to assign them duties.

12.48.3 The ruler is like a tree's high branches,

Though he appears above the people, he does not elevate himself.

12.48.4 and the common folk are like wild deer.

They are left free to achieve self-fulfillment.

12.48.5 They are upright without knowing this constitutes righteousness; they love each other without knowing this constitutes benevolence; they are honest without knowing this constitutes faithfulness; and they are fair without knowing this constitutes trustworthiness.

They abide by their original natures and just behave spontaneously, so none of this comes from selfconscious knowledge.

12.48.6 They move about like insects as they serve one another, but don't consider this doing a kindness.

Because they just engage in spontaneous behavior, actions don't provoke thanks.

12.48.7 Therefore, actions take place but no footprints are left behind,

Because the ruler can allow people to behave spontaneously, he leaves no footprints behind.[43]

12.48.8 and deeds are done but teachings are not made from them."

Because each person stays within the limits of his own allotted capacity, one does not transmit teachings to anyone else.

12.49.1 The filial son who fawns not on his parents, the loyal minister who flatters not his lord, are the best kinds of sons and ministers. However, if one agrees with whatever his parents say and approves of whatever they do, the common opinion of the world is that such a person is an unfilial son. If one agrees with whatever his lord says and approves of whatever he does, the common opinion of the world is that such a person is an unworthy minister. But can we be quite sure that this is so?

Since it simply goes against popular custom to obey lord and parents like this, common opinion is that it must be unworthy, but it is not quite sure where the real truth exactly lies.

12.49.2 Although someone agrees with whatever the common opinion of the world and approves of whatever it approves, such a one is still not declared a flatterer. So does this mean that common opinion is more strict than parents or that it is more respected than a lord?

This means that common opinion is neither more respected nor more strict than lord or parents, yet people obey it, and common opinion does not declare this flattery. Now since this clearly demonstrates that respect [for one's lord] and strictness [of one's parents] are insufficient to make people submit, that which makes people submit must lie even more with obeying common opinion. This is why the sage never estranges himself from his world but must "wax and wane at the proper moment."[44] Therefore, when a monarch, he behaves as a monarch, when a mere prince, he behaves as a prince. How could he possibly go against the common world and take a personal course of his own!

12.49.3 If someone is called a sycophant, he will suddenly show displeasure; if he is called a flatterer, he will flush with anger,

The common world, after all, regards as correct one who for the most part conforms, which is why when someone is called a sycophant or flatterer, he will flush with anger and not accept it.

12.49.4 even though he has been a sycophant and flatterer his whole life.

Even so, he does not question the truth of this, he just expects people to approve of him.

12.49.5 With appealing metaphors and attractive rhetoric, he gathers the masses to him, and, as long as he is consistent from start to finish and gets basic premises and details to agree, he is not found guilty.

Using such appealing metaphors and attractive rhetoric, he should be found guilty of sycophancy and flattery, yet the world continually allows him to attract people and gather the masses, indeed, as someone who conforms to common custom, thus he never is found guilty.

12.49.6 He lets robes hang loosely down,[45] displaying gorgeous colors, and feigns an expression by which to beguile the world, yet he never admits he is a sycophant and flatterer. As such, he is a fellow traveler of the common herd, using right and wrong as it does, yet he never admits he is just like everyone else. This is the ultimate of foolishness.

Since every member of the common world is completely foolish, such a one can't possibly fail to follow along.

12.49.7 He who realizes that he is a fool is not a great fool; he who realizes that he is deluded is not greatly deluded. The greatly deluded will for his whole life never be free from delusion; the great fool will for his whole life never achieve numinous wisdom [*ling*].

That the Dao of the sage is always the same but sovereigns leave different footprints is truly something that the deluded of the common world can never understand, which is why they follow and entrust themselves to them [the footprints].

12.49.8 If three people travel together and one is deluded, their destination can still be reached since the deluded constitute a minority, but if two of them are deluded, though they wear themselves out, never will they arrive since the deluded constitute a majority. Nowadays, because all in the world are deluded, although I might try to lead them in the right direction, I can't possibly succeed. Is this not sad!

Since all in the world are thus deluded, though I might persuade them to follow the path of the perfect Dao, I never can succeed. Therefore, it is only Yao and Shun, or Tang and Wu, that the prevalent mood of the time has them follow.

12.50.1 Great music has no appeal for villagers,

It is not esteemed by those in humble country lanes.

12.50.2 but if it is "Breaking Off Willow Branches" or "Brilliant Blossoms," they will laugh with loud delight.

When the common folk get a raucous tune, they all break out in laughter together.

12.50.3 For the same reason lofty words are not retained by the minds of the masses,

They don't keep them in mind.

12.50.4 and the reason perfect expressions don't appear from among them is because vulgar expressions dominate.

This is the reason why everyone in the world never has recourse to sagehood but always has recourse only to himself.

12.50.5 In such delusion, two will hesitate,[46] and so never arrive where they want to go.

Each trusts only himself so they know not where to go.

12.50.6 Now with all in the world deluded, although I might try to lead them in the right direction, how could I ever hope to do so! I know that I can't succeed, so if I tried to force them, I would be just another of the deluded. Therefore, it is better to let them go and not push them.

Since such a state exists, he just joins them.[47]

12.50.7 Since I don't push them, whom shall I trouble!

He prefers to let people suit their contemporary circumstances and does not try to force them out of delusion, so along with them he is spared a lifetime of anxiety.

12.50.10 When a ugly man [*li*] has a son born during the middle of the night, he immediately grabs a torch to examine him, anxious with fear that the son should resemble him.

Li [harsh, terrible] here means "ugly person." The text addresses how no one in the world wants to be ugly, since those who happen to be ugly either get pressed into harsh penal servitude or just become so deluded they lose their original natures. However, since the merely deluded inherently wish to recover their original natures, and the ugly inherently wish to become good, I should maintain unselfconscious action and thus allow all in the world to achieve self-transformation.[48]

12.51 A century-old tree was cut up to make an ox-shaped sacrificial wine vessel, patterns were painted on it in green and yellow, and the remaining chips thrown into a ditch. If you compare the ox-shaped vessel to the chips thrown into the ditch, there certainly is a difference between the beauty of the one and the ugliness of the other, but the same loss of original nature occurs with both. Likewise, between Robber Zhi, on the one hand, and Zeng Shen and Shi Qiu, on the other, there certainly is a difference between their practices of righteousness, but they all had the same loss of original nature. Moreover, one can lose one's original nature five ways:

> **The first is to let the five colors so confuse the eyes**
> **that they become clouded.**
> **The second is to let the five tones so confuse the ears**
> **that they are dulled.**
> **The third is to let the five odors so infume the nose**
> **that the sinuses are blocked.**

The fourth is to let the five flavors so muddle the mouth
that it is damaged.
The fifth is to let selection and rejection so unsettle the mind
that it races without rest.

Although these five all cause harm to life, Yang Zhu and Master Mo began to stretch up on tiptoes [make every effort] to promote them as the way to achieve fulfillment, but this is not what I call fulfillment. Their "fulfillment" means distress, so how can that be considered fulfillment? But if so, then a turtledove or an owl in a cage should also be thought to enjoy fulfillment. Moreover, when selection and rejection and tones and colors clog one's inner self, while leather and kingfisher feather caps, hand-held tablets, wide sashes, and long robes bind one's outer self, with inner selves completely penned in and outer selves bound in double fetters, such people, peering around from within these bonds, still think they enjoy fulfillment. If so, then criminals with arms tied and fingers in presses or tigers and leopards kept in cages should also be thought to enjoy fulfillment.

Notes

1. Cheng Xuanying: "*Yuan* [source] mean 'basis' or 'source' [*ben*]. In ruling people and things the true sovereign must make Virtue his model, for only then shall each and every thing achieve self-fulfillment, thus perfectly realizing its original nature." *Zhuangzi jishi*, 2: 404.
2. Cheng Xuanying's interpretation differs somewhat: "The great Dao begets things in such a way that they differ in innate nature, but if each is allowed to behave as it should all shall be completely fulfilled. Whether they run or fly all should fulfill their reason for existence [*yingyong*], though they are unaware how they do it, so why should they think any more about it! Therefore, if one [the ruler] looks at everything in terms of this principle, everything should fulfill its reason for existence perfectly." *Zhuangzi jishi*, 2: 405.
3. Cheng Xuanying: "Although he governs the people, in doing so he complies with their fundamental natures, so everyone abides by his own capabilities and all spontaneously do what is appropriate for them to do. Therefore, everything turns out the way it should and the whole world is well governed." *Zhuangzi jishi*, 2: 405.
4. Cheng Xuanying: "It is when one abides by his fundamental nature, which includes an innate skill, and does not rely on anything outside to do it that authentic craft occurs." *Zhuangzi jishi*, 2: 406.
5. Although Cheng Xuanying identifies the "Master" as Laozi (*Zhuangzi jishi*, 2: 407), the word more likely refers to Confucius; see Wang Shumin, *Zhuangzi jiaoquan*, 416–17, note 1.
6. Cheng Xuanying: "It [the Dao] carves the forms of everyone in such a way that the innate nature of each differs, so if each is permitted to abide by his fundamental allotted capacity, all alike shall be one with the Natural, which he [the ruler] should allow and not keep them apart from it. This is what is meant by 'great.'" *Zhuangzi jishi*, 2: 408; also, cf. 6.44.

7. Cheng Xuanying: "Only through fulfillment of virtuous conduct can one establish merit and succor the people." *Zhuangzi jishi*, 2: 408.
8. Cheng Xuanying: "Only if one can comply with the empty comprehensiveness of the Dao does virtuous conduct prove sufficient." *Zhuangzi jishi*, 2: 408.
9. Cheng Xuanying: "Slander and praise is all the same for him, as are glory and disgrace, so as he lets not the things of the world compromise his integrity, his virtue maintains complete perfection." *Zhuangzi jishi*, 2: 408.
10. Cf. 3.12.8 and 6.22.6.
11. This and the next line are based on *Laozi*, section 21: "Dark, oh, dim, oh, but within it some image is there. Dim, oh, dark, oh, but within it something is there. Abstruse, oh, indistinct, oh, but within it the essence of things is there." Richard John Lynn, *The Classic of the Way and Virtue*, 86–87.
12. Cheng Xuanying: "*Cheng* (gallop, race) here means 'indulge' [*zong*], and *su* (lodge, lodging) means 'tally with' or 'fulfill' [*hui*]. Since he thus embodies perfect emptiness, this allows him to respond to wants so they are perfectly met. Therefore, in timely fashion he can make use of people in compliance with their natures, respond to them in every possible way, the essential thing being to let them tally with and return [to their original natures] and not get stuck in one point of view. Therefore, whether great or small, whether superior or inferior, he reaches everyone no matter how far. He indulges those who come to him, complies with them and applies himself to the needs of the moment, and so always meets their wants, as if responding to illness with exactly the right medicine, perfectly in accord with the principles involved." *Zhuangzi jishi*, 2: 414.
13. Both Guo Xiang and Cheng Xuanying gloss Wangxiang, literally "no [mental] image," as "unselfconsciousness" [*wuxin*]. Although the *Zhuangzi jishi* and most other editions of the received *Zhuangzi* with Guo's commentary read as "Xiangwang" and not as "Wangxiang," it is more likely that "Wangxiang" is correct; see Wang Shumin, *Zhuangzi jiaoquan*, 425–26, note 7. As a variant, Wangxiang also can be found among editions of Guo's commentary; see Wang Shumin, *Guo Xiang Zhuangzi zhu jiaoji*, 3: 1b.
14. Cf. 1.8.1–1.9.5, 12.6–12.8.18, 24.51–24.61, and 28.1.
15. That is, as a paragon of intelligence, he inspired others to abandon their own original natures to emulate him. Cf. 8.1.6, Guo commentary.
16. Cheng Xuanying: "People had been losing their authenticity already by then for a long time, so he tried to use the art of selfconscious intelligence to recover his original state, but this resulted in his spontaneous natural endowment being lost even at a farther remove." *Zhuangzi jishi*, 2: 417.
17. Cheng Xuanying: "Since the sage is free of selfconscious mind, with resonant compliance he allows others to be others, but here because Nieque would take his own person as the fundamental basis of things and have the people gravitate to him, he would cause all in the world to change the shape of who they were [*yixing*] in submission to his influence. Why people lose their original natures is exactly because of this." *Zhuangzi jishi*, 2: 417. Interpreting *xing* [form, shape] as *shen* [person] follows the suggestion of Wang Shumin, *Zhuangzi jiaoquan*, 428, note 9. The myriad folk would be at odds either with each other or, as Cheng Xuanying suggests, with their "original natures" [*xing*].
18. Cheng Xuanying glosses "father" as "ruler" and "father of the father" as the sage-king Yao. Nieque could rule, but only by self-consciously following the footprints left by Yao, who ruled free of self-conscious mind. *Zhuangzi jishi*, 2: 419.
19. Cheng Xuanying: "If one uses intelligence to govern the people, although it would maintain order for the present, it would be sure to lead to chaos later." *Zhuangzi jishi*, 2: 419.

20. For Tian Heng, see 10.2.7. At court, ministers face north and rulers face south.
21. Cheng Xuanying identifies Hua with the Tang-dynasty Huazhou (present-day Hua county, Shaanxi). *Zhuangzi jishi*, 2: 420.
22. Cf. 33.15.1.
23. Cheng Xuanying: "To 'live like a quail' means to have no fixed abode, though some also say it indicates where the quail lives, that is, out in the wilderness." *Zhuangzi jishi*, 2: 421.
24. Cheng Xuanying: "A hatchling must lift its head to its mother to feed and thus is content." *Zhuangzi jishi*, 2: 421.
25. Cf. 8.6.5–8.6.6.
26. Guo quotes from 20.7. Cheng Xuanying: "Since he acts with tranquil detachment, he can successfully govern the infinite masses, and since he responds to things only as they happen, such reaction to the vicissitudes of the moment results in prosperity. Guo's comment that 'utterly without restraint he behaves freely' is contrary, I fear, to the meaning of the text." *Zhuangzi jishi*, 2: 422.
27. Cf. *Classic of Changes*, hexagram 49 (*Ge*, Radical Change), *Commentary on the Judgments*: "Just as Heaven and Earth make use of Radical Change so that the four seasons come to pass, so did Tang and Wu bring about Radical Change in the mandate to rule in compliance with the will of Heaven and in accordance with the wishes of mankind." Richard John Lynn, *The Classic of Changes*, 445.
28. Guo paraphrases from 11.7.1–11.7.2.
29. Cf. *Laozi*, section 19: "Repudiate sagehood and discard wisdom, and the people would benefit a hundredfold." Lynn, *The Classic of the Way and Virtue*, 82.
30. Cf. *Laozi*, section 32: "The Dao in its constancy is 'nameless.'" Lynn, *The Classic of the Way and Virtue*, 108.
31. Cf. *Laozi*, section 42: "The Dao begets the One; the One begets two; two begets three; and three beget the myriad things."
32. By denying any "knowledge that came later with it," Guo insists that the One did not selfconsciously bring itself into existence. Cf. 2.6, 23.30, and 23.38. Guo Xiang rejects the assertion that "nothingness" has the power to generate things, insisting rather that things generate themselves.
33. Cf. 2.12.13, 5.35.4, 8.2.4, 10.7.4, 17.27, and 33.8.2.
34. A slightly different parallel passage occurs in 7.11. Considerable disagreement exists over how the text of the *Zhuangzi* should be read here; see *Zhuangzi jishi*, 2: 428, and Wang Shumin, *Zhuangzi jiaoquan*, 439, note 4.
35. That is, people should be left undisturbed throughout their natural lives, neither distracted by disputation nor distressed by self-conscious thought, but "sages" such as Confucius want to inflict both on them. Cheng Xuanying: "Principle [the truth] both transcends disputation and can't be understood through the processes of thought. Ears are the basis of hearing [and auditory self-consciousness], which is why the text says they 'lack minds and ears.' Whether sentient or insentient, everything has a beginning and an end, which is why the text says they exist in masses. Since none can speak of it [principle, the truth] in words nor can understand it with the mind, why do you [Confucius] so often promote your monkey cleverness and advertise the clarity of your disputation, as if it were as obvious as if [the sun and moon] suspended in the sky! You make people model themselves on you, and how could this not be an error!" *Zhuangzi jishi*, 2: 428–29.
36. Jianglü Mian and Ji Che, apparently ancient worthies, are not identified in the sources; according to Lu Deming, "the Lord of Lu" might have been Duke Ding of Lu (r. 509–495 BCE). *Zhuangzi jishi*, 2: 430.

37. See 7.14–7.24.
38. Neither Guo Xiang nor Cheng Xuanying explains why such a one should have such feelings, but Lin Xiyi suggests that although "he has no selfconscious thought for the human world, he can't but help feel this way." *Zhuangzi Juanzhai kouyi*, 202.
39. Cheng Xuanying: " 'Mount' means use, and 'radiance' means wisdom. The Divine man of highest rank uses his wisdom to enlighten mankind, and, although he keeps shining like the sun and the moon, once he shines he himself disappears. He discards his body and dismisses his intelligence, and because both mind and body are gone, so the text says 'along with his body he ceases to exist.' " *Zhuangzi jishi*, 2: 443.
40. Guo's comment suggests that the Divine man, the sage ruler, trusts the people to govern themselves, thereby allowing *them* to realize and perfect their natural endowments and innate characters. However, Cheng Xuanying focusses on the Divine man himself: "Since he completely fulfills his natural endowment and perfectly realizes the innate character supplied with life, his sojourn between Heaven and Earth is never without the joy and happiness of spontaneous freedom. Once he realizes that the distinction between self and others is illusory, the myriad cares vanish." *Zhuangzi jishi*, 2: 443.
41. The "man of the Yu clan" is the scion of the Yu clan, the ancient sage-king Shun.
42. Cheng Xuanying notes that Guo Xiang understood Men Wugui's question to have been rhetorical: Wugui already knew that the world was in disorder when Shun began to govern it. *Zhuangzi jishi*, 2: 444.
43. The text of the *Zhuangzi* is ambiguous as to who does not leave footprints. Most later traditional and modern interpretations have it, contrary to Guo Xiang, that it is the people. Cheng Xuanying tries to reconcile both views: "The pristine simplicity of both ruler and people are perfectly pure, so those above and those below exist in harmony and peace, and because they act only in compliance with their original natures, they leave no footprints to be recorded." *Zhuangzi jishi*, 2: 446.
44. Cf. *Classic of Changes*, hexagram 55 (*Feng*, Abundance), *Commentary on the Judgments*: "As everything in Heaven and Earth waxes and wanes at the proper moment; is this not even truer for men, even truer for gods and spirits?" Lynn, *Classic of Changes*, 488.
45. Cf. *Classic of Changes*, "Commentary on the appended phrases" [*Xici zhuan*], Part Two: "The Yellow Emperor, Yao, and Shun let their robes hang loosely down, yet the world was well governed." Lynn, *Classic of Changes*, 78.
46. Lu Deming says that *fouzhong*, "*fou* liquid measure and *zhong* [2 x *fou*] liquid measure," is a scribal error for *chuizhong*, "hang the heel," explained as *chuizhong kongzhong*, "hang the heel in the air"; that is, "hesitate in midstep." The commentaries by Guo Xiang and Cheng Xuanying both support this reading. *Zhuangzi jishi*, 2: 451.
47. Cf. 16.4.2.
48. This assumes that physical ugliness can lead to moral ugliness (i.e., antisocial, criminal behavior). Another tradition, based on Lu Deming's reading of *li* as *lai*, "leper," is adopted by some later Chinese commentators, including Wang Xianqian, as well as some modern Japanese and Western translators; however, neither Guo Xiang nor Cheng Xuanying interpret it this way. *Zhuangzi jishi*, 2: 452. See also Wang Shumin, *Zhuangzi jiaoquan*, 467, note 7.

CHAPTER 13

TIANDAO [THE DAO OF HEAVEN]

13.1.1 Just as the Dao of Heaven operates in such a way that nothing is held back, which allows the myriad things to be produced [*cheng*], so the Dao of the thearchs [*di*] operated in such a way that nothing was held back, which induced the whole world to gravitate [*gui*] to them, and the Dao of the sage [*sheng*] operates in such a way that all within the seas submit [*fu*] to him.

These three ways all allow people to do as they please [*ziwu*] in following their own natures, attempting neither to lead nor impede them.[1]

13.1.2 One who understands Heaven is well versed in the ways of the sage and realizes the virtue of the ruler as it operates in all six directions and in all four seasons; he spontaneously acts [*ziwei*] in such a way that, void of sense and feeling [*meiran*], his quietude never fails.

Since he trusts to spontaneous action, though it operates in all six directions and all four seasons, his quietude is never harmed.

13.1.3 The quietude of the sage does not come about because quietude is supposed to be a good thing to do.

If one is quiet as a consequence of thinking it a good thing to do, agitation will occasionally occur.

13.1.4 It is because none of the myriad things are capable of disturbing his mind that he maintains his quietude.

As such, he remains spontaneously receptive [*zide*].

13.1.5 When water is still, the beard and eyebrows appear in it as if lit with bright candles, and its levelness is so perfectly precise that the great carpenter

takes it as his standard. Since if water is this clear when still, how much more clear should the essential spirit [*jingshen*] be when it is still! The mind of the sage is so still! It is the reflection of Heaven and Earth, the mirror of the myriad things.

To possess such a tool [*ju*] and trust to its spontaneous receptivity means that whatever it reflects shall always be penetrating clear.

13.1.6 Emptiness and quietude [*xujing*], disinterested serenity [*tiandan*], absolute quietude [*jimo*], and unselfconscious action, these constitute the equanimity [*ping*] of Heaven and Earth and the perfect realization of the Dao and its Virtue.[2]

Whenever something is not level or not perfect, it is the product of selfconscious action.

131.7 Therefore the ruler and the sage all reside at rest in them.

They are never agitated.

13.1.8 As such ones are at rest, they are empty; empty, they may be filled; filled, they are in proper order [*lun*].

"Proper order" [*lun*] means [to accord with] principle.

13.1.9 As such ones are empty, they are quiet [*jing*]; quiet, they can act; acting, they are successful.

They never lose that which allows them to act.

13.1.10 As such ones are quiet, they act unselfconsciously, and since they act unselfconsciously, those charged with duties fulfill their responsibilities.

It is because they act unselfconsciously that no matter what class of person, anyone with talent and ability can fulfill his duty. This it was said: "How majestic is the way Shun and Yu possessed the whole world without involving themselves in it!"[3] That is what is meant here.

13.1.11 Since they act unselfconsciously, they are leisurely and happy [*yuyu*]; leisurely and happy, anxiety and care can't find a place in them, thus their years of life last long.

When one seems "leisurely and happy" [*yuyu*], it is the appearance of carefree self-fulfillment.

13.1.12 Emptiness and quietude, disinterested serenity, absolute quietude, and unselfconscious action, these constitute the original nature of the myriad things.

Whenever one seeks to find original nature, it always emerges from unintentionality.

13.1.13 Using such understanding to face south was Yao the ruler, and using such understanding to face north was Shun the minister. To occupy the position of rulership with such understanding is the virtue of monarchs and the Son of Heaven, and to occupy a position of subordination with such understanding is to follow the Dao of the arcane sage [*xuansheng*] and the uncrowned king [*suwang*].[4]

This all indicates the perfection of unselfconscious action. One who possesses such a Dao, thus inducing the whole world to gravitate to him, and yet is denied the appropriate title of monarch is referred to as an "uncrowned king" for his innate nobility [*zigui*].

13.1.14 If one uses such understanding to live a life of seclusion, leisurely roaming among great and small rivers and lakes, recluses in the wilderness will yield in admiration. And if one uses such understanding to come forward to lead a life of engagement, bringing comfort to the world, his merit will be great, name illustrious, and the whole world shall become one.

This also comes next in order of importance. Thus it is that if such a one withdraws, he joins such people as Chao and Xu, and if such a one comes forward, he joins the ranks of Yi and Wang.[5] One who embodies unselfconscious action is indeed great, for what in the whole world would not be accomplished with it! Therefore, if the ruler refrains from performing the duties of the prime minister, this allows a Yi [Yin] or a [Lü] Wang to take charge and administer with quietude. If the prime minister refrains from doing what all the officials are supposed to do, all the officials will manage matters with quietude. If all the officials refrain from dealing with the duties of all the people, all the people will be content with their occupations. If all the people refrain from trying to exchange what he can do for what I can do, every he and I in the whole world will dwell in quietude and self-fulfillment [*zide*] will be had. Therefore, from the Son of Heaven to the common folk—even down to the insects—could any attempt be made to accomplish anything with selfconscious effort! This is the reason why the more unselfconscious action occurs, the more esteem is rendered.

13.1.15 In quietude, such a one is a sage; in action, a ruler.

When it is time to act, he acts; when it is time to stop, he stops.

13.1.16 Acting without selfconscious purpose, he is revered.

He is spontaneously revered by the people.

13.1.17 He is so plain and simple [*pusu*] that none in the world can compete with his beauty.

Beauty comparable to that of Heaven can only be the plain and simple.

13.1.18 When one has clear understanding of the virtue of Heaven and Earth, this is called the "Great Root" [*daben*] and the "Great Exemplar" [*dazong*], for it is to be in harmony with Heaven.

Heaven and Earth have as their virtue the power to act unselfconsciously. Therefore, when one understands this exemplary and fundamental truth [*zongben*], he never acts in opposition to Heaven and Earth.[6]

13.1.19 And this is how such a one keeps the whole world in balanced accord and achieves harmony with humankind.

To comply with Heaven is to resonate with humankind. Thus it is that one achieves perfect harmony with Heaven and complete harmony with humankind.

13.1.20 Harmony with humankind is called the "joy of benevolence," and harmony with Heaven is called the 'joy of Heaven."

When one complies with the joy of Heaven, ample shall be his joy.

13.2.1 Master Zhuang said, "My teacher! My teacher! Though it crushes the myriad things, it is not cruel.

It transforms and mixes them, which is why the text says it "crushes" [*ji*]. The crushing occurs spontaneously and is not caused by any brutal ruthlessness on the part of "my teacher" [the Dao].

13.2.2 Though its beneficence extends throughout a myriad ages, yet it is not benevolent.

Benevolence is just another name for universal love. But since it has nothing to do with love, there is no reason to call it "benevolent."

13.2.3 Though older than remote antiquity, it is not long-lived.

"Long-lived" just means an extremely long time. But since it is free from time, there is no reason to call it "long-lived."

13.2.4 It covers Heaven and carries Earth while it carves and shapes each and every physical form, yet it is not skillful.

"Skillful" just means the marvelous ability to make things. But since everything is done spontaneously, there is no reason to call it "skillful."

13.2.5 This is what the 'joy of Heaven' means.

Once no mindfulness of joy exists, joy becomes completely ample.

13.2.6 Thus it is said, 'When one knows the joy of Heaven, his life is a movement of Heaven, his death a transformation of things. In repose, his virtue is one with yin; in action, he pulses one with yang.' Therefore, one who knows the joy of Heaven stays free from Heaven's wrath, free from man's reproach, free from the bondage of things, and free from the censure of demons. Thus it is said, 'In action he is one with Heaven; in repose he is one with Earth.

Although he differs when either in action or repose, his freedom from self-conscious mind is always one and the same.

13.2.7 His entire mind tranquil, he thus rules the world in such a way that demons neither cause him trouble nor does his spirit [*hun*] ever tire. His entire mind tranquil, the myriad folk thus submit.' That is to say, his emptiness and quietude will spread to all of Heaven and Earth and permeate the myriad folk. This is what is meant by the joy of Heaven.

If one's own mind is always tranquil, this tranquility will permeate the minds of the myriad folk, and, if so permeated, they shall submit, but if not, they will rise in revolt.

13.2.8 The joy of Heaven is the mind of the sage by which he nurtures the entire world.

How can the mind of the sage nurture the entire world? It can only do so as the joy of Heaven!

13.3.1 The virtue of a true sovereign is such that he takes Heaven and Earth as his models, the Dao and its Virtue as his guiding principles, and unselfconscious action as his constant. Since he acts unselfconsciously, though he utilizes the entire world, he has something to spare.

"Something to spare" refers to his carefree leisure.

13.3.2 When it comes to those who practice selfconscious action, since they are used by the entire world, they can never provide enough for the task.

As for those who act selfconsciously, they are thoroughly eager to be used by him, and, since they are eager to be used by him, he can make them his ministers, and once made his ministers, they also contribute to his having "something to spare."

13.3.3 This is why the ancients esteemed unselfconscious action. It is the ruler who should act unselfconsciously. If his subordinates also practice it, they then share the same virtue as their ruler, which means they don't act as ministers. It is the subordinates who should act selfconsciously. If the ruler also practices it, then the ruler shares the same virtue as his subordinates, which means he does not act as a ruler.

As the craftsman practices unselfconscious action in carving wood, leaving the effort involved to the hatchet he employs, so the ruler above acts unselfconsciously in regard to the personal handling of matters, leaving the effort involved to the ministers he employs. It is up to ministers to attend to matters personally and up to the ruler to make use of his ministers, just as the hatchet is up to carving wood and the craftsman is up to employing his hatchet. When each is allowed to match its potential, inherent principle is naturally fulfilled; selfconscious effort has nothing to do with it. But once the ruler assumes the duties of his ministers, he no longer is a ruler, and once a minister controls the functions of a ruler, he no longer is a minister. Therefore, let each tend to his own responsibilities, and ruler and subordinates will all succeed and the principle of unselfconscious action shall be perfectly be realized.

13.3.4 The ruler must act unselfconsciously in making use of the world, and subordinates must act selfconsciously and be used by the world; such is the unalterable Dao.

The term "unselfconscious action" must be investigated. To "make use of the world" suggests that some dependence on action is still involved, but if this action can occur spontaneously so one acts only in compliance with his original nature, this then may be called "unselfconscious action." As for those used nowadays by the world, they also should be spontaneously receptive [to their responsibilities]. But since only those who occupy subordinate positions should handle matters personally, even if a minister were a Shun or a Yu, we reckon that such a one should still act with selfconsciously. Therefore, the ruler and his subordinates are clearly demarcated: the ruler resides in quietude and his ministers act selfconsciously. If we compare remote with later antiquity, whereas Yao and Shun just practiced unselfconscious action, Tang and Wu served as officials. Nevertheless, since each complied with his original nature and thus allowed his celestial mechanism to engage arcanely with things, whether they came earlier or later, whether they were rulers or subordinates, all of them [these four] acted unselfconsciously—how could they have ever acted selfconsciously![7]

13.3.5 Thus it was that although the wisdom of those who ruled the world in antiquity embraced all Heaven and Earth, they themselves engaged in no selfconscious deliberation. Although their eloquence could embellish the myriad things, they did not speak. Although no match for their ability could be found anywhere within the four seas, they did not themselves exercise it.

A ruler comes to grief if he fails to act unselfconsciously and instead assumes the duties of his ministers, which would have made it impossible for Jiu Yao to make his brilliant judgments and for Hou Ji to have sown his seeds.[8] As such, while his talented personnel are forced out of duties, the ruler would be overwhelmed by administration. Therefore, only when the ruler dons his tasseled cap and, with eyebrows relaxed and eyes shut, gives himself over to the world and allows everyone in the world to fulfill their innate capacity to do things, shall the ruler above and his subordinates below all act unselfconsciously. However, whereas the unselfconscious action of the ruler consists in making use of his subordinates, the unselfconscious action of subordinates consists in functioning spontaneously.

13.3.6 Heaven does not beget anything, yet the myriad things undergo transformation; Earth does not grow anything, yet the myriad things find nourishment.

In other words, all this happens spontaneously.

13.3.7 True sovereigns refrain from acting with effort, yet the whole world effectively functions.

Its efficacy is realized by the world itself.

13.3.8 Thus, it is said, nothing is more divine than Heaven, nothing is more bountiful than Earth, and nothing is greater than a true sovereign. And this is why it is also said that the virtue of the true sovereigns makes them companions to Heaven.

They are identical to Heaven and Earth in that they act unselfconsciously.

13.3.9 They ride Heaven and Earth as their vehicle and use the myriad folk to draw them at a gallop, for such is the Dao that allows one to make use of the masses.

13.4 The fundamental lies with the monarch, while minor ramifications lie with his subordinates. General strategy lies with the ruler, while details lie with his ministers. Deployment of the five weapons used by the three armies belongs to the minor ramifications of Virtue. The benefit of reward or harm of punishment, including the imposition of the five penalties, these belong to

the minor ramifications of civic education [*jiao*]. Ritual behavior and moral standards, distinctions between name and reality, deliberate consideration and selfconscious verification, these belong to the minor ramifications of governance. The sound of bells and drums accompanied by [dancers holding] pheasant feathers and oxtails, these belong to the minor ramifications of music. Wailing and sobbing while wearing hemp head band and waist sash, with elaborate or simple mourning clothes differentiated by kinship rank, these belong to the minor ramifications of grief. Only when these five categories of minor ramifications are prompted by the workings of the arts of the mind within the essential spirit, may they then be followed.

To the arts of the mind within the essential spirit belongs the fundamental source for the five categories of minor ramifications. If they are allowed to act spontaneously, the minor ramifications of these five will initiate themselves without prompting.

13.5.1 Such learning existed among the ancients, but it was not what they gave precedence to.

What they gave precedence to was the fundamental.

13.5.2 The sovereign precedes, and the minister follows; the father precedes, the son follows; the older brother precedes, the younger brother follows; the senior precedes, the junior follows; the man precedes, the woman follows; the husband precedes, the wife follows. That superiors should take priority over inferiors is the course of Heaven and Earth, which is why the sage took them as images to emulate [*xiang*].

In other words, although such precedence belongs to human affairs, each instance of it has its origin in the ultimate principle of things and is not formulated by the sage.[9]

13.5.3 Heaven is exalted and Earth is lowly, for such are the positions of the divine and bright. Spring and summer come first and autumn and winter come later, which is the course of the four seasons. Nurtured, the myriad things generate and grow from their incipient appearance each with its own physical form. All things that flourish and decline are subject to death, inherent to the flow of change and transformation. Although Heaven and Earth are both perfectly divine, since the exalted still takes priority over the lowly, how more likely such priority exists in the way of men!

This clarifies that the principle wherein the exalted takes priority over the lowly is something benevolence can't do without.

13.5.4 In the ancestral temple, the closer kin are venerated; at court, the higher ranked and titled are venerated; in villages, the older are venerated; among those who conduct affairs, the more worthy are venerated, for such is priority according to the Dao.

In other words, it is not just in ethical human relations that such [prioritized] veneration applies.

13.5.5 If one speaks of the Dao yet neglects its inherent priorities, it would not be the real Dao, and if one speaks of the Dao but not the real Dao, how could he grasp the real Dao!

The way the Dao may be grasped is through the priorities that exist in it.

13.6.1 This is why those in antiquity who understood the Great Dao first clarified Heaven and next addressed the Dao and its Virtue.

"Heaven" means Nature. Once people were clear about Nature, they attained its Dao.

13.6.2 Once the Dao and its Virtue was clarified, they next addressed benevolence and righteousness.

Once people attained the Dao, they lived in harmony since the principles [of benevolence and righteousness] spontaneously suited them.

13.6.3 Once benevolence and righteousness were clarified, they next addressed keeping to one's allotted place in life.

Once the principles [of benevolence and righteousness] spontaneously suited them, people no longer violated the limits of their natural allotment.

13.6.4 Once how one should keep to his allotted place in life was clarified, they next addressed actual person [*xing*] and title [*ming*].

Once people lived up to their natural allotment [and tried not to go further], everyone's title matched who they actually were.

13.6.5 Once actual person and title were clarified, they addressed how people should be used in compliance with their nature.

None were changed any further.

13.6.6 Once how people should be used in compliance with their nature was clarified, they next addressed forgiveness and excuse [*yuansheng*].

Because each person acted only according to his true nature, blame for wrongdoing was eliminated.[10]

13.6.7 Once forgiveness and excuse were clarified, they next addressed right and wrong.

Each should regard fulfillment of one's nature to be right and violation of one's nature to be wrong.[11]

13.6.8 Once right and wrong were clarified, they next addressed reward and retribution.

Reward and retribution are responses to success and failure. Whereas the Dao as it bears on perfect government is rooted in Heaven, its minor ramifications ultimately lie with these.[12]

13.6.9 Once reward and retribution were clarified, the stupid and the wise came to occupy appropriate places and the estimable and the lowly took rightful positions,

Every office was filled by someone whose talent was appropriate to it.

13.6.10 so that the benevolent and worthy as well as ne'er-do-wells were employed in accord with their original natures,

All were allowed to behave spontaneously within the capacities of their own original natures.

13.6.11 for they ensured that people were differentiated according to their capacities and that they followed what they were named to do.

People did not switch duties.

13.6.12 Thus people served their ruler,

Because assignments accorded with actual duties, people followed assignments and did not act in excess of actual duties.

13.6.13 managed subordinates, governed the common folk, and cultivated their own persons. They used neither selfconscious intelligence nor planning but were sure to submit [*gui*] to their natural endowments. This was called the "Great Peace," the perfection of government.

13.7.1 Since an ancient text states,[13] "there is actual person and there is title," [we know that] the distinction between actual person and title existed among the ancients—but they did not address this first. Those in antiquity who spoke of the Great Dao permitted themselves to take up actual person and title only at the fifth stage and permitted themselves to address reward and retribution only at the ninth stage.

From first clarifying Heaven, it took five stages until they reached actual person and title and nine stages until they reached reward and retribution, which is the right sequence of the natural order.

13.7.2 To have hastened straight to address actual person and title would have meant they were ignorant of the root; to have hastened straight to discuss reward and retribution would have meant they were ignorant of what is primary. One who inverts the Dao when he addresses it or violates the Dao when speaking of it will be governed by others. How could such a one govern others!

One who governs others must follow the right sequence.

13.7.3 To hasten to speak of actual person and title or reward and retribution indicates that one understands the tools of governing but not the Dao as it bears on governing.

Although the Dao as it bears on governing starts with the clarification of Heaven, this does not mean that one should discard reward and retribution but only that one must not get the sequence of what comes first and what later out of order.

13.7.4 As for one who may be used by the whole world but lacks the wherewithal to make use of the whole world, such a one should be called a sophist who grasps only single small details.

One who makes use of the whole world must have a thorough comprehension of the Dao in terms of its proper sequence.

13.7.5 Institutions and regulations relating to ritual behavior and moral standards as well as scrutiny and judgment as regards actual person and

title existed among the ancients, for it was by means of these that subordinates served rulers, but they were not the means by which rulers cultivated subordinates.

It is by entrusting such matters to all people of ability that the cultivation of subordinates is done.

13.8 Long ago, Shun asked Yao, "As Heavenly-endowed King, how do you use your mind?"

13.9.1 Yao answered, "I don't maltreat those whom no instruction can reach,

"Those whom no instruction can reach" [*wugao*] is a way to refer to the stupidly recalcitrant common folk.

13.9.2 neglect not the poverty-stricken common people,

He always gives succor to them.

13.9.3 and in grieving for the dead, I encourage orphans with praise and comfort widows. It is just in these ways that I use my mind."

13.10 To which Shun replied, "That is all well and good, but it not quite great enough."

13.11 Yao then said, "Well then what should I do?"

13.12.1 Shun replied, "Your virtue joined with Heaven, emerge with complete serenity,

Once one's virtue is joined one with Heaven, though emerged he remains serene.[14]

13.12.2 as the sun and moon do shine and the four seasons advance, like the regular occurrence of day and night, as clouds do move, so rain showers its blessings."

All these naturally happen without intent.

13.13.1 Yao then said, "How busily flustered I am!

He disparages himself for being so engaged with things.

13.13.2 You, sir, join with Heaven, whereas I join [am thoroughly engaged] with man."

13.14 As such, Heaven and Earth were thought great by the ancients, having been so praised equally by the Yellow Thearch as well as Yao and Shun. Therefore, as for those who rule the whole world, what, of course, should they do? They should behave as do Heaven and Earth, nothing more.

13.15 When Confucius was going to travel west to deposit his writings at the Zhou court, Zilu offered the advice, "According to what I have heard, there is a certain Lao Dan who was the Zhou court archivist but now has retired and returned to live at home. If you, sir, wish to deposit your writings there, you should try to see him and ask him about it."

13.16 Confucius then said, "Good suggestion."

13.17 But when he saw Lao Dan, he objected to it. Thereupon Confucius began to go through all the twelve classics so he could explain them.

13.18 But Lao Dan interrupted his exposition, saying, "Too tedious! I'd like to hear just about the essentials."

13.19 To which Confucius replied, "The essentials consist of benevolence and righteousness."
13.20 Lao Dan then said, "May I ask if benevolence and righteousness constitute one's original nature?"
13.21 Confucius replied, "Of course. If the noble man were not benevolent he should not be accomplished; if not righteous he should fail to provide for life. Benevolence and righteousness constitute the original nature of the authentic man—what else could it be?"
13.22 Lao Dan continued, "May I ask what you mean by 'benevolence' and 'righteousness'?"
13.23 Confucius replied, "One should take the happiness of others sincerely to heart and should love everyone impartially, this what 'benevolence' and 'righteousness' really mean."

This is what people usually mean by "benevolence" and "righteousness," so he [Master Zhuang] relies on this exchange between Confucius and Master Lao to correct it.

13.24.1 Lao Dan responded, "Ah! How dangerous, the last thing you said! Your 'one should love everyone,' is that not surely skewed!

Perfect benevolence consists in a straightforward approach that has nothing to do with love.[15]

13.24.2 To be impartial in this way is actually a matter of self-interest.

What the world means by "impartiality" is to discard self-interest [*si*] and love others, but one who so loves others does so because he wants others to love him, which is actually self-interest in the extreme and not the true impartiality [*gong*] that results from forgetting all about impartiality.

13.24.3 Would you, sir, wish to keep the whole world from losing its shepherd? Then like Heaven and Earth, whose basic nature is sure to follow constant ways, like the sun and moon, whose basic nature is sure to shine brightly, like the starry constellations, whose basic nature is sure to form up in ranks, like the birds and beasts, whose basic nature is sure to flock and herd, like the trees, whose basic nature is sure to stand tall,

All these are utterly self-sufficient.

13.24.4 you too, sir, trust freely in your virtue to act, keep in step with the Dao as you throw yourself into things, and you shall already be there!

He should not rely on "loving everyone impartially."

13.24.5 Why so energetically keep on promoting benevolence and righteousness, as if beating a drum were the way to catch a runaway?

This is not the way to get him.[16]

13.24.6 Ah! You, sir, are throwing the original nature of man into confusion!

If one loves only when the occasion for it occurs and practices righteousness no more than what is appropriate, this means such a one has forgotten all about benevolence and righteousness. But if one keeps them always in mind, he throws authenticity into confusion.

13.25.1 When Shi Chengqi went to see Master Lao, he asked, "When I heard, sir, that you were a sage, not at all put off by the distance of the journey, I have come in the wish to see you, and, though it took one hundred lodgings and the growth of thick calluses on my feet, I dared not rest. But now that I have observed you, I see that you are not a sage, for surplus vegetables lie here at the heaped earth from rat holes,

This means he does not cherish things.

13.25.2 and you reject the dim-witted, which shows a lack of benevolence.

He is not kind to those close to him.[17]

13.25.3 Things to wear and eat pile up before you endlessly,

Since he is perfectly satisfied, he always has more than enough.

13.25.4 yet you allow them to accumulate and set not a limit to them."

Since the mass of common folk gravitate to him, he just accepts what comes and is not petty about setting limits to it.[18]

13.26 Vacuously indifferent, Master Lao did not reply.

He did not allow what was said to concern his thoughts.

13.27 The next day when Shi Chengqi went to see him again, he said, "Yesterday I felt like ridiculing you, but now I feel utterly empty—why is that?"

He blames himself for the way he felt like ridiculing him, which is why he now feels bad.

13.28.1 Master Lao answered, "As for being someone with clever intelligence or divine sageliness, I think I have freed myself [*tuo*] from such considerations.

Tuo means "go beyond [*guoqu*]."

13.28.2 If yesterday you had called me an ox, I would have let you say I was an ox; if you had called me a horse, I would have let you say I was a horse.

He would have just agreed with what others called him.

13.28.3 But if there had been truth to it yet I refused to acknowledge it,

If there had been truth to it, he should have allowed no thought of praise or blame to enter his mind.

13.28.4 I would have suffered double harm.

Whether praise or blame, if either had made an impression on his mind, name and reality would get tangled together, thus causing double harm.[19]

13.28.5 But I yielded because my constant state is to yield;

"Yielded" refers to his humble bearing. It was because he did not let praise or blame harm him that he could refrain from altering the way he looked.

13.28.6 I did not yield by selfconsciously doing so.

If he acted with selfconscious effort, he could not have maintained a state of constant yielding.

13.29 Waddling like a goose, Shi Chengqi moved out of his shadow, then stepped carefully forward to ask, "How may I cultivate myself?"

13.30.1 Master Lao replied, "You look uneasily aloof,

In deportment he seems ill at ease.

13.30.2 while the look in your eyes is impetuous and rash,

He looks aggressive.

13.30.3 with your head haughtily held high,

Haughtily he shows off how fine he looks.

13.30.4 mouth set in a wide snarl,

He looks fiercely brave.

13.30.5 and your posture so impressively pumped up,

He holds himself full of self-importance and confidence.

13.30.6 that you look like a steed stopped only by its tether.

It is determined to run away.

13.30.7 Primed to act, you hold yourself fast,

He can't freely let himself go.

13.30.8 your release a crossbow trigger.

The speed with which he decides to pursue something or reject it is as fast as that.

13.30.9 In investigating things you are judgmental,

He clearly distinguishes right from wrong.

13.30.10 and you make your intelligence and cleverness appear so grand [*tai*].

"Grand" [*tai*] means that it exceeds what is in his fundamental nature.

13.30.11 You should consider that none of these is to be trusted.

To behave in these ten ways means that he does not trust in his natural endowment but instead lets himself be agitated by praise and blame; thus none of them belong to the way one should cultivate himself.

13.30.12 Were such a one as you to appear along the border, he would be called "bandit."

Such behavior as yours, indeed, is not that of an upright man.

13.31.1 The Master[20] said, "No matter how large, the Dao never comes to an end; no matter how small, it leaves nothing out. Therefore, it is universally sufficient for the myriad things. Ever expansive, there is nothing it does not contain; ever deep, it is unfathomable. Punishment and appeal to innate virtue [*de* (moral suasion)], benevolence and righteousness, are all the minor ramifications of spirit. Unless a Perfected one, who else could determine how they should be used? When a Perfected one possesses the world, is that, indeed, not a great thing! Nevertheless, even it is insufficient to entangle him.

Since such a one makes use of the world, he does not come to grief because of its great size.

13.31.2 All the world may contend for power, but he does not join in.

Serene, he just complies with circumstances.

13.31.3 Since he clearly knows what it is to be free from falsehood, he is not altered by advantage.[21]

Trusting to his authenticity, he sets forth unswervingly.

13.31.4 It is because he thoroughly penetrates to the authentic state of things that he can preserve his fundamental nature. Therefore, since he places himself outside Heaven and Earth and casts aside the myriad things, his spirit never suffers the least fatigue. In step with the Dao and merged with its Virtue, he rejects righteousness and benevolence,

He promotes the Dao and its Virtue.

13.31.5 dismisses rites and music,

He makes fundamental nature his guiding principle.

13.31.6 and in so doing the mind of the Perfected one achieves tranquility.

He finds tranquility in unselfconscious action.

13.32.1 What the world finds of value in the spoken word [*daozhe*][22] is the writing of them, but since writing is nothing more than the spoken word, it is really the spoken word that has value. What is of value in the spoken word is its meaning, and meaning has its referent. But the referent of meaning is impossible to convey in words. Nevertheless, since the world values words, it conveys them in writing. And even though the world values them, to me they deserve no such value, because what it finds valuable in them is not what is really valuable.

The really valuable always lies beyond ideas and words.

13.32.2 Thus it is, what can be seen when one looks are forms and colors; what one can hear when one listens are the names of things and sounds. What a pity that the people of the world assume that forms and colors or names and sounds provide sufficient means to grasp the true state of things! Now, since forms and colors or names and sounds are actually insufficient means to grasp the true state of things,

The grasp of the true state of things can only be done when one has forgotten all about words and shunned all writings.

13.32.3 Therefore,

He who knows does not speak;
He who speaks does not know.[23]

But how could the world ever understand this!

It would mean the rejection of learning and the elimination of knowledge.

13.33 Duke Huan was reading a book up in his hall. Wheelwright Bian [Lun Bian], who was down below the hall carving a wheel, put down his mallet and chisel, went up and asked Duke Huan, "May I be so bold as to ask, what the Duke is reading and whose words they are?"

13.34 The Duke replied, "They are the words of the sages."

13.35 "Are the sages alive?"

13.36 "They are already dead."

13.37 "If that is so, then what the Duke is reading is nothing more than the dregs and sediment of the ancients!"
13.38 Duke Huan then said, "How may a wheelwright criticize what I read! If you have an explanation, I shall excuse you, but, if you have none, you shall die."
13.39.1 Wheelwright Bian replied, "Being who I am, I'll look at it from the point of view of my own trade. When carving a wheel, if the angle of the chisel is too shallow, it will skid and not take hold, but if it is too steep, it will jam and not bite into the grain. To be neither too shallow nor too steep is to get it right with the hand as the mind resonates with it. Although this can't be explained in words, there is a knack which exists there between them [the hand and the mind], which I can't explain even to my son, and neither can my son learn it from me. Therefore, now I'm seventy, and old as I am I must keep on carving wheels.

That is, each person has his own fundamental nature, which teaching him can do nothing to augment.
13.39.2 The ancients along with all they could not transmit are already dead, so what you, my lord, are reading, is nothing more than the dregs and sediment of the ancients.

Things that happened in antiquity already vanished in antiquity. But even if they might be transmitted, how could the ancient ever be made to exist in the present! The ancient does not exist in the present, for things that happen in the present have already been subject to change. Therefore, it is only by shunning learning, following one's own nature, and changing with the times that one can attain perfection.

Notes

1. Cf. 18.4.3.
2. Cf. 15.3.1.
3. *Lunyu* (Analects), 8: 2487b.
4. Both epithets are often, but not always, applied to Confucius. *Su* in this sense means "simple and unadorned." Applied to the ideal ruler, whether "crowned" or not, this usage may derive ultimately from advice given to rulers in the *Laozi*, section 29: "embrace simplicity [*su*], embrace the uncarved block." Richard John Lynn, *The Classic of the Way and Virtue*, 82.
5. Chaofu, who supposedly lived at the time of the sage king Yao in remote antiquity, as did Xu You, who refused Yao's invitation to rule the world in his place, were both renowned recluses. By contrast, Yi Yin served Tang, the first king of Shang, and helped him overthrow the last king of Xia, the tyrant Jie; and Lü Wang served Wu, king of Zhou, and helped him overthrow the last king of Shang, the tyrant Zhou.
6. Cheng Xuanying: "Intelligence [literally "house of the spirit," *lingfu*] bright and still, power of scrutiny and judgment [*shenzhao*] pure and unadulterated, his virtue

in harmony with that of Heaven and Earth, such a one is sure to find his exemplary teacher [*zongjiang*] in the common folk and the root of his being [*genben*] in the myriad things. Arcanely merging with the Dao of Nature, he is thus in harmony with Heaven." *Zhuangzi jishi*, 2: 462.

7. It was in their original nature for King Tang, who had been the "minister" of King Jie of Xia, to overthrow him and found the Shang dynasty, and for King Wu, who had been the "minister" of King Zhou of Shang, to overthrow him and found the Zhou dynasty. Therefore, both acts of rebellion were accomplished through unselfconscious action, and although they were "ministers," Tang and Wu were also incipient rulers by nature.
8. Jiu Yao, also known as Gao Tao or Jiu Tao, was the legendary minister of justice, and Hou Ji, "Lord of Millet," was the legendary director of grains or minister of agriculture, both under Shun.
9. Cheng Xuanying: "The 'course of Heaven and Earth' refers to how spring and summer come first and autumn and winter come later, which is the course of the four seasons. Although Heaven and Earth are the largest of things, one is still superior, the other inferior, so how much less likely is it that such precedence does not exist among people! This was why the sage found images to emulate in the creative transformation of the Two Exemplars by observing the natural process inherent in the sequence of the four seasons. He was thus able to fix firmly the fundamental concept of ruler and minister and to rectify the essential Dao of father and son." *Zhuangzi jishi*, 2: 470. The wording of Guo's and Cheng's commentaries suggests that they both probably thought that the text of the *Zhuangzi* here alludes to the *Classic of Changes*; cf. "Commentary on the appended phrases" [*Xici zhuan*], Part Two: "When in ancient times Lord Bao Xi [Fu Xi] ruled the world as sovereign, he looked upward and observed the images in heaven and looked downward and observed the models that earth provided." Wang Bi: "When the sage made the *Changes*, there was no great thing he did not explore to the utmost and no small thing he did not thoroughly investigate. For great things he took images from Heaven and Earth and for small things he observed the markings on birds and beasts and what things were suitable for the land." Richard John Lynn, *Classic of Changes*, 78.
10. Cheng Xuanying: "*Yuan* means to forgive, and *sheng* means to excuse. Even though people were only used in compliance with their original natures, they still tended to transgress their limits. Therefore, it was appropriate that gracious mercy be dispensed and wrongdoing forgiven." *Zhuangzi jishi*, 2: 472.
11. Cheng Xuanying: "Even though mistakes were forgiven and crimes pardoned, people's minds gradually declined, so next they had to show them right and wrong as a warning to them." *Zhuangzi jishi*, 2: 472.
12. "Success" is "good," and "failure" is "bad." Cheng Xuanying: "Once right and wrong were clarified, success and failure were revealed. Therefore, good was rewarded and retribution exacted for evil in order to assist the common folk." *Zhuangzi jishi*, 2: 472. Both Guo and Cheng seem to have had in mind a passage in the *Yijing* (Classic of Changes), "Commentary on the appended phrases" [*Xici zhuan*], Part Two: "One uses the concept of the two to assist the common folk in the way they behave and to clarify the retribution and reward involved with failure and success." To which Wang Bi added the comment: "The two refer to failure and success. It is by using the concepts of failure and success that one may comprehensively assist the common folk in the way they behave. . . . The way this retribution and reward works is that when one is able to seize the right moment for something, he will enjoy good fortune, but if he goes against the principle involved, he will suffer misfortune." Lynn, *Classic of Changes*, 86.

13. Cheng Xuanying: "What is meant by 'a text' is some Daoist work, which was lost when the Qin burned books, so now no bamboo slips exist to verify what it was." *Zhuangzi jishi*, 2: 473.
14. Cheng Xuanying: "This refers to way one [a ruler] generates and nourishes: since his virtue is united with arcane Heaven, though his outward signs [footprints, *ji*] are manifest, his mind remains utterly serene." *Zhuangzi jishi*, 2: 476.
15. Cheng Xuanying: "The perfect one takes a straightforward approach in accord with principle, free of selfconscious mind or deliberate thought, yet you [Yao] keep in mind how you should love everyone—is that not a personal bias [*siqu*]! *Zhuangzi jishi*, 2: 479.
16. Cheng Xuanying: "Just as the louder the sound of the drum, the farther the runaway will take himself off, so the more benevolence and righteousness are promoted, the farther people will distance themselves from the Dao." *Zhuangzi jishi*, 2: 480.
17. Cheng Xuanying: "*Mei* [younger sister] should be read as *mei* [dim, dark; muddled]. Dim-witted disciples should be guided so they improve, but he rejects and refuses to teach them—how could this ever be called 'benevolence'!" *Zhuangzi jishi*, 2: 481.
18. Cheng Xuanying: "Once one possesses sagely virtue, it is to him that people gravitate. Therefore, such a one allows things they give him to mount up, not setting the least limits to them, and, oceanically generous and utterly unselfconscious, allows what is accumulated or dispersed to be entirely up to others." *Zhuangzi jishi*, 2: 482.
19. Cheng Xuanying: "If yesterday you called me an ox, I would have let you say I was an ox; if you had called me a horse, I would have let you say I was a horse—and not in the least opposed you. Although if it had really been an ox or a horse, these would have been the names for it. But if someone gives me such a name and I shun and reject it, this harms me twice over, for it is both a term of ridicule, on the one hand, and I am not actually an ox or horse, on the other. Even so, it is nothing to shun, let alone deny!" *Zhuangzi jishi*, 2: 483.
20. Cheng Xuanying: "Zhuang Zhou regards Master Lao as his teacher, thus he refers to him as 'Master.' " *Zhuangzi jishi*, 2: 486.
21. Cf. 5.4.4–5.4.5: "Since he clearly knows what it is to be free from falsehood, he isn't altered by things."
22. Cheng Xuanying: "*Daozhe* [that which is said] means the spoken word [*yanshuo*], and 'writing' is the written language." *Zhuangzi jishi*, 2: 489.
23. *Laozi*, section 56; Lynn, *The Classic of the Way and Virtue*, 157.

CHAPTER 14

TIANYUN [THE REVOLVING OF HEAVEN]

14.1.1 **Does Heaven revolve?**

It does not make itself revolve but just spontaneously moves.

14.1.2 **Does Earth stand still?**

It does not make itself stand still but spontaneously stays still.

14.1.3 **Do the sun and moon vie for position?**

They don't vie for position but spontaneously yield position to one another.

14.1.4 **What controls all this?**

14.1.5 **What maintains all this?**

Everything functions spontaneously.

14.1.6 **Disengaged itself, does something make all this go?**

If it were nothingness, it would lack the means to make things go; if it were existent, then each thing would have to be engaged in its own control. That being so, how could it possibly be that some disengaged thing makes things go! Each thing itself spontaneously moves—that's all there is to it!

14.1.7 **Might they have some inherent mechanism**
that inexorably works?
Or that that they operate in such a way
that they can't stop themselves?

They do so spontaneously, thus it is impossible to know how it happens.

14.1.8 Do the clouds make the rain?

Neither of the two can make the other happen; each occurs spontaneously.

> **What gives rise to them and makes them stop?**
> **What is itself disengaged**
> **Yet with indulgent pleasure incites them so?**
> **Winds arise in the north**
> **Then blow west, now east,**
> **Up there where they wander above,**
> **But what is it that so breathes in and out?**
> **Itself perfectly disengaged**
> **Yet fan-like wafts them back and forth?**
> **May I dare ask how all this happens?**

The question is posed to find out how all this spontaneity occurs.

14.2.1 Shaman Xian Chao[1] said, "Come, and I shall tell you. Heaven has six directions and five agents.

Whereas something of things in their familiar, superficial aspects might be known, if one continues to seek their sources all the way to their ultimate origin, it turns out that things occur spontaneously for no reason at all, and, since they occur spontaneously, it does not do the slightest good to ask why they occur—one should just comply with the way things are.

14.2.2 When rulers comply with them, order occurs, but when they oppose them, disaster results.

It is through emulation [of Heaven] that one becomes flexible [*kebian*], but inherent nature must not be violated.

14.2.3 When affairs throughout the nine regions are so conducted that good rule is fully realized and virtue proves universally sufficient, when they oversee the whole world in such a way that the whole world supports them, such rulers are called the "August on High."

This all results from their complying with spontaneity.

14.3 When Grand Steward Dang of the Shang[2] asked Master Zhuang about benevolence, Master Zhuang replied, "Tigers and wolves are benevolent."

14.4 "Why do you say that?"

14.5 Master Zhuang replied, "Since the fathers and cubs treat each other with intimacy, why should they not be thought benevolent?"

14.6 "Then may I ask about perfect benevolence."

14.7 Master Zhuang replied, "Perfect benevolence is to be utterly impartial."

"Utter impartiality" does not mean to be insipid in virtue. Consider how throughout the entire body, no partiality exists. The head is naturally above, the feet are naturally below, the organs are contained inside, and the skin and hair are outside. Whether outside or inside, above or below, superior or subordinate, the more or less valued, as far as the whole body is concerned, each part fulfills its responsibility to the utmost yet all remain utterly free of any intimate affection among them. This is how "perfect benevolence" proves its complete adequacy. Therefore, when it happens that those bound by the five degrees of familial relations or are members of the six blood relationships, whether sage or dull-witted, whether close or distant, never violate their allotted place in life anywhere in the world, this is all due to the spontaneous workings of the principles involved—so why go on to attribute it to a sense of partiality!

14.8 The Grand Steward responded, "I have heard that to be utterly impartial means that one does not love, and that one who loves not is unfilial. May one then say that perfect benevolence means one should be unfilial?"

14.9.1 Master Zhuang replied, "Not at all! Perfect benevolence is sublime! To speak of it in terms of filial piety is quite inadequate!

One must first reach the stage of having forgotten all about benevolence and filial piety before one may speak of its perfection.

14.9.2 What you have just said neither gets beyond 'filial piety' nor goes as far as [true] filial piety.

Because all names spring from inadequacy, one should get beyond the names "benevolence" and "filial piety" and cross beyond them to the realm where no names exist, for only there does one find perfection.

14.9.3 Now here is someone who goes south as far as Ying, where, when turning to the north, finds he can't see Dark Mountain [Mingshan]. Why is that? Because he has gone even farther away from it.

Dark Mountain is situated at the north end of the earth, and yet here someone goes south in order to see it. Perfect benevolence means to be utterly impartial, yet here is someone who tries to speak of it in terms of preferential love [*ren'ai*]. Therefore, just as Ying was there for the one to see while he was even the more removed from Dark Mountain, so the other might manifest benevolence and filial piety while even failing the more to achieve their ultimate principles.

14.9.4 Therefore, I say though being filial out of reverence is easy, to be filial out of love is hard; though being filial out of love is easy, to forget parents is hard; though to forget parents is easy, to make parents forget oneself is hard; though to make parents forget oneself is easy, to become completely unaware of all in the world is hard; though to become completely unaware of all in the world is easy, to have all in the world become unaware of oneself is hard.

When one practices perfect benevolence, it is like when all the joints in the body work well: one is never selfconscious of them. When a sage occupies the position of ruler he shuns all selfconscious effort and does absolutely nothing but allow each person his own self-fulfillment. And since each thus fulfills his capacity to do things, all things spontaneously go smoothly. The common folk thus all enjoy self-sufficiency, so who in the world could fail to forget oneself! And since everyone loses all selfconsciousness of self, where might any ruler for them be found? Such a state is referred to as being "completely unaware" [*jianwang*].[3]

14.9.5 If in virtue one discards Yao and Shun [as models] and does not exercise virtue deliberately,

Only when one has discarded Yao and Shun as models shall the virtue of a Yao or Shun be perfectly realized, but as long as one's mind remains connected to them, he shall fail to achieve self-realization.

14.9.6 he shall bestow rich benefits that last a myriad generations, but none in all the world shall be aware of it.

They [the benefits] perfectly tally with [the people's] constant sense of what is suitable.

14.9.7 So why just go on sighing deeply and talk about benevolence and filial piety!

This is to be [fish] lost amidst rivers and lakes that yet go on thinking about wetting one another with foam from the mouth.[4]

14.9.8 Filial piety and respect for one's elder brother, benevolence and righteousness, loyalty and trustworthiness, constancy and honesty, all these goad a person on and so enslave his virtue, thus they are not worthy of esteem. Therefore, I say that perfect nobility results when state conferred noble ranks and titles [*bing*] are discarded;

Bing here means "discard" [*chuqi*]. Esteem pertains to the self, so as even the self should be forgotten how much the more should state conferred noble ranks and titles! This is why the text states that "perfect nobility results when state conferred noble ranks and titles [*bing*] are discarded."

14.9.9 perfect wealth results when the wealth of the state is discarded;

Perfect wealth consists of self-sufficiency and nothing more. Therefore, one should forego the wealth of the whole world.[5]

14.9.10 perfect aspiration results when fame and reputation are discarded.

What perfect aspiration consists of is appropriateness [*shi*]. Once one obtains what is appropriate for him, all need for a benevolent and filial reputation vanishes.

14.9.11 As such, the Dao is unalterable."

This is because it discards the flower [*hua*] [outer show], yet retains the fruit [*shi*] [real substance].

14.10 Beimen Cheng asked the Yellow Thearch, "When you, oh Thearch, had the "Pool of Shaman Xian" [Xian Chi] performed out in the empty wilds,[6] a first hearing left me afraid, a second hearing left me limp, and a final hearing

left me thoroughly muddled. Perfectly serene and mind completely blank, I was utterly at a loss."

"Utterly at a loss" [*bu zide*] means to abide in forgetfulness [*zuowang*].

14.11.1 To which the Yellow Thearch replied, "You have just about got it!

I had it resonate with man,
Comply with Heaven,
Develop with proper ritual decorum,
Take form according to Grand Clarity [Taiqing].[7]

Looking at it from this perspective, we know that perfect music [*zhiyue*] does not designate some ordinary kind of music, for it must first comply with Heaven, resonate with Man, that is, derive from natural temperament and conform to innate character, and only then may it be expressed in sound and performed as composition. As such, "Pool of Shaman Xian" music had to wait upon the transformative power of the Yellow Thearch before it could take form.

14.11.2 For this perfect music, I first had it resonate with the way of the world, comply with natural principles, develop according to the five virtues, resonate with Nature, and then get in step with the four seasons and achieve great harmony with the myriad folk.[8]

As the four seasons arise in order,
The myriad things take life in turn,
As one thrives another declines,
So civil and military follow their constant course.

Now clear tone, now vibrato, yin and yang blended harmoniously,
Its sounds flowed richly forth.

It was with the tones of the pitch pipes of Nature, that he [the Yellow Thearch] filled all between Heaven and Earth, though he ensured that he did so with compliance and not by seizing the lead. As such, this perfect music was perfect throughout.

14.11.3 Now hibernating creepy-crawly creatures began to stir,
As I startled them with thunder.[9]

It is through their capacity for self-activation [*zizuo*] that they realize their potential to act.

14.11.4 No tail to its end,
No head to its beginning,

The cycle goes on forever.[10]

14.11.5 As soon as one dies, another comes alive,
As soon as one falls, another rises,
Capacity for constancy inexhaustible,

Since its constancy consists of change and transformation, its capacity for constancy is inexhaustible.

14.11.6 But not a single one can be relied on,
So this is why you became afraid.

When he first heard about inexhaustible change, he realized he could not use any particular instance of it to rely on, which was why he was filled with dread when he heard about it.[11]

14.12.1 A second time I had it
Resonate in harmony with yin and yang,
Illuminated with the light of sun and moon.

In other words, he used the Dao of Heaven.

14.12.2 Its notes might be

Either short or long,
Either soft or hard,
Each change and transformation
treated equally in the same way,
Uncontrolled by any precedent.

As they are treated equally in the same way by change and transformation, they are not controlled by precedent.

14.12.3 In valleys they filled valleys,
In hollows they filled hollows,

The Dao as it bears on perfect music reached absolutely everywhere.

14.12.4 As I blocked my apertures and guarded my spirit

That is, [as Master Lao says,] "block up your apertures."[12]

14.12.5 And let them find their own measure,

The "Great Cutter" [*dazhi*, the Dao] does not cut.

14.12.6 To undulate melodiously far and wide,

In other words, they spread out harmoniously.

14.12.7 And result in fame lofty and bright.

Since reputation here matches reality, they [the notes] are "lofty and bright."

14.12.8 Consequently,
Malign spirits with numinous powers quit not their darkness,[13]

They did not leave the place proper to them.

14.12.9 and sun, moon, and stars stayed their course.

They strayed not off their proper paths.

14.12.10 I let them stop when they reach their limits

He always stopped them [the notes] at the point where they could go no farther.

14.12.11 and let them flow on as long as it was not their place to stop.

He let them issue forth in step with change.

14.12.12 I might have wanted to deliberate about them, but they were impossible to know, wanted to distinguish what they were, but they were impossible to perceive, wanted to keep up with them, but this was impossible to do.

Thus it was that he just let them [the notes] freely go on transforming themselves.

14.12.13 So, mind utterly blank, I just abided in the boundlessly spacious Dao,

That is, in the immense reaches of impartiality.

14.12.14 and intoned the melody leaning on my withered parasol tree.

There was nothing else that he could do.[14]

14.12.15 I knew that my eyes would be exhausted by what I would try to see and my strength broken by what I was would try to pursue, and, as such, I was just not up to it!

In other words he realized that the extent of a person's selfconscious understanding has its own particular limit.

14.12.16 When the body is utterly void, it becomes perfectly compliant [*weiyi*], so when you became perfectly compliant, this was why you became limp.

When the body becomes completely void, one is freed from self, and, freed from self, one can be compliant [*weiyi*]. Compliantly, one trusts to one's nature, which results in a fearful sense of limpness.[15]

14.13.1 A third time I had it

Resonate using notes that banished limpness

Having created a sense of limpness, they then went on to banish limpness; such was their perfection.

14.13.2 And harmonize with the spontaneous workings of fate.

Whatever happens because of fate has nothing to do with selfconscious purpose, but in every case happens spontaneously.

14.13.3 They thus

Merged to spring forth like the ensemble sound of a forest,

Utterly unregulated in total disorder, their sound sprang forth as from a forest.

14.13.4 And like forest music were without form.

Perfect music conforms and does nothing more. Since such conformity is intrinsic to it, it has no form other than that.[16]

14.13.5 Spreading freely while not led,

They just spread themselves.

14.13.6 obscure and imperceptible they made no audible sound.

Such is perfect music.

14.13.7 When they moved, it was without direction,

How could it be that they moved only after a direction was set!

14.13.8 In repose, they resided in profound obscurity.

By this is meant "in utmost tranquility."

14.13.9 Now said to die,
Now said to live,
Now said to fruit,
Now said to flower,
They flowed along in random fluctuation,
No fixed score in control.

They changed and transformed in step with things.

14.13.10 But the common folk of the world doubt this and instead selfconsciously ascribe it to [*ji*] the sage.

It is clear that the sage acts in response to the world and does not take the lead.[17]

14.13.11 Since the sage thoroughly comprehends the innate character of things, he stays perfectly in step with fate.

One who has such possession of innate character and fate never fails in his reliance on them.

14.13.12 Without the celestial mechanism [one's original nature] so setting them, the five viscera are completely functional; this is a way of explaining what "Heavenly Music" means.

Once music is forgotten it becomes perfect in every way; it does not wait on perfection until it [one's celestial mechanism] sets it so.

14.13.13 Though no words can describe it, one's heart finds it a delight."

The heart finds delight in what suits it and not in what is said about something.

14.13.14 Long ago, Sire Flame [Yan shi, Shennong, the Divine Farmer] composed the following hymn:

Listen to it yet hear not its sound,
Look at it yet not see its form,
Though it fills all from Heaven to Earth
And embraces to the limits of the six directions.

You tried to hear it yet could not connect with it, which was why you became thoroughly muddled.

As such, this is the music without music, the perfection of music.

14.14.1 First, I had the music induce fear, and struck with such fear, you were as if beset by demons.

He listened with such fear that he could only feel he was beset by demons, for its great harmony was yet beyond reach.

14.14.2 Second, I then had it resonate with limpness, and you became so limp that this vanished.

Such outward signs gradually vanished.[18]

14.14.3 Finally, I had it resonate in total confusion, and you were so muddled that you became utterly stupid, so stupid that you attained the Dao, the Dao that can transport you in unity with it.

To be free from selfconsciousness is what "stupid" means, for with such stupidity, one attains perfection.

14.15 When Confucius travelled west to Wey, Yan Hui asked Grand Preceptor Jin, "What do you think of my master going there?"

14.16 Grand Preceptor Jin answered,[19] "Alas! How your master will exhaust himself!"

14.17 To which Yan Hui responded, "What do you mean?"

14.18.1 Grand Preceptor Jin replied, "Before straw dogs are ceremoniously displayed they are kept in bamboo boxes and wrapped in embroidered silk, and the ceremonial stand-in for the deceased purifies himself by fasting before offering them up. However, after such display they end up having their heads and backs trampled flat by passers-by, which then are collected by grass gatherers and burned as fuel. But if taken back and stored again in bamboo boxes and wrapped in embroidered silk, anyone who keeps them close at hand both on the road and at home, not only would fail to have proper dreams but is sure repeatedly to suffer harmful hallucinations [*mi*] because of them.

These things are to be discarded once they no longer serve their purpose, otherwise they will instead attract the anomalous and harmful.[20]

14.18.2 Now your master has also been collecting straw dogs once displayed by the former kings and has gathered disciples to bed down with them both on the road and at home, which is why he had a tree cut down because of him in Song, had to become a fugitive in Wey, and suffered distress while in Shang during the Zhou.[21] Were not these such occasions as he might have dreamt about? And when he was surrounded between Chen and Cai and, without cooked food for seven days, was on the border between life and death,[22] was this not an occasion he might have hallucinated about?

All these examples signify that one should just reject sagely wisdom and discard selfconscious knowledge so that one is not obstructed by them in the least. The "statues and rituals" of the former kings are means "employed at the times suitable for them." Once such times are past but these are not discarded, they then become anomalous and harmful to the people, for they serve as the impetus leading to forced conformity.[23]

14.19 For traveling on water nothing is better than a boat, and for traveling on land nothing is better than a cart. Whereas it is possible to use a boat to travel on water, if one tries to push one on land, even an entire lifetime of pushing won't move it more than a short distance. Are not antiquity and the present just like the water and the land? And are not Zhou and Lu just

like the boat and the cart? If one now tries to practice in the state of Lu what had gone on back during the Zhou, this is just like pushing a boat on the land: toil without accomplishment will surely mean harm for the person involved. Such a one still fails to grasp how one should act as does the infinitely changeable revolution, which allows one to resonate with things yet never be exhausted.

As over time the whole world differs, so rituals too change accordingly, which is why one [the ruler] should just comply with the people and stay free of all bonds. In this way, he shall without toil have accomplishment.

14.20.1 **Is it just you who has never seen a well sweep? Pull it down and down it goes; let it go and up it comes. It is pulled on by people and does not pull on them, so it can't be blamed by anyone for going up or down. So it was with the Three Thearchs and the Five Emperors, whose rites and regulations should be venerated, not because they preserved continuity but because they were congenial to order.**

Meeting the needs of the moment, they did nothing other than let the procedures of government respond accordingly.

14.20.2 **As such, how the rites and regulations of the Three Thearchs and the Five Emperors do seem like the haw, the pear, the orange, and the pomelo! Although these flavors are incompatible, they all are delicious.**

14.21.1 **Just so, rites and regulations should change in response to the times.**

What the one might have considered good another might have considered bad, which is why they [rites and regulations] should change to suit the times, for only then do they suit all occasions.

14.21.2 **Now, if you take a monkey and dress it in the clothes of the Duke of Zhou, it surely won't be satisfied until it has bitten them to pieces and ripped them all off.**

Take a look at how antiquity differs from the present, and you will see that it is just like how a monkey differs from the Duke of Zhou. Once upon a time, Xi Shi, feeling pain in her chest, frowned at her neighbors, but one of them, an ugly woman, when she saw this thought it made her beautiful, so on the way home she too held hand to chest and frowned at her neighbors. When the rich of the neighborhood saw her, they shut their doors tight and would not go out; when the poor saw her, they grabbed their wives and children and fled. Although that woman knew that frowning made Xi Shi beautiful, she failed to understand how the frown made her beautiful.

How much the more true this is for rites and regulations! To use them only when the time is right indicates a "Xi Shi," but if their time is past yet they are not discarded, this indicates an "ugly woman."

14.21.3 **Alas! How your master exhausts himself!"**[24]

14.22 **Confucius had lived all of fifty-one years yet had never heard the Dao. So he traveled south to Pei**[25] **to see Lao Dan.**

14.23 Lao Dan said, "You really came here? I have heard that you were a worthy of the north, so might you too have attained the Dao?" Confucius replied, "Not yet."

14.24 Master Lao then asked, "Where have you been seeking it?"

14.25 "I sought it in astronomical calculations [*dushu*], but after five years I still had not attained it."[26]

14.26 Master Lao continued, "Then where else did you seek it?"

14.27 "I sought it in the yin and yang, but after twelve years I still had not attained it."[27]

All of this conveys that Master Lao would have Confucius discard knowledge.

14.28.1 Master Lao then said, "Exactly! If the Dao could be presented, who would not present it to his sovereign! If the Dao could be offered, who would not offer it to his parents! If the Dao could be conveyed, who would not convey it to his brothers! If the Dao could be bestowed, who would not bestow it on his sons and grandsons! However, all this is impossible for no other reason than because no master exists within, so it does not linger,

If within the mind one's original nature [*zhi*] is not present to receive it,[28] though he hears the Dao, it will just pass him by.

14.28.2 and purity and truth [*zheng*] are lacking without, so it does not transmit.

Since no master exists within [anyone except the true sage], no one else is pure and true either, which is why it [the Dao] is not communicated.[29]

14.28.3 If that which may emerge from within is not received without, the sage does not let it go forth.

That which may emerge from within is the Dao of the sage. Only if there is someone without who may receive it does it go forth.

14.28.4 If that which may enter from without finds no master within, sageness won't abide there.

That which may enter from without refers to fulfillment of one's nature through learning. Although one's nature might be fulfilled through learning, one's original nature [*zhi*] must be present within, for if no such master is there, no place exists in which the sagely Dao [*shengdao*] may abide.

14.28.5 Fame is a public instrument,

Fame is something that may be used by anyone in the world.

14.28.6 which may not be grabbed at to excess.

To "grab at to excess" means to pretend to be more than one really is. Such grabbing at excess leads the whole world to fall into disorder

14.28.7 Benevolence and righteousness are but inns once used by the former kings,

They are like temporary lodgings.

14.28.8 in which one may stay for a night but not dwelled in long, for once conspicuous there one will incur much blame.

Benevolence and righteousness belong to one's inborn nature, but inborn nature is subject to change, so that of the present differs from long ago. Therefore, one should lodge with them [benevolence and righteousness] as if in transit, then leave them behind and thus preserve one's obscurity. However, if one is stuck with them as if attached to one place, he becomes conspicuous. Once conspicuous, he becomes pretentious, which then incurs much blame.

14.29.1 The Perfected one of antiquity found an expedient path via benevolence and a temporary lodging in righteousness, thereby allowing him to wander in the emptiness of spontaneous freedom, live off the land of rough provender, and finds a place for himself in the garden of no yield.

He changed [direction and lodging] according to the needs of the moment so left no permanent footprints behind.

14.29.2 "Spontaneous freedom" signifies unselfconscious action.

If he acted selfconsciously, it would violate benevolence and righteousness.

14.29.3 "Rough provender" signifies easily nourished.

Since he just took what plain and simple fare came his way, he was easily nourished.

14.29.4 "No yield" signifies not providing for others.

"No yield" means that such a one harms not his own person for the sake of others.

14.29.5 The ancients called this "wandering with presence authentic [*caizhen*].

To wander along just as one pleases, this signifies authentic presence [*zhencai*]. When one has authentic presence [*zhencai*], his appearance is free of pretention.[30]

14.30.1 One who considers wealth something good can't bear to yield his salary to others; one who considers prominence something good can't bear to yield his fame to others; one who loves power can't bear to share wielding it with others.

Never has anyone in the world fettered himself with something he considers bad but always instead sacrifices himself for what he considers good. One who sacrifices himself for what he considers good finds not a place for himself in the garden of no yield.

14.30.2 While grasping them such a one trembles, and when he lets them go he grieves.

One who grieves when he lets them go while he still grasps them can't help but tremble.

14.30.3 Yet he himself has not the least power of insight that allows him to see that not giving up these things leads to his being punished by Heaven.

In other words, because such a one knows only to keep going but not to stop, his natural endowment is thus lost, which is how he is punished.

14.30.4 Blame or favor, deprivation or bestowal, admonition or instruction, sparing of life or condemning to death, these eight are the instruments of governance. 14.30.5 But only one who complies with the great workings of change without interfering in any way is capable of using them. Thus it is said, "one who governs should himself be pure and true," for if his mind is not so prone he shall not find the gate of Heaven open to him.

If one holds fast to precedent and not allow for change, he will lose the correct [path, the Dao].

14.31.1 When Confucius went to see Lao Dan to tell him about benevolence and righteousness, Lao Dan said, "Winnowing chaff so blinds the eyes that the sky, the earth, and the four directions all seem out of position. If a mosquito or horsefly bites the skin, you sleep not the whole night.

Though it be little, augmentation by anything extraneous does great harm to one's original nature.

14.31.2 Benevolence and righteousness so viciously oppress one's mind that no greater confusion can beset it.

They are held in such esteem that people try to augment their original natures with them, hence confusion occurs.

14.31.3 My dear sir, if you would allow everyone in the world to maintain their own pristine nature,

Once original nature is safe and whole, benevolence and righteousness manifest themselves accordingly.

14.31.4 you, dear sir, would then act as the wind takes you, and since you would thus keep your virtue intact you would then prevail.

If he follows the wind as it spontaneously shifts, this would allow his virtue to sustain itself and thus remain intact. The Dao is as easy to maintain and as easy to practice as this.

14.31.5 So why go on wasting so much energy as if beating a drum to catch a fugitive?

That is, promoting benevolence and righteousness in order to dispose people to morality and ethics is like beating a drum to catch a fugitive—no way can these possibly succeed.[31]

14.31.6 The swan does not wash itself every day yet remains white; the crow does not darken itself every day yet remains black,

Their natural states are already adequate for each of them.

14.31.7 For the blackness or whiteness is in their pristine natures,

Both are just naturally so, not because they are disposed to be so.

14.31.8 so it does no good to dispute about them.

One who is perfectly adequate [in benevolence and righteousness] forgets all about fame and reputation, and once fame and reputation are forgotten, they [benevolence and righteousness] expand [*guang*].

14.31.9 But fame and reputation are matters of outward display so do no good when it comes to expanding [*guang*] them [benevolence and righteousness].

That is, a reputation for benevolence and righteousness always springs from inadequacy in them.

14.31.10 When sources dry up and fish find themselves stranded together on land, they spew moisture on each other and wet each other with foam from their mouths, but it would be better if they could just forget about one another in rivers and lakes."[32]

That is, only when people forget all about benevolence do they really become benevolent.

14.32 When Confucius returned from his visit to Lao Dan, he did not speak for three days, but then one of his disciples asked, "When you, sir, saw Lao Dan, you surely corrected him, but how did you do it?"

14.33.1 Confucius replied, "Finally, now in him I have seen a dragon! As when a dragon coalesces so he creates a physical body and as when it disperses so he forms patterns [*chengzhang*].

That is, Lao Dan was capable of change and transformation.[33]

14.33.2 He rides on clouds and mist and so provides nourishment in terms of yin and yang.

That is, since he operates without direction, his spontaneity is quite up to everything.

14.33.3 My jaw so dropped I could not even close my mouth [and my tongue so rose that I could not even stammer],[34] so what chance had I to correct Lao Dan!"

14.34 Zigong then said, "As such, can a man be still as a ceremonial stand-in for the deceased yet have the look of a dragon, be utterly silent yet sound like thunder,[35] so that when he starts to act he moves like Heaven and Earth? Could I too have an opportunity to see him?" Subsequently he went with an introduction from Confucius to see Lao Dan.

14.35 Lao Dan was then in his hall sitting with legs outstretched, ready to respond, so he said in a small voice, "My years have about all run out, so how would you now instruct and admonish me?"

14.36 Zigong said, "Although the Three Sovereigns[36] ruled the world differently from the Five Emperors,[37] their fame persists in the same way, yet you, sir, alone hold the view that they were not sages—why ever not?"

14.37 Lao Dan replied, "Young man, approach a little closer! Why do you say that they ruled differently?"

14.38 Zigong answered, "Yao yielded to Shun, and Shun yielded to Yu. Whereas Yu acted energetically on his own, Tang employed troops. Although King Wen obeyed Zhou and dared not revolt, King Wu rebelled against Zhou in defiance of him. This is why I say they differed."[38]

14.39.1 Lao Dan then said, "Young man, approach a little closer! I shall tell you how the Three Sovereigns and Five Thearchs ruled the world. The Yellow Thearch so ruled the world that the common folk were encouraged to such unity of mind that when those among them had a parent die, though they failed to wail, people did not discredit them.

If they had discredited them, this would have forced them to wail.

14.39.2 Yao so ruled the world that the common folk were encouraged to such bias of mind that when those among them regarded relatives in terms of diminishing kinship ties [*sha qisha*], people did not discredit them.

Sha [more generally "kill"] here means "diminish" [*jiang*], which refers to how the closeness of kinship ties is seen progressively to diminish [*jiangsha*].[39]

14.39.3 Shun so ruled the world that the common folk were encouraged to such a competitive state of mind that when pregnant women among them would give birth to a child in the tenth month, that child would be able to speak by the fifth month of life,

That is, teaching became as hurried as this.

14.39.4 and before it became a toddler it would know who was who.

"Who was who" means to distinguish among people. That pre-toddlers could already distinguish one person from another indicates how hurried competition in education had become.

14.39.5 This being so, people began to die young.

Since they no longer could merge other and self, they fixated on outdoing one another in differentiating gradations of kinship. As a result, they cut short their own natural lifespans.

14.39.6 Yu so ruled the world that the common folk were encouraged to such deviance of mind that people became cunning and amenable to the use of weapons.

That is, the reason why people were amenable to the use of weapons was because sedition already existed in the world.

14.39.7 So the killing of a robber was no longer the killing of a person.

Since robbers, of course, should die, people were willing to have them killed them, so it was not considered killing as such.[40]

14.39.8 Since people regarded themselves as this type or that, it was all just due to the way of the world.

Unable to regard all people as one, every person differentiated himself from others; this is what "people regarded themselves as this type or that" means. Such tendencies have lasted for hundreds of ages and meet now in the vicissitudes of the present. That the ruination reached such an extreme as this did not happen because of Yu, which is why the text says "it was all just due to the way of the world." That is, it was not impressions left by the sage's wisdom that inflicted chaos on the world, but the world itself that insisted on having such chaos.

14.39.9 At this, the whole world fell into panic, which prompted the rise of the Confucians and the Mohists.

And with this came the ruination of hundreds of ages.

14.39.10 What they first formulated may have been moral principles, but these now have reached the point where daughters are taken as wives.

That nowadays daughters are taken as wives and superiors and subordinates oppose one another happens not because what they first formulated lacked moral principles, but because what they did led to the ruination of such principles, culminating in such a state as this.

14.39.11 What else need be said!

Ruination arises from moral principles, thus there is nothing more to say.

14.39.12 I say to you that in ruling the world, although the Three Sovereigns and Five Thearchs have been said to have 'brought order to it,' they could not have caused it more disorder!

Inevitable ruination was the sure result.

14.39.13 Wisdom associated with the Three Sovereigns repels the light of the sun and moon above, acts contrary to the vital essence of mountains and streams below, and disrupts the effect of the four seasons in between. Wisdom associated with them, more lethal than the tail of a scorpion, is such that even the tiniest creature has failed to remain content with the innate tendencies of its own endowed nature, yet they consider themselves to have been sages! Was it not shameful, such lack of shame!"

14.40 Zigong was so shocked that he could just stand there ill at ease.

Zigong said at first that although Master Lao distinguished the Three Sovereigns from the Five Sovereigns, he wanted to judge them the same. But now that he perceived that Master Lao lumped the Five Thearchs together with the earlier Three Sovereigns in blanket condemnation, he lost the basis of what he had to say.

14.41.1 Confucius said to Lao Dan, "I have been studying the six classics, the *Odes*, *Documents*, *Rites*, *Music*, *Changes*, and *Spring and Autumn Annals*, for what I consider a long time, so I know full well how to explain them. Despite expounding to seventy-two morally recalcitrant rulers the Dao of the former kings and explaining to them the record of achievements of Dukes Zhou and Zhao, I have not been employed by a single ruler. How very difficult it is to persuade such men! Is it really so hard to explain the Dao?"

14.42.1 Master Lao replied, "How fortunate that you, sir, did not encounter a ruler who might really govern the world! The six classics are just footprints left behind by the former kings. Why should they be taken for the maker of such footprints!

The maker of such footprints is true nature. Footprints left by those who allowed people their true natures are what constitute the six classics.

14.42.2 What you, sir, are talking about is like such footprints. Footprints were produced when feet walked. Why should the footprints ever be taken for the walking itself!

Even more important for the present state of the world, he [Confucius] should realize that it was spontaneity that did the walking and the *Six Classics* that were the footprints made.

14.42.3 Just by looking at each other, white cormorants, without the movement of an eye, accomplish fertilization, and as for insects, when the male chirps upwind, the female just has to reply downwind to be fertilized.

Cormorants just have to look at each other with their eyes and insects just have to chirp and respond for both to beget offspring without depending on physical union. Therefore, the text uses the term "fertilized."

14.42.4 And since some species are such that the individual is both male and female, fertilization takes place that way.

Every male and female of the same species is capable of mutual response, but their ways of responding differ infinitely, but as long as one of the same species finds another, the fertilization is not difficult, which is why with some fertilization takes place even through distant resonance.

14.42.5 Original nature can't be changed; fated endowment can't be altered; time can't be stopped; and the flow of the Dao can't be obstructed.

Therefore, the Perfected one always complies with and allows them free flow.

14.42.6 If one attains to the Dao, no matter where he starts from he shall be up to it.

Although things transform in infinite ways, one shall be capable of dealing with them all.

14.42.7 But one lost to it will lack a place from which he can start."[41]

No matter in what circumstances, he will never be up to it.

14.43.1 Confucius did not go out for three months and then, when he again went to see him, he said, "I actually got it! Magpies hatch their young; fish depend on froth; the thread-waisted wasp transmutes.

That is, creatures are naturally endowed in such a way that each kind has its own sexual nature.

14.43.2 And once younger brother arrives, older brother howls.

That is, it is the nature of humans to neglect the older and cherish the younger, thus the older howls.

14.43.3 I have long failed to allow others be their own persons! Since I did not allow others to be their own persons, how could I have nurtured them!"

To allow others be their own persons is to allow them self-transformation. If one tries to influence them by spreading the six classics, he shall just alienate them.

14.43 Master Lao then said, "Right, you actually got it!"

Notes

1. Cheng Xuanying: "Shaman Xian was a *shenwu* (shaman with divine powers), who served as prime minister for [Shang emperor] Zhongzong (reigned 1535–1460 BCE). Chao was his given name." *Zhuangzi jishi*, 2: 496. However, another possibility is to read *chao* as a variant of *shao* (explain), which would result in "Shaman Xian explained, saying"; see Akatsuka Kiyoshi, *Sôji*, 1: 567–68. The pronunciation *chao* and not the usual *tiao* follows Lu Deming; see *Zhuangzi jishi*, 2: 496. Note that Shaman Xian is associated with the ancient music "Pool of Shaman Xian" [Xian Chi]; cf. 14.10, 18.20, and 33.6.
2. Cheng Xuanying: "After its demise Yin [Shang] continued on as [the domain of] Song. Therefore Shang here indicates the domain of Song. Grand steward [*dazai*] is the name of the man's office. His given name was Ying, and his personal name was Dang." *Zhuangzi jishi*, 2: 497.
3. Cheng Xuanying: "One [a ruler] who is completely unaware of all the world would discard a myriad chariots as if he were removing his shoes. When one makes all in the world completely unaware of [the ruler] himself [*wo*], it means that he makes use of the common folk day after day yet they are unaware of it. Such a one would let his sleeves hang down over clasped hands North of the Fen [Fenyang] or let his mind freely roam on Mount Guye, magnificent in the way he would yield rulership [to someone more worthy], for what he esteems is empty unawareness. All this characterizes one who is completely unaware of all the world." *Zhuangzi jishi*, 2: 500. "Oneself" [*wo*] appears in these passages in such a way that it is uncertain whether it refers to the ruler himself or each of the myriad folk individually, so perhaps a deliberate ambiguity is involved: in an utterly unselfconscious world, both people and ruler spontaneously perform functions and fulfill obligations free from deliberate purpose.
4. Cf. 6.10.1.
5. Cf. *Laozi*, section 33: "One who knows contentment is rich. One who knows contentment is himself not wanting for anything." Richard John Lynn, *The Classic of the Way and Virtue*, 111.
6. John S. Major, *Heaven and Earth in Early Han Thought: Chapters Three, Four, and Five of the Huainanzi*, 199: "It isn't clear what connection there might be between Shaman Xian (and his mountain) and the Pool of Xian, one of the 'six departments' of heaven. . . . The Pool of Xian is described as 'a park of water and fishes' . . . and . . . as being connected with the Jovian Year. *Xian* means 'broad,' so the Pool of Xian could also be translated as 'Broad Pool,' with no connection to Shaman Xian implied at all. It seems more likely, however, given the tendency of *Huainanzi* 4 and similar texts to locate the homes of mythic personages both in far-distant terrestrial places and among the stars, that the Pool of Xian is an astral projection of Shaman Xian Mountain." For Shaman Xian, see 14.2; also cf. 18.20 and 33.6.
7. "Grand Clarity" [*taiqing*] is written as *daqing*, with the same meaning, in the *Zhuangzi jizhi* ed, 2: 502; this is apparently a printing error, however, since Cheng Xuanying's commentary reads as *taiqing*; *Zhuangzi jishi*, 2: 503. Both terms are epithets of Heaven [*tian*].
8. Strong evidence exists that this passage, which translates thirty-five characters, is an interpolation from the commentary of Guo Xiang rather than the text of the *Zhuangzi* itself. See Wang Shumin, *Zhuangzi jiaoquan*, 513–14, note 7.
9. The notion that the sound of thunder brings things back to life after the dead of winter can be traced to the *Classic of Changes*, such as to the "Commentary on the appended phrases" [*Xici zhuan*], Part One: "It [the Dao] arouses things with claps of thunder,

moistens them with wind and rain. Sun and moon go through their cycles, so now it is cold, now hot." Richard John Lynn, *Classic of Changes*, 48.

10. Cf. *Laozi*, section 14: "Try to meet it, but you won't see its head. Try to follow it, but you won't see its tail, so hold on to the Dao of old to preside over what exists now." Lynn, *The Classic of the Way and Virtue*, 73.
11. Cheng Xuanying offers a different interpretation: "The ordering principle [*li*] of perfect unity [*zhiyi*] transcends both sight and hearing, so one can't rely on it through sound or form, which is why he listened in fear." *Zhuangzi jishi*, 2: 504.
12. Cf. *Laozi*, section 56: "Block up your apertures; close your door; blunt your sharpness." To this, Wang Bi adds the note, "Harbor simplicity [*zhi*, intrinsic nature] within you." Lynn, *The Classic of the Way and Virtue*, 151.
13. Cf. *Laozi*, section 60: "If one uses the Dao to oversee All Under Heaven, the malign spirits there will lose their numinous power." Lynn, *The Classic of the Way and Virtue*, 164.
14. Cf. 2.12 and 5.35. Cheng Xuanying: "With his immense capacity for emptiness, he forgot all about knowing and cut off all deliberate thought. Therefore, his body like a withered tree and mind like dead ashes, spontaneously free and acting unselfconsciously, he sang and chanted." *Zhuangzi jishi*, 2: 507. Another tradition of commentary, which reads "I" [*yu*] as a scribal error for "you" [*zi*], interprets the passage beginning with "I might have wanted to" as describing Beimen Cheng's bewildered reaction to the music, but Guo Xiang and Cheng Xuanying unequivocally read it as focusing on the Yellow Thearch himself.
15. It is only at this point that Guo's and Cheng's readings refocus on the effect that the music had on Beimen Cheng.
16. Cf. the spontaneity of the "pipes of Heaven and Earth" in 2.2. Cheng Xuanying: "The sounds of the forest pipes of Earth unselfconsciously form perfect music, which does nothing more than conform to natural endowment, so how could it have any additional form than that!" *Zhuangzi jishi*, 2: 508.
17. Cheng Xuanying: "*Ji* (inquire) here means 'selfconsciously lies with' [*liu*]. The way of the sage may be likened metaphorically to an echo in a deep, secluded valley or the image in a mirror, which when confronted by them one neither knows how they start nor how they stop. When things come to him [the sage], his response occurs in such a way that it is utterly unselfconscious, so how could it possibly be that he plans beforehand and then responds to the world with selfconscious concern [*liuxin*]! Therefore, whether he proceeds or rests is completely random, for no fixed score controls him. Nevertheless, the common folk of the world irrationally doubt that this is so." *Zhuangzi jishi*, 2: 509.
18. Cheng Xuanying: "Once he had again heard it, the way he thought became gradually enlightened. Therefore, as his fear limply withdrew the outward signs of it gradually vanished." *Zhuangzi jishi*, 2: 511.
19. Cheng Xuanying identifies Shi Jin as Taishi Jin [Grand Preceptor Jin] of the state of Lu, as does Lu Deming, quoting Li Yi; see *Zhuangzi jishi*, 2: 511.
20. Cheng Xuanying has it that such a person "won't only have bad dreams but also frequently suffer nightmares/sleep paralysis," but "bad dreams" pads the text, which literally reads "renders [him] incapable of dreaming," and, though Cheng's "nightmares/ sleep paralysis" [*yan*] is possible for *mi*, an interpretation by Luo Miandao is more likely: "*Mi* is the illness in which something [not really there] enters the eyes. Not only is one incapable of dreaming but also seems to see monsters and demons." *Nanhua zhenjing xunben*, 15: 246b. However, much controversy surrounds the text here; see Wang Shumin, *Zhuangzi jiaoquan*, 523, note 7.

21. Cheng Xuanying: "Once when traveling in Song, Confucius was lecturing his disciples beneath a great tree, which made Commander Huan Tui want to kill him, and after Confucius had fled, Huan Tui took hatred against the place where he had been seated, so had the tree cut down. . . . Once when Confucius was traveling in Wey, the people of Wey took an intense dislike to him, so they obliterated all impressions he left behind, for they found them completely useless. 'Shang' refers to the domain of the Yin dynasty [the Song domain at the time of Confucius], and 'Zhou' refers to this as it existed during the Eastern Zhou era. Confucius was once employed there as an official, which brought him nothing but grief. It was because he had gotten so bogged down in the footprints left by the sages that such bad things happened to him." *Zhuangzi jishi*, 2: 513.
22. Cheng Xuanying: "This happened just when King Zhao of Chu had engaged Confucius, when he, leading his disciples, had encamped in the countryside between Chen and Cai. Seeing how numerous they were, the people of Cai took them to be bandits and so raised troops to surround them. After seven days with provisions exhausted and no fires to cook food, his disciples were so starved that none could get to their feet. Since such grievous privation brought them so close to death, how could this not have been a nightmare brought about by already displayed straw dogs!" *Zhuangzi jishi*, 2: 513. Cf. 6.7.8, 20.15–20.16, 20.18, 20.24, 28.37, 28.40, 29.15, 29.17, and 31.19.
23. Cf. *Classic of Changes*, "Commentary on the appended phrases" [*Xici zhuan*], Part One: "The sages had the means to perceive the activities taking place in the world, and, observing how things come together and go smoothly, they then enacted statues and rituals accordingly." Wang Bi comments: "Statues and rituals are to be employed at the times suitable for them." Lynn, *Classic of Changes*, 57.
24. Cf. 14.16.
25. For the identification of Pei, Lu Deming quotes Sima Biao: "Master Lao was a native of Xiang in the state of Chen. Xiang now belongs to Hu district and is near Pei." *Zhuangzi jishi*, 2: 516. As such, Pei can be located east of present-day Luyi district city, Henan.
26. "Astronomical calculations" [*dushu*], literally "degree calculations," measure the rates of motion of heavenly bodies. Cheng Xuanying: "*Shu* (calculations) means the art of counting. Every three years requires one intercalary month, which indicates a lesser completion [*xiaocheng*] of the course of Heaven [*tiandao*], and every five years requires two intercalary months, which indicates a greater completion [*dacheng*] of the course of Heaven. And this is the reason why 'five years' occurs here. But the Dao isn't available to the art of numbers [*shushu*], which is why he [Confucius] had not yet attained it." *Zhuangzi jishi*, 2: 517. For the "art of numbers," see Fabrizio Pregadio, *The Encyclopedia of Taoism*, 116–17 and 405, where this "art" is associated with "astrology, choosing lucky days, *fengshui*" [landscape geomancy], as well as "astronomy, calendrics, and divination."
27. Cheng Xuanying: "Twelve years consists of a complete yin-yang cycle. That he had not attained the Dao is because he tried to obtain it through understanding the yin and yang, but the Dao isn't available through the yin and yang." *Zhuangzi jishi*, 2: 517.
28. Cf. 23.33, where Guo Xiang glosses *zhi* (original nature) as *zhu* (master); *Zhuangzi jishi*, 4: 807. Immediately afterward, Guo equates this "master" with "sage/sageness," the embodiment of the Dao.
29. So long as one is cursed with selfconscious mind, he can neither receive nor transmit the Dao. The text here and in 25.49 resonates with a passage in the *Chunqiu Gongyang zhuan* (*Spring and Autumn Annals*, the Gongyang tradition), Duke Xuan, third year (606 BCE), 2: 2278b: "Why must the sovereign join with his ancestor to offer sacrifice? If that which emerges from within lacks this compeer [*pi*], it will fail. If that which

enters from without is denied such a [co]master [of sacrifice], it won't stay." That is, if the ruler, the master of ritual sacrifice, fails to join in spirit with the first Zhou ancestor, needed as a cosacrificer, communication with Heaven fails and the sacrifice is in vain. Likewise, if no such cosacrificer exists to receive them, blessings from Heaven ("that which comes from without") won't linger to benefit Earth and man. Likewise, the *Zhuangzi* has it that only when the mind spontaneously and unselfconsciously joins with the Dao may one become a "master" to "receive" it, and as such become a true sage, a compeer of the Dao. The Dao then "lingers" with the sage, whose presence encourages people to escape from their self-conscious mind and recover their original nature. Among such people, the Dao transmits freely.

30. "Presence" translates *cai* (appearance, bearing, manner, mien). Although various editions of the *Zhuangzi* with Guo's commentary have "presence authentic" [*caizhen*] instead of "authentic presence" [*zhencai*], Wang Shumin, while remaining silent on *caizhen/zhencai* in the text of the *Zhuangzi* itself, concludes that *caizhen* in the commentary is the result of a copyist's error, and thus *zhencai* is the correct reading. *Guo Xiang Zhuangzi zhu jiaoji*, 3: 14a.
31. Cheng Xuanying: "Just as the louder the drum is beaten the farther the fugitive will run, so the more benevolence and righteousness are promoted the more morality and ethics will fail." *Zhuangzi jishi*, 2: 523.
32. Cf. 6.10.1.
33. Guo Xiang seems to have in mind two passages in the *Classic of Changes*: (1) "Commentary on the Appended Phrases" [*Xici zhuan*], Part One: "In Heaven this [process (interaction of *Qian* and *Kun*, yin and yang, and so on)] creates images, and on Earth it creates physical forms; this is how change and transformation manifest themselves." Lynn, *The Classic of Changes*, 47. (2) "Explaining the Trigrams" [*Shuo gua*]: "[The sages] determined . . . what the Dao of Man was, which they determined in terms of benevolence and righteousness. . . . They provided yin allotments and yang allotments, so their functions alternate between soft and hard; this is why the *Changes* forms its patterns [*chengzhang*] out of six positions." Lynn, *The Classic of Changes*, 120. That is, Master Lao appeared to Confucius as the manifestation of change and transformation as they occur in the very workings of Nature itself, revealed in the same way as the formation of hexagrams and likened to the ephemeral dragon.
34. The text in brackets appears as a textual variant only in the so-called *Jiangnan guzang ben* (Old edition preserved in the South). *Zhuangzi jishi*, 2: 525.
35. Cf. 11.4.4.
36. The three are Sire Suiren, Fu Xi, and Shennong.
37. The five are the Yellow Thearch, Zhuanxu, Di Ku, Yao, and Shun.
38. Cheng Xuanying: "Since two of them, Yao and Shun, should be counted among the Five Emperors, it is only those who came after Yu of the Xia whom he refers to as the 'Three Sovereigns.' Yao yielded to Shun, and Shun yielded to Yu. Yu expended his strength on water control, Tang employed troops to attack Jie, King Wen was imprisoned at Youli yet obeyed Xin of the Shang, King Wu forded [the Yellow River] at Meng Crossing [Mengjin] to revolt against Zhou of the Yin, so it could be said in a general way that the character [of their respective rules] differed." *Zhuangzi jishi*, 2: 527.
39. Cheng Xuanying: "In the practice of virtue, the Five Thearchs fell short of the Three Sovereigns, for they allowed father and son, older and younger brother to form stronger bonds of affection, and the prescription for them of progressively diminished [elaboration in] mourning clothes, which distinguish among closer and more distant kinship ties." *Zhuangzi jishi*, 2: 528.

40. Cheng Xuanying: "Since robbers and bandits were culpable criminals, in accord with principle their execution should be carried out in autumn, and, though such killing occurred, it was not considered killing. This was how the use of weapons was justified." *Zhuangzi jishi*, 2: 529. Similar passages occur in both the *Xunzi* (Sayings of Master Xun) and the *Mozi* (Sayings of Master Mo); see Knoblock, *Xunzi*, 3:131, and Ian Johnston, trans., *The Mozi: A Complete Translation*, 626–29. Affiliations between these texts and the *Zhuangzi* are complicated and extensive; see Wang Shumin, *Zhuangzi jiaoquan*, 543, note 10.
41. Cf. 11.33.21.

CHAPTER 15

KEYI [HONING THE WILL]

15.1 Here's one who keeps his will curbed, engages in high-minded behavior, stays aloof from the world, follows strange customs of his own, engages in haughty discourse and resent-filled censure, but all this serves nothing more than lofty ambition. Such is the person of learning who condemns the world from his mountain valley, someone fond of throwing his emaciated person into the watery abyss. Here's one who discourses on benevolence, righteousness, loyalty, trustworthiness, is reverent, temperate, yielding, and deferential, but all this serves nothing more than the cultivation of moral character. Such is the person of learning who would bring peace and order to the world, a teacher and instructor, someone fond of learning whether travelling or at home. Here's one who talks about great accomplishments, establishes a fine reputation, devotes himself to the decorum proper to sovereign and minister, rectifying the relationship between superior and inferior, but all this serves nothing more than government administration. Such is a person of learning at court, who honors his sovereign and strengthens his state, someone fond of maximizing accomplishments and annexing territory. Here's one who betakes himself to the marshes and ponds, dwells out in the empty wilderness, fishing or idling at home, and engages only in unself-conscious action, someone fond of rivers and lakes, being isolated from the world and living at leisure. Breathing in and out, *tshuaihuo*, exhaling the old and inhaling the new, bear-hanging and bird-stretching, all done just for the sake of longevity. Here's a learned person who does guiding-pulling

gymnastics, someone who nurtures his body, so what he is fond of is living as long as Pengzu.

Although what these several masters were fond of differed, each goes his own separate way to indulge freely in it. In doing so, they too all accomplish spontaneous free play. However, this results in nothing but individual self-fulfillment, so how could such as they ever comply with those who have no standing! It is when one fosters the myriad folk so each fulfills his own allotted capacity and violates not who he really is [*zishi*] that we may consign such a one to the ranks of those who don't use selfconscious effort to rule.

15.2.1 If one becomes lofty without honing the will, is cultivated without "benevolence" and "righteousness," achieves leisure without rivers and lakes, or becomes long-lived without guiding-pulling gymnastics,

This is what is called spontaneity.

15.2.2 then, oblivious to absolutely everything, such a one shall possess absolutely everything.

It is because one is oblivious to things that he may possess them. But if one selfconsciously tries to possess them, he shall fail to find recourse in oblivion. Therefore, real possession is had only if possession is free of possessiveness and only if one is oblivious to it.

15.2.3 Tranquilly unbiased and capacity infinite, all good things attend him.

If he honed himself in order to accomplish things, infinite capacity would be beyond his reach and all bad things would thus occur.

15.2.4 Such is the Dao of Heaven and Earth and the virtue of the sage.

That which applies unselfconscious action to the myriad things and so allows them self-generation are Heaven and Earth; just so, that which applies unselfconscious action to all the ways people behave and so allows their ways to lead to self-fulfillment is the sage.

15.3.1 Thus is it said, disinterested serenity, absolute quietude, and unselfconscious action constitute the equanimity of Heaven and Earth and the substance of the Dao and Virtue,

If one fails to practice unselfconscious action with absolute serenity, he jeopardizes his equanimity and loses his substance.

15.3.2 and it is also said, since the sage resides at rest in them, things are smooth and easy for him.[1]

Resting in disinterested serenity and absolute quietude, reposing in absolute nothingness and unselfconscious action, though such a one encounters vicissitudes of obstruction and danger, he is always secure and untroubled.

15.3.3 Finding things smooth and easy, he maintains disinterested serenity.

As adversity arises from selfconscious action and selfconscious action arises from adversity, so smooth and easygoing and disinterested serenity generate each other.

15.3.4 With things smooth and easy and maintenance of disinterested serenity, neither can concern for calamity invade him nor can pathogenic pneuma [*xieqi*] attack him.[2]

Tallying perfectly with them, such a one sets forth in step with the correct principles of things [*zhengli*].

15.3.5 His virtue thus remains whole and safe and his spirit suffers no depletion.

How can one who finds things not smooth and himself lacks serenity fail to harm his physical health! And virtue and spirit will both be destroyed within him.

15.4.1 Thus it is said, the life of the sage is but a movement of Heaven,

He acts only by giving himself over to spontaneity.

15.4.2 his death but a transformation of things.

Sloughing them off cicada-like, he is free of all bonds.[3]

15.4.3 In repose he shares the same virtue as the element yin; in movement he resonates with the element yang.

Whether in movement or repose, free of selfconscious mind, he complies perfectly with yin and yang.

15.4.4 He is neither a pathfinder to good fortune nor an initiator of misfortune, for he only reacts when stimulated to respond,

In nothing does he ever take the lead.

15.4.5 only moves when being pressed,

He only moves when the right moment arrives.

15.4.6 and only arises when it becomes inevitable.

To arise only in response to principle signifies that one can't help but do so.

15.4.7 Discarding knowledge and precedent, he abides by the principles of Heaven.

Since the principles of Heaven operate spontaneously, knowledge and precedent have no part to play among them.

15.4.8 Therefore, he incurs no Heaven-sent disaster,

Disaster occurs when one goes against Heaven.

15.4.9 is not fettered by things,

Fetters occur when one goes contrary to things.

15.4.10 suffers neither the censure of others,

Since he merges with all others, the masses are sure to find him in the right.

15.4.11 nor the punishment of demons.

Since he allows self-fulfillment equally to all, he remains free of punishment.[4]

15.4.12 His life proceeds as if he were floating; his death occurs as if he were taking a rest.

He just floats along, free of all attachments and cares.

15.4.13 He is free from selfconscious thought

He complies perfectly with the principles of Heaven.

15.4.14 and never schemes in advance.

He responds only when underlying principles perfectly apply.

15.4.15 Though indeed bright he himself does not shine.[5]

He realizes the whole world's potential for spontaneous brilliance; he need not himself shine.

15.4.16 Though indeed trustworthy he himself does not raise expectations.

He realizes the whole world's potential for spontaneous confidence; he need not himself raise expectations.[6]

15.4.17 He sleeps without dreaming and wakes without care.[7]

He is utterly free from desire.

15.4.18 His spirit is unadulterated,

He desires not a single thing.

15.4.19 and his soul tires not.

If beset by desire, it would tire.

15.4.20 for consisting of absolute nothingness and disinterested serenity it joins with the virtue of Heaven.

He thus joins his virtue, disinterested and serene, to that of Heaven and Earth.

15.5.1 Thus it is said, grief and joy are perversions of virtue; delight and anger are crimes against the Dao.

When things go as one likes, delight results; when things go against one's inclinations, anger results. As such, failure to keep delight and anger out of mind is a crime against the Dao.

15.5.2 Likes and dislikes err against virtue. Therefore, if free of grief and joy, the mind sustains perfection of virtue.

Because perfect virtue is always apt, the emotions are never affected.

15.5.3 If whole and complete and thus unchanging, it sustains perfection of quietude.

As long as it remains quiet and thus whole and complete, it can't change.

15.5.4 If free of all deviation, it sustains perfection of emptiness.

If the mind is completely steadfast in its emptiness, it won't be the slightest contrary.

15.5.5 If it engages not in relationships with others, it sustains perfection of serenity.

Such a one just lets others come to him of their own accord; the perfectly serene is free of inclination to form relationships with others.

15.5.6 If it stays free of contrariety, it sustains perfection of purity.

Adulterated by turbid desire, its capacity to comply will fail.

15.5.7 Thus it is said, just as the body if labored without rest becomes exhausted, so the spirit if used without cease becomes fatigued, and once fatigued it is thoroughly expends itself.

Everyone has a [limited] fundamental nature, which may not be violated.

15.6.1 It is the nature of water to be clear if not contaminated and level if not agitated, but if dammed up so it flows not, it surely fails to remain clear. As such, it is a symbol for the virtue of Heaven.

As a symbol for the virtue of Heaven, it signifies freedom from selfconscious mind and perfect merger with all things.

15.6.2 Thus it is said, absolutely pure, it is utterly uncontaminated,

Without exception it always acts in the most appropriate way,

15.6.3 tranquil in its singular totality, it does not vary,

and always stops exactly where it should.

15.6.4 perfectly serene, it acts without selfconscious purpose,

It just merges with everything, nothing more.

15.6.5 and in action, it moves as does Heaven.

If it acted to seek to fulfill desire, it would move as does man.

15.6.6 This is the way to nourish one's spirit. One who possesses a sword from Gan or Yue[8] stores it carefully in a case and dares not use it, for it is the most precious of treasures.

How much the less should one dare use his spirit lightly!

15.6.7 The essential spirit simultaneously flows forth in four directions, extending ultimately everywhere, stretching up to the borders of Heaven above and winding through all Earth below.

One who embodies as his essential spirit the infinite potential of Heaven and Earth and all the faculties [*shu*] of the myriad folk is just like this. As such, when one is given the power to function effectively as Heaven and Earth, he does nothing but allow himself to move as does Heaven. He does not use such power lightly.

15.6.8 Although for nurturing the myriad things no model may be made,

There is no fixed method for such nurturing.

15.6.9 The name for such a one is "Merges with the Thearchs."

Such a one merges with the Celestial Thearchs who eschew selfconscious effort.

15.7.1 The Dao of pristine purity is only attained by guarding the spirit, for by guarding it so it be not lost, one becomes one with the spirit.

By constantly guarding one's pristine simplicity with perfect quietude, not allowing any disturbance from without, he arcanely merges with it.

15.7.2 And once perfectly integrated wholly with one's vital essence, one can merge with the principles of Heaven.

"Vital essence" is a person's authenticity.

15.7.3 A folk adage has it that "The mass of common folk prize riches; learned persons of integrity prize fame; worthies esteem moral will; and sages value vital essence."

Achieving oneness with one's spirit has nothing to do with guarding; not being estranged from one's vital essence has nothing to do with valuing.

However, footprints left by them [the sages] were such that people labeled what they did "valuing" and "guarding."

15.7.4 Therefore, "natural simplicity" means one has allowed no adulteration; "pristine purity" means one has not allowed his spirit to be depleted.

If purity is maintained by not allowing depletion of spirit, even when undertaking joint operations requiring every kind of handling to keep up with all countless vicissitudes, then that is perfect purity. If natural simplicity is maintained by not allowing adulteration, even when one has a dragon's form and a phoenix's comportment, so handsome as to make an extraordinary appearance, then that is perfect natural simplicity. However, if one can't preserve his spontaneous original nature but allows himself to be adulterated by external ornamentation, even if it merely be the skins of dog or sheep, how could that ever be called pristine purity!

15.7.5 One who can embody pristine simplicity may be called an authentic man.

Notes

1. Cf. 13.1.
2. Cf. *Changes*, "Commentary on the appended phrases" [*Xici zhuan*], Part Two: "Did not the makers of the Changes become concerned about calamities?" Wang Bi comments, "If they had not become concerned about calamities, then it would have been sufficient for them to deal with things through effortless action." Richard John Lynn, *The Classic of Changes*, 87.
3. Cf. 2.30 end, Guo Xiang commentary.
4. Cf. 2.10 end, Guo Xiang commentary.
5. Cf. *Laozi*, section 58: "He is bright but does not shine." Richard John Lynn, *The Classic of the Way and Virtue*, 162.
6. Cheng Xuanying: "He adapts to the needs of the moment, the way a shadow follows a bodily form, so he is as trustworthy as the four seasons, which surely never err. He only responds when the moment is right, never raising expectations in advance." *Zhuangzi jishi*, 3: 541.
7. Cf. 6.4.1–6.4.2.
8. Cheng Xuanying: "Gan is the name of a stream, and Yue is the name of a mountain. Gan Stream and Mount Yue both produced fine swords. Another explanation is that Gan [a minor state absorbed by Wu] refers to Wu, that is, the two states, Wu and Yue, are what is meant here, for both produced famous swords, which is why their names are used." *Zhuangzi jishi*, 3: 545.

CHAPTER 16

SHANXING [MENDING ONE'S ORIGINAL NATURE]

16.1.1 Once they have mended original nature with conventional wisdom, people now seek to recover its initial state through the study of that conventional wisdom.

Having already regulated their original natures with conventional wisdom, such people now desire to recover the essence of their natural endowments by studying that conventional wisdom, but in seeking it in this way, they are ever more estranged from the Dao.

16.1.2 Having confused their desires with conventional wisdom, they now seek to perfect their understanding through selfconscious thought.

Already having confused their minds with desire, they now go on to seek understanding through selfconscious reflection, but the more their thinking is refined, the further they fall into error.

16.1.3 Let us call them people both obstructed and obscure.

As for those who suffer such obscurity, only if they abandon conventional wisdom and rid themselves of desire might they then be nearly there.

16.2.1 In antiquity those who governed with the Dao cultivated knowledge in tranquility.

Only in tranquility is knowledge not agitated, and if knowledge be not agitated, one's nature is not lost.[1]

16.2.2 They knew how to live but were free of knowing how to act with selfconscious purpose, so it may be said of them that they used knowledge to cultivate tranquility.

If one is free of the means to know how to act selfconsciously and just allows himself to know spontaneously, though he knows all about the myriad things, it is a matter of spontaneous receptivity tranquilly obtained.

16.2.3 With knowledge and tranquility mutually nourishing each another, harmony with principle emerged from their original natures.

When one knows but stays away from selfconscious action, no harm is done to one's tranquility. When one is tranquil and as such engages in unselfconscious action, no harm is done to one's knowledge. We can say of them that they mutually nourish each other. Since these two mutually nourish each other, how could the realization of one's allotted capacity working in harmony with principle ever occur otherwise!

16.2.4 Virtue means harmony, and the Dao means principles.

When one is in harmony, nothing fails to obtain; when one is with the Dao, nothing fails to accord with principle.

16.2.5 When one's virtue is such that he accepts absolutely everything, benevolence results.

This "accepts absolutely everything" does not mean that virtue creates benevolence but that the footprints of benevolence show up in the process.

16.2.6 When one's grasp of the Dao neglects no principle, righteousness results.

This "leaving no principle out" does not mean that the Dao creates righteousness, but that righteous merit [*yigong*] is manifest in the process.

16.2.7 When righteousness shines bright and people become close, loyalty results.

If righteousness shines bright but it does not lead to loyalty, then people become ever more estranged.[2]

16.2.8 When one is pure and honest within and as such reverts to his innate character, pleasure results.

When benevolence and righteousness burgeon forth within and one thus returns to trust to one's original state of mind, one's disposition is satisfied. When one's disposition is satisfied, the outward sign of this is pleasure.

16.2.9 When trustworthy behavior characterizes expression and posture and as such one complies with the forms of civility, ritual results.

When trustworthy behavior characterizes expression and posture and as such complies with the forms of civility [*jiewen*], the outward sign of this is ritual.

16.2.10 When ritual and pleasure are exercised with partiality,[3] the whole world suffers disorder.

If the behavior of one particular temperament and the pleasure experienced by one particular disposition were applied to the whole world, that one would gain but the myriad folk would lose.[4]

16.2.11 Such a one maintains himself pure and true [*zheng*] but keeps his own virtue hidden, thus his virtue does not impose itself on others. If it did so impose itself, all others would surely lose their own original natures.

If each maintained his own natural endowment pure and true yet kept his own virtue hidden, there would be no imposing this virtue on that virtue. If this virtue imposed itself on that virtue, how could others fail to lose their original nature!

16.3.1 People of antiquity existed in a chaotic, witless state and maintained a placid and detached relationship with the rest of the world. At that time, Yin and Yang interacted in peaceful harmony, the demonic and divine caused no trouble, the four seasons sustained their proper rhythm, the myriad creatures lived unhindered, no living thing died before its time, and although men had intelligence, they had no reason to use it.

All they did was give themselves over to spontaneity.

16.3.2 This may be called a state of perfect unity, for at that time no one acted with selfconscious purpose but only with unselfconscious spontaneity.

It was because everyone acted only with unselfconscious spontaneity that perfect unity prevailed.

16.4.1 But when such virtue declined,

The reason why such virtue declined was that true sages failed to succeed one another, so those in charge, incapable of unselfconscious action themselves, so admired the footprints left by unselfconscious action that it led to malpractice.

16.4.2 Suiren (Fire Maker) and Fu Xi came along and started in with selfconscious purpose to rule the world, which was why though they practiced compliance they were not one with it.

Once the world had lost unity, since people could not be liberated from delusion, they [rulers such as Suiren and Fu Xi] just let them go and did not push them, did nothing but comply with them.

16.4.3 When virtue declined further, Shennong and the Yellow Thearch came along and started in with selfconscious purpose to rule the world, which was why though they maintained peace they were not compliant.

They maintained peace only by using means they thought would maintain peace.[5]

16.4.4 When virtue declined even further, Tang and Yu came along and started in with selfconscious purpose to rule the world, initiating the tradition of government administration and moral inculcation, which dissipated purity and shattered pristine simplicity.

The sage, free of selfconscious mind, allows the world to fulfill itself, and all attempts to fulfill it by recourse to the superficial aspects of purity have nothing to do with true sagehood. Since the sage does nothing but allow the world to fulfill itself, what can he have to do with making the world acquire sageliness!

Therefore, though the footprints left by Heavenly Monarchs and Earthly Kings always kept changing from age to age, the Dao of the sage never fails to remain whole and intact.

16.4.5 This was abandoning the Dao to purvey goodness,

"Goodness" here is a term for doing more than what is appropriate. Therefore, when such goodness occurs, the Dao loses its integrity.

16.4.6 or imperiling virtue to fabricate behavior.

"Behavior" here means behaving in such a way that it violates original nature. Therefore, when such behavior is adopted, one is no longer pleased with one's innate virtue.

16.4.7 After that they abandoned their original natures and followed the dictates of selfconscious mind.

When the mind selfconsciously engages itself, original nature is abandoned.

16.4.8 Mind engaged with mind in selfconscious attention,

As minds of self and other vied in exercising foreknowledge, people no longer trusted to their original natures.[6]

16.4.9 but such knowledge proved inadequate to make the world tranquil.

Only by forgetting all about knowledge does tranquility occur.

16.4.10 After that they supplemented it with literary culture and augmented it with wide learning, but literary culture did away with its intrinsic basis and wide learning drowned the mind.

Literary culture and wide learning are but adornments to the mind's intrinsic basis.

16.4.11 And after that people began to be so deluded that they had no way to recover their innate natures or return to their original states [*chu*].

"Original state" [*chu*] means the root of one's natural endowment.

16.5.1 Looking at it from this point of view, as the world ruins the Dao, so the Dao ruins the world; that is, the world and the Dao ruin one another.

As long as the Dao functions without esteem, it can preserve the world, but because it preserves the world, the world accords it esteem. But once held in esteem, the Dao is thus ruined. The Dao can't prevent the world from according it esteem, while the world can't refrain from according the Dao esteem, which is why they ruin one another.

16.5.2 How then does a man of the Dao rouse the world! How then is the world roused by the Dao!

Only if free of esteem may such rousing and in turn being roused take place.[7]

16.5.3 If the Dao has no way to rouse the world and the world has no way to be roused by the Dao, even though a sage does not hide himself amidst mountains and woods, his virtue remains concealed.

Now, the reason why it would not remain concealed is because the rousing is done with selfconscious intent. So how should one do the rousing? One should do it so one stays free from esteem.[8]

16.6.1 One is really concealed because he does not try to conceal himself.

As long as one controls things while keeping himself concealed, the Dao and the world will rouse and in turn be roused, and what deliberate concealment is there to that!

16.6.2 Those in antiquity called learned recluses neither concealed their persons so to prevent being seen, stopped their words so to prevent them from getting about, nor kept their wisdom to themselves to prevent it from circulating, for this was a time beset by great error.

No one understood that to recover unity with things one should stop making footprints, but instead unity was sought by following footprints, so the more footprints were tracked down, the more unity was lost—this was the great error! Though they [learned recluses] might have come forward to cast light on things, might have begun to speak so their words got about, or might have manifested their wisdom so that it should circulate, how could any of these have led to the Dao's rousing, and in turn the world's being roused! It would instead only have led to them ruining one another![9]

16.6.3 If they had met with opportune times and so could have widely prevailed in the world, they would have recovered unity with things and thus left no footprints behind.

These were times characterized by tranquility and equanimity.

16.6.4 But as they met with inopportune times and so would have encountered great distress in the world,

These could not have been times characterized by tranquility and equanimity.

16.6.5 they sank their roots deep in utmost tranquility and just waited.

Although it was a world beset by problems, sages never lost their tranquility and equanimity; therefore, they sank their roots deep in utmost tranquility and just waited for the time when they could act spontaneously, and this was why the Dao was not ruined.

16.6.6 Such is the Dao as it bears on preserving one's person.

Never does it happen that persons so preserve themselves, yet the world is not roused.[10]

16.7.1 Those in antiquity who became persons of action did not embellish what they knew with eloquence.

They did nothing more than employ what they authentically knew.

16.7.2 They neither used what they knew to overtax the world

Their innate characters were indifferent to self-advantage.

16.7.3 nor used what they knew to overtax their virtue,

They did nothing more than keep to the limits of their own virtue.

16.7.4 But with exceptional detachment [*weiran*] just maintained their own proper states and since they continually reverted to their original natures, what further would they have done!

"With exceptional detachment" describes keeping to one's own proper state [*duzheng*].

16.7.5 The Dao for them was surely not for petty excursions,

They moved along the great smooth highway.

16.7.6 and their virtue surely was not involved with petty selfconscious distinctions [*xiaoshi*],

They intrinsically achieved great thoroughgoing comprehension [*datong*].

16.7.7 for petty selfconscious distinctions damage virtue, and petty excursions damage the Dao. Therefore, as it is said of them, they kept to their own proper states—that is all there was to it. Their perfection of joy consisted in achieving their aspirations.

If one achieves one's aspirations while maintaining his own mind apart in perfect balance [*yi*], free of predilection toward either grief or pleasure, this then is someone whose joy is perfect.

16.8.1 When those in antiquity are said to have achieved their aspirations, it refers not to such things as carriages and caps but only to the fact that for them nothing could have augmented their joy.

They were utterly content just to realize all the potential of their inner selves [*quan qinei*].

16.8.2 When those of the present are said to achieve their aspirations, it does refer to such things as carriages and caps. But carriages and caps are but accessories to the person and nothing to do with one's natural endowment. If by chance such things come one's way, they are but temporary lodgers. Regard them as temporary lodgers, for their arrival may not be prevented nor may their departure be stopped.

They are but accessories external to the person, so their gain or loss is irrelevant to the real self.

16.8.3 Therefore, one neither stretches one's aspirations because he is bestowed carriages and caps,

Indifferent to them and completely at ease, he is unaware they lodge with him.

16.8.4 nor bends himself to the rabble because he suffers poverty and reduced circumstances.

Unconcerned and self-fulfilled, he is unaware he is stricken with poverty.

16.8.5 One should be equally joyful whether with the one or with the other.

"The one" and "the other" refer respectively to carriages and caps on, the one hand, and poverty and reduced circumstances, on the other.

16.8.6 One thereby stays free of worry—that is all there is to it!

One should also shun the happiness that depends on pleasure.

16.8.7 Now, one is unhappy when such temporary lodgers depart, so looking at it from this point of view, although such things bring happiness, they never fail to cause turmoil.

People may be unhappy when such lodgers depart, but even their arrival means turmoil. This is because they let what is exterior to them alter their inner selves.

16.8.8 Thus it may be said, those who lose themselves for the sake of acquiring something or violate their original natures to conform to the rabble may be called people who get things upside down.

They nourish the outer and deplete the inner, which really gets things upside down.

Notes

1. Cheng Xuanying: "In antiquity, the sages governed person and state with the Dao and were sure to use tranquility as the way to cultivate authentic knowledge, which they did not allow to be agitated from without." *Zhuangzi jishi*, 3: 547.
2. Cheng Xuanying: "When moral principles become readily apparent, one's innate tendencies are led to moderation. Since people are then not self-righteous and arrogant, this results in their becoming close and caring." Note that Cheng glosses "loyalty" [*zhong*] as "moderation" [*zhong*]. *Zhuangzi jishi*, 3: 549.
3. Although the text of the *Zhuangzi* as it appears in the *Zhuangzi jishi* has *bian* [everywhere] instead of *pian* [partiality], it is obvious from both Guo's commentary and Cheng's subcommentary that the texts they saw had *pian*, Yu Yue observed; *Zhuangzi jishi*, 3: 550. *Pian* also occurs in several earlier well-known editions, including Lin Xiyi's *Zhuangzi Juanzhai kouyi*, 252, and Jiao Hong's (1541–1620) *Zhuangzi yi* (Wings to *Zhuangzi*), 5:45.
4. Cheng Xuanying: "If one who rules the world can't keep his mind empty in responding to things but instead obstinately holds to his own personal course, he is sure to become mired in magnificence and drown in dissolute pleasure. As such he just keeps on displaying straw dogs and so provokes disorder for the whole world." *Zhuangzi jishi*, 3: 550. Straw dogs are used in sacrifices as scapegoats to ward off evil, but once so used, they should be discarded. Reusing them is sure to provoke misfortune. Cf. 14.18.
5. Cheng Xuanying: "As the transformative power of virtue further declined, malpractices grew more severe, thus Shennong launched an attack against Gonggong and the Yellow Thearch went into battle with Chiyou, creating an aura of disaster that continued unabated as military activity repeatedly occurred. So by executing the vicious and exterminating the brutal, they tried to soothe the common folk and bring evil-doers to account. They muddled along in this way wishing to bring peace to the world, but were incapable of acting in compliance with the common folk." *Zhuangzi jishi*, 3: 552.
6. Cf. *Laozi*, section 38: "Foresight consists of the flower of the Dao and is thus the origin of duplicity. This why the really great one involves himself with its substance and not with its superficial aspects." Richard John Lynn, *The Classic of the Way and Virtue*, 119.
7. Cheng Xuanying: "Therefore, having internalized the Dao, the sage lifts his feet high as he steps through dusty worldliness, unwilling to use his great powers of arousal to rule the world. But then how may the world, afflicted with superficiality and artifice, be roused by the Dao of the sages?" *Zhuangzi jishi*, 3: 555.
8. Esteem occurs when the sage is recognized as a sage. Cheng Xuanying: "During the superficial last phase of an age, since the Dao becomes unfeasible, the Dao no longer

prevails in the world. When a sage who embodies the Dao lowers his steps into dusty worldliness, he so imperceptibly merges with the masses that no one knows he is there. He so conceals his sagely virtue that no one can see to make use of it. Though such a one even reside at court, how is it any different from his being out amidst the mountains and woods!" *Zhuangzi jishi*, 3: 555.

9. Cheng Xuanying: "Whereas they did not hid themselves to prevent being seen, though they were seen they did not mislead the mass of common folk; whereas they did not stop their words to prevent them from getting about, though bruited about they did not offend others; whereas they did not keep their wisdom to themselves to prevent it from circulating, though it circulated it did not confuse people. Because the times were beset with such absurd foolishness and fate had become so inhospitable, they just got in step with the vicissitudes of the world and thus kept their persons whole and safe far from harm." *Zhuangzi jishi*, 3: 556.
10. Cheng Xuanying: "To live in straitened circumstances yet always be happy, to be in great danger yet remain utterly calm, to act either openly or remain obscure in step with the vicissitudes of the moment, such behavior characterizes the Dao as it bears on preserving one's person." *Zhuangzi jishi*, 3: 556.

CHAPTER 17

QIUSHUI [AUTUMN FLOODS]

17.1.1 When the season of autumn floods arrives, all subsidiary streams pour their waters into the Yellow River, whose flow becomes so vast that from the banks and islets on the one side one can't distinguish oxen from horses on the other.

This addresses how wide it is.

17.1.2 Consequently the Earl of the Yellow River[1] was so elated and pleased with himself that he thought all splendors under heaven were vested in him. Following the current, he traveled east all the way to the North Sea, and when he there looked farther east but saw no end to the waters, he began to shake his head in perplexity, and with his gaze dazzled by the sight, he addressed the Sea God Ruo with a sigh, "As the proverb has it, 'though one has heard the Dao a hundred times, he still thinks no one is better than he'—which could be a saying meant exactly for me. Moreover, when some time ago I heard those who belittled Zhongni [Confucius] and disparaged the righteousness of Bo Yi,[2] at first I did not believe them. But now that I have seen your endless immensity with my own eyes, I realize that if I had not come to your gate I would have come to grief and been forever ridiculed by masters of the great method of the Dao."

Since he now knows how small he is and no longer can feel arrogant, he understands allotted capacity is something inherent, so the inclination to raise up on tiptoes and hope for something better has no part to play here.[3]

17.2.1 North Sea Ruo then said, "Just as one can't talk about the sea with a well frog, for it is restrained by its space or talk about ice with a summer insect,

for it is devoted to its season, one can't talk about the Dao with a bumpkin scholar, for he is bound by his doctrines.

The places creatures live safe and secure limits each in the way it thinks.

17.2.2 Now that you have come out from between your banks to gaze upon the great sea and realize how miserably small you are, it will be possible to talk with you about the Great Ordering Principle.

It is because he now understands what his allotted capacity is that Principle can be discussed with him.

17.2.3 Of all the waters of the world, none is greater than my sea. A myriad streams gravitate into me, and, though it is not known when this has ever ceased yet, I am never full. The Tail Gate [Weilü] drains me,[4] and, though it is not known when this ever stops, yet I am never empty. Spring and autumn I never fluctuate, and I have never known flooding or drying up. As such, by how much more I surpass the flow of the Yangzi and Yellow River is impossible to estimate. However, I have never made much of myself because my physical form is subordinate to Heaven and Earth and my pneuma is received from yin and yang, thus I am here within Heaven and Earth just as a pebble or tiny tree are found on a great mountain. Since I just keep to the view that I am a lesser thing, how could I go on making much of myself!

In taking the entire volume of all its tributaries and measuring it against that of the Yellow River, measuring that of the Yellow River against that of the sea, then measuring that of the sea against that of Heaven and Earth, to show that each has its own different volume, the way the drift of words starts here seems to draw an analogy for once one has seen how great the Yellow River is one then understands how small one is, but if one examines what it really means, this is not so. What causes trouble in the world is dissatisfaction [*buyi*].[5] Those whose embodiment is great arrogantly declare that those that are small need nothing more, whereas those whose substance is small, clods that they are [*kuairan*], declare that only the great have exactly enough. So it is that superiors and inferiors brag on the one hand and raise themselves up on tiptoes in hope on the other; either contemptuously looking down or enviously looking up, both to lose their true selves [*zishi*], which is how people in general become so deluded. To seek rectification of the deluded, such rectification is best served by first letting them take their differences perfectly into account, then have them comply with what is said about them: Since it is said that being great is to have exactly enough, this accordingly means that not a millet grain of difference exists between an autumn hair and even all Heaven and Earth; since it is said that being small is to need nothing more, this accordingly means all Heaven and Earth surpasses not even an autumn hair. Only then will the deluded have a way to find their way back, for if each recognizes his limits and people are content with their allotted capacities, those that do become spontaneous and free shall use their own steps to travel the wide open spaces of self-fulfillment. This is why Master Zhuang expressed his virtuous words as he did, but if explained the way the deluded do, the small and great will go on taking turns to contend one with the other, and such contention thus will never end. If when one sees someone great and thus feels discontent with being small, or if one sees someone with little and so regards himself as having much, such people, charging about within the confines of victory and defeat, will just aid and abet Heaven's innocent folk to become conceited and boastful—and how does this ever get at what Master Zhuang meant to say!

17.2.4 As for all the land within the Four Seas, does it not seem just like an anthill in a vast marsh! And if one calculates what the Middle Kingdom is compared to all the land within the Four Seas, does it not seem just like one grain of millet in an entire granary! We give the name myriad to the number of things, and mankind occupies but one place among them, and though people in masses may live throughout all Nine Divisions of the land, compared to all the grain and other foodstuffs produced and all the boats and carts used for transport, a man occupies just one place among these, so compared to all the myriad things, is he not just like the tip of a tiny hair on a horse's body!

Distinctions between small and great exist because each has his own inherent relative rank, so none should raise up on tiptoes toward another.

17.2.5 The succession of the Five Thearchs, the contention among the Three Sovereigns, the worries of benevolent men, or the labors of the capable and learned all amount to nothing more than this.

None should try to exceed his own individual limits.

17.2.6 Bo Yi refusal to serve was for the sake of reputation,[6] and Zhongni [Confucius] engaged in discourse in order to appear widely learned—this because they made much of themselves. And is this not just like you when before you made much of yourself regarding water!"

People have fixed limits, and even the most intelligent can't exceed them. Thus the text cites how both great and small fall short in order to clarify that the ultimate principle of things never differs.

17.3 The Earl of the Yellow River then said, "That being so, if I take Heaven and Earth to signify what is great and the tip of a tiny hair to signify what is small, would that do?"

17.4.1 North Sea Ruo replied, "Not at all, for things have no end of different capacities;

Each and every thing has its own unique capacity.

17.4.2 time never stops for them;

When they live and when die all depend on their span of time.

17.4.3 fate [*fen*] for them is inconstant;

Success and failure all depend on fate.[7]

17.4.4 and from beginning to end nothing ever stays the way it used to be.

This means renewal day after day.

17.4.5 Therefore, one of great intelligence observes things both in terms of the distant and the commonplace, so though he might be small, he has no sense of being too little,

Each one should be self-sufficient,[8]

17.4.6 or might be great but does not make much of himself,

and also would not have more than he needs.

17.4.7 for such a one realizes that things have no end of different capacities

Since he views things with comprehensive grasp, he realizes that whether distant or commonplace, great or small, each thing has its own innate capacity.

17.4.8 and clearly understands present and past.

Xiang [also "previously" or "toward"] here means "clearly" [*ming*], and "present and past" is the same as "past and present."[9]

17.4.9 Therefore, though his life is prolonged [*yao*], it depresses him not,

Yao ["distant"] here means "prolonged" [*chang*].

17.4.10 and if cut short [*duo*] neither rises up on tiptoe hoping for more,

Duo [fix, put in order] here is the same as "cut short" [*duan*].

17.4.11 for such a one realizes that time never stops.

Clearly understanding past and present, such a one realizes that change and transformation never stops when it comes to life and death, so thus is neither depressed when life is prolonged nor rises up on tiptoes in hope for more when it is cut short.

17.4.12 From scrutiny of how things wax and wane, he neither takes delight in gain nor feels grief at loss, for he understands the inconstancy of fate.

From his scrutiny of how things first wax then wane, he realizes that his fated share of gain is impermanent, so thus can lose all sense of grief or delight.

17.4.13 He has a clear grasp of the level path,

Living and dying follow the true path of daily renewal.[10]

17.4.14 thus he neither takes pleasure in being alive nor regards death as misfortune, 17.4.16 for he understands that from beginning to end, nothing ever stays the way it used to be.

Since he clearly grasps that things from beginning to end are renewed each passing day, he knows that one can't hold on to what he once was and remain that way. As such, he undergoes the new without shock and parts with the old without alarm and experiences the transformation from life to death as if were all the same.

17.4.15 Calculate what one might know and it compares not with what he does not know;

What each one knows has its individual limits.

17.4.16 calculate the time one is alive and it compares not with the time before he was born.

The time each one lives has its own number of years.

17.4.17 It is because one tries to exhaust the greatest of realms with the smallest of means that he brings such bewildered confusion on himself, which makes it impossible for him to achieve self-fulfillment.

Absolutely nothing is better than to remain content with the natural allotment with which one is endowed.

17.4.18 If we look at it this way, how can we still be sure that the tip of a hair is small enough to demarcate the smallest thing possible? Or how can we still be sure that Heaven and Earth are large enough to fill the greatest thing possible?"

If one seeks to be great with only small potential, he never shall achieve what is right for himself, but if one always remains content with his natural allotment, whether great or small, he shall be sufficient unto himself. One might have only the potential the size of the tip of a hair, but as long as he seeks not Heaven and Earth size achievements, anything more than he needs he shall discard as excess; one might have even the potential of Heaven and Earth, but as long as he feels no larger than an autumn hair, he shall regard his physical existence as cut just right for self-sufficiency. So how can one know that something small determines smallness or that something large determines greatness!

17.5 The Earl of the Yellow River then asked, "People who dispute such things all say, 'The utmost minute has no physical form, and the utmost great can't be encompassed.' Should we believe this is really so?"

17.6.1 North Sea Ruo replied, "To perceive the great with the minute [*jing*] won't get all of it; to perceive the minute with the great won't get it clearly.

Since what eyesight perceives has its usual limits, it can't see everything. Therefore, with something too large, it does not get all of it, and with something too small, it does not get it clear enough. As such, it is just that there are things that the eye does not capture and not that the utmost minute or the utmost great are actually without physical existence—how can it mean that the one has no physical form and the other can't be encompassed![11]

17.6.2 The minute is the smallest of the small, and the gigantic is the greatest of the great, thus they have different distinctions [*yibian*],

The large and the small differ, thus what distinguishes them can't be the same.

17.6.3 and this indicates the existence of physical features [*shi*].

If the one had no physical form and the other could not be encompassed, they would not have physical features that present such different distinctions.

17.6.4 Any reference to precise detail or coarse bulk is limited to [*qi*] something that has physical form.[12]

Since the one reveals precise detail and the other coarse bulk, they can't be without physical form.

17.6.5 That which is without physical form can't be formulated [*fen*] in numbers and that which can't be encompassed can't be fully accounted for by numbers. Though coarse bulk may be addressed in words and precise detail

reached by thought, what words can't address and thought can't reach is not limited to either coarse bulk or tiny size.

This can only be that which has no physical existence, and how could any coarse bulk or precise detail pertain to that! What can be spoken of or thought about involves existence, but here what is spoken of and thought about is without physical existence. Therefore, only when one seeks it beyond words and thought, thus entering a realm free of words and thought, may one reach it.[13]

17.7.1 Therefore, when the great one proceeds, he sets out not to harm people

The great one is free of selfconscious thought and thus, moving in step with Heaven, he lifts his feet and lets them fall only on auspicious ground—how could he ever set out on a path that harms people!

17.7.2 and so makes not much of his benevolence and favor [*en*].

Non-injurious [*wuhai*], he makes not much of himself for the favor he bestows.[14]

17.7.3 His actions are done not to confer benefit

He acts in resonance with principle, and principle intrinsically [*zi*] is non-injurious.

17.7.4 but finds nothing scornful in serving as a gate keeper.

He just trusts to what he can do and takes a position appropriate to it; it is not because he thinks it scornful that he looks for such an occupation.

17.7.5 Goods and belongings, he contends not for them

Let each person have the use of what is determined by natural allotment.

17.7.6 but makes not much of yielding them to others.

He uses no more than what is just right for him.

17.7.7 In the work he does, he borrows not help from others

Let each person be employed in what he trusts himself to do.

17.7.8 and makes not much of sustaining himself through his own efforts

He does no more than do what is sufficient for him.

17.7.9 but scorns not the corrupt and venal.

By fundamental nature [*li*], he is spontaneously free from desire.[15]

17.7.10 He might act differently from ordinary men

For him alone there is nothing he may do or may not do, as such he is different from ordinary men.[16]

17.7.11 but makes not much of being oddly eccentric.

Conforming to his fundamental nature, he is spontaneously different.

17.7.12 His behavior might conform to that of the masses,

He just follows what the masses do.

17.7.13 but he scorns not that of flatterers and sycophants

He is upright and straight by nature.[17]

17.7.14 All the ranks and emoluments of the world are not enough to urge him on; all the penalties and humiliations are not enough to shame him.

Things external to him find not a place in his mind.

17.7.15 He knows that right can't be divided from wrong, that the small and the great can't demarcate the one from the other.

This is why he arcanely unites them.

17.7.16 I have heard it said, 'The man of the Dao is unheralded;

It is by trusting people to do for themselves that people achieve self-fulfillment; thus he lets honor and rank gravitate to others, which is why he himself is unheralded.

17.7.17 perfect virtue is unsuccessful;[18]

"Success" is generated by "failure," so if one is always free of failure, the term "success" disappears.

17.7.18 and the great one has no self.'

He does nothing but trust people to do for themselves.[19]

17.7.19 Such is the perfection of complying with allotted capacity [*yuefen*]."

He complies with it in such a way that he perfectly fulfills his allotted capacity and thus achieves arcane fusion [*ming*]. Only someone who extends himself to the farthest reaches of that which has no form and is unencompassable can do such a thing.

17.8 The Earl of the Yellow River then asked, "Whether external to things or internal to them, how do demarcations come about between noble and base, between small and great?"

17.9.1 North Sea Ruo replied, "From the point of view of the Dao, there is nothing either noble or base about things.

Each is just sufficient unto itself [*zizu*].

17.9.2 From the point of view of people, one regards oneself as noble and others as mean.

Such trivialities are shuffled all together by the Dao and evened out.

17.9.3 From the point of view of the common and vulgar, nobility and baseness are not intrinsic to oneself.

This is what is meant by getting things upside down.[20]

17.9.4 From the point of view of differences in size, if something is great because it is deemed great, then none of the myriads of things would fail to be great; if something is small because it is deemed small, then none of the myriad things would fail to be small. But if we realize that Heaven and Earth may be as tiny as a grain of rice and that the tip of an autumn hair may be as large as a huge mountain, then what relativity in size means should become obvious.

Let that which is deemed great mean that it has just enough and let that which is deemed small mean that it has no more than it needs. As such, if something is designated "great" because being so means that it is sufficient to its inborn nature, then neither the tip of an autumn hair nor a huge mountain may change such a designation; if something is designated "small" because being so means that it has no more than it needs, then neither Heaven and Earth nor a tiny grain of rice have any reason to be called otherwise. If in viewing differences in size one does not follow this Dao, relative differences in sizes will so add to one another and the tiniest of things will so push each other out of the way that it will prove impossible to examine them.

17.9.5 From the point of view of salutary effect [*gong*], if something has it because it is deemed to have it, then none of the myriad things would fail to have it, but if something lacks it because it is deemed lacking, none of the myriad things would fail to lack it. But if we realize that for east and west to be in opposition, they can't do without one another, the allotment of salutary effect may thus be determined.

Nothing in all the world fails to stand in opposition to something else as other and self. As such, as other and self both tend to spontaneous function [*ziwei*], so do east and west find themselves in opposition. However, when an other and a self happen to be the lips and teeth, though lips and teeth never care for one another, when lips are gone the teeth grow cold. Thus it is that as the other [the lips] spontaneously function the salutary effect it has on the self [the teeth] is great, which means such opposed pairs can't do without one another. Therefore, if in spontaneously functioning things lacked such salutary effect, no salutary effect anywhere in the world could ever occur. It is because they can't do without one another and, as such, do have such salutary effect that salutary effect does occur throughout the world. If people abandon the salutary effect that occurs as spontaneous function and instead selfconsciously try to benefit one another, the more assiduous the benefit the more false and degraded it will be, and throughout the world enterprise shall come to naught and fundamental nature degenerate. This is how the salutary effect of things may be determined at any time.

17.9.6 From the point of view of predilection [*qu*], if someone is right because he deems himself right, then none of the myriad folk would fail to be right; if someone is wrong because he is deemed wrong, then none of the myriad folk would fail to be wrong. But if we realize that Yao and Jie each thought himself right and the other wrong, then what predilection in behavior [*qucao*] means should become obvious.

Since everyone deems himself right, no one fails to be right; since everyone deems the other to be wrong, no one fails to be wrong. But since no one fails to be wrong, no one is right either. And since no one fails to be right, no one is wrong either. Someone who was free of both right and wrong was Yao; someone who held to both right and wrong was Jie. However, both these monarchs could not take one another's place [*xiangwei*] because of the inherent natures with which they were endowed. Therefore, if we look at predilection in behavior all over the world as exemplified by Yao and Jie, why people can't take one another's place should become obvious.

17.10.1 Long ago, when Yao abdicated rule to Shun, he became emperor, but when Kuai abdicated rule to Zhi, it resulted in his destruction. Tang and Wu struggled and so became kings, but when Lord Bai[21] struggled, he perished.

When one complies with Heaven and is in resonance with the people, thus gaining the whole world, the footprints of this are manifested either as struggle or abdication. But if one strives after such footprints, it means that he has failed to grasp the reason such footprints occur, which is why the one was destroyed and the other perished.[22]

17.10.2 Looking at it in this way, the code of etiquette governing struggle or abdication, or the behavior of a Yao or a Jie, sometimes turns out noble and sometimes base, so it is impossible to consider them as constants. A roof beam or a house pillar can be used to break down a city wall but can't be used to stop up a small hole; this speaks to their different capacities. Qiji and Hualiu [famous steeds] could gallop one thousand tricents in a single day, but when it comes to catching rats, they are inferior to the wildcat; this speaks to their different skills. At night the owl catches fleas with the power to detect the tip of a hair, but when day comes, though it opens its eyes wide, it does not see hills or mountains; this speaks to differences in original nature.

It is by adapting to such differences and trusting to them that none of the myriad creatures ever fails to be equal to the moment.

17.10.3 Now do you still say that you are going to keep on being guided by what is 'right' and reject what is 'wrong,' and be guided by 'order' and reject 'disorder'? To do so is to fail to understand the principle of Heaven and Earth and everyone's innate tendency.

It is the principle of Heaven and Earth that the innate tendency in everyone to take what is of benefit to the self is "right," and what is disadvantageous to the self is "wrong," what suits one's nature is "order," and what harms one's sense of harmony is "disorder." However, people lack limits of contentment and the self lacks a constant sense of what is suitable. Since dissimilar natures discriminate differently, no guiding principle exists for "right" and "wrong." If I accept something as "right," this does not allow another to take it as "wrong," which is to know only one's own view and not appreciate the other's. This being the case, if one looks at things in terms of the Dao, nothing ever fails to be suitable. So if one entrusts things to the potter's wheel of Heaven and is comfortable to follow two such paths at once, no matter how different ways are and no matter how different things are, being the same for him all are beneficial.

17.10.4 This is like being guided by Heaven while denying Earth or being guided by yin while denying yang; that this is impossible to do is perfectly clear. Even so, those who say such things and never give up on them, if not stupid, must be liars.

Since Heaven and Earth as well as yin and yang exist only in paired opposition, and "right" and "wrong" as well as order and disorder generate each another's existence, which of them could ever be done away with!

17.10.5 Emperors and kings abdicated in different ways, and the three dynasties [Xia, Shang, and Zhou] had different means of succession. Those who were out of step with the times and defied the mood of the common folk we call usurpers; those who were in step with the times and complied with the mood of the common folk we call followers of righteousness. Oh, just be quiet, Earl of the Yellow River, for how could you ever understand what constitutes a noble or base family or a great or small household!"

What the mood of the common folk deems noble at other times is deemed base, and what the people think great in some other ages turns out in others to be thought small. Therefore, in complying with the footprints of the mood of the common folk, it can't but differ accordingly. This is why what happened during the times of the five emperors and three kings [the archs] differs in each case.

17.11 The Earl of the Yellow River then asked, "If that is so, then what should I do and what should I not do? After all, how should I know what to decline and what to receive, what to reject and what to accept?"

17.12.1 North Sea Ruo replied, "From the point of view of the Dao, what is 'noble,' and what 'base'! These are just names for relative status, the one giving way to the other.

The way of noble and base is such that they just chase each other around.

17.12.2 Hold not to a fixed goal [*zhi*], for this greatly obstructs your way to the Dao.

If one holds oneself inflexible, he shall not be at ease with the Dao.

17.12.3 What is 'little,' what 'much'! These are just names for amounts available, the one superseded by the other.

Depending on one's allotment, what one may thus use varies.

17.12.4 Hold not to one course of action, for this puts you at odds with the Dao.

If one can't keep in step with change, he shall not be equal to the Dao.

17.12.5 Be stern as a ruler should be with his state, one whose virtue is exercised impartially.

Be utterly impartial, that's all.

17.12.6 Be as aloof as the god of the soil when sacrificed to, one whose blessings are distributed impartially.

Be one whom all under Heaven may equally intreat.

17.12.7 Extend everywhere as do the endless reach of the four directions, for these have no boundaries to them.

Extend so widely that you are free from particularity of place.

17.12.8 If the myriad folk are universally cherished, who of them should expect special protection!

To shelter all the people is but to let them recover their natural allotments while interacting with all equally—and how has that anything to do with sheltering them with wide-spreading branches!

17.12.9 This is known as being 'directionless' [*wufang*].

Such a one is "directionless," thus he can take the myriad folk as his "direction."[23]

17.12.10 If the myriad folk are treated equally as one, who of them should be made too short, who too long!

Not a one should be denied sufficiency.[24]

17.12.11 Though the Dao has no beginning or end, people are subject to life and death.

The cycle of life and death is but an endless process of change, which neither begins nor ends.

17.12.12 So take it not on yourself to nurture [*cheng*] them,

There is no fixed procedure [*changchu*] for nurture.[25]

17.12.13 And, since it waxes and wanes, let not your position depend on your bodily form.

Use not your bodily form as means to keep your position, trying to maintain it without change.

17.12.14 For the years can't be suspended,

One may wish to suspend them to prevent their moving on, but this is impossible.

17.12.15 and time can't be stopped.

One may wish to stop it to make it stay, but this too is impossible.

17.12.16 Growth and decay, waxing and waning, when one ends the other begins.

Change and transformation make things new each day, never is what used to be kept the same.

17.12.17 This is how to talk about the way of the Great Truth [*dayi*] and its principles of the myriad things. One's life goes as if at a gallop or as if it had bolted.

One should just set about using it, that's all!

17.12.18 No action fails to produce change, no time fails to involve transition.

One thus should not persist in trying to keep things the same.

17.12.19 As for 'what should I do and what should I not do?' Well, what you really should do is just leave them alone to self-transform."

Were one to act or refrain from acting in regard to them, this would corrupt their self-transformation.

17.13 The Earl of the Yellow River then asked, "If that is so, then what is of value in the Dao?"

Due to it, self-transformation occurs.

17.14.1 North Sea Ruo replied, "One who comprehends the Dao must have insight into principle; one who has insight into principle must be clear about incipiency [*ji*]; one who is clear about incipiency shall not let himself be harmed by things.

One who comprehends the Dao knows that it has no power [*neng*], and since it has no power, how can it have given me life? I just came to life spontaneously, so since my four limbs and all other parts of my body, as well as my five viscera and essential spirit have been self-produced without it [the Dao] having made them, how could it have any designs on what happens to me after I came into being! One who has understanding of this principle is surely capable of shunning any knowledge that exceeds his allotted capacity and any inclination to try to extend his lifespan. Instead, riding change and resonating with incipiency, such a one lets nothing external harm his inner self, and since he himself is not harmed by things, this keeps him constantly whole.

17.14.2 If one be of perfect virtue, fire can't burn him, water can't drown him, cold and heat can't harm him, and wild birds and animals can't injure him.

Since his mind remains serene, danger is never dangerous to him, and since his state of mind [*yi*] never fails to suit circumstances [*shi*], trouble is never troublesome to him.

17.14.3 This does not mean that such a one makes light of these things,

Though his mind remains serene, it does not allow him to risk such things.

17.14.4 for he does distinguish between safety and danger,

He knows what can't be eluded.

17.14.5 is content with either misfortune or fortune,

He is content with whatever fate meets out to him.

17.14.6 and is cautious about whether to advance or retreat.

He judges whether advance or retreat would be bad for him.

17.14.7 Thus nothing can harm him.

Since he does not regard harm as harmful, nothing can harm him.

17.14.8 Thus it is said, 'Whereas what pertains to Heaven is internal, what pertains to the human is external.'

Whereas one's natural capacity [*tianran*] resides in the inner self, what natural capacity must comply with resides externally. Thus it is that it is stated in *The Great Exemplary Teacher*, "To know how Heaven acts and how man acts is to reach perfection,"[26] which clarifies that whether it be internal or external, one should in both aspects [*fen*] eschew selfconscious action [*feiwei*].

17.14.9 Virtue resides in what pertains to Heaven.

If one indulgently relies on knowledge, and it would recklessly corrupt his natural simplicity.

17.14.10 One who knows how Heaven acts and how man acts roots oneself in his natural endowment [*tian*] and stays within his capacity [*de*]

Such is naturally inherent knowledge that is used to act spontaneously [*zi-xing*] without exceeding one's allotted capacity. Therefore, though one acts in the external world, he always stays rooted in his natural endowment and stays within his capacity.

17.14.11 fluctuates between withdrawing or extending himself,

Only one who resonates with the incipiency of the moment possesses this flexibility [*bian*].

17.14.12 and, reverting to the prime directive [*yao*], speaks only out of its perfection [*ji*]."

Though knowledge involves the world and though engagement is with its myriad folk, such a one never violates the perfection of the prime directive. As such, the Dao of Heaven and man is kept entirely intact.

17.15 "What do you mean by 'Heaven'? What do you mean by 'man'?"

17.16.1 North Sea Ruo replied, "Oxen and horses have four legs, this is what I mean by 'Heaven.' Bridling horses and piercing oxen noses, this is what I mean by 'man.'

In the way men live, how can they not make oxen work for them or make horses carry them, and to do so not bridle them or pierce their noses? That oxen and horses refuse not to have noses pierces or be bridled is an inherently appropriate aspect of their natural fates [*tianming*], and since this conforms with their natural fates, even though dependent on the works of man, it is still rooted in Heaven.

17.16.2 Thus it is said,

> **Let not what pertains to Heaven be ruined by**
> **what pertains to man.**

Bridling and piercing are proper things to do, but if running the one or working the other is overdone, or if driving the one or making the other plod is done without proper limits, natural principles are thus ruined.

17.16.3 Let not allotted fate by ruined by deliberation.

One should not deliberately try to make them act as one would have them act, for how would this allow them to maintain their allotted fates!

17.16.4 Take not your potential and sacrifice it to reputation,

Since the amount of one's potential is a constant allotment, to sacrifice [*xun*] it for reputation is a fault of excess [*guo*].[27]

17.16.5 For if you carefully guard it and lose it not,

> **It may be said you revert to your authenticity."**

Authenticity is found within one's natural capacity.

17.17 The one-footed kui envies the millipede; the millipede envies the snake; the snake envies the wind; the wind envies the eye; and the eye envies the mind.

17.18 The kui said to the millipede, "Since I move by having to hop along on just one foot, I am no match for you, but now here you use a myriad feet to do it—how can you alone do that?"

17.19 The millipede replied, "That is not so. Have you not seen a spitter? As for the spittle, when big it is like pearls, and when tiny it is like mist, all mixed up together falling in numbers beyond count. Now when I activate my celestial mechanism, I know not why it happens as it does either."

17.20 The millipede said to the snake, "I use numerous feet to move but can't keep up with you who have no feet. Why is that?"

17.21 The snake replied, "Since I am moved by my celestial mechanism, how can I change that? So how could I ever use legs!"

As for the way creatures live, they live but know not how they live, and, thus alive they move, but how could they ever move because they know how to move! Therefore, feet know not how they move, eyes know not how they see, the mind knows not how it knows, but all just assiduously achieve self-fulfillment. As for the pace of movement or the reflective power of intelligence, whether one is capable or not, it never up to oneself. Yet the deluded wishing to secure their persons boast about their abilities and in doing so oppose their celestial mechanisms and harm their numinous vessels. The Perfected one realizes that one's celestial mechanism can't be changed, thus he abandons intelligence, discards selfconscious judgment, and, insubstantially unmindful of what he does, trusts to his own unselfconscious action. As a result, nothing the myriad folk might do is done without spontaneous freedom.

17.22 The snake said to the wind, "I move by shifting my backbone and ribs and thus have a visual shape. Now you roar up out of the North Sea, then roar along down to the South Sea, yet have no visual shape at all. How do you do that?"

17.23 The wind replied, "Right, I do roar up out of the North Sea, then roar along down to the South Sea, but I let myself be defeated just when a finger is raised to me or when a step is taken into me. Nevertheless, when it comes to snapping great trees and making houses fly away, I alone can do this. Therefore, by not trying to be victorious in many small things I manage to have great victories. To achieve great victories, only a sage can do this."

It allows its celestial mechanism to do as it likes, which shuns contention; as such, it tries not to be victorious in small things. However, the way to drive the myriad folk and control all the natural utility they have is to allow all this natural utility to achieve self-realization and the myriad folk their innate capacity to do things, for then none in all the world is denied spontaneous freedom. This is the way the sage achieves great victories.

17.24 When Confucius was traveling in Kuang, men of Song encircled him several ranks deep,[28] yet he did not cease [*chuo*][29] playing his zither and went on singing . Zilu went before him and asked, "How is it, Master, that you can amuse yourself so?"[30]

17.25.1 Confucius replied, "Approach and I shall tell you. That I have long tried to avoid adversity but not been spared it is due to fate; that I have long sought success but not found it is due to the times.

In order to elucidate that the times and fate are inherently apt, he uses what he says about seeking and avoiding as the vehicle to express it.

17.25.2 When it was Yao or Shun, there were no failed men in the entire world, but this was not due to their knowing how to be successful, and when it was Jie or Zhou, there were no successful men in the entire world, but this was not due to any failure of knowledge on their part—it was just that the dynamics of the age [*shishi*] made both inevitable.

Neither selfconscious effort nor belaboring of mind had anything to do with the adversity or success.

17.25.3 To travel on water yet flee not from sea serpents and dragons, such is the courage of the fisherman; to travel on land yet flee not from rhinos and tigers, such is the courage of the hunter; to look on death as life while bare blades clash before one, such is the courage of the martyred warrior.

Each of them remains content.

17.25.4 To know that adversity is a matter of fate and that success due to the times, to face great trouble and yet feel no fear, such is the courage of the sage.

The sage then never fails to be content.

17.25.5 You,[31] take it easy! For my fate has been determined for me."

Since one's fate may not be determined by oneself, there is nothing to exercise one's mind about. As for one who remains content with his fate, no matter what venture embarked on, he never fails to enjoy spontaneous freedom.

17.26 Not long afterwards the commander of the troops approached to apologize, "We mistook you for Yang Hu and thus surrounded you, but now we see that you are not he, so we beg your pardon so we may withdraw."

17.27 Gongsun Long posed a question to Mou of Wei,[32] "When young I studied the way of the former kings, and once grown up I knew to act with benevolence and righteousness. I joined the same and different, separated hardness from white, made so what was not so, affirmed the unaffirmable, vexed the hundred schools of thought, and confounded the disputation of all speakers. I considered myself nothing less than perfectly accomplished. But now that I have heard the words of Master Zhuang, I am perplexed at how strange they are. I know not whether my powers of debate fall short or if my understanding is not up to it, but now I have nothing to open my beak about. May I presume to ask what I can do about it?"

17.28.1 Prince Mou slouched again on his writing desk, heaved a great sigh, and looking up at the sky, laughed and said, "Is it just you who has not heard of the frog in the derelict well? It said to the great turtle of the Eastern Sea, "How pleased I am! I come out to jump along atop the railing of the well or go back in to rest in the edge where a tile is missing. When I go in the water, I let it reach my armpits and hold up my chin; when I trip about in the mud, I sink my feet into it and let my insteps disappear. When I look around at the bloodworms, crabs and tadpoles, none can equal what I can do. Moreover, I have hegemony over this entire pit of water and all the joy in straddling this dilapidated well—how perfect is that! Why don't you come in and take a look around some time!"

It seems like the little bird that is self-satisfied with its wild grass.[33]

17.28.2 When the great turtle of the Eastern Sea had not quite got its left foot in, its right knee was already stuck.

This clarifies how something large may not play about in something small—it is no fun at all to do so.

17.28.3 Thereupon, it hesitated and withdrew to tell the frog about the sea, "The distance of a thousand tricents is inadequate to encompass it, and a height of a thousand fathoms is inadequate to reach its entire depth. At the time of Yu, great flooding occurred nine years out of ten, yet its waters never increased. During the time of Tang, great drought occurred seven years out of eight, yet it shorelines never receded. Not to keep changing no matter how short or long the time, not to advance or recede regardless of how little or much the water, this likewise is the great joy of the Eastern Sea." At this, the frog in the dilapidated well, astonished and utterly confounded, was so bewildered that it lost all self-possession.

As something small, it so yearned to be large that it lost all self-possession.

17.29.1 "Moreover, though your intelligence is not even up to recognizing the boundaries between right and wrong, you still want to analyze what Master Zhuang has to say. This is like trying to have a mosquito carry a mountain on its back or a millipede race the Yellow River—you not at all equal to the task.

Since each person has his own unique allotted capacity, one can't by force equal what another has.

17.29.2 Furthermore, since your intelligence is not up to words that argue with such ultimate subtlety but is only comfortable with issues of temporary advantage, are you not just like the frog in the dilapidated well? Whereas at one moment he [Master Zhuang] is treading the Yellow Springs and the next has ascended to the Great Empyrean, for

Neither north nor south exists for him
As unobstructed in all directions
He dissolves into the unfathomable.

Neither east nor west exists for him
As he starts from arcane obscurity
To return on the great thoroughfare.

There is no place he fails to reach.[34]

17.29.3 On the other hand, here you are plotting and planning to find a way to analyze him and seek the means to dispute him.

Such a wanderer in the boundless is not caught by analysis or disputation.

17.29.4 This is simply to use a tube to peer at the sky or an awl to indicate the earth—are these not really too small! Get you gone!

Since he was not someone up to the task, it was right to dismiss him.

17.29.5 Furthermore, is it just you who has not heard of the boy from Shaoling who tried to learn how to walk in the Handan manner?[35] Not only did he fail to get the knack of how they did it there, he also forgot how he himself used to walk, so just had to crawl all the way home.[36]

Using a "this" to imitate a "that" results in the loss of both.

17.29.6 So if you don't go now, you shall both forget what you used to know as well as fail at what you are trying to learn."

17.30 Gongsun Long's mouth fell wide open and would not shut, and, with his tongue stuck to its roof, he hastily made his getaway.

17.31 Once when Master Zhuang was fishing in the Pu River, the King of Chu[37] dispatched two officers of state to go to him in advance and announce on his behalf, "I wish to burden you with the administration of my realm."

17.32 Master Zhuang held on to his pole and without turning his head said, "I have heard that in Chu there is a sacred tortoise, already dead for three thousand years, which is kept by the king wrapped in cloth and preserved in a bamboo hamper at the ancestral hall. As for this tortoise, would it rather be dead and have its bones left behind to be venerated or to be alive so it could drag its tail in the mud?"

17.33 The two officers of state replied, "It would rather be alive so it could drag its tail in the mud."

17.34 To which Master Zhuang said, "Get you gone! I am going to drag my tail in the mud!"

The nature of each is thus content.

17.35 When Master Hui was prime minister of Liang, Master Zhuang went to see him. Someone said to Master Hui, "Master Zhuang is coming because he wants to replace you as prime minister." At this, Master Hui was so afraid that he searched the capital for him three days and nights.

So he mustered troops and instructed them to do this.

17.36 Master Zhuang went to see him and said, "In the south there is a bird, whose name is phoenix fowl [*yuanchu*]. Do you know it? When the phoenix fowl flies out from the Southern Sea all the way up to the Northern Sea, it

perches on nothing but the paulownia tree, eats nothing but bamboo seed, and drinks nothing but sweet spring water. But then there was an owl that had just got a rotting rat, and as the phoenix fowl happen to pass by, it raised its head and, seeing it, cried out 'shoo.' Now do you want to shoo me away for the sake of this Liang state of yours?"

This addresses how the tastes of creatures are so different—each limited to what it desires.

17.37 Whilst Master Zhuang and Master Hui were walking about on Hao Bridge, Master Zhuang remarked, "The *shu* fish emerge to wander so free and easy, for such is the joy of fish."[38]

17.38 Master Hui then said, "You are not a fish, so wherein [*an*] can you know the joy of fish?"[39]

17.39 Master Zhuang replied, "You are not me, so wherein do you know that I don't know the joy of fish?"

By saying this, he wants to cast light on the proposition that because one is not another, he can't know that other: If, despite not being me, you still can know that I am not a fish, then it must be true that even though I am not a fish, I too can know the joy of fish.[40]

17.40 Master Hui then said, "I am not you, so I definitely don't know what it is to be you, but as you are definitely not a fish, this proves perfectly that you don't know what it is to be a fish."

Abandoning his original thesis, he tries to use nimble disputation to refute him.

17.41 Master Zhuang responded, "May I get back to your original thesis? When you said 'wherein do you know the joy of fish,' you already knew wherein I knew it but asked me anyway: I knew it above the Hao."

He gets back to Master Hui's original thesis, in which he said, "Since you are not a fish you have no means to know what it is to be one." Now [to paraphrase Master Zhuang], "You are not me yet still ask wherein do I know the joy of fish, which means that you know that I am not a fish, and if you know that I am not a fish, this in general means that mutual knowing [between self and other] is such that a this one can know a that one, and one need not depend on being a fish and only then know what it is to be a fish. Therefore I went back to what you said about wherein could I have known such a thing, which means that you already knew what I knew! But just when you persisted in interrogating me, I knew it exactly there above the Hao, so why did I have to depend on entering the water!" That creatures live where they feel safe and secure [*an*] is because Heaven and Earth can't exchange places and yin and yang can't interchange productive activities. Therefore, one living on land may by reference to how he feels safe and secure can know how those that live in water feel joy—there is nothing especially profound or mysterious about this at all![41]

Notes

1. Cheng Xuanying: "The Earl of the Yellow River, god of the river, is surnamed Feng and has Yi as his given name, . . . and he realized the Dao of a water immortal." *Zhuangzi jishi*, 3: 562.
2. Cf. 6.7.8, 8.6.6, 8.7.8, 17.2, 28.55, and 19.17.
3. Cf. 1.5. 2–1.5.4, Guo commentary.
4. The Tail Gate is the mythical hole in the seabed that drains the sea.
5. Cf. 16.4.6, Guo commentary.
6. Cf. 6.7.8, 8.6.6–8.6.7, 8.7.8, 17.1.2, 28.55–28.56, and 29.17.
7. Cheng Xuanying: "The fate [*fenming*] with which one is endowed is subject to continuous change at all times." *Zhuangzi jishi*, 3: 569.
8. Cheng Xuanying: "Thanks to great sagely intelligence, one observes things in terms of profound and far-reaching principles while scrutinizing the most commonplace of matters; therefore, though even if as small as the tip of a hair such a one feels self-sufficient with his fundamental nature and so has no sense of being too little." *Zhuangzi jishi*, 3: 569.
9. Cheng Xuanying: "Since such a one already realizes that great and small are not really great and small, he clearly understands that there is no past and present to past and present." *Zhuangzi jishi*, 3: 570. Cf. 6.16, where it is said of Buliang Yi, "Once she became aware of her perfect independence, she could free herself from past and present."
10. Cheng Xuanying: "He neither regards death as death nor life as life, because no gap exists between life and death—such is his clear grasp of the great path equally level for all." *Zhuangzi jishi* 3: 571.
11. Cheng Xuanying: "To look at something tremendously large with a tiny physical form will surely fail to get all of its far and wide expanse, thus one says it can't be encompassed. Likewise to peer at the most minute physical form with something tremendously large will surely fail to grasp it clearly, thus one says that it has no physical existence. But since neither is beyond the reach of that which has an object [the sense organ of sight, *youjing*], how can it mean that the one exceeds and the other fails to have physical existence!" *Zhuangzi jishi*, 3: 573. That is, in both cases, though in one case not grasped completely and in the other not grasped clearly, the eye still does see something.

    The "tiny physical form" and "something tremendously large" both seem to refer to the human viewer—tiny when trying to view all Heaven and Earth, huge when trying to view something minute.
12. Cf. 25.51.
13. Cheng Xuanying: "That which can be disputed or expounded are the coarse perceptual properties [*cufa*] of a thing, and that which can be attained through conceptual thought [*xinyi*] are the precise details of a thing. But that which even one with divine eloquence can't articulate and that which even one with the mind of a sage can't scrutinize is marvelous principle [*miaoli*], which must be sought beyond words and thought—and how must this be limited to something that falls between tiny size and coarse bulk!" *Zhuangzi jishi*, 3: 573.
14. Cheng Xuanying: "The kindness and favor he bestows is like the springtime sun that, though it acts everywhere, makes not much of itself for dispensing its grace and favor." *Zhuangzi jishi*, 3: 574.
15. Cheng Xuanying: "Thanks to embodying the arcane Dao, he is free from craving and desire and has nothing to do with either slavishly admiring the pure and honest or scorning the corrupt and venal." *Zhuangzi jishi*, 3: 575.

16. Cf. *Lunyu* (Analects), 18: 2530a: "As for me, I am different from them [selfconscious do-gooders], for I am free from I may and I may not."
17. Cheng Xuanying: "It is because he is loyal and steadfast by innate disposition that he treads not sinister paths; it isn't out of scorn for flatterers and sycophants that he becomes upright and straight." *Zhuangzi jishi*, 3: 576.
18. Cf. Cf. *Laozi*, section 38: "A person of superior virtue isn't virtuous, and this is why he has virtue. A person of inferior virtue never loses virtue, and this is why he lacks virtue." Richard John Lynn, *The Classic of the Way and Virtue*, 119.
19. Cheng Xuanying: "One who is a great sage responds to others with sympathetic resonance [*yougan siying*] and universally trusts people to do for themselves; as such he 'has no self.'" *Zhuangzi jishi*, 3: 577.
20. Cheng Xuanying: "Rank and honor, punishment and humiliation all happen by chance as events unfold, yet common, vulgar people rashly are provoked by them to joy or sorrow. When rank and honor come, they think it noble, for when they get them, they think it favor bestowed. But when they lose them they think it base, for in losing them they are humiliated. Thus since favor and humiliation come from outside of one, how could they ever think that nobility and baseness were intrinsic to oneself!" *Zhuangzi jishi*, 3: 578.
21. Lord Bai refers to Sheng, Lord of Bai, the grandson of King Ping of Chu (reigned 528–516 BCE); he rebelled in 479, but the rebellion was suppressed and Sheng committed suicide.
22. Cheng Xuanying: "Zhi refers to the minister of Yan, Zi Zhi [d. 314 BCE]. Kuai is the name of the king of Yan [r. 320–312 BCE]. Zi Zhi was the son-in-law of Su Qin [d. 284 BCE]. When Su Qin's younger brother Su Dai went as an emissary from Qi to Yan, he told King Kuai the story of how Yao tried to abdicate rule to Xu You, and so the king was made to abdicate rule to Zi Zhi. Although Zi Zhi then accepted, the people of Yan hated that he had taken over, and all refused to give him their allegiance, which resulted in three years of state-wide chaos. King Xuan of Qi, adopting the plan of Su Dai, raised an army and attacked Yan, with the result that King Kuai of Yan was killed outside the capital, and Zi Zhi was decapitated at court. As such, this brought an end to the state of Yan. How could it have been otherwise? It was because of trying to imitate the outward signs left behind by Yao and Shun that the disaster went so far as this. . . . Lord Bai's name was Sheng; he was the grandson of King Ping of Chu and the son of the crown prince Jian. On the advice of Fei Wuji, King Ping favored a woman from Qin [and her son Chen] and so became estranged from the crown prince, so the crown prince fled to Zheng, where he married a woman of Zheng who gave birth to Sheng. . . . [Later] because the people of Zheng had killed his father, Sheng asked for troops to exact revenge, but despite repeated requests it was not granted. Therefore, he raised troops on his own and led a revolt. When Chu dispatched Gao, Prince of She [*She gongzi* Gao], to attack him, Gao destroyed him, which is why the text says, 'when Duke Bo struggled, he perished.'" *Zhuangzi jishi*, 3: 580–81.
23. *Wufang* also has the sense of "boundlessness," "free of set methods," or "without method"; cf. 2.10, 7.24 (end), and 8.1 (Guo commentary).
24. Cf. 8.1 and 8.3.
25. Cheng Xuanying: "One should resonate with people free of set method, remain aloof, and allow them independent transformation. How could one possibly presume to raise and nurture them as a result of selfconscious intervention [*daidui*]!" *Zhuangzi jishi*, 3: 587.
26. Cf. 6.1.1.

27. The range of possible meanings for *xun* is a problem for translators; see 8.6, note 17. Here, Cheng Xuanying seems to interpret *xun* as pursue [*zhu*]: "Whereas the amount of reputation one may pursue [*xun*] is limitless, the amount one's inborn nature can achieve is limited, so if one uses one's limited potential to pursue ever more reputation, natural principle [*tianli*] is ruined and the amount naturally endowed [*xingming*] lost." *Zhuangzi jishi*, 3: 591.
28. Cf. 14.18.5 and 20.15.
29. Although the text has *chuo*, "trouble." commentary consensus, both traditional and modern, is that this is a phonetic loan for *chuo*, "cease." However, if "trouble," the line would read: "yet his playing the zither and singing were untroubled." *Zhuangzi jishi*, 3: 595.
30. Cheng Xuanying: "*Chuo* 'cease' means 'stop' [*zhi*]. 'Song' should be 'Wey,' for it is a textual error. Kuang was a district in Wey. The route Confucius took on his way from Lu to Wey went through Kuang district, which Yang Hu had attacked and pillaged the people there. Confucius looked like Yang Hu; moreover, Confucius' disciple Yan Ke had been with Yang Hu when he tried pillaged Kuang district and was now again serving as Confucius' driver. When the men of Kuang noticed that Confucius looked like Yang Hu and again saw Yan Ke serving as his driver, they declared that Confucius was Yang Hu, who had come again, and so mustered troops to surround him. But since Confucius was fully aware that fortune or misfortune were a matter of fate, he kept on playing and singing without cease." *Zhuangzi jishi*, 595. See also *Lunyu* (Analects), 9: 2490a and, for a more detailed and somewhat different account, see Sima Qian, *Shiji* (Records of the Grand Historian), *Kongzi shijia* (Hereditary House of Master Kong), 47: 1919.
31. Zilu is the personal name of Zhong You, here addressed simply as "You."
32. Cheng Xuanying: "Mou of Wei was a prince of Wei." *Zhuangzi jishi*, 3: 597. He is further identified in 28.32 as the prince of Zhongshan, Mou of Wei.
33. Cf. 1.6.5.
34. Although Guo Xiang seems to understand *datong* as being an epithet of the Dao, the "great thoroughfare," Cheng Xuanying interprets it and its context differently: "Such wisdom vanishes into unfathomable obscurity, where starting from the ultimate reach of profundity, courses through the profoundly arcane to return to the human realm, where it achieves great pervasive integration [*datong*] with people there." *Zhuangzi jishi*, 3: 602.
35. Shaoling was a district in the ancient state of Yan; Handan was the capital of the state of Zhao.
36. Cf. 24.24.9, Guo commentary.
37. Cheng Xuanying: "Pu is the name of a river, then under the jurisdiction of the Eastern Commandery, present-day Puyang district [Henan]. The 'King of Chu' was King Wei of Chu." *Zhuangzi jishi*, 3: 603.
38. Cheng Xuanying: "The Hao is the name of a stream in Zhongli prefecture in the Huainan region. . . . Where rock cuts across water a *liang* [bridge] is formed, but the text here may also refer to an actual bridge over the Hao River. . . . Fish move about in water, while birds perch on land; each complying with its inherent nature, they all enjoy spontaneous freedom. Master Zhuang was deft at understanding how the innate character of creatures was as it was [*wuqing suoyi*], thus he knew the joy of fish." *Zhuangzi jishi*, 3: 606. The *shu* may be identified with the *Hemiculter leucisculus*, the common sharpbelly or sawbelly of East and Southeast Asia, adult average size about 30 cm./12 in. Although the consensus of modern lexicography has *shu* for the name of the fish, traditional commentators suggest other pronunciations.

39. Cheng Xuanying: "Failing to embody the inherent nature of other creatures, Hui Shi presumptuously [*wang*] challenged him: Master Zhuang, you are not a fish, so wherein can you know the joy of fish?" *Zhuangzi jishi*, 3: 607.
40. Cheng Xuanying: "If I can't know what it is to be a fish because I am not a fish, since you are not me, wherein can you know what it is to be me? But if you are not me yet can still know what it is to be me, although I am not a fish, what prevents me from knowing what it is to be a fish? Master Zhuang turns Master Hui's argument back on him, which allows him to refute his objection." *Zhuangzi jishi*, 3: 607.
41. *An* here is translated "wherein" instead of the more usual "how" because a deliberate pun on the word is involved, which exploits the range of meanings of *an*: content, contentment, safe and secure, where, and wherein. "Wherein" can suggest both "how" and "where": Master Zhuang deliberately (and mischievously) misconstrues Master Hui's questioning so he has him asking, "Where do you know the joy of fish?" which leads to Master Zhuang's concluding remark, "I knew it there above the Hao."

CHAPTER 18

ZHILE [PERFECT JOY]

18.1.1 Is there anywhere in all the world that perfect joy may be had or not? Does any possibility exist to keep one's person alive or not? Only after one has forgotten about being happy shall one's joy be ample, and only after joy is ample shall one's person be preserved [*shencun*].[1] Should one act as if joy may be had? But perfect joy has nothing to do with being happy. Should one act as if joy may not be had? As such, one's person is thereby preserved and one shall be free of worry.

18.1.2 If so, how to do it? What to rely on? What to avoid and what to abide in? What to follow and what to shun? What is to enjoy and what is to dislike?

As for making any of these eight choices, none shall prove sufficient to keep one's person alive. Only by eschewing such choices and instead yielding to whatever one encounters shall one remain whole and safe.

18.2 What all in the world revere are wealth and honor, long life, and good reputation. What they delight in are personal security, rich flavors, good clothes, lovely colors, and fine music. What they despise are poverty and disgrace, early death, and ill repute. What distresses them are failure to achieve an easy life for their persons, failure to obtain rich flavors for their mouths, failure to secure good clothes for their bodies, failure to get lovely colors for their eyes, and failure to obtain fine music for their ears. If they fail to obtain these things, they worry so very much that it scares them. That this all happens for the sake of one's body, is truly foolish!

As far as all these are concerned, whereas losing them does no harm to one's body, obtaining them subjects original nature to harm. But now this is reversed and people think that not getting them is cause for distress—which is why it is deemed "foolish."

18.3.1 Those who would be wealthy exhaust themselves making assiduous effort to amass so much wealth that they can't use it all; though they do this for the body, they yet treat it as an outsider [*wai*].

One who treats the body as an intimate [*nei*] knows nothing but contentment.

18.3.2 Those who would be honored calculate night into day whether their reputations are good or not; though they do this for the body, they yet treat it as a stranger [*shu*].

Therefore, one who treats the body as a familiar [*qin*] finds self-fulfillment within his own person and nowhere else.

18.3.3 From the time one is born, one is afflicted with innate worry, and those with long life, so befuddled, worry all that time yet die not—how very distressing! Though they do this for the body, they yet treat it as distant [*yuan*] from them.

Only by casting life aside may one forget to worry; only by forgetting to worry may one live in joy; only by living in joy may one's body become one's own. And once it is one's own possession, "honor" becomes but the flourishing of self [*worong*].

18.3.4 Though the martyred warrior is seen by all the world as "good," that was not enough to keep him alive, so I know not whether such "goodness" is really good or not, for

> **Though considered good,**
> **It's not good enough to keep one alive,**
> **Though considered not good,**
> **It's good enough to keep others alive.**

"Goodness" has to suit circumstances, thus it not universally beneficial.

18.3.5 Thus it is said,

> **"If loyal remonstrance is unheeded**
> **Yield you thus and contend not."**

Only virtue governed by the mean [*zhongyong*] would be correct here.

18.3.6 Hence,

> **"Zixu so contended to the destruction of his body,[2]**
> **But had he not contended**
> **He would not have been made his reputation."**

So was there truly good in this or not?

Therefore, one should use compromise in the way he conducts himself.[3]

18.4.1 Now, as for how the common lot of mankind behave and what they enjoy, I again know not whether such enjoyment represents true joy or not. But I see that what the common lot of mankind enjoy, they hasten after en masse, so obsessed that it seems they can't stop themselves.

So hastening en masse after enjoyment is no way to avoid death.

18.4.2 Yet what they all call "enjoyment" I neither enjoy nor fail to enjoy.

Free from selfconscious involvement with things, he [Master Zhuang] just allows people to do as they please [*ziwu*].[4]

18.4.3 So is there joy or not? I take unselfconscious action [*wuwei*] to be true joy.

The joy of unselfconscious action means nothing other than freedom from worry.

18.4.4 But this is also what the common lot of mankind also finds distressing. Therefore, I say, perfect joy is to be free of joy, and perfect honor is to be free of honor.

The common lot of mankind finds that the sonorous sound of bells, gongs, and drums provides joy and that flattery and praise provides honor.

18.5.1 Throughout the world, right and wrong is really indeterminable. Nevertheless, it is by acting unselfconsciously that right and wrong may be determined.

I just act unselfconsciously and so allow all people in the world their own right and wrong, and, as each individual commits himself [*ziren*] to his own right and wrong, let these be determined that way.

18.5.2 As for the perfect joy in keeping oneself alive, only unselfconscious effort might just about ensure survival.

If the common folk enjoy sufficiency, this might come close to ensuring one's own survival.

18.5.3 Please let me try to explain:

> **By its unselfconscious effort Heaven stays pure,**
> **By its unselfconscious effort Earth stays serene.**

As for both, one is spontaneously pure and the other spontaneously serene; they don't achieve this by trying to make it so.

18.5.4 Thus it is that these two unselfconscious ones act in perfect accord, and the myriad things all undergo transformation.

As this spontaneous union takes place without intent all things thus experience transformation. But if there were intention to make this happen, at times obstruction would occur.

18.5.5 So dim, so dark,
They emerge from nothing at all!

They all just emerge spontaneously, never is any selfconscious effort involved to make them emerge.

18.5.6 So dim, so dark,

That it has no image!

No image exists for this unselfconscious force.[5]

18.5.7 And the myriad things in their variety and number

All procreate compliant to that unselfconscious force.

All just procreate themselves.

18.5.8 Thus I say, "Because Heaven and Earth act unselfconsciously, nothing fails to be done.

If they acted selfconsciously, there would be failure.

18.5.9 But who among men can attain unselfconsciousness?

If unselfconsciousness were attained, there would be no trying to be happy and perfect joy would be had.

18.6 When the wife of Master Zhuang died, Master Hui went to visit the bereaved, to find Master Zhuang then sitting on the floor with his legs stretched out, drumming on a tile basin and singing.

18.7 Master Hui said, "She lived with you, raised your children, and was your old wife, so it is bad enough that you don't lament her passing, yet you go on to drum on a tile basin and sing—is that not really going too far!"

18.8 Master Zhuang replied, "It is not so. When she first died, how could I not feel grief! But when I considered her beginning, originally she had no life; not only had she no life, she had no body; not only had she no body, she had no pneuma. Then, there mixed in the dim and dark a change occurred and her pneuma existed; her pneuma underwent change and her body existed; her body underwent change and she had life, and now with another change it led to her death. This is just like the way spring, summer, autumn, and winter progress through the four seasons. Now she rests in peace in the grand chamber of her tomb, so if, sobbing and blubbering, I had gone on lamenting her death, I should have thought that I had no understanding of fate; therefore, I stopped."

As long as he had not understood this, he felt grief, but once he realized the truth of it, he stopped. This was how he instructed those subject to emotions—that by this teaching they should reach the ultimate truth [*zhili*] involved and thereby unburden themselves of such entanglements.

18.9 While Disjointed Decrepit [Zhili Shu][6] was accompanying Slippery Decrepit [Gujie Shu][7] to take in the sights at the Mound of the Arcane Lord [Mingbo zhi qiu] and the Wastes of Kunlun [Kunlun zhi xu], where the Yellow Thearch took his ease,[8] suddenly a willow sprouted from his left elbow, which seems to have startled and annoyed him.[9]

18.10 Disjointed Decrepit asked, "Do you find it annoying?"

18.11 Slippery Decrepit replied, "Not at all—why should it annoy me! Life is something borrowed. That which is borrowed so it may produce life is but dust and dirt, and death follows life as does night the day. Now while you and I have been observing how transformation works, it so happened that

transformation caught up with me, so why should I go on being annoyed at that?"

Such a one might always initially appear subject to emotion, but then he grasps perfect principle and thus casts it aside. As it has been said, the self in its original nature is free from emotion, thus it feels no anxiety, but if subject to emotion, it consequently alienates itself from the realm of detachment and emancipation and instead gets lost and comes to grief in the land of sorrow or happiness.

18.12 On his way to Chu, Master Zhuang happened to see a hollow skull, dried up but still intact. Tapping it with his horse whip, he then asked, "Was it that greed for life made so you act against the principles of things that you came to this? Or did it happen that with the loss of your state you were put to death by an executioner's axe and so came to this? Or did you engage in evil ways and were so ashamed of the disgrace you brought upon your parents, wife and children that you came to this? Or did you suffer so much cold and hunger that you came to this? Or did your springs and autumns so mount up that they brought you to this?"

18.13 When he had finished speaking, he took the skull, made it his pillow, and lay down. In the middle of the night, the skull appeared in a dream and said, "The way you go on is like a sophist's discourse, and as for what you say, it all concerns entanglements suffered by the living—once dead there is none of this. Would you like to hear what the dead have to say?"

18.14 Master Zhuang replied, "Of course!"

18.15 The skull then said, "Once dead there are no rulers above, no subjects below, as well as no duties demanded by the four seasons, so one's springs and autumns last as do those of Heaven and Earth—even the pleasure enjoyed by a south-facing monarch can be no better than this."

18.16 Master Zhuang, incredulous, replied, "If I had the Director of Destinies [Siming] bring your body back to life, provide you with flesh and bones, and return to you your parents, wife, children, and the neighbors whom you knew, you would want that, wouldn't you?"

18.17 The skull sternly glared at him, knitted its brows, and said, "How could I cast aside the pleasures of a south-facing monarch and instead have to deal again with the toils of the living!"

According to an old saying, Master Zhuang loved death and hated life, but this is absolutely wrong! If it were so, what could he have meant by saying they were equal? What he meant by "equal" was that when alive, one should be content with life, and when dead, he should be content with death. Once one's feelings about life and death are one and the same, he shall be free from worrying about death while in the midst of life—that's all there is to it! This is what Master Zhuang meant.

18.18 When Yan Yuan was going to travel east to Qi, Confucius looked worried about it, so Zigong left his mat and inquired, "May your humble disciple

dare to ask, this going east to Qi makes you, Master, seem worried about it—why is that?"

18.19.1 Confucius replied, "How excellent that you ask about it! In the past Master Guan had a saying of which I really approve: 'Of bags, small ones can't contain something large; of ropes, short ones can't draw up water from deep wells.' In like manner, we take it that one's fated endowment has a particular composition, and one's physical form is suited for certain things, both of which may neither be diminished nor increased.

This is why one must comply with them—that's all there is to it!

18.19.2 I fear that Hui [Yan Yuan] will tell the Marquis of Qi about the Way of Yao, Shun, and the Yellow Thearch, and then add to this accounts of the Fire Maker [Suiren] and the Divine farmer [Shennong]. The Marquis will then try to attain to what they were within himself but will fail; failing, he will become perplexed, and once perplexed, he will kill.

Once he tries to attain to it within his own limits but fails, he will seek it outside them. If one renounces the limits within which he is bound and instead tries to attain to something outside them, how could he not but become perplexed!

18.20.1 Is it you alone who has not heard? Long ago, when a sea bird landed just outside the capital of Lu,[10] the Marquis of Lu went out in a chariot to welcome it and then feasted it in the ancestral temple, at which the *Nine Accords* [Jiu Shao] were played for the music and Great Sacrifice [Tailao] animals were provided for the meat. But the bird looked on with eyes muddled with worry and grief, daring not to eat one morsel of meat or imbibe one cup of drink, and so in three days was dead. This was to use what nourishes oneself to nourish a bird and not use bird nourishment to nourish a bird. To nourish a bird with bird nourishment, one had better let it roost in deep forests, roam amidst islets, float on rivers and lakes, feed on loach and chub, follow flights of its fellows to rest with them, and stay wherever it pleases [*weishe*]. Just the sound of the human voice is hateful to it, so how could cope with such hubbub and clamor as that! As for the "Pool of Shan Xian" [Xian Chi] or the *Nine Accords*, perform them out in the wilds of Dongting, and when birds hear them, they will fly away, wild beasts hear them, they will flee, fish hear them, they will go deep under, but when crowds of people hear them, they gather in circles upon circles to appreciate them. Fish stay in water to live, but if humans were to stay in water they would die. It is certainly since they differ so much from one another that their likes and dislikes are so different. This was why the sages of yore did not regard their capabilities as equal and did not assign people the same tasks.

They let each comply with his own innate nature [*qing*].

18.20.2 Names went no further than what was actually so and righteousness was enacted with suitability. This resulted in what is referred to as "things going smoothly and blessings sustained."

Because of such actuality and suitability, things went smoothly. Because personal nature was always fulfilled, blessings were sustained.[11]

18.21.1 When Master Lie while on a trip[12] was having a meal by the side of the road, he happened to see a hundred-year-old skull. He pulled aside the weeds, pointed at it, and said "As only you and I know, you have never died and I have never lived.

Each is happy with what is encountered.

18.21.2 So have you ever really been sad? Have I ever really been happy?"

As for what really constitutes happiness and sadness, there have never been fixed conditions.

18.22.1 How many species exist [*zhong you ji*]? [13]

The number of species [*zhongshu*] subject to change and transformation is beyond count.

18.22.2 Once access to water is had, this starts their continuity [*ji*].[14] Reaching the margin of water and soil, this produces frog's clothes, but when generated on mounds and heights, this produces plantains. When plantains have access to rich soil, they become crow's feet. The roots of crow's feet become grubs, and their leaves become butterflies. Butterflies last but a short time, then change into bugs that live under the stove. These are of exuviate form whose name is "camel cricket." After a thousand days, camel crickets become birds whose name is "dried leftover bones." The spittle of dried leftover bones becomes simi bugs, which then become "vinegar eaters." Midges are generated from vinegar eaters, locusts are generated from dayflies, and dwarf mosquitoes are generated from fireflies. When ferns couple with bamboo that long have not shooted, they produce green placid bugs. 18.22.8 Green placid bugs produce leopards, leopards produce horses, horses produce humans, and humans again revert to the activating force [*ji*]. The myriad things all emerge from the activating force, and all go back into it.

This addresses how the unitary pneuma [*yiqi*] results in myriads of physical forms, and though these are subject to change and transformation, it itself is free from life and death.

Notes

1. Cf. Richard John Lynn, *Laozi*, section 7; Richard John Lynn, *The Classic of the Way and Virtue*, 63: "He [the sage] puts aside his person, yet his person is preserved. Is this not because he is utterly free of self-interest?" To which Wang Bi adds the comment: "To be utterly free of self-interest [*wusi*] means to make no selfconscious effort for one's sake. Such a person will always find himself in front and his self preserved."

2. See appendix A, "Prefaces and Postscript," note 26.
3. Cheng Xuanying: "King Fuchai of Wu [ruled 495–473 BCE] was dissolute and unprincipled, so when Zixu loyally remonstrated with him, he met with ruthless execution, but if he had not so remonstrated, his reputation for loyalty would not have been made. Therefore, whether to remonstrate or not, whether it is good or not, is truly indeterminable." *Zhuangzi jishi*, 3: 611.
4. Cf. 13.1.1.–13.1.3, Guo commentary.
5. Cheng Xuanying: "The creative transformative power [*zaohua*] of the two exemplars creates things unselfconsciously. It is so dim and dark and so all mixed together that it is impossible to fathom. As for finding where things come from, no one knows the course of it. Try to discern its image, and one finds that there is absolutely nothing to see." *Zhuangzi jishi*, 3: 613. Cf. *Laozi*, section 21; Lynn, *The Classic of the Way and Virtue*, 86: "The Dao as such is but dim, is but dark." [Wang Bi:] " 'Dim' and 'dark' refer to the appearance of that which is formless and not attached to anything." Dark, oh, dim, oh, but within it some image is there. Dim, oh, dark, oh, but within it something is there." [Wang Bi:] "It [the Dao] originates things thanks to its formlessness and brings things to completion thanks to its freedom from attachments. The myriad things are originated and completed in this way yet don't know how it happens." By contrast, both the text of the *Zhuangzi* and remarks by Guo Xiang and Cheng Xuanying declare that the creative power of Heaven and Earth, the Dao itself, does not "cause" anything—rather, things transform themselves. Nothing is there to see—nothing is there at all.
6. Cf. 4.44.1.
7. Cf. 24.16.2.
8. Cheng Xuanying: "*Zhili* [disjointed] means separation from the body; thanks to enlightenment one becomes oblivious to one's physical body. *Gujie* is the same as *Guji* [slippery, elusive], and means elusively stand apart from; one becomes oblivious to conscious understanding once one has cast it aside. Wishing to express the frivolity and deceit of declining age the term 'decrepit' [*shu*] is used here. 'Arcane' [*ming*] means 'obscure' [*an*]; 'lord' [*bo*] means 'leader' [zhang], and *kunlun* means the human body. That is to say, it is the abstusity [*yaoming*] of divine wisdom [*shenzhi*] that makes one fit to be the leader of men, and such arcane profundity [*xuanyuan*] of Kunlun is found nearby within one's own human body. The irregularity of 'mound' and 'wastes' refers to the way one looks down on the common ways of the world, but the holy lord, Yellow Thearch, when casting the radiance of his wisdom over his domain, turned off his mind, gave wisdom a rest, and entrusted himself to the commonplace, which happens when one grasps the profound arcana of the perfect Dao. As such, this isn't at all distant, which is why the text uses this story of the two decrepit ones to get the meaning across." *Zhuangzi jishi*, 3: 616.
9. Cheng Xuanying: "The willow is a tree that grows easily, and such a tree here symbolizes a coffin, so it serves as an omen of approaching death. As the two decrepit ones come roaming to Kunlun in order to observe the workings of change and transformation, all of a sudden the left elbow of the one sprouts a willow, which so startles him that he seems inclined to find it annoying." *Zhuangzi jishi*, 3: 616.
10. Cf. 19.50.
11. Cheng Xuanying: "It is by complying with actuality that names evoke what is really so. Reputation thus should not exceed the reality of one's being and no attempt should be made to pursue reputation beyond that. Moreover, righteousness as such should be appropriate, that is, it should be enacted provisionally and adjusted according to circumstances, for it should stay within the limits of one's original nature and no attempt should be made to abandon oneself so to imitate others." *Zhuangzi jishi*, 3: 623.

12. This same passage, with variations, occurs in the *Liezi* (Sayings of Master Lie); *Liezi jishi*, 1: 11–18.
13. Two traditions of interpretation have argued over this brief question for centuries; one exemplified by Guo Xiang and Cheng Xuanying takes *zhong* as *zhonglei* (species) and *ji* as "how many"; the other regards *ji* (how many) as a variant of *ji* (activating force, incipiency, spring)—that is, the potential spring of life that inheres in things. This tradition begins with Sima Biao, who glosses *ji* as *zhaozhen* (portent), the subtle and mysterious incipiency that sages discern in the workings of Heaven and Earth; see *Zhuanzi jishi*, 3: 625. However, the latter was the minority view during premodern times and came to prominence only in the modern era, with the likes of Ma Xulun (1884–1970), in *Zhuangzi yizheng* (Documentary evidence for meanings in the *Zhuangzi*), in which he glosses *ji* as *zhong zhi jiwei er wanwu suoyou shengzhe* ("the most minute of seeds from which the myriad things are generated"), 18: 6a; and Hu Shi (1891–1962), in *Xian Qin mingxue shi* (History of logic in the pre-Qin era), 113, where he glosses *ji* as *jingwei de yuanzi* ("most miniscule atom") or *peiya* ("germ/gemmule"). Reading *zhong* as "seed" instead of "species" is also characteristic of this tradition.
14. The "seed" and "activating force" tradition of exegesis interprets *ji* (continuity) as some sort of water plant; see *Zhuangzi jishi*, 3: 625. Identification of the names of plants, insects, and animals that follow in this passage by commentators results in much contradiction and controversy, none of which seems to enhance understanding of the philosophical understanding of the passage as a whole. My own renditions are thus understandably rather arbitrary. However, for a more fanciful and witty rendition of the names, see Victor Mair's efforts in *Wandering on the Way: Early Daoist Tales and Parables of Chuang Tzu*, 172–73.

CHAPTER 19

DASHENG [UNDERSTAND LIFE]

19.1.1 One who understands the conditions of life [*sheng zhi qing*] strives not after that which one's life lacks the means to provide.

That which life lacks the means to provide are things outside one's allotted capacity.

19.1.2 One who understands the conditions of fate [*ming zhi qing*] strives not after that which one's intelligence can do nothing.

That about which one's intelligence can do nothing are matters beyond the reach of one's fate.

19.1.3 To nurture the body, the first prerequisite is to tend to its material needs, but even though material things exceed need, the body is not nurtured.

One should stay within one's allotted capacity, for then such material things are in balance with one's life, which as such enjoys sufficiency—but any excess does harm.

19.1.4 To maintain life, the first prerequisite is not to let it depart the body, but even when it has not departed, life may still be lost.

When efforts to safeguard one's body go to extremes, life is thus lost.

19.1.5 The coming of life can't be rejected, and its going can't be stopped.

Since it is not under the control of the self, it is useless to be concerned about it while it lasts

19.1.6 How very sad! The worldly thinks that nurturing the body is up to preserving life!

Therefore, the more nurtured, the more it is lost.

19.1.7 Yet nurturing the body is actually not up to preserving life.

The more substantially one nurtures it, the closer it brings one to the land of death.

19.1.8 Thus what is there in all the world worth trying!

Nothing would be better than just to let things go and trust to what happens.[1]

19.1.9 As for things though not worth trying yet one can't help doing, their doing is not to be avoided.

All spontaneous actions in accord with one's natural capacity emerge from the seat of ultimate principles, thus one can't avoid doing them. This is why one who excels at nurturing life complies and trusts to them.[2]

19.2.1 If one wishes to avoid so tending to the body, nothing is better than to abandon worldly concerns. Once worldly concerns are abandoned, one is free of entanglements; once free of entanglements, one is true and equitable [*zhengping*]; once true and equitable, one is reborn therewith; once reborn one is almost complete [*ji*].

"Reborn" means daily renewal. Once granted daily renewal, one's natural endowment may be completely realized.

19.2.2 But why is it worthwhile to abandon worldly affairs and why worthwhile to discard concerns for life? Once one has abandoned worldly affairs, the body is no longer strained; once one has discarded concerns for life, the vital essence is no longer depleted.

This is why one abandons and discards them.

19.2.3 With the body whole and safe and the vital essence restored, one becomes one with Heaven.

All is done without intent.[3]

19.2.4 Heaven and Earth are the father and mother of the myriad things.

It is because they act utterly impartially [*wusuo pianwei*] that they can treat the myriad things as their children.

19.2.5 Fusing together, they form physical bodies; separating, they form new beginnings.

Such forming occurs whatever condition things are in, for no constant condition ever exists for them.

19.2.6 If body and vital essence are not depleted, this means that one can change.

That is, such a one bonds perfectly with transformation.

19.2.7 As vital essence is rendered ever more vital, such a one returns to succor his natural endowment [*xiangtian*].

He returns to succor his natural endowment.[4]

19.3.1 Master Lie asked Pass Director Yin [Guan Yin],[5] "The Perfected one moves submerged in water yet drowns not,[6]

Since the mind of such a one is void, he can handle all actualities.

19.3.2 steps through fire yet suffers no heat, and conducts himself [*xing*] as superior to the myriad folk yet trembles not.

Conforming perfectly to circumstances, there is absolutely nothing that such a one can't do. But these are not things that ordinary folk may hope to make possible.

19.3.3 May I ask how he attains to this?"

19.4.1 Pass Director Yin replied, "It is a matter of safeguarding one's pure pneuma, not something exemplified by knowledge, skill, courage, or resolution. Sit down and I shall tell you about it. Though everyone has a distinct form or appearance, voice or countenance, all are still people, so what might distance one person from another?

Only one free of conscious mind may so distance himself.

19.4.2 And what might suffice to advance one to the front? For there is nothing here other than personal appearance [*se*].

But since they have the same sort of personal appearance, nothing suffices here for one to attain precedence over another.

19.4.3 As such, a person is created when no form exists and ceases to be when all means to transform are gone.

One always moves toward this absolute limit.

19.4.4 Once had this just goes on to exhaust its limits, so how can a person pause somewhere within it!

As it proceeds to its ultimate end, it may not be controlled by anyone.

19.4.5 But one who manages to stay within an unexceeded capacity,

Such a one stays within his received allotted capacity.

19.4.6 conceals himself in the endless thread of life [*ji*],

Such a one arcanely renews himself every day along with change and transformation.

19.4.7 roams throughout the myriad things from beginning to end,

"From beginning to end" means the ultimate extent of things.

19.4.8 is one with his original nature,

Embellishment would result in duplicity.

19.4.9 nourishes his pneuma,

Such a one does not use it consciously.

19.4.10 and remains united with his virtue,

Such a one does not separate himself from his original nature for the sake of others.

19.4.11 as such he stays in step with the creation of things.

The myriad things are all created with spontaneity.

19.4.12 If you can be like this, safeguarding of your natural endowment shall be complete and your spirit shall remain free of breaches—how then could any external thing find a way into it!"

19.5.1 When a drunk falls out of a carriage,[7] though it is going fast he does not die. He has the same bones and joints of others, but when it comes to getting hurt, he is different from them, for his spirit is perfectly whole. He was not even aware he was riding in a carriage, so when he fell out, he was not aware of that either. Alarm for life and death did not enter his breast, which is why such a one could be so at odds with things and yet feel no fear. Since he could achieve such perfect wholeness just thanks to drink,

It was because he was drunk that he lost awareness; he did not become unselfconscious [*wuxin*] spontaneously.

19.5.2 how much the better could one achieve such perfect wholeness from Heaven! The sage hides himself in Heaven, thus none can harm him.

He does not sneak looks out from within his own natural capacity, which is why the text says "hide."

19.5.3 One bent on revenge does not break a Ganjiang or a Moye.

Although a Ganjiang or a Moye [famous swords of antiquity] was used by his enemy, one bent on revenge does not try to break it, because he is free from selfconscious mind.

19.5.4 Even someone bad-tempered feels no resentment toward tiles that happen to fall on him.

Although tiles fall and keep hitting him, such a one never feels resentment, because he is utterly impartial.

19.5.5 This is because for such a one, everything in the world is equal.

Whenever inequality occurs, it is because of partiality.

19.5.6 Therefore, to avoid disorder brought about by wars of aggression and to avoid punitive policy involving mass slaughter, one should follow this Dao.

The Dao as it bears on freedom from prejudicial feeling is indeed great!

19.6.1 Initiate not what humans deem natural [*tian*] but instead initiate the natural in one's natural endowment [*tian*].

To know without reflection, this is what "initiate the natural" means; response only after consciously knowing, this is what "initiates the human" means. As such, "initiate the natural" signifies activation of one's original nature, and "initiates the human" signifies implementation of conscious knowledge.

19.6.2 Whereas one who initiates the natural invests life with virtue,

With activation of original nature, one handles people with perfect appropriateness and so is unmindful of doing anything to excess. This is what "invest life with virtue" means.

19.6.3 one who initiates the human thieves from life.

The way conscious knowledge is used is that one seeks it following a response to something, which belabored one endlessly. This is what "thieves from life" means.[8]

19.6.4 Suppress not the natural, and be not negligent toward the people,

If one acts only in conformity with his inherent nature, principles of human relationships [*renli*] too shall be kept whole and safe.

10.6.5 for by doing so it will just about restore the common folk to authenticity.

Why disasters visit the common folk and why inauthenticity arises always lie with the conscious use of knowledge, and never with the activation of original nature.

19.7.1 On his way to Chu, Zhongni [Confucius] saw when he was coming out through a wood a hunchback catching cicadas as if he were picking them by hand.[9] Zhongni said, "How skilled you are! Do you have a special way of doing this?"

He replied, "I do have a special way: Over five or six months, if I can balance two pellets without their falling, those I lose will be very few,

By balancing two pellets on top of a pole, this had him stop paying attention to how good his hand control was; consequently during that time, his losses were not more than a very few.

19.9.2 if I can balance three without their falling, those I lose will be one in ten,

Those lost were even fewer.

19.9.3 and if five without their falling, it is as if I were picking them by hand.

He reached such perfection in paying no attention that he no longer lost any.

19.9.4 Setting my body like a tree trunk with its limbs lopped off, I hold my arms like the branches of a dead tree.

Such was the perfection of his immobility.

19.9.5 Regardless of how great Heaven and Earth are and how numerous the myriad things, I am only aware of the cicada's wings. Perfectly free of agitation, I don't let any of the myriad things take the place of the cicada's wings, so how could I possibly not succeed!"

It is by putting all else out of mind that he achieves this.[10]

19.10 Confucius then turned and addressed his disciples, "With attention undivided one becomes focused in spirit—how well this applies to yon hunchback elder!"

19.11.1 Yan Yuan [Yan Hui] asked Confucius, "Once when I was crossing the gorge at Goblet Deep, the ferryman handled the boat as if someone divine.[11] So I asked him, 'Is it possible to learn how to handle a boat.' And he replied, 'A good swimmer can with practice.

This speaks to the fact that though a person might have it by original nature, he still must repeatedly practice it, for only then can he do it.

19.11.2 And if a diver, even though he has never seen a boat he could immediately do it.'

"Diver" means one who can dive like a diver duck to the bottom of the water.

19.11.3 But when I asked him why this was so, he would not tell me. May I dare ask what did this mean?"

19.12.1 Zhongni replied, "That a good swimmer can do it with practice is because he forgets all about the water.

By practicing one fulfills his nature; so it then becomes spontaneous.

19.12.2 As for a diver who has never seen a boat yet immediately can handle one, he would regard a gorge as if it were a hillock and the capsizing of a boat as if it were just a cart rolling backwards.

Since such a one regards a gorge as if it were a hillock, if he sees a boat capsizing in a gorge, for him it is like a cart rolling backward down a slope.

19.12.3 Innumerable capsizings and backward rolling might appear before him yet would fail to enter his chamber [*she*].

Though capsizings and backward rollings be many, he still is not mindful [*jinghuai*] of them, since his inborn nature is used to them.[12]

19.12.4 So what venture would not leave him composed!

Whatever such a one encounters, he is always composed.

19.12.5 When aiming for the sake of a tile, one shows off his skill; when aiming for the sake of a belt buckle, one is apprehensive; and when aiming for the sake of yellow gold, one is flustered.[13]

As what is at stake increases in value, the more one's mind covets it.

19.12.6 Though one's skill always remains the same, once something is coveted, importance shifts to the external, and once focus is on anything external, one's inner being becomes inept."

If one wishes to nourish life and keep one's inner being whole and safe, the only way to do this is to shun all coveting and placing of value on things.

19.13 When Tian Kaizhi[14] had an audience with Duke Wei of Zhou,[15] the Duke said to him, "I've heard that Zhu Shen studies life and that you, my master, have associated with him, what did you actually hear from him?"

To study life, such effort is just and proper.

19.14 Tian Kaizhi replied, "Since I then just wielded a broom and took care of the gate and courtyard, what could I have ever heard from the master!"

19.15 Duke Wei said, "Don't be so modest, Master Tian, for I wish to hear what he said."

19.16 Kaizhi replied, "I heard the master say, 'One good at nourishing life is like a shepherd who when he sees a laggard whips it.' "

19.17 Duke Wei then said, "What did he mean?"

19.18 Tian Kaizhi replied, "In Lu there was a certain Lone Leopard [Danbao] who lived among the crags, drank only water, and shared not in the advantages of living with others. Even at seventy he still had the complexion of an infant, but unfortunately he met a hungry tiger which killed and ate him. And as for a certain Zhang Yi, there was not a high gate or lowered door

curtain he did not run around to, yet at forty he contracted an internal fever and died.[16] Whereas Lone Leopard nourished his inner being but a tiger ate his outer self, Zhang Yi nourished his outer self but allowed sickness to attack his inner being. So these two fellows both failed to whip the laggard in them.

One who safeguards only one side of things so that it even exceeds the principles involved lags behind when it comes to reconciling and unifying both. So "to whip the laggard" means to oust what lags behind in him.

19.19.1 As Zhongni said,

Don't withdraw and then go on to hide yourself,

Hiding away already deals with one's inner being, so to withdraw even more exceeds what withdrawal should be.

19.19.2 Don't engage and then go on to display yourself,

Engaging already deals with one's outer self, so to engage even more exceeds what engagement should be.

19.19.3 But stand as a dead tree right in the middle.

Like a dead tree, unselfconsciously find what is just and proper, for this is such a stand.

19.19.4 If one is successful at these three, his repute will surely be all it should be.

His repute will be all it should be, for it will match who he really is.

19.19.5 The road is feared when just one out of ten might be killed, so fathers and sons, older and younger brothers warn one another that they must only set out on journeys in good-sized armed groups. Don't you even know this! But what one should also take warning about is when one is on his mat in sleeping attire or when eating and drinking. That people don't realize they should take warning about these is a great mistake!"

When just one out of ten might be killed, people greatly fear it, but when it comes to the harm caused by carnal desire, though any act might inevitably lead to the land of death yet none fail to risk it. As such, this is the worst kind of mistake.

19.20 The master of sacrifices to ancestors attired in black ceremonial robes approaches the piggery and addresses the hogs, "Why should you hate death? I shall feed you for three months, fulfill precepts for ten days, fast for three days, make you cushions of white rushes, and place your shoulders and rumps on carved cutting boards. Will you let this happen?" If planning for the hogs, he would say that it would be better to feed them with chaff and leave them in the pigpen. If planning for himself, he would say that for the time being, may my life enjoy the honors of official carriage and cap, and when I die, let me be borne on a ornamented hearse and lie in a canopied coffin—this is what he would have happen. If planning on behalf of the hogs, he would dispense

with such things, while planning for himself, he would have them, but how is he different from the hogs?"

Desire for enrichment leads to death of the body; here the principle is the same for both, for no difference exists between man and beast.

19.21 When Duke Huan was hunting in the marshes, with Guan Zhong as his driver,[17] he saw a demon. The Duke then grasped Guan's hand and said, "Father Zhong, what did you see?" But he replied, "I did not see anything."

19.22 After the Duke returned, he became so ill with worry and depression that for several days he did not go out. Huangzi Gaoao, one of the learned of Qi,[18] addressed him, "The Duke is but harming himself—how could a demon ever harm him! If the pneuma becomes so saturated with resentment that it disperses and recovers not, it becomes deficient. If it rises and does not abate, it makes one prone to anger; if it abates and does not rise, it makes one prone to forget; if it neither rises nor abates, it centers in the body and blocks the mind, and this makes one ill."

19.23 Duke Huan then said, "So be it, but do demons exist?"

19.24 He replied, "They do exist. In muddy puddles are found treaders [*lü*], and at stoves are found topknots [*jie*]. Thunderclaps [*leiting*] lurk in rubbish indoors, while below at the northeast side, doublets [*beia*] and fishy bugs [*guilong*] make this their place to hop. And below to the northwest, this is where overfull yangs [*yiyang*] dwell. In water are no-shapes [*wangxiang*], on hills horned dogs [*shen*], on mountains one-footers [*kui*], in the countryside wanderers [*panghuang*], and in marshes winders [*weiyi*]."[19]

19.25 The Duke then said, "May I ask what winders look like?"

19.26 Huangzi replied, "Winders are as big around as a wheel hub and as tall as a cart shaft is long. It wears a purple robe and a red cap. This is a creature that hates to hear the rumbling noise of chariot wheels, for if it does it holds its head in its two hands and stands still. To see it means that to be on the verge of becoming a hegemon."

19.27 Duke Huan happily laughed out loud and said, "That is the one I saw." Thereupon he adjusted his robe and cap and had Huangzi sit down with him. Before the day was over, his illness had left him without his being aware of it.

This passage explains, on the one hand, that if beset by worry, one thus endangers his life, this is due to ignorance, and, on the other, when disaster is avoided and original nature thus fulfilled, this occurs because one has penetrated the principles of things.

19.28 Ji Xingzi, who was rearing a fighting cock for the king,[20]

19.29 was asked after ten days, "Is the cock all ready?" he replied, "Not yet, for just now it is still full of empty pride and dependent on its pneuma."

19.30 After another ten days, he was again asked but said, "Not yet, for it still reacts to echoes and shadows."

19.31 After another ten days, he was again asked but said, "Not yet, for its look is still a glower, pumped up as it is with pneuma."

19.32 After yet another ten days, he was again asked, at which he said, "It is actually just about ready, for although other cocks might crow, they have no effect on it. To look at it, it seems a cock made of wood. Since its virtue is now perfectly realized, other cocks dare not answer but turn tail and run away."

This passage explains how nourishing may reach perfection, but even though such a one might have no external match, how much the better if perfection were spontaneously achieved [*ziquan*]!

19.33 Where Confucius was enjoying the sights at Lüliang[21] the waterfall hung down eighty yards, its spray billowed out for some forty tricents miles, so no tortoise, alligator, fish, or turtle could swim there. When he saw a brave man swimming in it, he thought he wanted to die because of some distress, so he sent his disciples to line up along the course of the current to rescue him. But after going several hundred paces, he just came out, and, with hair all disheveled, walked along singing as he sauntered there below the embankment.

19.34 Keeping pace with him, Confucius asked, "I first thought you were a demon but when I looked closely you turned out to be a man. May I presume to ask, do you have a special technique to tread water?"

19.35.1 The man replied, "No, I have no special technique. I began with what I first was [*gu*], matured with my original nature [*xing*], and became fully realized as my natural endowment [*ming*] would have it. Going under along with the swirls [*qi*] and emerging along with the whirls [*mi*],

To spin under as a grinding wheel goes around is what "swirl" [*qi*] means; to let oneself turn in circles and spurt out is what whirl [*mi*] means.

19.35.2 I follow the way the water goes and don't force myself on it.

He yields to the water and follows no intention of his own [*buren ji*].

19.35.3 This is how I tread it."

19.36 Confucius then asked, "What do you mean by 'I began with what I first was, matured with my original nature, and became fully realized as my natural endowment would have it?' "

19.37 He replied, "I was born on the land and so felt safe on the land; this is what I mean by 'what I first was.' I matured in water and so felt safe in water; this was what I mean by 'original nature.' I know not why I am as I am; this is what I mean by 'natural endowment.' "

This passage explains that as people have particular skills, if one manages to realize his skill and trusts to it, none in the whole world would suffer hardship. As such, free from hardship, one may tread the path that leads to live life to the full [*shengsheng*], and what might one then venture to do that is not a complete success!

19.38 When Woodworker Qing [Zi Qing][22] carved a bell stand and had finished it, those who saw it were so amazed that it seemed as if it were something demonic and divine. Then the Marquis of Lu went to see it and so asked him, "What artful technique did you use to make it?"

It did not seem as if it had been made by man.

19.39.1 He replied, "I am just an artisan, so what artful technique could I have! However, there is one thing about it, for when going to make a bell stand, I never risk wasting my pneuma and am sure to fast in order to still my mind. Once I fast for three days, I no longer have any concern for congratulation and reward, rank and emolument. When I have fasted for five days, I no longer have any concern for praise or disapproval, skill or bungling. Having fasted seven days, I become so immovable that I utterly forget I have four limbs and a physical body. By this time the court no longer exists for me,

Once one looks upon the court as if it did not exist, all thought about expectation and yearning ceases.

19.39.2 and my skill becomes so concentrated that all external distractions vanish.

All matters extraneous to one's original nature are discarded.

19.39.3 After that, I go among mountain trees. where I carefully examine their inherent natures, for it is only one perfect in body that allows me to see a bell stand in it. To such a one alone will I set my hand; otherwise I give it up.

He makes sure to select only one whose material is exactly right.

19.39.4 As such, I merge my natural endowment [*tian*] with its natural endowment [*tian*].

He allows no separation between the natural endowments [*ziran*] involved.

19.39.5 The reason why people suspect that my device is divine lies exactly here!"

It is because he complies completely with the marvelousness of the object that people suspect that it is made by a demon or the divine.

19.40 When Dongye Ji was demonstrating his driving to Duke Zhuang,[23] his advances and withdrawals were as straight as a marking line, and his swerves to left and right were as round as a compass curve. Duke Zhuang thought that even Zaofu[24] could not have surpassed him, so ordered him to go around in circles one hundred times and then return to him.

19.41 After Yan He[25] happened to come across him, he came in to see the Duke and said, "Ji's horses will break down." But the Duke kept his own counsel and did not reply.

19.42 A short time later, when they actually did break down and Ji had returned, the Duke asked, "How did you know it would happen?"

19.43 Yan He replied, "Though his horses had used up all their strength, he still sought more from them; this is why I said, 'they will break down.'"

This clarifies how the perfectly appropriate may not be exceeded.

19.44.1 The way Artisan Chui[26] scribed his marks was better than if using compass and square, for his fingers transformed so in harmony with things that he did not have to think about it. As such, his numinous tower [*lingtai*] kept its integrity and remained unfettered.

Despite Artisan Chui's great skill, he still conformed to compass and square, which speaks to the ease with which he complied with things.[27]

19.44.2 One forgets the feet when shoes fit perfectly, and forgets the waist when belt fits perfectly.

When the body in all its parts is fitted perfectly, one forgets all about the body.

19.44.3 When consciousness forgets all about right and wrong, the mind finds perfect fit.

Right and wrong are born from nothing other than such lack of fitness.[28]

19.44.4 When no change occurs in the inner self and one abides [*cong*] not by anything external, one so fits that he enjoys synchronicity with things [*shihui*].

If one is content with whatever is encountered, no such change or abiding ever occurs.

19.44.5 To begin with a perfect fit and never experience the absence of perfect fit is fitness had when one forgets all about being fitted perfectly.

As long as one is conscious of being fitted perfectly, one still is not quite fitted perfectly.

19.45 There was a certain Sun Xiu who, paying a call at his gate, complained to Pian Ziqing,[29] "Whatever village have I lived in has never called me uncultivated, and whatever trouble I have faced I have never been cited for lack of bravery. Nevertheless, fields I plant never have a good year, and rulers I have served have never done me any good. Though I am cast from country villages and driven from district towns, what crime have I committed against Heaven? Why have I encountered such a fate as this?"

19.46.1 Master Pian replied, "Is it you alone who has not heard of how the Perfected one conducts himself? He forgets all about his liver and gall bladder and is utterly unmindful of his ears and eyes,

Such a one unselfconsciously [*an*] gives himself over to spontaneity.

19.46.2 and, utterly aimless, wanders about beyond the dust and dirt,

All that is not one's true nature is dust and dirt.

19.46.3 enjoys spontaneous freedom with tasks from which he is utterly disengaged.

Anything done spontaneously is always a task from which one is utterly disengaged.

19.46.4 Such behavior is what is meant by 'He acts, yet does not make them dependent.

He just lets them follow their original natures; it is not to make them dependent that he acts.

19.46.5 He matures them, yet he is not their steward.'

He just allows them to mature themselves; it is not to be their steward that he matures them.[30]

19.46.6 Now you dress up your intelligence to amaze the stupid and morally cultivate yourself to show up the disgraced, parading such clarity and brilliance that you seem to be walking around holding up the sun and moon.[31] You have managed to keep your whole body intact, possess all your nine orifices, have not prematurely become deaf, blind, lame or crippled, as many other people have—you are indeed lucky! So how can you spare time to go on complaining about Heaven! Get you gone!"

19.47 After Master Sun had gone, Master Pian went back inside, sat for awhile, looked up to heaven, and sighed. A disciple asked him, "Master, why do you sigh?"

19.48 Master Pian replied, "Just now when Sun Xiu came, I told him about the virtue of the perfect men, but I fear that this so alarmed him that it will leave him utterly confounded."

19.49 The disciple then said, "You are mistaken. Was it right what Master Sun said and what you said wrong? But wrong surely can't confound right. Was it wrong what Master Sun said and what you said right? But he surely came here already confounded. So what more fault have you done him!"

19.50.1 Master Pian then said, "It's not like that at all. Long ago, when a bird landed just outside the capital of Lu,[32] the ruler of Lu was so pleased with it that he had a Great Sacrifice banquet prepared to feast it and had Nine Accords music performed to serenade it. At which the bird became so depressed that its eyes glazed over and it dared not eat or drink. This is what it means to use what nourishes oneself to nourish a bird. To nourish a bird with what nourishes a bird, one had better allow it to roost in deep forests, float on rivers and lakes, and feed on whatever it pleases [*weishe*], so it's the flatlands for it, nowhere else.

Each should have that which is suitable for it.

19.50.2 Now Sun Xiu is a common fellow of limited views and little experience of the world, so for me to explain things to him in simile and metaphor would be like giving a mouse a ride in a horse-drawn carriage or serenading a quail with bells and drums.[33] How could he not become even more alarmed than they!"

This passage explains that to be good at nurturing life, such perfection is attained by complying with what suits the natural allotment of each.

Notes

1. Cheng Xuanying: "Dashing around in the material realm after things is basically done to secure the needs of life, but since life may not be preserved by nurture, we know that in what the world works at, there is nothing worth trying!" *Zhuangzi jishi*, 3: 631.
2. Cheng Xuanying: "As for actions outside one's allotted capacity, these are not worth trying, but those within one's allotted capacity, one can't fail to do. The ways that eyes see, ears hear, feet move, and mind knows are endowments of one's original nature [*xingli*], and are done with unconscious effort, so one should not strive to avoid doing them." *Zhuangzi jishi*, 3: 631. Taken together, Guo and Cheng seem to relate "things though not worth trying yet one can't help doing" to "allotted capacity": one must see but not try to see more than he can see, hear but not try to hear more than he can hear, and know but not try to know more than he can know.
3. Cheng Xuanying glosses "becomes one with Heaven" as "become one with the virtue of the arcane way of nature [*xuantian*]." *Zhuangzi jishi*, 3: 632.
4. Cheng Xuanying's interpretation is more general: "It is by recovering one's original nature and recovering one's fundamental state that one becomes of assistance to the Way of nature." *Zhuangzi jishi*, 3: 633.
5. Cheng Xuanying: "As for Pass Director Yin, surname Yin, given name Xi, personal name Gongdu, he was Director of Hangu Pass and thus was known as 'Pass Director Authentic Man'; he was a disciple of Master Lao." *Zhuangzi jishi*, 3: 633.
6. The text from 19.2 to most of 19.5 appears, with only minor variations, in the *Liezi* (Sayings of Master Lie); *Liezi jishi*, 2: 48–50.
7. The same passage occurs, with minor variations, in the *Liezi* (Sayings of Master Lie); *Liezi jishi*, 2: 51.
8. Cf. *Laozi*, section 65; Richard John Lynn, *The Classic of the Way and Virtue*, 172: "Thus to use knowledge to govern the state is to bring about the theft of the state. . . . Not to use knowledge to govern the state is to enrich the state."
9. The same passage occurs with minor variations in the *Liezi* (Sayings of Master Lie); *Liezi jishi*, 2: 64–66.
10. Cf. 24.65.1.
11. The same passage occurs, but worded differently, in places in the *Liezi* (Sayings of Master Lie); *Liezi jishi*, 2: 59–61.
12. Cheng Xuanying glosses "chamber" [*she*] as "within the mind" [*xinzhong*]. *Zhuangzi jishi*, 3: 643.
13. "Aiming" refers to archery competition.
14. According to Cheng Xuanying, Tian was his surname and Kaizhi his given name. *Zhuangzi jishi*, 3: 645.
15. It is likely that this "Duke Wei of Zhou" may be identified as the son and heir of Duke Huan, who was the younger brother of King Kao of Eastern Zhou (r. 440–426 BCE); see Sima Qian, *Shiji*, *Zhou benji* (Basic Annals of Zhou), 4: 158.
16. Cheng Xuanying: "Surname Zhang and given name Yi, he too was a native of Lu. 'High gate' indicates a wealthy household, and 'lowered door curtain' means 'lowered bamboo screen' [*chuilian*]. Here it says that Zhang Yi was a mundane fellow who pursued worldly profit and that there was not a wealthy household with its high gate and lowered bamboo screen over vermillion door to which he did not rush around to pay his respects or offer congratulations and condolences. So his body became so worn out and spirit exhausted, so distressed and never rested, that an inner fever burst out in his back and he died." *Zhuangzi jishi*, 3: 646.

17. This is Duke Huan of Qi and Master Guan (d. 645 BCE).
18. According to Cheng Xuanying, Huangzi was his surname and Gaoao was his personal name; see *Zhuangzi jishi*, 3: 551.
19. Translations of these obscure demon names, more guesswork than not, can only be arbitrary. For other renderings, see Victor H. Mair, *Wandering On the Way: Early Taoist Tales and Parables of Chuang Tzu*, 181. For descriptions of the demons gleaned from commentaries, see A. C. Graham, *Chuang-Tzu: The Inner Chapters*, 192.
20. Where this same passage occurs with variations in the *Liezi* (Sayings of Master Lie); *Liezi jishi*, 2: 86, the king is identified as King Xuan of Zhou (r. 827/825–782 BCE).
21. The same passage appears, with variations, in the *Liezi* (Sayings of Master Lie), 2: 62–64. The name "Lüliang" probably means something like "Spine Precipice." Cheng Xuanying: "Lüliang is a watercourse name, identifications of which differ. One explanation is that it is where the Yellow River falls a tremendous distance at Lishi in Xihe [Shanxi], for its name is Lüliang; another explanation is that it refers to Longmen (Dragon Gate), located two hundred *li* from Puzhou [Shanxi], through which the Yellow River flows downstream over a waterfall, for its name is also Lüliang; yet another explanation is that it refers to the Lüliang in Pengcheng district [Jiangsu] in the state of Song." *Zhuangzi jishi*, 3: 656.
22. It is recorded in *Zuo's Commentary* to the *Spring and Autumn Annals*, fourth year of Duke Xiang [569 BCE]: "Woodworker Qing [Jiang Qing] addressed Ji Wenzi [Jisun Xingfu, d. 568 BCE], 'You are the chamberlain for ceremonials, yet since you have left the funeral rites for the duchess incomplete, you have not done all you should for our monarch. When he reaches his maturity, who will take the blame for this?' " *Chunqiu Zuozhuan zhengyi*, 29: 1932c. Therefore, it seems that this "Marquis of Lu" may be identified with Duke Xiang of Lu, and that Woodworker Qing lived during his reign.
23. Cheng Xianying identifies the duke as Duke Zhuang of Lu (r. 693–662 BCE). *Zhuangzi jishi*, 3: 660.
24. Although the received text says "even Wen could not have surpassed him," "Wen" seems to be a scribal error for Fu, for the same passage appears, with minor variants, in the *Lüshi chunqiu* (*Spring and Autumn Annals* of Master Lü), 19: 530, where the text reads "even Zaofu could not have surpassed him." Tradition has it that Zaofu, whose driving skills were of mythical proportions, was the charioteer of King Mu of Zhou (r. 956–918).
25. Cf. 4.30.1 and 28.11.
26. Cheng Xuanying identifies Artisan Chui as a marvelous craftsman who lived at the time of Yao. *Zhuangzi jishi*, 3: 662.
27. Cheng Xuanying: "He complied with things and followed them exactly, empty and bland with freedom from conscious mind; therefore, his numinous tower kept its absolute integrity and perfectly unfettered." *Zhuangzi jishi*, 3: 662.
28. When consciousness experiences no discomfort, it means that the mind finds whatever it encounters perfectly suitable—in other words, everything "fits it."
29. Cheng Xuanying identifies Sun Xiu as a native and Pian Ziqing as a worthy of the ancient state of Lu. *Zhuangzi jishi*, 3: 663.
30. Cheng Xuanying: "He interacts with people so to nurture them but does not make them dependent on his own efforts—how could nurture of the common folk ever be a matter of intentional management that makes them dependent on one! The passage quoted here comes from the *Scripture of Master Lao*." *Zhuangzi jishi*, 3: 664. Cf. *Laozi*, section 10; Lynn, *The Classic of the Way and Virtue*, 67.
31. Cf. 20.16.6.
32. Cf. 18.20.
33. Cf. 24.4.1.

CHAPTER 20

SHANMU [THE MOUNTAIN TREE]

20.1 When Master Zhuang was traveling in the mountains, he saw a great tree with limbs and foliage lush and thick, and though a woodcutter had stopped beside it, he refrained from harvesting it, so Master Zhuang asked him why. The woodcutter replied, "It has no use at all." Master Zhuang then said, "This tree, thanks to being worthless, has managed to live out its natural span of years."

20.2 After the Master emerged from the mountains, he took lodging at the home of an old friend, who, delighted, ordered a boy servant to kill a goose and cook it. But the boy, asking for advice, said, "One of them can honk, and one other can't honk, so I beg to ask which one do I kill?" His master replied, "Kill the one that can't honk."

20.3 The next day Master Zhuang's disciples asked him, "Yesterday that tree in the mountains because it was worthless managed to live out its natural span of years, but now this master's goose because it was worthless lost its life. Which position, Sir, would you take?"

20.4.1 Master Zhuang laughed and said, "I might position myself midway between worth and worthlessness, but though a position between worth and worthlessness might seem right, it's not, for one won't quite avoid trouble [*lei*] there.

He supposes that he might so position himself, but since it would not let him avoid trouble, he actually does not take a position there.

20.4.2 But one who makes the Dao and its Virtue his vehicle to wander about won't find this so, for:

> **Free from praise or censure,**
> **Now a dragon, now a snake,**
> **He transforms together with the moment,**
> **Unwilling to be any one particular thing.**
> **Now increasing now decreasing,**
> **He forms his size in harmonious accord.**

Since he wanders together with the First Ancestor of the myriad things, he let things be things and was not an other to things, so how then could he ever have got into trouble![1]

20.4.3 Such was the way the Divine Farmer and the Yellow Thearch did things.

Therefore, Master Zhuang also positions himself there.

20.4.4 But if one is concerned with the properties of the myriad things and the tradition of proper human relationships, he won't find this so, for:

> **Any joining shall be sundered apart,**
> **And any success shall turn into failure.**
> **His uprightness shall lead to harm,**
> **His nobility shall bring on suspicion.**
> **Any action he takes results in his destruction,**
> **And if worthy he shall provoke plots,**
> **If foolish he shall be easily deceived.**

So how could such a one ever manage to be sure!

20.4.5 Alas! Disciples, determine this: You have only the Dao and its Virtue before you!

Since one may not be sure, the position taken must not be one-sided. Only one who transforms in sync with the moment becomes capable of so interacting with change that he constantly enjoys success.

20.5 Market South Yiliao went to see the Marquis of Lu,[2] who looked worried. So Master Market South asked, "My lord looks worried, why is that?"

20.6 The Marquis of Lu replied, "I have studied the way of the former kings and cultivate the tasks of former sovereigns. I pay respects to the spirits and venerate worthies. Not for a moment do I neglect to do these things, yet I fail to avoid calamity. This is why I am worried."

20.7.1 Master Market South then said, "The method, my Lord, you use to avoid calamity is but superficial!

To maintain his person, he concerns himself assiduously about his state, thus innumerable matters fill him with worry. So the more he venerates worthies and engages in high-minded behavior, the more profound his worries about calamity become.

20.7.2 The luxuriously furred fox and the leopard with its spotted pattern live in mountain forests and dwell in cliffside caves; such is their repose. They prowl by night but lurk in dens by day; such is their caution. Though distressed by hunger and thirst, they still keep completely away from rivers and lakes where they might seek something to eat;[3] such is their resolve. But even so, they can't avoid the calamity of nets and traps—but what fault of theirs is that! It is their pelts that bring disaster on them. Now, is the state of Lu not your pelt, my lord? I beseech you, my lord, cut away your body, get rid of your pelt, cleanse your mind, discard desire, and wander about in the uninhabited wilds.

He wishes that he would free himself from his body, forget all about his state, and give himself over to self-transformation.

20.7.3 Nanyue[4] has a capital there whose name is Realm for Establishing Virtue.

He sets this in Nanyue so to choose a place far from Lu.

20.7.4 Its people are foolish and pristinely simple, with little regard for self and few desires. They know how to do things but know not to store against the future. When they give they seek no repayment. They neither know how to conform with righteousness nor to accord with civility. Since these people behave so freely as this, utterly without restraint, they tread the path of the great method.

Let each person step where his fundamental nature takes him so everyone spontaneously treads the way of the great method [of the Dao], for then its infinite method shall all be fulfilled; is that not indeed great!

20.7.5 With birth they find happiness, and with death they get a proper burial.

This means they abide in such a [happy] state from beginning to end.

20.7.6 I wish that you, my Lord, would rid yourself of your state, discard your common folk, and go there with the Dao as your guide."

What is said here about ridding himself of his state and discarding his common folk means that he should discard all concern for them.

20.8 His Lord then said, "The route there is far and dangerous, and also involves rivers and mountains. Since I have neither boat nor carriage, what can be done about it?

He actually takes him to mean that he wants him to go to Nanyue.

20.9.1 Master Market South replied,

"Appear ye not obstructive [*xingju*],

Xingju means "obstructive" [*zhiai*].[5]

20.9.2 Be ye not inflexible [*liuju*],

Liuju means "inflexible" [*zhishou*].

20.9.3 And let this be your carriage."

He should appear in balance [*yi*] with his people and let his mind transform in sync with them, for this is how to use the people as a vehicle to transport oneself.

20.10 His Lord responded, "The route there is remote and mysterious with no people along the way, so who will be my subordinates? I have no provisions and shall have nothing to eat, so how shall I manage to reach my destination?"

20.11.1 Master Market South replied, "Lessen your expenditures and make your desires few, for then even without provisions you will have enough.

That is to say, if one knows contentment, under no condition will he fail to have enough.

20.11.2 My Lord, may you ford rivers then float out on the sea, until your gaze no longer sees the shore and where you just keep going without knowing where it will end.

He should distance himself absolutely from desire [*qingyu*].

20.11.3 Once those who send you off have all returned from the shore,

Once the lord has eliminated all desire, his people all will again abide by their allotted capacities.

20.11.4 thenceforth, my Lord, you shall be far away!

Transcendent, he shall stand alone above his myriad folk.

20.11.5 For so it is, to possess others is to bring trouble on yourself,

In possessing others, one possesses them in the sense that he considers them his private property.

20.11.6 and to be possessed by others is to be beset by worry.

To be possessed by others means to be used by others.

20.11.7 Therefore, Yao neither possessed others nor was possessed by others.

Though he possessed all under Heaven, Yao entrusted everything to his officials and let the myriad folk do what they wanted and did not meddle with them. As such, he did not possess others. He just let things happen the way the common folk would have them happen, and so he himself was not made to work at it. As such, he was not used by others.

20.11.8 I wish, my Lord, to rid you of trouble and eliminate your worry, so that you may set yourself apart and wander about with the Dao in the realm of Great Nothingness [*damo*].

He wants to have him become completely serene and keep nothing in mind about possessing a state.

20.11.9 If someone in two boats doubled up is crossing a river and an empty boat comes along and collides with him, even a short-tempered man won't

get angry. But if there is a man aboard, he will shout to him to watch out. If that one shout is not heeded, he will shout again, and if that is ignored, will there not be a third shout, surely followed by verbal abuse! Before he was not angry, but now he is. Before he was empty, but now he is filled. If one can wander through the world empty of self, what can ever harm him!"

Though the world is ever changing, the way to avoid harm is to remain empty of self, which is always one and the same.

20.12 Once Beigong She[6] had collected taxes for Duke Ling of Wey [Wey Linggong] to make bells, he built an altar outside the gate of the outer city wall, and in three months had completed the upper and lower tiers of suspended bells.

20.13 When Prince Qingji [Wang Ziqing][7] saw them, he asked him, "What technique did you use to devise them?"

20.14.1 She replied, "Since it's a matter of staying within the One, I dare not devise anything.

Having serenely embraced the One, he dared not presume to devise anything to augment that.

20.14.2 For as I have heard,

> **'Though once carved and once polished,**
> **Revert again to pristine simplicity—**

He reverts to using his fundamental nature.

20.14.3 How insensible such intrinsic unawareness,

He gives himself over to nothing less than absolute guilelessness.

20.14.4 and how unconscious this intrinsic lack of reflection.

He is free of all predilection.

20.14.5 How people gather to me, and mindless am I
to send them off or welcome them hither—

He is absolutely indifferent to them.

20.14.6 Their coming I won't prevent, their going I won't stop.'

He just lets them be.

20.14.7 Thus I allow the dangerously bold to have their way,[8]

He complies with the strong.

20.14.8 go along with the concessively obsequious,

He has no attachments whatsoever.

20.14.9 and take advantage of those who use themselves up.

He makes use of those who can't help but be the way they are.

20.14.10 This is how I collected taxes from morn till night, yet had not the slightest trouble with it.

As usual he suffered no setback.

20.14.11 So how much the more this would be true for one who has access to the Dao!"

Serenely he adheres to nothing but instead takes advantage of the spontaneous behavior of everyone under Heaven—the path of great pervasive integration. As thus was said, "He surveyed it, applied himself to it / And in a few days finished it."[9]

20.15 When Confucius was surrounded between Chen and Cai without cooked food for seven days, Venerable Elder Ren [Taigong Ren] went to console him and said, "Are you going to die?" To which he replied, "Yes." "Do you hate death?" He replied again, "Yes."[10]

Since he has the same attitude toward like and hate, the sage is free of like and hate.

20.16.1 Ren then said, "I shall try to tell you about the way to avoid death. At the Eastern Sea there is a bird, whose name is Indolence [*yidai*]. It is such a bird that it just flaps slowly around, seemingly utterly inept, flying only when carried along by its fellows and only roosting when bullied into it by its brood.

Not only is it beset with such lethargy, it also is free of constant attachments.

20.16.2 Advancing, it never dares take the lead; when retreating, it never dares be last.

It always calmly positions itself in between.

20.16.3 As for food, it never dares eat first but is sure to wait its turn.

It just follows the others.

20.16.4 Therefore, a place within the flock is never denied it.

It stays together with the flock.

20.16.5 So outsiders never manage to harm it, which is how it avoids calamity.

Calamitous harm arises when one belabors intelligence to compete for advantage.

20.16.6 A straight tree is the first cut down,
And a sweet well is the first drained dry.

Thus is harm inherent in useful qualities.

20.16.7 What you mean to do is dress up your intelligence to amaze the stupid and morally cultivate yourself to show up the disgraced, parading such obvious brilliance that you seem to be walking around holding up the sun and moon,[11] so there is no such escape for you.

Even if minor differences are observed in you, you put yourself at odds with the mass of common folk, but if you were to merge with the Great Unity, you would not be any different from those of the world at large. Therefore, what you show off as obvious brilliance is actually but a reflection of tracks left behind by those who had arcanely so merged. And that you now rely of words to leave behind tracks of your own is why you have brought calamity on yourself here between Chen and Cai.[12]

20.16.8 In the past I once hear a man of great achievement say,

> **'One who boasts about himself has no merit.**
> **One whose merit is achieved finds it collapse.**
> **One whose reputation is attained sees it fail.'[13]**

One who relies on merit and reputation to think he is fully accomplished has never remained whole and safe.

20.16.9 Who is it that can rid himself of merit and reputation and thus rejoin the mass of common folk!

Since achievement of merit derives from the mass of common folk, one should rejoin them.

20.16.10 One in whom the Dao flows but knows it not,

Utterly ignorant of it, such a one just practices it spontaneously.

20.16.11 Able to practice it with ease yet does it not for reputation.

In all cases, he spontaneously succeeds at such practice with ease, and not because it may lead to fame and only then engages in it.

20.16.12 One so pure and innocent, so very ordinary
That he actually compares with the mad.

This is because he acts unselfconsciously.

20.16.13 He obliterates his tracks, discards his authority, and acts not for merit or reputation.

Since merit is achieved thanks to others, authority lies not with him, so any tracks that lead to fame, he gets rid of them all.

20.16.14 Therefore, he places no blame on others, and others too place no blame on him.

Since he lets others indulge their inclinations, everyone themselves become responsible for blame.

20.16.15 Since the Perfected one would be unknown, why do you, sir, delight in being known?"

Tranquilly indifferent and free from selfconscious involvement with things, such is the Perfected one.

20.17.1 Confucius then said, "Excellent!" He dismissed his associates, left his disciples behind, and escaped into a great marshland, where he wore animal furs and coarse clothing and ate acorns and chestnuts.

He partook of the delights had when one discards the human world.

20.17.2 He entered among beasts but did not agitate their herds, entered among birds but did not agitate their flocks.

Since he was as unselfconscious as the plants and trees, there was nothing about him for birds and beasts to fear.

20.17.3 Since even birds and beasts did not find him injurious, how much the less did men!

For as we know, he relied on words as much as he could to promote the trustworthiness of perfect sincerity, and by complying with others, he stayed away from places where he might suffer harm.

20.18 Confucius asked Master Sang Hu,[14] "I have twice been driven from Lu, had a tree cut down because of me in Song, had to become a fugitive in Wei, was completely frustrated in Shang and Zhou, and surrounded between Chen and Cai. As I encountered such calamities as these, my intimate associates became ever more estranged and my disciples and friends ever more scattered. Why has all this happened to me?"[15]

20.19.1 Master Sang Hu replied, "Is it you alone who has not heard of the man of Jia who fled?[16] Lin Hui abandoned a jade disk worth a thousand pieces of gold, yet carried his baby child on his back when he fled. Someone said to him, 'Was it for its monetary value [*bu*]? But the value of a child is very little!

Bu means monetary value [*caibo*].

20.19.2 Was it because of involvement [*lei*]? But a child means much involvement! So why did you abandon a jade disk worth a thousand pieces of gold but carry with you a child?' Lin Hui responded, 'My bond with the former was one of advantage, but the latter is a relationship due to nature. If the bond is one of advantage, when beset by poverty, misfortune, calamity, or harm, the one will abandon the other, but if the relationship is due to nature, when beset by poverty, misfortune, calamity, or harm, the one will hold the other close. For one to hold the other close and for one to abandon the other are certainly positions far apart! Furthermore,

> **While the way the noble man makes friends is**
> **as bland as water,**
> **The way the petty man makes friends is**
> **as sweet as rich wine.**

20.19.3 Because the way of the noble man is bland, his friendships remain close,

Because nothing of advantage is involved, the one is bland, and because they are in accord with the Dao, such friendships remain close.

but because the way of the petty man is sweet, his friendships don't last.

Because it is dressed up in advantage, the other is sweet, but advantage can't always endure, which is why with time such friendships don't last.

20.19.4 When a bond occurs without intent, it will part also without intent.' "

To bond spontaneously without intent creates a natural relationship, and when a bond is made without intent, any intent to part it shall always fail.

However, when a bond is made with an intent, some other intent will surely part it.

20.20 Confucius then said, "I humbly receive your instruction!" At that, he slowly moved off, seemingly aimless, and returned home, where he abandoned study and threw away his books. His disciples no longer bowed before him, but their love for him ever kept increasing.

This is because, plain and simple, he had cast off his trappings of benevolence.

20.21.1 On another day, Sang Hu said, "When Shun was about to die, he clearly admonished Yu, saying, 'Be ye warned! For your demeanor, nothing is better than accord [*yuan*], and for your inclinations, nothing is better than compliance [*shuai*].

Let your demeanor express compliance and comply with your inclinations—don't falsify them for the sake of advantage.

20.21.2 If in accord, no estrangement will result; if in compliance, no fatigue will occur.

As long as one's demeanor is not false, one shall always remain safe and whole; as long as one's inclinations are free of pretense, one shall always be at ease.

20.21.3 Then, not estranged and not fatigued, you need not seek embellishment on which your appearance depends, and when you seek not embellishment on which your appearance depends, needless to say, you need not depend on anything else.' "

Trust to your pristine simplicity, and as such, just go straight on ahead.

20.22 Master Zhuang, wearing coarse cloth that had been patched and just wearing sandals secured with string, went to pay a visit to the King of Wei,[17] who then asked him, "Why, Master, do you look so wretched as this?"

20.23.1 "Though I am poor, I am not at all wretched. When a gentleman has attained the Dao and its Virtue yet may not practice them, that is wretchedness; when his clothes are worn out and his footgear is full of holes, that indicates poverty, not wretchedness—what is referred to as 'not meeting with the right time.' Has your majesty never seen the leaping gibbon? Once it gets up into a nanmu, catalpa, or camphor tree, it clambers around amidst the branches with the greatest of ease, and not even a Yi or a Peng Meng[18] would escape being made cross-eyed!

Here meeting with the right time and attaining the right place, it relaxes on the long branches,[19] and, though they be great archers of antiquity, none can harm it.

20.23.2 But when it gets up into a thorny mulberry, a zizyphus, a trifoliate orange, or a wolfthorn berry tree, it moves precariously, looks about with mistrust, and trembles with terror. It is not that its bones and sinews have become cramped and are no longer supple but because it finds itself in a place not right for it, where it can't fully engage its abilities. If I now find myself

with a benighted ruler and perplexed ministers yet wish not to be wretched, how could I ever manage to do so? Proof of this is that Bi Gan had his heart cut out!"[20]

He was in a place not right for him yet tried to force it to be so, he was thus put to death.

20.24 When Confucius found himself in dire straits between Chen and Cai and went without cooked food for seven days, he rested his left hand on a dead tree and with his right hand beat time on a withered branch as he sang an ode to Sire Biao. He had an instrument but lacked a measured beat for it, had some music but lacked proper notes for it. However, the wood's sound and the human voice combined plaintively to match what was in his heart and mind.

20.25.1 Yan Hui, hands clasped together respectfully before him and eyes cast down, watched him covertly. Zhongni, fearing that Yan Hui's exaggerated view of him was growing too great and that his love for him causing too much grief, said, "Hui, it is easy not to be affected by the harm inflicted by Heaven,

This is only so if one remains content in the face of it.

20.25.2 but hard not to be affected by the benefits of man.

When things come unbidden, one finds it impossible to reject them.

20.25.3 Nothing begins that is not also an ending;

Something that may have begun today is something that ended yesterday. As such, what is called a "beginning" is nothing other than an ending—which indicates that change and transformation are endless.

20.25.4 in this Heaven and man are one and the same.

They both are naturally so.

20.25.5 So, the one who was just now singing, who was he?

Since that one had given himself over to spontaneity, the singer then was not the I [that I am now].

20.26 Yan Hui then asked, "May I presume to ask what is meant by 'it is easy not to be affected by the harm inflicted by Heaven?' "

20.27.1 Zhongni replied, "Hunger, thirst, cold, heat, and the obstacles of poverty, these are the doings of Heaven and Earth, emanated by the movement of fate.

These are impossible to evade.

20.27.2 By this I mean they happen together in conjunction with them.

What is meant is that such things happen utterly unconsciously in obedience to the laws of the Lord on High [*di*].[21]

20.27.3 A minister who serves his sovereign dares not evade his commands; therefore, since one upholds the way of the minister as attentively as this, how much more attentively should one treat Heaven!"

If one is content with whatever situation comes his way and does not regard harm as harm, by treating Heaven in this way he shall not be affected by harm.

20.28 Yan Hui then asked, "May I presume to ask what is meant by 'it is hard not to be affected by the benefits of man.'"

20.29.1 Zhongni replied, "When one is first employed, things go smoothly in all directions [*sida*],

One's interactions with people everywhere proceed smoothly is what "things go smoothly in all directions" [*sida*] means.

20.29.2 and rank and emolument at once endlessly come one's way.

Because everything goes smoothly, one's handling of things is judged brilliant and outstanding.

20.29.3 But these are advantages conferred by others and not intrinsically his own.

It is not that he tries to get them through his own efforts.

20.29.4 My fate depends on what is external to me.

A man's life surely depends externally on how fate has him interact with others; he is not like a tile or stone, which are nothing more than physical bodies.[22]

20.29.5 The noble man does not become a robber; the worthy man does not become a thief. So if I were to try to get them, what would that make me!

To rob or thieve means to get things for one's private benefit, but now when a worthy or noble man has rank and emolument come to him, he does not get them for his private benefit but just receives them—that is all there is to it.

20.29.6 Thus it is said, 'No bird is wiser than the swallow, for any place it spots as unsuitable it does not give a second glance. Even if it has to drop the food it carries, it will abandon it and flee.

Such is the speed with which it avoids disaster.

20.29.7 It fears men yet lives stealthily among them,

It is a creature that never tries to live apart from men, and so men give it shelter. That it fears men yet enters human dwellings is the reason why it is called wise.

20.29.8 who, as it were, maintain Altars of the Soil and Grain for them!'"

How much the more true this is for the Perfected one, for he arcanely unites with all people under Heaven, so everyone never tires of happily acclaiming him as leader and share their God of the Soil [She] with him and regard him as their Hou Ji. This shows how hard it is not to be affected by the benefits of man.

20.30 What do you mean by "nothing begins that is not also an ending"?

20.31.1 Zhongni answered, "As for the process that transforms the myriad things in such a way that we are unaware that one thing is replaced by another,

No one is aware of such changes.

20.31.2 how may we know when it ends, when it begins? One should do nothing other than just take things as they come."

Though such replacement takes place day and night, never does it reach an end, so one should take things just as they come.

20.32 And what do you mean by "Heaven and man are one and the same."

20.33.1 Zhongni answered, "That there is man is because of Heaven. That there is Heaven is also because of Heaven.

All mention of "Heaven" here should be understood as designating that which is naturally so without intent to be so.

20.33.2 That man can't possess Heaven is because it pertains to his inborn nature.

If we use the term "naturally so," it designates that which is naturally so, for how could a man intentionally acquire this naturally so-ness! Since one is just naturally so, it pertains to his inborn nature.

20.33.3 So the sage serenely allows his body to age until the end comes!"

Such a one is so serenely unconcerned, his body becomes perfectly one with change.

20.34.1 When Zhuang Zhou was wandering through Eagle Hill Park, he happened to see a strange-looking magpie approach from the south, its wingspan seven feet and its eyes an inch around. It brushed against Zhou's forehead and then settled amidst chestnut trees. Zhuang Zhou remarked, "What kind of bird is this! Wings so big it can't go far and eyes so big it does not see!" He then gathered up his robe and walked quickly toward it, his pellet catapult held at the ready, waiting for the right moment. But then he saw a cicada that had just found such a fine piece of shade that it became unmindful of its body, and a praying mantis took advantage of its cover and grabbed it. As it let itself thus be seen, it became unmindful of its own body.

Though it used a leaf to shield itself from the cicada, it was unmindful that its own body now could be seen by the strange-looking magpie.

20.34.2 And the strange-looking magpie, following after it, took advantage of it, but while it saw its own advantage, it became unmindful of its own body.

Its eyes could see, and its wings could let it escape; whereas these were features of its authentic nature, now that it saw an advantage to be had, it forgot all about them.

20.34.3 Zhuang Zhou then said with alarm, "Alas! How creatures surely cause one another trouble!

Since they try to take advantage of one another, they constantly cause one another trouble.

20.34.4 Just as these two brought it on one another."

As one coveted the other, something else coveted it.

20.34.5 He then threw aside his catapult, turned around, and ran, since a gamekeeper was in pursuit to accost him [*sui*].

Accost [*sui*] means to interrogate [*wen*] him.

20.35 Zhuang Zhou returned home and for three days was upset. Lin Ju went to attend him and asked, "Why, Master, have you been so very unhappy recently?"[23]

20.36.1 Zhuang Zhou replied, "While I was taking care of my physical body, I was unmindful of my person.

His person was among men, a world fraught with danger and adversity. In his physical body he promoted serenity and ease in such a world but failed to gauge what that world found appropriate—this is what the text means by "taking care of one's bodily existence but being unmindful of one's person."

20.36.2 Because I was looking into muddy water, it blurred my sight of what was in the clear deep pool.

Though he looked into it, it was unclear, and since it was the means by which he saw himself, he nearly forgot all about the Dao reflected in his mirror.[24]

20.36.3 Moreover, as I have heard my master [Master Lao] say, 'Whenever you enter a place follow the customs of that place.'

One should not violate its prohibitions.

20.36.4 Now when I was wandering about in Eagle Hill Park, I became unmindful of my own person, so when a strange-looking magpie brushed against my forehead, forgetting my authentic state, I wandered into the chestnut trees. The chestnut grove gamekeeper then accosted me as a poacher, which is why I have been upset."

His being accosted as a poacher is used [as a metaphor] to express how, in order to promote serenity and ease throughout the world, Master Zhuang relied on words to express his ideas, which had him actually vilifying Confucius, scorning Old Long Ears [Master Lao], while back in time he abused and attacked the Three Thearchs, and now in the present brought painful blame on his own person.

20.37 When Master Yang [Yangzi, Yang Zhu] was on his way to Song,[25] he lodged overnight at an inn, where the innkeeper had two concubines, one beautiful the other ugly, but he held the ugly one in esteem and disdained the beautiful one. When Master Yang asked the reason for this, a boy servant at the inn replied, "The beautiful one considers herself so beautiful that we aren't conscious she is beautiful, while the ugly one considers herself so ugly that we aren't conscious she is ugly."

20.38 Master Yang then said, "Disciples, remember this! If you act worthily yet stay free of all sense that you act worthily, where might you go that you were not loved!"

This means that one must never follow the path of self-conscious worth.

Notes

1. Cf. 11.31.3–11.31.4 and 22.35.8.
2. A certain Xiong Yiliao of Market South is mentioned in the *Commentary to the Spring and Autumn Annals*, in the sixteenth year of Duke Ai [479 BCE], so if this is the same person, it means that the marquis may be identified as Duke Ai of Lu (r. 494–467); see *Chunqiu Zuozhuan zhengyi*, 60: 2178a; also cf. 24.41.

3. This sentence, riddled with ambiguity and likely corrupt, has bedeviled commentators throughout the tradition well into modern times, a detailed account of which is found in Wang Shumin, *Zhuangzi jiaoquan*, 727, note 7. The reading here follows Wang's interpretive comments [*an*].
4. Nanyue (South of Yue) is likely a fanciful invention; it should not be identified with the later historical Nanyue (Southern Yue) kingdom (204–111 BCE).
5. The traditional commentaries, including that of Cheng Xuanying, reject or ignore Guo Xiang's gloss of *xingju* as "obstructive" [*zhiai*]; instead, they render it as "[appear] arrogant," which results in "Appear ye not arrogant." *Zhuangzi jishi*, 3: 674. Apparently, Guo wanted to contrast "obstructive" here with the "in balance" [*yi*] two lines below. And by "in balance," he seems to mean "be one with" or "interact with smoothly/without obstruction."
6. Whether Beigong is a surname or a cognomen is uncertain. Cheng Xuanying says that it is a surname and She a given name. However, the fourth-century commentator Li Yi says that Beigong, "North Palace," is a cognomen, which She acquired because he lived there. *Zhuangzi jishi*, 3: 676.
7. Several possibilities exist for the identification of Prince Qingji. Cheng Xuanying, following Li Yi, says that he was the son of the king of Zhou and a Grand Master [*dafu*] of that state, without identifying which king of Zhou was the father. Yu Yue, citing Huang Kan's (488–545) commentary on the *Lunyu* (Analects), suggests that the prince may be identified with Prince Sunjia, the grandson of King Ling of Zhou (r. 571–545 BCE), who at the time was a Grand Master residing in Wey, though he says that another possibility is Prince Chengfu, originally from Zhou, who had fled to Qi, where he held high office, citing a passage from the eleventh year of Duke Wen (616 BCE) in the *Zuozhuan* (*Spring and Autumn Annals, the Zuo tradition*).
8. Cf. *Laozi*, section 42; Richard John Lynn, *The Classic of the Way and Virtue*, 132: "The dangerously bold don't get to die a natural death, so I am going to use them as the fathers of my teachings."
9. These are two lines extracted from Ode 242, *Lingtai*, "Spirit Tower," *Daya* (Greater elegentiae), *Shijing* (Classic of Odes) in praise of King Wen of Zhou; see Zheng Xuan and Kong Yingda, *Maoshi zhengyi* (Correct meaning of the *Mao edition of the Odes*), 16.5:524c.
10. Cf. 6.7.8, 14.18.2, 20.18, 20.24, 28.37, 29.15, 29.17, and 31.19.
11. Cf. 19.46.6.
12. See 20.15.
13. Though the three lines seem attributed to Master Lao, only the first actually appears in the *Laozi*, in section 42; see Lynn, *The Classic of the Way and Virtue*, 93.
14. Cf. 6.25 and 6.59. It is uncertain whether Master Sang's given name was Hu or Yu. Cheng Xuanying: "Surname Sang and given name Yu, he was a recluse. When Confucius was serving as minister of justice [*sikou*] in Lu, people in Qi heard of it and so sent the Lu ruler gifts of singing girls and horses with beautifully colored coats, which estranged Confucius from his lord and got him banished from Lu. Though Song was the heir of the Yin, when Confucius was in Song and Zhou, he was not given office, which was why he said he was completely frustrated." *Zhuangzi jishi*, 3: 684. Since Confucius, a specialist in ritual, was a descendant of the dukes of Song, he would have expected to be given office while in Song, where rites honoring the Yin-Shang kings were then still maintained.
15. Cf. 6.7.8, 14.8.2, 20.15–20.16, 20.24, 28.37, 29.15, 29.17, and 31.19.
16. When the minor state of Jia was vanquished by Jin early during the Spring and Autumn era (771–476 BCE), its people fled as refugees.

17. This is King Hui of Wei/Liang (r. 370–319 BCE; until 344 BCE, he was Marquis Hui of Wei).
18. Yi and his disciple, Peng Meng, were renowned archers of remote antiquity.
19. "It relaxes on the long branches" translates *shen qi changzhi*. However, a kind of double pun might be involved here, for *shen* is also the name for the ninth of the earthly branches [*dizhi*], as well as "Monkey" in the Chinese zodiac. Therefore, reading *shen* as a putative or causative verb would result in "it finds the long branches a place for monkeys" or "it turns the long branches into branches for monkeys."
20. Cf. 4.10.1.
21. This is an anthropomorphic deity who sent blessings or calamities, gave or withheld protection, and was eventually replaced by "Heaven" [*tian*].
22. Cheng Xuanying: "Confucius was a sage who, subject to his fate, exercised his virtue externally to succor the common folk—not a matter for the physical body of a tile or stone to do." *Zhuangzi jishi*, 3: 692.
23. This text seems corrupt and has been amended; see *Zhuangzi jishi*, 3: 697–98, and Wang Shumin, *Zhuangzi jiaoquan*, 761–62, note 12.
24. "Mirror" is a metaphor for "mind": Master Zhuang was so distracted by the lure of personal advantage (i.e., shooting the big bird for food) that his mind became clouded to the extent that he lost sight of the true Dao that governs existence—truth that should always be present "reflected" in his mind.
25. The same passage occurs, with variants, in the *Liezi* (Sayings of Master Lie); *Liezi jishi*, 2: 81–82.

CHAPTER 21

TIAN ZIFANG

21.1 When Tian Zifang was sitting in attendance to Marquis Wen of Wei, he repeatedly praised Xi Gong.[1]

21.2 Marquis Wen asked, "This Xi Gong, is he your teacher?"

21.3 "No, he is my fellow villager; he often hits the mark in his remarks about the Dao, which is why I praise him."

21.4 Marquis Wen then asked, "That being so, do you not have a teacher?"

21.1.5 Zifang replied, "I do have a teacher."

21.6 "Who is your teacher?"

21.7 "Shunzi of East Wall [Dongguo Shunzi]."

21.8 "That being so, why do you never praise him?"

21.9.1 "Because he is authentic by innate nature [*weiren*].

He is utterly free of artifice.

21.9.2 Although he has the look of a man, he is one with Heaven.

Although his appearance is the same as any man, uniquely, he has given himself over to spontaneity.

21.9.3 It is his vacuous compliance [*xuyuan*] that preserves his authenticity,

Utterly vacuously, he complies with others; as such, his authenticity is not lost.

21.9.4 and his purity [*qing*] that allows him to yield to others.

One who makes himself pure does harm to great purity [*dajie*], but here it is his purity that lets him yield to others and remain one with Heaven.

21.9.5 If people are wicked [*wudao*], by just rectifying his appearance he awakens them to the error of their ways, which causes these intentions of theirs to vanish.

Utterly openminded in his pure vacuity [*qingxu*], all his has to do is rectify himself and people's wickedness [*wuxie*] spontaneously vanishes.

21.9.6 So how could I, Wuze, be worthy enough to praise him!

21.10.1 After Zifang had left him, Marquis Wen, so bewildered that he was bereft of speech for the whole rest of the day, then summoned before him his ministers standing in attendance on him, whom he addressed, "How profoundly mysterious is the way of the true sovereign [*junzi*] of perfect virtue! To start with I thought that the words of the sages and the practice of benevolence and righteousness were the ways to perfection, but now that I have heard of Zifang's teacher, my body has so come to pieces that I would not move, my mouth is so pinched that I would not speak!

He was drawing near to self-awareness [*zijue*].

21.10.2 For what I have been studying is no more than just mud dolls,

They were not things that actually exist.

21.10.3 and this state of Wei has become just an entanglement for me."

One whose understanding is most noble considers worldly greatness just a tangle of worry.

21.11 When Wenbo Xuezi[2] was on his way to Qi and took lodgings in Lu, a man of Lu asked to see him, but Wenbo Xuezi said, "That won't do, for I have heard that whereas the noble men of this central state know all about rites and regulations, they are stupid when it comes to understanding the human mind, so I wish not to see him."

21.12 Once he had reached Qi, he returned, and it was while lodging in Lu that the man again asked to see him, which prompted Wenbo Xuezi to say, "Once before he sought to see me, and now since he seeks to see me again, he must surely have a way to change my mind."

21.13 But after he went out to see his visitor, he went back in and sighed, and the next day when he saw him, he again just went back in and sighed. His servant then asked him, "Every time you see your visitor you have to come back in and heave a sigh—why is that?"

21.14.1 "As I first told you, 'People of this central state know all about rites and regulations but are stupid when it comes to understanding the human mind.' Before when he came to see me, his advancing and withdrawal were as precise as if done with a compass or a square, and he was poised just like a dragon, self-possessed just like a tiger.

Since his steps went round in circles, his footprints made a serpentine path.

21.14.2 He admonished me like a son, instructed me like a father. This was why I sighed.

The corrupt practices of rites and regulations are glossed over in such a way as this.

21.15.1 Zhongni went to see him but spoke not.

He already knew his mind.

21.15.2 So Zilu said, "Master, you have long wanted to see Wenbo Xuezi, but now when you saw him you did not speak—why is that?"
2.16 Zhongni replied, "With a man like this, as soon as my glance fell on him, it beheld the Dao there, as such, it would not do to put this into words."

With the cast of an eye, meaning was already conveyed, so there was nothing to be put into fine utterances about it.

21.17 Yan Yuan asked of Zhongni, "When you walk, I too walk; when you hasten, I too hasten; when you dash, I too dash. But when you run so fast that you leave even the dust behind, I can only stare after you."[3]
21.18 The Master then said, "Hui, what do you mean?"
21.19 "When you walk, I too walk, that is, when you speak, I too speak; when you hasten, I too hasten, that is, when you dispute, I too dispute; when you dash, I too dash, that is, when you talk about the Dao, I too talk about the Dao; when you run so fast that you leave even the dust behind and I can only stare after you, that is, you are believed even when you speak not; you deal with people utterly free of partiality; and though you have no official position, the common folk gather thickly before you. I don't understand how all this can be so—that is all there is to it!"
21.20.1 Zhongni replied, "Ah! How could we not look into this! There is no greater grief than death of the mind, for even the death of the person is second to it."

If the mind regards death as death, it hastens its own death. Increased speed toward death occurs because one brings about one's own death with grief. If one is free from grief, this stops, but when grief is there and the mind dies, the greatest of grief occurs.[4]

21.20.2 The sun emerges in the east and sets in the far west; without exception the myriad creatures follow the same example.

Everyone can see that.

21.20.3 Those with eyes and feet wait in attendance on it, for only with it is their potential realized and effectiveness had [*chenggong*].

Once the potential of eyes is realized, sight becomes effective; once the potential of feet is realized, movement becomes effective.[5]

21.20.4 When it rises, it "exists"; when it sets, it "perishes."

Just because people no longer see it, they think it perishes, but it does not really perish.

21.20.5 The myriad creatures are the same: they wait in attendance to die and wait in attendance to live.[6]

Wait in attendance on concealing darkness means "die"; wait in attendance to revealing light means "live," but actually neither death nor life occurs.[7]

21.20.6 Once I received this physical body, without change I wait for the end.

The existent does not have the capacity to change and become non-existent. Therefore, once one receives a physical body, it will never reach the end of its transformations.[8]

21.20.7 I model my behavior on things,

He himself is free from selfconscious mind.

21.20.8 day and night without break,

Constantly transforming, he is always new.

21.20.9 but I don't know how it will end.

He does not regard death as death.

21.20.10 Easily my physical body took shape.

Since it easily fulfills itself, why should anything more be done about it?[9]

21.20.11 I understand that fate is such that it is impossible to plan for it on the basis of what has happened before. It is in this way that I, Qiu, go forward day by day.

Not tied to what has happened before, he proceeds in step with change, making progress day by day.

21.21.1 I've linked my arm with yours all my life, yet now I've lost you; is that not sad?

Change and transformation can't be stopped by trying to hold them back. Therefore, although arm in arm they took care of one another, they still could not make them stop. If death is thought sad, this too may be thought sad, but people now never think this sad—why must they think death alone sad![10]

21.21.2 What you probably see in me is based on how I appear to you, but even after this is completely gone, you still seek it as if it still existed; this is to seek a horse in a deserted marketplace.

A deserted market is not a place where horses are left to wait, meaning that if one seeks something that once only existed in the past, it shall prove impossible to find ever again. Human life is just like a horse passing through a marketplace, in that it does not stop even for an instant, for the old is succeeded by the new, night and day without cease. *Zhu* (manifest) means "see" or "appear" [*jian*/*xian*], which is to say, "You probably do nothing more than just see me as I appear, but how I appear is something new each day. Therefore, what I was is now completely gone, so how can you find me as if I were still there?"

21.21.3 I would keep you in mind, but this is very easy to forget; you would keep me in mind but this is very easy for you to forget too.

Fu [serve] here has the sense of "keep in mind" [*sicun*]. "Very easy to forget" refers to how fast it passes away. That is to say, "you" are gone so suddenly that though it is my constant wish to keep you in mind, I can never keep up with it.

21.21.4 Nevertheless, why should you feel bad about this? Although the old me is forgotten, what one does not forget about me still exists.

"What one does not forget" refers to such continuance that results from daily renewal. Although you forget the old me, the new me has already arrived, and since this is never not an "I," why should I feel bad about it? Therefore, able to keep apart from the vulgar and mundane, such a one never fails to merge arcanely with things.

21.22.1 Confucius went to see Lao Dan, but Lao Dan had newly washed his hair, which he had all loose and disarrayed so it would dry, and he himself was so utterly still that he did not seem human.

He had reached the perfection of detached tranquility.

21.22.2 Confucius withdrew to await him, 21.22.3; shortly thereafter when he did see him, he said, "Was I seeing things or were you really like that? Before, sir, your body was as withered as a dead tree, as if you were detached from things and disassociated from men, and had placed yourself in utter isolation."

Once free of both mind and body he had gone beyond things.

21.23 Lao Dan replied, "I let my mind wander free in the beginning of things."

At their beginning, things don't quite exist, then suddenly exist; therefore, once he had wandered in the beginning of things, he understood that the existence of things is not a matter of their being made to exist, but that they come into existence by themselves.

21. 24 Confucius asked, "What do you mean by that?"

21.25.1 He replied, "The mind is so confounded by it that it fails to understand; the mouth is so tied by it that it fails to speak.

He wants to ensure that Confucius seeks it beyond words and conscious thought.

21.25.2 But I shall try to tell you what it is approximately.

He tries to use yin and yang to tell him how to imagine that which has no physical existence, nothing more than that, for he would never dare be entirely sure about it.

21.25.3 Perfect yin is entirely cold and wet [*susu*]; perfect yang is entirely hot and dry [*hehe*], yet such cold and wet emerge from Heaven, and such hot and dry emerge from Earth.

This speaks to the intercourse between them.[11]

21.25.4 Intercourse between the two results in complete harmony by which the myriad things come to life. Something might control all this, but no one has ever seen a physical form for it.

Since no one has ever seen a physical form that provides such control, it is clear that this happens all by itself.

21.25.5 Extinction and generation, times of repletion and times when sere, now dark night and now bright day, sun shifting and moon changing, daily such things happen,

Things never remain the same.

21.25.6 yet no one has ever seen what accomplishes all this.

Since all this happens by itself, there is no accomplishment to it.

21.25.7 Life has that from which things sprout.

They sprout from the not quite coalesced.

21.25.8 Death has that to which things return.

They return to a state of dissociation.

21.25.9 Beginnings and endings alternate with neither beginning nor end, and no one knows when they ever will exhaust themselves.

As has been said, "Try to meet it, but you won't see its head. Try to follow it, but you won't see its tail."[12]

21.25.10 If it be not this, what else could serve as the Progenitor of it all!"

21.26 Confucius then said, "May I ask how one wanders free in such a realm?"

21.27 Lao Dan replied, "Attaining this is to find perfect beauty and perfect happiness; one who attains to perfect beauty and wanders free in perfect happiness is known as a Perfected one."

Perfect beauty is had because he is free from the sense of beauty, and perfect happiness is had because he is free from the sense of happiness.

21.28 Confucius then said, "I wish to hear about the way to do this."

21.29.1 He answered, "Grass-eating beasts are not upset when they have to shift grassy wetlands; water insects are not upset when they have to shift waters, for in undergoing such minor changes, they lose not what is a major constant for them.

Life and death are also minor changes.

21.29.2 For so it is that joy or anger and sorrow or enjoyment never enter their thoughts.

This is because they know these are minor changes and not a loss of what are major constants for them.

21.29.3 Now the term 'all under Heaven' refers to the unity intrinsic to the myriad creatures. It is by achieving such unity and becoming one with it that one's four limbs and all other parts of one's body become just dust and dirt, and life and death, one's beginning and end, become just a day and night. As such, since none of these can trouble one, how much the less should gain or loss, good fortune or bad be paid any heed!

These become even less sufficient to cause worry.

21.29.4 One discards such things that adhere to one as if they were mud and mire, for he knows that one's person is of more value than what adheres to him.[13]

Since such a one understands that his person is of more value than that which adheres to him, he discards them as if he were just discarding mud. If one realizes that wherever changes of life or death place him, his self is always there, thus what is of value always exists.

21.29.5 Value lies in the self, which is thus not lost in change.

What is of value is the self, and because with such a one the self is bound together as one with change, no loss ever occurs.

21.29.6 Moreover, since such myriads of transformations never have an end, which among them should be sufficient to distress one's mind! One who has been practicing the Dao is set free [*jie*] from such things."

This is called to have one's "ties untied."[14]

21.30 Confucius then said, "Your virtue, Master, pairs you with Heaven and Earth, yet you still have to rely on perfect speech to cultivate the mind.[15] Were any among the noble men of antiquity able to free themselves from this?"

21.31 Lao Dan replied, "Not so. The way water gushes forth is due to its ability to do so naturally without conscious intent. Just so the Perfected one relates to his virtue in such a way that without cultivating it, people can't do without him.[16] Just so Heaven is naturally high, Earth naturally thick and deep, and sun and moon naturally bright—what need have they to cultivate themselves to such ends!

They achieve self-fulfillment without conscious effort.

21.32.1 After Confucius left he told Yan Hui all about it, saying "The way I relate to the Dao, am I not just like a vinegar midge [*xiji*]!

The term "vinegar midge" indicates a midge [*miemeng*] in an earthen vinegar jar.

21.32.2 If the Master had not lifted the lid for me, I would never have known all the greatness of heaven and Earth.

Comparing what I regard as the totality of things to that of Lao Dan is like comparing what is inside an earthenware jar to all of Heaven and Earth!

21.33 When Master Zhuang went to see Duke Ai of Lu, the duke said to him, "Lu has many Confucian learned men but few, sir, practice your method."

Lu had few Confucians.[17]

21.34 Master Zhuang then said, "Lu has few Confucians."

21.35 Duke Ai retorted, "Throughout the state of Lu there are many in Confucian dress, so why do you say few?"

21.36 Master Zhuang replied, "According to what I have heard, that Confucians wear a round cap signifies they understand destiny is decided by Heaven; that they wear square-nosed sandals signifies they understand the shape of Earth; and that they wear at the waist a penannular jade ring signifies that they decisively deal with matters as soon as they arise. The noble man may embody such a way but not necessarily engage in such dress, and one who engages in such dress does not necessarily understand such a way. Since you, my lord, thinks this is not so, why not issue an edict throughout your state: 'Anyone who dresses this way but fails to embody the way it signifies shall suffer the penalty of death!'

21.37 Subsequently, by the fifth day after Duke Ai had made the proclamation, no one in the state of Lu dared wear Confucian dress, except for one old

fellow who stood at the duke's gate in Confucian dress. The duke immediately summoned him and questioned him about the affairs of state, but though he taxed him with thousands of different points and used myriads of changing perspectives, he failed to stump him.

21.38 Master Zhuang then said, "So in all of Lu there is just this one man who really is a Confucian—can this be said to be 'many'!"

One whose inner self is replete with virtue attaches no adornment to his outer person.

21.39 Boli Xi did not allow thought of rank or emolument to enter his mind, thus he just feed cattle and, when the cattle grew fat, this made Duke Mu of Qin disregard his humble status and turn government over to him.[18] Then there was the Sire of Yu,[19] who, because he did not allow thought of life or death to enter his mind, had it in him to move others.

For one whose inner self is self-fulfilled worldly affairs turn out perfectly.

21.40 Lord Yuan of Song was going to have topographic maps painted, so when all his scribes arrived, they accepted the task and bowed, then queued up, licking brushes and mixing ink, with half their number stretching outside. But there was one scribe who arrived later, relaxed as can be and not hurrying at all. He accepted the task with a bow but did not queue up, but instead just went to his quarters. When the duke sent someone to see what he was doing, it seems he had removed his clothes and was sitting contentedly on the floor with his legs stretched out. Lord Yuan exclaimed, "This one will indeed do, for he is a true painter."

When the inner self is sufficient unto itself, the spirit is relaxed and thought is tranquil.

21.41.1 While King Wen was taking in the sights of Zang,[20] he saw an old fellow fishing, but his fishing line had no fishhook,

He just lives out the years of his life by living in the moment.

21.41.2 One who does fishing but uses not a fishhook

This means to be utterly without needs or desires.

21.41.3 does "constant fishing."

He does not allow thought of success or failure to cross his mind and, moment by moment, just goes on fishing.

21.42 King Wen, on the one hand, wanted to elevate him and turn government over to him but feared this would not set well with grand ministers and his elder kin, so, on the other, wanted to be finished with him and let him go, but could not bear to deny the heavenly to the common folk.[21] Thereupon, the next dawn he declared to his grand ministers, "Last night I dreamt I saw a superior man, dark in complexion, bearded and mustached, riding a piebald horse with hooves of ruddy cast, who ordered me, 'Entrust your government to the old fellow of Zang so the sufferings of the people might be alleviated!' "

21.43 The grand ministers reverently cried out, "It was the late king!"[22]
21.44 King Wen then said, "Just so, let us divine it."
21.45 The grand ministers responded, "Since it was an order from your father, the late king, Your Majesty has no other recourse—what further need is there to divine it!"
21.46.1 Consequently, he summoned the old fellow of Zang and turned government over to him, who, though he left regulations and laws unchanged, allowed no biased decrees to be issued. Three years later, when King Wen made a tour of inspection of his state, he discovered that the rank and file of officials scorned factional leadership and disbanded factions, that those in senior positions did not think of virtue in terms of success, and that issues of bushel and hamper measures dared not enter the four boundaries of the state [*zhonghu bugan ru yu sijing*]. Since the rank and file of officials scorned factional leadership and disbanded factions, they now exalted unity [*shangtong*].

This is just what is meant by "merges with the brilliant, and becomes one with the very dust."[23]

21.46.2 Since those in senior positions did not think of virtue in terms of success, they regarded all duties as one and the same.

If one tries to fulfill oneself in isolation, he becomes estranged from duties as a whole.

21.46.3 Issues of bushel and hamper measures dared not enter the four boundaries of the state, for all feudal lords had eschewed duplicity.

Because everyone in the world trusted one another, it was possible to "unify musical scales, units of length, weights, and measures [*lü du liang heng*]."[24]

21.47 King Wen thereupon made him his Grand Tutor, and, facing north, asked him, "Can my government be extended to the whole world?" The old man of Zang, seemingly confused, did not reply, then, vague as can be, took his leave. Appointed to office in the morning, by evening he had withdrawn, and for the rest of his life was never heard of again.

Since the accomplishment of such achievement was not due to himself, once it had been accomplished, he could not help but withdraw. Once the undertaking was realized, the renown attached to it could not but be discarded; to discard renown, he took himself off, for only then could the effect be extended to the whole world.

21.48 Yan Yuan then asked Zhongni, "Did even King Wen fall short? Moreover, why did he have to resort to a dream to bring this off?"
21.49.1 "Quiet! Don't say such things! King Wen was completely successful.

He entrusted things to his grand ministers and did not try to undertake them himself, which was why he achieved complete success.

21.49.2 And how could you criticize him in such terms! He just complied with the need of the moment."

"The need of the moment" refers to the attitude of the common folk. At the very moment between knowing what to do and not quite knowing what to do, King Wen accordingly blurted out what needed to be done, that is, what was in accord with the general attitude of the common folk.

21.50.1 Guard Against Bandits Lie [Lie Yukou, Master Lie] was demonstrating his archery to Elder Muddled None His Other [Bohun Wuren][25] and so drew his bow to the full [*yingguan*]

Yingguan means that he drew it fully to the arrowhead [*yidi*].

21.50.2 and had a cup of water placed on his elbow.

His left hand was solid as a rock, while his right hand was like a branch attached to a tree, so when his right hand let loose, the left hand was not aware of it, which is how a cup of water could be placed on his elbow.

21.50.3 As they went forth, arrowheads to arrows repeatedly joined,

As arrows were loosed off, arrow shafts and arrowheads went forth in such a way that they repeatedly stuck and joined together.

21.50.4 for joined arrows repeatedly took the place of one another.

Just as one arrow went off, but before it reached the target, another cup was placed on his elbow, which speaks to how marvelous was his dexterity.[26]

21.50.5 All the while he looked like a statue.

This indicates the epitome of immobility.

21.51 Elder Muddled None His Other then said, "This is shooting by trying to shoot; it is not shooting without trying to shoot. Let me climb a high mountain with you, where we risk dangerous rocks that overlook a hundred-fathom abyss—would you still be able to shoot then?

21.52 Thereupon, None His Other had him follow him up a high mountain to risk dangerous rocks that overlooked a hundred-fathom abyss. There he edged backwards until his feet hung out two inches over it. He then bowed to Guard Against Bandits to invite him come forward, but Guard Against Bandits prostrated himself on the ground, bathed in sweat down to his heels.

21.53.1 Elder Muddled None His Other addressed him thus, "Though a Perfected one may scrutinize Blue Heaven above and submerge himself in the Yellow Springs below or boldly do as he wants [*huichi*] to the far reaches of the eight directions, yet his spirit will undergo no change.

"Boldly do as he wants [*huichi*]" means about the same as "do as one wants [*zongfang*]." If the inner self is replete with virtue, one's spirit shall prove fully able to engage with the exterior world, so no matter whether near or far, however profound or deep, wherever he happens to be all shall be clear to him. As such, when distinguishing the incipient arrival of safety or danger, such a one remains spontaneously receptive, calm and at rest.

21.53.2 Now here you are, scared as can be, timidity of will shown in your eyes, your inner self in great danger, indeed!"

Since perfection of clarity is beyond him, he is beset with such fear as this and so fearful that he has lost most of his will—so how could he ever shoot now!

21.54 Jianwu asked Sun Shu'ao,[27] "Three times you were appointed chief minister but did not find it glorious and splendid; three times you were dismissed but displayed no look of regret. At first I had my doubts about you, but now seeing the nose on your face surrounded by such happy satisfaction, how is it that you alone can think like this?"

21.55.1 Sun Shu'ao replied, "How am I any better than any one else! 21.55.2 When it came my way, I could not refuse it, and when dismissed, I could do nothing to prevent it, so I reckon that since its gain or loss was not up to me, in no way should I look regretful–that's all there is to it! How am I any better than anyone else! I don't even know whether it [the respect involved] resides with others or resides with me. If it resides with others, it has nothing to do with me; if it resides with me, it has nothing to do with others.

Open and clear, thus utterly free of attachments, such a one arcanely unites other and self. As such, if it [the respect involved] resides with others, it is not he alone who loses it; if it resides with him, it is not he alone who preserves it.

21.55.2 I was just about to enjoy my leisure and contentment and go off to have a look all around, so what time do I have to bother about whether people esteem or despise me?"

21.56.1 When Zhongni heard about this, he said, "Authentic men of antiquity could not be swayed by the learned, could not be made to indulge by beautiful women, could not be intimidated by robbers, and could not be befriended by Fu Xi and the Yellow Thearch.

"Fu Xi" and "Yellow Thearch" are nothing more than slogans for accomplishment and not identical with those by whom accomplishment was done. As such, slogans for accomplishment are but distant reflections of the actual authors of accomplishment. That is why such names were insufficient reason to befriend them.

21.56.2 Life and death are, indeed, of great significance, but since they leave him utterly unmoved, how much the less would high rank and emolument be likely to move him! For such a one as this, his spirit would take him across high mountains without the least hitch, plunge him into deep springs without getting soaked, and allow him to occupy the most mean and insignificant position without becoming the least debased. It fills all Heaven and Earth, so the more he gives of it, the more he himself has.

When someone cuts off his flesh and skin for the sake of all the world, both others and self perish, but when one does nothing other than allow everyone self-fulfillment, this augments others without diminishing oneself. His spiritual radiance so fills Heaven and Earth that wherever he is he can do everything. Since wherever he is he can do everything, he does not diminish himself for the sake of others but instead releases them into the realm of self-fulfillment.

21.57.1 When the King of Chu was sitting with the Lord of Fan,[28] after a short time those in the entourage of the King of Chu said that Fan's destruction was marked in three ways.

That is, there were three portents of ruin [*wangzheng*].[29]

21.57.2 The Lord of Fan then said, "The destruction of Fan should prove insufficient to destroy what I would have exist.

This is because he would just let Fan go.

21.57.3 So if the demise of Fan should prove insufficient to destroy what I would have exist, then the preservation of Chu should prove insufficient to preserve what it would have exist."

One who would just let it go does not regard loss as loss; as such, it also means that for such a one, "preservation" should also prove insufficient to be thought preservation. Only if one is utterly void and free of self-importance shall constant existence [*changcun*] be had.

Notes

1. Cheng Xuanying: "Surnamed Tian, given name Wuze, and personal name Zifang, he was a worthy of the state of Wei and the teacher of Marquis Wen [r. 424–396 BCE], who was the seventh-generation descendent of Bi Wan [who founded the state of Wei in 661 BCE] and the father of Marquis Wu [r. 396–370 BCE]. The one surnamed Xi had the given name Gong; he too was a worthy of the state of Wei." *Zhuangzi jishi*, 3: 701.
2. Cheng Xuanying: "Surnamed Wen, given name Bo and personal name Xuezi, he was a man of Chu who cherished the Dao." *Zhuangzi jishi*, 3: 704.
3. Cf. 24.3.1.
4. Cf. 24.40.2.
5. Cheng Xuanying: "As one receives all parts of the body from the yin and yang, the capacity of eyes to see and feet to move is provided by creative transformation, so if they fail to wait in attendance on it, how could they ever realize their potential and become effective? Therefore, we know that life and death are not in human control." *Zhuangzi jishi*, 3: 708.
6. "Wait in attendance" translates *dai* or *youdai* (rendered as "dependency" elsewhere) in an attempt to convey both the sense of dependency—the myriad creatures are subject to the presence of the sun in order to see and walk properly (realize the potential of sight and movement)—and the sense of waiting for the sun to rise before such potential is realized. In the same way, creatures subject to dependency "wait" for life or death to happen, which are events "naturally" beyond their control. The sun is a metaphor for creative transformation, as Cheng Xuanying indicates immediately afterward: the process of the Dao, on which all creatures depend for their presence or absence in the world.
7. Cheng Xuanying: "The concealing darkness and revealing light that creatures experience both wait on [are subject to] creative transformation. Although 'concealing darkness' is an expression for 'death' and 'revealing light' an expression for 'life,' since the

rising and the setting of the sun don't actually signify life and death, why should 'concealing darkness' and 'revealing light' signify life and death for creatures?" *Zhuangzi jishi*, 3: 708.

8. That is, though it will undergo countless changes and transformations, it will always exist in some form or other. Cheng Xuanying makes a different point: "My physical body and personal nature are endowed by creative transformation. Once demarcations as to bright or stupid and good-looking or ugly occur, no further change or transformation are to take place, so all one can do is undeviatingly wait for the end, and as such finish out one's days. Just as it isn't up to the individual whether he is bright or stupid, good-looking or ugly, one should give oneself over to the principles governing life and death." *Zhuangzi jishi*, 3: 708–709.
9. Cheng Xuanying: " 'Easily' [*xunran*] means that it seems self-initiated [*zidong*]. Easily endowed with pneuma, the physical body takes shape; nothing causes it to be the way it is." *Zhuangzi jishi*, 3: 709.
10. Cheng Xuanying: "Confucius with Master Yan, sage and worthy, cultivated themselves together, close to one another as if arm in arm. But as change and transformation effected daily renewal, shift and flow rapidly occurred, so though they tried to hold firm, this was impossible to stop, so this arm-in-arm relationship suddenly gave way, and once the new prevailed, the old was lost to them. If he grieved because the old was lost, this could be profoundly sad for him." *Zhuangzi jishi*, 3: 710.
11. Cheng Xuanying: "*Susu* refers to the cold of yin-pneuma, and *hehe* refers to the heat of yang-pneuma. Here we find the yang within yin and the yin within yang becoming intimate, which accounts for such perfect harmonious intercourse [*jiaotai*]. *Zhuangzi jishi*, 3: 713. Cf. *Classic of Changes*, hexagram 11 (*Tai*, Peace), *Commentary on the Images*: " 'Heaven and Earth perfectly interact': this constitutes the image of Peace." Richard John Lynn, *The Classic of Changes*, 205.
12. This is an exact quote from *Laozi*, section 14; Richard John Lynn, *The Classic of the Way and Virtue*, 73.
13. It should be obvious from the context that what "[adheres] to one" is the aforementioned gain and loss, good fortune or bad.
14. Cf. 3.12.8.
15. Cheng Xuanying glosses "cultivate the mind" [*xiuxin*] as "cultivate the art/technique of the mind" [*xiu xinshu*]; that is, how to design, scheme, and plot; cf. 24.64.8.
16. Cf. 5.26.5.
17. Cheng Xuanying: "One might dress in order to project an image of virtue, but this does not alter the man himself. It is Master Zhuang's embodied knowledge that has him deride how few real Confucians are there. *Zhuangzi jishi*, 3: 717.
18. Cheng Xuanying: "Surnamed Meng and with personal name Boli Xi, he was a worthy of the state of Qin. Originally a native of Yu, when Yu was vanquished by Qin, he subsequently went to live in Qin, where at first he failed to find employment so, reduced to poverty and mean existence, he fed cattle, which became so very delightfully fat that he forgot all about wealth and honor. As such, no thought of rank or official salary entered his mind. When Duke Mu later discovered what a worthy he was, he turned governance of his state over to him, having no misgivings whatsoever, which is why the text states that he disregarded his humble status." *Zhuangzi jishi*, 3: 719.
19. Cheng Xuanying: "The Sire of Yu refers to Shun, whose clan took the surname Gui and whose personal name was Chonghua (Double Splendor)." *Zhuangzi jishi*, 3: 719.
20. Cheng Xuanying: "Zang is the name for the area adjacent to the Wei River [in Shanxi]." *Zhuangzi jishi*, 3: 720.

21. "Deny the heavenly' translates *wutian*. Cheng Xuanying: "He could not bear to have the common folk denied such shelter and protection, which was why he said they would be 'denied the heavenly.'" *Zhuangzi jishi*, 3:7: 721. *Tian* (Heaven, heavenly) should be understood as being short for *tianren*, "Heavenly man," a sage in perfect unity with the workings of Nature itself, and thus an absolutely perfect man to take charge of government.
22. "The late king" refers to Jili, the father of King Wen, who also was known as King Ji of Zhou.
23. This is an exact quote from *Laozi*, section 4: "The vessel of the Dao is empty, so use It but don't try to refill It. It is such an abyss, oh, that It appears to be the progenitor of the myriad things. It blunts the sharp, cuts away the tangled, merges with the brilliant, and becomes one with the very dust." Lynn, *The Classic of the Way and Virtue*, 57. That Guo quotes from this passage in the *Laozi* suggests that he had in mind Wang Bi's commentary on this *Laozi* passage, for Wang says "adhering strictly to the measures of one noble household can't keep that household whole, and adhering strictly to the measures of one state can't keep that state intact." This alludes in turn to one of the devices that the Chen family used to gain popular support and usurp power from the Jiang family in the ancient state of Qi: "Yanzi (Master Yan) said, 'This is Qi's last age. I may know nothing, but Qi will belong to the Chen family. The Duke abandons the common folk, and they find a new home with the Chen family. Qi for a long time has had four measures, *dou*, *ou*, *fu*, and *zhong*. . . . Ten *fu* equal one *zhong*. The Chen family doubles the size of the first three, so its *zhong* is very large. They lend in family measures but take returns in the state's measures.' " See *Chunqiu Zuozhuan zhengyi* (Correct meaning of Zuo's *Commentary on the Spring and Autumn Annals*), the third year in the reign of Duke Zhao (538 BCE), 2031a. By manipulating the size of measures, commodities from Chen lands were sold or loaned to the rest of Qi at large discounts—a certain way to win popular support, especially since the Qi state was then imposing heavy taxes and a harsh criminal code. However, here, as is made immediately afterward, such duplicity has vanished and universal trust prevails.
24. This is an exact quote from the *Shundian* (Canon of Shun) in the *Shangshu* (Venerated ancient documents) or *Shujing* (Classic of documents); see *Shangshu zhengyi* (Correct meaning of the venerated ancient documents), 3: 127b–127c.
25. The same passage occurs, with variations, in the *Liezi* (Master Lie); *Liezi jishi*, 2: 51–52.
26. Guo's interpretation, supported by Cheng Xuanying, was largely supplanted by Lin Xiyi and the later tradition of exegesis, which interprets the passage to mean that while one arrow was still in flight, another was already nocked on the bow. Moreover, Guo's odd comment that between each shot, a cup was placed on the elbow (which seems most unlikely) has also been rejected by the later commentary tradition and modern commentaries and translations. However, I think that Guo was right to describe Master Lie's skill as he did: he could repeatedly shoot so fast, never varying his grips on the bow and bowstring in the least, so that the arrowhead of the one behind split the notch of the arrow in front to form an unbroken line of joined arrows all the way to the target. This is a more fitting description of Master Lie's divine skill than merely saying that he could shoot off one arrow while the one before was still in flight—he could ride the wind, after all! Complicating matters, the text of both the *Zhuangzi* here and Guo's commentary is obviously corrupt in places, so establishing the most likely reading is quite difficult; see Wang Shumin, *Zhuangzi jiaoquan*, 796, notes 4 and 5, and *Guo Xiang Zhuangzi zhu jiaoji*, 4: 17a–17b. Master Lie's divine archery skill is echoed in another *Liezi* passage, *Liezi jishi*, 4: 139–40; see A. C. Graham, trans., *The Book of Lieh-Tzu*, 87 and 89, where note 1 elaborates on how such a feat was done.

27. Sun Shu'ao was a court minister of King Zhuang of Chu (r. 613–591 BCE).
28. This refers to King Wen of Chu (r. 689–677 BCE) and Marquis Xi of Fan, whose small state was originally a fief granted by the duke of Zhou.
29. Cheng Xuanying: "The three are [1] failure to revere the spirits, [2] to venerate the worthy, and [3] to take care of the people." *Zhuangzi jishi*, 3: 728. Chapter 15 of the *Hanfei zi* (Sayings of Master Hanfei), "*Wangzheng*" ("Portents of Ruin"), is devoted to such signs and omens. However, since the Lord of Fan, shown immediately afterward to have been an enlightened sage whose rule would not have resulted in such portents, the king's advisors were apparently fabricating justifications for Chu to take over Fan—which it soon does.

CHAPTER 22

ZHI BEIYOU [KNOWLEDGE WANDERS NORTH]

22.1 Knowledge wandered north up to Dark Waters, where he climbed Recluse Rise Hill and there happened to meet Not Conscious of What He Says [Wuwei Wei]. Knowledge said to Not Conscious of What He Says, "I have something I'd like to ask you. What should I think and how should I reflect on it so that I may know the Dao? What should I settle on and how should I deal with it so that I may find the Dao my refuge? What path should I take and how should I follow it so that I may attain the Dao?" Although he asked these three questions, Not Conscious of What He Says did not answer; it was not that he would not reply, he knew not how to reply.

22.2 Since Knowledge did not get any answer, he went back down south to White Waters, where he climbed to the summit of Wily Vacuity and there happened to see Crazy Intractable. Knowledge put the same questions to Crazy Intractable, but Crazy Intractable said, "Alas, I knew what you wanted and was going to tell you, but just as I was about to speak, I forgot what I wanted to say."

22.3 Since Knowledge did not get any answer, he went back to the imperial palace, where, in audience with the Yellow Thearch, he put the questions to him. The Yellow Thearch replied, "Don't think and reflect not and you shall begin to know the Dao. Settle on nothing and deal with nothing and you shall begin to find the Dao your refuge. Take no path and follow nothing and you shall begin to attain the Dao."

22.4 Knowledge then asked the Yellow Thearch, "You and I know this, but both those others did not know it, so who is right?"

22.5.1 The Yellow Thearch replied, "Not Conscious of What He Says was undoubtedly right, and Crazy Intractable seemed to get it, but you and I are nowhere near it, for

> **'He who knows does not speak.**
> **He who speaks does not know.'[1]**

Thus it is that 'the sage practices the teaching that is not expressed in words.'[2]

To give oneself over to its spontaneous practice, this is "the teaching that is not expressed in words."

22.5.2 The Dao can't be got at,

Since the Dao consists of what is just naturally so, it can't be got at through words.

22.5.3 and virtue can't be made perfect.

Because one does not lose virtue, he may be declared virtuous, but this so-called virtue is not perfect virtue.

22.5.4 Whereas benevolence can manipulate behavior and righteousness can curtail it, propriety begets mutual hypocrisy. Thus it is said, 'One resorts to virtue only after losing the Dao, resorts to benevolence only after losing virtue, resorts to righteousness only after losing benevolence, and resorts to propriety only after losing righteousness. Propriety consists of superficial aspects of the Dao and is thus the beginning of disorder.'[3]

Since propriety consists of fixed rules, it is the source from which coercion is born.

22.5.5 Thus it is also said, 'The pursuit of the Dao means having less each day.'[4]

Its superficiality and inauthenticity are diminished.

22.5.6 'Having less upon having less, eventually one reaches the point where one engages in no conscious action, yet nothing remains undone.'[5]

Once superficiality is all gone and only pristine simplicity is left perfectly intact, though one might act, no selfconscious effort is involved.

22.5.7 Since we now have become made-up things,

Once one loses that which he is, he becomes some made-up thing.

22.5.8 when we try to return to our origins, is that not indeed hard! One who would find that easy could only be a great one!

One who finds it easy to return to his origin could only be a great one, for a great one embodies and stays perfectly in step with change and transformation. Therefore, such a one finds transforming physically [*huawu*] not difficult.

22.6.1 Since life is the companion of death

One who understands the Dao of change and transformation does not regard life and death as different.

22.6.2 and death the beginning of life, who understands their endless thread!

Since they keep changing places with one another, one is not quite sure which is death and which life.

22.6.3 The life of a person is the coalescence of pneuma; whereas coalescence results in life, dispersal results in death.

Both involve coalescence; both involve dispersal.

22.6.4 So if life and death are companions, why be anxious any longer!

Such anxiety springs from regarding them as different.

22.6.5 Therefore, though the myriad things exist in such unity, those admired are deemed miraculous and extraordinary and those despised are deemed foul-smelling and rotten. But since the foul-smelling and rotten keep transforming back into the miraculous and extraordinary, and the miraculous and extraordinary keep transforming back into the foul-smelling and rotten, we may say that 'permeating all heaven and earth is just one single unified pneuma.'

Each person takes what he admires to be miraculous and extraordinary and what he despises to be foul-smelling and rotten. However, what is admired by another might be what I despise, and what I admire might be despised by another. Therefore, since the "miraculous and extraordinary" and the 'foul-smelling and rotten" just keep turning one into the other, what difference should then exist between life and death, between other and self!

22.6.6 The sage thus reveres unity of all things."

22.7 Knowledge then said to the Yellow Thearch, "When I asked Not Conscious of What He Says, he did not answer; it was not that he would not reply, he knew not how to reply. When I asked Crazy Intractable, just when he was about to tell me, he did not say anything; it was not that he would not tell me but just when about to tell me he forgot what he was going to say. But now when I asked you, you knew the answer, so why is this not near it?"

22.8 The Yellow Thearch relied, "As for the former, he was really right because he did not know; as for the latter, he really seemed to get it because he forgot what it was. You and I fail to get near it because we know the answer."

22.9 When Crazy Intractable heard about this, he thought that the Yellow Thearch knew just what to say.

The understanding of Nature is not had by anyone who says he knows what it is. Therefore, those [two] obscured themselves in the realm of speechlessness, and this is why the text first cites examples of not speaking and then later provisionally lets stand the Yellow Thearch's explanation. Nevertheless, how could one ever discern even the general meaning of such an obscure and mysterious entity as Nature!

22.10.1 Heaven and Earth possess great splendors yet speak not of them; the four seasons possess laws bright with wisdom yet discourse not on them; the myriad things possess perfect principles yet talk not of them.

This is exactly what Confucius meant when he said, "I wish that I need not speak."[6]

22.10.2 The sage finds his source in the great splendors of Heaven and Earth and has penetrating insight into the principles governing the myriad things, for this is the way the Perfected one acts unselfconsciously.

Such a one allows things to happen spontaneously [*ziwei*], that's all there is to it.

22.10.3 The great sage does not initiate,

He just uses things in compliance with their natures [*yinren*].

22.10.4 which is what is meant by "they observed Heaven and Earth."

They [the sages] observed the condition of things and made images out of those that seemed appropriate, no different from Heaven and Earth.[7]

22.11.1 Now, the utmost subtlety of his divine intelligence allows him to stay in step with their everchanging transformations.

These everchanging transformations just self-transform without interference from his divine intelligence.

22.11.2 When things have died or come to life, when they have taken a square shape or round, no one knows the root of all this [*gen*].

When the dead have died of their own accord, the living have come alive of their own accord, the round have become round of their own accord, and the square have become square of their own accord, it is because no agency ever activated their roots that no one knows what it is.

22.11.3 So it is that the myriad things in great abundance have persistently existed since antiquity.

How is it possible that they depended on something to be created and only then had existence!

22.11.4 Though the reach of the six directions is enormous, it never exceeds the scope of it [the Dao/self-transformation].[8]

To reckon what the reach of the six directions is within what is infinite is a crude and shallow thing to do.

22.11.5 As tiny as an autumn hair is, it depends on it [the Dao/self-transformation] to be fully formed.

As tiny as an autumn hair might be, it still depends on the non-nothing yet nothing [*feiwu yi wu*] to form its particular physicality [*zhi*].

22.11.6 Of all things under Heaven, not one fails to sink and float, so throughout life they are never again what they were before.

They are something new each day.

22.11.7 As fluctuations of yin and yang, the four seasons circulate so that each keeps its proper place.

They don't depend on anything to do this.

22.11.8 Unclear whether it exists or not,

As soon as it seems it might exist, it has already vanished.

22.11.9 Flowing like oil with no physical form yet divine,

If demarcated with physical form, it would not be divine.

22.11.10 though the myriad things are reared by it, they know it not.

It rears them but does not affect the root of their fundamental natures, therefore, they know not what it is that rears them.

22.12.1 When Front Teeth Missing [Nieque] asked Clothed [Piyi] about the Dao, Wear Clothes replied,

> **"If you rectify your appearance**
> **and see all things as one,**
> **The harmony of Heaven shall reach you.**
> **If you subdue your knowledge**
> **and see all measures as one,**
> **The divine shall come to dwell in you,**
> **Virtue shall be your beauty,**
> **The Dao shall be your home,**
> **And you, guileless as a new born calf,**
> **shall not seek why this is so!"**

22.13 Before he had finished speaking, Front Teeth Missing dozed off. Absolutely delighted, Piyi walked away singing

> **"Body like dry bones,**
> **Mind like dead ashes,**
> **Authentic his real knowledge,**
> **Eschewing precedent he handles things himself.**

He keeps pace perfectly with change.

> **Dim and dark as can be,**
> **Free from selfconscious mind,**
> **It's impossible to seek advice from him,**
> **So what kind of man is he!"**

He is one capable of independent transformation.

22.14 Shun asked a counselor, "Can one obtain the Dao and thus possess it?"[9]

22.15 The counselor replied, "Since your own person is not yours to keep, how can you possess the Dao?"

Your person is not something that you can possess, for clod-like [intrinsically], it just exists spontaneously all on its own [*ziyou*]. Since your person is not yours to possess, how much the less could you ever possess the Dao!

22.16 Shun then said, "So if my self is not mine to possess, who then does possess it?"

22.17.1 "It is but a physical body coalesced from Heaven and Earth. Your life is not yours to possess, for it is but something coalesced in harmony from Heaven and Earth. Your natural endowment is not yours to possess, for it is but something coalesced in compliance with Heaven and Earth.

If your self were possessed by you, then whether you be handsome or ugly or whether you live or die, should all be controlled by you. Now, when your pneuma coalesced so you might live, this was not something you could have prevented, and when your pneuma disperses so you die, this is not something you can stop. It is thus clear that since it is just something that coalesced to form itself, it is not your possession.

22.17.2 Sons and grandsons are not yours to possess, for they are but coalescences and sloughings-off of Heaven and Earth.

Their pneumas spontaneously coalesce [*weijie*] and, cicada-like, slough away.

22.17.3 Therefore, moving, be unaware of where you go; halting, be unaware of where you maintain yourself; eating, be unaware of what you taste.

If all these occur during a state of spontaneity, one is thus unaware of them.

22.17.4 Since all this is due to the vigorous waxing [*qiangyang*] of the pneuma of Heaven and Earth, how apart from that could one ever obtain and thus possess it!

"Vigorous waxing" [*qiangyang*] just means something similar to "action" [*yundong*]. If one understands the Dao in this way, such a one might just about be able to cast aside self and become unaware of life.

22.18 Confucius asked Old Longears [Master Lao], "Now that you are at leisure and are free, may I venture to ask about the perfect Dao?"

22.19 Old Long Ears replied: "You must fast and practice austerities. Flush away your mind, purify your essential spirit [*jingshen*], and destroy your selfconscious awareness. Although the Dao is so remote and obscure that it is impossible to discuss, I shall try to give you a rough summary of it.

22.20.1 The clear and bright grows from the obscure and dark
the ordered grows from the formless
and essential spirit grows from the Dao,

This all is used to clarify that these come to exist independently, free of dependence on anything else.

22.20.2 where the root of bodily form [*xingben*] grows from
this the most refined and subtle [*jing*].

Everything develops from the refined to the crude.

22.20.3 The myriad things beget one another
through bodily form.
Thus it is that
those with nine orifices are womb born,
and those with eight orifices are egg born.

This speaks to how though the myriad things beget one another through bodily form, they nevertheless all do so spontaneously. As such, womb and egg can't change kinds when they give birth, which makes it clear that spirit pneuma [*shenqi*] can't function selfconsciously.

22.20.4 Its coming leaves no footprints,
and it goes where there are no limits,
For, free of gate and dwelling place,
its immeasurable vastness extends everywhere.

It [the Dao], in accord with its spontaneous nature, wanders a path on which no footprints are left but where it leaves bodily forms throughout Heaven and Earth. Its essential spirit lodges beyond the bounds of the eight directions, this means since it is free of gate and dwelling place, its immeasurable vastness extends everywhere. As such, it plays freely throughout the six directions and stays perfectly in step with transformation itself.

22.20.5 As for those welcome it,

Their four limbs are strong and healthy,
thought processes precise and unimpeded,
and hearing and vision sharp and clear.
They exercise mind without effort,
and their response to things infinitely flexible.

If in life anyone welcomes this Dao, his inherent nature shall remain whole and safe and his essential spirit shall enjoy tranquility.

22.20.6 That Heaven can't but be high,
Earth can't but be broad,
Sun and moon can't but move,
and the myriad things can't but flourish,
for is this not due to the Dao!

This means that all these things can't but be as they are and are so spontaneously; it does not mean that the Dao can cause them to be this way.

22.21.1 And furthermore, since erudition is not necessarily understanding, and eloquence not necessarily wisdom, the sage forsakes both.

Such a one forsakes understanding and eloquence and instead gives himself over to spontaneity.

22.21.2 That which increases not if added to and decreases not if diminished is what the sage safeguards.

All there is to this is to allow each to maintain his true allotted capacity [*zhengfen*]. Hence such a one has no need of understanding or wisdom to act.

22.21.3 So vast and deep, it is like the ocean.

Its capacity seems infinite.

22.21.4 So majestic and mountainous, when finished it always starts again.

Staying perfectly in step with transformation it piles up infinite centuries, so it may be described as "majestic and mountainous."

22.21.5 Though it carries along the myriad things, it never is depleted.

Since it allows others to make the effort so it does not belabor itself, it never wears out.

22.21.6 As such, the way of the "noble man," is it not found outside himself!

It shall suffice to find it within one's own person.

22.21.7 The myriad things go to it to be sustained [*zi*] yet it never is depleted; is this not just what the Dao is!

As long as effort reverts to others, I myself am not depleted. This makes it clear that the way the Dao sustains things is by not sustaining them. This is why the text says, "is this not just what the Dao is!" This means that the perfect Dao is without merit, for only if it is without merit may it be called the "Dao."

22.22.1 In the Central States there is a man who lives there, who is neither yin nor yang

He is free of any reason for such biased reputation.

22.22.2 and who takes his place between Heaven and Earth where for the time being he is just a man.

Free and easy, he just lets himself go, content with whatever comes his way, utterly indifferent to a reputation for merit.

22.22.3 He is thus ready to return to the Progenitor.

He pursues not superfluous things.

22.22.4 Looking at it from its fundamentals, life is just a mute blob of a thing.

It is just a coalescence of pneuma.

22.22.5 Whether one has a long life or premature death, how much difference is there between them? It is time for a momentary chat—how is that long enough to judge whether Yao and Jie is right or wrong!

Since life and death are not sufficiently different, how much the less is the difference between long life and premature death!

22.22.6 Principles inhere in fruits of trees and plants.

No thing is without its principles; all that need happen is compliance with them.

22.22.7 Though human relationships are difficult, they have a way to integrate successfully.

Human relationships vary according to intelligence, which is why they are difficult.

However, so that the amounts of intelligence involved spontaneously mesh [*xiangchi*], all people should do is comply accordingly.[10]

22.22.8 When the sage has such encounters, he acts not contrary to them,

He complies with whom he encounters.

22.22.9 and when he might pass them by, he does not linger.

When it is suitable to pass them by, he passes them by.

22.22.10 To respond to things in accord [*tiao*] with them indicates virtue; to respond to them by adjusting [*ou*] oneself to them indicates the Dao.

Accord [*tiao*] and adjustment [*ou*] both mean harmony.

22.22.11 This is the way emperors flourish and kings arise.

This occurs in no other way.

22.23.1 One's lifetime between Heaven and Earth goes as quick as a white colt passing a crack—suddenly it is all over.

So it is not worth grieving about.

22.23.2 Suddenly as if gushed out, nothing fails to come forth but in this way; tranquilly as if flowing like oil, nothing fails to pass away but in this way.

"Come forth" and "pass away" is just another way to say "change and transformation," that is, never has anything under Heaven failed to undergo transformation.

22.23.3 One transformation and so one is born; another transformation and so one dies.

Both are occurrences of such transformation.

22.23.4 As living things find this sad,

Dead things don't feel sad.

22.23.5 so the human species grieves over it.

A dead species does not grieve.

22.23.6 But it is just the unravelling of one's heavenly endowed bag, the disintegration of one's heavenly endowed sack.

It is independent release [*dutuo*].

22.23.7 How it roils! How lithe it is!

Such is the mist and smoke of change and transformation.

22.23.8 With the evanescent soul and earth-bound soul leading the way and the body following them, it is the great return!

This all happens without any selfconscious effort or thought.

22.23.9 One goes from no physical form to physical form and from physical form to no physical form.

It is only from no physical form that physical form is realized, so any attempt to form it otherwise fails.

22.23.10 Although this is something that people commonly know,

Although they know it, they nevertheless can't just let such self-formation [*zixing*] happen but instead try to form it, thus failing for the most part.

22.23.11 it is not something of concern for one who will perfectly realize it.

If concerned, one won't perfectly realize it.

22.23.12 Although this is something that everyone commonly discusses,

Although they discuss it, since they still can't help but be concerned, they thus fail to realize it perfectly.

22.23.13 those who perfectly realize it don't discuss it,

Only one dispassionately unaware shall perfectly realize it.

22.23.14 and those who do discuss won't perfectly realize it.

22.23.15 Even the clearest eyesight has no chance of encountering it.

Only the perfection of unselfconsciousness [*anzhi*] will encounter it.

22.23.16 It is better to remain silent than to dispute about it. Since the Dao can't be heard, it is better to cover one's ears than listen. As such, this may be called the way to great attainment.

If one remains silent and covers his ears, this will free him from chasing after things; as such, this is the way to great attainment.

22.24 Ziqi of East Wall asked Master Zhuang, "Where is this so-called Dao found?"

22.25 Master Zhuang replied, "There is no place that it is not found."

22.26 Ziqi of East Wall then said, "If I knew exactly where, that would do."

He wants to have Master Zhuang name where it is.

22.27 Master Zhuang answered, "It is in the ants."

22.28 "How can it really be as low as that?"

22.29 "It is in the tares and weeds."

22.30 "How can it be even lower as that?"

22.31 "It is in the tiles and bricks."

22.32 "How can it even be as extremely low as that?"

22.33 "It is in the shit and piss."

22.34.1 To this Ziqi of East Wall did not respond. Master Zhuang then said, "The questions you pose, sir, really don't reach the essentials of it."

To cite its most salient and essential aspect, Master Zhuang said that there is no place that it is not found, but this seemed to puzzle Ziqi, who was not up to getting at its essentials.

22.34.2 When the inspector of markets asked a hog butchery manager why he stepped on the hogs [*xi*], [he replied] "the lower you go in the more there is."

Xi are large pigs. The hog butchery manager stepped on the pigs in order to know whether they were fat or lean, for the more he stepped on parts where it was difficult to find the fat, the more he discovered how basically fat the pigs were. Now, asking where the Dao was to be found, as things became ever more humble, it became increasingly clear that it was certain the Dao did not exist apart from anything.

22.34.3 Don't go on insisting that Nothingness exists apart from things.

If you insist on implying that Nothingness exists apart from things, then the Dao would not be universal, and if the Dao were not universal, it could not be the Dao.[11]

22.34.4 The perfect Dao is just like that, and great words are also the same.

They make clear that the Dao does not exist apart from things.[12]

22.34.5 The three epithets 'universal' [*zhou*], 'omnipresent' [*bian*], and 'total' [*xian*] are different terms for the same reality; what they indicate is one and the same.

22.35.1 Let's try wandering together in the Palace of Nothing At All, where merging into one with it, our discussion should conclude that absolutely no limit for it exists!

Wandering in phenomenal existence can't lead to universality, omnipresence, and totality. Hence it is only after merging as one with and discussing it can one realize that the Dao is absolutely everywhere. Only after realizing the Dao is absolutely everywhere can one expand to become free from selfconscious involvement with things and thus wander in its boundlessness.

22.35.2 Let's try practicing unselfconscious action together, for how still and placid, boundless and pure, harmonious and easeful we should be!

All this is thanks to unselfconscious action.

22.35.3 And void indeed should be our wills!

So still and quiet, they should be utterly free of intention.

22.35.4 Setting off without conscious purpose in such a way, we won't know where we shall arrive.

As long as the will remains still and quiet, they should not be aiming to go anywhere, and since they aim not to go anywhere, when they do go, they know not where they will arrive. But to set off with conscious purpose [*youwang*] means that before Principle acts, the will is already engaged.[13]

22.35.5 Going to and fro in such a way, we won't know where we shall stop.

In this way, they just let it happen.

22.35.6 Then when we have gone to and fro in such a way, we won't know when it will end.

As long as going to and fro depends not on conscious awareness [*zhi*], they won't fail to go to and fro, for going to and fro, as such, constitutes a constant principle of things, so how could they ever end!

22.35.7 We shall let ourselves go in the vast boundlessness [*pinghong*] there, into which great wisdom enters, unaware of where it ends.

Vast boundlessness [*xukong*] means perfect emptiness [*xukuo*]. Great wisdom will play about in unlimited vacuity as they set it free to tally with change and transformation—they thus are unaware of it.

22.35.8 That which makes things things has no boundaries with things.[14]

It is clear that "that which makes things things," means that things just become things all by themselves and are not caused by anything else. That things become things just by themselves is because of arcane fusion [*ming*].[15]

22.35.9 However, things do have boundaries—those known as "boundaries between things."

It is because things with boundaries can't act arcanely [*mingran*] when interacting with each other that these may truly be called "boundaries."

22.35.10 The boundaries that don't bound are those that bound the unbounded.

Although the "unbounded" is said to be "that which makes things," it is perfectly clear that things become things just all by themselves. Since "that which makes things" is actually not a thing at all, where could boundaries ever exist for that!

22.35.11 Although we speak of waxing and waning, declining and spoiling, that which brings about waxing and waning is not some waxer or waner; that which brings about declining and spoiling is not some decliner or spoiler; that which brings about roots and branches is not some rooter or brancher; and that which brings about accumulation and dispersal is not some accumulator or disperser.

Since it is already clear that that which makes things is not a thing, it should also be clear that things don't "make" themselves into things; as such, what is it then that makes them? All are just spontaneously so [*zier*].

22.36.1 Once while Supple Lotus Sweet [E Hegan] and Shennong were fellow disciples studying with Old Dragon Auspicious [Lao Longji], Shennong had closed his door and was leaning on his armrest to take a nap. About midday Supple Lotus Sweet opened his door and announced, "Old Dragon has died!" Shennong, still leaning on his armrest, heaved himself up with the aid of the staff, cast it aside with a clatter, and burst out laughing.

As he got up he suddenly realized that death was not worth getting alarmed about, which was why he cast aside his staff and burst out laughing.

22.36.2 He then said, "Because he knew how shallow and prejudiced, how arrogant and self-indulgent I am, this Heavenly man abandoned me and died. Alas, now it's all over with the Master, for he died without bequeathing any of his wild nonsense to me!"

Beginning with Jianwu on down, everyone thought perfect expression just wild nonsense so did not believe it. This is why, except for fellows such as Old Dragon and Lian Shu, no one else was worth mentioning..

22.37.1 When Covercrock Condole [Yangang Diao][16] heard about this, he said, "It is to those who embody the Dao that noble men all over the world attach themselves.

One who may be said to embody the Dao would be a progenitor and master [*zongzhu*] in human form.[17]

22.37.2 But as for the Dao, like the tip of an autumn hair, he had not got even one part in ten thousand of it.

The tip of an autumn hair is indeed tiny, it thus also indicates that he did not get one part in ten thousand of it.

22.37.3 Yet since even he knew enough to conceal his wild nonsense when he died, how much the more would someone do so who had really embodied the Dao!

It is clear that the perfect Dao can't be attained by words; it can only be attained spontaneously [*zide*].

22.37.4 Look for it but it has no form; listen for it but it has no sound. When people discuss it, they call it arcane mystery [*mingming*], but saying this about the Dao is not the real Dao."

Since even "arcane mystery" in the same way is still not the Dao, it is clear that no term exists for the Dao.

22.38 Thereupon, Grand Clarity [Taiqing] asked Eternity [Wuqiong], "Do you know the Dao?"

22.39 Eternity replied, "I don't know it."

22.40 So he went on to ask Unselfconsciousness [Wuwei], "Do you know the Dao?" And Unselfconsciousness said, "I know the Dao."

22.41 "Since you know the Dao, does even it have special aptitudes?"

22.42 "It has."

22.43 "What then are these special aptitudes?"

22.44 Unselfconsciousness then said, "I know that the Dao can make things noble and can make them mean, can make them coalesce and make them disperse. These are the special aptitudes I know about."

22.45 Grand Clarity, conveying what had been said, asked No Beginning [Wushi], "Since they answered in such ways, with Eternity not knowing and Unselfconscious knowing, who is right, who wrong?"

22.46 No Beginning replied, "Not knowing is deep while knowing is shallow. Not knowing it belongs to the inner; knowing it belongs to the outer."[18]

22.47 At that, Grand Clarity, caught between the two positions, sighed and said, "So not to know it is to know, and to know is not to know! But who knows how to know by not knowing!"

In every instance of grasping it [the Dao], is it never due to knowing, but only thanks to arcane fusion [*ming*] with it.

22.48.1 No Beginning responded, "The Dao can't be heard of, for what may be heard is not it; the Dao can't be seen, for what may be seen is not it; the Dao can't be spoken of, for what is spoken of is not it.

Therefore, accomplish this silently [*mocheng*] by staying within the realm of hearing not and seeing not, for only then shall one attain to it.[19]

22.48.2 Know that which forms forms does not take form.

Since forms spontaneously just take form by themselves, that which forms forms is no thing at all.

22.48.3 The Dao matches not any name."

Although there is the name "Dao," because it is no thing at all, it is impossible for any name to match it.

22.49.1 No Beginning then said, "The one who when asked about the Dao answered the question did not know the Dao, so though the other asked about the Dao, he still heard not what it was.

Since the one did not know, he asked. Whereas what was answered when asked was not the Dao, if the other had not answered, this would not have allowed the one who asked to attain it either. Therefore, although the one asked, he did not, after all, hear what it was.

22.49.2 Let no question be asked about the Dao; let no question about it be answered.

Abandon learning, cast aside teaching, and revert to a spontaneous and natural state of mind [*ziran zhi yi*].

22.49.3 If one asks what should not be asked, this is to ask in vain.

This is what is known as to "task in vain" [*zekong*]

22.49.4 If one answers what should not be answered, this will have nothing inside it.

If one's answer lacks truth and be false in content, it is extraneous.

22.49.5 To take what contains nothing and have it depend on questioning in vain, anyone who does such a thing neither observes the universe without nor understands the great source within himself, and thus neither crosses over Mount Kunlun nor fords the Great Void."

One who casually falls in with Heaven and Earth, wanders in emptiness, and crosses over great distances, thereby consorting with arcane mystery, just would not answer, nothing more!

22.50 Bright Clarity [Guanghui] asked Nonexistent [Wuyou], "Sir, do you have existence or do you not have existence?"

22.51 When he got no response, Bright Clarity carefully tried to see how he looked, but, as he was absolutely obscure and utterly void, though he looked at him all day long he saw him not, listened to him but heard him not, groped for him but grasped him not.

22.52 Bright Clarity then said, "How perfect! Who else could reach such a state as this! Though I can grasp the existence of non-existence, I can't quite grasp the non-existence of non-existence, and when it comes to grasping the non-existence of existence, where does ever reaching that come from!"

All of this indicates a state of mind in which learning has been utterly excluded. If thanks to the Dao one has so excluded it, then learning as such comes from within the fundamental essence of things. Therefore, one good at learning, is this not only one who does not try to learn!

22.53.1 The belt hook forger for the minister of war was all of eighty yet was never off even the slightest,

The force with which he pounded out hooks was not off by even the slightest amount.

22.53.2 so the minister asked him, "Is this because you are so skilled? Or do you have a special way of doing it?"

22.54 He replied, "It is what I concentrate on. From the time I was twenty I so liked to pound out hooks that I never looked at anything else, thus, if it were not a hook I heeded it not. As for this faculty of mine, I have long had access to it thanks to not consciously using it. So how much the more true this is for one who has the facility to do absolutely everything! What thing would not lend itself to him!"

He was free from selfconscious involvement with things, thus whenever something came his way, he always responded effectively to it.

22.55 Ran Qiu[20] asked of Zhongni [Confucius], "Is it possible to know what it was like before there were Heaven and Earth?"

22.56 Zhongni replied, "It is possible, for the past is just like the present."

He meant that since Heaven and Earth have always existed, there never was a time when they did not exist.

22.57 Since Ran Qiu was at a loss for anything more to ask , he withdrew, but the next day again went to see him to ask again, "Before, when I asked you 'Is it possible to know what it was like before there were Heaven and Earth,' you said, 'It is possible, for the past is just like the present.' Although this seemed clear to me then, now I am confused, so may I presume to ask what you meant?"

22.58.1 Zhongni replied, "When it seemed clear to you before, this was because it was with your spirit that you then first received it,

To await instructions with an empty mind, this is to receive with one's spirit.

22.58.2 but now that you are confused, is this not because you no longer seek it with your spirit?

If one seeks it consciously, on the contrary understanding shall remain beyond reach.

22.58.3 If they were not there in the past they would not exist now; they had no beginning so they will have no end.

Not only is it impossible for the non-existent to transform and become existent, it is impossible for the existent to transform and become non-existent. As such, although the existent in material form undergoes myriads of transformations, not once does it become non-existent. And since it does not even once become non-existent, never in the past has there been a time when they did not exist—they have thus always existed.

22.58.4 Is it possible to have sons and grandsons without there having already been sons and grandsons?"

He means that generations follow generations without end.

22.59.1 Before Ran Qiu could reply, Zhongni told him, "Enough! No need to respond! Don't cause death because of life!

Death becomes death only through independent transformation, not because life causes such death.

22.59.2 Don't make life into death because of death!

Life also becomes life only through independent transformation.[21]

22.59.3 Are life and death subject to dependency?

Only independent transformation is sufficient for them to happen.

22.59.4 Each has what is its own single state.

Life and death each on its own fully realizes its state [*chengti*].

22.59.5 Before there were Heaven and Earth, did something produce things? That which makes things things is no thing. It is impossible for things to appear before there were things, for things were still there. That things were still there is because they go on endlessly.[22]

What could possibly exist prior to things! I might have it that yin and yang were prior to them, but yin and yang themselves are just what we may call things. So what was there even prior to ying and yang? I might have it that Nature [*ziran*] was prior to them, but Nature means just things functioning spontaneously on their own. I might have it that the perfect Dao was there prior to it, but the perfect Dao consists of just perfect emptiness [*zhiwu*]. As such, it has no existence, so what could have been more prior to that? This being so, what then could have possibly existed prior to things! However, since things still come into existence without ever ending, it is clear that they just happen spontaneously and not because something makes them happen.

22.59.6 That the sage's love for mankind never comes to an end should also be understood in such terms."

It should be understood as spontaneity, for this is how such favor and grace flows on for age upon age yet never fails.

22.60 Yan Yuan [Yan Hui] asked Zhongni [Confucius], "I have heard you say, Master, 'Neither send anyone away nor welcome anyone hither.'[23] May I presume to ask how this is done [*qiyou*]?"[24]

22.61.1 Zhongni replied, "Men of antiquity transformed on the exterior but did not transform on the interior.

Since the mind allowed the physical form comply, physical appearance self-transformed accordingly.[25]

22.61.2 But men nowadays transform on the interior but don't transform on the exterior.

This is because the mind is contingent on physical form.[26]

22.61.3 One who transforms with things is unified with that which does not transform.[27]

As long as one remains constantly free of conscious mind, he is one with that which does not transform, which is the only way one can transform in step with things.

22.61.4 Such a one calmly accepts both their transformation and non-transformation,

Whether people transform or not, such a one just lets them be, for this is due to his freedom from conscious mind.

22.61.5 calmly mingles together with them,

Simply free of conscious mind, such a one just lets himself self-transform, neither sending people away nor welcoming them hither but just mingling in compliance with them.

22.61.6 and is sure not to do anything in excess of this."

He neither sends anyone away nor welcomes anyone hither; as such, since in all cases what such a one does is exactly enough, he stops at that.[28]

22.61.7 Sire Xiwei[29] let his park confine him, the Yellow Thearch let his garden confine him, Sire of Yu [Shun] let his palace confine him, and Tang and Wu let their chambers confine them.

This addresses how, free of selfconsciousness, they just let transformation take place, which gave all these sages a place to relax.

22.61.8 And such were the noble men among them, when it came to teachers of the Ru and Mo traditions, that they even took their rights and wrongs and mashed them together [*ji*], so how much more easily should they do so with those of the people of today!

"Mash together" [*ji*] means "reconcile" [*he*]. Confucian and Mohist teachers were the most difficult to reconcile in all the world, yet they, with their freedom from conscious mind, still reconciled them, so how much easier should they reconcile ordinary people![30]

22.61.9 When a sage abides with others, he harms them not.

This is because he is perfectly compliant.

21.61.10 That he harms not others means that others too can't harm him.

Such a one does nothing other than just keep to himself.

21.61.11 Only one free of any instance of harm can send away and welcome others.

Since such a one is free of conscious mind, he is perfectly compliant, and, perfectly compliant, does not ever try to send anyone away or welcome anyone hither—this meaning caps any sending away or welcoming that occurs.[31]

22.61.12 Oh, the mountains and forests. Oh, the wetlands and hinterlands. Filling me with joy, how they delight me!

Mountains and forests or wetlands and hinterlands never do me any good, yet they fill me with delight. This is delight that occurs without cause.

22.61.13 But before such delight ends, it is succeeded again by sorrow.

As delight occurs without cause, so one's sorrow happens also without cause, for whatever delights one is not worth feeling delight about, and whatever besets one with sorrow is not worth feeling sorrow about.

22.61.14 I can't ward off the coming of sorrow or delight, nor can I stop them from leaving. How sad! The people of this world just let things use them as if they were but places to stay.

Since they are unable to abide in forgetfulness and achieve self-fulfillment, they but provide a place for sorrow or delight to lodge.

22.61.15 They understand what they have encountered but don't understand what they have not encountered.

What their knowledge has encountered they understand, but what their knowledge has not encountered they don't understand.

22.61.16 They are able to do what they are capable of but are unable to do what they are incapable of.

What they are unable to do, they can't force themselves to be capable of. If one looks at it this way, control over whether one understands or does not understand or whether one is capable of something or not capable of something does not come from one's personal self but must tally with nothing other than what is in one's natural endowment.

22.61.17 To lack certain knowledge or lack certain capability is surely the unavoidable lot of men.

Each person who receives life has a certain allotted capacity.

22.61.18 To strive to avoid what people can't avoid, is that not also sad!

22.61.19 Perfect speech is to abandon speech; perfect action is to abandon action.

Each instance of either is always realized spontaneously.

22.61.20 To equate knowing with what is known is a shallow view indeed!

To try to succeed thanks to the application of knowledge is to pursue false learning, which is why it is "shallow."

Notes

1. *Laozi*, section 56; Richard John Lynn, *The Classic of the Way and Virtue*, 157.
2. *Laozi*, section 2; Lynn, *The Classic of the Way and Virtue*, 54.
3. *Laozi*, section 38; Lynn, *The Classic of the Way and Virtue*, 119; this is the exact quotation, except that the last sentence in the *Laozi* reads, "Propriety consists of the superficial aspects of loyalty and trust and is thus the beginning of disorder."
4. This is an exact quotation from Wang Bi's commentary on the *Laozi*, section 20, on the first passage: "Repudiate learning, and stay free of worry . . ." Lynn, *The Classic of the Way and Virtue*, 83.
5. This is an exact quote from the *Laozi*, section 48; see Lynn, *The Classic of the Way and Virtue*, 143.
6. *Lunyu* (Analects) 17: 2526a.
7. Cf. *Yijing* (Classic of Changes), "Commentary on the appended phrases" [*Xici zhuan*], Part One: "The sages had the means to perceive the mysteries of the world and, drawing comparisons to them with analogous things, made images out of those things that seemed appropriate." Richard John Lynn, *The Classic of Changes*, 56–57.
8. According to Cheng Xuanying, "its scope" [*qinei*] means "within the scope of the perfect Dao" [*zhidao zhi zhong*]; according to Lu Deming, it means "impossible to escape the bounds of self-transformation" [*buneng chu zihua*]. *Zhuangzi jishi*, 3: 736.

9. The same passage appears, with variations, in the *Liezi* (Sayings of Master Lie); *Liezi jishi*, 1: 33–35.
10. Cheng Xuanying: "Dangers and obstacles make it difficult for people to live in this world. However, if the noble and the mean, superiors and inferiors, mesh together hierarchically [*chici*] and people but comply accordingly, spontaneous agreement with the Dao occurs, analogous to the way fruits of trees and plants have principles inherent in them." *Zhuangzi jishi*, 3: 746.
11. Cheng Xuanying: "The term 'Nothingness' refers to the Dao with its unselfconscious force." *Zhuangzi jishi*, 3: 751.
12. Cheng Xuanying: "The expression 'perfect Dao' refers to Principle [*li*], and the expression 'great words' refers to teaching [*jiao*]. Just as Principle does not exist apart from things, so its teaching is universal and free of bias." *Zhuangzi jishi*, 3: 751.
13. In addressing this passage in the *Zhuangzi*, commentators variously equate Principle [*li*] with Nature [*tian*], Nothingness [*wu*], or the Dao, all of which suggests that Guo's gloss "to set off with conscious purpose [*youwang*] means that before Principle acts, the will is already engaged" can be restated as "to set off without conscious purpose means that as long as Principle/Nature (unselfconscious spontaneity)/Nothingness/Dao is allowed to act first while the individual will remains void (utterly unselfconscious), the individual, merged and perfectly one with the Dao, will find whatever he sets out to do will go well." See *Zhuangzi jishi*, 3: 753.
14. Cf. 22.59.5.
15. Cheng Xuanying interprets this passage differently: "One who can let things be things is the sage. Because the sage arcanely merges with the myriad things of phenomenal existence, he has no boundaries with things, between others and self." *Zhuangzi jishi*, 3: 753. Cf. 11.31.3–11.31.4.
16. The translation of Yangang Diao as "Covercrock Condole" is by Victor Mair; it can't be improved on; see *Wandering on the Way: Early Taoist Tales and Parables of Chuang Tzu*, 218.
17. "Progenitor and master" are epithets for the Dao; cf. Wang Bi, *Laozi zhilue* (Outline introduction to the *Laozi*), Lou Yulie, ed., *Wang Bi ji jiaoshi* (Critical edition of the works of Wang Bi, with explanatory notes), 159; Lynn, *The Classic of the Way and Virtue*, 30: "Thus, try to conceive of It [the Dao] as a thing, and It will turn out to be amorphous and complete; try to capture It as an image, and It will be utterly formless; try to hear It as tonality, and It will greet you as an inaudible sound; try to experience It as flavor, and It will have an indistinguishable taste. Thus It is capable of serving as the progenitor and master of things in all their different categories, of covering and permeating everything in Heaven and Earth, so that nothing is allowed to escape the warp of Its weave."
18. Cheng Xuanying: "Not knowing accords with principle, thus profound and arcane, it belongs to the inner, while knowing something is contrary to the Dao, thus crude and shallow, it belongs to the outer." *Zhuangzi jishi*, 3: 757.
19. Guo's statement seems to paraphrase the *Yijing* (Classic of Changes), "Appended Phrases" [*Xici zhuan*], Part One: "to accomplish things while remaining silent and to be trusted without speaking is something intrinsic to virtuous conduct." Lynn, *The Classic of Changes*, 68.
20. Cheng Xuanying: "Surnamed Ran and given name Qiu, he was a disciple of Zhongni [Confucius]." *Zhuangzi jishi*, 3: 762.
21. It seems that Guo Xiang's focus on noncausality had him ignore the obvious meaning of the text: it is an injunction not to let concern for life and fear of death result in worry that shortens one's life.

22. Cf. 22.35.8.
23. Cf. 7.26.11.
24. Although the characters for *qiyou* in the received text read as "this [way to] wander," Cheng Xuanying glosses it as *qi suoyou*, "from where does one start" or "how this is done." More evidence that *you*, "wander," should be corrected to *you*, "from," is provided by Wang Shumin; see *Zhuangzi jiaoquan*, 847–48, note 1.
25. Cheng Xuanying: "Men of antiquity were so pure and pristinely simple that many were one with the Dao. As such, their exterior physical appearance could conform to others while their interior minds remained steadfastly serene." *Zhuangzi jishi*, 3: 765.
26. Cheng Xuanying: "Because one's mind is thoroughly contingent on one's physical form, change and transformation are beyond its comprehension, so exterior appearance becomes false, and one is unable to comply with others." *Zhuangzi jishi*, 3: 765.
27. Cf. 25.10.3.
28. Cheng Xuanying: "Though such a one consistently complies with others, he also refrains from adding benevolence or mercy to what he does; as such, everyone stays within the limits of individual allotted capacity; thus self and other suffer no loss." *Zhuangzi jishi*, 3: 766.
29. Cf. 6.12.7.
30. Cheng Xuanying: " 'Mash together [*ji*]' means 'harmonize [*he*]'. The way Confucian and Mohist teachers refuted one another made them the most difficult to reconcile in all the world. However, noble men who were sages could still make them comply and be reconciled. So how much easier should they do so with people of the present age who are not Confucian or Mohist teachers! That they should make them comply [one with the other] and transform them—is this not just what one might expect!" *Zhuangzi jishi*, 3: 766.
31. Cheng Xuanying: "Only one who calmly accepts everyone as they are, so that others and self stay free from harm, can associate with others in such a way that it is clear that he neither tries to send anyone away or welcomes anyone." *Zhuangzi jishi*, 3: 767.

PART III

THE SAYINGS OF MASTER ZHUANG, THE MISCELLANEOUS CHAPTERS

CHAPTER 23

GENGSANG CHU

23.1.1 Among the disciples of Lao Dan was Gengsang Chu, who in particular attained his sagely way and, as such, he went north to dwell in the Rocky [Weilei] Mountains.[1] He dismissed those of his male servants who were ostentatiously intelligent and distanced himself from those of his female servants who were self-importantly benevolent.

"Ostentatiously" means to show off one's intelligence, and "self-importantly" means to take pride in one's benevolence.

23.1.2 He only had the unspoiled simple live with him

"Unspoiled simple" [*yongzhong*] means 'pristinely simple [*pu*].

23.1.3 and only had those who just worked hard as his servants.

"Just worked hard" means those who were "self-fulfilled" [*zide*].

23.1.4 Having dwelt there for three years, such a bountiful harvest occurred in the Rocky Mountains that the common folk of the Rocky Mountains said to one another, "When Master Gengsang first came, we were astonished and thought him strange.

They thought it strange that he had discarded wisdom and had just given himself over to stupidity.

23.1.5 Now, though reckoned by what he does by the day seems inadequate, reckoned by what he does by the year seems more than enough.

To be at one with the four seasons results in no immediate gain.

23.1.6 This just about makes him a sage! So why don't we make him our ceremonial stand-in for the deceased and dedicate our altar to him as deity of soil and grain?"

23.2.1 When Master Gengsang heard this, he faced south, seemingly displeased, and, when his disciples thought this strange, he said, "Disciples, why do you think me strange?

> **When the pneuma of spring starts up, all vegetation comes alive,**
> **And with the arrival of autumn, myriad treasures ripen.**

As for spring and autumn, how could they not but be this way! As such, they were set into motion by the Dao of Heaven.

The "coming alive" and "ripening" of spring and autumn always occur thanks to the Dao of Nature, thus it happens without intent.

23.2.2 I have heard that the Perfected one dwells corpse-like in his little room while the common folk rush energetically about unselfconscious of where they seem to be going.

They just spontaneously go forth, not prompted by selfconscious understanding.

23.2.3 Now that the common folk of Rocky Mountains are buzzing with rumor that they wish to sacrifice to me with ritual vessels as one of the worthies, but how could I let myself become such an exemplar for them?

He does not wish to become an exemplar for others.

23.2.4 This is why I am displeased, because of what Lao Dan had to say."

As Dan [Master Lao] said, "success is had and the task accomplished," but the common folk all say that this happens because of me, which means that now they at Rocky Mountains are at odds with this, which is why I am displeased.[2]

23.3 His disciples said, "This is not right! In a narrow, shallow ditch, great big fish have no room to turn around, yet little fish find it a place to swim circles in. On a hillock a few paces high a large beast would have nowhere to hide, yet the wily fox finds it a good place to be.

The disciples mean that a great one should have a rich salary.

23.3.2 Moreover, to honor the worthy, give office to the capable, and to give precedence to those who do good and provide benefit, it has ever been so since the ancient times of Yao and Shun, thus how much the more should the common folk of the Rocky Mountains do so! You, Master, too should heed them!"

23.4.1 Master Gengsang then said, "Young men, come near! Take a wild beast that could hold a carriage in its mouth, once on its own, away from the mountains, it would not avoid the peril of snare nets, or a fish that could swallow a boat, just let it be washed up high and dry and ants would cause it grief. This is why birds and beasts don't shun the heights and fish and turtles shun not the depths.

Only by avoiding benefit and staying far away from harm does one keep oneself perfectly intact.

23.4.2 One who would keep his body and life intact conceals himself and shuns not seclusion and obscurity—that's all there is to it!

If one allows himself to become entangled with wealth and official salary, he makes himself an obvious and easy target.

23.5.1 Moreover, what makes those two so worthy of praise!

By "those two," he means Yao and Shun.

23.5.2 They made distinctions that led to the boring of holes through garden walls and to rank weeds planting themselves.

By doing so, they caused people of later ages recklessly to bore holes and let perverse ways to plant themselves there.[3]

23.5.3 They singled out individual hairs to comb and counted grains of rice to cook.

That is, they went so far as "the points of awls and knives."[4]

23.5.4 What absolute clarity![5] But even so, what good can it do to save the world!

Only by merging with all in one integral whole, free of all effort at selfconscious control does such salvation occur.

23.5.5 Elevate the worthy and the people will harm one another with strife.

They will violate their fundamental natures for the chance of their being exalted.

23.5.6 Appoint the knowledgeable and the people will thieve from one another.

When one finds his authenticity inadequate and so would augment it with knowledge, this makes him a fraudulent imitation, and to seek one's livelihood as such a fraud, if this be not theft, what is it!

23.5.7 To deal with people in such ways does no good to improve the lives of the common folk, for they become so keen on benefiting themselves that sons would kill fathers, officials would kill sovereigns, some would commit robbery in broad daylight or tunnel through walls at high noon.

They no longer have consideration for anyone.

23.5.8 Let me tell you, great disorder surely took root in the time of Yao and Shun, and its branch tips will survive even after a thousand generations. After a thousand generations, there surely will be people devouring one another.

Because Yao and Shun left behind these footprints, presence and fraud afterwards spread so widely that such extreme evil as this occurred.[6]

23.6 Startled and embarrassed, Nanrong Chu sat up straight and said, "For someone like me who is already so old, what practice might I rely on to attain to what you say here?"

23.7.1 Master Gengsang replied,

"Keep your physical form intact,

One should guard one's natural allotment.

23.7.2 Embrace your life,

One should not try to grab more than his life's limits.

23.7.3 And don't let your thoughts wear you out
with their constant buzzing.

If you do this for three years, you may attain to what I say here."

23.8.1 Nanrong Chu then said, "The eye and its physical form, I can't make out the difference, yet the blind themselves can't see. The ear and its physical form, I can't tell the difference, yet the deaf can't themselves hear. The mind and its physical form, I can't make out the difference, yet the insane are incapable of comprehension.

Eyes and eyes, ears and ears, minds and minds, their physical forms may look alike but their capabilities differ, and as these are not equal, it is impossible to force those of one to conform to those of another.

23.8.2 If we compare the one physical form to the other, it too is open [*pi*], so is there anything to distinguish between them? But if either tries to match the other, it can't match."

It is not that they are closed.[7]

23.8.3 Now you have just told me,

> **'Keep your physical form intact,**
> **Embrace your life,**
> **And don't let your thoughts wear you out**
> **with their constant buzzing.'**

And though I strive to understand what you say, it only goes as far as my ears!"

It is because he had hitherto heard about the distinction among physical forms that he finds transformation so difficult.[8]

23.9 Master Gengsang replied, "I have nothing else to tell you. As it is said, 'The digger wasp can't transmute bean caterpillars, but though the Yue hen can't hatch swan eggs, the Lu hen certainly could.' If we compare the one hen to the other, it is not because the kind of innate potential of each differs that the one can do it but the other can't, but because the innate potential of each differs as to size. Now, the size of my innate potential is so small that it is not large enough to transform you, so why don't you go south and see Master Lao?"[9]

23.10 Carrying provisions with him, it took seven days and seven nights for Nanrong Chu to reach Master Lao's place.

23.11 Master Lao asked, "Have you come from Gengsang Chu's place?" And Nanrong Chu replied, "Yes."

23.12 Master Lao further asked, "Why have you come with such a crowd of people?" Startled, Nanrong Chu turned to look behind him.

[This is asked] because he has brought his three dilemmas along with him.

23.13 Master Lao then said, "Don't you know what I mean?" Ashamed, Nanrong Chu bowed his head, then, raising it, said with a sigh, "I've now lost track of how I should respond, for what I wanted to ask you escapes me."
23.14 Master Lao asked, "What do you mean?"
23.15 Nanrong Chu replied, "If unlearned, people would say that I am ignorant and stupid, but if learned, this repays me only with grief. If inhumane, I would harm people, but if humane, this repays me only with trouble. If unrighteous, I would injure others, but if righteous, this repays me only with anguish. How can I escape from all this? These three dilemmas are making me feel absolutely miserable. At the suggestion of Gengsang Chu, I wish to ask you what to do about it."
23.16 Master Lao then said, "A while ago when I looked at you right in the eyebrows and eyelashes, I discerned your inner self,[10] and now what you go on to say confirms it. You look panic-stricken and utterly at a loss, as if you were a child who had lost its parents or were trying to find something in the sea with a pole. You have utterly lost your bearings, absolutely at a loss at what to do! You want to return to your fundamental nature, but have no way to begin, how pitiful!" Nanrong Chu then asked permission to go back to his lodgings, where he tried to engage what was good in himself and to purge what was bad, but after ten days he was still making himself miserable, so again he went to see Master Lao.
23.17.1 Master Lao said, "How hard and anxiously you've worked at cleansing yourself! But your inner self so overflows with it that you still have what's bad in you. When one's outer is fettered, even the utmost dexterity fails to control it, so this blocks the inner; when one's inner is fettered, even the tightest grip fail to control it, so this blocks the outer.

"Block" [*jian*] means "shut down" [*guanjian*]. The ears and eyes constitute the "outer"/"without," and the techniques of the mind constitute the "inner"/"within." To keep one's bodily form whole and safe and preserve one's life, nothing is better than to become unselfconscious of the techniques of the mind and become unaware of the ears and eyes. When sights and sounds fetter the outer, the techniques of the mind are blocked within, and when desires and aversions fetter the inner, the ears and eyes fail without. Surely only if one is free from the sense of advantage and disadvantage can they [the inner and the outer] work smoothly together.

23.17.2 If the inner and the outer are thus fettered, even [one who aspires to] the Dao and its Virtue fails to control them, so how less likely can one who conducts himself apart from the Dao!"

Even one who tries to stay away from such fetters can't do it, so how less likely can one whose inner and outer are both fettered! When ears and eyes are dazzled and deluded without and the techniques of the mind float adrift within, even if one handled them with the utmost dexterity and managed them with the tightest of grasps, he would still fail to curb them.

23.18 Nanrong Chu then said, "When a villager gets sick and other villagers ask about it, if the sick one can talk about his illness and describe what it is like, this means he is not completely sick. For me to hear about the great Dao is like getting fed medicine that makes me feel sicker. All I want now is just to hear about the summary rules to preserve life."

23.19.1 Master Lao said, "The summary rules to preserve life are:

Can you embrace the One?

He should not lose his original nature.

23.19.2 And abandon it not?

He should ever return to his own potential.

23.19.3 Can you discern good fortune and misfortune
without tortoise shells or yarrow stalks?

If one behaves appropriately, good fortune results; if one exceeds one's limits, misfortune occurs—no need to divine about it.

23.19.4 Can you stay?

He should stay within his allotted capacity.

23.19.5 Can you stop?

He should not follow old footsteps.

23.19.6 Can you shun what is in others and seek only within yourself?

He should keep himself intact and not imitate others.

23.19.7 Can you be carefree?

He should not halt his steps.

23.19.8 Can you be childishly unaware?

He should be unconstrained.

23.19.9 Can you be an infant? 'That it can cry all day long yet never grow hoarse is because its bodily balance is perfect.'[11]

He lets sounds emerge spontaneously, not because he selfconsciously feels joy or anger.

23.19.10 That it can grab things all day long yet its hands never tire is because its virtue remains united.[12]

It lets hands grab spontaneously, not because it would get hold of something in particular.

23.19.11 That it can look at things all day without directing its gaze is because it feels no partiality for external things.

It lets eyes spontaneously look, not because it is attracted by the way something looks.

23.19.12 It moves but is unaware where it goes.

It lets its feet move spontaneously, free of selfconscious inclination.

23.19.13 It finds repose but is unaware of what it does,

It lets its body move freely, which thus acts to suit itself.

23.19.14 It complies with others as a snake wriggles compliantly to the ground,

This is how it so complies with them.

23.19.15 thus flows along as they flow.

As things flow, it too flows.

23.19.16 This then is all there is to the common rules to preserve life."

23.20 Nanrong Chu then asked, "But is this all there is to the virtue of a Perfected one?"

If he [Nanrong Chu] could reform himself and follow such advice, he would like to claim that he had the virtue of a Perfected one.

23.21.1 Master Lao replied, "No. This is merely what might be said to be the release of the ice-bound when ice melts. How could it amount to that?

"How could it amount to that!" Here he [Master Lao] clarifies that it [the virtue of a Perfected one] does not necessarily result.

23.21.2 Although the Perfected one joins with others in seeking food from the earth and joy from Heaven,

Having freed himself from his own mind, he at all times merges with everyone else.

23.21.3 he is not perturbed by others, neither for the sake of benefit nor to avoid harm, does nothing that appears strange to them, and neither does he plot with them nor selfconsciously engage in their endeavors. Carefree he lets things go; childishly unaware he lets them come. This is what I mean by 'this all there is to the common rules to preserve life.'"

23.22 "But is this then perfection?"

That is, could he himself reach perfection by following such advice?

23.23.1 "Not quite. As I've already said,

'Can you be an infant?'

He [Master Lao] does not mean that what he has said would not lead to perfection, for just being able to hear and learn what is said will fail as a way to reach perfection. If one does not reach perfection on one's own, though one may hear about what perfection is, this can only provide summary rules for it—and how could these ever provide the means to reach perfection! As such, one who tries to learn it will never reach perfection, and one who has attained perfection has not got it by learning it.

23.23.2 An infant acts but is unaware of what it does,
Moves but is unaware of where it goes,
Its body like a branch of dead wood
and mind like lifeless ashes.

23.23.3 As it is thus,

Calamity never touches it
Nor is it ever visited by good fortune,
So free of calamity and good fortune,
What human disaster shall ever befall it?"

Calamity and good fortune are born in loss and gain, and human disaster happens because of likes and dislikes. Now, utterly dispassionate as dead wood and lifeless ashes, neither penchant and aversion nor any sense of loss and gain have a way to reach it.

23.24.1 When the inner self [*yu*] is at peace and stable, it shines forth with the radiance of Heaven.

When one's inner virtue [*deyu*] is at peace and stable, it shines forth only with the radiance of Heaven and never with the light of human glory.

23.24.2 For one who shines forth with the radiance of Heaven, people appear as they really are and things appear as they really are.[13]

As the radiance of Heaven spontaneously shines forth, people appear as they really are, and things appear as they really are. Everything spontaneously appears to him as it really is and not just as something apart from him. Thus it is he has peace and stability.

23.24.3 Someone should so cultivate himself, for only then does one have constancy.

When someone cultivates himself, once he spontaneously succeeds then constant peace is the result.

23.24.4 Once one has constancy, people take shelter with him and Heaven aids him.

Such constancy and peace enable people to gravitate for shelter with him as if their own home and to have Nature provide him with help.

23.24.5 One with whom people take shelter is known as a "Commoner of Heaven" [*tianmin*], and one so aided by Heaven is known as a "Son of Heaven" [*tianzi*].

Emerged, such a one is a "Son of Heaven"; living privately, he is a "Commoner of Heaven." These two states are realized spontaneously by being utterly at peace—and never acquired by selfconscious effort.

23.25.1 A "learner" tries to learn what he can't learn; a "doer" tries to do what he can't do; a "disputer" tries to dispute what he can't dispute.

Whatever one can do, though he does it, he does not selfconsciously do it; though he practices it, he does not selfconsciously learn; though he discourses on it, he does not selfconsciously dispute.[14]

23.25.2 To know that one should stop at what one can't know is to have reached perfection.

What one is incapable of knowing, he can't force himself to know. Therefore, to stop at this point is to reach perfection.[15]

23.25.3 But anyone who fails to do so, the potter's wheel of Heaven will thwart.[16]

Whatever such a one has in mind to do, the doing is sure to fail, for the underlying principles involved will never allow him to succeed.

23.26.1 Use your physical body as a thing complete in itself,

Because it is complete in itself, use your physical body as it is formed.

23.26.2 activate your mind with no intentionality [*yu*] harbored within,

Just let your mind activate itself and don't let it start with selfconscious intention [*yu*]. "Selfconscious intention" means the same thing as *yidu*, "conjecture"/"estimation."

23.26.3 and interact with others while revering your inner self.

Just let principles spontaneously conduct your interaction with others, and slight not your inner self and instead revere others.

23.26.4 If such a one is still beset with a myriad of ill fortune, it would all be Heaven's doing

In the natural principles of things obstruction and facilitation are inherently present.

23.26.5 and not one's own fault.

It is when selfconscious action brings on ill fortune that it is one's own fault.

23.26.6 So this is insufficient to disturb one's self-realization [*cheng*],

Such a one is content with things as fate decrees, so his self-realization is not disturbed.

23.26.7 and fails to enter one's numinous tower.

"Numinous tower" is the mind, which, if clear and free-flowing, allows no sense of privation or tribulation to enter it.

23.26.8 The numinous tower has that which it grasps

"The numinous tower has that which it grasps" just means that it is not agitated by external things, so no "grasping" actually happens.

23.26.9 and should remain unaware of that which it grasps

If it were aware that it had something to grasp, it would try to grasp it.

23.26.10 and must not try to grasp it.

Because to try to grasp it would be to lose it.

23.27.1 If one sets forth without regard for the sincere self,

That is, if one sets forth to do something recklessly.

23.27.2 whatever he ventures to do shall never prove apt.

To set forth yet not start from the sincerity of the self, how should that ever prove apt!

23.27.3 He shall be inundated by affairs that he can't accommodate,

Such affairs can't be accommodated within his natural allotment.

23.27.4 it shall result in ever more failure.

Only if one starts from the sincerity of self shall he have success.[17]

23.27.5 If one does evil out where it is obvious, men will seize and punish him; if one does evil in obscurity and secrecy, ghosts will seize and punish him.

23.27.6 Only when one understands this for men and understands this for ghosts can he make his own way.

If one has a clear conscience for what he does both openly and in secret, he may make his own way without fear.

23.28.1 One who stays within his natural allotment [*quan*] acts without concern for fame.

Quan is the same as "natural allotment" [*fen*]. One who plays within the limits of his natural allotment acts not for the sake of fame.

23.28.2 One who exceeds the limits of his allotment fixes his will on getting all that he can get.

Whether something brings him increase or not is of such concern that he is willing to ruin himself in the attempt to become someone else.

23.28.3 One who acts without concern for fame just uses the radiance he has.

Such radiance is in his fundamental nature, thus he uses it.

23.28.4 One who fixes his will on getting all that he can get is just a merchant.

Even though he lacks something in himself, he tries to appropriate it elsewhere so he peddles it as his.

23.28.5 People see him standing on tiptoes, yet he thinks himself perfectly safe.

Although people already see how one who would get all he can get stands on tiptoes, yet he thinks he is perfectly safe.[18]

23.28.6 One who merges with others to the utmost [*qiong*] shall have others gravitate to him,

"To the utmost" [*qiong*] means "from beginning to end" [*zhongshi*].

23.18.7 but one who is only expeditious [*qie*] in his engagement with others will find that he can't provide shelter even for himself, so how could he ever provide shelter for others!

"Expeditious" [*qie*] describes one who, exceeding the limits of his allotment, stands on tiptoes. One who stands on tiptoes does not stand securely, so how could he shelter himself, and since he can't shelter himself, how could he ever shelter others! And since people don't obtain shelter, they just go away.[19]

23.28.8 One who can't shelter others has no intimates, which means that everyone is a stranger to him.

Since he can't shelter even his own person, even his own self is not a self to him, so how less likely is it that he have intimates! This is why everyone is a stranger to him.

23.28.9 No weapon can do more harm than the will; even a Moye would not be up to it.

The trouble that the will can stir up is worse than raging fire, crueler than freezing ice. Therefore, as a weapon it is more harmful than swords or halberds.

23.28.10 No enemies are greater than yin and yang, for nowhere in Heaven and Earth can one escape from them. 23.28.11 But it is not the yin and yang that cause the harm, but the mind that makes it so.

When the mind excites the pneuma, yin and yang are drawn to coagulate in all five viscera, so yin and yang are at their full everywhere, which means one can't escape them.

23.29.1 The Dao pervades all things, so disintegration [*fen*] means integration [*cheng*], and wholeness [*cheng*] means destruction.[20]

Integration and destruction have no constant status, yet the Dao pervades both.[21]

23.29.2 If one finds his allotment [*fen*] hateful, it is because the limits of his being [*bei*] are determined by it.

Such a one abides not by his own allotment but seeks to supplement it, which is why he finds his allotment hateful.[22]

23.29.3 If one finds the limits of his being hateful, he will try to supplement it with something.

When someone thinks his fundamental capacity is incomplete and so tries to supplement it with something, it means that he finds the limits of his being hateful. But since his fundamental capacity has been perfectly complete from the very beginning, why indeed should he hate it!

23.29.4 Because he transgresses his limits and returns not to them, his ghost shall be drawn forth.

Since he no longer returns to abide by the limits of his own allotment, his death is not far off.

23.29.5 If he gets something by transgressing them, it will mean that he has got death.

If he does not transgress them and so gets nothing, he will get life.

23.29.6 Done away with yet physically there, he might as well be one of the ghosts.

Since he has done away with his inborn nature, though he has this life of his, what difference is he from a ghost!

23.29.7 It is by making one's bodily existence seem to him non-existent that one's bodily existence is made secure.

Though one has a bodily form as such, if vacuously he can free himself from all selfconscious involvement with it, he shall live out his life to the full and keep his bodily form secure.

23.30.1 Its emergence is without a root;[23]

It just suddenly self-generates without root.

23.30.2 Its disappearance is without a hole.

It just suddenly self-terminates without stalk.

23.30.3 It bears fruit but is not located anywhere in particular; it has growth but is without beginning or end; it just emerges and bears fruit without any hole to emerge from.

This just means that what emerges is itself the fruit, and that it emerges without hole for the stem to emerge from.

23.30.4 That it bears fruit but is not located anywhere in particular signifies its universal scope.

"Universal scope" means the four directions and up and down, but the four directions and up and down are endless.

23.30.5 That it has growth with neither beginning nor end signifies its perpetuity.

"Perpetuity" means duration from past to present, but duration from past to present is infinite.

23.30.6 It is there in life; it is there in death; it is there in appearance; it is there in disappearance. Yet there is no discernible form ever to be seen.[24]

Life, death, appearance, disappearance, all occur suddenly and spontaneously. Since it does not come from anywhere, there is no discernible shape to be seen.

23.30.7 It is called the "Gateway of Heaven."

The Gateway of Heaven is a collective name for the myriad things. To refer to this as the Gateway of Heaven is like saying the "gateway of all subtleties."[25]

23.30.8 The gateway of Heaven has no physical existence [*wuyou*], thus the myriad things emerge from no physical thing [*wuyou*].[26]

Life and death, emerging and entering, spontaneously all just suddenly occur, not because something deliberately causes it to happen. Nevertheless, since things coalesce and disperse, vanish and appear, the terms "emerging" and "entering" are used. However, these are but terms, since after all neither emerging nor entering actually happens, for where is the gate through which they could occur? Therefore, there is nothing there to make a gate, and, since there is nothing there to make a gate, no gateway actually exists.

23.30.9 Since being [*you*] can't use its being to produce being,

Before something phenomenally extant is generated, what is there to produce any generation? Therefore, things must come into existence by themselves, for how could anything else cause them to exist!

23.30.10 it must emerge from no physical thing [*wuyou*],

This clarifies that being can't produce being and that being just produces itself; it does not mean that "nothingness" produces being, for if "nothingness" could produce being, how could it be called "nothingness"?

23.30.11 and "no physical thing" always means the same "no physical thing" throughout.

As the same "no physical thing" is involved throughout, this then is what "nothingness" always means. Thus it is clear that being just suddenly generates itself.

23.30.12 The sage conceals himself in this.

He just allows being to self-generate and does not generate generation.[27]

23.31.1 What the people of antiquity knew reached the ultimate. What was this ultimate that they reached? It was that things never yet existed

for them—this is the ultimate reached, the utmost perfection achieved, to which nothing can be added. Next came those for whom things existed,[28] but they tended to regard life as loss

They regarded their separateness [*san*] as loss, so would revert to the collective whole [*ju*].

23.31.2 **and to regard death as return.**

That is, again dissolve [into the whole].

23.31.3 **As such, the distinction [*fen*] had already occurred.**

Although they wanted to regard them [life and death] as equal, they had already made the distinction between them.

23.31.4 **Next came those who said, "At first, things did not exist, but then there was life, and with life suddenly there was death. We regard 'things don't exist' as the head, life as the torso, and death as the buttocks. Whoever understands that physical existence and non-existence, life and death, all should be guarded as one, I would be his friend."[29] Although these three differ, they all belong to the same royal clan,**

They either acknowledged that things existed but would have them not exist, or acknowledged that things existed but would be one with them, or distinguished among them but would regard them as all equal. This is why these views are referred to as the three [parts of the body]. Although these three [kinds of people] were somewhere between completely getting it and not completely getting it, they were all able to banish "it is" and "it is not" from their minds, which is why they are referred to as of "the same royal clan."

23.31.5 **such as the Zhao and the Jing, who were prominently capped for court, and the Jia clan [Jiashi], whose members were prominently enfoeffed, for they were not all the same either.**

Although these four were of the [same original] royal clan, it was by then no longer one, just as the three [kinds of people] mentioned above also had differentiated themselves.[30]

23.32.1 **When alive, one is as if but a mole on the skin [*yan*],**

One is just a coalescence of pneuma.

23.32.2 **but once one splits himself off, I say "so shifts affirmation."**

Once people split themselves off and have a sense of being separate, each will affirm what he regards as affirmable, but because such affirmation lacks all constancy, I say it "shifts."

23.32.3 **Although I've just tried to say how affirmation shifts, this is really not worth addressing.**

That affirmation shifts should have been readily apparent without my talking about it.

23.32.4 **Nevertheless, it is something that defies understanding.**

Without addressing how it shifts, its shifting can't be understood, which is why the attempt is made to talk about it.

23.32.5 At the great sacrifice at year's end, it both happens that the stomach and hooves of the ox may be detached yet may not be detached.

Each part of the beast is of use.[31]

23.32.6 Attendees may circulate throughout the ancestral temple but also should leave it to use the privy [*yan*] for the purpose involved.

Yan [bend over; hide; rest] means privy [*pingce*].[32]

23.32.7 In being "right," all such instances show how affirmation shifts.

The temple is for sacrificial feasting and banqueting, and the privy is for urinating and defecating. When urinating and defecating are involved, what was the "right" for the temple now shifts to the privy. Thus it is that the shift between "right" and "wrong" now goes this way, now that—who can ever make them constant! Therefore, the Perfected one rides on them in compliance and as such is always perfectly equal to them.[33]

23.33.1 Let me talk about how affirmation shifts. Affirmation is rooted in the awareness of existence,

However they might change and transform, people are never free of the awareness of existence, and with such sense of existence, whatever state they are in, therein it takes root.[34]

23.33.2 and takes knowledge as its teacher,

What people know may differ, but each lets what he knows serve as his teacher.

23.33.3 thus one rides on right and wrong,

One who rides on right and wrong should be free of the sense of right and wrong.

23.33.4 which results in engagement with name and reality.

When it comes to name and reality, each person has his own opinion of them.

23.33.5 This is why one thinks he is their steward [*zhi*].

Zhi means "steward" [*zhu*]. Since each person considers himself "right," this is enough to make him steward of "right" and "wrong."

23.33.6 Such a one would so have others think he is a person of integrity

Since everyone would have it that he is right, none really keep pace with it.

23.33.7 That he will even pay for integrity with his life.

Given what he holds dear, he does not really liberate himself from it [life].

23.33.8 For such a one as this, to be useful is considered wise, to be useless is thought stupid, so proficiency leads to fame, while incompetence brings disgrace.

He can't comply with the vicissitudes of life and so be content with them.

23.33.9 Such shifting of affirmation, which the people of today indulge in,

The people of remote antiquity were absolutely free from right and wrong, so how could such shifting ever have occurred to them!

23.33.10 makes them just cicadas and turtledoves agreeing to what they agree on.[35]

They mutually affirm what they agree on.

23.34.1 If one steps on someone's foot in the marketplace, one apologizes with "my careless blunder."

One apologizes by acknowledging he has made a careless mistake.

23.34.2 If on an older brother's, one reacts with solicitude.

That is, he just consoles him, with no words of apology.

23.34.3 If on a father's, absolutely nothing is done.

They [father and son] know full well that forgiveness is always amply there.

23.34.4 Therefore, it is said that perfect propriety occurs when others don't exist;

"When others don't exist" means that one regards all others as oneself. If one regards all others as oneself, neither offering apology nor giving forgiveness need occur—this the very perfection of propriety.

23.34.5 perfect righteousness occurs when people other than oneself don't exist;

When each person fulfills what is appropriate to his nature, everyone becomes the same "I."

23.34.6 perfect knowledge is free from selfconscious thought;

If one selfconsciously thinks about something and only then knows it, it is not spontaneous knowledge.

23.34.7 perfect benevolence is free from intimate relationships [*qin*];

It is analogous to that of the five viscera: without ever forming intimate relationships, their benevolent reciprocity is perfect.

23.34.8 and perfect trust may dispense with gold.

Gold or jade need only be used as security for petty trust, so perfect trust may dispense with them.

23.35.1 Eliminate confusions of the will,
Free yourself from entanglements of mind,
Cast aside fetters to one's virtue,
Break through obstructions to the Dao.

23.35.2 Distinction and wealth, eminence and honor, fame and advantage, these six all confuse the will. Demeanor [*rong*] and adjustment [*dong*], expression [*se*] and style [*li*], breath [*qi*] and mood [*yi*],[36] these six all entangle the mind. Aversion and desire, delight and anger, grief and joy, these six all fetter one's virtue. Rejection and acquiescence, acquisitiveness and beneficence, intelligence and talent, these six all obstruct the Dao. When these four sixes are not activated [*dang*] within the breast, this then is one's proper state [*zheng*], which results in tranquility. Tranquility then results in clarity, and clarity results in emptiness. Emptiness allows one to act without effort yet nothing fails to be done.[37]

"Activate" [*dang*] means "start up" [*dong*].

23.35.3 The Dao is the honor of virtue; life is the glory of virtue; original nature is the intrinsic basis of life. Movement of original nature is said to be action,

It is because original nature self-activates that it is referred to as "action," but only this is authentic action; it does not refer to selfconscious action.

23.35.4 but inauthenticity of action is said to be violation. Knowing either involves receptivity or involves selfconscious consideration. When knowing occurs unknowingly, it is just like the way we see.

That the eye can see is not because it selfconsciously tries to see. Just as it sees without selfconsciously seeing, one should know without selfconsciously knowing, for then action shall be spontaneous. But if one only acts after the onset of selfconscious thought, such knowing leads to inauthenticity.

23.35.5 When one acts only because it is inevitable, it is said to be out of virtue.

But if one acts to achieve some end, this forces action and violation results.

23.35.6 Movement that involves nothing but one's real self is said to render order.

If one acts in such a way as to imitate someone else, it results in disorder.

23.35.7 Names result in mutual opposition, but realities result in mutual compliance.

It is because such names as "other" and "self" exist that opposition occurs, but if each can but be who he really is, people shall be compliant.[38]

23.36.1 Whereas Archer Yi was skilled at hitting tiny targets but inept at getting people to deny him fame,

If he excelled at hitting targets, it meant he excelled at accruing fame; in principle these always go together.

23.36.2 the sage is skilled at the way of Heaven but inept at the way of men.

To allow things to go their natural course is the way of Heaven; to try to make them happen with selfconscious mind is the way of men.[39]

23.36.3 Skilled at the way of Heaven yet adept in dealing with men, only the Perfected one can do this.

If one is skilled at the way of Heaven, it means he is adept at dealing with men. Such a one is called a "Perfected one," and if a Perfected one, one is a sage.

23.36.4 Only a certain creature can be that creature, for only that creature has such an endowment from Heaven.

That it can continue being the creature it is depends on being able to fulfill the endowment it has from Heaven.

23.36.5 Does the Perfected one hate Heaven's endowment? Does he hate Heaven's endowment of others?[40] And even less [should he ask] "am I Heaven or am I man?"

Utterly free of selfconscious awareness, such a one always just lets things happen, which is why the text says he is "skilled at the way of Heaven."

23.37.1 If a sparrow happened to come upon Archer Yi, Yi would be sure to get it, for he had the power to do so.

If one relies on power to take creatures, they will surely try to flee.

23.37.2 But had he made the whole world a cage, sparrows would have had no place to flee.

Each and every creature in the world has its own interests, so if all interests are satisfied, why should any have reason to flee?

23.37.3 Thus it was that Tang caged Yi Yin with a kitchen, and Duke Mu of Qin caged Baili Xi with five goat skins. For no one can ever be caged except by using what appeals to his interests.[41]

23.38.1 The one-legged abandons adornment, for he has placed praise and blame beyond him.

Adornment is the means to decorate one's looks. Since the appearance of one whose foot has been cut off is already ruined by suffering such loss, he no longer cares whether he looks good or not, and this is why he abandons it and has nothing more to do with it.

23.38.2 A convict will climb any height without fear because he has cast aside all concerns for life or death.

Since he finds life worthless, he fears not death.

23.38.3 One so repeatedly cowed that he no longer feels shame becomes oblivious to what it is to be a man.

Such a one has lost all selfconsciousness of what people cherish.[42]

23.38.4 Oblivious to what it is to be a man, such a one has become a Heavenly man.

Once free of the mores of benevolence [*ren zhi qing*], one spontaneously becomes a "Heavenly man."

23.38.5 Therefore, only one who honored feels no delight or insulted feels no anger may share in the harmony of Heaven.

Even these, the one body ruined and the other a convict, may still share in the harmony of Heaven, so how more true this must be for those in their natural state [*ziran*]!

23.38.6 If he appears angry but is not angry [*bunu*], such anger comes from where no thought to anger exists [*bunu*]; if he appears to act but does not act [*wuwei*], such action comes from where no thought to act exists [*wuwei*].

This is what I previously meant by "nothingness can't generate phenomenal reality [the extant or "somethingness"] [*you*]; the extant can't be generated.[43]

23.38.7 If one wishes to be tranquil, he should get his pneuma in balance; if one wishes for divine powers, he should make his mind compliant. As for taking action [*youwei*], if one wishes to do what is appropriate, he should only comply with the inevitable, for the various kinds of inevitability are what constitute the Dao of the sage.

If one's pneuma is in balance, he is tranquil; if one's grasp of principles sufficiently render his mind compliant, his divine efficacy shall reach perfection; if one only complies with the inevitable, whatever action he takes shall always be appropriate. Therefore, the sage takes all this as his Dao—why should he ever try to discover unselfconscious action anywhere outside the "dim and dark"![44]

Notes

1. The Rocky [Weilei] Mountains, according to Cheng Xuanying and Li Yi, are variously located either in the ancient state of Lu or in the ancient region of Liangzhou (modern Shaanxi and Sichuan); see *Zhuangzi jishi*, 4: 770. For more on their possible location, see Wang Shumin, *Zhuangzi jiaoquan*, 857, note 3.
2. *Laozi*, section 17; Richard John Lynn, *The Classic of the Way and Virtue*, 78: "He [the perfect one] takes his time, oh, as he weighs his words carefully. And, when success is had and the task accomplished, the common folk all say, 'We just live naturally.' " Wang Bi: "When things happen 'naturally,' not the slightest prefiguring can be seen, so his [the perfect one's] intentions can't be discerned."
3. Guo Xiang apparently takes "garden walls" as a metaphor for the enclosure that surrounds and protects fundamental human nature, which, once breached, allows the seeds of perversity to enter. Cheng Xuanying elaborates: "So it was that the social mores of Yao and Shun were established extraneous to one's fundamental nature, their footprints serving as instructions that people were forced to emulate." *Zhuangzi jishi*, 4: 775.
4. Cf. *Chunqiu Zuozhuan zhengyi* (Correct meaning of the *Spring and Autumn Annals*, the Zuo tradition), 43: 2044b: "[As matters as small as] the points of awls and knives, would they [the people] all contend."
5. Cf. the "absolute clarity" of the stupid in 2.30.6.
6. The assertion here and in 24.54.1, that "benevolence" ultimately leads to such chaos and attendant famine that people are forced into cannibalism, argues directly against a passage in the *Mencius*: "When benevolence and righteousness are blocked, wild beasts are led to devour people and people are led to devour one another." *Mengzi zhushu*, 6B: 2714c.
7. Cheng Xuanying: "Although the two physical forms are both open, they can't achieve equivalence, which is the distinction between them." *Zhuangzi jishi*, 4: 779. Here, "physical forms" [*xing*] refers to the blind and nonblind eyes, the deaf and nondeaf ears, and the insane and the noninsane minds. Guo and Cheng indicate that being blind, deaf, or insane never results from just closing the eyes, ears, or mind, but rather comes from the fact that these organs fail to function. Both blind and nonblind eyes may be open, but only the nonblind can see; such is their nonequivalence, a nonequivalence that also holds for ears and minds.
8. Nanrong Chu understood the difference between the physical appearance of being able to see, hear, and comprehend and actual seeing, hearing, and comprehending, which implies that there exists not only a difference in kind (blind and nonblind, but example), but also a difference in degree: some people see better than others, hear better than others, or comprehend better than others. Here, he admits that although he has a mind, it is incapable of comprehending what Gengsang Chu has to say.

9. Cheng Xuanying: "The digger wasp with its tiny waist can transmute silkworms into its own offspring but can't so transmute those of the bean caterpillar. The Yue hen is small so can't hatch the eggs of the swan, but the Chu hen is large, so certainly could do it." *Zhuangzi jishi*, 4: 479.
10. Cf. 32.26.2, Guo commentary.
11. *Laozi*, section 55; Lynn, *The Classic of the Way and Virtue*, 156.
12. Cheng Xuanying: "That they tire not is because his pure bodily balance is merged with the perfect virtue of the arcane Dao." *Zhuangzi jishi*, 4: 787.
13. Most editions of the *Zhuangzi* don't include the phrase translated as "and things appear as they really are," but it seems to be a likely textual variant; see *Zhuangzi jishi*, 4: 792 and Wang Shumin, *Zhuangzi jiaoquan*, 887, note 2.
14. Cheng Xuanying: "As long as one's efforts stay within the limits of his natural allotment, though effort is made, it isn't selfconscious effort. Therefore, though he learns, it isn't selfconscious learning; though he acts, it isn't selfconscious acting; though he disputes, it isn't selfconscious disputing, for why should such a one go further and attempt something that exceeds the limits of his natural capacity or try to learn something that he is incapable of doing!" *Zhuangzi jishi*, 4: 792.
15. Cf. 2.14.26.
16. "The potter's wheel of Heaven" means the equitable principles of Nature; cf. 2.11.15.
17. Cheng Xuanying glosses "sincere"/"sincerity" [*cheng*] in this passage as "authentic"/"authenticity" [*zhen*]; *Zhuangzi jishi*, 4: 795.
18. Cheng Xuanying glosses "stand on tiptoes" as "be in danger." *Zhuangzi jishi*, 4: 797.
19. Cheng Xuanying: "Here one only expediently engages with others, muddling along pretending to care but really greedy for advantage and reputation, his greatest concern the need to aggrandize himself. But with his thoughts and emotions thus fixated on getting ahead, such a one is incapable of securing shelter for himself. And since he can't shelter himself, how could he ever shelter anyone else!" *Zhuangzi jishi*, 4: 797.
20. The phrase "wholeness means" [*cheng ye*] only appears in the text of the incomplete old handwritten scroll of the *Zhuangzi* owned by the Kōzanji in Japan, but that reading is identical to a similar passage, 2:11.7 and 2.11.8, which indicates that the text should be amended to read the same here. See *Zhuangzi jishi*, 1: 800, and Wang Shumin, *Zhuangzi jiaoquan*, 895, note 1.
21. Cf. 2.11.9.
22. Cheng Xuanying: "Glory or dishonor, longevity or early death are determined by one's endowment from Nature and exist in one's original allotment, thus one should revert to self for everything needed to complete his being. One who chases about outside his allotment in trying to supplement it lets his mind get involved with the realm of 'is' and 'isn't'—this all because he hates the allotment he has received." *Zhuangzi jishi*, 4: 799. The Guo and Cheng commentaries here abruptly shift from interpreting *fen* as "disintegration" to "original allotment," the logic of which seems to unfold this way: Following the disintegration [*fen*] of a certain integration [*cheng*], characterized by a particular allotment [*fen*], comes another integration [*cheng*] with its characteristic allotment [*fen*]. It is through such integration and disintegration that all things, including people, come into existence, persist for a time, then cease to exist. During a person's existence, the time of his integration [*cheng*], that existence is characterized by an individual natural allotment [*fen*], and with death, that integration [*cheng*] disintegrates [*fen*]. However, at the level of the myriad things and the unity of the Dao, *fen* signifies "separateness," which results from the disintegration of that unity. When particular *fen* disintegrate, they reintegrate with the collective whole [*ju*] of the myriad things.

23. The plant metaphor for the Dao here occurs, with similar wording, in the *Guanzi* (Sayings of Master Guan) of Guan Zhong (d. 645 BCE): "It is ever so that the Way / Has neither roots nor stalks, / Neither leaves nor blossoms. / Yet to all things gives life / And brings them to fruition / Is termed the Way." W. A. Rickett, trans., *Guanzi: Political, Economic, and Philosophical Essays from Early China* (vol. 2), 42.
24. Cf. 25.43.4.
25. Cf. *Laozi*, section 1: "These two [origin and mother] emerge together but have different names. Together we refer to them as mystery: the mystery upon mystery and gateway of all subtleties." Lynn, *The Classic of the Way and Virtue*, 52.
26. Cf. 12.18.2, Guo commentary.
27. Cheng Xuanying: "The sage of arcane virtue merges with authenticity and tallies with principle, so in them he conceals his spirit and hides his wisdom." *Zhuangzi jishi*, 4: 802.
28. The text here is identical with the beginning of 2.12.
29. Cf. 6.19, where the wording is almost identical.
30. Guo Xiang apparently understood Zhao, Jing, Jia, and Shi as four different clan family names, but this is far from certain because the Chu imperial clan consisted of three surnames, not four, and Jia might be a scribal error for Qu. However, Cheng Xuanying does not recognize Jia as a surname; he thinks only the names Zhao and Jing occur in the text: "Zhao, Qu, and Jing were the three surnames of the Chu imperial clan. Long ago Qu Yuan served as grand master of the three royal households [*sanlü dafu*], an office which managed the affairs of the three clans with their three surnames. This is what is referred to here. A lacuna occurs in the text, which explains why only the Zhao and Jing are mentioned. When young men from the nobility grew up, once they were capped, they wore court robes and caps. Each had an official rank and salary, and all served long terms in office. They were conferred surnames according to the names of their offices, which resulted in noble household clans. Once they achieved prominence thanks to meritorious deeds, they were ennobled and granted fiefs, which created branch family lines, and this explains why they no longer were of one [clan family]." Considerable disagreement exists within the commentary tradition over how to read this *Zhuangzi* passage; see *Zhuangzi jishi*, 4: 804, and Wang Shumin, *Zhuangzi jiaoquan*, 899–901, note 22.
31. Cheng Xuanying: "At the great sacrifice at year's end, the ox to be sacrificed shall be entirely intact, including even the four feet and five viscera, which should be displayed together with all the rest. Once the sacrifice is complete, the whole thing may then be divided up, thus separation now is the right thing to do. But before the sacrifice is complete it is forbidden to divide it up, for then separation isn't the right thing to do. Such is our understanding of 'right' and 'not right.' This is how affirmation shifts and so lacks all constancy." *Zhuangzi jishi*, 4: 805.
32. Cheng Xuanying: "Once the sacrificial ceremony is finished, the temple provides drink and sets out in its rooms the meat left over from the sacrifice. The attendees circulate throughout the interior of the temple, and after prolonged drinking and eating, needs must use the privy, which is why they go to the privy to urinate. When drinking and eating, the temple is considered 'right,' and when urinating, the privy is considered 'right.' Thus 'right' and 'wrong' lack all constancy—how could they ever be fixed!" *Zhuangzi jishi*, 4: 806.
33. Cf. 2.10.2.
34. Cheng Xuanying: "Only one who can lose all awareness of life and death may be free from right and wrong. As long as one is bogged down in awareness of existence, such a one shall cling to affirmation. But surely once awareness of existence is dispatched,

where then would affirmation lodge? Therefore, we know that how affirmation shifts is rooted in the awareness of existence." *Zhuangzi jishi*, 4: 807.

35. Cf.1.4.
36. Cheng Xuanying glosses these six as "demeanor" [*rongmao*], "behavior adjustment" [*biandong*], "expression of countenance" [*yanse*], "style of utterance" [*cili*], "breath regulation" [*qitiao*], and "selfconscious mood" [*qingyi*], all of which seem to refer to selfconsciousness of self as one interacts with others. "Breath regulation" is an important Daoist psychophysical cultivation technique, but here it probably refers to the selfconscious control of one's emotional response to people and things. See *Zhuangzi jishi*, 4: 810. The first four of the six also allude to a passage in the *Lunyu* (Analects), 8: 2486c: "The noble man finds three things in the way of conduct that are of particular value: he adjusts his demeanor so that it is far from callous and arrogant; he rectifies his expression of countenance so that it stays close to trustworthiness; he conducts his manner of speaking so that it is far from vulgar and unreasonable."
37. Cf. *Laozi*, section 37: "The Dao in its constancy engages in no selfconscious action, yet nothing remains undone." Lynn, *The Classic of the Way and Virtue*, 117.
38. Cheng Xuanying: "As long as the names 'other' and 'self' and 'right' and 'wrong' exist, such names create mutual opposition, but once 'other' and 'self' and 'right' and 'wrong' cease to exist, real selves exist in mutual compliance." *Zhuangzi jishi*, 4: 812.
39. Cheng Xuanying: "The first part starts the analogy, and this part completes it. While the sage marvelously tallies with the Natural and effectively matches creative transformation, he still gets everyone to remain unaware of him though they benefit on a daily basis." *Zhuangzi jishi*, 4: 813.
40. Cheng Xuanying: "As for the man of perfect virtue, since he does not examine his own divine efficacy, how could he ever loathe his own natural allotment [*sufen*] or hate the endowment of others! Surely he does nothing of the kind! He just complies with his own natural capacity—that's all there is to it!" *Zhuangzi jishi*, 4: 814.
41. Accounts differ whether five goat skins or a five-colored goat skin were involved. Cheng Xuanying: "Yi Yin, a slave assigned by Youshen to his daughter, was an excellent cook, who [accompanying the daughter when she was married to King Tang] to serve Tang was made responsible for cooking duties. Having recognized his worthiness, Tang, complying with Yi Yin's original nature, used his kitchen to cage him. Baili Xi had fallen into the hands of the Di barbarians, but, because they loved goat skins, Duke Mu of Qin ransomed him with five colored goat skins. Another account has it that because Baili Xi loved five-colored goat skin robes, his cognomen was "Master Five Rams." Therefore, the worthies Tang and Mu, both capable of appreciating men of learning, succeeded at recruiting these two men, whom them employed as fine assistants, for in both cases they acted in compliance with their [Yi Yin's and Baili Xi's] original natures, which is how they caged them." *Zhuangzi jishi*, 4: 815.
42. Cheng Xuanying: "he then becomes utterly oblivious to all sense of shame or gratitude, that is, he no longer is mindful of the way of ethical relations [*renlun*]." *Zhuangzi jishi*, 4: 816.
43. Cf. 12.18.2, Guo commentary. Cheng Xuanying: "One who can so appear angry and so appear to act is someone in whom no thought to anger [*bunu*] and no thought to act exist [*buwei*], for these spring from unselfconscious action [*wuwei*] and unselfconscious anger [*bunu*]. Therefore, we know that since such action originates in unselfconscious action and such anger originates in unselfconscious anger, such a one can embody the aptitude that when insulted allows him to feel no anger." *Zhuangzi jishi*, 4: 817. The interpretations here of the *Zhuangzi*, Guo's commentary, and Cheng's

subcommentary are predicated on understanding the *bu* in *bunu* and *wu* in *wuwei* to signify unintentionality and unselfconsciousness—the absence (*bu* or *wu*) of intention and selfconsciousness.

44. Cf. *Laozi*, section 14, where the Dao is referred to as the "dim and dark"; and section 21, where it states "The Dao as such is but dim, is but dark." Lynn, *The Classic of the Way and Virtue*, 73 and 86.

CHAPTER 24

XU WUGUI [EASYGOING THE FEARLESS]

24. 1 When, thanks to Nü Shang,[1] Xu Wugui obtained an audience with Marquis Wu of Wei, Marquis Wu, thinking him exhausted, said, "Sir, you seem ill! I suppose you are so worn out with hard life in mountain forests that it you are willing to pay me a visit."

24.2 Wugui replied, "It is I who should console you, my lord, for what is there, my lord, for you to console me about? If you persist in fulfilling your carnal desires and carrying on with your likes and dislikes, your naturally endowed life shall become emotionally diseased. But if you, my lord, were to banish carnal desires and shrink from likes and dislikes, your vision and hearing shall be diseased.

Carnal desires and likes and dislikes, it won't do either to keep them in or push them out.

24.2.3 I should console you, my lord, for what is there for you, my lord, to console me about!"

24.2.4 Marquis Wu was so disappointed that he did not reply.

He was displeased at what was said.

24.3 After a short pause, Xu Wugui continued, "I shall try to tell you how I judge dogs. Those of inferior quality stop once they have caught their fill, which is the virtue of wildcats; those of middling quality seem to be looking up at the sun;[2] those of superior quality seem to have forgotten that they as individuals exist. But the way I judge dogs is not up to how I judge horses. As I judge horses, those that go so straight as to match a carpenter's ink line, go in such curves as to match the curve of a hook, make squares as square as a carpenter's square, and make circles as round as a compass, though

these are horses of top state quality, they fall short of horses of world class quality. World class horses, which are of perfectly complete quality, seem as if worried and as if at a loss, as if they had forgotten their individual selves. Horses such as these run so fast that they leave even the dust behind, unaware of where they are."[3] Marquis Wu was then so delighted that he burst out laughing.

How does an authentic man get people to concur with what he says? The only way possible is if others find it pleasing.

24.4.1 When Xu Wugui came out, Nü Shang asked him, "How is it, sir, that you alone manage so to please my lord? The way I try to please him is, for the woof, to talk about the *Odes* [Shi], *Documents* [Shu], *Rites*[Li], and *Music* [Yue], and, for the warp, to talk about the *Metal Blocks* [Jinban] and *Six Bow-cases* [Liutao].[4] Measures of great merit that I have proposed are too numerous to count, yet my lord has never even smiled.

Since this is just "serenading a quail with bells and drums," it thus makes him sad.[5]

24.4.2 But what, sir, did you just now say to my lord that made him so pleased as that?"

24.5 Xu Wugui replied, "I merely told him about how I judge dogs and horses."

24.6 "Could it have been nothing more than that?"

24.7.1 "Have you not heard about the man banished to distant lands? After he had been gone from his own state for a few days, just to see someone he merely recognized was enough to make him happy.

Everyone longs for that which his fundamental nature finds pleasing.

24.7.2 After he had been gone from his own state for a full month, just to see someone from there whom he had seen just once was enough to make him happy. After he had been gone for a full year, just to see someone who looked like someone he knew was enough to make him happy. Is it not indeed so that the longer one is away from people, the more profoundly one longs for them! And if one flees to some desolate place, where brambles and pigweed choke stoat and weasel runs, and there wanders lost in the wilderness, were he to hear the thud of human footfalls, that would indeed make him happy! And would he not be even more happy to hear his brothers and relatives chatting and laughing at his side!

Were he to have such occasion for perfect happiness, it would make him overjoyed.

24.7.3 But long, indeed, has it been that no authentic man has talked and laughed at the side of our lord!"

This was why he had never smiled. The words of this authentic man reached his lord because they appealed to his fundamental nature, for getting them initially made him happy, but if he had been getting them over a long time, he would not have cared in the least."[6]

24.8 When Xu Wugui went to see Marquis Wu, the Marquis said, "Sir, living in mountain forests, subsisting on chestnuts and acorns and satisfying yourself with wild onions and chives, for the sake of that you have long scorned my company! But have you now grown so old that you seek the flavors of wine and meat? Or is it that you want to bring me blessings of the gods of soil and grain as well?"

24.9 Xu Wugui replied, "I have lived my whole life in poverty and humble circumstances and have never presumed to drink and sup my lord's wine and meat, but I have come to console you, my lord.

24.10 "What's that," said he, "how can you console me?"

24.11 "I shall console your spirit and body."

24.12 "What do you mean by that?"

24.13.1 Xu Wugui replied, "Nourishment provided by Heaven and Earth is one and the same for all.

They are not like this lord, whose selfishness is without limit.

24.13.2 Someone elevated high must not be thought to deserve more, and one who dwells in lowly circumstances must not be thought to deserve less. You, a single person as the master of ten thousand chariots, take the resources of your state's entire people to support the needs of your ears and eyes, nose and mouth,

As such, he acts contrary to the evenhandedness of Heaven and Earth.

24.13.3 but your spirit for its part does not permit it.

It is just his material being [*wu*] for its part that permits it.

24.13.4 But the spirit loves harmony and hates debauchery.

To share with the people promotes harmony, but selfish permissiveness results in debauchery.

24.13.5 And since debauchery is an illness, I have come to console you accordingly. It is only you, my lord, who has succumbed to such illness—why do you suppose that is?"

24.14 Marquis Wu said, "I have been wanting to see you, sir, for a long time. I wish to cherish my people and thus would practice righteousness [*yi*] and disband troops—how would that be?"

24.15.1 Xu Wugui replied, "It can't be done. Cherishing one's people is the start of doing them harm,

The outer sign [*ji*] of cherishing one's people is the esteem one enjoys from them. That he cherishes them for the sake of esteem means that his cherishing can only be false.

24.15.2 and to practice righteousness and disband troops is the root from which war springs.

If one practices righteousness and disbands troops, one's reputation will manifest itself, and once manifest, strife will arise. When strife arises, authenticity [*zhen*] is lost. Whether it be fathers and sons or rulers and ministers, all shall harbor prejudicial feelings [*qing*] and deceive one another. So even if one wishes to disband troops, how could that possibly do any good!

24.15.3 If, my lord, you go about things in this way, you are almost doomed to fail.

But if he were to follow unselfconscious action [*wuwei*] in doing things, he would be sure to succeed.

24.15.4 Every attempt to accomplish something praiseworthy [*mei*] becomes the instrument of evil [*e*].

If something praiseworthy is accomplished earlier, something false will appear later. This is why the accomplishment of something praiseworthy becomes the instrument of evil.

24.15.5 Although you, my lord, may practice benevolence [*ren*] and righteousness, this is tantamount to falsehood!

The people will continue such falsehood, unwilling to act authentically [*zhen*].

24.15.6 A discernible form [*xing*] certainly [*gu*] leads to copies being made of it.

As soon as benevolence and righteousness have discernible forms, counterfeits certainly will be made of them.

24.15.7 Accomplishment certainly will be flaunted [*fa*].

As soon as accomplishment occurs, it is flaunted [*xian*].[7]

24.15.8 Change [*bian*] will certainly lead to foreign wars.

Since original and constant nature [*changran*] will be thwarted.[8]

24.15.9 But, my lord, you must not have ranks of soldiers [*helie*] fill the spaces between your magnificent watch towers

"Ranks of soldiers" [*helie*] (literally, cranes arrayed) means deployment of troops, and "magnificent watch towers" [*liqiao*] means high-storied buildings.

24.15.10 nor foot soldiers [*tu*] and cavalry at the Temple of the Black Altar [Zitan zhi gong].

Foot soldiers are called *tu*. However, not only should he avoid practicing righteousness and cherishing his people, he should also refrain from massing troops and deploying fast horses.

24.15.11 Don't harbor tendencies that run contrary to success.

If he has tendencies that ran contrary to success, failure would result.

24.15.12 Don't use skill [*qiao*] to vanquish others.

He should preserve his own pristine simplicity [*pu*], allowing the pristine simplicity of each to realize its potential [*neng*], for then equality [*ping*] would result.

24.15.13 Don't use schemes to vanquish others.

He should follow his own authentic knowledge [*zhenzhi*], allowing the knowledge of each to realize its strength, for then equality [*jun*] would result.

24.15.14 Don't use warfare to vanquish others.

Respond [*ying*] to people with the Dao, and though people submit, it won't be called "vanquished."

24.15.15 If you kill the officers and people of another [ruler] and join his lands to yours in order to enhance your own personal interests and boost your individual spirit, in such a war it can't be known who would have good [*shan*] on his side or wherein such victory would lie.

Since it can't be known who would have good on his side, though such a one were to vanquish the other, it would not mean victory for himself.

24.15.16 If, my lord, you have to do something, cultivate sincerity [*cheng*] in your breast in order that may resonant [*ying*] with the innate tendencies [*qing*] of Heaven and Earth, and so don't do anything contrary.

If he can't help but do something, it would be best if he were to cultivate his own sincerity.

24.15.17 With that, since your people will have already escaped death, where would the need lie, my lord, to disband troops?"

This means that there would be no deployment of armed forces; it would not mean disbanding them.

24.16 When the Yellow Thearch went to see Big Steep Craggy [Dawei] at Mount Resting Place [Juci zhi shan],[9]

> **Bright Just Now [Fangming] was his carriage driver to the left,**
> **Cast Brilliance On All In the World [Changyu] his bodyguard to the right,**
> **As if Bow Strung [Zhangruo] and Overawe Many [Xipeng] led the horses,**
> **Kunhun [Primal Chaos] and Slippery Operator [Guji][10] brought up the rear,**
> **But reaching the wilds of Government Authority Banned [Xiangcheng],[11]**
> **The seven sages knew not where to go, and no one was there to ask the way.**

"Sage" is a name. Once a name is brought into being, that which it designates is lost; as such, though he wants to go to Big Steep Craggy, how could he ever succeed!

24.17 But then they happened to meet a boy who was tending horses, so they asked "Do you know Mount Resting Place?" He replied, "Yes."

24.18 "And do you know the location of Big Steep Craggy?" He said, "Yes."

24.19 The Yellow Thearch then said, "What an extraordinary young boy you are! Not only do you know Mount Resting Place, you also know the location of Big Steep Craggy! So may I ask you how to take care of all under Heaven?"

24.20.1 The boy replied, "Taking care of all under Heaven is just like what I do here, what more could there be to it!

If whatever happens one remains completely at ease, this is to be disengaged; as long as one remains disengaged one may thereby take care of all under Heaven.

24.20.2 Since I was little I wandered by myself everywhere within the reach of the six directions, for I was then handicapped with nearsightedness. But an elder instructed me, 'Ride in the chariot of the sun and wander about in the wilds of Government Authority Banned [Xiangcheng].'

Wander when the sun comes up and rest when the sun goes down.

24.20.3 And now, my handicap somewhat alleviated, I am trying again to wander, this time beyond the limits of the six directions. Well, taking care of all under Heaven, is just like doing that, nothing more, for what more could there be to it!"

To take care of all under Heaven, nothing is better than to let all have their own complete freedom, for once they all have their own complete freedom, what would anyone have to oppose! As such, though the ruler himself takes no conscious action, yet the people transform themselves.

24.21.1 The Yellow Thearch replied, "As for taking care of all under Heaven, this is certainly not any concern of yours, my son.

It is something for the people themselves to take care of.

24.21.2 Nevertheless, may I ask you how to take care of all under Heaven?"

One who allows the common folk their own self-fulfillment is sure to possess the Dao of it.

24.21.3 The boy declined to answer.

24.22.1 But when the Yellow Thearch again asked, the boy did reply, "As for taking care of all under Heaven, how is even that any different from tending horses? All one has to do is keep anything away that might harm the horses, nothing more than that!"

To strain horses beyond their allotted capacity is such harm.

24.22.2 The Yellow Thearch bowed twice, kowtowed, and then gave him the title "Heavenly Master" and withdrew.

Having made the Natural his master, he thus gave up trying to exceed his allotted capacity; as such, Big Steep Craggy was reached.

24.23 If something untoward occurs without the strategist predicting it, he is unhappy; if something starts and develops without the rhetorician proposing it, he is unhappy; if the perspicacious fails to have something to nitpick about, he is unhappy. As such, all allow themselves to be confined by external things.

It is because people can't find self-fulfillment within themselves but seek happiness in external things that they can be confined. Therefore, if each of them is allowed to be confined by what makes him happy, the myriad folk will spontaneously gravitate to one [i.e., a ruler] without being summoned, not because they are forced to do so.

24.24.1 Men who attract the attention of the age flourish at court; men who fairly treat the common folk thrive in office; brave and daring men throw

themselves into adversity; weaponed and armored men delight in warfare; men who emaciate themselves seek fame and reputation; legalistic men seek to broaden the reach of government; men immersed in ritual code use reference to ingratiate themselves; men of benevolence and righteousness value opportunities in social relationships.

It is because men are so unlike as this that those who fit these types can't change the way they do things.

24.24.2 If farmers did not have the tasks of dealing with plants and weeds, they would not be like one another; if merchants did not have the tasks concerned with the marketplace, they would not be like one another.

As long as they may do the same things, their tasks are the same, which is why they are like one another.

24.24.3 As long as the common folk have occupations that keep them busy from sunrise to sunset, they are encouraged.

It is because their occupations allow them to achieve their aspirations that they are encouraged.

24.24.4 As long as artisans have the opportunity to use skills relating to their tools and implements they will be robust.

Anything that does not involve their skills will find them indolent.

24.24.5 If wealth does not accumulate, the greedy become anxious.

It is when people get what they like that they are happy.

24.24.6 If they can't wield the maximum of power and influence, the arrogant and boastful are miserable. 24.24.7 Those who like to lord it over others delight in calamitous times.

Power and influence are born from calamitous times.

24.24.8 When such men encounter a time when they might be of use, they can't stop themselves from trying for it.

For all these various types of men, there is a time when each finds himself to be of use, and when that time for use arrives, they can't but try for it. But if they fail to encounter the right time, though they might wish to make themselves useful, how could this ever happen! This is why there is no constancy to eminence and lowliness.

24.24.9 Attempting to keep in step with the way the times are going, they all try to become what they are not by resorting to change.

As for a man's potential, each has his limit, which, like that of the four seasons, can't be changed. Therefore, if each man stays in accord with momentary things [*shiwu*] and complies with the sequence in which they occur,[12] then each, indeed, will prove of use, for this is how they [the seasons] comply with the year and as such stay in proper sequence. But to try to change one's basic nature is to reject the thing one is. To be a thing and yet try not to be that thing, if this does not lead to disaster, what does!

24.24.10 They so force their physical bodies and personal natures to gallop that they sink beneath the myriad folk, never to return home their entire lives—how sad!

This is to fail to keep within one's own capacity and instead use every possible trick to wrest advantage from the moment. As such, such men must try to crawl all their way home,[13] which is what is so sad.

24.25.1 Master Zhuang said, "If an archer hits the target without aiming, and we say he is a good shot, then anyone in the world may be Yi. Do you grant that?"

One who hits the target without aiming may be said to hit it by accident and so is not a good shot. If it is said that since one who hits the target by accident is a good shot, can it be granted that one may say that anyone in the world may be called a Yi? This means that it can't be so granted.

24.25.2 Master Hui replied, "I grant you that."

24.26.1 Master Zhuang went on to say, "In all the world there is no such thing as a common and impartial view of what is 'right,' so everyone regards as right what he thinks right, which means that anyone in the world can be a Yao. Do you grant that?"

If it may be said that one who hits the target by accident is a Yi, then anyone who comes up with his own individual and subjective "right" may be said to be a Yao. Master Zhuang with this makes it clear that one who hits the target by accident is not a Yi and that one who comes up with his own subjective "right" is not a Yao.

24.26.2 Master Hui replied, ""I grant you that."

24.27.1 Master Zhuang again went on, "However, as for Ru, Mo, Yang and Bing, these four,[14] together with you, make five, which one of you, after all, is right? Or perhaps it is someone like Stupid Scaredy [Lu Ju]? For a disciple of his said, 'I have attained your Way, master: I can bring a cauldron to boil in winter and in summer make ice.' To which Stupid Scaredy replied, 'This is simply to attract yang with yang and yin with yin; it is not what I mean by my Way. I shall demonstrate my Way to you.' To do this he tuned zithers, one of which he placed in the hall while setting the other in a side room. When he played the note *gong* on the one, the note *gong* resonated on the other, and when he played the note *jue* on the one, the note *jue* resonated on the other,[15] both times exactly in the same pitch.

All these too involve yang attracting yang, yet he perversely thought himself right.

24.27.2 Then at random he changed one string so that its pitch did not match any of the five notes,

That is, he changed it according to pitch.

24.27.3 so when he played it, all twenty-five strings on the other resonated.

As long as no note was played on the one, the other had nothing to resonate with, but once a note was played, the other would resonate only if it were the same note. Now, when he changed this one string, the twenty-five strings on the other all changed, for they tried to get in tune by vibrating either faster or slower.

24.27.4 Though there was nothing but a note to this, it still became the master of the other notes.

Although Stupid Scaredy used this to overawe his disciple, he did nothing more than make same resonate with same, which never proved that what he did was an expertise uniquely his.

24.27.5 Are not you all just like him?"

Each of the five masters considered his view of things to be his own unique view and considered what he thought right to be "right." As such, they too were no different from Stupid Scaredy when he tried to overawe his disciple—none could rise above the others.

24.28 Master Hui then said, "Just now Ru, Mo, Yang, and Bing were disputing with me, and, though they shook me with rhetoric and beat me down with shouts, they never refuted me, so how am I just like them?"

His assertion that "they never refuted me" just means that each of them just went on thinking himself right, yet Master Hui still wants to use this to prove he was best.

24.29.1 Master Zhuang replied, "A certain man of Qi sent his son to Song, his instructions to the gatekeeper there that he not be kept whole.

He sent his son away to a different state, where he had the gatekeeper there keep him, and, when he arrived, gave him free hand to see to it that his son's body did not remain intact. The man of Qi was as unkind as this, yet, since he thought himself right, he just went ahead and did it.[16]

24.29.2 But when he acquired some type of bronze bell, he would wrap it in cloth.

On the contrary, he regarded the way he cherished bells as right. He wrapped them in cloth out of fear they would be broken or damaged.

24.29.3 He never left the boundaries of his own state to get his lost [*tang*] son back—what a way to abandon his own kind!

"Lost" [*tang*] means abandon [*shi*]. He abandoned his own son and would not go any distance to get him back, which means he abandoned his own kind. Nevertheless, he never thought that he did wrong. How could a man so regard himself to be right that he becomes as confused and wrong as this!

24.29.4 Then there was the man of Chu, who while staying there lodged with a gatekeeper,

Both these men were stuck just where they then happen to be and so could not move to a higher position.

24.29.5 in the middle of the night, when no one was around, got into a fight with a boatman, so even before leaving the shore [*cen*] did enough to provoke hostility."

Cen (small hill) here means shore. In the middle of the night, just he himself boarded someone's boat and, before leaving the shore, got into a fight with him. This describes how these two men, of Qi and Chu, never considered themselves wrong. Now, as for how the five masters all considered themselves right, how are they any different from them!

24.30.1 Whilst Master Zhuang was sending someone off for burial and happened to pass by the grave of Master Hui, he turned to his entourage and said, "A man of Ying got a bit of plaster on the tip of his nose like a fly's wing, so he had Carpenter Shi slice it off. Wielding his axe with a sound like the wind, Carpenter Shi immediately sliced it off as requested.

He just shut his eyes and let his hand do as it would.

24.30.2 He removed all the plaster, yet the nose was unharmed. When Lord [Duke] Yuan of Song heard about this, he summoned Carpenter Shi and ordered him, 'Try to do this for me.' Carpenter Shi replied, 'As for me, I once could have sliced it off that way, but my chopping block has long been dead.' It has been since you died Master [Hui] that I too have had nothing to use as a chopping block—no one with whom to discuss things."

If it is not a chopping block that does not move or an interlocutor who has forgotten words, even the most perfect expression or the most marvelous slicing will be of no use.

24.31 When Guan Zhong fell ill, Duke Huan, going to see how he was,[17] said, "Your illness, Father Zhong, is so critical that we may not avoid saying that it will lead to the great illness [death]. Therefore, to whom may I now entrust my state?"

24.32. Guan Zhong replied, "To whom do you wish to entrust it?"

24.33 The duke replied, "Bao Shuya."

24.34 "He won't do. Though he is an excellent man of pure and honest character, he does not associate with people who are not up to his standards; moreover, once he hears of another's faults, he does not forget it for the rest of his life. If you were to let him govern your state, he would both restrict you above and act contrary to the interests of the common folk below. He would certainly offend you, My Lord, and that would not take long!"

24.35 "If that is so, who then would do?"

24.36.1 "If I must speak, then Xi Peng will do, for his character is such that he both would be unmindful of his eminence above and would let himself be constrained by subordinates below.

Though eminent, he would not be overbearing.

24.36.2 He is ashamed that he is not equal to the Yellow Thearch and pities those who are not equal to him.

Therefore, "no one is discarded."[18]

24.36.3 One who shares his virtue with others is called a sage, and one who shares his wealth with others is called a worthy. Though anyone who tries to overawe others with his worthiness never enjoys their support, anyone who humbles himself before others never fails to win their support. There are things within the state that such a one does not try to hear, and things within the family that such a one does not try to see. So if I must speak, Xi Peng will do."

If one were to hear and see all this, matters would converge on him and leave all his subordinates with nothing to set hand to or leg after. Therefore, he may set these all aside; but if he can't quite set them all aside, that would just about do it too.

24.37.1 When the King of Wu was boating on the Yangtze, he climbed a mountain teeming with monkeys. When all the monkeys saw him, they were so frightened that they abandoned what they were doing and fled, escaping into thick vegetation. But one monkey among them, nonchalant and cocky, went on with its grasping [branches] and scratching [*juesao*],[19] showing off how clever it was to the king. So the king shot at it, but it quickly grabbed them [*minji*],

Min here means "quick," and *ji* (receive) means "continually collect" [*xukuo*].

24.37.2 that is, the monkey grabbed the swift [*jie*] arrows out of the air.

Jie here means "swift." No matter how quickly the arrows were shot at it, the monkey could still grab them.

24.37.3 The king then ordered his entourage to shoot immediately at it, and the monkey, gripping one,[20] died.

24.38 The king turned to his friend Face That Doubts Not [Yan Buyi] and said, "This monkey showed off its skill and relied on its agility to taunt me, which brought it to such an end as this! Do you take warning! Alas! Don't let your face appear arrogant to others." When Face That Doubts Not returned home, he became the disciple of Keep Watch Sturdy [Dong Wu], who helped him with his facial expression. He shunned amusement and abjured prominence, and in three years everyone in the state praised him.

24.39 Ziqi of Southwall sat slumped on his writing table. Looking up, he slowly exhaled. Master Yan Cheng went in to see him and said, "Master, as a man you are extraordinary! Can your body really be made to look like a dried-up skeleton, your mind really made to seem like lifeless ashes?"[21]

24.40.1 "I used to live in a mountain cave, and it was at that time that Tian He[22] once came to see me, for which the entire people of Qi held three celebrations to congratulate him.

That he had managed to see Ziqi was considered such an honor.

24.40.2 I must first have had something for him, because he knew about me. I must certainly have been selling it, because he was going to trade on

it. If I did not have such a thing, how could he have known about it? If I had not been selling it, how could he have traded on it? Alas! I grieved how this man was bringing about his own death.[23] I then went on to grieve that I grieved for him, and then went even further to grieve about the grief I felt for grieving about him. It was after that that I began to distance myself from all this more each day.

Ziqi knew that he had not the wherewithal to save him and to try to do so would do just enough to harm himself. Therefore, as he began lamenting others with no sense of grief, his sense of grief gradually vanished, and, tranquilly freeing himself of conscious mind, he transformed his body into a dried-up skeleton—this is what is meant by "he distanced himself more each day."

24.41 When Zhongni [Confucius] went to Chu, the King of Chu ritually entertained him with wine. As Sun Shu'ao stood by holding a bronze goblet, Yiliao of South Market,[24] receiving the wine and offering a libation, said, "Oh man worthy of the ancients, let us, indeed, now have your words!"

When one so spoke in antiquity, it had to be at such a formal consultative gathering.

24.42.1 "I, Qiu, have heard words that are not said, but I have never quite spoken them myself.

Since the sage stays free of words, what he says are the words of the common folk. Therefore, the text has him refer to it as "words that are not said." But if he does use words to do his speaking, even though they come out of his own mouth, they are never words that he himself speaks.

24.42.2 But I shall now try to speak about such words.

He is going to take this opportunity to speak about staying free of words.

24.42.3 Yiliao of South Market juggled balls, and trouble between two factions was resolved; Sun Shu'ao sweetly slept holding a feather fan, and the people of Ying threw down their weapons.

These two masters put an end to dispute by keeping silent; they remained serenely disinterested and completely at ease, and yet armed conflict for the one and dispute for the other were spontaneously resolved.[25]

24.42.4 So I wish I had such a mouth three feet wide!"

As long as what is said is not one's own, even if one speaks all throughout his life, it is not to speak at all. This is why he wants to have a mouth three feet wide—even that would not be quite wide enough. When ordinary people keep their mouths shut, this never means they "don't speak."

24.43 Theirs [*bi*] I call the Dao that is not spoken [*dudao zhi Dao*],

"Theirs" [*bi*] refers to the two masters.

24.43.2 and mine [*ci*] I call disputation that is not said [*buyan zhi bian*].

"Mine" [*ci*] refers to Zhongni [Confucius].

24.43.3 Therefore, when virtue gathers in the unifying power of the Dao,

Although what the Dao consists of is infinitely changeable, to revert to it in an all-embracing way, nothing, after all, is better than spontaneous receptivity, for that brings one into unity with it.

24.43.4 and words stop at the point at which knowing no longer knows, that indeed perfectly does it.

When words stop at one's allotted capacity to use them, if that is not perfection, what is!

24.43.5 The way the Dao unifies things, virtue can't equal.

Each person just has his own spontaneous receptivity, none of which is equal, while the Dao is one with all.

24.43.6 So what knowing can't know, disputation can't designate,

Since it is not within the limits of one's capacity, one can't designate it.

24.43.7 To designate things the way the Confucians and Mohists do results in harm.

It is because the Confucians and the Mohists want to equal what they can't equal, and so denote what they can't denote, that they cause great harm.

24.43.8 Therefore, the way the sea rejects not waters that flow eastward into it signifies the greatest of perfections.

This clarifies that it is by accepting things without rejection that one's success is great.

24.43.9 The Sage embraces Heaven and Earth and his grace extends to all under Heaven, yet no one knows who he is.

Oceanically, his benevolence is universal.

24.43.10 This is why he lives free of noble title

Were he to have it, he would make nothing of it.

24.43.11 and dies free of posthumous name.

A posthumous name is a way to account for meritorious deeds, but since he credits not himself for his meritorious deeds, though a posthumous name is there for him, it is not his own to have.

24.43.12 Riches he does not amass,

This encouraged all the myriad folk to know contentment.

24.43.13 and fame he does not establish.

Since meritorious deeds are not attributed to him, fame gravitates to others.

24.43.14 This is what I mean by a "great one."

If he took credit and so was honored, that would make him petty!

24.43.15 Just as a dog is not considered good because it barks well, a man is not considered worthy because he talks well.

Worthiness emerges from one's fundamental nature; it is not a matter of how one speaks.

24.43.16 And as for being great, it is even more unlikely that one may achieve that by working at it.

How much less likely can one make oneself great!

24.43.17 Since trying to make oneself great is not a sufficient way to become great, how much less likely can one make himself virtuous!

Only spontaneously does one become virtuous.

24.43.18 As for the greatly endowed, none are greater than Heaven and Earth, yet what means did they ever try to use to make themselves as greatly endowed as that!

The great endowment of Heaven and Earth was not had by their seeking it.

24.43.19 One who is aware of his great endowment seeks it not, loses it not, abandons it not, and would not change himself for anyone else.

One who is aware of his great endowment casts not himself aside in order to try to be someone else. Therefore, he seeks it not, loses it not, and abandons it not.

24.43.20 As long as he reverts to self, he shall never be exhausted.

As long as one so reverts and safeguards his principle of self, his principle of self shall fulfill itself.

24.43.21 As long as he complies with what he has always been, he shall not wear away,

As long as he complies with his constant nature, he shall spontaneously fulfill himself and not wear away.

24.43.22 For a great one is that sincere.

Such a one spontaneously fulfills himself without trying to do so, which is why the text says that he is "that sincere."

24.44 Ziqi[26] had eight sons, whom he lined up before him. He then summoned Jiufang Yin and said, "Appraise my sons' physiognomies for me and determine who has an auspicious fate."

24.45 Jiufang Yin replied, "It is Kun who will have good fortune."

24.46 Pleasantly surprised, Ziqi asked, "How so?" "Kun will eat the same food as the sovereign of a state and do so for the rest of his life."

24.47 Desolated, Ziqi began to cry, saying, "Why should my son be brought to such an extreme as this?"

24.48 Jiufang Yin responded, "To eat the same food as the sovereign of the state means that such favor extends to the three generations of one's family, and even more so to the parents! But here you reject such good fortune, which means while your son is auspicious, you the father are not!"

24.49.1 Ziqi then said, "Yin, How could you manage to know this and yet think Kun should enjoy good fortune! All you know about is the wine and meat that would enter his nose and mouth, and what good is that when it comes to knowing where they come from! I was never a shepherd, yet a ewe was born in the southwest corner of my house, and I never liked hunting, yet a quail was born in the southeast corner of my house. You don't think that something to wonder at, why not?

The reason why one should wonder at this is because they appeared without reason or intention.

24.49.2 Where my son and I wander, we wander all through Heaven and Earth,

That is, they stay free from acting with intent.

24.49.3 And he and I chance to find [*yao*] our delight in Heaven and chance to find [*yao*] our food from Earth.

They just go along with what they receive from Heaven and Earth. *Yao* ["invite" or "seek"] here means *yu*, "chance to find."

24.49.4 He and I neither engage in conscious undertakings nor consciously plan anything, and thus are never surprised [*guai*] by things.

Guai here means *yi*, "find surprising." Since they constantly trust to their fundamental natures, utterly unconcerned, they function spontaneously.

24.49.5 He and I ride on the sincerity of Heaven and Earth and thus never find ourselves in opposition to things.

As such, they never engage in conscious undertakings.

24.49.6 He and I just go along perfectly at one with things and thus never consciously pursue what might be advantageous in them.

24.49.7 But now there is to be such a worldly reward for him as this!

It is when one performs a meritorious deed for others that people reward one. But if I don't perform any meritorious deed and yet they reward me, why should that happen?

24.49.8 Whenever a strange omen occurs, something strange is sure to happen. Danger! Since it can't be due to any fault of his or mine, Heaven probably ordained it!

Now, this strange omen occurred without anything strange happening, thus he knew that it was his son's ordained fate.

24.49.9 And that is why I began to cry."

If it had been something they were doing for such as this to happen, all that need be done is stop what they were doing, but if it spontaneously came without their doing anything, they could do nothing about it, which was why he cried over it.

24.50.1 Not long afterward, when he sent Kun on an errand to Yan, on the way he was captured by bandits. If his body had remained whole, it would be difficult to sell him, so they thought it better to mutilate him by cutting off a foot.

If he remained intact, they feared he would run away; thus they thought it better to cut off a foot and sell him mutilated.

24.50.2 Therefore, they cut off his foot and sold him in Qi, where he happened to be made the doorkeeper for Master Qu, thus for the rest of his life ate meat.[27]

24.51 When Front Teeth Missing happened to meet Xu You,[28] he asked, "Where are you going?"
24.52 He replied, "I am fleeing from Yao."
24.53 "What do you mean?"
24.54.1 "Well, Yao works so hard at promoting benevolence that I fear that he is thought ridiculous by all the world and that people of later ages will devour one another!

This happens because the "benevolent" vie so for esteem.[29]

24.54.2 The common folk are not difficult to gather to one. Cherish them, and they will feel close to you; benefit them, and they will arrive; praise them, and they will be encouraged, but cause them something they don't like, and they will scatter. Cherishing and beneficence emerge from benevolence and righteousness. Whereas few are those who cast aside benevolence and righteousness aside, many are those who make profit out of benevolence and righteousness. The practice of benevolence and righteousness is nothing other than, on the one hand, insincerity,

Once benevolence and righteousness are practiced, it will be done with deceit.

24.54.3 and on the other, utilized by the rapacious as a device.

When benevolence and righteousness appeared, the rapacious used them, as such, as devices to fulfill their ambitions.

24.54.4 Therefore, if the judgement of one man is used to benefit all in the world,

If benevolence and righteousness were allowed to emerge from the emotional expression of each individual, judgements concerning them would not be restricted to one man.

24.54.5 this is like using one and the same cut [*pie*] to make everyone look alike.

Pie [glance] here means "cut" [*ge*]. The myriad folk come in a myriad shapes, so if they are all cut [*ge*] with one and the same trim [*yiji*], there will be harm.

24.54.6 Yao knows how the worthy man benefits everyone in the world but knows not how such a one harms everyone in the world."

Only if one distances himself from worthiness will his worthiness not be a deceit.

24.55 There are the malleable and submissive, the opportunistic and improvident, and the feeble bent-overs.
24.56 Those known as the malleable and submissive learn what one teacher has to say, then, entirely shaped by it and utterly complying with it, pass it off as something they themselves have said and think that it is all that they themselves need, never realizing that there was never anything to it. And here, as such, are those called the malleable and submissive.

Since their thought is taken up entirely with teaching based on the appearance of things [*xingjiao*], how could they ever understand how we independently transform [*duhua*] in the realm of arcane obscurity [*xuanming*]!

24.57 The opportunistic and improvident behave like lice on a pig. They choose a place where bristles are sparse and make it their great palace and grand park, or find either some corner in the cloven hooves or there at the haunches among the nipples to make themselves a safe and handy dwelling. But they are utterly unaware that the butcher will, one day, with a brandish of the arm, spread out grass and light a smoky fire for the pig, where they and the pig are all singed.[30] As such, their comings or goings are bound by their situations. And here, as such, are those called the opportunistic and improvident.

People who lack the ability to keep in step freely with change [*tongbian*][31] steal moments of transient security and temporary advantage; they thus all might as well be lice on a pig.

24.58 As for the bent-over feebles, Shun was one. Mutton is not attracted to ants; it is the ants that are attracted to mutton—this because mutton is rank. It was because of Shun's rank behavior that the common folk happily submitted to him. This was why each of his three moves founded metropolises, and by the time he reached the desolation of Deng, he had more than a hundred thousand households with him. When Yao heard how worthy Shun was, he raised him from that desolate land, saying, "I hope this brings your beneficence to bear on us." By the time Shun was raised from that desolate land, he was already so old that his hearing and sight were in decline—yet he was unable to retire. And here, as such, are those called the bent-over feebles.

The body of a sage is no different from that of people in general. Therefore, though the use of his eyes and ears deteriorates, as for his spirit, it always remains whole and safe from beginning to end. But as for him, while still young he had not yet matured, and by the time he had reached old age he was in decline. Therefore, may we assume that this sage of sages had not even the time between dawn and breakfast for himself?

24.59.1 This is why the divine man hates it when multitudes gravitate to him.

It is just that multitudes gravitate to him of their own accord and not because he likes them to come.

24.59.2 For when multitudes come, discord occurs, and when discord occurs, it is no benefit to him.

This clarifies that when Shun took charge of the entire world, it was just something he could not help but do—how could it ever have led to accord and benefit to him!

24.59.3 Therefore, one should not get too close to anyone and not too distant from anyone, and, embracing his own virtue and allowing harmony to meld,

he complies with all in the world—such a one may be called an authentic man. To the ants he abandons knowledge, from the fish he gets his tactics, and to the mutton he abandons intention.[32]

As for the common folk, they enjoyed his beneficence, but for Shun, he just wore out his body.

24.60.1 Such a one uses his own eyes to see, his own eyes to hear, and uses his own mind to respond mentally to things.

As for these three, one can't do without such hearing, seeing, and conceptual thought [*xinyi*].

24.60.2 In this way, his levelings are as straight as a plumb line.

It is impossible to dispense with a plumb line, but such a one levels himself spontaneously.[33]

24.60.3 When change occur for him, he keeps perfectly in step with it.

Though he can't avoid making footprints, such a one maintains arcane unity [*xuanhui*] with things.

24.60.4 The authentic man of antiquity dealt with things by relying on the Natural

If one deals with things while abiding in disengagement from them, those things, as such, will be a success.

24.60.5 and tried not to get into the Natural through the ways of men.

But if one were to seek disengagement while engaging with things, such things would be done increasingly in vain.

24.60.6 As for the authentic man of antiquity, attaining it, he stayed alive and losing it, he died. But even when attained, he still might die, and even if lost, he still might live.

Whether alive or dead, whether attaining it [the Dao] or doing without it, each case just depends on where one is located. In life it is something to attain, and in death it might revert to something one does without, for there is never any constancy to it.

24.61 Medicine provides evidence for this: as for aconite, bellflower, gorgon nut, and pig's dung grass, when the time is just right, they each become an emperor such that no words could ever describe it!

Exactly when one of them is needed, such a one is far from worthless, but if it is not the right time for it, it is entirely without value. Value and worthlessness thus have their times—who could ever make them constant!

24.62 When Gou Jian took his three thousand troops with armor and shields and retired to perch atop Mount Kuaiji,[34] **only Zhong knew how his destruction could be turned into survival, but that same Zhong did not then realize how this would eventually bring him to grief.**[35] **As the saying goes, the owl's eyes have times suitable for them, and the crane's neck has occasions suitable for it, so they come to grief if they are deprived of such times and occasions [*jie*].**

Each is suited for use at particular times, and, since they can do nothing about their limitations, there are times when they fail. And because there are times when they fail, they come to grief. *Jie* [distinguish, set free] here means *qu* [deprive].

24.63.1 Thus it is said, when the wind passes over a river, loss for it should occur; when the sun passes over a river, loss for it should occur.

Things that have bodily form naturally get entangled with one another. It is only that which is beyond bodily form that is not worn down when ground upon.[36]

24.63.2 And even if we ask that the wind and sun just go on gripping the river together, the river would never be aware of their attack,

Though it really suffers loss, it is unaffected by it.

24.63.3 for, relying on its spring, it just keeps on flowing.

The reason why it is unaffected is not because it does not suffer loss but because, thanks to its spring, it just keeps on flowing.

24.63.4 It is water's tight grip on the land that gives it stability [*shen*];[37] it is the shadow's tight grip on the man that gives it stability; it is one thing's tight grip on another thing that gives it stability.

If one stays free from intention [*wuyi*], he will remain within his allotted capacity, and, as such, will have real stability.

24.64.1 Therefore, if the eye tries to see more than its clarity allows, it is in danger; if the ear tries to hear more than its capacity allows, it is in danger; if the mind tries to know more than it can pursue, it is in danger.

It is because such intentionality [*youyi*] knows no limit that danger occurs.

24.64.2 All faculties that one tries to increase beyond one's store of them lead to danger, and once such danger occurs, no chance is given to mend one's ways.

Therefore, one should respect what he can't do and but trust to his natural capacity [*tianran*].

24.64.3 Prolongations to disaster will thus keep piling up [*cui*].

Cui here means "gather" [*ju*]. As one can't free himself from selfconscious awareness, the duration of disaster will ever increase.

24.64.4 But if one reverses himself, though achievements will follow,

If one turns back to abide by his original nature, achievements will be accomplished without conscious effort [*buzuo*].

24.64.5 their fruition will take longer.

If one tries to hasten them, fruition won't occur.

24.64.6 Yet men consider them their personal treasures. Is that not pitiful!

"Personal treasures" means one's mental powers [*zhineng*].

24.64.7 This is why there is no end to the destruction of states and the slaughter of common folk,

All this is due to disaster that such persons [i.e., rulers and usurpers] bring on themselves.

24.64.8 and all because they know not to ask why this is so.

Though they know not to ask why this happens, it happens because of self-consciousness [*youxin*], yet they go on cultivating their minds in order to spar themselves from disaster.[38]

24.65.1 Where one's foot strikes the ground is just one step, but though a mere step, only after trusting to step where one has not yet stepped does one becomes adept at going farther afield. What one knows is but small, but though small, only after trusting to what one does not know does one come to understand what the Natural means.

It is only after one has forgotten all about Heaven and Earth and lost all awareness of the myriad things that one can focus all attention on the cicada's wings.[39] And how more true this is when it comes to understanding what the Natural means, for how could this ever be done unless one frees himself from conscious mind!

24.65.2 To know with great unity, to know with great yin, to know with great eye, to know with great equality, to know with great method, to know with great trust, and to know with great stability—this is to reach perfection. Great unity gives one comprehensive effect.

This is what the Dao does.[40]

24.65.3 Great yin frees one [*jie*].

As long as one uses only what is within his endowed capacity, every effort will be free from obstruction.[41]

24.65.4 Great eye allows one really to see.

To see things with everyone's eyes, that is, indeed, the great eye.

24.65.5 Great equality grants accord [*yuan*].[42]

If one both complies with one's fundamental nature and allows each person his own self-fulfillment, this is what "great equality" accomplishes.

24.65.6 Great method grants perfect realization [*ti*].[43]

Perfect realization allows each person to fulfill his own natural allotment, for in this way all practices everywhere achieve success, for such is what great method accomplishes.

24.65.7 Great trust grants attainment [*ji*].

Let no command be given to those who await orders that exceeds what they can do, for this makes for great trust.

24.65.8 Great stability grants control.

If one is sure not to agitate them, people become stable on their own. Therefore, one controls them with great stability, which is not to control them at all.

24.66.1 Everything has the Natural in it.

No thing has ever existed that did not have the Natural in it.

24.66.2 Compliance with it grants perspicacity [*ming*].[44]

Compliance with it results in such perspicacity that one is freed from conscious effort.

24.66.3 Arcane fusion [*ming*] with it gets at its pivotal essence [*shu*].

Although perfect principle [*zhili*] possesses the very crux of things [*youji*], one need but arcanely merge with it to get at its pivotal essence [*shuyao*].

24.66.4 From the beginning, "that" [*bi*] has been there.

What has been there from the beginning is "that." Therefore, abiding in it, I refrain from conscious effort.[45]

24.66.5 As such, one's understanding of it seems like not understanding it,

Since this understanding conforms to "that," and "that" just understands itself, and because such understanding achieves nothing, it seems as if no understanding occurs.

24.66.6 and such a one's knowing seems like not knowing.

This makes it clear that it is "that" that does the knowing.

24.66.7 Only when one ceases to have conscious awareness does one really know.

It is when the self no longer has conscious awareness that "that" [i.e., the Natural in each person] realizes how to become inherently useful [*ziyong*],[46] and once "that" is allowed to become inherently useful, no one in the world thus fails to know.

24.66.8 Examine it, and it seems it can't have limits,

Since it resonates with people as it suits them, it is infinitely changeable.

24.66.9 yet it can't fail to have limits.

It is limited to each according to one's allotted capacity.

24.66.10 Although it winds and slides, its realization [*shi*] is had.

Although the way it [the Natural] winds and slides for myriads of people, each and every one realizes it in his own way.

24.66.11 What it was originally the present does not replace,

Each person possesses it [the Natural] as he had it originally, for it is something that can't be exchanged.

24.66.12 and it can't be depleted.

It remains just right for each person to fulfill his allotted capacity.

24.66.13 As such, why may we not talk about it in some broad but essential way!

Let us discuss and propagate it, for it concerns the great crux of things [*daxian*].

24.66.14 And why not make inquiries into this! Why be so confused!

When we make inquiries into its broad essentials, we discover that it is within their absolute capacities for people to grasp the principle that one should forget oneself and trust others to do for themselves [*renwu*]. Why should there be any such confusion!

24.66.15 When people try to dispel confusion with non-confusion in order to recover non-confusion, they do this because they admire great non-confusion.

Such confusion is impossible to dispel. Therefore, to admire "great non-confusion" is the height of stupidity. This is why the sage leaves people to their own resources and great kings disassociate themselves from their own footprints, which leaves worldly opinion to create their fame.[47]

Notes

Victor Mair translates the title of this chapter, a surname and name, as "Ghostless Hsü"; see Victor H. Mair, trans., *Wandering on the Way: Early Taoist Tales and Parables of Chuang Tzu*, 237, but it is more likely that either (1) *gui* (ghost/spirit) is a rebus or phonetic loan character for *wei* (fear), resulting in "Xu the Fearless or (2) *gui* is short for *guize* (spirit blame), i.e., "one who knows the joy of Heaven [the Natural]. . . . is free from the censure of demons"; see 13.2.6 and *Zhuangzi jishi*, 2: 462. Moreover, a primary meaning of *xu* is "easygoing" or "relaxed," which seems to characterize the personality and behavior of Xu Wugui, whose name thus might be rendered "Easygoing the Fearless" or "Easygoing No Spirit Blame." The former is preferred here.

1. According to Cheng Xuanying, Nü Shang was the prime minister of Wei. *Zhuangzi jishi*, 4: 818.
2. Cheng Xuanying: "Temperament lofty and noble, they take long looks as if searching for the sun." *Zhuangzi jishi*, 4: 820.
3. Cf. 21.17.
4. Cheng Xuanying: "The Odes [Shi], Documents [Shu], Rites [Li], and Music [Yue] refer to the *Six Classics* [*Liujing*, including also the *Changes* (Yi) and the *Spring and Autumn Annals* (Chunqiu)]. The Metal Blocks [*Jinban*] and Six Bowcases [*Liutao*] are the titles of chapters in the *Documents of Zhou* [Zhoushu], though some say that these are esoteric mantic texts [*michen*]. . . . But let us say that it is the *Grand Duke's Treatise on the Art of War* [*Taigong bingfa*] that is meant, which means that the *Six Bowcases* are the *Civil* [Wen], *Martial* [Wu], *Tiger* [Hu], *Leopard* [Bao], and *Dragon* [Long]. 'Woof' [*heng*] implies 'far removed' and 'warp' [*zong*] implies 'near at hand'; Marquis Wu was fond of military things and disliked civil studies, which is why Nü Shang used the *Art of War* for the warp [tough material] and the *Six Classics* as the woof [soft material] of his presentations. If the 'Six Bowcases' should be identified with the six parts of the *Duke's Treatise on the Art of War*, *jinban* would not be the title of a work but an attribute of *Six Bowcases*: '[printed] on metal blocks.' " *Zhuangzi jishi*, 4: 821.
5. Cf. 19.50.5.
6. Cheng Xuanying: "Marquis Wu had longed to hear about dogs and horses for a very long time, just like that banished man and the refugee stuck in distant places who sorely missed their fellow villagers and family members. But now if talk by this authentic man had been instead of the *Six Classics* and the *Grand Duke's Treatise on the Art of War*, such chatting and laughing about it at his side would not have suited him at all—which fits with the above analogy perfectly." *Zhuangzi jishi*, 4: 824.
7. Cheng Xuanying takes *fa* [flaunt] in its original meaning of "attack"; namely, "launch a punitive expedition against": "Once accomplishment involving honor and rank occur, contention is sure to follow, which is reason for punitive expeditions [*zhengfa*]." *Zhuangzi jishi*, 4: 828.
8. Cheng Xuanying: "When one makes up a penal code, which brings about changes in usual ways, people will be sure to regard this as harm. As a result, this will extend to foreign enemies and will often involve fighting." *Zhuangzi jishi*, 4: 828.

9. Cheng Xuanying: "The Yellow Thearch's name was Xuanyuan. Big Steep Craggy is an epithet for the great Dao in all its vastness and its soaring emptiness and quietude. Another explanation is that it is the name of a Perfected one of antiquity. Resting Place is the name of a mountain located within the borders of Mi district, Yingyang [Henan], also called Mount Exalted Craggy [Taikui shan]. The Yellow Thearch, a sage though long arcanely merged with the ultimate principle of things for now wanted to dwell there and seek the arcane Dao [personified by the sage Big Steep Craggy], and thus avail himself of the footprints he [Big Steep Craggy] left behind at Resting Place." *Zhuangzi jishi*, 3: 830.
10. Cf. "Uncle Slippery Operator," 4.42; "Slippery Decrepit," 18.9; and "humorously cunning," 33.19.11. Moreover, in the *Guji liezhuan* (Biographies of Slippery Operators) in Sima Qian's *Shiji* (Records of the Grand Historian), *guji* has been variously translated as "comedians," "humorists," "jokesters," "buffoons," "clowns," or "comics," but these don't do justice to the term, for "slippery operators" used their rhetorical skills to undermine conventional assumptions about life and the world, to reform harmful behavior, and reverse wrong strategies. For a detailed analysis, see Richard John Lynn, "The Modern Chinese Word for Humour (*Huaji*) and Its Antecedents in the *Zhuangzi* and Other Early Texts," in Hans-Georg Moeller and Günter Wohlfart, ed., *Laughter in Eastern and Western Philosophies: Proceedings of the Académie du Midi*, 60–73.
11. It is likely that the *xiang* (assist) in "Xiangcheng" is written for *rang* (ban), so the place in the Yellow Emperor's journey isn't the actual place in Henan, but rather an invention of Master Zhuang, in keeping with the rest of the fanciful names. Note that all these names are translated differently by Victor Mair, who assumes an imaginary sky journey in which the Yellow Thearch in his sun chariot with entourage travels east to west, just as the sun appears to move, for all the names seem sky-related. I instead believe that all refer to attitude of mind, ways of knowing, and strategies of rulership; see Richard John Lynn, "The Modern Chinese Word for Humour," 61 and 68–69.
12. Cf. *Yijing* (Classic of Changes), "Appended phrases" [*Xici zhuan*], Part Two: "As a book, the *Changes* takes the plumbing of beginnings and the summing up of endings as its material. [Wang Bi: Material here means "embodiment" (of change, i.e., the hexagrams). A hexagram unites a concept as it progresses from its beginning to its end point.] The way the six lines mix in together is due to the fact that they are nothing other than momentary things [*shiwu*]. [Wang Bi: Each line depends on the moment. Things here means "events."]." Richard John Lynn, *Classic of Changes*, 90.
13. Cf. 17.29.6.
14. "Ru" (the Confucian) is Confucius, followed by Master Mo, Yang Zhu, and Bing, the personal name of Gongsun Long.
15. *Gong* (*do* or *C*) is the first note of the Chinese pentatonic scale, and *jue* (*mi* or *E*) the third.
16. A gatekeeper in ancient states was usually mutilated: a foot was amputated so he could not run away.
17. This same passage also appears, worded slightly differently, in the *Liezi* (Sayings of Master Lie); *Liezi jishi*, 6: 198–200, and with more variants in the *Guanzi* (Sayings of Master Guan); *Guanzi jiaozhu*, 2: 519–20.
18. Guo quotes from *Laozi*, section 27: "This is how the sage is always good at saving people, so no one is discarded. . . ." [Wang Bi:] "The sage does not establish punishments and names in order to impose restraints on the people. Nor does he create promotions and honors in order to cull out and discard the unworthy. He enhances the natural state of the myriad folk but does not serve as the starting point for them. Thus the text says, 'no one is discarded.'" Lynn, *The Classic of the Way and Virtue*, 101.

19. Cheng Xuanying glosses *juesao* (grasp at random) as "*tengzhi*" (fly and jump). *Zhuangzi jishi*, 4: 846.
20. Cheng Xuanying interprets "gripping" to mean that the monkey held on to a tree and died; more likely (and more dramatic), however, the monkey gripped the arrow that finally killed him as he died. *Zhuangzi zishi*, 4: 847.
21. Cf. 2.1.1–2.1.2.
22. Cheng Xuanying: "Tian and He are the surname and given name of the King of Qi." *Zhuangzi jishi*, 4: 849. As such, he may be identified as Duke Tai of Qi (d. 384), the ruler of Qi (404–384 BCE).
23. Cf. 21.20.1, Guo commentary. I suggest that Tian He sought out Ziqi, a hermit living in a mountain cave, because he thought such a person could impart the secret of longevity to him. This would explain why Ziqi initially grieved for him: Tian He was hastening his own death because of the worry that he must die.
24. Commentators have long noted the chronological inconsistencies of this passage: Sun Shu'ao served King Zhuang of Chu (r. 613–591 BCE) as prime minister and thus lived long before Confucius (551–479 BCE). "Yiliao of South Market" here seems to be referring to Xiong Yiliao, a warrior famous for valor and his skill at juggling, who also served under King Zhuang; however, Yiliao might also be identified with another man of the same name who appears in the *Zuozhuan*, sixteenth year of Duke Ai (479 BCE). Cf. 20.5, and see also *Zhuangzi jishi*, 4: 480, and Wang Shumin, *Zhuangzi jiaoquan*, 963, note 1.
25. Ying was the capital of Chu. Cheng Xuanying: "Sheng, Duke Bai of Chu, because he wanted to revolt found a way to kill Prime Minister Zixi [Lingyin Zixi]. Minister of War Ziqi [Sima Ziqi] then told him that Xiong Yiliao was a brave man, and if he could be brought on side, he could defeat 500 men all by himself. So the duke dispatched an emissary to get him to cooperate, but Yiliao just amused himself by juggling balls and refused to speak with the emissary. Though the emissary threated him with a sword, Yiliao never showed any alarm or fear. Not only did he ignore the order, he did not otherwise speak. Since Duke Bai did not get Yiliao on side, his revolt came to nothing—which is why the text states 'the trouble between the two factions was resolved.' . . . Shu'ao was self-possessed and learned in practical matters, understood principle, and was unaware of words. Holding a feather fan, he was so spontaneously receptive that he stopped the enemy state from invading, repulsing the enemy from a distance of more than a thousand *li*. The people of Chu, freed from trouble, cultivated civil virtues and abandoned all plans for war." *Zhuangzi jishi*, 4: 851.
26. Although Cheng Xuanying identifies this Ziqi as Minister of War Ziqi [Sima Ziqi], given the content of the passage, it is far more likely that this is Nanguo Ziqi. See *Zhuangzi jishi*, 4: 856.
27. Cheng Xuanying: "Master Qu was a rich man of Qi, who was market director [*jiezheng*] there. Once Kun had a foot cut off, he was sold into the household of that rich merchant of Qi, where he became the gatekeeper [*dangjie*, literally "faced the street"], so for the rest of his life ate meat." Lu Deming, in the *Jingdian shiwen*, has this to say: "Master Qu was a wealthy man of Qi, who was the market director there. He bought Kun and made him his personal representative [*zidai*], so for the rest of his life ate meat. Another source states that Master Qu was a butcher, so he and Kun, master and man, together ate meat." *Zhuangzi jishi*, 4: 860.
28. Cf. 1.8.1–1.9.5, 6.38–6.45, 12.6–12.8.18, and 28.1.
29. Cheng Xuanying: "Since the widespread practice of biased benevolence violates the virtues of simplicity and harmony, he fears that throughout the world, persons of learning

who have lost the Dao will bring about an age of even more superficial juggling morality. Following such footsteps in the future, the common folk will suffer famine, and once granaries are empty, they surely will devour one another. This is why he flees." *Zhuangzi jishi*, 4: 861.

30. The pig carcass is singed to remove the bristles.
31. Cf. *Yijing* (Classic of Changes), "Appended phrases" [*Xici zhuan*], Part One: "The means to know the future through the mastery of numbers is referred to as 'prognostication,' and to keep in step freely with change [*tongbian*] is referred to as 'the way one should act.' " [Wang Bi:] "When things reach their limit, they undergo change, and when change occurs, one should keep in perfect step with it. This is the dynamic that underlies the way one should act." Lynn, *Classic of Changes*, 54.
32. Cheng Xuanying: "He aspires not to the benevolence of [rank] mutton, so thus abandons knowledge of it to the ants [i.e., the common folk], engages not in rank behavior that morally transforms people, so thus abandons the intention to do so to the mutton [i.e., those who use benevolence and righteousness to effect moral suasion]. Casting benevolence and righteousness aside, he merges as one with the perfect Dao. It is because they wet one another with foam from their mouths to prevent harm [when waters dry up] but forget one another [when swimming freely] in rivers and lakes that he gets his tactics from the fish. It is to reprove Yu [Yao] and Shun for their rank behavior that the wording of this passage goes as far as this." *Zhuangzi jishi*, 4: 866. Also, cf. 6.10.1 and 14.31.11.
33. Cheng Xuanying: "Just as the plumb line unselfconsciously gets things straight, so the sage forgets all involvement with things and so equally is one with them [*pingdeng*]." *Zhuangzi jishi*, 4: 867.
34. Mount Kuaiji, now called Censer Peak [Xianglu shan], is located in Zhejiang, south of Hangzhou Bay and southeast of Shaoxing.
35. Cheng Xuanying: "Zhong was a Grand Master of Yue. When Gou Jian [the king of Yue] had suffered a great defeat [by the state of Wu in 494 BCE], with only three thousand troops fled up Mount Kuaiji [near Shaoxing, Zhejiang], total destruction seemed not far away. However, Zhong, who was really clever at devising secret schemes, turned this time of destruction into a chance for survival, pretending to conclude a peace treaty with Wu, which twenty years later led to Yue's conquest of Wu. However, though the crafty rabbit died, the fine hunting dog was cooked, so though the enemy state was vanquished, the loyal minister lost his life. If we analyze how this happened, after Wu was vanquished, . . . Grand Master Zhong did not flee [a purge of suspected disloyal officials], so was executed by Gou Jian. Though Zhong knew how to scheme how his state could survive on the verge of destruction, he did not know that this would lead to his personal grief and sure death." *Zhuangzi jishi*, 4: 869.
36. Cheng Xuanying: "Whereas the wind and sun consist of pneuma, the river has the stuff of physical form. Whatever has physical form or consists of pneuma can't avoid entanglements. So when wind blows or sun wears down [*lei*], there is sure to be loss and harm. However, it is because it [the river] relies on its [external, underground] spring that it can keep on going and remain unaffected. Likewise, after Wu was taken over by Yue, the strategic advisor [Zhong] should surely have relied on continuing meritorious contributions so that he would not have had to plan against getting executed later. Thus we know that if people are of advantage to one another, they are sure to cause one another harm." *Zhuangzi jishi*, 4: 869.
37. Cheng Xuanying glosses *shen* [comprehend, examine] as "stability" [*anding*]. *Zhuangzi jishi*, 4: 870.

38. "Cultivating the mind" [*xiuxin*] should be understood here as "cultivate the art/technique of the mind" [*xiu xinshu*]: how to scheme or plot; cf. 21.30.
39. Cf. 19.9.6.
40. Cheng Xuanying: "One is the ultimate yang number, and 'great unity' signifies Heaven (the Natural) in its comprehensive power to sustain all living things. Therefore, the text here says, 'comprehensive effect.' " *Zhuangzi jishi*, 4: 872.
41. Cheng Xuanying: " 'Great yin' is the earth. Since it bears everything unselfconsciously and indiscriminately, one should emulate it." *Zhuangzi jishi*, 4: 872.
42. Cheng Xuanying glosses "accord" [*yuan*] as "compliance" [*shun*]. *Zhuangzi jishi*, 4: 873.
43. Cheng Xuanying glosses *ti* as "perfect realization" [*tida*]. *Zhuangzi jishi*, 4: 873.
44. Cheng Xuanying glosses *ming* (bright, clear) as "perfect realization" [*tida*]. Zhuangzi jishi, 4: 874.
45. Cf. 2.8.1: "If it were not for that [*bi*], there would be no I; if there were no I, there would be nothing for it to endow, so it is, indeed, close by." Guo: " 'That' [*bi*] refers to Nature [*ziran*]. Since Nature begets me, I spontaneously generate. Therefore, this Nature is my own Nature, so how could it be thought something distant!" Although commentaries on and translations of 24.66.4 tend to interpret "beginning" [*chu*] as the "Great Beginning" [*taichu*], the very beginning of time and the universe, Guo Xiang insists that the Dao has always existed and always will: it is without beginning or end. Therefore, it is more likely that Guo takes "beginning" here to mean the beginning of existence of the figurative "I" or "self" of the narrative.
46. Cf. 2.11.10.
47. Cheng Xuanying: "Whereas no confusion is ever caused to sagely wisdom, such confusion does affect the mental state of ordinary people. If one uses the words of sagely wisdom to clear up the confusion of ordinary people, it won't occur to them to get back to their original meaning and recover their true essence, for they are unable to forget words once they get the meaning, but instead get stuck in the footprints sages leave behind. They so value words that clarify, that when these don't confuse, they think them 'great.' But this is just to admire them for the fact that they don't confuse—so how could they ever really manage to dispel confusion! We are advised again here to have nothing to do with such 'non-confusion.' " *Zhuangzi jishi*, 4: 875.

CHAPTER 25

ZEYANG

25.1 When Zeyang traveled to Chu, Yijie recommended him to the king, but since the king would not see him, Yijie went home.

25.2 Peng Yang then went to see Wang Guo[1] and said, "Why don't you recommend me to the king?"

25.3 Wang Guo answered, "I would not be as good as Lord Supervisor of Rest [Gong Yuexiu]."[2]

25.4 Peng Yang asked, "This Lord Supervisor of Rest, what does he do?"

25.5.1 "Winters, he spears turtles at the river; summers, he rests in the fastness of the forest, so when those who pass by ask him, he says, 'This is my home.'

He says this to restrain Peng Yang's penchant for advancement.

25.5.2 Since Yi Jie already could not help you, how much the less could I, for I'm not even his match! Yi Jie's character is such that, though he lacks moral goodness [*de*], he is perceptive and not self-permissive, and, as such, puts all his energy [*shen*] into securing relations with others; as such, he immerses himself in the world of wealth and honor.

He says that he neither loves wealth and honor as much as Yi Jie nor is as good at securing relations; he neither occupies his mind as much with forms and names nor use his knowledge as much to scramble upwards.

25.5.3 He does not assist others to enhance their virtue but instead assists them to waste it.

By assisting advancement illicitly, virtue weakens and reputation wastes.

25.5.4 And here is someone who, suffering cold, tries to borrow more clothes from the spring, someone who, suffering heat, tries to make winter return with its cold wind.

That is, since he himself [Wang Guo] complies with the pace of the four seasons, he can't move with the speed of Peng Yang.

25.5.5 The character of the King of Chu is such that, his bearing honorable and stern, he treats wrongdoers as merciless as a tiger. Who other than an eloquent man of upright morals could ever make him yield!

25.6.1 The sages of antiquity carried off their poverty in such a way that it made their family members forget they were poor.

Placidly free of desire and happily content with whatever came their way, they neither placed any value on extravagance nor regarded moral behavior as anything to bring them honor. Therefore, their family members knew not that poverty may cause them distress.

25.6.2 And behaved so when they prospered that it made kings and nobles forget their ranks and emoluments, which transformed them into humble and modest figures.

They took rank and emolument lightly and moral behavior seriously. Detached and aloof and situated in forgetfulness, they were utterly unconscious that honor had anything to do with them. Therefore, this had kings and nobles lose sight of what made them eminent.

25.6.3 Their attitude to things was such that they were happy with them just as they were.

They did not let themselves be distressed by things.

25.6.4 Their attitude toward people was such that they communed with them while protecting themselves from them.

Communing with others, they did not let themselves be lost.

25.6.5 Therefore, even sometimes without speaking they brewed harmony for people to drink.

When each person achieves self-fulfillment, this is harmony to drink—and why should that depend on words!

25.6.6 Just standing together with people, they brought about their transformation,

Watching the trend of popular custom, they fit in and followed it.

25.6.7 thus, as is proper for fathers and sons, they returned them to their rightful roles,

Enabling fathers to be fathers and sons be sons, they returned each to his proper role.

25.6.8 and they did what they did always with the very same tranquility.

Since what they did was always at one with the virtue of Heaven and Earth, tranquility never varied among them.

25.6.9 Compared to the minds of ordinary people, theirs were as far removed as this—which is why I say that you should wait upon Lord Supervisor of Rest."

He wants him to give up on the King of Chu and instead follow Supervisor of Rest, who, thanks to his serene and stable influence, will subdue his agitated mind.

25.7.1 The sage reaches the most abstruse

That is to say, arcane unity.

25.7.2 and joins in one body with absolutely everything.

Since there is no within or without for him, he looks on everything as the same.

25.7.3 Yet he knows not why he is this way, for it is due to his inborn nature.

Though such a one knows not why spontaneity makes him this way, if not inborn nature, what else could it be!

25.7.4 In reverting to destiny [fuming] and stirring to action, he takes Nature as his model.

Such stirring is spontaneous stirring and such action is spontaneous action, neither of which fails to return him to his destiny, where his own naturalness provides the model.[3]

25.7.5 People then follow his steps and give him the name [of sage].

This does not mean that it is to get that name that he deliberately leaves impressions of nobility, for he acts only when led by his fundamental nature; thus, the impressions he leaves are spontaneously noble, and, as a result, people can't deny him such a name.

25.7.6 Worry occurs due to conscious awareness so that one's actions constantly miss the incipient moment. One is thus foiled—and what can be done about it then!

When one acts with conscious awareness, cares and distress follow one upon the next.

25.8.1 When one is born good-looking, people serve as his mirror [*jian*], but if people don't tell, he won't know he is better-looking than others.

Jian is the same as *jing* (mirror). When one mirrors things impartially, people praise him [as a mirror]. But as for mirrors nowadays, how could knowing how to be a mirror ever make them mirrors! It is only when one is born with the ability to be a mirror that people should call such a one "mirror." The "if people don't tell one another, no one will know who is better looking than others" is a metaphor for the title "sage"—for it is a name given by others.

25.8.2 Whether he [the sage] knows or not, whether he hears or not, he never ceases to be joyful,

His mirroring is joyful because he is utterly impartial. Regardless of whether he knows about them or not, hears about them or not, when people come his way, he just mirrors them, and this is why he never ceases to be joyful. But if his mirroring were subject to what he hears or consciously knows, a time would come when it would fail.

25.8.3 and his love for people also never ceases, for it is due to his inborn nature.

If they were not loved by his inborn nature, how could he long continue to mirror them!

25.8.4 That "the sage loves people" is because people give him that reputation. If they did not tell him, he would not know that he loves people.

The sage is utterly free of love, just like a mirror. However, because his actions succor them, people give him that reputation. If people did not tell each other this, no one would know that he loved people.

25.8.5 So whether he knows or not, whether he hears or not, his love for people never ceases,

Void and tranquil, he treats the common folk like straw dogs, but because his way coincides with loving them, this can never cease. However, if his love for them were subject to what he hears or consciously knows, a time would come when it fails.

25.8.6 and his providing security to people also never ceases, for it is due to his inborn nature.

It is because such security is provided by his inborn nature that it can long last.

25.9.1 The old homeland, the old city, gazing upon it delights one so,

To get back what one used to have, as delightful as that can be, how much more delightful it is to get back [fulfill] one's inborn nature!

25.9.2 Even though its hills and knolls are closed in [*min*] by trees and vegetation.

Min [connect, hang] here means *he* (closed in).

25.9.3 And once having entered it, to find nine parts of ten still there, as delightful as that can be, how much more delightful to see what one had once seen, to hear what one had once heard!

To see what one had once seen, to hear what one had once heard, as delightful as that can be, how much more delightful it is to reembody one's original nature [*ti qiti*] and function again according to one's innate nature [*yong qixing*]!

25.9.4 Here is someone who can suspend ordinary people from a seventy-feet-high tower, and they still are at ease.

When ordinary people get used to something, even if is dangerous, they still are at ease, so how much the more so for a sage who has no sense of danger at all!

25.10.1 Sire Ren Xiang, by attaining to the empty center at the circle of things, was compliant and fulfilling.

Sire Ren Xiang was a sage king of antiquity who dwelt in that emptiness; as such, he complied with others and thus allowed them self-fulfillment.[4]

25.10.2 Joining with things, he had neither beginning nor end, so ceaseless and timeless was he.

Unconsciously he interacted with them.

25.10.3 Daily transforming with things, he was one with that which does not transform.[5]

Because he transformed day after day with things, he was always free from conscious self, and, because he was free from conscious self, he himself did not transform.

25.10.4 Why should one ever try to abandon that!

This addresses those who act with conscious intent—why not try to abandon doing such things?

25.10.5 But any such attempt to emulate the Natural will fail to emulate it.

It is only if free from any model may one succeed at emulating the Natural.

25.10.6 Such a one then just goes on trying along with everyone else—what would that do to address what need be done!

Although such a one tries to emulate the Natural, he still fails to avoid trying; as such, how could he ever be up to the task! Since one who tries to emulate the Natural is still inadequate to the task, how much more inadequate would one be who tries not to emulate the Natural!

25.10.7 For the sage, the Natural, man, the beginning, and things have never existed, and, since he just goes along as the world goes, he never fails. Since he already acts perfectly and thus never fails, for him to try to unite with it [the Natural]—what would that do!

It is because nothing exists for him that he attains arcane unity.

25.10.8 When Tang found Deng Heng serving as his gate keeper, he made him his tutor.

He tried to entrust all his officials to him, but he would have nothing to do with it.

25.10.9 Though he [Deng] let him take instruction from him, he did not confine him,

He let him gather it [i.e., his teaching] to him as he would, so it was not that he confined him with it; he let him freely divest himself of it as he would, so it was not that he released him from it.

25.10.10 for this is how, through compliance, one attains perfection. To do that, he let those in charge take on the title.

Though he was from the rank and file of functionaries, he could still comply with the natural way people react, so when Tang found him, this was why he let the title [of tutor] go to others and had the merit involved not reside with him.

25.10.11 Then such fame and superfluous ways of doing things both appeared to be theirs.

Famous ways of doing things are just footprints left behind from the past and not at all adequate. This is why the text says that one who is completely free of conscious mind will entrust rule to all his officials, for then fame and footprints should appear to be theirs.

25.10.12 Zhongni's "Be done with conscious deliberation"—to do that, [Deng] tutored him [King Tang].

Zhongni said, "In all the world, what need be pondered, what need be deliberated! Just be done with all conscious deliberation!" But even if the tiniest bit of deliberation remain, how could one ever achieve the state of imperturbable serenity and its infinite responsiveness, needed to assist the natural course of the myriad folk!

25.10.13 As Sire Rongcheng said, "Rid yourself of days, and years no longer exist.

Now, as long as years and days exist for someone, life and death exists for him as well. But once one is no longer aware of life and death, the count of years and days is gone as well.

25.10.14 When inner being is void, things external cease to exist."

If self and other cease to exist, both inner being and things external won't exist either.

25.11 Ying, king of Wei, made a treaty with Mou, Marquis Tian, but Marquis Tian violated it. Ying of Wei was furious and was going to dispatch someone to assassinate him.[6]

25.12 When "Rhinoceros Head" heard about this, he felt ashamed and said, "You, my lord, are the ruler of ten thousand war chariots, yet you use a commoner to exact revenge for you.[7] I request two hundred thousand soldiers to attack him for you, my lord. I shall take his people captive and confiscate his horses and cattle, which will make him so hot inside that it breaks out on his back. After this, I shall capture his capital, and when [Tian] Ji[8] breaks out and tries to flee, I shall hit him in the back so hard that it breaks his spine."

25.13 But when Master Ji [of Wei] heard about this, he felt ashamed and said, "If you were to have an eighty-foot city wall constructed and when it was all of eighty feet high, you turn around and have it torn down, this would be a bitter outcome for the convict laborers involved. Now, it has been seven years since you have raised troops, which has been the foundation of your kingly rule. Because Yan [Rhinoceros Head] is out to confuse you, you should not heed him."

25.14 When Master Hua heard about this, he thought it disgraceful and said, "The one who glibly says attack Qi is a troublemaker, and the other who glibly says don't attack is also a troublemaker. And one who says that both the one who advocates attacking and the other who is against attacking is also a troublemaker ."

25.15 The king then said, "If this is so, what am I supposed to do?"

25.16 "My lord, you should do nothing but seek the Dao."

25.17 When Master Hui heard about this, he arranged an audience for Dai Jinren[9] [with the king]. Dai Jinren said, "There is a creature called the snail, do you, my lord, know it?"

25.18 "Yes I do."

The snail is extremely tiny and has two horns.

25.19 "A country exists on the left horn of the snail which is called 'The Butters' [Chu] and a country exists on the right horn of the snail which is called 'The Crushers' [Man].[10] At times they fight over territory and go to war, one side leaving tens of thousands of prone corpses behind and the other side pursuing the enemy for up to fifteen days before it turns back."

If people really knew that what was fought over was as tiny as this, there would no longer be fighting anywhere in the world.

25.20 His Majesty said, "Pah! What empty talk is this!"

25.21 "Allow me to demonstrate, my Lord, the truth of it. Apply your imagination to the four directions and up and down—are there limits to how far it can reach?"

25.22 "It has no limits."

25.23 "Well, if you know how to let your mind wander around in the limitless, when it returns to lands to which one can actually travel, does it seem to you that they scarcely exist?"[11]

Where human footsteps can take you is what "to which one can actually travel" [*tongda*] means—that is, all then within the four seas.

25.24 "Yes, that is so."

Now, one naturally thinks all within the four seas to be big, but if one calculates its size in comparison to the limitless, it seems [so small] that it scarcely exists.

25.25 "Among those lands to which we can actually travel is Wei. In Wei is located the city of Liang, and in Liang is its sovereign. Is there any difference between this king and the chief of the Crushers?"

That is, the state of Wei is located somewhere within the four seas.

25.26 "There is no difference."

Both the king and the chief of the Crushers have a limited amount of resources. Since these are limited, it does not matter what their sizes are, for in size they both fall far short when compared to the limitless. Even if all Heaven and Earth could be placed again inside the limitless [doubled in size], it would all still count for nothing. So how much the less is it worth his while to go to war, this king who sits in Liang, Liang which is located there in Wei!

25.27 When his visitor left, the ruler was thoroughly disheartened, as if he had been utterly defeated.

He was distressed to realize that what he was going to fight over was so insignificant.

25.28 Once the visitor had left, Master Hui went to see the king, who said to him, "The visitor is such a great man that even the sages would fail to match him."

25.29 Master Hui replied, "If you blow even across a bamboo tube, you still get a flute-like sound, but if you blow across a sword hilt, you get but a niggardly noise. Though Yao and Shun are acclaimed by everyone, if you could have them speak in the presence of Dai Jinren, it would sound like such a niggardly noise."

They have never been worth listening to.

25.30. When Confucius travelled to Chu, he happened to lodge with a sauce vendor on Ant Hill, where, nearby, a husband and wife with their male and female servants climbed up as high as they could, which prompted Zilu to ask, "What is that crowd of people doing?"

25.31.1 Confucius replied, "He there is a sage-menial, buried amidst the common folk,

He is just the same as common folk.

25.31.2 who has hidden himself among field paths,

Here, putting oneself forward brings no personal glory, and drawing back is no cause to wither and die.

25.31.3 where, though fame all melts away,

He does away with all fame.

25.31.4 his will is inexhaustible.

25.31.5 His mouth may speak, but his mind never forms words.

What he says is always about the commonplace world.

25.31.6 He tends to be at odds with the world, and his mind disdains to go along with it.

He thinks differently from the worldly.

25.31.7 Since he is a man who can sink out of sight on dry land, might he not be Yiliao of Market South?"

"To hide amidst the people" has as metaphor "sink out of sight where there is no water."

25.32 Zilu then asked if he should go over and summon him.

25.33.1 Confucius replied, "Stop! He [*bi*] knows that it is clear [*zhu*] to me who he is, and that once arrived in Chu, he expects that I am sure to get the King of Chu to summon him, for he also thinks I am glib-tongued enough to do it.

Zhu (bright, clear, manifest) means *ming* (be clear about, clearly know).[12]

25.33.2 The attitude of someone like him to a flatterer would be shame to hear what he says, and even more shame to see him in person! And what makes you think he is still there?"

It is better to leave him alone to follow his own disposition.

25.34 Zilu then went to look for him, but his house was empty.

As expected, he had fled.

25.35.1 The border official of Tall Parasol Tree [Changwu] asked Master Lao,[13] "The way a ruler governs should not be slapdash, and the way he rules his people should not be erratic. In the past, when planting, I used to be slapdash in plowing, so the yield I got back was just as slapdash. And, since I used to be erratic in weeding, the yield I got back was just as erratic.

"Slapdash" and "erratic" indicate a frivolous way of doing things, with no attention to detail—not at all working up to one's allotted capacity.

25.35.2 But in recent years I changed to a careful and systematic method, that is, by deepening my plowing and harrowing meticulously. My yield has thus grown so bountiful that I have had more than enough to eat all year long."

Such achievement exhausted his entire allotted capacity, for nothing was not done to the utmost.[14]

25.36.1 When Master Zhuang heard this, he said, "By regulating their bodies and ordering their minds as people nowadays do, this is much like what the border official says, for they try to evade their natural endowment, depart from their fundamental nature, extinguish their innate character, and destroy their energy, for this is what everyone does.

Although such evasion, departure, extinction, and destruction are the extremes to which everyone goes, if each would just go up to his limits, what harm would that do!

25.36.2 Therefore, if one is slapdash with one's fundamental nature, this allows sprouts of desire and aversion to grow into reeds and rushes that choke the fundamental nature.

As reeds and rushes harm millet and rice, so desire and aversion injure one's true fundamental nature.

25.36.3 When reeds and rushes first sprout, they support one's body,

As support for the body spreads, the spirit is increasingly injured.

25.36.4 but they continue to deplete the fundamental nature.

Once desire and aversion begin to draw on the fundamental nature, they don't stop at what is appropriate for them.

25.36.5 Then festering and oozing break out together, haphazard where they emerge, so that the boils and pustules float on it, with all this accompanied by internal fever and clouding of the urine.

Such is the result of being slapdash. Therefore, to maintain the fundamental nature in good condition, how could one fail to maintain it in proper order to the utmost of his capacity!

25.37 While Bo Ju[15] was studying with Old Long Ears, he announced, "I request permission to go wandering about the whole world."

25.38 Old Long Ears replied, "Enough of that! The whole world is just like here."

25.39 When he again made the same request, Old Long Ears asked, "Where are you going to start from?"
25.40 "I shall start from Qi."
25.41.1 And when he reached Qi, seeing the body of an executed criminal there, he pushed it around so it stretched out flat. Covering it then with his court robes, he cried up to Heaven, "Oh Thou! Oh, Thou! The great calamity that is going to strike the entire world has Thou as the very first to encounter it! Be it said, 'Let no one steal!' Be it said, 'Let no one kill!'

"Kill people" and "great calamity" refer to things that shall happen from then on. Once this great calamity occurs, though injunctions be made that no one do such things, how could this ever prevent it!

25.41.2 Only after honor and disgrace get established does the disease they cause become apparent,

As long as everyone manages to achieve self-fulfillment, honor and disgrace don't exist, for it is when people become muddled about having it or not that honor and disgrace get established, and with the establishment of honor and disgrace, the honorable brag to the so-called disgraceful, and the disgraceful stand on tiptoes hoping to become the so-celled honorable. If such running back and forth between bragging and standing on tiptoes is not a disease, what is it!

25.41.3 and only after wealth and property gets amassed do disputes appear.

As long as people equate contentment with wealth, what is there for them to dispute!

25.41.4 Now then, with the establishment of that which causes people disease and the amassing of that which causes people to dispute, such misery is caused them that they have no time to rest, and, even if they try to avoid such an extreme, how could they ever succeed!

When those above have everything to please them, those below fail to be content with their fundamental allotted capacity.

25.42.1 The sovereign in antiquity attributed his success to his people and his failure to himself.

When the ruler fails at nothing, it is because the people achieve self-fulfillment.

25.42.2 When things went right, he attributed it to his people and when things went awry, he blamed himself.

When the ruler does nothing awry, the people rectify themselves.

25.42.3 Therefore, if even the body of one person were lost, he would retire and blame himself.

As for people's bodies or fundamental natures, what would people ever do themselves to lose them! They lose both because the ruler treats them so badly that such disasters occur; this is why he blamed himself.

25.42.4 Rulers nowadays are not like that at all, for they conceal what they do from the people so that their stupidity goes unrecognized.

When they violate the people's fundamental natures, it is concealed, but when they accommodate their fundamental natures, it is manifested. As such, what is manifested by the people is always recognized[16]

25.42.5 They significantly make things difficult, but then blame those who dare not [deal with them].

If things were made easy by the people, then all would dare.[17]

25.42.6 They make responsibilities too heavy and then punish those who can't bear them.

If their responsibilities were lightened, then all could bear them.

25.42.7 They make paths too long for those who take them, and then condemn the ones who fail to reach the end.

If made appropriate to the strength of the legs, all would reach the end.

25.42.8 They make the common folk exhaust their intelligence, who then continue on by practicing deceit.

By this they evade punishment and execution.

25.42.9 Since they practice much deceit on a daily basis, how could the gentry and common folk choose not to practice deceit themselves!

If rulers are moved to deceit day after day, how might the gentry and common folk ever manage to achieve authenticity!

25.42.10 When strength is insufficient, people practice deceit; when intelligence is insufficient, people become dishonest; when resources are insufficient, people become thieves. And when thieves and robbers ply their trade, who is it that may be blamed?

One should blame the ruler.

25.43.1 By the time Qu Boyu[18] reached sixty, he had transformed himself sixty times.

This was because he was both capable of complying with the ways of the world and was not bound by the distinction between other and self.

25.43.2 Though he never failed to start by considering something right, he would always finish by having to admit he was wrong.

He smoothly went along by complying with others, so kept changing in step with the way others were inclined.

25.43.3 So one never knew that what he now considered right was not what he had considered wrong for fifty-nine years.

The changes that people's inclinations undergo never come to an end.

25.43.4 A for the myriad things, it is there in life, but no one has seen its root; it is there in emergence, but no one has seen its gate.

With neither root nor gate, things come into existence all by themselves, and that's why no one has seen them. Only one who is utterly unmindful that he lives and has forgotten completely that he was born is enabled to see that this is its gate and this its stem.[19]

25.43.5 Everyone respects what his own knowing knows, but no one knows how to depend on knowledge that his own knowing knows not and only learns later. May we not call this great ignorance!

What I don't know, someone else will know. Therefore, if I use what others know, there is nothing that I won't know. But if I depend exclusively on just what I know, what I know will be extremely little. Now, if I depend not on what others know and respect only what I know, others won't tell me anything—and if that is not great ignorance, what is it!

25.43.6 Stop! Stop! For this gives you no place to shelter!

If you can't use [the knowledge of] others, it will leave you no place to shelter.[20]

25.43.7 This so-called "right," is it really right?

What one calls "right" is never the "right" of everyone in the world.

25.44 Zhongni [Confucius] asked the grand scribes, Big Bowcase [Taitao], Uncle Always Soaring [Bo Changqian], and Boar Hide [Xiwei],[21] "Duke Ling of Wey was a drinker who so sated himself with pleasure that he neglected state affairs, and was so addicted to hunting afield with net and harpoon arrow that he failed to interact with the other feudal lords when it was so appointed. Why then was he given the title 'Numinous Duke' [Linggong]?"

25.45 Big Bowcase responded, "It was because that was what he was."

Numinous [Ling] is the posthumous title conferred for disorderliness [*wudao*].[22]

25.46.1 Uncle Always Soaring added, "Duke Ling had three wives, with whom he bathed in the same tub.

For male and female to bathe together is a breach of decorum.

25.46.2. But when Shi Qiu entered the room holding an imperial offering for him, the duke seized the roll of silk [*bi*] to help him with it

Not only did he regard Qian as a worthy, here he was engaged in the meritorious talk of bring him an offering. The reason he seized the role of silk was to show him that he need not complete the ceremony, which exemplifies how serious he was with worthies. The role of silk [*bi*] was an imperial offering.

25.46.3 Although his uncouth behavior could be as awful as this, when he saw the worthy he became as serious as that, and this was why he was conferred 'Numinous Duke' as his posthumous title."

Here he wanted to amend the duke's reputation for uncouth personal behavior by referring to his serious treatment of worthies. Since the meaning of "numinous" is ambiguous, it may not mean "good." This is why Zhongni asked about it.

25.47.1 Boar Hide then said, "When Duke Ling died, since it was divined that it would be inauspicious to bury him in the graveyard of his forebears, it was then divined that to bury him on Sand Hill [Shaqiu][23] would be auspicious.

After digging down three or four yards, they found a stone coffin, and, when they washed it off to have a look, discovered on it an inscription, 'Without relying on his son, Duke Ling seizes this to make it his place of burial.' Duke Ling has thus been 'numinous' for a very long time."

"Son" refers to Kuaikui [Duke Zhuang of Wey], and what the inscription means is that without relying on his son, Duke Ling will seize this as his place. Since everyone has his fate determined beforehand, future events can be known, which means that whatever one does he can't help but do. Nevertheless, the stupid think that the doing lies with oneself—is not that absurd!

25.47.2 But how were those two ever capable of knowing what that meant!

They only knew what they saw had happened, but did not understand that what had happened was due to the spontaneous workings [of fate].

25.48 Narrow Understanding [Shaozhi] asked Great Impartial Harmonizer [Taigong Tiao], "What is meant by 'village vernacular?' "

25.49.1 Great Impartial Harmonizer replied, " 'Village vernacular' defines a social locale [*fengsu*] in which ten surnames and one hundred given names merge, the people involved merge their differences to be the same and detach themselves from such sameness to be different. Now, if you point at each of the many parts of a horse, none of these can be a 'horse' as such, yet when a horse is tethered in front of you, you assemble all its different parts and call it 'horse.' So it is that hills and mountains accumulate little by little and thus attain height, the Yangzi and Yellow River collect waters and thus attain great size, and the great one unites himself with all and thus is impartial.

Because he treats the whole world with utter detachment, the customs of the whole world become one and the same.

25.49.2 Therefore, that which enters from without has a master, but such a one is not rigid. That which emerges from within remains pure and true, and so no resistance occurs.

That which enters from without is the transformative power of the great one; that which emerges from within is the original nature of the common folk. Because the original nature of each person remains pure and true, the common folk are never recalcitrant. Since his transformative power is sure to work with perfect impartiality, such a master is free of rigidity. As such, he can merge villages and go on to unite the whole world, and by treating the myriad folk as one he resolves all differences.

25.49.3 As for the different pneuma of the four seasons, it is because they are not conferred by Nature that the seasons continue to form years.

It is because the different pneuma come into existence all by themselves that the seasons perpetually exist. If the seasons originally happened to lack them and depended on conferrals by Nature, at some time or other they would fail.

25.49.4 So is it with the different functions of the five official offices [*wuguan*], for as long as the ruler has no personal favorites, the state remains well-governed.

Since the different functions inherently possess resources of their own, the ruler should just leave them to it and not try to confer them with partiality.

25.49.5 And as long as the great one [the ruler] tries not to confer functions on the civil and the military, their virtues remain intact.

The civil is inherently the civil, and the military is inherently the military, and not because of anything the great one confers on them. But if their capabilities did derive from such conferrals, at some time or other they would fail. And how could this apply only to the civil and the military, for the fundamental nature of things in general is always like this.

25.49.6 The myriad creatures all differ in principle, and, since the Dao remains utterly detached, it deserves no recognition [*wuming*] here.

25.49.7 Deserving no recognition here,
It makes no selfconscious effort
Thus 'engages in no conscious action,
yet nothing remains undone.'[24]

Since recognition should go no further than what is actually so, this indicates that no selfconscious effort occurs. It is because each such realization of actuality occurs spontaneously that nothing remains undone.[25]

25.49.8 As the seasons have a beginning and end
so do worldly affairs change and transform.

Therefore, one who stays free of conscious mind is compliant in the same way.

25.49.9 Misfortune and fortune go around and around,
They flow continuously back and forth.

25.49.10 arriving so that one either has things go ill
or that they go well.

For this one things may go bad, but for that one they might go well.

25.49.11 For each pursues his own, each faces his own way,
Each has such trust in himself that he can't part with it.

25.49.12 So while one might think something correct,
for another it will be wrong.

What is correct for this one will be wrong for that one.

25.49.13 So be like the great marsh where
every kind of tree and plant is allowed its due.

Do not reject any resource.

25.49.14 And look at the huge mountain where
trees and rock merge into one great dais.

These form one and the same thing by merging their differences.

25.49.15 This is what is meant by 'village vernacular.' "

If you speak in village vernacular, everyone in the world will know what you mean.

25.50 Narrow Understanding then asked, "As such, if we say all this refers to the 'Dao,' would that do?"

25.51.1 Great Impartial Harmonizer replied, "Not at all! If we were to calculate the number of things that exist, it would not stop at ten thousand, but we still limit them to that number in the expression 'ten thousand things,' which is the term for an enormous number in conventional use.[26]

Just as things that may be counted are not actually limited to "ten thousand," this is even more true for that whose count is countless, so likewise we call this the "Dao" and that will have to do![27]

25.51.2 Heaven and Earth are the greatest of physical forms, yin and yang are the greatest of pneumas, all of which the Dao treats impartially.

It is able to penetrate all things, and as it penetrates all things impartially, if forced to use words for all this, we call it the "Dao."

25.51.3 Since this happens on such a vast scale, it may be referred to by this name.

This is what is meant by "the Dao that can be described in language."[28]

25.51.4 Since it already existed, how could it ever serve as its equivalent!

Because the name existed beforehand, there is no way it could serve as its equivalent.[29]

25.51.5 As such, if we use this name to determine what it is, it would be analogous to equating a dog with a horse—it falls that short from arriving at what it is."

Now, as for whether or not this name can determine what it [i.e., the Dao] is, it falls short by far, and this is why the text says that even "Dao" is inadequate. One must dwell in a realm free of names and free of language, for only then should one arrive at it. Whatever names there might be, this is why none can serve as its equivalent.

25.52 Narrow Understanding again asked,

> **"Within the four quarters and inside the six directions,**
> **What causes the myriad things to come into existence?"**

Asking this, he would have it said that it is the Dao that can generate them.

25.53.1 Great Impartial Harmonizer replied,

> **"As yin moon and yang sun in turn shine down,**
> **First enveloping them, then regulating them,**
> **The four seasons succeed one another,**
> **First begetting them, then killing them.**

This means that they are as they are due to spontaneity, which never fails to be productive.

25.53.2 As desire and aversion, attraction and rejection thus erupt,
Union of male and female herein begins its usual course.

Given such commonplace matters, the text speaks to the acceptance and rejection that closely arise with the yin moon and the yang sun alternately shining and the four seasons succeeding one another.

25.53.3 As safety and danger alternate, good fortune and bad
generate first one then the other,
Living long or going fast, coalescence and dispersal
thereby complete their course.
The match of such names with actualities may be noted,
And the most subtle essences involved recorded too.

But from this point on, we arrive at the Natural, and why the Natural is as it is, who knows why it is so!

25.53.4 Complying with successive governing principles of the seasons
And the alternating stimuli of impulses of the phases,
Things reach their limits and revert, when finished, start again,
For such are the properties of all things.[30]

The properties of all things are as they are because of their spontaneity, which never fails to supply them.

25.53.5 As far as words can reach, as far as thought can grasp,
these are limited to things and can go no further.

Since beyond things nothing further exists, words and thought can go no further than the limits of things.

25.53.6 One who looks to the Dao tries not to plumb the reason they perish,
tries not to find out wherein they arise.

Since such perishing and arising are both due to spontaneity, there is nothing to plumb or find out.

25.53.7 And this is where discussion must end."

Since it can go no further than spontaneity, there is nothing more to discuss.

25.54 Narrow Understanding then said,

> **"Jizhen's 'nothing does it' and Master Jie's 'it might be caused,'**
> **Of these axioms of the two masters,**
> **Which one correctly addresses the true state of things,**
> **Which one covers all the principles involved?"[31]**

Jizhen said, "the Dao never does it," and Master Jie said, "the Dao might cause it." "It might be caused" means that something causes the successful outcome of things.

25.55.1 Great Impartial Harmonizer replied,

"Cocks crow and dogs bark,
This is known by all men.
But even one with the greatest of knowledge
Cannot say in words how they self-transform,
And which, in thought, fail to conceive how it is done.

Things are inherently spontaneously so—it is not that they are made to have such capability. Looking at it from this point of view, what Jizhen said is correct.

25.55.2 Taking this into account, if we keep analyzing

Ever more minutely until it makes no sense at all,
Expanding so much that it's impossible to encompass,

Everything is not made so but is spontaneously so.

25.55.3 Whether 'it might be caused' or 'nothing does it,'
Neither frees one from the realm of things
And so ends up leading to error.

Although things may affect one another, they all do so spontaneously. Therefore, the assertion "nothing does it" does not quite make it to the realm where no things exist. All that is said here concerning things starts from "nothing does it" and goes on from there.

25.55.4 If 'it might be caused' then it is something actual,

It is caused by something actual.

25.55.5 And if it is 'nothing does it' then it is unreal.

Nothing causes it to be so.

25.55.6 As long as names and actualities are involved,
This is the realm of things.

It indicates the state in which names and actualities exist.

25.55.7 But once free of names and actualities,
We abide where things are void.

Even in the realm of things, their actuality is perfectly void.[32]

25.55.8 As long as one can speak of it or think of it,
What one says of it is ever more wide of the mark.

Therefore, only by seeking it beyond the reach of word and thought can one attain to it.

25.55.9 The not yet born cannot avoid it happening.

Since control over one's sudden self-generation is not up to oneself, the self cannot prevent it.

25.55.10 Once dead, the dead cannot go on living.

When self-termination suddenly occurs, the self cannot oppose it.

25.55.11 Although the distance between birth and death is not far,
The principle governing them cannot be discerned.

Although they are close inside one's own body, no one perceives that they occur spontaneously but instead tend to worry about it.

25.55.12 As for 'it might be caused' and 'nothing does it,'
These lend themselves to perplexity.

The people of the world are most perplexed by these two.

25.55.13 If we look for the origin [*ben*] of things,
It's infinitely far back to it,
And if we seek the end [*mo*] of things,
It comes at us unceasingly.
Infinite and unceasing,
Though no words exist for this,
It shares the same principle with things.

Since the principle of things is infinite, thought and words must be infinite too, which leaves one sharing the same principle with things.[33]

25.55.14 'It might be caused' and 'nothing does it'
Are rooted in language
And begin and end with things.

It [i.e., the Dao] is constantly free from intent, thus things just cause themselves to be so.

25.55.15 The Dao can neither be thought to exist nor thought not to exist.

Although the Dao cannot with intent cause existence, existence always goes on occurring spontaneously.

25.55.16 "Dao" serves as a name we expediently use for the way things carry on.

In order to address the way things carry on, we expediently name this the "Dao."

25.55.17 'It might be caused' and 'nothing does it' occupy just one corner of things, so what are they to the great method of the Dao!

They disclose one corner [*ju yiyu*] so that it may be known.[34]

25.55.18 For those to whom speaking seems adequate, speaking about it all day will entirely be about the 'Dao.'

Only seeking the Dao beyond thought and words will prove adequate.

25.55.19 For those to whom speaking seems inadequate, speaking about it all day long will entirely be about things.

As long as one cannot forget words and think consciously, it will prove inadequate.

25.55.20 'Dao' may be the ultimate spatial limit of things, but words are inadequate to convey what this is.

As the ultimate spatial limit of things, the Dao never does anything but operate spontaneously, so it lends itself neither to speaking nor not speaking.

25.55.21 So neither speak nor be silent, for all debate has limitations."

Since the Dao is limited to spontaneity, neither words nor silence may address what it is.

Notes

1. Cheng Xuanying: "[Zeyang's] surname was Peng, given name Yang, personal name Zeyang, a native of Lu who, traveling about serving feudal lords, at last entered Chu, where he wished to serve at the court of King Wen. . . . [Yi's] surname was Yi, given name Jie, and he was a minister of Chu. . . . Wang Guo was a worthy Grand Master of Chu." *Zhuangzi jishi*, 4: 876.
2. Cheng Xuanying: "Lord Supervisor of Rest [Gong Yuexiu] was the sobriquet of a recluse. The worthy man, Wang Guo, offended by how Peng Yang was so obsessed with greed for honor, thus lavishly praised the hermit in order to restrain Peng's penchant for quick advancement." *Zhuangzi jishi*, 4: 877.
3. Cf. Laozi, section 26: "To return to the root is called 'quietude,' which means to revert to one's destiny, and reversion to one's destiny is called 'constancy.' " [Wang Bi:] "When one returns to the root, he becomes quiet, which is why this state is called 'quietude' [*jing*]. When one is quiet, he reverts to his destiny [*ming*]. This is why this state is referred to as 'reversion to destiny.' When one reverts to his destiny, he fulfills the constant dimensions of his nature [*xing*] and destiny [*ming*], which is why this state is called 'constancy' [*chang*]." Richard John Lynn, *The Classic of the Way and Virtue*, 76.
4. Cheng Xuanying: "He complied with the true Dao and thus embodied the sublimity at the empty center of things. Therefore, his path was to comply with the mass of common folk and blend in with them." *Zhuangzi jishi*, 4: 885.
5. Cf. 22.61.3.
6. Cheng Xuanying: "Ying was the given name of King Hui of Wei. Marquis Tian was King Wei of Qi, given name Mou, who was the son of Duke Huan [of Qi] and a descendant of Tian Heng [Tian Chengzi, who became de facto ruler of Qi in 481 BCE], which was why he was called Marquis Tian. The two states, Wei and Qi, undertook a treaty not to attack one another, but not long after the treaty was concluded, King Wei violated it, which was why the Marquis of Wei became furious and was going to dispatch someone to assassinate him. The treaty was made in the twenty-sixth year in the rule of Marquis Wei of Qi and the eighth year in the rule of King Hui of Wei [381 BCE]. *Zhuangzi jishi*, 4: 888.
7. Cheng Xuanying: " 'Rhinoceros Head' [Xishou] is the name of an officer, like the "Brave as Tigers" [Huben] of the present day [head of the royal bodyguard]. The one who held this office was a descendent of the royal family, whose given name was Yan." However, this man is referred to in other sources usually as "Gongsun Yan." *Zhuangzi jishi*, 4: 889.
8. Cheng Xuanying: "His surname Tian and his given name Ji [fl. ca. 340 BCE], he was a Qi general." *Zhuangzi jishi*, 4: 890.
9. Cheng Xuanying identifies him as a worthy of the state of Liang; see *Zhuangzi jishi*, 4: 891.
10. "The Butters" translates *chu*, literally the way that a horned beast head-butts to attack or defend itself, and "The Crushers" translates *man*, literally the python, which crushes its prey. *Chu* and *man* are thus two antithetical styles of fighting, which are appropriate names for the two imaginary aggressive countries.

11. Cheng Xuanying: "After letting one's mind wander about in limitlessness, again compare it to all within the nine divisions of the world [China], speaking of its size, one can say that it seems so small that one is unsure whether it exists or not." *Zhuangzi jishi*, 4: 892.
12. Cheng Xuanying: "*Bi* (he) indicates Yiliao; *zhu* (clear) means *ming* (be clear about). He knows that Qiu [Confucius] recognizes him for a worthy sunk out of sight on dry land. He also knows that once arrived in Chu, he [Confucius] would recommend that the King of Chu summon him [Yiliao], for, as such, he takes Qiu [Confucius] to be a glib-tongued toady." *Zhuangzi jishi*, 4: 897.
13. According to Cheng Xuanying, "Tall Parasol Tree [Changwu] is a place name, likely fanciful, and Master Lao, whose surname was Qin, was a disciple of Confucius." *Zhuangzi jishi*, 4: 897.
14. "Nothing was not done to the utmost" translates *wusuo buzhi*, a well-documented textual variant for the *wuwei zhizhi* of the received edition, which would mean either "nothing was done to the utmost" or "the utmost/perfection of unselfconscious effort," neither of which fits the context. See *Zhuangzi jishi*, 4: 899, and Wang Shumin, *Guo Xiang Zhuangzi zhu jiaoji*, 4: 55.
15. Cheng Xuanying: "Bo was his surname, Ju his given name. A man who cherished the Dao, he was a disciple of Master Lao." *Zhuangzi jishi*, 4: 900.
16. The premodern commentary tradition is rife with different interpretations of this sentence, most of them based on rewording its text; see *Zhuangzi jishi*, 4: 903–4, and Wang Shumin, *Zhuangzi jiaoquan*, 1025, note 10. However, Guo Xiang's comment seems to make as much sense here as any of these alternative readings; moreover, it does not involve rewording the text. Let us have Cheng Xuanying have the last word: "Since all the laws and regulations they enact violate the people's fundamental nature, they conceal his culpability so that their stupidity and arrogance go unrecognized. As such, culpability shifts to the people in general." *Zhuangzi jishi*, 4: 903.
17. Cheng Xuanying: "When laws are difficult to adjudicate, enforcing them isn't easy. Therefore, it is certain they will be disobeyed, and this results in blame for it." *Zhuangzi jishi*, 4: 904. Commentaries by Guo Xiang and Cheng Xuanying suggest that the difficulties created by rulers result from harsh laws that are impossible to enforce, and as people evade them, the enforcers (officials high and low) are blamed for it. Conversely, if the people were allowed to regulate themselves, laws would be easy to enforce, leaving nothing that officials need dare.
18. Cheng Xuanying: "Surname Qu, given name Yuan, and personal name Boyu, he was a worthy grandee of Wey." *Zhuangzi jishi*, 4: 905.
19. The referent of "it" and "this" is the Dao; cf. 23.30.
20. Cheng Xuanying: ""Instead of concentrating on selecting and rejecting [what others know], it would be better to stop altogether, otherwise, one is sure to encounter disaster, with no place to shelter." *Zhuangzi jishi*, 4: 906. Guo Xiang and Cheng Xuanying seem at odds here: whereas Guo says the real issue here isn't extending one's own knowledge by accessing that of others but rather gaining the ability to hide oneself among people by sharing their common pool of knowledge, thereby merging anonymously with everyone else, Cheng argues that to abandon knowing altogether is the only way to remain safe.
21. Cf. 6.12.7.
22. Cheng Xuanying: "According to the rule for conferring posthumous titles established by the Duke of Zhou, one who is disorderly but causes no harm is deemed 'numinous.' 'Numinous' is thus the posthumous title for disorderliness." *Zhuangzi jishi*, 4: 907.

23. Cheng Xuanying: "Sand Hill [Shaqiu] is the name for a place north of the Mengjin River [north of present-day Luoyang]." *Zhuangzi jishi*, 4: 908.
24. This is an exact quote from the *Laozi*, section 48; see Lynn, *The Classic of the Way and Virtue*, 143.
25. Cheng Xuanying: "All creatures are different, for they diverge in accordance with their inherent natures. Some nest in trees, others dwell in holes in the earth, some run on the ground, other fly in the sky, but Nature's nurture is such that each and every one of them can support itself. Since each fulfills its own principle entirely by itself, it [the Dao] deserves no merit [*wugong*] here." *Zhuangzi jishi*, 4: 911.
26. Cf. 17.6.
27. Cheng Xuanying: "As for things that have physical existence, they are infinite in number, but when people nowadays speak of them, they limit them in the expression 'ten thousand things,' which sums up in general how numerous they are. It is the same for the marvelous truth of the void Dao, which by its nature is nameless, but for the sake of expediency we force the name 'Dao' on it, though it is inadequate to express what it really is." *Zhuangzi jishi*, 4: 913.
28. *Laozi*, section 1; Lynn, *The Classic of the Way and Virtue*, 51.
29. Cheng Xuanying: "Because it is expedient, we have had the term 'Dao,' but it won't do to use what has a name to match a truth for which there is no name; thus to use it as a match will miss the mark by far." *Zhuangzi jishi*, 4: 914.
30. Cheng Xuanying: "The four seasons go around and around, governing in succession, while impulses from the five phases act, taking charge in turn. When things reach their limit, they revert; when they finish, they start again, for such are the properties of all things, the principles involved all summed up here." *Zhuangzi jishi*,4: 915.
31. Cheng Xuanying: "Jizhen and Master Jie were both worthy of Qi. As they rambled about Jixia, people trusted these two worthies to clarify the principles of things." *Zhuangzi jishi*, 4: 916.
32. Cheng Xuanying: "If one's disposition [*qing*] is stuck with things, wherever he is things are always there, but if one's disposition is to give priority to their non-existence, wherever he is they always are non-existent. By this we know that the existent and the non-existent both reside in the mind and not external to it." *Zhuangzi jishi*, 4: 918.
33. Cheng Xuanying: "*Ben* (origin) refers to the past, and *mo* (end) refers to the future. Production and transformation throughout the past go back infinitely, so since there is no way to plumb where they began, how could thought ever reach that! If one gets into profound discussion about whether it [the Dao] is extant or not, he shall become so stuck and inflexible that he shall never escape from things, which explains why such a one shares the same principle with things." *Zhuangzi jishi*, 4: 918–19.
34. *Lunyu* (Analects), 7: 2482a: "The Master said, 'If it is not one eager, I don't inform; if it is not one who wants to speak but is at a loss for words, I don't reveal. If I disclose one corner [*ju yiyu]* but am not returned the other three, I don't repeat myself.'" Guo Xiang here suggests that "it might be caused" and "nothing does it," in disclosing one aspect of the issue, can light the way for those receptive enough to attain the great method of the Dao.

CHAPTER 26

WAIWU [EXTERNAL THINGS]

26.1.1 External things cannot be predicted. So it was that Guan Longfeng suffered execution, Bi Gan was killed, and Master Ji had to have it thought he was mad, E Lai died,[1] and Jie and Zhou perished.

The arrival of neither good nor bad can be predicted.

26.1.2 Absolutely all rulers want loyalty from their ministers, but that loyalty does not inevitably earn their trust. As such, Wu Yun was carried off on the current of the Yangzi and Chang Hong died in Shu, where his blood, kept for three years, turned into green jade.

These men reached the apex of good faith.

26.1.3 Absolutely all parents want obedience from their children, but that obedience does not inevitably earn their love. So it was that Xiaoji saddened and Zeng Shen sorrowed.[2]

This is why the Perfected one frees himself from conscious mind and so resonates with things that he always perfectly conforms with change.

26.1.4 When wood rubs against wood, it ignites; when metal keeps company with fire, it flows. But when yin and yang get out of order, all Heaven and Earth take such fright that thunder cracks and lightning bolts, so that fires up in the falling waters make blazing pagoda trees.

This is what is meant by "get out of order."

26.1.5 Just so, the two pitfalls of pleasure and grief give one no means to escape.

If one fails to forget all about his physical body, he must follow along with whatever befalls his body and mire himself in either grief or pleasure, with no good way out on either side.

26.1.6 As such, one becomes so fidgety with troubles that fulfillment is impossible.

As such affliction deepens, wherever one happens to be there trouble awaits, and since there are no ways to protect oneself, fulfillment is impossible.

26.1.7 With mind seemingly suspended between Heaven and Earth,

One's ardent hopes are that high and wide.

26.1.8 and happiness and gloom increasingly vexatious,

This is not clear and smooth going.

26.1.9 benefit and harm rub on one another,

This is why depletion fire syndrome [*neire*] afflicts one innards.

26.1.10 destroying the harmony of everyone with fire.

If everyone shunned benefit, harmony would be achieved, but as long as benefit and harm lodge in mind and heart, such harmony is destroyed by fire.

26.1.11 Moonlight surely does not vanquish a fire.

The one is big but dim, so it means much trouble, the other is small and bright, for it is made by one who knows to abide by his allotted capacity.[3]

26.1.12 Accordingly, by existing compliantly the Dao is fully realized.

Behave but compliantly and be not proud, cast aside your physical body and achieve self-fulfillment, for in this the Dao is fully realized.

26.2 When the family of Zhuang Zhou became poverty-stricken, he went to borrow grain from the Marquis Who Supervises the Yellow River [Jianhe Hou], who told him, "Of course! I just happen to be getting my fief tax payment soon, so what if I were to lend you three hundred pieces of gold?"

26.3.1 Flushed with anger, Zhuang Zhou replied, "On my way here yesterday a voice called out to me from the road, which turned out to be from a crucian carp. So I asked it, 'Come, Crucian Carp, what are you doing here?' And it replied, 'I am the Minister of Waves of the Eastern Sea. Might you have a little dipperful of water to keep me alive?' I replied, 'Of course, since I just happen to be on my way south to the kings of Wu and Yue, what if I were to redirect the course of West River to meet up with you?' Flushed with anger, the crucian carp said, 'Having lost my usual habitat, I have no place to stay, so all I need is a little dipperful of water to keep me alive. But now you propose this! I'd sooner be found as a dried fish in the market!' "

This means that as long as it accords with principle, it won't be too little, but if it does not accord with principle, though large, it will be to no avail.

26.4 The Prince of Ren had a huge hook and enormous line made, using fifty great bullocks for bait, and squatted atop Mount Kuaiji, where he fished every morning for an entire year without catching a single fish. Finally a giant fish took the bait and, dragging the huge hook with it, first dove down deep, then flapping duck-like, breached on its fins, which thrashed up waves as big as mountains. The seawater was so greatly agitated that it sounded like everything demonic and divine as it spread terror for a thousand tricents around. After the Prince of Ren landed the fish, he cut it up

and had it dried. From the Zhe River east and from Mount Cangwu north,[4] no one failed to gorge themselves on that fish. Afterwards, gossips of little talent in later generations all tell the story to shock one another. Well, they only take up pole and line to rush to some irrigation ditch to catch minnows, for to catch really big fish for them is impossible. They embellish their own stories as bait to catch some post of district magistrate, which shows that they are, indeed, a long way from great understanding. As such, anyone who has never heard of Sire Ren's people-oriented way of doing things is incapable of taking part in the management of things, for he is, indeed, a long way from that.

This means that because ambition varies in amount, as for who is right to manage things, depending on whether ambition is large or small, something is there suitable for each.

26.5 When some Confucians, equipped with the *Classic of Odes* and *Record of Rites*, were digging open a grave, a profoundly learned Confucian shouted down,

> **"The east now shows first light,**
> **So how is the work going?"**

26.6 A neophyte Confucian replied,

> **"We haven't removed the skirt and jacket yet,**
> **But there's a pearl in the mouth.**
> **Verily, as it is said in the *Odes*,**
> **'Green, green grows the wheat**
> **On your grave mound slopes.**
> **Since when alive you gave no alms,**
> **Why in death hold you a pearl in your mouth!'[5]**

Grab his hair at the temples and hold his beard tight, so I can use a hammer to break the jaw. Part his cheeks slowly, and don't damage the pearl in his mouth!"

The *Odes* and the *Rites* are sets of footprints left by the former kings. "But if one is not such a person, the Dao will not operate in vain."[6] Therefore, since the Confucians here appear to use them to do evil, such footprints are not sufficient guides.

26.7.1 While a disciple of Old Master Lai [Lao Laizi][7] was out gathering firewood, he happened to meet Zhongni [Confucius], and on returning reported, "There's a man out there whose upper body is long and lower body short.

Top half is long and bottom half short.

26.7.2 He is somewhat bent over, and his ears are toward the back of his head.

His ears are pulled back close to the back, and his upper body is bent over.

26.7.3 He looks as if he were trying to manage all within the four seas.

He looks utterly worn out, as if he were trying to manage the affairs of everyone else.

26.7.4 But I don't know to which clan he belongs."

26.8 Old Master Lai then said, "That's Kong Qiu, so tell him to come here."

26.9 When Zhongni arrived, he said, "Qiu, rid yourself of your haughty stance and your knowing expression, for then you might become a noble man."

He means that if Zhongni were able to lose all awareness of his body and rid himself of conscious understanding, he might then become a noble man.

26.10.1 Zhongni bowed and stepped back,

This signifies that he accepted the injunction.

26.10.2 and, face transformed with worry, asked, "Is it possible that my enterprise may make progress?"

He posed such a question in order to let Old Lai know that he has been unable to make progress.

26.11.1 Old Master Lai then said, "You can't endure the harm done to one age yet make light of the disaster you do to myriads of ages that follow.

What he does in one age leaves such footprints as to cause disaster for myriads of ages that follow. As such, he should not take this lightly.

26.11.2 Are you really so stupid, or does your plan just fall short?

If he just let people be, by fundamental nature they would not be stupid but just spontaneously exist all on their own, and that plan would never fail to be up to the task.

26.11.3 If you use kindness to make people happy, this may make you feel proud, but you will be loathed for it throughout life.

Being kind to them may make people happy, but not being kind provokes loathing. Because one cannot extend kindness to all, even one act of kindness will provoke loathing throughout your life.[8]

26.11.4 But men of middling intelligence are easily led in this way.

That is, since they are easily led, one should not carelessly be kind to them.[9]

26.11.5 They try to lead one another with reputation and form cliques by bending themselves to fit in [*yin*].

"Bend to fit in" [*yin*] is the *yin* in "wood straightener" [*yinkuo*]. It is "to lead" that this refers to.

26.11.6 Better than praising Yao and vilifying Jie, you should forget all about both and have nothing to do with [*bi*] the praised.

"Have nothing to do" [*bi*] means "block off" [*bisai*].

26.11.7 Opposition never fails to harm, and agitation never fails to pervert.

Compliance keeps one whole and safe, and quietude keeps one true.[10]

26.11.8 The sage hesitates to initiate anything, but in so doing always succeeds.

In doing things he never strays from fundamental nature; as such, all his efforts are successful.

26.11.9 But what about the way you convey things! After all, it's nothing but self-promotion!"

Self-promotion fails to convey anything else. As such, one should abandon this altogether and do entirely without it.

26.12 In the middle of the night, Lord Yuan of Song had a dream in which a man with hair hanging loose peeped in through some odd hidden door and said, "I am from the Zailu Abyss. As an envoy representing the Clear River[11] I was on my way to the abode of the Earl of the Yellow River when the fisherman Yu Qie caught me."

26.13 When Lord Yuan awoke and he had someone interpret what it meant, the prognostication was, "It is a divine tortoise."

26.14 The Lord then asked, "Among fishermen, is there a Yu Qie?"

26.15 His entourage replied, "There is."

26.16 "Order Yu Qie to come to court."

26.17 The next day when Yu Qie came to court, the Lord asked him, "What did you catch when fishing?"

26.18 "I caught a white turtle with my net, five feet around."

26.19 "Present your turtle."

26.20 When the turtle arrived, the Lord was of two minds whether to kill it or not; thus, being in doubt, had divination performed, with the result "to kill the turtle for divination would be auspicious." They then scooped out the turtle, and not one of the seventy-two bored holes gave a wrong prediction.

26.21 Zhongni observed, "The divine turtle could reveal itself in a dream to Lord Yuan, but it could not escape the net of Yu Qie. It knew how to keep the seventy-two holes bored in its shell free from erroneous prediction, but it could not avoid the disaster of having its shell scooped out. As such, knowledge has its problems, and for the divine there are things beyond its reach.

Such are the inadequacies of divine knowledge. Only one who serenely abides by his capacity and tries not to operate beyond it shall keep himself whole and safe.

26.21.2 Although one may have perfect knowledge, a myriad men will scheme against him.

Let him not employ that knowledge but use the schemes of the myriad masses.

26.21.3 Fish do not fear nets but fear pelicans.

It is because nets have no predilections that they catch fish.

26.21.4 So banish narrow understanding and let great intelligence shine.

Whereas narrow understanding arrogates to itself [*zisi*], great intelligence trusts to others.

26.21.5 Once "goodness" has been banished, one becomes spontaneously good.

Once "goodness" has been banished, there will be nothing in goodness to admire. And once there is nothing in goodness to admire, the good become spontaneously good without pretense.

26.21.6 When a child is born, it becomes able to speak without a master teacher, but does so just by being with those who can speak."

Going along unaware, it just becomes able without practicing, not because it longs for it and so studies others.

26.22 Master Hui said to Master Zhuang, "Master, what you say is useless."

26.23 Master Zhuang answered, "Only with one who understands the useless can one discuss the useful. Nowhere between Heaven and Earth fails to be both broad and great, yet what a man makes use of is only where his feet can stand. Even so, if one could insert his feet all the way down to place them atop the Yellow Springs, what use would that be to him?" Master Hui replied, "It would be of no use."

26.24 Master Zhuang then said, "Since this is so, it's indeed clear that the useless is useful."

The sage responds with the inner self, which springs forth in perfect accord with circumstances. It is the person himself, meaning the outer self, which makes things go smoothly, and, if things go smoothly, everything goes well. When the outer self is perspicacious, the inner self is put to use—such is the reciprocal principle involved.[12]

26.25.1 Master Zhuang said, "If a man has the ability to wander freely, can he yet make himself not wander? If a man can't wander freely, can he yet make himself wander?

What one can do by nature he can't help but do; what one cannot do by nature, he can't force himself to do. This is why the sage never tries to control anyone, for then all people can natural do what they do yet know not how they are able to do it.

26.25.2 As for people either disposed to take refuge in worldly ways or who act to break entirely with them, alas, is not it so, neither employs perfect knowledge or great virtue!

Only if there is access to such perfection and greatness, may anyone trust his disposition and actions or have faith in his singular abilities.

26.25.3 Even if they collapse and fall down, they do not turn back but, fast as fire, race along and never look back.

When it comes to what men like, avoiding neither right nor wrong, they go at it even if it's a question of life or death.

26.25.4 Although one may be in the relationship of ruler and subject, subject to time the world may change, leaving then no way to distinguish who is the lower.

That is how great harmony would take place.

26.25.5 Therefore, it is said, 'The Perfected one ceases not going with it.'"

Whatever such a one encounters, he complies with it, and that is how he can transform in step with whatever happens.

26.26.1 To venerate antiquity and belittle the present, this is the custom of the learned.

There's neither anything about antiquity to venerate nor anything about the present to belittle, yet the learned venerate antiquity and belittle the present, both of which misconstrue the basic nature of things.

26.26.2 However, if the present age were looked after as Sire Boar Hide did his, who of them could avoid being washed away!

In step with the moment, such a ruler would comply with the people, which then would wash them completely away.

26.26.3 It is only the Perfected one who can wander through the world without going awry,

Since such a one responds to what need be done at just the right moment, whatever situation he encounters he always finds him correct.

26.26.4 for by complying with the people, he does not lose himself.

The self is originally nonexistent [*benwu*], so how could I suffer its loss!

26.26.5 What he teaches is not learned,

Because such teaching complies with the fundamental nature of others, it is not something learned.

26.26.6 thus the intentions they follow are not his.

Because their intentions are spontaneous, they follow and use them; as such, each of the myriad folk keeps himself whole and safe.

26.27.1 Eyes if keen provide clear vision; ears if keen provide sharp hearing; nose if keen provides acute sense of smell; mouth if keen provides intense sense of taste; mind if sharp provides intelligence; intelligence if perceptive provides virtue. In general the Dao tends not to obstruction, but if obstructed, it chokes, and if the choking persists, pile-up occurs,

If what should go smoothly is obstructed, the principles involved fail to manifest themselves but pile up one atop the other.

26.27.2 and with such pile up all sorts of harm occur [*sheng*].

"Occur" [*sheng*] means "arise" [*qi*].

26.27.3 Creatures that have consciousness depend on breath,

Things that grow from roots not only lack consciousness but also depend not on breath.

26.27.4 but when this does not function properly [*duan*], it is no fault of nature.

"Work properly" [*duan*] means "is just right" [*dang*]. Breathing depends not on intelligence, but when it does depend on intelligence, it won't function properly, and if it does not function properly, it won't go smoothly. Therefore, intelligence depends on breath, and breathing does not depend on intelligence. As such, since control over the functions of intelligence and desire are subject to the individual, it does not inevitably result in a perfect match.

26.27.5 Although Nature's infusion of things ceases neither day nor night,

Its infusion of principle constantly operates.

26.27.6 when it comes to man, his conscious involvement blocks the conduit.

As long as one stays free of predilection and gives himself over to Nature, the conduit remains perfectly open.

26.27.7 The abdomen may be large and spacious [*lang*],

"Spacious" [*lang*] means empty and wide.

26.27.8 but the heart/mind has nature to roam freely in.

It may so roam because it is not attached.[13]

26.27.9 If the chambers of a house are not spacious enough, wife and her mother-in-law will quarrel.

They will argue about space.

26.27.10 Just so, if the mind has not nature to roam freely in, the six sense orifices [of eyes, ears, nose] will oppose one another [*rang*].

Rang means oppose [*ni*].

26.27.11 The reason why great forests, hills, and mountains are superior to men is because their spirits are never overburdened.

The natural principles that inhere in them just operate freely.

26.28.1 When one spills over with more virtues than he has, it is because of reputation.

The higher the reputation, the greater the benefits.

26.28.2 When one spills over with more of a reputation than is his due, it leads to violence.

Suppress violence, and one's reputation for goodness will exceed the virtues he has.[14]

26.28.3 When plans are scrutinized, urgency [*xian*] is involved.

Xian means urgency [*ji*]. Only after urgency arises are plans for it scrutinized.

26.28.4 Conscious thought is born of competition.

As long as one proceeds with equanimity, he shall stay free of conscious thought.

26.28.5 Obstruction [*chai*] is born of obstinacy.

Chai (firewood, brushwood; use brushwood to provide protection) here means "stop up" or "block" [*sai*].

26.28.6 Government laws and regulations result from the need to ease the life of the masses.

There is not just one way to ease the life of the masses, which is why government laws and regulations were established.

26.28.7 Just so, when spring rains arrive on time, vegetation grows robustly, and it is at this point that hoes and sickles begin cultivation.

When such things appear, there should always be reason for it.

26.28.8 Although more than half such vegetation is then razed to the ground, people don't realize that they do it.

Because what they are do springs from right principles, they are unaware that they do it.

26.29.1 Tranquility can remedy illness.

People are never without illness.

26.29.2 Massage can make aging pause.

People never fail to age.

26.29.3 Serenity can halt anxiety.

People are never without anxiety.

26.29.4 As such, although the troubled so concern themselves, they are not things that those who live at ease are ever concerned.

Such things are for those still troubled. Therefore, those who live at ease so transcend the need that they heed them not.

26.29.5 How the sage shakes up the people of the world, the Divine man never concerned himself.

"Divine man" means the same as "sage." "Sage" refers to the outer man; "divine" refers to the inner man.

26.29.6 How the worthy man shakes up the people of the world, the sage never concerns himself. How the noble man shakes up the state, the worthy never concerns himself. How the petty man stays in step with the times, the noble man never concerns himself.

When it comes to rushing around doing things, since each person has his allotted capacity, for each superior and inferior there is a place.

26.29.7 There was a man at Yan Gate,[15] whose parents had died, who was so good at appearing grief-stricken that he was ennobled as an officer of state. This led to his fellow villagers so pretending to be grief-stricken that half died.

He showed how filial he was in order to be admired, which took him far from his authentic self. Esteem for worthiness can cause such error as this!

26.29.8 When Yao tried to yield the whole world to Xu You, Xu You fled. When Tang tried to yield it to Wu Guang, Wu Guang found it an outrage.

When Ji Tuo heard of this, he led his disciples to live in seclusion at the Kuan River, which provoked great pity for him in the feudal lords. Three years later, in sympathy with him, Shentu Di fell to his death in the Yellow River.

Such turmoil so harmed their fundamental natures that they went so far as this.

26.29.9 The trap exists for the fish, but once the fish is caught, one forgets the trap. The snare exists for the hare, but once the hare is caught, one forgets the snare. Words exist for the idea, but once the idea is had, one forgets the words. Where, oh, where can I find someone who will forget words so I may have a word with him?

As for two sages who are free from selfconscious thought [*wuyi*], they both need have nothing to say.[16]

Notes

1. Cheng Xuanying: "E Lai was an obsequious courtier of King Zhou. Since he was utterly devoted to him, they both perished together." *Zhuangzi jishi*, 4: 921.
2. Cheng Xuanying: "Xiaoji was the son of Emperor Gaozong of Yin [King Wuding of Shang], who suffered such grief because of his stepmother that he died of despair. Despite Zeng Shen's perfect obedience, his parents so hated him that they often beat him, at times almost to death, which was the reason why he felt such sorrow." *Zhuangzi jishi*, 4: 921.
3. Cheng Xuanying: "Although the moon is big, its light is gentle and diffuse; although a fire is small, its gleam shines bright. This is a metaphor for someone whose aspirations are too large, is excessively greedy, and who knows not that he ought to abide by his allotted capacity." *Zhuangzi jishi*, 4: 923.
4. The Zhe is an ancient name for the Qiantang River, which flows past Hangzhou into Hangzhou Bay; Mount Cangwu is located in the Lingnan region of southeast China.
5. Cheng Xuanying: "Since this is an ode that is not included in the *Classic of Odes*, it must have been deleted a long time ago." *Zhuangzi jishi*, 4: 928.
6. *Yijing* (Classic of Changes), "Commentary on the appended phrases" [*Xici zhuan*], Part Two; Wang Bi: "One who understands how change operates will retain its essentials. This is why the text says: 'But if one is not such a person, The Dao will not operate in vain.' " Richard John Lynn, *The Classic of Changes*, 90.
7. Cheng Xuanying: "Old Master Lai was a worthy recluse of Chu who usually lived in seclusion on Mount Meng." *Zhuangzi jishi*, 4: 929. Mount Meng [Mengshan] is located in Mengyin district, northwest of Linyi, in Shandong.
8. Cheng Xuanying: "One may extend kindness to make people happy, but such kindness cannot extend to all. Therefore, many will feel they were treated with arrogance and disrespect. As such, if one uses kindness to win people's affection, it will be just the thing to make one the target of their ire. One thus becomes dishonored and reviled throughout life." *Zhuangzi jishi*, 4: 931.
9. Cheng Xuanying: "As for the most wise and the most stupid, their fundamental natures are impossible to change, and those of middling intelligence are easily led or repelled.

Therefore, hearing Yao praised, they lead one another around envying advantage and fame, and, hearing Jie condemned, they band together to conspire in secret." *Zhuangzi jishi*, 4: 931.

10. Cheng Xuanying: "If one acts in opposition to the fundamental nature of the people, it never fails to harm them. If one agitates one's mind, it never operates with true method [*zhengfa*]." *Zhuangzi jishi*, 4: 932.
11. The Clear River [Qingjiang] is a tributary of the Yangtze River in Hubei.
12. Cheng Xuanying: "With only enough space to plant the feet, one cannot move. Thus one must rely on more ground, for only then can the feet and legs be put to use; as such, the principle of the useless becomes clear. Let us thus cite the saying of Master Lao, 'Therefore this is how what is there provides benefit and how what is not there provides functionality.'" *Zhuangzi jishi*, 4: 936. Cheng quotes from the *Laozi*, section 11, to which Wang Bi comments: "That wood, clay, and wall can form these three things [wheel, vessel, and room] depends in all on achieving functionality [*yong*] through nothingness [*wu*]. In other words, [as for nothingness,] that what is there can be of benefit always depends on its achievement of functionality through what is not there." Richard John Lynn, *The Classic of the Way and Virtue*, 69.
13. The abdomen, the body cavity, contains all the viscera, including the heart, which was thought to be the seat of thought and emotion. As the "heart," that organ is attached there, but as the "mind," it is not confined to the abdomen but is free to wander through all the natural universe.
14. Cheng Xuanying: "*Bao* (violence) means killing and harming (*canhai*). Reputation is a tool of competition. Once reputations exceed what people deserve, they surely try to harm and kill one another. As it is said in the inner chapters, reputation leads to mutual strife." *Zhuangzi jishi*, 4: 942. Also, cf. 4.8.2.
15. "Yan Gate" refers to the east gate of the capital city of the ancient state of Song. *Zhuangzi jishi*, 4: 945.
16. Cheng Xuanying elaborates: "This is a composite analogy: Thought [*yi*] refers to marvelous principle [*miaoli*]. That one can catch a fish or a rabbit depends on the fish trap and the snare, but just as the fish trap and the snare are not really the fish and hare, so though one relies on words to grasp arcane principle [*xuanli*], the words used are not really arcane principle itself. And just as once the fish and hare are caught the trap and snare are forgotten, so once arcane principle is understood [*ming*] words used to describe it are abandoned. As for one who forgets words and so grasps principle [*li*], all it takes is a shared glance to know that the Dao is with him [*daocun*]. Such a one is truly rare and hard to find as this." *Zhuangzi jishi*, 4: 946.

CHAPTER 27

YUYAN [WORDS ATTRIBUTED TO OTHERS]

27.1.1 Words attributed to outsiders [*wai*] are effective nine times of ten,

If attributed to outsiders, nine out of ten are believed.

27.1.2 and weighty words seven of ten.

As for what is given weight to by common people of the world, seven out of ten words are believed.[1]

27.1.3 But goblet words [*zhiyan*] keep on appearing day after day in accord with Heaven's distinctions.

A goblet when full gets tipped and when empty is set upright—it does not just stay the same. How much the more this is true of words, for they change according to what they refer to. Since they but follow them [their referents], this is why the text says they "appear day after day." "Appear day after day" means "new each day." Since they are new each day, they fulfill what is naturally allotted to them, and because their natural allotments are thus fulfilled, they function harmoniously.[2]

27.2.1 Words attributed to outsiders are effective nine out of ten because one depends on someone else to say them.

If words come from oneself, the common run of people for the most part won't accept them, which is why one just attributes them to outsiders. Exchanges such as those between Jianwu and Lian Shu all involve such attributions.[3]

27.2.2 One's own father does not act as a matchmaker for a son, for if one's own father were to praise him, it would not be as effective as if someone not his father would do so.

When a father praises a son, truly many would not believe him, and even if some occasionally did believe him, he still would be doubted by those who are always suspicious. Therefore, he depends on someone else to do the talking.

27.2.3 So this is no fault of his own but the fault of others.

Although he himself is trustworthy, since those who are always suspicious won't accept what he says, he entrusts this to others to have it believed. The way to get people to hear things is as troublesome as this.

27.2.4 If an opinion is the same as one's own, one agrees with it, but if it does not agree with one's own, one rejects it.

Each regards the other to be wrong.

27.2.5 If the same as one's own, it is considered right, but if different from one's own, it is considered wrong.

When holders of three different opinions find themselves together and two who differ from each other argue that his should be accepted, though both are sure to differ from the one who does not argue, since each only believes what he himself thinks is right, how could they not but rely on the outsider!

27.3.1 Words held in respect are effective seven times of ten, because those who have already said them are the aged and wise.

Because they are from the aged and wise, ordinary people commonly hold them in respect, so even though they are not attributed to outsiders, seven out of ten are still believed.

27.3.2 This is just precedence in years. To treat [*qi*] them as elders though they lack the basics and details of the warp and woof of things does not really mean precedence.

They just precede people in years, but since such basics and details are extra to that, there is no reason to treat them so and thus no reason to give them precedence. *Qi* [expect, meet, wait for] here means "treat" [*dai*].

27.3.3 To be such a man yet lack anything to justify precedence over other men indicates lack of access to the Dao of man. Anyone who thus lacks access to the Dao of man may be said to be just a fusty old fellow.

Though such a one is just a fusty old fellow, yet common people all trust such a one, which shows how content they are with old ways of thinking and just follow established ways.

27.4.1 Just as goblet words appear day after day in accord with Heaven's distinctions, allow yours such continuous transformations [*manyan*], for this is how one may exhaust the limits of one's years.[4]

Since it is Nature that sets divisions, right and wrong thus have no master; since they have no master, they thus undergo continuous transformations, so who could ever fix what they are! Therefore, expansively free yourself from self-conscious involvement with things and just let them be, for this is how one may live out one's natural lifespan to the end.

27.4.2 No words equals equality,[5] but equality joined to words equals inequality, and words joined to equality equals inequality.

If one joins oneself to things and uses words for them from that point of view, "this" and "that," "what is" and "what is not" will readily self-adjust [*ziqi*]. But if, without complying with things, one tries to assign words to match [*qi*] them, one's "I" and the myriad things no longer are equally one [*qi*].

27.4.3 Therefore one says, "Let there be no words."

This is to say what someone else has said, so though there are these words, I actually would not say them.

27.4.4 Though one says, "Let there be no words," since one says them one's whole life, they are never not said.

Even if they were to come out of my own mouth, they would all be someone else's words.

27.4.5 So to go on about no words all one's life means that one never fails to speak.

Proof is they come out of my mouth.

27.4.6 There are grounds [*zi*] for it is acceptable, and there are grounds for it is not acceptable; there are grounds for it is so, and there are grounds for it is not so. Why is something so? It is so because it is deemed so. Why is something acceptable? It is acceptable because it is deemed acceptable. Why is something not acceptable? It is not acceptable because it is deemed not acceptable.

Zi (from, intrinsically, oneself) here means *you* (basis, cause, from, ground, reason). It is because they come from [*you*] the biased predilections of other and self that "acceptable" and "not acceptable" exist.

27.4.7 But things certainly do have that which makes them so, and things certainly have that which makes them acceptable.

Each thing is intrinsically so [*ziran*]; each thing is intrinsically acceptable [*zike*].

27.4.8 There is no thing that is not so; there is no thing that is not acceptable.

As a general piece of advice, do without [*wu*] "acceptable" and do without "not acceptable," for to do without "acceptable" and to do without "not acceptable" will get you there.[6]

27.4.9 Without goblet words that appear day after day in harmony with Heaven's distinctions, how could anyone manage to last as long as he should!

Only if one's words are adjusted to comply with things so they accord with natural divisions can one avoid an early death.

27.4.10 Though the myriad things all are from the same seed, they succeed one another in different forms.

Although they take one another's place thanks to change and transformation, if one traces their origin back to pneuma, it is all one and the same for them.

27.4.11 Beginnings and endings go around as if as a single ring,

What today is a beginning yesterday was yet again already an ending.

27.4.12 and no one understands the principle why this is so.

Since the principle functions spontaneously, no one understands it.

27.4.13 It is called the potter's wheel of Heaven; it is thanks to the potter's wheel of Heaven that Heaven's distinctions occur.

How could this potter's wheel ever make a mistake in the way it regulates, for all are natural distinctions!

27.5.1 Master Zhuang said to Master Hui, "Confucius by the age of sixty had transformed sixty times.

He transformed in accord with time.

27.5.2 What he had considered right at the beginning he ended by considering wrong,

As times change, so do the ways of the world. As for one who drives the people as his carriage lets his mind wander freely among them, how could such as he ever take issue with the ways of the world![7]

27.5.3 and we don't know but what he then now meant by 'right' is not what he had considered wrong when fifty-nine."[8]

Since change never stops, what is "right" can't remain constant

27.6 Master Hui then said, "Confucius worked at knowing things with diligence and determination."

What he meant was that Confucius knew things only after diligently committing them to memory and that he was incapable of self-transformation. This clearly demonstrates that Master Hui was not up to appreciating why the sage had such a far-reaching effect.

27.7.1 To this Master Zhuang responded, "Confucius left that all behind but then never said anything about it.

He replaced it with the spontaneity of change and transformation, not something that the power of knowledge can do. Thenceforth, in accord with the moment, he just trusted the people to do for themselves—but fabricated no doctrine about it.

27.7.2 As Confucius said, 'We receive our abilities from the Great Root and keep on living by restoring our spirit.'

If abilities and intelligence are belabored without restoring one's original spirit [*benling*], life would be lost.

27.7.3 But as singing should accord with the music scale so when one speaks it should accord with convention [*fa*].

As song should originate in the musical scale, so should speech emerge from convention. Since convention and the musical scale are created by the people, the sage accordingly just sets about using them. Therefore, though whatever he does never fails to be appropriate, he never talks about it nor consciously works at it.

27.7.4 So when it came to 'advantage' and 'righteousness' as well as 'good' and 'bad' and 'right' and 'wrong,' the only thing he did was just use [*fu*] the mouths of the people.

Fu (submit) here means "use" [*yong*]. I have nothing to say, so whatever I say is said by using the mouths of the people. The exposition of good and bad, right and wrong, advantage and righteousness has thus never come out of my own mouth.[9]

27.7.5 If people thus submitted in mind and so dared not stand in opposition, this would stabilize the world as it would be stabilized.

Since the mouth is the means to express the mind, he [Confucius] made use of the mouths of the people, and their minds were thus utilized by him. If I were to comply with the minds of the people, the minds of the people would trust me, so who then would stand in opposition to me! And if I were to stabilize the world by complying with its natural tendency to stability, what more would I have to do about it!

27.7.6 Enough! Enough! For I surely can't attain to the likes of him!"

By complying with them, he [Confucius] could drive the people as his carriage, thus there was nothing he could not attain.

27.8 When Master Zeng[10] took office a second time and then had another change of mind, he declared, "When I took office while my parents were still alive, I was happy with just a salary of three pecks, but now, as I take office a second time with a salary of three thousand bushels, it is too late [*bujǐ*], so I feel sad."

Jǐ [be up to, reach] is the same as *jí* [extend as far as].

27.9 A disciple asked Zhongni [Confucius], "As for someone like Shen, may we say that he was free from the fault of attachment [*xuan*]?"

Xuan, "suspended," here means *xi*, "attached." That is, since Shen served in office for the sake of his parents, he was free from the fault of attachment to salary.

27.10.1 Zhongni replied, "But he had actually been attached!

He was attached to a salary in order to support his parents.

27.10.2 If he had been free of attachment, could he have felt such sadness?

As long as one's parents are supported suitably, one should not worry about how this is implemented. If one can free himself from such attachment, he will care not about how noble or mean his circumstances are, but tranquilly and joyfully just do all that is right to support them with a pleasant disposition.

27.10.3 Such a one [*bi*] would have regarded three pecks and three thousand bushels as if they had been sparrows or mosquitoes flitting by in front of him."

"Such a one" [*bi*] indicates one free from attachment. One free from attachment looks upon honors and salary as so many mosquitoes and flies or birds flitting by in front of him—how could such a one feel either happy or sad about the difference between them!

27.11.1 Yan Cheng, Ziyou said to Ziqi of East Wall, "Since I heard your words, after the first year I became plain and simple [*ye*],

He placed power and privilege outside himself.

27.11.2 after the second I became compliant [*cong*],

He no longer acted on his own [*zizhuan*].

27.11.3 after the third I interchanged [*tong*],

He interchanged other with self.

27.11.4 after the fourth I became a thing,

He merged himself with other things.

27.11.5 after the fifth I was receptive [*lai*],

He achieved spontaneous receptivity [*zide*].[11]

27.11.6 after the sixth year the demonic had entered [*guiru*],[12]

He placed his physical body [*xinghai*] outside himself.[13]

27.11.7 after the seventh year I naturally accomplished things [*tiancheng*],

He never had to redo anything.

27.11.8 after the eighth year I had no sense of death, no sense of life,

Whatever was encountered he fell in with to his satisfaction.

27.11.9 and after the ninth year it was the Universal Wondrous [Damiao] for me."

"Wondrous" [*miao*] here means "the good" [*shan*]. Because good and bad are one and the same to him, no matter what he sets out to do, he never failed to merge arcanely with it. This speaks to how, after hearing about the Dao for a long time, one comes to understand the spontaneity of the pipes of Heaven, which leads one to mindlessly losing of all self-awareness; accordingly, mundane encumbrances disappear day by day to the point where they simply are all gone.

27.12.1 Life based on selfconscious action [*youwei*] leads to death.

To live by selfconscious action will lose one his life.

27.12.2 I urge you to be impartial, for your death will come from such a source [*zi*].[14]

"Source" [*zi*] is the same as *you* "for such a reason." It is because of selfconscious action that death occurs. Because he treats his life with partiality this has him act selfconsciously. Why he is urged to be impartial here is because his death will occur due to just such partiality.

27.12.3 Moreover, life is a yang state that does not happen for any reason.

Life as a yang state is the result of unselfconscious action that occurs absolutely without trace, mindlessly as an independent event [*duer*], and not at all for any reason.

27.12.4 And this is really so! As such, what should be suitable for you? What should be unsuitable for you?

What seems so is really so! Therefore, once the unsuitable becomes the not unsuitable, resulting in every state being suitable, all shall be suitable whatever state arrives.[15]

27.12.5 Heaven has its calendrical calculations, and Earth has places for people to settle in, so where else should I seek them?

All these are already self-sufficient unto themselves.[16]

27.12.6 Though no one knows how these will end, how could it not be due to fate?

Logically these [Heaven and Earth] surely end spontaneously [*zizhong*] and not because they are conscious about it, so how could it not be fated?

27.12.7 Though no one knows how these began, how could it have been subject to fate?

It is unknown why these are as they are, but to say that they are due to fate seems to imply that intentionality is involved, which is why the text goes on to reject the term "fate," in order to clarify that they happen spontaneously, for only then is the principle underlying fate fully realized [*mingli quan ye*].[17]

27.12.8 Since they [Heaven and Earth] have the means to resonate, how could the demonic [*gui*] not be involved?

Logically such resonance surely exists, as if it were conveyed by the numinous [*shenling*].

27.12.9 If they had no means to resonate, how could there be the demonic?

Logically they resonate spontaneously, for the resonance stems not from any reason; as such, though they resonate, nothing numinous is involved.

27.13 All the penumbras asked of Shadow: "A short time ago you were looking down, but now you look up. A short time ago you had your hair tied up, but now it hangs loose. A short time ago you were sitting down, but now you have gotten up. A short time ago you were walking, but now you are stopped. Why is this?"

27.14.1 Shadow said, "I'm just unselfconsciously moving around, so why ask me about it?

Its movement is spontaneous, so there is nothing to ask about.

27.14.2 It happens to me, but I don't know why.

It happens spontaneously, so it does not know why.

27.14.3 I am as a cicada shell, a snake slough.

A shadow seems like a bodily form but is not a bodily form.

27.14.4 In firelight or sunlight, I gather myself in, but when it is cloudy or when night comes, I fade away. Since it is questionable that I should have to depend on them [firelight or sunlight], how much less likely should I have to use what is there [a physical form] to depend on!

If we pursue this line of thought to its ultimate conclusion in determining what the shadow supposedly depends on, it turns out in the end that it depends on nothing at all, which makes the principle of independent transformation [*duhua*] manifestly obvious.[18]

27.14.5 When another thing arrives, I arrive with it, and when it goes, I leave with it. When it waxes vigorous, I wax vigorous with it. But as for this waxing vigorous, what further is there to ask about it?

The shadow simply waxes vigorously and moves about on its own, which accounts for its following some object around, which it does without intention, so it can't be asked about it.[19]

27.15 Yang Ziju [Yang Zhu] went to Pei, where, as Lao Dan was traveling west to Qin, he expected to meet him in the outskirts, but it was when he reached Liang that he encountered Master Lao.[20] Master Lao, in the middle of the road raising his face to Heaven, sighed and said, "At first I thought you could be taught, but now that seems impossible."

27.16 Yang Ziju did not reply, but when they reached lodgings, he brought to him water to wash, towel, and comb, and, removing his shoes outside the door, crawled forward on his knees into his presence, where he said, "Earlier I wanted to ask you, Master, for an explanation, but because you were then walking and had not the time, I dared not do so, but now since there is time, I beg to ask how I have gone wrong."

27.17.1 Master Lao replied,

> **"You have such an alarming look**
> **As you glare about that**
> **Who would ever dwell with you!**

"Alarming look as you glare about" [*suisui xuxu*] describes such a peremptory [*bahu*] appearance that, tending to fear trouble, people keep far away from you.

27.17.2 Great whiteness seems soiled,
Abundant virtue seems wanting."[21]

27.18 Yang Ziju, uneasy, changed countenance and said, "I have respectfully received your instruction."

27.19.1 Before when greeted at inns , the innkeeper held a mat for him, and his wife provided him with towel and comb. People staying at the inn left their mats in respect, and those tending to the cook stove left the stove.

His noble appearance made him so extraordinary that people feared and avoided him.

27.19.2 But when he was on his way back, people staying at inns competed with him for a place on a mat.

This was because he had rid himself of his boastful and arrogant demeanor.

Notes

1. "Weighty words" translates *zhongyan*, which Cheng Xuanying glosses as "that which is held in respect from local elders." Note that Guo Xiang also reads the term as "weighty words" [*zhongyan*], not as "repeated words" [*chongyan*]; see *Zhuangzi jishi*, 4: 947.
2. Cheng Xuanying: "A goblet when full gets tipped and when empty is set upright. Whether it is tipped or set upright depends on someone. Words uttered unselfconsciously, this is what 'goblet words' are. Therefore, one either does not speak or one's speech is done without any 'tipping' or 'being set upright.' Only then do words match what is naturally allotted to them." *Zhuangzi jishi*, 4: 947.

3. Cf. 1.10–1.13.
4. Cf. 2.32.4.
5. Cheng Xuanying: "For where principle is found there are no words, so to speak about it would miss the mark. Therefore, one should just keep to no words and let things maintain their own equality." *Zhuangzi jishi*, 4: 950.
6. This paraphrases a line from the *Lunyu* (Analects), 18: 2530a: "As for me, I am different from them, for I do without [*wu*] "acceptable" and do without "not acceptable." Most translations render *wu*, "do without," as something like "have no rigid views of."
7. Cf. 4.29.14.
8. Cf. 25.43.3.
9. Cheng Xuanying: "When it came to benevolence and righteousness, advantage and harm, good and bad, right and wrong, he [Confucius] explained their meaning commensurate with the mental capacities of those before him and as appropriate to the occasion. Though he repeated such sayings with his own mouth, this followed what earlier people had said. This then is how he used the mouths of the people." *Zhuangzi jishi*, 4: 954.
10. Master Zeng, given name Shen and personal name Ziyu, was a disciple of Confucius.
11. Cheng Xuanying interprets *lai* causatively, as "attract," "cause to come": "He had the multitudes gravitate to him [*zhonggui*]." *Zhuangzi jishi*, 4: 957. For Guo's "spontaneous receptivity" interpretation of *lai*, cf. 4.21.
12. Cf. 4.24.7.
13. Cheng Xuanying again differs from Guo: "He handled people by communing in spirit with them [*shenhui liwu*]." *Zhuangzi jishi*, 4: 957.
14. This passage has long been thought corrupt; much controversy has existed about how it should be read, and even how it should be parsed has been in doubt. See Wang Shumin, *Zhuangzi jiaoquan*, 1104, notes 12 and 13. Its reading here follows Guo's commentary.
15. Cheng Xuanying: "Since it is pneuma that gathers to produce life, it isn't worth being joyful about life; when pneuma disperses it results in death, so it isn't worth grieving over death. Once life and death are thus equal, grief and joy then vanish. Therefore, which state may one find suitable? Which state may one find unsuitable? Whichever one might find himself in can only be suitable." *Zhuangzi jishi*, 4: 958–59.
16. Cheng Xuanying: "According to calendrical calculations, astral phenomena decorate the sky, and the nine regions to the ends of the four directions provide the people with the means of support. Since every single aspect present in these creative transformative powers is absolutely perfect, where otherwise should I seek them?" *Zhuangzi jishi*, 4: 959.
17. My interpretation of this cryptic passage is assisted significantly by a gloss on it by Qian Mu (1895–1990): "The commentary states that if fate is governed by consciousness, it can't be spontaneous, which is why he [Guo Xiang] used principle [*li*] to elucidate 'fate' as the 'principle underlying fate' [*ming zhi li*], for which he especially coined the term 'principle of fate' [*mingli*]. 'Principle' may be used in this way to investigate the meaning of *tian* (Heaven, the Natural, spontaneity) in its all aspects. Since the images [in the *Classic of Changes*] effectively develop the sense of spontaneity involved, it won't do to discuss *tian* in terms of 'fate,' but the word 'principle' instead should be used exclusively. In his commentary to the *Changes*, Wang Bi had already said, 'Heaven [*tian*] indicates a form.' As for the two masters Wang and Guo, whenever they discuss anything 'natural' [*ziran*], the reason why they had to address it in terms of 'principle' is thus quite obvious." *Zhuang Lao tongbian* (General insights into the *Zhuangzi* and the *Laozi*), vol. 2, 494. "Heaven indicates a form" paraphrases a longer statement: "The term *tian* [Heaven] is the name for a form, a phenomenal entity;

the term *jian* [strength and dynamism: *Qian*] refers to that which uses or takes this form." *Qian* (Pure Yang, hexagram 1), *Commentary on the Judgments.* See Richard John Lynn, *The Classic of Changes*, 129. It is by conceiving of "fate" as the manifestation of "principle" that Guo understands how Heaven and Earth are both dependent and not dependent on fate, for it is innate principle that governs them both spontaneously. The same argument applies later to explain how Heaven and Earth resonate with man both with and without the vehicle of the numinous, for "the numinous" but refers to the workings of spontaneity.

18. Cheng Xuanying helps to make both the text of the *Zhuangzi* and Guo's comment more intelligible: "How much less likely [than the shadow being produced by sunlight or firelight] this should be if what I am supposedly dependent on is a physical form, for surely when there is no firelight or sunlight, a physical form can't produce a shadow, so this means that a shadow does not depend on a physical form either. Just as the production of a physical form does not depend on firelight or the sun, how could the production of a shadow depend on a physical form? This is why the text cites firelight and the sun to make it [physical form] less likely a possibility, which is how it makes it clear that we should know that a shadow does not depend on a physical form. Since even physical forms and shadows share no co-dependency, how much less should other things! From this we know further that all the myriad phenomenal entities are in each case the product of independent transformation." *Zhuangzi jishi*, 4: 961.
19. Cheng Xuanying: " 'Another thing' [*bi*] refers to a physical form [*xing*]. *Qiangyang* (wax vigorous) describes how something moves about. A physical form and a shadow may arrive and leave simultaneously, but since there is no reason for dependence, they both rely on their own independent transformation [*duhua*]. 'Principle [*li*] of independent transformation' is an absolutely marvelous descriptive term [*mingyan*] for it, and such a descriptive term and this exchange of question and answer bring out the meaning of it perfectly." *Zhuangzi jishi*, 4: 962.
20. The same passage occurs, with variants, in the *Liezi* (Sayings of Master Lie); *Liezi jishi*, 2: 80–81. Cheng Xuanying: "Pei refers to Pengcheng, present-day Xuzhou [Jiangsu]. . . . The state of Liang refers to the area around Bianzhou [present-day Kaifeng]. Yang Zhu was going south, and Master Lao was going west, so they happened to meet somewhere in the Liang and Song area [Henan], where in the outskirts he tried to talk with him." *Zhuangzi jishi*, 4: 962.
21. These two lines paraphrase the *Laozi*, section 41: "Great whiteness seems soiled. [Wang Bi: It is only by 'know[ing] the white yet sustain[ing] the black' that great whiteness can be achieved.] Vast virtue seems wanting. [Wang Bi: Vast virtue is filled with everything, for it is so capacious and formless that it can't be filled.]" Lynn, *The Classic of the Way and Virtue*, 132. Here, Master Lao chides Yang Zhu for parading his spotless character and showing off his virtue.

CHAPTER 28

RANGWANG [REFUSING RULERSHIP]

28.1 Yao tried to yield the whole world to Xu You, but Xu You would not accept it,[1] and when he tried to yield it to Zi Zhou Zhifu,[2] Zi said, "I could be up to that, but it so happens that I am so sick with distress and exhaustion that I am now trying to cure it, thus I have no time to spare for governing the whole world." To govern the whole world is of the utmost importance, yet he would not let it harm his life, so how much the less would he have allowed anything else to harm him! It is only someone who does not want to govern the whole world who may be entrusted with it.[3]

28.2 And when Shun tried to yield the whole world to Zi Zhou Zhibo, Zi said, "It so happens that I am so sick with distress and exhaustion that I am now trying to cure it, thus I have no time to spare for governing the whole world." Therefore, although the whole world is the great vessel, he would not exchange his life for it. This is how one who possesses the Dao differs from mundane people.

28.3 When Shun tried to yield the whole world to Shan Juan,[4] Shan said, "I stand at the very center of the whole universe. Winter days I wear skins and fur and summer days wear clothes of hemp. In spring I plow and plant, my body up to such toil; in autumn I harvest my crops, enough to allow me leisure and food. When sun comes up, I go to work; when sun sets, I rest. I enjoy such spontaneous freedom here between Heaven and Earth, where my heart and mind [*xinyi*] find self-fulfillment, why should I ever want to govern the whole world! Alas, how you fail to understand me!" Thereupon, refusing it, he left and went deep into the mountains, no one knows where.

28.4 When Shun tried to yield the whole world to his friend, Farmer of Stone Door [Shihu zhi Nong], he said, "How earnestly and diligently you conduct yourself! What a hard-working man!" But realizing that Shun's virtue had not quite reached perfection, carrying their possessions on his back and his wife carrying them on her head, they lead their children by the hand and went out to sea, never to return for the rest of their lives.

28.5 When the great King Danfu resided in Bin, the Di tribe attacked him.[5] He offered them skins and silk, but they would not accept them. Then he offered them dogs and horses, but they would not accept them. And finally he offered them pearls and jade, but they would not accept them either, for what they wanted was the land. Great King Danfu then said, "To dwell with the older brothers of people and have their younger brothers killed, to dwell with the fathers of people and have their sons be killed, this I can't bear to do. May all of you do your best to stay here, for what difference is there between being my subjects and being the subjects of the Di tribe! Moreover, I have heard that one should not use what provides nourishment [the land] to harm those whom it nourishes." Thereupon he took up his staff and set off, but his people in continuous procession followed him, and he consequently established his state below Mount Qi. Well, this great King Danfu may be said to have venerated life. One capable of venerating life, though noble and rich, would not let what nourishes the land bring harm on himself, or, though poor and lowly, would not let what might bring gain entangle himself in trouble. But people nowadays, respected and honored with high office, care only about losing it, and, if they see potential gain, they disregard how it might lead to loss of their lives. Is this not the height of folly!

28.6 Once the people of Yue had assassinated three successive generations of rulers, Crown Prince Sou [Wangzi Sou], realizing what danger he was in, fled to Cinnabar Caves [Danxue], leaving the state of Yu without a ruler. They could not find him when they first looked for him, but then traced him to Cinnabar Caves. When Crown Prince Sou would not come out, they smoked him out with wormwood and had him board the king's chariot. As Crown Prince Sou grabbed the chariot strap to pull himself up onto the chariot, he raised his face to the heavens and cried out, "Oh, to be a ruler, oh, to be a ruler, could not I alone have been spared!" It was not that Crown Prince Sou hated being a ruler, he hated the danger involved in being a ruler. Regarding a man like Crown Prince Sou, it may be said that he would not harm his life for the sake of having a state, which was certainly the reason why the people of Yue wanted to obtain him as their ruler.

28.7 While Han and Wei were fighting over land they both had invaded, Master Zihua went to see Marquis Zhaoxi and found him looking sad.[6] So Master Zihua said to him, "Now, if an oath were composed representing everyone in the world and set before you that stated, "Given that if one's left hand were to grab it, his right hand would wither, or if one's right hand were to grab it, his left hand would wither, anyone who does manage to grab it, we guarantee shall possess the whole world," would you be up to grabbing it?"

28.8 Marquis Zhaoxi replied, "I would not grab it."

28.9 Master Zihua went on, "Very good! Looking at it from this point of view, your two arms are more important to you than possessing the whole world, and your whole person should be still more important to you than your two arms. As Han is far and away less important than the whole world, what you are now fighting over is far and away even less important than is all of Han. My Lord, you are doing nothing but subjecting yourself to sorrow and bringing harm on your life by grieving over what you can't get!"

28.10 Marquis Zhaoxi then said, "Excellent! Many are those who have tried to instruct me, but never have I heard such words as these." Master Zihua may be said to have understood the difference between importance and insignificance.

28.11 When the ruler of Lu[7] heard that Yan He was someone who had attained the Dao,[8] he dispatched emissaries to go first with valuable gifts for him. Yan He happened to be at his humble gate, attired in rough hemp and feeding an ox, and as the emissaries from the ruler of Lu approached, he turned toward them. One of the emissaries then addressed him, "Is this the home of Yan He?" Yan He replied, "This is his home." But when the emissaries presented the gifts, Yan He said, "I fear that your instructions have been misunderstood, and you will be criminally liable, so you had better verify them." The emissaries then returned and, once they had verified things, came back again to look for him, but they just could not find him. Thus it was that people like Yan He truly despised riches and honor.

28.12 Therefore, as it has been said,

> The true essence of the Dao is for governing one's person,
> What remains from that is for governing the state and family,
> And the dregs left from that is for governing the whole world.

Looking at it from this point of view, the achievements of sovereigns are but matters of secondary importance to the sage, for they have nothing to do with keeping one's person whole and safe and don't nourish life. But mundane sovereigns nowadays mostly put their persons in danger and throw away their lives because they are obsessed with possessing things—is this not a pity! Whenever a sage takes action, he is sure to examine what he is about to do and how he is going to do it. Now, for instance, suppose someone uses the pearl that the Marquis of Sui had[9] as a pellet to shoot at a sparrow a thousand arm spans up in the air, everyone in the world would laugh at him. And why is that? Because what he uses is of great value and what he wants to get with it is insignificant. And is not life itself much more important than what the Marquis of Sui had!

28.13 Master Lie became so poverty stricken that he looked like he was starving.[10] One of his visitors informed Ziyang of Zheng[11] of this, "Lie Yukou happens to be a man who possesses the Dao, who lives in your state, Your Honor, but he now suffers privation. Is that not because Your Honor does not like such men?" Ziyang of Zheng immediately ordered officials to give him grain, but when Master Lie saw them, he bowed twice and refused it.

28.14 Once the officials had gone, Master Lie went inside, where his wife, beating her breast, said to him, "I have heard that the wife and children of someone who possesses the Dao all have it easy and enjoy life, but we instead look like we are going to starve. Now, His Honor, recognizing his injustice to you, tried to give you food, but you, husband, refused it. How could this not be but fate!"

28.15 Master Lie smiled and told her, "His Honor did not know me personally, but tried to give me grain because of what someone told him. And if he ever goes so far as to condemn me as a criminal, that again will be because of what someone told him. This is why I did not accept it." This all ended, as he had expected, with a commoner rising up and killing Ziyang.[12]

28.16 When King Zhao of Chu lost his state, sheep butcher Yue fled as one of his followers. When King Zhao regained his state, he proceeded to reward his followers, but when he came to sheep butcher Yue, Yue said, "When the great king, lost his state, I lost my sheep butchery, and when the great king, regained your state, I too regained my sheep butchery. Since my rank and emolument have already been restored to me, what further reward should I have!"

28.17 The king then said, "Force it on him."

28.18 Sheep butcher Yue said to this, "When the great king lost his state, it was not through any fault of mine, and when the great king regained his state, it was not due to any feat of mine. Therefore, I dare not accept any reward for it."

28.19 The king responded, "I would see him."

28.20 To this, sheep butcher Yue said, "According to the laws of Chu, one must have been richly rewarded for great service before obtaining such an audience, but neither was my intelligence up to saving the state nor my bravery up to facing the death-dealing enemy. When the Wu army entered Ying, fearing such dire straits, I fled from the enemy—it was not that I deliberately followed the great king. But now the great king wishes to ignore the law and break regulations so he can grant me audience—the likes of which I have never heard of anywhere in the whole world."

28.21 The king then told Minister of War Ziqi, "Although the position of sheep butcher Yue is humble and menial, his expression of moral meaning is quite higher than most. Ziqi, offer him on my behalf a position as one of the three banners."[13]

28.22 Sheep butcher Yue replied, "As for the position of one of the three banners, I know it carries more esteem than the trade of a butcher, and, since it comes with an emolument of ten thousand bushels of grain, I know that it means much more wealth than what the trade of butcher may earn. Nevertheless, how could I ever let greed for rank and emolument cause my lord to acquire a reputation for such reckless behavior! So I dare not accept and instead just want to return to my trade of butcher." And so, after all, he did not accept it.

28.23 When Yuan Xian[14] lived in Lu, it was in a ten-feet-square hovel thatched with living grass, its door of plaited saltbush only partial whole and hinged on a mulberry branch. Its two chambers had earthenware bottomless pots for windows and were blocked off from one another by coarse hemp cloth. It leaked above and was subject to seepage below. But there he sat upright, played his zither, and sang.

28.24 Zigong, his carriage drawn by great horses, his inner garment purple and his outer white, with his canopied carriage too big to enter the alley, went to see Yuan Xian. Yuan Xian, wearing a cap made of birch bark and slippers without heels bound on his feet, leaned on a goosefoot cane as he answered the door.

28.25 Zigong asked, "Oh sir, what distress you are in!"

28.26 To which Yuan Xian responded, "Whereas I hear that to have no assets is what one calls poverty, to study but fail to practice it is what one calls distress. Now, I am poor but not in distress." At that, Zigong drew back and looked ashamed.

28.27 Yuan Xian then said with a laugh, "To act in order to curry favor with the vulgar, to make friends for the sake of gain, to learn just in order to show off, to teach just to get something for yourself, to cloak evil deeds with benevolence and righteousness, and to adorn yourself with carriages and horses—these are all things I can't bear to do."

28.28 When Master Zeng was living in Wey, his tattered hemp robe lacked its outer cover, his face was mottled and puffy, and his hands and feet were heavily callused. For three days at a time he lit not a fire, and for ten years had not had clothes made. When he straightened his cap, the chin strap broke; when he pulled his lapels together, his elbows showed; when he put on his shoes, the heels split open. Dragging his shoes along, when he sang the Eulogies of Shang [Shang song], the sound filled Heaven and Earth as if it came from bronze bells or stone chimes. The Son of Heaven failed to get him as a minister, and the feudal lords failed to get him as a friend. As such, one who nourishes his will is unaware of his physical body, one who nourishes his physical body is unaware of the benefit to it, and one who attains the Dao is unmindful of it.

28.29 Confucius once said to Yan Hui, "Hui, come hither! Your family is so poor and lives in such humble conditions, why not take office?"
28.30 Yan Hui replied, "I am unwilling to take office, for I possess about eight acres of land outside the city wall, enough to provide us with congee, and about an acre and a half piece of land inside the city wall, enough to provide us with silk and hemp. I play the zither, which is enough to amuse myself, and my studies of your Dao, Master, is enough to give me joy—that is why I don't want to take office!"
28.31 Abased, Confucius, with changed expression, said, "How excellent are your aspirations! As I have heard, "One who knows contentment does not wear himself out for the sake of gain, one who carefully looks into what provides self-fulfillment fears not when loss occurs, and one whose inner self is cultivated feels no shame not to have an official position." I have been preaching such things for a long time, but only now, with you, Hui, have I seen them realized—and this is my reward!"
28.32 Mou, Prince of Zhongshan, asked of Master Chan: "Though my body may be out on the vast river reaches, my mind stays trapped below the palace gate towers of Wei—what can I do about it?"
28.33 Master Chan replied: "Value life more, for if you value life more, worldly advantage will then become unimportant."
28.34 Mou, Prince of Zhongshan, then said: "Though I realize this, I can't yet conquer myself."
28.35 Master Chan replied: "If you can't conquer yourself, yield to it and let no loathing befall your spirit, for, if you can't conquer yourself yet try to force yourself not to yield, this means that you will inflict a double injury on yourself, and no one who inflicts such double injury on himself is ever found among the long-lived."
28.36 Mou, Prince of Zhongshan, was the ruler of a state of ten thousand chariots, so it was more difficult for him to become a recluse among the cliffs and caves than for a gentleman of commoner status. Although he never attained the Dao, it can be said that he cherished the intention to do so.
28.37 When Confucius found himself in difficulties between Chen and Cai, he went without proper cooked food for seven days and had only stewed pigweed greens without grain to eat. Though he looked most sad, he still went on playing the zither and singing in his quarters. As Yan Hui foraged for vegetables, Zilu and Zigong talked with him, "Our master has twice been driven from Lu, was made a fugitive in Wei, had a tree cut down because of him in Song, suffered distress while in Shang and Zhou, and surrounded between Chen and Cai.[15] It would be no crime for anyone to kill him, and there is nothing to prevent anyone from insulting him, yet he goes on playing and singing, plucking his zither without missing a note. Can a noble man really be as free from shame as this?"

28.38 At a loss for what to say, Yan Hui reported this to Confucius, who pushed aside his zither, sighed deeply, and said, "You [Zilu] and Si [Zigong] are such shallow and narrow-minded fellows! Summon them to me, for I would speak to them."
28.39 When Zilu and Zigong had entered, Zilu said, "Such a situation as this may really be called 'difficulties'!"
28.40 Confucius replied, "What kind of talk is this! As long as the noble man stays in step with the Dao, things may be said to go smoothly for him; it is when one deprives himself of the Dao that he may be said to be in 'difficulties.' Now, embracing the Dao of benevolence and righteousness, I may have encountered these troubles in this an age of disorder, but how can that be construed as 'difficulties'! Therefore, since examination of my inner self tells me I have not deprived myself of the Dao, when faced with difficulties, I don't lose its virtues. As it is when cold weather is at its worst and frost and snow fall that we notice how lush the pine and cypress are, so it is that this crisis between Chen and Cai is for me a blessing!"
28.41 As Confucius then leisurely returned to his zither to play and sing, Zilu energetically grabbed a shield and began to dance, and Zigong exclaimed, "I did not know how high Heaven rose or how far down Earth went!"
28.42 Those in antiquity who attained the Dao were happy whether in difficulties or when things went smoothly, for their happiness had nothing to do with difficulties or smooth going. When the Dao manifests its virtue in someone, difficulties and smooth going become nothing more than the sequence of cold and heat or wind and rain. As such, Xu You found Yang in Yin delightful[16] and Count Bo [Gongbo] found self-fulfillment on Head of Gong [Gongshou].[17]
28.43 Shun tried to yield rule of the whole world to his friend, Northerner No Choice [Beiren Wuze],[18] who replied, "What a strange man the ruler is! When he dwelt amidst farmers and fields, he wandered off to the gates of Yao! And he does not stop at just that but now goes on to defile me with his disgraceful behavior. I am ashamed that he even came to see me!" Consequently, he threw himself into the Pure and Cool Abyss [Qingling yuan].[19]

Confucius said, "Of those who aspire to perfect benevolence, some even sacrifice their lives in order to keep benevolence intact, but none ever seek to stay alive at the expense of benevolence."[20] On the one hand, was the aspiration to pure detachment and to keep his lofty character far from the vulgar world, while on the other, was the sacrifice of his life to greed of gain. Therefore, he chose to renounce the whole world.
28.44 When Tang was going to attack Jie, he tried to consult with Bian Sui about strategy, but Bian Sui said, "It is not my business."
28.45 Tang then said, "Who could do it?"
28.46 "I don't know."

28.47 Tang also tried to consult Wu Guang about strategy, but Wu Guang said, "It is not my business."
28.48. Tang then said, "Who could do it?"
28.49 "I don't know."
28.50 "What about Yi Yin?"
28.51 "He is strong-willed and can put up with disgrace. I know nothing else about him."[21]
28.52 So Tang consequently discussed strategy for attacking Jie with him, and when Jie had been destroyed, he tried to yield rule to Bian Sui, but Bian Sui said, "When Your Majesty was going to attack Jie, you wanted to consult me about it—so you must have thought then that I was a traitor, but after having vanquished Jie, you now want to yield rule to me—so you must now think that I am greedy. I have been born into an age of disorder, and, on top of that, someone who lacks the Dao now keeps coming to defile me with his disgraceful behavior. I can't bear to keep listening to him any longer." At that, he threw himself into the Chou River and drowned.[22]
28.53 Tang also tried to yield rule to Wu Guang, saying to him, "The wise man plots; the valiant man follows through on it; and the humane man presides over the peace—this is the Dao of the ancients. My good sir, why not take the position?"
28.54 Wu Guang replied, "To depose one's sovereign is not righteous, to slaughter common folk is not humane, and to inflict trouble on others and reap benefits for oneself at their expense is not honest. I have heard it said, 'If it is not righteous, don't accept a salary for it; if the world lacks the Dao, don't tread on its soil.' So how much the worse than this is your trying to honor me! I can't bear to look on you any longer." Thereupon, he tied a big stone on his back and drowned himself in the Lu River.[23]

An old saying has it that people such as Bian Sui and Wu Guang regarded the world as if it were outside the six directions [*liuhe*, phenomenal reality], as something which people could not subject to scrutiny. But this is a mistake. One who regards the world lightly can't find anything important in it, and if it has nothing important in it, no soil is worth dying for. It was just because they did regard the world as outside the six directions that it was right to entrust it to the care of Yao, Shun, Tang, and Wu, for, tranquil and utterly without ties and as if caught up in a current, they simply followed the mass will of the people. Success or failure was of absolutely no concern to them, so how could they have done anything such as throw themselves [in a river to drown]! But as for these two [Bian Sui and Wu Guang], they died in order to win a good reputation and because they would have their lofty behavior honored—so it can never be said that they put themselves outside the world.

28.55 Long ago, at the rise of the Zhou, there were two men who lived in Guzhu,[24] whose names were Bo Yi and Shu Qi.[25] In conversation with one another, it was said, "We have heard that out west there is a man who seems to possess the Dao, so let us go and see if we can observe that in him." When they reached the north side of Mount Qi [Qishan],[26] King Wu, hearing of them, sent Uncle Dan [Shu Dan][27] to meet and form a covenant with them, to the effect "They are to be bestowed emoluments of the second order and appointed to offices of the first rank." This was anointed with sacrificial blood and buried.

28.56 The two men looked at one another and laughed, saying, "Oh! How strange! This is not what we would call the Dao. Long ago, when Divine Farmer [Shennong] possessed the world, though his sacrifices were done with the utmost reverence, he did not sacrifice to obtain good fortune. As for his people, though he ruled them with the utmost loyalty and sincerity, he made no demands on them. He was delighted to share governance and administration with them. He neither tried to fulfill himself by ruining others, try to elevate himself by debasing others, nor try to gain advantage for himself when hard times were met. Now that the Zhou has seen the disorder of the Yin, it has made all haste to take over the government, conspiring with those above, bribing those below, and resorting to military force to ensure its might. It sacrifices animals and makes covenants to create trust, touts its deeds to curry favor with the masses, and goes to war in its pursuit of gain—all of which suppresses disorder and exchanges it for violence. We have heard that the men of antiquity, when they met with an age of good order, did not shirk their responsibilities, and when they encountered an age of disorder, did nothing untoward to survive. Now, with the whole world utterly benighted and the virtue of the Zhou in decline, rather than besmirch our persons by joining the Zhou, it would be better if we maintained the purity of our conduct by shunning it completely." The two masters then went north to Mount Shouyang,[28] where they endured hunger and died there [*si yan*]. The attitude of men such as Bo Yi and Shu Qi toward riches and honor was such that as long as they could refuse, they surely refused them. With their lofty integrity and eccentric behavior, their sole delight was the exercise of will—thus they refused to serve the world. Such was the moral integrity of these two men.

The *Analects* say that Bo Yi and Shu Qi suffered hunger below Mount Shouyang;[29] it does not speak of their deaths. However, here where it is says "died there" *si yan*, it does so just to make clear that they endured hunger for the rest of their lives; it does not necessarily mean they starved to death [*esi*]. The general idea of this chapter is to cite ways of life dedicated to lofty refusal and remote retirement. As such, those inclined to take on such a way, although they be corrupt and deceitful, ride the thoroughfares of the capital, and have access to the imperial palace, the time still comes for them when, struck by grief on reaching the midcourse of life, they have to sigh in regret—and how much more true this is for people in general! Therefore, men such as Bo Yi and Xu You, who had the wherewithal to be a Hou Ji or a Xie or be the match of Yi Yi or Lü Wang, though they dwelled in mountain ravines, were known throughout the world. And although not all of them became aides to sage rulers, were they not higher than those who allowed themselves be covered by the dust and dirt of the impure world! Although what they did was difficult to do, the way they lived presents few evils; thus accounts of them deserve transmission. But if one asks, wherein lies the evil that Bo Yi and Xu You represent, I would say that the evil presented by Xu You is such that it may cause people to feign refusal as a means to seek advancement, which may go so far as to exhaust them completely. The example of Bo Yi's way of life is such that it may cause brutal and tyrannical rulers to become so wanton with their cruelty that no one dare oppose them. The evil inherent in the example of Yi Yin and Lü Wang is such that it may embolden corrupt and deceitful adventurers all over the world to rebel and revolt. Only if sages leave no footprints behind would there be no such evil. If we take "Yi Yin" and "Lü Wang" to be the footprints left by these sages, then "Bo Yi" and "Shu Qi" also represent footprints left by those sages. But what if we don't accept that "Bo Yi" and "Shu Qi" represent footprints left by sages? If so, then accounts of "Yi Yin" and "Lü Wang" don't represent sages either. It was because actual sages just let people behave spontaneously [*zixing*] that no footprints were left behind. As such, whereas those called "sages" themselves actually left no footprints, people were determined to find their footprints anyway, and once they found the footprints, they contrived to give them the name "sages." This is how "sages" became a name for those who left no footprints.

Notes

1. Cf. 1.8.1–1.9.5, 6.38–6.45, 12.6–12.8.18, 24.51–24.61.
2. Cheng Xuanying states that he was surnamed Zi, his given name was Zhou, and his personal name was Zifu. Lu Deming, citing Li Yi, says that this same man was also known as Zhibo. *Zhuangzi jishi*, 4: 965.
3. Cf. 11.4.2.
4. According to Cheng Xuanying, his surname was Shan and given name Juan, which was information apparently provided earlier by Li Yi. *Zhuangzi jishi*, 4: 966.
5. Cheng Xuanying identifies King Danfu as the father of King Ji [Jili] and the grandfather of King Wen of Zhou. *Zhuangzi jishi*, 4: 967. Bin was the ancient site of the Zhou clan in Shaanxi. The Di were an ancient non-Han people who lived in the north and northwest.
6. Cheng Xuanying identifies Zihua as a worthy of the state of Wei, and Zhaoxi as the Marquis of Han. *Zhuangzi jishi*, 4: 969.
7. Cheng Xuanying: "The ruler of Lu was Duke Ai of Lu, though some sources say it was Duke Ding of Lu." *Zhuangzi jishi*, 4: 971.
8. Cf. 4.30.1 and 19.41.

9. Cheng Xuanying: "The state of Sui was located near the Pu River, out of which came precious pearls. It so happened that a numinous snake once repaid a kindness by carrying one up in its mouth, which was obtained by the Marquis of Sui." *Zhuangzi jishi*, 4: 972.
10. The same passage occurs, with some variants, in the *Liezi* (Sayings of Master Lie); *Liezi jishi*, 8: 244–45, and in the *Lüshi chunqiu* (Spring and Autumn Annals of Master Lü), 16: 403–4.
11. Cheng Xuanying identifies Ziyang as the prime minister of Zheng. *Zhuangzi jishi*, 4: 973. This is corroborated in other sources, including the *Shiji* of Sima Qian, where Ziyan's surname is given as Si and his death reported to have occurred in 398 BCE. It is also reported here that Si Ziyang's followers assassinated the current ruler, Duke Xu, two years later. See *Shiji*, 15: 711.
12. *Lüshi chunqiu*, 19: 531: "Ziyang was extreme in his fondness for severity. When [a retainer] committed an offense by breaking his bow, fearing that he would be condemned to death, he took advantage of a mad dog scare to kill Ziyang—all because he was so extreme."
13. Cheng Xuanying: "The 'three banners' [*sanqi*] signified the 'three dukes' [*sangong*], which were also called 'jade tablets' [*gui*], meaning the three state ministers [*sanqing*], who all hold jade tablets, which is why the three state ministers were referred to as 'jade tablets.'" *Zhuangzi jishi*, 4: 974.
14. According to Cheng Xuanying, Yuan Xian was a disciple of Confucius, whose surname was Yuan, given name was Si, and personal name was Xian. *Zhuangzi jishi*, 4: 975.
15. Cf. 6.7.8, 14.18.2, 20.15, 20.18, 20.24, 29.15, 29.17, and 31.19.
16. Cf. 1.8.
17. Cheng Xuanying: "Count of Bo, given name He and grandson of a Zhou king, cherished the Dao and embraced its virtue. He had Gong as his fiefdom. At the troubled times of King Li of Zhou [r. ca. 877–841 BCE] when the position of Son of Heaven went vacant, knowing that Count Bo of Gong was worthy, the feudal nobles invited him to become king. Though he tried to decline, his refusal was not accepted, and so he did become king. Fourteen years later, when such a great drought struck the whole world that peoples' houses were even catching fire, a diviner declared, 'This is due to the evil influence of King Li.' So Count Bo of Gong was deposed and King Xuan [son of King Li, r. 827–782 BCE] was installed in his stead. Count Bo of Gong then retired to whence he had come and supported himself back in his original district. When he was made king, it did not make him happy, and when he was deposed, he resented it not. He went on to enjoy spontaneous freedom on Mount Hillhead [Qiushou shan]." *Zhuangzi jishi*,4: 983. "Head of Gong' was apparently another name for Mount Hillhead [Qiushou shan], located within the count's fiefdom of Gong, in the present-day Hui county, Henan.
18. Sources argue whether *beiren* is an attribute of Wuze, "northerner" (Cheng Xuanying), or a two-character surname, "Beiren" (Yu Yue, citing the *Guangyun* [Expanded rhymes, compiled 1007–1008]. See *Zhuangzi jishi*, 4: 984–85.
19. According to Cheng Xuanying, Qingling yuan was located in the Tang era Xi'e district, Nanyang commandery (present-day Nanyang city, Henan). *Zhuangzi jishi*, 4: 985.
20. Cf. *Lunyu* (Analects), *Lunyu zhushu* (Analects, with commentary and subcommentary), 15: 2517b: "For men who so aspire, men of benevolence, whereas none would ever seek to stay alive at the expense of benevolence, some will even sacrifice themselves in order to keep benevolence intact."
21. Cheng Xuanying: "His surname was Yi, given name Yin and personal name Zhi; he was a worthy who greatly assisted [the early Shang rulers] in successive reigns." *Zhuangzi jishi*, 4: 985.

22. The Chou River is located in what was Yingchuan commandery (antiquity-Tang), in present-day central Henan.
23. Cheng Xuanying: "The Lu River [Lushui] was then located within the boundaries of Beiping commandery in Liaoxi [present-day northeastern Hebei]." *Zhuangzi jishi*, 4: 987.
24. According to Cheng Xuanying, Guzhu was a state situated west of the Liao River [Liaoxi], and Lu Deming states that it was located within the Tang-era boundaries of Lingzhi district, east of the Liao River [Liaodong] (in the vicinity of present-day Tangshan city, Hebei). *Zhuangzi jishi*, 4: 987.
25. Cf. 6.7.8, 8.6.6–8.6.7, 8.7.8, 17.1.2, 17.2.6, 28.56, and 29.17. The story of Bo Yi and Shu Qi is presented at greater length and in more detail in *Lüshi chunqiu* (Spring and Autumn Annals of Master Lü), 12: 267–69.
26. Mount Qi was the site of the ancient Zhou capital, near present-day Baoji 寶雞, in western Shaanxi.
27. This is the Duke of Zhou (personal name Dan), the fourth son of King Wen of Zhou and the younger brother of King Wu of Zhou.
28. Cheng Xuanying identifies Mount Shouyang with Mount Shou, located south of Puzhou city near the Yellow River. *Zhuangzi jishi*, 4: 989.
29. *Analects* [Lunyu], 15: 2522b. Cf. 6.7.8, 8.6.6–8.6.7, 8.7.8, 17.1.2, 28.55, and 29.17.

CHAPTER 29

DAO ZHI [ROBBER ZHI]

29.1 Confucius was a friend of Beneath Willows Ji [Liuxia Ji],[1] whose younger brother was known as Robber Zhi. Robber Zhi, who had nine thousand men in his gang, which rampaged throughout the world, invaded and harassed the feudal domains, bored holes into houses and broke down doors, rustled people's cattle and horses, and abducted their wives and daughters. He was so greedy that he had no thought for his kin, gave no consideration to his parents or brothers, and made no sacrifice to his ancestors. Whatever region he passed through, those of major states stood guard at city walls and those of lesser states took refuge behind town and village walls, while myriads of the common folk were made to suffer by him.
29.2 Confucius then addressed Liuxi Ji, "One who is a father must be able to guide his son; one who is an older brother must be able to instruct his younger brother. If a father fails to guide his son, or an older brother fails to instruct his younger brother, then the bonds of father and son or older brother and younger brother are held in disrespect. Now while you, sir, known in our age as a man of talent and distinction, your younger brother is Robber Zhi. Though he has become the scourge of the entire world, you fail to instruct him. I shall take upon myself your shame and shall go on your behalf to persuade him to mend his ways."
29.3 Liuxia Ji replied, "Sir, you say that a father must be able to guide his son and an older brother must be able to instruct his younger brother. But what if a son does not obey his father's guidance or a younger brother does not accept his older brother's instruction, no matter how you, sir, argue it,

what good would it ever do! Moreover, Zhi's character is such that his mind works like a gushing wellspring, his thoughts fly around like a whirlwind, and he is strong enough to withstand any enemy, and disputatious enough to gloss over any wrong that he commits. Only if you comply with the way he thinks, is he pleased, but if you thwart his wishes, he is angered. It bothers him not to insult others by what he says. Therefore, sir, you simply must not go to him."

29.4 But Confucius did not heed him, and, with Yan Hui as his driver and Zigong on his right, went to see Robber Zhi, who just then was resting his men on the south side of Mount Tai and where he was having a meal of chopped human liver. Confucius got down from his carriage, approached, and, when he saw the receptions officer, said, "I am Kong Qiu of Lu. Having heard of the general's lofty sense of righteousness, I would like to pay him my reverent respects with all due ceremony."

29.5 The receptions officer went in to report, and on hearing it, Robber Zhi flew into a rage. Eyes gleaming like bright stars and hair bristling so as to raise the cap off his head, he exclaimed, "Is this not the Kong Qiu of Lu, who is so clever at deceiving people? Tell him for me, 'You swindle with words and make up phony stories, absurdly citing King Wen and King Wu. Wearing a tree branch cap on your head and girdling your ribs with the hide of a dead ox, you go on and on with your misleading sayings. You feed yourself without plowing, clothe yourself without weaving, but just flap your lips and rattle your tongue, arbitrarily sprouting your own rights and wrongs in order to confuse rulers all over the world and prevent its learned men from recovering their original natures. You absurdly fabricate notions of filial obedience and fraternal duty in the hope that you will gain the patronage of some enfoeffed lord or some wealthy and eminent personage. Your crime is so great it should be punished by death, so be quick and go back where you came from, otherwise, I shall have your liver added to my midday meal!' "

29.6 Confucius then again had a message conveyed to him, "Since I have the good fortune to be on close terms with your older brother Ji, I hope I may look upon your shoe ties."[2]

29.7 When the receptions officer again conveyed this, Robber Zhi said, "Have him come to me."

29.8 The Master then hurried in, avoided the mat set out for him, stepped quickly back, and bowed twice to Robber Zhi, who, angered greatly, stretched out his two legs, placed his hand on his sword, and glared at him. Growling like a nursing tigress, he said, "Qiu, come near! If what you have to say suits how I think, you shall live, but if it would thwart the way I think, you shall die."

29.9 Confucius responded, "I have heard that for all in the world there are three virtues: To become so grand and tall and incomparably good looking that everyone, whether young or old, noble or lowly, takes delight in you—this is superior virtue. To have netted such knowledge of Heaven and Earth that one can win arguments about everything—this is middling virtue. To be so brave and ruthless, so resolute and daring that one may muster and lead a great band of warriors—this is inferior virtue. Anyone with even one of these virtues has enough in him to face south and call himself 'solitary one.' Now you, general, combine all these three: You are six feet two inches tall, have a bright, shining face, lips as red as vivid cinnabar, teeth like arrayed cowrie shells, and your voice is pitched correctly to the yellow bell scale—yet you are known just as 'Robber Zhi'! I shall take upon myself this shame of yours, general, which you don't accept. If you would deign to listen to me, please send me south as an emissary to Yue and Wu, north to Qi and Lu, east to Song and Wei, and west to Jin and Chu. I shall have them construct for you a great wall several hundred tricents long, inside which is established a city of several hundred thousand households, and have you, general, honored as a feudal lord. To share a new start with all under Heaven, you shall put an end to fighting and demobilize all your men. You shall accept and nourish your brothers and make acceptable sacrifices to your ancestors. This is what a sagely man of talent and distinction should do, and what everyone in the world desires."

29.10 Greatly angered, Robber Zhi replied, "Qiu, come near! Anyone who lets himself be admonished by the promise of gain or reformed by mere words means he must be a common fellow, both ignorant and simple-minded. Now, my grand and tall physique, which people are delighted to see, is a virtue inherited from my parents, so even if you had not praised me for it, how could I not have known it!

29.11 Moreover, I have heard that anyone good at praising someone to his face will also be good at maligning him behind his back. Now here you are, haranguing me with the promise of a great city wall and multitudes of people, admonishing me with the promise of gain and trying to train me as if I were some dumb animal—but how long could I ever manage to keep such things! As for great city walls, none may be longer than one around the whole world, yet after Yao and Shun possessed the whole world, their sons and grandsons had not even enough land to stick in an awl, and after Tang and Wu had been established as sons of heaven, their later generations were completely exterminated. Was this not all because what they had gained was so great!

29.12 Moreover, what I have also heard that in ancient times, birds and beasts were so many and humans were so few that people all made nests and lived in trees to avoid them. During the day they gathered acorns and chestnuts, and when evening came they perched up in trees, which is why they were given the name 'Folk of Sire Have-a-Nest [Youchao shi].'[3] Also in ancient times, people knew not to wear clothes, so in summer they gathered much firewood and in winter warmed themselves with it, which is why they were known as the 'Folk who Knew How to Live.' During the age of the Divine Farmer [Shennong], lying down, people calmly slept, arising, they were utterly content, and though they knew their mothers, knew not their fathers. They dwelt together with the elk and deer, had something to eat by tilling the soil, had something to wear by weaving cloth, but had no mind at all to harm one another—for this was the ultimate realization of perfect virtue. However, the Yellow Thearch failed to attain such virtue, for he fought with Chiyou in the countryside of Zhuolu, where blood ran for a hundred tricents.[4] Then Yao and Shun worked at creating crowds of officials, Tang exiled his ruler [King Jie of Xia], and King Wu killed Zhou [the last ruler of Shang]. From then on, the weak have been bullied by the strong and the few savaged by the many. Ever since Tang and Wu all such men have been nothing but troublemakers.

29.13 Now here you go cultivating the Dao of King Wen and King Wu, manipulating opinion all over the world, so you can become teacher to all generations to come; using your fine-stitched robe and broad-waist sash, deceitful words and hypocritical behavior, to confuse and mislead rulers all over the world, so you can get wealth and honor from them. Since no robber is worse than you, why does the whole world not call you Robber Qiu instead of calling me Robber Zhi?

29.14 You used honeyed words to gratify Zilu so to make him your follower, persuading him to get rid of his high-peaked cap, unbuckle his long sword, and accept instruction from you. Everyone in the world says that you can stop violence and prevent wrongdoing, yet Zilu ended up with his attempt to kill the ruler of Wey, which, when it failed, resulted in his body being made into pickled mincemeat atop the East Gate of Wey.[5] So your teaching him seems to have fallen short.

29.15 Do you call yourself a man of talent and distinction, a sage? Yet you have twice been driven from Lu, had to become a fugitive in Wei, was completely frustrated in Qi, and surrounded between Chen and Cai,[6] so there is no place in all the world where you fit in! It was your instructing Zilu that brought on his disaster of being pickled as mincemeat. Above it does you no good, while below it does no good for others, so how is your Dao worth anything!

29.16 Of those whom the world elevates, none is more elevated than the Yellow Thearch, yet even he, failing to bring his virtue to complete perfection, went to war in the countryside at Zhuolu, where blood ran for a hundred tricents. Yao lacked parental love; Shun lacked filial obedience; Yu paralyzed half his body; Tang exiled his ruler; King Wu killed Zhou; and King Wen was incarcerated in Youli.[7] Although these six men are all elevated by the world, careful scrutiny of them reveals that each allowed gain to muddle his authenticity, and each forced himself to act contrary to his fundamental nature; as such, their conduct was actually quite shameful.

29.17 Those whom the world extolls as worthy men include Bo Yi and Shu Qi. Bo Yi and Shu Qi both declined the rulership of Guzhu and instead died of starvation on Mount Shouyang, where their flesh and bones went unburied. Bao Jiao made of his conduct an adornment while he reviled the world, yet died clinging to a tree.[8] When Shentu Di remonstrated with his lord to no avail, bearing a stone on his back, he threw himself into the Yellow River, where he was devoured by fishes and turtles.[9] Qie Zitui, promoted ever since as the epitome of loyalty, cut flesh from his own thigh to feed Duke Wen, but, later when Duke Wen ignored him, he was so angered that he let himself be burned to death clinging to a tree.[10] Weisheng[11] had arranged a tryst with a girl under a bridge, but when she never showed up, even as the water rose he would not leave, so died with his arms wrapped around a bridge pillar. These six men all were no different from flayed dogs, pigs in river currents, or calabash-toting beggars,[12] for all of them suffered for the sake of fame and regarded death lightly, neither giving thought to fundamental nature nor attending to long life.

29.18 Of those whom the world extolls as loyal ministers, none is extolled more than Prince Bigan and Wu Zixu, yet Zixu was drowned in the Yangtze and Bigan had his heart cut out. The world may once have extolled these two men as loyal ministers, but in the end they were ridiculed by all under Heaven. Considering what happened to all these mentioned above down to Zixu and Bigan, absolutely none are worth anyone's esteem.

29.19 As for evidence you are using to persuade me, when you tell me about the doings of the demonic, I can't know anything about that, and when you tell me about the doings of men, if you have nothing more than this, I have heard it all already.

29.20 Now I am going to tell you about human inclinations. The eyes want to see colors, the ears to hear sounds, the mouth to experience flavors, and the will [*zhiqi*] to have fulfillment. Superior longevity for a man is one hundred years, middling longevity is eighty, and inferior longevity is but sixty. Excepting when one is being cured of illness, engaged with funerals, or suffering worry and distress, during all this time he might have no more than four or five days per month when he may open his mouth for a laugh. Heaven and Earth may last forever, but there is a time when a man dies. Since as a vessel subject to time he is but assigned a slot in eternity, his life passes as suddenly as the flash of a thoroughbred racing past a crack in a wall. Anyone who fails to gratify the aspirations of his will or neglects to nourish his longevity can't possibly be in step with the Dao.

29.21 Everything you have to say I reject it all, so make all haste to go away back where you came from and say no more! Your Dao is muddled and frenetic, a cunningly deceitful, hypocritical affair, and not at all useful for perfecting one's authenticity, so what good is there in saying any more about it!"

29.22 Confucius then bowed twice and quickly fled. As he passed through the gate and mounted his carriage, grabbing for the reins three times but failed, his eyes so vacant that he lost his sight. Face like dead ashes, he propped himself on the crossbar and lowered his head, unable to breathe. On returning as far as just outside the east gate of Lu, he happened to meet Liuxia Ji, who said, "Just now I have been uneasy not having seen you for several days, and your carriage and horses look like you have been traveling, so could it be that you have gone to see Zhi?"

29.23 Confucius looked up at the sky and said with a sigh, "Yes, I have."

29.24 Liuxia Ji then said, "Could it be that Zhi was completely opposed to the way you thought, just as I predicted?"

29.25 "Yes, just so. I thus may be said to have cauterized myself without being taken ill, since I scurried about the tiger's head to tease him trying to plait its whiskers—I just about did not escape the tiger's jaws!"

29.26 Zizhang[13] asked Filled with Ill-gotten Gain [Man Goude], "Why not act morally? If you act immorally, people don't trust you, and if they don't trust you, they won't employ you. If they don't employ you, you get no benefit. As such, looking at it in terms of reputation and calculating it in terms of benefit, righteousness is really the right way to behave. But even if you disregard reputation and benefit and just reflect on it in your mind, as far as the way a man ought to act, he should not for a single day fail to act morally!"

29.27 Filled with Ill-gotten Gain replied, "Those without shame are the wealthy, and those most trusted are the prominent. So great reputation and benefit seem to lie with the shameless and the trusted. As such, looking at it in terms of reputation and calculating it in terms of benefit, trust is really the right way to go. But even if you disregard reputation and benefit and just reflect on it in your mind, as far as the way a man ought to act, he should but embrace his natural endowment!"

29.28 Zizhang continued, "Long ago, Jie and Zhou were honored as the Son of Heaven and had the whole world as their wealth, but if nowadays you were to say to a petty thief that he behaved like Jie and Zhou, he would look ashamed and think he did not deserve such a charge—so they are despised even by such a petty man as that. Zhongni and Mo Di were as poor as ordinary fellows, yet if nowadays you were to say to a prime minister that he was like Zhongni and Mo Di, he would change countenance, look embarrassed, and declare he was not worthy—so they are sincerely honored even by such a senior minister as that. Therefore, though one be as powerful as the Son of Heaven, he won't necessarily he honored, and though one be as poor as an ordinary fellow, he won't necessarily be despised, for the difference between honor and disdain depends on whether one's behavior is good or bad."

29.29 Filled with Ill-gotten Gain responded, "Whereas a petty thief gets arrested, a great robber gets to be a feudal lord, yet it is below a feudal lord's gate that righteous men gather. Long ago, Xiaobai, Duke Huan, killed his older brother and grabbed his wife as his own, yet Guan Zhong became his minister. Cheng, Lord Cheng of Tian,[14] killed his ruler and stole his state, yet Confucius accepted largess from him. In discussion they despised them, but in practice they lowered themselves beneath them. As such, the emotional biases of word and deed fought one another in their breasts—and was that not, indeed, real conflict! Therefore, it is written, 'Who is bad and who good? He who succeeds is the head, and he who fails is the tail.' "

29.30 Zizhang then said, "If you act immorally, it will make normal relations fail between close and distant kin; distinctions between noble and lowly will become meaningless, and order between older and younger will break down. How then can the five consanguinity norms [*wuji*] and six social positions [*liuwei*]make their distinctions?"[15]

29.31 Filled with Ill-gotten Gain went on, "Yao killed his oldest son and Shun exiled his mother's younger brother—are there any normal relations between close and distant kin here? Tang exiled Jie and King Wu killed Zhou—is there any distinction between noble and lowly here? King Ji usurped the succession and the Duke of Zhou killed his older brother[16]—is there any order between older and younger here? The hypocritical pronouncements of the Confucians and the universal love of the Mohists, what have they to do with distinctions made by the five consanguinity norms and six social positions?

20.32 Moreover, you are just concerned with reputation, and I am just concerned with gain; both reputation and gain neither accord with principle nor comply with the Dao. The other day when you and I laid our dispute before Nothing Tied [Wuyue], he said, 'Whereas the petty man sacrifices himself for wealth, the noble man sacrifices himself for reputation. How they change their innate characters and alter their fundamental natures may differ, but in rejecting who they are and sacrificing themselves for what they are not they are one and the same.' Therefore, as it is said,

Be not a petty man but
Revert to your natural endowment.
Be not a noble man but
Follow the principles of the Natural.
Whether crooked or straight,
Be guided by your natural capacity limits.
Looking straight at the four directions,

Wax and wane in step with the times.
Whether right or wrong,
Hold fast to your capacity for perfect realization [*yuanji*],
Fulfill your intentions all by yourself,
Shifting and fluxing with the Dao.
Neither stick to the same course,[17]
Nor try to augment your sense of righteousness,
For that will violate who you are.
Neither scamper after your wealth,
Nor sacrifice yourself for your success,
For that is to abandon your natural endowment.

29.33 Bi Gan had his heart cut out and Xixu his eyes removed—such disasters were brought on by loyalty.[18] Body upright [Zhigong] bore witness against his father[19] and Weisheng drowned to death—such calamities were brought on by trust. Master Bao withered away standing up, and Master Shen did not take care of himself—such harm was brought on by integrity. Confucius failed to see his mother, and Master Kuang would not see his father[20]—such violations were brought on by righteousness. It was because of these accounts, handed down in earlier ages and discussed throughout later times, that men became so honest and outspoken in speech and so steadfast in behavior that they brought such disasters on themselves and suffered such calamities."

This passage explains that when one elevates conduct, it becomes false, and when one ennobles the man, the man becomes inauthentic. Therefore, it is by depreciating one's conduct and humbling one's person that one perfects his inner self, for only after that shall one's conduct really be elevated and person ennobled.

29.34 Never Satisfied [Wuzu] said to Knows Harmony [Zhihe], "People in general have never refrained from seeking reputation and pursuing gain. If someone else is rich, people gravitate to him, and, gravitating to him, they thus abase themselves to him. Abasing themselves to him, they thus honor him. To have people abase themselves before and honor you is the way one may prolong life, comfort the body, and delight the mind. But now you alone don't think this way at all. Is this because you don't know enough how to do it? Or because, though your mind can handle it, you just don't have the strength to bring it off? And is this why you never forget to promote rectitude?"

29.35 Knows Harmony replied, "Suppose your sort of man, comparing himself to those who live at the same time as he and dwell in the same district, decides he is a real cut above the common and a far better man than his contemporaries, and that he on his own needs no moral guide by which to

scrutinize ancient and modern times and distinguish between right and wrong, but just lets himself change along with popular custom. But the common folk of the world cast aside what should be most important and reject what should be most honored as they just go about doing what they do.[21] But is not this not far removed from what you would say is the best way to prolong life, comfort the body, and delight the mind! Whether it's bad health that makes you miserable and grieve or good health that makes you pleased and happy, you don't recognize that this is due to your body; whether it's fear that makes you alarmed and anxious or delight that makes you cheerful and content, you don't recognize that this is due to your mind. You may be aware of doing what you do, but you don't know why you act as you do. As such, though you be as noble as the Son of Heaven and though for wealth you possess the entire world, you still would not avoid disaster."

29.36 Never Satisfied continued, "There is nothing that wealth does for a man that is not of benefit to him. It allows him to enjoy both everything good and beautiful and have the greatest power and influence—all of which your 'Perfected one' has no chance to attain and which your 'worthy man' has no chance to reach. He can employ the courage and strength of skilled warriors and thus become powerful; he can utilize the ingenuity and resourcefulness of others and thus seem immensely perceptive; he can engage the virtues of others and thus appear worthy and good. Although he rules not over a state, he is as awesome as a monarch-father. Moreover, music and beautiful women, fine flavors, and power and influence, neither does the mind have to be educated about these to enjoy them nor does the body have to follow some model to find contentment in them. Desire and aversion, what to avoid and what to go after, one certainly needs no teacher here, for it they are innate to one's fundamental nature. Let every in the world think me wrong, yet who can give such things up!"

29.37 Knows Harmony answered, "The reason that a wise man acts is because he is moved to do so by the common folk, whose standards he never violate. As such, as long as he has enough, he strives not for more, and since he shuns conscious action, he seeks outcomes. Only if he has not enough does he strive for more, thus he might contend with all around him but does not consider himself greedy. Only if he has too much does he decline more, thus he might decline the entire world, but does not consider himself temperate. The essence of greed or temperance is not imposed from without but consists of standards found on reflecting within. Such a one may have the power to become Son of Heaven yet depends not on his nobility to lord it over others, may have enough wealth to equal the entire world yet relies not on that wealth to taunt others. If he calculates that something may bring disaster on him or determines that it may work against him, realizing it would harm his inborn nature, he will desist and have nothing to do with it—and not because he expects it to give him an honorable reputation. When Yao and Shun were emperors and harmony was the result, they did not treat the world with benevolence, for they would not let praise for that harm their lives. And when Shan Juan and Xu You had the chance to become emperors and they rejected it, their refusal was no pretense, for they would not let such matters harm themselves. All these sought benefit and rejected harm, and the whole world praised them as worthies because of it. Although it's right that they have such reputations, they themselves did not encourage it."

29.38 Never Satisfied then said, "The only way sure to maintain their reputations was to make their bodies suffer and give up everything pleasant, hanging on to life in the strictures of poverty. As such, they might as well have been people who, though long sick and in great danger, managed not to die."

29.39 Knows Harmony concluded, "An equitable amount means good fortune, but too much means harm. This is true for all things, but especially so for assets and property. Rich men nowadays, with the music of bells and drums, pipes and flutes played for their ears, and their mouths stuffed with the taste of flesh both of pastured and penned animals as well as mellow and sweet wines, by which their senses are so roused that they utterly neglect their affairs; this, one may call confusion. They swell up with such loaded pneuma, like people climbing a height with a heavy load on their backs; this, one may call suffering. Their greed for wealth sickens them, and their greed for power exhausts them. At leisure when home they just indulge themselves, and their bodies grow so fat they overload; this, one may call disease. They desire such wealth that they keep striving to gain more; thus things so overflow that they seem walled in, knowing not how to escape. No matter how overloaded they become, they won't desist; this, one may call disgraceful. Although wealth piles up of no use to them, they are so enraptured by it they won't give up. Although their minds fill with worry and vexation, they keep striving for more and won't stop; this, one may call real distress. At home, they dread thieves who might rob or wheedle from them; abroad they fear harm from bandits and brigands. At home, they surround themselves with defensive towers, and when abroad don't dare go alone; this, one may call terrifying. These six are the most harmful things that can befall one in all the world, yet people forget all about them and know not to take them into consideration. But when such harms do beset them, though they try their natures to the utmost and exhaust their entire wealth, they fail to get back even a single day free of trouble. Therefore, looking for fame won't find it, and striving for gain won't get it, yet entangling both mind and body, people contend for them—is this not delusion!"

This passage explains that one who knows contentment always has enough.

Notes

1. Cheng Xuanying: "His surname was Zhan, given name Qin, and personal name Ji. Since he was the feudal governor of Liuxia district [in Lu], he was known as Liuxia Ji. But it was also said that it was because he actually dwelled beneath a willow tree that he had Beneath Willows [Liuxia] for his sobriquet. Since Zhan Qin lived at the time of Duke Zhuang of Lu [r. 693–662 BCE], more than one hundred years earlier than the lifetime of Confucius, when it says that he was his friend indicates that this account is a fable." *Zhuangzi jishi*, 4: 990. Zhan Qin or Zhan Huo, a sage-official of the state of Lu, is better known by his posthumous title, "Liuxia the Benevolent" [Liuxia Hui], and is supposed to have lived from 720–621 BCE.
2. Although the general meaning of this is obvious (it is a humble request to see Robber Zhi), the exact meaning has been much argued. Cheng Xuanying has this to say about it: "Since he dares not look him directly in the face, he but hopes to step inside his doorway curtain [*mu*]. But 'doorway curtain' in some texts is also rendered with the character *qi* (footprints), that is *lüji* (footprints). Confucius thus hopes to look where Robber Zhi leaves his footprints; that is, he would look 'below his feet' [*zuxia*; i.e., below one's superior, second person honorific]." Sima Biao also reads *mu* as *qi*, but he takes *qi* to mean *lüjie* (shoe ties): "He would look upon his shoe ties before returning whence he came." *Zhuangzi jishi*, 4: 992–93.
3. This primordial culture hero, the inventor of houses and buildings, is also supposed to have been the ruler of a state called "Chao" (Nest).
4. Cheng Xuanying: "Chiyou waged war five times fighting with the Yellow Thearch; blood thus ran for a hundred tricents." As for where battles took place, Lu Deming quotes Sima Biao: "Zhuolu is a place name for a city that used to exist some eighty tricents southeast of Shanggu commandery." *Zhuangzi jishi*, 4: 995. The fourth-century Shanggu of Sima Biao's day was located in the vicinity of the present-day Huailai district in Hebei.
5. Cheng Xuanying: "Zhong You [Zilu] hated evil intensely, so he tried to kill Kuaikui, the ruler of Wey, and when this failed, his body was made into pickled mincemeat. Robber Zhi thus used this to ridicule him." *Zhuangzi jishi*, 4: 997. Kuaikui was the given name of Duke Zhuang of Wey; cf. 4.30–4.31.
6. Cf. 6.7.8, 14.18.2, 20.15, 20.18, 28.37, 28.40, 29.17, and 31.19.
7. Cheng Xuanying: "That is, Yao did not hand over rule of the world to his son Danzhu. . . . Shun was hated by his father. . . . In managing the flood, Yu labored so hard, raked by wind and soaked by rain, that he became paralyzed, half his body useless to him. . . . Youli was the name of the Yin [Shang] prison. When King Wen fell foul of King Zhou, he was incarcerated in that prison for seven years in all before he was released." *Zhuangzi jishi*, 4: 997.
8. Cheng Xuanying: "Surname Bao and given name Jiao, he was a hermit of the Zhou era, who made his conduct an adornment and kept close guard on his own integrity. He shouldered firewood that he gathered himself, and the acorns he picked satisfied his need to eat. As such, he neither had progeny nor behaved as a proper subject toward the Son of Heaven, nor was friendly to feudal lords. When Zigong met him, he addressed him thus, 'I have heard that you refuse to tread on land where you disapprove of its government and accept no benefit from its ruler whom you think corrupt. But now here you do tread on such land and rely on it for benefit. How can this be?' Bao Jiao replied, 'I have heard that a man of integrity takes his entrance seriously but regards his withdrawal easy to do, and that a worthy man easily feels shame and regards death lightly.' Then, clinging to a tree, he just stood there until he withered away." *Zhuangzi jishi*, 4: 998.

9. Cf. 6.7.8.
10. Cheng Xuanying: "When Duke Wen of Jin, that is Chong'er [his given name], encountered the Concubine Li uprising, he fled to another state. On the way things became so bad and provisions so depleted that Qie Zitui cut off flesh from his own thigh to feed him. However, three days after the duke returned to Jin and was rewarding his followers with fiefs, he forgot all about Zitui. Zitui consequently composed an 'Ode on the Dragon and Snake,' which he inscribed on the palace gate, and then, filled with anger, ran away. Then the duke, ashamed and apologetic, pursued him as far as Mount Jie, where Zitui was hiding. The duke had fires lit to set the mountain ablaze to smoke him out, but when the fire reached him, he just clung to a tree, where he let the fire burn him to death." *Zhuangzi jishi*, 4: 998.
11. Lu Deming notes that the "Wei" of "Weisheng" is written not only with the character meaning "tail," but also with one meaning "tiny, subtle." *Zhuangzi jishi*, 4: 999.
12. That is, none of these dies a natural death.
13. Cheng Xuanying: "Zizhang was a disciple of Confucius. His surname was Zhuansun and given name Shi." *Zhuangzi jishi*, 4: 1002.
14. Lord Cheng of Tian was Chen Heng. However, the character *heng* (perseverance) became taboo during the early Western Han because it occurred in the name of Liu Heng (203–157 BCE), Emperor Wen (r. 180–157 BCE). Lord Cheng of Tian was subsequently known through the ages by two alternative names, Cheng Heng and Chen Chang.
15. Cheng Xuanying: "The *wuji* [the five consanguinity norms] are grandfather, father, self, son, and grandson, but this term also means the five phases [*wuxing*], metal, wood, water, fire, and earth, or the five cardinal virtues [*wude*], benevolence, righteousness, propriety, wisdom, and trust. The *liuwei* [six social positions] are sovereign, subject, father, son, husband, and wife, or father, mother, older brother, younger brother, husband, and wife." *Zhuangzi jishi*,4: 1004.
16. Cheng Xuanying: "King Ji was Jili, a son of King Tai of Zhou by a concubine, the father of King Wen. Since Taibo and Zhongyong [sons of the primary wife] refused the kingship, the young boy Jili was declared a son of a primary wife [so he could become king]. Guan and Cai were the older brothers of the Duke of Zhou, who wept as he had them condemned to death [for rebellion], which is why the text states that he killed them." *Zhuangzi jishi*, 4: 1005.
17. "Stick to the same course" translates *wuzhuan er xing*. However, Cheng Xuanying reads *zhuan* (turn from, waver) as it stands, and also glosses *wu zhuanxing* (don't let your course waver) as *wu zhuanzhi* (don't let your intention waver), so the line for him seems to mean that one should be resolute in following the Dao. This interpretation links this line to the previous one and not to the following one, as the majority of commentators and translators tend to do. For this to work, *zhuan* (waver) must be read as a scribal error for *zhuan* (exclusive, single-minded, one and the same). The parallel structure of the two lines ("neither-nor" lines) argues for the latter reading. See *Zhuangzi jishi*, 4: 1006, and Wang Shumin, *Zhuangzi jiaoquan*, 1202, note 18.
18. Cheng Xuanying: "When Bi Gan loyally remonstrated with King Zhou, Zhou said, 'I have heard that the heart of a sage has nine apertures,' and he then had his heart cut out so he could look at it. When Zixu loyally remonstrated with King Fuchai [of Wu, warning him of the threat posed by Yue], Fuchai had him killed, before which Zixu declared, 'After I am dead, remove my eyes and hang them on the East Gate of Wu so I can see Wu's destruction by Yue.' " This came to pass ten years later. *Zhuangzi jishi*, 4: 1007.

19. Cheng Xuanying: "When Zhigong's father stole a sheep, he bore witness against him." *Zhuangzi jishi*, 4: 1007.
20. Cheng Xuanying: "Confucius was so obsessed with footprints left by the sages that he went from state to state seeking official employment, so when his mother was dying, he did not get to see her. As for Master Kuang, his surname was Kuang, given name Zhang, and he was a native of Qi. He upbraided his father, who rejected what he said. Hated by his father, he went off to live in another town, where obsessed with benevolence and righteousness, which he studied with no thought to return. Thus when his father was on the verge of death, he did not get to see him." *Zhuangzi jishi*, 4: 1007–8.
21. Cheng Xuanying: "The 'most important' is life, and the 'most honored' is the Dao. The common run of people harm life and reject the Dao, and since everything done by them is follows this path, they remove themselves far from the Dao of long life." *Zhuangzi jishi*, 4: 1009.

CHAPTER 30

SHUOJIAN [DISCOURSE ON SWORDS]

30.1 In years past, King Wen of Zhao[1] was so fond of swords that swordsmen crowded in at his gate and he himself kept more than three thousand as retainers. These men day and night fought duels before him, and, though this left more than a hundred dead and wounded per year, he never tired of it. As this went on for three years, since his state was going into decline, the other feudal nobles began to plot against him.

30.2 Crown Prince Kui, worried that this was leading to disaster, called together his own retainers and declared, "Whoever can dissuade the king from so carrying on with swordsmen, I shall bequeath to him a thousand pieces of gold." His retainers replied, "Master Zhuang should be able to do this."

30.3 The Crown Prince then dispatched emissaries to offer the gold to Master Zhuang, but though Master Zhuang would not accept it, he returned together with the emissaries to see the Crown Prince, to whom he said, "What instructions would you have me carry out for which you offer a thousand pieces of gold?"

30.4 The Crown Prince replied, "Hearing that you, Master, were a wise sage, I respectfully offered a thousand pieces of gold as a present to defray your entourage, but now that you, Master, won't accept it, how dare I say anything more!"

30.5. Master Zhuang then said, "I have heard that the purpose for which the Crown Prince wished to use me was to deter the king from something he is very fond of. If I am sent up there to dissuade the King, but this only arouses his displeasure, down here, having failed the Crown Prince, I should be punished by death—so what good would gold do me then! But if up there I managed to dissuade the King and down here thus met the Crown Prince's wishes, what in the whole state of Zhao would I ask for yet fail to get!"

30.6 The Crown Prince continued, "Just so, but those that Our King admits to his presence are none but swordsmen."

30.7 Master Zhuang replied, "That's not a problem, for I am skilled at swordsmanship."

30.8 The Crown Prince objected, "Nevertheless, the swordsmen Our King admits to his presence all have disheveled hair sticking out at the temples, caps that droop with cap bands of plain pattern, and jackets short in the back. Their eyes glare and their speech sounds rough, for all this pleases Him. Now if you, Master, insist on wearing Confucian garb to see the King, the whole affair will go all wrong."

30.9 Master Zhuang answered, "Please have swordsman's clothes prepared for me." Three days later when the swordsman's clothes had been prepared, he went again to see the Crown Prince, who took him to see the King, who was waiting for him with his bare sword unsheathed. When Master Zhuang entered the door to the palace, he took his time, and, catching sight of the King, did not bow. The King then addressed him, "What is it you have to instruct and admonish me, now that you had the Crown Prince provide you with an introduction?"

30.10 "I heard that you, Great King, were fond of swordsmanship, so I have come to present myself to you with my sword."

30.11 "How good are you with your sword at dispatching others?"

30.12 "My sword dispatches one man every ten paces, and without pause goes on as such for a thousand tricents."

30.13 Greatly delighted with him, the king declared, "There is no one to rival you in the whole world!"

30.14 Master Zhuang replied, "The way to wield a sword is to show your opponent an opening, start to give him an advantage, then make your move after his but get there first. May I have a chance to demonstrate this for you?"[2]

30.15 The King replied, "Master, go rest at your lodgings, there await my command, and once I have arranged the competitions, I shall invite you to them."

30.16 He then tested his swordsmen's ability, which left more than sixty killed or wounded and from which he selected five or six men. Once he had dispatched these with their swords to stand by below the steps to the palace, he summoned Master Zhuang there, to whom he said, "Today as a test I am having these men try their swords against you."

30.17 Master Zhuang replied, "I have long hoped for this."

30.18 The King then asked, "The weapon you usually use, how long is it?"

30.19 "Any one that I use will do, but since I have three swords, it is up to the King which is used. But please first allow me to describe them to you before I am tested."

30.20 Agreeing, the King said, "I want to hear about the three swords."

30.21 "I have a Son of Heaven Sword, a feudal lord sword, and a commoner sword."

30.22 The King asked, "What do you mean by a 'Son of Heaven sword'?"

30.23 "A 'Son of Heaven Sword' uses the Valley of Yan [Yanxi] and Stone Wall [Shicheng] as its point, Mount Dai in Qi [Qi Dai] as its blade edge, Jin and Wei as its spine, Zhou and Song as its guard, and Han and Wei as its hilt.[3] It is bound by the four barbarian folk, enveloped by the four seasons, skirted by the Bohai, and girdled by the Chang Mountains [Changshan].[4] It controls things with the five phases and judges with punishment and moral suasion. It initiates with the force of yin and yang, sustains with the power of spring and summer, and takes action [*xing*] with the strength of autumn and winter.[5] Such a sword thrust straight ahead finds nothing to block it, raised up finds nothing to stop it, thrust down finds nothing to resist it, and wielded side to side finds nothing to withstand it. Above it cleaves the floating clouds, and below it cuts the meridians of Earth. Once this sword is used, it instils loyalty in the feudal lords and makes all under heaven submit. Such is a sword of the Son of Heaven."

30.24 King Wen, stunned and utterly at a loss, asked, "What do you mean by a 'feudal lord sword'?"

30.25 "A feudal lord sword uses wise and brave men as its point, honest and incorruptible men as its blade edge, worthy and good men as its spine, loyal and sagely men as its guard, and heroic and bold men as its hilt. Such a sword thrust straight ahead also finds nothing to block it, raised up also finds nothing to stop it, thrust down also finds nothing to resist it, and wielded side to side also finds nothing to withstand it. Above, it emulates round Heaven and so complies with the sun, moon, and stars; below, it emulates square Earth and so complies with the four seasons; in between, it conforms with the aspirations of the common folk and so brings peace and security to the four corners of the realm. Once this sword is used, it shakes the earth like a clap of thunder, so that everywhere within the four borders, none fail to submit in allegiance and obey the ruler's commands. Such is a sword of a feudal lord."

30.26 The King then asked, "What do you mean by a 'commoner's sword'?"

30.27 "A commoner's sword has disheveled hair sticking out at the temples, a cap that droop with cap band of plain pattern, and a jacket short in the back. Its eyes glare and its speech sounds rough. It fights with others in one's presence, above it cuts off heads and below it severs liver and lungs. Such is a sword of a commoner. No different from a fighting cock, for in just one day its life may be cut short, thus it is of no use to the affairs of state. Now you, great King, though you hold the position of a Son of Heaven, yet enjoy the sword of a commoner. May I venture to suggest that you, great King, should scorn such a thing."

30.28 The King then led him up to the palace, where his chef set out a meal, but the king kept pacing around, which led Master Zhuang to address him, "Great King, sit down quietly and calm yourself, for my presentation about swordsmanship is finished."

30.29 Consequently, King Wen did not leave his palace for three months, and all his swordsmen took death as the way out where they lodged.

Notes

1. King Wen of Zhao ruled from 298 to 266 BCE.
2. Cheng Xuanying: "The way to wield a sword is to do so with the Dao; as such, unaware of self and with mind emptied, one integrates himself perfectly with this thing so sharp; thus, while his opponent reacts only after he makes a move, he perceives what the opponent will do before he does it. That was the way Master Zhuang wielded a sword." *Zhuangzi jishi*, 4: 1019.
3. Cheng Xuanying: "The Valley of Yan is located in the state of Yan, and Stone Wall is a mountain range beyond the Great Wall. Since both these sites are to the north, they serve as the point of the sword. Dai the [Eastern] Marchmount in the state of Qi is located to the east, which makes it the sword's blade edge. . . . The two states, Jin and Wei, border on Zhao, thus form the spine, and the two states, Zhou and Song, border on it to the south, thus are its guard. . . . The two states, Han and Wei are to the west, so they form the hilt." *Zhuangzi jishi*, 4: 1020–21.
4. Cheng Xuanying identifies the Chang Mountains [Changshan] as the Northern Marchmount [Beiyue], Mount Heng. *Zhuangzi jishi*, 4: 1021.
5. Cheng Xuanying: "Yin and yang initiate [*kaipi*], spring and summer sustain [*weichi*], and autumn and winter exercise severe and destructive powers [*susha*], for such is the Natural Dao." *Zhuangzi jishi*, 4: 1021.

CHAPTER 31

YUFU [THE OLD FISHERMAN]

31.1 When Confucius was wandering through Black Curtains Forest, he sat down for a rest at Apricot Terrace. There, as his disciples read, he accompanied himself on the zither and sang a song, and had not quite reached midpoint when a fisherman left his boat and approached. Beard and eyebrows brilliantly white, long hair hanging loose and sleeves flapping about, he came up the bank and when reaching dry land stopped, and there listened, resting his left hand on a knee and cupping his chin with his left hand. Once the song ended, he beckoned Zigong and Zilu, and the two came over to him.

31.2 The wayfarer pointed to Confucius and inquired, "Who might that fellow over there be?"

31.3 Zilu answered him, "A noble man from Lu."

31.4 Then when the wayfarer asked what clan his was, Zilu said, "He is of the clan Kong."

31.5 "This Kong clansman, how does he handle things?"

31.6 When Zilu did not respond, Zigong said, "Clansman Kong by nature is devoted to loyalty and honesty and exemplifies benevolence and righteousness. He enhances rites and music and differentiates social relationships. Above, he serves the present sovereign with loyalty; below, he dedicates himself to the moral transformation of the common folk. As such, he is going to be of benefit to everyone in the world. This is how clansman Kong handles things."

31.7 And he again asked , "Is he a ruler who has some territory?"

31.8 Zigong replied, "No."

31.9 "Is he the assistant to some marquis or king?"

31.10 Zigong replied, "No."

31.11 The wayfarer then laughed and turned back, saying as he walked away, "As benevolence goes, he may be benevolent, but I fear that won't spare him disaster. By such stress of mind and strain on his body he endangers his authenticity. Alas! How very far he has separated himself from the Dao!"

31.12 Zigong then went back and reported all this to Confucius, who then pushed his zither aside, rose to his feet, and declared, "This man surely is a sage!" He then went down to look for him, and on reaching the edge of the wetlands, found him about to take up his scull and guide the boat away. Seeing him on looking back, he turned around towards him. Confucius then retreated a short distance, bowed twice, and advanced up to him.

31.13 The wayfarer asked, "What do you want from me?"

31.14 Confucius replied, "A short time ago you, sir, made some suggestive remarks but then went away. Unworthy as I am, I failed to understand what you meant, and now deferentially wait in the hope that you would be so kind as to drop a few words that might, after all, assist me."

31.15 "Ah! How very keen you are to learn!"

31.16 Confucius then bowed twice, stood up straight, and said, "I have been studying since my youth, right up to now, my sixty-ninth year! But I have never succeeded in hearing the consummate teaching [*zhijiao*], so how could I now dare not humble myself with open mind before you!"

31.17 "Things of the same category follow one another, things with the same tonality resonate together.[1] This is a certain principle of nature. Please allow me to elucidate what I have and use this to design how you should engage with things.[2] What you engage in are human affairs. If the Son of Heaven, feudal lords, grand ministers, and common folk are allowed to govern themselves, that is government at its finest. But when these four fail to keep to their own positions, no disorder can be greater than that! When officials tend to their own duties and people just worry about their own affairs, no encroachment on what others do will occur. Therefore, fields lying barren, houses leaking, clothing and food insufficient, wives and concubines failing to get along together, and young and old failing to observe proper order—these are things that the common folk worry about. Not being equal to one's duties, not tending properly to official business, failing to be pure and honest, one's subordinates wasting time and being lazy, not having one's merit recognized, failure to have rank and emolument—these are things that grand ministers worry about. Lacking loyal domain officials, domain and great families beset by chaos and confusion, craftsmen and artisans ineptitude, inferior quality of tribute articles, tardiness to spring and autumn audiences, failing to comply with the son of heaven—these are things that feudal lords worry about. Yin and yang in discord, unseasonable cold and heat, which harm the common folk, feudal lords rebelling and replacing one another through usurpation, which devastate the general populace, rites and music out of order, resources found wanting, social relationships in disorder, debauchery among the common folk—these are things that the Son of Heaven worries about. Now you, sir, above neither have the power of a monarch or of feudal lord's position, nor below have the authority that goes with the office of a high official, yet you usurp the right not only to enhance rites and music but also to differentiate social relationships in order to effect the moral transformation of the common folk—are you not just too meddlesome!

31.18 Moreover, people are beset by eight flaws and human affairs are subject to four dangers, all of which we can't fail to examine. To involve yourself in matters not your own, this is called encroachment [*zong*]; to wheedle in where people are indifferent to you, this is called obsequiousness [*ning*]; to speak so to pander to another's wishes, this is called flattery [*chan*]; to speak up for another whether he is right or wrong, this is called sycophancy; to enjoy speaking of another's faults, this is called captiousness [*chan*]; to break up friendships and estrange relatives, this is called wickedness [*zei*]; to praise or deceive in order to damage others, this is called maliciousness [*te*]; to ignore the difference between good and evil but embrace both while feigning the right expression to get what you want, this is called treachery [*xian*]. These eight flaws externally disrupt the lives of others and internally harm one's self. The noble man does not befriend those that have them, and the enlightened ruler does not appoint such men to office either. What I mean by the four kinds of dangers are the following: To be so fond of managing great affairs as to change and modify things in order to help yourself to a good name, this is called cupidity [*dao*]; to arrogate duties by insisting that you alone know how, thereby misappropriating what belongs to others to your own use, this is called greed [*tan*]; to see your errors but not correct them and to hear rebuke but let them become even more severe, this is called obstinacy [*hen*]; to approve of others only if they agree with you and, if they disagree, even though they are good, denigrate them, this is called arrogance [*jin*]. As such, these are the four dangers. Once one is able to rid himself of these eight flaws and not behave in these four dangerous ways he may just then be open to instruction."

31.19 Confucius abashed, sighed, bowed twice, stood up straight, and said, "I have twice been driven from Lu, was made a fugitive in Wei, had a tree cut down because of me in Song, and surrounded between Chen and Cai, but know not what errors I committed that I should have met with these four occasions of vilification."[3]

31.20 The wayfarer, seemingly distressed, changed expression and said, "How very hard it is to get you to understand! There was a man who so feared his shadow and so hated his footprints that he tried to run away from them, but the more he raised his feet, the more footprints he left behind, and the quicker he ran, the closer the shadow stuck to him. Thinking he was still too slow, he ran ever faster without pausing to rest, used up all his strength, and died. He did not realize that he could lose his shadow by just remaining in the shade and put an end to his footprints by just remaining still—how very stupid was he! You, sir, scrutinize the scope of benevolence and righteousness, examine the edge between same and difference, carefully observe the alterations of activity and rest, comply with proper measures for receiving and giving, regulate inclinations to like and loathe, conform with the right times for delight or anger, yet you almost did not escape from such occasions! If you had assiduously cultivated your own person, carefully guarded your own authenticity, and turned things over to others, you would not have brought such trouble on yourself! But even now you fail to cultivate your own person but seek to have others do it—is this not getting involved with external matters!"

31.21 Confucius, abashed, then asked, "May I presume to inquire what you mean by 'authenticity'?"

31.22 "Authenticity is the perfect realization of pure sincerity [*jingcheng*]. If neither pure nor sincere, one can't affect others. Thus it is, when one forces himself to sob, though he may seem grieved, is not sad; when one forces anger, though he may seem stern, is not imposing; when one forces affection, though he smiles, is not in accord. It is one who feels authentic grief, who, though silent, is really sad; it is one who feels authentic anger, who, though he shows it not, is really imposing; it is one who feels authentic affection, who, though he smiles not, is really in accord. If one has authenticity within, his spirit is sure to have affective power without, which is why authenticity is venerated. Its efficacy for the principles of human relationships is such that, in serving parents, it creates loving care between children and parents, in serving one's sovereign, it creates loyalty and steadfastness; in wine drinking, it creates merriment and joy; in mourning, it creates grief and sorrow. For loyalty and steadfastness, merit is most important; for wine drinking, joy is most important; for mourning, sorrow is most important; for serving parents, submission [*shi*] is most important. For meritorious achievement at its finest, one need not follow one and the same footsteps. If one serves one's parents with submission, it matters not how it is done. If one does wine drinking with joy, one need not choose particular vessels for it. If one mourns with sorrow, it matters not what ritual is used. Whereas ritual is the product of popular custom, authenticity is endowed by the Natural, and being natural itself, may not be altered. This is why sages emulate the Natural, venerate authenticity, and are bound not by popular custom. Since the stupid get this backwards, neither can they emulate the Natural nor succor others. Since they know not to venerate authenticity and slavishly subject themselves to the vagaries of custom, they are inadequate. What a pity that you sank so young into human hypocrisy and came so late to hear about the great Dao!"

31.23 Confucius again bowed twice, stood up straight, and said, "That I had the chance to meet you today seems a blessing from Heaven. If, sir, you would not be too embarrassed to include me among your servitors and teach me personally, may I presume to inquire where your lodgings may be found? I beg this thereby I may receive your instruction and at last learn about the great Dao."

31.24 The wayfarer replied, "I have heard it said, if it is someone fitting to go with, go with him, even unto the marvelous Dao, but if it is not someone fitting to go with, someone ignorant of the way there, take care not to go with him, for then no disaster will befall you. Sir, make you every effort! Now I have to leave you. Now I have to leave you." Accordingly, he sculled his boat away, guiding it through the green reeds.

31.25 Though Yan Yuan had turned the carriage around and Zilu held out the carriage strap to him, Confucius paid no heed but waited there by the water for the ripples to subside, and only when he no longer heard the sound of the scull did he venture to climb on board.

31.26 Walking beside the carriage, Zilu addressed him, "For as long as I have had the chance to serve you, Master, I have never seen you on meeting someone become so awestruck as this. When rulers of ten thousand chariots and sovereigns of a thousand chariots meet you, master, they never fail to share their courts with you and treat you with the ceremony of an equal, yet you still have a haughty expression for them. But now, when this old fisherman stood across from you with scull in hand, you bent your waist like a sharp-angled stone chime and as he spoke kept responding to him with bows—is this not rather going too far? Since all your disciples now find your behavior so strange, how was it that the old fisherman could get you to behave so?"

31.27 Leaning over the carriage crossbar, Confucius sighed and said, "How very hard it is to enlighten you! You may have immersed yourself in ritual and righteousness for such a long time but still fail to rid yourself of a blunt and mean-spirited mind. Come closer and I shall tell you: To meet an elder and fail to treat him with respect violates propriety; to meet a worthy and fail to honor him shows lack of benevolence. If someone were not a Perfected one, he would fail to make others feel humble before him, but if one so humbled were not pure, he would fail to realize his authenticity, and, as such, would long bring harm on himself. What a pity! No greater disaster can befall anyone than to lack benevolence, yet you alone insist it is all right for you. Moreover, since the Dao is the source of all things, whereas those

that lose it die, those that attain it live. Whereas to go against it when handling affairs results in failure, to comply with it results in success. Therefore, wherever the Dao resides, the sage venerates it. Now, in regard to the Dao, the old fisherman may be said to possess it, so how dare I not treat him with respect!"

This chapter tells how one who achieves leisure without rivers and lakes can humble himself before a man of the rivers and lakes.[4] As for Confucius's taking things as they came [*fangren*], how could this have only been so for the old fisherman? Flowing everywhere in all directions, he was universal in scope, which even included creepy crawly things, for everything got his complete concern. Moreover, he was ready to give his life to investigate principles to the utmost. As such, this was how he cultivated the Dao of the Perfected one.

Notes

1. Cf. *Yijing* (Classic of Changes), *Wenyan* (Commentary on the words of the text) to Qian (Pure Yang, hexagram 1): "The Master says: 'Things with the same tonality resonate together; things with the same material force [*pneuma*] seek out one another. Water flows to where it is wet; fire goes to where it is dry. Clouds follow the dragon; wind follows the tiger. The sage bestirs himself, and all creatures look to him. What is rooted in Heaven draws close to what is above; what is rooted in Earth draws close to what is below. Thus each thing follows its own kind." Richard John Lynn, *The Classic of Changes*, 137.
2. Cheng Xuanying: "The tiger roars thus the wind quickens; the dragon soars thus clouds spread. Since natural principles are involved, this is certain to be so! Therefore, the old fisherman, as a great sage, may elucidate the perfect Dao to Confucius, for such a sage and such a worthy interact with each other with 'the same tonality' and so 'resonate together.' As such, he elucidates the otherworldly Dao, which he has attained, and uses this to design how Confucius should go about his worldly enterprise." *Zhuangzi jishi*, 4: 1028.
3. Cf. 14.18.3 and 20:18.
4. Cf. 15.2.1.

CHAPTER 32

LIE YUKOU

32.1 As Lie Yukou [Master Lie] was on his way to Qi, but when he turned back halfway there, he happened to meet Elder Muddled Dim to Others [Bohun Wuren],[1] who asked, "Why do you turn back?"

32.2 "I became alarmed."

32.3 "What made you alarmed?"

32.4.1 "By the time I had eaten at ten congee vendors,

This means at places where congee was sold.

32.4.2 at five of them I was served first."

He said this is what alarmed him.

32.5 Elder Muddled Dim to Others then asked, "Since this is what happened, why did it alarm you?"

32.6.1 "If one fails to free himself from an appearance of inner sincerity,

The external self appears to boast of it.[2]

32.6.2 detected in one's physical appearance, it gives one a splendid appearance,

He behaves as if he were pandering to others, which gives him a splendid appearance.

32.6.3 and if by that outer appearance, one so dominates the minds of others

That is, if one lacks enough inner resources to gain the submission of others.

32.6.4 that it makes them no longer care about venerating their elders,

When the domination of others springs from one's inner resources, it makes them venerate their elders with profound feeling.

32.6.5 one thus gets crushed by such calamity that ensues.

This means that if one uses a fine appearance to influence others, it will be the cause of disastrous confusion.

32.6.6 Since congee vendors have only congee as fare for customers, their margins are not much and profits are meager. As such, though their authority is insignificant, they yet treat me this way!

With authority so insignificant and profits so meager, how could they but try to prevail upon me for something.

32.6.7 So how much more true would this be for the ruler of a myriad chariot state! For body worn out for his state and knowledge exhausted by affairs, he would burden me with those affairs and charge me with getting them done. And that is why I became alarmed."

32.7 Elder Muddled Dim to Others then said, "Excellent, indeed, how you look at it! But as long as you dwell in your self, people will fasten on to you!"

If one fails to put all physical existence out of mind, wherever he might be, he shall have people fasten on to him. "Fasten on to" [*shou*] means gather and fasten on to [*jushou*].

32.8 A short time later, when he went to visit him and found shoes filling the space outside his door, Elder Muddled Dim to Others just stood there facing north, staff fixed upright and jaw propped on it. After standing awhile, he went away without a word.

32.9 When his porter reported this to Master Lie, carrying his shoes and running after him barefoot, exclaimed, "Master, since you came, had you not a prescription for me?"

32.10.1 "Be done with it! I tried to tell you that people would fasten on to you, and, just as I said, they have fastened on to you. It's not that you can make people fasten on to you, but that you cannot make people not fasten on to you.

If one gives himself over to equanimity and just lets transformation happen, no stirring of others will occur and no one will come to him for help. As such, people won't fasten on.

32.10.2 What use is it to you to stir up people beforehand so that you appear extraordinary!

He prematurely bestowed kindness on people, but as such kindness depended not on them, bringing it out beforehand was extraordinary.

32.10.3 Since they are sure to have a response, this agitates your own fundamental nature—and nothing more need be said of that!

Since he is sure that they will respond, his own fundamental nature is provoked into agitation.

32.10.4 Those who associate with you
won't go on to tell you this,
But their petty words are all poison for you.

None of them understand, none aware,
so who among them may do for you!

Fastidiousness and ingenuity enter one as such petty words.

32.10.5 The clever wear out and the learned grow sad,
But the utterly inept has nothing to seek,
So just eats his fill and ambles about,
Drifting like an untethered boat,
Vacantly wending to and fro."

One who stays free from such skills can be only a sage. Beyond such a one right down to the "insects," there is not a one who, utterly unselfconscious of his skills, just lets everyone be.[3]

32.11.1 When Mitigate [Huan][4] of the state of Zheng recited his lessons [*shen-yin*] in the land of the Fur Coat Clan [Qiushi],

Shenyin (wail, groan) here means "chant."

32.11.2 it only [*zhi*] took three years for him to become a Confucian.

Zhi (only, merely) means the same as "just" [*shi*].

32.11.3 As the Yellow River spreads its enriching moisture for nine tricents, his blessings extended to his three consanguinity clans. He made his younger brother into a Mohist, and when as Confucian and Mohist they debated, their father sided with Pheasant [Di].

"Pheasant" [Di] was the name of Mitigate's younger brother.[5]

32.11.4 Ten years later when Mitigate took his own life, his father dreamt that he said to him, "Since I was the one who made your son a Mohist, why don't you take a look at my grave, where I have been making cypress cones?"

It was because Mitigate was so chagrined with his father for siding with his younger brother that he was moved to take his own life. So after he died and appeared in the dream, it meant that having been able to make himself into a Confucian, he also transformed his younger brother into a Mohist. Although he was the one who transformed his younger brother, his younger brother could yield to him. He was thus such a good teacher that it led to the chagrin that took his life, and his ultimate achievement of finest sincerity resulted in his making cypress cones.

32.12.1 When the Creator [*zaowuzhe*] rewards man, it does not reward what is due to the man but rewards what is due to the man's natural endowment.

From here on, we have the words of Master Zhuang. Reward for what is accomplished by accumulated practice is due to one's fundamental nature and not due to conscious effort. As such, the accomplishments of study are achieved exclusively by one's fundamental nature—how could they ever be achieved by conscious effort![6]

32.12.2 It was because of who he was that allowed him to become that.

Since he [Pheasant] had that fundamental nature of his, this allowed him to become thoroughly proficient at that [Mohism].[7]

32.12.3 Here, a man thought he had something that differentiated him from others, and because of that despised his father.

According to the text, Mitigate praised himself for his Ruism, claiming that it was an accomplishment of accumulated study, not realizing that it was actually the natural bent of his fundamental nature. Based on this accomplishment, he despised others and did not spare even his father. If he had been one who had done away with his self and thus set forth with equanimity, he would have not allowed esteem or contempt to violate proper human relationships.

32.12.4 Given that when people tried to drink at the Qi people's well and were pulled away,[8] I thus say that in the world of today, everyone is a Mitigate.

It is by sinking a well that one accesses a spring. It is by recitation that one accesses fundamental nature. If no spring existed, there would be no reason to sink a well. If fundamental nature did not exist, there would be no reason to recite, yet everyone in the world forgets that springs and fundamental natures are natural and only recognize the minor accomplishments of sinking and reciting, which they brag to have had—is not this absurd!

32.12.5 Therefore, since a person of virtue regarded this as ignorance, how much more so would one who had attained the Dao!

That he saw that Mitigate was all wrong about what he thought he had learned was because his father could spontaneously just know it—because he was acting unselfconsciously at the time.

32.12.6 The ancients referred to this as punishment befitting one who tries to evade Heaven.

To regard abilities determined by one's natural endowment as one's personal accomplishments is to try to evade Heaven. As such, this brings such a one punishment.

32.13.1 The sage is content with what contents him and tries not to find contentment in what does not content him.

The sage is neither contented nor discontented, for he just complies with the mind of ordinary folk.

32.13.2 The ordinary man tries to find contentment in what does not content him and is discontent with what contents him.

What constitutes contentment differs from person to person, for that is the way ordinary people are.[9]

32.14 Master Zhuang said, "To know the Dao is easy, but to refrain from speaking of it is hard. Whereas to know and yet not speak of it is to be with Heaven, to know and speak of it is to be with man. Men of antiquity were with Heaven and were not with man."

Even if one knew everything in all Heaven and Earth, he could never cite anything to define it; all one can do is resonate with it to the full extent of his capacity.

32.15 When Red Overflow [Zhu Pingman] learned how to butcher dragons from Dissect for Profit [Zhili Yi], he paid for it with a thousand pieces of gold, the entire family fortune. It took him three years to perfect his technique, but then no one had any use for his skill.

The value of a business lies in its suitability, which is utterly lacking in such an esoteric accomplishment.

32.16.1 The sage looks on certainties as uncertainties, which is why he resorts not to arms.

Even though in principle [*li*] something is certain, he still regards it as uncertain, which indicates perfect compliance [*zhishun*]—so where is the need for arms here!

32.16.2 But everyone in general regards what is uncertain as certain, which is why they often resort to arms.

Even though in principle something is not quite certain, they still regard it as certain, and it is because each regards his views as certain that conflicts arise.

32.16.3 And because they comply with the course of arms, their actions tend to be inherently covetous.

If people always complied with their natures, they would be content, and, being content, would covet nothing.

32.16.4 Those who rely on arms perish.

One who rules dispassionately [*tiandan*] and so "uses them only when there is no choice" never perishes.[10]

32.17.1 What the petty man knows is nothing more than packages and missives.

Packages are used for gifts and missives are used to convey respects; to these instruments of giving gifts and conveying respects petty knowledge is sacrificed.

32.17.2 Though he wears out his essential spirit in mean and superficial matters,

Since he only muddles through petty duties, what he achieves is insignificant.

32.17.3 he wants to lead people to universal relief, devoid of physical existence and at one with the great unity. As such, utterly baffled by space and time, he burdens himself physically without ever getting to know the great source of all things.

Though he has only the intelligence of the petty man, he wants to lead people to universal relief. Traversing nothingness and engaging great distances, his ambitions are so great that his spirit is worn out. Body thus burdened, he becomes so baffled and is utterly lost to the truth.

32.17.4 But as for the Perfected one, he returns his spirit to that which has no beginning and happily merges himself arcanely with the land of nothing at all, flowing like water into formlessness, draining away into great purity.

Quiescently, such a one acts unselfconsciously, thus allowing himself to move in step with Heaven.

32.17.5 How very sad! You exercise your intelligence only with the merest trifles,

What he achieves with his intelligence are but trifles.

32.17.6 thus know not great serenity!

It is by allowing one's fundamental nature great serenity that one may so arrive.

32.18 Among the men of Song there was Cao Shang, who was sent by the King of Song[11] as an emissary to Qin. When he set forth, he received several carriages, but the king there was so pleased with him that he added on a hundred more carriages. After he returned to Song, he went to see Master Zhuang and said to him, "To dwell in a poor, narrow lane or miserable alley, living poverty-stricken in pleated sandals, with scrawny neck and sallow complexion, I am not good at that at all. But to be given a hundred carriages by just getting the ruler of a myriad chariots to realize one thing, that's what I am good at."

Only by humbly serving below does one achieve lofty goals. It is only by achieving lofty goals that emolument increases. As such, the lofty and broad, the serene and content, have no thought for honor and glory.

32.19 Master Zhuang replied, "When the king of Qin falls ill, he summons a physician, who, if he lances a boil successfully, is rewarded with one carriage; if one licks his piles, he is rewarded with five carriages—the more demeaning the service, the more carriages is the reward. How did you, sir, treat his piles? How did you get so many carriages? Sir, get you gone!"

32.20 Duke Ai of Lu asked Yan He, "Were I to make Zhongni [Confucius] the constant trunk of human affairs [zhengan],[12] would my state be healed?"

32.21.1 "Beware [*ji*]! Danger lies with Zhongni!

"Beware" [*ji*] means "danger" [*wei*]. A Perfected one brings about safety and security by ensuring the tranquility of the common folk. But as soon as such a one becomes a "constant trunk of human affairs," he leaves his noble footprints for future myriads of generations to follow, causing people to vie one with the other to adorn themselves with benevolence and righteousness—carving and painting feathers already naturally colorful.[13] Not only will the common folk be put in danger, Perfected ones also will have no way to provide safety and security.

32.21.2 For it will come to pass [*fangqie*] that people will embellish feathers by painting them,

In general when the expression *fangqie* is used, it always indicates people of later generations, who, embellishing and painting, abide not by their authenticity.

32.21.3 conduct affairs with florid, empty rhetoric, and perversely distort meaning,

He will make those who conduct human affairs in later generations do so falsely and render the way they think perverse.

32.21.4 suppress their fundamental natures in overseeing the common folk, and not even realize they are not being honest.

Rulers of later generations will so admire long-lasting paths laid down by Zhongni that they will suppress their fundamental natures, distort themselves, and use deception and falsehood to preside over the common folk. Superiors and subordinates will emulate such practices and not even know they are doing it.

32.21.5 Since they would thus receive him [Confucius] in mind and let him take charge of their spirits, what good would that be for rulers!

If you now place him in charge of the people, later generations of common folk will not just follow him in body, but also will let him into their minds and let him take over. As such, they become no longer capable of finding self-fulfillment in their own natural embodiments.

32.21.6 Does what suits them suit you?

"They" [*bi*] are the common folk. "You" [*ru*] is Duke Ai. There is that which suits just them and there is that which just suits you, so if you and they copy each other, all lose authenticity—something already verified.[14]

32.21.7 Will you yourself be nourished?

Copying them is not the way to nourish yourself.[15]

32.21.8 Such error is certainly possible.

It can't possibly be the right thing to do[16]

32.21.9 Now, if this makes common folk abandon their authentic selves and instead emulate false ways, this is not the right way to oversee them. Since this leads to the disquiet of later generations, it would be better to stop it,

It is clear that he does not refer to the present age.

32.21.10 for it would make rule impossible."

Rule accords not with falsehood, which is why the sage does not rule this way.[17]

32.22.1 Failing to be unmindful that one provides for people is not the way Heaven spreads its blessings.

As long as one remains aware that he spreads blessings, this does not treat the myriad folk like straw dogs.[18]

32.22.2 Even merchants don't join such ranks.

How much more true for the noble man!

32.22.3 Though because of duties one must join such ranks, in spirit one does not.

If one can provide blessings and because of duties cannot but join such ranks, while one is not unmindful of it, the mind should disregard it. This is the everyday attitude of people in general.

32.23.1 For external punishment there is metal and wood.

"Metal" refers to cutters, saws, and the executioner's axe; "wood" refers to flogging sticks and wooden shackles.

32.23.2 For internal punishment there is agitation and sense of error.

As long as one remains tranquil and behaves properly, neither externally nor internally shall punishment befall him.

32.23.3 When a night prowler is subject to external punishment, metal and wood interrogate him.

One not touched by the light of day is a night prowler.

32.23.4 One subject to punishment internally has yin and yang gnaw at him.

When agitation drives one to exceed his allotted place in life, nature-pneuma [*xingqi*] is harmed internally, as metal and wood interrogate his external person.

32.23.5 As for avoiding both external and internal punishment, only the authentic man can do this.

As long as one is not an authentic man, who can stay within the limits of his allotted place in life, he is sure to suffer punishment both externally and internally—just don't ask how much.

32.24.1 Confucius said, "The minds of men in general are more dangerous than mountains or rivers and more difficult to know than Heaven. Whereas Heaven has its seasons of spring, summer, autumn, winter and times of sunrise and sunset, as for man, he keeps his face under thick wraps and his disposition deep inside. Therefore, he may seem honest and respectful yet be conceited and self-satisfied, seem capable yet be unworthy, seem at a loss yet be thoroughly proficient, seem determined yet be lazy, or seem slack yet be intense.

That is, man's disposition and appearance are as contradictory as this.

32.24.2 As such, though he may go to righteousness as if he thirsted for it, he flees from it as if it burned him.

Though one may be hard to know, he still never fails to leave footsteps behind.

32.24.3 Therefore, for the noble man, send him on a distant mission to see how loyal he is, dispatch him near at hand to see how respectful he is, burden him with troubles to see how capable he is, ask him suddenly about something to see how knowledgeable he is, set an urgent deadline for him to see how reliable he is, entrust him with funds to see how benevolent he is with them, tell him he is in danger to see how much integrity he has, get him drunk on wine to see how well he conducts himself, and involve him in mixed company to see how he handles attraction to women. With the application of these nine tests the unworthy man will be caught out.

Whereas the noble man is easily discerned, the unworthy man is hard to identify. However, once one sees how someone handles himself, sees what his motives are, spies out what makes him content, sees what path he has taken, he may well be known.

32.25.1 As for Zheng Kaofu,[19]

> **Receiving his first appointment, he bowed,**
> **Receiving his second appointment, he hunched over,**
> **Receiving his third appointment, he bent way down**
> **And departed, clinging to a wall.**
> **Who would dare not follow his example!**

That is, one would not dare fail to humble himself by following his example.

32.25.2 But if it's an ordinary man [*erfu*],

> **Receiving his first appointment, he becomes arrogant and conceited,**
> **Receiving his second appointment, he dances about in his carriage,**
> **Receiving his third appointment, he has people call him "Regal Uncle."**
> **So which one of these behaves like Tang or Xu!**

Erfu means an ordinary man. Tang refers to Yao, and Xu refers to Xu You. This line means, of the ordinary man and Kaofu, who it is that behaves like Tang and Xu?

32.26.1 There is no greater affliction than virtue deliberately undertaken.

When one does something virtuous with conscious deliberation, it is not true virtue. True virtue suddenly occurs all by itself, unaware that it is virtuous.

32.26.2 But suppose the mind has eyelashes,

If the mind is commanded to do something virtuous, it might seem able to do so. But when the mind is directed to look itself right in the eyebrows and eyelashes,[20] inauthenticity has already reached an extreme.

32.26.3 when it has eyelashes and so looks within oneself, one such look inward and failure occurs.

Once one tries an exploratory shot into its arcane darkness and tries to use its depths to undertake something, both mind and undertaking fail.

32.26.4 There are five kinds of evil virtue, foremost of which is "endogenous virtue" [*zhongde*].What is meant by "endogenous virtue"? One who practices endogenous virtue thinks himself good and vilifies [*bi*] anyone who doesn't practice his kind of virtue.

Bi means "vilify" [*zi*]. When one considers oneself right and others wrong, it won't be just one whom such a one attacks, which is why this is the foremost of evils. But if one is free of the tendency to think himself good, such a one accedes to what is right for the myriad folk, and, when no one has to give up what seems right to himself, everyone in the whole world will want to support him [such a ruler].

32.27.1 Misery involves eight extremes; success involves three necessities; punishment involves the six repositories. Beauty, fine beard, tall height, great stature, sturdiness, elegance, bravery, and daring, when one has more of all these eight than do others, they bring him misery.

Misery comes from being saddled with responsibilities. However, it never happens in all the world that misery comes from being deficient in these qualities—one always brings distress on oneself by having a surplus of them.

32.27.2 Be a hanger-on [*yuanxun*], bow and scrape [*yanyang*], and be timid [*kunwei*]—as if inferior to others—these three all bring complete success.

A "hanger-on" [*yuanxun*] is someone who progresses by using others as his walking sticks;[21] one who "bows and scrapes" [*yanyang*] is unable to handle things easily himself; to be timid [*kunwei*] is to cringe. People marked in these three ways may not be entrusted with responsibilities and so, attached as assistants to others, are sure to enjoy success.

32.27.3 But knowledge and intelligence get one involved in the external world;

If engaged externally, they do infinite harm to one's inner self.

32.27.4 acts of bravery provoke much enmity;

It is timidity and quietude by which the self is made more secure.

32.27.5 and benevolence and righteousness incite much reproach.

Everyone in the world hopes for love, but in loving people, one will not be universal; as such, he incites much reproach.

32.27.6 Whereas one who masters the conditions of life is wonderfully wise [*kui*],

Kui as such is the condition of great serene understanding.

32.27.7 one who masters knowledge is fragmented [*xiao*].

Xiao means *shisan* [fragmented].

32.27.8 Whereas one who masters long life keeps in step with it,

Such a one merges perfectly and is one with transformation.

32.27.9 one who masters short life runs up against it.

Such a one understands it only as he finds himself in each interval of it.

32.28 After a man was granted an audience by the King of Song and presented with ten carriages, pumped with pride, he showed them off to Master Zhuang.

32.29 Master Zhuang said, "By the Yellow River there was a man of poor family who depended on plaiting artemisia for sustenance, but when his son dove into the depths, he found a pearl worth a thousand pieces of gold. His father then said to him, 'Take a rock and smash it! A pearl worth a thousand pieces of gold must have been kept under the jaws of a black dragon down in the nine strata depths, and you surely came on it while it was asleep. If it had been awake, what tiny part of you would still exist!'

Now, there deep in the state of Song, is it not just such a nine strata deep? And the ferocity of the King of Song, is it not just the same as the black dragon's? That you were able to get carriages was surely because you came on him while he was asleep. If the King of Song had been awake, you would have been torn to shreds!"

When someone is conferred wealth and honor, it must comply with the hopes and aspirations of the common folk. But if one depends on outlandish advice to ride on the ruler's highway, if one tries to make the ruler's mind to think like a child, a perspicacious ruler would not present such a one with anything. Therefore, if the ruler has someone to praise, it must be verified, that is, if it is not in opposition to his people and they all say "elevate him." It was in agreement with the hopes and aspirations of the common folk that things were thus done with the straight and true Dao during the Three Dynasties of antiquity.

32.30 When some ruler offered a position to Master Zhuang, Master Zhuang replied to the emissary, "Have you seen a sacrificial ox? It is dressed in embroidered silk and fed with fresh grass and beans, but when it is led into the royal ancestral temple, though it might wish to be a calf on its own again, how could that ever happen!"

Whereas here one who loved life so feared becoming a sacrificial victim that he refused a position, when the skull heard about life, it knit its brows [in displeasure].[22] Thus it was that though the conditions of life and death differed, each spontaneously adjusted accordingly [*zidang*].

32.31 When Master Zhuang was about to die, his disciples wanted to give him a magnificent funeral, but he said, "I shall have Heaven and Earth as my inner and outer coffins, the sun and moon as my joined jade discs, the stars as my pearls and jades, and the myriad things as my grave objects. How might my funerary furnishings not be complete! For what could possibly be added to them!"

32.32 His disciples replied, "We are afraid that ravens and kites will eat you."

32.33 "Above ground I'd be eaten by ravens and kites, and below ground I'd be eaten by mole crickets and ants—why be so partial as to snatch me away from the former to give to the latter!

32.34.1 If you try to judge impartially with your own partiality, such impartiality won't be impartial.

Instead of using one's own particular sense of impartiality to judge the myriad things impartially, it would be better to entrust impartiality to the myriad things themselves.

32.34.2 If you try to confirm [*zheng*] what something is with your own sense of confirmation, such confirmation won't be true confirmation.

"Confirm" [*zheng*] means resonate [*ying*]. If one fails to abide by a spontaneous resonance with the myriad things but instead tries to resonate with them using his own point of view, he is sure to experience disjuncture.

32.34.3 One who thinks himself perspicacious becomes nothing but the servant of others.

Since one who holds fast to his own views often becomes such a servant, how can he ever make others his servants!

32.34.4 It is one of divine spirit who truly may confirm things.

Only by giving oneself over entirely to the divine can such perfect compliance be had; as such, no undertaking he attempts ever fails to resonate.

32.34.5 Of old, it has been so that the consciously perspicacious is no match for the divine.

What the consciously perspicacious manages to attain goes only so far as things of physical existence, but for the perfectly compliant, there is no near or far, nothing obscurely hidden, since everything is available to one capable of spontaneous receptivity.

32.34.6 Yet the stupid rely on their own point of view to fit in with people, so their efforts only reach them externally—is that indeed not sad!"

When one is perfectly compliant, he lets the way he functions spring from others and thereby conceals himself among them. But if one relies on his own point of view and insists it is right, though he may wish to fit in with people, his efforts only reach them externally.

Notes

1. The same passage, with some variations, appears in the *Liezi* (Sayings of Master Lie); *Liezi jishi*, 2: 76–79. For more on Bohun Wuren, see 5.9.1.
2. Cheng Xuanying: "As long as he remained aware of the wisdom filling his inner self, he could not free himself from a sense of it, and, since he was revered by others accordingly, this so alarmed him that he returned home." *Zhuangzi jishi*, 4: 1037.
3. "Insects" here must be interpreted figuratively to mean the most humble of people.
4. Cf. *Yijing* (Classic of Changes), *Commentary on the Images* to *Zhongfu* (Inner Trust, hexagram 61): "[T]he noble man evaluates criminal punishments and mitigates [*huan*] the death penalty." To which Wang Bi adds the comment, "When trust emerges from within, even one who makes mistakes can find exoneration." Richard John Lynn, *The Classic of Changes*, 524. I suggest that Guo Xiang connects this passage in the *Classic of Changes* with the name Fu, and with it turns Confucian trust (sincerity) on its head: the ultrasincere noble man, who yields to his father for years before chagrin condemns him to death, cannot mitigate his own self-imposed death sentence.
5. "Pheasant" [Di] is also the given name of Mozi, Master Mo, but commentaries, including those by Guo Xiang and Cheng Xuanying, do not identify the younger brother in this account with the founder of Mohism.
6. Cheng Xuanying: "A person's intelligence is endowed by creative transformation and depends not on learning from a teacher. As such, since the benefits of learning supplement one's Dao endowment, the reward is due to one's natural endowment and not due to one's accomplishments. By this we know that Pheasant had a Mohist nature, which he did not get from Mitigate, so when Mitigate said that it was he who taught him it, was he not in error!" *Zhuangzi jishi*, 4: 1043.

7. Cheng Xuanying: "He, Pheasant, had a Mohist fundamental nature from the start, which is why he became an accomplished Mohist. If his fundamental nature was pristine and void, study would never have accomplished this. And why should this apply only to the Mohist Pheasant, for everyone it is so!" *Zhuangzi jishi*, 4: 1044.
8. Cheng Xuanying: "At a well that the people of Qi had successfully sunk, travelers tried to draw up water to drink, but those in charge of the well hoarding the water pulled them away by the hair, stopping them." *Zhuangzi jishi*, 4: 1044.
9. Cheng Xuanying: "To try to learn what one cannot do is an attempt to find contentment in what does not content. Discontentment with one's fundamental capacity [*sufen*] leads to discontentment with what should constitute contentment." *Zhuangzi jishi*, 4: 1045.
10. Cf. *Laozi*, section 31: "Weapons are instruments of ill omen; they are not the instruments of the noble man, who uses they only when there is no choice. It is best to be utterly dispassionate [*tiandan*] about them, and, even if they bring victory, one should not praise them." Richard John Lynn, *The Classic of the Way and Virtue*, 107.
11. Following Sima Biao, Cheng Xuanying identifies the king as King Yan of Song, Song Kang, who seized the throne of Song in 329 BCE and died in 286 BCE *Zhuangzi jishi*, 4: 1049.
12. Cf. *Yijing* (Classic of Changes), *Wenyan* (Commentary on the words of the text) to *Qian* (Pure Yang, hexagram 1): " 'Constancy' [*zhen*] is the very trunk [*gan*] of human affairs." Lynn, *The Classic of Changes*, 130.
13. That is, to "gild the lily."
14. Guo's interpretation here, with which Cheng Xuanying is in complete agreement, seems unlikely. The later commentary tradition, beginning largely with Lin Xiyi, takes *bi* to refer not to the common folk, but to Confucius: "What suits him, is it for you?"
15. Alternatively, "Copying him [Confucius] won't do you any good."
16. Cheng Xuanying: "To take up such footprints left by loyalty and steadfastness and mistakenly follow them, it can't possibly be the right thing to do." *Zhuangzi jishi*, 4: 1052.
17. Cheng Xuanying: "To discard oneself and imitate someone else, this is not the way the sage rules." *Zhuangzi jishi*, 4: 1052.
18. Cf. 25.8.4–25.8.5.
19. Cheng Xuanying: "*Kao* means 'accomplished' [*cheng*], and *fu* signifies 'great' [*da*]. Since he achieved great virtue and followed the correct path, he was called Zheng Kaofu, namely, the tenth-generation ancestor of Confucius, who was a Grand Master of the State of Song." *Zhuangzi jishi*, 4: 1057.
20. Cf. 23.16. Much controversy surrounds interpretation of this passage, but the meaning as it is worded seems best: "when the mind has eyelashes" simply means when the mind is imagined as the faculty of sight. To look at someone right in the eyebrows and eyelashes is to examine one's facial expression closely to "see" what is in his mind, and when the mind does this to itself, it cannot help but be acutely self-conscious. Being self-conscious, whatever act of virtue is intended, cannot possibly be spontaneous and natural; that is, "authentic."
21. The closest expression to this in English is "ride/hang onto someone's coattails."
22. Cf. 18.16–17.

CHAPTER 33

TIANXIA [ALL UNDER HEAVEN]

33.1.1 All over the world we find many who practice the art of government, and each one of them thinks what his consists of cannot be added to. But what was known among the ancients as the art of the Dao, where, after all, is it now found? I say, "Where is it not found!"

They just did what they had to do, so it was authentic practice, and since what they did was authentic practice, they acted unselfconsciously—and what could be added to that!

33.1.2 If you ask, "Whence is the divine bestowed? Whence does such intelligence come?" "The sage possesses the means of his own production; the true sovereign possesses the means of his own completion.

Divine intelligence is bestowed only in the course of one [sage/true sovereign] responding to some task.

33.1.3 It is always the One that is the source."

All one has to do is revert to the root, embrace the One, and refrain from embellishing the external self, for this is how the sage and true sovereign are produced and completed.

33.2.1 One not separated from the progenitor is called a heavenly man; one not separated from his vital essence is called a divine man; and one not separated from his authenticity is called a Perfected one. One who makes Heaven his progenitor, makes virtue his basis, and makes the Dao his gate, who has incipient insight into change and transformation, such a one is called a sage.

All these four names refer to just one kind of man and differ only in what they say of him.

33.2.2 One who uses benevolence to provide for mercy, uses righteousness to provide for moral principles, uses ritual to provide for behavior, and uses music to provide for harmony, who is suffused with the fragrance of compassion and benevolence, such a one is called a noble man.

The rough footprints left by using these four are what the worthy man and the noble man keep in mind.

33.2.3 To use legal determinants to allot place in life, to use names to designate exemplars, to use consultation for verification, and to use examination for judgement, all done precisely as if summing up one, two, three, and four, thereby ensuring that all officialdom mesh properly together, that government service is constant, that clothing and food are major concerns, that crops thrive and be stored against future need, that the old and weak, the orphaned and widowed, be kept in mind, and that everyone be provided with nourishment and care—these are principles for the people.

Since these are principles for the people, sages and worthies do not violate them.

33.3.1 How comprehensive they were, those men in antiquity!

"Men in antiquity" means those given the four names, as mentioned above.

33.3.2 Companions of divine intelligence and pure distillations of Heaven and Earth, they fostered the myriad things, brought perfect harmony to all under Heaven, and extended favor and grace to all common folk. Utterly clear about the fundamental system, their specifics were tied to it.

Since the fundamental system was clear to them, their specifics never deviated from it.

33.3.3 They understood everything perfectly in all six directions and in all four seasons, whether small or large, fine or coarse—there was no place in which they were not engaged.

This is how they were "comprehensive."

33.3.4 Their intelligence, inherent in such systematic details, is still greatly available to us in records of old laws and regulations passed down through the ages.

As for what can be discerned of their intelligence in the details of these systematic details, although much of it remains, it is already alien and extraneous.

33.3.5 As for the remains of it in the *Odes*, *Documents*, *Rites*, and *Music*, many learned men and tableted officials in Zou and Lu[1] were able to discern it.

They were just able to discern the footprints left by it, and how should that ever represent how they were made!

33.3.6 The *Odes* were used to express heartfelt inclinations; the *Documents* were used to relate events; the *Rites* were used to prescribe behavior; the *Music* was used to convey harmony; the *Changes* was used to describe the interaction of yin and yang, and the *Spring and Autumn Annals* was used

to account for titles and status. All such norms, disseminated throughout the world, have become firmly established in the states of the Central Plain, where, in the doctrines of all the various philosophers, they are often cited since they correspond.

Since all these are nothing more than accounts based on footprints left by men of antiquity, they can never again provide constant correspondence.[2]

33.4.1 **Then the whole world suffered great upheaval,**[3]

This happened because people tried to use such footprints, which provided absolutely no guidance at all.

33.4.2 **for even sages and worthies did not understand them.**

To discern what such footprints were was not even easy for them.

33.4.3 **The Dao with its virtue lost its unity,**

All the various philosophers drilled holes in it.[4]

33.4.4 **and many all over the world grasped what they thought was its unity,**

Everyone trusted to his own biased view of it and thus failed to get the whole of it.

33.4.5 **for they searched for it in terms of what satisfied them.**

The true sage sums up the overall inclinations of the common folk and, conforming to them, creates rules and regulations accordingly. As such, since the common folk entrust their inclinations to this summation, they become utterly unmindful of their own likes and dislikes. In doing so, as with all people of the age, they achieve complete serenity. Upheaval is the opposite of all this: while people indulge themselves in what pleases them for the moment, noble families apply their own rules and standards, so states enact different modes of governance and noble families follow different customs.

33.4.6 **Just as how the ears, eyes, nose, and mouth all have powers of perception that cannot be interchanged, so it is with the skills of the philosophers, all of whom have particular strengths, which at different times prove useful.**

Since what they are strong at differs, they cannot always be used.

33.4.7 **Nevertheless, none are inclusive, none are comprehensive, for each sees things only from one angle,**

Therefore, when it comes to universal application, they all fail.

33.4.8 **so when it comes to assessing the merits of Heaven and Earth and analyzing the principles underlying the myriad things,**

Since each has recourse only to one angle, they have to assess and analyze.

33.4.9 **even if we examine the perfection of the ancients, few could fully grasp the merits of Heaven and Earth and fill the measure of divine intelligence.**

How much the less can these one angle fellows do!

33.4.10 **This is why the Dao of sageliness within and kingliness without has become so dark that it is quite obscure, so obstructed that it no longer manifests itself.**

This is why the perfect man is so hard to find.

33.4.11 Everyone all over the world makes what he wants of it and then uses that to devise his own doctrine. How distressing it is that the various philosophers keep on going their own ways and do not turn back, for as such they are sure never to join with it! Learned men of later ages see neither the pure simplicity of Heaven and Earth nor how the ancients embodied their great essence,

"Great essence" means that each one of them reverted to his roots and so embraced the One; as such, that signifies the pure simplicity of Heaven and Earth.

33.4.12 so the arts of the Dao were rendered asunder [*lie*] all over the world.

"Render asunder" means "split apart" [*fenli*]. As the arts of the Dao degenerated into malpractice, each snatched his doctrine from them, which some used to gain mastery over others. This meant that people separated themselves from their original natures in order to follow their superiors—as such, their natural endowments were lost.

33.5.1 As for not foisting extravagance on later ages, not treating the mass of common folk wastefully, and not trying to shine with institutions and regulations,

If one works too hard and is too frugal, one becomes exhausted, which is why one should not try to shine.

33.5.2 but rectifying [*jiao*] oneself as if with a straight-line marker

"Rectify" [*jiao*] means "treat strictly" [*li*].

33.5.3 and taking precautions against hard times,

It is because one works hard and is frugal that he has more than enough goods, which is how to take precautions against hard times.

33.5.4 there is some of all this in the arts of the Dao as followed by the ancients. Mo Di and Qin Huali, hearing of such habits, delighted in them, but they made people do too much with what should be done and made them conform too much with what should be avoided.

They no longer estimated what the mass of common folk could do.

33.5.5 They formulated a "no music" policy, justifying it as "reduction of expenditure." Alive, people should not sing; dead, they were denied grave clothes. Master Mo both advocated universal love and communal profit and opposed fighting.

When goods are inadequate, fighting is thought the right thing to do. Now, Master Mo would have the common folk all practice hard work and frugality, so each would have enough, which results in them thinking fighting was the wrong thing to do.

33.5.6 His way was opposed to anger.

However, he was too hard on himself.

33.5.7 Moreover, though he loved learning and was erudite, he did not tolerate difference.

Since he thought himself right, he wanted to make everyone just like him.

33.5.8 Therefore, he did not share the former kings' way to conformity.

The former kings allowed their multitudes to be as different from them as they liked; as such, they got all their people to conform, without knowing how they managed to do so.

33.5.9 And he would abolish the rites and music of the ancients.

He hated them for their extravagance and waste.

33.6.1 The Yellow Thearch had the "Pool of Shaman Xian" [Xianchi]; Yao had the "Great Stanzas" [Da Zhang]; Shun had the "Great Prominence" [Da Shao]; Yu had the "Great Xia" [Da Xia]; Tang had the "Great Flow" [Da Huao]; King Wen had the music for the Majesty Harmonious Academy; King Wu and the Duke of Zhou composed the "Martial." Funerary rites among the ancients had different ceremonies for the noble and the base and different degrees of status for superiors and inferiors. The Son of Heaven was placed inside seven nested coffins, feudal lords in five, grand masters in three, and officers of state in two. But now Master Mo takes exception to all this and would make it the law to ban singing among the living and, for the dead, would have no grave clothes and only three-inch paulownia plain wooden caskets with no outer coffins. Since he teaches this to people, I fear he does not really love them; since he practices this himself, he surely does not love himself.

Everyone regards what suits his potential and what accords with his innate tendencies as worthy of love.[5] But now to make toil and frugality the law and as such have people practice them to great excess, even if one tried to enforce this on the world leniently, it would not at all be the way to love them.

33.6.2 I do not quite accuse Master Mo of ruining the Dao,

But his way does not represent the Dao and its virtue.

33.6.3 nevertheless, if people would sing but are forbidden to sing, would cry but are forbidden to cry, would be joyful but are forbidden to rejoice, how can this really suit them?

Although this might have worked for Mo, it does not suit the innate tendencies of the myriad folk.

33.6.4 Since for him life means toil and death is of little significance, his way is thoroughly arid [*hu*].

"Arid" [*hu*] means utterly lacking enriching qualities.

33.6.5 Since it causes people grief and to feel sad, its practice is difficult to perform, so I am afraid it cannot serve as the Dao of the sage.

The Dao of the sage allows the common folk happiness; it is fulfilling their nature that makes them happy, and, being happy, the whole world is free from trouble.

33.6.6 If something is contrary to the mind of the world, the world will not bear it. Although Master Mo may on his own bear it, how could the entire

world ever do so! And since it brings such trouble on the world, it is, indeed, far from the way of true kingship.

The true king must share the same happy state of mind of all in the world and set about doing things only in union with the people.

33.7.1 **Yet Master Mo declared, "Long ago when Yu channelled the flood, he cut in the Yangzi and Yellow River, making them conduits to the four barbarian borders through all the nine regions, as well as creating three hundred named mountains, three thousand tributaries, and small streams beyond count. Yu himself wielded wicker pannier and dredge, so by the time this nine-fold matrix of rivers for the whole world existed, there was no down left on his calves and no hair on his shins. Though drenched with heavy rains and riddled with fierce winds, he managed to establish the myriad states. Yu was a great sage yet allowed his body to be worn out for the sake of whole world like this."**

Master Mo saw nothing other than that Yu wore out his body, never perceiving that this perfectly suited his fundamental nature.

33.7.2 **Mohists of later ages for the most part dressed themselves in skins and coarse cloth, wore wooden clogs and straw sandals, rested neither day nor night, and thought that wearing themselves out was the very best they could do.**

That is, wearing oneself out, for them, was the perfect way to grasp principle.

33.7.3 **So they say, "If we cannot measure up to this, we fail to follow the way of Yu, so are not worthy to be called Mohists."**

Though it is no longer the right time for it, they still maintain his way—that's how the practice of Mohism works.

33.8.1 **Although disciples of Xiangli Qin, followers of Wu Hou, and such southern Mohists as Ku Huo, Ji Chi, and Deng Ling all chanted Mohist scriptures, they held different views and accused each other of departing from Mohist teachings.**

Since each of them stuck exclusively to his own point of view, their positions were incompatible. As such, even within the Mohist tradition there were differences among adherents.

33.8.2 **They vilified each other in their debates about "white" and "hard" or "sameness" and "difference," and they countered each other in their arguments over the disparity between "odd" and "even." A giant here becomes a sage.**

A "giant" is one who proves most able to debate what he thinks "right," whereby making others fall into step behind him.

33.8.3 **All of them wanted to become such a master [*shi*]**

Shi [ceremonial stand-in for the deceased] here means "master" [*zhu*].

33.8.4 **and hoped their teachings would carry on in later ages. However, until now who has won out has not been settled.**

That is, they want to carry on this tradition of the "giant."

33.9.1 The ideas of Mo Di and Qin Huali may have been right,

It was their ideas about not being extravagant and wasteful and taking precautions against hard times that were right.

33.9.2 but their practice of them was wrong.

This happened because they took them too far.

33.9.3 So all this means is that Mohists in later ages insisted on wearing themselves out so that no down was left on their calves and no hair on their shins, as they egged each other onwards. Theirs is the best possible way to disorder

No greater disorder can result than when the people are thwarted and their fundamental natures are harmed.

33.9.4 and the worst possible way to good government.

To let the mass of common folk live as it suits their fundamental natures is the best possible way. Now, Mohism does just the opposite. Thus, it is the worst possible way.

33.9.5 Nevertheless, Master Mo was one of the good, fine men in all the world,

What was really good about him was how he stressed that the sage or worthy should not be contrary. However, he could not teach this to others.

33.9.6 and his like will not be found.

He is matchless.

33.9.7 Though he labored 'til he withered away, he never gave up.

This was what really constituted his goodness.

33.9.8 He was certainly a talented and learned man!

But he lacked corresponding virtue.

33.10.1 Be not entangled in worldly commonalities, do not adorn yourself with things, be not contrary to others, and be not recalcitrant [*zhi*] toward the mass of common folk,

Zhi (recalcitrant) here mean "thwart" [*ni*].

33.10.2 but wish for the peace and stability of the whole world so common people may preserve their lives and, when support for others and self is sufficient, wish not for more than that.

One should not dare to have more than enough.

33.10.3 Be pure of heart, for the arts of the Dao in antiquity are found exactly here. Song Xing and Yin Wen,[6] hearing of such habits, delighted in them, and had caps fabricated in the shape of Mount Hua to distinguish themselves.

The top and base of Mount Hua are equally flat.[7]

33.10.4 They had it that the fundamental starting point for associations among the myriad folk should be their distinct bounded places in life.

They did not wish them to treat each other wrongly.[8]

33.10.5 When they addressed the contents of the mind, they called it "workings of the mind," and would calm and moderate it to effect communal happiness, thereby bringing good order to all within the four seas.

They did their best to make people calm and moderate, in order to bring about social union, so that good order would then result in harmony.

33.10.6 Just give us someone like that to be ruler.

The two masters sought to find someone like that to establish as the ruler of men.

33.10.7 When they were insulted, they felt no shame,

They were so concerned about the survival of the common folk.

33.10.8 for they would spare the common folk from fighting, and so tried to prohibit aggression and to have troops stand down. Thus, saving the world from war.

This is what calm and moderate good order means.

33.10.9 They travelled with this all over the world, persuading those above and teaching those below. Although no one in all the world accepted it, they just went on and on about it and never gave up.

Just so does the principle of being calm and moderate operate.

33.10.10 Thus, it was said, "Those above and those below were sick of seeing them, yet they did their best to be seen."

This is what was meant by "they felt no shame."

33.11.1 Nevertheless, they tried to do too much for others and tried to do too little for themselves.

Since they failed to comply with their own self-transformation but instead did all they could to comfort others, such efforts were too heavy for them to bear.

33.11.2 They said, "Just give us five pints of rice and that will be enough,

This clearly shows that they did too little for themselves.

33.11.3 for we fear our teachers will fail to get their fill; although we, their disciples, go hungry, we do not forget all the people in the world."

Song and Yin called all the people in the world their teachers and called themselves their disciples.

33.11.4 They rested neither day nor night, saying "We are sure to survive!"

They meant that the common folk were sure to recompense them.

33.11.5 How proud their plans, these saviors of the world!

This chides them for the lofty and grand image they projected.

33.11.6 They said, "The noble man neither engages in exacting scrutiny

He deals with things in a tolerant and forgiving way.

33.11.7 nor for his sake does he rely on others."

He is sure to make his own efforts.

33.11.8 If something was of no benefit to the whole world, it was clear to them that it would be better just not to do it.

Such is the way saviors of the world behave.

33.11.9 They dealt with the external by prohibiting aggression and having troops stand down and dealt with the internal by keeping desires slight and few; whether this involved something great or small or something fine or coarse, their practices just went this far but no further.

They were never able to traverse the void and engage its vast emptiness.

33.12.1 Be public-oriented but not cliquish, amiable but impartial, decisive but not at all domineering,

That is, let each act to suit himself.

33.12.2 tend as do others and stay free from dualism,

It is when one can tend as others tend that he is one with them.

33.12.3 heed not conscious deliberation, scheme not with knowledge, be not preferential in regard to things, but go forth in tandem with them, for the arts of the Dao in antiquity are found somewhat here. Peng Meng, Tian Pian, and Shen Dao,[9] hearing of such habits, delighted in them. They had it that the fundamental starting point should be that the myriad things all be regarded as equal, about which they said, "Heaven can cover them but cannot carry them; Earth can carry them but cannot cover them; the Dao can embrace them but cannot discriminate among them. From this we know that for each of the myriad things, it is sometimes suitable, sometimes unsuitable. Therefore we say, 'if one prefers, he fails to be universal.' "

Only by regarding everything as suitable may one be universal.[10]

33.12.4 Teaching will not get you there, but the Dao leaves no one behind.

One only gets there by allowing one's original nature to fulfill itself.

33.13.1 Therefore, Shen Dao discarded knowledge, rid himself of self, and submitted to the inevitable. He regarded treating others with cool detachment as a principle of the Dao.

"Cool detachment" [*lengtai*] is like "compliant non-interference" [*tingfang*].

33.13.2 He said, "Once one knows that he does not know and thus realizes how shallow his knowing is, even then he remains close to harm."

Since the capacity to know is meager, one fails to realize it should just operate spontaneously. That's why, even though one knows it is meager, it still keeps one close to harm.

33.13.3 Elusive and wily, he avoided responsibility and scorned how everyone in the world esteemed the worthy.

Unwilling to shoulder them as his responsibility, he instead would have everyone in the world each take responsibility for themselves, for once they themselves were allowed to do this, none would unreasonably continue to esteem "the worthy."

33.13.4 Easygoing and uninhibited, he engaged in no good works, for he would not want the world to think he was a great sage,

He wanted to wipe out his footprints to ensure that people would not keenly pursue him.

33.13.5 and, in hammering their sharp points smooth, he would follow the twists and turns that people took.

Although this legalist was marvelous, he still would pound people with hammers; as such, he never merged imperceptibly with them.[11]

33.13.6 Casting right and wrong aside, he managed momentarily to avoid responsibility and, not led by conscious deliberation, was unconscious of past or future.

Unable to know whether something was right or wrong, or whether it was something past or yet to come, eyes thus, so clouded, he just did as it pleased his fundamental nature and somehow temporarily avoided the troubles of the moment.

33.13.7 He was sublimely self-possessed—that's all there was to it!

True to his nature, he was utterly detached.

33.13.8 He would only move if pushed, only set forth if pulled.

This is what is meant by "submitted to the inevitable."

33.13.9 Like the turning of a whirlwind, like the spinning of a feather as it falls, like the revolving of a millstone, he kept himself intact and free from error, never at fault whether active or passive—and thus was never blamed for anything. Why was that? As something unaware, he avoided the troubles involved with establishing oneself and from the entanglements incumbent on using conscious knowledge. Whether active or passive, he never deviated from the principles of things. Thus, to the end of his life he stayed free from praise.

Troubles arise from praise, and praise arises from having established oneself.

33.13.10 Therefore he said, "All I want is to become a thing unaware and have no need to become a worthy or sage,

Only after one has become a sage can he rid himself of knowledge and precedent and abide by the principles of Nature. Therefore, the stupid and the wise find their proper places, the noble and mean fill positions right for them, and the sage and the unworthy follow their natural tendencies. Nevertheless, he says that he has no need to become a worthy or sage, which indicates that he fails to understand the Dao.

33.13.11 for only the senseless clod does not lose the Dao."

Saying such things as trying to make himself unaware like a clod of earth or just be an ordinary thing all signifies that he had no way to attain the Dao, for the Dao is not biased toward anything.

33.13.12 The heroic and talented ridiculed him to each other, saying "The Dao of Shen Dao is not for the conduct of the living but principles whereby people might bring about death.

Only after one has rid himself of knowledge and comes to abide by his innate nature does divine intelligence clearly shine forth and one thus becomes a worthy sage. And yet he said that one has to be a clod of earth not to violate the

Dao. If a man is like a clod of earth, if that is not death, what is it! This is why the heroic and talented ridiculed him.

33.13.13 It is thus appropriate that we find him so bizarre."

He was not in accord with the perfect Dao, so they thought him bizarre.

33.14.1 It was the same with Tian Pian. When he studied with Peng Meng, what he attained was not taught by him.

He attained the Dao of self-empowerment.

33.14.2 The teacher of Peng Meng said, "Men of the Dao in antiquity were so perfect that nothing was 'right' and nothing 'wrong'—that was simply all there was to it.

This is what is meant by taking the myriad things to be equal as the fundamental starting point.

33.14.3 Since they raised a wind like a headwind [*huoran*], how could that ever be captured in words!"

It was the sound made by a headwind.[12]

33.14.4 He was so often contrary to others that no one paid any attention to him,

He did not abide by the aspirations of the common folk.

33.14.5 but he just had to try to make people smooth.

Even though he would establish laws, these would make people smooth so they had no sharp points.

33.14.6 What he called the Dao was not the Dao, and what he called "correct" [*wei*] could not help but be wrong.

"Correct" [*wei*] means "right" [*shi*].

33.14.7 Although Peng Meng, Tian Pian, and Shen Dao did not understand the Dao,

There is no place where the Dao does not exist, yet they say that it is only a senseless clod that does not lose the Dao; as such; they did not understand it.

33.14.8 nevertheless in general they all managed to hear something of it.

But they did not attain it.

33.15.1 Take the root as essence and things as coarse, regard however much one gathers as not enough,

Only by giving it away to all in the world does one have enough.[13]

33.15.2 and reside alone tranquilly at one with one's divine intelligence, for these are found among the arts of the Dao in antiquity. Pass Director Yin and Old Longears, hearing of such habits, were so delighted with them that they used [the doctrine] "things never exist" to establish them [as teachings].

What power can the non-existent have to establish anything! If "they used 'things never exist' to establish them," this clearly means that anything that exists just establishes itself.[14]

33.15.3 They maintained that the great unity was in charge, assumed compliance, softness, modesty, and humility for the outer self, and devoted the

inner self to a perfect vacuity innocent of harm for the myriads of common folk.

Beginning with Heaven and Earth and extending all the way to the myriad folk, everything just spontaneously realizes itself, nothing more, with no other agency involved—is this not to maintain that the great unity is in charge!

33.16.1 **Pass Director Yin [Guan Yin] said, "Let nothing stay with you,**[15]

When things come, just respond, and once response occurs, retain nothing of them, for then success follows others away from you.

33.16.2 **for then the figures of others may manifest themselves.**

Think not that you are right, but instead yield to the myriads of common folk, for then the figures of others may manifest themselves.

33.16.3 **Let your action be like water,**
Your tranquility like a mirror.
Your response like an echo.

Be constantly dispassionate.

33.16.4 **Be so indistinguishable that you seem not there,**
So still that you reflect with absolute clarity,
And join with others in such perfect harmony,
That how you got there is utterly lost to you.

One who maintains such constant wholeness is unaware how it is achieved.

33.16.5 **Never lead others but always follow them."**

33.17.1 **Old Longears said, "He who knows his maleness yet sustains his femaleness will be a river valley for all under Heaven. He who knows his whiteness [innocence] yet sustains disgrace will be a catchment valley for all under Heaven."**[16]

If each person is allowed to sustain his own allotted capacity, calm quietude will reign—that's all there is to it. One should stay free of maleness and whiteness, for are not maleness and whiteness just means to flaunt one's own superiority and dominance! As for flaunting one's own superiority and dominance, how can one thus fail to know that such exceeding one's allotted capacity endangers one's life! Therefore, the ancients did not pursue limitless knowledge but did nothing other than sustain the limits of their own allotted capacities. As such, their original natures remained whole and safe; once their original natures were whole and safe, they were able to reach all under Heaven; and once they were able to reach all under Heaven, people gravitated to them as if they were river valley catchments.

33.17.2 **Although others all seek to be first, such a one alone chooses to be last,**

Strive not against the myriads of common folk, for only then will all under Heaven never flag in their happy support for you—which is why one should put himself last.

33.17.3 saying, "I accept such humiliation."

Such designations as "female," "disgrace," "last," and "lowly" are all said by people to be humiliating.

33.17.4 Although others all seek to be full,

They only understand how advantageous it is to have things and never realize how useful to have nothing can be.

33.17.5 he alone chooses to be empty.

He sustains utter emptiness for himself as he waits upon repletion for the mass of common folk.

33.17.6 Since he hoards not for himself, surplus occurs,

Since he allows all the myriad folk to maintain themselves [*zishou*], he will not be troubled by their suffering want.

33.17.7 a single towering mountain of surplus!

By this is meant a self-sufficiency that is unique.

33.17.8 The way he conducts himself is leisurely and no waste of effort.

Acting for the sake of benefit to the common folk, he has things accomplished according to the four seasons and always in tandem with the principles of the Dao; as such, he is spared haste and wastes no effort.

33.17.9 Acting unselfconsciously, he scorns expertise.

Expertise involves selfconscious action, harmful to self-fulfillment of the numinous vessel. Therefore, acting unselfconsciously, he conforms to their self-generation and allows for their self-fulfillment, which allows each of the myriad folk free to act spontaneously. If, just as a spider can weave its web, every individual were to realize his inherent capabilities, no one would feel the need to esteem Artisan Chui.

33.17.10 Although others all seek good fortune, he alone keeps his wholeness intact by yielding,

By yielding [*weishun*] to perfect truth [*zhili*], he always keeps his wholeness intact. Thus, he has no good fortune to seek, as he already has all the good fortune he needs.[17]

33.17.11 saying, "Just let me avoid blame somehow or other."

Since he yields to others, others do not get to blame him for anything.

33.17. 12 He takes profundity as his root

Since principles are rooted in the farthest reach of the Great Beginning, he may not be called "shallow."

33.17.13 and frugality as his rule,

He shuns excess.

33.17.14 saying, "If rigid, one will be destroyed

If one is perfectly compliant, even metal or stone will not feel hard, but if one is obstinately contrary, even water or air will not feel soft. If perfectly compliant, one will be whole and safe, but if obstinately contrary, one will be destroyed—this is the true principle of it all.

33.17.15 and if sharp one, will be made blunt."

"Sharp" means insatiable assertiveness.[18]

33.17.16 Since he is always magnanimous toward others

If each person is allowed to sustain his own allotted capacity, he will have his own means of support.

33.17.17 and never encroaches on them, he may be said to have reached absolute perfection.

He keeps their original natures whole and safe.

33.18 Pass Keeper Yin and Old Longears—how magnificent those authentic men were!

33.19.1 Utterly quiescent and intangible, evanescent as change and transform,

This is to keep in step with the transformation of things.

33.19.2 alive with them or dead with them, they interacted with Heaven and Earth with divine intelligences so set forth!

That is, they gave themselves over to transformation.

33.19.3 Utterly witless, where would they go? Utterly vague, where would they head off to?

They were free of any particular way of thinking.

33.19.4 Though the myriads of things embrace and envelop, not a one was an adequate source to which to revert.

Therefore, everything holds to its own place.[19]

33.19.5 Since the arts of the Dao in antiquity are found somewhat here, hearing of such habits, Zhuang Zhou was so delighted with them that he used outlandish language to expound them in fantastic accounts, which were phrased to connote endless meaning. Though at times self-indulgent, he was not biased and so did not appear to take sides.

He was not anxious about making others see what he meant.

33.19.6 Because he thought the people of the world were so mired in stupidity that it was impossible to talk seriously with them, he used goblet words [*zhiyan*] for their unending connotations,

He found people so entangled with forms and names that if he had used a serious style of discourse, they would have thought it crazy and would not have believed it, so he did not give them that.

33.19.7 weighty words for their ready credibility, and words attributed to others for their broad impact. All on his own, he wandered back and forth with the essential spirit of Heaven and Earth—while never treated the myriads of common folk with the least arrogance.

His words communicated the ultimate principles of things and perfectly suited the naturally endowed lives of the myriads of common folk.

33.19.8 He did not censure others in terms of right or wrong

Since he himself had nothing to do with right or wrong, he just let others follow these two paths at once.

33.19.9 and just situated himself with the common run of humanity.

He joined his physical form to the common crowd of others.

33.19.10 Although what he wrote is both odd and unusual, it has such congenial appeal that it does no harm.

After all, since it is in accord with the way things are, it does no harm.

33.19.11 Although his discourse is uneven, it is so unconventional and unusual that it is well worth reading.[20]

Since it does not entirely deal with events of his own time, it is "uneven."[21]

33.19.12 That work of his is so rich in real meaning that there can be no end to it.

This describes how copious are its contents.

33.19.13 Above, he roamed with the Creator [*zaowuzhe*], while below he was friends with those who put life and death beyond them and who had no sense of beginning or ending. His access to the root was vast and wide open, so broad and deep that it was utterly unimpeded. His relationship with the Progenitor may be said to have been so harmonious that, above, he was completely commensurate with it. As such, the way he resonated with transformation and thus gained an understanding of things, though the principles involved are inexhaustible, when they came to him he did not set them aside. He is so boundless, so abstruse, that he has never been fully understood!

Master Zhuang here fluently discussed himself with equanimity, no differently than when he discussed others. In my opinion, his discourse is clearly so very broad and deep that even when Yu had fine speech to praise, how could he have been dissatisfied with this![22]

33.20 Hui Shi, extremely versatile, had enough books to fill five carts, but his way was confused and erroneous, and his sayings also miss the point. His lengthy scrutiny of things resulted in such notions as, "I call that which is so very large that nothing exists outside it 'The Greatest Singularity' and that which is so very small that nothing exists within it 'The Smallest Singularity.' That which has no thickness cannot pile up but may be thousands of tricents wide. The sky may be as low as the earth, and a mountain may be as level as a marsh.[23] Just as the sun is at noon, it starts to set. Just as a thing is born, it starts to die. Great similarity is different from small similarity, so I call this 'the small similarity and difference.' The myriad things are both all the same and all different, so I call this 'the great similarity and difference.' 'The direction south is both limitless and limited, so I might set out for Yue today yet arrive yesterday.'[24] 'Linked rings can be separated.' 'I know where the center of the whole world is: it is north of Yan and south of Yue.' 'Have universal love for the myriad things, for Heaven and Earth form one body.' "

33.21 Since Hui Shi thought this a great achievement, he showed it all over the world so to enlighten the rhetoricians—and rhetoricians all over the world

amused each other with: "Eggs have feathers and three legs"; "Ying City contains the whole world"; "A dog may be considered a sheep"; "Horses have eggs"; "Frogs have tails"; "Fire is not hot"; "Mountains emerge from mouths"; "Wheels do not leave treads on the ground"; "Eyes do not see"; "Pointing to things does not reach them, yet such pointing never ceases";[25] "Turtles are longer than snakes"; "A carpenter's square is not square"; "One cannot make a circle with a compass"; "A chisel does not fit around its handle"; "A flying bird's shadow does not move"; "An arrowhead-tipped arrow may be swift but there is a time when it neither moves or stops"; "A dog is not a canine"; "A tan horse and a jet-black ox make three"; "A white dog is black"; "An orphaned colt never had a mother"; "If you start with a stick a foot long and remove half of what remains daily, it will never in a myriad ages be all gone." Rhetoricians used these to respond to Hui Shi, never running out of them throughout their lives.

33.22 Such rhetoricians as Huan Tuan and Gongsun Long ornamented the minds of men and changed the way they thought. They could vanquish men in speech but could not make their minds submit—such were the limitations of the rhetoricians. Hui Shi used his wits to dispute with others on a daily basis, standing out as especially bizarre compared to other rhetoricians in the world—such were his fundamental characteristics.

33.23 However, according to what Hui Shi himself said, he thought he was most worthy, asking, in all the world is there anyone more grand! Although he harbored great ambitions, he was essentially incompetent. In the South there was an eccentric fellow called Huang Liao,[26] who asked him why the sky did not fall or the earth sink, and what caused the wind, rain, thunder, and lightning. Hui Shi, responding without hesitation and replying without reflection, started talking about all the myriads of things, going on and on without cease. But then, as if all that was still too little, he augmented it with his bizarre assertions. He regarded opposition to others as his true way and vanquishing them the means to make a name for himself. As such, he interacted badly with everyone. Weak in inner virtue but strong in the examination of things, his way was off in a corner by itself. Looking at Hui Shi's powers from point of view of Heaven and Earth, his were the labors of a mosquito or gadfly—what possible use are they to others! But that he should be counted as singularly important is still possible, but I say that if only he had honored the Dao more—how close he was! Hui Shi was unable to find peace for himself with such doings but instead never quit squandering himself in the pursuit of the myriad things, so in the end just became famous as a fine rhetorician—what a pity! Hui Shi's talents were utterly wasted without achieving anything, for he kept on chasing the myriad things with no turning back, as if he was trying to wear an echo out with his own voice, or trying to beat his own shadow in a race—how very sad!

Earlier when I had not yet read *The Sayings of Master Zhuang* myself, I had occasion to hear people discussing things who argued about what "a stick a foot long" and "linked rings" meant, which they all said were from the sayings of Master Zhuang. I consequently thought that Master Zhuang belonged to the tradition of the rhetoricians. Now I must say that this chapter, which compares and critiques various philosophical masters, on reaching this section, states that their way is confused and contradictory and what they say misses the mark entirely—so I now realize how heeding rumor can harm the truth. But to my way of thinking, I must say that his sayings also lack any practical value in governing the state, so truly his may be called useless talk. However, fat meat, wheat flour, and milled rice eaters [i.e., the elite] all enjoy playing around with what he has to say—some even wear themselves out making aphorisms from it. Moreover, those who can dispute names and realities and are good at analyzing principles use his sayings to convey his spirit and render his thought more systematic. As such, they are transmitted to posterity where they work to ensure that mankind's original nature is spared immorality—and is not this more worthy than gambling and chess playing![27] Therefore, since this is still an open question, I leave it up to those who are fond of such things.

Notes

1. Zou and Lu were the states in which the traditions of Mencius and Confucius flourished.
2. That is, the "footprints," once made, never again correspond to the act of making them.
3. The argument expressed in 33.4.1–33.4.12 is echoed in *Huainanzi*; see *Huainanzi jiaoshi*, 2: 195; Roth et al., *The Huainanzi: A Guide to the Theory and Practice of Government in Early Han China*, 94.
4. To drill holes into the Dao is the same as drilling holes into Hundun, (Primal Chaos); see 7.27.
5. Cf.1.3.1, Guo commentary.
6. Cheng Xuanying: "Surnamed Song and given name Xing, and surnamed Yin and given name Wen, they both lived at the time of King Xuan of Qi [r. 329–301 BCE] and both were itinerants in Jixia. Song composed a work in one volume and Yin composed a work in two. Both also served as teachers to the common folk there, which earned them a good reputation." *Zhuangzi jishi*, 4: 1082.
7. The top and base of Mount Hua, located in Shaanxi east of Xi'an, both look equally flat from a distance; the caps, shaped in the same way, suggest unbiased fairness and lofty equanimity. See the comments of Cheng Xuanying and Lu Deming in *Zhuangzi jishi*, 4: 1083.
8. Cheng Xuanying: "*You* 'forgive' here means 'bounded place' [*quyu*], and *shi* 'starting point' means 'basis' [*ben*]. They established a doctrine of names [*mingjiao*] for the social interaction among people so that the myriads were all assigned distinct places—this served as their basis." *Zhuangzi jishi*, 4: 1083. Much controversy surrounds this passage, and alternative readings abound; for example, see Wang Shumin, *Zhuangzi jiaoquan*, 1322–23, note 8.

9. Cheng Xuanying: "Surnamed Peng and given name Meng, surnamed Tian and given name Pian, and surnamed Shen and given name Dao, all were learned recluses of the state of Qi, were itinerants at Jixia, and each wrote books in several volumes. Since they by nature conformed with natural law, when they heard of such habits, they were utterly delighted." *Zhuangzi jishi*, 4: 1087. All these men were active during the second half of the fourth century BCE until the first quarter of the third century BCE.
10. Cf. 2.11.5–2.11.6.
11. Cheng Xuanying: "To 'hammer' means whip or beat, that is, inflict corrective punishment. 'Twists and turns' is a way of saying 'change and transformation.' In order that at different times he could go on using beatings as corrective punishment, he kept up with how times changed. Therefore, able to stay in step with change and transformation, he did not stubbornly stick to fixed ways." *Zhuangzi jishi*, 4: 1089.
12. Cheng Xuanying: "*Huoran* describes something that happens very quickly. Men of the Dao in antiquity, of empty and freely receptive mind, were so utterly unselfconscious that they encompassed all Heaven and Earth and no longer had anything to do with right and wrong. The transformative power of their actions worked as fast as the wind, gone in a moment, so how could they have left behind any sagely footprints to follow, anything to grasp and record in words!" *Zhuangzi jishi*, 4: 1092.
13. Cf. 12.13.2.
14. Cheng Xuanying: "To establish them as their teaching, they always did so by combining them with 'things never exist' as their principal doctrine." *Zhuangzi jishi*, 4: 1094. That is, "things never exist" means "things should never exist": one should always stay free of the conscious awareness of and deliberate involvement with things.
15. Pass Director Yin's saying also occurs in *Liezi* (Sayings of Master Lie); *Liezi jishi*, 4: 144–45. Cf. John Knoblock and Jeffrey Riegel, *The Annals of Lü Buwei*, 90–91.
16. Cf. *Laozi*, section 28: "He who knows the male [his maleness] yet sustains the female [his femaleness] will be a river valley for all under Heaven. . . . He who knows the white yet sustains the black will be a model for all under Heaven. . . . He who knows glory yet sustains disgrace will be a valley for all under Heaven." Richard John Lynn, *The Classic of the Way and Virtue*, 103.
17. Cf. *Laozi*, section 22: "Stepping aside keeps one's wholeness intact." Wang Bi comments: "Avoid flaunting yourself, and your brilliance will remain unimpaired." "Stepping aside" translates *qu* (literally "curved"), a sense suggested by Momoi Hakuroku's reading of the passage: "According to Wang's commentary, what is kept whole is one's brilliance, so *qu* must be the *qu* of *pianqu* [out of the way], and if one is out of the way, he is sure to be obscure [*an*]. If a person steps aside [i.e., out of the way], his whole being will fully shine forth." Quoted in Hatano Tarō, *Rōshi Dōtokukyō kenkyū* (Researches on *The Classic of the Way and Virtue* of Laozi), 161. See also Lynn, *The Classic of the Way and Virtue*, 88–90.
18. Cf. *Laozi*, section 4: "It [the Dao] blunts the sharp, cuts away the tangled, merges with the brilliant, and becomes one with the very dust." Lynn, *The Classic of the Way and Virtue*, 57.
19. Cheng Xuanying: "As it embraces everything and envelops all material existence, nothing ever exists apart from the Dao, so where else may things revert to their roots?" *Zhuangzi jishi*, 4: 1099. This muddled passage seems to paraphrase the *Laozi*, section 16, with Wang Bi's commentary: "Their attainment of emptiness absolute and their maintenance of quietude guileless." [Wang Bi:] "In other words, 'Attainment of emptiness' refers to the state of absolute guilelessness, and 'maintenance of quietude' refers to the state of perfect genuineness." "The myriad things interact." [Wang Bi:] "This refers to

their behavior and growth." "I, as such, observe their return." [Wang Bi:] "With emptiness and quietude, one observes their eternal return. Everything that exists arises from emptiness, and action arises from quietude. Thus, although the myriad things interact together, they all ultimately return to emptiness and quietude, which is the state of absolute guilelessness." "All things flourish, but each reverts to its roots." [Wang Bi:] "Each returns to where it began" "To return to the root is called 'quietude,' which means to revert to one's destiny, and reversion to one's destiny is called 'constancy.' " [Wang Bi:] "When one returns to the root, he becomes quiet, which is why this state is called 'quietude.' When one is quiet, he reverts to his destiny. This is why this state is referred to as 'reversion to destiny.' When one reverts to his destiny, he fulfills the constant dimensions of his nature and destiny, which is why this state is called 'constancy.'" Lynn, *The Classic of the Way and Virtue*, 75–76.

20. Cf. 5.18.2.
21. Cheng Xuanying: "The term 'uneven' refers to how it is sometimes fictional and sometime actual—the discourse is not consistently maintained. 'Unconventional and bizarre' is something like 'humorously cunning' [*guji*]. Although he used fables and parables to convey matters, the eras involved are now from one time, now another. Moreover, he uses the unconventional and bizarre in such humorously cunning ways that it is really well worth reading." *Zhuangzi jishi*, 4: 1101. Cf. "Uncle Slippery Operator," 4.42, and "Slippery Decrepit," 18.9.
22. See *Shangshu zhengyi* (Correct meaning of the venerated ancient documents), *Da Yu mo* ("Counsels of the Great Yu"), 4: 137b: "Yu praised such splendid words, saying. . . ."
23. This statement is reminiscent of a passage in the *Guanzi*, 1: 6b; W. Allyn Rickett, *Guanzi: Political and Philosophical Essays from Early China*, vol. 1, 72.
24. Cf. 2.8.24.
25. "Pointing to things does not reach them, yet such pointing never ceases" translates *zhi buzhi zhi bujue*, which obviously alludes to Gongsun Long's *Zhiwu lun* ((Treatise on designating things [in terms of attributes]), a chapter in the *Gongsun Longzi* (Sayings of Master Gongsun Long). Much controversy surrounds not only the meaning of the chapter as a whole, but also the meaning of *zhi*, whose range of meanings include "finger," "to point," " indicate," "elucidate," "attribute," "mean," and "meaning." I suggest that *zhi buzhi zhi bujue* might best be understood as, "Even though any human attempt to indicate what things really are is sure to fail, people still continue to do it," as if the assignment of names to and the descriptions of things really can account for the things themselves. However, for a detailed account of other possibilities and the complexity of the problems involved, see A. C. Graham, *Later Mohist Logic, Ethics, and Science*, 457–68.
26. Cheng Xuanying: "Dwelling in the South, surnamed Huang and given name Liao, he did not associate with the common run of people. A sojourner different from others, he wandered about in the otherworldly and was a true worthy." *Zhuangzi jishi*, 4: 1113.
27. *Lunyu* (Analects), 17: 2526b: "Someone who stuffs himself with food all day long without ever employing his mind is real trouble! Is not even playing at gambling games or chess more worthy than that!" The "someone who stuffs himself with food" echoes the "fat meat, wheat flour, and milled rice eaters" in Guo's comment.

APPENDIX A

PREFACES AND POSTSCRIPT

Prefaces that appear at the beginning of the *Zhuangzi jishi* (Collected commentaries to the *Zhuangzi*), and a postface attributed to Guo Xiang

A.1 Preface to *Zhuangzi jishi* (Collected commentaries to the *Zhuangzi*)

Wang Xianqian

When Master Guo Zijing [Guo Qingfan (1844–1896)] had completed his *Collected commentaries to the Zhuangzi*, he presented it to me for my perusal. However, it so happened that it was this year that the disturbance caused by the Eastern Barbarians occurred,[1] so as I complied with his request, I had to sigh, saying Oh, how Master Zhuang grasped the inevitable inherent in the mean! When he was beset with worldly obstacles from which there was no means of rescue, his spirit still happily wandered in limitless vastness, and, having examined things, no matter how great or small, and having investigated Heaven and Earth from beginning to end, astonished by all this, he had to put it into words. As Zou Yan [late fourth century BCE] said, "What the learned refer to as the Central States occupy only one part of the eighty-one parts of the whole world, and beyond the Sacred Region of the Crimson Realm [the Central States] there are nine regions in their own right, each surrounded by a small sea and with a great ocean all around the periphery."[2] And as Hui Shi [Huizi] said, "I know where the center of the whole world is; it is north of Yan and south of Yue,"[3] for which Master Zhuang praised him, while he himself told of such things as Shu and Hu boring holes in Hundun [Primal Chaos] until he died.[4] He spoke as if he saw the future beforehand and could deduce the final outcome. What an extraordinary man! When Zigong would make a well sweep to lift water, the old man on the south side of the Han River laughed at him.[5] The ingenuity involved in mechanical devices nowadays is ten thousand times that of a well sweep. If Master Zhuang were to see them, what would he make of them? When the Butters and the Crushers fought over territory between the snails horns, they left tens of thousands of corpses lying around, the victor pursuing the loser for ten days.[6] And who knows how many Butters and Crushers are around today. And what would Master Zhuang make of them?

Thus it was that for the Yellow Thearch to rule he had to deal with Chiyou,[7] and for Yao to rule he had to deal with Congzhi, Zong, Kuai, and Xu'ao.[8] These were not good things for the Yellow Thearch and Yao to have done. Nevertheless, since they wanted to empty those states and punish those people, there is no doubt that they were incapable of ruling with emptiness and quietude [*xujing*]. As for Master Zhuang himself, he sought out such a method but failed to get it, so he went and established a solitary existence out in the measureless wilds, where he would have the good fortune to keep himself whole and lead a happy existence. How was he ever up to dealing with the whole world! Moreover, although his book enjoyed great prominence in later ages, when the Jin [265–420] expanded it into the learning of the arcane [*xuanxue*], it gave no relief from the disastrous miasma emanating from the barbarian Jie,[9] and when the Tang [618–907] venerated it as a "true classic," it did nothing to rescue it from the disaster brought on by An [An Lushan (d. 757) and Shi [Shi Siming (d. 761)].[10] It was just as a cure for the licentiousness and extravagance of rulers and as a means to mitigate decadence and cupidity that it might have provided occasional help. However, the way it is written is yet so absolutely marvelous that Master Guo has taken endless delight in it. Consequently, he has compiled this work of collected commentaries on it, "adding on textual support and augmenting it with erudition."[11] If Master Zhuang could see it, would it not have him say, "Yet this is but the dregs of what I mean"![12] Nevertheless, just as except for the footprints, how could we ever see where one has stepped, so except for such dregs, how could we ever perceive the beauty of antiquity? For this work, Master Guo plays the role of the son of "Ink as Aid," which makes all those in the world nothing other than grandsons of "Repetitive Reciter."[13]

Twentieth year of the Guangxu era, a *jiawu* year [1894],
Winter, twelfth month, composed by this humble junior,
Wang Xianqian of Changsha.

A.2 Preface to *Zhuangzi zhu* (Commentary to the *Zhuangzi*)

Guo Xiang, Zixuan, from Henan

We can say of Master Zhuang that he did indeed understand the underlying basis of things [*ben*]. As such, he never kept wild talk about it to himself. His words are those of one who responds to things in a unique way but fails to identify with them. Since he so responded but failed to identify with them, his words may be apt but have no practical use, and since what he says fails to address practical matters, though lofty it has no application. A gap certainly exists between one such as he who quietly refrains from action and one who does start to act but only because it is inevitable—for him, it may be said his awareness is unselfconscious. When mind functions in terms of unselfconscious action, one responds as he is immediately affected, his response varying according to the moment involved. Such a one speaks only with utmost caution. As such, he forms one body with transformation and, flowing through a myriad ages, arcanely merges with things. How could such a one just playfully talk about otherworldly things only in terms of his own individual experience! Therefore, though Master Zhuang fails to be canonical, he is still the absolute best of all the non-canonical philosophers. However, although he himself never quite embodied it, his words do reach perfection, for they thoroughly reveal the cosmic order of Heaven and Earth, perfectly comply with the nature of the myriad things, completely comprehend the transformations attending life and death, thus clarifying the Dao as it bears on sage within and ruler without. Above he knows that the creator does not exist, and below he knows that things that do exist are self-created. His words are great and grand, their meaning an arcane marvel that reaches the perfect Dao by fusing subtlety with meaningful elegance. Calm and self-possessed, he is disengaged but not arrogant.

Thus, as the *Zhuangzi* says, people in a perfect age were "unselfconscious of what conforms to righteousness . . . [and] utterly without restraint behaved freely and thus tread the great method [of the Dao]."[14] "Happy their mouths were full of food, they wandered about drumming on their full bellies."[15] The ultimate reach of perfect benevolence lies in utter impartiality, and the complete realization of filial piety and paternal compassion lies in forgetting all about both.[16] Let rites and music return to the potentiality of self,[17] and let loyalty and trustworthiness shine forth with the light of Heaven.[18] If one uses such light, pristine simplicity[19] will fulfill itself. As a result, the numinous vessel[20] will work its independent transformation in the realm of arcane obscurity, its wellspring running deep and strong. Therefore, however much incessant waves might surge and high winds bluster, all becomes calm when people can live as it suits their natures and the aspirations of the common folk are met. Their meanness is converted into magnanimity, their sufferings alleviated, and, without any increased effort to shed them, all their conceit and boasting disappears in the process.

Therefore, if one reads this book, he will transcend the common world to realize that he already has what is appropriate in himself. He will cross over Mount Kunlun and ford the Great Void to wander at ease in the Garden of the Dim and the Dark. Even the insatiably greedy and the rashly ambitious will for a time pick from its overabundant fragrant blossoms, savor its brimming richness of flavor, and lose himself amidst its sounds and images. Therefore, such a one will have enough expanded thought and sensibilities to achieve a state of mind in which physical existence is forgotten and self-fulfillment achieved. So how much the more capable of this will be one who plumbs the profundities of mind and makes sport of longevity! Profound and far-sighted, such a one abandons the dusty world and finds his way back to the arcane fulfillment of limits.

A.3 Postscript [*houyu*] to the *Zhuangzi* by Guo Xiang[21]

Learning esteems it a virtue to make fulfillment of one's nature easy to understand, and does not hold the ability to study heterodox doctrines in high regard. Nevertheless, Master Zhuang's great talent is known throughout the world, and his work truly is so replete with exceptional phrasing and splendid expression that his "true words seem false." Therefore, scholars stuck in just one narrow corner of learning cannot understand the broad thrust of his meaning, and instead rashly inserted wild stories into it. As for chapters such as *Eyi* [Blocked Chess Move], *Yixiu* [Mind on Teacher's Salary], *Weiyan* [Cautionary Words], *Youfu* [Swimming Duck], and *Zixu*,[22] in general all clever interpolations, if counted in make up three parts of ten of all the texts.[23] Some are forced into familiar terms, while others altered so as to be more fantastic. Some resemble the *Shanhai jing* (Classic of mountains and waters), and others are like *zhanmeng shu* (works of dream interpretation). Some come from the *Huainan* (Master of Huainan), while others dispute about names and reality. Joined to elegant language, they drive on as teams of paired dragons and snakes.[24] Moreover, their style is superficial and illogical, utterly failing to say anything profound and are simply impossible to understand. It makes one feel as if *Kun* (Impasse) were followed by *Meng* (Juvenile Ignorance) since one gets so stuck in one place that the gist is completely lost.[25] How could this ever be the way to get at what Master Zhuang meant! Therefore, I deleted all such texts and included none of them here and, instead, editing the best, I brought together all the important things he said, in a total of thirty-three chapters. The Grand Historian said: "Master

Zhuang's given name was Zhou, a native of Meng district in the state of Song, who once served in the Office of Lacquer Manufacture and was a contemporary of King Hui of Wei [r. 370–334 BCE], King Xuan of Qi [r. 319–301], and King Wei of Chu [r. 339–329]."[26]

A.4 *Jingdian shiwen xulu* (Exegesis of classics and scriptures, explanation of the contents), *Zhujie chuanshu ren* (Annotators and transmitters), *Introduction to Zhuangzi yinyi* (Pronunciation and meaning of the *Zhuangzi*) by Lu Deming (556–627)

Master Zhuang's surname was Zhuang and his given name was Zhou, though the Grand Historian [Sima Qian] said that it was Zixiu. He was a native of Meng district in the state of Liang. At the time of the Six States,[27] he served as a clerk in the Office of Lacquer Manufacture. He was a contemporary of King Hui of Wei [r. 370–334 BCE], King Xuan of Qi [r. 319–301], and King Wei of Chu [r. 339–329], and Li Yi[28] says that he was contemporary with King Min of Qi [r. 357–320]. Qi and Chu once invited him to become their prime minister, but he declined both. People at the time all highly esteemed the art of rhetorical persuasion, but Master Zhuang kept himself apart and approached such matters with noble integrity. Carefree and relaxed, he achieved self-fulfillment. Keeping in the same vein as the teachings of Master Lao, he wrote a book of more than ten thousand words and which just dealt with spontaneous freedom, the natural, unselfconscious action and regarding all things equal. For the most part, he conveys what he wants to say in parables, which he uses to set forth principles, so he cannot be censured on the basis of what is literally said in the text.

However, though Master Zhuang's vast talent enjoys universal renown, the meaning of his writing is so brilliant and profound, in that its "true words that seem false,"[29] that no one can understand the gist of its overall meaning. Later people "added feet"[30] to it so its true meaning was gradually lost, which is why Guo Zixuan said, "People of limited talent who could handle just one aspect of things rashly inserted wild stories into it so that cleverly concealed interpolations such as the *Eyi* [Blocked Chess Move], *Yixiu* [Mind on Teacher's Salary], *Weiyan* [Cautionary Words], *Youfu* [Swimming Duck], and *Zixu* chapters came to make up three parts of ten of the text as a whole."

The *Zhuangzi* in fifty-two chapters listed in the dynastic bibliography in the *History of the former Han* [206 BCE–24 CE] by Ban Gu (32–92), the *Hanshu yiwen zhi*, is the work to which Sima Biao [240–306] and Mengshi [Master Meng, name and dates unknown] later wrote commentaries. It contains much strange and incredible material, sometimes resembling the *Shanhai jing* [Classic of Mountains and Waters (compiled probably in the third century BCE) and sometimes works concerned with dream divination. As such, these commentators selected and rejected parts based on their opinion of them. Although the inner chapters are the same for all versions, as for the rest of the work, some have the outer chapters but lack the miscellaneous chapters, and it is only Zixuan's [Guo Xiang's] commentary edition that entirely captures Master Zhuang's real meaning, which is why it is universally admired. When Xu Xianmin [Xu Mian (344–397) and Li Hongfan [Li Gui (early fourth century)] prepared their pronunciation editions, they both used Guo Xiang's version, and I too now use it as the base text here.

[Lu now lists the known editions of the Zhuangzi of his day:] the Cui Zhuan [later third century] commentary edition in twenty-seven chapters. Cui was a native of Qinghe commandery [in present-day Hebei)] and held the office of court gentleman of consultation under the Jin dynasty. This work consists of seven inner chapters and twenty outer chapters. The Xiang Xiu [ca. 221–ca. 300] commentary edition was in twenty-six chapters and twenty fascicles, which is also known as a work in twenty-seven or twenty-eight chapters. This version also lacks the miscellaneous chapters but has been provided with pronunciation notes in three fascicles. There was also the Sima Biao [240–306] commentary edition in fifty-two chapters. Sima Biao's personal name was Shaotong; he was a native of Henei commandery [northern Henan] and held the office of director of the palace library under the Jin dynasty. This work consists of seven inner chapters, twenty-eight outer chapters, fourteen miscellaneous chapters, explications in three parts, and it has been provided with pronunciation notes in three fascicles. The Guo Xiang commentary edition was in thirty-three fascicles and thirty-three chapters. Guo's personal name was Zixuan; he was a native of Henei commandery and served as a recorder for a princedom grand mentor under the Jin dynasty. This work consists of seven inner chapters, fifteen outer chapters, eleven miscellaneous chapters, and it has been provided with pronunciation notes in three fascicles. The Li Yi [later third-early fourth centuries] collected exegeses edition was in thirty fascicles and thirty chapters. Li's personal name was Jingzhen; he was a native of Xiangcheng in Yingzhou [present-day central Henan] and held the office of adjutant to the counselor-in-chief [*chengxiang canjun*] under the Jin dynasty. He gave himself the sobriquet Xuandao zi [Master of the Arcane Dao]. It is also known as a work in thirty-five chapters, and it has been provided with pronunciation notes in one fascicle. The Master Meng commentary edition was in fifty-two chapters. It is unknown who this Meng was. The Wang Shuzhi elucidation of the meaning edition was in three fascicles. Wang's personal name was Muye; he was a native of Langye [modern Donghai in Jiangsu] and lived as a scholar recluse during the Song dynasty [420–479]. He also wrote a commentary to it. The Li Gui pronunciation edition was in one fascicle, the Xu Mian pronunciation edition in three fascicles.

A.5 Preface to *Zhuangzi shu* (Sub-commentary to the *Zhuangzi*) by Cheng Xuanying, of the Tang, Master of Doctrine at the Xihua Temple

The *Zhuangzi* provides the means to explain the deep root of the Dao and its Virtue [*daode*], to elucidate the marvelous purport of the twofold arcane, to find carefree happiness in the disinterested serenity of unselfconscious action, and to cast light on the profound mystery of independent transformation. It renders all nine schools of thought mute as it comprehensively addresses everything all philosophers might say. It actually serves as the consummate teaching for human life and truly renders subtle truths that lie outside the appearance of things. Its author's surname is Zhuang, given name Zhou and personal name Zixiu. He was born in Meng district, Suiyang [present-day Shangqiu county, Henan], in the state of Song. He honored Changsang Gongzi as his teacher, and he himself became known as the Immortal of Nanhua. Since he lived at the beginning of the Warring States era [403–221 BCE], when the Zhou dynasty was in its final decline, he lamented how the common folk were poverty stricken and was troubled by the decline of the Dao and its virtue. Therefore, making a fervent resolution to do something about it, he wrote this work. Since its words are so great and far-ranging and its purport so profound and far-reaching, involving things that inferior persons of learning would not have heard of, how could someone who is shallow in knowledge and insight ever attempt to study it!

The term "master" is used because it is an address signifying praise and honor, for the ancients called teachers "master." That the address "master" also appears in the title of this book is not just to provide an overall name to its three collections of chapters, but also to serve as a title that conforms to names of works of philosophy in general. In the term "inner chapters," "inner" is a designation that stands in opposition to "outer," and "chapters" is used here to mean a book. The ancients removed the green outer layer of bamboo to make bamboo writing slips and used soft leather thongs to tie them together. Such books formed chapters just as we today join paper together to form fascicles. Thus, it was that Yuankai [Du Yu (222–284)] said, "Major events were recorded on large bamboo or wooden slips, but for lesser matters only small bamboo or wooden slips were used."[31] Just so the "inner" essentially addresses foundational principles, and the "outer" tells of the footprints left by the doing of things. Although matters might seem obvious, without principles they will not be understood, and since principle is latent in all things, it manifests itself in absolutely everything, so it is necessary at the start to clarify marvelous principle, and this is why this is addressed first in the inner chapters.

The principles addressed in the inner chapters are profound. Therefore, chapter titles are provided that are separate from the text. Guo Xiang always adds explanations for such titles immediately below them, as he does for "Spontaneous Free Play" and "On Regarding All Things Equal." From then on, it is the first two characters of the texts that are selected as chapter titles, such as for "Webbed Toes" and "Horses' Hooves." The expression "spontaneous free play" has elicited disparate explanations throughout ancient and modern times. If we now consider all these in general terms, three basic interpretations take shape. The first: Gu Tongbo [Gu Huan (fl. 420–479)][32] said, "*Xiao* 'leisurely move' means *xiao* 'dispel,' 'remove,' and *yao* 'distant,' 'remote' is the same as *yuan* 'far and wide.' One completely removes all entanglement with selfconscious action and gains a far-reaching vision of the principle of unselfconscious action. Since this is how one should play with things, it is referred to as 'spontaneous free play.'" The second: Zhi Daolin [Zhidun (314–366)] said, " 'Let things be things and be not an other to things.'[33] Thus it is that spontaneous freedom depends not on the self. Arcanely resonating with things, one makes speed without hurrying; as such, far and wide, nothing fails to be accomplished. Since this is how one should play with the world, it is referred to as 'spontaneous free play.'"[34] The third: Muye [Wang Shuzhi (ca. 420–ca. 479)] said, " 'Spontaneous free play' probably is a term for liberated self-fulfillment. Perfect virtue so fills one's inner being that at no time does one fail to be fitting and in doing so forgets all personal involvement with things as he resonates with them, so no venture fails to go smoothly. Since this is how one should play with the world, it is referred to as 'spontaneous free play.'"[35]

The inner chapters cast light on the basis of principles; the outer chapters address how these are manifest in events; and the miscellaneous chapters cast light on how to manage affairs. Although the inner chapters cast light on the basis of principles, this is always in conjunction with their manifestation in events, and although the outer chapters cast light on such manifestation in events, marvelous principle is given very much attention here as well. However, interpretation of how the text establishes its teachings and why such section divisions exist depends on which of many different theories one might follow.

The reason why the "Spontaneous Free Play" chapter is placed right at the beginning is because it addresses how the person of learning, fully realizing the Dao, is so intelligent and resourceful in wisdom and virtue that whatever he does it is always fitting, and however he interacts with things, it is always with spontaneous freedom. This is why "spontaneous freedom" is used in the name for it. The sage, free of dependency, reflects the secret workings of nature as if he were a mirror. Since such a one understands the two kinds of wisdom that address the expedient and the fundamentally real, he can discern the grand equality that pervades all possible realms of existence. This is why the "On Regarding All Things Equal" chapter is placed next. Once one can point to a single horse to indicate the sum total of Heaven and Earth, discern all things as an undifferentiated whole, and allow the intelligence to concentrate and become still, he can as such take care of himself and nurture life. This is why the "The Mastery of Nurturing Life" chapter is placed next. Once one has forgotten both good and evil, allows external conditions and one's awareness of them to merge marvelously together, and gives oneself over to transformation and keeps in step with change, he can as such engage with the human world. This is why the "The Ways of the World" chapter is placed next. Since one's inner virtue fills one completely, one can render that virtue disjointed and use it externally to interact with others in such a way that one can keep in step with their ups and downs. Since this deals with the arcane tally between the inner and the outer, the "Tally of Virtue Replete" chapter is placed next. As still water acts as a mirror, one should interact with others unselfconsciously, forget virtue and physical form, and effect a perfect communion of inner being and outer conditions. One can as such foster success in everyone. This is why the "The Great Model Teacher" is placed next. True sages of antiquity understood Heaven and understood man, sharing the same merit as creation itself. One resonates with others only if one is tranquil, and after that he can control everyone and everything. This is why the "Fit to Be Sovereigns" chapter is placed next.[36] Beginning with the "Webbed Toes" chapter on, all chapters take the first two characters of their texts as titles. Since no other meaning is attached to them, I shall not list any more of them here.

Moreover, of eminent scholars from antiquity on, as well as recluses of the Han to the Jin eras, none failed to tarry in pleasure in it, providing explanation of words and expressions. Although their interpretations of meaning cannot be faulted, they still also display fine rhetoric and can penetrate the hidden meaning. I, Xuanying, without regard to my own mediocrity and ignorance, applied myself to the study of it while still young, and so for thirty years I have examined it meticulously and thought deeply about it. Based on the commentary to thirty chapters written by Zixuan [Guo Xiang], I have prepared a sub-commentary for each chapter, which amounts to a total of thirty chapters.[37] Although the way it expresses things is repeatedly careless and awkward, it does to some extent communicate my thoughts and realize my intentions. Daring not to make it a bequest to later generations, I have merely done nothing more than make this record to cope with my forgetfulness.

Notes

1. The "Eastern Barbarians" were the Japanese. The Sino-Japan War, which was disastrous for China, began in July 1894 and continued into 1895.
2. This quotation is presented as if it were Zou Yan's own words, but Wang Xianqian is actually paraphrasing Sima Qian's (ca. 145–ca. 86 BCE) summary of Zou Yan's cosmology as presented in Sima Qian, *Shiji*, 74: 2344.
3. Yan is the most northern of the states, and Yue the most southern, Thus, there is no center of the world. It is wherever one happens to be. See 33.20.
4. See 7.27.
5. See 12.25–12.27.
6. See 25.19.
7. See 29.12.
8. See 2.15.
9. The Jie, a branch of the Xiongnu, had occupied northern Shanxi during the Wei and Western Jin eras, and after expanding and consolidating with other elements of the Xiongnu, drove the Jin out of north China in 316 with the capture of Luoyang, forcing it to reestablish itself in the south, deprived of its heartland in the Yellow River basin.
10. The great rebellion of 755, led by An Lushan (d. 757) and Shi Siming (d. 761), devastated the Tang; though the dynasty did not fall, it was much weakened and never recovered its former glory.
11. See 16.4.8.
12. See 13.37.
13. See 6.18.2.
14. See 20.7.8.
15. See 9.5.1.
16. See 14.7–14.9.
17. Although texts of Guo's preface in different editions prefer to write *yi'neng*, " Already able," instead of *ji'neng*, "potentiality of self," *ji'neng* seems the more likely reading, for here Guo turns a statement in the *Analects* of Confucius upside down; see *Lunyu zhushu* (Analects, with commentary and subcommentary) , 12: 2502c: "If one conquers the self and recovers propriety, benevolence results." However, the possibility remains that the expression is *yi'neng* after all, in which case the line should read: "Let rites and music return to what is already one's potential."
18. Cf. 23.24.1: "When the inner self is at peace and stable, such a one shines forth with the light of Heaven."
19. The concept of pristine simplicity, the "uncarved block," figures prominently in the *Laozi*, sections 15, 19, 28, 32, and 37; see Richard John Lynn, *The Classic of the Way and Virtue*, 74, 82, 103, 108, 109, and 118.
20. Cf. *Laozi*, section 29: "all under Heaven is the numinous vessel, which cannot be acted on. One who acts on it will destroy it; one who tries to grasp it will lose it." Wang Bi makes it clear that the sage ruler, as the steward of the numinous vessel, must allow it to develop in its own way: "The myriad folk follow Nature in forming their natures. This is why one can act in accordance with them but not act upon them, can identify with them but not interfere with them. People have their constant nature, so if one tries to create something artificial out of them, he is sure to destroy them. People have their own comings and goings, so if one tries to grasp them, he is sure to lose them." Lynn, *The Classic of the Way and Virtue*, 105.

21. The *Kōzanji hon Sōji* (Kōzan [High Mountain] Temple edition of the *Zhuangzi*) had been preserved at that temple near Kyoto since the Kamakura period (1185–1333), and it is likely to have been inscribed during the Southern Song (1127–1278). It consists of fragments of a *Zhuangzi Guo Xiang zhu* (The *Zhuangzi*, with commentary by Guo Xiang), seven of the *Waipian* (Outer chapters) and *Zapian* (Miscellaneous chapters): *Gengsang Chu* , chapter 23), *Waiwu* (External Things, chapter 26), *Yuyan* (Parables and Allegories, chapter 27), *Rangwang* (Refusing Rulership, chapter 28), *Shuojian* (Discourse on swords, chapter 30), *Yufu* (The Old Fisherman, chapter 31), and *Tianxia* (All Under Heaven, chapter 33). The Guo Xiang postscript is added directly after the end of the commentary to chapter 33 and for the most part appears to be an explanation of why the work consists of thirty-three chapters and ends there. See Takeuchi Yoshio, *Rōshi to Sōshi* (the *Laozi* and *Zhuangzi*), 128–29; Wang Shumin, "*Ba Riben Gaoshan si jiuchao juanzi ben Zhuangzi canjuan* (Postscript to the incomplete old hand-written scroll edition of the *Zhuangzi* owned by the Kōzanji in Japan)," *Zhongyang yanjiuyuan lishi yuyan yanjiusuo jikan* 22 (1951), 161–70, text of the postscript recorded on 166; Fukunaga Mitsuji, trans., *Sōji* (*Zhuangzi*), *zatsuhen ge* (Miscellaneous chapters, part 2) (vol. 6), 258–59; Livia Knaul, "Lost *Chuang-Tzu* Passages," *Journal of Chinese Religions* 10 (1982), 53–79.
22. *Zixu* may have been the title of a chapter concerned with Wu Yun, personal name Zixu, the famous general and chief minister of the state of Wu, who, when he continued to give good but unwelcome advice to the king of Wu was ordered to commit suicide in 482 BCE.
23. These two sentences also appear, worded slightly differently, in Lu Deming's "Preface to *Zhuangzi yinyi* (Pronunciation and meaning of the *Zhuangzi*)," *Jingdian shiwen* (Textual explications for classics and scriptures), where they are attributed to Guo Xiang; see section A.4 of this appendix.
24. That is, they mix great with small, significant with petty.
25. *Kun* (Impasse) and *Meng* (Youthful Ignorance) are the forty-seventh and fourth hexagrams in the *Classic of Changes*: hindrance and obstruction, resulting in a continued failure to understand.
26. This passage is worded slightly differently in Sima Qian, *Shiji* (Records of the Grand Historian), 63: 2143.
27. The Six States, during the Warring States era (475–221 BCE), were Qi, Chu, Yan, Han, Zhao, and Wei, all located east of the Hangu Pass in Henan.
28. Li Yi, who seems to have been an earlier contemporary of Guo Xiang, authored a *Zhuangzi jijie* (Collected interpretations of the *Zhuangzi*), which seems lost since the Tang era and survives only in fragments quoted in other works, Lu Deming's included.
29. Lu quotes the *Laozi*, section 78; Lynn, *The Classic of the Way and Virtue*, 1: 187.
30. See Liu Xiang (ca. 77–ca. 6 BCE), ed., *Zhanguo ce* (Intrigues of the warring states), 4: 17b–18a, where the story is told of the retainers who held a contest for a goblet of wine, the one who finished drawing a snake on the ground first would win the wine; when one finished first, being so far ahead, decided to add feet to it, he had to forfeit the wine—since snakes do not have feet." "Adding feet" became a cliché for ruining something by overdoing it.
31. Du Yu (222–285), preface to *Chunqiu jingzhuan jijie* (Collected exegeses on the *Spring and Autumn Annals*, classic and commentary), included in Du Yu and Kong Yingda (574–648), *Chunqiu Zuozhuan zhengyi* (Correct meaning of the *Spring and Autumn Annals*, the Zuo tradition), 1: 1704b.

32. Cheng Xuanying refers to Gu Huan as Gu Tongbo because Gu once resided at the Tongbo guan (Abbey of the Paulownias and Cypresses) on Mount Tiantai. This short passage from Gu's writings seems to have survived only as quoted by Cheng Xuanying.
33. Cf. 20.4.2.
34. The *Zhishi xiaoyao lun* (Master Zhi's discussion of spontaneity) has long been lost; this quotation is from a longer excerpt preserved in Liu Jun's (462–521) commentary to Liu Yiqing's (403–444) *Shishuo xinyu*; see *Shishuo xinyu*, part 4: *Wenxue* (Letters and learning), 32, A.2: 220; cf. Richard B. Mather, trans. *Shih-shuo Hsin-yü: A New Account of Tales of the World, by Liu I-ch'ing*, 116.
35. Wang Shuzhi, who lived during the Song era of the Southern dynasties (420–479), is known to have authored a *Zhuangzi yishu* (Subcommentary on the meaning of the *Zhuangzi*) in three fascicles, which has long been lost. The quotation here seems from that work.
36. Cheng notes the connection between the resonance that a ruler should have with his subjects and his fitness to rule.
37. The number "thirty" should be regarded as approximate in each of these three instances.

APPENDIX B

LOST WORKS ATTRIBUTED TO GUO XIANG

1. *Laozi zhu* 老子注 (Commentary to the *Laozi* [Sayings of Master Lao])

Guo Xiang is among the sixty-one commentators to the *Daode jing* (Scripture of the Dao and Its Virtue) of Master Lao listed by Du Guangting 杜光庭 (850–933) in his preface (dated 901) to *Daode zhenjing guangsheng yi* 道德真經廣聖義 (Explications expanding upon the sage's [Emperor Xuanzong] commentary to the *True Scripture of the Dao and Its Virtue*).[1] Moreover, in chapter 4 of this work, which begins supposedly with a preface by Tang Emperor Xuanzong 玄宗, Li Longji 李隆基 (685–762), a comment attributed to Guo is added to the explication provided by Du Guangting:

> 及乎窮理盡性，閉緣息想，處實行權，坐忘遺照，損之又損，玄之又玄，此殆不可得而言傳者矣。其教圓，其文約，其旨暢，其言邇，故游其廊廡者，皆自以為升堂睹奧，及研精覃思，然後知其於秋毫之端，萬分未得其一也。**Tang Emperor Xuanzong: "But as for examining principles in it [the *Daodejing*] to the utmost and entirely getting at its nature, if one closes down perception, halts ratiocination, engages with its substance provisionally, situates oneself in forgetfulness and banishes judgement, having thus less upon less, one may attain the arcane upon arcane, but this probably cannot be transmitted in words. Though its teaching is consummate, its text is spare; though its meaning is far-reaching, its words are plain and familiar. Consequently, those who wander only to its outer galleries all mistakenly think they have ascended its main hall and peered into its secrets. It is only after one has examined carefully and**

pondered deeply does he realize that his understanding but compares to the end of an autumn hair; that is, he has not got one part in ten thousand of it!" Du Guangting: 沉研鑽極。考情運思。探道之奧。極道之源。箋註詮疏。以求聖人之旨。所得之理逾少。聖人之意逾深 。"To penetrate as far as possible through exhaustive investigation, to determine concepts by examining innate truths, and to explore the hidden mysteries of the Dao to try to get at its original essence, commentary and explication are thus used to find out what the Sage [Master Lao] meant, but the less such truths are grasped the more profound the Sage's meaning appears." 郭象曰。秋毫之端細矣。又未得其萬分之一也。秋毫者。兔秋所生之毛也。端者。末也。Guo Xiang: "The end of an autumn hair is, indeed, tiny, thus one does not get even one part in ten thousand. An 'autumn hair' refers to the fur that a hare grows in autumn, and 'end' means tip."[2]

Whether Guo's comment comes from his lost *Laozi* commentary or from some other piece in his lost collected works is impossible to determine. It does not correspond to anything in his *Zhuangzi* commentary. Here follow the five fragments of Guo's commentary copied into Du's work:

Laozi **3:** 是以聖人之治。虛其心。 實其腹 **"Therefore the way the sage governs is to keep their minds/hearts empty and their bellies full."** 郭曰。 其惡改盡。 諸善自生。 懷道抱一。 淳和內足。 實其腹也。 Guo Xiang: "Once entirely changed from evil ways, every goodness spontaneously grows in them; as such, they internalize the Dao and embrace the One. Simple and mild, they are inwardly content—this is what is means by 'keep their bellies full.' "[3]

Laozi **4:** 湛兮似或存 **"Its depth is so deep, oh, that it seems somehow to exist (*cun*)."** 郭象曰。存在也。道湛然安靜。古今不變。終始一。故曰。存存而無物。故曰似也。Guo Xiang: "*Cun* means "be present" (*zai*). The Dao is so deep that it is utterly quiet, utterly still. It never changes from past to present, and though beginning and endings occur, it stays one and the same. As such, we say it exists, but its existence has no materiality; as such, "it seems to exist."[4]

Laozi **10:** 生而不有 **"He [the sage ruler] gives them life, yet he possesses them not."** 郭曰 。氤氳合化。 庶物從生。顯仁藏用，即有爲跡。功不歸己。 故曰不有。Guo Xiang: "It is by the blending and transformation of the generative powers [of the Dao] that all things accordingly have life. Manifested in benevolence and hidden in functioning, this results in 'footprints' made, but such accomplishments should not be ascribed to the ruler himself."[5]

The sage ruler governs just as the Dao functions in nature. "Manifested" and "hidden" allude to the *Xici zhuan* (Commentary on the appended phrases),

Part One, in the *Classic of Changes*: "It [the Dao] is manifested in benevolence and hidden within its functioning." Wang Bi: "It gives succor to the myriad things; this is why the text says: 'It is manifested in benevolence.' It functions on a daily basis, but they are unaware of it; this is why the text says: 'It is . . . hidden within its functioning. . . . Although the sages embody the Dao and apply it as function. . . . they may have success without hindrance throughout the whole world, but, as a consequence, there are always outward signs [i.e., "footprints"] to the way they bring things to pass."[6]

Laozi **24:** 自矜者不長 **"One filled with self-importance does not last long."**郭象曰。

矜誇自恃不解忘功。衆所不與。故不長也。Bragging and conceited, such a one fails to understand that he should free his mind of all thought of merit. It is because no one gets along well with him that he "does not last long."[7]

Laozi **39:** 谷得一以盈。**"Valleys can be filled by having obtained the One."** 郭象曰。谷。川谷也。谷川得一。故能泉源流潤。溪壑盈滿。 Guo Xiang: "Valleys means river valleys. When river valleys obtain the one [unify waters], as fountainheads they spread nourishing moisture, their stream basins fully replete."[8]

2. ***Zhuangzi yin*** **莊子音 (Pronunciation [of names and terms] in the** ***Zhuangzi*****)**

莊子音三卷郭象撰 : three-fascicle edition attributed to Guo Xiang is listed in *Suishu Jingji zhi* 隋書經籍志 (History of the Sui, treatise on classics and scriptures).[9] This same information is repeated in Zheng Qiao (1104–1162), *Tongzhi* (Comprehensive history of institutions).[10] Although these two bibliographies list the *Zhuangzi yin* as a separate work, Lu Duming (556–627), in his *Jingdian shiwen* (Explicating the texts of scriptures and classics), lists it as the last part of the *Zhuangzi* edition that he uses as base text: 郭象注三十三卷三十三篇。字子玄河内人晉太傅主簿内篇七外篇十五雜篇十一為音三卷 "The Guo Xiang commentary edition in thirty-three fascicles and thirty-three chapters: His personal name Zixuan, he was a native of Henei commandery and served as a recorder for a princedom grand mentor under the Jin dynasty. This work consists of seven inner chapters, fifteen outer chapters, eleven miscellaneous chapters, and a *Weiming* (Managing Pronunciation) in three fascicles."[11] Apparently this last three-fascicle section either was later detached from the edition that Lu knew or was already also circulating at the time as a separate text. In either case, it does not seem to have survived beyond the Tang.

3. *Lunyu tilue* 論語體略 (**Essentials of the** ***Lunyu*** **[Analects]**):

論語體略二卷晉太傅主簿郭象撰 "Two-fascicle edition by the Recorder for the grand mentor Guo Xiang of the Jin," listed in *Suishu Jingji zhi* 隋書經籍志 (History of the Sui, treatise on classics and scriptures), *Suishu*, 32: 936: 晉太傅主簿郭象著。論語體略二卷 。"Two-fascicle edition by the Recorder for the grand mentor Guo Xiang of the Jin," listed in *Jiu Tangshu jingji zhi* 舊唐書經籍志 (Old history of the Tang, treatise on classics and scriptures), 46: 1982. Two-fascicle edition listed in *Xin Tangshu yiwen zhi* 新唐書藝文志 (New history of the Tang, biographical treatise), 57: 1444. *Qinding siku quanshu zongmu* (Comprehensive catalog of the complete *FourTreasuries Library*, authorized by His Majesty), records Guo Xiang among the commentators included in the *Lunyu yishu* 論語義疏 (Explications and expository commentaries to the *Analects*) of Huang Kan 皇侃 (488–545).[12] This work has been lost in China since the Southern Song dynasty but it was preserved in Japan, where it was published in an amended edition by Nemoto Sonshi 根本遜志 (1699–1764) in 1750, a copy of which made its way to China about 1770, where, after considerable editing, it was included in the *Siku Quanshu* during the 1780s with the title *Lunyu jijie yishu* 論語集解義疏 (Collected explications and expository commentaries to the *Analects*). Another early edition was published in Guangzhou in 1873 by the Yuedong Shuju 粵東書局 in the series *Gujing jie huihan* 古經解彙函 (Explications of the classics collections casket), and a convenient moveable-type punctuated edition was published in 1923 by the *Kaitokudō kinenkai* 懐徳堂記念會 in Osaka.[13] The *Lunyu jijie* 論語集解 was compiled by He Yan 何晏 (193–249)[14] and includes commentaries by Kong Anguo 孔安國 (156–74 BCE), Bao Xian 包咸 (7 BCE–65 CE), a certain Master Zhou 周氏 (first century), Ma Rong 馬融 (79–166), Zheng Xuan 鄭玄 (127–200), Chen Qun 陳群 (d. 236), Wang Su 王肅 (195–256), and Zhousheng Lie 周生烈 (195–256). Huang Kan's *yishu* (expository commentaries) includes, besides nine fragments of Guo Xiang's *Lunyu Tilue* (Essentials of the *Analects*), excerpts from twelve other commentaries, all by Western Jin– and Eastern Jin–era (265–419) figures, the best known of which are probably Li Chong 李充 (d. ca. 362) and Yuan Hong 袁宏 (ca. 328–376). The passages from Guo's *Lunyu tilue* (Essentials of the *Analects*) quoted and analyzed next[15] are taken from Ma Guohan 馬國翰 (1794–1857), ed., *Yuhan Shanfang jiyi shu* 玉函山房輯佚書 (Fragments of lost works gathered at the Jade Casket Studio) (1874), *Jingbian Lunyu lei* 經編論語類 (Confucian Classics division, *Analects* category), case 5, vol. 3. Ma gleaned these fragments from Huang's *Lunyu jijie yishu* and collected them under the title *Lunyu tilue*, to which he added a preface, part of which reads: 此編隋經籍志。唐藝文志並云二卷。陸德明釋文序錄不著目。蓋其書在唐時惟秘閣有之。世少傳者。今則散佚。皇侃義疏引凡九節輯爲一卷。考象嘗注莊子。襲取向秀之言。頗爲世所詬病。解說經義度亦未必盡有心得。然江熙集解列論語十三家有郭象。。。。其言與衛瓘范甯諸人同採。蓋亦有

表見於當時者。今玩其佚說。不離元[玄]宗。而尚自暢達。晉人經解。取備一家。聊寄妮古之意云爾。象別有論語隱。亦佚。考訂另錄。次此卷後。 "Although this work is listed in both the Sui *jingji zhi* and the Tang *yiwenzhi* as consisting of two fascicles, it does not appear listed in the *Preface* to Lu Deming's *Jingdian shiwen*, because by the Tang surely only the imperial library had a copy and opportunities for public circulation were scarce. Now scattered and though lost, I have taken the nine passages from it included in Huang Kan's *Lunyu yishu* (Explications and Expository Commentaries to the *Analects*) and gathered them in one fascicle. . . . The vocabulary Guo chooses to use is similar to that of Wei Guan (220–291) and Fan Ning (339–401) and, as such, also exhibits features representative of the writing in that age. Now savoring these long lost remarks of his, I find they do not stray from the tradition of arcane Daoist thought (*xuanzong*) and even go on to develop it further. Therefore, for explications of the Confucian classics by people of the Jin, take these to represent one particular master and for a time indulge in his ancient way of thinking."

1. From *Lunyu* (Analects), "Conduct Government," part 2 (*Weizheng dier* 爲政第二): 子曰。爲政以德。譬如北辰居其所。而衆星共之。钟谦钧。**"The Master said, 'If one conducts government with virtue, he shall be like the pole star that keeps to its own place while all other stars pay court to it.' "** Guo: 萬物皆得性謂之德。夫爲政者奚事哉。得萬物之性。故云德而已也。得其性。則歸之。失其性則違之。"When the myriad folk all can fulfill their natures, this is what is meant by 'virtue'—and what has 'conduct government' to do with that! Only when the myriad folk are allowed to fulfill their nature may it be said to be 'virtue.' If they are allowed to fulfill their natures, they gravitate to one [a ruler], but if they are made to violate their natures, they turn against him."[16]

"Virtue" (*de* 德) in these texts rarely simply means moral virtue or goodness, but it usually refers to such qualities of human character and behavior as efficacy, power, potential, potency, force, or strength—all of which can underlie moral goodness.

2. From "Conduct Government" part 2 (*Weizheng dier* 爲政第二): 子曰。導之以政。齊之以刑。民免而無恥。導之以德。齊之以禮。有恥且格。**"The Master said, 'Guide them with government and regulate them with punishment, and the common folk will evade both without shame, but lead them with virtue and regulate them with propriety, and they will have a sense of shame and become rectified.'"** Guo: 政者。立常制以正民者也。刑者。興法辟以割制物者也。制有常則可矯。法辟興則可避。可避則違情而苟免。可矯則去性而從制。從制外正而心內未服。人懷苟免則無恥于物。其於化不亦薄乎。故曰。民免而無恥也。德者。得其性者也。禮者。體其情也。情有所恥。而性有所本。得其性則本至。體其情則知恥。知恥

則無刑而自齊。本至則無制而自正。是以導之以德。齊之以禮。有恥且格。"Government" means establishing invariable rules, which are used to rectify the common folk, and "punishment" means promoting criminal law, which is used to determine innocence and guilt. When rules are invariable, people can feign compliance, and when criminal law is promoted, people can evade it. But being able to evade it, they violate innate character to avoid trouble. Capable of pretense, one casts off one's original nature to comply with the rules. One's outer self may be rectified by complying with the rules, but no submission occurs in the innermost heart. If one harbors the intention to avoid trouble, he will have no sense of shame when it comes to others. As far as moral transformation is concerned, is this not a flimsy way to go about it! Therefore, the text says, "the common folk will evade both without shame." "Virtue" allows them to embody their original natures, and "propriety" allows them to realize the potential of their innate characters. Innate character has its own sense of shame, and original nature has its own source of being. When one fulfills his original nature, its source provides perfection, and when one embodies his innate character, he has a sense of shame. With this sense of shame, one regulates himself without threat of punishment, and with one's source providing perfection, one rectifies himself without need for rules. This is how "one leads them with virtue and regulates them with propriety, and they have a sense of shame and become rectified."[17]

The key terms here are "violate innate character" [*weiqing*], "abandon original nature" [*quxing* 去性] (16.4.7), "fulfill one's nature" [*de(qi)xing* 得(其)性] (1.6.2, 1.7.16, 9.3.4, 13.6.7, 25.9.1, and 33.6.5), "self-adjust" [*ziqi* 自齊] (2.13.5 and 27.4.2), and "govern oneself," "self-rectification," or "self-rectify" [*zizheng* 自正] (2.31.2, 2.31.5, 2.31.6, 5.8.4, 7.17.1, 11.22.3, and 25.42.2), all of which appear in Guo's commentary to the *Zhuangzi*. Although *weiqing*, "violate innate character," does not occur, the closely related term "violate original nature" [*weixing*] appears in conjunction with *quxing*, "abandon original nature," in *Shanxing* (chapter 16), a passage lamenting the loss of early man's pristine unself-consciousness as purposeful statecraft arose and the Dao was abandoned (16.4.6). Fulfillment of an original, fundamental, innate personal nature thus depends on maintaining an unself-conscious state of mind. Purposeful rulership, itself self-defeating, also affects the ruled, for such "corruption" starts at the top and works downward: the self-consciousness of the ruler undermines the pristine unself-consciousness of all the people below him, who, as individuals, no longer are left to fulfill their own natures and embody their own characters.

3. From "Transmit but [not Originate]," part 7 (*Shuer diqi* 述而第七): 子在齊聞韶。三月不知肉味。曰：不圖爲樂之至於斯也。**"When the Master was in Qi, he heard the music of Shao, which for three months made him unaware of the taste of meat. He said, 'I never thought performance of this music would reach such a place'!"** Guo: 傷器存而道廢。得有聲而無時。"He was

aggrieved that though the phenomenon existed, its Dao had been lost, for he experienced the sound of the one but had no opportunity for the other."[18]

Although this short comment by Guo seems not to relate directly to anything in his *Zhuangzi* commentary, the meaning is obvious: The ruler of Qi was oblivious to the Dao, yet he had music played that exemplified the sagely rule of Yao and Shun. Confucius was grieved that such music could be played in such a "Dao-less" place. We should also note that Guo's opposition of "phenomenon" [*qi* 器] and Dao is derived from a passage in the *Yijing* (Classic of Changes), *Xici Zhuan* 係辭傳 (Commentary on the appended phrases), part 1: "Therefore what is prior to physical form pertains to the Dao, and what is subsequent to physical form pertains to concrete objects [qi], the phenomenal world."[19]

4. From "Tai Bo," part 8 (*Tai Bo diba* 泰伯第八): 子曰：禹吾無間然矣。**The Master said, "As for Yu, I have no way to tell him apart."** Guo: 堯舜禹相承。雖三聖故一堯耳。天下化成則功美漸去。其所因循常事而已。故史籍無所稱。仲尼不能間。故曰。禹吾無間然矣。"Yao, Shun, and Yu, who succeeded one another as three sages, actually amount to just one 'Yao.' But as transformation and perfection of the world occurred, praise for what they were accomplishing gradually ceased, for they complied with things in such a way that it seemed just ordinary behavior, which is why historical records say nothing about it. Because Confucius could not distinguish him [from Yao and Shun], he said, 'As for Yu, I have no way to tell him apart.' "[20]

Guo's comment here to seems to be based on a longer passage in his *Zhuangzi* commentary, in *Tiandi* (chapter 12), where Yu attempts to yield rule to Bocheng Zigao, who refuses, part of which states: 夫禹時三聖相承，治成德備，功美漸去，故史籍無所載，仲尼不能間，是以雖有天下而不與焉，斯乃有而無之也。故考其時而禹爲最優，計其人則雖三聖，故一堯耳。時無聖人，故天下之心俄然歸啟。夫至公而居當者，付天下於百姓。 "By the time of Yu, the three Sage Kings [Yao, Shun, and Yu] had succeeded one another, and as governance reached perfection and virtue was fully realized, praise for what they were accomplishing gradually ceased, which is why historical accounts record nothing of this, thus Confucius could not distinguish among them. Therefore, although they possessed the world, they did not concern themselves with it; that is, they possessed it but regarded it as naught. Those who hitherto investigated those times regarded Yu as the best, and reckoned that these men were three sages, but actually they were all just one 'Yao.' As long as there were no sages, the minds of all in the world gravitated back to their pristine state, and, utterly impartial, someone [among them] took his rightful place [as ruler], who gave the world to the common folk." (12.17)

Although Yao, Shun, and Yu became names for the creators of ideal worldly rule, they do no good but much harm, because, as models, they inevitably lead to imitation, which in turn perverts the innate natural self so that the individual loses his authenticity and the good society is undermined. Such perversion affects the whole natural fabric of society: people try to overreach themselves, fomenting greed, dishonesty, exploitation of others, and, on a large scale, war and the slaughter of thousands.

5. From "Those Who First Advanced," part 11 (*Xianjin di shiyi* 先進第十一): 顏淵死。子哭之慟。從者曰。子慟矣。子曰。有慟乎。非夫人之爲慟而誰爲慟。**"When Yan Yuan [Yan Hui] died, the Master wailed with such profound grief that his disciples said, "How profoundly you feel!" "Do I feel such profound emotion? If I did not feel such profound feeling for this man, for whom would I feel it?"** Guo: 人哭亦哭。人慟亦慟。蓋無情者與物化也。"As others wailed, he too wailed, and as others felt profound emotion, he too felt it, for, utterly impartial, he transformed himself in step with others."[21]

To be effective, the sage must blend in with people and become indistinguishable from them. However extraordinary he might be, he must seem utterly ordinary, for only then can he prevent his "footsteps" from being followed and thus spare people from perverting their natural selves by emulating a "false" model—for all human models, as such, are false. However, the sage never consciously merges with others, for, whatever he does, it is done unself-consciously and with complete spontaneity.

6. From "Xian Asked," part 14 (*Xian wen di shisi* 憲問第十四): 子路問君子。子曰：修己以敬。曰：如斯而已乎。曰：修己以安人。曰：如斯而已乎。曰：修己以安百姓。修己以安百姓。堯舜其猶病諸。**"Zilu asked about the noble man. The Master said, 'He cultivates himself to be reverent.' 'Is that all there is to it?' 'He cultivates himself to bring contentment to his people.' 'Is that all there is to it?' 'He cultivates himself to bring contentment to the common folk, something that even Yao and Shun found hard to do.'"** Guo: 夫君子者不能索足。故修己者索己。故修己者僅可以內敬其身。外安同己之人耳。豈足安百姓哉。百姓百品。萬國殊風。以不治治之。乃得其極。若欲修己以治之。雖堯舜必病。況君子乎。今堯舜非修之也。萬物自無爲而治。若天之自高。地之自厚。日月之明。雲行雨施而已。故能夷暢條達。曲成不遺而無病也。"Even the 'noble man' is incapable of sufficient self-reflexivity for this. 'Cultivates himself" means self-reflexivity. Therefore, since such self-cultivation internally can only result in reverence for his own person and externally can only bring contentment to people of his own kind, how could it ever suffice to bring contentment to all the common folk! The common folk consists of all kinds of different people, and the whole world in all its parts follows divergent customs, so only when it is governed by not governing will it reach utmost perfection. If one wishes to govern it by cultivating himself, even Yao or Shun would have found this hard to do, so how much more so would a 'noble man.' Now, we see that Yao and Shun had nothing to do with such cultivation but just let the myriad folk engage in their own non-purposeful actions and thus govern themselves—just as the sky stays up high all by itself, the land maintains its bulk all by itself, the sun and moon stay bright, and

clouds move so rain dispenses its blessings. Thus, it is that one with complete composure is utterly unobstructed and, regardless of what possible means he uses, without exception finds that he encounters no hardship at all."[22]

A close parallel occurs in Guo's *Zhuangzi* commentary to a passage in *Qiwu lun* (chapter 2):夫時之所賢者爲君。才不應世者爲臣。若天之自高。地之自卑。首自在上。足自居下。豈有遞哉。雖無錯於當而必自當也。"-Those who the times regard as worthies become rulers; those whose talents fail to answer the need of the age become subjects. As Heaven is naturally high and Earth is naturally low, so the head is naturally located above and the feet are naturally located below, so how could they take turns replacing each other! Though they make no effort to fulfill duties, each is sure to fulfill duties spontaneously." (2.8.12)

7. From "Duke Ling of Wei," part 15 (*Wei Linggong di shiwu* 衛靈公第十五): 子曰。吾之於人。誰毀誰譽。如有可譽者。其有所試矣。斯民也。三代之所以直道而行也。**"The Master said, 'In my relation to others, whom do I blame, whom praise? If there is any that may be praised, there is a way to verify it, that is, by recourse to the common folk, for it was by recourse to them that the Three Dynasties were conducted by the straight and proper Dao.'"** Guo: 無心而付之天下者。直道也。有心而使天下從己者。曲法者也。故直道而行者。毀譽不出於區區之身。善與不善。信之百姓。故曰：吾之於人。誰毀誰譽。如有所譽。必試之斯民也。 "Whereas to be free of conscious mind and so give oneself over to the world is to follow the straight and proper Dao, to be of self-conscious mind and try to make the world follow one is to pervert its method. This is why one should conduct things by the straight and proper Dao. Praise or blame should not be based on finicky personal views, for whether one is good or not should be verified by recourse to the common folk. Therefore, the text states, 'In my relation to others, whom do I blame, whom praise? If there is any that may be praised, there is a way to verify it, that is, by recourse to the common folk, for it was by recourse to them that the Three Dynasties were conducted by the straight and proper Dao.' "[23]

A close parallel occurs in a commentary passage in *Lie Yukou* (chapter 32): 夫取富貴。必順乎民望也。若挾奇說。乘天衢。以嬰人主之心者。明主之所不受也。故如有所譽。必有所試。於斯民不違。僉曰舉之。以合萬夫之望者。此三代所以直道而行之也。"When someone is conferred wealth and honor, it must comply with the hopes and aspirations of the common folk. But if one depends on outlandish advice to ride on the ruler's highway, if one tries to make the ruler's mind to think like a child, a perspicacious ruler would not present such a one with anything! Therefore, if the ruler has someone to praise, it must be verified, that is, if it is not in opposition to his people and they all say, 'elevate him.' It was in agreement with the hopes and aspirations of the common folk that things were thus done with the straight and true Dao during the Three Dynasties of antiquity." (32.29).

8. From "Duke Ling of Wei," part 15 (*Wei Linggong di shiwu* 衛靈公第十五): 子曰。吾嘗終日不食終夜 不寢以思。無益。不如學也。**"The Master said, "I once did not eat for a whole day and did not sleep for a whole night, all in order to think, but it proved worthless. It would have been better to study."** Guo: 聖人無詭教。而云不寢不食以思者何。夫思而後通。習而後能者。百姓皆然也。聖人無事。而不與百姓同事。事同則形同。是以見形以爲己異。故謂聖人亦必勤思而力學。此百姓之情也。故用其情以教之。則聖人之教。因彼以教彼。安容詭哉。"The sage shunned any divergent teaching, yet here says that he did not sleep or eat in order to think. Why was that? To understand only after thinking, to gain mastery only after studying, this is the way common folk all behave. Although the sage should remain disengaged and not deal with things as do the common folk, if he seems to engage with things as they do, his behavior resembles theirs. Therefore, since the way he looks might make people regard him as different from them, it is said that even a sage must diligently think and study hard. Such behavior fits with how common folk tend to behave, so he teaches them in terms of those tendencies. In other words, how the sage teaches consists of teaching others by adapting himself to them—so why should any divergent teaching be involved here!"[24]

Whereas "disengagement" (*wushi* 無事) is an essential aspect of sagehood, the sage, to hide his "footprints," must blend in and merge with people in general, becoming thus indistinguishable from them. This is what Guo would have Confucius do here. *Wushi*, "disengagement," occurs more than a dozen times in Guo's *Zhuangzi* commentary, always signifying "free from self-conscious effort," but since ordinary people do not behave like that, the sage, to appear like them, must, paradoxically, seem to be engaged and to make a conscious effort. Various passages, both in the *Zhuangzi* and in Guo's commentary, describe how the true sage conceals himself, lest he leave "footprints" behind to lead astray the unwary common run of humanity.

9. From "Yang Huo," part 17 (*Yang Huo di shiqi* 陽貨第十七): 孔子曰。諾。吾將仕矣。**"Confucius said, 'Agreed. I shall take office.' "** Guo: 聖人無心。仕與不仕隨世耳。陽虎勸仕。理無不諾。不能用我。則我無自用。此直道而應者也。然危遜之理。亦在其中也。"The sage, free from self-conscious mind, in taking or not taking office, just complies with the ways of the world. When Yang Hu urged him to take office, since it was the right thing to do, he could not but agree. If the world cannot use me, I should refrain from trying to get myself used, for this is the way to follow the straight and proper Dao and resonate with others. However, the principle underlying 'being stern' and 'being conciliatory' is also implied herein."[25]

"Free from selfconscious mind" [*wuxin*] appears fifty-seven times in Guo's *Zhuangzi* commentary. An example specifically involving "the sage" appears in *Shanxing* 繕性 (chapter 16): 聖人無心。任世之自成。成之淳薄。皆非

聖也。聖能任世之自得耳，豈能使世得聖哉！故皇王之跡，與世俱遷，而聖人之道未始不全也。"The sage, free of selfconscious mind, allows the world to fulfill itself, and all attempts to fulfill it by recourse to the superficial aspects of purity have nothing to do with true sagehood. Since the sage does nothing but allow the world to fulfill itself, what can he have to do with making the world acquire sageliness! Therefore, though the footprints left by Heavenly Monarchs and Earthly Kings always kept changing from age to age, the Dao of the sage never fails to remain whole and intact." (16.4.4).

4. *Lunyu yin* 論語隱 (What is hidden in the *Lunyu* [Analects])

論語隱一卷，郭象撰 "*Lunyu yin*, author Guo Xiang, one fascicle" is listed in *Suishu Jingji zhi* 隋書經籍志 (History of the Sui, treatise on classics and Scriptures).[26]

論語隱一卷 郭象 見七錄 "*Lunyu yin*, author Guo Xiang, one fascicle" is listed in Ding Guojun 丁國鈞 (died 1919), *Bu Jinshu yiwenzhi* 補晉書藝文志 (Supplement to the bibliographical treatise in the *Jinshu* [History of the Jin]).[27]

In his *Jingyi kao* 經義考 (Studies on the meaning of the classics), Zhu Yizun 朱彝尊 (1629–1709) states: "As for the *Lunyu yin* 論語隱 (What is hidden in the *Analects*), the *Qilu* 七錄 (Seven-part catalogue) [of Ruan Xiaoxu 阮孝緒 (479–536)] records a one-fascicle edition and that it is lost." [28] Later in the same fascicle, Zhu addresses another work on the *Analects*: 論語隱義。隋志不載。但有其注載七錄。未審即是郭象論語隱否。 "A *Lunyu yinyi* is not listed in the Sui bibliographic treatise, but there is a *zhu* (commentary) version listed in the *Qilu*. However, investigation has yet to determine whether or not this really refers to the *Lunyu yin* of Guo Xiang." Zhu then adds: 太平御覽載隱義文云。衛蒯聵亂。子路興師往。有狐黯者當師。曰。子欲入邪。曰。然。黯從城上下麻繩鉤子。路半城問曰。為師邪。為君邪。曰。在君為君。在師為師。黯因投之。折其左股。不死。黯開城欲殺之。子路目如明星之光曜。黯不能前。謂曰。畏子之目。願覆之。子路以衣袂覆目。黯遂殺之。"The *Taiping yulan* records a passage from the *Lunyu yinyi*: 'When Kuaikui caused chaos in Wey, Zilu [Zhong You (542–480), a disciple of Confucius] raised troops and went there, where a certain Gu An, who was in command of troops, asked, 'Does Zilu wish to enter?' Zilu replied 'Yes, I do.' An then had a hempen rope lowered, and when Zilu had been raised halfway up the city wall, An asked him, 'Are you a military commander or a gentleman?' He replied, 'In the capacity of a gentleman I am a gentleman, and when in the capacity of a military commander, I am a military commander.' Thus, at that An dropped him, which broke his left leg but did not kill him. An then came out the city gate intending to kill him, but Zilu's bright star-like eyes so flashed that An was unable to approach him. Therefore, he said to Zilu, 'I fear your eyes, so be so good as to cover them.' Zilu then covered his eyes with the sleeve of his robe, and An killed him."[29] A collation note is added at this point by the modern editors: 王謨有輯本。“There exists a collected fragments edition by Wang Mo [ca. 1731–1817].”[30] This refers to a brief work included in Wang's *Han-Wei yishu chao* (Fragments copied from lost works of the Han and Wei eras). In his preface to the three passages of *Lunyu yinyi* fragments, Wang states: 如御覽白帖所引不過若衡波魯定公記之類。亦可以備聖門軼事少資談柄。故仍鈔出白帖一條御覽二條。“Although these passages extracted from the *Yulan* and *Baitie*[31] seem merely to be of the same category as *Chongbo* [*zhuan*] (Chronicle of Chengbo) and *Lu Dinggong ji* (Record of Duke Ding of Lu) [i.e., anecdotal tales], they still may provide a few sources to serve as subjects of discussion concerning of Confucius, his disciples, and tradition. Therefore, I have copied out one passage from the *Baitie* and two passages from the *Yulan*.”[32] The first passage copied by Wang from the *Taiping yulan* is the one already quoted above; the second passage is from the *Lunyu yinyi zhu*: 孔子至蔡。解于客舍。 夜人有取孔子一隻履去。盜者置屐于受盜家。 孔子屐長一尺四寸。與凡人屐異。“When Confucius reached Cai, he stayed at an inn. That night someone stole one of his shoes, but when the thief brought the shoe to the receiver of stolen goods, it was discovered that the length of Confucius's shoe was one *chi* four *cun* long [almost fourteen inches], quite different from the shoes of usual people.”[33] The passage from the *Baitie* is as follows: 齊桓公北伐中山還。倚柱歎目。天下珍物悉易得。 未得人肉食。 易牙歸。斷其兒兩手。以啖君。 “When Duke Huan of Qi (r. 685–643 BCE) returned after attacking the state of Zhongshan, leaning against a pillar, he said with a sigh, 'Although rare things all over the world are easy for me to get, I have never managed to get human flesh to eat.' At that [the cook] Yiya went home and cut off the hands of his son for his lord to eat.”[34]

Ma Guohan, preface of *Lunyu yinyi zhu* 論語隱義注 (Commentary to explications of what is hidden in the *Analects*): 論語隱義注一卷。撰人姓名闕考。隋書經籍志有當語隱一卷。郭象撰。又有論語隱義注二卷。並云亡。朱太史彝尊經義考。於論語隱論語隱義注外。別出隱義云。隋志不載。但有其注載七錄。未審即郭象論語隱否。案。郭書以隱名。茲云隱義注者。疑是後人衍象義而注之。唐藝文志稱義注隱。誤倒其文也。注疏不見稱述。惟白帖太平御覽引凡二[三]節。或題隱義。或題隱義注。其語鄙俚似小說。與郭氏體略不類。應皆是注者以異聞附益。茲從朱說。取次體略之後。並題隱隱義注。仍梁隋之舊目也。 “Although no research is available as to who the author was of the *Lunyu yinyi zhu*, the *Suishu jingji zhi* lists a *Lunyu yin* in one fascicle by Guo Xiang, as well as a *Lunyu yinyi zhu* in two fascicles, adding that both are lost. [Ma's note] Court historian Zhu Yizun in *Jingyi kao*: 'Guo's work is simply entitled *Lunyu yin*, but this work has the title *Lunyu yinyi zhu*, I suspect that some later person expanded on Guo Xiang's work and wrote a commentary to it. The *Tang yiwenzhi* calls it *Lunyu yizhu yin*, which mistakenly transposes the text of the title. Nothing is now seen of these commentary versions, and only the *Baitie* and *Taiping yulan* contain quotations of these three passages, either taken from the *yinyi* or from the *yinyi zhu*. The language involved is rather vulgar, like that of popular tales, not at all like that of Master Guo in his *Essentials of the Analects*; as such, they all must be odd material added by the commentators.' In accordance with what Zhu has to say, I place these excerpts after the *Essentials* and give them the titles *Lunyu yin* and *Lunyu yinyi zhu*."

5. *Guo Xiang ji* 郭象集 (Collected works of Guo Xiang)

The *History of the Sui*, *Jingji zhi* (Treatise on classics and scriptures) lists: 晉太傅主簿郭象集二卷。 梁五卷。錄一卷。"Collected works of Jin dynasty Taifu zhupu (Recorder for the Grand Mentor) Guo Xiang in two fascicles; the Liang dynasty [(502–557] edition of his works is known to have consisted of five fascicles, with one fascicle table of contents."[35] The *Jingji zhi* in the *Jiu Tangshu* (Old History of the Tang) lists an edition of Guo's collected works in five fascicles,[36] as does the *Yiwen zhi* in the *Xin Tangshu* (New History of the Tang).[37] In all three lists, the Guo Xiang *ji* is followed immediately by the entry *Xi Hanji* 嵇含集 (Collected works of Xi Han [236–306]) in ten fascicles, which suggests that the two works were linked in some way. The *Qinding siku quanshu zongmu* is more explicit, for it contains a reference to Guo's collected works in a note to an entry on the *Nanfang caomu zhuang* 南方草木狀 (Description of plants and trees of the south) that is attributed to Xi Han 嵇含, which follows the mention of Xi Han's collected works in ten fascicles: 隋志云。其集已亡。但附載郭象集下。舊唐志仍著錄。"The Sui treatise states that this collection was already lost by then, for it had only been appended to the collected works of Guo Xiang. The treatise in the *Old History of the Tang* records the same information."[38] By the Sui, Xi Han's works seem thus to have become detached from Guo's and lost, with only Guo's own works preserved into the Tang era.

The sources record three titles of lost works by Guo that may have been included in the *Guo Xiang ji*: (1) *Zhiming youji lun* 致命由己論 (Resultant fate depends on the individual self, a discourse), which, given its title, was likely included in another work; (2) the *Beilun* 碑論 (Tombstone discourses), in twelve chapters that could have circulated independently from the *Guo Xiang ji*; and (3) *Lun Xi Shao* 論嵇紹 (a discussion of Xi Shao [253–304]).

Zhiming youji lun (Resultant fate depends on the individual self, a discourse) and *Beilun* 碑論 (Tombstone discourses) as a whole both seem to have been concerned with fate, mortality, and death. Evidence for the *Zhiming youji lun*, at least, comes from reference to a later work, the *Bianming lun* 辯命論 (Disquisition on fate) of Liu Jun 劉峻 (462–521): 蕭遠論其本而不暢其流。子玄語其流而未詳其本。"Xiaoyuan [Li Kang 李康 (ca. 190–ca. 240)] discussed its [i.e., fate's] origin but failed to carry through with its ramifications. Zixuan [Guo Xiang] addressed its ramifications but did not quite treat its origin with sufficient clarity." To which Li Shan 李善 (d. 689) commented: 李蕭遠作運

命論。言治亂在天。故曰。論其本。郭子玄作致命由己之論。言吉凶由己。故曰。語其流。濟良注同。“In composing his *Yunming lun* 運命論 (Discourse on fate), Li Xiaoyuan [Li Kang] states that whether order or chaos occurs depends on Heaven, which is why Liu said that Li addressed its origin. In composing his *Zhiming youji lun* (How fate works depends on the individual self), he states that good fortune or bad depends on the individual self, which is why Liu said that Guo addressed its ramifications. The comments by Ji and Liang [Lü Yanji 呂延濟 (act. ca. 718) and Liu Liang 劉良 (act. ca. 718)] are the same.”[39] That Guo is here reported to have said that fate depends on the individual self (*youji* 由己) seems, at first glance, to be at odds with his insistence, clearly stated in his commentary to the *Zhuangzi*, that 命非己制，故無所用其心也。夫安於命者，無往而非逍遙矣，故雖匡陳羑里，無異於紫極閒堂也。“Since one's fate may not be controlled by oneself, there is nothing to exercise one's mind about. As for one who remains content with his fate, no matter what venture embarked on he never fails to enjoy spontaneous freedom.” However, *youji* 由己 and *fei jizhi* 非己制 are not at all incompatible, for as Wang Xiaoyi, among others, have pointed out, “self” means the original, inherent, natural self that one is endowed by Heaven (i.e., the Natural). As such, one's fate is inherently determined as it comes from the composition of the individual natural self. In other words, the individual self cannot “control” one's fate but is, in fact, subject to it; that is what the *youji* in *Zhiming youji lun* means.[40]

Evidence for the *Lun Xi Shao* 論嵇紹 (A discussion of Xi Shao [253–304]) comes from the *Taiping yulan* 太平御覽: 王隱晉書曰。郭象河南人。為東海太傅主簿。象著文稱。嵇紹父死在非罪。曾無耿介。貪位。而死闇主。義不足多。曾以問郗公曰。王褒之父。亦非罪死。褒猶辭徵。紹不辭用。誰爲多少。郗公曰。王勝於嵇。或曰魏晉所殺。子皆仕宦。何以無非也。荅曰。殛鯀興禹。禹不辭興者。以鯀犯罪也。若以時君所殺爲當耶。則同於禹。以不當耶。則同於嵇。又曰。世皆以嵇見危授命。荅曰。紀信代漢高之死可謂見危授命。如嵇偏善其一可也。以備體論之。則未得也。“In the *Jinshu* (History of the Jin) by Wang Yin [ca. 275–ca. 352], it is stated: ‘Among his writings Guo Xiang from Henan says that although Xi Shao's father [Xi Kang 嵇康 (223–262)] died innocent of crime, there was nothing upright and outstanding about Xi Shao himself in the least, since, greedy for high office, he died sacrificing himself for a dolt of a ruler [Emperor Hui (r. 290–306), Sima Zhong 司馬衷 (259–306)]; as such, he should not be considered a person of much integrity. So Guo once asked Master Xi, “Wang Bao's father also died innocent of crime, whereas Bao refused even to protest, Xi Shao did not refuse office, so which one showed more integrity.” Master Xi replied, ‘Wang was better that Xi.’ ‘Some say, “Those killed during the Wei and Jin all tended to be serving officials, so how could they have been entirely innocent!” ’ ” Master Xi answered, ‘When Gun was executed and Yu elevated, the reason why Yu did not refuse elevation was because Gun had committed crime. If because of circumstances an execution by a ruler is just, this is like what happened with Yu; if not just, then it is like what happened to Xi Kang.' To which Guo replied, 'The whole world is of the opinion that Xi when faced with danger sacrificed his life.' Master Xi answered, When Ji Xin sacrificed his life for Gao of Han, now that can really be called 'faced with danger sacrificed his life.' As for Xi Kang, the only thing that may be said of him is that he was obsessed with goodness. However, this does not quite cover the issue as a whole.' "[41]

Xi Shao's father Xi Kang was executed on the order of Sima Zhong's grandfather, Sima Zhao 司馬昭 (211–265). "Master Xi" is Xi Jian 郗鑒 (269–339). Gun 鯀, Yu's father, was ordered by Yao to control the flood, but when he failed, Yao, in some versions of the myth, had him executed and replaced by Yu, who was successful. Ji Xin 紀信 (d. 204 BCE) was one of the generals of Liu Bang 劉邦 (256–195 BCE) (later Han emperor Gaozu 漢高祖). When Liu was besieged in Xingyang 滎陽 (Henan) by Xiang Yu 項羽, Ji Xin volunteered to act as a decoy to help Liu escape, and so he rode out of the city in Liu's chariot, disguised as Liu, to offer surrender. This deceived Xiang Yu long enough to allow Liu to escape. Xiang then had Ji Xin burned to death.

Notes

1. Du Guangting, *Daode zhenjing guangsheng yi*, preface 2: 2b.
2. Du Guangting, *Daode zhenjing guangsheng yi*, 4: 4b–5a.
3. Gu Huan 顧歡 (420–483), ed. (attributed), *Daode zhenjing zhushu* 道德真經注疏 (Commentaries and subcommentaries to the *Daode zhenjing* [The True Scripture of the Dao and Its Virtue]), 1: 13a.
4. Li Lin (twelfth century), comp. *Daode jing qushan ji* (Collection of the best comments on the *Scripture of the Dao and Its Virtue*) (preface dated 1172), 1: 15a.
5. Gu Huan, *Daode zhenjing zhushu*, 1: 21a.
6. Richard John Lynn, *The Classic of Changes*, 54.
7. Li Lin, comp., *Daode jing qushan ji*, 4: 12b.
8. Li, *Daode jing qushan ji*, 6: 9a.
9. *Suishu*, 34: 1001.
10. Zheng Qiao, *Tongzhi* (Comprehensive history of institutions), 67: 1b.
11. Lu Deming, *Jingdian shiwen*, 1: 40a–40b.
12. *Qinding siku quanshu zongmu*, 35: 6b.
13. See Takahashi Hitoshi, *Rongo giso no kenkyū* 研究 (A study of the *Lunyu yishu*) (Tokyo: Sōbunsha 創文社, 2013). The *Lunyu jijie yishu* is also included in the *Zhibuzu zhai congshu* 知不足齋叢書 (Collectanea compiled at the Knows Not Enough Studio), ed. Bao Tingfu 鮑廷博 (1728–1814).
14. For the relationship between the *Lunyu jijie* and *xuanxue* 玄學 (arcane learning) thought, see John Makeham, "He Yan, *Xuanxue*, and the Editorship of the *Lunyu Jijie*," *Early Medieval China* 5 (1999), 1–35.

15. The following account of nine passages from Guo's commentary to the *Analects* and their affiliation with his *Zhuangzi* commentary is derived from a more detailed study published recently; see Richard John Lynn, "Guo Xiang's Theory of Sagely Knowledge as Seen in his *Essentials of the Analects* (*Lunyu Tilue* 論語體略)."
16. *Lunyu tilue*, 1a; *Lunyu jijie yishu*, 1: 17b–18a.
17. Guo Xiang 郭象, *Lunyu tilue*, 1a–1b; He Yan 何晏 and Huang Kan 皇侃, *Lunyu jijie yishu*, 1: 18b–19a.
18. Guo, *Lunyu tilue*, 1b–2a; He and Huang, *Lunyu jijie yishu*, 4: 7b–8a.
19. Lynn, *The Classic of Changes*, 67.
20. Guo, *Lunyu tilue*, 2a; He and Huang, *Lunyu jijie yishu*, 4: 37b–38a.
21. Guo, *Lunyu tilue*, 2a–2b; He and Huang, *Lunyu jijie yishu*, 6: 5b.
22. Guo, *Lunyu tilue*, 2b–3a; He and Huang, *Lunyu jijie yishu*, 7: 46a–46b.
23. Guo, *Lunyu tilue*, 3a–3b; He and Huang, *Lunyu jijie yishu*, 8: 11b–12a.
24. Guo, *Lunyu tilue*, 3b; He and Huang, *Lunyu jijie yishu*, 8: 13b–14a.
25. Guo, *Lunyu tilue*, 4a; He and Huang, *Lunyu jijie yishu*, 9: 3b and 9: 3b. Cf. *Analects*, *Xian wen di shisi* 憲問第十四 (part 14: Xian asked): 邦有道。危言危行。邦無道。危行言遜."When the state follows the Dao, be stern in words and be stern in action. When a state is without the Dao, be stern in action but conciliatory in words." *Lunyu* (Analects), 14: 2510a.
26. *Suishu jingji zhi* (History of the Sui, treatise on classics and Scriptures), *Suishu*, 32: 936.
27. Ding Guojun, *Bu Jinshu yiwenzhi* (Supplement to the bibliographical treatise in the history of the Jin), 1: 23.
28. Zhu Yizun, *Dianjiao buzheng Jingyi kao* (Studies on the meaning of the classics, punctuated, collated, amended and corrected). 6: 614.
29. Li Fang (925–996) et al., ed., *Taiping yulan* (Encyclopedia published during the Taiping Xingguo era [976–983], perused by His Majesty), *juan* 366, 4: 54.
30. Zhu, *Dianjiao buzheng Jingyi kao*, 6: 634–35.
31. *Baitie* (Bai's noteboards) is part of the *Bai Kong liutie* 白孔六帖 (Six noteboards of Bai and Kong), a *leishu* 類書 (literally, "classified writings" and "encyclopedias" in Western sources). Its brief title is *Baishi liutie* 白氏六帖, and its full title is *Baishi jingshi shilei liutie* 白氏經史事類六帖 (Six noteboards of Master Bai's classified matters in the classics and history); this part of the work is attributed to Bai Juyi 白居易 (772–846). The part entitled *Kongshi liutie* 孔氏六帖 (Master Kong's six noteboards) was compiled by Kong Chuan孔傳 (1065–1139).
32. Wang Mo 王謨 (ca. 1731–1817), ed., *Han-Wei yishu chao* (Fragments copied from lost works of the Han and Wei eras), *Jingyi disi ji* 經翼第四集 (Works assisting the classics, the fourth collection), Preface, 1a and text, 1a.
33. Li, *Taiping yulan*, *juan* 698, 6: 472.
34. Wang, *Han-Wei yishu chao*, *Jingyi disi ji*, 1b; *Bai Kong liutie*, 30: 29a.
35. *Suishu jingji zhi* (History of the Sui, treatise on classics and Scriptures), *Suishu*, 35: 1063.
36. *Jiu Tangshu*, 47: 2061.
37. *Xin Tangshu*, 60: 1584.
38. *Qinding quanshu zongmu*, 70: 24b.
39. Xiao Tong (501–531), comp., *Wenxuan* (Selections of refined literature), 54: 2345–46.
40. Wang Xiaoyi, "Guo Xiang *mingyun ji qi yiyi* 郭象命運論及其意義 (Guo Xiang's theory of fate and its meaning), 19.
41. Li, *Taiping yulan*, *juan* 445, 4: 690.

APPENDIX C

XIANG XIU AND GUO XIANG COMMENTS COMPARED

I. Included in Xiang's commentary but not in Guo's (forty-eight places)

1.8 堯讓天下於許由曰：「日月出矣而爝火不息其於光也不亦難乎 **When Yao tried to yield the whole world to Xu You, he said, "When the sun or the moon has come out but torches [*juehuo*] remain unextinguished, will it not be difficult for them to furnish light"?** 向云爝火人所然火也 Xiang says, [*Juehuo*] means fires that people set alight. (*Jingdian shiwen*, 26: 4b)

2.1.1 南郭子綦隱机而坐仰天而嘘 **Ziqi of Southwall sat slumped on his writing table. Looking up, he slowly exhaled [*xu*], . . .** 嘘向云息也 Xiang says *Xu* means that he took a breath. (*Jingdian shiwen*, 26: 7b)

2.7.12 樂出虛，蒸成菌。**Music comes from emptiness, steamy air forms mushrooms [*chengjun*].** 成菌向云結也 As for *chengjun*, Xiang says that it means "produces them." (*Jingdian shiwen*, 26: 9b)

2.23.4 猨猵狙以爲雌 **Apes regard dog's head monkeys as proper mates.** 向云猨猵狙以爲雌 Xiang says, As for apes, they regard dog's head monkeys as proper mates. (*Jingdian shiwen*, 26: 12b)

2.25.2 大澤焚而不能熱河漢沍而不能寒 **The Great Marshland might blaze, yet he cannot be burned; the Yellow and Han Rivers might freeze [*hu*], yet he cannot be chilled** 向云沍凍也 Xiang says that *hu* means freeze. (*Jingdian shiwen*, 26: 12b)

2.26.1 瞿鵲子問乎長梧子曰吾聞諸夫子 **Master Startled Magpie asked Master Tall Parasol Tree, "I have heard it from you, Master. . . .** 向云夫子瞿

鵲之師 Xiang says that "You, Master" refers to Startled Magpie's teacher. (*Jingdian shiwen*, 26: 13a)

2.26.7 夫子以爲孟浪之言 **You, Master, thought these rash and simplistic words** 向云孟浪音漫瀾無所趣舍之謂 Xiang says that *Menglang [məijŋhlaŋh]* sounds like *manlan* [*manhlanh*][1] and means "nothing to accept or reject about them." [i.e., they are meaningless]. (*Jingdian shiwen*, 26: 13a)

2.27 長梧子曰：是黃帝之所聽熒也 **2.27.1 Master Tall Parasol Tree replied: "Since it would have been perplexing to hear [*tingying*] them even if they came from the Yellow Thearch. . . ."** 向司馬云聽熒疑惑也 Xiang and Sima [Biao] both say that *tingying* means perplexing. (*Jingdian shiwen*, 26: 13a)

2.33 罔兩問景曰曩子行今子止曩子坐今子起何其無特操與 **Penumbra asked Shadow: "A short time ago you were moving, but now you are stopped. A short time ago you were sitting, but now you are standing up. How you lack independent control [*wu tecao*]!** 向云無持者行止無常也 Xiang says that the expression "lack control" [*wuchizhe*] means movements are irregular. Note: The entry here says "no independent . . ." [*wute*], and yet Xiang's commentary reads as "no control" [*wuchi*]. Thus, the text that Xiang knew read as *wu chicao*, "lacks control." See the note for 2.33, text of the translation.

3.2 砉然嚮然，奏刀騞然，莫不中音。合於桑林之舞，乃中經首之會。**Matched a sharp sound of rending, as he played his knife, swishing in and out, always in perfect tune, right in step for the Mulberry Grove Dance and in perfect rhythm with the Jingshou Melody.** 向司馬云咸池樂章也 Xiang and Sima [Biao] both say that it [Jingshou] is a piece of "Pool of Shaman Xian" music. (*Jingdian shiwen*, 26: 15a)

4.17.2 易之者，皞天不宜。**As for those who think this should be easy, bright Heaven [*haotian*] will not accommodate them."** 向云皞天自然也 Xiang says that *haotian* means Nature [*ziran*]. (*Jingdian shiwen*, 26: 17b–18a)

4.24.8 是萬物之化也禹舜之所紐也伏戲几蘧之所行終而況散焉者乎 **This is the transformation of the myriad things, out of which Yu and Shun made bonds, and which Fu Xi and Ji Qu used to practice their entire lives.** 向云古之帝王也 Xiang says that he [Ji Qu] was a sovereign of antiquity. (*Jingdian shiwen*, 26: 18a)

4.29.4 獸死不擇音氣息茀然 **When wild beasts die, they do not choose the sounds they make and their breath [*qixi*] is filled with pent-up fury.** 向本作誋器云誋 The Xiang edition [of the *Zhuangzi*] writes it [*qixi*] as *xiqi* 誋器 and says that it means *xi*, 'breath. (*Jingdian shiwen*, 26: 19a)

4.39 匠石覺而診其夢 **When Carpenter Shi awoke, he divined [*zhen*] what the dream meant.** 司馬向云診占夢也 Sima [Biao] and Xiang both say that *zhen* means to divine a dream. (*Jingdian shiwen*, 26: 20a)

4.44.1 支離疏者頤隱於臍肩高於頂會撮指天 **Disjointed Shu was such a man that his chin was hidden in his navel, his shoulders were higher than the top of his head, and his topknot pointed straight up to Heaven.** 向云兩肩

竦而上會撮然也 Xiang says that his two shoulders both jutted up like a hair topknot. (*Jingdian shiwen*, 26: 21a)

4.44.1 挫鍼治繲足以餬口 **By doing sewing and laundry [*zhixie*] he managed to feed himself.** 司馬云浣衣也向同 Sima [Biao] says that [*zhixie*] means laundry, and Xiang says the same. (*Jingdian shiwen*, 26: 21b)

6.4.5 眾人之息以喉屈服者其嗌言若哇 **When the throat makes the breath of ordinary men waver and quaver, it so stifles their words that they choke over them.** 向云喘悸之息以喉爲節言情欲奔競所致 Xiang says that breath that comes in palpitations and pants is trapped by the throat, signifying that one is beset by desire run amuck. (*Jingdian shiwen*, 26: 25a)

6.8.3 與乎其觚而不堅也 **How [*yuhu*] carefree and easy he might have been in his independence, yet he did not cling to it.** 向云疑貌 Xiang says that [*yuhu*] expresses a state of doubt. The text here is amended by Huang Zhuo, *Jingdian shiwen huijiao* (Exegesis of classics and scriptures, collected collations), 26: 227. (*Jingdian shiwen*, 26: 26a)

6.20.2 曰偉哉夫造物者 **[Master Yu] said, How great [*wei*] the Creator is. . . .** 向云美也 Xiang says that [*wei*] means splendid. (*Jingdian shiwen*, 26: 28b)

6.22.4 安時而處順哀樂不能入也此古之所謂縣解也 **Content with my time, I abide in compliance, so neither grief nor joy can intrude on me. This the ancients called "ties untied" [*xuanjie*].** 向云縣解無所係也 Xiang says that *xuanjie* means free from attachments. (*Jingdian shiwen*, 26: 29a)

6.23.2 倚其戶與之語曰偉哉造化又將奚以汝爲將奚以汝適以汝爲鼠肝乎 **Leaning on the doorway, he addressed Master Lai thus: "How great the creator is! What is he going to make out of you next? And what path is he going to have you follow? Will he make you into a rat's liver [*shugan*], or will he make you into a bug's arm?"** 向云委棄土壤而已 Xiang says that as for "rat's liver," this means just a discarded piece of dirt, nothing more. (*Jingdian shiwen*, 26: 29a)

6.37.16 造適不及笑獻笑不及排 **Searching for answers is not as good as a good [*xian*]laugh, and having a laugh is not as good as just going along with things.** 向云獻善也 Xiang says that *xian* means good. (*Jingdian shiwen*, 26: 30a)

7.1 齧缺問於王倪四問而四不知 **Front Teeth Missing, in questioning Wang Ni, asked four questions, but Wang knew not how to answer any of the four.** 向云事在齊物論中 Xiang says that this matter appears in [chapter 2 of this book] *Qi wu lun* (On Regarding All Things Equal). (*Jingdian shiwen*, 26: 31b)

7.14.2 列子見之而心醉 **But when Master Lie saw her, his mind became drunk.** 向云迷惑於其道也 Xiang says that this means he was utterly bewildered by her way. (*Jingdian shiwen*, 26: 32b) The variant 迷惑其道也, "He found her way bewildering," is quoted in the commentary of Zhang Zhan (fourth century) to the *Liezi* (Sayings of Master Lie); see Yang Bojun, ed., *Liezi jishi* (Collected explanations of sayings of Master Lie), 2: 70. It is also appears as such among the commentaries to Yan Yanzhi (384–456), *Wujun yong* 五君詠 (Song of the five noble men); see *Wenxuan* (Selections of refined literature), 21: 1010.

7.17.1 列子入泣涕沾襟以告壺子壺子曰鄉吾示之以地文萌乎 **Master Lie then went back in and, tears soaking his lapels, reported this to Master Hu, but Master Hu said, "What I have showed her was myself as outer signs of the Earth. . . .** 向秀曰塊然若土也 Xiang Xiu says, "He was clod-like as if dirt." (*Liezi jishi*, 2: 72)

7.25.1 然後列子自以爲未始學而歸三年不出 **After this, Master Lie thought that he had never learned anything and so went home, which he did not leave for three years, . .** 向秀曰棄人事之近務也 Xiang Xiu says, "He set human affairs aside and tended to household duties." (*Liezi jishi*, 2: 76)

7.25.1 爲其妻爨 **where he cooked for his wife . . .** 向秀曰遺恥辱 Xiang Xiu says, "He lost all sense of shame." (*Liezi jishi*, 2: 76)

8.2.1 是故駢於明者亂五色淫文章青黃黼黻之煌煌非乎 **Therefore, if a "web" were added to vision, would this not [*fei hu*] throw the five colors into confusion, cause licentious enjoyment of designs, emblems, and green and yellow colorful embroidery that bedazzle the eye!** 向云非乎言是也 Xiang says that "would this not" [*feihu*] means that it is so. (*Jingdian shiwen*, 27: 2a)

8.2.1 而離朱是已 **All this is only so [*shiyi*] because of Li Zhu!** 向云猶是也 Xiang says that "this is only so" is equivalent to "this is so." (*Jingdian shiwen*, 27: 2a)

8.2.3 駢於辯者纍瓦結繩竄句遊心於堅白同異之閒而敝跬譽無用之言非乎 **Those who add a "web" to their powers of disputation pile up tiles and tie knots in ropes in ever changing rhetoric as their minds wander amidst "hard," "white," "identical," and "difference," but do they not just wear themselves out for the sake of these useless words that provide such limited [*kui*] fame!** 向崔本跬作趌向丘氏反云近也 In the Cui [Zhuan] and Xiang [Xiu] editions, *kui* (half a pace, short distance, limited) is written as *gui* (step half a pace). Xiang says [*gui*] should be pronounced with the initial *qiu* [*khuw*] combined with the final *shi* [*dẓiə.'*,] and that it means "near."

10.4.1 聖人不死大盜不止 **As long as sages do not die, great robbers will not cease, . . .** 向云聖人不死言守故而不日新牽名而不造實也大盜不止不亦宜乎 Xiang says that "As long as sages do not die" refers to those who hold fast to precedent and forgo daily renewal, who, enticed by fame, fail to behave honestly. As such, is it not fitting that "great robbers will not cease"! (*Jingdian shiwen*, 27: 7b)

10.4.2 爲之斗斛以量之則並與斗斛而竊之 **If bushels and pecks are used for measuring, the robber will steal with bushels and pecks** 向云自此以下皆

所以明苟非其人雖法無益 Xiang says that from this point on, everything clarifies that if one wrongly takes what is not his, even if legal, no good will come of it. (*Jingdian shiwen*, 27: 7b)

19.5.1 是故忤物而不慴 . . . **which is why such a one could be so at odds with things and yet feel no fear** 向秀曰遇而不恐也 Xiang Xiu says, "Such encounters do not make him afraid." (*Liezi jishi*, 2: 51)

19.5.2 而況得全於天乎 . . . **how much the better could one achieve such perfect wholeness from Heaven!** 向秀曰得全於天者自然無心委順至理也 Xiang Xiu says, "One who achieves such perfect wholeness from Heaven is spontaneously free from conscious mind and thus perfectly in accord with the ultimate principle of things." (*Liezi jishi*, 2: 51)

23.5.7 日中穴坏[阫] . . . **tunnel through walls [*peia*] at high noon** 向音裴云阫牆也言無所畏忌 According to Xiang, *peia* sounds like *peib* [*bəj*], and he says that *peia* is a wall. The text means that such as they have no scruples or fear. (*Jingdian shiwen*, 28: 2b)

23.9 越雞不能伏鵠卵 . . . **though the Yue hen cannot hatch swan eggs, . .** 司馬向云小雞也 Sima [Biao] and Xiang both say that [the Yue hen] is a small fowl . . . 魯雞固能矣 **the Lu hen certainly could.** 向云大雞也 Xiang says that [the Lu hen] is a large fowl. (*Jingdian shiwen*, 28: 3a)

23.16 揭竿而求諸海也 . . . **trying to find something in the sea with a pole.** 向云言以短小之物欲測深大之域也 Xiang says that this means trying to use something short in length to fathom the depth of some vast realm. (*Jingdian shiwen*, 28: 3a)

23.17.2 而況放道而行者乎 . . . **so how less likely can one who merely tries to act in conformity with [*fanga*] the Dao!** 向方往反云依也). Xiang has it that *fanga* [puaŋ[h]] should be pronounced with the initial *fangb* [*puaŋ*] combined with the final *wang* [*wuaŋ'*] and says that "conformity with" [fang[a]] means "rely on."

24.57 濡需者豕蝨是也擇疏鬣自以爲廣宮大囿奎蹄曲隈 **The opportunistic and improvident behave like lice on a pig. They choose a place where bristles are sparse and make it their great palace or grand park, or find in the cloven hooves and where hams curve [*quwei*], or at the haunches among the nipples a safe and handy dwelling.** 向云股間也 Xiang says that [*quwei*] means at the hams. (*Jingdian shiwen*, 28: 12b)

24.58 舜有羶行百姓悅之故三徙成都至鄧之虛而十有萬家 **It was because of Shun's rank behavior that the common folk happily submitted to him. This was why each of his three moves founded metropolises, and by the time he reached the desolation of Deng, he had more than a hundred thousand households with him.** 向云邑名 Xiang says that [Deng] is a district name. (*Jingdian shiwen*, 28: 12b)

24.58 堯聞舜之賢舉之童土之地 **When Yao heard how worthy Shun was, he raised him from that desolate land [*tongtu*]** . . . 向云童土地無草木也

Xiang says that [*tongtu*] means devoid of plants and trees. (*Jingdian shiwen*, 28: 12b)

25.10.8 湯得其司御門尹登恆爲之傅之 When Tang found Deng Heng serving as his gatekeeper [*menyin*], he made him his tutor. 向云門尹官名登恒人名 Xiang says that *menyin* is the name of an offical position and that Deng Heng is a man's name. (*Jingdian shiwen*, 28: 14b–15a)

26.5 儒以詩禮發冢大儒臚傳 When some Confucians, equipped with the *Classic of Odes* and *Record of Rites*, were digging open a grave, a profoundly learned Confucian shouted down [*lu*] to them . . . 向云從上語下曰臚 Xiang says that the term for speaking down to those below from above is *lu*. (*Jingdian shiwen*, 28: 19a)

33.8.2 以巨子爲聖人 A giant [*juazi*] here becomes a sage. 向崔本作鉅向云墨家號其道理成者爲鉅子若儒家之碩儒 **The Cui [Zhuan] and Xiang editions read *ju*b [instead of *ju*a]. Xiang says that the Mohists call one accomplished in the principles of their way a "grand master" [*jubzi*], just like the "grand literatus" [*shuoru*] of the Confucians. (*Jingdian shiwen*, 28: 36b)**

Texts not included in the Guo Xiang thirty-three-chapter edition:

Cf. 6.24.6 成然寐蘧然覺。So I just peacefully go to sleep, / and wake up pleasantly surprised. 向崔本此下更有發然汗出一句云無係則津液通也 In the Cui [Zhuan] and Xiang editions, immediately following the above line is added a four-character line, "Flowing easily I sweat," about which Xiang notes: since he is free of attachments, his bodily fluids flow freely. (*Jingdian shiwen*, 26: 29b) The following passage from the first chapter of the *Liezi* (Sayings of Master Lie), *Tianrui* 天瑞 (Auspices of Heaven), includes from Zhang Zhan's commentary a quote from the commentary of Xiang Xiu to the *Zhuangzi*, perhaps associated with *Zhuangzi*. **2.5–2.6** 故生物者不生化物者不化 **Therefore, that which generates things is not generated, and that which transforms things is not transformed.** 莊子亦有此言向秀注曰吾之生也非吾之所生則生自生耳生生者豈有物哉故不生也吾之化也非物之所化則化自化耳化化者豈有物哉無物也故不化焉若使生物者亦生化物者亦化則與物俱化亦奚異於物明夫不生不化者然後能爲生化之本也 The *Zhuangzi* also contains this text, about which the commentary of Xiang Xiu states, "My generation is not caused by me; such generation just generates itself. For generation to generate, how can anything material be involved! Therefore, it is not anything material. My transformation is not caused by me. Such transformation just transforms itself. For transformation to transform, how can anything material be involved! Therefore, it is without material substance [*wuwu*]. If that which generates things were also subject to generation and that which transforms things were also subject to transformation, how could it differ from material things? It is thus clear that only something subject to neither generation nor transformation may serve as the root source of generation and transformation." (*Liezi jishi*, 1: 4) Guo Xiang's view here is significantly different: whereas Xiang has it that the generator of things [*shengwuzhe*], the source or initiator of material existence, exists but is itself immaterial, Guo insists that no such generator exists, because for him, no existence is possible apart from material reality, phenomenal, and material existence; see also **2.5** and **22.59.5**.

汝逢衣徒也 **You are one of those fellows who wear a seamed gown [*fengyi*].** 向云[逢衣]儒服寬而長大者 Xiang says that a [*fengyi*] is Confucian garb, which is both loose fitting and quite long. (*Liezi jishi*, 2: 67) The term "seamed gown" [*fengyi*] does not appear in the received thirty-three-chapter text of the *Zhuangzi*.

Wang Shumin: "Of the above forty-eight places, the last three are not associated with the main text of Guo's version of the *Zhuangzi*, so he, of course, could not have said anything about them. As for the first forty-five, which only occur as excerpts from Xiang's commentary, Master Guo did not take a single word from them, so how can we see here any plagiarism of Xiang's commentary? Moreover, passages cited in *Zhuangzi shiwen* and Zhang Zhan's commentary to the *Liezi* that come only from Xiang's commentary means these are that many the more not included in Master Guo's commentary, and those cited there that only come from Master Guo's commentary means these are that many the more certainly not included in Master Xiang's commentary."[2]

II. Xiang and Guo comments differ completely (thirty places)

1.15.5 則夫子猶有蓬之心也夫 **So, after all, you have a mugwort plant for a mind, do you not!** (Guo) 蓬非直達者也. Mugwort is not a plant that grows straight and attains length. (Xiang) 向云蓬者短不暢曲士之謂. Xiang says that the mugwort signifies something short and does not spread, and it just twists around in the ground. (*Jingdian shiwen*, 26: 7a)

2.28.4 爲其脗合 **To muddle in perfect union with them, . . .** (Guo) 脗然無波際之謂也. To seem indistinct and unsettled [*chuna*] is used to describe water when no distinction exists between one wave and another. (Xiang) 向音脣云若兩脣之相合也. Xiang has it that *chuna* sounds like *chun*[b] [*ẓwin*] and says that it means to fit together like the two lips. 置其滑涽 **. . . accept their disorderliness, . . .** (Guo) 滑涽紛亂 . . . but such disorderliness is so chaotic that. . . . (Xiang) (instead of *huahun* 滑涽, the Xiang edition of the *Zhuangzi* has *mihun*汨昏) 向云汨昏未定之謂. Xiang says that *mihun* means "indeterminate." (*Jingdian shiwen*, 26: 13a)

2.33 罔兩問景曰 **Penumbra asked Shadow** (Guo) 罔兩景外之微陰也. A penumbra is the faint aura of darkness around the outside of a shadow. (Xiang) 向云景之景也. Xiang says that a penumbra is the shadow of a shadow. (*Jingdian shiwen*, 26: 14a)

3.4.5 官知止而神欲行 **When sense and knowledge stop, the divine is ready to act.** (Guo) 司察之官廢縱心而順理. As the senses which govern scrutiny quit working, he loosens his mind and accords with principle. (Xiang) 向云從手放意無心而得謂之神欲 Xiang says that to act freely with spontaneous inclination, utterly free of conscious mind, is what "the divine is ready" means. (*Jingdian shiwen*, 26: 15a)

4.5.1 回聞衛君其年壯其行獨 **I [Yan Hui] have heard that the ruler of Wei, young and dynamic, acts out of personal motives, . . .** (Guo) 不與民同欲也. He does not share in the common aspirations of his people. (Xiang) 向云與人異也. Xiang says that he regards himself as different from his people. (*Jingdian shiwen*, 26: 16b)

4.25.9 我其內熱與 **How hot my insides are!** (Guo) 所饌儉薄而內熱飲冰者誠憂事之難非美食之爲也. What he eats is frugal fare, yet his insides become so hot he drinks ice water, which means that he truly is worried about the difficulty of his task—and not that it is caused by rich food. (Xiang) 向云食美食者必內熱. Xiang says that it is someone who eats rich food whose insides become hot. (*Jingdian shiwen*, 26: 18b)

6.5.3 翛然而往翛然而來而已矣 **Carefree [*xiaoran*] he went as carefree he came—that was all there was to it.** (Guo) 寄之至理故往來而不難也. Since he entrusted himself to the ultimate principle of things, his going and coming were no problem to him. (Xiang) 向云翛然自然無心而自爾之謂. Xiang says that *xiaoran* means naturally free from conscious mind, and thus functioning spontaneously. (*Jingdian shiwen*, 26: 25b)

6.8.5 邴邴乎其似喜乎 **How carefree [*bingbing*]he was—seemingly so happy!** (Guo) 至人無喜暢然和適故似喜也. The Perfected one did not experience happiness, but because he was so free from care and in such harmony with things that he did seem happy. (Xiang) 向云 [邴邴]喜貌. Xiang says that [*bingbing*] is the appearance of happiness. (*Jingdian shiwen*, 26: 26a)

6.8.6 崔乎其不得已乎 **How absolute [*cui*] he was in circumstances inevitable!** (Guo) 動靜行止常居必然之極. His activity and behavior were always governed by the absolutely inevitable. (Xiang) 向云[崔]動貌. Xiang says that [*cui*] is to appear dynamic. (*Jingdian shiwen*, 26: 26a)

6.41 意而子曰雖然吾願遊於其藩 **Master Yier said, "Nevertheless, I would still like to wander along the edges of this realm [*fan*]."** (Guo) 不敢復求涉中道也且願遊其藩傍而已. He dares not try again to take up the way through its center and wants nothing more than to try to wander along the margins of this realm. 司馬向皆云[藩]崖也. Sima [Biao] and Xiang both say that [*fan*] means "boundaries." (*Jingdian shiwen*, 26: 30b)

7.15.1 壺子曰吾與汝既其文未既其實而固得道與眾雌而無雄而又奚卵焉 **Master Hu replied, "What I have conveyed to you so far is entirely the outer form of it but not yet all its inner substance, so are you sure that you really have mastered the Dao? You might have all the hens but no rooster,**

so then what fertile eggs might you get from them? (Guo) 言列子之未懷道也. That is, Master Lie has not yet fully internalized the Dao. (Xiang) 向秀曰夫實由文顯道以事彰有道而無事猶有雌無雄耳今吾與汝雖深淺不同然俱在實位則無文相發矣故未盡我道之實也此言至人之唱必有感而後和者也. Xiang Xiu says, "As inner substance is revealed in outer form, so the Dao is manifest in concrete performance. Therefore, to possess the Dao yet have no concrete performance to show for it is just like having hens but no rooster. Now, although you and I possess it in different degrees and levels of its inner substance should accordingly be in us both, you actually manifest no signs of its outer form. Therefore, you must still fail to realize fully the substance of my Dao. That is to say, when a perfected one sings out, resonance must occur before harmony takes place." (*Liezi jishi*, 2: 71)

7.25.2 於事無與親 **In regard to affairs, he had no preferences, . . .** (Guo) 唯所遇耳. He just took things as he encountered them. (Xiang) 向秀曰無適無莫也. Xiang Xiu says, "He was not for or against anything" (*Liezi jishi*, 2: 76). Cf. *Lunyu* (Analects), 4: 2471b: 君子之於天下也無適也無莫也義之與比, "The noble man in relation to all in the world is not for or against anything—he just aligns himself with what is right."

7.25.3 彫琢復朴 **From the carved and polished he returned to pristine simplicity, . . .** (Guo) 去華取實. He rejected gorgeous elaboration and adopted unadorned simplicity. (Xiang) 向秀曰雕瑑 [variant 琢] 之文復其真朴則外事去. Xiang Xiu says, "Returning to authentic simplicity from carved and polished decoration meant that worldly affairs ceased to concern him." (*Liezi jishi*, 2: 76)

7.25.6 以是終 **And in unity with everyone he lived out his life thus to the end.** (Guo) 使物各自終. He allowed all others to live out their natural lives to the end. (Xiang) 向秀曰遂得道也. Xiang Xiu says, "He consequently attained the Dao." (*Liezi jishi*, 2: 76)

10.3.6 竭川非以虛谷而谷虛夷丘非以實淵而淵實聖人已死則大盜不起, . . . **As valleys empty when rivers run dry, as chasms are filled when hills are leveled, so once sages die great robbers no longer arise, . . .** (Guo) 竭川非以虛谷而谷虛夷丘非以實淵而淵實絕聖非以止盜而盜止故止盜在去欲不在彰聖知. Rivers dry up not to make valleys empty, but valleys do become empty; hills are leveled not to make chasms filled, but chasms do become filled; sages are rejected not to bring an end to robbers, but robbers still come to an end. Therefore, bringing an end to robbers depends on the elimination of desire and not on the promulgation of sagely wisdom. (Xiang) 向云事業日新新者爲生故者爲死故曰聖人已死也損其名歸真而忘其塗則大盜息矣. Xiang says that as long as they engaged in new enterprises day after day, it meant that they were alive, but once all this was in the past, it meant that they were dead. This is why the text says, "once sages die." It is by disparaging their reputations, recovering one's own authenticity, and forgetting the paths that they followed that great robbers cease. (*Jingdian shiwen*, 27: 27a–27b)

19.1.2 達命之情者不務知之所無柰何 **19.1.2 One who understands the conditions of fate [*ming*] strives not after that about which intelligence can do nothing.** (Guo) 知之所無柰何者命表事也. That about which one's intelligence can do nothing are matters beyond one's fated endowment [*ming*]. (Xiang) 向秀曰命盡而死者是. Xiang Xiu says, "When one's fate has reached its end and death occurs—such matters as that." Xiang's commentary is quoted in Zhang Junfang 張君房 (ca. 961–ca. 1042), ed., *Yunji qiqian* 雲笈七籤 (Seven lots from the bamboo book hamper of the clouds), 32: 3a. Note: Whereas Guo understands *ming* as "fated endowment," Xiang takes it to mean "one's fated span of years." Cheng Xuanying supports Guo's reading. See *Zhuangzi jishi*, 19: 630.

19.3.2 蹈火不熱行乎萬物之上而不慄 **[The Perfected one] steps through fire yet suffers no heat and conducts himself as superior to the myriad folk yet trembles not.** (Guo) 至適故無不可耳非物往可之. Conforming perfectly to circumstances, there is absolutely nothing that such a one cannot do. But these are not things that ordinary folk can set out to do. (Xiang) 向秀曰天下樂推而不厭非吾之自高故不慄者也. Xiang Xiu says, "When 'all under Heaven happily promote him without ever tiring of it,' it is not something he is arrogant about, and this is why he 'trembles not.' " (*Liezi jishi*, 2: 49) Cf. *Laozi*, section 66; Richard John Lynn, *The Classic of the Way and Virtue*, 173: "Therefore all under Heaven happily promote him without ever tiring of it. It is because he does not contend that none among all under heaven can contend with him."

19.11.1 顏淵問仲尼曰吾嘗濟乎觴深之淵津人操舟若神問焉曰操舟可學邪曰可善游者數能 **Yan Yuan [Yan Hui] asked Confucius, "Once when I was crossing the gorge at Goblet Deep, the ferryman handled the boat as if someone divine. So I asked him, 'Can one learn how to handle a boat this way?' And he replied, 'A good swimmer can with repetition [*shuo*].'** (Guo) 言物雖有性亦須數習而後能耳. This speaks to the fact that though a person has it by original nature, he still must repeatedly [*shuo*] practice, for only then can he do it. (Xiang) 向秀曰其數自能也言其道數必能不懼舟也. Xiang Xiu says, "His skill [*shu*] is an innate capability, which means that such skill [*daoshu*] gives him the ability not to fear boats" (*Liezi jishi*, 2: 60). Note: Whereas Lu Deming assigns the pronunciation *shuo* 朔 [*ṣaɨwk*] to "數 here" (*Jingdian shiwen*, 26: 26a), meaning repetition/repeatedly (which is as Guo reads it), Xiang obviously reads it as *shu* [*ṣuə.'*], meaning "skill."

23.1.1 He [Gengsang Chu] dismissed those of his male servants who were ostentatiously knowledgeable and distanced himself from those of his female servants who were self-importantly [*qieran*] benevolent. (Guo) 其臣之畫然知者去之，其妾之挈然仁者遠之. (Guo) 畫然飾知挈然矜仁. "Ostentatiously" means to show off one's knowledge, and "self-importantly" [*qieran*] means to take pride in one's benevolence. (Xiang) 向云知也 Xiang says that [*qieran*] means "astute," "clever, "know all about" [*zhi*] (*Jingdian shiwen*, 28:

1a–1b). Note: Xiang, then, would have read the passage as "and distanced himself from those of his female servants who knew all about benevolence" (i.e., were astute or clever in manipulating benevolence).

23.1.2 擁腫之與居 **He only had the unspoiled simple live with him** (Guo) 擁腫朴也 "Unspoiled simple" [*yongzhong*] means "pristinely simple" [*pu*].

23.1.3 and only had those who just worked hard as his servants. (Guo) 鞅掌自得 "Just worked hard" means those who were "self-fulfilled." (Xiang) 向云二句朴纍之謂 Xiang says that the two lines mean "bound to pristine simplicity." (*Jingdian shiwen*, 28: 1b)

23.1.5 今吾日計之而不足歲計之而有餘 **Now, though if reckoned by the day his accomplishments seem inadequate, reckoned by the year they seem more than adequate.** (Guo) 夫與四時俱者無近功. Conforming with the four seasons results in no immediate gain. (Xiang) 向云無旦夕小利也 順時而大穰也. Xiang says that just for one day, not even little benefit occurs, but if one complies with the right amount of time, a great yield is had. (*Jingdian shiwen*, 28: 1b)

23.5.3 簡髮而櫛數米而炊 **They singled out individual hairs to comb and counted grains of rice to cook.** (Guo) 理錐刀之末也. That is, they concerned themselves with [matters as small as] "the points of awls and knives." (Xiang) 向云理於小利也. Xiang says that they concerned themselves with things of little benefit. (*Jingdian shiwen*, 28: 2b)

23.8.4 趎勉聞道達耳矣 **And though I strive to understand what you say, it only goes as far as my ears!** (Guo) 早聞形隔故難化也. Having just heard how one physical form differs from another, he thus finds it impossible to change. (Xiang) 崔向云僅達於耳未徹入於心也. Cui [Zhuan] and Xiang say that it only reaches his ears and fails to penetrate his mind. (*Jingdian shiwen*, 28: 3a)

23.17.1 夫外韄者不可繁而捉將內揵 **When one's outer is fettered, even the utmost dexterity fails to control it, so this blocks the inner.** (Guo) 揵關揵也. "Block" [*jian*] means "shut down" [*guanjian*]. (Xiang) 向云閉也. Xiang says that [*jian*] means "closed." (*Jingdian shiwen*, 28: 3b)

23.19.8 能侗[侗]然乎 **Can you be like a child [*tong*]?** (Guo) 無節礙也. He should be unconstrained. (Xiang) 向敕動反云直而無累之謂. Xiang says [*tong*] [*dəwŋ*] should be pronounced with the initial *chi* [*trhik*] combined with the final *dong* [*dəwŋ'*], and it means "free of entanglements." (*Jingdian shiwen*, 28: 3b)

24.66.10 頡滑有實 **Although it winds and slides [*xiehua*], its realization is had.** (Guo) 萬物雖頡滑不同而物物各自有實也. Although the way it [the Natural] winds and slides [*xiehua*] for myriads of people, each and every one realizes it in his own way. (Xiang) 向云頡滑謂錯亂也. Xiang says that *xiehua* means "in disorder." (*Jingdian shiwen*, 28: 13b)

26.28.3 謀稽乎誸 **When plans are scrutinized, urgency [*xiana*] is involved.** (Guo) 誸急也急而後考其謀. *Xiana* means urgency [*ji*]. Only after urgency arises are plans for it scrutinized. (Xiang) 向本作弦云堅正也. The Xiang edition [of the *Zhuangzi*] writes *xiana* as *xian*[b] [bowstring, musical instrument string, archer], and Xiang says that it means "firm and upright." (*Jingdian shiwen*, 28: 20b) Note: Xiang's reading results in a different translation: "Let plans be scrutinized, so they be firm and upright."

Wang Shumin: "In not a one of the thirty places cited above do the Guo and Xiang commentaries match, so even if the Xiang commentary still existed in its entirety today, the places where Guo's commentary differed from it ought not to stop with these, yet the *Shishuo* and *Jinshu* both state that Master Guo 'composed his own commentary to only two chapters, "Autumn Floods" and "Perfect Joy," and modified just one chapter, "Horses' Hooves." ' This implies that Guo's commentary should not differ in any way in any of the other chapters other than these three. [Given the above evidence,] I do not know what this could be based on to say such a thing!"[3]

III. Similar comments by Xiang and Guo (thirty-two places)

1.0 (Guo) 夫小大雖殊而放於自得之場則物任其性事稱其能各當其分逍遙一也豈容勝負於其間哉. Although the small and the great differ, as long as they let themselves go in the realm of self-fulfillment, creatures shall abide by their natures, their behavior shall correspond to their abilities, and each shall fulfill its allotted capacity, for spontaneous free play is the same for all. How could success or failure have any place here!

1.7.13 若夫乘天地之正而御六氣之辯以遊無窮者彼且惡乎待哉 **But if one conveys himself on the rectitude of Heaven and Earth, rides the interactions among the six pneumas, and so roams about endlessly, on what would such a one then ever need to depend?** (Guo) 苟有待焉則雖列子之輕妙猶不能以無風而行故必得其所待然後逍遙耳而況大鵬乎夫唯與物冥而循大變者爲能無待而常通豈自通而已哉又順有待者使不失其所待所待不失則同於大通矣. But subject to dependency, even Master Lie with his easy and marvelous manner could not travel without the wind. Thus, he had to have access to something on which to depend before he could enjoy spontaneous freedom. And how much the more this is true for the great Peng! Only one who arcanely merges with things and abides with great transformation can be free from dependency and thus always keep in step with things. How could this ever be just the result of self-made success and nothing more! As for one who also complies with that on which he depends and never lets such dependency fail, as long as it fails not, he remains one with the great thoroughfare [the Dao].

The following passage is quoted in Liu Yiqing (403–440), *Shishuo xinyu* (A new account of tales of the world), with commentary by Liu Jun 劉俊 (462–521), *Shang zhi xia* 上之下 (first fascicle, part 2), and *Wenxue disi* 文學第四 (Letters and scholarship, part 4), 22b–23a: 向子期郭子玄逍遥義曰夫大鵬之上九萬尺鷃之起榆枋小大雖差各任其性苟當其分逍遥一也然物之芸芸同資有待得其所待然後逍遥耳唯聖人與物冥而循大變為能無待而常通豈獨自通而已又從有待者不失其所待不失則同於大通矣. Concerning the meaning of spontaneous free play, Xiang Ziqi [Xiang Xiu] and Guo Zixuan [Guo Xiang] say, "Whereas the great Peng rises ninety thousand and the little quail rises just to an elm or a sandalwood, although there is a difference in their size, each abides by its nature, and as long as each fulfills its allotted capacity, access to spontaneous free play is one and the same for them. However, although creatures are diverse and varied, they equally must depend on something on which to rely, and only after they manage to access such dependence may they enjoy spontaneous free play. Only the sage, who arcanely merges with things and abides with great transformation, can stay free from dependency and yet always keep in step with things. And how could this ever just be the result of self-made success and nothing more! As for one who also complies with that on which he depends and never lets such dependency fail, as long as it fails not, he remains one with the great thoroughfare [the Dao]." Wang Shumin concludes that since the passage is attributed in the *Shishuo xinyu* to both Xiang Xiu and Guo Xiang, it must have originally appeared in Xiang's annotated version of the text (*Zhuangxue guankui*, 122). However, since the wording differs in places and considerable rearrangement is involved, Guo did more than just copy Xiang's commentary.

1.1.2 是鳥也海運則將徙於南冥 **This is such a bird that, spiraled by the sea, it goes to move its abode to the South Sea.** (Guo) 非冥海不足以運其身非九萬裏不足以負其翼. As only the dark sea has the means to convey the Kun's body, so only ninety thousand tricents of wind have the means to support the Peng's wings. 向秀云非海不行故曰海運. Xiang Xiu says that if it were not for the sea, it would not move, which is why the text says "spiraled by the sea" (*Jingdian shiwen*, 26: 1b). Although somewhat similar, Guo's comment is more specific and detailed.

1.13.2 是其言也猶時女也 **How correct his words are, just like a maiden's.** (Guo) 謂此接輿之所言者自然爲物所求辦知之聾盲者爲無此理. This means that these words of Jieyu naturally are just what people ask for. However, one whose understanding is deaf and blind will say it is nonsense. 向云時女虛靜柔順和而不喧未嘗求人而爲人所求也. Xiang says that a maiden, impassive and quiet, gentle and yielding, is so congenial that she never confront others. She never asks anything of others, but it is to her that others apply (*Jingdian shiwen*, 26: 5b). Whereas Xiang's comment focuses entirely on explaining why the words of a "maiden" are so appealing, Guo's goes on to address the failure to appreciate them.

2.5 子綦曰夫吹萬不同而使其自己也咸其自取怒者其誰邪 **Ziqi said, "They blow through the myriad things differently since they allow them all**

to act on their own." (Guo) 故天者萬物之總名也 Therefore, "Heaven" is the general term for the myriad things, . . . (Xiang) 善哉向生之言曰天者何萬物之總名人者何天中之一物 How splendid are Master Xiang's words, which say, "What is 'Heaven'? It is the general term for the myriad things. What is 'man'? He is one creature among that 'Heaven.' " Xiang Xiu's note is quoted by Luo Han 羅含 (Junzhang 君章) (292–372), in *Gengsheng lun* 更生論 (Treatise on rebirth), Sengyou 僧祐 (445–518), ed., *Hongming ji* 弘明集 (Collection spreading the light [of Buddhism]), 5: 27b. Wang Shumin points out that since the *Zhuangzi* passage involved is not recorded, it is uncertain if Xiang's text is actually associated with that passage. (*Zhuangxue guankui*, 123)

3.1.1 吾生也有涯 **For our lives there is a limit.** (Guo) 所稟之分各有極也. For one's allotted capacity, each has its own limits. (Xiang) 向秀曰生之所稟各有涯也. Xiang Xiu says, "For the life with which one is endowed, each has its own limit. (*Yunji qiqian*, 32: 3a) Whereas Guo conceives of the length of life as part of one's allotted capacity, Xiang focuses entirely on the length of life.

3.1.3 以有涯隨無涯殆已 **To pursue the limitless / With the limited, / Here lies nothing but danger** [*dai*]. (Guo) 以有限之性尋無極之知安得而不困哉. To seek knowledge that has no limits with a nature that has limits—how could anyone ever manage not to bring trouble on himself doing this! (Xiang) 向云疲困之謂. Xiang says that [*dai*] means fatigue (*Jingdian shiwen*, 26: 14b). Unable to decide on whether *dai* means danger or fatigue, Cheng Xuanying says, 形勞神弊而危殆者也. "One's body will be so belabored and spirit so worn out that he puts himself in danger." *Zhuangzi jishi*, 1: 116.

3.1.4 已而爲知者殆而已矣 **To be in such a state and yet keep on trying to know, / Here lies nothing but danger!** (Guo) 已困於知而不知止又爲知以救之斯養而傷之者真大殆也. Already in trouble because of knowledge, yet one knows not to stop but brings ever more knowledge to bear in order to rescue his situation. This is how one injures life through attempting to nurture it, for this truly means great danger. (Xiang) 向秀曰已困於智矣又爲以攻之者又殆矣. Xiang Xiu says, "Already fatigued because of knowledge, one uses ever more of it to cope with his situation, which makes for even more fatigue. (*Yunji qiqian*, 32: 3a) Wang Shumin, considering that Xiang's text should be more like Guo's, declares it corrupt and corrects it to 已困於智矣又爲智以救之者又大殆矣, "Already fatigued because of knowledge, yet one uses ever more of it to rescue his situation, which makes for even more fatigue" (*Zhuangxue guankui*, 123). However, either way, Guo's text expands on what Xiang's says and seems the richer for it.

3.4.5 官知止而神欲行 **When sense and knowledge** [*guanzhia*] **stop, the divine is ready to act** [*shenyu*]. (Guo) 司察之官廢縱心而順理. As the senses which govern scrutiny quit working, this sets the mind free so that it accords with principle. (Xiang) 向音智專所司察而後動謂之官智. Xiang has it that [*zhia*] [*triăh/trih*] sounds like *zhib* [*triăh/trih*] [and says that] what is activated only after that which controls scrutiny takes control is what the term *guanzhib* means (*Jingdian shiwen*, 26: 15a). As such, Xiang Xiu seems to understand "what is activated" to mean knowledge controlled by the senses. It is uncertain if this is exactly what his text means, for the wording seems confused and ambivalent. The meaning of Guo's text, by contrast, is much clearer. Note also that in this context, *zhia* 知 and *zhib* 智 are interchangeable.

4.17.1 仲尼曰齋吾將語若有而爲之其易邪 **Zhongni replied: "Fast! That's what I have to tell you! But to apply yourself to it, do you think this an easy [*yi*] thing to do?** (Guo) 夫有其心而爲之者誠未易也 To apply oneself to it with selfconscious mind would certainly never make it easy. (Xiang) 向崔云輕易也. Xiang and Cui [*Zhuan*] both say that *yi* means "easy" (*Jingdian shiwen*, 26: 17b). Since *yi* can also mean "change," the Xiang/Cui text makes clear that here, *yi* means "easy." However, *yi* meaning "easy" surely is obvious from the context; as such, the comment seems inane. On the other hand, Guo's comment addresses the large issue that conscious mind is an obstacle to such ease.

4.24.4 瞻彼闋者虛室生白 **4.24.4 Look there behind that closed door into the empty chamber where radiance lives.** (Guo) 夫視有若無虛室者也虛室而純白獨生矣. Look and it seems nothing is there, but only in an empty chamber does pure radiance exist independently. (Xiang) 向秀曰虛其心則純白獨著. Xiang Xiu says, "When one empties his mind, pure radiance appears." Xiang's text is quoted in Li Shan's 李善 (630–690) commentary to Xi Kang 嵇康 (223–262), *Yangsheng lun* 養生論 (Treatise on nurturing life); see also *Wenxuan* (Selections of refined literature), 53: 2293. Although both Xiang and Guo equate the mind empty of conscious thought with ultimate perception and wisdom, Guo adds an essential element of his own, self-generated independence, as an attribute of the sagely mind. Cf. 22.20.1, Guo's comment.

4.33.3 時其飢飽達其怒心 **He keeps track of the times it [the tiger] is hungry or full, and so gets at what makes its mind angry.** (Guo) 知其所以怒而順之. Knowing what makes it angry, he complies with it. (Xiang) 向秀曰達其心之所以怒而順之. Xiang Xiu says, "Understanding what makes its mind angry, he complies with it." (*Liezi jishi*, 2: 58)

4.34.2 適有蚊虻僕緣 **But if by chance mosquitoes or gadflies swarm onto it [a horse], . . .** (Guo) 僕僕然群著馬. They irritatingly swarm onto the horse. (Xiang) 向云僕僕然蚉蝱緣馬稠概之貌. Xiang says this describes the horse irritatingly beset with thick swarms of mosquitoes and gadflies. (*Jingdian shiwen*, 26: 19b)

7.15.2 而以道與世亢必信夫故使人得而相汝 **Yet you [Master Lie] take such a way and flaunt it at the world, determined to be trusted, which allowed this person to examine your physiognomy.** (Guo) 未懷道則有心有心而亢其一方以必信於世故可得而相之. As he had not quite internalized the Dao, he still remained selfconscious, and selfconsciously flaunted one aspect of it, determined that he would be trusted by the world, which is why he could be judged physiognomically. (Xiang) 向云亢其一方以必信於世故可得而相. Xiang says that he flaunted one aspect of it, determined that he would be trusted by the world, which is why physiognomical judgement could be had (*Liezi jishi*, 2: 71). Guo's reference to self-consciousness enhances the explanation of why Master Lie left himself open to physiognomical judgment, expanding on what Xiang says.

7.17.1 列子入泣涕沾襟以告壺子壺子曰鄉吾示之以地文萌乎不震不正 **Master Lie then went back in and, tears soaking his lapels, reported this to Master Hu, but Master Hu said, "What I have showed her was myself as outer signs of the Earth, as does a bud neither stirring nor governed.** (Guo) 萌然不動亦不自正與枯木同其不華濕灰均於寂魄此乃至人無感之時也夫至人其動也天其靜也地其行也水流其止也淵默淵默之與水流天行之與地止其於不爲而自爾一也今季咸見其尸居而坐忘即謂之將死睹其神動而天隨因謂之有生誠能應不以心而理自玄符與變化升降而以世爲量然後足爲物主而順時無極故非相者所測耳此應帝王之大意也. Like a bud motionless, which still does not govern itself, he is a match for an old tree not in flower or for the wet ashes equal to a forlorn earthbound soul, for such is the state of a Perfected one free of thoughts and feelings. A perfected one acts as does Heaven, is quiescent as is Earth, moves as does water, and is still as is the silence of the abyss. Whether the abyss is still or the water flows, whether Heaven acts or Earth rests are all identical in that they are free from intent and function spontaneously. Now Ji Xian saw him there like a corpse abiding in forgetfulness and so said that he was about to die, but if she had seen how his spirit moved in compliance with Heaven, she would have said that he still had life to live. One who truly can respond to things without using selfconscious mind and whose comprehension spontaneously tallies arcanely with them, one who takes the measure of the world in step with increases and decreases arising from change and transformation, only such a one is up to mastery over them and can infinitely comply with the demands of the moment. Therefore, he is not someone whom a physiognomist may examine. Here we have the basic gist of "Fit to be Sovereigns." (Xiang) 向秀曰萌然不動亦不自止與枯木同其不華死灰均其寂魄此至人無感之時也夫至人其動也天其静也地其行也水流其湛也淵嘿淵嘿之與水流天行之與地止其於不為而自然一也今季咸見其尸居而坐忘即謂之將死見其神動而天隨便為之有生苟無心而應感則與變升降以世為量然後足為物主而順時無極耳豈相者之所覺哉. Xiang Xiu says, "Like a bud motionless yet not keeping itself still he is a match. . . . it is only such a one who is up to mastery over them and can infinitely comply with the demands of the moment. How could he ever be a subject whom a phsiognomist would understand! (*Liezi jishi*, 2: 72). Not only are the two commentaries keyed to two different texts of the *Zhuangzi* (see the note to Guo's commentary to 7.17.1), Guo's commentary is worded somewhat differently at the beginning and end, and it is slightly longer. Nevertheless, most of it follows Xiang's text exactly.

7.19.1 列子入以告壺子壺子曰鄉吾示之以天壤 **Master Lie then went back in and reported this to Master Hu, but Master Hu said, "What I have showed her was my natural earthbound aspect, . . .** (Guo) 天壤之中覆載之功見矣比之地文不猶外乎此應感之容也. Amidst Heaven and Earth, his effectiveness at covering and bearing up [as does the Dao] was apparent. Although comparable to signs of the Earth, does this not still signify an outer aspect? But this is how he looks when he reacts and responds. (Xiang) 向秀曰天壤之中覆載之功見矣比地之文不猶外乎 (*Liezi jishi*, 2: 73). Although the text is exactly the same in Xiang's commentary except for the subordination marker *zhi* 之, which links 地 to 文, Guo's comment also extends to another sentence, which relates Master Hu's appearance to his virtues.

7.19.2 名實不入 **into which neither reputation nor benefit enter, . . .** (Guo) 任自然而覆載則天機玄應而名利之飾皆爲棄物也. As he gives himself over to spontaneity, thus covering and bearing up, it is his celestial mechanism that arcanely responds to things, which means the trappings of reputation and gain have all really become discarded waste (Xiang) 任其自然而覆載則名利之飾皆爲棄物 (*Liezi jishi*, 2: 73). The only difference is the *ye* 也, indicating the intensifier "really" at the end of Guo's comment.

7.19.4 是殆見吾善者機也嘗又與來 **She probably saw that the good in me was this activating force.** (Guo) 機發而善於彼彼乃見之. When activating force started up, it did him good, and so she saw it (Xiang) 向秀曰有善於彼彼乃見之明季咸之所見者淺矣. Xiang Xiu says, "It did him good, and so she saw it. This clarifies that what Ji Xian saw was only superficial." (*Liezi jishi*, 2: 73)

7.21.1 壺子曰吾鄉示之以太沖莫勝 **Master Hu said, "What I then showed her was that my great emptiness had no room for victory.** (Guo) 居太沖之極浩然泊心而玄同萬方故勝負莫得厝其間也. He dwells in the infinite capacity of great emptiness, in whose oceanic vastness he moors his mind, where it unites arcanely with its infinite methods; as such, victory or defeat finds no place in it. (Xiang) 向秀曰居太沖之極皓然泊心玄同萬方莫見其迹 (*Liezi jishi*, 2: 73). Xiang Xiu says, "He dwells in the infinite capacity of great emptiness, in whose oceanic vastness he moors his mind, where it unites arcanely with its infinite methods, so no one sees the footprints he leaves behind." (*Liezi jishi*, 2: 73)

7.21.3 鯢桓之審爲淵止水之審爲淵流水之審爲淵淵有九名此處三焉 **A whale-swirled whirlpool gathered to form my abyss, then still waters gathered to form my abyss, and then flowing water gathered to form my abyss. Though the abyss exists in nine kinds, here I distinguished only three of them, . . .** (Guo) 淵者靜默之謂耳夫水常無心委順外物故雖流之與止鯢桓之與龍躍常淵然自若未始失其靜默也夫至人用之則行捨之則止行止雖異而玄默一

焉故略舉三異以明之雖波流九變治亂紛如居其極者常淡然自得泊乎忘爲也. The abyss signifies quiet passivity. Water always behaves unselfconsciously, so accommodates itself to whatever is outside it. Therefore, whether it flows or is still, whether swirled by whale or made to leap by dragon, abyss-like it always is just as it was before, never losing its quiet passivity. When a Perfected one is called upon, he acts; when he is set aside, he desists. Although such acting and desisting differ, they are identical in their quiet passivity. Therefore, he cited in brief these three different states to illustrate what he meant. Although the flow of water exists in nine different transformations, still and disturbed all mixed up together, one who dwells in infinite capacity will always placidly achieve self-fulfillment and moor himself in unselfconscious effort. (Xiang) 向秀曰夫水流之與止鯢旋之與龍躍常淵然自若未始失其靜默也. Xiang Xiu says, "Whether water flows or is still, whether swirled by a whale or made to leap by a dragon, abyss-like it always is just as it was before, never losing its quiet passivity" (*Liezi jishi*, 2: 75). Guo Xiang elaborates considerably on Xiang's core statement.

7.24.1 壺子曰鄉吾示之以未始出吾宗 **Master Hu said, "What I had already showed her never revealed my Progenitor.** (Guo) 雖變化無常而常深根冥極也. Although his change and transformation occurred without constancy, he always remained deeply rooted in the arcane ultimate. (Xiang) 向秀曰雖進退同羣而常深根寧極也. Xiang Xiu says, "Although he advanced or withdrew together with the crowd, he always remained deeply rooted in the utmost tranquility" (*Liezi jishi*, 2: 75). Guo significantly replaces "tranquility" in his commentary with his quintessential term "the arcane."

7.24.2 吾與之虛而委蛇 **I was so empty, with her, wriggling as compliant as a snake is to the ground . . .** (Guo) 無心而隨物化. Unselfconsciously he kept transforming in step with external conditions. (Xiang) 向秀曰無心以隨變也. Xiang Xiu says, "He unselfconsciously stayed in step with change." (*Liezi jishi*, 2: 75)

7.24.4 因以爲弟靡因以爲波流故逃也 **As such, I became utterly flexible, and, as such, I drifted one with the current—and that was why she ran away.** (Guo) 變化頹靡世事波流無往而不因也夫至人一耳然應世變而時動故相者無所措其目自失而走此明應帝王者無方也. He freely submits to change and transformation, drifts in step with the affairs of the world, so in nothing he ventures does he fail to comply. Though a Perfected one remains integrally one, he resonates with worldly vicissitudes and so acts in step with them. Therefore, the physiognomist had nothing to set her eyes on and, losing self-possession, just ran away. This illustrates how someone fit to be a sovereign stays free of set methods. (Xiang) 向秀曰變化頹靡.世事波流.無往不因.則為之非我.我雖不為.而與羣俯仰.夫至人一也.然應世變而時動.故相者無所用其心.自失而走者也. (Xiang) Xiang Xiu says, "He freely submits to change and

transformation, drifts in step with the affairs of the world, so in nothing he ventures does he fail to comply. As such, whatever he does, it does not arise from his self. Although he himself takes no conscious action, he still gets along with the crowd. Though a perfected one remains integrally one, he resonates with worldly vicissitudes and so acts in step with them. Therefore, since the physiognomist had nothing to exercise her mind on, she lost self-possession and ran away." (*Liezi jishi*, 2: 76)

7.25.4 塊然獨以其形立 **Clod-like to stand alone in his physical form, . . .** (Guo) 外飾去也. All external trappings have been eliminated. (Xiang) 向秀曰則外事去矣. Xiang Xiu says, "That is, all things external to him had been eliminated." (*Liezi jishi*, 2: 76)

7.25.5 紛而封哉 **Though engaged in turmoil he kept himself gathered together, . . .** (Guo) 雖動而真不散也. Although he acted, his authenticity remained intact. (Xiang) 向秀曰真不散也. Xiang Xiu says, "His authenticity remained intact." (*Liezi jishi*, 2: 76)

10.7.6 自三代以下者是已舍夫種種之民而悅夫役役之佞釋夫恬淡無爲而悅夫啍啍之意啍啍已亂天下矣 **Ever since the Three Dynasties it has only been thus; the pristinely simple common folk are abandoned but cunning sharpers are favored; peaceful unselfconscious action is abolished and intent fostered by continuous harangue is preferred. It is just this continuous harangue that has so confused the world!** (Guo) 啍啍以己誨人也. "Continuous harangue" means to use one's own resources to instruct others. (Xiang) 向秀曰以智誨人之貌. Xiang Xiu says, "[Continuous harangue] describes using what one knows to instruct others." Xu Miao 徐邈 (344–397), *Zhuangzi jiyin* 莊子集音 (Collected pronunciation glosses for the *Zhuangzi*), fragments reprinted in Zhang Yongquan 張涌泉, ed., *Dunhuang jingbu wenxian heji* 敦煌經部文獻合集 (Collection of documents from Dunhuang, classics and scriptures section), 9: 4711.

12.40.3 手撓顧指四方之民莫不俱至此之謂聖治 **He but lifts his hand to point, turns his head to look, and common folk from the four quarters without exception all come to him. This is called the government of the sage.** (Guo) 言其指麾顧眄而民各至其性也任其自爲故. This means with the wave of his finger or the turn of his head, each and every one of the common folk perfectly fulfills his original nature, for he allows them to act on their own. (Xiang) 向云顧指者言指麾顧盼而治也. Xiang says that "turns his head to look" means that all he has to do to govern is use a wave of his finger or the turn of his head. (*Jingdian shiwen*, 27: 15b)

16.8.8 故曰喪己於物失性於俗者謂之倒置之民 **Thus, it may be said, those who lose themselves for the sake of acquiring something or violate their original natures to conform to the rabble may be called people who get things upside down.** (Guo) 營外虧內甚倒置也. They nourish the outer and deplete the inner, which really gets things upside down. (Xiang) 向云以外易内可謂倒置. Xiang says that to let one's inner self be altered by external things may be said to get things upside down. (*Jingdian shiwen*, 27: 24b)

19.1.1 達生之情者不務生之所無以爲 **One who understands the conditions of life strives not after that which one's life lacks the means to provide.** (Guo) 生之所無以爲者分外物也. That which life lacks the means to provide are things outside one's allotted capacity. (Xiang) 向秀曰生之所無以為者性表之事也. Xiang Xiu says, "That which life lacks the means to provide are things outside one's original nature." (*Yunji qiqian*, 32: 3a)

19.4.2 夫奚足以至乎先是色而已 **And what might suffice to advance one to the front? For there is nothing here other than personal appearance.** (Guo) 同是形色之物耳未足以相先也. But since they have the same sort of personal appearance, nothing suffices here for one to attain precedence over another. (Xiang) 向秀曰同是形色之物耳未足以相先也以相先者唯自然也. Xiang Xiu says, "But since they have just the same sort of personal appearance, nothing suffices here for one to attain precedence over another. It is only natural endowment that provides for precedence over another." (*Liezi jishi*, 2: 49)

19.11.2 若乃夫沒人則未嘗見舟而便操之也 **And if a diver, even though he has never seen a boat, he could immediately do it.** (Guo) 沒人謂能鶩沒於水底. "Diver" means one who can dive like a diver duck to the bottom of the water. (Xiang) 向秀曰能鶩沒之人也. Xiang Xiu says, "This is one who can dive like a diver duck to the bottom of the water." (*Liezi jishi*, 2: 60)

23.5.7 之數物者不足以厚民民之於利甚勤子有殺父臣有殺君正晝爲盗日中穴坏 **To deal with people in such ways does no good to improve the lives of the common folk, for they become so keen on benefiting themselves that sons would kill fathers, officials would kill sovereigns, some would commit robbery in broad daylight or tunnel through walls at high noon.** (Guo) 無所復顧. They no longer have consideration for anyone. (Xiang) 向[坏]音裴云坏牆也言無所畏忌. Xiang has it that *peia* [*phəj*] sounds like *peib* [*bəj*] and says that it is a wall. The passage means that they are without fear or scruples. (*Jingdian shiwen*, 28: 2b)

27.14.1 景曰搜搜也奚稍問也 **Shadow said, "I'm just unselfconsciously moving around [*sousou*], so why ask me about it?"** (Guo) 運動自爾無所稍問. Its movement is spontaneous, so there is nothing to ask about. (Xiang) 向云[搜搜]動貌. Xiang says that *sousou* describes its movement. (*Jingdian shiwen*, 28: 22a)

Wang Shumin: "As for the thirty-two places cited above, Guo's commentary is certainly based on Xiang's commentary, but Guo also either deleted or added something to Xiang's to formulate what he himself had to say. He did not merely 'edit the wording' and do nothing more."[4]

上舉三十二條，郭注固本於向注，但復有所損益，以自成說，非僅點定文句而已。

IV. Comments by Xiang and Guo almost identical wording (twenty-eight places)

1.15.1 莊子曰夫子固拙於用大矣宋人有善爲不龜手之藥者世世以洴澼絖爲事 **Master Zhuang said: "You certainly are inept when it comes to putting great things to use. There was a man of Song who excelled at making salve to prevent hands from chapping and splitting [*guishou*], and, generation after generation, his family made bleaching silk its occupation.** (Guo) 其藥能令手不拘坼故常漂絮於水中也. Because this salve could render hands resistant to chapping and splitting [*juche*], one could keep on bleaching silk in the bleaching solution. (Xiang) 向云[龜手]拘坼也. Xiang says that *guishou* means *juche*. (*Jingdian shiwen*, 26: 6b)

2.4.8 厲風濟則眾竅爲虛 **When such a fierce wind [*lifeng*] passes by, all the hollows become empty.** (Guo) 濟止也烈風作則眾竅實及其止則眾竅虛虛實雖異其於各得則同. "Has past" means stop. When a fierce wind [*liefeng*] acts up, all the hollows are filled, but when it stops, all the hollows become empty. Although to be full or empty constitutes a difference, as for the potentiality of each, it is always the same (Xiang) 向郭云烈風. Xiang and Guo both say that a [*lifeng*] is a [*liefeng*]. (*Jingdian shiwen*, 26: 8b)

2.4.9 而獨不見之調調之刁刁乎 Is it just you who hasn't seen how it makes things sway and shake, rustle and swish? (Guo) 調調刁刁刀刀動搖貌也言物聲既異而形之動搖亦又不同也動雖不同其得齊一耳豈調調獨是而刁刁獨非乎. "Sway and shake" and "rustle and swish" describe how things look in agitation. That is, not only are the sounds of things different, the kind of agitation their bodily forms undergo also differ. Although their movements differ, they achieve an overall uniformity. So how could "sway and shake" ever be singled out as "correct" or "rustle and swish" as "incorrect"! (Xiang) 向云調調刁刁皆動搖貌. Xiang says that "sway and shake" and "rustle and swish" both describe how things look in agitation. (*Jingdian shiwen*, 26: 8b)

2.8.24 未成乎心而有是非是今日適越而昔至也 **However, for right and wrong to exist without first being formed in the mind would be like leaving today for Yue and yet arriving there yesterday** [*xi*], . . . (Guo) 今日適越昨日何由至哉？未成乎心是非何由生哉明夫是非者群品之所不能無故至人兩順之. If one were to go to Yue today, how could one arrive yesterday [*zuori*]? If not first formed in the mind, where could right and wrong come from? It is obvious that right and wrong, as such, are things that all kinds of people cannot do without. Therefore, the Perfected one follows along the course of both at once. (Xiang) 向云昔者昨日之謂也. Xiang says that *xi* means *zuori*. (*Jingdian shiwen*, 26: 10a)

3.4.4 方今之時臣以神遇而不以目視 **And now, I encounter it with my spirit and do not see it with my eyes.** (Guo) 闇與理會. He arcanely fuses with the principle involved. (Xiang) 向云暗與理會謂之神遇. Xiang says that arcane fusion with the principle involved is what "encounter it with my spirit" means. (*Jingdian shiwen*, 26: 15a)

3.4.11 而況大軱乎 **. . . so how much the less likely a big bone [*gu*]!** (Guo) 軱戾大骨衄刀刃也. "Big bone" [*gu*] here means to clash with a big bone, which would defeat the knife edge. (Xiang) 向郭云軱戾大骨也. Xiang and Guo say that *gu* means to clash with a big bone. (*Jingdian shiwen*, 26: 15b)

3.6.1 公文軒見右師而驚曰是何人也惡乎介也 **When Gongwen Xuan saw the Commander of the Right, he was startled to say: "What kind of man are you? How is it that you have one foot [*jie*]?** (Guo) 介偏刖之名. *Jie* is a term for having one foot cut off. (Xiang) 向郭云[介]偏刖也. Xiang and Guo say that [*jie*] is to have one foot cut off. (*Jingdian shiwen*, 26: 15b–16a)

3.7.1 澤雉十步一啄百步一飲不蘄畜乎樊中 **The wild pheasant takes a peck every ten steps, a drink every hundred steps, and it does not beg to be raised in a cage [*fan*].** 蘄求也樊所以籠雉也夫俯仰乎天地之間逍遙乎自得之場固養生之妙處也又何求於入籠而服養哉. *Qi*, "beg," means "seek," and *fan*, "cage," is something in which to confine a pheasant. Starting and stopping anywhere in Heaven and Earth, enjoying spontaneous freedom in the open fields of self-fulfillment, all this certainly indicates a marvelous situation for nurturing life, so why should it seek further to enter a cage and so submit to being raised! (Xiang) 李云[樊]藩也所以籠雉也向郭同. Li [Yi][5] says that a *fan* is the fence used to cage a pheasant. Xiang and Guo say the same. (*Jingdian shiwen*, 26: 16a)

4.5.5 死者以國量乎澤若蕉 **As for his dead, he reckons his state a marsh and they the grasses and weeds [*jiao*] in it.** (Guo) 舉國而輸之死地不可稱數視之若草芥也. He mobilizes his entire state's population and conveys it to the land of death, so the dead, impossible to count, he regards as just so much grasses and weeds [*caojie*]. (Xiang) 向云[蕉]草芥也. Xiang says that *jiao* means "grasses and weeds." (*Jingdian shiwen*, 26: 16b)

4.41 南伯子綦遊乎商之丘見大木焉有異結駟千乘隱將芘其所藾其枝所陰可以隱芘千乘者也 **When Senior of the South Ziqi was wandering on a hill in Shang he saw there a great tree that was different from others. A thousand chariots with teams of four horses could have found shade in the shadow it cast.** (Guo) 其枝所陰可以隱芘千乘者也. The shadow cast by its branches could provide shade for a thousand carriages. (Xiang) 向云蔭也可以蔭芘千乘也李同. Xiang says that its shadow could provide shade for a thousand chariots. Li [Yi] says the same. (*Jingdian shiwen*, 26: 20b)

5.14.1 魯有兀者叔山無趾踵見仲尼 **In Lu, Shushan, known as No-Toes, who had had his feet cut, repeatedly [*zhong*] went to see Zhongni.** (Guo) 踵頻也. *ZhongZhong*, "repeatedly, means *pin*, "frequently." (Xiang) 向郭云[踵]頻也. (*Jingdian shiwen*, 26: 23a)

(Guo) 踵頻也. *Zhong* (often) means *pin* (frequently. (Xiang) 向郭云頻也. It means frequently. (*Jingdian shiwen*, 26: 23a)

6.6.3 其顙頯 **His forehead juts out [*kuia*].** (Guo) 頯大朴之貌. Juts out [*kuia*] gives him the look of the great uncarved block. (Xiang) 向本[頯]作頯云頯然大朴貌. The Xiang edition [of the *Zhuangzi*] writes *kuia* with the character *kuib*, and he says that jutting out gives it the look of the great uncarved block. (*Jingdian shiwen*, 26: 25b)

6.18.1 於謳聞之玄冥 **Singing heard it from Arcane Obscurity.** (Guo) 玄冥者所以名無而非無也. Arcane Obscurity is a name for that which is nothingness and yet not nothingness. (Xiang) 向郭云所以名無而非無也. Xiang and Guo say that it [Arcane Obscurity] is a name for that which is nothingness and yet not nothingness. (*Jingdian shiwen*, 26: 28a)

6.22.1 曰亡予何惡浸假而化予之左臂以爲雞予因以求時夜 **"Not at all, why should I resent it? If my left arm gradually evolves into a rooster, I shall thus demand of it the hour that ends the night. . . .** (Guo) 浸漸也夫體化合變則無往而不因無因而不可也. *Qin*, "soak," means "gradually" [*jian*]. Since such a one embodies transformation and merges with change, wherever they lead him he is sure to comply, and wherever such compliance leads it will suit. (Xiang) 向云漸也. Xiang says that *qin* "soak" means "gradually" [*jian*]. (*Jingdian shiwen*, 26: 29a)

7.14.1 鄭有神巫曰季咸知人之死生存亡禍福壽夭期以歲月旬日若神鄭人見之皆棄而走 **In Zheng there was a shaman with divine powers named Ji Xian, who knew if one would live or die, survive or perish, whether enjoy good fortune or suffer misfortune, live long or die young—predicting the year, month, and day of the month as if godlike. When the people of Zheng saw her, they avoided her and ran away.** (Guo) 不憙自聞死日也. They did not like to hear the day of their own deaths. (Xiang) 向秀曰不喜自聞死日也. Xiang Xiu says, "They did not like to hear the day of their own deaths." (*Liezi jishi*, 2: 70)

7.17.2 是殆見吾杜德機也嘗又與來 **So she probably saw me in a state of sealed-up vitality. Try to bring her here again."** (Guo) 德機不發曰杜. Vitality unexpressed is said to be "sealed up." (Xiang) 向秀曰德幾不發故曰社也. Xiang Xiu says, "Since his vitality was unexpressed, it was said to be sealed up." (*Liezi jishi*, 2: 72)

7.21.2 是殆見吾衡氣機也 **. . . so she probably saw me with activating force in balanced pneuma.** (Guo) 無往不平混然一之以管闚天者莫見其涯故似不齊. No venture of his is done without equanimity, for he merges with all in one integral whole. No one who peers at the sky through a tube ever sees its limits, which is why he seems irregular to her. (Xiang) 向秀曰無往不平混然一之以管窺天者莫見其崖故以不齊也. Xiang Xiu says, "No venture of his is done without equanimity, for he merges with all in one integral whole. No one who peers at the sky through a tube ever sees its limits, which is why he seems irregular to her." (*Liezi jishi*, 2: 73)

7.24.3 不知其誰何 **. . . that she did not know what kind of a person I was.** (Guo) 汎然無所係也. He so overflowed that there was nothing by which he could be bound. (Xiang) 向秀曰汎然無所係. Xiang Xiu says, "He was so adrift that there was nothing by which he could be bound." (*Liezi jishi*, 2: 75)

7.25.1 然後列子自以爲未始學而歸三年不出爲其妻爨食豕如食人 **After this, Master Lie thought that he had never learned anything and so went home, which he did not leave for three years, where he cooked for his wife and fed the pigs as one would feed people.** (Guo) 忘貴賤也. He forgot about all distinctions between noble and base. (Xiang) 向秀曰忘貴賤也. Xiang Xiu says, "He forgot about all distinctions between noble and base." (*Liezi jishi*, 2: 76)

11.4.6 從容無爲而萬物炊累焉 **And utterly at ease, he acts free of selfconscious purpose, at which the myriad things for him become freely drifting dust.** (Guo) 若游塵之自動. They seem just like drifting dust freely moving about on its own. 向郭云如埃塵之自動也. Xiang and Guo say that they are like dust freely moving on its own. (*Jingdian shiwen*, 27: 9b)

16.4.8 心與心識 **Mind engaged with mind in knowledge** [*shi*], . . . (Guo) 彼我之心競爲先識無復任性也. As minds of self and other vied to be first in exercising knowledge [*shi*], people no longer trusted their original natures. (Xiang) 向本作職云彼我之心競為先職矣郭注既與向同則亦當作職也 The Xiang edition [of the *Zhuangzi*], instead of *shi*, "knowledge," writes *zhi*, "performance of duties," and says that minds of self and other vied to be first in the performance of duties. Since Guo's commentary was identical to Xiang's, it also should be written with *zhi*, "performance of duties" (*Jingdian shiwen*, 27: 24a). Wang Shumin concludes in *Zhuangzi jiaoquan*, 572, note 12, that because *shi* and *zhi* were used interchangeably in antiquity, the reading for both commentaries should be *shi*, "knowledge," and rejects Lu Deming's assertion that the texts should read as *zhi*.

17.4.8 證曏今故 **. . . and clearly understands present and past.** (Guo) 曏明也今故猶古今. *Xiang* [also "previously" or "toward"] here means "clearly," and "present and past" is the same as "past and present" (Xiang) 向郭云[曏]明也. Xiang and Guo say that [*xiang*] means "clearly." (*Jingdian shiwen*, 27: 25b)

19.4.1 關尹曰是純氣之守也非知巧果敢之列居予語女凡有貌象聲色者皆物也物與物何以相遠 **Pass Director Yin replied, "It is a matter of safeguarding one's pure pneuma, not something exemplified by knowledge, skill, courage, or resolution. Sit down and I shall tell you about it. Though everyone has a distinct form or appearance, voice, or countenance, all are still people, so what might distance one person from another?** (Guo) 唯無心者獨遠耳. Only one free of conscious mind may so distance himself. (Xiang) 向秀曰唯無心者獨遠耳. Xiang Xiu says, "Only one free of conscious mind may so distance himself." (*Liezi jishi*, 2: 49)

19.5.1 彼得全於酒而猶若是 **Since he could achieve such perfect wholeness just thanks to drink, . . .** (Guo) 醉故失其所知耳非自然無心者也. It was because he was drunk that he lost awareness; it was not that he became unselfconscious spontaneously. (Xiang) 向秀曰醉故失其所知耳非自然無心也. Xiang Xiu says, "It was because he was drunk that he lost awareness; he did not become unselfconscious spontaneously. (*Liezi jishi*, 2: 51)

19.9.1 曰我有道也五六月累丸二而不墜則失者錙銖 **The other replied, "I do have a special way: Over five or six months, if I can balance two pellets without their falling, those I drop will be very few, . . .** (Guo) 累二丸於竿頭是用手之停審也故其承蜩所失者不過錙銖之閒也. Balancing two pellets on top of a pole stops him from paying heed to his hand control, so during that time the caught cicadas he dropped did not amount to more than a very few. (Xiang) 向秀曰累二丸而不墜是用手之停審也故承蜩所失者不過錙銖之間耳. Xiang Xiu says, Balancing two balls so they do not fall stops him from paying heed to his hand control, so during that time the caught cicadas he dropped did not amount to more than a very few.(*Liezi jishi*, 2: 65)

23.5.1 且夫二子者又何足以稱揚哉 **Moreover, what makes those two so worthy of praise!** (Guo) 二子謂堯舜. By "those two," he means Yao and Shun. (Xiang) 向崔郭皆云堯舜也. Xiang, Cui [Zhuan], and Guo all identify them as Yao and Shun. (*Jingdian shiwen*, 28: 2b)

23.17.1–23.17.2 老子曰汝自洒濯熟哉鬱鬱乎然而其中津津乎猶有惡也夫外韄者不可繁而捉將內揵內韄者不可繆而捉將外揵 **Master Lao said, "How hard and anxiously you've worked at cleansing yourself! But your inner self so overflows with it that you still have what's bad in you. When one's outer is fettered, even the utmost dexterity fails to control it, so this blocks the inner. When one's inner is fettered, even the tightest grip [*mou*] fails to control it, so this blocks the outer.** (Guo) 偏韄由不可況外內俱韄乎！將耳目眩惑於外而心術流蕩於內雖繁手以執之綢繆以持之弗能止也. Even one who tries to stay away from such fetters cannot do it, so how less likely can one whose inner and outer are both fettered! When ears and eyes are dazzled and deluded without and the techniques of the mind float adrift within, even if one manages to handle them with the utmost dexterity and with the tightest of grips [*choumou*], he will still fail to curb them. (Xiang) 崔向云[繆]綢繆也. Cui [Zhuan] and Xiang say that [*mou*] means "the tightest of grips" [*choumou*]. (*Jingdian shiwen*, 28: 3b)

33.14.3 其風窢然惡可而言 **Since they raised a wind like a headwind, how could that ever be captured in words!"** (Guo) 逆風所動之聲. It was the sound made by a headwind. (Xiang) 向郭云[窢]逆風聲. Xiang and Guo say that [*huo*] is the sound a headwind. (*Jingdian shiwen*, 28: 37b)

2.22.2 庸詎知吾所謂知之非不知邪 **How can I know that what I mean by "I know it" is not really that "I do not know it"?** (Guo) 夫蛣蜣之知在於轉丸而笑蛣蜣者乃以蘇合爲貴. What the dung beetle knows pertains to rolling pellets, but those who laugh at the dung beetle themselves regard storax as something of great value. (Xiang) 向秀曰蛣蜣之知在於轉丸. Xiang Xiu says, "What the dung beetle knows pertains to rolling pellets." Xiang's comment is recorded in Dai Tong 戴侗 (ca. 1200–1284), *Liushu gu* 六書故 (Origins of the six categories of characters), 20: 12b. However, when the exact same text is recorded in Wu Shu 吳淑 (947–1002), *Shilei fu zhu* 事類賦註 (Rhapsodies on categorized matters, with commentary), 30: 3b, it is ascribed not to Xiang's commentary but to the text of the *Zhuangzi* itself: 莊子曰 蛣蜣之智在於轉丸. The same attribution to the *Zhuangzi* also occurs in Zhu Mu 祝穆 (d. ca. 1255), *Gujin shiwen leiju* 古今事文類聚 (Classified compendium based on events and writings), 48: 18b, and in Zhiyuan 智圓 (976–1022), *Niepan jing shu sande zhigui* 涅槃經疏三德指歸 (Three virtues outline to the commentary to the *Mahāparinirvāṇa-sūtra*), 1: 318a. Wang Shumin concludes that the text that was included in Guo's commentary but also attributed to Xiang is actually from a lost version of the *Zhuangzi.* Either Xiang and Guo both incorporated it into their respective commentaries or scribal error placed it there during recension. Wang Shumin cites other such examples, but there is no need to repeat them here.[6]

Wang Shumin: "As for the twenty-eight places cited above, it cannot be denied that Guo's commentary copies the Xiang commentary, but even then slight differences exist, for phrase and sentences are not always exactly the same. . . . The *Shishuo* and *Jinshu* both state that the "Autumn Floods" chapter was commented on only by Guo, but according to the *Jingdian shiwen* one comment on that chapter [17.4.8] is also attributed to Xiang Xiu. In fact, commentaries at times by chance just happen to turn out the same, so they all inevitably contain such examples. . . . From discrepancies between the commentary texts by these two masters large differences in meaning can also be deduced."

IV. Other evidence for Guo's authorship of the commentary (one passage)

The expression "Make the two modes his vehicles [*cheng liangyi*] is attributed not to Xiang Xiu, but to Guo Xiang, in the *Beitang shuchao* (Excerpts from books in the Northern Hall), edited by Yu Shinan (558–638), 69: 2b. Also see 1.12.3, Guo commentary: "Thus, it is that he makes the two modes [the *yin* and *yang*] his vehicles [*cheng liangyi*] and drives the six climatic phenomena, identifies with the mass of common folk, and urges on the myriad things."

Notes

The material gathered here is based on Wang Shumin, *Zhuangxue guankui* 莊學管窺 (Studies of the *Zhuangzi*, limited views), 113–30.

1. Early middle Chinese pronunciation is according to Edwin G. Pulleyblank, *Lexicon of Reconstructed Pronunciation in Early Middle Chinese, Late Middle Chinese, and Early Mandarin.*

2. Wang, *Zhuangxue guankui*, 118.
3. Wang, *Zhuangxue guankui*, 121.
4. Wang, *Zhuangxue guankui*, 126.
5. Li Yi 李頤 [later third–early fourth centuries] compiled a version of *Zhuangzi jijie* 莊子集解 (*Zhuangzi*, collected exegeses), consisting of thirty fascicles according to the *Suishu jingji zhi* 隋書經籍志 (*History of the Sui*, bibliographic treatise) or twenty fascicles according to the *Jiu Tangshu jingji zhi* 舊唐書經籍志 (*Old History of the Tang*, bibliographic treatise).
6. See Wang, *Zhuangxue guankui*, 129–30.

APPENDIX D

SIMA QIAN, "BIOGRAPHY OF MASTER ZHUANG"

Master Zhuang was a native of Meng whose given name was Zhou, and who once served as a local official in Meng at Lacquer Garden [Qiyuan]. He was a contemporary of King Hui of Liang and King Xuan of Qi. There was nothing into which did not look, but his fundamental ideas reverted to the words of Master Lao, and as a result his writings in over a hundred thousand words for the most part consist of metaphors and allegories for them. He wrote "The Old Fisherman [Yufu]," "Robber Zhi [Dao Zhi]," and "Ransack Chests [Quque]" to criticize the followers of Confucius and to clarify the thought of Master Lao. Chapters such as "Master Kangsang of Weilei Mountain" [Gengsang Chu] were all fictional fabrications.[1] Yet he excelled at style and diction and at clarifying the principles underlying events through analogy, which he used to excoriate the Confucians and the Mohists. Even the most erudite scholars of the age could not defend themselves against him. His words unrestrained flowed as a great ocean just to please himself. Therefore, from rulers to high officials no one could make use of his talents. King Wei of Chu heard that Zhuang Zhou was a worthy man, so he sent a messenger with rich gifts to induce him to come, offering to appoint him minister. Zhuang Zhou laughed and said to the messenger from Chu, "A thousand gold pieces is great profit and a ministership is certainly a noble position, but have you not seen the sacrificial ox used in the suburban sacrifices? After being raised for several years, it is dressed in patterned embroidery so that it may be led into the great temple. At this juncture, though it might wish to be a solitary piglet, how could that ever happen? Leave quickly, sir, do not contaminate me!

I would prefer to enjoy myself playing in a filthy ditch than be held in fetters by the ruler of a kingdom. I will never take office for as long as I live, for it is by doing so that I can be happy as I please!"[2]

The Grand Historian states: "Since what Master Lao esteemed was the Dao, absolute nothingness [*xuwu*], and resonating [*ying*] with change and transformation [*bianhua*] in non-purposeful action [*wuwei*], the work that he wrote is deemed so marvellously subtle that it is hard to understand. Master Zhuang separated Dao from Virtue [*de*], and though indulging in wide-ranging exposition, in his essential thought he always reverted to the Natural [*ziran*]. Shen Buhai [ca. 400–337 BCE] constantly strove to improve himself and applied all effort to the study of the relationship between name and reality. Han Fei [ca. 280–233 BCE] stretched out the carpenter's ink line to judge matters [judged matters only in terms of explicit law] and clarified the difference between right and wrong, but this reached such an extreme of brutal severity that he lacked all sense of mercy. However, though all of them founded their thought on Dao and Virtue, Master Lao was certainly the most profound and comprehensive of them.[3]

Notes

1. The *Shiji suoyin* (Explicating obscurities in the *Records of the Historian*) of Sima Zhen (early eighth century) reads "Weilei xu" and "Kangsang zi" as two separate chapters of the *Zhuangzi*, the former chapter identified with the sayings of a disciple of Master Lao, known only as someone who supposedly lived on Weilei Mountain, and the latter chapter identified with Master Gengsang. However, the *Shiji zhengyi* (Correct meaning of the Records of the Historian) of Zhang Shoujie, with a preface dated 737, parses and interprets the text as rendered previously, "Master Kangsang of Weilei Mountain," which is exactly how Gengsang Chu, though with variant characters, is identified at the very beginning of the *Gengsang Chu* chapter in the Guo Xiang's recension (23.1); see *Shiji*, 63: 2144.
2. Sima Qian, *Shiji* (Records of the Grand Historian), 7: 2143–2145.
3. Sima Qian, *Shiji*, 7: 2156.

GLOSSARY OF TERMS

an	content, contentment; safe and secure, safety and security; where; wherein 安
	obscure 暗
anding	stability 安定
baifei	hundred negations 百非
bao	preserve 葆
	violence 暴
beia	side doublets 倍阿
beiren	northerner 北人
ben	basis; origin; original nature; underlying basis of things 本
benwu	originally nonexistence/originally nonexistent 本無
benyuan	root source 本原
bi	another thing; he; it; [the] other; such a one; that; they; theirs 彼
	cover, shelter 蔽
	have nothing to do with 閉
	vilify 吡
bing	discard 并
biran	certainty, inevitability 必然

biran zhi ji	the absolutely inevitable 必然之極
bisai	block off 閉塞
bosai zhi chou	gambling chips 博塞[賽]之籌
bu	monetary value 布
bu zide	had no access to myself 不自得
budeyi	because it is inevitable; there is no alternative 不得已
buwu	not used as a thing 不物
cai	appearance, bearing, manner, mien 采
	innate abilities, innate talents; resources 才
	natural utility 材
caibo	monetary value 財帛
caide	talents and virtues 才德
caili	analytical thinking 才理
caizhen	presence authentic 采真
cen	small hill 岑
chai	firewood, brushwood; use brushwood to provide protection; obstruction 柴
chaiqiao	firewood 柴樵
chang	prolonged 長
cheng	accomplished; be produced; completely whole; fulfill, fulfillment; perfectly realize; potential realized; integration; (realizable) potential; (fully) realize(d); success, successful 成
	sincere, sincerity 誠
chenggong	success 成功
cheng liangyi	makes the two modes [yin and yang] his vehicles 乘兩儀
chengran	peacefully 成然
chengsi	get worried 成思
chengxiang canjun	adjutant to the chancellor 丞相參軍
chengxiang zhubu	recorder for the chancellor 丞相主簿
chi	linear measurement (about nine inches) 尺
chilun	arguments 持論
chongyan	repeated words 重言
chu	butt 觸
chugui	unconventional and bizarre 諔詭
chuizhong	hang the heel 垂踵

chuizhong kongzhong	hang the heel in the air; hesitate in midstep 垂腳空中
chuo	cease 輟
	trouble 惙
chuqi	discard 除棄
ci	mine; this 此
cili	style of utterance 辭理
cong	abide by; compliant; follow/go after; from 從
congshi zhonglang	palace guard administrator 從事中郎
cui	pile up 萃
da	great; large 大
dai	depend, dependency; subject to; treat; wait in attendance on 待
dang	accord with, apt; appropriate; conform to; equal to the moment; fundamental nature; inherently right; just right; knack; live up to; make correspondences; match; right (action); suitable; what is appropriate 當
	activate, activated 盪
Dao	Dao; Way 道
dao	way 道
Daojia	adherents of philosophical Daoism/literati Daoism 道家
dashan	great mountain 大山
datong	great pervasive integration; great thoroughfare [the Dao] 大通
de[*qi*]*xing*	fulfill one's nature 得[其]性
di	thearch 帝
ding	male domestic servant 丁
dou	ancient dry measure 豆
du	governor, supervisor 督
duan	beginning; end; extremity 端
	cut short 短
	function properly 股
dumai	governor tract 督脈
duo	cut short; fix; put in order 掇
e	bad; evil; ugly 惡
er	common subordinate conjunction; you 而

eryi	two exemplars 二儀 (Heaven and Earth, yin and yang)
esi	starve to death 餓死
fa	attack; convention; flaunt; launch punitive expedition; law; method(s); natural law; phenomenal construct; standard(s) 法
fanfu	go to and fro 反覆
fangqie	come to pass 方且
fei jizhi	fate may not be controlled by oneself 非己制
feiyou	nonexistent (*abhāva*); rejection of existence 非有
fen	allotted place in life; aspect; natural allotment; disintegration; distinction; formulated;
	divisions; separate, separatedness 分
feng	wind 風
fenli	split apart 分離
fouzhong	*fou* liquid measure and *zhong* (2 x *fou*) liquid measure 缶鍾
fu	ancient dry measure (= 4 or 5 *ou* 區) 釜[鬴]
	correspond; tally with 符
	submit; use 服
	wheel struts 輔
fuju	wheel struts and wheel 輔車
ge	cut; trim 割
gong	first note of the Chinese pentatonic scale 宫
gongfu	princely court 公府
gu	matter; reason 故
guai	strange 怪
guanjian	shut down 關揵
gui	demon, demonic ghost; spirit; the demonic 鬼
	jade tablet 珪
guigen	revert to one's roots 歸根
guilong	fishy bug 鮭蠪 (kind of demon)
guize	spirit blame 鬼責
guji	buffoons, clowns, comedians, comics; elusive; humorists; slippery; tricksters 滑[骨]稽
guoqu	go beyond 過去
he	reconcile 和

hehe	entirely hot and dry 赫赫
helie	ranks of soldiers (literally, cranes arrayed) 鶴列
houyu	postscript 後語
hu	ancient dry measure "bushel" 斛
	arid 縠
huangmen shilang	gentleman in attendance of the yellow gate; supervising secretary of the chancellery 黃門侍郎
huben	"brave as tigers" 虎賁 (head of the royal bodyguard)
hui	cloudy 晦
huizhao	light of wisdom 惠[慧]照
huntianyi	armillary sphere 渾天儀
hunyuan	Amorphous Origin 混元
ji	achievement; footsteps/prints; impressions; manifestation; objective traces, outward sign, tracks 跡[迹]
	activating force; incipient movment; inward spring; crossbow mechanism 機
	steep; danger 圾
	collect; receive 給
	continuity 繼
	gather together 積
	how many; just about do 幾
	mash together 韲
	receive 給
	urgency 急
jiafu	quasi-diametral struts 夾輔
jian	block 揵
	choose, choice; simplify 簡
	firm; to persist 堅
	gradually 漸
	mirror 鑒[鑑]
	see 見
jiandu	awareness of/be aware of one's perfect independence 見獨
jiang	diminish 降
	take, take along, lead; send off 將

jiangsha	diminish progressively 降殺
jiao	rectify 矯
jiaotai	perfect harmonious intercourse 交泰
jiaowei	commandant 校尉
jiawu	artificial 假物
jie	deprive; distinguish; set free 解
	one foot cut off 介
	swift 捷
	topknot (kind of demon) 髻
jiegu	explanatory comments 解詁
jijie	collected exegesis 集解
jiju gan dai	centipedes relish snakes 蝍蛆甘帶
jiju qian dai	the centipede uses its pincers on the snake 蝍蛆鉗帶
jiliao	complete realization, completely realize; complete usage; exhaust, exhaustion 盡
	without physical form or substance 寂寥
ji'neng	potentiality of self 己能
jing	boundary, limit; scope 竟
	canonical 經
	external conditions; external world; realm(s) 境
	minute; vital essence 精
	mirror 鏡
	quiet, quietude 靜
jingjie	realms of perceptual objects (*viṣaya*) 境界
jingmo	quiet passivity 靜默
jingnei	attend to worldly conventions 經內
jingqi	essential pneuma 精氣
jingshen	essence and spirit; essential spirit 精神
jingwei de yuanzi	most miniscule atom 精微的原子
jiren	eccentric individual 畸人
jishu	infinite aptitude 極數
jiu	try to get close 就
jiwei	self effort 己爲
jiwu	entrust oneself to the people; use the people as a vehicle 寄物

jixi	accumulated practice 積習
ju	aggregate, aggregation; coalescence; collective whole; gather 聚
jue	cut off; reject, rejection 絕
	third note of the Chinese pentatonic scale 角
juesao	grasp at random 攫搔
jushou	gather and fasten on to 聚守
kongwu	absolute nothingness 空無
kui	cheekbones; juts out; look of the great uncarved block 頯
	one-footer 夔 (kind of demon)
kuiran	high and handsome/magnificent; *kui*-like 頯然
kunwei	timid 困畏
lai	leper 癩
lei	bondage; entangle, entanglements; involvement; trouble ; wear down 累
leiting	thunderclap (kind of demon) 雷霆
lengran	cool and collected 冷然
lengtai	cool detachment 泠汰
li	advantage, advantageous; benefit, beneficial; sharp 利
	civility; propriety; rites, ritual, ritual behavior 禮
	fundamental nature; logically; moral principles; natural principles [of behavior or things]; reason, rationally, reasoned discourse; "right" 理
	harsh; in danger; terrible; treat strictly; ugly man 厲
	principle 理
	tricent (one-third mile, one-half kilometer) 里
liang	bridge 梁
liangyi	兩儀 Heaven and Earth; the two modes, yin and yang
lie	render asunder 裂
lingtai	numinous tower 靈臺
liqi	sharp instruments 利器
liuhe	six directions 六合
liuji	absolute reach of the six directions 六極
liuwei	six social positions 六位
longsha	elaborate and spare 隆殺

lü	conscious deliberation; powers of ratiocination 慮
	treader (kind of demon) 履
lüji	footprints 履跡
lüjie	shoe ties 履結
ma	counter 碼
	horse 馬
mi	get something in the eye; hallucinations 眯
miao	wondrous 妙
miaodang	marvelous aptness 妙當
mie	do away with 滅
min	quick 敏
ming	allotted life span, destiny; fate, fated; fated endowment, natural endowment 命
	be clear about; bright; clarification, clarify; clearly; clearly know; perspicacity; understand 明
mingjiao	doctrine of names 名教
mingshi	role befitting reputation名尸
mingxing	obscure and chaotic; greatest of esteem 溟涬
mo	end 末
mu	curtain 幕
naonao	chaotic, random; spontaneous behavior 撓撓
neizai chaoyue	immanent transcendence 內在超越
neizai yiyuanlun	immanent monism 內在一元論
neng	ability; capability; potential 能
ni	boundary; limit 倪
	disobedient, disobey; move in the opposite direction; oppose, opposition; thwart 逆
ning	obsequiousness 佞
ou	ancient dry measure (= 4 or 5 *dou* 豆) 區
pan	boundary end, limit 畔
panghuang	wanderer 彷徨 (kind of demon)
peiya	germ, gemmule 胚芽
peng	mugwort 蓬
pie	cut; glance 覕
pingce	privy 屏廁
pingcui	stable essence 平粹

pinping	appraisal of personal character 品評
pu	pristine simplicity, pristinely simple; uncarved block 樸/朴
qi	adjust; equality; equally one and the same; match; stabilize 齊
	concrete objects; phenomenon; the phenomenal world 器
	pneuma 氣
	shoelaces 綦
qian	pincers; use pincers 鉗
qianshi	foresight 前識
qiangyang	wax vigorous 強陽
qian xin	add firewood 前薪
qie	expeditious 且
qijing bamai	the eight extraordinary tracts [channels, meridians] 奇經八脈
qimu	mother of pneuma 氣母
qing	attitude; bias; disposition; emotional bias; emotional involvement; emotions; facts [of the matter]; conditions; inclinations;
	innate character/nature; natural inclination; predilection; prejudicial feelings; innate properties; innate tendencies; true state 情
qingci qiuzhi	the most sublime meaning expressed in the clearest of diction 清辭遒旨
qingtan	pure conversation 清談
qingyan	pure discourse [of arcane learning] 清言
qiong	difficulties; exhaust, use up completely; grasp completely 窮
qipin	seventh rank in government 七品
qisuo	one's authentic state 其所
qi suoyou	from where does one start; how this is done 其所由
qiu	hill; earthen ridge between fields 丘
qiwu	the [twenty-four] seasonal pneuma and all things 氣物
qiyou	how this is done; this [way to] wander 其遊[由]
qu	circuitous 曲
quan	contract; tally; natural allotment 券

quxing abandon original nature 去性

ren benevolence 仁

ru you 汝

ruo if; as if, like; you 若

sai block; stop up 塞

sha partition 殺

shao explain 紹

shen the divine, divine power, divinity; energy; god; the numinous; spirit 神

horned dog 莘 (kind of demon)

person 身

shengui greatest of esteem 甚貴

shenji divine/spiritual mechanism 神機

shenren divine man 神人

shenyin 呻吟 recite lessons

shi abandon 失

affirm; approve; correct; right; this, this one; this is such; it; it is; it is so; what is 是

authentic substance; full; real, fullfill oneself; inner self; reality, realization, really; who one really is 實

begin; essence, fundamental starting point; initial state; origin 始

capacity to do things; matter 事

corpse; ceremonial stand-in for the deceased; master, arbiter 尸

time is right, situation; timely, timeliness 時

shisan fragmented 釋散

shou fasten on to 守

shouben maintenance of original nature 守本

shu ailanthus, tree of Heaven 樗

fish: Hemiculter leucisculus, sharpbelly or sawbelly 儵

siju four propositions, tetralemma 四句

siju fenbie the fourfold propositional distinctions, the fourfold negation 四句分別

sikong minister of works 司空

sikong yuan section administrator in the ministry of works 司空掾

silü	selfsconscious ratiocination 思慮
sima	major 司馬
situ	minister of education 司徒
situ yuan	section administrator in the ministry of education 司徒掾
song	send off 送
su	white simplicity 素
sufen	fundamental capacity 素分
sui	accost 誶
tai	great; too much 太
	nag; worn out horse 駘
	peaceful, grand 泰
taichong	great empty vessel 太沖
taichu	great beginning 泰[太]初
taiding	great quietude 泰定
taifu	senior tutor 太傅
taifu zhubu	recorder for the senior tutor 太傅主簿
taiji	Great Ultimate 太極
taiqing	grand clarity 太清
taisu	grand basis 太素
taiwei	defender-in-chief 太尉
tang	lost 唐
ti	body, embodiment; embody; physical body/ embodiment;
	embody; original nature; perfect realization; substance 體
tian	Heaven; light of Heaven; natural endowment; nature; the Natural 天
tiandan	utterly dispassionate 恬淡
tiandao	course of Heaven; Dao of Heaven 天道
tianjun	potter's wheel of Heaven 天均
tianren	heavenly man 天人
tingfang	compliant non-interference 聽放
tongbian	foot soldier 徒
	keep in step freely with change 通變
waizai chaoyue	external transcendence 外在超越

wang	ban; destroy, lose; perish 亡
wanglai	come and go 往來
wangxiang	no-shape 罔象 (kind of demon)
wei	correct 韙
	danger 危
weiqing	violate innate character 違情
weishun	yield 委順
weiyi	winder 委蛇 (kind of demon)
wu	be/do without;emptiness,empty; free from; lose; non-existent, nonexistence;nothing; nothingness; without" 無
	detest, detestation; hate, hateful 惡
	material being; others; people; other things 物
wudao	be without/lack the Dao; disorderliness, disorderly; wicked 無道
wude	five virtues: 五德 benevolence [*ren* 仁], righteousness [*yi* 義], propiety [*li* 禮],
	wisdom, [*zhi* 智], trustworthiness [*xin* 信] 德
wufang	the boundlessly, boundlessness; free of set methods/ without method;
	the infinitely changeable; unruly 無方
wuguan	the five sense organs [*wuguan* 五官]: eyes [*mu* 目], nose [*bi* 鼻], tongue [*she* 舌], mouth [*kou* 口], ears [*er* 耳]
wuji	five consanguinity norms 五紀; the term also means the five phases 五行 and the five cardinal virtues 五德
wuqing	dispassionate; freedom from prejudicial feeling, impartially; free of/without the predilection to 無情
	five emotions 五情: joy [*xi* 喜], anger [*nu* 怒], sorrow [*ai* 哀], pensiveness [*si* 思], fear [*kong* 恐] (variants include worry [*you* 憂],
	pleasure [*le* 樂], fondness [*hao* 好], hate [*wu* 惡], and love [*ai* 愛], among others)
wushi	disengagement 無事
wusi	impartial; utterly free of self-interest 無私
wusuo buzhi	nothing was not done to the utmost 無所不至

wuwei.	act unself-consciously; do without intent; unself-conscious effort/force 無爲
wuwei zhizhi	nothing was done to the utmost; the utmost/perfection of unself-conscious effort 無爲之至
wuwu	has no materiality 無物
wuxin	free from conscious mind; unself-consciously, unself-consciousness 無心
wuxing	five agents/phases 五行: wood [*mu* 木], fire [*huo* 火], earth [*tu* 土], metal [*jin* 金], water [*shui* 水]
wuye	five humors 五液: sweat [*han* 汗], nasal mucus [*ti* 涕], tears [*lei* 淚], saliva [*yan* 涎], spittle [*tuo* 唾]
wuzang	five viscera 五臟: heart [*xin* 心], liver [*gan* 肝], spleen [*pi* 脾], lung [*fei* 肺], kidney [*shen* 腎]
wuzhuan er xing	stick to the same course 無轉而行
xi	attached, attachments, bonds 係
	breathe; breath; breather (rest) 息
	crack, gap, gapped, space; intermittent; leisurely 郤
	enter; make combinations 襲
	hog 狶
xian	flaunt; revealing light 顯
	treachery 險
	urgency 諴
xianfang	relaxed 閒放
xiang	lend assistance 襄
xiangying	mutual consonance; resonate with 相應
xiao	dispel; remove 銷
	filial piety 孝
	fragmented 肖
	leisurely move 逍
xiaocheng	lesser completions 小成
xichou	gambling chips 戲籌
xin	evidence; trust, trustworthy, trustworthiness 信
	self-conscious mind; heart; heart/mind; heart and mind; mind; state of mind; temperament 心
Xinruxue	New Confucianism 新儒學
xing	application; conduct oneself; move; progress; take action; walk 行

	bodily form; discernible form/shape; demeanor; physical appearance/existence/ form/state 形
	whetstone 硎
xingju	appear arrogant; obstructive 形倨
xingshen	physical forms and animating spirits 形神
xiongde	virtue of viciousness 凶德
xiqu	gapped and circuitous 郤曲
xishou	rhinoceros head 犀首 (head of royal bodyguard; office held by Gongsun Yan)
xu	beginning 緒
	easygoing, relaxed 徐
	empty, emptiness; illusory; vacuity, void 虛
	field ditch; occlusion, occluded 洫
xuan	black profundity 玄
xuanli	arcane principles 玄理
xuanmiao	arcane marvels 玄妙
xuantian	arcane way of nature 玄天
xuantong	arcane unity, arcanely unite; arcanely identify with 玄同
xuanxue	arcane thought 玄[元]學
xuanzong	arcane tradition 玄[元]宗
xun	abide with, comply with, in compliance with; keep in step with 循
	pursue; sacrifice (oneself/something for); self-sacrifice 殉
xunzhuo	smoke and singe 熏灼
xuwu	pure nothingness 虛無
yan	bend over; hide; privy; rest 偃
yanshu	shrew mole 偃[鼴]鼠
yanyang	bow and scrape 偃佒
yao	distant; prolonged; remote 遙
	invite, see 邀
yi	in balance; interact with smoothly/without obstruction 夷
	good purpose; meaning; signify; moral justice, moral meaning; righteous, righteousness 義
	suitable, suitability 宜
	surprised 異

ying	seek; strive for 營
yingguan	draw bow to the full
yinkuo	wood straightener 隱括
yishu	explications and expository commentaries 義疏
yiyang	overfull yang 泆陽 (kind of demon)
you	actuality; being; everything extant, existent; material/ physical existence; possess, possessions; something; somethingness 有
	basis; cause; from; ground; for such a reason 由
youdai	dependency, dependent; wait in attendance on 有待
youji	fate depends on the individual self 由己
youqi	mirages; moving vapors 遊[游]氣
youwei wu	person of self-conscious effort 有爲物
youyu	have both feet 有與
	rain 雨
yu	chance to find 遇
yuan	accord 緣
	section administrator 掾
yuanqi	primordial undifferentiated pneuma 元氣
yuanxun	hanger-on 緣循
yulu	recorded conversations 語錄
zaohua	Former-and-Transformer 造化
zaowuzhe	Creator 造物者
zhangju shiyi	phrase and passage interpretive comments 章句釋義
zhangshi	chief executive 長史
zhaozhen	portent; subtle and mysterious incipiency 兆朕
zhencai	authentic presence 真采
zheng	confirm 徵
	governed; pure and true; rational; rectify; rectitude; standard; true 正
zhengdao	correct path, correct way 正道
zhengqi	correct pneuma 正氣
zhenren	authentic man 真人
zhenshi	stone probes 針石
zhi	aspiration, aspire to; determination, determined to; intend, intention; will 志

	attain, attainment; epitome; perfect, perfection; perfect realization, perfectly done, perfectly fulfill; realize 至
	attribute; elucidate; finger; indicate; mean/meaning; to point 指
	conscious thought/understanding; self-conscious awareness, expertise; intelligence; knowing; knowledge;
	halt, pause, stay, stop 止
	intrinsic nature of things; particular physicality; steward 質
	knowledgeable; perspicacity;wisdom, wise 知/智
	merely, only 衹
	recalcitrant 忮
zhi buzhi zhi bujue	pointing to things does not reach them, yet such pointing never ceases 指不至至不絕
zhili	disjointed 支離
	perfect principle, perfectly realized principle, ultimate principle of things; perfect/ultimate truth 至理
zhiyan	goblet words 卮言
zhiyin	one who knew what I was playing 知音
zhi zai	should be determined to, should intend to, should set one's will on 志在
zhong	ancient dry measure "hamper" (about 2.5 bushels) 鍾[鈌]
	seed; species 種
zhong you ji	How many species exist? 種有幾
zhong zhi jiwei er wanwu suoyou shengzhe	the most minute of seeds from which the myriad things are generated 種之極微而萬物所由生者
zhonglei	species 種類
zhongshu	number of species 種數
zhongwei	superintendent of the capital 中尉
zhu	base text; guiding principle; master; steward 主
	bright, clear, manifest 著
	commentary 注
	pursue 逐
zhubu	recorder 主簿

zhuanshi	usurp autocratic power 專勢
zhuo	clumsy; unskilled 拙
zhuo de qian xing	pull up their virtues and try to boost their original natures 擢德攓性
zi	assistance; resources 資
	from; grounds; intrinisically; myself/oneself, the person himself; source 自
	you 子
	vilify 訾
zide	spontaneous receptivity; 自得
zihua	self-transform; undergo moral transformation spontaneously 自化
ziqi	self-adjust 自齊
ziran	intrinsically/naturally so; the Natural, Nature; natural endowment/state; spontaneity, spontaneous workings; spontaneously 自然
ziran pingjun zhi li	the natural principle of equality 自然均平之理
ziruo	completely at ease; go one's own unhindered way; just as before 自若
zisheng	self-generate, self-generation 自生
zizheng	govern/rectify oneself, self-rectification, self-rectify 自正
zizhi	keeping itself still 自止
zizu	one's own feet; self-satisfied; self-sufficiency, self-sufficient, sufficient unto itself 自足
zong	be soft on, soft material; indulge, pamper; vertical; warp 縱[從]
zongfang	do as one wants 縱放

GLOSSARY OF PROPER NOUNS

Ai	艾 (district in the ancient domain of Lirong 驪[麗]戎, present-day Lintong district 臨潼, Xi'an, Shaanxi)
All Under Heaven (Tianxia)	天下 (chapter 33)
An Lushan (d. 757)	安祿山
Analects (Lunyu)	論語
Arcane Numinous (Mingling)	冥靈
Arcane Obscurity (Xuanming)	玄冥
Argumentation (Chigou	喫詬
Artisan Chui (Gong Chui)	工倕 (skilled artisan of the time of Yao)
As if Bow Strung (Zhangruo)	張若
Autumn Floods (Qiushui)	秋水 (chapter 17)
Baima lun	白馬論 (Treatise on the White Horse)
Ban Biao	班彪 (3–54)
Ban Gu	班固 (32–92)
Ban Zhao	班昭 (ca. 49–ca. 120)
Bao Jiao	鮑焦 (ancient hermit of the Zhou era)
Bao Shuya	鮑叔牙 (Qi official during the rule of Duke Huan, contemporary and friend of Guan Zhong)
Bao Xian (7 BCE–65 CE)	包咸

Baopu zi neipian	抱朴子內篇 (Master who embraces simplicity, Inner Chapters, by Ge Hong)
Beigong She	北宮奢 (tax collector for Duke Ling of Wey)
Beiji	北極 (Extreme North)
Beilun	碑論 (Tombstone Discourses)
Beipin jun	北平郡 (Beiping commandery)
Bi Gan	比干 (younger half-brother by a concubine of the father of King Zhou of Yin [Shang])
Bi Wan	畢萬 (founded the state of Wei in 661 BCE)
Bian Sui	卞隨 (hermit at the time of King Tang of Shang)
Bianming lun	辯命論 (Disquisition on Fate), by Liu Jun 劉峻 (462–521)
Bianzhou	汴州 (present-day Kaifeng)
Big Bowcase (Taitao)	大弢 (grand scribe, interlocutor of Confucius)
Big Steep Craggy (Dawei)	大隗
Bin	邠 (ancient city in Shaanxi)
Black Palace (Xuangong)	玄宮
Bo Ju	柏[栢]矩 (disciple of Master Lao)
Bo Yi	伯夷 (hermit at the time of the Shang-Zhou transition)
Boar Hide (Xiwei)	狶韋 (grand scribe, interlocutor of Confucius, mythical hero, perhaps the same figure as Hog Hide)
Bocheng Zigao	伯成子高 (feudal lord at the time of Yao)
Body Upright (Zhigong)	直躬
Bohuang	伯皇 (monarch of remote antiquity)
Bole	伯樂, surname Sun 孫, given name Yang 陽, personal name Bole, expert judge of horses at the time of Duke Mu of Qin 秦穆公 (r. 659–621 BCE)
Boli Xi	百里奚 (personal name, "Hundred Tricent Servant," of a man surnamed Meng 孟, a worthy of Qin)
Bright Clarity (Guanghui)	光曜
Bright Just Now (Fangming)	方明
Buliang Yi	卜梁倚 (woman ascetic of remote antiquity)
Butters (Chu)	觸

Cai	蔡 (ancient state; name of the second older brother of the Duke of Zhou)
Cangwu	蒼梧 (located in the Lingnan 嶺南 region of southeast China）
Cao Shuang (d. 249)	曹爽
Carpenter Shi (Jiang Shi)	匠石
Cast Brilliance on All in the World (Changyu)	昌宇
Chang'an	常安 (modern Xi'an 西安, Shaanxi)
Chang Hong (d. 492 BCE)	萇弘
Chang Ji	常季 (surnamed Chang, given name Ji, a worthy of Lu; perhaps a disciple of Confucius)
Chang Mountains (Changshan)	常山 (Northern Marchmount 北嶽[岳], Mount Heng 恆山)
Changsang Gongzi	長桑公子 (teacher of Master Zhuang)
Changshui	長水 (district southwest of Luoyang)
Chao, Shaman Xian (Xian Chao)	咸袑 (supposedly lived in the mid-second millenium BCE)
Chaofu	巢父 (cowherd of remote antiquity, worthy hermit, Father Chao)
Chen	陳 (ancient state)
Chen Heng	陳恆[恒] (grand master of Qi, Lord Cheng of Tian 田成子, became de facto ruler of Qi in 481 BCE)
Chen Qun (d. 236)	陳群
Chen Shou (233–297)	陳壽
Cheng Xuanying (ca. 600–ca. 660)	成玄英
Chiba Unkaku (1727–1792)	千葉芸閣
Chiyou	蚩尤 (tribal leader of remote antiquity, opponent of the Yellow Thearch)
Chizhang Manji	赤張滿稽 (sage who lived at the Shang-Zhou transition)
Chongbo [zhuan]	衡波[傳] (*Chronicle of Chongbo*)
Chongyou lun	崇有論 ("On venerating material existence," by Pei Wei)
Chou River	稠[裯]水
Chu	楚 (ancient state)

Cinnabar Caves (Danxue)	丹穴
Classic of Odes (Shijing)	詩經
Clear River	清江 (tributary of the Yangzi in Hubei)
Clothed (Piyi)	被衣
Cloud General (Yun Jiang)	雲將
Commander of the Right (Youshi)	右師 (in the ancient state of Song 宋)
Congzhi	叢枝 (ancient tribal state)
Count of Bo (Gong Bo)	共伯 (given name He 和)
Crazy Intractable (Kuangqu)	狂屈
Crown Prince Sou (Wangzi Sou)	王子搜 (of Yue)
Crushers (Man)	蠻
Cui Qu	崔瞿 (interlocuter of Laozi)
Cui Zhuan (late third–early fourth centuries)	崔譔
Curbing Ambition (Keyi)	刻意 (chapter 15)
Da nan yangsheng lun	答難養生論 (Rejoinder to the refutation of "On nurturing life")
Dao of Heaven (Tiandao)	天道 (chapter 13)
Da Yu mo	大禹謨 (Councels of the Great Yu)
Da Zuang lun	達莊論 (On understanding Master Zhuang, by Ruan Ji)
Dahui Zonggao (1089–1163)	大慧宗杲 (Chan Master)
Dai Jinren	戴晉人 (worthy of the state of Liang at the time of King Hui of Wei)
Danzhu	丹朱 (son of Yao)
Daolun	道論 ("On the Dao," a lost work by He Yan)
Dapeng	大彭 (one of the Five Tyrants)
Dashan	大山 ("Great Mountain" = Mount Tai)
Dating	大庭 (monarch of remote antiquity)
Daya	大雅 (greater elegentiae)
Da Yu mo	大禹謨 ("Counsels of the Great Yu")
Deng Heng	登恆 (tutor of King Tang of Shang)
Deng Ling	鄧陵 (later Mohist)
Di	狄 (ancient northern non-Han tribe)
Di Hong	帝鴻 (alternative name for the Yellow Thearch)

Discourse on Swords (Shuojian)	說劍 (chapter 30)
Disjointed Baggy (Zhili Shu)	支離疏 (identified with the following)
Disjointed Decrepit (Zhili Shu)	支離叔 (identified with the preceding)
Dissect for Profit (Zhili Yi)	支離益
Distrust Origin (Yishi)	疑始
Divine Farmer (Shennong)	神農 (mythical hero who invented agriculture)
Doleful Camelback (Ai Taituo/Aitai Tuo)	哀駘它[佗/駝]
Dongguo Shunzi	東郭順子 (worthy of the state of Wei during the rule of Marquis Wen)
Donghai	東海 (present-day southeast Shandong)
Dongmen Wu	東門吳
Dongye Ji	東野稷 (chariot driver in the ancient state of Lu)
Dongyi	東夷 (Eastern Barbarians, the Japanese)
Duke Ai of Lu	魯哀公 (r. 494–467 BCE)
Duke Bai of Chu (Chu Baigong)	楚白公 (given name Sheng 勝, d. 479 BCE)
Duke Ding of Lu (Lu Dinggong)	魯定公 (r. 509–495 BCE)
Duke Gong of Lu (Lu Gonggong)	魯恭公 (contemporary of King Xuan of Chu 楚宣王 [r. 369–340 BCE])
Duke Huan of Eastern Zhou (Dong Zhou Huangong)	東周桓公 (the younger brother of King Kao)
Duke Huan of Qi (Qi Huangong)	齊桓公 (personal name Xiaobai 小白, r. 685–643 BCE)
Duke Jian of Qi (Qi Jiangong)	齊簡公 (r. 484–482 BCE)
Duke Ling of Wey (Wey Linggong)	衛靈公 (r. 534–493 BCE)
Duke Mu of Qin	秦穆公 (r. 659–621 BCE)
Duke of Zhou	周公 (personal name Dan 旦, the fourth son of King Wen of Zhou and the younger brother of King Wu of Zhou)
Duke Ping of Jin (Jin Pinggong)	晉平公 (r. 557–532 BCE)
Duke Tai of Qi	齊太公 (r. 404–384 BCE, surname and given name Tian He 田和[禾]; the King of Qi)

Duke Wei of Zhou (Zhou Weigong) — 周威公 (son and heir of Duke Huan, the younger brother of King Kao of Eastern Zhou)

Duke Wen of Jin — 晉文公 (given name Chong'er 重耳, r. 636–628 BCE)

Duke Wen of Lu (Lu Wengong) — 魯文公 (r. 626–609 BCE)

Duke Xi of Lu (Lu Xigong) — 魯僖公 (r. 659–627 BCE)

Duke Xian of Jin (Jin Xiangong) — 晉獻公 (r. 676–651 BCE)

Duke Xiang of Lu (Lu Xianggong) — 魯襄公 (r. 572–542)

Duke Xu of Zheng — 鄭繻公 (r. 422–396 BCE)

Duke Yuan of Song (Song Yuangong) — 宋元公 (r. 531–517 BCE) = Lord Yuan of Song, 宋元君

Duke Zhuang of Lu (Lu Zhuanggong) — 魯莊公 (r. 693–662 BCE)

Duke Zhuang of Wey — 衛莊公 (son and heir of Duke Ling of Wey, given name Kuaikui 蒯聵, r. 480–478 BCE)

Du Yu (222–285) — 杜預 (personal name Yuankai 元愷)

E Lai — 惡來 (obsequious courtier of King Zhou 紂 of Shang)

Earl of the Yellow River (Hebo) — 河伯

Eastern Marchmount (Dongyue) — 東嶽 (Taishan, Mount Tai)

Easygoing the Fearless (Xu Wugui) — 徐無鬼 (chapter 24)

Elder Muddled None His Other (Bohun Wuren) — 伯昏無人

Eternity (Wuqiong) — 無窮

External Things (Waiwu) — 外物 (chapter 26)

Eyi — 閼弈 (Blocked Chess Move)

Fang Qian (1805–1868) — 方濳

Fang Xuanling (578–648) — 方玄齡

Fan Ning (339–401) — 范甯

Father Chao — *see* Chaofu

Fei Wuji — 費無忌 (minister of Chu at the time of King Ping of Chu)

Feng Mengzhen (1546–1605)	馮夢禎
Feng Qi (1915–1995)	馮契
Feng Yi	馮夷 (invested as the Earl of the Yellow River, Hebo 河伯)
Feng Youlan (Fung Yu-lan)	馮友蘭
Fenshui	汾水 (Fen River, tributary of the Yellow River in Shanxi)
Fit to be Sovereigns (Ying Diwang)	應帝王 (chapter 7)
Flame Thearch (Yan di)	炎帝
Front Teeth Missing (Nieque)	齧缺
Fu Xi	伏戲 (mythical sage-king)
Fu Yue	傅說 (star spirit)
Funiao fu	鵩鳥賦 (Houlet rhapsody)
Fuyan	傅巖 (ancient location in Henan, native place of Fu Yue)
Ganjiang	干將 (name of ancient sword)
Gao You (ca. 168–212)	高誘
Gaoshi zhuan	高士傳 (Traditions of lofty scholars [scholars who spurn official appointment])
Gaozong	高宗 (Eminent ancestor)
Garden of the Dim and Dark (Huhuang zhi ting)	惚怳之庭
Ge Hong (283–343)	葛洪 (author of *Baopuzi* and *Shenxian zhuan*)
Gengsang Chu	庚桑楚 (chapter 23)
Gong	共 (ancient district, present-day Hui county 輝縣, Henan)
Gong Ziqi	宮之奇 (minister of the state of Yu 虞)
Gonggong	共工 (minister of waters for Yao)
Gongsun Long	公孫龍 (325–250 BCE, personal name Bing 秉, rhetorician, associated with the doctrine of names 名教)
Gongsun Longzi	公孫龍子 (Sayings of Master Gongsun Long)
Gongsun Yan	公孫衍 (held the office of Rhinoceros Head [Xishou 犀首])
Gongwen Xuan	公文軒 (a native of the ancient state of Song)
Gou Jian	*see* King Gou Jian of Yue

Government Authority Banned	*see* Xiangcheng
Grand Obscurity (Hong Meng)	鴻蒙
Great Brightness (Taihao)	太昊 (epithet of Fu Xi)
Great Cedrela (Dachun)	大椿
Great Clod (Dakuai)	大塊[凷, 块]
Great Exemplary Teacher (Da Zongshi)	大宗師 (chapter 6)
Great Flow (Da Huo)	大濩 (ancient music)
Great Impartial Harmonizer (Taigong Tiao)	大公調
Great Prominence (Da Shao)	大韶 (ancient music)
Grand Clarity (Taiqing)	泰清
Great Stanzas (Da Zhang)	大章 (ancient music)
Great Unity (Taiyi)	太一
Great Void (Taixu)	太虛
Great Xia (Da Xia)	大夏 (ancient music)
Gu Huan (fl. 420–479)	顧歡 (Gu Tongbo 顧桐柏)
Gu Jiegang (1893–1980)	顧頡剛
Guan	管 (the eldest brother of the Duke of Zhou)
Guangyun	廣韻 (Expanded rhymes, compiled 1007–1008)
Guan Longfeng	關龍逢 (worthy minister of King Jie of Xia)
Guan Zhong (d. 645 BCE)	管仲 (Master Guan 管子, "Father Zhong," prime minister of Duke Huan of Qi, r. 685–643 BCE)
Guanzi	管子 (Sayings of Master Guan 管子)
Guardians of the East (Dongwei)	東維
Gui	嬀 (clan surname of Shun)
Gui Youguang (1507–1571)	歸有光
Guiguzi	鬼谷子 (Demon Valley Master)
Guji liezhuan	滑[骨]稽列傳 (Traditions of Slippery Operators)
Gujing jie huihan	古經解彙函 (Explications of the classics collections casket)
Gukong lun	骨空論 (Discussion of the bone orifices)
Gun	鯀 (father of Yu)
Guo	虢 (Spring and Autumn–era state)

Guo Qingfan (1844–1896)	郭慶藩 (sobriquet Zijing 子靜)
Guo Xiang (d. 312)	郭象 (personal name Zixuan 子玄)
Guo Xiang ji	郭象集 (Collected works of Guo Xiang)
Guye	姑射 (mythical mountain)
Guzhu	孤竹 (ancient state located in what is present-day Tangshan city, Hebei)
Han	漢 (ancient state)
Handan	邯鄲 (capital of the ancient state of Zhao 趙)
Hangu Pass	函谷關 (between upper Yellow River and Wei valleys and North China Plain)
Hanshi waizhuan	韓詩外傳 (Outer commentary on the *Classic of Poetry* by Han Ying)
"Hanshu jueyi"	漢書抉疑 (Resolving doubtful passages in *History of the Former Han*)
Hanshu yiwen zhi	漢書藝文志 (Dynastic bibliography in *History of the Former Han*)
Han Ying (fl. ca. 150 BCE)	韓嬰
Hao	濠 (river)
Hata Tei (1761–1831)	秦鼎 (Sōrō 滄浪)
Hattori Nankaku (1683–1759)	服部南郭
He Yan (190–249)	何晏 (personal name Pingshu 平叔)
Head of Gong (Gongshou)	共首(Mount Hillhead, Qiushou shan 丘首山, where the count of Bo retired)
Heaven and Earth (Tiandi)	天地 (chapter 12)
Skyroot (Tiangen)	天根
Hebei	河北 (province; old county name in Henan)
Heguanzi	鶡冠子 (Pheasant Cap Master)
Henei	河內 (ancient commandery)
Hexu	*see* Sire Ardent Attractor of Followers
Hog Hide (Shiwei)	豕韋 (one of the Five Tyrants, perhaps the same figure as Boar Hide)
Hongnong	弘農 (Han-Tang prefecture, in present-day western Henan)
Horses' Hooves (Mati)	馬蹄 (chapter 9)
Hu	虎 (Tiger, one of the six parts of the *Grand Duke's Treatise on the Art of War*)

Huailu	懷來 (district in Hebei)
Huainan	淮南 (region)
Huainan zi	淮南子 (Master of Huainan)
Huan Dou	讙兜 (alternative name of Primal Chaos [Hundun])
Huangdi suwen	黃帝素問 (The Yellow Thearch's familiar conversations)
Huangfu Mi (215–282)	皇甫謐
Huang Kan (488–545)	皇侃
Huang Liao	黃繚 (ancient eccentric worthy of the South)
Huangzi Gaoao	皇子告敖 (interlocutor of Duke Huan of Qi)
Huan Tuan	桓魋 (commander in Song who wanted to kill Confucius)
	桓團 (rhetorician and contemporary of Gongsun Long)
Huayin	華陰 (county in Han-Tang-era Hongnong prefecture, Henan)
Hu Buxie	狐不偕 (worthy at the time of Yao)
Hui (county)	輝縣 (Henan)
Huiyuan (334–416)	慧遠
Huizi, Hui Shi (380–305 BCE)	惠子, 惠施 (Master Hui)
Hu Shi (1891–1962)	胡適
Hundun	渾沌 (Primal Chaos)
Indolence (Yidai)	意怠 (mythical bird of the Eastern Sea)
Ink as Aid (Fumo)	副墨
Ji	棘 (minister of King Tang of Shang)
	箕 (Sagittarius)
	for surname 嵇, *see* Xi
Jia	假 (ancient state)
	甲 (surname)
Jia Mi	賈謐 (nephew of Jia Nanfeng)
Jian	建 (crown prince of Chu)
Jia Nanfeng (257–300)	賈南風
Jianglü Mian	將閭葂 (worthy of remote antiquity)
Jianwu	肩吾 (god of Taishan)
Jiao	角 (Spica)

Jiao Hong (1540–1620)	焦竑 (compiler of Laozi yi 老子翼 [Wings to *Laozi*] and Zhuangzi yi 莊子翼 [Wings to *Zhuangzi*])
Jiashi	甲氏 (Jia clan)
Jia Yi (200–169 BCE)	賈誼
Ji Che	季徹 (worthy of remote antiquity)
Ji Chi	已齒 (later Mohist)
Jie	解 (Expiation Sacrifice)
	桀 (last Xia king)
	羯 (Xiongnu branch)
Jieyu	接輿 (personal name of Lu Tong 陸通, a crazy hermit in the ancient state of Chu)
Jiezi	接子 (Master Jie)
Jili	季歷 (father of King Wen, also known as King Ji of Zhou)
Jin	晉 (ancient state)
Jinshu	(*History of the Jin*), by Wang Yin 王隱 (ca. 275–ca. 352)
Jin Wen	晉文 (one of the Five Tyrants)
Jinban	金板[版] (Metal Blocks)
Jing	景 (one of the Chu royal clan names)
Jingbian Lunyu lei	經編論語類 (Confucian Classics division, Analects category)
Jingdian shiwen	經典釋文(Explications of the texts of scriptures and classics)
Jingshan	荊山 (Mount Jing in Henan)
Jingshi	荊氏 (district in the ancient state of Song 宋)
Jinyun	縉雲 (summer [war] minister of the Yellow Thearch; clan of that name)
Jinzhen	季真
Ji Qu	几蘧 (mythical hero)
Ji Tuo	紀他 (hermit at the time of King Tang)
Ji Wenzi	季文子 (Jisun Xingfu 季孫行父, d. 568 BCE)
Ji Xian	季咸 (shaman of Zheng 鄭)
Ji Xin (d. 204 BCE)	紀信 (gave his life for Emperor Gaozu of the Han, Liu Bang 劉邦 [256–195 BCE])
Ji Xingzi	紀渻子, worthy who lived at the time of King Xuan of Zhou)

Jishan	箕山 (in present-day Zhili)
Jiufang Yin	九方歅 (physiognomist)
Jiu Yao	咎繇 (also known as Gao Tao 皋陶 or Jiu Tao 咎陶, minister of justice to Shun)
Jixia	稷下 (ancient place name, located in present-day Linzi 臨淄 district, Shandong)
Ju Boyu	蘧伯玉 (personal name Yuan 瑗)
Juliang	據梁 (strongman of remote antiquity)
Kaitokudō kinenkai	懷德堂記念會
Kang	亢 (Virgo)
Kanpi	堪坏 (god who lives in the Kunlun mountains)
Keep Watch Sturdy (Dong Wu)	董梧 (teacher of Yan Buyi)
King Danfu	*see* King Tai of Zhou
King Fuchai of Wu	吳王夫差 (r. 495–473 BCE)
King Gou Jian of Yue	越王勾踐 (r. 496–465 BCE)
King Hui of Wei/Liang	魏/梁惠王, given name Ying 罃 (r. 370–319 BCE; until 344 BCE Marquis Hui of Wei 魏惠侯)
King Ji of Zhou	*see* Jili
King Jing of Zhou	周敬王 (r. 519–476 BCE)
King Kao of Eastern Zhou	東周考王 (r. 440–426 BCE)
King Kuai of Yan	燕噲王 (r. 320–312 BCE)
King Li of Zhou	周厲王 (r. ca. 877–841 BCE)
King Ling of Zhou	周靈王 (r. 571–545 BCE)
King Min of Qi	齊愍王 (r. 300–284 BCE)
King Mu of Zhou	周穆王 (r. 956–918 BCE)
King Nan of Zhou	周赧王 (r. 314–256 BCE)
King of Qi	*see* Duke Tai of Qi
King Ping of Chu	楚平王 (r. 528–516 BCE)
King Tai of Zhou	周太[大]王 (postumous title conferred on "Old Duke Danfu" 古公亶父, father of King Ji [Jili] and grandfather of King Wen of Zhou)
King Tang of Shang	商湯王 (r. 1675–1646 BCE)
King Wei of Chu	楚威王 (r. 339–329 BCE)
King Wei of Qi	齊威王, given name Mou 牟 (r. 356–320 BCE)
King Wen of Chu	楚文王 (r. 689–677 BCE)
King Wen of Zhao	趙文王 (r. 298–266 BCE)

King Wen of Zhou	周文王 (1152–1056 BCE, founder of the Zhou dynasty)
King Wuding of Shang	商武丁王 (temple name Gaozong 殷高宗, r. 1324–1264 BCE)
King Xuan of Qi	齊宣王
King Xuan of Zhou	周宣王 (r. 827–782 BCE)
King Yan of Song	宋偃王 (r. 329–286 BCE, also known as Song Kang 宋康)
King Zhao of Chu	楚昭王 (r. 515–489 BCE)
King Zhuang of Chu	楚莊王 (r. 613–591 BCE)
Knowledge (Zhi)	知
Knowledge Wanders North (Zhi beiyou)	知北遊 (chapter 22)
Knows Harmony (Zhihe)	知和
Kong Anguo (156–74 BCE)	孔安國
Kong Qiu	孔丘 (Confucius)
Kongtong	空同 (mountain in Liangzhou, Gansu)
Kong Yingda (574–648)	孔穎達
Kongzi jiayu	孔子家語 (School Teachings of Confucius)
Kongzi shijia	孔子世家 (Hereditary House of Master Kong)
Kuai	膾 (ancient tribal state at the time of Yao)
Kuaiji	會稽 (Mount Kuaij, now called Censer Peak [Xianglu shan 香爐山], located south of Hangzhou Bay and southeast of Shaoxing in Zhejiang)
Kuaikui	*see* Duke Zhuang of Wey
Kuang	匡 (a district in Wey 衛)
Kuan River	窾水
Kuang Zhang	匡章 (native of Qi, obsessed with Ru morality)
Ku Huo	苦獲 (later Mohist)
Kun	鯤 (giant mythical fish)
	梱 (son of Nanguo Ziqi)
Kunlun	崑崙 (Kunlun mountains)
Kunlun zhi xu	崑崙之虛 [墟] (Wastes of Kunlun)
Kunwu	昆吾 (one of the Five Tyrants)
Langye	琅邪 [瑯琊] (modern Donghai in Jiangsu)
Lao Dan	老聃 (Old Longears, Master Lao, Laozi 老子)

Lao Jun 老君 (epithet of Master Lao)

Lao Laizi 老萊子 (Old Master Lai, a contemporary of Confucius, a worthy recluse of Chu who lived in seclusion on Mount Meng)

Laozi zhu 老子注 (Commentary to the *Laozi*), a lost work by Guo Xiang

Leopard (Bao) 豹 (one of the six parts of the *Grand Duke's Treatise on the Art of War*)

Let Things Freely Be (Zaiyou) 在宥 (chapter 11)

Lian Shu 連叔 (ancient sage, interlocutor of Jianwu)

Liang 梁 (ancient state)

Liangzhou 梁州 (ancient region, modern Shaanxi and Sichuan)

涼州 (place name in Gansu)

Liaodong 遼東 (east of the Liao River)

Liao River 蓼水

Liaoxi 遼西 (west of the Liao River)

Liaoxi 遼西 (northeastern present-day Hebei)

Li Chong (d. ca. 362) 李充

Lie Yukou 列禦寇 (chapter 32)

Liezi 列子 (The sayings of Master Lie)

Li Gui (early fourth century) 李軌 (personal name Hongfan 弘範)

Liji 麗姬 (Imperial Concubine Li)

Li Kang (ca. 190–ca. 240) 李康

Li Longji (685–762) 李隆基, Tang emperor Xuanzong 玄宗

Lilu 栗陸 (monarch of remote antiquity)

Lingtai 靈臺 ("Spirit Tower," *Classic of Odes* 242)

Lingzhi 令支 (Tang-era district in the vicinity of present-day Tangshan, Hebei)

Lin Hui 林回 (worthy of the ancient state of Jia)

Lin Ju 藺且 (disciple of Confucius)

Lin Xiyi (1193–1271) 林希逸

Lin Yunming (jinshi of 1658) 林雲銘

Li Shan (d. 689) 孝善

Lishi 離石 (Shanxi place name)

Liu Bang 劉邦 (Emperor Gaozu of the Han [256–195 BCE])

Liu Heng	劉恆[恒] (203–157 BCE), Han Emperor Wen 漢文帝 (r. 180–157 BCE)
Liujia zhi yaozhi	六家之要指 (Essentials of the six jia)
Liu Jun (462–521)	劉峻 (personal name Xiaobao 孝標)
Liu Liang (act. ca. 718)	劉良
Liu Qia （dates unknown）	劉洽
Liu Ruoyu (1926–1986)	劉若愚 (James J. Y. Liu)
Liutao	六弢[韜] (Six Bowcases)
Liu Xiang (79–8 BCE)	劉向
Liu Xiaobiao (462–521)	劉孝標
Liu Yan (dates unknown)	劉演
Liu Yiqing (403–444)	劉義慶 (Prince Kang of Linchuan 臨川康王 , author of *Shishuo xinyu*)
Liu Yu (265–311)	劉輿
Lixu	驪畜 (monarch of remote antiquity)
Li Yi (fourth century)	李頤 (personal name Jingzhen 景真 and sobriquet Xuandaozi 玄道子, Master of the Arcane Dao)
Li Zhu (Li Lou)	離朱 (離婁, ancient exemplar of keen eyesight)
Long	龍 (Dragon, one of the six parts of the *Grand Duke's Treatise on the Art of War*)
Longmen	龍門 (Dragon Gate)
Lord Bai	*see* Sheng, Lord of Bai
Lord Cheng of Tian	田成子, *see* Cheng Heng
Lord of Millet [Hou Ji]	后稷 (director of grains for Shun and first ancestor of the Zhou people)
Lord on High (*di*)	帝 (anthropomorphic deity who sent blessings or calamities, gave or witheld protection, eventually replaced by *tian* 天)
Lord Supervisor of Rest (Gong Yuexiu)	公閱休
Lord Yuan of Song	宋元君 (*see* Duke Yuan of Song)
Lu	魯 (ancient state)
Lü Buwei (d. 235 BCE)	呂不韋
Lu Deming (556–627)	陸德明
Lu Dinggong ji	魯定公記 (Record of Duke Ding of Lu)
Lüliang	呂梁 ("Spine Precipice," watercourse name)
Lun Xi Shao	論嵇紹 (a discussion of Xi Shao)

Lunyu tilue	論語體略 (Essentials of the *Lunyu* [*Analects*]), a lost work by Guo Xiang
Lunyu yin	論語隱 (What is hidden in the Lunyu [*Analects*]), a lost work by Guo Xiang
Luoyang	洛陽 (Henan, Western Jin capital)
Lu River	瀘水 (present-day northeastern Hebei)
Lüshi chunqiu	呂氏春秋 (*Spring and Autumn Annals of Master Lü*, by Lü Buwei)
Lü Wang	呂望 (minister of King Wu of Zhou)
Lü Yanji (act. ca. 718)	呂延濟
Majesty Harmonious Academy (Biyong)	辟雍 (academy of King Wen)
Man Goude	滿苟得 (Filled with Ill-Gotten Gain)
Mao Qiang	毛嬙 (famous beauty of the ancient state of Yue)
Maoshi	毛詩 (Mao edition of the Odes)
Ma Rong (79–166)	馬融
Marquis of Lu	*see* Duke Xiang of Lu
Marquis of Qi	齊侯 (Duke Jing of Qi 齊景公 [r. 547–490 BCE])
Marquis Wen of Wei	魏文侯 (r. 424–387 BCE)
Marquis Who Supervises the Yellow River (Jianhe Hou)	監河侯 Marquis Wu of Wei
Marquis Xi of Fan	凡僖侯 (the marquis of a state vanquished during the rule of King Wen of Chu [689–677 BCE])
Marquis Zhouxi of Han	韓昭僖侯 (r. 362–333 BCE)
Master Cattail Clothes (Piyi zi)	被衣子
Master Chan	瞻子 (worthy of the state of Wei during the Warring States era)
Master Commoner Clothes (Puyi zi)	蒲衣子
Master Craftsman Yan	偃師 (ancient maker of automaton)
Master of Eastwall (Dongguo zi)	東郭子綦
Master Guan	*see* Guan Zhong
Master Guangcheng	廣成子 (Vast Fulfillment, epithet of Laozi)
Master Hu	壺子, given name Lin 林 (Native of the ancient state of Zheng, teacher of Master Lie)

Master Hua	華子 worthy minister of Wei at time of King Hui)
Master Hui	*see* Huizi
Master Ji	季子 (worthy minister of the state of Wei at the time of King Hui)
Master Ji	箕子 (given name Xuyu 胥餘, worthy minister of King Zhou of the Yin [Shang])
Master Kangsang of Weilei Mountain	畏累[壘]虛[墟]亢桑子
Master Kuang	*see* Music Master Kuang
Master Lie (Liezi)	列子 (given name Yukou 禦寇 "Guard Against Bandits")
Master Market South	熊宜僚 (of Market South 市南), (1) served King Zhuang of Chu; (2) served King Hui of Chu 楚惠王 (r. 488–432 BCE)
Master Min	閔子 (given name Sun 損, personal name Ziqian 子騫, a native of Lu and disciple of Confucius)
Master Mo (Mozi)	墨子 (Mo Di 墨翟 [ca. 470–ca. 391 BCE])
Master Sang Hu (Sang Yu)	子桑戶[雽] (桑雩) (a recluse and interlocutor of Confucius)
Master Tall Parasol Tree (Changwu zi)	長梧子 Master Yan
Master Yier	意而子 (worthy of remote antiquity)
Master Yu	子輿 (worthy of remote antiquity)
Master Zeng	曾子 (given name Shen 參 and personal name Ziyu 子輿, disciple of Confucius)
Master Zhou (first century)	周氏
Mastery of Nurturing Life (Yangsheng zhu)	養生主 (chapter 3)
Ma Xulun (1884–1970)	馬敘倫
Meng	蒙 (district in the ancient state of Liang)
Meng Crossing (Mengjin)	孟[盟]津 (of the Yellow River in Henan)
Mengshi	孟氏 (Meng, an early commentator of the Zhuangzi)
Mengsun Cai	孟孫才 (worthy of the state of Lu)
Mengzi	孟子 (Mencius)
Men Wugui	門無鬼 (sage who lived at the Shang-Zhou transition)
Mi	密 (district in Yingyang 滎陽, Henan)

Mianxue	勉學 (Encouragement to learning), part 8 of *Yanshi jiaxun*
Mindless (Wangxiang)	罔象 (literally "no image")
Ming dan lun	明膽論 (On elucidating courage, by Xi Kang)
Mitigate (Huan)	緩
Momoi Hakuroku (1637–1716)	桃井白鹿
Morita Shūhō (d. 1815)	杜多秀峰
Mound of the Arcane Lord (Mingbo zhi qiu)	冥伯之丘
Mountain Tree (Shanmu)	山木 (chapter 20)
Mount Exalted Craggy (Taikui shan)	泰隗山
Mount Hua	華山 (Western Marchmount 西嶽 in Shaanxi)
Mount Meng (Mengshan)	蒙山 (located in present-day Mengyin 蒙陰 district, northwest of Linyi, 臨沂, Shandong)
Mount Resting Place (Juci zhi shan)	具茨之山
Mount Tai (Taishan)	泰山 (the Eastern Marchmount 東嶽 in Shandong)
Mount Yin	殷山
Mou, Prince of Zhongshan	中山公子牟 (Prince of Zhongshan Mou of Wei, in the Warring States era)
Moye	鏌鋣 (name of ancient sword)
Mozi	墨子 (Master Mo)
Mou Zongsan (1909–1995)	牟宗三
Music Master Kuang (Shi Kuang)	師曠 (ancient exemplar of keen hearing)
Must Practice (Xuyi)	需役
Nameless Man (Wuming Ren)	無名人
Nan yangsheng lun	難養生論 (Refutation of "On nurturing life")
Nanbo Zikui	南伯子葵 (= Nanbo Ziqi)
Nanbo Ziqi	南伯子綦 (Senior of the South Ziqi)
Nanfang caomu zhuang	南方草木狀 (Description of plants and trees of the South)
Nanguo Ziqi	南郭子綦 (Southwall Ziqi = Nanbo Ziqi)
Nanhua Xianren	南華仙人 (epithet of Master Zhuang)
Nanrong Chu	南榮趎 (disciple of Gengsang Chu)

Nanyue	南越 "South of Yue" (imaginary realm); (ancient kingdom, southern Yue [204–111 BCE])
Narrow Understanding (Shaozhi)	少知
Neipian	內篇 (Inner Chapters)
Nemoto Sonshi (1699–1764)	根本遜志
Niexu	聶許 (Whispered Approval)
Nine Accords (Jiu Shao)	九韶 (court music of the time of Shun)
Northern Marchmount	*see* Chang Mountains
Northerner No Choice (Beiren Wuze)	北人無擇
North Sea Simulacrum (Bohai Ruo)	北海若
Nü Yu	女偊 (Woman Loner)
Old Fisherman (Yufu)	漁夫 (chapter 31)
On Regarding All Things Equal (Qiwu lun)	齊物論 (chapter 2)
Ouyang Jianshi (268–300)	歐陽堅石
Overawe Many (Xipeng)	謵朋
Pang Pu (1928–2015)	龐朴
Pan Tao (d. 311)	潘滔
Pao Ding	庖丁 (Cook Ding)
Pass Director Yin (Guan Yin)	關尹 (surname 尹, given name Xi 喜, personal name Gongdu 公度)
Pei	沛 (Pengcheng, present-day Xuzhou [Jiangsu])
Pei Chuo	裴綽 (younger brother of Pei Kai and father of Pei Xia)
Pei Kai (237–291)	裴楷 (personal name Jishu 季舒)
Pei Miao (dates unknown)	裴邈
Pei Qi 裴啟 (second half of fourth century	裴啟 (author of the *Yulin* (Grove of anecdotes)
Pei Songzhi (372–451)	裴松之
Pei Wei (267–300)	裴頠
Pei Xia (dates unknown)	裴遐 (son of Pei Chuo, nephew of Pei Kai)
Peng	鵬 (a giant mythical bird)
Pengcheng	彭城 (place name in the ancient state of Song [modern Jiangsu])

Peng Meng	逄蒙 (ancient archer)
	彭蒙 (a learned recluse of Qi 齊 and itinerant at Jixia 稷下)
Peng Yang	彭陽 (personal name Zeyang 則陽 , native of Lu, intinerant official who lived at the time of King Wen of Chu)
Pengzu	彭祖 (ancient sage who lived 800 years)
Perfect Joy (Zhile)	至樂 (chapter 18)
Pheasant (Di)	翟 (Mitigate's younger brother)
Pian Dun (d. 329)	卞敦
Pian Ziqing	扁慶子
Primal Chaos (Hundun or Kunhun)	混沌/昆閽
Primal Chaos (Hundun)	混沌/渾沌 (Emperor of the Center)
Prime Minister Zixi (Lingyin Zixi)	令尹子西 (d. 481 BCE, prime minister of King Hui of Chu 楚惠王 [r. 488–432 BCE])
Prince Chengfu (late seventh century BCE)	王子成父
Princeling	*see* Wangni
Prince Qingji	王子慶忌 (identified both with Prince Sunjia and Prince Chengfu of Qi)
Prince Sunjia	王孫賈 (grandson of King Ling of Zhou)
Prince Xiao of Liang	梁孝王 (enfoeffed 168–144 BCE)
Pu River	濮水 (vicinity of Puyang 濮陽, Henan)
Puzhou	蒲州 (Shanxi place name)
Qi	齊 (ancient state)
Qian	乾 (Pure Yang, hexagram 1)
Qian Mu	錢穆 (1895–1990)
Qi Dai	齊岱 (Mount Dai in Qi, the Eastern Marchmount 東嶽[岳], Mount Tai 泰山)
Qi Huan	齊桓 (one of the Five Tyrants)
Qinghe	清河 (commandery located in present-day Hebei)
Qingling yuan	清泠淵 (Pure and cool abyss)
Qin Huali	禽滑釐 (disciple of Mozi)
Qin Xiu	秦秀
Qin Yi	秦失[佚] (sage, friend of Master Lao)
Qiongqi	窮奇 (alternative name of Gonggong)

Qishan	岐山 (Mount Qi, ancient site of the Zhou capital)
Qiu	丘 (personal name of both Confucius and Changwu)
Qiushi	裘氏 (Fur Coat Clan)
Qiushou shan	丘首山 (Mount Hillhead, also known as Head of Gong, 共首)
Qixie	齊諧 (Comic Stories of Qi)
Qiyuan	漆園 (Office of Lacquer Manufacture)
Qu	屈 (one of the royal Chu clan names)
Qu Boyu	蘧伯玉 (surname Qu, given name Yuan 瑗, and personal name Boyu, a worthy grandee of Wey)
Qu Gong	渠公 (Master Qu, a wealthy merchant of Qi and market director, perhaps a butcher as well)
Qu Yuan (340–278 BCE)	屈原
Quque zi	瞿鵲子 (Master Startled Magpie)
Quyuan	曲轅 (Crooked Shaft)
Rangcheng	攘城 (Government Authority Banned)
Ransack Chests (Quque)	胠篋 (chapter 10)
Record of Rites (Li)	禮
Refusing Rulership (Rangwang)	讓王 (chapter 28)
Ren Jiyu (1916–2009)	任繼愈
Ren Xiang	冉相 (Sire Ren Xiang)
Repairing Original Nature (Shanxing)	繕性 (chapter 16)
Repetitive Reciter (Luosong)	洛誦
Revolving of Heaven (Tianyun)	天運 (chapter 14)
Rhinoceros Head (Xishou)	犀首
Rizhong Shi	日中始 (Sire Midday Start)
Robber Zhi (Dao Zhi)	盜跖 (chapter 29)
Rocky Mountains (Weilei)	畏壘 [猥/嵔壘, 畏纍])
Rongcheng	容成 (monarch of remote antiquity)
Ru and Ying	汝潁 (two rivers in Henan)
Ruan Ji (210–263)	阮籍 (personal name Sizong 嗣宗)
Ruan Xiaoxu (479–536)	阮孝緒

Ruan Yuan (1764–1849)	阮元
Ruo	若 (Simulacrum, god of the North Sea)
Sanmiao	三苗 (domain of Taotie)
Sanwei	三峗 (a mountain on the border to the far west at the time of Yao)
Sanxuan	三玄 (Three arcane classics)
School of Names (Mingjia)	名家
Seeing Distinct (Zhanming)	瞻明
Sengzhao (384–414)	僧肇
Shaguang	少廣 (mythical mountain at the Extreme West [Xiji])
Shaman Xian	*see* Wu Xian
Shan Bao	單豹 (ancient sage-hermit who lived in the state of Lu)
Shang	商 (alternative name for the ancient state of Song 宋)
Shangqiu	商丘 (present-day Suiyang 睢陽, in Shangqiu county, Henan)
Shangshu	尚書 (Venerated ancient documents) also known as the *Shujing* 書經 (Classic of documents)
Shang song	商頌 (Eulogies of Shang)
Shang (Yin)	商 (殷) (dynasty)
Shangyu	賞譽 (Appreciation and praise), *Shishuo xinyu*, part 8
Shanhai jing	山海經 (Classic of mountains and waters)
Shan Juan	善卷 (ancient sage-hermit)
Shan Tao (205–283)	山濤 (personal name Juyuan 巨源)
Shanxi	山西 (province)
Shanzhou	陝州 (old place name in Henan)
Shaohao	少昊[皞] (mythical emperor, son of the Yellow Thearch)
Shaoling	壽陵 (district in the ancient state of Yan 燕)
Shaqiu	沙丘 (Sand Hill, where Duke Ling of Wey was buried)
She	社, god of the soil
She gongzi Gao	葉公子高 (Gao, Prince of She)
Sheji	社稷 (Altars of the Soil and Grain)

Shen Dao	慎到 (learned recluse of Qi 齊 and itinerant at Jixia 稷下)
Sheng, Lord of Bai (d. 479 BCE)	勝白公 (grandson of King Ping of Chu 楚平王 [r. 528–516 BCE])
Sheng wu aile lun	聲無哀樂論 (On neither grief nor joy exists in music, by Xi Kang)
"Shen Guo pian"	申郭篇 (On exonerating Guo)
Shennong	*see* Divine Farmer
Shentu Di	申徒狄 (contemporary of Ji Tuo, in the time of King Tang of Shang)
Shentu Jia	申徒嘉 (disciple of Bohun Wuren [Elder Muddled None His Other])
Shenxian zhuan	神仙傳 (Traditions of divine immortals, by Ge Hong)
Shi	詩 (Odes, classic of poetry)
Shi Chengqi	士成綺 (interlocutor of Master Lao)
Shi Jiao (ca. 390–330 BCE)	尸佼
Shi Qiu	史鰌[鰍], also known as Shi Yu 史魚 (minister of Duke Ling of Wey 衛靈公)
Shi Siming (d. 761)	史思明
Shicheng	石城 (Stone Wall)
	石戶之農 (Farmer of Stone Door)
Shiji	史記 (*Records of the Grand Historian*)
Shiji suoyin	史記索隱 (Explicating Obscurities in the *Records of the Historian*) of Sima Zhen 司馬貞 (early eighth century)
Shiji zhengyi	史記正義 (Correct meaning of the *Records of the Historian*) of Zhang Shoujie 張守節 (preface dated 737)
Shishuo xinyu	世說新語
Shizi	尸子 (Sayings of Master Shi, by Shi Jiao)
Shoushan	首山 (Head Mountain, Henan)
Shouyang	首陽 (mountain, also called Mount Shou 首山, located south of Puzhou city, Shanxi, near the Yellow River)
Shu	儵 (Quick, emperor of the Southern Sea)
Shu	書 (Documents or Classic of documents)
Shu Dan	*see* Duke of Zhou

Shuer	述而 (Transmit but [not Originate]), *Analects*, part 7
Shujing	書經 (Classic of documents) also known as *Shangshu* (Venerated ancient documents)
Shun	舜 (ancient sage-king, of the clan Gui, 媯, which originated in Youyu, his personal name Chonghua 重華 (Double Splendor)
Shundian	(Canon of Shun) 舜典 in the *Shangshu* 尚書 (Venerated ancient documents) or *Shujing* 書經 (Classic of documents)
Shuoyuan	說苑 (Garden of persuasions)
Shu Qi	叔齊 (hermit at the time of the Shang-Zhou transition)
Shu Xiang (d. ca. 528 BCE)	叔向 (statesman of Jin 晉)
Sima Biao (240–306)	司馬彪 (personal name Shaotong 紹統)
Sima Chi (284–313)	司馬熾 (Emperor Huai of Jin 晉懷帝, r. 307–311)
Sima Qian (ca. 145–ca. 86 BCE)	司馬遷
Sima Tan (ca. 165–110 BCE)	司馬談
Sima Ying (279–306)	司馬穎 (Prince of Chengdu 成都王, younger brother of Jin Emperor Hui, regent and crown prince)
Sima Yu (278–300)	司馬遹 (son of Sima Zhong, crown prince [290–300])
Sima Yue (d. 311)	司馬越 (Prince Yue of Donghai 東海王)
Sima Zhao (211–265)	司馬昭 (Emperor Wen of Jin 晉文帝 [r. 264–265])
Sima Zhong (259–306)	司馬衷 (Emperor Hui of Jin 晉惠帝 [r. 290–306])
Sima Ziqi	司馬子期 (Chu 楚, Minister of War Ziqi [d. 481 BCE])
Siming	Director of Destinies 司命
Simple Dimwit (Chun Mang)	諄芒
Singing (Ou)	謳
Sire Ardent Attractor of Followers (Hexu Shi)	赫胥氏 (monarch of remote antiquity)
Sire Biao (Biao Shi)	猋氏 (may be identified with Shennong)
Sire Flame (Yan Shi)	焱氏
Sire Have-a-Nest (Youchao Shi)	有巢氏

Sire Primal Chaos	*see* Hundun and Primal Chaos
Sire of Yu (Yu Shi)	虞氏 (epithet of Shun)
Si Ziyang	駟子陽 (d. 398 BCE, prime minister of the state of Zheng during the reign of Duke Xu 繻公)
Slippery Operator (Guji)	滑[骨]稽
Slippery Operator Decrepit (Gujie shu)	滑介叔
Song	宋 (ancient state)
Song Rongzi	宋榮子 (ca. 370–ca. 292 BCE, also Song Rong 榮, Song Xing 鈃, or Song Keng 牼)
Song Xing	宋鈃 (Jixia 稷下, in Qi 齊, scholar, late fourth century BCE)
Spontaneous Free Play (Xiaoyao you)	逍遙遊 (chapter 1)
Stone Wall (Shicheng)	石城
Stupid Scaredy (Lu Ju)	魯遽
Su Dai	蘇代 (younger brother of Su Qin)
Sudden (Hu)	忽 (emperor of the Northern Sea)
Sui	隨 (ancient state located in the Han River Basin in what is now Suizhou 隨州, Hubei)
Suiren	燧人 (Fire Maker, mythical hero who invented fire making)
Suiyang	睢陽 (located in Shangqiu 商丘 county, Henan)
Sun Fengyi (fl. ca. 1801)	孫馮翼
Sun Shi (962–1033)	孫奭
Sun Shu'ao	孫叔敖 (court minister of King Zhuang of Chu)
Sun Xiu	孫休
Sun Zichan	孫子產 (given neme Qiao 僑 and personal name Zichan, worthy of Zheng, disciple of Bohun Wuren [Elder Muddled None His Other])
Su Qin (d. 284 BCE)	蘇秦 (political strategist in the Warring States era)
Tai Bo	泰伯, *Analects*, part 8
Taibo	太伯 (first son of King Tai of Zhou)
Taigong bingfa	太公兵法 (*Grand Duke's Treatise on the Art of War*)
Tail Gate (Weilü)	尾閭 (mythical hole in the seabed that drains the sea)

Taishi jian	太師箴 (Admonitions of the Grand Tutor, by Xi Kang)
Tall Parasol Tree (Changwu)	長梧 (fanciful place name)
Tally of Virtue Replete (Dechong fu)	德充符 (chapter 5)
Tang	*see* King Tang of Shang
Tang Junyi (1909–1978)	唐君毅
Tangshan	唐山 (city in Hebei)
Tang Yongtong (1893–1964)	湯用彤
Taotie	饕餮 (enfoeffed by Yao with the domain of Sanmiao)
Temple of the Black Altar (Zitan zhi gong)	緇[錙]壇之宮
Thearch Ku (Di Ku)	帝嚳 (one of the five emperors of remote antiquity)
Tian He	*see* Duke Tai of Qi
Tian Heng (Tian Chengzi)	*see* Chen Heng
Tian Ji (fl. ca. 340 BCE)	田忌 (Qi general)
Tian Kaizhi	田開之 (interlocuter of Duke Wei of Zhou)
Tian Pian	田駢 (learned recluse of Qi 齊 and itinerant at Jixia 稷下)
Tian Zifang	田子方 (worthy of the state of Wei during the rule of Marquis Wen; given name Wuze 無擇, personal name Zifang 子方)
Tian Zifang	田子方 (chapter 21)
Tong	潼 (town located in Huayin county, Hongnong prefecture in the Han-Tang era, present-day Henan)
Tongbo guan	桐柏觀 (Abbey of the paulownias and cypresses on Mount Tiantai)
Tong Lao lun	通老論 (On understanding Master Lao, by Ruan Ji)
Triple Voidance (Canliao)	參寥
Uncle Always Soaring (Bo Changqian)	伯常騫 (grand scribe, interlocutor of Confucius)
Uncle Slippery Operator (Gujie Shu)	滑介叔
Understand Life (Dasheng)	達生 (chapter 19)

Valley of Yan (Yanxi) 燕谿
Venerable Elder Ren (Taigong Ren) 太公任
Waipian 外篇 (Outer Chapters)
Wang Bao (90–51 BCE) 王褒
Wang Bi (226–249) 王弼 (personal name Fusi 輔嗣)
Wang Fuzhi (1619–1692) 王夫之
Wang Guo 王果 (worthy grand master of Chu at the time of King Wen)
Wang the Nag (Wang Tai) 王駘
Wangni (Princeling) 王倪 (teacher of Front Teeth Missing)
Wang Rong (234–305) 王戎
Wang Shuzhi (ca. 420–ca. 479) 王叔之 (personal name Muye 穆夜)
Wang Su (195–256) 王肅
Wang Xianqian (1842–1918) 王先謙
Wang Yan (256–311) 王衍 (personal name Yifu 夷甫)
Wang Yin (ca. 275–ca. 352) 王隱
Ways of the World (Renjian shi) 人間世 (chapter 4)
Webbed Toes (Pianmu) 駢拇 (chapter 8)
Wei 魏 (ancient state, one of the six states of the Warring States era)
尾 (Scorpio)
Wei Guan (220–291) 衛瓘
Wei Linggong 衛靈公 (Duke Ling of Wei), *Analects*, part 15
Weiyan 危言 (Cautionary words)
Weiyin 爲音 (Managing pronunciation)
Weizheng 爲政 (Conduct government), *Analects*, part 2
Wei Zhengtong (1927–2018) 韋政通
Wen 文 scribal error for fu 父, in the name Zaofu 造父 (ancient charioteer)
Wen 文 (Civil, one of the six parts of the *Grand Duke's Treatise on the Art of War*)
Wenbo Xuezi 溫伯雪子 (a man of Chu who cherished the Dao, supposedly during the time of Confucius)
Wenhui Jun 文惠君 (Lord Wenhui)

Wenshi zhuan	文士傳 (Traditions of Literary Men), Zhang Yin 張隱 (late fourth century) and Zhang Zhi 張騭 (act. ca. 401), ed.
Wenxuan	文選 (Selections of refined literature)
Wenxue	文學 (Letters and learning), *Shishuo xinyu*, part 4
Wenyan	文言 (Commentary on the words of the text)
Wenzi	文子 (Master Wen)
Western Marchmount	*see* Mount Hua
Wey	衛 (ancient state)
Wheelwright Bian (Lun Bian)	輪扁
Whirlwind (Yuanfeng)	苑風
Whispered Approval (Niexu)	聶許
Woodworker Qing (Zi Qing/Jiang Qing)	梓慶/匠慶 (woodworker in the ancient state of Lu)
Words Attributed to Others (Yuyan)	寓言 (chapter 27)
Worrier Apprehensive (Cui Qiu)	崔瞿
Wu	武 (Martial, one of six parts of the *Grand Duke's Treatise on the Art of War*; music composed by King Wu and the Duke of Zhou)
Wuba	五伯[霸] (Five tyrants of the Xia, Shang, and Zhou eras)
Wu Guang	務光 (noble and learned scholar at the time of King Tang of Shang)
Wugui	無鬼 (No Demons)
Wu Hou	五侯 (follower of Mozi in the Warring States era)
Wu She (d. 522 BCE)	伍奢 (grand master of the state of Chu)
Wushi	無始 (No Beginning)
Wuwei Wei	無爲謂 (Not Conscious of What He Says)
Wu Xian	巫咸 (Shaman Xian)
Wuyou	無有 (Nonexistant)
Wuyue	無約 (Nothing Tied)
Wu Yun (d. 484 BCE)	伍員 (personal name Zixu 子胥 or Xuyu 胥餘, son of Wu She)
Wuzhuang	無莊 (beauty of remote antiquity)
Wuzhuo Miaozong (1095–1170)	無著妙總 (nun and Chan Master)

Wuzu	無足 (Never Satisfied)
Xi Gong	谿工 (worthy of the state of Wei during the rule of Marquis Wen)
Xi Han (236–306)	嵇含
Xi Jian (269–339)	郗鑒
Xi Kang (223–262)	嵇康 (personal name Shuye 叔夜)
Xi Peng	隰朋 (worthy of the state of Qi who lived at the time of Duke Huan and Guan Zhong)
Xi Shao (253–304)	嵇紹
Xi Shi	西施 (famous beauty who lived at the time of King Fuchai of Wu)
Xi Wang Mu	西王母 (Queen Mother of the West)
Xia	夏 (ancient dynasty)
Xiahou Xuan (209–254)	夏侯玄
Xian wen	憲問 (Xian asked), *Analects*, part 14
Xianchi	咸池 ("Pool of Shaman Xian," ancient music)
Xiangcheng	襄城 (located in present-day central Henan); (Government Authority Banned = Rangcheng 攘城)
Xiangli Qin	相里勤 (disciple of Mozi during the Warring States era)
Xiang Xiu (ca. 223–ca. 275)	向秀
Xiang Yu (232–202 BCE)	項羽
Xianjin	先進 (Those who first advanced), *Analects*, part 11
Xiao Jiefu (1924–2008)	蕭萐父
Xiaoji	孝己 (son of King Wuding of Shang)
Xiaoming	小明 (Little brightness)
Xiaoya	小雅 (Lesser elegentiae)
Xici zhuan	繫辭傳 (Commentary on the appended phrases)
Xie	契 (first ancestor of the Yin-Shang people)
Xi'e	(Tang-era district, Nanyang commandery 南陽郡, present-day Nanyang city, Henan)
Xie Jiang (995–1039)	謝絳 (personal name Xishen 希深)
Xie Kun (282–324)	謝鯤 (personal name Youyu 幼輿)
Xihe	西河 (Shanxi place name)
Xihua si	西華寺 (Xihua Temple)
Xingyang	滎陽 (Henan)

Xinxu	新序 (Newly edited accounts, of Liu Xiang)
Xiongnu	匈奴 (ancient nomadic people)
Xiong Yiliao	*see* Master Market South
Xu'ao	胥敖 (ancient tribal state at the time of Yao)
Xuan Ni	宣尼 (= Baocheng xuan Ni Gong 褒成宣尼公, "Exalted Ni, Duke of Consummate Perfection," epithet of Confucius)
Xuanyuan	軒轅 (name of the Yellow Thearch; also listed as a monarch of remote antiquity)
Xuchang	許昌 (district 100 miles southwest of Luoyang)
Xu Fuguan (1904–1982)	徐複觀
Xu Mian (344–397)	徐邈 (personal name Xianmin 仙民)
Xun Can (ca. 209–ca. 237)	荀粲 (personal name Fengqian 奉倩)
Xun Kai (d. 324)	荀闓
Xun Kuang	荀況
Xunzi	荀子 (Sayings of Master Xun) of Xun Kuang
Xu Shen (ca. 55–ca. 149)	許慎
Xu You	許由 (personal name Zhongwu 仲武, worthy hermit who lived at the time of Yao)
Xuyu	胥餘 (given name of Master Ji 箕子; also identified with Wu Yun 伍員, given name Ziyu 子胥)
Xuzhou	徐州 (in Jiangsu)
Yan	燕 (ancient state)
Yan Buyi	顏不疑 ("Face That Doubts Not," friend of the king of Wu)
Yan Cheng, Ziyou	顏成子游 (surname Yan 顏, given name Yan 偃, postumous title Cheng 成, personal name Ziyou 子游, disciple of Nanguo Ziqi)
Yan Gate	演門 (east gate of the capital city of the ancient state of Song)
Yangcheng	陽成 (place name in Henan)
Yang Hu	陽虎 (despot of Lu 魯, contemporary of Confucius)
Yang Huo	陽貨 (Yang Huo), *Analects*, part 17
Yang Shen (1488–1559)	楊慎
Yangsheng lun	養生論 (On nurturing life)

Yang Xianrong (d. 322)	羊獻容 (wife of Jin Emperor Hui, became empress dowager after his death)
Yang Zhu (370–319 BCE)	楊朱 personal name Ziju 子居
Yang Ziju	陽子居 (identified with Yang Zhu 楊朱)
Yan He	顏闔 (worthy of the state of Lu)
Yan Hui [Yan Yuan] (521–481 BCE)	顏回 [= 顏淵] (native of Lu, disciple of Confucius)
Yan Ke	顏剋[刻] (disciple/driver of Confucius)
Yan Shigu (581–645)	顏師古 (personal name Zhou 籀, author of the definitive commentary on the *Hanshu*)
Yanshi jiaxun	顏氏家訓 (Family instructions for the Yan clan)
Yantou Quanhuo (828–887)	巖頭全奯 (Chan master)
Yan Yanzhi (384–456)	顏延之
Yan Youqin (early seventh century)	顏游秦 (son of Yan Zhitui and uncle of Yan Shigu, author of *Hanshu jueyi*)
Yan Yuan	*see* Yan Hui
Yan Zhitui (531–591)	顏之推
Yao	堯 (ancient sage-king)
Yao Nai (1732–1815)	姚鼐
Yecheng	鄴城 (modern Handan 邯鄲, Hebei)
Yellow Thearch (Huangdi)	黃帝
Yi	易 (*Changes, Classic of Changes*)
Yi	羿 (ancient archer)
Yifu	意賦 （"Rhapsody on the way to think," by Yu Ai)
Yi Jie	夷節 (minister of Chu at the time of King Wen)
Ying	郢 (capital of the ancient state of Chu)
Yingchuan	潁川 (place name in central Henan)
Yingyang	滎陽 (prefecture in Henan)
Yin-Shang	殷商 (dynasty, 1600–1059 BCE)
Yin Wen	尹文 (Jixia 稷下 in Qi 齊, scholar, late fourth century BCE)
Yinyi	隱義 ("Explanation of its [*Zhuangzi*] hidden meaning")
Yixiu	意脩 (Mind on Teacher's Salary)
Yiya	易牙
Yi Yi	夷逸 (ancient recluse)

Yi Yin	伊尹 (surname Yi, given name Yin, personal name Zhi 贄, a worthy of the early Shang dynasty)
Yonghuai shi	詠懷詩 (Poems singing my feelings, by Ruan Ji)
Youdu	幽都 (far-northern place where Gonggong was banished by Yao)
Youfu	游鳧 (Swimming Duck)
Youhu	有扈 (ancient tribal state)
Youli	羑里 (Yin [Shang] prison in which King Wen was incarcerated)
Yu	禹 (Xia sage-king)
	虞 (fiefdom that Shun received from Yao; state in the Spring and Autumn era)
Yu Ai (262–311)	庾敳 (personal name Shanfu 山甫)
Yuan Hong (ca. 328–376)	袁宏
Yuan Xian	原憲 (disciple of Confucius, surname Yuan, given name Si 思, personal name Xian)
Yu Chun	庾純 (uncle of Yu Ai, personal name Mofu 謀甫)
Yue	越 (ancient state)
	樂 (Music, classic of music)
	說 (sheep butcher who lived at the time of King Zhao of Chu [r. 515–489 BCE])
Yuedong Shuju	粤東書局
Yu Er (seventh century BCE)	俞兒 (connoisseur of flavors)
Yu Jiaxi (1884–1955)	余嘉錫
Yulin	語林 (Grove of anecdotes, by Pei Qi)
Yunming lun	運命論 (Discourse on fate), by Li Kang 李康 (ca. 190–ca.240)
Yupian	玉篇 (Tablets of jade)
Yuqiang	禺強 (water god, also called Yujing 禺京)
Yu Qie	余且 (mythical fisherman)
Yushan	羽山 (Mount Yu, straddles the Shandong-Jiangsu border)
Yu Xingshi (b. 1930)	余英時
Yu Yue (1821–1907)	俞樾
Yu Zhong	虞仲 (ancient recluse)
Yuzhou	豫州 (Western Jin province comprising Henan and northern Hubei)

Zailu	宰路 (mythical abyss)
Zang Rongxu (415–488)	臧榮緒 (author of lost *Jinshu*)
Zaofu	造父 (ancient charioteer)
Zapian	雜篇 (Miscellaneous Chapters)
Zeng Shen	曾參 (disciple of Confucius; he taught Kong Ji 孔伋, grandson of Confucius, who in turn was the teacher of Mencius 孟子)
Zeyang	則陽 (chapter 25; *see* also Peng Yang)
Zhang Junmai (1886–1969)	張君勱 (Carsun Chang)
Zhanguo ce	戰國策 (Intrigues of the Warring States)
Zhang Yi	張毅 (ancient native of Lu)
Zhang Zhan	張湛 (fl. 350–400)
Zhao	趙 (ancient state)
	昭 (one of the Chu royal clan names)
Zhao Qi (d. 201)	趙歧
Zhao Wen	昭文 (virtuoso zither player of antiquity)
Zhe	制/淛/浙 (ancient name for the Qiantang 錢塘 River, which flows past Hangzhou into Hangzhou Bay)
Zheng	鄭 (ancient state)
Zheng Xuan (127–200)	鄭玄
Zhidun (314–366)	支遁, personal name Daolin 道林
Zhili Shu	*see* Disjointed Baggy (Zhili Shu) and Disjointed Decrepit (Zhili Shu)
Zhiming youji lun	致命由己論 (Resultant fate depends on the individual self, a discourse),
Zhishi xiaoyao lun	支氏逍遙論 (Master Zhi's discussion of spontaneity)
Zhiwu lun	指物論 (Treatise on designating things [in terms of attributes])
Zhong	種 (Grand Master 大夫 in the state of Yue at the time of King Gou Jian [r. 496–465 BCE])
Zhonghuang	中央 (monarch of remote antiquity)
Zhongli	鍾離 (prefecture name in Huainan region)
Zhongni	仲尼 (personal name of Confucius)
Zhongyang	中央 (monarch of remote antiquity)
Zhongyong	仲雍 (second son of King Tai of Zhou)
Zhou	紂 (last Shang king)

Zhou benji	周本紀 (Basic annals of Zhou)
Zhousheng Lie (195–256).	周生烈
Zhoushu	周書 (Documents of Zhou)
Zhouyi Xiangshi yi	周易向氏義 (Master Xiang's explications of the *Changes of the Zhou*)
Zhouyuan	周原 (ancient capital of the Zhou, in the vicinity of present-day Baoji 寶雞, in western Shaanxi)
Zhuangzi	莊子 (Master Zhuang, Zhuang Zhou 莊周)
Zhuangzi jie	莊子解 (Interpretation of the *Zhuangzi*), by Li Yi 李頤
Zhuangzi jijie	莊子集解 (Collected interpretations of the *Zhuangzi*), by Wang Xianqian 王先謙
Zhuangzi jishi	莊子集釋 (Collected commentaries to the *Zhuangzi*), by Guo Qingfan 郭慶藩
Zhuangzi quewu	莊子闕誤 (Omissions and errors in the text of the *Zhuangzi*), by Yang Shen 楊慎
Zhuangzi yin	莊子音 (Pronunciation [of names and terms] in the *Zhuangzi*)
Zhuangzi yishu	莊子義疏 (Subcommentary on the meaning of the *Zhuangzi*), by Wang Shuzhi 王叔之
Zhuanxu	顓頊 (Emperor Gaoyang 高陽, the Black Emperor 玄帝)
Zhuolu	涿鹿 (ancient city near where Chiyou fought with the Yellow Thearch)
Zhu Pingman	朱泙漫 (Red Overflow)
Zhurong	祝融 (monarch of remote antiquity)
Zhu Shen	祝腎 (ancient Daoist adept)
Zi Zhi (d. 314 BCE)	子之 (prime minister of Yan)
Zi Zhou Zhifu	子州支父 (hermit at the time of Yao, surnamed Zi 子, given name Zhou 州, personal name Zifu 支父, also known as Zhibo 支伯)
Zichan	*see* Sun Zichan
Zigong	子貢 (personal name of Duanmu Si 端木賜, disciple of Confucius)
Zilao	子牢 (Master Lao, surname Qin 琴, disciple of Confucius)
Zilu	子路 (personal name of Zhong You 仲由 (542–480, disciple of Confucius)

Ziqi of Southwall (Nanguo Ziqi)	南郭子綦
Zixiu	子休 (personal name of Zhuang Zhou; given name according to Sima Qian)
Zixu	子胥 (*see* Wu Yun)
Ziyang	*see* Si Ziyang
Ziyou	子游 (disciple of Confucius)
Zizhang	子張 (personal name of Zhuansun Shi 顓孫師, disciple of Confucius)
Zong	宗 (ancient tribal state at the time of Yao)
Zou Mengyang (1575–1643)	鄒孟陽
Zou Yan (later fourth century BCE)	騶衍
Zou Yang (d. 120 BCE)	鄒陽
Zunlu	尊盧 (monarch of remote antiquity)
Zuozhuan	左傳 (*Spring and Autumn Annals*, the Zuo tradition）

BIBLIOGRAPHY

Primary Sources

Bai Juyi 白居易 (772–846), and Kong Chuan 孔傳 (1065–1139), ed. *Bai Kong liutie* 白孔六帖 (Six noteboards of Bai and Kong). *Wenyuange siku quanshu* ed.

Ban Gu 班固 (32–92). *Hanshu* 漢書 (History of the former Han). Beijing: Zhonghua shuju, 1975.

Baoyantang miji 寶顏堂秘笈 (Secret book hamper from the hall where Yan [Zhenqing 顏真卿 (704–784)] is treasured). Ed. Chen Jiru (1558–1639). Shanghai: Wenming shuju, 1922.

Beitang shuchao 北堂書鈔 (Excerpts from books in the Northern Hall). Ed. Yu Shinan 虞世南 (558–638). Collation and commentary by Kong Guangtao 孔廣陶 (1832–1890). 1888 Nanhai Kongshi sanshi you san wanjuan tang 三十有三萬卷書堂wood block ed. Reprint. Beijing: Xueyuan chubanshe 學苑出版社, 1998.

Cefu Yuangui 冊府元龜 (Prime perspicacious tortoise guide to the storehouse of letters) (1005–1013). , ed. Wang Qinruo 王欽若 et al. *Wenyuange siku quanshu* ed.

Chen Jiang 陳絳 (*jinshi* 1544). *Jinlei zi* 金罍子 (Master of the golden wine jar). 1616 wood block ed.

Chen Jiru 陳繼儒 (1558–1639). *Xu kuangfu zhi yan* 續狂夫之言 (Supplement to the words of a crazy fellow). *Baoyantang miji* ed.

Chen Yumo 陳禹謨 (1548–1618). *Pianzhi* 駢志 (Extraneous records). *Wenyuange siku quanshu* ed.

Chen Zhensun 陳振孫 (ca. 1183–1262). *Zhizhai shulu jieti* 直齋書錄解題 (Annotated library catalog from the Studio of Strightforward Sincerity). Shanghai: Shanghai guji chubanshe, 1987.

Chunqiu Gongyangzhuan zhushu 春鞦公羊傳注疏 (Commentaries and sub-commentaries to the *Spring and Autumn Annals* with the commentary of Gongyang). *Shisanjing zhushu* ed.

Chunqiu Zuozhuan zhengyi 春秋左傳正義 (Correct meaning of the *Spring and Autumn Annals* with *Zuo's Commentary*). *Shisanjing zhushu* ed.

Chuxue ji 初學記 (Notes for beginning studies). Ed. Xu Jian 徐堅 (659–729) et al. *Wenyuange siku quanshu* ed.

Congshu jicheng chubian 叢書集成初編 (Grand compendium of collectanea, first series). Ed. Wang Yunwu 王雲五 (1888–1979). Shanghai: Shangwu yinshuguan, 1935–1940.

Dahui Zonggao 大慧宗杲 (1089–1163). *Dahui Pujue chanshi yulu* 大慧普覺禪師語錄 (Recorded conversations of Chan Master Dahui Pujue). *Taishō shinshū Daizōkyō* ed.

Dai Tong 戴侗 (ca. 1200–1284). *Liushu gu* 六書故 (Origins of the six categories of characters). *Wenyuange siku quanshu* ed.

Daozang. See *Zhengtong Daozang*.

Ding Guojun 丁國鈞 (d. 1919). *Bu Jinshu yiwenzhi* 補晉書藝文志 (Supplement to the bibliographical treatise in the *Jinshu* [History of the Jin]). *Congshu jicheng chubian* ed.

Du Guangting 杜光庭 (850–933). *Daode zhenjing guangsheng yi* 道德真經廣聖義 (Explications expanding upon the sage's [Emperor Xuanzong's] commentary to the *True Scripture of the Dao and Its Virtue*). *Zhengtong Daozang* ed.

Du Yu 杜預 (222–285) (commentary) and Kong Yingda 孔穎達 (574–648) (subcommentary). *Chunqiu Zuozhuan zhengyi* 春秋左傳正義 (Correct meaning of the *Spring and Autumn Annals*, the Zuo tradition). *Shisanjing zhushu* ed.

Ershiwushi bubian 二十五史補編 (Supplements to the twenty-five dynastic histories). 6 vols. Shanghai: Kaiming shudian, 1937.

Fang Bao 方苞 (1668–1749). *Shiji zhu buzheng* 史記注補正 (Supplements and corrections to annotations of the *Records of the Historian*). *Guangya shuju ke* 廣雅書局刻 wood block ed. of 1888.

Feng Mengzhen (1546–1605). *Kuaixue tang ji* 快雪堂集 (Literary collection from the Sudden Snow Hall). *Siku quanshu cunmu congshu* ed. 四庫全書存目叢書.

Gao Sisun 高似孫 (ca. 1160–ca. 1220). *Zilue* 子略 (Summary of the philosophers). *Wenyuange siku quanshu* ed.

Ge Hong 葛洪 (283–343). *Baopuzi neipian jiaoshi* 抱朴子內篇校釋 (Master who embraces simplicity, Inner Chapters, collation, and annotation). Ed. Wang Ming 王明. Beijing: Zhonghua shuju, 1988. Reprint, 1996.

Ge Hong. *Baopu zi waipian jiaojian* 抱朴子外篇校箋 (Master who embraces simplicity, outer chapters, collation and annotation). *Xinbian zhuzi jicheng* 新編諸子集成 (New edition of the *Grand Compendium of the Philosophers*). Ed. Yang Mingzhao 楊明照. First Collection 第一輯. Beijing: Zhonghua shuju, 1991.

Ge Hong. *Shenxian zhuan* 神仙傳 (Traditions of divine transcendents).

Gongsun Longzi 公孫龍子 (Sayings of Master Gongsun Long [with the commentary of Xie Xishen 謝希深]). *Sibu beiyao* ed.

Guangya conshu 廣雅叢書 (Broad and elegant collectanea). Ed. Xu Shaoqi 徐紹棨 (1879–1948). Guangzhou, China: Guangya shuju, 1920.

Guanzi 管子 (Master Guan). Commentary by Fang Xiaoling 方玄齡 (579–648). *Wenyuange siku quanshu* ed.

Gu Huan 顧歡 (420–483), ed. (attributed), *Daode zhenjing zhushu* 道德真經注疏 (Commentaries and subcommentaries to the *Daode zhenjing* [The true classic of the Dao and virtue]). *Zhengtong Daozang* ed.

Gui Youguang (1507–1571). *Nanhua zhenjing pingzhu* 南華真經評註 (Commentary and marginal comments to the *True Classic of the* [authentic man] *of Nanhua*). 1624 wood block ed.

Guo Qingfan 郭慶藩 (1844–1896), comp. *Zhuangzi jishi* 莊子集釋 (Collected explanations of *Master Zhuang*). *Xinbian zhuzi jicheng* 新編諸子集成 (New edition of the *Grand Compendium of the Philosophers*). First Collection 第一輯. Beijing: Zhonghua shuju, 1961. Reprint. 1997.

Guo Xiang 郭象. *Lunyu tilue* 論語體略 (Essentials of the *Analects*). *Yuhan Shanfang jiyi shu* ed.

Han Ying 韓嬰 (fl. ca. 150 BCE), ed. *Han shi waizhuan* 韓詩外傳 (Outer commentary to the *Classic of Poetry* by Master Han). *Sibu congkan*.ed.

Hatano Tarō 波多野太郎. *Rōshi Dōtokukyō kenkyū* 老子道德經研究 (Researches on *The Classic of the Way and Virtue* of *Laozi*). Tokyo: Kokuho kankō kai, 1979.

He Ning 何寧, comp. *Huainanzi jishi* 淮南子集釋 (Collected explanations of the *Master of Huainan*). *Xinbian zhuzi jicheng* 新編諸子集成 (New edition of the *Grand Compendium of the Philosophers*). First Collection 第一輯. Beijing: Zhonghua shuju, 1998.

He Xiu 何休 (129–182) and Xu Yan 徐彥 (late ninth–early tenth century). *Chunqiu Gongyang zhuan zhushu* 春秋公羊傳注疏 (Commentary and subcommentary to *Spring and Autumn Annals*, the Gongyang tradition). *Shisanjing zhushu* ed.

He Yan 何晏 (193–249) and Xing Bing 邢昺 (932–1010). *Lunyu zhushu* 論語注疏 (*Analects*, with commentaries and subcommentaries). *Shisanjing zhushu* ed.

He Yan 何晏, and Huang Kan 皇侃 (488–545). *Lunyu jijie yishu* 論語集解義疏 (Collected explications and expository commentaries to the *Analects*). *Wenyuange siku quanshu* ed.

Huainan honglie jie 淮南鴻烈解 (Grand and luminous [book] of Huainan, with explanations). *Sibu congkan* ed.

Huangdi yinfu jing jie 黃帝陰符經解 (Explications of the Yelow Thearch's scripture of the hidden accordance). *Wenyuange siku quanshu* ed.

Huangfu Mi 皇甫謐. *Gaoshi zhuan* 高士傳 (Traditions of lofty scholars [scholars who spurned official appointment]. *Sibu beiyao* ed.

Huang Huaixin, ed. *Heguanzi jiaozhu* 鶡冠子校注 (Pheasant cap master, collated with commentary). Beijing: Zhonghua shuju, 2014.

Hu Yinglin 胡應麟 (1551–1602). *Sibu zhenge* 四部正譌 (Correct guide to forgeries in the four branches of literature). Included in *Xiaoshi shanfang bicong* 小室山房筆叢 (Collectanea of jottings from the Little House mountain lodge). *Guangya congshu* ed.

Jiao Hong 焦竑 (1540–1620). *Jiaoshi bisheng* 焦氏笔乘 (Brush vehicle of Master Jiao). *Congshu jicheng chubian* ed.

Ji Kang. See Xi Kang.

Jin shu 晉書 (History of the Jin era). Ed. Fang Xuanling 方玄齡 (579–648). Beijing: Zhonghua shuju, 1974.

Jiu Tangshu 舊唐書 (Old History of the Tang). Ed. Liu Xu劉昫 (888–947) et al. Beijing: Zhonghua shuju, 1975.

Kong Anguo 孔安國 (commentary) and Kong Yingda 孔穎達 (sub-commentary). *Shangshu zhengyi* 尚書正義 (Correct Meaning of the Venerated Documents). *Shisanjing zhushu* ed.

Liezi 列子 (Sayings of Master Lie), with the commentary of Zhang Zhan 張湛 (fourth century CE). *Sibu beiyao* ed.

Li Fang 李昉 (925–996), et al., ed., *Taiping yulan* taiping 太平御覽 (Encyclopedia published during the Taiping [Xingguo] era [976–983], perused by His Majesty). Shijiazhuang: Hebei jiaoyu chubanshe 河北教育出版社, 1994. Reprint. 2000.

Li Lin 李霖 (twelfth century), comp. *Daode jing qushan ji* 道德真經取善集 (Collection of the best comments on the Classic of the Way and Virtue) (preface dated 1172). *Zhengtong Daozang* ed.

Lin Xiyi 林希逸 (ca. 1210–ca. 1273). *Zhuangzi Juanzhai kouyi jiaozhu* 莊子鬳齋口義校注 (Juanzhai's vernacular explications of the *Zhuangzi*, collated with commentary [by Zhou Qicheng 周啟成]). Beijing: Zhonghua shuju, 1997.

Lin Yunming 林雲銘. *Biaozhu Zhuangzi yin* 標註莊子因 (The causes and reasons underlying the *Zhuangzi*, with exegesis). Supplemental exegesis by Hata Tei 秦鼎 (Hata Sōrō 秦滄浪 [1761–1831]) and explanations by Tōjō Tamotsu 東條保. Osaka: Matsumura Kyūbei 松村九兵衛, 1890. Reprint. Taipei: Lantai shuju 蘭臺書局, 1975.

Liu Xiang (79–8 BCE), ed. *Shuoyuan zhenbu* 說苑斟補 (Garden of persuasions, supplemented judiciously). Ed. and ann. Liu Wendian 劉文典 (1889–1958). *Liu Wendian quanji* ed.

Liu Xiang, ed. *Xinshu jiaoshi*新序校釋 (Newly edited accounts, collated and explicated). Ed. Shi Guangying 石光瑛 and Chen Xin 陳新. Beijing: Zhonghua shuju, 2009.

Liu Xiang, ed. *Zhanguo ce jiaozhu* 戰國策校注 (Intrigues of the states, collated with commentary). Commentary by Bao Biao 鮑彪 (ca. 1100–1146) and Wu Shidao 吳師道 (1283–1344). *Sibu congkan chubian* ed.

Liu Yiqing 劉義慶 (403–444). *Shishuo xinyu jianshu* 世說新語箋疏 (A new account of tales of the world, collation and commentary). Original commentary by Liu Jun 劉俊 (462–521). Collation and new commentary by Yu Jiaxi 余嘉錫 (1884–1955). Ed. Zhou Zumo 周祖謨. Beijing: Zhonghua shuju, 1983.

Liu Zhiji 劉知幾 (661–721). *Shitong* 史通 (Comprehensive account of historiography). *Wenyuange siku quanshu* ed.

Liu Zongzhou 劉宗周 (1578–1645). *Renpu leiji* 人譜類記 (Classified records of human behavior). *Wenyuange siku quanshu* ed.

Lu Deming 陸德明 (556–627). *Jingdian shiwen* 經典釋文 (Textual explications for classics and scriptures). *Wenyuange siku quanshu* ed.

Lunyu. See He Yan.

Luo Miandao 羅勉道. *Nanhua zhenjing xunben* 南華真經循本 (Tracing the original meaning of the *True classic of the* [*Authentic Man*] *of Nanhua*). *Zhengtong Daozang* ed.

Lüshi chunqiu jishi 呂氏春秋集释 (Collected explanations of *Spring and Autumn Annals of Master Lü*). Compiled by Xu Weiyu 許維遹, ed. Liang Yunhua 梁運華. *Xinbian zhuzi jicheng* 新編諸子集成 (New edition of the *Grand Compendium of the Philosophers*). First Collection 第一輯. Beijing: Zhonghua shuju, 1985. Reprint. 2010.

Lu Yitian (*jinshi* 1836). *Lenglu zashi* 冷廬雜識 (Sundry notices from Cold Hermitage). *Xuxiu siku quanshu* ed.

Ma Duanlin 馬端臨 (1254–1323). *Wenxian tongkao* 文獻通考 (Comprehensive examination of documentary sources). *Wenyuange siku quanshu* ed.

Ma Guohan 馬國翰 (1794–1857), ed., *Yuhan Shanfang jiyi shu* 玉函山房輯佚書 (Fragments of lost works gathered at the Jade Casket Studio). Jinan: Huanghua guan shuju皇華館書局, 1874.

Mengzi. See Zhao Qi.

Qian Zeng 錢曾 (1629–1701). *Dushu minqiu ji* 讀書敏求記 (Record of my earnest search through reading books). 1726 wood block ed.

Qinding siku quanshu zongmu tiyao 欽定四庫全書總目提要 (Comprehensive catalog of the complete Four Treasuries Library, authorized by His Majesty) (1781–1783). Ji Yun 紀昀 (1724–1805) (editor-in-chief). *Wenyuange siku quanshu* ed.

Ruan Ji 阮籍 (210–263). *Ruan Ji ji jiaozhu* 阮籍集校注 (Collected works of Ruan Ji, collated and annotated). Ed. Chen Bojjun 陳伯君. Beijing: Zhonghua shuju, 1987.

Sanguo zhi. See Chen Shou.

Shijing. See Zheng Xuan and Kong Yingda.

Shinsan dainihon zokuzōkyō 新纂大日本續藏經 (Newly revised great Japan supplement to the Buddhist canon). Ed. Kōshō Kawamura河村孝照 et al. Tokyo: Kokusho kankōkai, 1980–1984.

Shisanjing zhushu 十三經注疏 (Commentaries and subcommentaries on the thirteen classics). Ed. Ruan Yuan 阮元. 1815 woodblock ed. Reduced facsimile ed. Taipei: Shijie shuju, 1963. Reprint. Shanghai: Guji chubanshe, 1997.

Shuoyuan. See Liu Wendian.

Sibu beiyao 四部備要 (Essential works from the four categories of literature [Confucian classics, philosophy, history, and belles-lettres]). Ed. Gao Yehou 高野侯 et al. Shanghai: Zhonghua shuju, 1927–1931. Reprint. Taipei: Zhonghua shuju, 1966–1975.

Sibu congkan chubian 四部叢刊初編 (Collectanea of the four categories of literature, first series). Ed. Zhang Yuanji 張元濟 et al. Shanghai: Shangwu yinshuguan (Commercial Press), 1919–1922. Reprint. 1932–1936.

Siku quanshu. See *Yingyin wenyuange siku quanshu*.

Siku quanshu cunmu congshu 四庫全書存目叢書 (Collectanea of works listed in the catalog for [but not included in the] Four Treasuries Library). Ji'nan: Ji-Lu shushe, 1997.

Siku weishoushu jikan 四庫未收書輯刊 (Collectanea of works not included in the Four Treasures Library). Beijing: Beijing chubanshe, 1997–2000.

Sima Biao 司馬彪 (240–306). *Zhuangzi zhu* 莊子注 (Commentary to *Zhuangzi*). Ed. Sun Pingyi 孫馮翼. Beijing: Zhonghua shuju, 1991.

Sima Qian 司馬遷 (ca. 145–ca. 86 BCE). *Shiji* 史記 (Records of the Grand Historian). Beijing: Zhonghua shuju, 1975.

Suishu 隋書 (History of the Sui). Ed. Wei Zheng 魏徵 (580–643). Beijing: Zhonghua shuju, 1973.

Taishō shinshū Daizōkyō 大正新修大藏經 (Chinese Buddhist canon newly revised during the Taishō era). Ed. Takakusu Junjirō (1866–1945) and Watanabe Kaikyoku (1872–1933). Tokyo: *Daizō shuppan kabushiki kaisha* 大藏出版株式会社, 1924–1934.

Tang Qiu 湯球 (1804–1881), ed. *Jiujia jiu jinshu jiben* 九家舊晉書輯本 (Collection of fragments of old histories of the Jin era by nine authors). *Congshu jicheng chubian* ed.

Wang Bi 王弼 (226–249) and Kong Yingda (574–648). *Zhouyi zhengyi* 周易正義 (Correct meaning of the *Changes of the* Zhou). *Shisanjing zhushu* ed.

Wang Chang王昶 (1725–1806). *Chunrong tang ji* 春融堂集 (Literary collection from Spring Warmth Hall). *Xuxiu siku quanshu* ed.

Wang Liqi 王利器 (1912–1998). *Wenzi shuyi* 文子疏義 (*Master Wen*, with commentary explications). Beijing: Zhonghua shuju, 2000.

Wang Mo 王謨 (ca. 1731–1817), ed. *Han-Wei yishu chao* 漢魏遺書鈔 (Fragments copied from lost works of the Han and Wei eras). Shanghai: Shanghai guji chubanshe, 1996.

Wang Su 王肅 (195–256), ed. *Kongzi jiayu* 孔子家語 (School sayings of Confucius). *Congshu jicheng chubian* ed.

Wang Xianqian 王先謙 (1842–1918), ed. *Xunzi jijie* 荀子集解 (Master Xun, collected explications). *Xinbian zhuzi jicheng* 新編諸子集成 (New edition of the *Grand Compendium of the Philosophers*). First Collection 第一輯. Beijing: Zhonghua shuju, 1988.

Wang Xianqian. *Zhuangzi jijie* 莊子集解 (*Master Zhuang*, collected explications). *Xinbian zhuzi jicheng* 新編諸子集成 (New edition of the *Grand Compendium of the Philosophers*). First Collection 第一輯. Beijing: Zhonghua shuju, 1999.

Wang Yinglin 王應麟 (1223–1296). *Kunxue jiwen* 困學紀聞 (Record of information about learning painfully acquired). *Wenyuange siku quanshu* ed.

Wan Sitong 萬斯同 (1638–1702). *Jin jiang xiang dachen biao* 晉將相大臣表 (Chronological table of Jin-dynasty generals, ministers, and high officials). *Ershiwushi bubian* ed.

Wenyuange siku quanshu. See *Yingyin Wenyuange siku quanshu.*

Wenzi. See Wang Liqi.

Wudeng huiyuan 五燈會元 (Combined sources for the five lamps). Ed. Dachuan Puji 大川普濟 (1179–1253). *Shinsan dainihon zokuzōkyō* ed.

Wuqiubei zhai Zhuangzi jicheng xubian 無求備齋莊子集成續編 (Collectanea of works on the *Zhuangzi* from the Has Everything with Nothing to Seek Studio, second series). Ed. Yan Lingfeng 嚴靈峰 (1903–1999). Taipei: Yiwen yinshuguan, 1974.

Wu Shu 吳淑 (947–1002). *Shilei fu zhu* 事類賦註 (Rhapsodies on categorized matters, with commentary). *Wenyuange siku quanshu* ed.

Xiang Xiu (ca. 223–ca. 275). *Zhouyi Xiangshi yi* 周易向氏義 (Master Xiang's explications of the *Changes of the Zhou*). *Yuhan Shanfang jiyi shu* ed.

Xiao Tong 蕭統 (501–531), ed. *Wenxuan* 文選 (Selections of refined literature). Commentary by Li Shan 李善 (630–690). Shanghai: Shanghai guji chubanshe, 1986.

Xiaoshi shanfang bicong. See Hu Yinglin.

Xie Zhaozhe謝肇淛 (1567–1624). *Wenhai pisha* 文海披沙 (Sand sifted for gold in the sea of letters). *Xuxiu siku quanshu* ed.

Xi Kang 嵇康 (223–263). *Xi Kang ji jiaozhu* 嵇康集校注 (Collected works of Xi Kang, collated and annotated). Ed. and ann. Dai Mingyang 戴明揚. Beijing: Renmin wenxue chubanshe, 1962.

Xin Tangshu 新唐書 (New history of the Tang). Ed. Ouyang Xiu 歐陽修 (1007–1072) and Song Qi 宋祁 (998–1061). Beijing: Zhonghua shuju, 1975.

Xu Fuhong許富宏, ed. *Guigu zi jijiao jizhu* 鬼谷子集校集注 (Master of Demon Valley, collected collations and commentaries). Xinbian zhuzi jicheng xubian 新編諸子集成續編 (New edition of the *Grand Compendium of the Philosophers*, supplement edition). Beijing: Zhonghua shuju, 2008. Reprint. 2010.

Xunzi. See Wang Xianqian.

*Xuxiu siku quanshu*續修四庫全書 (Supplement to the four treasures library). Ed. Gu Tinglong 顧廷龍 (1904–1998). Shanghai: Shanghai guji chubanshe, 2002.

Yang Bojun 楊伯峻 (1909–1992), ed. *Liezi jishi* 列子集释 (Collected Explanations of *Liezi*)). Beijing: Zhonghua shuju, 1979.

Yan Kejun 嚴可均, ed. *Quan Shanggu Sandai Qin Han Sanguo Liuchao wen* 全上古三代秦漢三國六朝文 (Complete prose of remote antiquity, the three eras, Qin, Han, Three Kingdoms, and Six Dynasties). Beijing: Zhonghua shuju, 1958. Reprint. 1995.

Yan Lingfeng 嚴靈峰, ed. *Wuqiubeizhai Lao Lie Zhuang sanzi jicheng bubian* 無求備齋老列莊三子集成補編 (Collectanea of works on the three masters, *Laozi*, *Liezi*, and *Zhuangzi*, from the Has Everything with Nothing to Seek Studio, supplementary series). Taipei: Chengwen chubanshe, 1982.

Yan Lingfeng. *Wuqiubeizhai Zhuangzi jicheng chubian* 無求備齋莊子集成初編 (Collectanea of works on the *Zhuangzi* from the Has Everything with Nothing to Seek Studio, first series). Taipei: Yiwen yinshuguan, 1972.

Yan Lingfeng. *Wuqiubeizhai Zhuangzi jicheng xubian* 無求備齋莊子集成續編 (Collectanea of works on the *Zhuangzi* from the Has Everything with Nothing to Seek Studio, second series). Taipei: Yiwen yinshuguan, 1974.

Yan Zhitui 顏之推 (531–591). *Yanshi jiaxun* 顏氏家訓 (Family instructions for the Yan clan). *Sibu congkan chubian* ed.

Yao Nai 姚鼐 (1731–1815). *Xibao xuan wenji* 惜抱軒文集 (Collected Prose from the Cherished Embrace Studio). *Xuxiu siku quanshu* ed.

Yao Nai. *Zhuangzi zhangyi* 莊子章義 (Meaning of the *Zhuangzi*, arranged by section). *Wuqiubei zhai Zhuangzi jicheng xubian* ed.

Yingyin Wenyuange siku quanshu 影印文淵閣四庫全書 (Photo facsimile reprint of the Wenyuan Pavilion copy of the Four Treasuries Library). Taipei: Shangwu yinshuguan, 1983–1986. Reprint. Shanghai: Shanghai guji chubanshe, 1987.

Yiwen leiju 藝文類聚 (Compendium of arts and letters). Ed. Ouyang Xun 歐陽詢 (557–641). *Wenyuange siku quanshu* ed.

Yuan Shouding 袁守定 (1705–1782). *Zhanbi congtan* 佔畢叢談 (Collected discussions for casual reading). *Siku weishoushu jikan* ed.

Yuding peiwen yunfu 御定佩文韻府 (Pendant literary culture treasury of rhymes, authorized by His Majesty [Kangxi]). Ed. Chen Tingjing 陳廷敬 (1638–1712) and Zhang Yushu 張玉書 (1642–1711). *Wenyuange siku quanshu* ed.

Yuhan Shanfang jiyi shu. See Ma Guohan.

Yu Yue 俞樾 (1827–1909). *Zhuangzi pingyi* 莊子平議 (Equitable discussions of the *Zhuangzi*). *Wuqiubeizhai Zhuangzi jicheng xubian* ed.

Zhang Junfang 張君房 (ca. 961–ca. 1042), ed. *Yunji qiqian* 雲笈七籤 (Seven lots from the Bamboo Book Hamper of the Clouds). *Wenyuange siku quanshu* ed.

Zhang Shuangdi 張雙棣, *Huainanzi jiaoshi* 淮南子校釋 (*Master of Huainan*, collated and explicated). Beijing: Beijing daxue chubanshe, 1997; revised and enlarged ed. 2013.

Zhang Yongquan 張涌泉, ed. *Dunhuang jingbu wenxian heji* 敦煌經部文獻合集 (Collection of documents from Dunhuang, classics and scriptures section). 10 vols. Beijing: Zhonghua shuju, 2008.

Zhao Qi 趙歧 (commentary) and Sun Shi 孫奭 (subcommentary). *Mengzi zhushu* 孟子注疏 (*Mencius*, with commentary and subcommentary). *Shisanjing zhushu* ed.

Zheng Qiao鄭樵 (1104–1162). *Tongzhi* 通志 (Comprehensive history of institutions). *Wenyuange siku quanshu* ed.

Zhengtong Daozang 正統道藏 (The Zhengtong-era [1436–1449] edition of the *Daoist Canon*). Shanghai: Shangwu yinshuguan, 1923–1926. Reprint. Taipei: Xinwenfeng, 1995.

Zheng Xuan 鄭玄 (commentary) and Kong Yingda. (correct meaning). *Liji zhengyi* 禮記正義 (Correct Meaning of the *Record of Ritual*). *Shisanjing zhushu* ed.

Zheng Xuan. *Maoshi zhengyi* 毛詩正義 (Correct meaning of the *Mao edition of the Odes*). *Shisanjing zhushu* ed.

Zhibuzu zhai congshu 知不足齋叢書 (Collectanea compiled at the Knows Not Enough Studio). Ed. Bao Tingfu 鮑廷博 (1728–1814). Shanghai: Shanghai gushu liutongchu yingyin 上海古書流通處影印, 1921.

Zhiyuan 智圓 (976–1022). *Niepan jing shu sande zhigui* 涅槃經疏三德指歸 (Three virtues outline to the commentary to the *Mahāparinirvāṇa-sūtra*). *Taishō shinshū Daizōkyō* ed.

Zhouyi. See Wang Bi and Kong Yingda.

Zuozhuan. See Du Yu and Kong Yingda.

Zhu Mu祝穆 (d. ca. 1255), Fu Dayong 富大用 (fl. ca. 1326), Zhu Yuan 祝淵 (1614–1645), ed. *Gujin shiwen leiju* 古今事文類聚 (Classified collection based on events and writings). *Wenyuange siku quanshu* ed.

Zhu Yizun 朱彝尊 (1629–1709). *Dianjiao buzheng jingyi kao* 點校補正經義考 (Studies on the meaning of the classics, punctuated, collated, amended and corrected). Ed. Xu Weiping 許維萍,Feng Xiaoting 馮曉庭 and Jiang Shuichuan 江永川 Taipei: Zhongyang yanjiuyuan Zhongguo wenzhe yanjiusuo choubeichu 中央研究院中國文哲研究所籌備處, 1997.

Secondary Sources in Chinese and Japanese

Akatsuka Kiyoshi 赤塚忠 (1913–1983). *Sōji* 莊子 (*Zhuangzi*). 2 vols. Tokyo: Shūeisha, 1974. (*Zenshaku kanbun taikei* 全釈漢文大系, 16–17).

Chen Suzhen 陳蘇鎮. "*Sima Yue yu Yongjia zhi luan* 司馬越與永嘉之亂 (Sima Yue and the turmoil of the Yongjia era [307–313])." *Beijing daxue xuebao* 北京大學學報 (*Zhexue shehui kexue baoban* 哲學社會科學版) 1 (1989): 117–23.

Fang Yong 方勇. *Zhuangzi xueshi* 莊子學史 (History of *Zhuangzi* studies). 3 vols. Beijing: Renmin chubanshe, 2008.

Feng Youlan 馮友蘭 (Fung Yu-lan, 1895–1990). *Zhongguo zhexueshi xinbian* 中國哲学史新编 (History of Chinese philosophy, new edition). 3 vols. Beijing: Renmin chubanshe, 1998. Reprint 2001.

Fukunaga Mitsuji 福永光司 (1918–2001). "*Kaku Shō no Sōji kaishaku* 郭象の莊子解釈 (Guo Xiang's interpretation of the *Zhuangzi*)." *Tetsugaku kenkyū* 哲学研究 37, no. 2–37, no. 3 (1954), 46–62; 167–77.

Fukunaga Mitsuji. "*Kaku Shō no Sōjichū to Shō Shū no Sōjichū: Kaku Shō tōsetu setsuni suite no gimon* 郭象の莊子注と向秀の莊子注：郭象盜窃説についての疑問 (Guo Xiang's *Zhuangzi* commentary and Xiang Xiu's *Zhuangzi* commentary: Doubts concerning the Guo Xiang plagiarism theory)." *Tōhō gakuhō* 東方学報 36 (1964): 187–215.

Fukunaga Mitsuji. *Sōji* 莊子 (*Zhuangzi*). 6 vols. Tokyo: Asahi shinbunsha, 1966–1967. Reprint. 1992.

Guan Feng 關鋒 (1919–2005). *Zhuangzi neipian yijie he pipan* 莊子內篇譯解和批判 (Interpretation and critique of the Inner Chapters of the *Zhuangzi*). Beijing: Zhonghua shuju, 1961.

Guan Feng. "*Zhuangzi wai zapian chutan* 莊子外雜篇初探 (Preliminary investigation of the Outer and Miscellaneous Chapters of the *Zhuangzi*)." In Zhexue yanjiu bianjibu 哲學研究編輯部, ed., *Zhuangzi zhexue taolun ji* 莊子哲學討論集 (Collected essays on the philosophy of the *Zhuangzi*) (Beijing: Zhonghua shuju, 1961), 62–98.

Jiang Longxiang 姜龍翔. "*Xiang Xiu benti sixiang shangque* 向秀本體思想商榷 (Deliberating Xiang Xiu's ontology)." *Donghua renwen xuebao* 東華人文學報 15 (2009): 39–67.

Kang Zhongqian 康中乾. *Cong Zhuangzi dao Guo Xiang: Zhuangzi yu Zhuangzi zhu bijiao yanjiu* 從莊子到郭象: 莊子與莊子注比較研究 (From the *Zhuangzi* to Guo Xiang: Comparative study of the *Zhuangzi* and *Commentary to Zhuangzi*). Beijing: Renmin chubanshe, 2013.

Liu Kunsheng 劉坤生. "*Shilun daojia zhexue yu ziran de guanxi jiqi biaoda fangfa* 試論道家哲學與自然的關係及其表達方法:「三玄」通論之一 (On the relationship between the philosophy of the Daoists and the Natural, including their manner of philosophical expression: General discussion of the 'Three Arcane Works,' part 1)." *Wuhan daxue xuebao* (*Zhexue shehui kexue ban*) 武漢大學學報 (哲學社會科學版) 3 (1999): 53–58.

Liu Pansui 劉盼遂 (1896–1966). "*Shishuo xinyu jiaojian* 世說新語校箋 (A new account of tales of the world, collation and commentary)," *Guoxue luncong* 國學論叢 (Collected essays on Chinese studies) 1, no. 4 (1939): 65–110.

Liu Xiaogan 劉笑敢. *Zhuangzi zhexue jiqi yanbian* 莊子哲學及其演變 (Philosophy of the *Zhuangzi* and its evolution). Beijing: Zhongguo shehui kexue chubanshe, 1988.

Lu Guolong 盧國龍. *Guo Xiang pingzhuan: lixing de qiangkui* 郭象評傳：理性的薔薇 (Critical biography of Guo Xiang: Rose of rationality). Liuzhou, Guangxi, China: Xinhua shudian, 1996. Reprint. 1997.

Qian Mu 錢穆 (1895–1990). *Zhuang Lao tongbian* 莊老通辨 (General insights into the *Zhuangzi* and the *Laozi*). (*Qian Binsi xiansheng quanji* 錢賓四先生全集 [Complete works of Mister Qian Binsi]), vol. 7. Taipei: Lianjing聯經, 1998.

Seki Masao 関正郎. *Sōji no shisō to sono kaishaku: Kaku Shō Sei Gen'ei* 荘子の思想とその解釈: 郭象 成玄英 (The thought of the *Zhuangzi* and its interpretation: Guo Xiang and Chen Xuanying). Tokyo: Sanseidō, 1999.

Takahashi Hitoshi 高橋均, *Rongo giso no kenkyū* 論語義疏の研究 (A study of the *Lunyu yishu*). Tokyo: Sōbunsha, 2013.

Takeuchi Yosio 武内義雄 (1866–1966). *Rōshi genshi: fu Shoshi kōryaku*老子原始: 附諸子攷略 (*Laozi*, origins: *Brief Examination of the Philosophers* appended). Tokyo: Kōbundō shobo, 1926.

Takeuchi Yoshio. *Rōshi to Sōshi* 老子と荘子 (Master Lao and Master Zhuang). Tokyo: Iwanami Shoten, 1930.

Tang Junyi. *Ru Dao Shi yu neizai chaoyue wenti* 道儒釋與內在超越問題 (Issues concerning Ruism [Confucianism], Daoism, and Buddhism and imminent transcendence). Nanchang, China: Jiangxi renmin chubanshe, 1991.

Tang Yijie 湯一介 (1927–2014). *Guo Xiang* 郭象. Taipei: Dongda tushu, 1999.

Tang Yijie. *Guo Xiang yu Wei-Jin xuanxue* 郭象與魏晉玄學 (Guo Xiang and arcane learning in the Wei-Jin period). Beijing: Beijing daxue chubanshe, 2000.

Tang Yijie. *Neizai chaoyue zhi lu* 內在超越之路 (The road to immanent transcendence). Beijing: Zhongguo guangbo dianshi chubanshe, 1992.

Tang Yijie. *Ru Dao Shi yu neizai chaoyue wenti* 儒道釋與內在超越問題 (Issues concerning Ruism [Confucianism], Daoism, and Buddhism and imminent transcendence). Nanchang, China: Jiangxi jiaoyu chubanshe, 1991.

Tang Yongtong 湯用彤 (1893–1964). *Tang Yongtong quanji* 湯用彤全集 (Complete works of Tang Yongtong). Ed. Wang Shuhua 王書華. 7 vols. Shijiazhuang, China: Hebei renmin chubanshe, 2000.

Tang Yongtong. *Wei-Jin xuanxue lungao* 魏晉玄學論稿 (Draft discussions of arcane learning in the Wei-Jin era). Beijing: Renmin chubanshe, 1957. Reprint. Shanghai: Shanghai guji chubanshe, 2001.

Teraoka Ryūgan 寺岡竜含. *Tonkōbon Kaku Shō chū Sōshi Nanka shinkyō kenkyū sōron* 敦煌本郭象注莊子南華真経研究総論 (An introduction to research on the Dunhuang edition of Guo Xiang's commentary to the *Classic of the* [true man of] *Nanhua of Zhuangzi*). Fukui 福井, Japan: Fukui kanbun gakkai, 1966.

Teraoka Ryūgan. *Tonkōbon Kaku Shō chū Sōshi Nanka shinkyō kōkanki* 敦煌本郭象注莊子南華真経校勘記 (Record of collating a critical edition of the Dunhuang edition of Guo Xiang's commentary to the *Classic of the* [true man of] *Nanhua of Zhuangzi*). Fukui 福井, Japan: Fukui kanbun gakkai, 1961.

Teraoka Ryūgan 寺岡竜含, ed. *Tonkōbon Kaku Shō chū Sōshi Nanka shinkyō shūei* 敦煌本郭象注莊子南華真経輯影 (Photographic facsimile edition of the Dunhuang edition of Guo Xiang's commentary to the *Classic of the* [true man of] *Nanhua of Zhuangzi*). Fukui 福井, Japan: Fukui Kanbun gakkai, 1966.

Wang Baoxuan 王葆玹. *Xuanxue tonglun* 玄學通論 (General survey of arcane learning). Taipei: Wunan tushu, 1996.

Wang Shumin王叔岷 (1914–2008). "*Ba Riben Gaoshan si jiuchao juanzi ben Zhuangzi canjuan* 跋日本高山寺舊鈔卷子本莊子殘卷 (Postscript to the incomplete old hand-written scroll edition of the *Zhuangzi* owned by the Kōzanji in Japan)." *Zhongyang yanjiuyuan lishi yuyan yanjiusuo jikan* 中央研究院歷史語言研究所季刊 22 (1951): 161–70.

Wang Shumin. *Guo Xiang Zhuangzi zhu jiaoji* 郭象莊子注校記 (Guo Xiang's commentary to the *Zhuangzi*, with collation notes). Shanghai: Shangwu yinshuguan, 1950. Reprint. Taipei: Zhongyang yanjiuyuan lishi yuyan yanjiusuo中央研究院歷史語言研究所, 1993.

Wang Shumin. *Zhuangxue guankui* 莊學管闚莊學管窺 (Studies of the *Zhuangzi*, limited views). Beijing: Zhonghua shuju, 2007.

Wang Shumin. *Zhuangzi jiaoquan* 莊子校詮 (Collation and interpretation of the *Zhuangzi*). Taipei: Zhongyang yanjiuyuan lishi yuyan yanjiusuo 中央研究院歷史語言研究所, 1988. Reprint. 1999.

Wang Shumin. "*Zhuangzi Xiang Guo yitong kao* 莊子向郭注異同考" (Investigation of differences and similarities in Xiang's and Guo's commentaries to *Zhuangzi*). *Zhongyang tushuguan guankan fukan*中央圖書館館刊復刊 (*National Central Library Bulletin*) 1, no. 4 (1947): 1–8.

Wang Xiaoyi 王曉毅. "Guo Xiang *mingyun ji qi yiyi* 郭象命運論及其意義 (Guo Xiang's theory of fate and its meaning). *Wen shi zhe* 文史哲 (*Journal of Literature History and Philosophy*) 6, no. 291 (2005): 19–24.

Wang Xiaoyi. *Guo Xiang pingzhuan fu Xiang Xiu pingzhuan* 郭象評傳附向秀評傳 (Critical biography of Guo Xiang with critical biography of Xiang Xiu appended). Nanjing, China: Nanjing daxue chubanshe, 2006.

Xu Jialu 許嘉璐 and An Pinqiu 安平秋, ed., *Ershisi shi quanyi: Shiji* 二十四史全譯: 史記 (Complete translation [into modern Chinese] of the twenty-four histories: Records of the Historian). Beijing: Hanyu dacidian chubanshe, 2004.

Wu Chengshi 吳承仕 (1884–1939). *Jingdian shiwen xulu shuzheng* 經典釋文序錄疏證 (Prefatory treatise to textual explications for classics and scriptures, critical annotations). Beiping: Zhongguo shuyuan, 1933. Reprint. Beijing: Zhonghua shuju, 2008.

Yang Mingzhao 楊明照 (1909–2003). "*Guo Xiang Zhuangzi zhu shifou qie zi Xiang Xiu jiantao* 郭象莊子注是否竊自向秀檢討" (Critical discussion of whether or not Guo Xiang stole his commentary of the *Zhuangzi* from Xiang Xiu), *Yanjing xuebao* 燕京學報 (*Yenching Journal of Chinese Studies*) 28 (1940): 71–88, 301–2.

Zhang Gengguang 張耿光, trans. and ann. *Zhuangzi* 莊子. Taipei: Taiwan guji chuban, 2004.

Zhao Yixin 趙義鑫. "*Jin Huaidi, Sima Yue yu Xin Jin zhongshu zhengquan de bengkui* 晉懷帝、司馬越與西晉中樞政權的崩潰 (Jin emperor Huai, Sima Yue, and the collapse of Western Jin central state power)." *Leshan shifan xueyuan xuebao* 樂山師範學院學報 (*Journal of Leshan Normal University*) 33, no. 1 (2018): 74–81.

Zhu Qingzhi 朱慶之. "*Yema yizheng* 野馬義證 (Evidence for interpretation of the expression "wild horses")." *Guhanyu yanjiu* 古漢語研究 7 (1990): 17–18.

Works in Western Languages

Aimes, Roger T. *Confucian Role Ethics: A Vocabulary*. Hong Kong: Chinese University Press, 2011.

Aimes, Roger T. "Getting Past Transcendence: Determinacy, Indeterminacy, and Emergence in Chinese Natural Cosmology." In *Transcendence, Immanence, and Intercultural Philosophy*, ed. Nahum Brown and William Franke, 3–67. Cham, Switzerland: Palgrave Macmillan, 2018.

Arendrup, Birthe. "The First Chapter of Guo Xiang's Commentary to *Zhuang Zi*: A Translation and Grammatical Analysis." *Acta Orientalia*, 36 (1974): 311–415.

Birrell, Anne. *Chinese Mythology: An Introduction*. Baltimore: John Hopkins University Press, 1993.

Brooks, E. Bruce, and A. Taeko Brooks. *The Original Analects: Sayings of Confucius and His Successors*. New York: Columbia University Press, 1998.

Brown, Nahum, and William Franke, ed. *Transcendence, Immanence, and Intercultural Philosophy*. Cham, Switzerland: Springer Nature, 2018.

Bumbacher, Stephan. "Reconstructing the *Zhuang zi*: Preliminary Considerations." *Asiatische Studien/Études Asiatiques* 70, no. 4 (2016): 611–74.

Chan, Alan K. L. "Sage Nature and the Logic of Namelessness." In *Philosophy and Religion in Early Medieval China*, ed. Alan K. L. Chan and Yuet-Keung Lo, 23–52. Albany: State University of New York Press, 2010.

Chan, Wing-tsit. *A Source Book in Chinese Philosophy*. Princeton, NJ: Princeton University Press, 1963.

Davis, Timothy M. *Entombed Epigraphy and Commemorative Culture in Early Medieval China*. Boston: Brill, 2015.

Defoort, Carine. "The 'Transcendence' of *Tian*." (Review of *Law and Morality in Ancient China: The Silk Manuscripts of Huang-Lao*. By Randall Peerenboom. New York: SUNY, 1993). *Philosophy East and West*, 44, no. 2 (April 1994): 347–68.

Di Cosmo, Nicola, ed. *Military Culture in Imperial China*. Cambridge, MA: Harvard University Press, 2009.

Dien, Albert E., and Keith Nathaniel Knapp, ed. *The Cambridge History of China. Vol. 2: The Six Dynasties, 220–589*. Cambridge: Cambridge University Press, 2019.

Fung, Yu-lan (Feng Youlan). *Chuang Tzu: A New Selected Translation with an Exposition of the Philosophy of Kuo Hsiang*. Shanghai: Commercial Press, 1933. Reprint. New York: Paragon Book Reprint Corp. 1964.

Giles, Herbert A., trans. *Chuang Tzu, Taoist Philosopher and Chinese Mystic*. London: Allen & Unwin, 1926. Reprint. 1961.

Graham, A. C., trans. *The Book of Lieh-Tzu*. London: John Murray, 1960. Reprint. New York: Columbia University Press, 1990.

Graham, A. C., trans. *Chuang-tzu: The Seven Inner Chapters and Other Writings from the Book Chuang-tzu*. Boston: Allen & Unwin, 1981.

Graham, A. C. "How Much of *Chuang Tzu* Did Chuang Tzu Write?" In *Studies in Classical Chinese Thought*, ed. Henry Rosemont, Jr. and Benjamin I. Schwartz, 459–501. Chico, CA: American Academy of Religion, 1980.

Graham, A. C. *Later Mohist Logic, Ethics, and Science*. Hong Kong: Chinese University Press, 1978.

Hall, David L., and Roger T. Ames. *Thinking Through Confucius*. Albany: State University of New York Press, 1987.

Henricks, Robert G. *Philosophy and Argumentation in Third-Century China: The Essays of Hsi K'ang*. Princeton, NJ: Princeton University Press, 1983.

Heubel, Fabian. "Immanente Transzendenz im Spannungsfeld von europäischer Sinologie, kritischer Theorie und zeitgenössischem Konfuzianismus" [Immanent transcendence as a field of controversy in European sinology, critical theory, and contemporary Confucianism]. *Polylog: Zeitschrift für interkulturelles Philosophieren* 26 (2011): *Selbstkultivierung und Politik im zeitgenössischen Konfuzianismus* (Self-cultivation and politics in contemporary Confucianism), 125–65.

Hoffert, Brian H. "*Chuang Tzu*: The Evolution of a Taoist Classic." PhD diss., Harvard University, 2001.

Holzman, Donald. *Poetry and Politics: The Life and Works of Juan Chi (A.D. 210–263)*. Cambridge: Cambridge University Press, 1976.

Holzman, Donald. *La vie et la pensée de Hi K'ang*. Leiden, Netherlands: Brill, 1957.

Hsiao, Kung-Kung-ch'üan [Xiao Gongquan]. *A History of Chinese Political Thought. Volume 1: From the Beginnings to the Sixth Century A.D.* Trans. Frederick W. Mote. Princeton, NJ: Princeton University Press, 1979.

Hucker, Charles O. *A Dictionary of Official Titles in Imperial China*. Stanford, CA: Stanford University Press, 1985.

Hummel, Arthur W., ed. *Eminent Chinese of the Ch'ing Period*. 2 vols. Washington, DC: United States Government Printing Office, 1944.

Idema, Wilt and Beata Grant. *The Red Brush: Writing Women of Imperial China*. Cambridge, MA: Harvard University Asia Center, 2007.

Johnston, Ian, trans. *The Mozi: A Complete Translation*. New York: Columbia University Press, 2010.

Jullien, François. *La propension des choses: Pour une histoire de l'efficacité en Chine* [The propensity of things: For a history of efficiency in China]. Paris: Seuil, 1992.

Kim, Ha Tai. "Transcendence Without and Within: The Concept of *T'ien* in Confucianism," *International Journal for Philosophy of Religion* 3, no. 3 (Fall 1972): 146–60.

Klein, Esther. "Were There 'Inner Chapters' in the Warring States? A New Examination of Evidence About the *Zhuangzi*," *T'oung Pao*, Second Series, 96, no. 4/5 (2010): 299–369.

Knaul, Livia (Livia Kohn). "Lost *Chuang-tzu* Passages." *Journal of Chinese Religions* 10 (1982): 53–79.

Knechtges, David R. *Wen Xuan or Selections of Refined Literature: Vol. III: Rhapsodies on Natural Phenomena, Birds and Animals, Aspirations and Feelings, Sorrowful Laments, Literature, Music, and Passions*. Princeton, NJ: Princeton University Press, 1996.

Knechtges, David R., and Chang Taiping, ed. *Ancient and Early Medieval Chinese Literature: A Reference Guide*. 4 vols. Leiden, Netherlands: Brill, 2014.

Knoblock, John, trans. *Xunzi: A Translation and Study of the Complete Works*. Stanford, CA: Stanford University Press, 1988–1994.

Knoblock, John, and Jeffrey Riegel, trans. *The Annals of Lü Buwei*. Stanford, CA: Stanford University Press, 2000.

Kohn, Livia. *Early Chinese Mysticism: Philosophy and Soteriology in the Taoist Tradition*. Princeton, NJ: Princeton University Press: 1992.

Legge, James, trans. *The Sacred Books of China: The Texts of Taoism*. Oxford: Clarendon Press, 1891. Reprint. New York: Dover Publications, 1962.

Lin, Yutang, trans. *Chuangtse*. Taipei: World Book, 1957.

Liu, Xiaogan. *Classifying the Zhuangzi Chapters*. Trans. William E. Savage. Ann Arbor: University of Michigan, Center for Chinese Studies, 1994.

Liu, Xiaogan, ed. *Dao Companion to Daoist Philosophy*. Dordrecht, Netherlands: Springer, 2015.

Loewe, Michael. *The Men Who Governed Han China: Companion to a Biographical Dictionary of the Qin, Former Han and Xin Periods*. Leiden, Netherlands, and Boston: Brill, 2004.

Lynn, Richard John, trans. *The Classic of Changes: A New Translation of the I Ching as Interpreted by Wang Bi*. New York: Columbia University Press, 1994.

Lynn, Richard John, trans. *The Classic of the Way and Virtue: A New Translation of the Tao-te ching of Laozi as Interpreted by Wang Bi*. New York: Columbia University Press, 1999.

Lynn, Richard Lynn. "Guo Xiang's Theory of Sagely Knowledge as Seen in His *Essentials of the Analects* (*Lunyu Tilue* 論語體略)." In *Dao Companion to Xuanxue*, ed. David Chai, 393–410. Dordrecht, Netherlands: Springer, 2020.

Lynn, Richard John. "The Modern Word for Humour (*Huaji*) and Its Antecedents in the *Zhuangzi* and Other Early Texts." In *Laughter in Eastern and Western Philosophies: Proceedings of the Académie du Midi*, ed. Hans-Georg Moeller and Günter Wohlfart, 60-73. Freiburg im Breisgau: Verlag Karl Albern, 2010.

Mair, Victor H., trans. *Wandering on the Way: Early Taoist Tales and Parables of Chuang Tzu*. Honolulu: University of Hawai'i Press, 1998.

Major, John S. *Heaven and Earth in Early Han Thought: Chapters Three, Four, and Five of the Huainanzi*. Albany: State University of New York Press, 1997.

Major, John S., Sarah A. Queen, Andrew Seth Meyer, Harold D. Roth, Michael Puett, and Judson Murray, trans. and ed. *The Huainanzi: A Guide to the Theory and Practice of Government in Early Han China*. New York: Columbia University Press, 2010.

Makeham, John. "He Yan, *Xuanxue*, and the Editorship of the *Lunyu Jijie*." *Early Medieval China* 5 (1999): 1–35.

Mather, Richard B. "The Controversy over Conformity and Naturalness During the Six Dynasties." *History of Religions* 9, no. 2/3 (Nov. 1969–Feb. 1970): 160–80.

Mather, Richard B., trans. *Shih-shuo Hsin-yü: A New Account of Tales of the World, by Liu I-ch'ing*. Minneapolis: University of Minnesota Press, 1976. Reprint Ann Arbor: University of Michigan Center for Chinese Studies, 2002.

Montaigne, Michel de. *The Complete Essays of Montaigne*. Translated by Donald M. Frame. Stanford, CA: Stanford University Press, 1957. Reprint. 2002.

Needham, Joseph, and Wang Ling. *Science and Civilization in China, Vol. 4: Physics and Physical Technology; Part II: Mechanical Engineering*. Cambridge: Cambridge University Press, 1965.

Peerenboom, Randall. *Law and Morality in Ancient China: The Silk Manuscripts of Huang-Lao*. Albany: State University of New York Press, 1993.

Pohl, Karl-Heinz. " 'Immanent Transcendence' in the Chinese Tradition: Remarks on a Chinese (and Sinological) Controversy." In *Transcendence, Immanence, and Intercultural Philosophy*, ed. Nahum Brown and William Franke, 103–23. Cham, Switzerland: Springer Nature, 2018.

Pulleyblank, Edwin G. *Lexicon of Reconstructed Pronunciation in Early Middle Chinese, Late Middle Chinese, and Early Mandarin*. Vancouver: University of British Columbia Press, 1991.

Rickett, W. Allyn, trans. *Guanzi: Political and Philosophical Essays from Early China*. Princeton, NJ: Princeton University Press, Vol. 1, 1985, Vol. 2, 1998.

Robinet, Isabelle. "Kouo Siang ou le monde comme absolu (Guo Xiang or the world as absolute)." *T'oung Pao*, Second Series, 69:1/3 (1983), 73–107.

Schipper, Kristofer. *The Taoist Body*. Translated by Karen C. Duval. Foreword by Norman Girardot. Berkeley, CA: University of California Press, 1993.

Swartz, Wendy. *Reading Philosophy, Writing Poetry: Intertextual Modes of Making Meaning in Early Medieval China*. Cambridge, MA: Harvard Asian Center, 2018.

Tu Weiming. *Centrality and Commonality: An Essay on Confucian Religiousness*. Albany: State University of New York Press, 1993.

Van den Stock, Ady. " 'Immanent Transcendence': Toward a Genealogical Analysis of a Key Concept in the Philosophy of Mou Zongsan (1909–1995)." *Asian Philosophy* 31, no. 2 (2021): 195–209.

Watson, Burton, trans. *Chuang-tzu: The Complete Works*. New York: Columbia University Press 1968.

Wawrytko, Sandra A., and Youru Wang. *Dao Companion to Chinese Buddhist Philosophy*. Dordrecht: Springer, 2018.

Ziporyn, Brook A. "Guo Xiang: The Self-So and the Repudiation-cum-Reaffirmation of Deliberate Action and Knowledge." In *Dao Companion to Daoist Philosophy*, ed. Xiaogan Liu, 397–423. Dordrecht, Netherlands: Springer, 2015.

Ziporyn, Brook A. *The Penumbra Unbound: The Neo-Taoist Philosophy of Guo Xiang*. Albany: State University of New York Press, 2003.

Zücher, Erik. *The Buddhist Conquest of China: The Spread and Adaptation of Buddhism in Early Medieval China*. 2 vols. Leiden, Netherlands: E. J. Brill, 1959.

INDEX

TRANSLATIONS FROM THE ASIAN CLASSICS

Major Plays of Chikamatsu, tr. Donald Keene 1961

Four Major Plays of Chikamatsu, tr. Donald Keene. Paperback ed. only. 1961; rev. ed. 1997

Records of the Grand Historian of China, translated from the Shih chi of Ssu-ma Ch'ien, tr. Burton Watson, 2 vols. 1961

Instructions for Practical Living and Other Neo-Confucian Writings by Wang Yang-ming, tr. Wing-tsit Chan 1963

Hsün Tzu: Basic Writings, tr. Burton Watson, paperback ed. only. 1963; rev. ed. 1996

Chuang Tzu: Basic Writings, tr. Burton Watson, paperback ed. only. 1964; rev. ed. 1996

The Mahābhārata, tr. Chakravarthi V. Narasimhan. Also in paperback ed. 1965; rev. ed. 1997

The Manyōshū, Nippon Gakujutsu Shinkōkai edition 1965

Su Tung-p'o: Selections from a Sung Dynasty Poet, tr. Burton Watson. Also in paperback ed. 1965

Bhartrihari: Poems, tr. Barbara Stoler Miller. Also in paperback ed. 1967

Basic Writings of Mo Tzu, Hsün Tzu, and Han Fei Tzu, tr. Burton Watson. Also in separate paperback eds. 1967

The Awakening of Faith, Attributed to Aśvaghosha, tr. Yoshito S. Hakeda. Also in paperback ed. 1967

Reflections on Things at Hand: The Neo-Confucian Anthology, comp. Chu Hsi and Lü Tsu-ch'ien, tr. Wing-tsit Chan 1967

The Platform Sutra of the Sixth Patriarch, tr. Philip B. Yampolsky. Also in paperback ed. 1967

Essays in Idleness: The Tsurezuregusa of Kenkō, tr. Donald Keene. Also in paperback ed. 1967

The Pillow Book of Sei Shōnagon, tr. Ivan Morris, 2 vols. 1967

Two Plays of Ancient India: The Little Clay Cart and the Minister's Seal, tr. J. A. B. van Buitenen 1968

The Complete Works of Chuang Tzu, tr. Burton Watson 1968

The Romance of the Western Chamber (Hsi Hsiang Chi), tr. S. I. Hsiung. Also in paperback ed. 1968

The Manyōshū, Nippon Gakujutsu Shinkōkai edition. Paperback ed. only. 1969

Records of the Historian: Chapters from the Shih chi of Ssu-ma Ch'ien, tr. Burton Watson. Paperback ed. only. 1969

Cold Mountain: 100 Poems by the T'ang Poet Han-shan, tr. Burton Watson. Also in paperback ed. 1970

Twenty Plays of the Nō Theatre, ed. Donald Keene. Also in paperback ed. 1970

Chūshingura: The Treasury of Loyal Retainers, tr. Donald Keene. Also in paperback ed. 1971; rev. ed. 1997

The Zen Master Hakuin: Selected Writings, tr. Philip B. Yampolsky 1971

Chinese Rhyme-Prose: Poems in the Fu Form from the Han and Six Dynasties Periods, tr. Burton Watson. Also in paperback ed. 1971

Kūkai: Major Works, tr. Yoshito S. Hakeda. Also in paperback ed. 1972

The Old Man Who Does as He Pleases: Selections from the Poetry and Prose of Lu Yu, tr. Burton Watson 1973

The Lion's Roar of Queen Śrīmālā, tr. Alex and Hideko Wayman 1974

Courtier and Commoner in Ancient China: Selections from the History of the Former Han by Pan Ku, tr. Burton Watson. Also in paperback ed. 1974

Japanese Literature in Chinese, vol. 1: *Poetry and Prose in Chinese by Japanese Writers of the Early Period*, tr. Burton Watson 1975

Japanese Literature in Chinese, vol. 2: *Poetry and Prose in Chinese by Japanese Writers of the Later Period*, tr. Burton Watson 1976

Love Song of the Dark Lord: Jayadeva's Gītagovinda, tr. Barbara Stoler Miller. Also in paperback ed. Cloth ed. includes critical text of the Sanskrit. 1977; rev. ed. 1997

Ryōkan: Zen Monk-Poet of Japan, tr. Burton Watson 1977
Calming the Mind and Discerning the Real: From the Lam rim chen mo of Tsoṇ-kha-pa, tr. Alex Wayman 1978
The Hermit and the Love-Thief: Sanskrit Poems of Bhartrihari and Bilhaṇa, tr. Barbara Stoler Miller 1978
The Lute: Kao Ming's P'i-p'a chi, tr. Jean Mulligan. Also in paperback ed. 1980
A Chronicle of Gods and Sovereigns: Jinnō Shōtōki of Kitabatake Chikafusa, tr. H. Paul Varley 1980
Among the Flowers: The Hua-chien chi, tr. Lois Fusek 1982
Grass Hill: Poems and Prose by the Japanese Monk Gensei, tr. Burton Watson 1983
Doctors, Diviners, and Magicians of Ancient China: Biographies of Fang-shih, tr. Kenneth J. DeWoskin. Also in paperback ed. 1983
Theater of Memory: The Plays of Kālidāsa, ed. Barbara Stoler Miller. Also in paperback ed. 1984
The Columbia Book of Chinese Poetry: From Early Times to the Thirteenth Century, ed. and tr. Burton Watson. Also in paperback ed. 1984
Poems of Love and War: From the Eight Anthologies and the Ten Long Poems of Classical Tamil, tr. A. K. Ramanujan. Also in paperback ed. 1985
The Bhagavad Gita: Krishna's Counsel in Time of War, tr. Barbara Stoler Miller 1986
The Columbia Book of Later Chinese Poetry, ed. and tr. Jonathan Chaves. Also in paperback ed. 1986
The Tso Chuan: Selections from China's Oldest Narrative History, tr. Burton Watson 1989
Waiting for the Wind: Thirty-Six Poets of Japan's Late Medieval Age, tr. Steven Carter 1989
Selected Writings of Nichiren, ed. Philip B. Yampolsky 1990
Saigyō, Poems of a Mountain Home, tr. Burton Watson 1990
The Book of Lieh Tzu: A Classic of the Tao, tr. A. C. Graham. Morningside ed. 1990
The Tale of an Anklet: An Epic of South India—The Cilappatikāram of Iḷaṅkō Aṭikaḷ, tr. R. Parthasarathy 1993
Waiting for the Dawn: A Plan for the Prince, tr. with introduction by Wm. Theodore de Bary 1993
Yoshitsune and the Thousand Cherry Trees: A Masterpiece of the Eighteenth-Century Japanese Puppet Theater, tr., annotated, and with introduction by Stanleigh H. Jones Jr. 1993
The Lotus Sutra, tr. Burton Watson. Also in paperback ed. 1993
The Classic of Changes: A New Translation of the I Ching as Interpreted by Wang Bi, tr. Richard John Lynn 1994
Beyond Spring: Tz'u Poems of the Sung Dynasty, tr. Julie Landau 1994
The Columbia Anthology of Traditional Chinese Literature, ed. Victor H. Mair 1994
Scenes for Mandarins: The Elite Theater of the Ming, tr. Cyril Birch 1995
Letters of Nichiren, ed. Philip B. Yampolsky; tr. Burton Watson et al. 1996
Unforgotten Dreams: Poems by the Zen Monk Shōtetsu, tr. Steven D. Carter 1997
The Vimalakirti Sutra, tr. Burton Watson 1997
Japanese and Chinese Poems to Sing: The Wakan rōei shū, tr. J. Thomas Rimer and Jonathan Chaves 1997
Breeze Through Bamboo: Kanshi of Ema Saikō, tr. Hiroaki Sato 1998
A Tower for the Summer Heat, by Li Yu, tr. Patrick Hanan 1998
Traditional Japanese Theater: An Anthology of Plays, by Karen Brazell 1998
The Original Analects: Sayings of Confucius and His Successors (0479–0249), by E. Bruce Brooks and A. Taeko Brooks 1998
The Classic of the Way and Virtue: A New Translation of the Tao-te ching of Laozi as Interpreted by Wang Bi, tr. Richard John Lynn 1999
The Four Hundred Songs of War and Wisdom: An Anthology of Poems from Classical Tamil, The Puṟanāṉūṟu, ed. and tr. George L. Hart and Hank Heifetz 1999
Original Tao: Inward Training (Nei-yeh) *and the Foundations of Taoist Mysticism*, by Harold D. Roth 1999

Po Chü-i: Selected Poems, tr. Burton Watson 2000
Lao Tzu's Tao Te Ching: *A Translation of the Startling New Documents Found at Guodian*, by Robert G. Henricks 2000
The Shorter Columbia Anthology of Traditional Chinese Literature, ed. Victor H. Mair 2000
Mistress and Maid (Jiaohongji), by Meng Chengshun, tr. Cyril Birch 2001
Chikamatsu: Five Late Plays, tr. and ed. C. Andrew Gerstle 2001
The Essential Lotus: Selections from the Lotus Sutra, tr. Burton Watson 2002
Early Modern Japanese Literature: An Anthology, 1600–1900, ed. Haruo Shirane 2002; abridged 2008
The Columbia Anthology of Traditional Korean Poetry, ed. Peter H. Lee 2002
The Sound of the Kiss, or The Story That Must Never Be Told: Pingali Suranna's Kalapurnodayamu, tr. Vecheru Narayana Rao and David Shulman 2003
The Selected Poems of Du Fu, tr. Burton Watson 2003
Far Beyond the Field: Haiku by Japanese Women, tr. Makoto Ueda 2003
Just Living: Poems and Prose by the Japanese Monk Tonna, ed. and tr. Steven D. Carter 2003
Han Feizi: Basic Writings, tr. Burton Watson 2003
Mozi: Basic Writings, tr. Burton Watson 2003
Xunzi: Basic Writings, tr. Burton Watson 2003
Zhuangzi: Basic Writings, tr. Burton Watson 2003
The Awakening of Faith, Attributed to Aśvaghosha, tr. Yoshito S. Hakeda, introduction by Ryūichi Abé 2005
The Tales of the Heike, tr. Burton Watson, ed. Haruo Shirane 2006
Tales of Moonlight and Rain, by Ueda Akinari, tr. with introduction by Anthony H. Chambers 2007
Traditional Japanese Literature: An Anthology, Beginnings to 1600, ed. Haruo Shirane 2007
The Philosophy of Qi, by Kaibara Ekken, tr. Mary Evelyn Tucker 2007
The Analects of Confucius, tr. Burton Watson 2007
The Art of War: Sun Zi's Military Methods, tr. Victor Mair 2007
One Hundred Poets, One Poem Each: A Translation of the Ogura Hyakunin Isshu, tr. Peter McMillan 2008
Zeami: Performance Notes, tr. Tom Hare 2008
Zongmi on Chan, tr. Jeffrey Lyle Broughton 2009
Scripture of the Lotus Blossom of the Fine Dharma, rev. ed., tr. Leon Hurvitz, preface and introduction by Stephen R. Teiser 2009
Mencius, tr. Irene Bloom, ed. with an introduction by Philip J. Ivanhoe 2009
Clouds Thick, Whereabouts Unknown: Poems by Zen Monks of China, Charles Egan 2010
The Mozi: A Complete Translation, tr. Ian Johnston 2010
The Huainanzi: A Guide to the Theory and Practice of Government in Early Han China, by Liu An, tr. and ed. John S. Major, Sarah A. Queen, Andrew Seth Meyer, and Harold D. Roth, with Michael Puett and Judson Murray 2010
The Demon at Agi Bridge and Other Japanese Tales, tr. Burton Watson, ed. with introduction by Haruo Shirane 2011
Haiku Before Haiku: From the Renga Masters to Bashō, tr. with introduction by Steven D. Carter 2011
The Columbia Anthology of Chinese Folk and Popular Literature, ed. Victor H. Mair and Mark Bender 2011
Tamil Love Poetry: The Five Hundred Short Poems of the Aiṅkuṟunūṟu, tr. and ed. Martha Ann Selby 2011
The Teachings of Master Wuzhu: Zen and Religion of No-Religion, by Wendi L. Adamek 2011
The Essential Huainanzi, by Liu An, tr. and ed. John S. Major, Sarah A. Queen, Andrew Seth Meyer, and Harold D. Roth 2012
The Dao of the Military: Liu An's Art of War, tr. Andrew Seth Meyer 2012
Unearthing the Changes: Recently Discovered Manuscripts of the Yi Jing *(I Ching) and Related Texts*, Edward L. Shaughnessy 2013

Record of Miraculous Events in Japan: The Nihon ryōiki, tr. Burton Watson 2013
The Complete Works of Zhuangzi, tr. Burton Watson 2013
Lust, Commerce, and Corruption: An Account of What I Have Seen and Heard, *by an Edo Samurai*, tr. and ed. Mark Teeuwen and Kate Wildman Nakai with Miyazaki Fumiko, Anne Walthall, and John Breen 2014; abridged 2017
Exemplary Women of Early China: The Lienü zhuan *of Liu Xiang*, tr. Anne Behnke Kinney 2014
The Columbia Anthology of Yuan Drama, ed. C. T. Hsia, Wai-yee Li, and George Kao 2014
The Resurrected Skeleton: From Zhuangzi to Lu Xun, by Wilt L. Idema 2014
The Sarashina Diary: *A Woman's Life in Eleventh-Century Japan*, by Sugawara no Takasue no Musume, tr. with introduction by Sonja Arntzen and Itō Moriyuki 2014; reader's edition 2018
The Kojiki: *An Account of Ancient Matters*, by Ō no Yasumaro, tr. Gustav Heldt 2014
The Orphan of Zhao *and Other Yuan Plays: The Earliest Known Versions*, tr. and introduced by Stephen H. West and Wilt L. Idema 2014
Luxuriant Gems of the Spring and Autumn, attributed to Dong Zhongshu, ed. and tr. Sarah A. Queen and John S. Major 2016
A Book to Burn and a Book to Keep (Hidden): Selected Writings, by Li Zhi, ed. and tr. Rivi Handler-Spitz, Pauline Lee, and Haun Saussy 2016
The Shenzi Fragments: *A Philosophical Analysis and Translation*, Eirik Lang Harris 2016
Record of Daily Knowledge *and* Poems and Essays: *Selections*, by Gu Yanwu, tr. and ed. Ian Johnston 2017
The Book of Lord Shang: Apologetics of State Power in Early China, by Shang Yang, ed. and tr. Yuri Pines 2017; abridged edition 2019
The Songs of Chu: An Ancient Anthology of Works by Qu Yuan and Others, ed. and tr. Gopal Sukhu 2017
Ghalib: Selected Poems and Letters, by Mirza Asadullah Khan Ghalib, tr. Frances W. Pritchett and Owen T. A. Cornwall 2017
Quelling the Demons' Revolt: A Novel from Ming China, attributed to Luo Guanzhong, tr. Patrick Hanan 2017
Erotic Poems from the Sanskrit: A New Translation, R. Parthasarathy 2017
The Book of Swindles: Selections from a Late Ming Collection, by Zhang Yingyu, tr. Christopher G. Rea and Bruce Rusk 2017
Monsters, Animals, and Other Worlds: A Collection of Short Medieval Japanese Tales, ed. R. Keller Kimbrough and Haruo Shirane 2018
Hidden and Visible Realms: Early Medieval Chinese Tales of the Supernatural and the Fantastic, compiled by Liu Yiqing, ed. and tr. Zhenjun Zhang 2018
A Couple of Soles: A Comic Play from Seventeenth-Century China, by Li Yu, tr. Jing Shen and Robert E. Hegel 2019
The Original Meaning of the Yijing: *Commentary on the* Scripture of Change, by Zhu Xi, tr. and ed. Joseph A. Adler 2019
Plum Shadows and Plank Bridge: Two Memoirs About Courtesans, Mao Xiang and Yu Huai, tr. and ed. Wai-yee Li 2020
The Diary of 1636: The Second Manchu Invasion of Korea, Na Man'gap, tr. with introduction by George Kallander 2020
Top Graduate Zhang Xie: The Earliest Extant Chinese Southern Play, tr. and introduced by Regina S. Llamas 2020
In the Shelter of the Pine: A Memoir of Yanagisawa Yoshiyasu and Tokugawa Japan, by Ōgimachi Machiko, tr. G. G. Rowley 2021

GPSR Authorized Representative: Easy Access System Europe, Mustamäe tee 50, 10621 Tallinn, Estonia, gpsr.requests@easproject.com

www.ingramcontent.com/pod-product-compliance
Lightning Source LLC
Chambersburg PA
CBHW031041110726
47900CB00003B/770

* 9 7 8 0 2 3 1 1 2 3 8 7 7 *